ABA·LSAC

━ OFFICIAL GUIDE TO ━

ABA-APPROVED LAW SCHOOLS

Produced by the Law School Admission Council
and the American Bar Association

2006 EDITION

Editors

Wendy Margolis, Director of Communications, LSAC

Bonnie Gordon, Editor and Producer, LSAC

Joe Puskarz, Manager of Publications, ABA

David Rosenlieb, Data Specialist, ABA

The Law School Admission Council (LSAC) is a nonprofit corporation whose members are more than 200 law schools in the United States and Canada. It was founded in 1947 to coordinate, facilitate, and enhance the law school admission process. The organization also provides programs and services related to legal education. All law schools approved by the American Bar Association (ABA) are LSAC members. Canadian law schools recognized by a provincial or territorial law society or government agency are also included in the voting membership of the Council.

The services provided by LSAC include the Law School Admission Test (LSAT); the Law School Data Assembly Service (LSDAS); the Candidate Referral Service (CRS); software including ADMIT-M admission office software; and various publications and LSAT preparation tools. The LSAT, LSDAS, and CRS are provided to assist law schools in serving and evaluating applicants. LSAC does not engage in assessing an applicant's chances for admission to any law school; all admission decisions are made by individual law schools.

LSAT; *The Official LSAT PrepTest*; ADMIT-M; and LSAC are registered marks of the Law School Admission Council, Inc. Law School Forums is a service mark of the Law School Admission Council, Inc. *The Official LSAT SuperPrep; 10 Actual, Official LSAT PrepTests; 10 More Actual, Official LSAT PrepTests; The Next 10 Actual, Official LSAT PrepTests; The New Whole Law School Package; ABA-LSAC Official Guide to ABA-Approved Law Schools;* and LSDAS are trademarks of Law School Admission Council, Inc.

Law School Admission Council fees, policies, and procedures relating to, but not limited to, test registration, test administration, test score reporting, misconduct and irregularities, and other matters may change without notice at any time. Up-to-date Law School Admission Council policies and procedures are available at *www.LSAC.org*, or you may contact our candidate service representatives.

Table of Contents

Introduction

The *Official Guide to ABA-Approved Law Schools* is a joint effort of the Law School Admission Council (LSAC) and the American Bar Association's Section of Legal Education and Admissions to the Bar (ABA).

The Law School Admission Council is a nonprofit corporation that was founded in 1947 to coordinate, facilitate, and enhance the law school admission process. LSAC provides numerous programs and services related to legal education. All law schools approved by the American Bar Association are LSAC members. Canadian law schools recognized by a provincial or territorial law society or government agency are also included in the voting membership of LSAC.

The American Bar Association is the national organization of the legal profession. The Council of the Section of Legal Education and Admissions to the Bar of the ABA is identified by the US Department of Education as the "nationally recognized accrediting agency for professional schools of law."

The information contained in this book is collected separately by the ABA and LSAC from the 188 ABA-approved law schools that are also members of the Law School Admission Council. The two organizations agreed to combine this wealth of information to provide a comprehensive resource for data and descriptions about ABA-approved law schools.

Although no book or website can substitute for direct contact with admission offices, professors, students, alumni, and prelaw advisors, this guide can inform the process of deciding whether, and where, to attend law school. This guide is designed to provide prospective law school applicants with basic information in a simple format that will facilitate comparisons among schools. In addition to statistics on all ABA-approved law schools, this book contains information intended to help individuals prepare for the rigors and costs associated with attending law school.

The ABA collects quantitative data as part of the accreditation process using questionnaires completed annually during the fall academic semester. Standard 509 of the *Standards: Rules of Procedure for Approval of Law Schools*, as adopted by the ABA House of Delegates in August 1996, states: "A law school shall publish basic consumer information. The information shall be published in a fair and accurate manner reflective of actual practice."

The data collected in the ABA annual questionnaire and published in this guide satisfy a law school's obligation to provide basic consumer information under Standard 509. The data are certified as fair and accurate by the dean of the law school.

LSAC collects admission profile data and school descriptions each fall as a service to its member schools and to prospective law school applicants. The information provided by the law schools to LSAC in no way affects the ABA accreditation process and is not meant to satisfy a law school's publication requirements under Standard 509.

Neither the LSAC nor ABA condones, approves, or sanctions use of the data contained in this book to rank law schools. Both organizations disapprove of any and all rankings. The deans of 178 law schools have published the following statement regarding rankings:

> The idea that all law schools can be measured by the same yardstick ignores the qualities that make you and law schools unique, and is unworthy of being an important influence on the choice you are about to make. As the deans of schools that range across the spectrum of several rating systems, we strongly urge you to minimize the influence of rankings on your own judgment. In choosing the best school for you, we urge you to get information about all the schools in which you might have some interest. … Law schools may all have met the same standards of quality to become accredited, but they are quite different from each other. The unique characteristics of each law school will inform you why one school may be best for you and another school best for someone else. We want you to make the best choice for you.

The information contained in this edition of the *ABA/LSAC Official Guide to ABA-Approved Law Schools* was collected in fall 2004. Some of the information, including ABA-accreditation status, may change; check the website of the ABA Section of Legal Education and Admissions to the Bar—*www.abanet.org/legaled*—for updates. Neither the ABA nor LSAC conducts an audit to verify the accuracy of the information submitted by the respective institutions.

Chapter 1: Being a Lawyer

■ Lawyers and Their Skills

Law practice is so diverse that it is not possible to describe the so-called typical lawyer. Each lawyer works with different clients and different legal problems. Ordinarily, certain basic legal skills are required of all lawyers. They must know:

- how to analyze legal issues in light of the existing state of the law, the direction in which the law is headed, and relevant policy considerations;

- how to synthesize material in light of the fact that many issues are multifaceted and require the combination of diverse elements into a coherent whole;

- how to advocate the views of groups and individuals within the context of the legal system;

- how to give intelligent counsel on the law's requirements;

- how to write and speak clearly; and

- how to negotiate effectively.

Reading and Listening

Lawyers must be able to take in a great deal of information, often on topics about which they are unfamiliar. The ability to digest information from lengthy, dense texts is essential. Equally important is the ability to listen to clients and understand their unique issues and concerns.

Analyzing

Lawyers must be able to determine the fundamental elements of problems. They spend much time discerning the nature and significance of the many issues in a particular problem. In every issue, the lawyer must study the relationship between each element in order to arrive at an answer, result, or solution.

Synthesizing

Lawyers must learn that because of the complexities of many issues and the number of laws either directly or tangentially relevant, they must be able to pull together in a meaningful, focused, cogent manner often large amounts of material.

Advocating

As an advocate, the lawyer's role is to represent his or her client's particular point of view and interests as vigorously as possible. The American judicial system assumes that equitable solutions will emerge from the clash of opposing interests. The success of this adversarial system of American law depends upon the talents and training of the lawyers who work as advocates within it. Lawyers must be able to use their advocacy skills to marshal evidence and present arguments as to why a particular outcome is desirable.

Counseling

Lawyers also spend a good deal of their time giving clients legal advice. Few ventures in the modern world can be undertaken without some understanding of the law. Through their knowledge of what the law involves, lawyers advise clients about partnerships, decisions, actions, and many other subjects. In many cases, the lawyer's role as a counselor serves as much to prevent litigation as to support it.

Writing and Speaking

Whether in the courtroom or the law office, lawyers must be effective communicators. If lawyers could not translate thoughts and opinions into clear and precise English, it would be difficult for the law to serve society. After all, the law is embodied in words, and many of the disputes that give birth to laws begin with language—its meaning, use, and interpretation. Litigation leads to written judicial opinions; congressional enactments are recorded as printed statutes; and even economic transactions must be expressed as formal, written contracts.

Negotiating

One of the lawyer's primary roles is reconciling divergent interests and opinions. When the parties to a proposed transaction disagree, the lawyer, acting as a facilitator, may be able to help them negotiate to a common ground. Although the client's interests are a lawyer's first priority, often those interests are served best after compromise and conciliation have paved the way to an equitable settlement. Because lawyers are trained to see the implications of alternative courses of action, they are often able to break an impasse.

■ Fields of Law

Lawyers are central figures in the life of a democratic country. They may deal with major courtroom cases or minor traffic disputes, complex corporate mergers or straightforward real estate transactions. Lawyers may work for giant industries, small businesses, government agencies, international organizations, public interest groups, legal aid offices, and universities—or they may work for themselves. They represent both the impoverished and the wealthy, the helpless and the powerful. Lawyers may work solo, in a small group, or in a large law firm.

About 72.9 percent of American lawyers are in private practice, most in small, one-person offices and some in large firms. Roughly 8.2 percent of the profession work for government agencies, 9.5 percent work for private industries and associations as salaried lawyers or as managers, 1.1 percent work for legal aid or as public defenders, and 1 percent are in legal education. (About 4.6 percent are retired or inactive.) Many lawyers develop expertise in a particular field of law. Large law firms that provide a full range of legal services tend to employ more specialists. The solo practitioner, who must handle a variety of problems alone, may have greater opportunity to work in several areas. Of course, there are lawyers in large firms who maintain general practices, and lawyers in one-person offices who concentrate on a particular legal issue. Both specialized and general practice can be rewarding. One offers the satisfaction of mastering a particular legal discipline, and the other the challenge of exploring new fields. Following are brief descriptions of selected areas of specialization, though there are many areas of the law that can rightly fall into more than one category.

Corporate and Securities Law

The corporate lawyer helps clients conduct their business affairs in a manner that is efficient and consistent with the law. The responsibilities of a corporate lawyer can range from preparing the initial articles of incorporation and bylaws for a new enterprise to handling a corporate reorganization under the provisions of federal bankruptcy law. Examples of other areas of corporate law practice include (but are not limited to) contract, intellectual property, legislative compliance, and liability matters.

Securities law is an extremely complex area that almost always requires the services of a specialist. Lawyers who acquire this specialty are involved with the formation, organization, and financing of corporations through securities such as stock, as well as mergers, acquisitions, and corporate takeovers.

Criminal Law

Criminal defense lawyers represent clients accused of crimes. Their public counterparts are the prosecutors and district attorneys who represent the interests of the state in the prosecution of those accused of crimes. Both types of criminal lawyers deal with fundamental issues of the law and personal liberty. They defend many of the basic rights considered crucial to the preservation of a free and just society.

Environmental and Natural Resources Law

Environmental law was born out of widespread public and professional concern about the fate of our natural resources. Lawyers in this field may tackle legal and regulatory issues relating to air and water quality, hazardous waste practice, natural gas transportation, oil and gas exploration and development, electric power licensing, water rights, toxic torts, public land use, marine resources, and energy trade regulation. They may work directly for governmental agencies that address environmental problems or represent corporations, public interest groups, and entities concerned about protecting the environment.

Family and Juvenile Law

Family, or domestic relations, law is concerned with relationships between individuals in the context of the family. Many lawyers who practice this kind of law are members of small law firms or are solo practitioners. They specialize in solving problems that arise among family members and in creating or dissolving personal relationships through such means as adoption or divorce.

Health Law

The practice of health law encompasses many different disciplines. Lawyers in this field can be in the private bar or at government agencies. Health lawyers can represent hospitals, physician groups, health maintenance organizations (HMOs), or individual doctors, among many others. Government health lawyers can investigate fraud, deal with Medicare policy and compliance, or can oversee public health policy. Many health lawyers are engaged in the business of healthcare, spending significant time in mergers and acquisitions, tax law, employee benefits, and risk management issues. The impact of technology on health care has been great with health lawyers helping to guide their clients through intellectual property, biomedicine, and telemedicine issues. Other health lawyers specialize in bioethics and clinical ethics representing universities and other research academic centers.

Intellectual Property Law

Intellectual property law is concerned with the protection of inventors' rights in their discoveries, authors' rights in their creations, and businesses' rights in their identifying marks. Often, an intellectual property lawyer will specialize in a particular area of the law. For example, for those attorneys with a technical background, patent law is a way to combine one's scientific and legal background into one practice. A copyright attorney counsels authors, composers, and artists on the scope of their rights in their creations, and even personal identities, negotiates contracts, and litigates to enforce these rights. In recent years, copyright law has also focused on technological advances, particularly developments in electronic publishing. Additionally, in today's global economy, intellectual property issues are at the forefront of international trade negotiations.

International Law

International law has grown significantly as a field of practice, reflecting the increasing interdependence of nations and economies. Public international law provides a limited range of job opportunities, particularly with national governments or international institutions or with public interest bodies. Immigration and refugee law also assumes increasing importance as more people move more frequently across national boundaries for business, tourism, or permanent resettlement. Private international law may offer more extensive employment opportunities, either through law firms or for corporations, banks, or telecommunications firms. Fluency in another language or familiarity with another culture can be a decided advantage for law school graduates who seek to practice in the international arena.

Tax Law

In the past 50 years, the importance and complexity of federal, state, and local taxes have necessitated a specialty in this field of law. It is one area of the law where change is constant. The federal Internal Revenue Code and its associated regulations are now several thousand pages in length. New statutes, court decisions, and administrative rulings are issued frequently, and the tax lawyer must be alert to these changes. Economic planning usually includes attention to taxes, and the tax lawyer often assists clients in understanding and minimizing their tax liabilities.

Civil Rights

Many lawyers entered law school wishing ultimately to work in the field of civil rights—the area of law that is concerned with the balance of governmental power and individual liberties. Although the number of full-time jobs in this field is relatively small, many lawyers whose principal practices are in other fields are able to work in this area by taking cases on a pro bono basis. Full-time civil rights attorneys often work for nonprofit, public interest law firms, or as part of a larger firm with a diverse practice.

Chapter 2: Becoming a Lawyer

A legal education is both challenging and rewarding. You will develop your analytical, synthesizing, creative, and logical thinking skills, and you will strengthen your reading and debating abilities. A legal education is necessary to become a lawyer in the United States, but it is also excellent preparation for many other careers, both because of the framework for organizing knowledge it provides and the analytical approach it brings to problems. Many teachers, business people, and writers first obtained a legal education before pursuing careers other than law.

■ Preparing for Law School

Statement on Prelaw Preparation

What follows are excerpts from a statement on preparation for legal education drafted by the Prelaw Committee of the ABA Section of Legal Education and Admissions to the Bar. It addresses the course of study and skills necessary to obtain admission into law school and to be a successful lawyer.

Students who are successful in law school, and who become accomplished attorneys or use their legal education successfully in other areas of professional life, come to their legal education from widely differing educational and experiential backgrounds. As undergraduate students, some have majored in subjects that are traditionally considered paths to law school, such as history, English, philosophy, political science, economics, or business. Other successful law students, however, have focused their undergraduate studies in areas as diverse as art, music theory, computer science, engineering, nursing, or education. Many law students enter law school directly from their undergraduate studies and without having had any substantial work experience. Others begin their legal education significantly later in life, and they bring to their law school education the insights and perspectives gained from those life experiences.

Thus the ABA does not recommend any particular group of undergraduate majors or courses that should be taken by those wishing to prepare for legal education; the law is too multifaceted, and the human mind too adaptable, to permit such a linear approach to preparing for law school or the practice of law. Nonetheless, there are important skills and values, and significant bodies of knowledge, that can be acquired prior to law school and that will provide a sound foundation for a sophisticated legal education. Even though a student may well be able to acquire in law school some specific fundamental skills and knowledge that the student's prelaw school experience has not provided, the student who comes to law school lacking a broad range of basic skills and knowledge will face an extremely difficult task.

Prospective law students should also consult closely with the prelaw advisor at their undergraduate institution. That individual may be able to assist current students in selecting courses or professors that will particularly assist in developing the skills and knowledge foundation that is emphasized in this statement. Taking difficult courses from demanding instructors is the best generic preparation for legal education. The prelaw advisor can also assist current and former students in choosing law schools to which to apply that are appropriate in light of a prospective student's interests and credentials. Finally, prospective law students should also consult the publications and admissions personnel of the schools to which they are considering applying for any specific recommendations that individual schools may have concerning preparation for law school.

Skills and Values

The core skills and values that are essential for competent lawyering include analytic and problem-solving skills, critical reading abilities, writing skills, oral communication and listening abilities, general research skills, task organization and management skills, and the values of serving faithfully the interests of others while also promoting justice.* Thus, individuals who wish to prepare adequately for legal education, and for a career in law or for other professional service that involves the use of lawyering skills, should seek educational, extracurricular, and life experiences that will assist them in developing those attributes. Some brief comments about each of the listed skills and values follow.

Analytic and Problem-Solving Skills
Students should seek courses and other experiences that will engage them in critical thinking about important issues, that will engender in them tolerance for uncertainty, and that will give them experience in structuring and evaluating arguments for and against propositions that are susceptible to reasoned debate. Students also should seek courses and other experiences that require them to apply previously developed principles or theories to new situations and that demand that they develop solutions to new problems. The law school experience will develop and refine those crucial skills, but one must enter law school with a reasonably well developed set of analytic and problem-solving abilities.

Critical Reading Abilities

Preparation for legal education should include substantial experience at close reading and critical analysis of complex textual material, for much of what law students and attorneys do involves careful reading and sophisticated comprehension of judicial opinions, statutes, documents, and other written materials. As with the other skills discussed, the requisite critical reading abilities may be acquired in a wide range of experiences, including the close reading of complex material in literature, political or economic theory, philosophy, or history. The particular nature of the materials examined is not crucial; what is important is that law school not be the first time that a student has been rigorously engaged in the enterprise of carefully reading and understanding, and critically analyzing, complex written material of substantial length. Potential law students should also be aware that the study and practice of law require the ability to read and assimilate large amounts of material, often in a short period of time.

Writing Skills

Those seeking to prepare for legal education should develop a high degree of skill at written communication. Language is the most important tool of a lawyer, and lawyers must learn to express themselves clearly and concisely. Legal education provides good training in writing, and particularly in the specific techniques and forms of written expression that are common in the law. Fundamental writing skills, however, should be acquired and refined before one enters law school. Those preparing for legal education should seek as many experiences as possible that will require rigorous and analytical writing, including preparing original pieces of substantial length and revising written work in response to constructive criticism.

Oral Communication and Listening Abilities

The ability to speak clearly and persuasively is another skill that is essential to success in law school and the practice of law. Lawyers also must have excellent listening skills if they are to understand their clients and others with whom they must interact daily. As with writing skills, legal education provides excellent opportunities for refining oral communication skills, and particularly for practicing the forms and techniques of oral expression that are most common in the practice of law. Before coming to law school, however, individuals should seek to develop their basic speaking and listening skills, such as by engaging in debate, making formal presentations in class, or speaking before groups in school, the community, or the workplace.

General Research Skills

Although there are many research sources and techniques that are specific to the law, an individual need not have developed any familiarity with these specific skills or materials before entering law school. However, the individual who comes to law school without ever having undertaken a project that requires significant library research and the analysis of large amounts of information obtained from that research will be at a severe disadvantage. Those wishing to prepare for legal education should select courses and seek experiences that will require them to plan a research strategy, to undertake substantial library research, and to analyze, organize, and present a reasonably large amount of material. A basic ability to use a personal computer is also increasingly important for law students, both for word processing and for computerized legal research.

Task Organization and Management Skills

The study and practice of law require the ability to organize large amounts of information, to identify objectives, and to create a structure for applying that information in an efficient way in order to achieve desired results. Many law school courses, for example, are graded primarily on the basis of one examination at the end of the course, and many projects in the practice of law require the compilation of large amounts of information from a wide variety of sources, frequently over relatively brief periods of time. Thus those entering law school must be prepared to organize and assimilate large amounts of information in a manner that facilitates the recall and application of that information in an effective and efficient manner. Some of the requisite experience can be obtained through undertaking school projects that require substantial research and writing, or through the preparation of major reports for an employer, a school, or a civic organization.

Serving Others and Promoting Justice

Each member of the legal profession should be dedicated both to the objectives of serving others honestly, competently, and responsibly, and to the goals of improving fairness and the quality of justice in the legal system. Those thinking of entering this profession would be well served by having some significant experience, before coming to law school, in which they devoted substantial effort toward assisting others. Participation in public service projects or similar efforts at achieving objectives established for common purposes can be particularly helpful.

Knowledge

In addition to these fundamental skills and values, there are some basic areas of knowledge that are important to a sophisticated legal education and to the development of a competent attorney. As law becomes more pervasive in our society, an increasingly broad range of knowledge and information from other disciplines become relevant in order to have a full appreciation of the legal system in general, to understand how disputes might be resolved, to understand and apply various legal principles and standards, and to appreciate the context in which a legal problem or dispute arises. Some of the types of knowledge that are most useful, and that would most pervasively affect one's ability to derive the maximum benefit from legal education, include the following:

- A broad understanding of history, particularly American history, and the various factors (social, political, economic, and cultural) that have influenced the development of the pluralistic society that presently exists in the United States;

- A fundamental understanding of political thought and theory, and of the contemporary American political system;

- A basic understanding of ethical theory and theories of justice;

- A grounding in economics, particularly elementary microeconomic theory, and an understanding of the interaction between economic theory and public policy;

- Some basic mathematical and financial skills, such as an understanding of basic precalculus mathematics and an ability to analyze financial data;

- A basic understanding of human behavior and social interaction; and

- An understanding of diverse cultures within and beyond the United States, of international institutions and issues, and of the increasing interdependence of the nations and communities within our world.

As law has become more woven into the fabric of our society, and as that society is increasingly influenced by disparate national and global forces, a broad knowledge base is essential for success in law school and for competence in the legal profession. Knowledge of specific areas of law can and will be acquired during a good legal education, but students must come to law school with much fundamental knowledge upon which legal education can build.

*These core skill and value areas are drawn, in substantial part, from the Statement of Skills and Values contained in the 1992 Report of the American Bar Association Task Force on Law Schools and the Profession, *Legal Education and Professional Development—An Educational Continuum.*

■ Other Resources

For a selected list of books, audiocassettes, and video programs pertaining to legal education and the legal profession, see Resources for the Prelaw Candidate, Appendix D, or go to Law School Resources/Resources for the Prelaw Candidate on LSAC's website, *www.LSAC.org.* Also included in the list are biographies and books on jurisprudence and legal issues.

■ The Juris Doctor Degree

ABA-approved law schools generally require three years of full-time study to earn the Juris Doctor (JD) degree. Most schools with part-time programs require four years of part-time study to earn the JD degree. Most law schools share a common approach to training lawyers. However, they differ in the emphasis they give to certain subjects and teaching methods, such as opportunities for independent study, legal internships, participation in clinical programs, and involvement with governmental affairs.

Law school can be an intense, competitive environment. Students have little time for other interests, especially during the first year of law school. The ABA requires that no full-time student hold an outside job for more than 20 hours a week. Most schools encourage their students to become totally immersed in reading, discussing, and thinking about the law.

The First Year

The newness of the first year of law school is exciting for many and anxiety-provoking for almost all. Professors expect you to be prepared in class, but in most courses, grades will be determined primarily from examinations administered at the end of the semester or, at some schools, the end of the year. The professor may give little feedback until the final examination.

The Case Method Approach

The "case method" is what first-year law students are likely to find least familiar. By focusing on the underlying principles that shape the law's approach to different situations, you will learn to distinguish among subtly different legal results and to identify the critical factors that determine a particular outcome. Once these distinctions are mastered, you should be able to apply this knowledge to new situations.

The case method involves the detailed examination of a number of related judicial opinions that describe an area of law. You will also learn to apply the same critical analysis to legislative materials and scholarly articles. The role of the law professor is to provoke and stimulate. For a particular case, he or she may ask questions designed to explore the facts presented, to determine the legal principles applied in reaching a decision, and to analyze the method of reasoning used. In this way, the professor encourages you to relate the case to others and to distinguish it from those with similar but inapplicable precedents. In order to encourage you to learn to defend your reasoning, the professor may adopt a position contrary to the holding of the case.

Because this process places much of the burden of learning on the student, classroom discussions can be exciting. They are also demanding. However uninformed, unprepared, or puzzled you may be, you will be expected to participate in these discussions.

The Ability to Think

The case method reflects the general belief that the primary purpose of law school is not to teach substantive law but to teach you to think like a lawyer. Teachers of law are less concerned about rules and technicalities than are their counterparts in many other disciplines. Although the memorization of specifics may be useful to you, the ability to be analytical and literate is considerably more important than the power of total recall. One reason for this approach to legal education is that in our common-law tradition, the law is constantly evolving and changing; thus, specific rules may quickly lose their relevance.

Law is more an art than a science. The reality lawyers seek in analyzing a case is not always well-defined. Legal study, therefore, requires an attentive mind and a tolerance for ambiguity. Because many people believe incorrectly that the study of law involves the memorization of rules in books and principles dictated by learned professors, law schools often attract those people who especially value structure, authority, and order. The study of law does not involve this kind of certainty, however; complex legal questions do not have simple legal solutions.

The Curriculum

As a first-year law student, you will follow a designated course of study that may cover many of the following subjects:

- **Civil procedure**—the process of adjudication in the United States; i.e., jurisdiction and standing to sue, motions and pleadings, pretrial procedure, the structure of a lawsuit, and appellate review of trial results.

- **Constitutional law**—the legislative powers of the federal and state governments, and questions of civil liberties and constitutional history, including detailed study of the Bill of Rights and constitutional freedoms.

- **Contracts**—the nature of enforceable promises and rules for determining appropriate remedies in case of nonperformance.

- **Criminal law and criminal procedure**—bases of criminal responsibility, the rules and policies for enforcing sanctions against individuals accused of committing offenses against the public order and well-being, and the rights guaranteed to those charged with criminal violations.

- **Legal method**—students' introduction to the organization of the American legal system and its processes.

- **Legal writing**—research and writing component of most first-year programs; requires students to research and write memoranda dealing with various legal problems.

- **Property law**—concepts, uses, and historical developments in the treatment of land, buildings, natural resources, and personal objects.

- **Torts**—private wrongs, such as acts of negligence, assault, and defamation, that violate obligations of the law.

In addition to attending classes, you may be required to participate in a moot court exercise in which you take responsibility for arguing a hypothetical court case.

After the first year, you will probably have the opportunity to select from a broad range of courses. Generally, you will take courses in administrative law, civil litigation, commercial law, corporations, evidence, family law, professional responsibility, taxation, and wills and trusts before completing your degree. These universal courses are basic to legal education. Every law school supplements this basic curriculum with additional courses, such as international law, environmental law, conflict of laws, labor law, criminal procedure, and jurisprudence.

Opportunities to Practice What Is Learned

Legal education is primarily academic, in that students devote most of their time to mastering general concepts and principles that shape the law. Most schools offer a variety of professional skills courses as well. Through clinical programs, law schools offer students direct experience in legal practice. These programs allow second- and third-year students to render counseling, undertake legislative drafting, participate in court trials and appeals, and do other legal work for academic credit. Schools differ in the range and variety of practical education they offer, but the benefits of integrating this experience with theoretical study are well established.

Extracurricular Activities

Student organizations greatly supplement classroom learning. Typically, these organizations are dedicated to advancing the interests of particular groups of law students, such as black, women, or Hispanic students; or to promoting greater understanding of specific legal fields, such as environmental or international law; or to providing opportunities for involvement in professional, social, and sports activities.

A unique feature of American law schools is that law students manage and edit most of the legal profession's principal scholarly journals. Membership on the editorial staffs of these journals is considered a mark of academic distinction. Selection is ordinarily based on outstanding academic performance, writing ability, or both, as discussed on page 22 of this book.

■ Admission to the Bar

The Bar Examination*

In order to obtain a license to practice law, almost all law school graduates must apply for bar admission through a state board of bar examiners. Most often this board is an agency of the highest state court in the jurisdiction, but occasionally the board is connected more closely to the state's bar association. The criteria for eligibility to take the bar examination or to otherwise qualify for bar admission are set by each state.

Licensing involves a demonstration of worthiness in two distinct areas. The first is competence. For initial licensure, competence is ordinarily established by a showing that the applicant holds an acceptable educational credential (with rare exception, a JD degree) from a law school that meets educational standards, and by achieving a passing score on the bar examination.

The most common testing configuration consists of a two-day bar examination, one day of which is devoted to the Multistate Bar Examination, a standardized 200-item test covering six areas (Constitutional Law, Contracts, Criminal Law, Evidence, Real Property, and Torts). The second day of testing is typically comprised of locally crafted essays from a broader range of subject matters; however, in a growing number of states, nationally developed tests, such as the Multistate Essay Examination and the Multistate Performance Test, are used to round out the test.

In addition, almost all jurisdictions require that the applicant present an acceptable score on the Multistate Professional Responsibility Examination, which is separately administered three times each year.

The second area of inquiry by bar examiners involves the character and fitness of applicants for a law license.

In this regard, bar examiners seek background information concerning each applicant that is relevant to the appropriateness of granting a professional credential. Because law is a public profession, and because the degree of harm a lawyer lacking the necessary character or fitness can inflict is substantial, decisions about who should be admitted to practice law are made carefully by bar examining boards.

Boards of bar examiners in most jurisdictions expect to hear from prospective candidates during the final year of law school. Bar examinations are ordinarily offered at the end of February and July, with considerably more applicants taking the summer test because it falls after graduation from law school.

Some boards offer or require law student registration at an earlier point in law school. This preliminary processing, where available, permits the board to review character and fitness issues in advance.

As state-specific information is so important (and so variable) in the lawyer-licensing process, law students should contact the board of bar examiners in the jurisdiction(s) in which they are most likely to practice law.

*This section was written by Erica Moeser, President of the National Conference of Bar Examiners (NCBE).

General Information

Lawyers may practice only in the state or states where they are members of the bar in good standing. However, many states will admit a lawyer to its bar if the lawyer has been admitted to the bar of another state and has practiced law actively for a certain number of years. This is known as "motion admission." Courts often grant temporary bar admission to out-of-state lawyers for the duration of a specific case.

Many states have student practice rules that, in conjunction with students' academic programs, admit advanced law students who are under the close supervision of an admitted lawyer. A few states require law students to register with the board of bar examiners before graduation or, in some cases, soon after they are enrolled in law school, if they intend to practice in those states. So, if you're planning to attend law school, you should check the bar admission requirements for those states in which you may wish to practice after graduation.

Federal courts set their own standards for admission. It is a common requirement for federal district court admission that the lawyer be admitted to the bar in the state in which the federal district is located or, for the applicant to have one good state court admission.

Some state bar associations inquire about the law school admission records of those seeking admission to the bar. You should keep and maintain complete copies of all law school application records throughout the admission cycle and your law school career.

All states accept graduation from an ABA-approved law school as meeting the state's education requirement for eligibility to sit for the bar examination. A number of states have special rules that accept other forms of legal education as sufficient. A good source of information regarding bar admission requirements is the latest edition of the *NCBE/ABA's Comprehensive Guide to Bar Admission Requirements*, which is available online at *www.abanet.org/legaled*. It should also be available in any law school library or can be ordered through the ABA Service Center at 1.800.285.2221. If you would like additional information relating to bar admissions about a specific state, please contact the appropriate authority in that state. Also, you may want to visit the websites for NCBE (*www.ncbex.org*), the ABA (*www.abanet.org/legaled*), and LSAC (*www.LSAC.org*).

Distance Education

Educating a student for a Juris Doctor degree is a professional education of a most distinct variety. During a law school education, a student is expected to participate in a learning community to develop skills and knowledge that will advance the legal system, society, and the student's career. This law school experience involves interaction with faculty and fellow students outside the classroom as well as in class. Students also learn from each other by inquiry and challenge, review, and study groups.

ABA-approved law schools may not offer a JD degree program that is online or done through correspondence study. ABA-approved law schools may grant credit hours for distance education courses, but no more than 4-credit hours in any term, and no more than 12-credit hours toward the JD degree. Students should be aware that studying law by correspondence or other distance education programs would limit the ability to sit for the bar in many states.

Bar Associations

Bar associations are membership organizations designed to raise the standards of the legal profession and to encourage professional unity. Each state has its own bar association. There are also a variety of national, state, local, and special-interest bar associations. Many bar associations sponsor programs intended to broaden the availability of legal services and to familiarize the public with the legal profession. They also conduct extensive continuing legal education programs to help members update their skills and their knowledge of the law.

The American Bar Association (ABA) is the largest national organization of attorneys in the United States with 405,348 members. The ABA sponsors a number of programs dealing with legal education, law reform, judicial selection, and professional responsibility. The ABA also publishes the "Model Rules of Professional Conduct," a set of regulations governing ethical standards in the practice of law. Attorneys who violate such standards are subject to censure, suspension, or disbarment by the state bar admitting authorities.

Additionally, there are local and national chapters of bar associations for lawyers from minority groups. Among them are the National Bar Association, National Hispanic Bar Association, National Asian and Pacific American Bar Association, and the Native American Bar Association. For more information on events sponsored by these organizations, go to *www.LSAC.org* or contact the LSAC Office of Minority Affairs at *mile@LSAC.org*.

Chapter 3: The Law School Admission Process

■ How Law Schools Determine Whom to Admit

It is very difficult to predict with certainty which individuals will perform well in law school, so admission committees seek the most qualified from the pool of applicants. In order to be fair, schools rely heavily upon selection criteria that bear on expected performance in law school and can be applied objectively to all candidates. Law schools consider a variety of factors in admitting their students, and no single qualification will independently guarantee acceptance or rejection. The two factors that all candidates present, prior academic performance and the LSAT score, are fundamental to the admission process.

The most difficult admission decisions are those regarding candidates who are neither so well qualified nor so deficient as to present a clear-cut case for acceptance or rejection. These applicants constitute the majority of the applicant pool at many law schools.

Criteria That May Be Considered by Law School Admission Committees

- Undergraduate grade-point average

- LSAT score

- Undergraduate course of study

- Graduate work, if any

- College attended

- Improvement in grades and grade distribution

- College curricular and extracurricular activities

- Ethnic/racial background

- Individual character and personality

- Letters of recommendation

- Writing skills

- Personal statement or essay

- Work experience or other postundergraduate experiences

- Community activities

- Motivation to study and reasons for deciding to study law

- State of residency

- Obstacles that have been overcome

- Past accomplishments and leadership

- Anything else that stands out in an application

■ The Law School Admission Test (LSAT)

All American Bar Association (ABA)-approved law schools and many non-ABA-approved law schools require applicants to take the LSAT as part of the admission process.

The test consists of five 35-minute sections of multiple-choice questions, in three different item types. Four of the five sections contribute to the test taker's score. One of the five sections is typically used to pretest new test items and to preequate new test forms. The placement of this section, which is commonly referred to as the variable section, is varied for each administration of the test. A 35-minute writing sample is administered at the end of the test. LSAC does not score the writing sample. Copies of the writing sample are sent to all law schools to which you apply.

The score scale for the LSAT is 120 to 180. Some schools place greater weight than others on the LSAT; most law schools do evaluate your full range of credentials.

What the Test Measures

The LSAT is designed to measure skills that are considered essential for success in law school: the reading and comprehension of complex texts with accuracy and insight; the organization and management of information and the ability to draw reasonable inferences from it; the ability to think critically; and the analysis and evaluation of the reasoning and arguments of others.

The three multiple-choice question types in the LSAT are:

Reading Comprehension Questions
These questions measure your ability to read, with understanding and insight, examples of lengthy and complex materials similar to those commonly encountered in law school work. The reading comprehension items consist of passages of approximately 450 words, each followed by five to eight questions that test reading and reasoning abilities.

Analytical Reasoning Questions
These questions are designed to measure your ability to understand a structure of relationships and to draw logical conclusions about that structure. You are asked to make deductions from a set of statements, rules, or conditions that describe relationships among entities such as persons, places, things, or events. They simulate the kinds of detailed analyses of relationships that a law student must perform in solving legal problems.

Logical Reasoning Questions
These questions are designed to evaluate your ability to understand, analyze, criticize, and complete a variety of arguments. Each logical reasoning question requires you to read and comprehend a short passage, then answer one or two questions about it. The questions test a variety of abilities involved in reasoning logically and thinking critically.

Important Note Regarding Changes to the LSAT Writing Sample

Beginning with the June 2005 LSAT, the time allotted for the unscored writing sample increases from 30 to 35 minutes, the writing space increases from one to two pages, the directions have been revised, and each test taker will be randomly assigned one of two different kinds of writing prompt. One kind is new to the LSAT. The other is very similar to the kind of writing prompt that has previously been administered with the LSAT and that has appeared in official LSAT preparation materials produced prior to June 2005. For more information, see the *2005–2006 LSAT & LSDAS Information Book* or go to the LSAT information at *www.LSAC.org*.

Your Score as a Predictor of Law School Performance

The LSAT, like any admission test, is not a perfect predictor of law school performance. The predictive power of an admission test is limited by many factors, such as the complexity of the skills the test is designed to measure and the unmeasurable factors that can affect students' performances, such as motivation, physical and mental health, or work and family responsibilities.

In spite of these factors, the LSAT compares very favorably with admission tests used in other graduate and professional fields of study. (For additional information about the predictive value of LSAT scores, refer to the 2005–2006 edition of the *LSAT & LSDAS Information Book*.)

Test Preparation

Most law school applicants familiarize themselves with test directions and question types, practice on sample tests, and study the information available on test-taking techniques and strategies. Although it is difficult to say when examinees are sufficiently prepared, very few people achieve their full potential without some preparation.

You should be so familiar with the instructions and question types that nothing you see on the test can delay or distract you from thinking about how to answer a question. At a minimum, you should review the descriptions of the question types in the *LSAT & LSDAS Information Book* and on LSAC's website and simulate the day of the test by taking a practice test that includes a writing sample under actual time constraints. Taking a practice test under timed conditions helps you to estimate the amount of time you can afford to spend on each question in a section and to determine the question types for which you may need additional practice.

LSAC publishes a variety of materials to help you prepare for the LSAT. See the ad toward the back of this book, or visit LSAC's website—*www.LSAC.org*.

Academic Record

Undergraduate performance is generally an important indicator of how someone is likely to perform in law school. Hence, many law schools look closely at college grades when considering individual applications.

Course selection also can make a difference in admission evaluations. Applicants who have taken difficult or advanced courses in their undergraduate study often are evaluated in a more favorable light than students who have concentrated on easier or less advanced subjects.

Many law schools consider undergraduate-performance trends along with a student's numerical average. Thus, they may discount a slow start in a student's undergraduate career if he or she performs exceptionally well in the later school years. Similarly, admission committees may see an undergraduate's strong start followed by a mediocre finish as an indication of less potential to do well in law school. Candidates are advised to comment on irregular grade trends in their personal statement.

Grade Conversion Table

LSDAS Conversion				Grades as Reported on Transcripts	
4.0 Scale	A to F	1 to 5	100-0*	Four Passing Grades	Three Passing Grades
4.33	A+	1+	98-100	Highest Passing Grade (4.0)	Highest Passing Grade (4.0)
4.00	A	1	93-97		
3.67	A-	1-	90-92		
3.50	AB				
3.33	B+	2+	87-89	Second Highest Passing Grade (3.0)	Middle Passing Grade (3.0)
3.00	B	2	83-86		
2.67	B-	2-	80-82		
2.50	BC				
2.33	C+	3+	77-79	Third Highest Passing Grade (2.0)	Lowest Passing Grade (2.0)
2.00	C	3	73-76		
1.67	C-	3-	70-72		
1.50	CD				
1.33	D+	4+	67-69	Lowest Passing Grade (1.0)	
1.00	D	4	63-66		
0.67	D-	4-	60-62		
0.50	DE or DF				
0.00	E and F	5	Below 60	Failure (0.0)	Failure (0.0)

*In some instances, a school's numeric grading scale might be converted differently than shown here.

■ Additional Admission Decision Factors

Law schools consider more than academic records and LSAT scores when evaluating applicants. Some of the most important factors are discussed below.

Letters of Recommendation

The most effective letters of recommendation are those from professors who have known you well enough to write with candor, detail, and objectivity about your academic and personal achievements and potential. Work supervisors also can write in support of your application. Letters that compare you to your academic peers are often considered the most useful. Most schools do not consider general, unreservedly praiseworthy letters helpful. Some schools do not require letters at all, and some of those schools will not read letters of recommendation if they receive them.

Work Experience

Law schools want diverse, interesting classes, representative of a variety of backgrounds. A candidate who applies to law school several years after completing his or her undergraduate education, and who has demonstrated an ability to succeed in a nonacademic environment, is sometimes more motivated than one who continues his or her education without a break. In fact, only about 40 percent of law students enter directly from college.

Interviews

In general, interviews are not a part of the law school admission process. You are encouraged to visit law schools to gather information, and often an appointment with admission personnel will be a part of the visit. The purpose of your conversation with the admission staff usually will be informational rather than evaluative and will not become a part of your admission file. An occasional school will grant an interview, and some may even request it, but, in general, you should not count on an interview as a means to state your case for admission; this is best done in the personal statement.

Graduate or Professional Study

Prior success or failure in other graduate or professional school work, including other law schools, may also be a factor in the admission committee's decision. In any case, you are required to report such work to any law school to which you apply.

Minority Applicants

Ethnic diversity is essential to the study of law, and greatly benefits the law class, the law school, and the legal profession. All law schools actively seek students who are members of minority groups and strongly encourage minority applicants. (See chapter 6 for further details on minority recruitment and enrollment.)

International Applicants

Students from other countries are enrolled at US law schools, most frequently in graduate programs (usually called LLM programs) that are designed to meet the needs of people who already hold a recognized law degree from another country but want to learn about the legal system of the United States.

Procedures and requirements for foreign applicants for the JD or LLM programs vary from school to school. You should contact the individual schools that interest you to learn about each school's particular requirements. Most schools will ask applicants for whom English is not their native language to take a standardized test such as the Test of English as a Foreign Language (TOEFL) or the Test of Written English (TWE). Each school sets its own standard for required minimal scores on the tests.

Some schools may use a credential-evaluation service to translate documents, inspect them for authenticity, and evaluate a student's grades and degrees for US admission committees. The student is responsible for the cost of this service, and some law schools will require you to use a specific service.

For candidates applying to post-JD programs (LLM, SJD, and other similar degrees), the LSAC offers a credential assembly service that collects, authenticates, and distributes all transcripts and TOEFL scores to each law school where the applicant submits an application. Most law schools with post-JD programs for international students subscribe to this service, but candidates should check with individual schools before registering. Detailed information about the service is available at *http://LLM.LSAC.org*.

Foreign students must also demonstrate the ability to pay for schooling in this country in order to apply for a student visa (F-1 form). You may be asked to complete a certification of finances form from the law school; if the school is satisfied that the student can pay, it will issue a form (I-20) to submit to the Immigration and Naturalization Service (INS) as part of your application for a student visa. Because of the time required to process entry visas, international applicants are encouraged to apply for admission as early in the process as possible.

Foreign students may be eligible for institutional grants and loans, but are ineligible for federal loans, and (in most schools) are required to have a US cosigner for private loans. Contact the financial aid office at the schools to which you are applying for more details.

Your Personal Essay

Each candidate to law school has something of interest to present. Maybe you've had some experience, some training, or some dream that sets you apart from others. Law schools want to recruit men and women who are qualified for reasons beyond grades and scores. The essay or personal statement in your application is the place to tell the committee about yourself.

In general, your evaluation of actual experiences and past accomplishments has more value to the committee than speculation about future accomplishments. Also, if you have overcome a serious obstacle in your life to get where you are today, by all means let the admission committee know about it. Any noteworthy personal experience or accomplishment may be an appropriate subject for your essay; however, be sure to do more than just state it. Describe your experience briefly but concretely, and why it had value to you, whether it is a job, your family, a significant accomplishment, or your upbringing. You are simultaneously trying to add information and create structure. Be brief, be factual, be comprehensive, and be organized.

You are a storyteller here. You want a living person—you—to emerge. The statement is your opportunity to become vivid and alive to the reader, and it is an opportunity to demonstrate your ability to write and present a prose sample in a professional manner.

■ Assessing Yourself Realistically

When selecting law schools to which you will apply, the general philosophy is that you should have a threefold plan: dream a little, be realistic, and be safe. Most applicants have no trouble selecting dream schools —those that are almost, but not quite, beyond their grasp—or safe schools—those for which admission is virtually certain. A common strategic error made by applicants is failure to evaluate realistically their chances for admission to a particular law school. The admission data and law school admission profile grids in this book are helpful sources, along with the information at *www.LSAC.org*, because the data are provided by the law schools directly to the ABA and LSAC.

Use the Admission Profile Grids in This Book

Check your qualifications against the admission profiles of the law schools that interest you. Most schools publish a grid that indicates the number of applicants with LSAT scores and GPAs like yours who were admitted in the most recent admission year. This gives you a general sense of your competitiveness at that school. These charts will help you determine which schools are your dream schools, your realistic schools, and your safe schools. If your profile meets or exceeds that of a school, it is likely that that school will be as interested in admitting you as you are in being admitted. Other statistics are contained in the school's ABA data, so that material should be read with care as well. A few words of caution: First, law schools consider many other factors beyond the LSAT score and GPA, as described in the previous section ("Additional Admission Decision Factors"), and the grids and data about these credentials only give you part of the story. Second, you should make your final decision about where you will apply only after obtaining additional qualitative information from each school. Third, the data in the grids are from a previous application year and may not reflect fluctuations in applicant volume that affect admission decisions.

Research Specific Law Schools That Interest You

Other sources of information include:

- **The school's admission office.** This is a good source for general information about the school and your chances for admission. Do not hesitate to request admission counseling. Be sure to obtain current catalogs from each law school you are considering.

- **Your college or university prelaw advisor.** Your prelaw advisor can often provide you with reliable information about which law schools fit your personal profile. He or she may also be able to tell you which law schools have accepted students from your school in the past and provide you with an overview of the admitted students' credentials. This will help you to determine how law schools have treated applicants from your school in the recent past.

- **Law School Forums.** The Law School Forums, organized by the Law School Admission Council, are excellent opportunities to talk with law school representatives from around the country in one central, urban location—usually a hotel exhibit hall. Recent forums have been held in Atlanta, Boston, Chicago, Dallas, Houston, Los Angeles, New York City, San Francisco Bay Area, and Washington, DC. In 2004, 178 ABA-approved law schools participated in the forums, and 14,100 people registered as attendees. Because the costs of traveling to a number of law schools can be expensive, many prospective law students find the forums to be the most productive means of gathering information and making school contacts. Forum admission is free; for dates and locations of 2005 Law School Forums, see the ad toward the back of this book, or visit LSAC's website—*www.LSAC.org*. Forum preregistration is also available on the LSAC website.

- **School representatives and alumni.** Take advantage of opportunities to talk with law school representatives and alumni. When you talk with alumni, remember that law schools sometimes change fairly quickly. Try to talk to a recent graduate or to one who is active in alumni affairs and therefore knowledgeable about the school as it is today.

- **School visits.** Law schools encourage you to visit. You can learn a surprising amount about a school from talks with students and faculty members. Many law schools have formal programs in which a currently enrolled student will take you on a tour of the campus and answer your questions. Such a firsthand experience can be quite valuable in assessing how you would fit into the school.

- **The Internet.** The websites of LSAC—*www.LSAC.org* —and the ABA—*www.abanet.org/legaled*—provide links to the websites of ABA-approved law schools.

Keep Your Options Open

Flexibility is a key word in the law school admission process. Keep your options open. Even during the early stages of the admission process, you should continually reevaluate your prospects and prepare alternative plans. For example, don't set your sights on only one law school and one plan of action. You could severely limit your potential and your chance to practice law.

Chapter 4: Applying to Law School

■ Working with LSAC: Registering for the LSAT and the LSDAS

The Law School Admission Council (LSAC) administers the LSAT and serves as a liaison for much of the communication between you and the law schools. The LSDAS provides a means of centralizing and standardizing undergraduate academic records to simplify the law school admission process. The LSDAS prepares a report for each law school to which you apply. LSDAS registration includes law school report preparation, letter of recommendation and transcript processing, and access to electronic applications for all ABA-approved law schools.

Comprehensive information about the LSAT and LSDAS can be found at the LSAC website, *www.LSAC.org*. The quickest and easiest way to register for both the LSAT and the LSDAS is online. If you need to obtain a paper registration form, call 215.968.1001.

Planning Ahead for Law School Deadlines

Most law schools have a variety of application requirements and deadlines that you must meet to be considered for admission. If you are applying to a number of schools, the various deadlines and requirements can be confusing. It probably will be helpful if you set up a detailed calendar that will remind you of when and what you must do to complete your applications.

In registering for the LSAT, be sure to give yourself enough time to select a convenient testing location and prepare for the test. You also should determine whether each law school in which you are interested will accept scores from the February LSAT administration, which is the last test date in each admission cycle.

Below is a chart listing all scheduled test administrations, including alternate dates for Saturday Sabbath observers, along with corresponding deadlines and fees.

■ Basic LSAT Date and Deadline Information (2005–2006)

All scheduled administrations of the LSAT, both for regular test takers and test takers who are Saturday Sabbath observers, are listed below along with corresponding regular registration deadlines. Dates shown represent postmark deadlines for mail registrations and receipt deadlines for telephone and online registration. The basic fee for the LSAT is $115 (published test centers only). For complete information on deadlines and fees for late registrations and nonpublished test centers (domestic and foreign), partial refunds, and early score reporting, please refer to LSAC's website at *www.LSAC.org*. You can also find information in the current *LSAT & LSDAS Information Book*, or call LSAC at 215.968.1001.

	Test Dates			
■ Regular	Monday, June 6, 2005	Saturday, Oct. 1, 2005	Saturday, Dec. 3, 2005	Saturday, Feb. 4, 2006 Nondisclosed*
■ Saturday Sabbath Observers		Thursday, Sept. 29, 2005 Nondisclosed*	Monday, Dec. 5, 2005 Nondisclosed*	Monday, Feb. 6, 2006 Nondisclosed*
■ Score by E-mail	June 27, 2005	Oct. 24, 2005	Jan. 3, 2006	Feb. 27, 2006
■ Score Report mailed (approx.)	July 5, 2005	Oct. 31, 2005	Jan. 5, 2006	March 3, 2006
Regular Registration Deadline (mail, telephone, and online)				
■ Domestic	May 3, 2005	Aug. 30, 2005	Nov. 1, 2005	Jan. 3, 2006
■ Foreign	April 29, 2005	Aug. 26, 2005	Oct. 28, 2005	Dec. 30, 2005

*Persons who take a nondisclosed test receive only their scores. They do not receive their test questions, answer key, or individual responses.

◼ The Law School Data Assembly Service (LSDAS)

The LSDAS provides a means of centralizing and standardizing undergraduate academic records to simplify the law school admission process (for US law schools only). Nearly all American Bar Association-approved law schools (and some non-ABA-approved schools) require that applicants use the Law School Data Assembly Service. Canadian law schools do not participate in the LSDAS and do not require its use.

The LSDAS prepares a report for each law school to which you apply. There is a registration fee for the LSDAS, as well as a fee for each law school report (go to *www.LSAC.org* for current fees). Your LSDAS registration includes law school report preparation, letter of recommendation and transcript processing, and access to electronic applications for all ABA-approved law schools.

The law school report contains information that the schools use, along with your application, personal essay, letters of recommendation, and other criteria, to make their admission decisions. Information contained in the report includes

- an undergraduate academic summary;

- copies of all undergraduate, graduate, and law/professional school transcripts;

- LSAT scores and writing sample copies; and

- copies of letters of recommendation processed by LSAC.

Fee Waivers

Fee waivers are available for the LSAT, LSDAS, and *Official LSAT SuperPrep*. For US citizens, US nationals, or permanent resident aliens of the United States with an Alien Registration Receipt Card (I-151 or I-551), fee waivers can be authorized by LSAC or LSAC-member law schools, which are listed on our website and in the *Information Book*. Canadian citizens must submit their fee waiver request to a Canadian LSAC-member law school even if they plan to apply for admission to a US law school. Fee waivers cannot be granted by financial aid offices of undergraduate institutions, non-LSAC-member law schools, prelaw advisors, or any other individual or organization. Go to *www.LSAC.org* or any ABA-approved law school admission office for additional information about fee waivers.

◼ The Admission Process

Law school applicants can expect that the admission process will be competitive. Nationally, there are more applicants than spaces available in first-year classes, and this means that, at some law schools, there will be considerable competition for seats. However, it is probably true that, if you assess your credentials accurately, your likelihood of admission to an ABA-accredited law school is strong.

The Importance of Complete Files

Remember that law schools require complete files before making their decisions. A law school will consider your file complete when it has received your application form, LSDAS Law School Report (or LSAT Law School Report if the law school does not require the LSDAS), letters of recommendation (if required), any requirements unique to the particular school, and application fee.

Rolling Admission

Many law schools operate what is known as a rolling admission process: The school evaluates applications and informs candidates of admission decisions on a continuous basis over several months, usually beginning in late fall and extending to midsummer for waiting-list admissions.

Even if you have not yet taken the LSAT, it might be helpful to submit your application early so that your LSDAS file can be sent to law schools as soon as your test score is available. The earlier you apply, the more places the school is likely to have available. Most schools try to make comparable decisions throughout the admission season, even those that practice rolling admission. Still, it is disadvantageous to be one of the last applicants to complete a file. Furthermore, the more decisions you receive from law schools early in the process, the better able you will be to make your own decisions, such as whether to apply to more law schools or whether to accept a particular school's offer.

Applying to More Than One School

The average applicant applies to 5.3 law schools. You should be sure to place your applications at schools representing a range of admission standards. Even if you have top qualifications, you should apply to at least one safety school where you are almost certain of being admitted. This is your insurance policy. If you apply to a safety school in November, and are accepted in January or February, you may be disappointed but not panicked if you are later denied admission by your top choices.

The Preliminary Review of an Application

Applicants whose qualifications more than fulfill the school's admission standards are usually accepted by an admission committee during the first round of decisions. Candidates whose credentials fall below the school's standards are usually denied admission.

Most applications are not decided upon immediately. They are usually reviewed by a committee that bases its admission decision on many facets of each application (see "How Law Schools Determine Whom to Admit," page 10).

The length of time it takes the committee to review an application varies; consult the individual law schools to which you apply.

Waiting Lists

If you have strong qualifications, but you do not quite meet the competition of those currently being admitted at a particular law school, you may be placed on a waiting list for possible admission at a later date. The law school will send you a letter notifying you of its final decision as early as April or as late as July.

Many schools rank students who are on the waiting list. Some law schools will tell you your rank. If a law school doesn't tell you, you might ask the admission office how many students have been placed on the waiting list.

Seat Deposits

Many law schools use seat deposits to help keep track of their new classes. For example, a typical fee is $200, which is credited to your first-term tuition if you actually register at the school; if you don't register, the deposit may be forfeited or partially returned. A school may require a larger deposit around July 1, which is also credited to tuition. If you decline the offer of admission after you've paid your deposit, a portion of the money may be refunded, depending on the date you actually decline the offer. At some schools, you may not be refunded any of the deposit.

The official position of the Law School Admission Council is:

Except under early decision plans, no law school should require an enrollment commitment of any kind, binding or non-binding, to an offer of admission or scholarship prior to April 1. Admitted applicants who have submitted a timely financial aid application should not be required to commit to enroll by having to make a nonrefundable financial commitment until notified of financial aid awards that are within the control of the law school.

Ethical Conduct in Applying for Law School

The practice of law is an honorable, noble calling. Lawyers play an important role in society by serving both their clients' needs and the public good. Your submission of an application for admission to law school is your first step in the process of becoming a lawyer. Now is the time, as you take this first, important step, to dedicate yourself to a personal standard for your conduct that consists of the highest levels of honesty and ethical behavior.

The legal profession requires its members to behave ethically in the practice of law at all times, in order to protect the interests of clients and the public. You must understand that those who aspire to join the legal profession will be held to the same high standards for truth, full disclosure, and accuracy that are applied to those who practice law. The legal profession has set standards for ethical conduct by lawyers through the adoption of the Model Rules of Professional Conduct and the Code of Professional Responsibility by the American Bar Association (ABA). Similarly, law schools have set standards for ethical conduct by law school applicants through the Law School Admission Council (LSAC). These standards are known as the *LSAC Rules Governing Misconduct and Irregularities in the Admission Process*. Just as lawyers are required to study, understand, and comply with the ABA's ethical standards, law school applicants are expected to read, understand, and comply with LSAC's ethical standards.

If you fail to comply with LSAC's ethical standards, you may be barred from admission to law school. If you fail to disclose required information on your law school application, or if you engage in misconduct during the admission process that is discovered after you enroll in law school or start to practice law, you may face more serious sanctions. Take the time, right now, to read LSAC's statement on misconduct and irregularities in the admission process presented below.

Misconduct and Irregularities in the Admission Process

The Law School Admission Council has established procedures for dealing with instances of possible candidate misconduct or irregularities on the LSAT or in the law school admission process. Misconduct or irregularity in the admission process is a serious offense with serious consequences. Intent is not an element of a finding of misconduct or irregularity. Misconduct or irregularity is defined as the submission, as part of the law school admission process, including, but not limited to, regular, transfer, and visiting applications, of any information that is false, inconsistent, or misleading, or the omission of information that may result in a false or misleading conclusion, or the violation of any regulation governing the law school admission process, including any violation of LSAT test center regulations.

Examples of misconduct and irregularities include, but are not limited to, submission of an altered or a nonauthentic transcript; submission of an application containing false, inconsistent, or misleading information; submission of an altered, nonauthentic, or unauthorized letter of recommendation; falsification of records; impersonation of another in taking the LSAT; switching of LSAT answer sheets with another; taking the LSAT for purposes other than applying to law school; copying on, or other forms of cheating on, the LSAT; obtaining advance access to test materials; theft of test materials; working, marking, erasing, reading, or turning pages on sections of the LSAT during unauthorized times; submission of false, inconsistent, or misleading information to the Law School Data Assembly Service (LSDAS); false, inconsistent, or misleading statements or omissions of information requested on the LSAT & LSDAS Registration Form or on individual law school application forms; falsification of transcript information, school attendance, honors, awards, or employment; or providing false, inconsistent, or misleading information in the financial aid/scholarship application process. A charge of misconduct or irregularity may be made prior to a candidate's admission to law school, after matriculation at a law school, or after admission to practice.

When alleged misconduct or irregularity brings into question the validity of LSAC data about a candidate,

the school may be notified of possible data error, and transmission of LSAT scores and LSDAS reports will be withheld until the matter has been resolved by the Law School Admission Council's Misconduct and Irregularities in the Admission Process Subcommittee. The Council will investigate all instances of alleged misconduct or irregularities in the admission process in accordance with the *LSAC Rules Governing Misconduct and Irregularities in the Admission Process.*

A subcommittee representative will determine whether misconduct or an irregularity has occurred. If the subcommittee representative determines that a preponderance of the evidence shows misconduct or irregularity, then a report of the determination is sent to all law schools to which the individual has applied, subsequently applies, or has matriculated. Notation that a misconduct or irregularity report is on file is also included on LSAT & LSDAS Law School Reports. Such reports are retained indefinitely. In appropriate cases, state and national bar authorities and other affected persons and institutions may also receive notification. Individual law schools and bar authorities determine what action, if any, they will take in response to a finding of misconduct or irregularity. Such action may include the closing of an admission file, revocation of an offer of admission, dismissal from law school through a school's internal disciplinary channels, or disbarment. Thus, a finding of misconduct or irregularity is a very serious matter. More information regarding misconduct and irregularity procedures may be obtained by writing to: Law School Admission Council Misconduct and Irregularities in the Admission Process Subcommittee 662 Penn Street, Box 40, Newtown, PA 18940-0040.

Chapter 5: Choosing a Law School

For some people, the choice of which law school to attend is an easy one. Applicants tend to select the schools they perceive to be the most prestigious or those which offer a program of particular interest, or the greatest amount of financial support. Some need to stay in a particular area perhaps because of family or job obligations, and will choose nearby schools with part-time programs.

However, the majority of applicants will have to weigh a variety of personal and academic factors to come up with a list of potential schools. Once you have a list, and more than one acceptance letter, you will have to choose a school. Applicants should consider carefully the offerings of each law school before making a decision. The quality of a law school is certainly a major consideration; however,

estimations of quality are very subjective. Factors such as the campus atmosphere, the school's devotion to teaching and learning, and the applicant's enthusiasm for the school also are very important. Remember that the law school is going to be your home for three years. Adjusting to law school and the general attitudes of a professional school is difficult enough without the additional hardship of culture shock. Don't choose a law school in a large city if you can't bear crowds, noise, and a fast pace. And, if you've lived your entire life in an urban environment, can you face the change you will experience in a small town? You also may want to ask yourself if you are already set in an unshakable lifestyle or if you are eager for a new environment.

■ Ranking Law Schools

Law Schools and Reputation

Many people will tell you to apply to the schools that take students in your GPA and LSAT ranges, and then enroll in the best one that accepts you. Law school quality can be assessed in a number of ways.

There is a hierarchy of law schools based on reputation, job placement success, strength of faculty, and the prestige of the parent institution (if there is one). In fact, a study done at one university suggests that undergraduate students perceive schools not only in terms of a hierarchy but also in terms of hierarchical clusters. In other words, certain schools are grouped together in terms of equivalent quality and prestige. Also, there are books or magazine articles that assign law schools purported numerical quality rankings.

However, according to the ABA:

> No rating of law schools beyond the simple statement of their accreditation status is attempted or advocated by the official organizations in legal education. Qualities that make one kind of school good for one student may not be as important to another. The American Bar Association and its Section of Legal Education and Admissions to the Bar have issued disclaimers of any law school rating system. Prospective law students should consider a variety of factors in making their choice among schools.[1]

Since there is no official ranking authority, you should be cautious in using such rankings. The factors that make up a law school's reputation—strength of curriculum, faculty, career services, ability of students, quality of library facilities, and the like—don't lend themselves to quantification. Even if the rankings were

more or less accurate, the school's reputation is only one factor among many for you to consider.

What's in a Name?

While going to a "name" school may mean that you will have an easier time finding your first job, it doesn't necessarily mean that you will get a better legal education than if you go to a lesser-known law school. Some schools that were at their peaks years ago are still riding on the wave of that earlier reputation. Others have greatly improved their programs and have recruited talented faculty but have not yet made a name for themselves.

Once admitted, applicants should consider a variety of factors, such as the contacts you may acquire at a school in the area where you hope to practice, the size of the school, and cost. The substantive differences between schools should be your focus when making this important choice rather than the school's reputed ranking.

The Parent University

About 90 percent of ABA-approved law schools are part of a larger university. The reputation of an undergraduate school may influence the reputation of the law school so you might want to investigate the college before committing to the law school.

In addition, there may be some advantages to attending a law school that is part of a university. Such law schools may have more options for joint-degree programs or for taking a non-law school course or two. They also may have more academic and social activities, campus theater groups, sports teams, and everything else that comes with university life. Perhaps most important, the university can act as a support system for the law school by providing a wealth of facilities, including student housing and support for career services.

National, Regional, and Local Schools

A national school will generally have an applicant population and a student body that draws almost indistinguishably from the nation as a whole and will have many international students as well. A regional school is likely to have a population that is primarily from the geographic region of its location, though many regional schools have students from all over the country; a number of regional schools draw heavily from a particular geographical area, yet graduates may find jobs all over the country. Generally speaking, a local school is drawing primarily on applicants who either come from or want to practice in the proximate area in which the school is located. Many local law schools have excellent reputations and compete with the national schools in faculty competence, in research-supporting activities, and in resources generally. Check the school's catalog or talk with the admission and placement staff to get a clear breakdown on where their students come from and where they are finding jobs.

[1] The American Bar Association Standards for Approval of Law Schools, General Information of the Council for the Section of Legal Education and Admissions to the Bar, Number 8, "Rating of Law Schools," p. 146, American Bar Association, Chicago, IL, 2001

■ Evaluating Law Schools

The best advice on how to select a law school is to choose the school that is best for you. The law schools invest substantial time and effort in evaluating prospective students, and applicants should evaluate law schools with equivalent care. The following are some features to keep in mind as you systematically evaluate law schools. (Costs and other financial criteria are not included below; they are discussed in chapter 9.)

Each listing in this guide provides school-specific information in the following categories as well.

Enrollment/Student Body

The academic qualifications of the student body are important to consider. It's a good idea to select a law school where you will be challenged by your classmates. Use the admission profile grids in this book to check the LSAT scores and GPAs for the previous year's entering class. Try to select a school where your averages will not be significantly different from those of your fellow law students. Because of the important role of student participation in law school classes, your legal education might not be as rewarding as it could be if you are not challenged by your classmates.

You might also inquire about the diversity of the student body. Are a majority of the students the same age, race, sex, and so on? Remember, differences among students will expose you to various points of view; this will be an important aspect of your law school education.

Find out how many students are in a typical class. Much of the learning in law school depends on the quality of class discussion. Small classes provide essential interaction; large classes (and the Socratic method) provide diversity, challenge, and a good mix of reactions, opinions, and criticism.

It is also important to find out the total number of students enrolled at the school. Not surprisingly, the larger law schools tend to offer a larger selection of courses. Of course, more doesn't always mean better, and no one student has time to take all the courses offered at a large school. However, if you think you want to sample a wide range of courses, you are apt to have more opportunity to do so at a law school with a large faculty.

Part of the law school learning experience takes place after class with fellow students and with members of the faculty. Check to see whether faculty and students are on campus for a substantial part of the day.

Larger schools may also offer more extracurricular programs, greater student services, and a larger library. However, faculties and administrators at smaller schools may be able to give students more attention, and students at smaller schools may experience greater camaraderie. The size of a school is a personal consideration. Some students thrive in large schools; others prefer a smaller student community. Ask yourself which kind of student you are.

Faculty

You will undoubtedly want to assess the faculties of the law schools you are considering. School catalogs will give you some idea of the backgrounds of the full-time faculty—what specialties they have, what they have published, and their public service activities. If the catalog tells you only where degrees were earned, ask for more information. You may also want to check the latest edition of the Association of American Law Schools' *Directory of Law Teachers*, which is available at law school libraries. It may help you to know that some members of the faculty have interests similar to your own.

Is the faculty relatively diverse with respect to race, ethnic background, gender, degrees in other fields, and breadth of experience? A faculty with diverse backgrounds will have various points of view and experiences. This diversity will enrich your legal education, broaden your own point of view, and help prepare you for the variety of clients you will work with after law school.

How many full-time professors teach how many students—that is, what is the faculty/student ratio?

Although some of the most prestigious law schools are famous for their large sections in the introductory courses, they also provide smaller classes, clinics, simulations, and seminars in advanced subjects. According to the *ABA Standards: Rules of Procedure for Approval of Law Schools*, it is not favorable to have a full-time faculty to full-time student ratio of 30 to 1 or more.

Are some of the teachers recognized as authorities in their respective fields through their writings and professional activities? Law school catalogs and websites vary widely regarding information about faculty. Some merely list each faculty member's name along with schools attended and degrees earned. Others may provide details about publications, professional activities, and noteworthy achievements, particularly when an individual is an authority in his or her field.

Are there visiting professors, distinguished lecturers and visitors, symposiums and the like at the schools you are considering? Law school lectureship programs are a good means of presenting the knowledge and views of academics outside of the particular law school you attend.

The Library and Other Physical Facilities

Chances are you will spend more time in the library than anywhere else, so take stock of the library before you enroll. There are several factors to consider when assessing a law school library: the quality of its holdings, cataloging methods, access to electronic databases, participation in library networks for information retrieval, staff, facilities, and the hours the library is available to students.

Whether it has 250,000 volumes or 2.5 million volumes tells you little about the actual usefulness of the library. It may have an unfathomable number of volumes, but many of them may be outdated, irrelevant, or not readily available to students. All ABA-approved law schools must maintain a library that has the research materials considered essential for the study of law. Beyond that, find out if the school has any special collections, subscribes to computerized legal research services, or participates in interlibrary loan networks. Also, find out how many copies of essential materials are available, particularly for large classes.

Find out about the quality of the library's professional staff. Is there an adequate number of reference librarians for the number of students and faculty being served? Is the staff helpful?

Be sure the library has an adequate number of comfortable seats with at least enough carrels to accommodate a reasonable number of students at any given time. Either in the library or elsewhere in the law building, there should be suitable space for group study and other forms of collaborative work.

Because you will need to spend much of your time in the library, make sure its hours will accommodate just about any schedule you might have. While it is not necessary for a library to be open around the clock, it should be open before classes begin each day and remain open well into the night with a professional library staff on hand to assist students.

Access to technology should not only be available in the library, but throughout the law building, so that students can use computers to retrieve information outside the actual library space.

Curriculum

The range and quality of academic programs is one of the most important factors to consider when choosing a law school.

Almost all law schools follow the traditional first-year core curriculum of civil procedure, criminal law, contracts, legal research and writing, torts, and property (see chapter 2). Do not assume that all law schools have programs that suit your personal needs and special interests. If you don't have any specific interests in mind—and many beginning students don't—try to make sure the school offers a wide range of electives so that you will have many options. A thorough grounding in basic legal theory will enable you to apply the principles learned to any area of law to which they pertain.

In fact, you shouldn't overemphasize your search for specialties; most law students are not specialists when they graduate, nor do they need to be. Generally speaking, new lawyers begin to find their specialties only in the second to fifth years of their careers. A well-rounded legal education is the best preparation for almost any career path you take. The schools' catalogs and the descriptions in this book will tell you a good deal about academic programs. You may also wish to ask school representatives questions such as: Does the school offer a variety of courses, or is it especially strong in certain areas; what sizes are the classes; are seminars and small-group classroom experiences available; and are there ample opportunities for developing writing, researching, and drafting skills?

Beyond the content of law school courses, other academic program considerations may be of interest to you as a prospective law student.

Special Programs and Academic Activities

Joint-Degree Programs

Joint-degree programs allow you to pursue law school and graduate degrees simultaneously. Almost every combination is available at some institutions. Among the more popular degrees are the JD/MBA and the JD/MA in such areas as economics or political science. For details, check the individual school listings in this book or check the law school's recruitment materials.

Master of Laws (LLM) Programs and Special-Degree Programs

Many law schools offer advanced degrees that allow students to take graduate-level law courses. The LLM degree is quite common and usually is tailored to individual interests. Some schools offer master of laws degrees with particular concentrations, such as a master of laws in taxation and master of comparative law. Students may enroll in LLM programs only after having received the JD degree.

A few schools also offer very specific, special-degree programs. Some of these specialties include a Doctorate in Civil Law, Doctor of Juridical Science, and Doctor of Jurisprudence and Social Policy. Finding out what types of advanced degrees a law school offers may help you determine the emphases of the school. (See appendix B for a listing of post-JD programs.)

Part-Time and Evening Programs

Part-time programs may be offered either in the evening or the day. For the past 10 years, approximately 17 percent of law students have been enrolled in part-time programs. The conventional wisdom is that if you are financially able to attend law school full-time, you ought to do so.

Part-time programs generally take four years to complete instead of three years. If you wish to enroll in such a program, you may be limiting your choice of law schools somewhat, since less than half of the law schools offer part-time programs.

Clinical Programs and Moot Court Competitions

Many law schools offer students authentic experiences as lawyers by involving them with clients and providing opportunities to rehearse trial and appellate advocacy in trial team and moot court competitions. It is important that students become adept at using interviewing, counseling, research, advocacy, and negotiation skills.

The best clinical programs involve students in actual legal situations, simulations of such situations, or a combination of both, either at the school itself or in the community. Clinical programs at some schools offer a team-teaching approach; practical, professional skills are taught along with traditional classroom theory. In this manner, faculty can advise and work closely with students.

Student Journals

Most law schools have a law review—a journal of scholarly articles and commentaries on the law—and other student-edited scholarly journals. Writing for the journals of a school can be important to both your legal education and your career in law. Thus, evaluating the journals at a particular law school may be worthwhile when trying to choose the right school to attend.

Traditionally, student journal editors are chosen on the basis of academic standing, but writing ability, regardless of class rank, may also be a criterion. Today, a growing number of schools select journal editors by holding a competition in which students submit a previously assigned writing sample to the current editorial board. If you are on a journal, employers may assume you are either one of the brightest in your class, or an outstanding writer—or both.

If possible, check the journals of the schools you are considering. The character of the journal may be a reflection of the character of the institution that supports it.

Order of the Coif

Many law schools have a chapter of the Order of the Coif, a national honor society for outstanding students. Students are elected to Coif on the basis of scholarship and character. Check to see if the schools you are considering include such a chapter.

Academic Support Programs

Programs for students who need or who are expected to need assistance with legal analysis and writing are offered by most law schools. Students are invited to participate in these programs on the basis of either their entering credentials or their actual law school performance. This assistance may be offered in the summer prior to beginning law school, during the academic year, or both. The aim of academic support programs is to ensure that students have an equal opportunity to compete in law school. For further information about academic assistance programs, consult the admission office at the law school.

Student Organizations

You can also tell something about a law school's intellectual resources and its students by the number and range of student associations and organizations sponsored on campus. Many schools have chapters of the American Bar Association-Law Student Division; a student bar association; associations for minority groups, such as the Asian, Black, Hispanic, and Native American law student associations; and associations based on religious affiliations. Some, but not all, schools sponsor an environmental law society, a gay and lesbian law student society, a legal assistance society, a postconviction assistance project, an ACLU group, a federalist society, a volunteer income-tax assistance program, a law student spouses' club, an international law society, a law and technology society, or a client-counseling society. Determine which associations are important to you and check individual law school catalogs to see which law schools offer what you need.

Career Services and Employment

One of the tests of a good law school is the effort the institution makes to help its students and graduates understand their career options and find satisfying employment. Planning a career in law requires students to integrate their legal education and personal goals in the context of the employment marketplace. Some students begin law school with a clear idea of how they expect to use their legal education (although they may change their minds along the way). Others are uncertain, or see a number of tempting possibilities. The career services office, faculty, and alumni of the school are valuable resources in the process of understanding and selecting among the many opportunities available to lawyers.

The first role of the career services office is to educate students about career opportunities in all sectors, including government and public service, law firms of all sizes and specialties, corporations, and so forth. To accomplish such a task, a law school may arrange panel presentations, meetings with practicing lawyers in different fields, and a library of career information materials. Career services professionals also collect and distribute vital information and resources, teach students job-search strategies, such as effective interviewing skills and employment research, and discuss students' individual interests, options, and presentation.

In performing all of these tasks, the career services office becomes a major marketing and outreach program for its law school and a valuable resource for both law students and graduates as they chart their career paths. One of the most visible career services provided by many law schools is the opportunity to interview with employers on campus for summer and full-time jobs. Ideally, the recruiters should represent a broad range of legal options (small and large firms, government agencies, public interest groups, corporate law departments) and sufficient geographic diversity to meet your needs. Be aware that the number of recruiters at the law school does not necessarily reflect the range of options open to students.

In most schools, only a small percentage of the class gets jobs through on-campus interviewing. Therefore, it is important to investigate the additional support provided by the career services staff and the experiences of the school's students and graduates in finding jobs.

Career services offices are concerned about all students, not just those at the top of the class rankings. Most spend a great deal of time and effort working with students individually and marketing the school to potential employers in order to increase students' options. Here are some questions you may want to ask about a school's career services:

- What programs does the school offer to introduce students to career options? Do they seem interesting, relevant, and timely?

- Are the career-counseling professionals accessible, respected, well-qualified, and supportive?

- Are the school's faculty and graduates involved in educating students about their career options?

- What types of employers, and how many, recruit on-campus each year? What are the average number of interviews and offers per student? What percentage of students obtain jobs through the on-campus interviewing process?

- What positions have graduates taken in recent years? What jobs do students take during the summers? In what locales do students and graduates work? Are these employment profiles changing?

- What are the average or median salaries for the school's graduates?

- What percentage of students have accepted positions by graduation; within six months of graduation?

- Does the school offer career counseling and information for its graduates?

Chapter 6: Opportunities in Law for Minority Men and Women

■ A Career in Law for Minority Group Members

The legal profession is cognizant of the minority exclusion and underrepresentation that has historically pervaded American society. The legal system, which greatly values and benefits from multicultural perspectives, acknowledges the importance of diverse legal representation. A law career provides a singular opportunity to effect change both on an individual level—by representing the interests of a client—and on a global level—by setting policy or establishing a precedent in the governmental or business arenas.

Although minority participation in law school and the legal profession has increased over the last three decades, more can and is being done to attract minority men and women to the profession. Outreach efforts by the legal system can and do counteract the shortage of minority lawyers. So does the realization on the part of minority men and women that law can be a rewarding and fulfilling career.

Acquiring a Legal Education

Individual law schools and legal organizations have worked hard to assure continued progress toward alleviating the historic shortage of minority lawyers. For example, the Law School Admission Council established a Minority Affairs Committee, which thus far has spent in excess of $3 million on projects designed to increase the number of minority men and women who attend law schools. The American Bar Association adopted a law school standard calling for specific commitments to provide full opportunities for members of minority groups. The Association of American Law Schools also requires that member schools provide full opportunities in legal education for minorities and has programs to increase the number of minority faculty.

A legal education can provide you with considerable opportunity. You will have spent approximately three years thinking critically, reading broadly, and debating forcefully, and these skills are worthwhile in most everything you do.

Admission to Law School

Admission to law school is competitive—sometimes very competitive. However, getting into law school may be less difficult than you expect. Because there are many law schools and varied admission requirements, it is advisable for you to do sufficient research and be selective. Read and reread the information in this book and study law school catalogs.

Get advice from as many people as you can, including a prelaw advisor, an academic counselor, a minority affairs advisor, and a practicing lawyer.

Let the law schools you have selected know that you are interested. Often a school will have a specific program, a minority organization, designated personnel, or a law student to provide assistance for minority applicants.

Don't be intimidated by the law school admission process. The schools take all aspects of candidates' applications into account when they evaluate them. Personal and educational background are considered, as are undergraduate records, LSAT scores, and letters of recommendation. It is to your advantage to include information on your racial or ethnic identity (even if not requested on the application); such information helps to present a complete picture of you. Similarly, interesting life experiences and past employment experiences also count.

For information on the number and percentages of specific minority students and specific minority faculty at ABA-approved law schools, consult the individual school data pages and "Key Facts for Minority Law School Applicants" on the following pages.

Once You Are in Law School

Once you are in law school, you will encounter a difficult but manageable academic program. Very often minority student groups will advise, assist, and support newcomers. Most minority students perform successfully in law school; they are also able to make effective use of their law degrees, whether practicing law or following other career avenues.

	Total # students (Full-time and Part-time)	American Indian/Alaskan Native		Asian/Pacific Islander		Black/African American		Mexican American		Puerto Rican		Hispanic		Total # and % Minority Students		Total Full-time Faculty, Fall	Total Full-time Faculty, Spring	Total # and % Full-time Minority Faculty, Fall		Total # and % Full-time Minority Faculty, Spring		Total # Part-time Minority Faculty, Fall	Total # Part-time Minority Faculty, Spring
	#	#	%	#	%	#	%	#	%	#	%	#	%	#	%	#	#	#	%	#	%	#	#
Alabama																							
Alabama	536	5	0.9	6	1.1	34	6.3	1	0.2	0	0.0	3	0.6	49	9.1	37	40	10	21.3	11	22.0	3	3
Samford	540	4	0.7	4	0.7	30	5.6	0	0.0	0	0.0	5	0.9	43	8.0	22	23	3	13.0	3	12.5	1	2
Arizona																							
Arizona	464	20	4.3	46	9.9	22	4.7	28	6.0	2	0.4	24	5.2	142	30.6	30	30	6	18.8	7	21.9	1	3
Arizona State	594	36	6.1	35	5.9	24	4.0	53	8.9	1	0.2	19	3.2	168	28.3	53	57	8	14.5	8	13.6	0	0
Arkansas																							
Arkansas-Fayetteville	474	11	2.3	15	3.2	68	14.3	1	0.2	0	0.0	5	1.1	100	21.1	29	29	5	16.1	4	12.9	1	1
Arkansas-Little Rock	464	6	1.3	8	1.7	29	6.3	1	0.2	0	0.0	6	1.3	50	10.8	21	23	3	13.0	5	20.0	4	3
California																							
California-Berkeley	880	10	1.1	170	19.3	46	5.2	61	6.9	0	0.0	39	4.4	326	37.0	51	52	7	11.9	7	11.7	3	4
California-Davis	563	4	0.7	130	23.1	15	2.7	49	8.7	0	0.0	14	2.5	212	37.7	35	36	13	37.1	13	36.1	2	4
California-Hastings	1239	4	0.3	307	24.8	24	1.9	41	3.3	4	0.3	34	2.7	414	33.4	45	47	13	28.3	11	22.9	53	29
California-Los Angeles	943	14	1.5	153	16.2	42	4.5	68	7.2	1	0.1	5	0.5	283	30.0	69	68	11	13.9	9	11.7	1	3
California Western	934	10	1.1	96	10.3	19	2.0	51	5.5	3	0.3	22	2.4	201	21.5	38	35	8	19.5	8	21.6	3	1
Chapman	521	4	0.8	97	18.6	5	1.0	16	3.1	1	0.2	15	2.9	138	26.5	22	22	3	13.6	3	13.6	3	6
Golden Gate	853	3	0.4	151	17.7	36	4.2	19	2.2	0	0.0	35	4.1	244	28.6	31	29	10	26.3	10	27.8	13	11
Loyola Marymount	1331	9	0.7	301	22.6	61	4.6	85	6.4	3	0.2	53	4.0	512	38.5	62	63	15	23.4	15	23.1	5	8
Pacific, McGeorge	1104	10	0.9	129	11.7	21	1.9	18	1.6	3	0.3	40	3.6	221	20.0	92	92	12	12.6	11	11.6	3	4
Pepperdine	720	2	0.3	72	10.0	25	3.5	14	1.9	0	0.0	12	1.7	125	17.4	29	27	4	13.8	4	14.8	1	4
San Diego	1030	7	0.7	158	15.3	23	2.2	54	5.2	7	0.7	41	4.0	290	28.2	53	56	6	10.3	6	9.8	3	2
San Francisco	716	4	0.6	119	16.6	43	6.0	26	3.6	3	0.4	28	3.9	223	31.1	32	26	8	25.0	6	23.1	8	6
Santa Clara	976	9	0.9	262	26.8	48	4.9	0	0.0	0	0.0	95	9.7	414	42.4	38	38	8	15.4	10	18.9	2	2
Southern California	630	0	0.0	133	21.1	55	8.7	50	7.9	0	0.0	21	3.3	259	41.1	40	38	4	9.5	4	10.0	11	23

	Total # students (Full-time and Part-time)	American Indian/Alaskan Native		Asian/Pacific Islander		Black/African American		Mexican American		Puerto Rican		Hispanic		Total # and % Minority Students		Total Full-time Faculty, Fall	Total Full-time Faculty, Spring	Total # and % Full-time Minority Faculty, Fall		Total # and % Full-time Minority Faculty, Spring		Total # Part-time Minority Faculty, Fall	Total # Part-time Minority Faculty, Spring
	#	#	%	#	%	#	%	#	%	#	%	#	%	#	%	#	#	#	%	#	%	#	#
Southwestern	967	11	1.1	198	20.5	46	4.8	64	6.6	4	0.4	32	3.3	355	36.7	43	44	8	16.3	10	20.0	6	2
Stanford	514	7	1.4	55	10.7	44	8.6	58	11.3	5	1.0	4	0.8	173	33.7	45	44	10	18.9	11	20.4	0	0
Thomas Jefferson	833	2	0.2	68	8.2	17	2.0	42	5.0	5	0.6	16	1.9	150	18.0	23	26	1	4.3	2	7.7	2	1
Whittier	1006	6	0.6	186	18.5	62	6.2	53	5.3	2	0.2	71	7.1	380	37.8	38	37	5	13.2	5	13.5	4	6
Colorado																							
Colorado	502	15	3.0	36	7.2	20	4.0	20	4.0	2	0.4	8	1.6	101	20.1	25	25	7	28.0	6	24.0	0	0
Denver	1162	56	4.8	65	5.6	66	5.7	64	5.5	0	0.0	0	0.0	251	21.6	62	58	13	20.6	12	20.3	5	8
Connecticut																							
Connecticut	687	4	0.6	44	6.4	40	5.8	5	0.7	17	2.5	36	5.2	146	21.3	42	36	4	8.7	3	7.7	3	2
Quinnipiac	655	2	0.3	20	3.1	12	1.8	0	0.0	0	0.0	10	1.5	44	6.7	32	33	3	8.1	3	7.9	0	1
Yale	581	1	0.2	74	12.7	49	8.4	19	3.3	8	1.4	29	5.0	180	31.0	61	58	11	16.9	10	16.1	5	5
Delaware																							
Widener	1150	1	0.1	56	4.9	66	5.7	0	0.0	0	0.0	12	1.0	135	11.7	41	41	5	9.8	5	9.8	0	3
District of Columbia																							
American	1485	6	0.4	188	12.7	109	7.3	26	1.8	9	0.6	89	6.0	427	28.8	75	75	12	15.8	12	15.8	13	10
Catholic	951	4	0.4	78	8.2	43	4.5	6	0.6	9	0.9	36	3.8	176	18.5	41	42	9	18.4	8	16.0	4	7
District of Columbia	220	1	0.5	14	6.4	71	32.3	0	0.0	2	0.9	14	6.4	102	46.4	15	16	7	46.7	7	43.8	10	10
George Washington	1578	8	0.5	168	10.6	143	9.1	0	0.0	0	0.0	137	8.7	456	28.9	85	87	13	14.0	14	14.7	26	24
Georgetown	1936	4	0.2	187	9.7	179	9.2	11	0.6	6	0.3	70	3.6	457	23.6	102	102	14	13.3	15	14.3	8	3
Howard	518	2	0.4	18	3.5	441	85.1	0	0.0	0	0.0	16	3.1	477	92.1	23	22	20	80.0	19	79.2	14	20
Florida																							
Barry	524	3	0.6	20	3.8	31	5.9	0	0.0	0	0.0	52	9.9	106	20.2	18	20	1	4.8	2	8.7	1	2
Florida	1153	4	0.3	61	5.3	86	7.5	0	0.0	0	0.0	112	9.7	263	22.8	60	66	8	11.9	7	9.6	5	3
Florida A&M	289	2	0.7	6	2.1	109	37.7	0	0.0	0	0.0	37	12.8	154	53.3	16	16	14	70.0	14	70.0	0	0
Florida Coastal	904	12	1.3	16	1.8	77	8.5	2	0.2	2	0.2	28	3.1	137	15.2	36	36	5	13.9	5	13.9	2	2
Florida International	284	1	0.4	9	3.2	30	10.6	0	0.0	0	0.0	120	42.3	160	56.3	14	14	11	55.0	11	50.0	2	4
Florida State	748	7	0.9	33	4.4	50	6.7	0	0.0	3	0.4	63	8.4	156	20.9	46	45	6	13.0	5	11.1	3	1

	Total # students (Full-time and Part-time) #	American Indian/Alaskan Native #	%	Asian/Pacific Islander #	%	Black/African American #	%	Mexican American #	%	Puerto Rican #	%	Hispanic #	%	Total # and % Minority Students #	%	Total Full-time Faculty, Fall #	Total Full-time Faculty, Spring #	Total # and % Full-time Minority Faculty, Fall #	%	Total # and % Full-time Minority Faculty, Spring #	%	Total # Part-time Minority Faculty, Fall #	Total # Part-time Minority Faculty, Spring #
Miami	1186	4	0.3	37	3.1	79	6.7	0	0.0	0	0.0	139	11.7	259	21.8	49	46	10	17.5	11	19.6	17	20
Nova Southeastern	963	2	0.2	29	3.0	68	7.1	7	0.7	18	1.9	168	17.4	292	30.3	49	51	11	20.4	11	19.6	6	7
St. Thomas	721	2	0.3	32	4.4	54	7.5	11	1.5	13	1.8	190	26.4	302	41.9	22	22	3	12.0	3	12.0	15	16
Stetson	931	7	0.8	29	3.1	63	6.8	10	1.1	12	1.3	80	8.6	201	21.6	41	45	6	14.6	6	13.3	3	4
Georgia																							
Emory	685	0	0.0	57	8.3	59	8.6	0	0.0	0	0.0	36	5.3	152	22.2	40	41	4	8.5	5	10.2	3	0
Georgia	690	2	0.3	24	3.5	86	12.5	0	0.0	0	0.0	12	1.7	124	18.0	33	31	2	4.9	2	5.1	1	1
Georgia State	681	4	0.6	35	5.1	66	9.7	0	0.0	0	0.0	15	2.2	120	17.6	33	34	4	11.1	4	10.5	3	6
Mercer	424	4	0.9	13	3.1	36	8.5	1	0.2	2	0.5	1	0.2	57	13.4	25	26	3	12.0	3	11.5	2	2
Hawai'i																							
Hawai'i	324	8	2.5	178	54.9	6	1.9	1	0.3	2	0.6	2	0.6	197	60.8	17	21	6	33.3	8	32.0	9	10
Idaho																							
Idaho	301	3	1.0	16	5.3	4	1.3	4	1.3	0	0.0	1	0.3	28	9.3	17	18	2	11.1	2	10.5	0	0
Illinois																							
Chicago	596	3	0.5	91	15.3	41	6.9	16	2.7	5	0.8	32	5.4	188	31.5	50	47	4	6.6	6	10.3	1	3
Chicago-Kent	1073	5	0.5	91	8.5	56	5.2	18	1.7	5	0.5	24	2.2	199	18.5	65	66	3	4.5	3	4.5	7	8
DePaul	1111	4	0.4	72	6.5	66	5.9	0	0.0	0	0.0	76	6.8	218	19.6	49	51	9	17.3	8	14.8	4	1
Illinois	679	4	0.6	114	16.8	51	7.5	0	0.0	0	0.0	50	7.4	219	32.3	39	39	4	8.7	6	12.5	4	3
John Marshall	1407	6	0.4	79	5.6	66	4.7	27	1.9	2	0.1	33	2.3	213	15.1	55	54	7	12.5	8	14.5	15	17
Loyola-Chicago	847	2	0.2	69	8.1	44	5.2	11	1.3	1	0.1	19	2.2	146	17.2	37	35	4	10.8	3	8.6	12	7
Northern Illinois	324	2	0.6	27	8.3	36	11.1	28	8.6	0	0.0	0	0.0	93	28.7	15	15	6	33.3	7	38.9	1	0
Northwestern	780	3	0.4	113	14.5	52	6.7	56	7.2	1	0.1	0	0.0	225	28.8	52	52	9	9.9	9	9.8	2	11
Southern Illinois	390	1	0.3	13	3.3	6	1.5	4	1.0	0	0.0	0	0.0	24	6.2	23	24	0	0.0	1	3.8	3	0

Chapter 6: Opportunities in Law for Minority Men and Women

	Total # students (Full-time and Part-time)	American Indian/Alaskan Native		Asian/Pacific Islander		Black/African American		Mexican American		Puerto Rican		Hispanic		Total # and % Minority Students		Total Full-time Faculty, Fall	Total Full-time Faculty, Spring	Total # and % Full-time Minority Faculty, Fall		Total # and % Full-time Minority Faculty, Spring		Total # Part-time Minority Faculty, Fall	Total # Part-time Minority Faculty, Spring
	#	#	%	#	%	#	%	#	%	#	%	#	%	#	%	#	#	#	%	#	%	#	#
Indiana																							
Indiana-Bloomington	637	1	0.2	38	6.0	38	6.0	26	4.1	0	0.0	0	0.0	103	16.2	38	40	3	7.9	4	10.0	0	0
Indiana-Indianapolis	893	1	0.1	32	3.6	60	6.7	17	1.9	9	1.0	15	1.7	134	15.0	47	43	5	9.8	5	10.6	3	2
Notre Dame	553	4	0.7	38	6.9	32	5.8	8	1.4	6	1.1	26	4.7	114	20.6	28	30	3	10.3	2	6.5	2	1
Valparaiso	559	2	0.4	13	2.3	24	4.3	6	1.1	2	0.4	12	2.1	59	10.6	27	26	1	3.6	1	3.7	0	0
Iowa																							
Drake	473	1	0.2	15	3.2	20	4.2	7	1.5	0	0.0	0	0.0	43	9.1	21	20	2	8.7	2	9.1	1	3
Iowa	712	9	1.3	38	5.3	32	4.5	38	5.3	0	0.0	0	0.0	117	16.4	44	44	5	10.6	6	12.0	0	0
Kansas																							
Kansas	524	12	2.3	36	6.9	22	4.2	0	0.0	0	0.0	42	8.0	112	21.4	28	31	4	12.9	4	11.8	1	1
Washburn	462	9	1.9	13	2.8	21	4.5	9	1.9	1	0.2	6	1.3	59	12.8	26	24	7	25.0	6	23.1	0	0
Kentucky																							
Kentucky	420	1	0.2	2	0.5	22	5.2	0	0.0	0	0.0	1	0.2	26	6.2	21	21	1	4.8	0	0.0	0	0
Louis D. Brandeis, Louisville	385	1	0.3	12	3.1	12	3.1	2	0.5	0	0.0	4	1.0	31	8.1	21	21	2	9.5	2	9.5	1	3
Northern Kentucky	580	5	0.9	5	0.9	22	3.8	0	0.0	0	0.0	9	1.6	41	7.1	23	22	3	12.5	3	13.0	0	1
Louisiana																							
Louisiana State	656	2	0.3	10	1.5	61	9.3	0	0.0	0	0.0	9	1.4	82	12.5	33	33	4	9.5	8	18.6	2	3
Loyola-New Orleans	803	5	0.6	26	3.2	78	9.7	0	0.0	39	4.9	15	1.9	163	20.3	37	39	9	24.3	10	25.6	0	2
Southern	464	0	0.0	3	0.6	294	63.4	0	0.0	0	0.0	3	0.6	300	64.7	28	28	17	60.7	17	60.7	15	15
Tulane	977	7	0.7	49	5.0	77	7.9	9	0.9	7	0.7	27	2.8	176	18.0	43	41	5	9.4	3	5.9	1	1
Maine																							
Maine	278	1	0.4	7	2.5	5	1.8	0	0.0	1	0.4	2	0.7	16	5.8	12	10	0	0.0	0	0.0	0	0
Maryland																							
Baltimore	987	5	0.5	39	4.0	136	13.8	0	0.0	0	0.0	22	2.2	202	20.5	34	33	12	30.8	12	31.6	51	61
Maryland	772	2	0.3	72	9.3	106	13.7	2	0.3	3	0.4	22	2.8	207	26.8	54	50	11	20.4	10	20.0	6	4

	Total # students (Full-time and Part-time)	American Indian/Alaskan Native		Asian/Pacific Islander		Black/African American		Mexican American		Puerto Rican		Hispanic		Total # and % Minority Students		Total Full-time Faculty, Fall	Total Full-time Faculty, Spring	Total # and % Full-time Minority Faculty, Fall		Total # and % Full-time Minority Faculty, Spring		Total # Part-time Minority Faculty, Fall	Total # Part-time Minority Faculty, Spring
	#	#	%	#	%	#	%	#	%	#	%	#	%	#	%	#	#	#	%	#	%	#	#
Massachusetts																							
Boston College	795	0	0.0	79	9.9	41	5.2	10	1.3	4	0.5	26	3.3	160	20.1	47	45	10	19.6	11	22.0	7	7
Boston	858	2	0.2	127	14.8	36	4.2	7	0.8	7	0.8	31	3.6	210	24.5	58	43	4	6.7	4	8.9	1	1
Harvard	1694	11	0.6	203	12.0	173	10.2	35	2.1	9	0.5	45	2.7	476	28.1	127	114	19	13.0	18	12.7	1	1
New England	1101	1	0.1	63	5.7	39	3.5	8	0.7	9	0.8	22	2.0	142	12.9	29	29	3	10.3	4	13.8	4	1
Northeastern	619	7	1.1	71	11.5	45	7.3	0	0.0	2	0.3	41	6.6	166	26.8	27	28	8	29.6	7	25.0	3	3
Suffolk	1667	6	0.4	101	6.1	42	2.5	0	0.0	0	0.0	45	2.7	194	11.6	70	71	9	11.8	9	11.7	3	5
Western New England	585	0	0.0	18	3.1	28	4.8	0	0.0	0	0.0	16	2.7	62	10.6	23	25	4	14.3	3	10.3	0	0
Michigan																							
Ave Maria	302	6	2.0	15	5.0	8	2.6	3	1.0	3	1.0	17	5.6	52	17.2	18	18	3	13.0	3	13.0	0	0
Detroit Mercy	604	0	0.0	5	0.8	28	4.6	0	0.0	0	0.0	11	1.8	44	7.3	25	23	3	12.0	3	13.0	1	1
Michigan	1182	29	2.5	124	10.5	72	6.1	0	0.0	0	0.0	75	6.3	300	25.4	61	46	6	8.7	5	9.1	1	1
Michigan State	1117	5	0.4	44	3.9	57	5.1	14	1.3	0	0.0	2	0.2	122	10.9	38	37	5	12.8	5	13.2	1	0
Thomas M. Cooley	2868	9	0.3	176	6.1	431	15.0	52	1.8	22	0.8	87	3.0	777	27.1	81	71	10	11.8	10	13.3	23	12
Wayne State	723	11	1.5	36	5.0	72	10.0	3	0.4	0	0.0	13	1.8	135	18.7	27	26	4	12.9	3	10.0	0	0
Minnesota																							
Hamline	714	5	0.7	33	4.6	31	4.3	0	0.0	0	0.0	27	3.8	96	13.4	31	29	5	14.7	5	15.6	3	3
Minnesota	817	7	0.9	77	9.4	18	2.2	2	0.2	1	0.1	26	3.2	131	16.0	47	45	8	16.7	7	14.9	3	5
St. Thomas	361	4	1.1	26	7.2	14	3.9	1	0.3	1	0.3	8	2.2	54	15.0	20	19	2	10.0	1	5.3	1	3
William Mitchell	1078	5	0.5	47	4.4	42	3.9	5	0.5	2	0.2	16	1.5	117	10.9	34	33	5	14.7	5	15.2	37	39
Mississippi																							
Mississippi	581	3	0.5	3	0.5	48	8.3	0	0.0	0	0.0	2	0.3	56	9.6	22	22	5	16.1	5	16.1	0	0
Mississippi College	454	1	0.2	0	0.0	36	7.9	0	0.0	0	0.0	3	0.7	40	8.8	17	17	2	11.8	2	11.8	0	1

	Total # students (Full-time and Part-time)	American Indian/Alaskan Native		Asian/Pacific Islander		Black/African American		Mexican American		Puerto Rican		Hispanic		Total # and % Minority Students		Total Full-time Faculty, Fall	Total Full-time Faculty, Spring	Total # and % Full-time Minority Faculty, Fall		Total # and % Full-time Minority Faculty, Spring		Total # Part-time Minority Faculty, Fall	Total # Part-time Minority Faculty, Spring
	#	#	%	#	%	#	%	#	%	#	%	#	%	#	%	#	#	#	%	#	%	#	#
Missouri																							
Missouri-Columbia	437	4	0.9	11	2.5	24	5.5	0	0.0	0	0.0	4	0.9	43	9.8	24	25	2	8.0	3	11.5	0	1
Missouri-Kansas City	528	6	1.1	15	2.8	17	3.2	4	0.8	0	0.0	5	0.9	47	8.9	23	23	1	4.0	1	4.0	1	1
St. Louis	877	0	0.0	26	3.0	36	4.1	0	0.0	0	0.0	20	2.3	82	9.4	35	36	4	9.5	3	7.0	2	0
Washington	756	7	0.9	71	9.4	47	6.2	3	0.4	1	0.1	8	1.1	137	18.1	46	45	4	8.5	4	8.7	9	3
Montana																							
Montana	241	11	4.6	2	0.8	1	0.4	0	0.0	1	0.4	0	0.0	15	6.2	15	14	2	12.5	2	13.3	0	0
Nebraska																							
Creighton	478	3	0.6	10	2.1	10	2.1	11	2.3	0	0.0	7	1.5	41	8.6	24	23	3	12.0	3	12.5	1	1
Nebraska	408	3	0.7	10	2.5	12	2.9	10	2.5	0	0.0	0	0.0	35	8.6	23	22	2	8.7	2	9.1	0	0
Nevada																							
William S. Boyd	467	2	0.4	49	10.5	14	3.0	19	4.1	0	0.0	16	3.4	100	21.4	26	26	7	24.1	7	24.1	1	1
New Hampshire																							
Franklin Pierce	428	0	0.0	47	11.0	15	3.5	2	0.5	0	0.0	11	2.6	75	17.5	20	20	1	4.5	1	4.5	0	1
New Jersey																							
Rutgers-Camden	793	1	0.1	48	6.1	38	4.8	4	0.5	9	1.1	22	2.8	122	15.4	35	36	3	6.4	3	6.1	6	4
Rutgers-Newark	810	4	0.5	102	12.6	114	14.1	5	0.6	38	4.7	39	4.8	302	37.3	33	42	10	27.8	10	22.2	3	4
Seton Hall	1234	5	0.4	100	8.1	56	4.5	2	0.2	24	1.9	60	4.9	247	20.0	54	58	13	23.6	13	22.0	9	10
New Mexico																							
New Mexico	342	33	9.6	6	1.8	12	3.5	78	22.8	0	0.0	0	0.0	129	37.7	27	25	11	35.5	11	37.9	2	3
New York																							
Albany	755	1	0.1	48	6.4	36	4.8	1	0.1	10	1.3	14	1.9	110	14.6	38	36	4	9.5	3	7.5	1	1
Brooklyn	1518	2	0.1	223	14.7	60	4.0	8	0.5	16	1.1	48	3.2	357	23.5	65	60	4	6.2	5	8.3	4	5
Buffalo, SUNY	741	5	0.7	52	7.0	46	6.2	0	0.0	1	0.1	30	4.0	134	18.1	48	49	5	9.3	4	7.3	3	10
Cardozo	1037	2	0.2	106	10.2	43	4.1	0	0.0	11	1.1	53	5.1	215	20.7	51	50	2	3.8	4	7.5	1	2
City U of NY	447	2	0.4	52	11.6	51	11.4	5	1.1	13	2.9	31	6.9	154	34.5	30	30	15	44.1	14	41.2	8	8
Columbia	1239	8	0.6	160	12.9	111	9.0	43	3.5	13	1.0	25	2.0	360	29.1	94	62	13	13.4	8	12.3	5	9

Number and Percentage of Minority Students

Number and Percentage of Minority Faculty

Chapter 6: Opportunities in Law for Minority Men and Women

Number and Percentage of Minority Students / Number and Percentage of Minority Faculty

	Total # Students (Full-time and Part-time)	American Indian/Alaskan Native		Asian/Pacific Islander		Black/African American		Mexican American		Puerto Rican		Hispanic		Total # and % Minority Students		Total Full-time Faculty, Fall	Total Full-time Faculty, Spring	Total # and % Full-time Minority Faculty, Fall		Total # and % Full-time Minority Faculty, Spring		Total # Part-time Minority Faculty, Fall	Total # Part-time Minority Faculty, Spring
	#	#	%	#	%	#	%	#	%	#	%	#	%	#	%	#	#	#	%	#	%	#	#
Cornell	593	2	0.3	113	19.1	45	7.6	13	2.2	8	1.3	8	1.3	189	31.9	46	48	3	6.5	3	6.3	0	2
Fordham	1522	6	0.4	165	10.8	90	5.9	6	0.4	22	1.4	93	6.1	382	25.1	71	68	13	17.3	15	20.8	13	14
Hofstra	1018	4	0.4	61	6.0	61	6.0	0	0.0	0	0.0	57	5.6	183	18.0	44	44	6	13.6	5	11.4	0	2
New York Law	1542	5	0.3	112	7.3	94	6.1	6	0.4	13	0.8	53	3.4	283	18.4	52	51	8	14.3	7	12.7	3	3
New York	1360	0	0.0	133	9.8	119	8.8	9	0.7	9	0.7	63	4.6	333	24.5	101	102	17	13.7	15	12.0	8	7
Pace	774	0	0.0	55	7.1	26	3.4	4	0.5	9	1.2	23	3.0	117	15.1	36	35	4	10.8	4	11.1	1	2
St. John's	961	2	0.2	83	8.6	63	6.6	8	0.8	7	0.7	40	4.2	203	21.1	43	46	8	18.6	8	16.7	2	4
Syracuse	792	6	0.8	55	6.9	34	4.3	9	1.1	6	0.8	30	3.8	140	17.7	39	34	7	14.3	4	9.1	4	3
Touro	755	4	0.5	56	7.4	75	9.9	0	0.0	0	0.0	44	5.8	179	23.7	32	30	3	8.6	3	9.1	3	1
North Carolina																							
Campbell	369	4	1.1	7	1.9	16	4.3	1	0.3	3	0.8	7	1.9	38	10.3	16	15	2	11.8	1	6.3	0	0
Duke	640	4	0.6	56	8.8	66	10.3	0	0.0	0	0.0	20	3.1	146	22.8	45	41	4	8.2	4	8.9	4	2
North Carolina	710	12	1.7	39	5.5	93	13.1	0	0.0	0	0.0	23	3.2	167	23.5	36	36	6	16.2	6	16.2	5	9
North Carolina Central	437	14	3.2	5	1.1	197	45.1	0	0.0	2	0.5	2	0.5	220	50.3	17	17	11	61.1	11	57.9	6	6
Wake Forest	480	0	0.0	11	2.3	30	6.3	0	0.0	0	0.0	26	5.4	67	14.0	33	32	8	20.0	6	15.4	2	0
North Dakota																							
North Dakota	203	4	2.0	1	0.5	3	1.5	4	2.0	0	0.0	0	0.0	12	5.9	8	7	1	10.0	1	11.1	0	0
Ohio																							
Akron	569	0	0.0	12	2.1	25	4.4	0	0.0	0	0.0	11	1.9	48	8.4	25	25	2	8.0	3	12.0	1	0
Capital	787	1	0.1	13	1.7	62	7.9	0	0.0	0	0.0	13	1.7	89	11.3	31	30	4	11.1	4	11.8	0	4
Case Western	708	3	0.4	63	8.9	27	3.8	1	0.1	1	0.1	9	1.3	104	14.7	41	38	9	17.6	8	16.7	40	49
Cincinnati	382	2	0.5	25	6.5	32	8.4	0	0.0	2	0.5	3	0.8	64	16.8	25	22	5	17.9	5	20.0	1	6
Cleveland State	747	1	0.1	30	4.0	50	6.7	0	0.0	0	0.0	23	3.1	104	13.9	42	39	3	7.1	3	7.7	1	0
Dayton	544	4	0.7	27	5.0	23	4.2	5	0.9	1	0.2	10	1.8	70	12.9	26	25	4	15.4	4	16.0	1	1

	Total # students (Full-time and Part-time)	Number and Percentage of Minority Students															Total Full-time Faculty, Fall	Total Full-time Faculty, Spring	Number and Percentage of Minority Faculty						
		American Indian/Alaskan Native		Asian/Pacific Islander		Black/African American		Mexican American		Puerto Rican		Hispanic		Total # and % Minority Students				Total # and % Full-time Minority Faculty, Fall		Total # and % Full-time Minority Faculty, Spring		Total # Part-time Minority Faculty, Fall	Total # Part-time Minority Faculty, Spring
	#	#	%	#	%	#	%	#	%	#	%	#	%	#	%	#	#	#	%	#	%	#	#
Ohio Northern	318	1	0.3	5	1.6	19	6.0	0	0.0	0	0.0	4	1.3	29	9.1	19	18	1	5.3	1	5.6	0	0
Ohio State	747	2	0.3	66	8.8	54	7.2	9	1.2	2	0.3	22	2.9	155	20.7	41	42	8	17.8	8	17.4	0	2
Toledo	517	0	0.0	12	2.3	20	3.9	0	0.0	0	0.0	6	1.2	38	7.4	29	29	2	6.9	2	6.9	0	0
Oklahoma																							
Oklahoma	519	44	8.5	16	3.1	26	5.0	10	1.9	0	0.0	1	0.2	97	18.7	27	28	4	11.8	4	11.4	0	0
Oklahoma City	684	39	5.7	25	3.7	29	4.2	32	4.7	0	0.0	0	0.0	125	18.3	24	23	3	10.7	3	11.1	1	2
Tulsa	618	42	6.8	10	1.6	18	2.9	19	3.1	0	0.0	0	0.0	89	14.4	20	22	3	13.6	3	12.5	1	1
Oregon																							
Lewis & Clark	742	14	1.9	68	9.2	18	2.4	20	2.7	5	0.7	18	2.4	143	19.3	41	42	3	6.5	3	6.7	1	0
Oregon	529	6	1.1	32	6.0	14	2.6	12	2.3	1	0.2	20	3.8	85	16.1	21	21	4	16.7	5	20.0	1	1
Willamette	466	8	1.7	18	3.9	4	0.9	4	0.9	0	0.0	6	1.3	40	8.6	21	22	3	11.5	4	14.8	0	1
Pennsylvania																							
Duquesne	611	0	0.0	10	1.6	16	2.6	0	0.0	0	0.0	4	0.7	30	4.9	24	24	3	11.1	3	11.1	1	0
Penn State, Dickinson	622	1	0.2	37	5.9	41	6.6	0	0.0	26	4.2	10	1.6	115	18.5	30	28	5	13.2	5	13.9	2	1
Pennsylvania	833	6	0.7	89	10.7	61	7.3	7	0.8	8	1.0	51	6.1	222	26.7	53	55	5	8.9	5	8.6	8	10
Pittsburgh	722	1	0.1	28	3.9	54	7.5	3	0.4	0	0.0	8	1.1	94	13.0	44	39	6	13.0	5	11.9	3	3
Temple	1053	5	0.5	99	9.4	81	7.7	8	0.8	10	0.9	21	2.0	224	21.3	49	48	12	24.5	12	25.0	8	12
Villanova	762	3	0.4	64	8.4	29	3.8	0	0.0	0	0.0	34	4.5	130	17.1	35	34	4	9.3	5	11.4	2	3
Widener	513	1	0.2	18	3.5	11	2.1	0	0.0	0	0.0	11	2.1	41	8.0	19	21	0	0.0	1	4.3	1	0
Puerto Rico																							
Inter American	758	0	0.0	0	0.0	0	0.0	0	0.0	755	99.6	1	0.1	756	99.7	22	23	25	100.0	26	100.0	38	30
Pontifical Catholic	490	0	0.0	0	0.0	0	0.0	0	0.0	489	99.8	0	0.0	489	99.8	23	22	24	100.0	23	95.8	14	18
Puerto Rico	714	0	0.0	0	0.0	0	0.0	0	0.0	709	99.3	1	0.1	710	99.4	24	22	24	92.3	22	84.6	29	22
Rhode Island																							
Roger Williams	630	4	0.6	31	4.9	15	2.4	1	0.2	0	0.0	13	2.1	64	10.2	23	24	2	6.7	2	6.5	1	1

	Total # students (Full-time and Part-time) #	American Indian/Alaskan Native #	%	Asian/Pacific Islander #	%	Black/African American #	%	Mexican American #	%	Puerto Rican #	%	Hispanic #	%	Total # and % Minority Students #	%	Total Full-time Faculty, Fall #	Total Full-time Faculty, Spring #	Total # and % Full-time Minority Faculty, Fall #	%	Total # and % Full-time Minority Faculty, Spring #	%	Total # Part-time Minority Faculty, Fall #	Total # Part-time Minority Faculty, Spring #
South Carolina																							
South Carolina	754	0	0.0	4	0.5	50	6.6	0	0.0	0	0.0	9	1.2	63	8.4	33	34	2	5.9	2	5.7	0	0
South Dakota																							
South Dakota	251	4	1.6	5	2.0	1	0.4	1	0.4	0	0.0	4	1.6	15	6.0	12	11	0	0.0	0	0.0	0	0
Tennessee																							
Memphis	443	1	0.2	6	1.4	43	9.7	0	0.0	0	0.0	0	0.0	50	11.3	22	21	2	9.1	1	4.8	1	2
Tennessee	452	1	0.2	3	0.7	52	11.5	0	0.0	0	0.0	4	0.9	60	13.3	30	30	7	23.3	7	23.3	1	2
Vanderbilt	632	2	0.3	35	5.5	78	12.3	0	0.0	0	0.0	26	4.1	141	22.3	33	32	7	18.9	6	16.7	5	3
Texas																							
Baylor	426	1	0.2	20	4.7	3	0.7	18	4.2	0	0.0	6	1.4	48	11.3	21	21	1	4.8	1	4.8	0	0
Houston	1103	9	0.8	116	10.5	33	3.0	41	3.7	0	0.0	40	3.6	239	21.7	37	34	8	14.3	7	13.5	2	0
South Texas	1254	8	0.6	97	7.7	58	4.6	58	4.6	5	0.4	55	4.4	281	22.4	48	43	4	8.2	4	9.3	4	5
SMU Dedman	841	9	1.1	58	6.9	42	5.0	8	1.0	0	0.0	46	5.5	163	19.4	43	43	8	17.8	10	22.2	2	2
St. Mary's	786	9	1.1	27	3.4	17	2.2	147	18.7	2	0.3	26	3.3	228	29.0	28	29	7	20.6	8	22.9	24	18
Texas	1493	10	0.7	103	6.9	71	4.8	174	11.7	0	0.0	58	3.9	416	27.9	69	62	7	9.7	6	9.1	5	8
Texas Southern	628	3	0.5	37	5.9	307	48.9	129	20.5	0	0.0	18	2.9	494	78.7	34	34	30	83.3	30	83.3	6	10
Texas Tech	683	5	0.7	15	2.2	17	2.5	79	11.6	0	0.0	0	0.0	116	17.0	29	28	6	20.7	6	21.4	3	3
Texas Wesleyan	684	7	1.0	38	5.6	46	6.7	43	6.3	0	0.0	11	1.6	145	21.2	22	22	2	7.7	2	7.7	6	5
Utah																							
Brigham Young	484	8	1.7	21	4.3	7	1.4	11	2.3	0	0.0	24	5.0	71	14.7	22	19	3	13.6	3	15.8	2	1
Utah	402	5	1.2	15	3.7	2	0.5	6	1.5	1	0.2	7	1.7	36	9.0	26	23	6	19.4	5	17.9	1	0
Vermont																							
Vermont	545	6	1.1	17	3.1	40	7.3	1	0.2	0	0.0	24	4.4	88	16.1	26	24	0	0.0	0	0.0	0	2

	Total # students (Full-time and Part-time)	Number and Percentage of Minority Students													Total Full-time Faculty, Fall	Total Full-time Faculty, Spring	Number and Percentage of Minority Faculty						
		American Indian/Alaskan Native		Asian/Pacific Islander		Black/African American		Mexican American		Puerto Rican		Hispanic		Total # and % Minority Students				Total # and % Full-time Minority Faculty, Fall		Total # and % Full-time Minority Faculty, Spring		Total # Part-time Minority Faculty, Fall	Total # Part-time Minority Faculty, Spring
	#	#	%	#	%	#	%	#	%	#	%	#	%	#	%	#	#	#	%	#	%	#	#
Virginia																							
Appalachian	369	3	0.8	8	2.2	14	3.8	0	0.0	1	0.3	7	1.9	33	8.9	16	16	3	18.8	3	18.8	0	0
George Mason	723	5	0.7	59	8.2	24	3.3	0	0.0	0	0.0	23	3.2	111	15.4	35	28	1	2.9	1	3.6	4	4
Regent	511	2	0.4	13	2.5	42	8.2	0	0.0	0	0.0	15	2.9	72	14.1	20	19	5	21.7	5	23.8	0	1
Richmond	478	1	0.2	16	3.3	20	4.2	0	0.0	0	0.0	4	0.8	41	8.6	26	26	4	13.3	3	10.0	4	1
Virginia	1100	4	0.4	92	8.4	71	6.5	0	0.0	0	0.0	13	1.2	180	16.4	67	72	7	10.4	5	6.9	1	5
Washington and Lee	399	3	0.8	21	5.3	36	9.0	1	0.3	0	0.0	3	0.8	64	16.0	31	33	4	12.9	4	12.1	1	1
William & Mary	585	3	0.5	22	3.8	43	7.4	0	0.0	0	0.0	10	1.7	78	13.3	31	28	5	16.1	5	17.9	3	2
Washington																							
Gonzaga	628	7	1.1	42	6.7	3	0.5	24	3.8	0	0.0	0	0.0	76	12.1	27	27	2	7.4	3	11.1	0	0
Seattle	1102	17	1.5	122	11.1	44	4.0	24	2.2	9	0.8	20	1.8	236	21.4	51	46	11	21.2	11	23.4	4	3
Washington	552	17	3.1	64	11.6	14	2.5	1	0.2	0	0.0	7	1.3	103	18.7	42	43	7	14.9	7	14.3	0	5
West Virginia																							
West Virginia	464	2	0.4	6	1.3	18	3.9	1	0.2	0	0.0	3	0.6	30	6.5	22	23	4	17.4	4	16.0	0	0
Wisconsin																							
Marquette	721	3	0.4	21	2.9	23	3.2	1	0.1	0	0.0	7	1.0	55	7.6	32	29	3	9.1	2	6.7	1	3
Wisconsin	851	16	1.9	63	7.4	72	8.5	44	5.2	12	1.4	16	1.9	223	26.2	55	52	10	15.9	10	16.7	12	15
Wyoming																							
Wyoming	229	4	1.7	2	0.9	1	0.4	3	1.3	2	0.9	4	1.7	16	7.0	12	12	2	16.7	3	25.0	0	0

Chapter 7: ABA's Role in the Accreditation Process

The ABA Role in General

Law schools approved by the American Bar Association (ABA) provide a legal education that meets a minimum set of standards as promulgated by the ABA. Every jurisdiction in the United States has determined that graduates of ABA-approved law schools are able to sit for the bar in their respective jurisdictions. The role that the ABA plays as the national accrediting body has enabled accreditation to become unified and national in scope rather than fragmented, with the potential for inconsistency, among the 50 states, the District of Columbia, the Commonwealth of Puerto Rico, and other territories.

Since its inception in 1878, the American Bar Association has been concerned with improving the quality of legal education. Following numerous studies of the educational programs available in the late 1880s and early 1900s, it was determined that a national process must be developed for ensuring the quality of the education of the prospective lawyer. Consequently, in 1921, the ABA adopted a statement for minimum standards of legal education and instituted a policy of publishing a list of law schools that complied with those standards.

As of February 2005, a total of 191 institutions are approved by the American Bar Association: 190 confer the first degree in law (the JD degree); the other ABA-approved school is the US Army Judge Advocate General's School, which offers an officer's resident graduate course, a specialized program beyond the first degree in law. One of the 191 ABA-approved law schools (Widener) also has a branch campus. Nine of the law schools are provisionally approved: Appalachian School of Law, Ave Maria School of Law, Barry University School of Law, University of the District of Columbia School of Law, Florida A&M University College of Law, Florida International University College of Law, John Marshall Law School (Atlanta), University of St. Thomas School of Law (Minnesota), and Western State University College of Law.

With an increase in the number of approved law schools, total JD enrollment in approved schools has gone from approximately 98,042 students in 1972 to 140,376 in the fall of 2004. In that same period, enrollment of women increased from 11,878 to 67,438 and minority enrollment increased from 6,730 to 29,536.

The Council, the Standards, and the Accreditation Committee

The Council of the ABA Section of Legal Education and Admissions to the Bar is the US Department of Education recognized accrediting agency for programs that lead to the first professional degree in law. The law school approval process established by the Council is designed to provide a careful and comprehensive evaluation of a law school and its compliance with the *Standards: Rules of Procedure for Approval of Law Schools*. A current copy of the Standards is available on the Section's website at *www.abanet.org/legaled*. Those Standards are reviewed frequently to ensure that they focus on matters that are central to quality legal education. The Council, which ultimately adopts the Standards, has established an extensive process to seek comment on the Standards and possible revisions to the Standards by law school deans, law faculty, university presidents, leaders of the bar and judiciary, and others interested in legal education.

Decisions concerning the approval of a law school and its compliance with the Standards are ultimately made by the Council of the Section of Legal Education and Admissions to the Bar. The Council is comprised of 21 voting members, no more than 10 of whom may be law school deans or faculty members. Other members of the Council include judges, practicing attorneys, one law student, and at least three "public" members who are neither lawyers nor employees of a law school. The Accreditation Committee, which exercises oversight of schools that have been approved by the Council and makes recommendations to the Council concerning a school's application for approval, is similarly constituted.

The Council and the Accreditation Committee are assisted by the 11-person full-time staff of the Office of the Consultant on Legal Education and Admissions to the Bar. Dean John A. Sebert has served as Consultant since September 2000.

Provisional Approval

A law school may not apply for provisional approval by the ABA until it has been in operation for one year. Schools considering applying for provisional approval are strongly encouraged to contact the Office of the Consultant as early as possible, and well before the year in which the school applies for provisional approval. The Consultant or other senior members of the Consultant Office staff meet with representatives of schools seeking provisional approval and provide them with extensive information about the *Standards: Rules of Procedure for Approval of Law Schools* and the accreditation process.

A school must apply for provisional approval after classes have begun in the fall term and before October 15, so that a full site evaluation can be properly scheduled for late in the fall or early in the spring term. The school is required to develop an extensive self-study, which describes the school in detail, contains a critical evaluation of the school's strengths and weaknesses, establishes goals for the school's future progress, and identifies the means of achieving those goals. The school also completes a Site Evaluation Questionnaire that provides much of the information that a site evaluation team needs to ascertain the basic facts concerning the school and its operation.

The Office of the Consultant appoints a site evaluation team of six or seven persons to undertake a site evaluation of the school. The team chairperson is always an experienced site evaluator and often—but not always—a present or former law school dean. The team usually consists of one or two academic law school faculty members, a law librarian, one faculty member with an expertise in professional skills instruction (clinic, simulation skills, or legal writing), one judge or practitioner, and one university administrator who is not a member of a law faculty.

The site evaluation team carefully reviews the materials the school has provided and visits the school for a three-day period, often from Sunday afternoon through Wednesday morning. During that visit the team meets with the dean and other leaders of the faculty and law school administration, with the president and other university administrators (or, in the case of a free-standing law school, with the leadership of the board of trustees), and tries to have one member of the team meet individually with every member of the faculty. The team also visits as many classes as it can during its visit in order to make judgments concerning the quality of instruction, holds an open meeting with students, and meets with student leaders. In addition, the team meets with alumni and members of the bar and judiciary who are familiar with the school.

At the end of the visit (usually on Wednesday morning), the team meets with the dean and the president (or board chair) to provide an oral report of the team's findings. Shortly after leaving the school, the team drafts and finalizes an extensive written site evaluation report. The report covers all aspects of the school's operation, including faculty and administration, the academic program, the student body and their success on the bar examination and in placement, student services, library and information resources, financial resources, and physical facilities and technological capacities.

The site evaluation team does not make judgments or reach conclusions as to whether the school complies with the Standards. Those judgments are made by the Accreditation Committee and, ultimately, the Council. The role of the site evaluation team is to provide a factual report that accurately and completely describes the situation of the school and that provides a comprehensive basis for the judgments that must be made by the Accreditation Committee and the Council.

The site evaluation report is sent to the Office of the Consultant. Then the report is sent to the school, which is given the opportunity to provide written corrections of any factual errors and other comment on the site report. Then the report is sent to the Accreditation Committee, which holds a hearing at which representatives of the school applying for provisional approval appear. After the hearing, the Accreditation Committee makes its recommendation concerning provisional approval to the Council.

A school that applies for provisional approval must establish that it "is in substantial compliance with each of the Standards and presents a reliable plan for bringing the school into full compliance with the Standards within three years after receiving provisional approval." The burden is on the school to establish that it fulfills these requirements. If the Accreditation Committee concludes that a school is in substantial compliance with the Standards and that the school has a reliable plan for coming into compliance, the Committee will recommend that the Council grant provisional approval. If the Committee concludes either that the school is not in substantial compliance or does not have a reliable plan to come into full compliance in three years, it will recommend against provisional approval.

When a school seeks provisional approval, the final decision on the school's application is made by the Council. The Accreditation Committee's findings of fact are binding on the Council unless those findings are not supported by substantial evidence in the record, but the Accreditation Committee's conclusions and recommendations are not binding on the Council.

If the decision of the Council is to grant provisional approval, that decision is transmitted to the House of Delegates for its concurrence or for nonconcurrence and referral back to the Council. If the decision of the Council is to deny provisional approval, the school has the right to appeal to the House of Delegates and ask the House to refer the matter back to the Council. If the House concurs with a Council decision to grant provisional approval, the school immediately becomes provisionally approved. If the House refers the matter back to the Council, the application process continues with the Accreditation Committee and the Council again reviewing the school to determine whether it meets the standards for provisional approval. In the event of a referral back by the House, the Council's decision after the second referral back is final.

A school that is provisionally approved is entitled to all the rights of a fully approved law school. Similarly, graduates of provisionally approved law schools are entitled to the same recognition that is accorded graduates of fully approved schools.

Obtaining Full Approval

Once a school has obtained provisional approval, it remains in provisional status for at least three years. Unless extraordinary circumstances justify an extension, a school may not remain in provisional status for more than five years. In order to be granted full approval, a school must demonstrate that it is in full compliance with each of the standards; substantial compliance does not suffice. Again, the burden is upon the school to establish full compliance.

During a school's provisional status, the progress of the school is closely monitored. It is visited by a site evaluation team once each year. After each such site visit, a site evaluation report is submitted to the school and the Accreditation Committee. The Committee reviews the site report and the school's response and sends the school a letter that indicates any areas where the Committee concludes the school does not yet fully comply with the Standards.

In the year in which a school is considered for full approval, the process is identical to that undertaken in connection with an application for provisional approval. Decisions on full approval are made only by the Council, in reviewing the findings, conclusions, and recommendations of the Accreditation Committee. The role of the House of Delegates in reviewing Council decisions on full approval is identical to the House's role concerning decisions on provisional approval.

Oversight of Fully Approved Schools

After a school is granted full approval, it undergoes a full site evaluation in the third year after full approval, and then a full sabbatical site evaluation every seven years. The site evaluation process and the review of the site report by the Accreditation Committee is very similar to that described in connection with a school's application for provisional approval.

The Accreditation Committee's actions upon review of a site report on a fully approved school are likely to take one of three forms. If the Committee concludes that the school fully complies with all the standards, it writes the school with that conclusion and indicates that the school remains on the list of approved schools. In the remainder of the cases, the Committee will conclude either that the school does not appear to comply with one or more of the standards, or that the Committee lacks sufficient information to determine whether or not the school complies. In either case the Committee's action letter will indicate with specificity the standard or standards with which the school does not comply, or as to which the Committee lacks sufficient information to determine compliance, and will ask the school by a specified time to provide the information necessary to enable the Committee to determine compliance or to indicate what steps the school has taken to bring itself into compliance.

Chapter 8: Pro Bono Legal Services

Written by the ABA Standing Committee on Pro Bono and Public Service

When society confers the privilege to practice law on an individual, he or she accepts the responsibility to promote justice and to make justice equally accessible to all people. Thus, all lawyers should aspire to render some legal services without fee or expectation of fee for the good of the public (*pro bono publico*). Prospective students should be mindful of this responsibility when considering law as a career. When choosing a law school, they should evaluate whether a particular school will supply the necessary foundation for achieving their goals relating to pro bono. Many schools offer service opportunities through structured pro bono programs. The ABA Standards for Approval of Law Schools encourages schools to provide opportunities for students to participate in pro bono activities.

The Need for Pro Bono Service

The responsibility to perform pro bono services sets the legal profession apart from other societal roles. Pro bono opportunities offered by law schools teach students that for the economically disadvantaged, the inability to obtain legal services for basic needs can have dire consequences. Students learn firsthand that for many people, pro bono legal assistance is vital to maintaining minimum levels of basic needs, such as government benefits, income, shelter, utilities, child support, and physical protection. The special skills they develop during law school can significantly benefit the underprivileged. Both law students and lawyers should place greater emphasis on their ethical responsibility to provide pro bono services, in order to bridge the rapidly growing gap between the legal needs of those who cannot afford legal services and the resources available to meet those needs.

Pro Bono Opportunities in Law School

Some law schools offer pro bono opportunities, either through established, structured programs or unsuper-

vised, unstructured programs. Typically, the opportunities cover a wide range of areas, such as family law, children's issues, consumer fraud, AIDS-related problems, housing, immigration, taxation, environmental law, criminal defense, elder law, and death penalty appeals. Pro bono legal service is currently mandatory in approximately 30 law schools. These schools may require a specific number of hours of pro bono legal service as a condition of graduation (e.g., 20–75 hours), or they may require a combination of pro bono legal service, clinical work, and community-based volunteer work. Law schools with voluntary rather than mandatory pro bono service policies encourage students to assist lawyers and legal aid organizations by offering incentives, such as awards at graduation or special notations on law school transcripts, or by making pro bono an important part of a school's culture.

Benefits of Pro Bono Programs in Law School

Pro bono programs help students develop professionalism and an understanding of a lawyer's responsibility to the community. Participation facilitates student involvement in the community and increases the availability of legal services to needy populations. Students also benefit by increasing their knowledge and marketability, gaining practical experience, developing skills, enhancing their reputations, and exploring alternative career opportunities.

Support for Pro Bono and Public Service in Law School

Other organizations also support pro bono and public service in law school, including The Public Service Law Network Worldwide (PSLawNet, formerly Pro Bono Students America/PBSA), the National Association for Public Interest Law (NAPIL), and the Association of American Law Schools (AALS).

Chapter 9: Financing Your Legal Education

■ The Cost of a Legal Education

Legal education is an investment. It can be an expensive one. The cost of a three-year law school education could exceed $150,000. Tuition alone can range from a few thousand dollars to more than $30,000 a year. When calculating the total cost of attending law school, you also have to include the cost of housing, food, books, transportation, and personal expenses. Law schools will determine the student expense budget for you. Today, approximately 80 percent of law school students rely on education loans as their largest source of financial aid for law school. Loans from governmental and private sources at low and moderate interest rates may be available to qualified students.

Financial Aid: A Student's Responsibility

The first step in applying for financial aid for law school is to complete the Free Application for Federal Student Aid (FAFSA), available online at *fafsa.ed.gov*, from your college or university financial aid office, or from the law school to which you are applying. This is a free form and you need not pay to file it. The FAFSA is a need analysis tool developed by the US Government, Department of Education. It asks for information about you and your spouse's income, assets, and other financial resources. The information you provide on the financial aid form will be used to compute how much you and your spouse should contribute toward your legal education. Many schools require copies of annual federal tax returns to verify financial information; some schools also require students to fill out a supplemental form to be considered for institutional aid. Once the analysis is completed, the financial aid officer at the school can determine what types of aid you will need—such as scholarships, grants, loans, or work-study—to pay your law school expenses.

A brochure published by the Law School Admission Council, *Financial Aid for Law School: A Preliminary Guide*, is available at most law school financial aid offices and at *www.LSAC.org*. For complete and individualized information on financing your law school education, contact the financial aid office at the individual law school(s) to which you apply.

Determining How You Will Pay

There are three basic types of financial aid:

- **Scholarships, Grants, and Fellowships**—Depending on the school's policies, these types of awards—which do not have to be repaid—are given according to need and/or merit. Their availability is quite limited, and they are usually awarded by the law schools

themselves. The law schools' admissions and financial aid offices can give you more information.

- **Federal Work-Study**—Federal Work-Study is a program that provides funding for students to work part time during the school year and full time during the summer months. Students sometimes may work on campus in a variety of settings or in off-campus nonprofit agencies. Additional information is available from any law school financial aid office.

- **Loans**—Education loans may be awarded directly by the school or through other private agencies. The largest student loan programs are funded or guaranteed by the federal government. Some are awarded on a need basis, while others are not need-based. Federal student loans are usually offered at interest rates lower than consumer loans, and the repayment of principal and interest usually begins after the end of your educational program. Private education loans are offered at market rates. Some types of private loans will require a credit check.

Debt Management

An education loan is a serious financial obligation that must be repaid. Dealing with this long-term financial obligation can be made easier through the implementation of sound debt management practices—both while you are in law school and following your graduation.

Credit History
Private loans are approved on the basis of a student's credit. Lenders will analyze your credit report before they approve the loan. Most offer prequalification services on the Internet or by phone. If you have a poor credit history, you may be denied a loan. If there is a mistake on your credit report—and there are often mistakes—you will want adequate time to correct the error. It would be wise to clear up errors or other discrepancies before you apply for a private loan.

You may want to obtain a copy of your credit report so that you can track and clear up any problems. You can order a copy by calling a national credit reporting company or accessing its website. Such companies include Experian (888.397.3742; *www.experian.com*), Equifax (800.685.111; *www.equifax.com*), or TransUnion (800.916.8800; *www.transunion.com*).

Living on the Student Expense Budget
While loans may be available to students with good credit histories, the question of how much to borrow is often asked. The maxim, "live like a student now or you

will live like a student later" is a good one to remember. Although students may borrow up to the limit of the school-determined Student Expense Budget, loans do have to be paid back. Consider tracking your current spending habits and compare them to the budgets at schools of your choice. Look into having a roommate. Learn to cook; food expenses are often budget-busters. For example, $5 a day for lunch totals $25 weekly, $100 monthly, and so on. If you have to borrow to pay for lunch, the real cost is in the neighborhood of $8 a day. Bring a lunch rather than buying one. While law school may be an excellent long-term investment, paying loans in the short term can be a real burden. Remember, not all lawyers can earn the highest reported salaries.

If possible, you should pay off any outstanding consumer debt before entering law school. Student expense budgets do not allow the use of federal education loan funds to pay for prior consumer debt. Entering law school with no credit card debt will make living on your budget easier. Most federal and private education loans allow you to defer payment while you attend law school at least half time. Interest on subsidized loans does not accrue, while unsubsidized and private loans accrue interest while you are in law school. Be sure to inform your prior lenders that you have returned to school.

Loan Default or Delinquency

These two terms are often confused: neither is good. Delinquency occurs when you have begun repayment on a loan or other obligation and have missed one or more payment dates; default generally occurs when a delinquency goes beyond 150–180 days.

Delinquencies appear on credit records and may hinder you from qualifying for an education loan that requires a credit check. Defaults are even more serious and are likely to prevent you from receiving federal financial aid as well as disqualifying you for most other education loans. If you are in a default status, you must take steps to change your status if you wish to apply for a federally guaranteed loan for law school. Contact the servicer of your loan(s) for more information on this subject.

Planning Ahead: Repayment of Your Loan

Your income after law school is an important factor in determining what constitutes manageable payments on your education loans. Although it may be difficult to predict what kind of job you will get (or want) after law school, or exactly what level of salary you will receive, it is important that you make some assessment of your goals for the purpose of sound debt management. In addition to assessing expected income, you must also

create a realistic picture of how much you can afford to pay back on a monthly basis and maintain the lifestyle that you desire. You may have to adjust your thinking about how quickly you can pay your loans back, or how much money you can afford to borrow, or just how extravagantly you expect to live in the years following your graduation from law school.

Your education loan debts represent a serious financial commitment which must be repaid. A default on any loan engenders serious consequences, including possible legal action against you by the lender and/or the government.

Law school graduate debt of $80,000 amounts to almost $1,000 a month on a 10-year repayment plan. Most lenders offer graduated and income-sensitive repayment plans that lower monthly payment amounts but increase the number of years of repayment. Federal Loan Consolidation allows students to repay their Federal Stafford Loans and Ford Federal Direct Student Loans on an extended repayment schedule, lasting up to 30 years. Many lenders have good websites with loan repayment and budget calculators.

Strategies for Graduates Seeking Public Interest Careers

Students who seek to work in public service or the public interest sector of the profession face special challenges in financing their legal educations. Salaries for such jobs are comparatively low. Students graduating from law school with the average amount of indebtedness may find that the median entry-level public service or public interest salary ($37,500 for 2003 graduates) will not provide the resources needed to repay their law school loans and cover their basic living expenses. Even among the graduates who can and do take such positions, many are forced to leave after only two to three years of employment, having exhausted their ability to repay their loans (let alone pay rent) on such low salaries.

Students can employ a number of strategies to make it easier (or possible) to pursue a career in the public service or interest sectors. First, students can borrow less during law school (e.g., attend a lower tuition institution; follow some of the debt management strategies mentioned in this chapter). Students may also take advantage of programs developed at some law schools to relieve the debt burden for students interested in public interest careers, including fellowships, scholarships, and loan repayment assistance programs (LRAPs). LRAPs provide financial aid to law school graduates, typically those working in the public interest sector, government, or other lower-paying legal fields. In most cases, this aid is given to graduates in the form of a forgivable loan to help them repay their annual educational debt. Upon completion of the required service obligation, schools will forgive or cancel these loans for program participants.

The number of law schools sponsoring LRAPs is limited: as of December 2004, approximately 81 law schools sponsored such programs. The funding for these programs is limited, so that most schools are unable to provide assistance to all applicants.

LRAPs are also administered by state bar foundations, public interest legal employers, and federal and state governments to assist law graduates in pursuing and remaining in public interest jobs. The federal government offers some options to assist graduates seeking legal careers in public service, including the Income Contingent Repayment option (ICR) of the William D. Ford Federal Direct Loan Program. The income-contingent repayment option is available to all borrowers with federal direct loans and borrowers who consolidate their federally guaranteed loans into Federal Direct Consolidation Loans. Congress created ICR to enable graduates who have high educational debt to take lower-paying community service or public service jobs. The ICR limits annual loan repayment obligations to an affordable percentage of a borrower's income. Any remaining debt is forgiven after 25 years of payments under the ICR plan.

For more information about loan repayment assistance programs or ICR, visit *www.abalegalservices.org/lrap* or *www.equaljusticeworks.org*.

Chapter 10: Finding a Job

■ Employment Prospects

Because the number of practicing lawyers in the United States continues to increase, it may become more difficult for recent graduates to find jobs in some fields and in certain parts of the country. Opportunities will vary from locality to locality and among legal disciplines. Future lawyers may have to devote considerable time and energy to secure a first job that they consider acceptable. Competition for certain positions will continue to be intense, while opportunities in other fields may expand.

Future demand for people with legal training is almost impossible to predict. Demand for legal services is substantially influenced by the state of the economy. Rising caseloads in the nation's courts and continuing federal and state regulation suggest that the need for lawyers is growing. Whether this expanding need will match or fall short of the parallel growth in the number of practicing lawyers is a question no one can answer with certainty. Lawyers with outstanding academic credentials will continue to obtain desirable positions.

The legal profession itself may adapt to changing job markets by encouraging the entry of lawyers into relatively new fields of law, such as environmental law, intellectual property law, immigration law, and other fields. In addition, certain parts of the country are underrepresented by lawyers.

Career Satisfaction

A job search strategy requires careful self-assessment in much the same way as a school search strategy does. A legal career should meet the interests, abilities, capacities, and priorities of the individual lawyer. Career satisfaction is a result of doing what you like to do, and being continually challenged by it. It is up to you to determine what skills you are comfortable using, and to discern which skills are required in the specialties or types of practice you are considering.

Gathering Information

Take advantage of any programs and workshops offered by the career services office at your law school. (See page 23 for more on the role of the career services office.) Place your name on file in the office, and be sure to maintain contact with the staff even after you leave school. The National Association for Law Placement (NALP) is an important source of information (see page 843 for details). Both employers and students are guided in the employment process by NALP's Principles and Standards for Law Placement and Recruitment Activities. These guidelines are promulgated to ensure that students have an adequate opportunity to make decisions about offers of employment without undue pressure and that employers will receive responses from students in a timely manner. Copies of the Principles and Standards are available through each law school or by contacting NALP.

This chapter includes a number of charts and graphs compiled by NALP that provide current information relating to employment of law school graduates.

■ Graduates Acquire Jobs at Various Times

The search for a full-time job is a process that is dictated not only by the effort and commitment of the candidate but also by the unique recruiting practices of various types of employers. Large firms tend to be more structured and predictable than smaller firms.

Summer Clerkship May Lead to First-Year Associate Offer

Some law firms (typically the large firms which can predict their needs well in advance) interview on campus in the fall to hire students for the following summer. If a student's performance is acceptable and the hiring needs of the firm have remained consistent with the size of the summer class, the student may receive an offer for a full-time job following graduation. Students receiving such offers make a decision on whether to accept such an offer during the fall of their third year of law school.

Some government agencies (typically Department of Justice and other large agencies) have honors programs which work in a similar manner, although few of those agencies actually conduct on-campus interviews.

Employers Hire in Spring from Third-Year Class

Smaller private practice employers and a significant number of public interest and government agencies interview and hire third-year law students during the spring of the student's third year. This timetable enables them to predict more accurately their hiring needs and offers both employers and students an additional semester of law school for hiring/career decisions.

Judicial Clerkships Are a Source of Postgraduation Employment

Jobs as clerks for judges at the local, state, or federal level provide postgraduate employment for about 12 percent of law graduates. These job offers typically encompass one or two years and provide invaluable experience in the court system. Judicial clerks balance the advantages of the clerkship experience with the delay of entering full-time practice.

■ Graduates Choose Jobs According to Interests

Members of each graduating class acquire full- and part-time jobs with an array of public and private, legal and nonlegal organizations. Although most graduates obtain jobs as attorneys, not all do. One kind of nonattorney job is a "JD preferred" position, requiring a Juris Doctor and substantial use of legal skills and training. Examples of jobs for which a JD is preferred (and may even be required) include corporate contracts administrator, alternative dispute resolution specialist, government regulatory analyst, FBI special agents, jobs with legal publishers, and jobs in law school career services offices. Other professional but nonlegal jobs do not require a Juris Doctor and may or may not make specific use of legal skills and background. Law graduates have in the past obtained legal, nonlegal, and full- and part-time jobs from the following general types of employers:

- **Private Practice**—includes all positions within a law firm, including solo practitioner, associate, law clerk, paralegal, and administrative or support staff.

- **Public Interest**—includes positions funded by the Legal Services Corporation and others providing civil, legal, and indigent services as well as positions with nonprofit advocacy or cause-related organizations.

- **Government**—includes all levels and branches of government, including public defender and prosecutor positions, positions with the military, and all other agencies, such as the Small Business Administration, state or local transit authorities, congressional committees, law enforcement, and social services.

- **Judicial Clerkship**—a one- or two-year appointment clerking for a judge on the federal, state, or local level.

- **Business and Industry**—includes positions in accounting firms, insurance companies, banking and financial institutions, corporations, companies and organizations of all sizes, such as private hospitals, retail establishments, consulting and public relations firms, political campaigns, trade associations, and labor unions.

- **Academic**—includes work as a law professor, law librarian, administrator, or faculty member in higher education or other academic settings, including elementary and secondary schools.

- **Nonlegal Careers for Lawyers**—Law-trained individuals pursue a wide variety of careers, and the skills discussed in the first section of this chapter provide excellent training for law school graduates who pursue directions outside the practice of law itself. Lawyers work in the media; as teachers of college, graduate school, and law school; and in law enforcement, public relations, foreign service, politics, and administration.

■ *Jobs & JD's*—Research from NALP

The charts, tables, and copy in this section were adapted with permission from *Jobs & J.D.'s: Employment and Salaries of New Law Graduates, Class of 2003* (NALP). More than 92 percent of all 2003 graduates from ABA-accredited law schools reported employment status, and salary information was reported for 65 percent of those employed full time.

■ Types of Employment

Class of 2003[†]
(as of February 15, 2004)

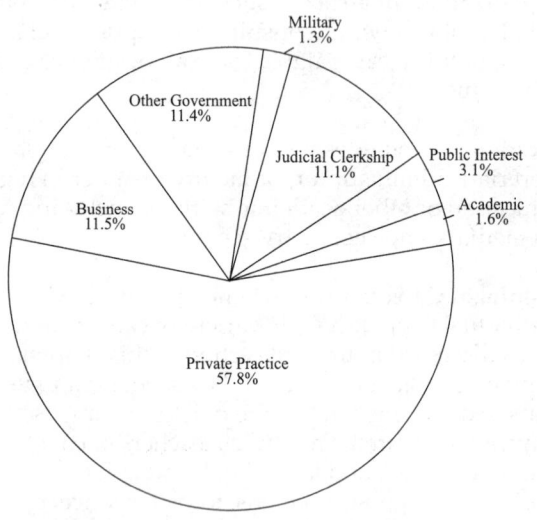

Military 1.3%
Other Government 11.4%
Judicial Clerkship 11.1%
Public Interest 3.1%
Business 11.5%
Academic 1.6%
Private Practice 57.8%

[†]Based on 31,812 jobs.
Note: The category for unknown employer type, representing 2.1% of jobs, is not shown.

■ Salary as an Employment Factor

The national median salary for the class of 2003 was $55,000. This compares with $60,000 for the class of 2002 and is the first decrease in the median since 1992. The decrease not withstanding, this number has essentially doubled since 1985, when a national median was first compiled, with much of that increase occurring since the mid-nineties.

The highest-paying jobs were the exception rather than the rule: Although salaries of more than $75,000 accounted for 34 percent of salaries reported, salaries of $55,000 or less were more common, accounting for just over half of salaries. This is in spite of the fact that since 1996 the share of salaries of more than $70,000 has more than doubled, from 15 percent to 38 percent, while the

proportion of salaries which were $40,000 or less decreased from 53 percent to 21 percent.

The vast majority of graduates—89 percent of those for whom employment status was known—were employed as of February 15, 2004. This rate is virtually unchanged from that for the prior year; in the last five years the employment market for new law school graduates has remained relatively strong, standing at or above the 89 percent employment rate mark.

Median Starting Salaries

	Private Practice	Business	Government
Atlanta	$100,000	$55,000	$48,000
Boston	$125,000	$65,500	$40,000
Chicago	$125,000	$63,500	$41,548
Dallas	$110,000	$56,500	$48,000
Houston	$100,000	$75,000	$48,500
Los Angeles	$125,000	$70,000	$52,500
New York City	$125,000	$69,500	$49,000
Philadelphia	$105,000	$71,000	$44,000
San Francisco	$125,000	$68,000	$52,000
Washington, DC	$125,000	$50,000	$48,800

Note: Figures reflect full-time jobs only

Note: The median is the mid-point in a ranking of salaries reported. However, because so many reported salaries are identical and especially cluster at round dollar amounts, such as $50,000, the median should generally be interpreted as the point at which half the salaries are at or above that figure and half are at or below it.

Differences in Salary Medians by Job and Employer Type

	Bar Passage Required	JD Preferred	Other Professional
All Types	$55,000	$50,000	$57,000
Academic	$40,000	$40,000	$41,500
Business	$58,000	$60,000	$65,000
Private Practice	$80,000	$45,000	$45,500
Government	$42,611	$43,000	$50,000
Public Interest	$37,500	$40,000	$40,000

Note: Figures reflect full-time jobs only.

■ Geography as an Employment Factor

Geographic considerations provide yet another perspective on the placement of new law graduates.

Jobs by City
The 20 cities reporting the largest number of jobs accounted for 43 percent of all jobs with a known location. Of these 20 cities listed in the table at right, 13 correspond to the 20 largest cities in terms of population. The three largest cities in the country—New York, Los Angeles, and Chicago—continue to be major employment centers for new law graduates.

Seven of the 20 cities providing the most jobs, however, are not among the largest cities in the country. Some of these, such as Cleveland and St. Louis, are older industrial cities that have been eclipsed in population by the rapidly growing cities of the south and west. Even though Washington, DC, no longer ranks as one of the 20 largest cities in terms of population, its importance in the legal job market is unlikely to diminish. Not surprisingly, New York City accounts for by far the largest number of jobs with location reported, just over nine percent of the total.

Jobs by State
States vary widely in the number of jobs each provides, again reflecting the distribution of the total population. However, the top 10 states in terms of total reported jobs taken by law graduates have remained the same over the past six years, with New York and California consistently ranked first and second.

Number of Jobs by Region*—Full- and Part-time Jobs
Number of Jobs = 30,900

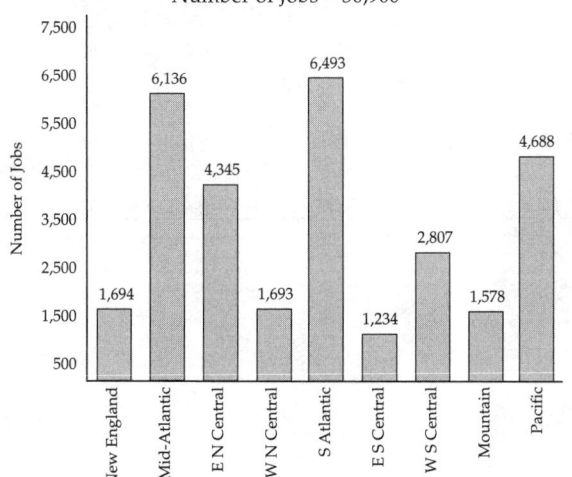

Note: Jobs in foreign locations—232 jobs—are not shown.

*See page 46 for US Census Bureau Regions

Cities with the Largest Number of Jobs Reported

City	Number of Jobs
New York	2,828
Washington, DC	1,667
Chicago	1,331
Los Angeles	1,005
Houston	745
Boston	641
Philadelphia	527
Atlanta	501
San Francisco	475
Dallas	449
Minneapolis/St. Paul	391
Miami	351
Seattle	343
San Diego	340
Cleveland	334
St. Louis	307
Columbus	268
Pittsburgh	264
Phoenix	228
Indianapolis	220

Place of Work Versus Place of School
Nationally, about 78 percent of jobs were accepted by graduates who had attended law school in the same region. Comparing the location of graduates' law school training with the location of their first job provides an understanding of the extent to which each geographic market attracts and absorbs graduates from within that market. The data collected here (see page 46) do not allow for various factors (such as the perceived attractiveness of each market and individual preferences) to be isolated. Nonetheless, the data can provide insights into geographic variations in the employment market for new law graduates and two components of that market —the supply of new graduates and the demand for new graduates. The accompanying table shows that regions with the highest percentage of jobs going to regional graduates are also the regions where the total supply of graduates exceeded the number of jobs taken by the largest margin. This finding suggests that there is a correlation between a region's supply of graduates and the extent to which employers hired from that supply.

States in Which the Largest Number of Jobs Were Taken
1998–2003

Rank	1998	1999	2000	2001	2002	2003
1	New York	New York	New York	New York	New York	New York
2	California	California	California	California	California	California
3	Texas	Texas	Texas	Texas	Texas	Texas
4	Illinois	Illinois	Washington, DC	Washington, DC	Washington, DC	Illinois
5	Washington, DC	Washington, DC	Illinois	Illinois	Illinois	Florida
6	Florida	Florida	Florida	Florida	Florida	Washington, DC
7	Pennsylvania	Pennsylvania	Pennsylvania	Pennsylvania	Pennsylvania	Pennsylvania
8	Ohio	Ohio	Ohio	Ohio	Ohio	Ohio
9	Massachusetts	Massachusetts	Massachusetts	Massachusetts	Massachusetts	Massachusetts
10	New Jersey	New Jersey	New Jersey	New Jersey	New Jersey	New Jersey

Jobs and Graduates by Region (see boxed table below)

Region

	New England	Mid-Atlantic	East North Central	West North Central	South Atlantic	East South Central	West South Central	Mountain	Pacific	Total
Graduates with Known Employment Status	3,052	5,952	5,703	2,249	7,371	1,408	3,399	1,467	5,186	35,787
Graduates with Known Job Location[†]	2,613	5,070	4,946	1,943	6,344	1,290	2,822	1,258	4,382	30,900
Jobs Reported in Region	1,694	6,136	4,345	1,693	6,493	1,234	2,807	1,578	4,688	30,668
Graduates Staying in Region	1,343	4,333	3,718	1,442	4,865	959	2,399	1,019	3,793	23,871
Percentage of Jobs to Region Graduates	79.3	70.6	85.6	85.2	74.9	77.7	85.5	64.6	80.9	77.8
Percentage of Graduates Staying in Region	51.4	85.5	75.2	74.2	76.7	74.3	85.0	81.0	86.6	77.3
Ratio of Graduates to Jobs	1.80	0.97	1.31	1.33	1.14	1.14	1.21	0.93	1.11	1.17

[†]Includes foreign locations

US Census Bureau Regions

	Region	States Included
1.	New England	CT, ME, MA, NH, RI, VT
2.	Mid-Atlantic	NJ, NY, PA
3.	East North Central	IL, IN, MI, OH, WI
4.	West North Central	IA, KS, MN, MO, NE, ND, SD
5.	South Atlantic	DE, DC, FL, GA, MD, NC, SC, VA, WV
6.	East South Central	AL, KY, MS, TN
7.	West South Central	AR, LA, OK, TX
8.	Mountain	AZ, CO, ID, MT, NV, NM, UT, WY
9.	Pacific	AK, CA, HI, OR, WA

Career Placement and Bar Passage Chart

| | Career Placement | | | | | | | | | | | | | | Bar Passage* | | |
| | Employment Status | | | | | Type of Employment | | | | | | Location | | | | | |
	% Employment Status Known	% Employed	% Pursuing Graduate Degree	% Unemployed - Seeking	% Unemployed - Not Seeking	% in Law Firms	% in Business & Industry	% in Government	% in Public Interest	% in Judicial Clerkships	% in Academia	% Employed in State	% Employed in Foreign Nations	# States where employed	State where most take exam	% Pass rate for first-time test takers	% State's overall pass rate for first-time test takers
Alabama																	
Alabama	100.0	90.9	4.9	2.4	1.8	71.1	6.0	12.8	1.3	7.4	1.3	76.5	0.0	11	AL	92	81
Samford	99.4	92.9	2.6	3.2	1.3	79.3	4.8	5.5	0.7	9.0	0.7	70.3	0.0	12	AL	89	81
Arizona																	
Arizona	99.3	85.3	5.3	6.0	3.3	43.0	4.7	24.2	4.7	21.9	1.6	68.7	0.0	17	AZ	93	77
Arizona State	93.8	86.7	3.3	2.2	7.7	47.1	14.0	24.2	1.9	10.2	2.5	82.2	0.0	16	AZ	76	77
Arkansas																	
Arkansas-Fayetteville	98.0	91.8	5.1	3.1	0.0	64.4	10.0	1.1	14.4	6.7	4.4	74.4	0.0	9	AR	78	79
Arkansas-Little Rock	96.2	85.3	7.8	4.9	2.0	47.1	16.1	18.4	2.3	12.6	3.4	83.9	0.0	8	AR	86	79
California																	
California-Berkeley	100.0	92.3	1.8	2.2	3.6	66.0	1.2	7.5	5.9	16.2	1.6	70.8	2.0	19	CA	89	60
California-Davis	100.0	82.7	2.5	6.2	8.6	55.2	6.0	14.2	7.5	5.2	0.0	77.6	0.7	8	CA	80	60
California-Hastings	94.8	92.2	1.8	1.5	4.5	69.0	5.7	8.7	4.9	5.4	1.9	89.1	0.5	13	CA	76	60
California-Los Angeles	100.0	85.0	0.0	3.1	12.0	75.5	2.9	5.4	6.5	7.2	1.1	85.2	0.7	13	CA	89	60
California Western	93.6	86.9	0.9	10.0	2.3	65.6	9.4	9.9	3.1	5.2	1.0	68.7	2.1	20	CA	62	60
Chapman	97.9	90.4	2.1	5.3	2.1	41.2	36.5	5.9	2.4	7.1	4.7	90.6	1.2	6	CA	54	60
Golden Gate	91.6	62.5	2.5	2.5	32.5	60.0	12.0	10.7	5.3	5.3	6.7	88.0	0.0	7	CA	29	60
Loyola Marymount	100.0	94.6	0.5	3.5	1.5	67.6	16.2	5.7	6.0	1.0	2.1	94.5	0.0	13	CA	68	60
Pacific, McGeorge	100.0	94.8	0.9	0.9	3.4	53.8	15.4	21.7	2.7	3.2	1.8	86.4	0.0	15	CA	68	60
Pepperdine	99.0	80.9	3.5	12.6	3.0	68.9	11.8	5.6	0.0	3.1	3.1	78.3	0.0	17	CA	70	60
San Diego	94.7	89.1	7.5	2.6	0.7	65.1	13.0	10.1	5.0	3.4	0.8	86.1	0.0	18	CA	79	60
San Francisco	96.7	90.4	0.6	8.4	0.6	57.8	10.6	13.0	1.9	3.1	1.2	85.7	0.0	6	CA	64	60
Santa Clara	98.3	81.6	1.8	14.2	2.5	46.1	11.3	8.3	1.7	3.0	0.9	83.5	0.4	15	CA	66	60
Southern California	100.0	96.7	1.0	0.5	1.9	69.5	18.2	4.9	3.9	1.5	2.0	88.2	0.5	15	CA	79	60
Southwestern	88.7	90.4	0.0	2.7	6.9	55.9	14.1	11.2	1.2	0.6	0.0	94.7	0.0	9	CA	57	60
Stanford	99.5	97.9	1.0	0.5	0.5	64.9	3.7	2.1	2.7	26.6	0.0	44.7	2.1	24	CA	90	60
Thomas Jefferson	74.5	90.5	2.9	4.8	1.9	53.7	22.1	5.3	1.1	7.4	1.1	68.4	2.1	20	CA	47	60
Whittier	97.4	86.2	1.6	9.0	3.2	53.4	29.4	7.4	4.9	1.2	3.7	88.3	1.2	14	CA	30	60
Colorado																	
Colorado	97.3	90.3	0.7	5.6	3.5	41.5	10.0	16.2	5.4	23.8	3.1	70.0	0.8	25	CO	86	75
Denver	99.7	92.4	6.4	0.5	0.8	51.0	21.2	12.4	2.2	9.4	1.1	80.4	0.3	30	CO	69	75

| | Career Placement | | | | | | | | | | | | | | Bar Passage* | | |
| | Employment Status | | | | | Type of Employment | | | | | | Location | | | | | |
	% Employment Status Known	% Employed	% Pursuing Graduate Degree	% Unemployed - Seeking	% Unemployed - Not Seeking	% in Law Firms	% in Business & Industry	% in Government	% in Public Interest	% in Judicial Clerkships	% in Academia	% Employed in State	% Employed in Foreign Nations	# States where employed	State where most take exam	% Pass rate for first-time test takers	% State's overall pass rate for first-time test takers
Connecticut																	
Connecticut	97.6	95.8	0.6	3.0	0.6	49.1	15.7	11.3	3.8	18.9	1.3	64.8	0.0	17	CT	88	81
Quinnipiac	96.4	86.1	2.3	9.7	1.9	40.9	23.1	19.9	1.1	8.6	1.1	73.7	0.5	11	CT	81	81
Yale	99.5	94.9	2.8	1.4	0.9	46.8	2.4	2.4	4.9	42.0	1.5	5.4	3.4	30	NY	95	75
Delaware																	
Widener	90.4	84.0	1.9	11.0	3.0	35.7	20.4	14.5	0.0	19.5	1.8	24.4	0.0	7	PA	58	76
District of Columbia																	
American	99.0	90.3	5.4	1.8	2.6	42.8	21.0	17.8	5.1	11.3	2.0	47.3	0.8	28	MD	70	71
Catholic	99.7	88.3	1.0	7.6	3.1	37.7	19.1	23.0	3.1	15.2	1.9	47.9	0.0	21	MD	65	71
District of Columbia	94.1	84.4	9.4	0.0	6.2	37.0	18.5	11.1	22.2	7.4	3.7	44.4	0.0	11	MD	35	71
George Washington	100.0	96.6	0.5	2.5	0.5	56.5	7.4	17.3	2.6	12.4	0.5	46.8	0.5	34	MD	80	71
Georgetown	97.8	90.4	0.3	1.5	7.8	62.9	2.2	9.8	3.4	10.5	0.7	34.2	1.5	33	NY	92	75
Howard	96.6	95.6	1.8	2.7	0.0	46.3	21.3	19.4	5.6	5.6	1.9	41.7	0.0	25	MD	54	71
Florida																	
Barry	94.0	84.1	1.6	3.2	11.1	41.5	26.4	24.5	1.9	0.0	5.7	96.2	0.0	3	FL	43	76
Florida	99.8	88.4	6.0	3.9	1.6	55.8	6.8	22.3	1.6	4.7	1.6	79.3	0.3	19	FL	79	76
Florida A&M	0.0	0.0	0.0	0.0	0.0	0.0	0.0	0.0	0.0	0.0	0.0	0.0	0.0	0			
Florida Coastal	100.0	93.6	0.8	4.0	1.6	53.8	21.4	18.8	3.4	1.7	0.9	81.2	0.0	14	FL	77	76
Florida International	0.0	0.0	0.0	0.0	0.0	0.0	0.0	0.0	0.0	0.0	0.0	0.0	0.0	0			
Florida State	98.0	89.8	5.3	0.4	4.5	45.5	5.5	35.0	3.2	5.0	0.5	88.2	1.4	11	FL	81	76
Miami	91.4	92.8	3.7	2.2	1.2	65.7	9.1	16.2	3.0	4.0	0.3	80.5	0.3	19	FL	80	76
Nova Southeastern	82.6	83.7	2.4	13.1	0.8	57.8	15.2	17.5	0.9	2.4	0.9	87.2	0.5	9	FL	58	76
St. Thomas	90.3	77.9	8.6	8.6	5.0	64.2	11.0	13.8	4.6	1.8	2.8	89.0	0.0	10	FL	57	76
Stetson	98.7	90.5	3.0	4.3	2.2	56.2	7.6	28.6	1.4	3.8	2.4	90.0	0.0	13	FL	80	76
Georgia																	
Emory	100.0	90.3	2.3	4.6	2.8	61.0	7.7	14.4	1.0	10.3	1.0	41.0	0.0	28	GA	93	83
Georgia	98.0	94.0	3.5	2.0	0.5	60.8	6.3	10.1	3.7	16.4	2.1	84.1	0.0	15	GA	90	83
Georgia State	98.2	89.0	2.4	5.5	3.0	63.0	10.3	15.8	0.7	8.2	2.1	90.4	0.0	11	GA	91	83
Mercer	98.7	93.2	4.8	2.0	0.0	72.3	5.8	12.4	0.7	7.3	0.7	78.8	0.7	9	GA	84	83
Hawai'i																	
Hawai'i	98.6	90.3	6.9	1.4	1.4	29.2	10.8	15.4	1.5	40.0	1.5	86.2	1.5	5	HI	91	86
Idaho																	
Idaho	100.0	85.3	6.3	7.4	1.1	40.7	4.9	21.0	1.2	25.9	6.2	65.4	0.0	11	ID	76	80
Illinois																	
Chicago	100.0	96.2	0.0	1.4	2.4	74.4	1.5	3.4	3.0	16.3	1.5	40.4	0.5	28	IL	97	84
Chicago-Kent	98.9	89.3	1.8	2.6	6.3	65.8	11.9	16.9	0.4	2.9	2.1	87.2	0.0	21	IL	88	84
DePaul	99.3	83.1	2.1	11.3	3.5	58.9	15.7	16.5	2.5	1.3	3.0	87.3	0.8	18	IL	73	84
Illinois	100.0	94.6	1.5	1.5	2.5	67.2	8.3	9.9	1.6	10.9	2.1	71.9	2.1	21	IL	97	84
John Marshall	98.4	82.4	2.6	14.4	0.6	58.1	12.4	19.0	3.5	3.9	1.6	88.0	0.0	16	IL	69	84

	Career Placement														Bar Passage*		
	Employment Status					Type of Employment						Location					
	% Employment Status Known	% Employed	% Pursuing Graduate Degree	% Unemployed - Seeking	% Unemployed - Not Seeking	% in Law Firms	% in Business & Industry	% in Government	% in Public Interest	% in Judicial Clerkships	% in Academia	% Employed in State	% Employed in Foreign Nations	# States where employed	State where most take exam	% Pass rate for first-time test takers	% State's overall pass rate for first-time test takers
Loyola-Chicago	99.1	92.0	2.4	1.4	4.2	55.9	14.4	20.5	1.5	7.7	0.0	87.2	0.5	14	IL	88	84
Northern Illinois	99.0	93.7	1.0	5.2	0.0	48.9	13.3	23.3	3.3	2.2	1.1	78.9	0.0	10	IL	83	84
Northwestern	100.0	95.0	0.9	0.0	3.5	73.1	5.1	3.2	1.9	16.2	0.5	44.0	2.3	24	IL	98	84
Southern Illinois	97.1	89.0	5.0	4.0	2.0	66.3	4.5	21.3	2.2	4.5	1.1	62.9	0.0	15	IL	78	84

Indiana

Indiana-Bloomington	99.5	81.6	4.7	1.4	12.3	54.9	8.7	14.5	2.9	9.8	5.8	51.4	0.0	21	IN	86	79
Indiana-Indianapolis	100.0	88.6	1.6	9.8	0.0	51.2	19.4	17.5	4.1	2.8	2.8	84.3	0.9	15	IN	79	79
Notre Dame	97.7	96.0	2.3	1.7	0.0	68.7	4.2	9.0	1.8	15.1	1.2	11.4	1.8	34	IL	97	84
Valparaiso	89.3	86.2	1.8	10.1	1.8	63.8	7.4	12.8	1.1	7.4	4.3	52.1	0.0	16	IN	79	79

Iowa

Drake	87.5	94.1	2.5	3.4	0.0	58.9	16.1	11.6	1.8	7.1	0.9	64.3	0.9	15	IA	80	86
Iowa	100.0	93.5	5.6	0.9	0.0	54.6	9.3	14.4	4.6	13.0	1.4	29.6	0.9	29	IA	93	86

Kansas

Kansas	95.4	84.9	0.0	13.7	1.4	48.4	18.5	18.5	3.2	7.3	2.4	38.7	1.6	23	KS	84	83
Washburn	98.4	88.6	4.1	4.1	3.3	51.4	12.8	18.3	9.2	6.4	1.8	72.5	0.0	13	KS	78	83

Kentucky

Kentucky	100.0	96.0	4.0	0.0	0.0	59.5	6.6	11.6	3.3	18.2	0.8	78.5	0.8	16	KY	86	79
Louis D. Brandeis, Louisville	100.0	94.7	2.7	2.7	0.0	56.1	14.0	22.4	1.9	3.7	1.9	78.5	0.9	11	KY	77	79
Northern Kentucky	97.0	96.9	0.0	3.1	0.0	47.9	23.4	12.8	1.1	12.8	2.1	53.2	0.0	6	KY	77	79

Louisiana

Louisiana State	95.1	86.9	4.0	8.5	0.6	64.7	3.9	7.2	0.0	24.2	0.0	83.0	0.0	13	LA	73	61
Loyola-New Orleans	100.0	84.4	7.1	1.3	7.1	50.3	21.2	9.5	2.1	16.4	0.5	66.7	0.5	19	LA	60	61
Southern	88.8	90.5	5.3	2.1	2.1	52.3	2.3	12.8	1.2	26.7	2.3	82.6	0.0	6	LA	34	61
Tulane	96.6	87.3	5.1	4.1	3.5	57.2	6.5	7.2	3.3	10.5	0.0	22.5	1.1	30	LA	70	61

Maine

Maine	100.0	86.9	4.9	6.6	1.6	43.4	13.2	9.4	3.8	24.5	1.9	66.0	1.9	14	ME	64	71

Maryland

Baltimore	82.6	86.6	1.0	10.5	1.9	37.0	10.5	17.1	2.2	21.5	2.2	74.0	0.0	7	MD	67	71
Maryland	98.8	83.7	7.1	1.6	7.5	36.0	15.6	18.0	2.8	24.6	2.8	66.4	0.9	18	MD	78	71

Massachusetts

Boston College	98.2	96.3	1.5	1.5	0.7	67.2	5.7	8.4	3.8	14.5	0.4	45.4	0.4	24	MA	90	82
Boston	99.7	94.6	3.7	0.0	1.7	66.7	3.6	8.6	5.0	14.0	2.2	31.2	1.1	31	MA	91	82
Harvard	99.5	97.7	1.9	0.2	0.2	67.0	3.0	2.7	4.1	22.3	0.9	10.9	3.4	37	NY	96	75
New England	93.1	83.4	3.9	11.8	0.9	48.2	16.8	20.4	4.7	5.8	2.1	62.8	1.0	24	MA	70	82
Northeastern	100.0	90.2	1.6	7.1	1.1	40.0	18.8	6.7	16.4	16.4	1.8	65.5	0.6	18	MA	88	82
Suffolk	98.7	88.8	1.1	9.5	0.6	52.6	21.7	14.5	1.0	6.9	2.4	83.3	0.5	21	MA	81	82
Western New England	88.7	81.4	2.5	14.4	1.7	30.2	32.3	16.7	5.2	11.5	3.1	37.5	0.0	20	MA	65	82

| | Career Placement | | | | | | | | | | | | | | Bar Passage* | |
| | Employment Status | | | | | Type of Employment | | | | | | Location | | | | | |
	% Employment Status Known	% Employed	% Pursuing Graduate Degree	% Unemployed - Seeking	% Unemployed - Not Seeking	% in Law Firms	% in Business & Industry	% in Government	% in Public Interest	% in Judicial Clerkships	% in Academia	% Employed in State	% Employed in Foreign Nations	# States where employed	State where most take exam	% Pass rate for first-time test takers	% State's overall pass rate for first-time test takers
Michigan																	
Ave Maria	100.0	90.8	0.0	6.2	3.1	47.5	10.2	16.9	5.1	16.9	3.4	42.4	1.7	19	MI	93	75
Detroit Mercy	90.3	85.7	3.6	8.3	2.4	62.5	13.9	9.7	2.8	4.2	6.9	95.8	2.8	2	MI	69	75
Michigan	99.7	92.8	3.1	1.1	3.1	61.3	4.2	5.4	5.7	22.2	1.2	14.1	0.9	36	NY	95	75
Michigan State	95.7	89.4	4.0	4.0	2.5	55.6	14.6	17.4	1.7	6.2	1.7	66.3	0.0	22	MI	85	75
Thomas M. Cooley	80.6	77.1	3.4	19.0	0.6	46.7	15.1	19.1	1.5	11.4	4.0	48.5	1.1	28	MI	51	75
Wayne State	100.0	89.6	1.1	9.3	0.0	64.0	13.4	11.6	4.9	4.3	1.2	95.7	1.8	3	MI	83	75
Minnesota																	
Hamline	92.9	81.9	2.8	8.3	6.9	44.9	25.4	11.0	5.1	11.9	0.0	77.1	0.0	20	MN	82	89
Minnesota	99.6	97.6	1.6	0.0	0.8	52.1	12.5	10.0	6.7	15.4	0.0	62.1	1.7	27	MN	98	89
St. Thomas	0.0	0.0	0.0	0.0	0.0	0.0	0.0	0.0	0.0	0.0	0.0	0.0	0.0	0			
William Mitchell	77.8	84.4	1.3	12.5	1.8	55.0	18.0	10.6	1.6	13.2	1.6	91.0	0.5	12	MN	90	89
Mississippi																	
Mississippi	100.0	91.8	5.7	1.9	0.6	72.4	2.8	7.6	0.7	13.8	2.8	69.7	0.0	14	MI	91	92
Mississippi College	100.0	98.4	0.8	0.8	0.0	71.1	3.3	7.4	0.8	17.4	0.0	81.0	0.0	4	MI	87	92
Missouri																	
Missouri-Columbia	100.0	92.1	2.8	3.4	1.7	56.4	8.0	25.8	0.6	4.9	1.2	84.0	0.0	12	MO	84	84
Missouri-Kansas City	100.0	84.2	4.5	11.3	0.0	68.7	9.8	19.6	0.0	1.8	0.0	75.9	0.9	9	MO	88	84
St. Louis	100.0	93.0	0.0	1.5	5.5	64.0	16.1	8.6	4.3	4.3	2.7	82.3	0.0	15	MO	78	84
Washington	97.6	96.7	2.9	0.0	0.4	68.2	4.7	12.3	6.4	5.5	0.4	32.2	0.8	33	MO	89	84
Montana																	
Montana	98.8	79.3	11.0	8.5	1.2	44.6	7.7	15.4	1.5	29.2	0.0	63.1	0.0	16	MT	76	82
Nebraska																	
Creighton	100.0	91.2	3.4	2.7	2.7	57.0	20.0	11.1	0.7	6.7	3.7	53.3	0.0	20	NE	74	82
Nebraska	98.4	84.2	4.2	5.8	5.8	44.6	15.8	21.8	6.9	5.9	5.0	68.3	1.0	19	NE	95	82
Nevada																	
William S. Boyd	100.0	78.8	0.8	12.9	7.6	39.4	17.3	21.2	2.9	17.3	1.0	91.3	0.0	5	NV	57	65
New Hampshire																	
Franklin Pierce	98.5	82.4	5.3	2.3	9.9	53.7	11.1	8.3	3.7	8.3	2.8	28.7	5.6	22	NH	57	63
New Jersey																	
Rutgers-Camden	93.2	95.5	0.9	2.7	0.9	35.2	13.8	7.1	0.5	41.0	0.0	64.8	0.0	16	NJ	79	73
Rutgers-Newark	97.7	89.2	1.9	4.2	4.7	46.3	7.9	6.8	3.2	34.7	1.1	68.4	0.0	10	NJ	72	73
Seton Hall	97.9	91.9	0.9	6.6	0.6	30.4	14.7	7.8	1.3	41.8	0.3	82.7	0.0	15	NJ	79	73
New Mexico																	
New Mexico	99.0	92.2	1.9	3.9	1.9	49.5	5.3	29.5	2.1	10.5	2.1	80.0	2.1	14	NM	88	86

| | Career Placement | | | | | | | | | | | | | | Bar Passage* | | |
| | Employment Status | | | | | Type of Employment | | | | | | Location | | | | | |
	% Employment Status Known	% Employed	% Pursuing Graduate Degree	% Unemployed - Seeking	% Unemployed - Not Seeking	% in Law Firms	% in Business & Industry	% in Government	% in Public Interest	% in Judicial Clerkships	% in Academia	% Employed in State	% Employed in Foreign Nations	# States where employed	State where most take exam	% Pass rate for first-time test takers	% State's overall pass rate for first-time test takers
New York																	
Albany	100.0	93.5	1.6	3.7	1.2	44.8	19.1	19.1	2.2	7.8	1.7	83.0	0.4	14	NY	67	75
Brooklyn	100.0	91.7	1.4	1.8	5.1	63.4	16.0	10.6	2.0	7.8	0.2	88.0	0.2	17	NY	83	75
Buffalo, SUNY	96.6	85.8	8.0	3.1	3.1	58.0	16.6	13.5	6.2	3.1	2.6	81.9	1.6	17	NY	74	75
Cardozo	99.3	85.0	4.3	5.6	5.0	66.8	12.5	11.7	2.0	5.9	1.2	81.2	3.1	13	NY	86	75
City U of NY	74.4	83.3	1.0	6.2	9.4	23.7	17.5	20.0	31.2	3.7	2.5	71.2	1.2	8	NY	55	75
Columbia	100.0	97.1	0.0	2.2	0.7	80.2	1.5	1.8	3.3	13.1	0.3	71.4	2.3	24	NY	96	75
Cornell	100.0	97.7	0.6	1.7	0.0	75.7	1.7	3.5	1.7	12.1	2.3	60.1	0.6	21	NY	93	75
Fordham	98.4	98.3	0.5	0.0	1.2	76.5	10.3	5.0	1.4	4.3	0.5	82.0	1.0	17	NY	85	75
Hofstra	93.7	86.0	5.9	2.1	5.9	65.5	12.3	12.8	1.0	5.9	1.5	83.3	0.5	10	NY	64	75
New York Law	93.1	92.0	0.9	4.8	2.3	50.2	13.3	11.1	3.4	6.5	0.9	68.7	0.3	14	NY	71	75
New York	100.0	97.1	0.7	0.7	1.6	70.0	2.5	2.7	9.8	14.4	0.5	66.4	2.5	30	NY	97	75
Pace	96.5	86.7	1.0	8.7	3.6	46.7	21.9	14.8	2.4	5.3	1.8	77.5	0.0	6	NY	71	75
St. John's	98.2	91.7	0.0	2.5	5.8	63.4	14.2	17.3	0.8	3.1	0.4	88.2	0.4	15	NY	85	75
Syracuse	95.9	86.9	4.7	4.7	3.8	55.6	10.7	13.2	2.4	14.6	1.0	43.9	1.5	30	NY	80	75
Touro	95.7	73.3	2.2	24.4	0.0	63.6	15.2	14.1	6.1	1.0	0.0	91.9	1.0	4	NY	61	75
North Carolina																	
Campbell	95.9	97.8	1.1	1.1	0.0	74.7	1.1	14.3	1.1	7.7	1.1	93.4	1.1	5	NC	90	76
Duke	100.0	98.4	1.0	0.0	0.5	72.3	2.1	5.3	0.5	18.6	1.1	11.2	1.1	27	NY	99	75
North Carolina	99.4	91.1	3.5	2.5	2.9	61.2	7.0	10.5	4.5	15.7	1.0	52.4	0.3	24	NC	85	76
North Carolina Central	88.4	90.8	1.3	6.6	1.3	60.9	10.1	11.6	15.9	1.4	0.0	87.0	0.0	5	NC	70	76
Wake Forest	95.0	94.0	3.3	2.6	0.0	59.9	9.9	7.0	1.4	16.2	1.4	44.4	0.0	22	NC	87	76
North Dakota																	
North Dakota	98.5	92.2	1.6	3.1	3.1	52.5	6.8	16.9	8.5	15.3	0.0	44.1	3.4	8	ND	75	78
Ohio																	
Akron	97.7	83.7	1.6	12.4	2.3	47.2	19.4	20.4	3.7	6.5	0.9	79.6	0.9	14	OH	84	79
Capital	98.1	89.5	2.4	4.3	3.8	48.1	23.5	19.3	2.7	3.7	2.7	85.6	0.0	14	OH	59	79
Case Western	98.5	94.8	3.6	0.0	1.5	57.6	11.4	11.4	4.9	5.4	4.3	59.8	1.6	19	OH	83	79
Cincinnati	99.3	94.0	4.5	1.5	0.0	54.0	13.5	12.7	7.1	7.9	3.2	71.4	0.0	17	OH	87	79
Cleveland State	96.9	91.8	1.4	5.9	0.9	55.4	20.8	12.4	2.0	7.4	2.0	90.1	0.0	13	OH	71	79
Dayton	93.3	93.7	0.0	5.4	0.9	61.9	17.1	11.4	1.0	6.7	1.0	67.6	1.0	18	OH	83	79
Ohio Northern	97.2	94.3	2.9	2.9	0.0	60.6	9.1	13.6	1.5	9.1	3.0	34.8	0.0	22	OH	75	79
Ohio State	96.3	91.5	5.2	2.4	0.9	59.1	10.9	16.1	2.6	9.8	1.6	69.4	2.1	20	OH	91	79
Toledo	98.1	96.2	0.0	3.8	0.0	50.0	17.6	20.6	1.0	2.9	2.9	63.7	1.0	14	OH	80	79
Oklahoma																	
Oklahoma	89.6	85.0	2.0	10.2	2.7	61.6	4.0	22.4	4.8	4.0	3.2	72.8	0.0	11	OK	91	82
Oklahoma City	100.0	79.5	0.8	18.1	1.6	59.4	11.9	20.8	0.0	0.0	2.0	70.3	0.0	10	OK	65	82
Tulsa	98.1	78.6	7.5	13.8	0.0	68.8	16.0	13.6	0.8	0.8	0.0	65.6	0.0	20	OK	86	82
Oregon																	
Lewis & Clark	95.9	91.5	2.6	2.1	3.7	48.0	14.5	19.1	11.0	6.4	1.2	67.1	0.0	19	OR	77	78
Oregon	95.8	85.7	8.7	4.3	1.2	44.2	11.6	11.6	4.3	19.6	8.7	57.2	0.0	18	OR	77	78
Willamette	100.0	86.8	4.4	4.4	4.4	50.8	17.8	16.1	1.7	9.3	0.8	61.9	0.8	16	OR	76	78

	Career Placement — Employment Status					Career Placement — Type of Employment						Career Placement — Location			Bar Passage*		
	% Employment Status Known	% Employed	% Pursuing Graduate Degree	% Unemployed - Seeking	% Unemployed - Not Seeking	% in Law Firms	% in Business & Industry	% in Government	% in Public Interest	% in Judicial Clerkships	% in Academia	% Employed in State	% Employed in Foreign Nations	# States where employed	State where most take exam	% Pass rate for first-time test takers	% State's overall pass rate for first-time test takers
Pennsylvania																	
Duquesne	97.8	95.1	1.6	2.2	1.1	55.5	19.7	9.2	2.9	12.7	0.0	87.9	0.0	9	PA	70	76
Penn State, Dickinson	98.8	90.2	1.8	2.5	5.5	53.1	8.8	13.6	4.8	17.0	0.0	63.9	0.0	16	PA	87	76
Pennsylvania	100.0	97.6	0.8	0.0	1.6	69.0	2.1	3.8	3.3	21.8	0.0	27.2	1.3	20	NY	92	75
Pittsburgh	99.2	90.2	2.1	3.0	4.7	63.2	14.6	7.1	1.9	8.5	2.4	72.6	0.5	23	PA	81	76
Temple	96.2	95.1	0.0	3.3	1.6	51.0	15.9	13.5	5.9	9.7	1.7	75.7	0.3	16	PA	83	76
Villanova	99.6	90.6	4.7	3.9	0.9	58.3	12.8	9.5	2.8	15.6	1.4	64.0	0.9	16	PA	83	76
Widener	99.0	88.0	1.0	10.0	1.0	39.8	12.5	23.9	0.0	22.7	0.0	68.2	0.0	7	PA	68	76
Puerto Rico																	
Inter American	95.8	94.0	2.7	2.7	0.5	49.7	7.0	18.7	3.5	8.8	1.8	99.4	0.0	2	PR	44	54
Pontifical Catholic	93.2	86.8	1.5	11.8	0.0	33.9	8.5	38.1	0.8	2.5	0.0	0.0	0.0	0	PR	44	54
Puerto Rico	33.5	82.7	0.0	15.4	1.9	55.8	9.3	16.3	0.0	16.3	2.3	95.3	0.0	2	PR	71	54
Rhode Island																	
Roger Williams	80.4	80.0	1.1	17.8	1.1	47.2	15.3	15.3	5.6	12.5	1.4	62.5	0.0	11	RI	68	67
South Carolina																	
South Carolina	97.7	93.5	4.7	0.9	0.9	57.0	5.0	11.0	1.0	26.0	0.0	85.0	1.5	14	SC	82	78
South Dakota																	
South Dakota	100.0	84.6	3.8	9.6	1.9	38.6	2.3	22.7	0.0	34.1	0.0	84.1	0.0	6	SD	73	76
Tennessee																	
Memphis	99.2	96.2	2.3	0.8	0.8	76.4	7.1	7.1	0.8	8.7	0.0	90.6	0.0	9	TN	88	81
Tennessee	97.5	87.9	1.3	2.5	8.3	75.4	6.5	5.1	2.2	10.1	0.7	68.1	0.0	16	TN	88	81
Vanderbilt	99.5	95.1	2.2	0.5	2.2	66.1	4.0	10.9	1.7	16.7	0.0	23.6	2.3	32	TN	82	81
Texas																	
Baylor	99.4	94.3	3.8	0.6	1.3	79.9	6.0	6.0	0.0	7.4	0.0	91.3	0.7	10	TX	94	80
Houston	100.0	89.7	1.8	5.5	3.0	70.4	16.0	3.3	3.3	4.5	2.5	96.3	0.0	5	TX	88	80
South Texas	94.4	81.9	2.0	14.8	1.3	71.9	10.4	10.8	1.2	3.6	0.4	96.4	0.0	6	TX	73	80
SMU Dedman	96.9	89.5	2.7	4.1	3.6	69.5	7.6	9.6	2.0	7.1	1.0	86.3	0.0	15	TX	92	80
St. Mary's	83.4	76.2	2.8	10.5	10.5	60.1	10.9	15.2	4.3	3.6	0.0	83.3	2.9	4	TX	71	80
Texas	100.0	95.5	1.0	0.8	2.7	62.3	7.1	11.8	4.5	11.8	1.7	75.4	1.3	34	TX	93	80
Texas Southern	88.0	91.8	2.7	5.5	0.0	49.3	11.9	1.5	6.0	3.7	2.2	81.3	1.5	13	TX	49	80
Texas Tech	91.3	98.5	0.5	1.0	0.0	70.6	7.1	17.3	0.5	4.6	0.0	97.0	0.0	4	TX	85	80
Texas Wesleyan	94.7	85.4	1.4	13.2	0.0	54.5	13.0	17.9	2.4	1.6	2.4	95.9	0.0	6	TX	76	80
Utah																	
Brigham Young	100.0	94.5	1.8	1.2	2.4	56.1	10.3	13.5	2.6	15.5	1.9	44.5	0.6	21	UT	98	92
Utah	97.5	93.2	3.4	1.7	1.7	55.0	16.5	16.5	1.8	9.2	0.9	71.6	0.0	13	UT	88	92
Vermont																	
Vermont	100.0	86.9	5.9	3.3	3.9	36.1	20.3	17.3	6.8	14.3	1.5	30.8	3.0	35	VT	71	80

| | Career Placement | | | | | | | | | | | | | | | Bar Passage* | |
| | Employment Status | | | | | Type of Employment | | | | | | Location | | | | | |
	% Employment Status Known	% Employed	% Pursuing Graduate Degree	% Unemployed - Seeking	% Unemployed - Not Seeking	% in Law Firms	% in Business & Industry	% in Government	% in Public Interest	% in Judicial Clerkships	% in Academia	% Employed in State	% Employed in Foreign Nations	# States where employed	State where most take exam	% Pass rate for first-time test takers	% State's overall pass rate for first-time test takers
Virginia																	
Appalachian	63.6	85.7	0.0	11.9	2.4	69.4	11.1	0.0	0.0	19.4	0.0	44.4	0.0	11	VA	52	72
George Mason	100.0	94.0	2.2	0.5	3.3	48.5	14.6	17.5	4.7	9.9	4.7	52.0	1.8	14	VA	72	72
Regent	88.9	80.0	2.5	15.0	2.5	32.3	26.0	21.9	4.2	5.2	9.4	47.9	0.0	19	VA	53	72
Richmond	97.5	91.8	4.4	1.9	1.9	55.2	20.0	11.0	0.7	13.1	0.0	0.0	0.0	0	VA	77	72
Virginia	100.0	96.6	1.1	0.3	2.0	76.2	1.2	4.8	3.0	13.4	0.0	13.1	1.5	33	VA	93	72
Washington and Lee	99.1	91.3	1.7	2.6	4.3	49.5	6.7	11.4	1.9	28.6	0.0	24.8	0.0	24	VA	79	72
William & Mary	98.8	89.9	4.2	1.2	4.8	46.4	13.2	17.9	2.6	18.5	1.3	38.4	0.7	25	VA	77	72
Washington																	
Gonzaga	100.0	76.9	8.4	4.9	9.8	41.8	19.1	21.8	3.6	11.8	1.8	50.0	0.9	20	WA	74	74
Seattle	100.0	94.7	4.0	0.0	1.3	35.6	33.1	18.0	4.6	6.7	2.1	89.1	0.0	11	WA	72	74
Washington	98.7	87.5	7.2	0.0	5.3	51.1	7.5	16.5	6.0	14.3	3.8	79.7	0.0	13	WA	85	74
West Virginia																	
West Virginia	94.4	94.1	3.0	0.7	2.2	52.0	6.3	9.4	1.6	23.6	5.5	84.3	0.8	9	WV	73	72
Wisconsin																	
Marquette	91.7	95.2	0.5	3.7	0.5	70.8	12.4	6.2	2.2	6.2	2.2	78.1	1.1	17	WI	100	79
Wisconsin	95.7	95.1	2.5	0.8	1.6	64.1	10.8	13.9	1.7	8.7	0.9	52.4	1.3	22	WI	100	79
Wyoming																	
Wyoming	98.4	85.0	3.3	5.0	6.7	39.2	11.8	17.6	3.9	23.5	0.0	54.9	2.0	13	WY	60	65

*Bar Passage data are for the Summer 2003 and Winter 2004 exams.

New England

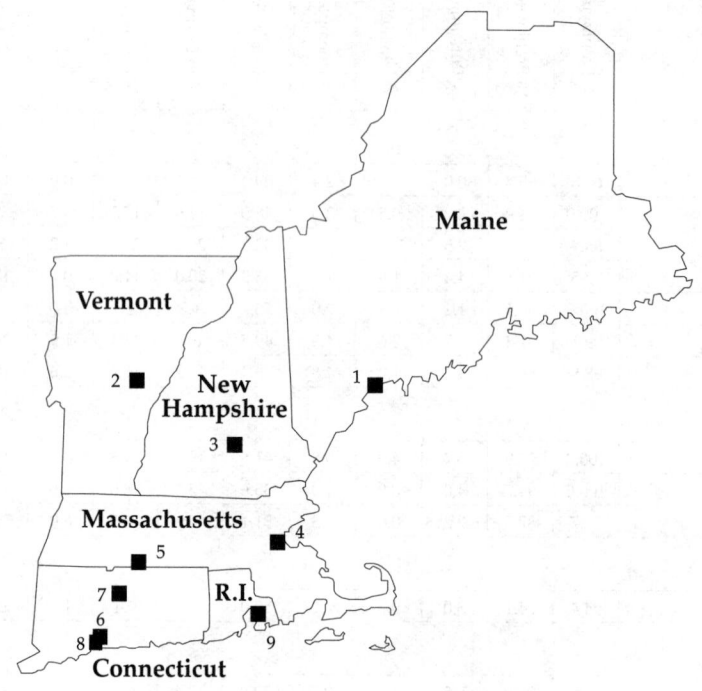

Maine
1. **Portland—Population: 64,249**
    Maine—Enrollment: 271/7

Vermont
2. **South Royalton—Population: 750**
    Vermont—Enrollment: 545/0

New Hampshire
3. **Concord—Population: 40,687**
    Franklin Pierce—Enrollment: 422/6

Massachusetts
4. **Boston—Population: 589,141**
    Boston College—Enrollment: 795/0
    Boston University—Enrollment: 858/0
    Harvard (Cambridge, MA)—Enrollment: 1,694/0
    New England—Enrollment: 738/363
    Northeastern—Enrollment: 619/0
    Suffolk—Enrollment: 1,063/604

5. **Springfield—Population: 152,082**
    Western New England—Enrollment: 401/184

Connecticut
6. **Hamden—Population: 53,200**
    Quinnipiac—Enrollment: 467/188
7. **Hartford—Population: 121,578**
    Connecticut—Enrollment: 531/156
8. **New Haven—Population: 123,626**
    Yale—Enrollment: 580/1

Rhode Island
9. **Bristol—Population: 22,469***
    Roger Williams—Enrollment: 477/153

"Enrollment" represents the numbers of total full-time/total part-time students unless otherwise indicated.

*Population information is derived from the US Bureau of the Census, Population Division, Washington, DC. Data are accurate as of the 2000 Census. City populations reflect the number of people residing in the city proper, not the metropolitan area which would include outlying suburbs as well. Donald P. Racheter, director of the prelaw program at Central College, also contributed data for these regional maps.

Northeast

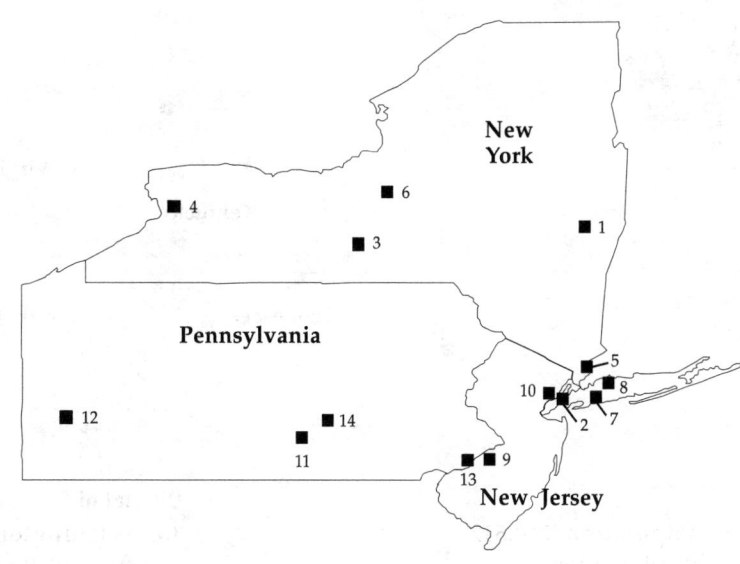

New York
1. **Albany—Population: 95,658**
   Albany—Enrollment: 703/52
2. **New York City—Population: 8,008,278**
   Brooklyn—Enrollment: 1,148/370
   Cardozo, Yeshiva University—Enrollment: 963/74
   City U. of NY—Enrollment: 439/8
   Columbia—Enrollment: 1,239/0
   Fordham—Enrollment: 1,164/358
   New York Law School—Enrollment: 1,180/362
   New York University—Enrollment: 1,360/0
   St. John's (Jamaica, NY)—Enrollment: 759/202
3. **Ithaca—Population: 29,287**
   Cornell—Enrollment: 593/0
4. **Buffalo—Population: 292,648**
   Buffalo, State U. of NY—Enrollment: 737/4
5. **White Plains—Population: 53,077**
   Pace—Enrollment: 529/245
6. **Syracuse—Population: 147,306**
   Syracuse—Enrollment: 781/11
7. **Hempstead—Population: 56,554**
   Hofstra—Enrollment: 872/146
8. **Huntington—Population: 18,403**
   Touro—Enrollment: 489/266

New Jersey
9. **Camden—Population: 79,904**
   Rutgers–Camden—Enrollment: 579/214
10. **Newark—Population: 273,546**
    Rutgers–Newark—Enrollment: 561/249
    Seton Hall—Enrollment: 863/371

Pennsylvania
11. **Carlisle—Population: 17,970**
    Penn State, Dickinson—Enrollment: 622/0
12. **Pittsburgh—Population: 334,563**
    Duquesne—Enrollment: 406/205
    Pittsburgh—Enrollment: 722/0
13. **Philadelphia—Population: 1,517,550**
    Pennsylvania—Enrollment: 833/0
    Temple—Enrollment: 803/250
    Villanova (Villanova, PA)—Enrollment: 762/0
14. **Harrisburg—Population: 48,950**
    Widener—Enrollment: 341/172

Midsouth

Kentucky
1. **Lexington—Population: 260,512**
   Kentucky—Enrollment: 420/0
2. **Louisville—Population: 530,000**
   Louis D. Brandeis—Enrollment: 291/94
3. **Highland Heights—Population: 6,554**
   Northern Kentucky—Enrollment: 302/278

West Virginia
4. **Morgantown—Population: 26,809**
   West Virginia—Enrollment: 456/8

Virginia
5. **Arlington—Population: 189,453**
   George Mason—Enrollment: 396/327
6. **Virginia Beach—Population: 425,257**
   Regent—Enrollment: 439/72
7. **Richmond—Population: 197,790**
   Richmond—Enrollment: 478/0
8. **Charlottesville—Population: 45,049**
   Virginia—Enrollment: 1,100/0
9. **Lexington—Population: 6,867**
   Washington and Lee—Enrollment: 399/0
10. **Williamsburg—Population: 11,998**
    William & Mary—Enrollment: 585/0
11. **Grundy—Population: 1,105**
    Appalachian—Enrollment: 364/5

Maryland
12. **Baltimore—Population: 651,154**
    Baltimore—Enrollment: 656/331
    Maryland—Enrollment: 607/165

District of Columbia
13. **Washington, DC—Population: 572,059**
    American—Enrollment: 1,193/292
    Catholic—Enrollment: 667/284
    District of Columbia—Enrollment: 220/0
    George Washington—Enrollment: 1,311/267
    Georgetown—Enrollment: 1,551/385
    Howard—Enrollment: 517/1

Delaware
14. **Wilmington—Population: 72,664**
    Widener—Enrollment: 681/469

Tennessee
15. **Memphis—Population: 650,100**
    Memphis—Enrollment: 421/22
16. **Knoxville—Population: 173,890**
    Tennessee—Enrollment: 452/0
17. **Nashville—Population: 545,524**
    Vanderbilt—Enrollment: 632/0

North Carolina
18. **Buies Creek—Population: 2,215**
    Campbell—Enrollment: 369/0
19. **Durham—Population: 187,035**
    Duke—Enrollment: 610/30
    North Carolina Central—Enrollment: 338/99
20. **Chapel Hill—Population: 48,715**
    North Carolina—Enrollment: 710/0
21. **Winston-Salem—Population: 185,776**
    Wake Forest—Enrollment: 462/18

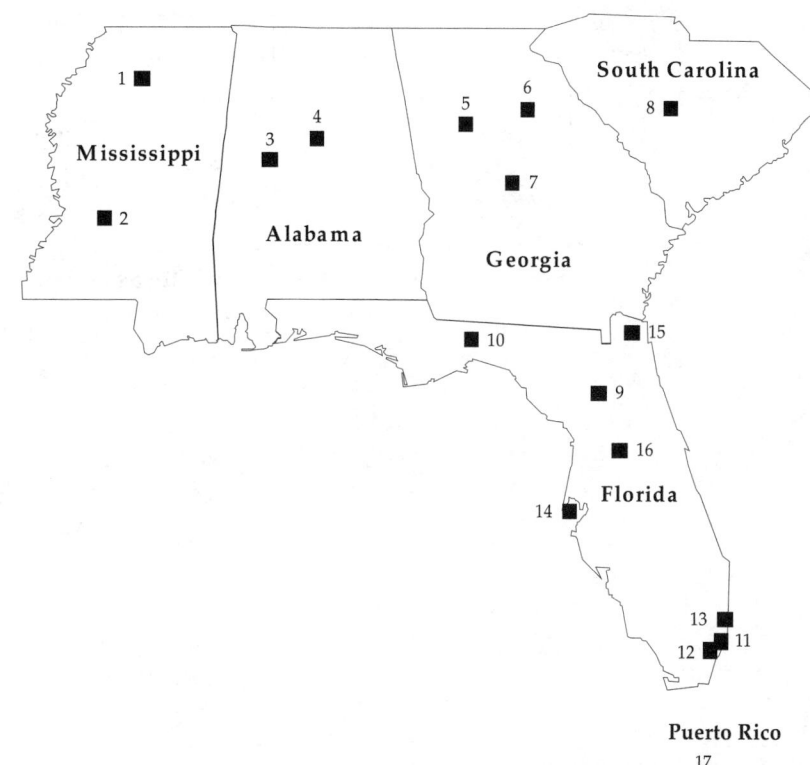

Mississippi

1. **Oxford—Population: 11,756**
   Mississippi—Enrollment: 581/0
2. **Jackson—Population: 184,256**
   Mississippi College—Enrollment: 454/0

Alabama

3. **Tuscaloosa—Population: 77,906**
   Alabama—Enrollment: 536/0
4. **Birmingham—Population: 242,820**
   Samford—Enrollment: 535/5

Georgia

5. **Atlanta—Population: 416,474**
   Emory—Enrollment: 685/0
   Georgia State—Enrollment: 498/183
6. **Athens—Population: 100,266**
   Georgia—Enrollment: 690/0
7. **Macon—Population: 97,255**
   Mercer—Enrollment: 422/2

South Carolina

8. **Columbia—Population: 116,278**
   South Carolina—Enrollment: 751/3

Florida

9. **Gainesville—Population: 95,447**
   Florida—Enrollment: 1,153/0
10. **Tallahassee—Population: 150,624**
    Florida State—Enrollment: 748/0

11. **Miami—Population: 362,470**
    Florida International—Enrollment: 174/110
    St. Thomas—Enrollment: 721/0
12. **Coral Gables—Population: 42,249**
    Miami—Enrollment: 1,157/29
13. **Ft. Lauderdale—Population: 152,397**
    Nova—Enrollment: 770/193
14. **Gulfport—Population: 12,527**
    Stetson—Enrollment: 747/184
15. **Jacksonville—Population: 735,617**
    Florida Coastal—Enrollment: 647/257
16. **Orlando—Population: 185,951**
    Barry—Enrollment: 351/173
    Florida A&M—203/86

Puerto Rico

17. **San Juan—Population: 434,374**
    Inter American—Enrollment: 445/313
    Puerto Rico—Enrollment: 431/283
18. **Ponce—Population: 186,475**
    Pontifical Catholic—Enrollment: 329/161

South Central

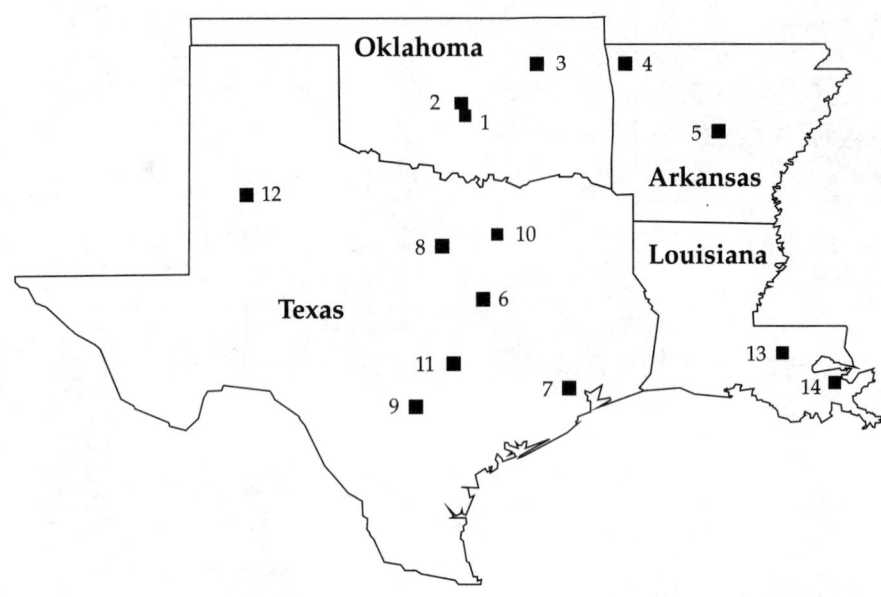

Oklahoma

1. **Norman—Population: 95,694**
   Oklahoma—Enrollment: 519/0
2. **Oklahoma City—Population: 506,132**
   Oklahoma City—Enrollment: 490/194
3. **Tulsa—Population: 393,049**
   Tulsa—Enrollment: 502/116

Arkansas

4. **Fayetteville—Population: 58,047**
   Arkansas–Fayetteville—Enrollment: 474/0
5. **Little Rock—Population: 183,133**
   Arkansas–Little Rock—Enrollment: 319/145

Texas

6. **Waco—Population: 113,726**
   Baylor—Enrollment: 426/0
7. **Houston—Population: 1,953,631**
   Houston—Enrollment: 906/197
   South Texas—Enrollment: 958/296
   Texas Southern—Enrollment: 628/0
8. **Fort Worth—Population: 534,694**
   Texas Wesleyan—Enrollment: 423/261

9. **San Antonio—Population: 1,144,646**
   St. Mary's—Enrollment: 786/0
10. **Dallas—Population: 1,188,580**
    SMU Dedman—Enrollment: 702/139
11. **Austin—Population: 656,562**
    Texas—Enrollment: 1,493/0
12. **Lubbock—Population: 199,564**
    Texas Tech—Enrollment: 683/0

Louisiana

13. **Baton Rouge—Population: 227,818**
    Louisiana State—Enrollment: 639/17
    Southern—Enrollment: 410/54
14. **New Orleans—Population: 484,674**
    Loyola–New Orleans—Enrollment: 633/170
    Tulane—Enrollment: 975/2

Mountain West

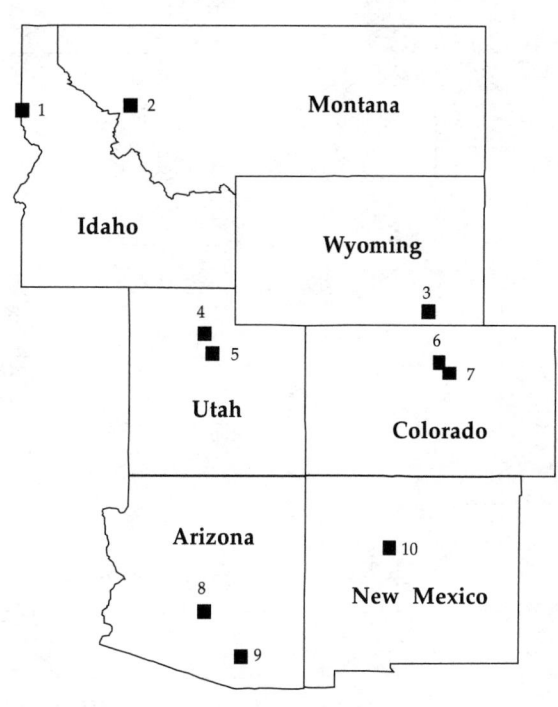

Idaho
1. **Moscow—Population: 21,291**
   Idaho—Enrollment: 301/0

Montana
2. **Missoula—Population: 57,053**
   Montana—Enrollment: 241/0

Wyoming
3. **Laramie—Population: 27,204**
   Wyoming—Enrollment: 229/0

Utah
4. **Salt Lake City—Population: 181,743**
   Utah—Enrollment: 402/0
5. **Provo—Population: 105,166**
   Brigham Young—Enrollment: 483/1

Colorado
6. **Boulder—Population: 94,673**
   Colorado—Enrollment: 502/0
7. **Denver—Population: 554,636**
   Denver—Enrollment: 852/310

Arizona
8. **Tempe—Population: 158,625**
   Arizona State—Enrollment: 594/0
9. **Tucson—Population: 486,699**
   Arizona—Enrollment: 464/0

New Mexico
10. **Albuquerque—Population: 448,607**
    New Mexico—Enrollment: 342/0

Far West

California

1. **Berkeley—Population: 102,743**
   California–Berkeley—Enrollment: 880/0
2. **Davis—Population: 60,308**
   California–Davis—Enrollment: 563/0
3. **Orange—Population: 128,821**
   Chapman—Enrollment: 453/68
4. **Los Angeles—Population: 3,694,820**
   California–Los Angeles—Enrollment: 943/0
   Loyola—Enrollment: 1,000/331
   Pepperdine—Enrollment: 720/0
   Southern California—Enrollment: 630/0
   Southwestern—Enrollment: 660/307
5. **Sacramento—Population: 407,018**
   Pacific, McGeorge, U. of—Enrollment: 721/383
6. **San Diego—Population: 1,223,400**
   California Western—Enrollment: 808/126
   San Diego—Enrollment: 772/258
   Thomas Jefferson—Enrollment: 622/211

7. **San Francisco—Population: 776,733**
   University of California–Hastings—
   Enrollment: 1,238/1
   Golden Gate—Enrollment: 667/186
   San Francisco—Enrollment: 590/126
8. **Santa Clara—Population: 102,361**
   Santa Clara—Enrollment: 747/229
9. **Costa Mesa—Population: 108,724**
   Whittier—Enrollment: 670/336
10. **Stanford—Population: 13,315**
    Stanford—Enrollment: 514/0

Hawai'i

11. **Honolulu—Population: 371,657**
    Hawai'i—Enrollment: 324/0

Nevada

12. **Las Vegas—Population: 478,434**
    Nevada–Las Vegas—Enrollment: 304/163

Northwest

Washington
1. **Seattle—Population: 563,374**
   Washington—Enrollment: 552/0
   Seattle—Enrollment: 847/255
2. **Spokane—Population: 195,629**
   Gonzaga—Enrollment: 604/24

Oregon
3. **Portland—Population: 529,121**
   Lewis & Clark—Enrollment: 533/209
4. **Salem—Population: 136,924**
   Willamette—Enrollment: 461/5
5. **Eugene—Population: 137,893**
   Oregon—Enrollment: 529/0

Midwest

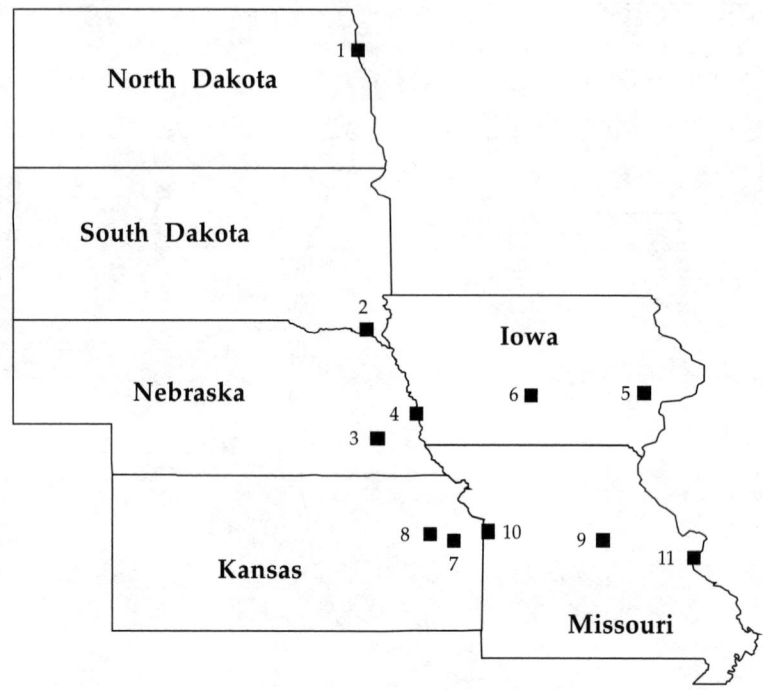

North Dakota
1. Grand Forks—Population: 49,321
    North Dakota—Enrollment: 203/0

South Dakota
2. Vermillion—Population: 9,765
    South Dakota—Enrollment: 248/3

Nebraska
3. Lincoln—Population: 225,581
    Nebraska—Enrollment: 405/3
4. Omaha—Population: 390,007
    Creighton—Enrollment: 455/23

Iowa
5. Iowa City—Population: 62,220
    Iowa—Enrollment: 712/0
6. Des Moines—Population: 198,682
    Drake—Enrollment: 454/19

Kansas
7. Lawrence—Population: 80,098
    Kansas—Enrollment: 524/0
8. Topeka—Population: 122,377
    Washburn—Enrollment: 462/0

Missouri
9. Columbia—Population: 84,531
    Missouri–Columbia—Enrollment: 435/2
10. Kansas City—Population: 441,545
    Missouri–Kansas City—Enrollment: 487/41
11. St. Louis—Population: 348,189
    St. Louis—Enrollment: 642/235
    Washington University—Enrollment: 752/4

Great Lakes

Minnesota

1. **Minneapolis—Population: 382,618**
    Minnesota—Enrollment: 817/0
    St. Thomas—Enrollment: 361/0
2. **St. Paul—Population: 287,151**
    Hamline—Enrollment: 515/199
    William Mitchell—Enrollment: 653/425

Wisconsin

3. **Madison—Population: 208,054**
    Wisconsin—Enrollment: 800/51
4. **Milwaukee—Population: 596,974**
    Marquette—Enrollment: 563/158

Michigan

5. **Lansing—Population: 119,128**
    Thomas M. Cooley—Enrollment: 475/2,393
    Michigan State—Enrollment: 894/223
6. **Detroit—Population: 951,270**
    Detroit, Mercy—Enrollment: 407/197
    Wayne State—Enrollment: 537/186
7. **Ann Arbor—Population: 114,024**
    Michigan—Enrollment: 1,182/0
    Ave Maria—Enrollment: 302/0

Illinois

8. **Chicago—Population: 2,896,016**
    Chicago—Enrollment: 596/0
    Chicago–Kent—Enrollment: 804/268
    DePaul—Enrollment: 776/335
    John Marshall—Enrollment: 1,046/361
    Loyola–Chicago—Enrollment: 604/243
    Northwestern—Enrollment: 780/0
9. **DeKalb—Population: 39,018**
    Northern Illinois—Enrollment: 313/11
10. **Champaign—Population: 67,518**
    Illinois—Enrollment: 679/0
11. **Carbondale—Population: 20,681**
    Southern Illinois—Enrollment: 389/1

Indiana

12. **South Bend—Population: 107,789**
    Notre Dame—Enrollment: 553/0
13. **Valparaiso—Population: 27,428**
    Valparaiso—Enrollment: 513/46
14. **Indianapolis—Population: 781,870**
    Indiana–Indianapolis—Enrollment: 623/270
15. **Bloomington—Population: 69,291**
    Indiana–Bloomington—Enrollment: 635/2

Ohio

16. **Toledo—Population: 313,619**
    Toledo—Enrollment: 344/173
17. **Cleveland—Population: 478,403**
    Case Western Reserve—Enrollment: 689/19
    Cleveland State—Enrollment: 494/253
18. **Akron—Population: 217,074**
    Akron—Enrollment: 350/219
19. **Ada—Population: 5,582**
    Ohio Northern—Enrollment: 318/0
20. **Columbus—Population: 711,470**
    Capital—Enrollment: 474/313
    Ohio State—Enrollment: 747/0
21. **Dayton—Population: 166,179**
    Dayton—Enrollment: 543/1
22. **Cincinnati—Population: 331,285**
    Cincinnati—Enrollment: 382/0

	Application Fee ($)	Admission Fall 2004 — Full-time 75% GPA	FT 25% GPA	FT 75% LSAT	FT 25% LSAT	FT # Accepted	FT # of Matriculants	Part-time 75% GPA	PT 25% GPA	PT 75% LSAT	PT 25% LSAT	PT # Accepted	PT # of Matriculants	Total # Accepted	Total # of Matriculants	Student Body # Full-time	SB # Part-time	SB % Men	SB % Women	SB % Minorities	Faculty # Full-time	Fac # Part-time	Fac % Men	Fac % Women	Student/Faculty Ratio	# Credits Required for JD	Tuition Resident, Full-time	Nonresident, Full-time	Resident, Part-time	Nonresident, Part-time	Official Guide Page #	Grid included •
Alabama																																
Alabama	25	3.70	3.10	163	159	318	171	0.00	0.00	0	0	0	0	318	171	536	0	63.1	36.9	9.1	37	34	74.1	25.9	12.1	90	8,130	16,802	0	0	82	•
Samford	50	3.49	2.90	157	154	380	170	3.16	2.69	157	152	6	4	386	174	535	5	61.9	38.1	8.0	22	23	79.6	20.4	20.4	90	23,758	23,758	14,255	14,255	622	•
Arizona																																
Arizona	50	3.69	3.27	164	157	471	155	0.00	0.00	0	0	0	0	471	155	464	0	50.0	50.0	30.6	30	27	60.3	39.7	12.9	85	12,597	21,577	0	0	98	•
Arizona State	50	3.74	3.16	162	155	627	211	0.00	0.00	0	0	0	0	627	211	594	0	53.4	46.6	28.3	53	22	76.8	23.2	9.8	87	12,380	20,900	0	0	102	•
Arkansas																																
Arkansas-Fayetteville	0	3.68	3.06	159	150	331	162	0.00	0.00	0	0	0	0	331	162	474	0	54.0	46.0	21.1	29	10	67.4	32.6	13.8	90	8,694	17,274	0	0	106	•
Arkansas-Little Rock	0	3.76	3.13	157	152	173	90	3.56	2.95	157	149	81	58	254	148	319	145	50.2	49.8	10.8	21	40	55.9	44.1	16.5	90	8,317	16,549	6,199	12,079	110	•
California																																
California-Berkeley	75	3.90	3.63	168	161	771	270	0.00	0.00	0	0	0	0	771	270	880	0	39.2	60.8	37.0	51	55	62.9	37.1	14.4	85	21,531	33,776	0	0	150	•
California-Davis	75	3.72	3.39	164	160	843	194	0.00	0.00	0	0	0	0	843	194	563	0	43.3	56.7	37.7	35	13	66.0	34.0	14.3	88	21,224	33,469	0	0	154	•
California-Hastings	75	3.73	3.40	165	160	1,398	427	0.00	0.00	0	0	0	0	1,398	427	1238	1	45.8	54.2	33.4	45	183	57.8	42.2	22.9	86	20,919	33,119	0	0	158	•
California-Los Angeles	75	3.84	3.47	168	163	987	308	0.00	0.00	0	0	0	0	987	308	943	0	51.1	48.9	30.0	69	16	73.0	27.0	11.6	87	22,123	33,168	0	0	162	•
California Western	45	3.47	2.95	157	152	1,156	306	3.26	2.86	156	151	68	24	1,224	330	808	126	49.6	50.4	21.5	38	34	60.0	40.0	19.5	89	28,920	28,920	20,450	20,450	166	•
Chapman	60	3.47	3.00	158	154	595	181	0.00	0.00	0	0	0	0	595	181	453	68	49.7	50.3	26.5	22	35	66.7	33.3	18.9	88	27,941	27,941	19,217	19,217	190	•
Golden Gate	60	3.43	2.92	155	151	1,145	298	3.22	2.64	156	150	122	59	1,267	357	667	186	42.6	57.4	28.6	31	68	54.7	45.3	21.2	88	26,000	26,000	18,640	18,640	318	•
Loyola Marymount	50	3.58	3.14	159	156	932	343	3.55	2.94	162	155	120	79	1,052	422	1000	331	53.6	46.4	38.5	62	55	64.3	35.7	16.4	87	29,828	29,828	20,022	20,022	398	•
Pacific, McGeorge	50	3.46	2.88	160	156	865	255	3.45	2.86	156	152	178	106	1,043	361	721	383	51.7	48.3	20.0	92	58	67.3	32.1	8.8	88	29,275	29,275	19,481	19,481	550	•
Pepperdine	50	3.71	3.31	161	157	879	250	0.00	0.00	0	0	0	0	879	250	720	0	49.2	50.8	17.4	29	45	64.8	35.2	19.7	88	29,690	29,690	0	0	562	•
San Diego	50	3.60	3.19	164	160	1,144	245	3.37	2.96	159	156	230	107	1,374	352	772	258	55.0	45.0	28.2	53	39	72.5	27.5	14.8	85	30,796	30,796	21,896	21,896	626	•
San Francisco	60	3.54	2.98	162	157	997	190	3.43	2.88	160	157	125	67	1,122	257	590	126	49.3	50.7	31.1	32	35	65.3	34.7	17.5	86	29,057	29,057	20,785	20,785	630	•
Santa Clara	75	3.61	3.23	160	156	1,433	250	3.52	3.12	159	154	167	74	1,608	324	747	229	49.1	50.9	42.4	38	24	53.1	46.9	19.7	86	30,750	30,750	21,525	21,525	634	•
Southern California	70	3.76	3.54	167	163	1,376	203	0.00	0.00	0	0	0	0	1,376	203	630	0	52.1	47.9	41.1	40	54	62.3	37.7	13.1	88	36,025	36,025	0	0	662	•
Southwestern	50	3.64	3.13	157	153	769	253	3.52	3.07	156	151	147	94	916	347	660	307	48.7	51.3	36.7	43	18	69.3	30.7	16.7	87	28,600	0	18,150	0	674	•
Stanford	65	3.94	3.77	172	166	390	166	0.00	0.00	0	0	0	0	390	166	514	0	52.9	47.1	33.7	45	22	65.4	34.6	9.5	86	34,230	0	0	0	678	

School	Application Fee ($)	FT 75% GPA	FT 25% GPA	FT 75% LSAT	FT 25% LSAT	FT # Accepted	FT # of Matriculants	PT 75% GPA	PT 25% GPA	PT 75% LSAT	PT 25% LSAT	PT # Accepted	PT # of Matriculants	Total # Accepted	Total # of Matriculants	SB # Full-time	SB # Part-time	SB % Men	SB % Women	SB % Minorities	Fac # Full-time	Fac # Part-time	Fac % Men	Fac % Women	Student/Faculty Ratio	# Credits Required for JD	Resident, Full-time	Nonresident, Full-time	Resident, Part-time	Nonresident, Part-time	Official Guide Page #	Grid included
Thomas Jefferson	35	3.35	2.67	157	150	936	223	3.32	2.65	157	149	136	58	1,072	281	622	211	59.5	40.5	18.0	23	27	63.0	37.0	27.6	88	26,950	26,950	16,950	16,950	722	
Whittier	50	3.35	2.69	155	150	836	297	3.34	2.74	154	149	174	93	1,010	390	670	336	46.7	53.3	37.8	38	52	53.2	46.8	19.6	87	27,790	27,790	16,690	16,690	798	•
Colorado																																
Colorado	65	3.84	3.45	164	159	679	166	0.00	0.00	0	0	0	0	679	166	502	0	48.4	51.6	20.1	25	19	64.4	35.6	16.7	89	10,737	26,329	0	0	214	•
Denver	60	3.46	2.81	162	153	700	246	3.48	2.86	158	148	122	90	822	336	852	310	50.4	49.6	21.6	62	71	63.1	36.2	14.2	90	23,308	23,308	16,640	16,640	238	•
Connecticut																																
Connecticut	30	3.58	3.13	164	160	461	126	3.61	3.15	160	156	161	64	622	190	531	156	50.2	49.8	21.3	42	34	70.7	29.3	12.3	86	15,388	31,780	10,774	22,214	222	•
Quinnipiac	40	3.54	2.98	156	152	547	154	3.41	2.88	154	150	136	76	683	230	467	188	52.8	47.2	6.7	32	33	66.7	33.3	15.4	86	30,280	30,280	21,340	21,340	578	•
Yale	70	3.96	3.79	175	168	246	189	0.00	0.00	0	0	0	0	246	189	580	1	55.8	44.2	31.0	61	43	70.3	29.7	7.9	82	36,490	36,490	0	0	828	•
Delaware																																
Widener	60	3.42	2.84	155	151	764	221	3.41	2.71	153	148	337	170	1,101	391	681	469	52.4	47.6	11.7	41	47	59.1	40.9	20.1	87	26,870	26,870	20,170	20,170	802	•
District of Columbia																																
American	65	3.61	3.22	162	159	2,002	366	3.68	3.09	160	156	285	94	2,287	460	1193	292	40.6	59.4	28.8	75	119	63.0	36.5	15.4	86	31,108	31,108	21,837	21,837	90	•
Catholic	60	3.52	3.05	160	155	763	233	3.39	2.88	158	152	186	77	949	310	667	284	49.8	50.2	18.5	41	53	69.8	30.2	17.4	84	30,185	0	21,820	0	186	•
District of Columbia	35	3.41	2.82	154	148	248	81	0.00	0.00	0	0	0	0	248	81	220	86	39.1	60.9	46.4	15	19	56.8	43.2	12.2	90	7,135	14,135	0	0	250	
George Washington	70	3.78	3.45	166	162	N/A	393	3.65	3.22	164	160	N/A	119	2,066	512	1311	267	53.7	46.3	28.9	85	181	69.1	30.9	14.6	84	32,620	32,620	22,940	22,940	302	•
Georgetown	70	3.80	3.43	170	166	2,143	453	3.71	3.18	166	160	190	130	2,333	583	1551	385	54.2	45.8	23.6	102	105	75.7	24.3	14.8	83	33,055	33,055	24,200	24,200	306	•
Howard	60	3.49	2.86	156	148	488	158	0.00	0.00	0	0	0	0	488	158	517	1	34.7	65.3	92.1	23	16	50.0	50.0	18.8	88	16,895	16,895	0	0	346	•
Florida																																
Barry	50	3.27	2.72	151	146	422	173	3.32	2.66	152	147	317	68	739	241	351	173	52.9	47.1	20.2	18	17	61.4	38.6	21.5	90	24,600	24,600	18,450	18,450	122	•
Florida	30	3.81	3.35	161	155	813	418	0.00	0.00	0	0	0	0	813	418	1153	0	52.3	47.7	22.8	60	34	63.1	36.9	15.9	88	7,168	26,475	0	0	270	•
Florida A&M	20	3.33	2.77	150	143	143	87	3.37	2.67	151	146	51	33	194	120	203	86	39.8	60.2	53.3	16	0	56.5	43.5	13.5	90	7,274	26,696	5,365	19,608	274	
Florida Coastal	50	3.38	2.71	153	149	1,722	347	3.32	2.85	152	147	251	86	1,973	433	647	257	53.5	46.5	15.2	36	29	50.7	49.3	18.9	87	23,410	23,410	18,920	18,920	278	•
Florida International	20	3.51	2.88	156	152	139	65	3.46	2.83	156	151	64	47	203	112	174	110	56.3	43.7	56.3	14	8	67.6	32.4	14.7	90	7,129	25,751	5,092	18,395	282	•
Florida State	20	3.65	3.29	161	156	828	243	0.00	0.00	0	0	0	0	828	243	748	0	53.1	46.9	20.9	46	30	60.2	39.8	13.9	88	7,504	27,517	0	0	286	•
Miami	50	3.59	3.16	160	155	1,754	426	3.51	3.20	166	161	14	3	1,768	429	1157	29	53.3	46.7	21.8	49	100	68.1	31.9	20.0	88	29,458	29,458	21,812	21,812	430	•

Chapter 12: Key Facts About ABA-Approved Law Schools

	Application Fee ($)	Admission Fall 2004 Full-time 75% GPA	FT 25% GPA	FT 75% LSAT	FT 25% LSAT	FT # Accepted	FT # of Matriculants	Part-time 75% GPA	PT 25% GPA	PT 75% LSAT	PT 25% LSAT	PT # Accepted	PT # of Matriculants	Total # Accepted	Total # of Matriculants	Student Body # Full-time	SB # Part-time	SB Men %	SB Women %	SB Minorities %	Faculty # Full-time	Fac # Part-time	Fac Men %	Fac Women %	Student/Faculty Ratio	# Credits Required for JD	Tuition Resident, Full-time	Nonresident, Full-time	Resident, Part-time	Nonresident, Part-time	Official Guide Page #	Grid included •
Nova Southeastern	50	3.32	2.79	152	148	0	299	3.17	2.72	153	146	0	60	746	359	770	193	50.3	49.7	30.3	49	56	58.6	41.4	15.3	90	23,873	23,873	17,905	17,905	522	•
St. Thomas	45	3.26	2.58	153	148	788	274	0.00	0.00	0	0	0	0	788	274	721	0	55.2	44.8	41.9	22	47	57.7	42.3	27.3	90	24,700	24,700	0	0	614	•
Stetson	55	3.66	3.16	157	151	727	299	3.41	2.73	157	149	123	72	850	371	747	184	46.9	53.1	21.6	41	47	60.0	40.0	17.7	88	24,940	24,940	17,240	17,240	682	•
Georgia																																
Emory	70	3.62	3.27	165	161	1,016	215	0.00	0.00	0	0	0	0	1,016	215	685	0	49.1	50.9	22.2	40	21	63.9	36.1	14.2	90	32,772	32,772	0	0	266	•
Georgia	30	3.82	3.35	164	157	580	235	0.00	0.00	0	0	0	0	580	235	690	0	49.4	50.6	18.0	33	13	68.9	31.1	17.4	88	7,978	25,084	0	0	310	•
Georgia State	50	3.62	3.08	160	156	506	183	3.68	3.00	163	157	71	47	577	230	498	183	50.4	49.6	17.6	33	15	58.3	41.7	15.6	90	6,112	20,306	5,696	18,698	314	•
Mercer	50	3.63	3.05	158	154	375	143	0.00	0.00	0	0	0	0	375	143	422	2	54.2	45.8	13.4	25	9	65.1	34.9	14.4	91	25,450	25,450	0	0	426	•
Hawai'i																																
Hawai'i	60	3.64	3.08	160	154	230	100	0.00	0.00	0	0	0	0	230	100	324	0	45.1	54.9	60.8	17	21	56.5	43.5	15.9	89	11,529	19,689	0	0	334	•
Idaho																																
Idaho	50	3.68	3.06	158	153	270	113	0.00	0.00	0	0	0	0	270	113	301	0	58.5	41.5	9.3	17	5	66.7	33.3	14.8	88	7,572	15,592	0	0	350	•
Illinois																																
Chicago	65	3.78	3.47	171	167	750	192	0.00	0.00	0	0	0	0	750	192	596	0	55.5	44.5	31.5	50	18	74.1	25.9	9.9	105	34,419	34,419	0	0	194	•
Chicago-Kent	60	3.64	3.14	162	157	987	280	3.41	2.94	158	154	224	101	1,211	381	805	268	53.7	46.4	18.5	65	79	68.5	31.5	12.5	87	27,696	27,696	20,240	20,240	198	•
DePaul	60	3.54	2.97	161	156	1,132	262	3.41	3.01	156	153	312	102	1,444	364	776	335	48.6	51.4	19.6	49	41	60.0	40.0	17.0	86	27,710	27,710	18,000	18,000	242	•
Illinois	40	3.64	3.12	165	160	676	228	0.00	0.00	0	0	0	0	676	228	679	0	58.2	41.8	32.3	39	25	70.3	29.7	14.4	90	15,888	28,224	0	0	354	•
John Marshall	50	3.35	2.74	156	152	1,073	392	3.30	1.30	155	151	244	130	1,317	522	1046	361	58.6	41.4	15.1	55	109	71.8	28.2	19.5	90	26,756	26,756	19,140	19,140	374	•
Loyola-Chicago	50	3.58	3.17	162	159	565	174	3.45	2.85	159	153	131	75	696	249	604	243	45.6	54.4	17.2	37	104	54.1	45.9	17.2	86	28,440	28,440	21,390	21,390	402	•
Northern Illinois	50	3.59	2.94	158	153	391	102	3.77	2.69	151	146	5	3	396	105	313	11	46.3	53.7	28.7	15	8	66.7	33.3	17.7	90	10,504	18,850	0	0	506	•
Northwestern	80	3.78	3.47	170	166	774	245	0.00	0.00	0	0	0	0	774	245	780	0	51.7	48.3	28.8	52	54	61.0	39.0	12.5	86	35,896	35,896	0	0	514	•
Southern Illinois	50	3.64	3.15	156	151	291	129	0.00	0.00	0	0	0	0	291	129	389	1	64.1	35.9	6.2	23	14	53.2	46.8	14.1	90	9,004	24,184	0	0	666	•
Indiana																																
Indiana-Bloomington	35	3.74	2.97	164	158	952	202	0.00	0.00	0	0	0	0	952	202	635	2	58.4	41.6	16.2	38	9	67.7	32.3	13.9	88	13,045	25,875	0	0	358	•
Indiana-Indianapolis	45	3.70	3.14	158	152	368	201	3.52	2.88	158	150	106	85	474	286	623	270	52.7	47.3	15.0	47	33	62.4	37.6	14.2	90	11,661	24,472	7,402	15,667	362	•
Notre Dame	55	3.77	3.26	167	162	516	178	0.00	0.00	0	0	0	0	516	178	553	0	55.9	44.1	20.6	28	33	67.9	32.1	15.6	90	30,140	30,140	0	0	518	•
Valparaiso	50	3.62	3.01	155	150	581	164	3.48	2.91	150	145	42	25	623	189	513	46	49.0	51.0	10.6	27	19	62.5	37.5	16.8	90	25,282	25,282	15,766	15,766	746	•

School	Application Fee ($)	FT 75% GPA	FT 25% GPA	FT 75% LSAT	FT 25% LSAT	FT # Accepted	FT # Matriculants	PT 75% GPA	PT 25% GPA	PT 75% LSAT	PT 25% LSAT	PT # Accepted	PT # Matriculants	Total # Accepted	Total # Matriculants	SB # Full-time	SB # Part-time	SB % Men	SB % Women	SB % Minorities	Fac # Full-time	Fac # Part-time	Fac % Men	Fac % Women	Student/Faculty Ratio	# Credits Required for JD	Tuition Resident Full-time	Tuition Nonresident Full-time	Tuition Resident Part-time	Tuition Nonresident Part-time	Official Guide Page #	Grid included
Iowa																																
Drake	40	3.67	3.12	157	153	481	168	0.00	0.00	0	0	3	3	484	171	454	19	50.1	49.9	9.1	21	17	65.9	34.1	18.5	90	22,550	22,550	0	0	254	•
Iowa	50	3.82	3.32	163	156	494	248	0.00	0.00	0	0	0	0	494	248	712	0	52.4	47.6	16.4	44	14	62.2	37.8	13.5	90	12,348	26,556	0	0	370	•
Kansas																																
Kansas	50	3.80	3.28	160	153	313	167	0.00	0.00	0	0	0	0	313	167	524	0	55.7	44.3	21.4	28	20	63.2	36.8	15.6	90	8,725	16,573	0	0	378	•
Washburn	40	3.60	2.95	156	151	370	157	0.00	0.00	0	0	0	0	370	157	462	0	55.4	44.6	12.8	26	20	67.3	32.7	14.8	90	10,766	17,682	0	0	770	•
Kentucky																																
Kentucky	50	3.81	3.33	162	156	397	144	0.00	0.00	0	0	0	0	397	144	420	0	56.2	43.8	6.2	21	17	70.5	29.5	16.7	90	10,268	19,868	0	0	382	•
Louis D. Brandeis, Louisville	45	3.63	3.16	159	154	229	97	3.70	2.94	158	149	67	37	296	134	291	94	46.8	53.2	8.1	21	11	66.7	33.3	14.0	90	9,200	20,760	7,680	17,300	390	•
Northern Kentucky	30	3.57	3.09	157	152	252	104	3.50	2.85	154	149	181	120	433	224	302	278	56.2	43.8	7.1	23	17	59.6	40.4	17.6	90	9,240	20,184	7,700	16,820	510	•
Louisiana																																
Louisiana State	25	3.76	3.25	158	151	473	213	0.00	0.00	0	0	0	0	473	213	639	17	48.3	51.7	12.5	33	28	78.7	20.0	16.4	97	11,650	20,746	0	0	394	•
Loyola-New Orleans	40	3.63	3.16	156	151	593	215	3.53	3.00	154	147	87	57	680	272	633	170	47.8	52.2	20.3	37	17	77.6	22.4	17.6	90	27,746	27,746	18,716	18,716	406	•
Southern	25	3.25	2.66	149	144	251	148	3.25	2.55	151	144	53	46	304	194	410	54	51.9	48.1	64.7	28	18	54.9	45.1	13.3	96	5,724	10,324	3,604	5,904	670	•
Tulane	60	3.73	3.28	163	158	1,055	300	0.00	0.00	0	0	0	0	1,055	300	975	2	49.7	50.3	18.0	43	26	75.3	24.7	18.8	88	31,210	31,210	31,210	0	734	•
Maine																																
Maine	50	3.54	3.15	158	153	271	85	0.00	0.00	0	0	0	0	271	85	271	7	44.6	55.4	5.8	12	10	60.0	40.0	19.1	90	14,114	22,514	9,470	15,070	410	•
Maryland																																
Baltimore	60	3.56	2.97	155	151	729	252	3.57	3.01	156	151	155	93	884	345	656	331	49.2	50.8	20.5	34	84	68.7	31.3	21.4	90	7,165	12,786	594	1,000	118	•
Maryland	60	3.75	3.31	162	155	438	221	3.54	3.02	161	150	48	34	486	255	607	165	44.6	55.4	26.8	54	56	60.7	39.3	11.1	85	16,253	27,532	12,311	20,771	418	•
Massachusetts																																
Boston College	65	3.75	3.43	166	162	1,298	259	0.00	0.00	0	0	0	0	1,298	259	795	0	49.4	50.6	20.1	47	29	58.7	41.3	14.1	85	31,596	31,596	0	0	130	•
Boston	65	3.76	3.45	165	162	1,329	291	0.00	0.00	0	0	0	0	1,329	291	858	0	49.4	50.6	24.5	58	26	75.6	24.4	12.9	84	31,408	31,408	0	0	134	•
Harvard	75	3.94	3.73	175	169	834	554	0.00	0.00	0	0	0	0	834	554	1694	0	56.0	44.0	28.1	127	32	71.0	29.0	11.3	80	34,568	0	0	0	330	
New England	50	3.45	2.91	154	150	1,074	256	3.38	2.77	152	147	243	138	1,317	394	738	363	45.4	54.6	12.9	29	72	59.0	41.0	28.0	84	22,475	0	16,875	0	474	•
Northeastern	65	3.62	3.19	162	157	921	223	0.00	0.00	0	0	0	0	921	223	619	0	38.8	61.2	26.8	27	28	55.0	45.0	19.1	103	31,281	31,281	0	0	502	•

Chapter 12: Key Facts About ABA-Approved Law Schools

School	Application Fee ($)	FT 75% GPA	FT 25% GPA	FT 75% LSAT	FT 25% LSAT	FT # Accepted	FT # Matric	PT 75% GPA	PT 25% GPA	PT 75% LSAT	PT 25% LSAT	PT # Accepted	PT # Matric	Total # Accepted	Total # Matric	SB # Full-time	SB # Part-time	SB % Men	SB % Women	SB % Minorities	Fac # Full-time	Fac # Part-time	Fac % Men	Fac % Women	Student/Faculty Ratio	# Credits Req. for JD	Tuition Res. Full-time	Nonres. Full-time	Res. Part-time	Nonres. Part-time	Official Guide Page #	Grid included
Suffolk	60	3.50	3.00	159	154	1,042	356	3.40	2.90	158	152	275	186	1,317	542	1063	604	49.6	50.4	11.6	70	65	73.0	27.0	17.4	84	29,980	29,980	22,486	22,486	686	•
Western New England	50	3.41	2.80	157	151	565	141	3.03	2.65	152	147	109	53	674	194	401	184	53.2	46.8	10.6	23	18	67.3	32.7	18.9	88	27,060	27,060	20,002	20,002	794	•
Michigan																																
Ave Maria	50	3.49	2.78	161	152	541	146	0.00	0.00	0	0	0	0	541	146	302	0	69.5	30.5	17.2	18	9	65.8	34.2	14.0	90	27,500	27,500	0	0	114	
Detroit Mercy	50	3.47	2.90	152	147	461	162	3.48	3.01	152	148	138	70	599	232	407	197	53.0	47.0	7.3	25	23	67.9	32.1	17.9	90	12,828	12,828	8,838	8,838	246	•
Michigan	60	3.77	3.44	169	164	1,098	381	0.00	0.00	0	0	0	0	1,098	381	1182	0	55.9	44.1	25.4	61	23	64.9	35.1	16.0	80	29,358	34,358	0	0	434	
Michigan State	50	3.58	3.08	159	154	755	234	3.54	2.95	155	149	142	89	897	323	894	223	55.9	44.1	10.9	38	45	68.4	31.6	22.8	88	23,156	23,156	16,540	16,540	438	•
Thomas M. Cooley	0	3.39	2.67	151	144	2,616	387	3.29	2.66	148	142	305	1,041	2,921	1,428	475	2393	51.2	48.8	27.1	81	184	62.3	37.3	21.1	90	22,160	22,160	15,840	15,840	718	•
Wayne State	50	3.71	3.32	158	152	512	184	3.52	3.06	159	151	44	26	556	210	537	186	51.7	48.3	18.7	27	20	64.9	35.1	20.4	86	12,707	25,418	6,869	13,648	786	•
Minnesota																																
Hamline	40	3.63	3.14	158	152	435	159	3.56	3.00	155	147	133	74	568	233	515	199	43.4	56.6	13.4	31	44	61.4	38.6	17.4	88	23,858	23,858	17,190	17,190	326	•
Minnesota	60	3.81	3.48	166	160	716	270	0.00	0.00	0	0	0	0	716	270	817	0	55.4	44.6	16.0	47	66	58.9	41.1	14.5	88	17,948	28,042	0	0	442	•
St. Thomas	50	3.66	3.08	160	152	365	147	0.00	0.00	0	0	0	0	365	147	361	0	46.0	54.0	15.0	20	29	61.1	38.9	15.0	88	24,842	24,842	0	0	618	
William Mitchell	45	3.67	3.14	158	153	742	214	3.57	3.04	157	147	81	106	823	320	653	425	49.8	50.2	10.9	34	200	58.0	42.0	22.9	86	24,550	24,550	17,780	17,780	816	•
Mississippi																																
Mississippi	40	3.79	3.30	159	153	387	170	0.00	0.00	0	0	0	0	387	170	581	0	56.5	43.5	9.6	22	7	71.1	28.9	22.0	90	7,210	13,380	360	669	446	•
Mississippi College	50	3.48	2.99	154	149	401	183	0.00	0.00	0	0	0	0	401	183	454	0	65.0	35.0	8.8	17	23	67.4	32.6	22.3	90	17,672	17,672	0	0	450	•
Missouri																																
Missouri-Columbia	50	3.72	3.22	161	157	319	145	0.00	0.00	0	0	0	0	319	145	435	2	60.6	39.4	9.8	24	7	63.6	36.4	15.2	89	12,117	23,073	8,788	16,614	454	•
Missouri-Kansas City	50	3.63	3.14	156	151	447	197	3.62	3.25	156	150	19	14	466	211	487	41	52.5	47.5	8.9	23	32	67.7	32.3	18.6	91	13,342	25,456	9,033	17,109	458	•
St. Louis	55	3.75	3.32	160	154	673	234	3.62	3.07	156	151	123	79	796	313	642	235	48.9	51.1	9.4	35	35	67.5	32.5	18.9	91	27,250	0	19,890	0	606	
Washington	70	3.70	3.20	167	162	802	238	0.00	0.00	0	0	0	0	802	238	752	4	58.3	41.7	18.1	46	60	64.7	35.3	13.6	85	33,189	33,189	0	0	782	•
Montana																																
Montana	60	3.68	3.18	158	153	188	83	0.00	0.00	0	0	0	0	188	83	241	0	53.5	46.5	6.2	15	9	70.4	29.6	13.4	90	8,710	17,415	0	0	462	•
Nebraska																																
Creighton	45	3.72	3.20	156	151	501	162	3.56	2.64	153	145	11	6	512	168	455	23	55.6	44.4	8.6	24	18	67.3	26.5	16.3	94	22,312	22,312	14,448	14,448	230	•
Nebraska	25	3.83	3.43	159	152	346	130	0.00	0.00	0	0	0	1	346	131	405	3	54.7	45.3	8.6	23	20	68.6	31.4	14.8	96	8,998	20,612	0	0	466	•

School	Grid included	Official Guide Page #	Tuition Nonresident, Part-time	Tuition Resident, Part-time	Tuition Nonresident, Full-time	Tuition Resident, Full-time	# Credits Required for JD	Student/Faculty Ratio	Faculty % Women	Faculty % Men	Faculty # Part-time	Faculty # Full-time	Student % Minorities	Student % Women	Student % Men	Student # Part-time	Student # Full-time	Total # of Matriculants	Total # Accepted	PT # of Matriculants	PT # Accepted	PT 25% LSAT	PT 75% LSAT	PT 25% GPA	PT 75% GPA	FT # of Matriculants	FT # Accepted	FT 25% LSAT	FT 75% LSAT	FT 25% GPA	FT 75% GPA	Application Fee ($)
Nevada																																
William S. Boyd		470	10,916	5,716	15,078	7,833	86	13.2	41.9	58.1	7	26	21.4	46.9	53.1	163	304	150	265	45	50	152	160	2.94	3.68	105	215	154	160	3.28	3.73	40
New Hampshire																																
Franklin Pierce	•	294	0	0	25,274	25,274	84	17.8	25.0	75.0	37	20	17.5	42.1	57.9	6	422	159	570	0	0	0	0	0.00	0.00	159	570	150	156	3.00	3.50	55
New Jersey																																
Rutgers-Camden	•	594	19,254	13,318	23,755	16,724	84	17.2	38.5	61.5	40	35	15.4	38.8	61.2	214	579	252	544	101	N/A	156	161	3.02	3.68	151	N/A	159	163	3.20	3.60	50
Rutgers-Newark	•	598	19,105	13,169	23,556	16,525	84	18.3	33.9	64.5	21	33	37.3	43.1	56.9	249	561	284	730	78	117	152	159	2.83	3.45	206	613	153	162	3.00	3.61	50
Seton Hall	•	642	21,914	21,914	29,950	29,950	85	17.1	36.6	63.4	84	54	20.0	44.2	55.8	371	863	344	1,199	155	497	152	156	2.87	3.48	189	702	158	162	2.91	3.52	65
New Mexico																																
New Mexico	•	478	0	0	19,901	7,567	86	10.6	43.6	56.4	11	27	37.7	55.3	44.7	0	342	120	243	0	0	0	0	0.00	0.00	120	243	150	159	3.09	3.68	40
New York																																
Albany	•	86	22,602	22,602	30,093	30,093	87	16.2	45.5	54.5	28	38	14.6	50.1	49.9	52	703	235	732	0	0	0	0	0.00	0.00	235	732	151	157	3.07	3.55	50
Brooklyn	•	142	24,788	24,788	32,975	32,975	86	17.8	39.0	61.0	62	65	23.5	48.8	51.2	370	1148	491	1,295	188	319	158	160	3.00	3.43	303	976	161	164	3.11	3.57	65
Buffalo, SUNY		146	0	0	19,522	13,422	90	12.8	36.4	62.7	51	48	18.1	52.4	47.6	4	737	244	517	0	0	0	0	0.00	0.00	244	517	152	158	3.07	3.66	50
Cardozo	•	178	32,950	32,950	32,950	32,950	84	16.5	24.4	75.6	66	51	20.7	47.9	52.1	74	963	349	1,185	74	125	157	161	3.19	3.62	275	1,060	161	166	3.14	3.64	65
City U of NY	•	206	0	0	13,481	8,731	91	12.3	54.7	45.3	13	30	34.5	66.9	33.1	8	439	153	474	0	0	0	0	0.00	0.00	153	474	148	154	2.95	3.56	50
Columbia		218	0	0	37,256	37,256	83	11.2	29.4	70.6	62	94	29.1	44.7	55.3	0	1239	374	1,187	0	0	0	0	0.00	0.00	374	1,187	167	173	3.50	3.83	70
Cornell		226	0	0	35,342	35,342	84	10.8	37.1	62.9	14	46	31.9	48.1	51.9	0	593	191	879	0	0	0	0	0.00	0.00	191	879	164	168	3.43	3.76	70
Fordham	•	290	24,963	24,963	33,216	33,216	83	16.4	33.8	66.2	126	71	25.1	46.9	53.1	358	1164	479	1,467	163	245	160	163	3.21	3.66	316	1,222	163	167	3.37	3.78	65
Hofstra	•	338	22,408	22,408	31,440	31,440	87	18.5	26.3	73.8	30	44	18.0	47.0	53.0	146	872	381	1,458	113	225	151	156	2.87	3.51	268	1,233	155	159	3.06	3.68	60
New York Law	•	482	28,050	28,050	36,480	36,480	86	22.7	39.4	60.0	92	52	18.4	52.5	47.5	362	1180	496	2,057	134	305	151	155	2.90	3.46	362	1,752	154	157	3.06	3.54	60
New York	•	486	0	0	36,768	36,768	82	11.2	31.0	69.0	56	101	24.5	46.8	53.2	0	1360	441	1,628	0	0	0	0	0.00	0.00	441	1,628	167	172	3.57	3.85	75
Pace	•	546	23,457	23,457	31,224	31,224	84	16.0	45.8	54.2	31	36	15.1	59.9	40.1	245	529	256	882	77	159	151	155	2.91	3.38	179	723	154	157	3.11	3.56	65
St. John's	•	602	22,900	22,900	30,500	30,500	86	17.3	28.9	71.1	42	43	21.1	47.8	52.2	202	759	308	1,097	73	175	153	157	3.05	3.66	235	922	158	163	3.13	3.62	60
Syracuse	•	690	27,518	27,329	31,642	31,642	87	16.8	35.0	63.8	24	39	17.7	46.5	53.5	11	781	250	783	1	1	0	0	0.00	0.00	249	782	152	156	3.15	3.56	50

School	App Fee ($)	FT 75% GPA	FT 25% GPA	FT 75% LSAT	FT 25% LSAT	FT # Accepted	FT # Matric	PT 75% GPA	PT 25% GPA	PT 75% LSAT	PT 25% LSAT	PT # Accepted	PT # Matric	Total # Accepted	Total # Matric	SB # FT	SB # PT	SB Men %	SB Women %	SB Minorities %	Fac # FT	Fac # PT	Fac Men %	Fac Women %	S/F Ratio	# Credits JD	Res FT Tuition	Nonres FT Tuition	Res PT Tuition	Nonres PT Tuition	Official Guide Page #	Grid
Touro	50	3.32	2.74	153	150	546	200	3.37	2.62	152	148	138	73	684	273	489	266	54.4	45.6	23.7	32	17	66.7	33.3	17.3	87	25,660	25,660	20,000	20,000	730	•
North Carolina																																
Campbell	50	3.50	3.01	157	152	249	143	0.00	0.00	0	0	0	0	249	143	369	0	53.4	46.6	10.3	16	12	79.4	20.6	19.2	90	22,252	22,252	0	0	170	•
Duke	70	3.83	3.38	169	162	869	219	0.00	0.00	0	0	0	0	869	219	610	30	54.8	45.2	22.8	45	30	58.9	41.1	11.7	84	34,574	0	0	0	258	•
North Carolina	65	3.79	3.40	164	157	613	239	0.00	0.00	0	0	0	0	613	239	710	0	48.9	51.1	23.5	36	28	66.3	33.8	16.4	86	11,118	23,036	0	0	490	•
North Carolina Central	40	3.46	2.93	150	143	263	138	3.63	3.17	157	150	41	34	304	172	338	99	40.7	59.3	50.3	17	11	43.2	56.8	19.8	88	3,891	15,751	3,891	15,751	494	
Wake Forest	60	3.60	3.15	165	160	493	157	0.00	0.00	0	0	0	0	493	157	462	18	55.4	44.6	14.0	33	12	63.2	36.8	12.0	89	26,400		0	0	766	•
North Dakota																																
North Dakota	35	3.62	3.21	154	148	167	74	0.00	0.00	0	0	0	0	167	74	203	0	51.2	48.8	5.9	8	7	56.0	44.0	21.2	90	7,032	14,900	0	0	498	•
Ohio																																
Akron	0	3.67	2.82	161	156	366	106	3.62	2.89	157	152	120	68	486	174	350	219	58.2	41.8	8.4	25	27	60.7	39.3	16.5	88	12,896	20,332	10,462	16,411	78	•
Capital	35	3.61	3.02	156	150	485	188	3.51	2.93	156	150	136	92	621	280	474	313	51.3	48.7	11.3	31	35	71.4	28.6	18.3	86	22,540	22,540	16,100	16,100	174	•
Case Western	40	3.53	3.04	161	157	808	209	3.50	2.96	157	156	0	19	808	228	689	19	60.0	40.0	14.7	41	71	65.9	34.1	14.2	88	28,276	28,276	11,826	11,826	182	•
Cincinnati	35	3.80	3.24	162	157	416	129	0.00	0.00	0	0	0	0	416	129	382	0	51.6	48.4	16.8	25	29	67.2	32.8	12.7	90	14,084	26,190	10,040	13,822	202	•
Cleveland State	35	3.61	3.13	156	152	460	173	3.54	2.88	155	149	102	74	562	247	494	253	54.5	45.5	13.9	42	26	61.6	38.4	13.3	90	13,052	17,969	0	0	210	•
Dayton	0	3.45	2.89	154	150	730	219	0.00	0.00	0	0	0	0	730	219	543	1	56.3	43.8	12.9	26	23	59.6	40.4	17.4	87	24,174	24,174	0	0	234	•
Ohio Northern	40	3.62	3.02	156	149	424	120	0.00	0.00	0	0	0	0	424	120	318	0	50.3	49.7	9.1	19	7	68.8	31.3	14.0	87	22,790		0	0	526	•
Ohio State	40	3.77	3.32	162	156	634	237	0.00	0.00	0	0	0	0	634	237	747	0	53.4	46.6	20.7	41	15	64.4	35.6	15.2	88	14,405	27,237	0	0	530	•
Toledo	40	3.76	3.07	159	153	251	86	3.37	2.86	155	151	123	104	374	190	344	173	56.7	43.3	7.4	29	17	63.3	36.7	13.5	89	12,852	23,096	10,177	18,286	726	•
Oklahoma																																
Oklahoma	50	3.84	3.37	160	153	321	172	0.00	0.00	0	0	0	0	321	172	519	0	51.6	48.4	18.7	27	12	72.5	27.5	16.0	90	9,386	18,652	0	0	534	•
Oklahoma City	50	3.50	2.72	154	148	645	169	3.22	2.68	152	146	120	77	765	246	490	194	58.0	42.0	18.3	24	18	65.4	34.6	21.5	90	24,230	24,230	16,400	16,400	538	•
Tulsa	30	3.56	3.00	154	148	501	216	3.47	2.85	159	150	34	17	535	233	502	116	61.0	39.0	14.4	20	38	63.9	36.1	22.7	88	22,777	22,777	15,967	15,967	738	•
Oregon																																
Lewis & Clark	50	3.51	2.99	164	158	836	197	3.61	3.08	164	155	67	39	903	236	533	0	51.2	48.8	19.3	41	29	57.6	42.4	13.6	86	25,334	25,334	19,004	19,004	386	•
Oregon	50	3.64	3.27	160	155	650	184	0.00	0.00	0	0	0	0	650	184	529	0	59.2	40.8	16.1	21	19	60.0	40.0	20.9	85	16,156	20,458	0	0	542	•
Willamette	50	3.57	3.13	158	153	504	181	0.00	0.00	0	0	0	0	504	181	461	5	59.4	40.6	8.6	21	10	73.7	26.3	18.3	90	24,280	0	0	0	808	

School	Application Fee ($)	Full-time 75% GPA	Full-time 25% GPA	Full-time 75% LSAT	Full-time 25% LSAT	Full-time # Accepted	Full-time # Matriculants	Part-time 75% GPA	Part-time 25% GPA	Part-time 75% LSAT	Part-time 25% LSAT	Part-time # Accepted	Part-time # Matriculants	Total # Accepted	Total # Matriculants	SB # Full-time	SB # Part-time	SB % Men	SB % Women	SB % Minorities	Fac # Full-time	Fac # Part-time	Fac % Men	Fac % Women	Student/Faculty Ratio	# Credits Required for JD	Tuition Resident Full-time	Tuition Nonresident Full-time	Tuition Resident Part-time	Tuition Nonresident Part-time	Official Guide Page #	Grid included
Pennsylvania																																
Duquesne	50	3.61	3.20	157	153	319	166	3.68	3.28	157	154	59	35	378	201	406	205	52.7	47.3	4.9	24	25	70.4	29.6	18.8	86	22,865	22,865	17,724	17,724	262	•
Penn State, Dickinson	60	3.50	3.08	157	154	699	176	0.00	0.00	0	0	0	0	699	176	622	0	53.9	46.1	18.5	30	44	66.3	33.7	17.3	88	25,650	25,650	0	0	554	•
Pennsylvania	70	3.81	3.45	171	166	826	257	0.00	0.00	0	0	0	0	826	257	833	0	55.0	45.0	26.7	53	60	69.1	30.9	13.1	89	34,988	34,988	0	0	558	•
Pittsburgh	55	3.64	3.05	162	157	670	248	0.00	0.00	0	0	0	0	670	248	722	0	54.4	45.6	13.0	44	43	67.7	32.3	13.7	88	19,074	27,970	0	0	566	•
Temple	60	3.62	3.17	163	158	1,149	257	3.58	3.02	160	156	120	74	1,269	331	803	250	51.9	48.1	21.3	49	109	62.9%	37.1%	16.5	87	13,312	22,800	10,752	18,342	694	•
Villanova	75	3.69	3.25	162	157	921	247	0.00	0.00	0	0	0	0	921	247	762	0	50.8	49.2	17.1	35	41	62.4	37.6	18.1	87	26,380	26,380	0	0	758	
Widener	60	3.52	2.89	152	149	309	132	3.48	2.75	153	150	99	54	408	186	341	172	53.4	46.6	8.0	19	18	60.5	39.5	19.9	87	26,870	26,870	20,170	20,170	804	•
Puerto Rico																																
Inter American	63	3.27	2.93	144	139	206	146	3.53	3.13	142	136	180	102	386	248	445	313	47.8	52.2	99.7	22	39	61.8	35.3	24.7	92	13,227	13,227	10,767	10,767	366	•
Pontifical Catholic	75	3.58	2.93	139	133	172	129	3.50	2.82	138	131	116	63	288	192	329	161	46.7	53.3	99.8	23	14	81.4	16.3	15.8	94	12,736	0	9,074	0	570	•
Puerto Rico	15	3.78	3.30	149	143	135	130	3.80	3.31	149	143	82	66	217	196	431	283	42.9	57.1	99.4	24	31	63.9	36.1	21.5	92	2,395	3,570	1,720	3,570	574	•
Rhode Island																																
Roger Williams	60	3.54	2.91	155	150	542	200	3.41	2.67	154	147	101	48	643	248	477	153	48.6	51.4	10.2	23	18	55.9	44.1	20.9	90	24,410	24,410	17,400	17,400	590	•
South Carolina																																
South Carolina	60	3.70	3.22	160	156	480	238	0.00	0.00	0	0	0	0	480	238	751	3	55.3	44.7	8.4	33	0	84.6	15.4	20.8	90	14,288	28,704	606	1,206	650	•
South Dakota																																
South Dakota	35	3.65	2.93	156	150	169	73	0.00	0.00	0	0	0	0	169	73	248	3	56.2	43.8	6.0	12	1	83.3	16.7	17.4	90	7,498	15,230	3,749	7,615	654	•
Tennessee																																
Memphis	25	3.61	3.00	158	154	123	121	3.64	3.05	158	154	14	13	137	134	421	22	57.1	42.9	11.3	22	17	65.9	34.1	16.5	90	8,286	23,046	7,850	21,270	422	•
Tennessee	15	3.83	3.39	161	155	316	156	0.00	0.00	0	0	0	0	316	156	452	0	50.2	49.8	13.3	30	37	58.8	35.0	12.6	89	8,396	21,384	0	0	698	•
Vanderbilt	50	3.80	3.50	166	164	763	227	0.00	0.00	0	0	0	0	763	227	632	0	52.1	47.9	22.3	33	26	68.7	31.3	16.0	88	32,194	32,194	0	0	750	•
Texas																																
Baylor	40	3.87	3.45	162	157	549	164	0.00	0.00	0	0	0	0	549	164	426	0	53.5	46.5	11.3	21	10	81.1	18.9	16.9	126	24,470	24,470	0	0	126	•
Houston	70	3.70	3.30	161	158	810	271	3.71	3.01	161	157	70	54	880	325	906	197	50.9	49.1	21.7	37	52	71.4	28.6	23.3	90	13,313	20,093	7,229	9,941	342	•

Chapter 13: ABA-Approved Law Schools

This chapter is designed to provide consumers with basic information in a simple format that will facilitate the consideration of ABA-approved law schools. Please note that applicants should not use this information as the sole source regarding application and admission. Rather, this book should supplement other avenues of evaluating respective schools, including making direct contact with admission officers, professors, students, alumni, or prelaw advisors.

The following section includes four pages of text and numerical data about each of the 188 ABA-approved law schools conferring the first degree in law (the JD degree). The two pages of numerical data about each school were compiled from questionnaires completed during the fall 2004 academic semester and submitted by ABA-approved law schools to the ABA's Consultant on Legal Education as part of the accreditation process. The completed questionnaires provided to the Consultant's Office are certified by the dean of each law school. Each certification is submitted to the Consultant's Office as an assurance that the information provided accurately reflects prevailing conditions at the law school for which the certification is given. The Consultant's Office, however, does not directly audit the information submitted by the respective institutions on an annual basis.

The information contained in this book is only a small portion of what is collected in the questionnaire for accreditation purposes. Each page is divided into different segments as discussed below. In addition, many of the same data are displayed on the charts in the next section to facilitate side-by-side comparisons.

In addition to the two pages of numerical data, each law school provides two pages of descriptive text to LSAC. LSAC edits these text pages for style and formatting, but does not verify the descriptive information provided by the schools. As part of this two-page spread, most schools provide admission profile grids that illustrate admission prospects based on a combination of LSAT score and GPA. The data in these grids are based on 2004–2005 academic year admission decisions as reported by the schools to LSAC. The grids are intended to be indicative of the admission profile of last year's entering law school classes; they should not be interpreted as predictors of the likelihood of admission for any applicant.

LSAC collects admission profile data and school descriptions each fall as a service to its member schools and to prospective law school applicants. The information provided by the law schools to LSAC in no way affects the ABA accreditation process.

■ School Name

The law schools are arranged in alphabetical order by each institution's primary name. Please note that some schools are known by more than one name. A law school that has completed at least one full year of successful operation may apply for provisional approval. A law school is granted provisional approval when it establishes that it substantially complies with *Standards: Rules of Procedure for Approval of Law Schools* and gives assurances that it will be in full compliance with all of the Standards within three years after receiving provisional approval. It is the ABA's view that students at provisionally approved law schools and persons who graduate while a school is provisionally approved are entitled to the same recognition as students and graduates of fully approved law schools. Schools listed in this publication with *Provisional* to the right of their name were provisionally approved as of February 2005. John Marshall Law School (Atlanta) and Western State University College of Law were granted provisional approval by the Council of the ABA Section of Legal Education and Admissions to the Bar. This approval came too late to include information about the law schools in this edition of the *ABA/LSAC Official Guide to ABA-Approved Law Schools*.

The Basics

The Basics section contains a variety of general information, sorted into the categories listed below.

Type of school: All ABA-approved law schools are either public or private. *Public* means that the school receives money from the state in which the school is located. *Private* indicates the school is not operated by the state.

Term: Indicates whether the school operates on a semester, quarter, or trimester system.

Application deadline: Not all schools have specific deadlines for admission applications. If the item was left blank in the questionnaire completed by the school, it generally means that the school considers applications on a continual basis until the class is filled.

Application fee: Fee charged by most law schools for processing an application for admission.

Financial aid deadline: Indicates the deadline for the school's financial aid form. (The school deadline may not be the same as federal and state deadlines.) If the item was left blank in the questionnaire completed by the school, it generally means that the school considers financial aid applications on a continuing basis.

Can first year start other than fall? Indicates whether the school has an entering class other than in the fall term.

Student to faculty ratio: Indicates the number of students relative to the number of instructors for the fall term. The ratio is calculated by comparing faculty full-time equivalency (FTE) to FTE of JD enrollment. A general definition of faculty FTE is as follows: Total full-time faculty plus additional instructional resources. Additional instructional resources include administrators who teach, as well as part-time faculty. Teaching administrators and part-time faculty are included in the faculty FTE at differing weighted factors ranging from .2 to .7. FTE of JD enrollment is calculated as follows: full-time JD enrollment plus two-thirds of part-time JD enrollment less enrollment in semester-abroad programs. For a detailed definition of the ABA's student/faculty ratio, please consult the ABA's *Standards: Rules of Procedure for Approval of Law Schools* at *www.abanet.org/legaled*.

Student housing: Indicates whether there is housing restricted to law students and whether there is graduate housing for which law students are eligible.

Faculty and Administrators

This section of the two-page spread contains detailed information on the number, gender, and race of the teachers at the school for both semesters. For fall, the information is reported as of October 1, 2004; for spring, the information is an estimate. It should be noted that some schools may have lower part-time numbers in the fall semester because at their school most of the part-time instruction occurs in the spring semester. The five categories of faculty are mutually exclusive. Teachers on leave or sabbatical are not included in the full-time faculty count for the term they are on leave. The *Full-time* row indicates tenured or tenure-track faculty. *Other Full-time* indicates nontenured professional skills instructors and nontenured legal writing instructors. *Deans, librarians, & others who teach* are law school administrators who teach at least halftime. Administrators who neither teach nor hold faculty rank are not included in these numbers. Administrators who teach are typically at the school and available to students during the entire year. For this reason they are counted in fall and spring regardless of their teaching load. *Part-time* during the fall semester includes adjuncts, permanent part time, faculty from another unit, part-time professional skills, and emeritus part time. The *Total* row combines figures from the *Full-time* row through the *Part-time* row.

JD Enrollment and Ethnicity

This section represents the JD enrollment by ethnic category, gender, first-year student, and full-time/part-time status. Students are classified for purposes of enrollment statistics on the basis of whether they are carrying a full load in the division in which they are enrolled. Minority group enrollment is the total enrollment of students who classify themselves as African American, American Indian or Alaskan Native, Asian or Pacific Islander, Mexican American, Puerto Rican, and other Hispanic American. Although Puerto Rican law students enrolled in the three approved law schools in Puerto Rico are not classified as minority students in the "Survey of Minority Group Students Enrolled in JD Programs in Approved Law Schools," they are counted as minorities in all other areas. Nonresident alien students (foreign nationals) and students whose ethnicity is unknown or unspecified are not included as minority students.

JD Degrees Awarded: This indicates the total number of JD degrees awarded during the 2003–2004 academic year.

Curriculum

All information in this category is based on the 12-month period beginning at the close of the prior academic year (e.g., June 2003 through May 2004). In courses where there was enrollment by both full-time and part-time students, schools were asked to classify each of those courses as full-time or part-time based on time of day and relative enrollment of full-time and part-time students. Some schools that have a part-time program experienced difficulty providing curriculum information which distinguished between full-time and part-time. In those cases, the part-time column contains zeros. A *small section* means a section of a substantive law course, which may include a legal writing component; small section does not mean a legal writing section standing alone. The *number of classroom course titles beyond the first-year curriculum* refers only to classroom courses offered the previous year, not to clinical or field placement possibilities. If a title is offered in both the full-time program and part-time program, the school could count it once in each column. *Seminars* are defined as courses requiring a written work product and having an enrollment limited to no more than 25. A *simulation course* is one in which a substantial portion of the instruction is accomplished through the use of role playing or drafting exercises, for example, trial advocacy, corporate planning and drafting, negotiations, and estate planning and drafting. *Faculty-supervised clinical courses* are those courses or placements with other agencies in which full-time faculty have primary professional responsibility for all cases on which students are working. *Field placements* is a term in which someone other than full-time faculty has primary responsibility to the client; they are frequently called externships or internships. Schools were also asked not to double count a single course by classifying it both as full-time and part-time. *Number involved in law journals* and *number involved in moot court or trial competitions* reflected those students beyond the first year who participated in those activities during the previous year regardless of whether the student received credit.

Tuition and Fees

- *Full-time*: Represents the full-time tuition (plus annual fees) for the academic year for a typical first-year student.

- *Part-time*: Represents the part-time tuition (plus annual fees) for the academic year for a typical first-year student. Please note that some schools elected to report part-time tuition on a "per credit hour" basis.

Living Expenses

This represents the 2004–2005 academic year total living expenses (room, board, etc.) and book expenses for full-time, single, resident students "Living on campus," "Living off campus," and "Living at home." Tuition and fee charges are not included. The figures are used in analyzing law student budgets for loan purposes. Many schools use the same budget amount for all three categories.

GPA and LSAT Scores

This section of the two-page spread contains statistics on the 2004 entering class. All persons in the particular category, regardless of whether they were admitted through any special admission program rather than through the normal admission process, were included. The admission year was calculated from October 1, 2003 through September 30, 2004. Schools that admit in the spring and/or summer were to include those students in the totals. Figures on matriculants include all students who attended at least one class during the first week of the term in which they were admitted. For a small number of schools, applications and admitted applicants are not identified by the school as full-time or part-time. Therefore, "N/A" appears under the full-time and part-time columns, and the total application and admission offers were entered under the total column.

Percentiles of GPA and LSAT: The GPA and LSAT scores represent the 75th and 25th percentile of the entering class. For example, one-quarter (25 percent) of the first-year class has credentials that are *below* the number given for the 25th percentile. Three-quarters (75 percent) of the first-year class has credentials that are *below* the number given for the 75th percentile. For example, if a school reports a 25th/75th percentile GPA—3.01/3.47, then 25 percent of this first-year class had a GPA of *less than* 3.01, while 75 percent of this class had a GPA of *less*

than 3.47. The same principle holds for 25th/75th percentile LSAT score.

Grants and Scholarships

This indicates the number and percentage of students receiving internal grants or scholarships from law school or university sources. External grants such as state grants are not included. The percentage for full time and part time are based on the total number of full-time and part-time JD students, respectively. The total column percentage is based on total JD enrollment. Zeros are reported where a school did not provide data. The data represent information from the previous academic year.

Informational and Library Resources

This section of the two-page spread contains basic information about the law library. In addition, it contains brief information about the physical size of the school and the number of computers available.

- *Number of volumes and volume equivalents*: "Volumes" refers to a physical unit of any printed, typewritten, mimeographed, or processed work contained in one binding or portfolio, cataloged, classified, or otherwise made ready for use, and which is held by the law school at the end of the 2003–2004 fiscal year. "Volume equivalents" is also the number held at the end of the 2003–2004 fiscal year. Volume equivalents are computed as follows: Microfiche, six fiche = 1 volume. Microfilm, 1 roll = 5 volumes.

- *Titles:* Each item for which a separate shelf bibliographic unit record has been made.

- *Active serial subscriptions:* Subscriptions where pieces/parts/updates have been received on a regular or irregular basis.

- *Study seating capacity inside the library:* Number of study seats available for library users.

- *Professional librarians:* Number of professional librarians, including librarians who teach or hold faculty rank.

- *Hours per week library is open:* Number of hours per week that professional staff are on duty in the library.

- *Wired connections available to students:* Number of open, wired, network connections available to students or, if the library has a wireless network, the number of simultaneous users accommodated within.

- *Networked computers available for use by students:* Number of workstations in law school or library computer labs, plus workstations in the library for users that are not in computer labs.

- *Simultaneous wireless users:* Number of simultaneous users accommodated within.

- *Require computer:* Indicates whether the school requires students entering the law school to have a computer.

JD Attrition (Prior Year)

Attrition percentages were based on fall 2003 enrollment. *Academic* attrition, for this purpose refers to those students not continuing their legal studies between October 1, 2003 and October 1, 2004. *Other* attrition may include transfers, health, financial, and students who leave for other reasons.

Employment

This section represents statistics on the employment status of the 2003 graduating class six months after graduation. The employment percentages are based on the graduates whose employment status was "known." Hence, for the schools reporting a large percentage of graduates for whom the employment status is unknown, the percentage reported may not be a very accurate reflection of the actual percentage of the class as a whole. *Type of employment* and geographic location percentages are based on the number of students employed.

Bar Passage Rates

This section refers to numbers and percentages of 2003 graduates who took the summer 2003 and the February 2004 examinations. The states' overall pass rates for first-time takers were obtained by an independent survey of each state bar authority with the assistance of the National Conference of Bar Examiners. Bar examination passage rates vary considerably from state to state, and for first-time and repeat test takers. For this book, schools reported data for the jurisdiction(s) in which they had the largest number of first-time takers; overall, that accounted for approximately 75 percent of all graduates in 2004. Reporting the second highest jurisdiction was optional. Wisconsin allows graduates of the University of Wisconsin Law School and Marquette University Law School to exercise the "diploma privilege" and be admitted to the bar without taking the examination.

■ Applicant Profiles

Applicant profiles are provided by some schools to give candidates information about the number of applicants and admitted applicants in each cell. For various reasons, the total number of applicants and admitted applicants do not equal the official totals that appear on the ABA data pages in this book.

The purpose of the applicant profiles is to provide information about the LSAT/GPA credentials of applicants and admitted applicants to the schools that provide the profiles. You will note that some schools provide alternatives to the grid format for their profile or no profile at all.

The University of Akron School of Law

150 University Avenue
Akron, OH 44325-2901
Phone: 800.4.AKRON.U or 330.972.7331; Fax: 330.258.2343
E-mail: lawadmissions@uakron.edu; Website: www.uakron.edu/law

ABA
Approved
Since
1961

The Basics

Type of school	Public
Term	Semester
Application deadline	3/1
Application fee	$0
Financial aid deadline	3/1
Can first year start other than fall?	No
Student to faculty ratio (fall)	16.5 to 1
Does the university offer:	
housing restricted to law students?	No
graduate housing for which law students are eligible?	Yes

Faculty and Administrators

	Total		Men		Women		Minorities	
	Fall	Spr	Fall	Spr	Fall	Spr	Fall	Spr
Full-time	25	25	17	16	8	9	2	3
Other Full-time	0	0	0	0	0	0	0	0
Deans, librarians, & others who teach	4	4	3	3	1	1	0	0
Part-time	27	21	14	8	13	13	1	0
Total	56	50	34	27	22	23	3	3

Curriculum

	Full-time	Part-time
Typical first-year section size	41	58
Is there typically a "small section" of the first-year class, other than Legal Writing, taught by full-time faculty	No	No
If yes, typical size offered last year	0	0
# of classroom course titles beyond 1st year curriculum	84	

# of upper division courses, excluding seminars with an enrollment:	Under 25	59
	25-49	27
	50-74	26
	75-99	4
	100+	0

# of seminars	21	
# of seminar positions available	539	
# of seminar positions filled	195	82
# of positions available in simulation courses	578	
# of simulation positions filled	309	155
# of positions available in faculty supervised clinical courses	264	
# of faculty supervised clinical positions filled	73	19
# involved in field placements	55	13
# involved in law journals	35	17
# involved in moot court or trial competitions	40	11
# of credit hours required to graduate	88	

JD Enrollment and Ethnicity

	Men		Women		Full-time		Part-time		1st-year		Total		JD Degs. Awd.
	#	%	#	%	#	%	#	%	#	%	#	%	
African Amer.	13	3.9	12	5.0	16	4.6	9	4.1	11	6.1	25	4.4	10
Amer. Indian	0	0.0	0	0.0	0	0.0	0	0.0	0	0.0	0	0.0	0
Asian Amer.	8	2.4	4	1.7	8	2.3	4	1.8	6	3.3	12	2.1	1
Mex. Amer.	0	0.0	0	0.0	0	0.0	0	0.0	0	0.0	0	0.0	0
Puerto Rican	0	0.0	0	0.0	0	0.0	0	0.0	0	0.0	0	0.0	0
Hispanic	7	2.1	4	1.7	7	2.0	4	1.8	7	3.9	11	1.9	2
Total Minority	28	8.5	20	8.4	31	8.9	17	7.8	24	13.3	48	8.4	13
For. Nation.	0	0.0	0	0.0	0	0.0	0	0.0	0	0.0	0	0.0	0
Caucasian	254	76.7	194	81.5	272	77.7	176	80.4	132	72.9	448	78.7	135
Unknown	49	14.8	24	10.1	47	13.4	26	11.9	25	13.8	73	12.8	42
Total	331	58.2	238	41.8	350	61.5	219	38.5	181	31.8	569		190

Tuition and Fees

	Resident	Nonresident
Full-time	$12,896	$20,332
Part-time	$10,462	$16,411

Living Expenses

Estimated living expenses for singles

Living on campus	Living off campus	Living at home
$13,134	$13,134	$13,134

The University of Akron School of Law

*ABA
Approved
Since
1961*

GPA and LSAT Scores

	Total	Full-time	Part-time
# of apps	2,379	1,928	451
# of admits	486	366	120
# of matrics	174	106	68
75% GPA	3.65	3.67	3.62
25% GPA	2.85	2.82	2.89
75% LSAT	159	161	157
25% LSAT	154	156	152

Grants and Scholarships (from prior year)

	Total		Full-time		Part-time	
	#	%	#	%	#	%
Total # of students	624		393		231	
Total # receiving grants	184	29.5	166	42.2	18	7.8
Less than 1/2 tuition	55	8.8	44	11.2	11	4.8
Half to full tuition	25	4.0	23	5.9	2	0.9
Full tuition	77	12.3	72	18.3	5	2.2
More than full tuition	27	4.3	27	6.9	0	0.0
Median grant amount			$9,310		$2,000	

Informational and Library Resources

# of volumes and volume equivalents	285,355
# of titles	60,744
# of active serial subscriptions	3,224
Study seating capacity inside the library	302
# of professional librarians	5
Hours per week library is open	95
# of open, wired connections available to students	5
# of networked computers available for use by students	62
# of simultaneous wireless users	840
Require computer?	N

JD Attrition (from prior year)

	Academic	Other	Total	
	#	#	#	%
1st year	11	19	30	16.0%
2nd year	6	3	9	4.1%
3rd year	0	1	1	0.6%
4th year	0	1	1	2.0%

Employment

	Total	Percentage
Employment status known	129	97.7
Employment status unknown	3	2.3
Employed	108	83.7
Pursuing graduate degrees	2	1.6
Unemployed seeking employment	16	12.4
Unemployed not seeking employment	3	2.3

Type of Employment

# employed in law firms	51	47.2
# employed in business and industry	21	19.4
# employed in government	22	20.4
# employed in public interest	4	3.7
# employed as judicial clerks	7	6.5
# employed in academia	1	0.9

Geographic Location

# employed in state	86	79.6
# employed in foreign countries	1	0.9
# of states where employed	14	

Bar Passage Rates

Jurisdiction		Ohio	
Exam	Sum 03	Win 04	Total
# from school taking bar for the first time	88	25	113
School's pass rate for all first-time takers	82%	92%	84%
State's pass rate for all first-time takers	81%	72%	79%

The University of Akron School of Law

Office of Admissions, 150 University Avenue
Akron, OH 44325-2901
Phone: 800.4.AKRON.U or 330.972.7331; Fax: 330.258.2343
E-mail: lawadmissions@uakron.edu; Website: www.uakron.edu/law

■ Introduction

Located just 45 minutes south of Cleveland, The University of Akron (UA) is one of the 50 largest universities in the country. UA is a comprehensive research and teaching university with degree programs ranging from the associate to the doctoral level. Founded in 1870, UA has celebrated over 130 years of academic excellence while forging ahead to meet the complex needs of today's students.

The Akron School of Law was founded in 1921 and merged with UA in 1959. More than 6,000 students have graduated from the law school. The School of Law has alumni practicing throughout the US and abroad. It is accredited by the ABA and is a member of the AALS.

■ Admission

In order to be considered for admission, the applicant must submit the application form and personal statement. The $35 fee is waived for online applications. The applicant must also take the LSAT and register for the LSDAS before the file may be sent to the Admission Committee. An applicant may apply during his/her final year of undergraduate studies. The bachelor's degree must be conferred prior to law school matriculation. Decisions are made on a rolling basis as soon as the files are complete. Priority deadline: March 1. For more details on admission, please see our website at *www.uakron.edu/law.*

Students enrolled in an ABA-accredited law school may apply for transfer or transient status. A law student who has completed not more nor less than one year (approx. 30 semester credit hours) and is in good academic standing may apply for transfer. A law student who has the dean's permission to visit for one or two semesters may apply for transient status. Consult *www.uakron.edu/law* for details.

■ Tuition/Fees and Financial Aid [annual]

First-year students are considered for full or partial scholarships. No application is required. Most of the fall 2004 entering day class received scholarship assistance. Merit- and need-based loans are available. File FAFSA early.

■ Physical Facilities

The law building includes a 1987 addition to the library and a 1993 addition to the original structure. The university's $200 million New Landscape for Learning campus improvement program includes a new Student Union, Student Recreation Center, Student Affairs Building, academic buildings, and parking decks. Approximately 30 acres of new green space were added to campus to create a more park-like setting. The law school is within one block of the Akron Municipal Court, the Court of Common Pleas, and the Ninth District Court of Appeals. The Federal Court is a few blocks from campus. While the law school is in the downtown Akron area, the campus is a green one bordered by grassy areas, decorative plantings, and fountains.

■ Intellectual Property Center

Patent, trademark, trade secret, copyright, and cyber law are among the many topics covered in the Intellectual Property Law program. Staffed by three full-time faculty, supplemented by four full-time and additional part-time faculty with special expertise, Akron's IP program is one of the most extensive in the nation. Twenty-two IP courses are offered either every year or every other year, and more than six additional courses are planned.

In addition, Akron offers the only **LLM degree in IP** in Ohio and is one of only 17 in the nation. This one-year graduate program provides law graduates with an opportunity to begin or continue a specialization in IP.

■ Curriculum/Special Programs

The first-year curriculum is traditional in content, using traditional and innovative interactive pedagogies. The upper-class curriculum is varied between basic courses and specialty courses, and also focuses on interactive learning pedagogies and development of crucial lawyering skills. All law students are eligible to participate in the programs offered and the services provided by the Office of Academic Success Programs. The director of academic success programs counsels students on study techniques, learning styles, time management, and other topics related to academic success. A comprehensive writing program designed to enhance students' skills in research, exposition, drafting, and argumentation is an integral part of the curriculum.

Four Juris Doctor (JD) Tracks: Litigation, business, taxation, and general. Other specialty areas include criminal, intellectual property, international, and labor and employment.

Four Joint Degrees: JD/Master in Business Administration, JD/Master of Science and Management Human Resources, JD/Master in Taxation, and JD/Master in Public Administration. JD/Master of Applied Politics *pending.*

Two Certificate Programs: Intellectual Property and Litigation.

LLM graduate law degree: Intellectual Property.

Competition Teams

Students have a number of opportunities to sharpen their litigation skills by participating in regional and national mock trial, moot court, and negotiation competitions. Our litigation teams have had almost unparalleled success in competitions throughout the US and Europe, including placing first nationally in 2004 in the Association of Trial Lawyers of America; placing second nationally in 2004, Best Advocate, and first nationally in 2003 in the National Institute for Trial Advocacy; and placing Best Advocate, second in the region, and fourth nationally in 2004 in the National Black Law Students Association Thurgood Marshall Mock Trial Competition.

Legal Clinic

Students represent clients in court, at trial, and on appeal. A variety of opportunities for clinical training are offered. Programs offered include Appellate Review; Clinical Seminar; Criminal, Judicial, and Public External Placements; Inmate Assistance Program; Transactional Clinic for New Businesses; and Trial Litigation Clinic.

Student Activities and Leadership

Our more than 15 active law student organizations include *Akron Law Review*, Black Law Students Association, Environmental Law Society, Gay-Straight Law Alliance, Intellectual Property and Technology Law Association, International Law Society, Law Association for Women, Public Interest Law Society, Student Bar Association, and more. Elections for leadership positions are held each year for day and evening students.

Library

On the cutting edge of technology, Akron students enjoy a wireless network and an affordable laptop program. The law library contains 285,000+ volumes. Students have access to 40.2 million library items and 8.7 million unique titles that may be delivered through OhioLink. Students have access to 3.8 million library items through UA libraries catalog. In addition, students have access to many full text resources including 6,000 journals, 5.3 million articles, and 19,000 e-books.

Students receive free e-mail and free web access and can create free web pages through the university. Of course, law students receive free access to LexisNexis and Westlaw.

Career Planning and Placement

The Career Planning and Placement director counsels law students on résumé writing, job searches, interview skills, and preparation for entrance into the legal profession. On-campus interviews, off-campus interviews, a minority clerkship program, an attorney-student mentor program, employment-related seminars, and career fairs are also coordinated through this office. Akron's extensive law alumni database enables the career planning office to assist students with networking opportunities nation-wide. This office assists in the placement of students in law-related positions during summer sessions and upper-division years. In addition, graduates receive placement assistance, on request, throughout their careers. Akron's reputation for excellence in legal education and resulting high bar passage facilitates competitive placements for students and graduates in all areas of practice.

Applicant Profile

The University of Akron School of Law

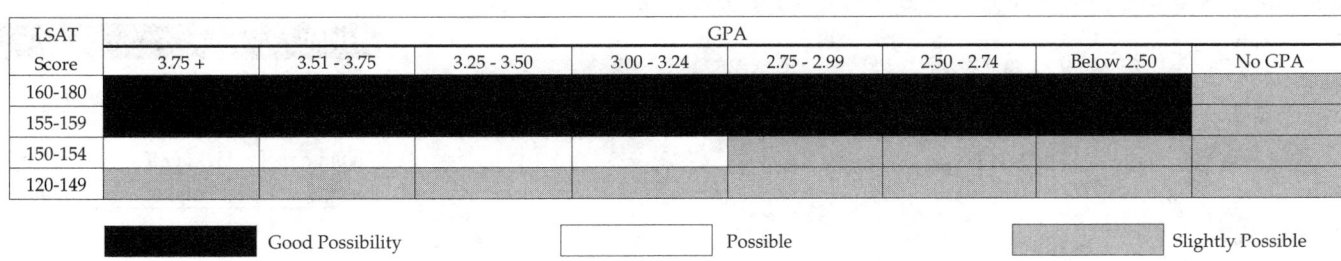

The University of Alabama School of Law

Box 870382
Tuscaloosa, AL 35487
Phone: 205.348.5440; Fax: 205.348.3917
E-mail: admissions@law.ua.edu; Website: www.law.ua.edu

ABA
Approved
Since
1926

The Basics

Type of school	Public
Term	Semester
Application deadline	3/1
Application fee	$25
Financial aid deadline	
Can first year start other than fall?	No
Student to faculty ratio (fall)	12.1 to 1
Does the university offer:	
housing restricted to law students?	No
graduate housing for which law students are eligible?	Yes

Faculty and Administrations

	Total		Men		Women		Minorities	
	Fall	Spr	Fall	Spr	Fall	Spr	Fall	Spr
Full-time	37	40	25	29	12	11	5	6
Other Full-time	10	10	3	3	7	7	5	5
Deans, librarians, & others who teach	4	4	4	4	0	0	0	0
Part-time	34	33	31	31	3	2	3	3
Total	85	87	63	67	22	20	13	14

Curriculum

	Full-time	Part-time
Typical first-year section size	57	0
Is there typically a "small section" of the first-year class, other than Legal Writing, taught by full-time faculty	No	No
If yes, typical size offered last year	0	0
# of classroom course titles beyond 1st year curriculum	120	
# of upper division courses, excluding seminars with an enrollment: Under 25	91	
25-49	27	
50-74	11	
75-99	1	
100+	4	
# of seminars	18	
# of seminar positions available	216	
# of seminar positions filled	197	0
# of positions available in simulation courses	308	
# of simulation positions filled	291	0
# of positions available in faculty supervised clinical courses	88	
# of faculty supervised clinical positions filled	83	0
# involved in field placements	64	0
# involved in law journals	127	0
# involved in moot court or trial competitions	163	0
# of credit hours required to graduate	90	

JD Enrollment and Ethnicity

	Men #	Men %	Women #	Women %	Full-time #	Full-time %	Part-time #	Part-time %	1st-year #	1st-year %	Total #	Total %	JD Degs. Awd.
African Amer.	15	4.4	19	9.6	34	6.3	0	0.0	14	8.1	34	6.3	11
Amer. Indian	5	1.5	0	0.0	5	0.9	0	0.0	2	1.2	5	0.9	2
Asian Amer.	6	1.8	0	0.0	6	1.1	0	0.0	2	1.2	6	1.1	2
Mex. Amer.	0	0.0	1	0.5	1	0.2	0	0.0	0	0.0	1	0.2	0
Puerto Rican	0	0.0	0	0.0	0	0.0	0	0.0	0	0.0	0	0.0	0
Hispanic	2	0.6	1	0.5	3	0.6	0	0.0	1	0.6	3	0.6	1
Total Minority	28	8.3	21	10.6	49	9.1	0	0.0	19	11.0	49	9.1	16
For. Nation.	0	0.0	0	0.0	0	0.0	0	0.0	0	0.0	0	0.0	0
Caucasian	310	91.7	177	89.4	487	90.9	0	0.0	153	89.0	487	90.9	162
Unknown	0	0.0	0	0.0	0	0.0	0	0.0	0	0.0	0	0.0	0
Total	338	63.1	198	36.9	536	100.0	0	0.0	172	32.1	536		178

Tuition and Fees

	Resident	Nonresident
Full-time	$8,130	$16,802
Part-time	$0	$0

Living Expenses

Estimated living expenses for singles

Living on campus	Living off campus	Living at home
$12,184	$13,048	$10,382

The University of Alabama School of Law

*ABA
Approved
Since
1926*

GPA and LSAT Scores

	Total	Full-time	Part-time
# of apps	1,339	1,339	0
# of admits	318	318	0
# of matrics	171	171	0
75% GPA	3.70	3.70	0.00
25% GPA	3.10	3.10	0.00
75% LSAT	163	163	0
25% LSAT	159	159	0

Grants and Scholarships (from prior year)

	Total		Full-time		Part-time	
	#	%	#	%	#	%
Total # of students	550		550		0	
Total # receiving grants	190	34.5	190	34.5	0	0.0
Less than 1/2 tuition	65	11.8	65	11.8	0	0.0
Half to full tuition	51	9.3	51	9.3	0	0.0
Full tuition	53	9.6	53	9.6	0	0.0
More than full tuition	21	3.8	21	3.8	0	0.0
Median grant amount			$5,438		$0	

Informational and Library Resources

# of volumes and volume equivalents	562,995
# of titles	109,325
# of active serial subscriptions	3,340
Study seating capacity inside the library	535
# of professional librarians	7
Hours per week library is open	110
# of open, wired connections available to students	10
# of networked computers available for use by students	70
# of simultaneous wireless users	210
Require computer?	N

J.D. Attrition (from prior year)

	Academic	Other	Total	
	#	#	#	%
1st year	4	6	10	5.5%
2nd year	0	3	3	1.6%
3rd year	0	1	1	0.6%
4th year	0	0	0	0.0%

Employment

	Total	Percentage
Employment status known	164	100.0
Employment status unknown	0	0.0
Employed	149	90.9
Pursuing graduate degrees	8	4.9
Unemployed seeking employment	4	2.4
Unemployed not seeking employment	3	1.8

Type of Employment

# employed in law firms	106	71.1
# employed in business and industry	9	6.0
# employed in government	19	12.8
# employed in public interest	2	1.3
# employed as judicial clerks	11	7.4
# employed in academia	2	1.3

Geographic Location

# employed in state	114	76.5
# employed in foreign countries	0	0.0
# of states where employed	11	

Bar Passage Rates

Jurisdiction	Alabama			Mississippi		
Exam	Sum 03	Win 04	Total	Sum 03	Win 04	Total
# from school taking bar for the first time	158	15	173	8	17	25
School's pass rate for all first-time takers	94%	80%	92%	100%	100%	100%
State's pass rate for all first-time takers	83%	72%	81%	92%	91%	92%

The University of Alabama School of Law

Box 870382
Tuscaloosa, AL 35487
Phone: 205.348.5440; Fax: 205.348.3917
E-mail: admissions@law.ua.edu; Website: www.law.ua.edu

■ Introduction

The University of Alabama School of Law, the only public law school in Alabama, offers students a nationally recognized, progressive legal education. The law school has served as the training ground for state and national leaders of the legal profession, business, and government. Law students are provided with an abundance of cultural, academic, and athletic opportunities through the university. The law curriculum is traditional but diverse, with Alabama law emphasized only in select elective courses. Although the faculty's first priority is teaching, the professors are actively engaged in scholarly research and writing. Alabama is accredited by the ABA and the AALS.

■ Library and Physical Facilities

The law school building, which sits on 23 acres on the University of Alabama's campus in Tuscaloosa, was designed by Edward Durell Stone, who was the architect for the Museum of Modern Art, the US Embassy in New Delhi, and the Kennedy Center for Performing Arts, to name a few. The building is graphic evidence of the school's dynamic growth and progressive spirit. The Bounds Law Library provides users with a substantial research collection of Anglo-American and international legal materials. The library includes a computer lab, students' study carrels, and the Hugo Black Study, the Howell Heflin Conference Room, and the Payne Special Collections Room. The school is on a wireless network.

■ Special and Summer Programs

The clinical programs enable law students to gain valuable practical experience in interviewing clients, preparing cases, and participating in courtroom presentations. During the second and third years, students can choose to participate in the Elder Law, Civil (student legal and domestic violence), Capital Defense, or Public Defender Clinics.

The externship program offers students practical experience while receiving credit. Externships are available during the summer and the second and third academic year. The law school's Public Interest Institute awards grants to encourage students to participate in the area of public interest and honors students who perform public interest work.

The joint JD/MBA program offers select students an opportunity to earn both an MBA and JD in four years. The Graduate Program for International Students provides a limited number of international lawyers an opportunity to earn an LLM degree.

The law school also offers two summer programs at the University of Fribourg in Fribourg, Switzerland, and the Australian National University in Canberra, the capital of Australia. Students may earn four to five credit hours in the Switzerland program and five credit hours in the Australian program. Both programs include a course surveying the host country's national law and a comparative doctrinal course. Summer school is open to students who have completed the first year.

■ Admission

A student must obtain a bachelor's degree at an accredited institution before enrolling but may apply during his or her senior year. Applicants must take the LSAT, preferably in June or October in the year preceding enrollment, and register for the LSDAS for transcript analysis. Transcripts must show all schools attended. Application materials are available in August each year and accepted as early as September 1. March 1 is the application deadline. Applications are processed on a rolling basis; thus, applicants are encouraged to submit competitive applications early. The two most significant factors for admission are the undergraduate GPA and LSAT score. The law school believes that the law school experience is enriched by a diverse group of students. The Admissions Committee also considers other factors, such as honors, activities, work or service experience, difficulty of undergraduate courses, writing ability, trends in academic performance, leadership qualities, and history of overcoming adversity. Written letters of recommendation are not required, but if sent, the law school recommends that letters be submitted through the LSAC service. Personal interviews are not required. Students are admitted only for the fall semester and only for full-time study.

■ Student Activities

A broad range of student activities adds to the students' law school experience. Student organizations represent diverse interests. These include the Student Bar Association, Black Law Students Association, Alabama Public Interest Law Association, Civil Rights Students Association, Dorbin Association (women's support group), Law Students for Choice, Gay-Straight Alliance, Environmental Law Society, International Law Students Association, Business Law Society, Criminal Law Student Association, Defense Lawyers Association, Future Trial Lawyers Association, Christian Legal Society, Sports and Entertainment Law Society, and Latin American Law Association.

The School of Law also offers numerous writing opportunities. The *Alabama Law Review*, a nationally recognized law journal, is edited by students and devotes substantial space to national and state issues. *The Journal of the Legal Profession* and the *Law and Psychology Review* are also student-edited law journals.

Moot court and trial advocacy teams have enjoyed exceptional success over the years. The law school sponsors teams in several moot court, specialty, and trial advocacy competitions. The moot court and trial advocacy teams have won many team and individual awards in both regional and national competitions.

Expenses and Financial Aid

The majority of students enrolled in the School of Law finance their legal education through loans, savings, earnings, or contributions from their families. Scholarships are awarded to over 35 percent of the law students. Applicants are considered automatically for first-year scholarships, which are typically based on factors such as GPA and LSAT performance, and may be based on other factors such as economic need. As part of the scholarship program, outstanding nonresident students may receive a nonresident fee waiver. Scholarships sometimes are renewable during the second and third years—depending upon funding, the student's need, and whether the recipient maintains stated levels of academic achievement. Following acceptance by the law school, each admitted student who applies for federal aid through the Free Application for Federal Student Aid (FAFSA) receives a financial aid packet from the university's Financial Aid Office. Information on loans can be obtained by contacting Student Financial Aid, the University of Alabama, Box 870162, Tuscaloosa, AL 35487-0162. Phone: 205.348.6756; *www.financialaid.ua.edu*. Applicants

should complete the FAFSA form as soon after January 1 as possible, and may apply online at *www.fafsa.ed.gov*.

Career Services

The Career Services Office assists students in their efforts to find employment. The office provides individual career counseling, group presentations, speaker programs, and library and database resources. Seminars are presented on résumé writing, interviewing techniques, and job-search techniques to help students refine their job-search skills. Extensive on-campus interviewing occurs. The law school also participates in job fairs in Atlanta, New York City, Chicago, and Washington, DC. The employment rate within nine months of graduation was 97 percent for the class of 2003.

Housing

The University of Alabama maintains residence halls and apartment units for students; however, most law students live off campus. The cost of living in Tuscaloosa for a single law student ranges from approximately $500 to $1,100 per month. For information on university housing, students must contact the Office of Residential Life, The University of Alabama, Box 870399, Tuscaloosa, AL 35487-0399. Phone: 205.348.6676 or e-mail: *reslife@sa.ua.edu*.

Applicant Profile

The University of Alabama School of Law
This grid includes only applicants who earned 120-180 LSAT scores under standard administrations.

LSAT Score	GPA								
	3.75 +	3.50 - 3.74	3.25 - 3.49	3.00 - 3.24	2.75 - 2.99	2.50 - 2.74	2.25 - 2.49	2.00 - 2.24	Below 2.00
175-180									
170-174									
165-169									
160-164									
155-159									
150-154									
145-149									
140-144									
135-139									
130-134									
125-129									
120-124									

Good Possibility   Possible   Unlikely

This graph is to be used as a general guide only. Nonnumerical factors are strongly considered for applicants. The law school encourages applicants to contact the Admission Office with questions.

Albany Law School of Union University

80 New Scotland Avenue
Albany, NY 12208
Phone: 518.445.2326; Fax: 518.445.2369
E-mail: admissions@mail.als.edu; Website: www.als.edu

*ABA
Approved
Since
1930*

The Basics

Type of school	Private
Term	Semester
Application deadline	3/1
Application fee	$50
Financial aid deadline	
Can first year start other than fall?	No
Student to faculty ratio (fall)	16.2 to 1
Does the university offer:	
housing restricted to law students?	No
graduate housing for which law students are eligible?	No

Curriculum

		Full-time	Part-time
Typical first-year section size		90	0
Is there typically a "small section" of the first-year class, other than Legal Writing, taught by full-time faculty		Yes	No
If yes, typical size offered last year		50	0
# of classroom course titles beyond 1st year curriculum		111	
# of upper division courses, excluding seminars with an enrollment:	Under 25	52	
	25-49	23	
	50-74	14	
	75-99	5	
	100+	7	
# of seminars		31	
# of seminar positions available		558	
# of seminar positions filled	445		0
# of positions available in simulation courses		242	
# of simulation positions filled	242		0
# of positions available in faculty supervised clinical courses		88	
# of faculty supervised clinical positions filled	88		0
# involved in field placements	217		0
# involved in law journals	176		0
# involved in moot court or trial competitions	69		0
# of credit hours required to graduate		87	

Faculty and Administrators

	Total		Men		Women		Minorities	
	Fall	Spr	Fall	Spr	Fall	Spr	Fall	Spr
Full-time	38	36	19	19	19	17	4	3
Other Full-time	4	4	0	0	4	4	0	0
Deans, librarians, & others who teach	7	8	3	3	4	5	1	1
Part-time	28	24	20	18	8	6	1	1
Total	77	72	42	40	35	32	6	5

JD Enrollment and Ethnicity

	Men		Women		Full-time		Part-time		1st-year		Total		JD Degs. Awd.
	#	%	#	%	#	%	#	%	#	%	#	%	
African Amer.	8	2.1	28	7.4	32	4.6	4	7.7	11	4.4	36	4.8	16
Amer. Indian	0	0.0	1	0.3	1	0.1	0	0.0	0	0.0	1	0.1	0
Asian Amer.	18	4.8	30	7.9	46	6.5	2	3.8	24	9.7	48	6.4	5
Mex. Amer.	1	0.3	0	0.0	1	0.1	0	0.0	0	0.0	1	0.1	0
Puerto Rican	5	1.3	5	1.3	10	1.4	0	0.0	3	1.2	10	1.3	3
Hispanic	7	1.9	7	1.9	13	1.8	1	1.9	6	2.4	14	1.9	5
Total Minority	39	10.3	71	18.8	103	14.7	7	13.5	44	17.7	110	14.6	29
For. Nation.	10	2.7	4	1.1	13	1.8	1	1.9	4	1.6	14	1.9	4
Caucasian	323	85.7	299	79.1	578	82.2	44	84.6	195	78.6	622	82.4	189
Unknown	5	1.3	4	1.1	9	1.3	0	0.0	5	2.0	9	1.2	2
Total	377	49.9	378	50.1	703	93.1	52	6.9	248	32.8	755		224

Tuition and Fees

	Resident	Nonresident
Full-time	$30,093	$30,093
Part-time	$22,602	$22,602

Living Expenses

Estimated living expenses for singles

Living on campus	Living off campus	Living at home
N/A	$12,299	$7,999

Albany Law School of Union University

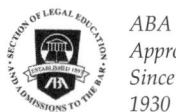

ABA Approved Since 1930

GPA and LSAT Scores

	Total	Full-time	Part-time
# of apps	2,307	2,307	0
# of admits	732	732	0
# of matrics	235	235	0
75% GPA	0.00	3.55	0.00
25% GPA	0.00	3.07	0.00
75% LSAT	0	157	0
25% LSAT	0	151	0

Grants and Scholarships (from prior year)

	Total		Full-time		Part-time	
	#	%	#	%	#	%
Total # of students	790		717		73	
Total # receiving grants	317	40.1	289	40.3	28	38.4
Less than 1/2 tuition	234	29.6	210	29.3	24	32.9
Half to full tuition	80	10.1	76	10.6	4	5.5
Full tuition	3	0.4	3	0.4	0	0.0
More than full tuition	0	0.0	0	0.0	0	0.0
Median grant amount			$5,600		$4,200	

Informational and Library Resources

# of volumes and volume equivalents	640,589
# of titles	99,523
# of active serial subscriptions	3,203
Study seating capacity inside the library	472
# of professional librarians	7
Hours per week library is open	104
# of open, wired connections available to students	877
# of networked computers available for use by students	105
# of simultaneous wireless users	0
Require computer?	N

JD Attrition (from prior year)

	Academic	Other	Total	
	#	#	#	%
1st year	17	19	36	11.8%
2nd year	1	8	9	3.7%
3rd year	1	4	5	2.2%
4th year	0	0	0	0.0%

Employment

	Total	Percentage
Employment status known	246	100.0
Employment status unknown	0	0.0
Employed	230	93.5
Pursuing graduate degrees	4	1.6
Unemployed seeking employment	9	3.7
Unemployed not seeking employment	3	1.2

Type of Employment

	Total	Percentage
# employed in law firms	103	44.8
# employed in business and industry	44	19.1
# employed in government	44	19.1
# employed in public interest	5	2.2
# employed as judicial clerks	18	7.8
# employed in academia	4	1.7

Geographic Location

	Total	Percentage
# employed in state	191	83.0
# employed in foreign countries	1	0.4
# of states where employed		14

Bar Passage Rates

Jurisdiction	New York		
Exam	Sum 03	Win 04	Total
# from school taking bar for the first time	215	12	227
School's pass rate for all first-time takers	67%	50%	67%
State's pass rate for all first-time takers	78%	58%	75%

Albany Law School of Union University

80 New Scotland Avenue
Albany, NY 12208
Phone: 518.445.2326; Fax: 518.445.2369
E-mail: admissions@mail.als.edu; Website: www.als.edu

■ Why Albany Law School?

The only law school in the capital of New York State, Albany Law School is a private, highly selective law school.

Our location in the governmental and economic center of upstate New York and western New England translates into unprecedented opportunities for internships, field placements, and clinical experiences in the diverse agencies and corporations around the Capital Region.

Our world-class faculty are dedicated and accessible to students. Our law centers, in-house legal clinic, and field placement program provide myriad opportunities for students to gain hands-on legal experience working with the most respected members of the bar. Albany Law School is positioned to provide you with a uniquely comprehensive legal education.

■ The Academic Experience

From your first day at Albany Law School you will be challenged by a rigorous academic curriculum.

As a first-year student, you acquire the skills that will become the foundation of your legal education. As part of our innovative Introduction to Lawyering course, you will represent a plaintiff or defendant in a simulated case where you conduct legal research, draft motions and memorandum, and participate in client interviews and negotiations. The class culminates with each student presenting an oral argument before some of the Capital Region's most notable attorneys, who preside as appellate court justices.

As a second- and third-year student, you have the opportunity to focus your studies in one of 15 concentrations and complement course work by participating in one of 6 clinical projects, more than 140 field placement internships, and study-abroad programs. Students also have the option to pursue a joint degree with an area graduate school, allowing you to earn a JD and master's degree in four years.

■ Real-Life Experience

Our groundbreaking legal centers and clinical programs provide valuable hands-on experience.

You work alongside committed clinical faculty and practicing attorneys to assist low-income clients with legal problems related to chronic health conditions, disabilities, domestic violence, disputes with the Internal Revenue Service, and securities arbitration matters. And you work with prosecutors, members of the judiciary, and experienced attorneys through our field-placement program.

You interact with the leaders in New York state government and the visionaries building New York's

high-technology base through the programs at the Government Law Center (GLC) and the Science and Technology Law Center.

In the GLC, you conduct research; contribute to publications; and participate in conferences and special projects that promote the study of the problems facing government, policy analysis, and public service.

You can provide legal services to start-up ventures and early stage technology companies throughout New York by working with attorneys at the Science and Technology Law Center.

■ Your Career

From your first week at school, our Career Planning Office helps you develop a career plan and supports you throughout your job search. Professional career counselors help you define career goals, craft résumés and cover letters, prepare for interviews, and compare employment offers.

Job fairs, information sessions, workshops, and panel discussions on a variety of employment related topics occur almost daily. Career Planning hosts more than 1,200 interviews each year and conducts off-campus interview programs in metropolitan areas, including New York City and Boston, specifically for Albany Law School students. Our alumni frequently participate in the Career Planning activities.

Our graduates find employment in law firms, government agencies, public interest organizations, and businesses in New York City, Boston, and other major metropolitan areas throughout the country. The employment rate for the class of 2003 was 93 percent compared to the national average of 88.9 percent.

■ Our Community

Our community of approximately 700 students and 52 full-time faculty is close-knit. We welcome students and faculty with diverse talents, backgrounds, and interests and provide a supportive environment for the pursuit of scholarship, teaching, and public service.

Albany Law School's faculty members contribute to the national dialogue on important legal topics via symposia, law reviews, and the media.

Our students come to Albany Law School from around the globe. The small size of our student body fosters a supportive atmosphere and an environment that encourages camaraderie among students and frequent contact between students and faculty.

Fifty percent of our students are women and 18 percent are members of a minority group. Fifty-three percent of our fall 2004 entering class graduated from college a year or more before entering Albany Law School and 11 percent graduated five or more years before entering law school and had a career in another profession before attending law school.

■ Student Life

You have dozens of opportunities to participate in student organizations and activities around specific academic, professional, social, cultural, or athletic interests.

Three student-edited journals, the *Albany Law Review,* the *Albany Law Journal of Science and Technology,* and the *Albany Law Environmental Outlook,* offer cocurricular research and writing opportunities.

Our nationally recognized Moot Court Program enables you to develop skills in trial advocacy, appellate advocacy, client counseling, and negotiating while competing in both intramural and interscholastic competitions.

The Capital Region boasts museums, galleries, restaurants, shops, theaters, nightclubs for every taste, arenas that host professional sporting events, and performing arts centers that attract national acts. The Adirondack, Berkshire, and Catskill Mountains offer skiing, camping, hiking, and water sports. And metropolitan centers New York City, Boston, and Montreal are within an easy drive.

■ Our Campus

Albany Law School's facilities are designed to support legal education in the twenty-first century.

The open design of the 53,000-square-foot Schaffer Law Library—a federal depository library—provides an inviting environment with seating for hundreds of students. Book and microfilm collections number more than half a million volumes, and the library supplements its collection with online databases and legal research systems, including LexisNexis and Westlaw.

The Law School's main building, known as the 1928 Building, houses state-of-the-art lecture halls, seminar-style classrooms, a modern paperless moot courtroom, and "smart" classrooms with wireless Internet access and advanced audio, video, computing, and conferencing systems.

A 45,000-square-foot building built in 2000 houses the Law School's clinic, law centers, and administrative offices, as well as several classrooms—including a high-tech distance learning classroom.

■ Admission and Financial Aid

As part of our ongoing commitment to institutional excellence, we have committed nearly $4 million in scholarship assistance. Approximately 35 percent of first-year students receive scholarships which average $20,000 for each year of study.

When evaluating each individual application, the Admissions Committee considers LSAT, undergraduate grade-point average, strength of the undergraduate institution, rigor of the undergraduate program, and life experience. The committee seeks to enroll a student body that enriches the educational experience of all of its members. The committee also seeks to provide future members of the bar who both reflect the diversity of society and are sensitive to it.

Approximately 90 percent of our students qualify for need-based federal, state, and/or institutional funds via grants, loans, or part-time employment to assist in meeting educational expenses.

Applicant Profile

Albany Law School of Union University

LSAT Score	GPA								
	3.75 +	3.50 - 3.74	3.25 - 3.49	3.00 - 3.24	2.75 - 2.99	2.50 - 2.74	2.25 - 2.49	2.00 - 2.24	Below 2.00
166 and up									
162-165									
158-161									
154-157									
150-153									
146-149									
142-145									
138-141									
137 and below									

Likely   Possible   Unlikely

American University, Washington College of Law

4801 Massachusetts Avenue, NW, Suite 507
Washington, DC 20016
Phone: 202.274.4101; Fax: 202.274.4107
E-mail: wcladmit@wcl.american.edu; Website: www.wcl.american.edu

ABA Approved Since 1940

The Basics

Type of school	Private
Term	Semester
Application deadline	3/1
Application fee	$65
Financial aid deadline	3/1
Can first year start other than fall?	No
Student to faculty ratio (fall)	15.4 to 1
Does the university offer:	
housing restricted to law students?	No
graduate housing for which law students are eligible?	Yes

Faculty and Administrators

	Total		Men		Women		Minorities	
	Fall	Spr	Fall	Spr	Fall	Spr	Fall	Spr
Full-time	75	75	36	35	39	40	12	12
Other Full-time	1	1	1	1	0	0	0	0
Deans, librarians, & others who teach	5	5	3	3	2	2	2	2
Part-time	119	96	86	71	32	24	13	10
Total	200	177	126	110	73	66	27	24

Curriculum

		Full-time	Part-time
Typical first-year section size		78	86
Is there typically a "small section" of the first-year class, other than Legal Writing, taught by full-time faculty		Yes	Yes
If yes, typical size offered last year		45	45
# of classroom course titles beyond 1st year curriculum		281	
# of upper division courses, excluding seminars with an enrollment:	Under 25	122	
	25-49	48	
	50-74	26	
	75-99	11	
	100+	4	
# of seminars		135	
# of seminar positions available		2,545	
# of seminar positions filled		1,464	262
# of positions available in simulation courses		518	
# of simulation positions filled		370	68
# of positions available in faculty supervised clinical courses		244	
# of faculty supervised clinical positions filled		218	26
# involved in field placements		198	13
# involved in law journals		322	13
# involved in moot court or trial competitions		36	1
# of credit hours required to graduate		86	

J.D. Enrollment and Ethnicity

	Men #	Men %	Women #	Women %	Full-time #	Full-time %	Part-time #	Part-time %	1st-year #	1st-year %	Total #	Total %	JD Degs. Awd.
African Amer.	35	5.8	74	8.4	82	6.9	27	9.2	30	6.6	109	7.3	31
Amer. Indian	2	0.3	4	0.5	4	0.3	2	0.7	3	0.7	6	0.4	1
Asian Amer.	57	9.5	131	14.9	156	13.1	32	11.0	52	11.4	188	12.7	46
Mex. Amer.	9	1.5	17	1.9	20	1.7	6	2.1	14	3.1	26	1.8	8
Puerto Rican	4	0.7	5	0.6	8	0.7	1	0.3	4	0.9	9	0.6	2
Hispanic	36	6.0	53	6.0	77	6.5	12	4.1	33	7.2	89	6.0	15
Total Minority	143	23.7	284	32.2	347	29.1	80	27.4	136	29.7	427	28.8	103
For. Nation.	2	0.3	7	0.8	7	0.6	2	0.7	4	0.9	9	0.6	10
Caucasian	458	76.0	591	67.0	839	70.3	210	71.9	318	69.4	1049	70.6	219
Unknown	0	0.0	0	0.0	0	0.0	0	0.0	0	0.0	0	0.0	10
Total	603	40.6	882	59.4	1193	80.3	292	19.7	458	30.8	1485		342

Tuition and Fees

	Resident	Nonresident
Full-time	$31,108	$31,108
Part-time	$21,837	$21,837

Living Expenses

Estimated living expenses for singles

Living on campus	Living off campus	Living at home
$16,700	$16,700	$16,700

American University, Washington College of Law

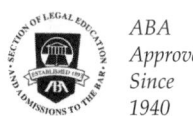

*ABA
Approved
Since
1940*

GPA and LSAT Scores

	Total	Full-time	Part-time
# of apps	9,287	8,159	1,128
# of admits	2,287	2,002	285
# of matrics	460	366	94
75% GPA	3.63	3.61	3.68
25% GPA	3.19	3.22	3.09
75% LSAT	162	162	160
25% LSAT	157	159	156

Grants and Scholarships (from prior year)

	Total		Full-time		Part-time	
	#	%	#	%	#	%
Total # of students	1,389		1,118		271	
Total # receiving grants	435	31.3	423	37.8	12	4.4
Less than 1/2 tuition	385	27.7	373	33.4	12	4.4
Half to full tuition	22	1.6	22	2.0	0	0.0
Full tuition	20	1.4	20	1.8	0	0.0
More than full tuition	8	0.6	8	0.7	0	0.0
Median grant amount			$8,000		$1,400	

Informational and Library Resources

# of volumes and volume equivalents	529,718
# of titles	208,030
# of active serial subscriptions	6,667
Study seating capacity inside the library	677
# of professional librarians	10
Hours per week library is open	119
# of open, wired connections available to students	1,723
# of networked computers available for use by students	225
# of simultaneous wireless users	3,155
Require computer?	N

JD Attrition (from prior year)

	Academic	Other	Total	
	#	#	#	%
1st year	0	35	35	8.7%
2nd year	0	1	1	0.2%
3rd year	0	0	0	0.0%
4th year	0	0	0	0.0%

Employment

	Total	Percentage
Employment status known	391	99.0
Employment status unknown	4	1.0
Employed	353	90.3
Pursuing graduate degrees	21	5.4
Unemployed seeking employment	7	1.8
Unemployed not seeking employment	10	2.6

Type of Employment

# employed in law firms	151	42.8
# employed in business and industry	74	21.0
# employed in government	63	17.8
# employed in public interest	18	5.1
# employed as judicial clerks	40	11.3
# employed in academia	7	2.0

Geographic Location

# employed in state	167	47.3
# employed in foreign countries	3	0.8
# of states where employed		28

Bar Passage Rates

Jurisdiction	Maryland			New York		
Exam	Sum 03	Win 04	Total	Sum 03	Win 04	Total
# from school taking bar for the first time	123	27	150	79	8	87
School's pass rate for all first-time takers	73%	56%	70%	78%	63%	77%
State's pass rate for all first-time takers	73%	62%	71%	78%	58%	75%

American University, Washington College of Law

4801 Massachusetts Avenue, NW, Suite 507
Washington, DC 20016
Phone: 202.274.4101; Fax: 202.274.4107
E-mail: wcladmit@wcl.american.edu; Website: www.wcl.american.edu

■ Introduction

American University Washington College of Law offers opportunity for the study of law in the center of the nation's legal institutions. The law school is minutes from downtown Washington, but at the same time offers the facilities and ambiance of a campus environment in one of the city's most beautiful residential neighborhoods.

Founded in 1896 by two women, the law school is national in character. It is committed to the development of the intellectual abilities, professional values, and practical skills required to prepare lawyers to practice in an increasingly complex and transnational world. The school is noted for the accessibility of faculty and administration to its students.

■ Library and Physical Facilities

Located in a residential area of Northwest Washington, DC, the Washington College of Law is one-quarter mile from American University's 78-acre campus and just seven metro stops from downtown.

The two-story library is the heart of the complex and seats over 600 students. Approximately half of the total seats are equipped with data ports so a student can plug in a portable computer and have access to all Internet and campus-wide research databases. For students who do not have laptops, there are approximately 80 networked desktop computers available for use. The law school implemented wireless networking providing data connectivity virtually anywhere within the building, including the library. There are also five networked laser printers dedicated to supporting student printing. The library collection includes European Community and US Government depositories and the Baxter Collection in International Law. Students also have access to the university's library, the Library of Congress, specialized agency libraries, and other area law libraries to which the school is electronically linked.

■ Curriculum

The law school offers full- and part-time programs leading to the JD degree, which is awarded after satisfactory completion of 86 credit hours, 34 of which are prescribed. All degree candidates must also fulfill an upper-level writing requirement. While a modified version of the Socratic method is the dominant form of teaching in the first year, faculty increasingly employ such methodologies as role-playing, simulations, and small group collaborative exercises. The goal is to develop the skills of critical analysis, provide perspectives on the law and lawyering, and deepen understanding of fundamental legal principles. In the Legal Rhetoric program, basic legal research and writing skills are taught to groups of students by full-time faculty (23 students per section) and practicing attorneys (12 students per section). In the second and third years, students elect a course of study drawing from advanced courses, seminars, independent research, externships, and clinical programs. Students are exposed to a variety of teaching approaches by the law school's distinguished full-time tenured and tenure-track faculty and our many adjunct professors.

■ Special Programs

While many of the advanced courses are taught in a traditional classroom setting, a variety of other innovative teaching modes are available to enhance research skills and provide professional training. The Washington College of Law enjoys a national reputation for clinical education. Second-year and third-year students may participate in the Civil Practice Clinic for both full- and part-time students, the Community and Economic Development Law Clinic, the International Human Rights Law Clinic, and the Intellectual Property Law Clinic; third-year students may also develop their lawyering abilities in the Criminal Justice Clinic, the DC Law Students in Court Clinic, the Domestic Violence Clinic, and the Tax Clinic. The Women and the Law program also includes a clinical component in which students represent indigent women in family law cases in the District of Columbia courts. This program also offers several public-education projects each year and is designed to integrate women's legal studies into the overall curriculum and to heighten awareness about legal issues affecting women.

- **Dual-Degree Programs**—American University offers three domestic dual-degree programs for students seeking to enhance their law degree with additional graduate coursework. Complementing the law school's nationally recognized curriculum in international law, the university offers a combined JD/MA in International Affairs with the School of International Service. The JD/MBA with the Kogod School of Business prepares students to meet the demanding aspects of business-oriented practice. The JD/MS in Justice, Law, and Society with the School of Public Affairs offers a thorough understanding of how law intersects with theories of justice and justice systems in our society. The Washington College of Law recently established three international dual-degree programs in Ottawa, Canada; Paris, France; and Madrid, Spain. Program participants complete two years in the United States and two years abroad.

The externship program places upper-level students in many governmental, nonprofit, and public interest entities throughout the DC metropolitan area. Field components, taken simultaneously with a seminar, include such areas as securities and commodities markets regulation. In addition, the law school offers a summer course in the Federal Regulatory Process that provides an intensive analysis of the federal regulatory process through lectures and optional field placements in a myriad of federal agencies and nonprofit organizations.

Graduate study is available leading to either an LLM or SJD degree in International Legal Studies or Law and Government.

■ Admission

Applicants to the law school are admitted on the strength of their entire academic and related record. The faculty admission committee gives primary emphasis to the undergraduate record, LSAT scores, and other major accomplishments and achievements, whether academic, work-related, or extracurricular. The benefits the school derives from racial, ethnic, cultural, and geographical diversity among its students are considered in admission decisions. Members of disadvantaged and minority groups are encouraged to apply. Admission to the law school is highly competitive and operates on a modified rolling admission basis, so early application is strongly encouraged.

■ Student Activities

The *American University Law Review*, the *International Law Review*, the *Administrative Law Review*, the *Journal of Gender, Social Policy & the Law,* and *The Human Rights Brief* are edited and published by students selected on the basis of scholarship and creative research. The Moot Court Board sponsors intraschool competitions for first-year and upper-level students and selects representatives for a number of interschool competitions, including the National Moot Court Competition. There are more than 40 active student organizations, including the Black Law Students Association, the Women's Law Association, the Environmental Law Society, the Hispanic Law Students Association, the Asian Pacific American Law Students Association, the National Lawyers Guild, the Equal Justice Foundation, the Federalist Society, the Lambda Law Students Association, the International Law Society, and Law and Government Society.

■ Career Services

Staffed by six full-time counselors, the Office of Career Services provides individual assistance to students on career counseling and the techniques of job searching. The office arranges for both on- and off-campus recruitment for summer and permanent legal positions and participates in a variety of hiring consortia, including the Boston Lawyer's Group, the New Hampshire Job Fair, the Delaware Minority Job Fair, regional Black Law Students Association fairs, and the ABA Business Law Section Career Forum. In addition, the office has expanded its recruitment efforts to include regional programs in New York, Boston, Atlanta, and Southern California.

Applicant Profile

American University, Washington College of Law
This grid includes only applicants who earned 120-180 LSAT scores under standard administrations.

LSAT Score	3.75 +		3.50 - 3.74		3.25 - 3.49		3.00 - 3.24		2.75 - 2.99		2.50 - 2.74		2.25 - 2.49		2.00 - 2.24		Below 2.00		No GPA		Total	
	Apps	Adm	Apps	Adm	Apps	Adm	Apps	Adm	Apps	Adm	Apps	Adm	Apps	Adm	Apps	Adm	Apps	Adm	Apps	Adm	Apps	Adm
175-180	1	1	4	4	2	1	2	2	1	1	2	1	0	0	1	0	0	0	0	0	13	10
170-174	11	11	11	11	17	16	12	11	12	8	7	4	4	1	1	0	0	0	1	0	76	62
165-169	67	66	129	118	111	97	99	76	52	25	29	5	14	0	4	0	0	0	6	1	511	388
160-164	270	245	537	439	485	302	365	144	178	30	78	16	36	4	11	0	2	0	13	3	1975	1183
155-159	403	102	787	134	819	90	578	52	268	22	119	10	60	3	15	1	5	0	22	0	3076	414
150-154	223	22	455	42	558	67	463	55	238	18	126	5	46	0	23	1	3	0	24	1	2159	211
145-149	52	3	146	3	237	5	215	4	145	0	82	0	49	1	19	0	2	0	20	2	967	18
140-144	17	0	44	0	64	1	90	1	89	0	54	0	30	0	20	0	6	0	15	0	429	2
135-139	2	0	12	0	26	0	21	0	31	0	22	0	14	0	11	0	3	0	9	0	151	0
130-134	1	0	0	0	3	0	7	0	12	0	5	0	6	0	7	0	0	0	2	0	43	0
125-129	0	0	0	0	2	0	3	0	4	0	1	0	1	0	0	0	1	0	1	0	13	0
120-124	0	0	0	0	0	0	0	0	1	0	1	0	0	0	0	0	0	0	0	0	2	0
Total	1047	450	2125	751	2324	579	1855	345	1031	104	526	41	260	9	112	2	22	0	113	7	9415	2288

Apps = Number of Applicants
Adm = Number Admitted
Reflects 99% of the total applicant pool.

Appalachian School of Law

Post Office Box 2825
Grundy, VA 24614
Phone: 800.895.7411 (toll free) or 276.935.4349; Fax: 276.935.8261
E-mail: aslinfo@asl.edu; Website: www.asl.edu

ABA Approved Since 2001

The Basics

Type of school	Private
Term	Semester
Application deadline	7/1
Application fee	$50
Financial aid deadline	7/1
Can first year start other than fall?	No
Student to faculty ratio (fall)	19.9 to 1
Does the university offer:	
housing restricted to law students?	No
graduate housing for which law students are eligible?	No

Faculty and Administrators

	Total		Men		Women		Minorities	
	Fall	Spr	Fall	Spr	Fall	Spr	Fall	Spr
Full-time	16	16	8	8	8	8	3	3
Other Full-time	0	0	0	0	0	0	0	0
Deans, librarians, & others who teach	5	5	3	3	2	2	0	0
Part-time	3	1	2	1	1	0	0	0
Total	24	22	13	12	11	10	3	3

Curriculum

		Full-time	Part-time
Typical first-year section size		106	0
Is there typically a "small section" of the first-year class, other than Legal Writing, taught by full-time faculty		Yes	No
If yes, typical size offered last year		35	0
# of classroom course titles beyond 1st year curriculum		36	
# of upper division courses, excluding seminars with an enrollment:	Under 25	13	
	25-49	7	
	50-74	5	
	75-99	3	
	100+	6	
# of seminars		6	
# of seminar positions available		120	
# of seminar positions filled		90	0
# of positions available in simulation courses		200	
# of simulation positions filled		193	0
# of positions available in faculty supervised clinical courses		0	
# of faculty supervised clinical positions filled		0	0
# involved in field placements		138	0
# involved in law journals		28	0
# involved in moot court or trial competitions		21	0
# of credit hours required to graduate		90	

JD Enrollment and Ethnicity

	Men		Women		Full-time		Part-time		1st-year		Total		JD Degs. Awd.
	#	%	#	%	#	%	#	%	#	%	#	%	
African Amer.	6	2.6	8	5.8	14	3.8	0	0.0	7	4.9	14	3.8	4
Amer. Indian	2	0.9	1	0.7	3	0.8	0	0.0	1	0.7	3	0.8	1
Asian Amer.	4	1.7	4	2.9	8	2.2	0	0.0	0	0.0	8	2.2	0
Mex. Amer.	0	0.0	0	0.0	0	0.0	0	0.0	0	0.0	0	0.0	0
Puerto Rican	1	0.4	0	0.0	1	0.3	0	0.0	1	0.7	1	0.3	0
Hispanic	3	1.3	4	2.9	7	1.9	0	0.0	2	1.4	7	1.9	0
Total Minority	16	7.0	17	12.2	33	9.1	0	0.0	11	7.7	33	8.9	5
For. Nation.	0	0.0	0	0.0	0	0.0	0	0.0	0	0.0	0	0.0	1
Caucasian	209	90.9	119	85.6	323	88.7	5	100.0	125	88.0	328	88.9	87
Unknown	5	2.2	3	2.2	8	2.2	0	0.0	6	4.2	8	2.2	0
Total	230	62.3	139	37.7	364	98.6	5	1.4	142	38.5	369		93

Tuition and Fees

	Resident	Nonresident
Full-time	$20,150	$0
Part-time	$0	$0

Living Expenses

Estimated living expenses for singles

Living on campus	Living off campus	Living at home
N/A	$14,795	N/A

Appalachian School of Law

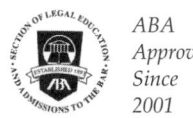

*ABA
Approved
Since
2001*

GPA and LSAT Scores

	Total	Full-time	Part-time
# of apps	990	990	0
# of admits	464	464	0
# of matrics	145	145	0
75% GPA	3.30	3.30	0.00
25% GPA	2.62	2.62	0.00
75% LSAT	152	152	0
25% LSAT	146	146	0

Grants and Scholarships (from prior year)

	Total		Full-time		Part-time	
	#	%	#	%	#	%
Total # of students	355		350		5	
Total # receiving grants	205	57.7	205	58.6	0	0.0
Less than 1/2 tuition	145	40.8	145	41.4	0	0.0
Half to full tuition	52	14.6	52	14.9	0	0.0
Full tuition	8	2.3	8	2.3	0	0.0
More than full tuition	0	0.0	0	0.0	0	0.0
Median grant amount			$4,375		$0	

Informational and Library Resources

# of volumes and volume equivalents	188,225
# of titles	112,761
# of active serial subscriptions	3,384
Study seating capacity inside the library	232
# of professional librarians	6
Hours per week library is open	91
# of open, wired connections available to students	412
# of networked computers available for use by students	27
# of simultaneous wireless users	0
Require computer?	N

JD Attrition (from prior year)

	Academic	Other	Total	
	#	#	#	%
1st year	6	24	30	20.1%
2nd year	2	3	5	4.6%
3rd year	0	0	0	0.0%
4th year	0	0	0	0.0%

Employment

	Total	Percentage
Employment status known	42	63.6
Employment status unknown	24	36.4
Employed	36	85.7
Pursuing graduate degrees	0	0.0
Unemployed seeking employment	5	11.9
Unemployed not seeking employment	1	2.4

Type of Employment

	Total	Percentage
# employed in law firms	25	69.4
# employed in business and industry	4	11.1
# employed in government	0	0.0
# employed in public interest	0	0.0
# employed as judicial clerks	7	19.4
# employed in academia	0	0.0

Geographic Location

	Total	Percentage
# employed in state	16	44.4
# employed in foreign countries	0	0.0
# of states where employed	11	

Bar Passage Rates

Jurisdiction	Virginia			Tennessee		
Exam	Sum 03	Win 04	Total	Sum 03	Win 04	Total
# from school taking bar for the first time	23	0	23	9	0	9
School's pass rate for all first-time takers	52%		52%	78%		78%
State's pass rate for all first-time takers	75%	60%	72%	81%	79%	81%

Appalachian School of Law

Post Office Box 2825
Grundy, VA 24614
Phone: 800.895.7411 (toll free) or 276.935.4349; Fax: 276.935.8261
E-mail: aslinfo@asl.edu; Website: www.asl.edu

■ Introduction

The Appalachian School of Law (ASL) opened its doors in 1997 and received provisional approval from the ABA in 2001. ASL's location, nestled in the mountains of southwestern Virginia, provides a peaceful and scenic setting for the study of law. The small size assures an individualized education and creates the opportunity for students to make their own contribution to building a new institution. ASL's commitment to community service is a special and important feature that reinforces and gives context to the academic program.

The following statement of purpose was written by representatives of the students, faculty, staff, and administration of ASL: *The Appalachian School of Law exists to provide opportunity for people from Appalachia and beyond to realize their dreams of practicing law and bettering their communities. We attract a qualified, diverse, and dedicated student body, many of whom will remain in the region after graduation and serve as legal counselors, advocates, judges, mediators, community leaders, and public officials. We offer a nationally recruited, diverse, and well-qualified faculty; a rigorous program for the professional preparation of lawyers; and a comprehensive law library. The program emphasizes professional responsibility, dispute resolution, and practice skills. The ASL community is an exciting, student-centered environment that emphasizes honesty, integrity, fairness, and respect for others. We also emphasize community service and staff and faculty development. At the same time, we are a full participant in our community, serving as a resource for the people, the bar, and other institutions of the region.*

■ Curriculum

The curriculum at ASL is structured to give students the skills and knowledge to succeed. Students receive intensive instruction in legal research, writing, analysis, and other skills essential to the practice of law through ASL's Legal Process program and required upper-level skills courses. During the summer, between the first and second years, each student will serve an externship with a judge, prosecutor, or other government lawyer, or legal services organization. Recent placements have included externships in the chambers of justices of the supreme courts in North Carolina, Tennessee, and Virginia, and with the United States Department of Justice and Environmental Protection Agency. The second-year curriculum provides required courses in the subject areas law students are typically expected to master and lawyers are universally expected to understand well. The third-year curriculum will provide additional required courses in critical subject areas mixed with skill courses in a wide array of subjects. Alternative dispute resolution and professional responsibility are infused throughout the curriculum.

ASL also offers an Academic Success program, designed to assist students with the development and refinement of the skills necessary to make a successful transition to the study of law.

■ Community Service

ASL's vision is to educate community leaders. We emphasize community service as a central aspect of professional responsibility and provide a variety of service opportunities to our students. To demonstrate the commitment of the legal profession to public service, as well as to enhance the program of legal education at ASL, students at ASL are required to complete 25 hours of community service each semester in a project of their choosing. ASL's community service program was saluted as a national model by former Attorney General Janet Reno.

Although students are able to structure their community service to meet their own individual preferences and schedules, ASL assists students in making time for these projects by scheduling one afternoon each week that students may devote to community service projects. Projects sponsored by ASL in recent years include a conflict resolution program taught by our students in public elementary schools; a county mapping project in which our students engage in property research and mapping; work with Buchanan Neighbors United, a group that provides housing repairs to improve substandard housing; a community recycling project; and a gender bias study of the Virginia state court system. Students also are invited to develop alternative projects to satisfy their service obligations.

■ Faculty

ASL's expanding faculty currently consists of 20 full-time professors and a talented group of adjunct professors drawn from the region's bench and bar. The full-time faculty offers an unusual depth of private and governmental practice experience, as well as experience teaching at other law schools. The ranks of the faculty include former law clerks to federal and state court judges, government officials, and partners in small and large private law firms. In addition to being dedicated classroom professors, the ASL faculty also has published a variety of scholarly works in areas ranging from constitutional law to legal ethics to business and commercial matters.

■ Students and Student Organizations

ASL enjoys the support and enthusiasm of a dedicated student body. The entering class usually numbers around 125. Students come to Grundy not only from the immediate region but from across the country and abroad. Frequent "college coffee" events provide an informal opportunity for students, faculty, and staff to get together.

The student body elects a Student Bar Association. Students may participate in numerous student organizations, in the *Appalachian Journal of Law*, and on moot court, trial advocacy, and ADR competition teams. ASL has a Family Resource Network for the spouses, partners, and family of law students. ASL also has a speaker series that brings a number of distinguished speakers to campus.

■ Facilities

ASL is housed in two buildings on a 3.5-acre campus located near the town center of Grundy. The classroom and office building was extensively renovated for the law school in 1997 into a state-of-the-art law school facility and has won an award from the American Institute of Architects. The classroom building is constructed around an open quadrangle that serves as an informal gathering place for the ASL community. The library was extensively renovated during 1998. The building provides a modern, well organized, and technologically advanced library.

Students have access to the Internet through connections to the ASL network that are available in most of ASL's classrooms and at all tables and carrels in the library.

■ Admission and Financial Aid

ASL accepts for admission those students who will benefit from a challenging curriculum in a caring environment.

Admission decisions are not based on a single criterion, but rather each item will be considered in relation to the applicant's total qualifications. Besides the usual undergraduate transcripts and LSAT score, other considerations include an applicant's graduate work, character, work history, professional promise, personal commitment, recommendations, life experience, and other nonacademic achievements. Students can apply online at ASL's website. We are happy to discuss our admission process and criteria with potential applicants at any time.

ASL also offers a Pre-Admission Summer Opportunity (PASO) program for students who may have the potential to succeed as law students and lawyers, but whose skills and talents may not be reflected fully by the traditional measures of the LSAT and undergraduate performance. PASO is a four-week program during July that provides participants an opportunity to experience law school coursework and gives an opportunity for the faculty to evaluate the students' performance to assess their ability to succeed in law school. Participants who fail to demonstrate potential to successfully complete ASL's three-year legal education program will not be offered admission. In 2003, about 50 percent of PASO participants were offered admission to the fall entering class.

While most students will depend on federal student loans to finance a legal education, ASL does offer both merit- and need-based scholarships. Merit-based scholarships are based on entering LSAT and GPA credentials, and the application for admission serves as the application for a merit scholarship.

Applicant Profile

Appalachian School of Law

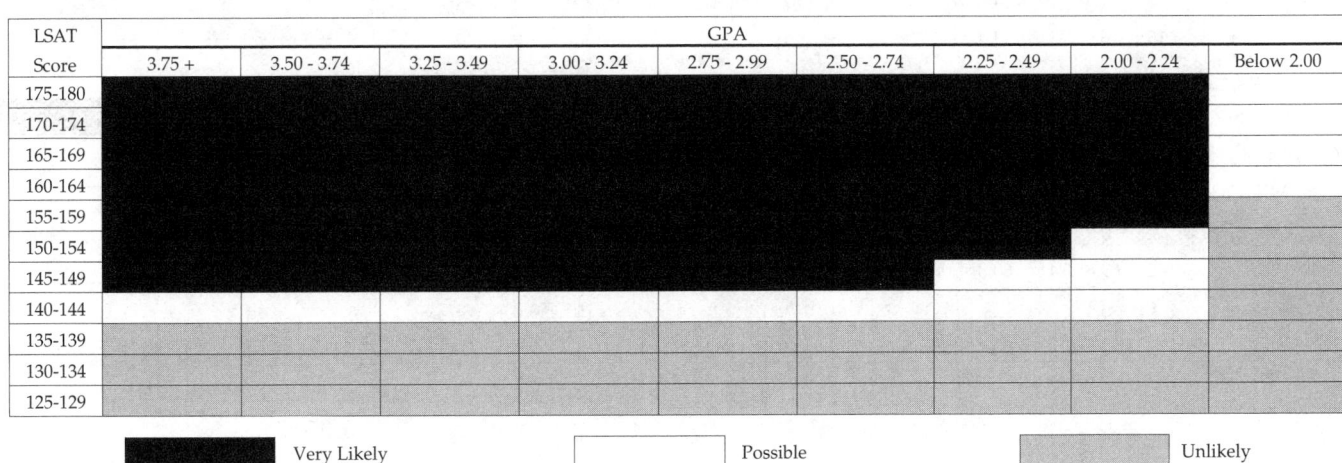

LSAT Score	GPA								
	3.75 +	3.50 - 3.74	3.25 - 3.49	3.00 - 3.24	2.75 - 2.99	2.50 - 2.74	2.25 - 2.49	2.00 - 2.24	Below 2.00
175-180									
170-174									
165-169									
160-164									
155-159									
150-154									
145-149									
140-144									
135-139									
130-134									
125-129									

Very Likely · Possible · Unlikely

This grid represents data for 100% of the applicant pool for fall 2004 admission. It does not reflect the possibility of invitation to participate in the Pre-Admission Summer Opportunity Program. This chart is to be used as a general guide only. Nonnumerical factors are strongly considered for all applicants.

The University of Arizona James E. Rogers College of Law

PO Box 210176, 1201 E Speedway
Tucson, AZ 85721-0176
Phone: 520.621.3477; 520.621.9949; Fax: 520.621.9140
E-mail: admissions@law.arizona.edu; Website: www.law.arizona.edu

ABA Approved Since 1930

The Basics

Type of school	Public
Term	Semester
Application deadline	2/15
Application fee	$50
Financial aid deadline	3/1
Can first year start other than fall?	No
Student to faculty ratio (fall)	12.9 to 1
Does the university offer:	
housing restricted to law students?	No
graduate housing for which law students are eligible?	Yes

Faculty and Administrators

	Total		Men		Women		Minorities	
	Fall	Spr	Fall	Spr	Fall	Spr	Fall	Spr
Full-time	30	30	20	19	10	11	6	7
Other Full-time	2	2	1	1	1	1	0	0
Deans, librarians, & others who teach	4	3	1	1	3	2	1	1
Part-time	27	40	16	32	11	8	1	3
Total	63	75	38	53	25	22	8	11

Curriculum

	Full-time	Part-time
Typical first-year section size	78	0
Is there typically a "small section" of the first-year class, other than Legal Writing, taught by full-time faculty	Yes	No
If yes, typical size offered last year	26	0
# of classroom course titles beyond 1st year curriculum	99	
# of upper division courses, excluding seminars with an enrollment: Under 25	75	
25-49	28	
50-74	4	
75-99	4	
100+	3	
# of seminars	40	
# of seminar positions available	541	
# of seminar positions filled	433	0
# of positions available in simulation courses	363	
# of simulation positions filled	273	0
# of positions available in faculty supervised clinical courses	88	
# of faculty supervised clinical positions filled	77	0
# involved in field placements	40	0
# involved in law journals	104	0
# involved in moot court or trial competitions	68	0
# of credit hours required to graduate	85	

JD Enrollment and Ethnicity

	Men		Women		Full-time		Part-time		1st-year		Total		JD Degs. Awd.
	#	%	#	%	#	%	#	%	#	%	#	%	
African Amer.	10	4.3	12	5.2	22	4.7	0	0.0	5	3.2	22	4.7	5
Amer. Indian	10	4.3	10	4.3	20	4.3	0	0.0	7	4.5	20	4.3	5
Asian Amer.	15	6.5	31	13.4	46	9.9	0	0.0	16	10.3	46	9.9	8
Mex. Amer.	14	6.0	14	6.0	28	6.0	0	0.0	11	7.1	28	6.0	11
Puerto Rican	0	0.0	2	0.9	2	0.4	0	0.0	2	1.3	2	0.4	1
Hispanic	11	4.7	13	5.6	24	5.2	0	0.0	8	5.2	24	5.2	10
Total Minority	60	25.9	82	35.3	142	30.6	0	0.0	49	31.6	142	30.6	40
For. Nation.	2	0.9	3	1.3	5	1.1	0	0.0	1	0.6	5	1.1	0
Caucasian	162	69.8	141	60.8	303	65.3	0	0.0	92	59.4	303	65.3	119
Unknown	8	3.4	6	2.6	14	3.0	0	0.0	13	8.4	14	3.0	0
Total	232	50.0	232	50.0	464	100.0	0	0.0	155	33.4	464		159

Tuition and Fees

	Resident	Nonresident
Full-time	$12,597	$21,577
Part-time	$0	$0

Living Expenses

Estimated living expenses for singles

Living on campus	Living off campus	Living at home
$11,590	$13,330	$7,010

The University of Arizona James E. Rogers College of Law

ABA Approved Since 1930

GPA and LSAT Scores

	Total	Full-time	Part-time
# of apps	2,376	2,376	0
# of admits	471	471	0
# of matrics	155	155	0
75% GPA	3.69	3.69	0.00
25% GPA	3.27	3.27	0.00
75% LSAT	164	164	0
25% LSAT	157	157	0

Grants and Scholarships (from prior year)

	Total #	Total %	Full-time #	Full-time %	Part-time #	Part-time %
Total # of students	475		475		0	
Total # receiving grants	385	81.1	385	81.1	0	0.0
Less than 1/2 tuition	229	48.2	229	48.2	0	0.0
Half to full tuition	95	20.0	95	20.0	0	0.0
Full tuition	3	0.6	3	0.6	0	0.0
More than full tuition	58	12.2	58	12.2	0	0.0
Median grant amount			$4,250		$0	

Informational and Library Resources

# of volumes and volume equivalents	421,001
# of titles	94,535
# of active serial subscriptions	4,400
Study seating capacity inside the library	368
# of professional librarians	9
Hours per week library is open	99
# of open, wired connections available to students	90
# of networked computers available for use by students	33
# of simultaneous wireless users	750
Require computer?	N

JD Attrition (from prior year)

	Academic #	Other #	Total #	Total %
1st year	1	1	2	1.3%
2nd year	0	4	4	2.6%
3rd year	1	2	3	1.8%
4th year	0	0	0	0.0%

Employment

	Total	Percentage
Employment status known	150	99.3
Employment status unknown	1	0.7
Employed	128	85.3
Pursuing graduate degrees	8	5.3
Unemployed seeking employment	9	6.0
Unemployed not seeking employment	5	3.3

Type of Employment

	Total	Percentage
# employed in law firms	55	43.0
# employed in business and industry	6	4.7
# employed in government	31	24.2
# employed in public interest	6	4.7
# employed as judicial clerks	28	21.9
# employed in academia	2	1.6

Geographic Location

	Total	Percentage
# employed in state	88	68.7
# employed in foreign countries	0	0.0
# of states where employed	17	

Bar Passage Rates

Jurisdiction	Arizona		
Exam	Sum 03	Win 04	Total
# from school taking bar for the first time	91	14	105
School's pass rate for all first-time takers	96%	79%	93%
State's pass rate for all first-time takers	78%	74%	77%

The University of Arizona James E. Rogers College of Law

PO Box 210176, 1201 E Speedway
Tucson, AZ 85721-0176
Phone: 520.621.3477; 520.621.9949; Fax: 520.621.9140
E-mail: admissions@law.arizona.edu; Website: www.law.arizona.edu

■ Introduction

The University of Arizona James E. Rogers College of
Law, the oldest law school in Arizona, has a rich and
distinguished history. The college is an integral part of
the University of Arizona, one of the nation's leading
research institutions and most spirited campuses. The
College of Law has a national reputation for providing
its students a high quality education in a collegial,
friendly, and intellectually challenging atmosphere.
The college is located in Tucson, an environmentally
unique and culturally rich city of 800,000, which is home
to an active legal and judicial community. The college is
approved by the ABA, has been a member of the AALS
since 1931, and has a chapter of the Order of the Coif.

■ The College

The identity of the college is shaped by several key
components. First, its size enables students and faculty
to learn in a congenial atmosphere. A school of about
480 students (460 JD students and 20 LLM students),
32 full-time faculty, and many visiting scholars and
lecturers provides an environment for intellectual and
personal growth and genuine community. Arizona offers
a favorable faculty to student ratio (1 to 13), which
enables full-time faculty to teach first-year classes in
sections as small as 25 students. Second, the college has
an outstanding, diverse faculty who are gifted teachers
and nationally recognized scholars. The faculty includes
exceptional teachers and scholars in a broad range of
legal specialties. Third, the college is a leader in promoting the interdisciplinary study of law and society by
collaborating with world class departments at the University of Arizona and by supporting 10 dual-degree
programs. Fourth, the college's commitment to an affordable tuition structure enables students to pursue legal
education without assuming overwhelming debt burden.
Fifth, the college attracts students of intelligence, energy,
and commitment. The JD student body of 460 represents
over 160 different undergraduate and graduate schools,
many nationalities, diverse ethnic and cultural groups,
and unique work, volunteer, and personal achievements.
Finally, the college nurtures an ethic of public service and
community involvement through volunteer activities for
students, faculty, and staff organized by the College
Community Service Board and aimed at improving the
lives of members of the Tucson community.

■ Library and Physical Facilities

The Rogers College of Law occupies a modern building
which was expanded and refurbished in 1997, and which
is fully wheelchair accessible. The Rountree Hall clinical

facility is adjacent to the law school. Both buildings are
part of the 350-acre campus of the University of Arizona,
located in central Tucson. The law library is one of the
foremost legal research facilities in the Southwest. In
addition to a strong Anglo-American collection, the
library has nationally recognized collections in Mexican,
Latin American, and water law. Students also have
access to the resources of the Arizona Health Sciences
Center Library and university libraries. The law library is
a fully networked, technologically sophisticated facility
that is constantly evolving to meet research needs.

■ Curriculum

The college has committed substantial faculty resources
to the first-year curriculum and the development of
research and writing skills. Each first-year student meets
in a section of 25 students in one of the first-semester
courses and shares all other classes with that group of
students. Students enroll in a three-unit Legal Analysis,
Writing, and Research class of 13 in the second semester.
Students must also complete a special writing seminar
during the second or third year.

After completing the first-year requirements, students
have considerable flexibility in determining second- and
third-year coursework. The college offers a rich variety
of courses taught by nationally recognized faculty.

In 2003, the college's nationally recognized Trial
Advocacy Program won the Emil Gumpert Award from
the American College of Trial Lawyers, awarded
annually to the best trial advocacy program in the US.
The college also has numerous clinical opportunities that
combine classroom instruction and field placements in
criminal defense and prosecution, child advocacy,
domestic violence, immigration and indigenous peoples'
law, and the judicial clerking program. The Arizona
Supreme Court convenes annually at the college and
hears arguments on cases under review. The college
awards academic credit for congressional and executive
agency internships in Washington, DC, a state legislative
internship, a university attorney internship, and
internship programs with the Navajo, Pascua Yaqui, and
Tohono O'Odham tribal governments.

The JD degree is normally completed in six semesters
of full-time study; a cumulative grade-point average of
2.0 is required to graduate.

■ Dual-Degree and LLM Programs

The College of Law joins with other colleges at the University of Arizona to offer interdisciplinary study and
dual-degree programs in the following areas: JD/PhD
programs in Philosophy, Psychology, and Economics;
JD/MA programs in Economics, American Indian

The University of Arizona James E. Rogers College of Law

Studies, Latin American Studies, and Women's Studies; a JD/MBA; a JD/MPA; and a JD/MS in Management/Finance. Law students with a 2.75 GPA or better can take six units of coursework in another department and transfer that work to the College of Law for elective credit. The college offers two one-year LLM programs in International Trade Law and in Indigenous Peoples Law and Policy.

■ Admission

Admission to the College of Law is very selective. There are two routes to admission: through the Presumptive process and through the Admission Committee. In the Presumptive process, all applicants are initially ranked according to an index score generated by combining the cumulative undergraduate GPA and LSAT score. Some applicants, selected primarily according to their index rankings, are admitted after a complete administrative review of their files. In the Admission Committee process, a portion of the remaining applicants are selected for further review by the Admission Committee. In making decisions, the committee considers all information, including the nature and rigor of undergraduate experience; graduate education; work and travel experience; unique talents, interests, or accomplishments; extracurricular activities; substantial community or public service; distinctive ethnic or cultural backgrounds; or other circumstances which have influenced the candidate's life or given him/her direction. The college is committed to enrolling students who bring diverse perspectives and encourages applications from minority, disadvantaged, and disabled candidates and candidates who bring varied life experiences to the

educational process. The deadline for completed applications, including transcripts, LSAT scores, and two letters of recommendation, is February 15. To complete a timely application, applicants must take the LSAT no later than the February of the year of expected enrollment.

■ Tuition and Financial Aid

The tuition structure of the University of Arizona affords students the opportunity to pursue a legal education of outstanding quality without extraordinary debt burden. Tuition and fees for JD students for the 2004–2005 year was $12,598 for Arizona residents and $21,578 for nonresidents. The College of Law awarded over $2.4 million in merit- and need-based scholarships to JD students in 2004–2005.

■ Student Activities

The *Arizona Law Review* and the *Arizona Journal of International and Comparative Law* are well-known, student operated, and edited scholarly journals on current legal problems. The students in the moot court and trial advocacy programs participate in national and state appellate advocacy competitions. The student body is self-governing through the Student Bar Association, and students participate in making law school policy by serving as voting members of student-faculty committees. There are over 25 law student organizations that are an important part of institutional and student life. College-sponsored community service projects are an important element in cultivating collaboration among students, faculty, and staff.

Applicant Profile

The University of Arizona James E. Rogers College of Law
This grid includes only applicants with 120-180 LSAT scores earned under standard administrations.

LSAT Score	GPA 3.75 +		3.50 - 3.74		3.25 - 3.49		3.00 - 3.24		2.75 - 2.99		2.50 - 2.74		2.25 - 2.49		2.00 - 2.24		Below 2.00		No GPA		Total	
	Apps	Adm	Apps	Adm	Apps	Adm	Apps	Adm	Apps	Adm	Apps	Adm	Apps	Adm	Apps	Adm	Apps	Adm	Apps	Adm	Apps	Adm
175-180	0	0	1	1	1	1	0	0	1	0	0	0	1	1	0	0	0	0	0	0	4	3
170-174	6	5	7	6	5	4	4	4	2	1	1	0	2	0	2	1	0	0	0	0	29	21
165-169	23	22	35	32	40	33	17	12	14	5	7	4	2	0	1	0	0	0	1	0	140	108
160-164	85	61	99	61	135	52	64	20	44	5	20	2	13	0	3	0	0	0	2	2	465	203
155-159	118	18	153	20	193	25	106	10	59	8	37	3	12	0	2	0	0	0	3	1	683	85
150-154	67	4	111	9	120	5	117	4	63	3	24	0	15	0	2	0	0	0	4	0	523	25
145-149	27	0	58	1	66	0	61	3	32	0	27	0	18	1	4	0	0	0	4	0	297	5
140-144	8	0	22	0	28	0	39	0	27	0	17	0	10	0	3	0	0	0	1	0	155	0
135-139	0	0	7	0	9	0	5	0	14	0	4	0	4	0	3	0	0	0	4	0	50	0
130-134	0	0	1	0	1	0	1	0	1	0	2	0	1	0	1	0	0	0	0	0	8	0
125-129	0	0	0	0	0	0	0	0	1	0	0	0	0	0	0	0	0	0	0	0	1	0
120-124	0	0	0	0	0	0	0	0	0	0	0	0	0	0	1	0	0	0	0	0	1	0
Total	334	110	494	130	598	120	414	53	258	22	139	9	78	2	22	1	0	0	19	3	2356	450

Apps = Number of Applicants   Adm = Number Admitted   Reflects 99% of the total applicant pool.

Arizona State University College of Law

Box 877906
Tempe, AZ 85287-7906
Phone: 480.965.6181
Website: www.law.asu.edu

The Basics

Type of school	Public
Term	Semester
Application deadline	2/15
Application fee	$50
Financial aid deadline	2/15
Can first year start other than fall?	No
Student to faculty ratio (fall)	9.8 to 1
Does the university offer:	
housing restricted to law students?	No
graduate housing for which law students are eligible?	Yes

Faculty and Administrators

	Total		Men		Women		Minorities	
	Fall	Spr	Fall	Spr	Fall	Spr	Fall	Spr
Full-time	53	57	40	42	13	15	8	8
Other Full-time	2	2	2	2	0	0	0	0
Deans, librarians, & others who teach	5	6	3	3	2	3	0	0
Part-time	22	25	18	22	4	3	0	0
Total	82	90	63	69	19	21	8	8

Curriculum

	Full-time	Part-time
Typical first-year section size	99	0
Is there typically a "small section" of the first-year class, other than Legal Writing, taught by full-time faculty	Yes	No
If yes, typical size offered last year	36	0
# of classroom course titles beyond 1st year curriculum	111	
# of upper division courses, excluding seminars with an enrollment: Under 25	73	
25-49	26	
50-74	6	
75-99	4	
100+	0	
# of seminars	36	
# of seminar positions available	501	
# of seminar positions filled	354	0
# of positions available in simulation courses	289	
# of simulation positions filled	279	0
# of positions available in faculty supervised clinical courses	75	
# of faculty supervised clinical positions filled	73	0
# involved in field placements	185	0
# involved in law journals	85	0
# involved in moot court or trial competitions	25	0
# of credit hours required to graduate	87	

JD Enrollment and Ethnicity

	Men #	Men %	Women #	Women %	Full-time #	Full-time %	Part-time #	Part-time %	1st-year #	1st-year %	Total #	Total %	JD Degs. Awd.
African Amer.	5	1.6	19	6.9	24	4.0	0	0.0	9	4.3	24	4.0	7
Amer. Indian	14	4.4	22	7.9	36	6.1	0	0.0	9	4.3	36	6.1	8
Asian Amer.	16	5.0	19	6.9	35	5.9	0	0.0	11	5.2	35	5.9	6
Mex. Amer.	24	7.6	29	10.5	53	8.9	0	0.0	19	9.0	53	8.9	14
Puerto Rican	1	0.3	0	0.0	1	0.2	0	0.0	1	0.5	1	0.2	1
Hispanic	11	3.5	8	2.9	19	3.2	0	0.0	7	3.3	19	3.2	4
Total Minority	71	22.4	97	35.0	168	28.3	0	0.0	56	26.5	168	28.3	40
For. Nation.	9	2.8	4	1.4	13	2.2	0	0.0	6	2.8	13	2.2	2
Caucasian	237	74.8	176	63.5	413	69.5	0	0.0	149	70.6	413	69.5	127
Unknown	0	0.0	0	0.0	0	0.0	0	0.0	0	0.0	0	0.0	0
Total	317	53.4	277	46.6	594	100.0	0	0.0	211	35.5	594		169

Tuition and Fees

	Resident	Nonresident
Full-time	$12,380	$20,900
Part-time	$0	$0

Living Expenses

Estimated living expenses for singles

Living on campus	Living off campus	Living at home
$14,003	$14,003	$14,003

Arizona State University College of Law

ABA
Approved
Since
1969

GPA and LSAT Scores

	Total	Full-time	Part-time
# of apps	2,987	2,987	0
# of admits	627	627	0
# of matrics	211	211	0
75% GPA	3.74	3.74	0.00
25% GPA	3.16	3.16	0.00
75% LSAT	162	162	0
25% LSAT	155	155	0

Grants and Scholarships (from prior year)

	Total		Full-time		Part-time	
	#	%	#	%	#	%
Total # of students	529		529		0	
Total # receiving grants	251	47.4	251	47.4	0	0.0
Less than 1/2 tuition	165	31.2	165	31.2	0	0.0
Half to full tuition	52	9.8	52	9.8	0	0.0
Full tuition	2	0.4	2	0.4	0	0.0
More than full tuition	32	6.0	32	6.0	0	0.0
Median grant amount			$1,500		$0	

Informational and Library Resources

# of volumes and volume equivalents	410,422
# of titles	117,819
# of active serial subscriptions	3,999
Study seating capacity inside the library	538
# of professional librarians	9
Hours per week library is open	111
# of open, wired connections available to students	44
# of networked computers available for use by students	80
# of simultaneous wireless users	600
Require computer?	N

JD Attrition (from prior year)

	Academic	Other	Total	
	#	#	#	%
1st year	5	10	15	8.4%
2nd year	0	9	9	5.3%
3rd year	0	4	4	2.2%
4th year	0	0	0	0.0%

Employment

	Total	Percentage
Employment status known	181	93.8
Employment status unknown	12	6.2
Employed	157	86.7
Pursuing graduate degrees	6	3.3
Unemployed seeking employment	4	2.2
Unemployed not seeking employment	14	7.7

Type of Employment

	Total	Percentage
# employed in law firms	74	47.1
# employed in business and industry	22	14.0
# employed in government	38	24.2
# employed in public interest	3	1.9
# employed as judicial clerks	16	10.2
# employed in academia	4	2.5

Geographic Location

	Total	Percentage
# employed in state	129	82.2
# employed in foreign countries	0	0.0
# of states where employed	16	

Bar Passage Rates

Jurisdiction	Arizona		
Exam	Sum 03	Win 04	Total
# from school taking bar for the first time	143	18	161
School's pass rate for all first-time takers	77%	72%	76%
State's pass rate for all first-time takers	78%	74%	77%

Arizona State University College of Law

Box 877906
Tempe, AZ 85287-7906
Phone: 480.965.6181
Website: www.law.asu.edu

■ Introduction

Founded in 1967, the College of Law at Arizona State University boasts a strong general law curriculum supported by four lead programs and an outstanding teaching faculty. Phoenix is the largest metropolitan area in the country to have only one ABA fully accredited law school. Students are attracted by the quality of legal education available, a commitment to innovative teaching and scholarship, reasonable tuition, and low student/ faculty ratio. A busy calendar of distinguished scholars, jurists, and public officials enriches the student experience and fosters a strong sense of community among the faculty. The College of Law combines the best traditions of American legal education with innovative programs supported by strong community partnerships.

■ Library and Physical Facilities

The College of Law is composed of Armstrong Hall and the John J. Ross-William C. Blakley Law Library and is set on the eastern edge of the university's beautiful 700-acre campus. Armstrong Hall's classrooms are fully accessible to disabled students. The Willard H. Pedrick Great Hall serves not only as a courtroom for annual visits from the Ninth Circuit Court of Appeals, the Arizona Supreme Court, the Navajo Supreme Court, and the Arizona Court of Appeals, but also as a location for campus events. The Ryan C. Harris Courtroom is a state-of-the-art facility specially designed for trial advocacy classes. Armstrong Hall also houses a legal clinic; the Center for the Study of Law, Science, and Technology; the Indian Legal Program; the Committee on Law and Philosophy; the ABA *Jurimetrics* journal; as well as the Cohen Student Center and Sidebar Café. The Ross-Blakely Law Library hosts 3 computer labs, totaling 40 computers, a well-staffed help desk, 12 public terminals, and LexisNexis and Westlaw training. Both Armstrong Hall and the Ross Blakely Law Library are fully equipped with a wireless network; most study rooms have Ethernet access.

■ Curriculum

The College of Law offers one of the best student/ teacher ratios in the country (under 10 to 1) and a wide variety of courses. More than half of the classes in the second and third year have fewer than 25 students. It has a joint JD/MBA program as well as a joint program offering a JD/PhD in Justice Studies. The college takes full advantage of its unique relationship to Phoenix by offering over 80 externship opportunities.

■ Center for the Study of Law, Science, and Technology

Founded in 1984, the Center for the Study of Law, Science, and Technology is the oldest and largest law and science center in the country. It offers certificate programs in Intellectual Property, Health Care Law, and Environmental Law. Each year 10 entering students are invited to become Center Scholars and participate in special activities designated to give a unique experience to those with a special interest in law and science. Center faculty and students edit and co-publish, with the American Bar Association, the prestigious, peer refereed *Jurimetrics: The Journal of Law, Science, and Technology*, the oldest and most widely circulated journal in the field of law and science.

■ Indian Legal Program

The Indian Legal Program enjoys a position of national preeminence. The Indian Legal Program coordinates a certificate program offering more than a dozen courses in Indian law as well as coursework in areas such as natural resources and environmental law, employment law, administrative law, and tax law designed to provide the necessary foundation for practice in Indian law. An extraordinary faculty and long-term partnerships with tribal governments contribute to the strength and reputation of the College of Law in this critical area.

■ Clinical Programs

The Clinical Program is one of the most comprehensive in the nation. Most students participate in at least one of four "live client" clinics: Criminal Practice, Public Defender, Civil Practice, and the Lodestar Mediation Clinic. The Technology Ventures Clinic brings law students together with students from other colleges to assist an agency of the university in assessing, preparing, and implementing technology transfers. The new Indian Legal Clinic trains students for practice in state, federal, and tribal courts, and offers practical experience in the application of fundamental principles of Indian law to issues affecting Native American communities.

■ Committee on Law and Philosophy

Composed of law faculty and liberal arts and sciences faculty, the committee creates and maintains an active intellectual community specializing in criminal law theory, punishment, forgiveness, constitutional interpretation, human rights theory, law and literature, law and religion, and political obligation. The committee sponsors and hosts conferences, lectures, courses, and seminars.

■ Student Activities

The Student Bar Association and almost 30 other student organizations sponsor numerous activities. Upper-level students publish the *Arizona State Law Journal*. Most students volunteer time and talent through student-coordinated pro bono organizations, and pro bono hours are awarded at graduation as part of each student's official record. Students direct the moot court program and participate in national and international moot court competitions.

■ Admission

Admission to the College of Law is highly selective. Among the factors influencing the admission decision are undergraduate and previous graduate education, LSAT score, trend of college grades, course-selection patterns, quality and grading patterns of undergraduate institutions, work or other nonacademic experience, and cultural or socioeconomic background. Transfer applications are considered on a space-available basis for students with excellent records. Students from minority groups are encouraged to apply. Students from diverse cultural, ethnic, and racial backgrounds enrich the College of Law community and ultimately increase the number of minority lawyers in the country.

■ Career Services

The Career Services Office provides individual assistance to students and alumni seeking employment. The office conducts an extensive program of on-campus interviews during the fall and spring semesters with law firms and governmental agencies. Services also include a computerized job line and alumni bulletin, a resource library, and workshops on résumé writing, interviewing, and job-search techniques.

■ LLM Program

The groundbreaking Master of Laws in Biotech and Genomics is the first degree of its kind in the nation, which explains the overwhelming attention it received from applicants and the national media following announcement of its inception. It provides students in-depth study of the scientific and policy aspects of genomics. Through classroom instruction and guided independent study, LLM candidates explore the laws that enable and constrain the development, control, and application of biotechnology and genomics, including areas such as public health law, agricultural law and policy, and intellectual property. Forensic science and ethical constraints upon the various contemplated uses are also important elements of the program.

Applicant Profile

Arizona State University College of Law
This grid includes only applicants with 120-180 LSAT scores earned under standard administrations.

LSAT Score	3.75 +		3.50 - 3.74		3.25 - 3.49		3.00 - 3.24		2.75 - 2.99		2.50 - 2.74		2.25 - 2.49		2.00 - 2.24		Below 2.00		No GPA		Total	
	Apps	Adm	Apps	Adm	Apps	Adm	Apps	Adm	Apps	Adm	Apps	Adm	Apps	Adm	Apps	Adm	Apps	Adm	Apps	Adm	Apps	Adm
175-180	0	0	0	0	1	1	1	1	0	0	0	0	0	0	0	0	0	0	0	0	2	2
170-174	4	4	4	4	1	1	2	2	3	3	0	0	2	2	0	0	0	0	0	0	16	16
165-169	26	25	25	24	23	22	10	10	14	13	5	3	1	1	1	0	1	1	0	0	106	99
160-164	65	61	86	71	108	76	65	44	51	23	20	6	19	6	1	0	1	0	3	1	419	288
155-159	117	50	151	26	189	24	133	19	87	15	46	4	17	1	5	0	1	0	3	1	749	140
150-154	87	11	157	13	189	12	196	11	112	3	53	2	18	1	8	1	2	0	3	1	825	55
145-149	38	7	82	2	120	8	97	3	77	0	51	0	31	0	11	0	0	0	5	0	512	20
140-144	7	1	29	0	37	2	55	2	50	0	26	1	18	0	6	0	1	0	5	0	234	6
135-139	1	0	13	0	9	0	15	0	17	0	9	0	6	0	7	0	1	0	3	0	81	0
130-134	0	0	1	0	1	0	2	0	1	0	5	0	5	0	2	0	0	0	0	0	17	0
125-129	0	0	0	0	0	0	0	0	2	0	0	0	3	0	0	0	0	0	1	0	6	0
120-124	0	0	0	0	0	0	0	0	0	0	0	0	0	0	1	0	0	0	0	0	1	0
Total	345	159	548	140	678	146	576	92	414	57	215	16	120	11	42	1	7	1	23	3	2968	626

Apps = Number of Applicants
Adm = Number Admitted
Reflects 99% of the total applicant pool.

University of Arkansas School of Law

Robert A. Leflar Law Center
Fayetteville, AR 72701
Phone: 479.575.3102; Fax: 479.575.3937
E-mail: ualawad@uark.edu; Website: law.uark.edu/

ABA Approved Since 1928

The Basics

Type of school	Public
Term	Semester
Application deadline	4/1
Application fee	$0
Financial aid deadline	
Can first year start other than fall?	No
Student to faculty ratio (fall)	13.8 to 1
Does the university offer:	
housing restricted to law students?	No
graduate housing for which law students are eligible?	Yes

Faculty and Administrators

	Total		Men		Women		Minorities	
	Fall	Spr	Fall	Spr	Fall	Spr	Fall	Spr
Full-time	29	29	17	17	12	12	5	4
Other Full-time	2	2	1	1	1	1	0	0
Deans, librarians, & others who teach	5	5	4	4	1	1	0	0
Part-time	10	13	9	12	1	1	1	1
Total	46	49	31	34	15	15	6	5

Curriculum

		Full-time	Part-time
Typical first-year section size		76	0
Is there typically a "small section" of the first-year class, other than Legal Writing, taught by full-time faculty		No	No
If yes, typical size offered last year		0	0
# of classroom course titles beyond 1st year curriculum		73	
# of upper division courses, excluding seminars with an enrollment:	Under 25	67	
	25-49	21	
	50-74	7	
	75-99	2	
	100+	4	
# of seminars		11	
# of seminar positions available		165	
# of seminar positions filled		131	0
# of positions available in simulation courses		198	
# of simulation positions filled		180	0
# of positions available in faculty supervised clinical courses		132	
# of faculty supervised clinical positions filled	76		0
# involved in field placements	37		0
# involved in law journals	47		0
# involved in moot court or trial competitions	42		0
# of credit hours required to graduate		90	

JD Enrollment and Ethnicity

	Men #	Men %	Women #	Women %	Full-time #	Full-time %	Part-time #	Part-time %	1st-year #	1st-year %	Total #	Total %	JD Degs. Awd.
African Amer.	26	10.2	42	19.3	68	14.3	0	0.0	28	17.4	68	14.3	10
Amer. Indian	4	1.6	7	3.2	11	2.3	0	0.0	1	0.6	11	2.3	5
Asian Amer.	4	1.6	11	5.0	15	3.2	0	0.0	7	4.3	15	3.2	2
Mex. Amer.	1	0.4	0	0.0	1	0.2	0	0.0	1	0.6	1	0.2	0
Puerto Rican	0	0.0	0	0.0	0	0.0	0	0.0	0	0.0	0	0.0	0
Hispanic	5	2.0	0	0.0	5	1.1	0	0.0	2	1.2	5	1.1	1
Total Minority	40	15.6	60	27.5	100	21.1	0	0.0	39	24.2	100	21.1	18
For. Nation.	2	0.8	0	0.0	2	0.4	0	0.0	0	0.0	2	0.4	1
Caucasian	213	83.2	158	72.5	371	78.3	0	0.0	121	75.2	371	78.3	100
Unknown	1	0.4	0	0.0	1	0.2	0	0.0	1	0.6	1	0.2	0
Total	256	54.0	218	46.0	474	100.0	0	0.0	161	34.0	474		119

Tuition and Fees

	Resident	Nonresident
Full-time	$8,694	$17,274
Part-time	$0	$0

Living Expenses

Estimated living expenses for singles

Living on campus	Living off campus	Living at home
$12,699	$12,699	$3,000

University of Arkansas School of Law

*ABA
Approved
Since
1928*

GPA and LSAT Scores

	Total	Full-time	Part-time
# of apps	1,282	1,282	0
# of admits	331	331	0
# of matrics	162	162	0
75% GPA	3.68	3.68	0.00
25% GPA	3.06	3.06	0.00
75% LSAT	159	159	0
25% LSAT	150	150	0

Grants and Scholarships (from prior year)

	Total		Full-time		Part-time	
	#	%	#	%	#	%
Total # of students	458		458		0	
Total # receiving grants	141	30.8	141	30.8	0	0.0
Less than 1/2 tuition	39	8.5	39	8.5	0	0.0
Half to full tuition	58	12.7	58	12.7	0	0.0
Full tuition	36	7.9	36	7.9	0	0.0
More than full tuition	8	1.7	8	1.7	0	0.0
Median grant amount			$6,047		$0	

Informational and Library Resources

# of volumes and volume equivalents	282,810
# of titles	186,093
# of active serial subscriptions	3,498
Study seating capacity inside the library	343
# of professional librarians	7
Hours per week library is open	115
# of open, wired connections available to students	18
# of networked computers available for use by students	58
# of simultaneous wireless users	500
Require computer?	N

JD Attrition (from prior year)

	Academic	Other	Total	
	#	#	#	%
1st year	3	25	28	16.9%
2nd year	2	0	2	1.2%
3rd year	0	0	0	0.0%
4th year	0	0	0	0.0%

Employment

	Total	Percentage
Employment status known	98	98.0
Employment status unknown	2	2.0
Employed	90	91.8
Pursuing graduate degrees	5	5.1
Unemployed seeking employment	3	3.1
Unemployed not seeking employment	0	0.0

Type of Employment

# employed in law firms	58	64.4
# employed in business and industry	9	10.0
# employed in government	1	1.1
# employed in public interest	13	14.4
# employed as judicial clerks	6	6.7
# employed in academia	4	4.4

Geographic Location

# employed in state	67	74.4
# employed in foreign countries	0	0.0
# of states where employed	9	

Bar Passage Rates

Jurisdiction	Arkansas		
Exam	Sum 03	Win 04	Total
# from school taking bar for the first time	64	14	78
School's pass rate for all first-time takers	80%	71%	78%
State's pass rate for all first-time takers	83%	70%	79%

University of Arkansas School of Law

Robert A. Leflar Law Center
Fayetteville, AR 72701
Phone: 479.575.3102; Fax: 479.575.3937
E-mail: ualawad@uark.edu; Website: law.uark.edu/

■ Introduction

The University of Arkansas School of Law is located on the main university campus at Fayetteville, a city of 58,000 in northwest Arkansas. The School of Law was established in 1924 and has continuously sought to provide high quality legal education in a university community. In 1926, the School of Law was approved by the ABA, and, in 1927, the school became a member of the AALS.

■ Enrollment/Student Body

Although approximately 75–80 percent of the students are Arkansas residents, others are from every part of the United States. Since the school has no undergraduate course prerequisites, the academic backgrounds and nonacademic experiences of students are varied.

■ Library and Physical Facilities

The law library has over 273,000 volumes and volume equivalents. Students are trained in the techniques of computer-assisted legal research as well as in the traditional research methods. The law library is a federal and state depository for government documents.

■ Curriculum

The primary function of the University of Arkansas School of Law is to prepare lawyers who will render the highest quality of professional service to their clients, who are interested in and capable of furthering legal process and reform, and who are prepared to fill the vital role of the lawyer as a community leader. The school offers a full-time, three-year program leading to the JD degree. The degree is conferred upon satisfactory completion of 90 semester hours, including 42 hours of required courses. The first-year curriculum is required. A broad selection of elective second- and third-year courses is available. Students who have completed the first year of law school may earn up to 12 semester hours of credit in summer school, and graduation can be accelerated one semester by summer coursework. The School of Law offers a joint JD/MBA program with the College of Business Administration. If a student is accepted into both programs, a maximum of six hours of approved upper-level elective law courses may be used on duplicative credit toward the MBA degree, and a maximum of six hours of approved graduate courses in business administration may be used as duplicative credit toward the JD degree. The Department of Political Science, the graduate school, and the School of Law cooperate in offering a dual-degree program that allows a student to pursue the MPA and the JD degrees concurrently. Students must be

admitted to the MPA program, the School of Law, and the dual-degree program. The School of Law and the Department of Political Science provide a dual JD/MA in International Law and Politics. This program's students must be admitted both to the School of Law and the Graduate School, Department of Political Science. The Graduate Program in Agriculture Law provides opportunities for advanced study, creative research, and specialized professional training in this rapidly developing area of law. The program is designed to prepare a small number of carefully selected attorneys as specialists in the legal problems of agriculture production, distribution, and marketing. Applicants for admission as candidates for the Master of Laws (LLM) in Agricultural Law must have earned a JD or LLB degree from a fully accredited law school in the United States. Graduates from a law school in another country may be admitted upon the approval of the Agricultural Law Programs Committee.

■ Admission

First-year students are admitted in the fall and only for full-time study. Prior to enrolling in the School of Law, applicants must have completed all requirements for an undergraduate degree from an accredited four-year college. Admission is based on the applicant's LSAT score and undergraduate GPA. In a small percentage of cases, additional criteria such as vocational or professional experience, graduate work, ethnicity, and progressive improvement in college work are considered by a faculty admission committee. Preference is given to Arkansas residents; for the current status of this preference, contact the school. A nonrefundable tuition deposit is required of all admitted candidates. The law school's application deadline is April 1 of the year in which admission is sought. Applicants must take the LSAT no later than February. Applications completed after April 1 will be considered only on a space-available basis.

■ Housing

Housing for single students is available in campus dormitories; apartments are also available for married students. Applicants should write to the Housing Office, University of Arkansas, Fayetteville, AR 72701. A variety of private off-campus housing is available in Fayetteville and surrounding communities, within easy commuting distance of the law school.

■ Student Activities

The *Arkansas Law Review* is a legal periodical published quarterly by the students of the School of Law in cooperation with the Arkansas Bar Association. Candidates for the *Review* are selected on the basis of scholarship and writing ability. The *Journal of Food Law and Policy* is a legal periodical published twice a year by students of the School of Law. Candidates for the *Journal* are selected from the second- and third-year law classes by the editorial board on the basis of scholarship and writing ability. Students in their second and third years are encouraged to compete in an intramural moot court competition, and Arkansas students participate in national moot court competitions. The University of Arkansas School of Law also participates in the ABA Law Student Division Client Counseling Competition. The law school operates a legal aid clinic providing counseling and representation for university students and indigent persons seeking legal assistance. An Arkansas Supreme Court Rule permits senior law students, upon certification and under supervision, to appear in court on a no-fee basis. The Student Bar Association sponsors a variety of academic and social activities. All students are also eligible for membership in the Law Student Division of the Arkansas Bar Association. Three of the largest national legal fraternities, Delta Theta Phi, Phi Alpha Delta, and Phi Delta Phi, maintain active chapters at the school. The Women's Law Student Association was organized to provide an opportunity for women to discuss and work with common professional interests and problems. Members of the Arkansas Chapter of Black Law Students Association work as a collective body to inform black students of the availability and advantages of a legal education, to promote the academic success of black law students at Arkansas, and to increase the awareness and commitment of the legal profession to the black community.

■ Expenses and Financial Aid

Students are expected to make sufficient financial arrangements for the first year of study without the necessity of seeking employment. All law students are required to be full-time students. All financial aid in the form of Perkins Loans (formerly NDSL), higher education loans, and work-study grants is processed by the University of Arkansas Office of Student Financial Aid, University of Arkansas, Fayetteville, AR 72701. Merit scholarships are awarded to some entering students. Applications for a limited number of other scholarships are distributed following fall registration in August.

■ Career Planning and Placement

The law school maintains an Office of Career Planning and Placement with a full-time, highly qualified director and staff to assist and advise students and graduates. Services offered by the office include on-campus interviews for permanent and summer employment; individual career counseling sessions; workshops and handbooks regarding résumé preparation, interviewing skills and techniques, and job searches; panels of lawyers who present programs on a variety of topics; a jobs bulletin; and a comprehensive placement library. The office also maintains employment and bar passage statistics.

Applicant Profile Not Available

University of Arkansas at Little Rock, William H. Bowen School of Law

1201 McMath Avenue
Little Rock, AR 72202-5142
Phone: 501.324.9434; Fax: 501.324.9433
E-mail: lawadm@ualr.edu; Website: www.law.ualr.edu

*ABA
Approved
Since
1969*

The Basics

Type of school	Public
Term	Semester
Application deadline	4/15
Application fee	$0
Financial aid deadline	3/1
Can first year start other than fall?	No
Student to faculty ratio (fall)	16.5 to 1
Does the university offer:	
housing restricted to law students?	No
graduate housing for which law students are eligible?	No

Faculty and Administrators

	Total		Men		Women		Minorities	
	Fall	Spr	Fall	Spr	Fall	Spr	Fall	Spr
Full-time	21	23	11	11	10	12	3	5
Other Full-time	2	2	0	0	2	2	0	0
Deans, librarians, & others who teach	5	5	3	3	2	2	0	0
Part-time	40	28	24	19	16	9	4	3
Total	68	58	38	33	30	25	7	8

Curriculum

	Full-time	Part-time
Typical first-year section size	75	53
Is there typically a "small section" of the first-year class, other than Legal Writing, taught by full-time faculty	No	No
If yes, typical size offered last year	0	0
# of classroom course titles beyond 1st year curriculum	87	
# of upper division courses, excluding seminars with an enrollment: Under 25	84	
25-49	24	
50-74	8	
75-99	2	
100+	0	
# of seminars	18	
# of seminar positions available	277	
# of seminar positions filled	150	67
# of positions available in simulation courses	339	
# of simulation positions filled	217	80
# of positions available in faculty supervised clinical courses	103	
# of faculty supervised clinical positions filled	70	5
# involved in field placements	0	1
# involved in law journals	48	5
# involved in moot court or trial competitions	25	6
# of credit hours required to graduate	90	

JD Enrollment and Ethnicity

	Men		Women		Full-time		Part-time		1st-year		Total		JD Degs. Awd.
	#	%	#	%	#	%	#	%	#	%	#	%	
African Amer.	5	2.1	24	10.4	17	5.3	12	8.3	13	8.5	29	6.3	3
Amer. Indian	4	1.7	2	0.9	5	1.6	1	0.7	0	0.0	6	1.3	0
Asian Amer.	4	1.7	4	1.7	6	1.9	2	1.4	3	2.0	8	1.7	2
Mex. Amer.	0	0.0	1	0.4	1	0.3	0	0.0	0	0.0	1	0.2	0
Puerto Rican	0	0.0	0	0.0	0	0.0	0	0.0	0	0.0	0	0.0	0
Hispanic	3	1.3	3	1.3	5	1.6	1	0.7	2	1.3	6	1.3	5
Total Minority	16	6.9	34	14.7	34	10.7	16	11.0	18	11.8	50	10.8	10
For. Nation.	0	0.0	0	0.0	0	0.0	0	0.0	0	0.0	0	0.0	1
Caucasian	217	93.1	197	85.3	285	89.3	129	89.0	135	88.2	414	89.2	94
Unknown	0	0.0	0	0.0	0	0.0	0	0.0	0	0.0	0	0.0	0
Total	233	50.2	231	49.8	319	68.8	145	31.3	153	33.0	464		105

Tuition and Fees

	Resident	Nonresident
Full-time	$8,317	$16,549
Part-time	$6,199	$12,079

Living Expenses

Estimated living expenses for singles

Living on campus	Living off campus	Living at home
$12,382	$12,382	$12,382

University of Arkansas at Little Rock, William H. Bowen School of Law

ABA
Approved
Since
1969

GPA and LSAT Scores

	Total	Full-time	Part-time
# of apps	1,055	898	157
# of admits	254	173	81
# of matrics	148	90	58
75% GPA	3.68	3.76	3.56
25% GPA	3.05	3.13	2.95
75% LSAT	157	157	157
25% LSAT	151	152	149

Grants and Scholarships (from prior year)

	Total		Full-time		Part-time	
	#	%	#	%	#	%
Total # of students	451		315		136	
Total # receiving grants	119	26.4	99	31.4	20	14.7
Less than 1/2 tuition	44	9.8	39	12.4	5	3.7
Half to full tuition	48	10.6	42	13.3	6	4.4
Full tuition	10	2.2	7	2.2	3	2.2
More than full tuition	17	3.8	11	3.5	6	4.4
Median grant amount			$7,347		$3,900	

Informational and Library Resources

# of volumes and volume equivalents	279,724
# of titles	86,228
# of active serial subscriptions	3,664
Study seating capacity inside the library	381
# of professional librarians	6
Hours per week library is open	98
# of open, wired connections available to students	0
# of networked computers available for use by students	64
# of simultaneous wireless users	300
Require computer?	N

JD Attrition (from prior year)

	Academic	Other	Total	
	#	#	#	%
1st year	9	9	18	10.2%
2nd year	2	7	9	6.3%
3rd year	1	3	4	3.6%
4th year	0	0	0	0.0%

Employment

	Total	Percentage
Employment status known	102	96.2
Employment status unknown	4	3.8
Employed	87	85.3
Pursuing graduate degrees	8	7.8
Unemployed seeking employment	5	4.9
Unemployed not seeking employment	2	2.0

Type of Employment

	Total	Percentage
# employed in law firms	41	47.1
# employed in business and industry	14	16.1
# employed in government	16	18.4
# employed in public interest	2	2.3
# employed as judicial clerks	11	12.6
# employed in academia	3	3.4

Geographic Location

	Total	Percentage
# employed in state	73	83.9
# employed in foreign countries	0	0.0
# of states where employed	8	

Bar Passage Rates

Jurisdiction	Arkansas		
Exam	Sum 03	Win 04	Total
# from school taking bar for the first time	76	25	101
School's pass rate for all first-time takers	87%	84%	86%
State's pass rate for all first-time takers	83%	70%	79%

University of Arkansas at Little Rock, William H. Bowen School of Law

1201 McMath Avenue
Little Rock, AR 72202-5142
Phone: 501.324.9434; Fax: 501.324.9433
E-mail: lawadm@ualr.edu; Website: www.law.ualr.edu

■ Introduction

The Bowen School of Law is located in the heart of metropolitan Little Rock, the Arkansas state capital. Little Rock is the seat of the state government as well as the center of the business, technology, financial, and legal communities. Opportunities for law-related employment are plentiful. The Bowen School of Law is fully accredited by the American Bar Association and is a member of the Association of American Law Schools. The small student body provides students an opportunity to learn and simultaneously build a sense of community.

■ Admission

The Bowen School of Law values diversity and seeks a student body with varied backgrounds, experiences, ideas, goals, and lifestyles because we believe this improves the quality of education. With the goal of admitting diverse, highly qualified students, we structure our admission process so we thoroughly evaluate every application. Approximately 140 students enroll annually with around 20 percent of the students being nonresidents. April 15 is the deadline for priority admission; however, we encourage applicants to complete their applications well before this date.

We would like to encourage your interest in the Bowen School of Law. We schedule Pre-Law Visitation Days approximately once a month, providing prospective students an opportunity to tour the facilities, attend a class, meet with faculty and students, and have their questions answered. Please contact Linda Ahlen at 501.324.9896 or Assistant Dean Wood at *rkwood@ualr.edu* to register for a Pre-Law Visitation Day.

■ Clinical Programs

The Bowen School of Law has three legal clinics. These provide students the opportunity to practice law, under supervision, while learning. Additionally, the school and the students are left with the satisfaction of giving back to the community through meeting the legal needs of underserved populations.

Tax Clinic: Students handle cases for real people who are involved in disputes with the Internal Revenue Service. Students conduct client interviews, gather facts, research tax laws, formulate action plans, prepare written protests, negotiate, and litigate. Educational goals include developing familiarity with tax rules and procedures and the ethical considerations in tax practice.

Mediation Clinic: This clinic includes training both in mediation and negotiation skills. The students conduct actual mediations involving special education issues, families in need of services cases, small claims court

cases, juvenile delinquency cases, and other types of conflicts. The special education mediation is a new project for the clinic. It will educate law students on the intricacies of special education cases as well as provide invaluable aid to special education students, their parents, and school personnel regarding their mutual rights and responsibilities.

Litigation Clinic: Students in this clinic handle a number of cases, which often involves them presenting their cases in Arkansas courts. The specific types of cases handled include divorce, paternity, guardianship, abuse/neglect, and delinquency. Students develop their litigation skills while experiencing and analyzing the law as well as engaging in direct client interaction.

■ Facilities and Library

The Bowen School of Law has truly one of the finest law school facilities in the nation. Originally constructed in the 1930s to house the state's medical school, the six-story building was completely renovated in 1992 to create modern law classrooms and courtrooms while preserving the traditional exterior.

The law school recently renovated its technology by adding state of the art equipment, including making its courtrooms and classrooms computerized. Additionally, the entire law school now has wireless Internet access.

The spacious facility contains over 150,000 square feet, which is fully accessible to those with disabilities. Additionally, the Bowen School of Law provides students with a private parking lot. The four-story library is state of the art. It contains two computer labs and wireless Internet access available throughout all four floors. Private study carrels along with plenty of comfortable group study rooms are available for our students.

Our students are provided with mailboxes, lockers, and e-mail accounts. Several indoor and outdoor balconies and lounges provide students ample space for studying and relaxing. One lounge even includes a video game system for that brief escape from law studies.

■ Academic Program

The Bowen School of Law offers a traditional curriculum that blends theory with practice. As part of this emphasis, Evidence and Lawyering Skills are required upper-level courses. In Lawyering Skills, students interview clients and witnesses, draft pleadings and interrogatories, and try a mock case before a judge and jury. Numerous electives are available for second- and third-year students to explore their particular field of interest, whether that is corporate and partnership taxation, health law, internet law, legislative externships,

University of Arkansas at Little Rock, William H. Bowen School of Law

or one of many other choices. Currently, there are four joint-degree programs available: the JD/MBA, the JD/MPA, JD/MPH, and the JD/MD. The Bowen School of Law offers both a full-time division and a part-time division. Students in the part-time division usually complete the program in four years.

■ Cost and Financial Aid

Comparatively, the Bowen School of Law provides a great educational value at a relatively low cost. Many nonresidents obtain resident status after six months, and the school offers a number of nonresident scholarships to reduce tuition to the in-state amount. The Bowen School of Law offers a number of scholarships both prior to enrollment and after enrollment. The largest number of scholarships are part of the Bowen Scholar Program, which provides full tuition and fees. Information about the various scholarship opportunities can be obtained

from the school's website. The school also participates in the Federal Family Education Loan and Federal College Work-Study programs.

■ Activities

There are numerous opportunities for students at the Bowen School of Law to become involved in activities, including service on the *UALR Law Review* and the Moot Court Board. A few examples of our many organizations on campus include the Student Bar Association, American Bar Association, Arkansas Bar Association, Arkansas Women's Lawyers Association, Black Law Students Association, Hispanic Law Students Association, Environmental Law Society, Christian Legal Society, Criminal Law Society, Federalist Society, Overton Inn of Court, International and Foreign Law Association, Young Democrats, Young Republicans, and a legal fraternity.

Applicant Profile

University of Arkansas at Little Rock, William H. Bowen School of Law
This grid includes only applicants who earned 120-180 LSAT scores under standard administrations.

LSAT Score	3.75 +		3.50 - 3.74		3.25 - 3.49		3.00 - 3.24		2.75 - 2.99		2.50 - 2.74		2.25 - 2.49		2.00 - 2.24		Below 2.00		No GPA		Total	
	Apps	Adm	Apps	Adm	Apps	Adm	Apps	Adm	Apps	Adm	Apps	Adm	Apps	Adm	Apps	Adm	Apps	Adm	Apps	Adm	Apps	Adm
175-180	0	0	0	0	0	0	0	0	0	0	0	0	0	0	0	0	0	0	0	0	0	0
170-174	0	0	0	0	1	0	0	0	0	0	1	1	0	0	0	0	0	0	0	0	2	1
165-169	2	2	2	1	1	1	3	3	2	1	0	0	1	1	1	0	0	0	0	0	12	9
160-164	9	8	6	4	8	6	3	2	9	8	3	2	0	0	2	0	1	0	2	0	43	30
155-159	17	12	15	9	19	14	23	12	25	15	14	6	5	2	2	1	1	1	1	0	122	72
150-154	31	21	30	17	52	23	45	15	41	2	31	3	15	1	11	1	1	0	6	0	263	83
145-149	17	11	31	14	62	11	73	5	42	3	36	0	18	0	6	0	1	0	9	0	295	44
140-144	6	1	12	1	28	1	35	2	29	0	28	2	10	1	9	0	3	0	9	0	169	8
135-139	0	0	5	0	14	0	11	0	12	0	12	0	10	0	5	0	4	0	9	0	82	0
130-134	0	0	0	0	4	0	4	0	5	0	6	0	1	0	4	0	1	0	3	0	28	0
125-129	0	0	0	0	0	0	0	0	1	0	1	0	0	0	0	0	1	0	1	0	4	0
120-124	0	0	0	0	0	0	0	0	0	0	0	0	0	0	0	0	0	0	1	0	1	0
Total	82	55	101	46	189	56	197	39	166	29	132	14	60	5	40	2	13	1	41	0	1021	247

Apps = Number of Applicants
Adm = Number Admitted
Reflects 95% of the total applicant pool.

Ave Maria School of Law

3475 Plymouth Road
Ann Arbor, MI 48105
Phone: 734.827.8063; Fax: 734.622.0123
E-mail: info@avemarialaw.edu; Website: www.avemarialaw.edu

ABA
Approved
Since
2002

The Basics

Type of school	Private
Term	Semester
Application deadline	4/1
Application fee	$50
Financial aid deadline	6/1
Can first year start other than fall?	No
Student to faculty ratio (fall)	14.0 to 1
Does the university offer:	
housing restricted to law students?	No
graduate housing for which law students are eligible?	No

Faculty and Administrators

	Total		Men		Women		Minorities	
	Fall	Spr	Fall	Spr	Fall	Spr	Fall	Spr
Full-time	18	18	12	12	6	6	3	3
Other Full-time	5	5	0	0	5	5	0	0
Deans, librarians, & others who teach	6	6	5	5	1	1	0	0
Part-time	9	8	8	5	1	3	0	0
Total	38	37	25	22	13	15	3	3

Curriculum

		Full-time	Part-time
Typical first-year section size		45	0
Is there typically a "small section" of the first-year class, other than Legal Writing, taught by full-time faculty		Yes	No
If yes, typical size offered last year		45	0
# of classroom course titles beyond 1st year curriculum		58	
# of upper division courses, excluding seminars with an enrollement:	Under 25	43	
	25-49	7	
	50-74	3	
	75-99	0	
	100+	0	
# of seminars		9	
# of seminar positions available		144	
# of seminar positions filled		106	0
# of positions available in simulation courses		139	
# of simulation positions filled		83	0
# of positions available in faculty supervised clinical courses		0	
# of faculty supervised clinical positions filled		0	0
# involved in field placements		40	0
# involved in law journals		25	0
# involved in moot court or trial competitions		31	0
# of credit hours required to graduate		90	

JD Enrollment and Ethnicity

	Men		Women		Full-time		Part-time		1st-year		Total		JD Degs. Awd.
	#	%	#	%	#	%	#	%	#	%	#	%	
African Amer.	3	1.4	5	5.4	8	2.6	0	0.0	4	2.7	8	2.6	0
Amer. Indian	5	2.4	1	1.1	6	2.0	0	0.0	4	2.7	6	2.0	0
Asian Amer.	9	4.3	6	6.5	15	5.0	0	0.0	11	7.5	15	5.0	0
Mex. Amer.	3	1.4	0	0.0	3	1.0	0	0.0	2	1.4	3	1.0	1
Puerto Rican	1	0.5	2	2.2	3	1.0	0	0.0	2	1.4	3	1.0	0
Hispanic	13	6.2	4	4.3	17	5.6	0	0.0	12	8.2	17	5.6	0
Total Minority	34	16.2	18	19.6	52	17.2	0	0.0	35	24.0	52	17.2	1
For. Nation.	8	3.8	2	2.2	10	3.3	0	0.0	4	2.7	10	3.3	2
Caucasian	168	80.0	72	78.3	240	79.5	0	0.0	107	73.3	240	79.5	50
Unknown	0	0.0	0	0.0	0	0.0	0	0.0	0	0.0	0	0.0	0
Total	210	69.5	92	30.5	302	100.0	0	0.0	146	48.3	302		53

Tuition and Fees

	Resident	Nonresident
Full-time	$27,500	$27,500
Part-time	$0	$0

Living Expenses

Estimated living expenses for singles

Living on campus	Living off campus	Living at home
$19,037	$19,037	$19,037

Ave Maria School of Law

ABA
Approved
Since
2002

GPA and LSAT Scores

	Total	Full-time	Part-time
# of apps	793	793	0
# of admits	541	541	0
# of matrics	146	146	0
75% GPA	3.49	3.49	0.00
25% GPA	2.78	2.78	0.00
75% LSAT	161	161	0
25% LSAT	152	152	0

Grants and Scholarships (from prior year)

	Total		Full-time		Part-time	
	#	%	#	%	#	%
Total # of students	222		222		0	
Total # receiving grants	179	80.6	179	80.6	0	0.0
Less than 1/2 tuition	9	4.1	9	4.1	0	0.0
Half to full tuition	70	31.5	70	31.5	0	0.0
Full tuition	81	36.5	81	36.5	0	0.0
More than full tuition	19	8.6	19	8.6	0	0.0
Median grant amount			$11,864		$0	

Informational and Library Resources

# of volumes and volume equivalents	453,833
# of titles	175,613
# of active serial subscriptions	4,235
Study seating capacity inside the library	285
# of professional librarians	5
Hours per week library is open	100
# of open, wired connections available to students	569
# of networked computers available for use by students	53
# of simultaneous wireless users	0
Require computer?	N

JD Attrition (from prior year)

	Academic	Other	Total	
	#	#	#	%
1st year	3	6	9	9.1%
2nd year	0	1	1	1.5%
3rd year	0	0	0	0.0%
4th year	0	0	0	0.0%

Employment

	Total	Percentage
Employment status known	65	100.0
Employment status unknown	0	0.0
Employed	59	90.8
Pursuing graduate degrees	0	0.0
Unemployed seeking employment	4	6.2
Unemployed not seeking employment	2	3.1

Type of Employment

	Total	Percentage
# employed in law firms	28	47.5
# employed in business and industry	6	10.2
# employed in government	10	16.9
# employed in public interest	3	5.1
# employed as judicial clerks	10	16.9
# employed in academia	2	3.4

Geographic Location

	Total	Percentage
# employed in state	25	42.4
# employed in foreign countries	1	1.7
# of states where employed	19	

Bar Passage Rates

Jurisdiction	Michigan			Florida		
Exam	Sum 03	Win 04	Total	Sum 03	Win 04	Total
# from school taking bar for the first time	28	1	29	6	0	6
School's pass rate for all first-time takers	93%	100%	93%	100%		100%
State's pass rate for all first-time takers	77%	71%	75%	76%	75%	76%

Ave Maria School of Law

3475 Plymouth Road
Ann Arbor, MI 48105
Phone: 734.827.8065; Fax: 734.622.0123
E-mail: info@avemarialaw.edu; Website: www.avemarialaw.edu

■ Introduction

Ave Maria School of Law is a national Catholic law school committed to preparing lawyers to practice with the highest degree of integrity and professional skill. Ave Maria students have enrolled from 45 states and almost 200 colleges and universities. Having the benefit of a student-faculty ratio of approximately 14 to 1, Ave Maria students are consistently challenged to reflect critically on the law, the principles that undergird it, and their role within the legal system.

To provide this distinctive legal education, Ave Maria has recruited some of the finest faculty members in the country. The faculty includes nationally recognized scholars and talented up-and-coming scholars. The faculty prepares students to practice at the highest level and to succeed on bar exams throughout the country. Ave Maria's bar pass rate has been the highest in Michigan for the past two years.

Ave Maria encourages applications from students of all faiths who seek a distinctive legal education enriched by the Catholic faith and the Catholic intellectual tradition, a tradition that contains a rich heritage of legal thought.

■ Enrollment/Student Body

While many students come to Ave Maria directly from their undergraduate institutions, others have earned postgraduate degrees and have work experience in fields including business, medicine, engineering, military service, and education. Undergraduate schools represented in Ave Maria's student body include Princeton, Cornell, University of Pennsylvania, University of Chicago, Boston College, Duke, Notre Dame, UCLA, and many other fine schools.

■ Faculty

The Ave Maria School of Law faculty includes nationally recognized scholars and accomplished teachers. Their legal scholarship contributes to the development of the law and serves as a fundamental means to enhance their teaching. Indeed, the faculty sees teaching as its primary vocation. Ave Maria provides a quality legal education by challenging students to consider law, what underlies it, and whether the law should be as it is. Ave Maria continuously adds renowned scholars and legal professionals to its faculty.

■ Library/Physical Facilities

The Ave Maria library provides excellent print and online resources as well as a plethora of electronic databases. The library houses more than 440,000 volumes and volume equivalents.

Ave Maria School of Law is housed in a beautifully appointed 84,500-square-foot building designed by renowned architect Alden B. Dow. The building contains classrooms with cutting-edge technology, a moot court room, student offices, and indoor and outdoor community space for student gatherings. All classrooms, student carrels, and group study rooms are connected to the Internet.

■ Curriculum

Ave Maria School of Law awards the Juris Doctor degree after three years of full-time residential day study. The law school requires 90 credit hours for graduation, including a core curriculum of 60 credit hours. Ave Maria ensures that students gain a clear, practical, and comprehensive understanding of the law. Ave Maria professors use a variety of teaching methods, including the Socratic method, lectures, group discussions, and writing assignments. The favorable student-faculty ratio optimizes the benefits associated with these teaching methods.

■ Admission

Ave Maria enrolls talented individuals from diverse backgrounds who seek a rigorous and distinctive legal education. To this end, Ave Maria evaluates applicants from a whole-person perspective and considers many factors, including work experience, activities, background, obstacles overcome, accomplishments, undergraduate and graduate school records, Law School Admission Test (LSAT) scores, letters of reference, and the applicant's personal statement. Ave Maria recognizes that a diverse student body, drawn from throughout the United States and internationally, enriches the educational atmosphere.

■ Student Activities

By providing opportunities for interaction among students, faculty, and the legal community, Ave Maria ensures a vibrant, professional atmosphere and a constructive law school experience. A five-day Orientation Program, a Distinguished Lecture Series, conferences, and the Ave Maria Mentor Program, together with a challenging and comprehensive curriculum, provide Ave Maria students with an exceptional law school experience. A multitude of student organizations offer students the opportunity to pursue their specific areas of interest and augment their law school education.

Career Services/Placement

In addition to meeting with students individually, Ave Maria's Career Services Office presents informational sessions, workshops, speakers, and panel discussions to assist students with career planning. Ave Maria's first three classes have received clerkships from 14 federal court judges, three state supreme court justices, and one state appellate court judge, as well as positions with law firms, government agencies, corporations, academia, and nonprofit organizations.

Learning Beyond the Classroom

Ave Maria students gain hands-on experience through the law school's Clinical and Externship Programs. The Asylum and Immigrant Rights Law Clinic enables students to assist in the representation of persons seeking asylum through affirmative procedures or in removal proceedings. Ave Maria's Externship Program offers students firsthand experience in a variety of practice settings while earning academic credit.

Expenses/Financial Aid

Ave Maria strives to ensure that cost will not prevent any worthy student from attending. Accordingly, Ave Maria offers a generous scholarship program, including full-tuition scholarships. These scholarships are automatically renewed each year if the student maintains a minimum cumulative grade-point average of 3.0. A full-time Financial Aid Director is available to students as they assess their financial needs and apply for student loans.

Housing

Ave Maria's 11-acre campus does not include housing, but is within walking distance of neighborhoods with apartments, condominiums, and homes. Two apartment complexes and a condominium complex, located within a mile of the law school, house most of the students. Additionally, students have access to parking spaces at the law school and convenient curbside parking.

Applicant Profile

Ave Maria School of Law
This grid includes only applicants who earned 120-180 LSAT scores under standard administrations.

LSAT Score	3.75 +		3.50 - 3.74		3.25 - 3.49		3.00 - 3.24		2.75 - 2.99		2.50 - 2.74		2.25 - 2.49		2.00 - 2.24		Below 2.00		No GPA		Total	
	Apps	Adm	Apps	Adm	Apps	Adm	Apps	Adm	Apps	Adm	Apps	Adm	Apps	Adm	Apps	Adm	Apps	Adm	Apps	Adm	Apps	Adm
175-180	0	0	0	0	0	0	0	0	0	0	1	1	0	0	0	0	0	0	0	0	1	1
170-174	1	1	2	2	1	1	0	0	2	2	0	0	1	1	0	0	0	0	1	1	8	8
165-169	11	11	6	6	10	9	7	6	4	3	1	1	1	1	2	2	0	0	2	2	44	41
160-164	27	27	31	30	24	20	15	14	27	26	8	7	7	7	2	2	1	1	5	4	147	138
155-159	26	26	24	23	40	39	32	30	19	16	15	12	7	7	6	4	3	1	11	6	183	164
150-154	9	7	26	23	26	23	28	23	32	31	23	19	10	6	11	9	2	1	9	7	176	149
145-149	3	1	11	6	16	6	19	6	10	1	10	4	10	1	3	2	0	0	4	3	86	30
140-144	1	0	5	0	10	0	13	0	11	0	12	1	6	0	1	0	1	0	4	0	64	1
135-139	2	0	6	0	7	0	9	0	11	0	5	0	9	0	0	0	1	0	6	0	56	0
130-134	1	0	0	0	1	0	2	0	1	0	2	0	1	0	2	0	0	0	0	0	10	0
125-129	0	0	0	0	0	0	0	0	3	0	2	0	0	0	0	0	0	0	3	0	8	0
120-124	0	0	0	0	0	0	0	0	0	0	0	0	0	0	0	0	0	0	1	0	1	0
Total	81	73	111	90	135	98	125	79	120	79	79	45	52	23	27	19	8	3	46	23	784	532

Apps = Number of Applicants
Adm = Number Admitted
Reflects 97% of the total applicant pool.

University of Baltimore School of Law

1420 North Charles Street
Baltimore, MD 21201
Phone: 410.837.4468; Fax: 410.837.4450
E-mail: lwadmiss@ubalt.edu; Website: law.ubalt.edu

ABA Approved Since 1972

The Basics

Type of school	Public
Term	Semester
Application deadline	4/15
Application fee	$60
Financial aid deadline	4/1
Can first year start other than fall?	No
Student to faculty ratio (fall)	21.4 to 1
Does the university offer:	
housing restricted to law students?	No
graduate housing for which law students are eligible?	No

Faculty and Administrators

	Total Fall	Total Spr	Men Fall	Men Spr	Women Fall	Women Spr	Minorities Fall	Minorities Spr
Full-time	34	33	21	22	13	11	9	9
Other Full-time	5	5	2	2	3	3	3	3
Deans, librarians, & others who teach	11	11	8	8	3	3	3	3
Part-time	84	91	61	64	23	27	51	61
Total	134	140	92	96	42	44	66	76

Curriculum

	Full-time	Part-time
Typical first-year section size	68	68
Is there typically a "small section" of the first-year class, other than Legal Writing, taught by full-time faculty	No	No
If yes, typical size offered last year	0	0
# of classroom course titles beyond 1st year curriculum	247	
# of upper division courses, excluding seminars with an enrollment: Under 25	169	
25-49	29	
50-74	7	
75-99	2	
100+	1	
# of seminars	17	
# of seminar positions available	533	
# of seminar positions filled	227	198
# of positions available in simulation courses	518	
# of simulation positions filled	239	263
# of positions available in faculty supervised clinical courses	112	
# of faculty supervised clinical positions filled	75	15
# involved in field placements	51	0
# involved in law journals	273	43
# involved in moot court or trial competitions	45	6
# of credit hours required to graduate	90	

JD Enrollment and Ethnicity

	Men #	Men %	Women #	Women %	Full-time #	Full-time %	Part-time #	Part-time %	1st-year #	1st-year %	Total #	Total %	JD Degs. Awd.
African Amer.	59	12.1	77	15.4	65	9.9	71	21.5	37	10.7	136	13.8	41
Amer. Indian	0	0.0	5	1.0	3	0.5	2	0.6	1	0.3	5	0.5	3
Asian Amer.	17	3.5	22	4.4	24	3.7	15	4.5	17	4.9	39	4.0	7
Mex. Amer.	0	0.0	0	0.0	0	0.0	0	0.0	0	0.0	0	0.0	0
Puerto Rican	0	0.0	0	0.0	0	0.0	0	0.0	0	0.0	0	0.0	0
Hispanic	13	2.7	9	1.8	17	2.6	5	1.5	10	2.9	22	2.2	8
Total Minority	89	18.3	113	22.6	109	16.6	93	28.1	65	18.8	202	20.5	59
For. Nation.	5	1.0	6	1.2	8	1.2	3	0.9	3	0.9	11	1.1	3
Caucasian	330	67.9	341	68.1	472	72.0	199	60.1	229	66.4	671	68.0	188
Unknown	62	12.8	41	8.2	67	10.2	36	10.9	48	13.9	103	10.4	21
Total	486	49.2	501	50.8	656	66.5	331	33.5	345	35.0	987		271

Tuition and Fees

	Resident	Nonresident
Full-time	$7,165	$12,786
Part-time	$594	$1,000

Living Expenses

Estimated living expenses for singles

Living on campus	Living off campus	Living at home
N/A	$16,500	$9,500

University of Baltimore School of Law

ABA
Approved
Since
1972

GPA and LSAT Scores

	Total	Full-time	Part-time
# of apps	2,921	2,345	576
# of admits	884	729	155
# of matrics	345	252	93
75% GPA	3.53	3.56	3.57
25% GPA	2.80	2.97	3.01
75% LSAT	155	155	156
25% LSAT	150	151	151

Grants and Scholarships (from prior year)

	Total		Full-time		Part-time	
	#	%	#	%	#	%
Total # of students	972		669		303	
Total # receiving grants	70	7.2	57	8.5	13	4.3
Less than 1/2 tuition	56	5.8	47	7.0	9	3.0
Half to full tuition	0	0.0	0	0.0	0	0.0
Full tuition	0	0.0	0	0.0	0	0.0
More than full tuition	14	1.4	10	1.5	4	1.3
Median grant amount			$5,000		$3,100	

Informational and Library Resources

# of volumes and volume equivalents	346,227
# of titles	31,727
# of active serial subscriptions	3,380
Study seating capacity inside the library	339
# of professional librarians	11
Hours per week library is open	110
# of open, wired connections available to students	29
# of networked computers available for use by students	33
# of simultaneous wireless users	700
Require computer?	N

JD Attrition (from prior year)

	Academic	Other	Total	
	#	#	#	%
1st year	17	0	17	5.1%
2nd year	5	3	8	2.8%
3rd year	0	2	2	0.7%
4th year	2	0	2	3.0%

Employment

	Total	Percentage
Employment status known	209	82.6
Employment status unknown	44	17.4
Employed	181	86.6
Pursuing graduate degrees	2	1.0
Unemployed seeking employment	22	10.5
Unemployed not seeking employment	4	1.9

Type of Employment

	Total	Percentage
# employed in law firms	67	37.0
# employed in business and industry	19	10.5
# employed in government	31	17.1
# employed in public interest	4	2.2
# employed as judicial clerks	39	21.5
# employed in academia	4	2.2

Geographic Location

	Total	Percentage
# employed in state	134	74.0
# employed in foreign countries	0	0.0
# of states where employed	7	

Bar Passage Rates

Jurisdiction	Maryland		
Exam	Sum 03	Win 04	Total
# from school taking bar for the first time	170	71	241
School's pass rate for all first-time takers	65%	70%	67%
State's pass rate for all first-time takers	73%	62%	71%

University of Baltimore School of Law

1420 North Charles Street
Baltimore, MD 21201
Phone: 410.837.4468; Fax: 410.837.4450
E-mail: lwadmiss@ubalt.edu; Website: law.ubalt.edu

■ Introduction

Founded in 1925, the University of Baltimore is one of 13 institutions in the university system of Maryland. The School of Law has a distinguished history of offering high quality legal education in a vibrant urban environment that provides a wide range of opportunities for students to put their legal knowledge into practice. In both day and evening divisions, the school offers a comprehensive curriculum that gives students core substantive and procedural classes, as well as excellent training in legal skills. A broad selection of elective courses completes the curriculum. The school's midtown location puts it only 18 blocks from Baltimore's Inner Harbor, Oriole Park at Camden Yards, and the Baltimore Ravens' PSInet Stadium. Also nearby are state and federal courts, large law firms, and government offices. The School of Law is accredited by the American Bar Association and is a member of the Association of American Law Schools.

■ Library and Physical Facilities

The library's permanent collection contains approximately 317,000 books and bound volume equivalents. The collection includes the published reports of federal and state courts, statutes, administrative materials, and secondary materials such as treatises, legal encyclopedias, digests, citators, form books, looseleaf services, and law reviews. The library staff believes that technology should not be considered separate from the study and practice of law. To that end, professional reference librarians are available to students seven days a week. Legal research courses teach students how to use the computer-assisted legal systems, as well as how to access the library's many resources on CD-ROM. The library's two computer labs are open to law students during library hours and provide access to word processing, LexisNexis, Westlaw, the Internet, online catalogs, and other resources.

■ Joint Degrees

The School of Law offers six joint degrees: JD with MBA, MPA, MS in Criminal Justice, MS in Negotiations and Conflict Management, LLM in Taxation, and the PhD in Policy Science.

■ Special Programs

Areas of Concentration—The School of Law has an innovative curriculum that allows students to develop an area of study focused on one or more areas of the law, while still providing them with the basic first-year curriculum and many electives. Students may take courses in one of 13 areas of concentration: Business Law, Criminal Practice, Electronic Commerce, Environmental Law, Estate Planning, Family Law, General Practice, Intellectual Property, International and Comparative Law, Litigation and Advocacy, Public Interest Law, Real Estate Practice, and Theories of the Law.

The University of Baltimore Center for Families, Children, and the Courts—focuses on reforming state courts into more appropriate forums for the resolutions of family legal crises.

The Center for International and Comparative Law—promotes the study and understanding of international and comparative law and the political and economic institutions that support the international legal order. The center places special emphasis on environmental law, human rights, intellectual property, and international business transactions.

The Stephen L. Snyder Center for Litigation Skills—supports and enhances the acclaimed litigation skills training of the School of Law through a variety of programs and activities, including lectures by prominent lawyers and judges, special conferences, and litigation research.

Clinical, Advocacy, and Internship Programs—Professional development is fostered through clinics in which students represent individuals and organizations in litigation and transactional matters. Clinics include the **Appellate Practice Clinic**, which enables students to brief and argue a case in the Maryland Court of Special Appeals; the **Civil Clinic**, which focuses on such issues as consumer protection, public benefits cases, and landlord-tenant disputes; the **Community Development Clinic**, which represents nonprofit community organizations in a variety of housing, economic, social, and cultural development areas; the **Criminal Practice Clinic**, in which students handle misdemeanor and felony matters in the district and circuit courts; the **Disability Law Clinic**, which provides representation to patients in involuntary commitment hearings; the **Family Law Clinic**, where students represent low income clients seeking child custody, support, divorce, and protection from domestic violence; and the **Tax Clinic**, which enables students to represent low income clients before the Internal Revenue Service and the US Tax Court. **Internship Programs** give students experience clerking for academic credit in the public and private sector, including positions in the executive, legislative, and judicial branches of state and local governments.

Law reviews, journals, and other periodicals give students an opportunity to hone their skills in research, analysis, and writing. *The University of Baltimore Law Review, Journal of Environmental Law,* and *Intellectual Property Law Journal* offer in-depth analysis of issues of current concern to practitioners and judges alike. The *Law Forum* specializes in articles that trace developing trends in the law.

■ Admission

The School of Law has established an admission policy designed to obtain a diverse and well-qualified student body. In evaluating applicant files, the Admission Committee considers not only the cumulative undergraduate grade-point average and the LSAT score, but also nontraditional factors that may be relevant in determining an applicant's ability to succeed in law school. Applicants are encouraged to discuss fully in a personal statement any such factors they wish the committee to consider in evaluating their application.

■ Expenses and Financial Aid

The university's Financial Aid Office administers federal, state, and institutional loan programs. First-year and transfer applicants are advised to apply for financial aid well in advance of the April 1 deadline. Law scholarships are awarded by the School of Law on the basis of the same traditional and nontraditional factors considered for admission. Financial need is not required for scholarships, although it is a factor. Applicants should submit scholarship forms and a copy of the FAFSA they filed with the Financial Aid Office to the Office of Admission.

■ Career Services

Six months after graduation, 87 percent of the class of 2003 was employed. (Note: The percentage is the total number employed of those seeking employment.) The Career Services Center is dedicated to assisting law students in articulating, developing, and attaining their professional goals. The Career Services Center provides career counseling, offers a broad array of programs and workshops, maintains an extensive resource library, and is online with both LexisNexis and Westlaw.

Applicant Profile

University of Baltimore School of Law
This grid includes only applicants who earned 120-180 LSAT scores under standard administrations.

LSAT Score	GPA																		
	3.75 +		3.50 - 3.74		3.25 - 3.49		3.00 - 3.24		2.75 - 2.99		2.50 - 2.74		2.25 - 2.49		2.00 - 2.24		Below 2.00		No GPA		Total	
	Apps	Adm	Apps	Adm	Apps	Adm	Apps	Adm	Apps	Adm	Apps	Adm	Apps	Adm	Apps	Adm	Apps	Adm	Apps	Adm	Apps	Adm
175-180	0	0	0	0	0	0	0	0	0	0	0	0	0	0	0	0	0	0	0	0	0	0
170-174	1	1	1	0	0	0	1	0	1	0	1	1	2	0	0	0	0	0	0	0	7	2
165-169	3	1	5	1	4	1	4	0	2	0	2	0	4	2	1	0	0	0	0	0	25	5
160-164	11	4	19	5	15	0	25	6	23	4	16	2	11	2	7	2	0	0	2	0	129	25
155-159	34	11	43	18	73	19	77	32	62	24	34	9	34	1	11	3	3	0	3	0	374	117
150-154	46	21	120	44	142	57	160	43	157	27	101	12	48	2	25	2	2	0	12	4	813	212
145-149	26	1	94	10	157	11	162	11	146	8	100	2	57	2	24	1	4	0	17	0	787	46
140-144	12	0	36	0	61	0	106	0	112	0	71	0	60	1	27	0	10	0	9	0	504	1
135-139	6	0	15	0	25	1	31	0	40	1	28	0	29	0	16	0	7	0	7	0	204	2
130-134	0	0	1	0	5	0	11	0	16	0	21	0	10	0	7	0	3	0	2	0	76	0
125-129	0	0	0	0	1	0	4	0	6	0	3	0	2	0	2	0	1	0	0	0	19	0
120-124	0	0	0	0	0	0	0	0	2	0	1	0	0	0	0	0	0	0	1	0	4	0
Total	139	39	334	78	483	89	581	92	567	64	378	26	257	10	120	8	30	0	53	4	2942	410

Apps = Number of Applicants
Adm = Number Admitted
Reflects 99% of the total applicant pool.

Barry University Dwayne O. Andreas School of Law

6441 East Colonial Drive
Orlando, FL 32807
Phone: 321.206.5600; Fax: 321.206.5662
E-mail: lawinfo@mail.barry.edu; Website: www.barry.edu/law

ABA Approved Since 2002

The Basics

Type of school	Private
Term	Semester
Application deadline	4/1
Application fee	$50
Financial aid deadline	4/15
Can first year start other than fall?	No
Student to faculty ratio (fall)	21.5 to 1
Does the university offer:	
housing restricted to law students?	No
graduate housing for which law students are eligible?	No

Faculty and Administrators

	Total		Men		Women		Minorities	
	Fall	Spr	Fall	Spr	Fall	Spr	Fall	Spr
Full-time	18	20	12	14	6	6	1	2
Other Full-time	3	3	0	0	3	3	0	0
Deans, librarians, & others who teach	6	6	3	3	3	3	2	2
Part-time	17	12	12	9	5	3	1	2
Total	44	41	27	26	17	15	4	6

Curriculum

		Full-time	Part-time
Typical first-year section size		80	80
Is there typically a "small section" of the first-year class, other than Legal Writing, taught by full-time faculty		No	No
If yes, typical size offered last year		0	0
# of classroom course titles beyond 1st year curriculum		72	
# of upper division courses, excluding seminars with an enrollment:	Under 25	65	
	25-49	36	
	50-74	9	
	75-99	2	
	100+	1	
# of seminars		4	
# of seminar positions available		44	
# of seminar positions filled		24	17
# of positions available in simulation courses		202	
# of simulation positions filled		61	68
# of positions available in faculty supervised clinical courses		16	
# of faculty supervised clinical positions filled		1	12
# involved in field placements		5	3
# involved in law journals		6	3
# involved in moot court or trial competitions		11	6
# of credit hours required to graduate		90	

JD Enrollment and Ethnicity

	Men		Women		Full-time		Part-time		1st-year		Total		JD Degs. Awd.
	#	%	#	%	#	%	#	%	#	%	#	%	
African Amer.	15	5.4	16	6.5	17	4.8	14	8.1	18	6.9	31	5.9	3
Amer. Indian	1	0.4	2	0.8	2	0.6	1	0.6	2	0.8	3	0.6	0
Asian Amer.	11	4.0	9	3.6	16	4.6	4	2.3	14	5.4	20	3.8	3
Mex. Amer.	0	0.0	0	0.0	0	0.0	0	0.0	0	0.0	0	0.0	0
Puerto Rican	0	0.0	0	0.0	0	0.0	0	0.0	0	0.0	0	0.0	0
Hispanic	29	10.5	23	9.3	31	8.8	21	12.1	19	7.3	52	9.9	12
Total Minority	56	20.2	50	20.2	66	18.8	40	23.1	53	20.4	106	20.2	18
For. Nation.	0	0.0	0	0.0	0	0.0	0	0.0	0	0.0	0	0.0	0
Caucasian	192	69.3	159	64.4	244	69.5	107	61.8	185	71.2	351	67.0	58
Unknown	29	10.5	38	15.4	41	11.7	26	15.0	22	8.5	67	12.8	8
Total	277	52.9	247	47.1	351	67.0	173	33.0	260	49.6	524		84

Tuition and Fees

	Resident	Nonresident
Full-time	$24,600	$24,600
Part-time	$18,450	$18,450

Living Expenses

Estimated living expenses for singles

Living on campus	Living off campus	Living at home
N/A	$15,100	$15,100

Barry University Dwayne O. Andreas School of Law

*ABA
Approved
Since
2002*

GPA and LSAT Scores

	Total	Full-time	Part-time
# of apps	1,500	1,245	255
# of admits	739	422	317
# of matrics	241	173	68
75% GPA	3.29	3.27	3.32
25% GPA	2.71	2.72	2.66
75% LSAT	151	151	152
25% LSAT	147	146	147

Grants and Scholarships (from prior year)

	Total #	Total %	Full-time #	Full-time %	Part-time #	Part-time %
Total # of students	410		233		177	
Total # receiving grants	219	53.4	172	73.8	47	26.6
Less than 1/2 tuition	169	41.2	127	54.5	42	23.7
Half to full tuition	48	11.7	43	18.5	5	2.8
Full tuition	2	0.5	2	0.9	0	0.0
More than full tuition	0	0.0	0	0.0	0	0.0
Median grant amount			$6,000		$3,300	

Informational and Library Resources

# of volumes and volume equivalents	257,593
# of titles	107,624
# of active serial subscriptions	1,688
Study seating capacity inside the library	326
# of professional librarians	9
Hours per week library is open	98
# of open, wired connections available to students	0
# of networked computers available for use by students	29
# of simultaneous wireless users	512
Require computer?	N

JD Attrition (from prior year)

	Academic #	Other #	Total #	Total %
1st year	28	18	46	26.1%
2nd year	0	4	4	3.6%
3rd year	2	2	4	4.0%
4th year	1	0	1	4.2%

Employment

	Total	Percentage
Employment status known	63	94.0
Employment status unknown	4	6.0
Employed	53	84.1
Pursuing graduate degrees	1	1.6
Unemployed seeking employment	2	3.2
Unemployed not seeking employment	7	11.1

Type of Employment

# employed in law firms	22	41.5
# employed in business and industry	14	26.4
# employed in government	13	24.5
# employed in public interest	1	1.9
# employed as judicial clerks	0	0.0
# employed in academia	3	5.7

Geographic Location

# employed in state	51	96.2
# employed in foreign countries	0	0.0
# of states where employed	3	

Bar Passage Rates

Jurisdiction	Florida		
Exam	Sum 03	Win 04	Total
# from school taking bar for the first time	39	22	61
School's pass rate for all first-time takers	44%	41%	43%
State's pass rate for all first-time takers	76%	75%	76%

Barry University Dwayne O. Andreas School of Law

6441 East Colonial Drive
Orlando, FL 32807
Phone: 321.206.5600; Fax: 321.206.5662
E-mail: lawinfo@mail.barry.edu; Website: www.barry.edu/law

■ A Growing Presence in Higher Education

Founded in early 1993, the University of Orlando School of Law admitted its first class in 1995. In March of 1999, the School of Law became a part of Barry University, a Catholic international university located in Miami Shores, Florida. The affiliation is an extremely positive one, since both administrations have the same focus—to offer quality academics grounded in a strong ethical foundation with the goal of preparing qualified, competent practicing attorneys.

The School of Law is situated on a beautiful 20-acre campus in East Orlando, about 15 minutes from downtown. The School of Law facilities include a two-story, 20,000-square-foot Law Center building; a 9,000-square-foot Moot Court building; a 9,000-square-foot classrooms and faculty offices building; and a 36,000-square-foot law library.

■ The Perfect Venue for Your Legal Education

Central Florida is one of the fastest growing areas in the country. The region's major industry today is tourism. A host of attractions bring millions of visitors into central Florida each year. Just an hour away are the Kennedy Space Center and the beaches of the Atlantic.

Orlando is a major commercial center; many national corporations have headquarters in the city. The area is fast becoming a television and motion picture production center.

Central Florida provides a wealth of firsthand exposure to the practice of corporate and entertainment law, as well as juvenile and criminal law. The Advisory Board is composed of many prominent central Florida attorneys, judges, government officials, and others in the community. Their community affiliations enhance the networking and career opportunities available to Barry's students.

Central Florida enjoys a year-round subtropical climate and offers a wide range of cultural and recreational activities. Accommodations in the immediate area include fully furnished or unfurnished apartments as well as a wide range of single-family dwellings. Orlando has a large number of hotels and executive lodges that offer reduced rates on a weekly or monthly basis.

Orlando is the ideal venue to pursue your legal education.

■ Mission and Goals of the School of Law

Barry University School of Law seeks to offer a quality legal education in a caring environment that will enable its graduates to apply the skills and knowledge they have acquired to their own personal development and to the good of society through the competent and ethical practice of law. The School of Law seeks to provide a learning environment that challenges students to accept intellectual, personal, ethical, spiritual, and social responsibilities. The school commits itself to assuring a religious dimension in an atmosphere of religious freedom and to providing community service.

■ An Overview

The School of Law educates students to become responsible lawyers, trained to assume an active role in the legal community. Students are trained to act in strict accord with the highest ethical standards and to exercise their professional skills competently, with sensitivity to the needs and concerns of their clients.

The School of Law offers a three-year daytime program structured for full-time students. The School of Law also offers a four-year extended studies program in the evening to accommodate working adults or anyone who is unable to pursue full-time study.

Students at the School of Law have many opportunities to experience the "law-in-action" concept, both in the classroom and through practical application. Small classes foster a collegial student/professor relationship and enable the School of Law to provide legal education at its best.

Through the in-house Children and Families Clinic, Barry students gain solid practical experience working with clients involved in actual cases. Barry Law also offers a wealth of externship opportunities to allow students to further develop their skills as emerging attorneys while working in various venues. Externship placement currently includes opportunities in the following areas: civil government, civil poverty, judicial, mediation, public defender, and state attorney.

Mindful of the need for qualified and caring attorneys to work with disadvantaged children and families, Barry Law now offers a certificate program in this vital area of law. Students may earn a certificate of specialization in Children and Families Law at graduation once the core and elective course requirements for this certificate are met. Another emerging area of emphasis at Barry Law is Sports and Entertainment Law. Finally, a wealth of elective offerings allow Barry students to develop their legal knowledge and skills in many different areas.

■ Juris Doctor

The School of Law offers the Juris Doctor (JD) degree. All students in the program must complete 90 semester hours of study in areas that are essential to the understanding and practice of law. Students in the fall entering class must complete required courses in subjects that provide a common core of understanding in the law. Students may choose from a wide variety of electives to meet the remaining requirements necessary for graduation.

■ Program Objective

The School of Law combines traditional and innovative teaching methods to provide a dynamic, professional program. The JD curriculum is designed to develop students' analytical ability, communication skills, and understanding of the codes of professional responsibility and ethics that are central to the practice of law. The faculty utilizes a variety of teaching methods, including simulations and role-playing. Seminars and advanced courses provide close interaction with faculty.

Barry Law emphasizes research and writing proficiency from the first day of class. Armed with a strong foundation in research and writing, Barry Law students gain an advantage in the legal market place.

■ American Bar Association Accreditation

Barry University School of Law was provisionally approved by the ABA on February 4, 2002. With provisional approval, Barry law school students and graduates are entitled to the same recognition given to students and graduates of fully approved law schools. As such, graduates may sit for the bar exam in Florida and almost all jurisdictions in the United States. The ABA accreditation process is rightfully designed to be a rigorous one in order to assure quality legal education among approved schools. All new law schools emerging from this careful scrutiny and meeting nationally established standards are first granted provisional approval by the ABA. A law school may be reviewed for full approval only after it has been provisionally approved for at least two years and not exceeding five years. Barry University is devoting all necessary resources to not only meet, but exceed, the standards for full approval within the designated time period.

Each student should determine if the state in which he/she intends to practice has special bar admission requirements, including, but not limited to, domicile, filing notice of intent to practice before entering law school, certification of character and fitness, and law school curriculum.

■ Graduation Requirements

To be eligible to receive the degree of JD, a student must (1) complete 90 academic credits of instruction with a cumulative grade-point average of 2.0 or above; (2) earn a cumulative grade-point average of 1.8 for all required courses and a passing grade in each of the required courses; (3) successfully complete the writing requirement; (4) complete a minimum of 60 out of 90 academic credits in residence at Barry University School of Law; (5) successfully complete the pro bono requirement; (6) satisfy all financial obligations to Barry University, and; (7) be approved by the faculty for graduation.

Applicant Profile

Barry University Dwayne O. Andreas School of Law

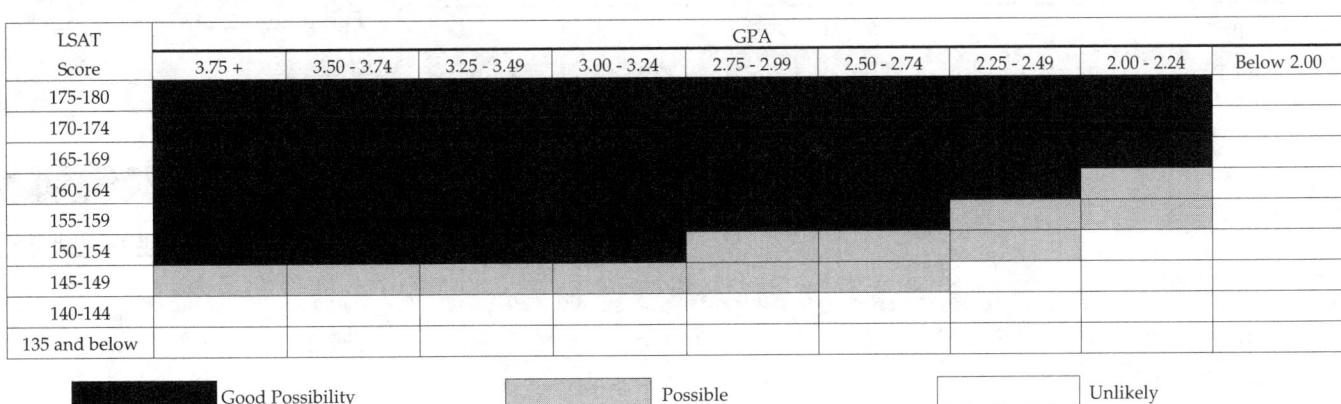

LSAT Score	GPA								
	3.75 +	3.50 - 3.74	3.25 - 3.49	3.00 - 3.24	2.75 - 2.99	2.50 - 2.74	2.25 - 2.49	2.00 - 2.24	Below 2.00
175-180									
170-174									
165-169									
160-164									
155-159									
150-154									
145-149									
140-144									
135 and below									

Good Possibility   Possible   Unlikely

Baylor University School of Law

1114 South University Parks Drive, One Bear Place No. 97288
Waco, TX 76798
Phone: 800.BAYLOR.U, 254.710.1911; Fax: 254.710.2316
E-mail: Heather_Creed@baylor.edu; Website: law.baylor.edu

*ABA
Approved
Since
1931*

The Basics

Type of school	Private
Term	Quarter
Application deadline	11/1 2/1 3/1
Application fee	$40
Financial aid deadline	
Can first year start other than fall?	Yes
Student to faculty ratio (fall)	16.9 to 1
Does the university offer:	
housing restricted to law students?	No
graduate housing for which law students are eligible?	Yes

Faculty and Administrators

	Total		Men		Women		Minorities	
	Fall	Spr	Fall	Spr	Fall	Spr	Fall	Spr
Full-time	21	21	18	18	3	3	1	1
Other Full-time	0	0	0	0	0	0	0	0
Deans, librarians, & others who teach	6	6	3	3	3	3	0	0
Part-time	10	25	9	24	1	1	0	0
Total	37	52	30	45	7	7	1	1

Curriculum

	Full-time	Part-time
Typical first-year section size	63	0
Is there typically a "small section" of the first-year class, other than Legal Writing, taught by full-time faculty	Yes	No
If yes, typical size offered last year	51	0
# of classroom course titles beyond 1st year curriculum	76	

# of upper division courses, excluding seminars with an enrollment:	Under 25	74
	25-49	38
	50-74	15
	75-99	9
	100+	1

# of seminars	5	
# of seminar positions available	97	
# of seminar positions filled	97	0
# of positions available in simulation courses	1,321	
# of simulation positions filled	1,321	0
# of positions available in faculty supervised clinical courses	8	
# of faculty supervised clinical positions filled	8	0
# involved in field placements	92	0
# involved in law journals	71	0
# involved in moot court or trial competitions	53	0
# of credit hours required to graduate	126	

J.D. Enrollment and Ethnicity

	Men		Women		Full-time		Part-time		1st-year		Total		JD Degs. Awd.
	#	%	#	%	#	%	#	%	#	%	#	%	
African Amer.	2	0.9	1	0.5	3	0.7	0	0.0	2	1.3	3	0.7	1
Amer. Indian	1	0.4	0	0.0	1	0.2	0	0.0	0	0.0	1	0.2	0
Asian Amer.	9	3.9	11	5.6	20	4.7	0	0.0	8	5.1	20	4.7	1
Mex. Amer.	8	3.5	10	5.1	18	4.2	0	0.0	4	2.5	18	4.2	10
Puerto Rican	0	0.0	0	0.0	0	0.0	0	0.0	0	0.0	0	0.0	0
Hispanic	3	1.3	3	1.5	6	1.4	0	0.0	4	2.5	6	1.4	0
Total Minority	23	10.1	25	12.6	48	11.3	0	0.0	18	11.5	48	11.3	12
For. Nation.	0	0.0	0	0.0	0	0.0	0	0.0	0	0.0	0	0.0	0
Caucasian	205	89.9	173	87.4	378	88.7	0	0.0	139	88.5	378	88.7	126
Unknown	0	0.0	0	0.0	0	0.0	0	0.0	0	0.0	0	0.0	0
Total	228	53.5	198	46.5	426	100.0	0	0.0	157	36.9	426		138

Tuition and Fees

	Resident	Nonresident
Full-time	$24,470	$24,470
Part-time	$0	$0

Living Expenses

Estimated living expenses for singles

Living on campus	Living off campus	Living at home
$13,191	$16,449	$16,593

Baylor University School of Law

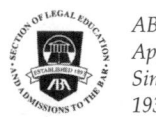

*ABA
Approved
Since
1931*

GPA and LSAT Scores

	Annual Fall	Spring	Summer	Total
# of apps	2,323	1,137	525	4,051
# of admits	301	136	112	549
# of matrics	63	55	46	164
75% GPA	3.97	3.77	3.76	3.87
25% GPA	3.74	3.40	3.31	3.45
75% LSAT	164	159	161	162
25% LSAT	159	156	154	157

Grants and Scholarships (from prior year)

	Total		Full-time		Part-time	
	#	%	#	%	#	%
Total # of students	440		440		0	
Total # receiving grants	399	90.7	399	90.7	0	0.0
Less than 1/2 tuition	287	65.2	287	65.2	0	0.0
Half to full tuition	85	19.3	85	19.3	0	0.0
Full tuition	8	1.8	8	1.8	0	0.0
More than full tuition	19	4.3	19	4.3	0	0.0
Median grant amount			$3,300		$0	

Informational and Library Resources

# of volumes and volume equivalents	220,009
# of titles	26,069
# of active serial subscriptions	2,195
Study seating capacity inside the library	279
# of professional librarians	5
Hours per week library is open	112
# of open, wired connections available to students	721
# of networked computers available for use by students	58
# of simultaneous wireless users	300
Require computer?	N

JD Attrition (from prior year)

	Academic	Other	Total	
	#	#	#	%
1st year	3	23	26	13.7%
2nd year	1	6	7	4.5%
3rd year	0	1	1	1.1%
4th year	0	0	0	0.0%

Employment

	Total	Percentage
Employment status known	158	99.4
Employment status unknown	1	0.6
Employed	149	94.3
Pursuing graduate degrees	6	3.8
Unemployed seeking employment	1	0.6
Unemployed not seeking employment	2	1.3

Type of Employment

# employed in law firms	119	79.9
# employed in business and industry	9	6.0
# employed in government	9	6.0
# employed in public interest	0	0.0
# employed as judicial clerks	11	7.4
# employed in academia	0	0.0

Geographic Location

# employed in state	136	91.3
# employed in foreign countries	1	0.7
# of states where employed	10	

Bar Passage Rates

Jurisdiction	Texas		
Exam	Sum 03	Win 04	Total
# from school taking bar for the first time	107	31	138
School's pass rate for all first-time takers	95%	90%	94%
State's pass rate for all first-time takers	83%	69%	80%

Baylor University School of Law

1114 South University Parks Drive, One Bear Place No. 97288
Waco, TX 76798
Phone: 800.BAYLOR.U, 254.710.1911; Fax: 254.710.2316
E-mail: Heather_Creed@baylor.edu; Website: law.baylor.edu

■ Introduction

Baylor University School of Law is a private,
ABA-approved law school and is a member of the
Association of American Law schools. Formally
organized in 1857, Baylor law school is the oldest law
school in Texas and is located on the campus of Baylor
University in Waco, Texas. Waco is located in central
Texas, has a population of over 200,000, and offers a
diverse and rich array of cultural and recreational
opportunities, as well as very moderate living costs.

Baylor law school stands at the forefront of
practice-oriented law schools nationally. Baylor is
singularly clear about its mission—to equip students upon
graduation to practice law effectively and ethically. That is
the key difference. Students are trained and mentored in
all facets of law, including theoretical analysis, practical
application, legal writing, advocacy, professional
responsibility, and negotiation and counseling skills.

■ Enrollment

Baylor law school is small by choice, with entering
classes of approximately 65 students in the spring, 30 in
the summer, and 65 in the fall. Baylor law school has a
target student population of 400. We keep our program
small because, at Baylor, we are interested in producing
quality, not quantity. In 2004, the entering classes
included 16 percent minority students.

■ Faculty

Baylor law school is first a teaching school, and one of
the few law schools in the nation in which the granting
of tenure is primarily based upon a professor's teaching
effectiveness. Faculty members hold degrees from law
schools and universities throughout the nation. One of
the distinctive features of the faculty is that professors
maintain unrestricted hours for student consultation.

Faculty members are experts in their areas and have
substantial practical experience. They produce a
significant amount of legal scholarship, which results in
their demand as speakers at legal institutes and civic
functions. Every professor is available for lending advice
and guidance in all academic, professional, and other
matters of concern to students.

■ Facilities and Technology

The new home of Baylor law school, the award-winning
Sheila and Walter Umphrey Law Center, was dedicated
in 2002. At every stage of the design of the Law Center,
the most important goal was to put teaching first. The
building houses every facility a modern law school

requires: classrooms that are unsurpassed as teaching
facilities; an advocacy suite, including state-of-the-art
courtrooms that provide the optimum environment for
advocacy training—Baylor's centerpiece of excellence; a
large, two-story appellate advocacy courtroom/class-
room; a library with comfortable study and seating space
in several impressive reading rooms overlooking the
Brazos River; and faculty offices that support the faculty
mentoring, which is the hallmark of our program.

Technology permeates the Law Center, including data
and electric ports at virtually every seat in the building,
along with a concurrent wireless network. Classrooms
are equipped with cutting-edge technology, including
audio, video, and Internet access. The automatic cameras
in the courtrooms can be aimed at a desired location in
the room through use of joystick controllers mounted in
the console tabletops. The law school uses a
sophisticated course-management system that allows the
faculty to post assignments, syllabi, and course
announcements and provides discussion boards.

■ Trial Advocacy Program

Procedure is the tool of the trial lawyer and Practice
Court is an ultra-intensive study of civil procedure. In
addition to the science of procedure, students will learn
the art of trial advocacy in a rigorous and tough
six-month program of skills training during the third
year of law school. Students try lawsuits from beginning
to end. This course prepares you to be a competent,
responsible, and ethical lawyer.

■ Curriculum and Special Programs

The required curriculum is structured to provide a logical progression for legal study from fundamental legal
doctrine in first-year courses to increasingly more
sophisticated and complex second- and third-year
courses. The challenging curriculum, along with the
opportunity to perform specialized lawyering tasks
under the direct supervision of accomplished lawyers,
prepares students for the rigors of any type of modern
legal practice. Additionally, students have the opportunity to complete a more concentrated course of study
and training in six areas of interest: general civil litigation, business litigation, business transactions, criminal
practice, estate planning, and administrative practice.

There are three joint degrees: JD/MBA, JD/MTax, and
JD/MPPA.

■ Admission

The law school has three entering classes—spring
(February), summer (May), and fall (August). Each class

has far more applications than seats available, however, admission to the spring or summer classes is slightly less competitive than admission to the fall class.

The Admission Committee considers each application in its entirety and considers many factors beyond test scores and undergraduate GPA. Such factors include employment experience, demonstrated leadership potential, cocurricular and extracurricular activities, ethnicity, academic performance trends, undergraduate major, caliber of undergraduate school, life experience, circumstances of particular disadvantage, and any other relevant information submitted by the applicant. Any factors the applicant would like for the Admission Committee to take into consideration should be addressed in a personal statement.

■ Scholarships and Financial Aid

Numerous academic-merit scholarships are awarded to entering students based upon their UGPA and LSAT score. Additionally, special scholarships are awarded to persons with evidence of academic achievement despite significant disadvantage. The law school also participates in the nationally recognized financial aid programs. Texas residents are eligible for the Texas Tuition Equalization Grant.

■ Student Life

Students will find a stimulating variety of enjoyable student activities and organizations that will enhance their

legal education. Students can compete interscholastically with Baylor's nationally recognized mock trial and moot court teams. Students can hone their writing and legal scholarship abilities by being a member of the *Baylor Law Review*, which is a legal periodical published quarterly by the students under the supervision of faculty. Baylor law school also offers a wide array of "special interest" student organizations focused on particular areas of law.

■ Career Services

The Career Services Office is committed year-round to providing students the support and resources they need in pursuing their chosen career paths. Baylor graduates enjoy a 98 percent placement rate; and graduates are placed throughout the nation in private practice in large and small firms, government agencies, judicial clerkships, public interest organizations, and public and private corporations.

The director of the Career Services Office is a lawyer and a graduate of Baylor law school. The director provides extensive one-on-one training on job-search techniques, interview skills, job strategies, and résumé and cover letter writing techniques. The office also coordinates an extensive on-campus interview program, and posts over 1,200 job listings from law firms, government agencies, corporations, and public interest groups.

Applicant Profile

Baylor University School of Law
This grid includes only applicants who earned 120-180 LSAT scores under standard administrations.

LSAT Score	GPA 3.75 +		3.50 - 3.74		3.25 - 3.49		3.00 - 3.24		2.75 - 2.99		2.50 - 2.74		2.25 - 2.49		2.00 - 2.24		Below 2.00		No GPA		Total	
	Apps	Adm	Apps	Adm	Apps	Adm	Apps	Adm	Apps	Adm	Apps	Adm	Apps	Adm	Apps	Adm	Apps	Adm	Apps	Adm	Apps	Adm
175-180	0	0	0	0	0	0	0	0	0	0	0	0	0	0	1	0	0	0	0	0	1	0
170-174	3	3	5	5	5	5	2	2	1	1	1	0	0	0	0	0	0	0	0	0	17	16
165-169	22	22	22	18	21	19	15	11	4	3	3	0	1	0	0	0	0	0	0	0	88	73
160-164	114	101	91	40	107	12	40	4	32	1	20	0	7	0	0	0	0	0	3	2	414	160
155-159	182	41	188	5	181	1	95	0	43	0	27	0	14	0	4	0	0	0	5	0	739	47
150-154	69	0	97	0	119	1	108	0	54	0	37	0	14	0	5	0	1	0	2	0	506	1
145-149	25	0	48	0	55	0	63	0	44	0	35	0	8	0	3	0	0	0	2	0	283	0
140-144	7	0	15	0	43	0	45	0	33	0	28	0	14	0	3	0	0	0	1	0	189	0
135-139	3	0	6	0	10	0	14	0	17	0	10	0	13	0	4	0	1	0	1	0	79	0
130-134	0	0	1	0	1	0	3	0	5	0	1	0	2	0	2	0	1	0	2	0	18	0
125-129	0	0	0	0	0	0	0	0	0	0	1	0	0	0	0	0	0	0	1	0	2	0
120-124	0	0	1	0	0	0	0	0	0	0	0	0	0	0	0	0	0	0	0	0	1	0
Total	425	167	474	68	542	38	385	17	233	5	163	0	73	0	22	0	3	0	17	2	2337	297

Apps = Number of Applicants   Adm = Number Admitted   Reflects 99% of the total fall applicant pool.

Boston College Law School

885 Centre Street
Newton, MA 02459
Phone: 617.552.4350; Fax: 617.552.2917
E-mail: bclawadm@bc.edu; Website: www.bc.edu/law

ABA
Approved
Since
1932

The Basics

Type of school	Private
Term	Semester
Application deadline	3/1
Application fee	$65
Financial aid deadline	3/15
Can first year start other than fall?	No
Student to faculty ratio (fall)	14.1 to 1
Does the university offer:	
housing restricted to law students?	No
graduate housing for which law students are eligible?	No

Faculty and Administrators

	Total		Men		Women		Minorities	
	Fall	Spr	Fall	Spr	Fall	Spr	Fall	Spr
Full-time	47	45	26	24	21	21	10	11
Other Full-time	4	5	1	2	3	3	0	0
Deans, librarians, & others who teach	12	12	3	3	9	9	0	0
Part-time	29	38	24	25	5	13	7	7
Total	92	100	54	54	38	46	17	18

Curriculum

	Full-time	Part-time
Typical first-year section size	90	0
Is there typically a "small section" of the first-year class, other than Legal Writing, taught by full-time faculty	Yes	No
If yes, typical size offered last year	34	0
# of classroom course titles beyond 1st year curriculum	148	
# of upper division courses, excluding seminars with an enrollment: Under 25	101	
25-49	32	
50-74	11	
75-99	11	
100+	3	
# of seminars	44	
# of seminar positions available	703	
# of seminar positions filled	492	0
# of positions available in simulation courses	796	
# of simulation positions filled	687	0
# of positions available in faculty supervised clinical courses	109	
# of faculty supervised clinical positions filled	108	0
# involved in field placements	71	0
# involved in law journals	173	0
# involved in moot court or trial competitions	133	0
# of credit hours required to graduate	85	

JD Enrollment and Ethnicity

	Men		Women		Full-time		Part-time		1st-year		Total		JD Degs. Awd.
	#	%	#	%	#	%	#	%	#	%	#	%	
African Amer.	13	3.3	28	7.0	41	5.2	0	0.0	13	5.0	41	5.2	16
Amer. Indian	0	0.0	0	0.0	0	0.0	0	0.0	0	0.0	0	0.0	1
Asian Amer.	36	9.2	43	10.7	79	9.9	0	0.0	32	12.4	79	9.9	26
Mex. Amer.	6	1.5	4	1.0	10	1.3	0	0.0	7	2.7	10	1.3	0
Puerto Rican	1	0.3	3	0.7	4	0.5	0	0.0	2	0.8	4	0.5	0
Hispanic	14	3.6	12	3.0	26	3.3	0	0.0	11	4.2	26	3.3	14
Total Minority	70	17.8	90	22.4	160	20.1	0	0.0	65	25.1	160	20.1	57
For. Nation.	4	1.0	11	2.7	15	1.9	0	0.0	3	1.2	15	1.9	7
Caucasian	261	66.4	260	64.7	521	65.5	0	0.0	162	62.5	521	65.5	201
Unknown	58	14.8	41	10.2	99	12.5	0	0.0	29	11.2	99	12.5	10
Total	393	49.4	402	50.6	795	100.0	0	0.0	259	32.6	795		275

Tuition and Fees

	Resident	Nonresident
Full-time	$31,596	$31,596
Part-time	$0	$0

Living Expenses

Estimated living expenses for singles

Living on campus	Living off campus	Living at home
N/A	$16,315	$16,315

Boston College Law School

*ABA
Approved
Since
1932*

GPA and LSAT Scores

	Total	Full-time	Part-time
# of apps	7,835	7,835	0
# of admits	1,298	1,298	0
# of matrics	259	259	0
75% GPA	3.75	3.75	0.00
25% GPA	3.43	3.43	0.00
75% LSAT	166	166	0
25% LSAT	162	162	0

Grants and Scholarships (from prior year)

	Total #	Total %	Full-time #	Full-time %	Part-time #	Part-time %
Total # of students	816		815		1	
Total # receiving grants	403	49.4	403	49.4	0	0.0
Less than 1/2 tuition	253	31.0	253	31.0	0	0.0
Half to full tuition	148	18.1	148	18.2	0	0.0
Full tuition	0	0.0	0	0.0	0	0.0
More than full tuition	2	0.2	2	0.2	0	0.0
Median grant amount			$10,000		$0	

Informational and Library Resources

# of volumes and volume equivalents	438,588
# of titles	67,166
# of active serial subscriptions	3,822
Study seating capacity inside the library	649
# of professional librarians	10
Hours per week library is open	105
# of open, wired connections available to students	1,213
# of networked computers available for use by students	146
# of simultaneous wireless users	1,950
Require computer?	N

JD Attrition (from prior year)

	Academic #	Other #	Total #	Total %
1st year	0	16	16	5.7%
2nd year	1	2	3	1.2%
3rd year	0	0	0	0.0%
4th year	0	0	0	0.0%

Employment

	Total	Percentage
Employment status known	272	98.2
Employment status unknown	5	1.8
Employed	262	96.3
Pursuing graduate degrees	4	1.5
Unemployed seeking employment	4	1.5
Unemployed not seeking employment	2	0.7

Type of Employment

	Total	Percentage
# employed in law firms	176	67.2
# employed in business and industry	15	5.7
# employed in government	22	8.4
# employed in public interest	10	3.8
# employed as judicial clerks	38	14.5
# employed in academia	1	0.4

Geographic Location

	Total	Percentage
# employed in state	119	45.4
# employed in foreign countries	1	0.4
# of states where employed	24	

Bar Passage Rates

Jurisdiction	Massachusetts		
Exam	Sum 03	Win 04	Total
# from school taking bar for the first time	151	3	154
School's pass rate for all first-time takers	90%	100%	90%
State's pass rate for all first-time takers	82%	82%	82%

Boston College Law School

Office of Admissions, 885 Centre Street
Newton, MA 02459
Phone: 617.552.4350; Fax: 617.552.2917
E-mail: bclawadm@bc.edu; Website: www.bc.edu/law

■ Introduction

Since its founding in 1929, Boston College Law School
has earned a national reputation for educational excellence and the highest standards of professionalism while
fostering a unique spirit of community among its students,
faculty, and staff. The diverse curriculum is designed to
help students develop the skills and knowledge needed to
adapt successfully to changes in society and the legal
profession. Boston College Law School is located on an
attractive 40-acre campus in Newton, Massachusetts, just
minutes from downtown Boston. It is fully accredited
and has a chapter of Order of the Coif, the prestigious
national law school honorary society.

■ Library and Physical Facilities

The Law School is the sole academic unit on Boston
College's Newton campus. It consists of three interconnected buildings. Stuart House contains administrative
and faculty offices as well as classrooms and a cafeteria.
The law library accommodates 560 people and provides a
technologically advanced environment for study and
research. The East Wing, opened in 1999, includes five
state-of-the-art lecture halls with data connections to every
seat for use of computers. It also houses a greatly expanded
Office of Career Services and student organization spaces,
including the Curtin Public Interest Center.

All academic, administrative, library, and service
facilities are accessible to physically challenged persons.

■ Curriculum

The faculty of Boston College Law School strongly
believes in the importance of a general legal education
designed to enable graduates to adapt to the changing
demands of law practice. Areas of particular focus
include constitutional law, business law, dispute
resolution, environmental law, family law, international
law, intellectual property law, and clinical programs.

In the first year, all students take traditional courses,
including Civil Procedure, Constitutional Law, Contracts,
Property Law, and Torts, as well as Legal Research
and Writing and an innovative skills course titled
Introduction to Lawyering and Professional
Responsibility. More than 100 courses offered in the
second and third years are elective.

■ Clinical Programs

The Law School is committed to making clinical
experiences available to all students who desire them.
At the **Boston College Legal Assistance Bureau** (LAB),
students assume responsibility for representation of

indigent clients through the **Civil Litigation,
Homelessness**, and **Women and the Law Clinics**.

Students in the **Criminal Justice Clinic** prosecute or
defend criminal cases in state court. **The Judge and the
Community Courts** class examines the interaction
between the local court and the community it serves. The
Judicial Process course includes clinical placement with
a specific Superior Court justice. In **Juvenile Rights
Advocacy**, students advocate for troubled youth and
work toward juvenile justice policy reform. In the
Immigration Law Clinic, students advise clients and
work on administrative and appellate litigation under
the supervision of practicing attorneys.

■ Externships

The **Semester in Practice** program offers individually
designed placements with judges, government agencies,
public interest organizations, and law firms in the greater
Boston area. The **Attorney General Program** provides an
intensive full-year clinical experience in the Government
Bureau of the Massachusetts Office of the Attorney
General. The **International Criminal Tribunals** (ICT)
offer a unique opportunity to work on-site at the criminal
tribunal established by the UN Security Council in The
Hague, Netherlands. The **London Program** has both
academic and experiential components. The program
provides students with a critical insight into comparative
legal institutions with special emphasis on international
regulatory process, whether in environmental or securities
regulation, antitrust, intellectual property, or human rights.

■ Student Activities

Selected students may participate in the following writ-
ing programs: *Boston College Law Review, Boston College
Environmental Affairs Law Review, Boston College Interna-
tional and Comparative Law Review, Boston College Third
World Law Journal*, and the *Uniform Commercial Code
Reporter-Digest*.

Boston College Law School supports several annual
moot court competitions that help students develop
writing, courtroom-advocacy, and client-counseling
skills. Over the years, Boston College has performed
extremely well in the regional and national competitions,
which are judged by faculty, state, and federal judges,
and practicing attorneys.

■ Admission

The Law School has no minimum cutoff either for GPA
or LSAT. Academic achievement and LSAT scores are
extremely significant, but work and professional experience, college extracurricular activities, the quality of

recommendations, and the personal statement also play an important role in decision making.

In evaluating the undergraduate record, class rank as well as courses taken are considered. If the LSAT has been taken more than once, scores are averaged unless a compelling reason is presented for considering a particular score. Consideration is given to the LSAT if the applicant has a history of academic achievement despite poor standardized test scores.

■ Minorities and Affirmative Action

Boston College Law School strongly encourages applications from qualified minority, disabled, or other students who have been socially, economically, or culturally disadvantaged. Each applicant is evaluated in an effort to ensure that all relevant credentials are favorably considered. The Law School has been very successful both in admitting minority and special students and in retaining them to graduation. Both academic support and minority student mentor programs are available.

■ Expenses and Financial Aid

The Financial Aid Office administers federal and private loan programs, the College Work-Study program, and the law school scholarship and grant programs. The Law School also offers a Loan Repayment Assistance program providing financial assistance to graduates taking lower-paying positions in government, nonprofit

corporations, and legal services programs. Each year, several entering students are designated Public Service Scholars because of their demonstrated commitment to public service law.

All applicants for financial aid must file the FAFSA (Free Application for Federal Student Aid) and the online Need Access financial aid application. Processed electronic data should be received in the Office of Financial Aid by March 15.

■ Housing

Housing assistance is provided through the university's Office of Off-Campus Housing. Applicants seeking resident assistantships should write the University Housing Office, Boston College, Chestnut Hill, MA 02467.

■ Career Services

The Office of Career Services is dedicated to helping students make the transition from law student to employed professional. The range of opportunities for graduates spans virtually the entire spectrum of legal practice. Each year more than 1,000 prospective employers solicit applications from Boston College law students. In 2003, approximately 332 law firms, government agencies, corporations, and public interest organizations from 27 states interviewed Boston College students as part of off-campus recruiting programs. Our 10,400 alumni are presently practicing in 50 states and 19 foreign countries.

Applicant Profile

Boston College Law School
This grid includes only applicants who earned 120-180 LSAT scores under standard administrations.

LSAT Score	3.75 +		3.50 - 3.74		3.25 - 3.49		3.00 - 3.24		2.75 - 2.99		Below 2.75		No GPA		Total	
	Apps	Adm	Apps	Adm	Apps	Adm	Apps	Adm	Apps	Adm	Apps	Adm	Apps	Adm	Apps	Adm
175-180	8	8	9	9	8	3	8	5	3	1	3	1	0	0	39	27
170-174	53	47	73	55	63	34	42	14	21	2	13	1	3	2	268	155
165-169	289	243	381	224	309	93	166	18	62	3	43	3	7	3	1257	587
160-164	527	192	868	158	641	55	332	19	124	6	69	2	23	8	2584	440
150-159	478	20	773	29	732	22	501	11	231	3	145	1	42	1	2902	87
140-149	63	3	107	4	157	1	134	1	96	0	71	0	22	0	650	9
Below 140	4	0	13	0	21	0	10	0	22	0	25	0	4	0	99	0
Total	1422	513	2224	479	1931	208	1193	68	559	15	369	8	101	14	7799	1305

Apps = Number of Applicants
Adm = Number Admitted
Reflects 99% of the total applicant pool.

Boston University School of Law

765 Commonwealth Avenue
Boston, MA 02215
Phone: 617.353.3100; Fax: 617.353.0578
E-mail: bulawadm@bu.edu; Website: www.bu.edu/law

*ABA
Approved
Since
1925*

The Basics

Type of school	Private
Term	Semester
Application deadline	3/1
Application fee	$65
Financial aid deadline	3/1
Can first year start other than fall?	No
Student to faculty ratio (fall)	12.9 to 1
Does the university offer:	
housing restricted to law students?	No
graduate housing for which law students are eligible?	Yes

Faculty and Administrators

	Total		Men		Women		Minorities	
	Fall	Spr	Fall	Spr	Fall	Spr	Fall	Spr
Full-time	58	43	40	31	18	12	3	3
Other Full-time	2	2	2	2	0	0	1	1
Deans, librarians, & others who teach	4	4	3	3	1	1	0	0
Part-time	26	33	23	25	3	8	1	1
Total	90	82	68	61	22	21	5	5

Curriculum

	Full-time	Part-time
Typical first-year section size	88	0
Is there typically a "small section" of the first-year class, other than Legal Writing, taught by full-time faculty	Yes	No
If yes, typical size offered last year	44	0
# of classroom course titles beyond 1st year curriculum	120	

# of upper division courses, excluding seminars with an enrollment:		
	Under 25	56
	25-49	27
	50-74	12
	75-99	7
	100+	5

# of seminars	56	
# of seminar positions available	1,010	
# of seminar positions filled	785	0
# of positions available in simulation courses	338	
# of simulation positions filled	309	0
# of positions available in faculty supervised clinical courses	170	
# of faculty supervised clinical positions filled	149	0
# involved in field placements	55	0
# involved in law journals	330	0
# involved in moot court or trial competitions	173	0
# of credit hours required to graduate	84	

JD Enrollment and Ethnicity

	Men		Women		Full-time		Part-time		1st-year		Total		JD Degs. Awd.
	#	%	#	%	#	%	#	%	#	%	#	%	
African Amer.	16	3.8	20	4.6	36	4.2	0	0.0	13	4.5	36	4.2	7
Amer. Indian	2	0.5	0	0.0	2	0.2	0	0.0	0	0.0	2	0.2	0
Asian Amer.	61	14.4	66	15.2	127	14.8	0	0.0	41	14.2	127	14.8	14
Mex. Amer.	2	0.5	5	1.2	7	0.8	0	0.0	3	1.0	7	0.8	3
Puerto Rican	3	0.7	4	0.9	7	0.8	0	0.0	2	0.7	7	0.8	1
Hispanic	17	4.0	14	3.2	31	3.6	0	0.0	8	2.8	31	3.6	16
Total Minority	101	23.8	109	25.1	210	24.5	0	0.0	67	23.3	210	24.5	41
For. Nation.	10	2.4	17	3.9	27	3.1	0	0.0	10	3.5	27	3.1	8
Caucasian	313	73.8	308	71.0	621	72.4	0	0.0	211	73.3	621	72.4	184
Unknown	0	0.0	0	0.0	0	0.0	0	0.0	0	0.0	0	0.0	0
Total	424	49.4	434	50.6	858	100.0	0	0.0	288	33.6	858		233

Tuition and Fees

	Resident	Nonresident
Full-time	$31,408	$31,408
Part-time	$0	$0

Living Expenses

Estimated living expenses for singles

Living on campus	Living off campus	Living at home
$15,422	$15,422	$10,672

Boston University School of Law

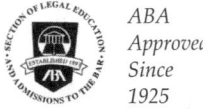

*ABA
Approved
Since
1925*

GPA and LSAT Scores

	Total	Full-time	Part-time
# of apps	6,165	6,165	0
# of admits	1,329	1,329	0
# of matrics	291	291	0
75% GPA	3.76	3.76	0.00
25% GPA	3.45	3.45	0.00
75% LSAT	165	165	0
25% LSAT	162	162	0

Grants and Scholarships (from prior year)

	Total		Full-time		Part-time	
	#	%	#	%	#	%
Total # of students	807		807		0	
Total # receiving grants	367	45.5	367	45.5	0	0.0
Less than 1/2 tuition	76	9.4	76	9.4	0	0.0
Half to full tuition	260	32.2	260	32.2	0	0.0
Full tuition	0	0.0	0	0.0	0	0.0
More than full tuition	31	3.8	31	3.8	0	0.0
Median grant amount			$15,000		$0	

Informational and Library Resources

# of volumes and volume equivalents	653,826
# of titles	167,063
# of active serial subscriptions	5,116
Study seating capacity inside the library	691
# of professional librarians	8
Hours per week library is open	102
# of open, wired connections available to students	0
# of networked computers available for use by students	110
# of simultaneous wireless users	500
Require computer?	N

JD Attrition (from prior year)

	Academic	Other	Total	
	#	#	#	%
1st year	0	4	4	1.5%
2nd year	0	2	2	0.7%
3rd year	1	2	3	1.2%
4th year	0	0	0	0.0%

Employment

	Total	Percentage
Employment status known	295	99.7
Employment status unknown	1	0.3
Employed	279	94.6
Pursuing graduate degrees	11	3.7
Unemployed seeking employment	0	0.0
Unemployed not seeking employment	5	1.7

Type of Employment

# employed in law firms	186	66.7
# employed in business and industry	10	3.6
# employed in government	24	8.6
# employed in public interest	14	5.0
# employed as judicial clerks	39	14.0
# employed in academia	6	2.2

Geographic Location

# employed in state	87	31.2
# employed in foreign countries	3	1.1
# of states where employed	31	

Bar Passage Rates

Jurisdiction	Massachusetts			New York		
Exam	Sum 03	Win 04	Total	Sum 03	Win 04	Total
# from school taking bar for the first time	121	8	129	113	10	123
School's pass rate for all first-time takers	93%	75%	91%	91%	90%	91%
State's pass rate for all first-time takers	82%	82%	82%	78%	58%	75%

Boston University School of Law

765 Commonwealth Avenue
Boston, MA 02215
Phone: 617.353.3100; Fax: 617.353.0578
E-mail: bulawadm@bu.edu; Website: www.bu.edu/law

■ Introduction

Boston University School of Law offers one of the finest legal educations in the nation, attracting students from all over the country and abroad. A pioneer in American legal education, the school was founded in 1872 on the principles that legal education should be open to all men and women of ability without regard to background or beliefs, and that it should balance theory and analysis with practical training. Today, the school's innovative curriculum combines theoretical courses, clinical train- ing, and specialized offerings—including concentrations, dual degrees, and semesters abroad. The full-time faculty of distinguished scholars and teachers ranks among the most productive in the nation's law schools. The students represent a range of educational backgrounds, ethnicities, races, age groups, and employment histories —evidence of the school's "open door" admission policy, a firm part of its tradition for over 130 years.

The city of Boston is a great place to study the law and launch a career. BUSL's location presents students with enormous opportunities. They can gain invaluable experience while in school, whether or not they intend to stay in Boston, through myriad job and internship opportunities which flow from Boston's unique status as a major business, financial, and legal center. Boston is home to many high-tech, start-up companies and is also a leading center in health care. In addition, Boston, as the state capital, is an active government center at both the federal and state levels, making it a laboratory for clinics, pro bono volunteering, and externships.

■ Faculty

BUSL faculty come from a range of backgrounds— including six Supreme Court clerks and numerous fed- eral court of appeals clerks—and from several schools of legal thought, such as law and economics and feminist legal theory. They are not only the leading scholars in their fields, but they excel inside the classroom as well.

■ Curriculum

Not only does BUSL offer an exceptionally strong teach- ing faculty, but it also offers one of the widest ranges of academic opportunities available at any American law school. At BUSL, students can explore virtually any area of law from among the school's 150 classes and seminars. They can concentrate and focus their studies in any of five important fields—business organizations and finance law, health law, intellectual property law, interna- tional law, and litigation and dispute resolution—and thus design a curriculum around courses that prepare them for exciting work in specific areas of interest.

Students can also expand beyond law by pursuing any of 10 dual-degree programs, combining law study with graduate coursework in a program that leads to a JD and a master's degree. Those dual degrees are JD/MBA, JD/MBA in Health Care Management, JD/MA in Historic Preservation, JD/MA in International Relations, JD/MS in Mass Communication, JD/MA in Philosophy, JD/MPH in Public Health, and JD/MSW in Social Work. Students interested in tax or banking can earn a combined JD/master of laws (LLM) degree in these fields on an accelerated seven-semester basis.

Students at BUSL can also immerse themselves in a foreign legal culture for a semester, studying international and comparative law in one of BUSL's eight semester-long study abroad programs. Programs offered in 2004–2005 are University of Buenos Aires (Argentina); Université Jean Moulin, Lyon 3 (France); Université Panthéon-Assas, Paris II (France); St. Catherine's College, University of Oxford (United Kingdom); Leiden University (The Netherlands); Tel Aviv University (Israel); University of Florence (Italy); University of Hong Kong (China); or Bucerius Law School (Germany).

For hands-on practical training, BUSL has been recognized for having some of the finest clinical offerings in the country. The clinical faculty is among the most experienced in American legal clinical education. Students can gain valuable experience through one of these clinics: Civil Litigation, Criminal Trial Advocacy, Legal Externship, Judicial Internship, and the Legislation Clinic.

■ Career Development

The BUSL Career Development Office is committed to helping each law student see all the possibilities that a BUSL degree affords them. The office offers a comprehensive program of services to students and alumni—from personal counseling to instructional workshops and events, to print and online resources and tools. First-year students benefit from the expertise of a diverse range of career advisors in the office and can participate in numerous workshops to hone job search skills. Alumni assist students through the Career Assistance Program and the young alumni mock interview program.

BUSL offers an extensive on- and off-campus recruiting program. Each year, more than 570 law firms, government agencies, public interest organizations, and corporations from all regions of the United States recruit BUSL students at specialty job fairs. Over 180 employers from 23 states come to campus to interview students; about 200 more meet BUSL students through eight regional job fairs, and many more advertise positions through the Career Development Office. Starting salaries of BUSL graduates entering the private sector are among the highest in the nation ($125,000, median private sector). The geographic reach of BUSL graduates is extremely broad, with 38 percent locating in the New England region—an obvious stronghold—and the other 62 percent spread throughout the south, west, and mid-Atlantic region.

■ Financial Aid

Boston University School of Law is committed to making a legal education affordable for its students. Through scholarship awards, federal and private loans, and work-study awards, the School of Law provides funding for over 80 percent of its enrolled J.D. students.

A significant pool of scholarship funds is awarded every year based on both financial need and academic merit. Because Boston University School of Law's scholarship resources are among the largest of all law schools, we are able to assist more than 45 percent of our enrolled students with some form of scholarship aid.

A small number of applicants who demonstrate outstanding academic achievement are recognized through the Dean's Scholar Program, which offers awards covering full tuition and fees. These awards are based solely on merit and do not require an application separate from the application for admission. The School of Law is also committed to upholding the diversity of its student body. It offers several scholarship programs intended to achieve this goal. Students applying through the regular financial aid application process will be considered for all types of aid available.

The Office of Financial Aid encourages all applicants to observe the March 1 financial aid application deadline, to follow the directions for application carefully, and to check with the financial aid office to ensure the completeness of their financial aid files.

Applicant Profile

Boston University School of Law
This grid includes only applicants who earned 120-180 LSAT scores under standard administrations.

LSAT Score	3.75 + Apps	Adm	3.50 - 3.74 Apps	Adm	3.25 - 3.49 Apps	Adm	3.00 - 3.24 Apps	Adm	2.75 - 2.99 Apps	Adm	2.50 - 2.74 Apps	Adm	2.25 - 2.49 Apps	Adm	2.00 - 2.24 Apps	Adm	Below 2.00 Apps	Adm	No GPA Apps	Adm	Total Apps	Adm
175-180	9	9	4	4	5	3	5	3	1	0	1	0	1	0	0	0	0	0	0	0	26	19
170-174	35	34	53	52	43	33	33	9	21	0	9	0	4	0	0	0	0	0	4	1	202	129
165-169	157	153	248	232	224	158	145	12	65	3	29	0	13	0	4	0	1	0	6	3	892	561
160-164	336	171	628	247	502	64	295	9	101	1	45	0	13	0	7	0	0	0	28	5	1955	497
155-159	232	19	394	14	447	16	259	8	102	1	33	1	19	0	1	0	0	0	20	0	1507	59
150-154	108	8	188	6	228	9	190	5	90	1	43	0	14	0	3	0	3	0	21	0	888	29
145-149	32	2	61	0	96	0	84	0	61	0	23	0	18	0	2	0	2	0	6	0	385	2
140-144	12	0	18	0	36	0	41	0	27	0	20	0	6	0	4	0	1	0	5	0	170	0
135-139	1	0	9	0	20	0	9	0	9	0	6	0	6	0	5	0	1	0	2	0	68	0
130-134	0	0	4	0	0	0	3	0	6	0	6	0	1	0	3	0	0	0	3	0	26	0
125-129	0	0	0	0	0	0	0	0	2	0	0	0	1	0	0	0	0	0	2	0	5	0
120-124	0	0	0	0	0	0	0	0	0	0	0	0	1	0	0	0	1	0	0	0	2	0
Total	922	396	1607	555	1601	283	1064	46	485	6	215	1	97	0	29	0	9	0	97	9	6126	1296

Apps = Number of Applicants
Adm = Number Admitted
Reflects 99% of the total applicant pool.

Brigham Young University—J. Reuben Clark Law School

340 JRCB, Box 28000
Provo, UT 84602-8000
Phone: 801.422.4277; Fax: 801.422.0389
E-mail: admissions@lawgate.byu.edu; Website: www.law2.byu.edu/Law_School/

ABA Approved Since 1974

The Basics

Type of school	Private
Term	Semester
Application deadline	2/1
Application fee	$50
Financial aid deadline	6/1
Can first year start other than fall?	No
Student to faculty ratio (fall)	18.3 to 1
Does the university offer:	
housing restricted to law students?	No
graduate housing for which law students are eligible?	No

Faculty and Administrators

	Total		Men		Women		Minorities	
	Fall	Spr	Fall	Spr	Fall	Spr	Fall	Spr
Full-time	22	19	17	15	5	4	3	3
Other Full-time	0	0	0	0	0	0	0	0
Deans, librarians, & others who teach	12	12	8	8	4	4	0	0
Part-time	26	33	16	25	10	8	2	1
Total	60	64	41	48	19	16	5	4

Curriculum

		Full-time	Part-time
Typical first-year section size		106	0
Is there typically a "small section" of the first-year class, other than Legal Writing, taught by full-time faculty		Yes	No
If yes, typical size offered last year		52	0
# of classroom course titles beyond 1st year curriculum		120	
# of upper division courses, excluding seminars with an enrollment:	Under 25	45	
	25-49	4	
	50-74	8	
	75-99	6	
	100+	4	
# of seminars		52	
# of seminar positions available		1,150	
# of seminar positions filled		649	0
# of positions available in simulation courses		285	
# of simulation positions filled		282	0
# of positions available in faculty supervised clinical courses		174	
# of faculty supervised clinical positions filled	158		0
# involved in field placements		258	0
# involved in law journals		283	0
# involved in moot court or trial competitions	183		0
# of credit hours required to graduate		90	

JD Enrollment and Ethnicity

	Men		Women		Full-time		Part-time		1st-year		Total		JD Degs. Awd.
	#	%	#	%	#	%	#	%	#	%	#	%	
African Amer.	6	2.0	1	0.5	7	1.4	0	0.0	5	3.3	7	1.4	1
Amer. Indian	7	2.4	1	0.5	8	1.7	0	0.0	0	0.0	8	1.7	1
Asian Amer.	10	3.4	11	5.9	21	4.3	0	0.0	7	4.7	21	4.3	10
Mex. Amer.	7	2.4	4	2.1	11	2.3	0	0.0	6	4.0	11	2.3	1
Puerto Rican	0	0.0	0	0.0	0	0.0	0	0.0	0	0.0	0	0.0	0
Hispanic	16	5.4	8	4.3	24	5.0	0	0.0	9	6.0	24	5.0	5
Total Minority	46	15.5	25	13.3	71	14.7	0	0.0	27	18.0	71	14.7	18
For. Nation.	11	3.7	6	3.2	17	3.5	0	0.0	11	7.3	17	3.5	96
Caucasian	239	80.7	157	83.5	395	81.8	1	100.0	112	74.7	396	81.8	45
Unknown	0	0.0	0	0.0	0	0.0	0	0.0	0	0.0	0	0.0	0
Total	296	61.2	188	38.8	483	99.8	1	0.2	150	31.0	484		159

Tuition and Fees

	Resident	Nonresident
Full-time	$7,200	$10,780
Part-time	$0	$0

Living Expenses

Estimated living expenses for singles

Living on campus	Living off campus	Living at home
$13,250	$13,060	$9,710

Brigham Young University—J. Reuben Clark Law School

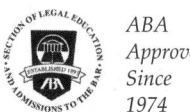

ABA
Approved
Since
1974

GPA and LSAT Scores

	Total	Full-time	Part-time
# of apps	985	985	0
# of admits	247	247	0
# of matrics	151	150	1
75% GPA	3.86	3.86	0.00
25% GPA	0.53	3.53	0.00
75% LSAT	166	166	0
25% LSAT	160	160	0

Grants and Scholarships (from prior year)

	Total		Full-time		Part-time	
	#	%	#	%	#	%
Total # of students	483		483		0	
Total # receiving grants	243	50.3	243	50.3	0	0.0
Less than 1/2 tuition	208	43.1	208	43.1	0	0.0
Half to full tuition	20	4.1	20	4.1	0	0.0
Full tuition	14	2.9	14	2.9	0	0.0
More than full tuition	1	0.2	1	0.2	0	0.0
Median grant amount			$1,500		$0	

Informational and Library Resources

# of volumes and volume equivalents	472,188
# of titles	166,937
# of active serial subscriptions	4,447
Study seating capacity inside the library	879
# of professional librarians	9
Hours per week library is open	105
# of open, wired connections available to students	605
# of networked computers available for use by students	36
# of simultaneous wireless users	1,000
Require computer?	Y

JD Attrition (from prior year)

	Academic	Other	Total	
	#	#	#	%
1st year	0	0	0	0.0%
2nd year	0	0	0	0.0%
3rd year	0	0	0	0.0%
4th year	0	0	0	0.0%

Employment

	Total	Percentage
Employment status known	164	100.0
Employment status unknown	0	0.0
Employed	155	94.5
Pursuing graduate degrees	3	1.8
Unemployed seeking employment	2	1.2
Unemployed not seeking employment	4	2.4

Type of Employment

# employed in law firms	87	56.1
# employed in business and industry	16	10.3
# employed in government	21	13.5
# employed in public interest	4	2.6
# employed as judicial clerks	24	15.5
# employed in academia	3	1.9

Geographic Location

# employed in state	69	44.5
# employed in foreign countries	1	0.6
# of states where employed		21

Bar Passage Rates

Jurisdiction	Utah			California		
Exam	Sum 03	Win 04	Total	Sum 03	Win 04	Total
# from school taking bar for the first time	57	24	81	18	3	21
School's pass rate for all first-time takers	100%	92%	98%	83%	67%	81%
State's pass rate for all first-time takers	93%	87%	92%	63%	47%	60%

Brigham Young University—J. Reuben Clark Law School

340 JRCB, Box 28000
Provo, UT 84602-8000
Phone: 801.422.4277; Fax: 801.422.0389
E-mail: admissions@lawgate.byu.edu; Website: www.law2.byu.edu/Law_School/

■ Introduction

Since its founding just over 30 years ago, the J. Reuben Clark Law School at Brigham Young University has been distinguished by the strength of its program and the accomplishments of its graduates. With 10 of its graduates having clerked for the US Supreme Court, the Law School has an enviable placement record throughout the United States in all branches of the legal profession. The Law School's relatively small entering class of 150 lends itself to individualized instruction, while the university with its 30,000 students, provides all the athletic, cultural, and social opportunities that a student may expect from a larger school. The Law School is fully accredited by the American Bar Association, is a member of the Association of American Law Schools, and has a chapter of the Order of the Coif.

■ Library and Physical Facilities

The Howard W. Hunter Law Library is one of the most technologically advanced law libraries in the world. It houses 475 individual study carrels with full Internet and LAN computer connectivity (hardwired and wireless). Thus each student in his or her private study space has access to electronic resources that include Westlaw, LexisNexis, and the growing Hunter Law Library Electronic Reserve, including archives of past examinations. The Ashton Legal Research Training Lab provides state-of-the-art facilities for advanced legal research and related computer training. Printers and copy machines for student use are available on all library floors. The law library also contains 17 group study rooms (three of which are family support rooms to assist parents who need to view closed-circuit broadcasts of classes), spacious casual seating, and office and research space for the Law School's three scholarly journals, two advocacy programs, and the Student Bar Association. Specialized rooms are dedicated to video viewing, interactive video, microforms, and television hookups. A 24-hour-access reference library is available to students. The library houses a collection of over 450,000 volumes or volume equivalents. Via interlibrary loan, students have access to many more titles found in the catalogs and collections of over 167 other worldwide institutions that, like the Hunter Library, subscribe to the Research Library Information Network (RLIN).

■ Faculty and Curriculum

The combination of the small entering class size and our internationally renowned faculty creates unique opportunities for learning. Together they seek to meet the challenge of making a difference worldwide as they engage in joint research, publishing, and advocacy. The objective of the Law School's curriculum is to maximize the students' mastery of legal reasoning and legal methods while teaching a core of the basic substantive rules of the law. Over 65 courses and 20 seminars are offered each year by a faculty of 34 full-time members and 32 additional adjunct faculty members. In addition, the Law School provides opportunities for students to develop practical skills through international and US externships with private law firms, corporations, and agencies, as well as public defenders, legal services, city and county attorneys, judges, attorneys general, and guardians ad litem. Students receive one credit for each 50 hours of work.

■ The Rex E. Lee Advocacy Program

It is not enough for lawyers to know the law. They must also synthesize complex information, analyze and formulate strategy, predict outcomes, and present information persuasively. The Rex E. Lee Advocacy Program administers a required course for first-year law students in the essential skills of legal writing, research, analysis, and oral advocacy. Students receive individualized attention during one-on-one conferences with instructors and teaching assistants and in small classes. The Legal Writing Center provides additional instruction and assistance to students through individual writing conferences and online resources. In the Advocacy Program, students learn and practice the critical skills that bring success in both law school and the profession.

■ International Center for Law and Religion Studies

The BYU International Center for Law and Religion Studies promotes freedom of religion by studying and disseminating information on the laws, principles, and institutions affecting the interaction of state and religion throughout the world. The center works with scholars, government leaders, nongovernment groups, and religious organizations from a variety of countries and faith traditions, playing an important role in promoting religious liberty and the accompanying relationships between governments and religious organizations.

■ World Family Policy Center

The World Family Policy Center participates in major United Nations conferences and sponsors important international conferences on family policy. The center seeks to provide balanced, solidly researched, pro-family education to member states and institutions within the United Nations system.

Brigham Young University—J. Reuben Clark Law School

The Schooley Mediation Program

The Schooley Mediation Program trains interested law students to become certified mediators. The program includes actual client experiences in juvenile victim-offender cases, small claims court, domestic cases, landlord-tenant disputes, and others.

The Externship Program

The Law School provides a five-week academic externship program as a capstone experience for students at the completion of their first year. This program places first-year students with judges, outstanding law firms, corporations, public interest groups, and governmental organizations throughout the world. During the summer of 2004, 168 students externed with 197 employers earning an average of four units of law school credit. Twenty-four placements were out of the country, and many of the domestic externships involved international aspects.

The Academic Success Program

The Academic Success Program (ASP) is designed to help students adjust to and meet the rigorous demands of a legal education. The ASP offers legal skills workshops with personal feedback, weekly tutorial sessions in each first-year course, individual tutoring, and one-on-one legal writing instruction to all students upon request and by deans' referral.

Cocurricular Programs

The objective of the cocurricular program at the Law School is to make law review-quality experience available to larger numbers of students. Comparable standards of excellence in research, writing, and editing are offered in five programs: the *Brigham Young University Law Review*, the Board of Advocates Moot Court, Trial Advocacy, the *BYU Journal of Public Law*, and the *Brigham Young University Education and Law Journal*.

Career Services

The Career Services Office (CSO) is available to all students and graduates seeking employment. The CSO offers two legal career-planning courses featuring skills training and presentations by practicing attorneys who participate as guest lecturers. It also publishes a *Professional Development Handbook, Job Hunt Book*, and *Judicial Clerkship Handbook* and maintains a web page with links for both students and employers. About 98 percent of the graduates who are seeking work accept employment within nine months after graduation, and graduates are placed in all 50 states and several foreign countries. The CSO brings firms to campus every year for on-campus interviews and has interviewing events and job fairs in DC, New York, Southern California, and Nevada.

Applicant Profile

Brigham Young University—J. Reuben Clark Law School
This grid includes only applicants who earned 120-180 LSAT scores under standard administrations.

LSAT Score	3.75 +		3.50 - 3.74		3.25 - 3.49		3.00 - 3.24		2.75 - 2.99		2.50 - 2.74		2.25 - 2.49		2.00 - 2.24		Below 2.00		No GPA		Total	
	Apps	Adm	Apps	Adm	Apps	Adm	Apps	Adm	Apps	Adm	Apps	Adm	Apps	Adm	Apps	Adm	Apps	Adm	Apps	Adm	Apps	Adm
175-180	1	1	0	0	0	0	0	0	0	0	0	0	0	0	0	0	0	0	0	0	1	1
170-174	11	11	6	6	4	4	1	1	1	1	0	0	1	0	0	0	0	0	0	0	24	23
165-169	46	44	34	32	17	10	9	2	2	0	0	0	0	0	0	0	0	0	0	0	108	88
160-164	61	35	75	34	43	11	25	2	11	0	2	0	0	0	1	0	0	0	5	0	223	82
155-159	65	17	68	4	52	1	35	2	16	0	5	0	3	0	2	0	0	0	2	0	248	24
150-154	32	2	50	6	37	0	33	3	24	1	6	0	2	0	0	0	0	0	2	0	186	12
145-149	12	0	19	0	15	0	16	0	17	0	6	1	5	0	0	0	1	0	6	0	97	1
140-144	1	0	3	0	9	0	6	0	8	0	0	0	2	0	1	0	0	0	4	0	34	0
135-139	0	0	2	0	1	0	3	0	3	0	3	0	1	0	0	0	0	0	3	0	16	0
130-134	0	0	1	0	1	0	0	0	0	0	0	0	1	0	1	0	1	0	0	0	5	0
125-129	0	0	0	0	0	0	0	0	2	0	0	0	0	0	0	0	0	0	1	0	3	0
120-124	0	0	0	0	0	0	0	0	0	0	0	0	0	0	0	0	0	0	0	0	0	0
Total	229	110	258	82	179	26	128	10	84	2	22	1	15	0	5	0	2	0	23	0	945	231

Apps = Number of Applicants
Adm = Number Admitted
Reflects 99% of the total applicant pool.

Brooklyn Law School

250 Joralemon Street
Brooklyn, NY 11201-9846
Phone: 718.780.7906; Fax: 718.780.0395
E-mail: admitq@brooklaw.edu; Website: www.brooklaw.edu

ABA Approved Since 1937

The Basics

Type of school	Private
Term	Semester
Application deadline	
Application fee	$65
Financial aid deadline	3/15
Can first year start other than fall?	No
Student to faculty ratio (fall)	17.8 to 1
Does the university offer:	
housing restricted to law students?	Yes
graduate housing for which law students are eligible?	No

Faculty and Administrators

	Total		Men		Women		Minorities	
	Fall	Spr	Fall	Spr	Fall	Spr	Fall	Spr
Full-time	65	60	36	33	29	27	4	5
Other Full-time	0	0	0	0	0	0	0	0
Deans, librarians, & others who teach	9	9	4	4	5	5	1	1
Part-time	62	74	43	46	19	28	4	5
Total	136	143	83	83	53	60	9	11

Curriculum

	Full-time	Part-time
Typical first-year section size	57	42
Is there typically a "small section" of the first-year class, other than Legal Writing, taught by full-time faculty	Yes	No
If yes, typical size offered last year	40	0
# of classroom course titles beyond 1st year curriculum	155	
# of upper division courses, excluding seminars with an enrollment: Under 25	149	
25-49	55	
50-74	24	
75-99	10	
100+	19	
# of seminars	55	
# of seminar positions available	983	
# of seminar positions filled	798	77
# of positions available in simulation courses	964	
# of simulation positions filled	656	207
# of positions available in faculty supervised clinical courses	321	
# of faculty supervised clinical positions filled	302	19
# involved in field placements	390	33
# involved in law journals	175	7
# involved in moot court or trial competitions	71	9
# of credit hours required to graduate	86	

J.D. Enrollment and Ethnicity

	Men #	Men %	Women #	Women %	Full-time #	Full-time %	Part-time #	Part-time %	1st-year #	1st-year %	Total #	Total %	JD Degs. Awd.
African Amer.	25	3.2	35	4.7	28	2.4	32	8.6	18	3.7	60	4.0	24
Amer. Indian	0	0.0	2	0.3	1	0.1	1	0.3	1	0.2	2	0.1	1
Asian Amer.	75	9.7	148	20.0	176	15.3	47	12.7	77	15.7	223	14.7	45
Mex. Amer.	4	0.5	4	0.5	6	0.5	2	0.5	4	0.8	8	0.5	0
Puerto Rican	5	0.6	11	1.5	10	0.9	6	1.6	4	0.8	16	1.1	3
Hispanic	20	2.6	28	3.8	37	3.2	11	3.0	13	2.7	48	3.2	20
Total Minority	129	16.6	228	30.8	258	22.5	99	26.8	117	23.9	357	23.5	93
For. Nation.	4	0.5	12	1.6	13	1.1	3	0.8	5	1.0	16	1.1	10
Caucasian	644	82.9	501	67.6	877	76.4	268	72.4	367	75.1	1145	75.4	350
Unknown	0	0.0	0	0.0	0	0.0	0	0.0	0	0.0	0	0.0	1
Total	777	51.2	741	48.8	1148	75.6	370	24.4	489	32.2	1518		454

Tuition and Fees

	Resident	Nonresident
Full-time	$32,975	$32,975
Part-time	$24,788	$24,788

Living Expenses

Estimated living expenses for singles

Living on campus	Living off campus	Living at home
$17,433	$17,433	$6,904

Brooklyn Law School

ABA
Approved
Since
1937

GPA and LSAT Scores

	Total	Full-time	Part-time
# of apps	5,620	4,822	798
# of admits	1,295	976	319
# of matrics	491	303	188
75% GPA	3.52	3.57	3.43
25% GPA	3.07	3.11	3.00
75% LSAT	163	164	160
25% LSAT	159	161	158

Grants and Scholarships (from prior year)

	Total		Full-time		Part-time	
	#	%	#	%	#	%
Total # of students	1,515		1,132		383	
Total # receiving grants	671	44.3	602	53.2	69	18.0
Less than 1/2 tuition	617	40.7	553	48.9	64	16.7
Half to full tuition	50	3.3	45	4.0	5	1.3
Full tuition	4	0.3	4	0.4	0	0.0
More than full tuition	0	0.0	0	0.0	0	0.0
Median grant amount			$8,659		$4,581	

Informational and Library Resources

# of volumes and volume equivalents	534,591
# of titles	164,064
# of active serial subscriptions	3,729
Study seating capacity inside the library	665
# of professional librarians	10
Hours per week library is open	108
# of open, wired connections available to students	1,973
# of networked computers available for use by students	133
# of simultaneous wireless users	900
Require computer?	N

JD Attrition (from prior year)

	Academic	Other	Total	
	#	#	#	%
1st year	5	33	38	7.6%
2nd year	2	0	2	0.4%
3rd year	1	1	2	0.5%
4th year	1	0	1	1.3%

Employment

	Total	Percentage
Employment status known	492	100.0
Employment status unknown	0	0.0
Employed	451	91.7
Pursuing graduate degrees	7	1.4
Unemployed seeking employment	9	1.8
Unemployed not seeking employment	25	5.1

Type of Employment

# employed in law firms	286	63.4
# employed in business and industry	72	16.0
# employed in government	48	10.6
# employed in public interest	9	2.0
# employed as judicial clerks	35	7.8
# employed in academia	1	0.2

Geographic Location

# employed in state	397	88.0
# employed in foreign countries	1	0.2
# of states where employed	17	

Bar Passage Rates

Jurisdiction	New York		
Exam	Sum 03	Win 04	Total
# from school taking bar for the first time	425	12	437
School's pass rate for all first-time takers	84%	75%	83%
State's pass rate for all first-time takers	78%	58%	75%

Brooklyn Law School

250 Joralemon Street
Brooklyn, NY 11201-9846
Phone: 718.780.7906; Fax: 718.780.0395
E-mail: admitq@brooklaw.edu; Website: www.brooklaw.edu

■ The Law Campus

Situated at the junction of the Brooklyn Heights Historic District, the Brooklyn Civic Center, and downtown Brooklyn, Brooklyn Law School boasts a location unrivaled for its legal, cultural, and historical character. Students share their environs with federal and state judges, government officials, and lawyers in private practice, many of them alumni. Within a few-block radius are the US District Court; US Bankruptcy Court; US Attorney's Office; the NYS Supreme Court, Appellate Division, and Family Court; the Brooklyn District Attorney; the Kings County Surrogate's Court; the NYC Civil and Criminal Courts; The Legal Aid Society; and numerous law firms. These are our laboratories, a backdrop for learning few schools can replicate.

■ Renaissance Brooklyn

Multibillion-dollar construction projects have recast downtown Brooklyn as the city's third business hub, after Wall Street and midtown Manhattan. Here, moreover, is Brooklyn's most charming neighborhood, Brooklyn Heights. Overlooking New York Harbor and lower Manhattan, the Heights is where you will find much of our campus. Brooklyn Heights is the first New York City neighborhood designated a historic district, many of its original townhouses, brownstone mansions, carriage houses, churches, and public buildings survive, some registered as national historic landmarks. Many of our students and faculty live here in residence halls or in private apartments and homes. Nearby neighborhoods—Carroll Gardens, Cobble Hill, and Park Slope—also offer convenient, affordable housing.

■ Manhattan at Our Doorstep

Minutes away is the financial, legal, business, and cultural crossroads of the world: Manhattan. Proximity to Wall Street gives students easy access to school-year externships and summer jobs with major law firms and financial institutions. Students enjoy a great campus in a dynamic urban environment softened by a sense of community. This is New York City on a human scale—Manhattan without the hassle.

■ Building for the New Millennium

In recent years, BLS has undertaken $118 million in capital improvements to serve its needs well into the 21st century. The focal point of our campus is the 11-story addition to our main building. Work continues on a 360-bed residence hall scheduled to open in fall 2005. Our 78,000-square-foot library, one of the largest and most modern in the city, includes more than 535,000 volumes, 5 computer labs, 26

group study rooms, and seating for nearly 700. In addition to about 90 computer workstations, we provide over 1,900 other student accessible network connections throughout our main building as well as 900 wi-fi connections.

■ Our Faculty: Diverse, Brilliant, and User Friendly

Our 69 full-time faculty members comprise one of the largest faculties in New York. They are joined by approximately 130 adjuncts, including many distinguished judges, practitioners, and corporate counsel. They are extraordinarily talented and, above all, superb teachers. Shaping public policy, making law in the community at large, they are also prolific authors. They are recognized nationally and globally for their scholarship in such areas as Commercial and Bankruptcy Law, Corporate and Securities Law, Evidence, Health Care, Information Privacy and Internet Law, Intellectual Property, International Business Law, Human Rights, Product Liability, and Women's Rights. BLS offers a congenial community. Its learning environment, while rigorous and challenging, remains supportive and nurturing. A desirable student-faculty ratio of 17.8:1 facilitates this dynamic. Faculty members are accessible to students in a way that few faculties are. There is a strong correlation between the priority we assign to teaching and mentoring and the fact that, since 1993, our average passing rate of 83 percent was 5 percent ahead of the state-wide rate for first-time takers of the New York State Bar examination.

■ Our Students: The Best and the Brightest

A recent entering class included students from 31 states, the District of Columbia, and 15 foreign countries who earned degrees from more than 165 universities and colleges, including many of the nation's most prestigious. Sixty-nine percent completed undergraduate work at least one year before enrolling here. Forty-five percent of the 2004 entering class had LSAT scores in the top 10 percent nationwide; the median LSAT score was in the top 12 percent. Minorities represented 24 percent of that class; just under half of the students were women.

■ Our Alumni: Accomplished and Accessible

One of the great strengths of BLS is the size, stature, and loyalty of our more than 16,750 graduates in 48 states, 2 US territories, and 20 foreign countries, one of the largest alumni families of any law school.

■ The Career Center

Our Career Center is staffed by seven attorney-counselors and an attorney dedicated to job development/employer relations. Job listings are readily available to students and graduates via Internet. Over the past three years, we have averaged a 97 percent employment rate nine months after graduation, ranking us among the top law schools nationwide. For current salary information, see *www.brooklaw.edu/career/empstats/*.

■ First-Year Program of Study

Day students take one core course in a seminar section of about 40 students, allowing for significant individualized skills training. Our goal is to help students cultivate the ability to think clearly, analyze problems thoroughly and carefully, and to recognize that no "legal" issue exists in a social, philosophical, economic, or political vacuum. Students participate in a Legal Writing Program structured to develop fully their writing abilities. An Academic Success Program combining an early-start summer course with a series of support workshops helps students reach their potential. This contributes to our exceptionally high retention rate between the first and second year.

■ Upperclass Program of Study: The Art and Craft of Lawyering

Our upperclass curriculum is designed to bridge the law school/law practice gap and to make law school something that students enjoy, not merely endure. Students create individualized programs, choosing from over 200 electives in 19 concentrations and areas of interest. Over 75 percent of fulltime and about 60 percent of all students participate in one or more of our 23 in-house and externship clinics, including over 400 students placed in a recent year in judicial chambers, law offices, and government agencies through our large externship programs. Simulation courses enroll some 950 students annually.

■ Beyond the Core Curriculum

We are consistently recognized as among the country's top law schools in supporting public interest law. The **Edward V. Sparer Public Interest Law Fellowship Program** has exposed some 320 students to a broad range of legal work in public interest organizations nationwide and abroad. Our **International Business Law Fellowship Program** is a rewarding educational experience for those pursuing careers in that field. We sponsor three student-edited journals: the *Brooklyn Law Review*, the *Journal of Law and Policy*, and the *Brooklyn Journal of International Law*. Our **Moot Court Program**, one of the finest in the nation, garnered 62 top honors—including 18 national championships—in recent competitions. Keeping pace with the movement toward interdisciplinary study, our *Center for the Study of Law, Language, and Cognition* explores the legally relevant areas of linguistics and psychology. A **Center for Health, Science, and Policy** engages students in the legal issues and public policy concerns confronting health care organizations. A joint-degree option allows students to earn master's degrees in business administration, city and regional planning, public administration, urban planning, political science, or library and information science. Finally, we offer summer study-abroad programs in Italy and China.

Applicant Profile

Brooklyn Law School
This grid does not differentiate between full-time and part-time applicants/admit offers. It includes only applicants who earned 120-180 LSAT scores under standard administrations; it does not include applicants who took the LSAT under nonstandard conditions.

LSAT Score	GPA 3.75 +		3.50 - 3.74		3.25 - 3.49		3.00 - 3.24		2.75 - 2.99		2.50 - 2.74		2.25 - 2.49		2.00 - 2.24		Below 2.00		No GPA		Total	
	Apps	Adm	Apps	Adm	Apps	Adm	Apps	Adm	Apps	Adm	Apps	Adm	Apps	Adm	Apps	Adm	Apps	Adm	Apps	Adm	Apps	Adm
175-180	0	0	0	0	1	1	3	2	1	1	0	0	0	0	0	0	0	0	0	0	5	4
170-174	13	12	12	10	20	17	11	8	7	6	7	5	2	0	1	0	0	0	0	0	73	58
165-169	55	47	67	56	85	74	55	52	33	25	19	10	9	1	5	0	1	0	6	2	335	267
160-164	163	122	265	202	283	190	242	136	97	42	70	24	25	5	8	0	0	0	6	1	1159	722
155-159	196	22	344	51	421	65	319	58	170	21	80	7	52	0	15	0	1	0	3	0	1601	224
150-154	104	1	229	2	302	3	297	6	174	0	105	4	51	2	13	0	1	0	6	0	1282	18
145-149	42	0	91	0	122	0	148	0	98	0	57	0	32	0	13	0	3	0	6	0	612	0
140-144	13	0	34	0	59	0	67	0	62	0	46	0	29	0	13	0	3	0	3	0	329	0
135-139	5	0	12	0	20	0	25	0	26	0	28	0	16	0	6	0	3	0	1	0	142	0
130-134	3	0	1	0	5	0	11	0	8	0	11	0	5	0	8	0	1	0	1	0	54	0
125-129	0	0	1	0	1	0	3	0	1	0	2	0	6	0	1	0	0	0	4	0	19	0
120-124	0	0	0	0	0	0	0	0	0	0	1	0	0	0	1	0	0	0	0	0	2	0
Total	594	204	1056	321	1319	350	1181	262	677	95	426	50	227	8	84	0	13	0	36	3	5613	1293

Apps = Number of Applicants   Adm = Number Admitted   Reflects 99% of the total applicant pool.

University at Buffalo Law School, The State University of New York (SUNY)

309 John Lord O'Brian Hall
Buffalo, NY 14260
Phone: 716.645.2907; Fax: 716.645.6676
E-mail: law-admissions@buffalo.edu; Website: www.law.buffalo.edu

ABA Approved Since 1936

The Basics

Type of school	Public
Term	Semester
Application deadline	3/15
Application fee	$50
Financial aid deadline	3/1
Can first year start other than fall?	No
Student to faculty ratio (fall)	12.8 to 1
Does the university offer:	
housing restricted to law students?	Yes
graduate housing for which law students are eligible?	Yes

Faculty and Administrators

	Total		Men		Women		Minorities	
	Fall	Spr	Fall	Spr	Fall	Spr	Fall	Spr
Full-time	48	49	28	29	20	20	5	4
Other Full-time	6	6	1	1	5	5	0	0
Deans, librarians, & others who teach	5	5	4	4	1	1	0	0
Part-time	51	90	36	58	14	31	3	10
Total	110	150	69	92	40	57	8	14

Curriculum

	Full-time	Part-time
Typical first-year section size	80	0
Is there typically a "small section" of the first-year class, other than Legal Writing, taught by full-time faculty	Yes	No
If yes, typical size offered last year	40	0
# of classroom course titles beyond 1st year curriculum	195	
# of upper division courses, excluding seminars with an enrollment: Under 25	145	
25-49	54	
50-74	17	
75-99	3	
100+	1	
# of seminars	36	
# of seminar positions available	494	
# of seminar positions filled	431	0
# of positions available in simulation courses	1,958	
# of simulation positions filled	1,676	0
# of positions available in faculty supervised clinical courses	115	
# of faculty supervised clinical positions filled	115	0
# involved in field placements	39	0
# involved in law journals	232	0
# involved in moot court or trial competitions	74	0
# of credit hours required to graduate	90	

JD Enrollment and Ethnicity

	Men		Women		Full-time		Part-time		1st-year		Total		JD Degs. Awd.
	#	%	#	%	#	%	#	%	#	%	#	%	
African Amer.	15	4.2	31	8.0	46	6.2	0	0.0	17	7.0	46	6.2	21
Amer. Indian	2	0.6	3	0.8	5	0.7	0	0.0	3	1.2	5	0.7	2
Asian Amer.	28	7.9	24	6.2	52	7.1	0	0.0	25	10.2	52	7.0	10
Mex. Amer.	0	0.0	0	0.0	0	0.0	0	0.0	0	0.0	0	0.0	0
Puerto Rican	0	0.0	1	0.3	1	0.1	0	0.0	0	0.0	1	0.1	1
Hispanic	8	2.3	22	5.7	30	4.1	0	0.0	10	4.1	30	4.0	11
Total Minority	53	15.0	81	20.9	134	18.2	0	0.0	55	22.5	134	18.1	45
For. Nation.	0	0.0	0	0.0	0	0.0	0	0.0	0	0.0	0	0.0	0
Caucasian	249	70.5	277	71.4	523	71.0	3	75.0	153	62.7	526	71.0	163
Unknown	51	14.4	30	7.7	80	10.9	1	25.0	36	14.8	81	10.9	28
Total	353	47.6	388	52.4	737	99.5	4	0.5	244	32.9	741		236

Tuition and Fees

	Resident	Nonresident
Full-time	$13,422	$19,522
Part-time	$0	$0

Living Expenses

Estimated living expenses for singles

Living on campus	Living off campus	Living at home
$11,729	$11,729	$11,729

University at Buffalo Law School, The State University of New York (SUNY)

ABA
Approved
Since
1936

GPA and LSAT Scores

	Total	Full-time	Part-time
# of apps	1,444	1,444	0
# of admits	517	517	0
# of matrics	244	244	0
75% GPA	3.66	3.66	0.00
25% GPA	3.07	3.07	0.00
75% LSAT	158	158	0
25% LSAT	152	152	0

Grants and Scholarships (from prior year)

	Total		Full-time		Part-time	
	#	%	#	%	#	%
Total # of students	744		743		1	
Total # receiving grants	627	84.3	627	84.4	0	0.0
Less than 1/2 tuition	473	63.6	473	63.7	0	0.0
Half to full tuition	0	0.0	0	0.0	0	0.0
Full tuition	117	15.7	117	15.7	0	0.0
More than full tuition	37	5.0	37	5.0	0	0.0
Median grant amount			$2,950		$0	

Informational and Library Resources

# of volumes and volume equivalents	554,116
# of titles	107,826
# of active serial subscriptions	6,650
Study seating capacity inside the library	526
# of professional librarians	11
Hours per week library is open	102
# of open, wired connections available to students	70
# of networked computers available for use by students	91
# of simultaneous wireless users	460
Require computer?	N

JD Attrition (from prior year)

	Academic	Other	Total	
	#	#	#	%
1st year	0	9	9	3.7%
2nd year	0	4	4	1.6%
3rd year	1	1	2	0.8%
4th year	0	0	0	0.0%

Employment

	Total	Percentage
Employment status known	225	96.6
Employment status unknown	8	3.4
Employed	193	85.8
Pursuing graduate degrees	18	8.0
Unemployed seeking employment	7	3.1
Unemployed not seeking employment	7	3.1

Type of Employment

	Total	Percentage
# employed in law firms	112	58.0
# employed in business and industry	32	16.6
# employed in government	26	13.5
# employed in public interest	12	6.2
# employed as judicial clerks	6	3.1
# employed in academia	5	2.6

Geographic Location

	Total	Percentage
# employed in state	158	81.9
# employed in foreign countries	3	1.6
# of states where employed	17	

Bar Passage Rates

Jurisdiction	New York		
Exam	Sum 03	Win 04	Total
# from school taking bar for the first time	197	12	209
School's pass rate for all first-time takers	74%	67%	74%
State's pass rate for all first-time takers	78%	58%	75%

University at Buffalo Law School, The State University of New York (SUNY)

309 John Lord O'Brian Hall
Buffalo, NY 14260
Phone: 716.645.2907; Fax: 716.645.6676
E-mail: law-admissions@buffalo.edu; Website: www.law.buffalo.edu

■ Introduction

Long recognized as the leading public law school in the Northeast, the University at Buffalo Law School, the only law school in the SUNY system, continues to provide students with cutting-edge legal tools to formulate their legal education. This education allows students to gain the practical skills necessary in today's ever-changing legal community.

Located in Amherst, New York—a suburb of Buffalo—the Law School has a small-school feel with all the advantages of a large university, including access to other professional and graduate departments, Division 1 sports, a Fine Arts Center, Slee Concert Hall, and numerous other academic, social, and cultural opportunities. The City of Buffalo offers great skiing, great sailing, major-league sports, a first-rate orchestra, many professional theaters, a lively club scene, and access to Canada, all within minutes of the Law School. You can live comfortably, not to mention affordably, in Buffalo, the second largest city in New York.

■ Library and Physical Facilities

The Law School is housed in John Lord O'Brian Hall, a seven-story building recently renovated to include a state-of-the-art courtroom that provides students with an opportunity to watch judges and lawyers in action. Other new facilities include classrooms, apartments, and an elegant student lounge. The library is the core of the Law School, occupying six of the seven floors.

The law library follows the Law School's commitment to providing students with exceptional research and writing skills by assigning librarians to each research and writing instructor. This enables first-year law students to gain one-on-one instruction in various research methods.

■ Curriculum

The Law School provides a comprehensive curriculum while affording students a broad range of curricular options, practical coursework, and special programs. The Buffalo curriculum emphasizes the study of law in its social context, and a large number of interdisciplinary courses and programs support this emphasis. A strong clinical education program is closely tied to the core curriculum and enhances the optional concentrations. Current concentration subjects include Family Law, Finance Transactions, Affordable Housing and Community Development Law, Environmental Law, Civil Litigation, Criminal Law, Health Law, Law and Social Justice, International Human Rights Law, Employment and Labor Law, and Technology and Intellectual Property Law.

Instruction is offered in two semesters from early September to May, including a January bridge term, and a summer session from mid-May to mid-July. Six full-time semesters or five full-time semesters plus two summer sessions are required for graduation.

In addition to standard first-year subjects, the first year includes a course in legal profession and ethics, as well as small practice-oriented classes in the spring semester. These courses afford an introduction to the social and economic context of the legal system and to legal institutions and processes.

Beyond the first year, students are required to complete 58 semester credit hours of work, including at least one seminar. The upper-division program is wholly elective. Second- and third-year students may choose from a full spectrum of survey and advanced courses covering the main fields of public and private law; a very rich selection of seminars and small group courses in special or emerging areas of law study and research; and clinics and simulations devoted to professional skills training.

■ Special Programs

Clinical Program—The Law School is committed to programs that emphasize interdisciplinary study and applications of law. The clinical program is distinguished in that the skills training is coordinated with substantive law courses to give students theoretical understanding of practical issues. Students serve clients and conduct research and fieldwork in such areas as economic development, affordable housing, family violence, criminal law, disability and education law, elder law, and securities law.

Dual-Degree Programs—The school also has an extensive dual-degree program, which permits students to earn credit toward a master's or PhD degree and the JD. In recent years, the most active dual-degree programs have been with political science, management, philosophy, public health, legal information and management and analysis, social work, sociology, and economics. Special programs can be arranged with other departments.

Bridge Term—Second- and third-year students can enroll in up to three one-credit bridge courses taught by experienced lawyers and judges, giving students a window into current issues in practice.

■ Admission

The Law School admits first-year students only in the fall semester; transfer and visiting students in both fall and spring. Application deadline: March 15. LSAT and LSDAS are required.

University at Buffalo Law School, The State University of New York (SUNY)

Because quantitative factors—GPA and LSAT—may not accurately reflect a student's potential for law school success, the Admissions Committee pays close attention to the qualitative factors presented in an application. These factors include, but are not limited to, personal statements, character traits, recommendations, work experience, and writing ability. If an application reveals that the applicant has been educationally, socially, economically, or otherwise disadvantaged, the Admissions Committee will review the application for signs of achievement that should lead to success in law school.

■ Student Activities

There are ample extracurricular activities for students to get involved in. The Student Bar Association, an elected representative body, oversees all law school student organizations. The Moot Court Board sponsors mock appellate practice competitions; *The Opinion* is the student newspaper; the *Buffalo Law Review* is a professional journal edited by students; and there are specialty journals in environmental law, affordable housing and community development law, intellectual property, criminal law, human rights law, and social policy concerning women.

■ Expenses and Financial Aid

UB is able to offer a state-subsidized tuition to New York residents and a reasonable out-of-state tuition charge. In-state tuition—$12,170; out-of-state—$18,270. Estimated additional expenses—$11,000–12,000.

This results in overall educational expenses that are less than half the cost of many law schools. Dean's tuition waivers are available to students demonstrating high academic achievement, and state aid is offered on a need basis to qualified students. Some UB law students are able to fund their education through the use of the Stafford Federal Loan Program without seeking additional private loans.

■ Career Services

The Law School's Career Services Office (CSO) should become every law student's first point of reference as he or she begins a job search. In addition to providing job search and résumé services for third-year and LLM students, the CSO also aids first- and second-year students in conducting their summer job searches.

Over the last several years, the placement rate of eligible graduates who have been employed in legal work or enrolled in an advanced-degree program within nine months of graduation has been 98 percent. While Buffalo and New York City continue to employ the greatest number of our graduates, several northeastern states, including Washington, DC; southern states (Florida, Georgia, North Carolina); western states (California, Arizona); and midwestern states are presenting an increase in opportunities for our graduates. For more information about career services, contact the office: telephone 716.645.2056; fax 716.645.7336; e-mail *law.careers@buffalo.edu*.

Applicant Profile

University at Buffalo Law School, The State University of New York
This grid includes only applicants who earned 120-180 LSAT scores under standard administrations.

LSAT Score	GPA 3.75 +		3.50 - 3.74		3.25 - 3.49		3.00 - 3.24		2.75 - 2.99		2.50 - 2.74		2.25 - 2.49		2.00 - 2.24		Below 2.00		No GPA		Total	
	Apps	Adm	Apps	Adm	Apps	Adm	Apps	Adm	Apps	Adm	Apps	Adm	Apps	Adm	Apps	Adm	Apps	Adm	Apps	Adm	Apps	Adm
175-180	0	0	0	0	0	0	1	1	0	0	0	0	1	1	0	0	0	0	0	0	2	2
170-174	0	0	0	0	1	1	1	1	0	0	0	0	0	0	1	1	0	0	0	0	3	3
165-169	3	3	8	8	5	5	9	9	0	0	6	6	4	3	1	0	0	0	0	0	36	34
160-164	15	15	22	22	24	24	20	20	11	10	10	6	5	4	2	0	0	0	1	1	110	102
155-159	35	35	55	55	79	66	54	40	33	13	22	9	17	7	5	2	1	0	6	6	307	233
150-154	39	29	87	49	82	24	82	18	52	5	40	5	20	2	5	1	1	0	5	4	413	137
145-149	16	4	46	12	72	9	55	9	48	3	23	1	33	0	5	1	1	0	4	2	303	41
140-144	7	0	16	1	39	0	34	0	31	0	18	0	12	0	6	0	2	0	6	0	171	1
135-139	1	0	3	0	8	0	12	0	9	0	18	0	12	0	3	0	1	0	3	0	70	0
130-134	0	0	0	0	4	0	4	0	3	0	6	0	3	0	2	0	2	0	0	0	24	0
125-129	0	0	0	0	3	0	0	0	1	0	2	0	3	0	0	0	0	0	0	0	9	0
120-124	0	0	1	0	0	0	0	0	0	0	1	0	0	0	0	0	0	0	0	0	2	0
Total	116	86	238	147	317	129	272	98	188	31	146	27	110	17	30	5	8	0	25	13	1450	553

Apps = Number of Applicants   Adm = Number Admitted   Reflects 99% of the total applicant pool.

University of California, Berkeley School of Law (Boalt Hall)

5 Boalt Hall
Berkeley, CA 94720-7200
Phone: 510.642.2274
E-mail: admissions@law.berkeley.edu; Website: www.law.berkeley.edu

ABA Approved Since 1923

The Basics

Type of school	Public
Term	Semester
Application deadline	2/1
Application fee	$75
Financial aid deadline	3/2
Can first year start other than fall?	No
Student to faculty ratio (fall)	14.4 to 1
Does the university offer:	
housing restricted to law students?	No
graduate housing for which law students are eligible?	Yes

Faculty and Administrators

	Total		Men		Women		Minorities	
	Fall	Spr	Fall	Spr	Fall	Spr	Fall	Spr
Full-time	51	52	36	37	15	15	7	7
Other Full-time	8	8	3	3	5	5	0	0
Deans, librarians, & others who teach	10	10	4	4	6	6	1	1
Part-time	55	62	35	43	20	19	3	4
Total	124	132	78	87	46	45	11	12

Curriculum

		Full-time	Part-time
Typical first-year section size		90	0
Is there typically a "small section" of the first-year class, other than Legal Writing, taught by full-time faculty		Yes	No
If yes, typical size offered last year		30	0
# of classroom course titles beyond 1st year curriculum		203	
# of upper division courses, excluding seminars with an enrollment:	Under 25	101	
	25-49	34	
	50-74	6	
	75-99	11	
	100+	15	
# of seminars		36	
# of seminar positions available		864	
# of seminar positions filled		495	0
# of positions available in simulation courses		365	
# of simulation positions filled		331	0
# of positions available in faculty supervised clinical courses		152	
# of faculty supervised clinical positions filled	136		0
# involved in field placements		101	0
# involved in law journals		238	0
# involved in moot court or trial competitions	66		0
# of credit hours required to graduate		85	

JD Enrollment and Ethnicity

	Men		Women		Full-time		Part-time		1st-year		Total		JD Degs. Awd.
	#	%	#	%	#	%	#	%	#	%	#	%	
African Amer.	17	4.9	29	5.4	46	5.2	0	0.0	15	5.5	46	5.2	15
Amer. Indian	4	1.2	6	1.1	10	1.1	0	0.0	1	0.4	10	1.1	1
Asian Amer.	60	17.4	110	20.6	170	19.3	0	0.0	53	19.5	170	19.3	52
Mex. Amer.	24	7.0	37	6.9	61	6.9	0	0.0	18	6.6	61	6.9	10
Puerto Rican	0	0.0	0	0.0	0	0.0	0	0.0	0	0.0	0	0.0	0
Hispanic	13	3.8	26	4.9	39	4.4	0	0.0	9	3.3	39	4.4	8
Total Minority	118	34.2	208	38.9	326	37.0	0	0.0	96	35.3	326	37.0	86
For. Nation.	0	0.0	0	0.0	0	0.0	0	0.0	0	0.0	0	0.0	0
Caucasian	151	43.8	212	39.6	363	41.3	0	0.0	117	43.0	363	41.3	159
Unknown	76	22.0	115	21.5	191	21.7	0	0.0	59	21.7	191	21.7	77
Total	345	39.2	535	60.8	880	100.0	0	0.0	272	30.9	880		322

Tuition and Fees

	Resident	Nonresident
Full-time	$21,531	$33,776
Part-time	$0	$0

Living Expenses

Estimated living expenses for singles

Living on campus	Living off campus	Living at home
$18,780	$18,780	$18,780

University of California, Berkeley School of Law (Boalt Hall)

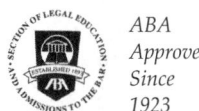

ABA Approved Since 1923

GPA and LSAT Scores

	Total	Full-time	Part-time
# of apps	7,704	7,704	0
# of admits	771	771	0
# of matrics	270	270	0
75% GPA	0.00	3.90	0.00
25% GPA	0.00	3.63	0.00
75% LSAT	0	168	0
25% LSAT	0	161	0

Grants and Scholarships (from prior year)

	Total		Full-time		Part-time	
	#	%	#	%	#	%
Total # of students	924		924		0	
Total # receiving grants	671	72.6	671	72.6	0	0.0
Less than 1/2 tuition	538	58.2	538	58.2	0	0.0
Half to full tuition	89	9.6	89	9.6	0	0.0
Full tuition	17	1.8	17	1.8	0	0.0
More than full tuition	27	2.9	27	2.9	0	0.0
Median grant amount			$6,600		$0	

Informational and Library Resources

# of volumes and volume equivalents	867,899
# of titles	265,696
# of active serial subscriptions	8,007
Study seating capacity inside the library	401
# of professional librarians	17
Hours per week library is open	100
# of open, wired connections available to students	181
# of networked computers available for use by students	168
# of simultaneous wireless users	1,000
Require computer?	N

JD Attrition (from prior year)

	Academic	Other	Total	
	#	#	#	%
1st year	0	4	4	1.4%
2nd year	0	8	8	2.6%
3rd year	0	0	0	0.0%
4th year	0	0	0	0.0%

Employment

	Total	Percentage
Employment status known	274	100.0
Employment status unknown	0	0.0
Employed	253	92.3
Pursuing graduate degrees	5	1.8
Unemployed seeking employment	6	2.2
Unemployed not seeking employment	10	3.6

Type of Employment

# employed in law firms	167	66.0
# employed in business and industry	3	1.2
# employed in government	19	7.5
# employed in public interest	15	5.9
# employed as judicial clerks	41	16.2
# employed in academia	4	1.6

Geographic Location

# employed in state	179	70.8
# employed in foreign countries	5	2.0
# of states where employed	19	

Bar Passage Rates

Jurisdiction	California		
Exam	Sum 03	Win 04	Total
# from school taking bar for the first time	213	15	228
School's pass rate for all first-time takers	91%	67%	89%
State's pass rate for all first-time takers	63%	47%	60%

University of California, Berkeley School of Law (Boalt Hall)

5 Boalt Hall
Berkeley, CA 94720-7200
Phone: 510.642.2274
E-mail: admissions@law.berkeley.edu; Website: www.law.berkeley.edu

■ Introduction

Learning law at Boalt Hall means joining a stimulating intellectual community that is part of a tradition of academic excellence, professional leadership, and public service. Boalt's location in the San Francisco Bay Area, with influences from Silicon Valley and the Pacific Rim, provides an unparalleled opportunity to study at one of the world's leading institutions of legal education and research. Boalt's academic program includes specialized study in business, law, and economics; environmental law; law and technology; international legal studies; comparative legal studies; and social justice. The curriculum is complemented by research centers and clinical programs that provide real client work. Boalt offers a broad three-year curriculum leading to the JD degree and postgraduate programs leading to LLM and JSD degrees. The interdisciplinary Jurisprudence and Social Policy (JSP) program leads to MA and PhD degrees. Boalt is a member of AALS and is ABA-approved.

■ Location

UC Berkeley is a beautiful 1,232-acre campus bordered by wooded rolling hills. Berkeley is known for its intellectual, social, and political engagement. With its global population, rich diversity of arts, and sense of political adventure, Berkeley reflects and affects the rest of the country. Yet, it is an intimate city of friendly neighborhoods, renowned restaurants, coffeehouses, bookstores, parks, and open spaces. Across the bay lies San Francisco, home to internationally recognized museums, opera, ballet, symphony, and restaurants. The mild climate makes outdoor activities possible year-round.

■ Students

Boalt seeks a student body with a broad set of interests, backgrounds, life experiences, and perspectives. The intellectual excellence, varied interests, and backgrounds of the students are among Boalt's great strengths. Students received undergraduate degrees from more than 100 universities, about half at schools outside California.

■ Faculty

Boalt's faculty members are internationally recognized experts in the law, from law and technology to youth violence and juvenile justice to environmental law. They include recipients of 15 Fulbright and 20 Guggenheim fellowships and a MacArthur "genius" grant, as well as authors of casebooks used worldwide. Lecturers are drawn from prominent law firms and institutions.

■ Library and Physical Facilities

The law library contains more than 700,000 volumes and is one of the finest law collections in the world. Its holdings include the Robbins Religious and Civil Law Collection of approximately 360,000 titles in ecclesiastical, civil, comparative, and international law, and extensive collections of foreign, comparative, human rights, and environmental law. It is also a US government depository and is linked to the UC system's holdings of more than seven million volumes. The law library provides online databases, three computer labs with Internet access, four spacious reading rooms, and a photocopying service. Multimedia capabilities are available. Wireless networks are accessible in some reading rooms and at the cafe.

Boalt is composed of three adjoining buildings (and two courtyards) with classrooms, seminar rooms, auditoriums, the law library, a lounge, a reception room, a cafe, dining and study areas, and offices.

■ Housing

The campus Housing Office offers apartments, rental listings, residence halls, and student family apartments. International House accommodates students from the United States and abroad.

■ Admission

Requirements: Bachelor's degree, LSAT, and LSDAS; application fee: $75; deadline: February 1 (early application strongly preferred).

Applicants' LSAT scores and undergraduate grade-point averages (GPAs) are important criteria to evaluate academic ability. Applicants may use the mean LSAT percentile and undergraduate GPAs of the previous year's admitted applicant pool as a guide for assessing their chances of admission. Because Boalt takes other factors into account in making admission decisions, higher or lower scores and grades neither ensure nor preclude admission.

■ Student Activities

Students edit and publish 11 legal periodicals: *African-American Law and Policy Report, Asian Law Journal, Berkeley Business Law Journal, Berkeley Journal of Employment and Labor Law, Berkeley Journal of International Law, Berkeley La Raza Law Journal, Berkeley Technology Law Journal, Berkeley Women's Law Journal, Boalt Journal of Criminal Law, California Law Review,* and *Ecology Law Quarterly.*

More than 50 student groups focus on a variety of interests.

University of California, Berkeley School of Law (Boalt Hall)

■ JD Curriculum

Boalt's broad and innovative curriculum is one of the most dynamic among law schools. Opportunities for study in specific areas of the law connect you to Boalt's renowned faculty members. The first-year curriculum includes Civil Procedure, Contracts, Criminal Law, Legal Research and Writing, Property, Torts, Written and Oral Advocacy, and two elective courses. The flexible second- and third-year curriculum offers a variety of legal topics and course styles, including seminars, individual and group research projects, clinical work, and judicial externships. Students may work on clinical projects providing direct legal services to clients or work with lawyers on large cases or legal matters. The Center for Clinical Education, Boalt's in-house clinical facility, offers the Death Penalty Clinic, the International Human Rights Law Clinic, and the Samuelson Law, Technology & Public Policy Clinic. The East Bay Community Law Center is the community-based component of the program. Other clinical opportunities include the Domestic Violence Clinic and field placements.

■ Financial Aid

Requirements: Boalt Hall Financial Aid Application (optional); FAFSA need analysis form; deadline for priority consideration: March 2.

The law school seeks to provide need-based financial aid sufficient to permit any admitted student to attend. A majority of the students at Boalt Hall receive some form of financial aid.

The financial aid awarded by UC Berkeley's Financial Aid Office is need-based and includes mostly federal student loans. The financial aid awarded by Boalt Hall includes federal student loans and other campus-based awards such as work study. Additionally the law school administers a variety of grants and scholarships based on financial need and/or need and academic merit.

■ Career Services

The Office of Career Services is a resource for students, alumni, and prospective employers. It operates one of the largest on-campus recruitment programs in the country, provides opportunities for legal employment, and maintains an online job database of positions available throughout the nation. The staff conducts career counseling, résumé workshops, and programs on traditional and nontraditional law careers in the private and public sectors.

Applicant Profile Not Available

University of California, Davis School of Law (King Hall)

400 Mrak Hall Drive
Davis, CA 95616-5201
Phone: 530.752.6477
E-mail: lawadmissions@ucdavis.edu; Website: www.law.ucdavis.edu

ABA
Approved
Since
1968

The Basics

Type of school	Public
Term	Semester
Application deadline	2/1
Application fee	$75
Financial aid deadline	3/2
Can first year start other than fall?	No
Student to faculty ratio (fall)	14.3 to 1
Does the university offer:	
housing restricted to law students?	No
graduate housing for which law students are eligible?	Yes

Faculty and Administrators

	Total		Men		Women		Minorities	
	Fall	Spr	Fall	Spr	Fall	Spr	Fall	Spr
Full-time	35	36	22	22	13	14	13	13
Other Full-time	0	0	0	0	0	0	0	0
Deans, librarians, & others who teach	5	5	3	3	2	2	1	1
Part-time	13	23	10	18	3	5	2	4
Total	53	64	35	43	18	21	16	18

Curriculum

		Full-time	Part-time
Typical first-year section size		65	0
Is there typically a "small section" of the first-year class, other than Legal Writing, taught by full-time faculty		Yes	No
If yes, typical size offered last year		32	0
# of classroom course titles beyond 1st year curriculum		71	
# of upper division courses, excluding seminars with an enrollment:	Under 25	31	
	25-49	20	
	50-74	8	
	75-99	3	
	100+	8	
# of seminars		21	
# of seminar positions available		343	
# of seminar positions filled	272		0
# of positions available in simulation courses		405	
# of simulation positions filled	373		0
# of positions available in faculty supervised clinical courses		183	
# of faculty supervised clinical positions filled	113		0
# involved in field placements		99	0
# involved in law journals		64	0
# involved in moot court or trial competitions	105		0
# of credit hours required to graduate		88	

JD Enrollment and Ethnicity

	Men		Women		Full-time		Part-time		1st-year		Total		JD Degs. Awd.
	#	%	#	%	#	%	#	%	#	%	#	%	
African Amer.	6	2.5	9	2.8	15	2.7	0	0.0	2	1.0	15	2.7	5
Amer. Indian	0	0.0	4	1.3	4	0.7	0	0.0	1	0.5	4	0.7	1
Asian Amer.	48	19.7	82	25.7	130	23.1	0	0.0	46	23.6	130	23.1	43
Mex. Amer.	21	8.6	28	8.8	49	8.7	0	0.0	14	7.2	49	8.7	10
Puerto Rican	0	0.0	0	0.0	0	0.0	0	0.0	0	0.0	0	0.0	0
Hispanic	4	1.6	10	3.1	14	2.5	0	0.0	3	1.5	14	2.5	5
Total Minority	79	32.4	133	41.7	212	37.7	0	0.0	66	33.8	212	37.7	64
For. Nation.	2	0.8	5	1.6	7	1.2	0	0.0	0	0.0	7	1.2	2
Caucasian	128	52.5	158	49.5	286	50.8	0	0.0	102	52.3	286	50.8	98
Unknown	35	14.3	23	7.2	58	10.3	0	0.0	27	13.8	58	10.3	26
Total	244	43.3	319	56.7	563	100.0	0	0.0	195	34.6	563		190

Tuition and Fees

	Resident	Nonresident
Full-time	$21,224	$33,469
Part-time	$0	$0

Living Expenses

Estimated living expenses for singles

Living on campus	Living off campus	Living at home
N/A	$13,174	N/A

University of California, Davis School of Law (King Hall)

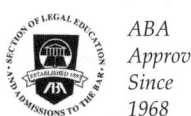

ABA
Approved
Since
1968

GPA and LSAT Scores

	Total	Full-time	Part-time
# of apps	4,439	4,439	0
# of admits	843	843	0
# of matrics	194	194	0
75% GPA	3.72	3.72	0.00
25% GPA	3.39	3.39	0.00
75% LSAT	164	164	0
25% LSAT	160	160	0

Grants and Scholarships (from prior year)

	Total		Full-time		Part-time	
	#	%	#	%	#	%
Total # of students	571		571		0	
Total # receiving grants	461	80.7	461	80.7	0	0.0
Less than 1/2 tuition	455	79.7	455	79.7	0	0.0
Half to full tuition	0	0.0	0	0.0	0	0.0
Full tuition	0	0.0	0	0.0	0	0.0
More than full tuition	6	1.1	6	1.1	0	0.0
Median grant amount			$5,850		$0	

Informational and Library Resources

# of volumes and volume equivalents	434,714
# of titles	92,705
# of active serial subscriptions	4,439
Study seating capacity inside the library	375
# of professional librarians	8
Hours per week library is open	78
# of open, wired connections available to students	0
# of networked computers available for use by students	89
# of simultaneous wireless users	350
Require computer?	N

JD Attrition (from prior year)

	Academic	Other	Total	
	#	#	#	%
1st year	0	15	15	7.8%
2nd year	0	1	1	0.5%
3rd year	0	3	3	1.6%
4th year	0	0	0	0.0%

Employment

	Total	Percentage
Employment status known	162	100.0
Employment status unknown	0	0.0
Employed	134	82.7
Pursuing graduate degrees	4	2.5
Unemployed seeking employment	10	6.2
Unemployed not seeking employment	14	8.6

Type of Employment

	Total	Percentage
# employed in law firms	74	55.2
# employed in business and industry	8	6.0
# employed in government	19	14.2
# employed in public interest	10	7.5
# employed as judicial clerks	7	5.2
# employed in academia	0	0.0

Geographic Location

	Total	Percentage
# employed in state	104	77.6
# employed in foreign countries	1	0.7
# of states where employed	8	

Bar Passage Rates

Jurisdiction	California		
Exam	Sum 03	Win 04	Total
# from school taking bar for the first time	145	3	148
School's pass rate for all first-time takers	81%	0%	80%
State's pass rate for all first-time takers	63%	47%	60%

University of California, Davis School of Law (King Hall)

Admissions Office, 400 Mrak Hall Drive
Davis, CA 95616-5201
Phone: 530.752.6477
E-mail: lawadmissions@ucdavis.edu; Website: www.law.ucdavis.edu

■ Introduction

The School of Law at the University of California, Davis, was founded in 1965. It is accredited by the American Bar Association and is a member of the Association of American Law Schools. The law school building, King Hall, was named for Dr. Martin Luther King Jr. in recognition of his efforts to bring social and political justice to disadvantaged peoples. A statue of Dr. King is located in the law school lobby.

The Davis campus is 20 minutes from Sacramento and a little over an hour from San Francisco, within easy reach of the major recreational areas of Lake Tahoe. The campus occupies 3,600 acres within the college town of Davis, where the law school is well-known for its commitment to community among students and faculty as well as its cutting edge scholarship and teaching.

The close proximity to the state capitol and the Bay Area provide the opportunity for a well-rounded educational experience. The campus also offers a full range of graduate and professional programs.

■ Library and Physical Facilities

All faculty offices, classrooms, and the law library are housed in King Hall on the Davis campus. It has a moot courtroom, a pretrial-skills laboratory, a large computer lab, study carrels, student journal offices, lounges, an infant care co-op, and offices for student organizations, and it is easily accessible to disabled students. Unique to King Hall, every law student is given a key to the building allowing access to the facilities around the clock.

All first-year students are assigned to carrels, and books can be charged to carrels. The library is a federal and California documents depository.

All classrooms have state-of-the-art audiovisual and multimedia equipment. Wireless Internet access is available throughout the building.

The law school's clinical programs are housed in law offices a short distance from King Hall.

■ Curriculum

The law school offers a three-year, full-time program in law leading to the Juris Doctor degree and postgraduate programs leading to an LLM and an MA in International Commercial Law (MICL). At King Hall, a faculty with a national reputation for excellent scholarship and teaching is combined with an outstanding and diverse student body. This year each first-year section has less than 70 students. Each student is taught at least one of the required first-year courses in small sections of 25-35 students. The first year begins with a weeklong introductory course and includes courses in legal research and writing. Upper-division

courses may be selected within broad areas of concentration such as criminal justice, business and taxation, civil litigation, estate planning and taxation, labor and employment law, environmental law, human rights and social justice law, immigration law, intellectual property, international law, and public law. Students may also combine JD studies with a master's or MBA degree.

■ Special Programs

King Hall is renowned for its excellent clinical programs. Students have the opportunity to work under the supervision of practicing lawyers in civil rights, immigration law, environmental law, family law, tax law, employment relations, public interest law, legislative, judicial, prison law, and criminal justice administration. Students also participate in judicial externships in trial and appellate courts.

The Immigration Law Clinic, in which students have as a resource the best immigration law faculty in the United States, allows students to assist immigrants facing deportation. Students prepare clients and their case for hearings.

King Hall has an integrated civil rights curriculum, including a substantive course in civil rights law and clinics representing clients in federal civil rights cases, both at the trial and appellate level. Students participating in the Civil Rights Clinic are certified to appear in federal court, where they represent people who might otherwise have no counsel, and gain firsthand experience in constitutional litigation.

First-year students engage in oral argument as a part of the required legal research and writing course. This provides basic preparation for participation in the formal Moot Court Program, which emphasizes appellate advocacy. Skills courses cover the major elements of both litigation and nonlitigation practice. These include pretrial skills (interviewing, counseling, and document drafting), negotiation, mediation, and alternative dispute resolution, and introductory and advanced trial practice courses.

Students in the Public Interest Law Program receive a certificate based on required coursework, practical experience, and community service. Students in the Environmental Law Program receive a certificate for completion of an environmental curriculum.

■ Admission

The Admission Committee seeks students of diverse backgrounds and interests. The entire application is carefully reviewed with consideration given to many factors, including undergraduate grades, LSAT score, economic and other disadvantages, advanced studies, work experience, extracurricular and community activities, maturity, and commitment to the study of law. Residency is not a

University of California, Davis School of Law (King Hall)

factor in the admission process. An Open House for prospective applicants takes place in October and Information Sessions are held October through January. Guided tours can be arranged.

■ Student Life

King Hall is renowned for its wonderful sense of community. The student body is small compared to that of most law schools, which lessens competition among a highly qualified student cohort. Students work well with each other, faculty, administrators, and staff. Cooperation and collegiality are the hallmark of student life at King Hall.

Faculty and administrators have an open-door policy for students. Student/faculty relations are good. Alumni of the School of Law look back fondly on their law school years.

An academic support program is available to students in the first-year class. There are four student-run journals: the *UC Davis Law Review* and specialized journals in International Law, Environmental Law, and Juvenile Justice Law.

Students sit on the student-faculty Educational Policy, Faculty Appointments, and Admission Committees. There are about 30 active student organizations encompassing a wide variety of interests.

■ Expenses and Financial Aid

The School of Law Financial Aid Office, located in King Hall, is available for the exclusive use of law students.

All financial aid services, from entrance through graduation, are administered at the law school. The law school Financial Aid Office administers all nationally recognized aid programs, such as Perkins Loan and Work Study, and participates in the Federal Direct Student Loan Program. University student loan and grant funds are available for child care. The Free Application for Federal Student Aid (FAFSA) must be submitted by March 2 of the year in which admission is sought. FAFSA applications are accepted after that date, but are not considered for grant or Perkins loan funding.

■ Housing

A wide variety of reasonably priced housing is available in the community. The university maintains on-campus apartments for students and student families.

■ Career Services

The office successfully assists students in securing rewarding summer and post-JD positions. Career Services presents speakers and training workshops geared to student needs and to the hiring cycles of various segments of the legal and law-related job markets. Close to 150 employers visit the school to interview students, and advertise many positions through the office. Students also have access to many professional opportunities through job fairs, online nationwide listings, and other sources.

Applicant Profile

University of California, Davis School of Law (King Hall)
This grid includes only applicants who earned 120-180 LSAT scores under standard administrations

LSAT Score	3.75 +		3.50 - 3.74		3.25 - 3.49		3.00 - 3.24		2.75 - 2.99		2.50 - 2.74		2.25 - 2.49		2.00 - 2.24		Below 2.00		No GPA		Total	
	Apps	Adm	Apps	Adm	Apps	Adm	Apps	Adm	Apps	Adm	Apps	Adm	Apps	Adm	Apps	Adm	Apps	Adm	Apps	Adm	Apps	Adm
175-180	1	1	3	3	4	3	1	1	4	1	1	0	0	0	0	0	0	0	0	0	14	9
170-174	18	17	19	18	27	22	14	10	7	1	6	0	0	0	0	0	0	0	2	1	93	69
165-169	76	74	124	111	116	75	61	18	41	2	21	1	3	0	3	0	0	0	7	5	452	286
160-164	181	123	352	171	332	60	201	18	86	0	44	0	11	1	2	0	0	0	18	4	1227	377
155-159	200	36	337	24	364	9	216	3	104	2	46	0	10	0	3	0	1	0	21	1	1302	75
150-154	101	5	181	11	199	5	188	2	90	0	38	1	12	0	8	0	1	0	14	0	832	24
145-149	24	0	63	0	84	1	85	1	35	0	29	0	15	0	3	0	1	0	12	0	351	2
140-144	10	0	15	0	32	0	36	0	22	0	24	0	11	0	4	0	0	0	5	0	159	0
135-139	0	0	4	0	6	0	7	0	14	0	11	0	3	0	3	0	0	0	7	0	55	0
130-134	0	0	1	0	1	0	4	0	2	0	4	0	4	0	4	0	0	0	2	0	22	0
125-129	0	0	0	0	0	0	1	0	0	0	0	0	1	0	0	0	0	0	1	0	3	0
120-124	0	0	0	0	0	0	0	0	0	0	0	0	0	0	0	0	0	0	0	0	0	0
Total	611	256	1099	338	1165	175	814	53	405	6	224	2	70	1	30	0	3	0	89	11	4510	842

Apps = Number of Applicants   Adm = Number Admitted   Reflects 99% of the total applicant pool.

University of California, Hastings College of the Law

200 McAllister Street
San Francisco, CA 94102
Phone: 415.565.4600; Fax: 415.565.4863
E-mail: admiss@uchastings.edu; Website: www.uchastings.edu

*ABA
Approved
Since
1939*

The Basics

Type of school	Public
Term	Semester
Application deadline	3/1
Application fee	$75
Financial aid deadline	3/1
Can first year start other than fall?	No
Student to faculty ratio (fall)	22.9 to 1
Does the university offer:	
housing restricted to law students?	Yes
graduate housing for which law students are eligible?	Yes

Faculty and Administrators

	Total		Men		Women		Minorities	
	Fall	Spr	Fall	Spr	Fall	Spr	Fall	Spr
Full-time	45	47	30	32	15	15	13	11
Other Full-time	1	1	1	1	0	0	0	0
Deans, librarians, & others who teach	8	8	4	4	4	4	1	1
Part-time	183	158	102	82	81	76	53	29
Total	237	214	137	119	100	95	67	41

Curriculum

	Full-time	Part-time
Typical first-year section size	105	0
Is there typically a "small section" of the first-year class, other than Legal Writing, taught by full-time faculty	Yes	No
If yes, typical size offered last year	53	0
# of classroom course titles beyond 1st year curriculum	133	

# of upper division courses, excluding seminars with an enrollment:		
Under 25	123	
25-49	34	
50-74	15	
75-99	28	
100+	4	

# of seminars	50	
# of seminar positions available	1,012	
# of seminar positions filled	710	0
# of positions available in simulation courses	946	
# of simulation positions filled	806	0
# of positions available in faculty supervised clinical courses	320	
# of faculty supervised clinical positions filled	250	0
# involved in field placements	254	0
# involved in law journals	301	0
# involved in moot court or trial competitions	267	0
# of credit hours required to graduate	86	

JD Enrollment and Ethnicity

	Men		Women		Full-time		Part-time		1st-year		Total		JD Degs. Awd.
	#	%	#	%	#	%	#	%	#	%	#	%	
African Amer.	8	1.4	16	2.4	24	1.9	0	0.0	5	1.2	24	1.9	16
Amer. Indian	1	0.2	3	0.4	4	0.3	0	0.0	1	0.2	4	0.3	1
Asian Amer.	126	22.2	181	26.9	307	24.8	0	0.0	106	24.8	307	24.8	75
Mex. Amer.	18	3.2	23	3.4	41	3.3	0	0.0	16	3.7	41	3.3	16
Puerto Rican	0	0.0	4	0.6	4	0.3	0	0.0	1	0.2	4	0.3	1
Hispanic	11	1.9	23	3.4	33	2.7	1	100.0	11	2.6	34	2.7	12
Total Minority	164	28.9	250	37.2	413	33.4	1	100.0	140	32.8	414	33.4	121
For. Nation.	13	2.3	15	2.2	28	2.3	0	0.0	18	4.2	28	2.3	1
Caucasian	265	46.7	292	43.5	557	45.0	0	0.0	188	44.0	557	45.0	187
Unknown	125	22.0	115	17.1	240	19.4	0	0.0	81	19	240	19.4	87
Total	567	45.8	672	54.2	1238	99.9	1	0.1	427	34.5	1239		396

Tuition and Fees

	Resident	Nonresident
Full-time	$20,919	$33,119
Part-time	$0	$0

Living Expenses

Estimated living expenses for singles

Living on campus	Living off campus	Living at home
$19,400	$19,400	$19,400

University of California, Hastings College of the Law

*ABA
Approved
Since
1939*

GPA and LSAT Scores

	Total	Full-time	Part-time
# of apps	7,176	7,176	0
# of admits	1,398	1,398	0
# of matrics	427	427	0
75% GPA	3.73	3.73	0.00
25% GPA	3.40	3.40	0.00
75% LSAT	165	165	0
25% LSAT	160	160	0

Grants and Scholarships (from prior year)

	Total		Full-time		Part-time	
	#	%	#	%	#	%
Total # of students	1,231		1,225		6	
Total # receiving grants	911	74.0	911	74.4	0	0.0
Less than 1/2 tuition	860	69.9	860	70.2	0	0.0
Half to full tuition	51	4.1	51	4.2	0	0.0
Full tuition	0	0.0	0	0.0	0	0.0
More than full tuition	0	0.0	0	0.0	0	0.0
Median grant amount			$4,300		$0	

Informational and Library Resources

# of volumes and volume equivalents	688,787
# of titles	209,714
# of active serial subscriptions	7,969
Study seating capacity inside the library	1,295
# of professional librarians	11
Hours per week library is open	102
# of open, wired connections available to students	469
# of networked computers available for use by students	155
# of simultaneous wireless users	1,800
Require computer?	N

JD Attrition (from prior year)

	Academic	Other	Total	
	#	#	#	%
1st year	2	12	14	3.3%
2nd year	6	19	25	5.9%
3rd year	1	2	3	0.8%
4th year	0	0	0	0.0%

Employment

	Total	Percentage
Employment status known	399	94.8
Employment status unknown	22	5.2
Employed	368	92.2
Pursuing graduate degrees	7	1.8
Unemployed seeking employment	6	1.5
Unemployed not seeking employment	18	4.5

Type of Employment

# employed in law firms	254	69.0
# employed in business and industry	21	5.7
# employed in government	32	8.7
# employed in public interest	18	4.9
# employed as judicial clerks	20	5.4
# employed in academia	7	1.9

Geographic Location

# employed in state	328	89.1
# employed in foreign countries	2	0.5
# of states where employed	13	

Bar Passage Rates

Jurisdiction	California		
Exam	Sum 03	Win 04	Total
# from school taking bar for the first time	359	22	381	0
School's pass rate for all first-time takers	78%	36%	76%
State's pass rate for all first-time takers	63%	47%	60%

University of California, Hastings College of the Law

200 McAllister Street
San Francisco, CA 94102
Phone: 415.565.4600; Fax: 415.565.4863
E-mail: admiss@uchastings.edu; Website: www.uchastings.edu

■ Introduction

Since its founding in 1878 as the University of California's first school of law, Hastings College of the Law has been at the center of the legal community in the West. In addition to pursuing legal practices that cover the entire spectrum of law, some 450 Hastings graduates sit as judges on the California bench.

Located in San Francisco's Civic Center, UC Hastings provides students with unparalleled access to legal institutions. The California Supreme Court, California Court of Appeal, and the US Court of Appeals for the Ninth Circuit are nearby. Two blocks away is City Hall, as well as superior and municipal courts. With its central location and strong community links to many of the Bay Area's multicultural neighborhoods, UC Hastings offers students an educational experience that is virtually unlimited in its scope and diversity.

■ Library and Physical Facilities

The law library houses an extensive collection of federal and California documents for which UC Hastings is an official depository. The breadth and depth of the library's collection and its state-of-the-art computer-assisted research capabilities draw local attorneys, court personnel, and government agency employees to use the library's resources.

■ Curriculum

The UC Hastings curriculum offers a broad spectrum of courses, from those that are fundamental to all forms of practice to those that reflect increased specialization. After three years of successful study, the student will receive a Juris Doctor degree, conferred by the Regents of the University of California.

Students must complete six semesters in residence, earn 86 semester units, pass all required courses, and earn a cumulative grade-point average of at least C (2.00). The program is designed for full-time students; new students are admitted only at the beginning of the fall semester.

■ Special Programs

- **Legal Education Opportunity Program**—Initiated in 1969, the Legal Education Opportunity Program (LEOP) was designed to assist students in excelling academically at UC Hastings. Students admitted through LEOP are offered a number of academic support services throughout their three years of study, beginning with orientation for incoming students and ending with a supplemental bar review course. To be eligible for LEOP, applicants must complete the LEOP application that includes questions regarding cultural, economic, educational, familial, geographic, linguistic, physical, or social issues or circumstances affecting preparation for law school.
- **Exchange Programs and Institutes**—As part of the second- and third-year course of study, students at UC Hastings have the opportunity to participate in student-exchange programs with Bocconi University of Milano, Italy; Leiden University, The Netherlands; University of Copenhagen, Denmark; University of London and University College of London, England; University of Heidelberg, Germany; and Vermont Law School. Students may also participate in programs offered by UC Hastings Institute: our Center for Local and State Government, our Center for International Justice and Human Rights, and our Center for Negotiation and Dispute Resolution.
- **Joint-degree Program**—UC Hastings students may participate in a joint-degree program between the college and another graduate program in a law-related discipline, such as public policy or business administration. To qualify, students must have completed the first-year curriculum with a grade-point average of 2.5 or higher. A maximum of 12 credits may be transferred to Hastings from a joint-degree program.
- **Judicial Externships**—Judicial externships offer semester-long placements with judges in the US Court of Appeals, US District Courts, US Magistrate Court, California Supreme Court, California Court of Appeal, and San Francisco Superior Court. To qualify, a student needs a minimum grade-point average of 2.5 and successful completion of prerequisites, which vary depending on the court in which the student will work.
- **Upper-division Concentrations**—UC Hastings' large full-time and adjunct faculty has enabled the college to develop comprehensive curricular offerings in specific areas of the law that lead to concentrations. The concentrations include Civil Litigation, International Law, Tax Law, Public Interest Law, and Family Law.

■ Cocurricular and Student Activities

Second-year students may earn academic credit by working on one of six law journals: *Hastings Communication and Entertainment Law Journal, Hastings Constitutional Law Quarterly, Hastings International and Comparative Law Review, Hastings Law Journal, Hastings Women's Law Journal,* and *West-Northwest Journal of Environmental Law and Policy.*

Beyond the first-year moot court requirements, UC Hastings offers Appellate Advocacy as a second-year elective. Students write a brief and present oral arguments based on the record of an actual case pending in the California or the United States Supreme Court.

Second- and third-year students represent UC Hastings in a number of state, national, and international advocacy competitions.

The Civil Justice Clinic, Criminal Practice Clinic, Workers' Rights Clinic, Local Government Clinic, Immigrants' Rights Clinic, Environmental Law Clinic, and Legislation Clinic offer students valuable experience in criminal and civil practice under the supervision of practicing attorneys and faculty.

The governing organization of the student body is the Associated Students of the University of California, Hastings. Additionally, students participate in approximately 50 different student groups.

■ Financial Aid

Typically, more than 80 percent of UC Hastings' students receive financial assistance from college-administered sources. Scholarship awards are made to recognize and encourage the achievement, service, and professional promise of students.

In addition, students who pursue qualifying public interest and government sector employment may receive loan repayment assistance after graduation through the Public Interest Career Assistance Program (PICAP).

■ Housing

On-campus housing is available at McAllister Tower, a 24-story building. The 250 apartments include efficiencies, studios, one-bedroom and a few two-bedroom apartments. Students with families are clustered together to provide mutual support and companionship. The Off-Campus Housing Office provides current listings in San Francisco and the Bay Area, as well as sample leases and other helpful publications.

■ Career Services

As a part of its commitment to students and alumni, UC Hastings offers one of the most comprehensive law career services offices in the West. Students are assisted in clarifying their legal focus, acquiring job search strategies, and honing interviewing techniques.

UC Hastings lists a large volume of part-time and summer jobs for current students and alumni. Through the fall and spring, close to 400 employers visit the campus to interview students for both summer associate positions and permanent postgraduation employment. An additional 200–300 employers from throughout the nation participate in the recruit-by-mail program.

Applicant Profile

University of California, Hastings College of the Law
This grid includes only applicants who earned 120-180 LSAT scores under standard administrations.

LSAT Score	3.75 +		3.50 - 3.74		3.25 - 3.49		3.00 - 3.24		2.75 - 2.99		2.50 - 2.74		2.25 - 2.49		2.00 - 2.24		Below 2.00		No GPA		Total	
	Apps	Adm	Apps	Adm	Apps	Adm	Apps	Adm	Apps	Adm	Apps	Adm	Apps	Adm	Apps	Adm	Apps	Adm	Apps	Adm	Apps	Adm
175-180	5	5	6	6	7	6	4	2	5	3	1	0	0	0	1	0	0	0	0	0	29	22
170-174	26	23	45	42	53	47	35	17	14	0	10	3	2	0	2	0	0	0	3	2	190	134
165-169	128	119	219	199	218	143	101	11	74	6	29	0	11	1	6	0	1	0	12	11	799	490
160-164	297	227	573	258	531	72	332	15	155	2	66	1	21	0	9	0	0	0	24	10	2008	585
155-159	265	47	497	33	513	17	356	16	175	2	75	1	24	0	7	0	1	0	28	2	1941	118
150-154	131	7	255	11	283	14	267	1	145	0	76	0	21	0	12	0	4	0	13	0	1207	33
145-149	39	1	87	3	122	0	147	0	84	0	42	0	21	0	7	0	0	0	19	0	568	4
140-144	17	0	16	0	45	0	59	0	45	0	31	0	18	0	5	0	0	0	8	0	244	0
135-139	1	0	5	0	15	0	20	0	20	0	15	0	8	0	5	0	0	0	3	0	92	0
130-134	0	0	5	0	2	0	2	0	3	0	8	0	5	0	3	0	0	0	1	0	29	0
125-129	0	0	0	0	0	0	2	0	1	0	1	0	1	0	0	0	1	0	0	0	6	0
120-124	0	0	0	0	0	0	0	0	0	0	0	0	0	0	0	0	0	0	0	0	0	0
Total	909	429	1708	552	1789	299	1325	62	721	13	354	5	132	1	57	0	7	0	111	25	7113	1386

Apps = Number of Applicants
Adm = Number Admitted
Reflects 99% of the total applicant pool.

University of California at Los Angeles (UCLA) School of Law

71 Dodd Hall, Box 951445
Los Angeles, CA 90095-1445
Phone: 310.825.4041
E-mail: admissions@law.ucla.edu; Website: www.law.ucla.edu

ABA
Approved
Since
1950

The Basics

Type of school	Public
Term	Semester
Application deadline	2/1
Application fee	$75
Financial aid deadline	3/2
Can first year start other than fall?	No
Student to faculty ratio (fall)	11.6 to 1
Does the university offer:	
housing restricted to law students?	No
graduate housing for which law students are eligible?	Yes

Faculty and Administrators

	Total		Men		Women		Minorities	
	Fall	Spr	Fall	Spr	Fall	Spr	Fall	Spr
Full-time	69	68	52	50	17	18	8	7
Other Full-time	10	9	5	5	5	4	3	2
Deans, librarians, & others who teach	5	5	3	3	2	2	0	0
Part-time	16	30	13	21	3	9	1	3
Total	**100**	**112**	**73**	**79**	**27**	**33**	**12**	**12**

Curriculum

	Full-time	Part-time
Typical first-year section size	76	0
Is there typically a "small section" of the first-year class, other than Legal Writing, taught by full-time faculty	Yes	No
If yes, typical size offered last year	38	0
# of classroom course titles beyond 1st year curriculum		132

# of upper division courses, excluding seminars with an enrollment:		
Under 25		69
25-49		33
50-74		12
75-99		10
100+		7

# of seminars		33
# of seminar positions available		584
# of seminar positions filled	542	0
# of positions available in simulation courses		79
# of simulation positions filled	79	0
# of positions available in faculty supervised clinical courses		304
# of faculty supervised clinical positions filled	285	0
# involved in field placements	52	0
# involved in law journals	260	0
# involved in moot court or trial competitions	130	0
# of credit hours required to graduate		87

JD Enrollment and Ethnicity

	Men		Women		Full-time		Part-time		1st-year		Total		JD Degs.
	#	%	#	%	#	%	#	%	#	%	#	%	Awd.
African Amer.	18	3.7	24	5.2	42	4.5	0	0.0	13	4.2	42	4.5	11
Amer. Indian	7	1.5	7	1.5	14	1.5	0	0.0	5	1.6	14	1.5	4
Asian Amer.	58	12.0	95	20.6	153	16.2	0	0.0	52	16.9	153	16.2	59
Mex. Amer.	31	6.4	37	8.0	68	7.2	0	0.0	16	5.2	68	7.2	25
Puerto Rican	1	0.2	0	0.0	1	0.1	0	0.0	1	0.3	1	0.1	1
Hispanic	4	0.8	1	0.2	5	0.5	0	0.0	2	0.7	5	0.5	1
Total Minority	119	24.7	164	35.6	283	30.0	0	0.0	89	29.0	283	30.0	101
For. Nation.	1	0.2	0	0.0	1	0.1	0	0.0	1	0.3	1	0.1	0
Caucasian	245	50.8	191	41.4	436	46.2	0	0.0	131	42.7	436	46.2	139
Unknown	117	24.3	106	23.0	223	23.6	0	0.0	86	28.0	223	23.6	88
Total	482	51.1	461	48.9	943	100.0	0	0.0	307	32.6	943		328

Tuition and Fees

	Resident	Nonresident
Full-time	$22,123	$33,168
Part-time	$0	$0

Living Expenses

Estimated living expenses for singles

Living on campus	Living off campus	Living at home
N/A	$18,609	$10,821

University of California at Los Angeles (UCLA) School of Law

ABA
Approved
Since
1950

GPA and LSAT Scores

	Total	Full-time	Part-time
# of apps	7,260	7,260	0
# of admits	987	987	0
# of matrics	308	308	0
75% GPA	3.84	3.84	0.00
25% GPA	3.47	3.47	0.00
75% LSAT	168	168	0
25% LSAT	163	163	0

Grants and Scholarships (from prior year)

	Total		Full-time		Part-time	
	#	%	#	%	#	%
Total # of students	962		962		0	
Total # receiving grants	501	52.1	501	52.1	0	0.0
Less than 1/2 tuition	457	47.5	457	47.5	0	0.0
Half to full tuition	19	2.0	19	2.0	0	0.0
Full tuition	25	2.6	25	2.6	0	0.0
More than full tuition	0	0.0	0	0.0	0	0.0
Median grant amount			$6,440		$0	

Informational and Library Resources

# of volumes and volume equivalents	619,403
# of titles	223,967
# of active serial subscriptions	8,322
Study seating capacity inside the library	774
# of professional librarians	14
Hours per week library is open	97
# of open, wired connections available to students	1,620
# of networked computers available for use by students	128
# of simultaneous wireless users	0
Require computer?	N

JD Attrition (from prior year)

	Academic	Other	Total	
	#	#	#	%
1st year	0	14	14	4.6%
2nd year	0	3	3	0.9%
3rd year	0	1	1	0.3%
4th year	0	0	0	0.0%

Employment

	Total	Percentage
Employment status known	326	100.0
Employment status unknown	0	0.0
Employed	277	85.0
Pursuing graduate degrees	0	0.0
Unemployed seeking employment	10	3.1
Unemployed not seeking employment	39	12.0

Type of Employment

	Total	Percentage
# employed in law firms	209	75.5
# employed in business and industry	8	2.9
# employed in government	15	5.4
# employed in public interest	18	6.5
# employed as judicial clerks	20	7.2
# employed in academia	3	1.1

Geographic Location

	Total	Percentage
# employed in state	236	85.2
# employed in foreign countries	2	0.7
# of states where employed	13	

Bar Passage Rates

Jurisdiction	California			New York		
Exam	Sum 03	Win 04	Total	Sum 03	Win 04	Total
# from school taking bar for the first time	270	14	284	19	3	22
School's pass rate for all first-time takers	89%	79%	89%	100%	100%	100%
State's pass rate for all first-time takers	63%	47%	60%	78%	58%	75%

University of California at Los Angeles (UCLA) School of Law

Law Admissions Office, 71 Dodd Hall, Box 951445
Los Angeles, CA 90095-1445
Phone: 310.825.4041
E-mail: admissions@law.ucla.edu; Website: www.law.ucla.edu

■ Introduction

The School of Law is set on the beautiful UCLA campus, located in the foothills of the Santa Monica Mountains. Our location provides ready access to the exciting city of Los Angeles, while at the same time offering students a refuge from urban life.

■ Library

The renovated and expanded law library gives UCLA law students a spacious, electronically equipped facility for quiet study and reflection.

■ Admission

All applicants must have a baccalaureate degree from an accredited university or college of approved standing and must take the LSAT no later than the December administration. Students are admitted for the fall semester only.

Admission is based primarily on proven outstanding academic and intellectual ability measured largely by the LSAT and the quality of undergraduate education as determined by not only the GPA, but also by such factors as the breadth, depth, and rigor of the undergraduate educational program. The Admissions Committee may also consider whether economic, physical, or other hardships and challenges have been overcome. Distinctive programmatic contributions, community or public service, letters of recommendation, work experience, career achievement, language ability, and career goals (with particular attention paid to the likelihood of the applicant representing underrepresented communities) are also factors taken into consideration.

UCLA accepts transfer applications into the second-year class from students with excellent first-year credentials from an ABA-accredited law school. Transfer applications are available online in May and due in early July.

■ Residency

Applicants admitted to the law school as nonresident students (for tuition purposes) are eligible to be considered for resident classification if certain eligibility requirements are met. Most nonresident law students achieve residency status during the second year of law school.

■ Financial Aid

Financial Aid assistance is available in the form of scholarships, need-based grants, and educational loans. The FAFSA must be filed by March 2. The Financial Aid Summary should be submitted with the law school application, both of which are due on or before February 1.

■ Curriculum

The law school offers a three-year, full-time course of study leading to a Juris Doctor degree. Evening, summer, or part-time programs are not offered. UCLA differs from many other institutions in that it invests major resources in its first-year Lawyering Skills Program. This program combines the beginning of skills training, such as client interviewing and counseling, with traditional legal research and writing.

As a requirement for graduation, each student must complete a Substantial Analytic Writing (SAW) project during the second or third year of law school.

The Clinical Education Program provides extensive and rigorous practical training through simulated and actual client contact. Examples of clinical courses regularly offered are the Environmental Law Clinic; Trial Advocacy; Doing Business in China; and Interviewing, Counseling, and Negotiation.

The LLM Master of Laws Program at UCLA is a one-year graduate program with a comparative law focus designed exclusively for outstanding graduates from foreign law schools.

The Doctor of Juridical Science (SJD) is a highly selective degree program designed for those pursuing careers as teachers and scholars of law. Applicants must hold a JD degree or foreign equivalent and an LLM degree (or be enrolled in a program leading to an LLM degree).

■ Special Programs

The Public Interest Law and Policy Program marks a distinct break with the way schools have traditionally trained lawyers for public interest careers. This program, which has a limited enrollment of 25 students, builds on the array of public interest oriented courses, programs, and activities. Participants take a special section of Lawyering Skills and participate in a first-year workshop, advanced seminars, and extracurricular programs.

The Corporate Law Program gives second- and third-year law students a coherent program of focused coursework in an important practice area.

The Critical Race Studies Concentration is available to second- and third-year students. This specialization is appropriate for law students who seek advanced study in areas such as race and the law, critical race theory, civil rights, public policy, and other legal practice areas that are likely to involve working with racial minority clients and communities or working to combat inequalities.

The Williams Project is the nation's first think tank dedicated to the field of sexual orientation law and public policy. The project supports legal scholarship, legal research, policy analysis, and education regarding sexual

University of California at Los Angeles (UCLA) School of Law

orientation discrimination and other legal issues that affect lesbian and gay people.

The law school also has a full-time, semester-long Judicial and Agency Externship Program. Nonprofit and government agency placements are primarily in Los Angeles, New York, San Francisco, and Washington, DC; judicial externships are with federal judges in Los Angeles.

■ Academic Support

UCLA School of Law is a recognized leader in academic support, providing assistance to students both before matriculation and throughout their law school careers.

■ Joint Degrees

UCLA School of Law offers preapproved programs that lead to a joint Juris Doctor and Master's degrees in Afro-American Studies, American Indian Studies, Business Administration, Public Health, Public Policy, Social Welfare, and Urban Planning.

■ Student Activities

Students edit and publish the *UCLA Law Review, þPacific American Law Jouqnal, Chicano/Latino Law Review, UCLA Pacific Basin Law Journal, Entertainment Law Review, UCLA Journal of Environmental Law and Policy, UCLA Journal of Islamic & Near Eastern Law, UCLA Journal of Law and Technology, Dukeminier Journal of Sexual Orientation & Law, UCLA Women's Law Journal, The Indigenous Peoples Journal of Law, Culture and Resistance*, and the *UCLA Journal of International and Foreign Affairs*. Diverse student interests are represented in more than 30 student organizations. The Moot Court Honors Program is open to all second-year students and offers a large and effective program of mock appellate advocacy. There is a very active Student Bar Association. Students publish a law school newspaper, and participate in a student/faculty musical.

■ Housing

Many housing options are open to UCLA School of Law students. There are university-owned apartments for single graduate students, single students who are parents, and married students with or without children. Also available for rent are privately owned apartments as well as rooms and guesthouses in neighboring homes.

■ Career Services

The Office of Career Services coordinates on-campus interviews and other career fairs with approximately 400 interviewers from law firms, corporations, government agencies, and public interest organizations who visit the school annually.

The office offers private counseling sessions to students and alumni. It also sponsors educational programs and receptions, including a practice specialty series with practitioners, a mock-interview program, a government reception and information fair, and a small/midsize law firm reception.

In the Class of 2003, there was a 96.5 percent employment rate nine months after graduation.

Applicant Profile

University of California at Los Angeles (UCLA) School of Law
This grid includes only applicants who earned 120-180 LSAT scores under standard administrations.

LSAT Score	3.75 +		3.50 - 3.74		3.25 - 3.49		3.00 - 3.24		2.75 - 2.99		2.50 - 2.74		2.25 - 2.49		2.00 - 2.24		Below 2.00		No GPA		Total	
	Apps	Adm	Apps	Adm	Apps	Adm	Apps	Adm	Apps	Adm	Apps	Adm	Apps	Adm	Apps	Adm	Apps	Adm	Apps	Adm	Apps	Adm
175-180	20	20	20	19	14	9	9	4	6	1	2	0	0	0	0	0	0	0	0	0	71	53
170-174	104	99	134	108	104	49	50	6	13	0	9	0	1	0	1	0	0	0	6	1	422	263
165-169	351	281	439	149	310	41	130	4	62	0	22	1	14	0	3	0	0	0	17	4	1348	480
160-164	452	44	744	37	485	27	257	9	96	0	52	0	11	0	3	0	1	0	38	0	2139	117
155-159	253	10	415	14	372	14	232	8	111	1	51	0	17	0	6	0	1	0	30	0	1488	47
150-154	118	4	212	8	192	3	191	5	88	0	41	0	25	0	8	0	0	0	20	0	895	20
145-149	38	0	95	0	80	0	97	0	62	0	44	0	19	0	6	0	2	0	13	0	456	0
140-144	15	0	15	0	50	0	50	0	41	0	28	0	13	0	9	0	1	0	10	0	232	0
135-139	3	0	6	0	11	0	15	0	18	0	13	0	8	0	5	0	0	0	4	0	83	0
130-134	0	0	2	0	4	0	5	0	2	0	7	0	4	0	5	0	2	0	2	0	33	0
125-129	0	0	0	0	0	0	2	0	0	0	1	0	5	0	1	0	0	0	2	0	11	0
120-124	0	0	0	0	0	0	0	0	0	0	1	0	1	0	0	0	0	0	0	0	2	0
Total	1354	458	2082	335	1622	143	1038	36	499	2	271	1	118	0	47	0	7	0	142	5	7180	980

Apps = Number of Applicants   Adm = Number Admitted   Reflects 99% of the total applicant pool.

California Western School of Law

225 Cedar Street
San Diego, CA 92101
Phone: 800.255.4252 ext. 1401; Bulletin requests: 619.525.7083; Fax: 619.615.1401
E-mail: admissions@cwsl.edu; Website: www.californiawestern.edu

ABA
Approved
Since
1962

The Basics

Type of school	Private
Term	Trimester
Application deadline	4/1 11/1
Application fee	$45
Financial aid deadline	2/11 4/8 10/7
Can first year start other than fall?	Yes
Student to faculty ratio (fall)	19.5 to 1
Does the university offer:	
housing restricted to law students?	No
graduate housing for which law students are eligible?	No

Faculty and Administrators

	Total		Men		Women		Minorities	
	Fall	Spr	Fall	Spr	Fall	Spr	Fall	Spr
Full-time	38	35	24	22	14	13	7	7
Other Full-time	3	2	1	1	2	1	1	1
Deans, librarians, & others who teach	10	10	4	4	6	6	1	1
Part-time	34	27	22	18	12	9	3	1
Total	85	74	51	45	34	29	12	10

Curriculum

	Full-time	Part-time
Typical first-year section size	82	0
Is there typically a "small section" of the first-year class, other than Legal Writing, taught by full-time faculty	No	No
If yes, typical size offered last year	0	0
# of classroom course titles beyond 1st year curriculum	116	
# of upper division courses, excluding seminars with an enrollment: Under 25	113	
25-49	40	
50-74	14	
75-99	12	
100+	9	
# of seminars	32	
# of seminar positions available	730	
# of seminar positions filled	512	66
# of positions available in simulation courses	1,666	
# of simulation positions filled	1,225	100
# of positions available in faculty supervised clinical courses	118	
# of faculty supervised clinical positions filled	39	4
# involved in field placements	155	16
# involved in law journals	67	6
# involved in moot court or trial competitions	41	2
# of credit hours required to graduate	89	

JD Enrollment and Ethnicity

	Men #	Men %	Women #	Women %	Full-time #	Full-time %	Part-time #	Part-time %	1st-year #	1st-year %	Total #	Total %	JD Degs. Awd.
African Amer.	5	1.1	14	3.0	9	1.1	10	7.9	4	1.4	19	2.0	6
Amer. Indian	7	1.5	3	0.6	7	0.9	3	2.4	2	0.7	10	1.1	1
Asian Amer.	41	8.9	55	11.7	84	10.4	12	9.5	32	11.0	96	10.3	22
Mex. Amer.	24	5.2	27	5.7	39	4.8	12	9.5	14	4.8	51	5.5	18
Puerto Rican	0	0.0	3	0.6	1	0.1	2	1.6	0	0.0	3	0.3	2
Hispanic	9	1.9	13	2.8	20	2.5	2	1.6	9	3.1	22	2.4	4
Total Minority	86	18.6	115	24.4	160	19.8	41	32.5	61	21.0	201	21.5	53
For. Nation.	7	1.5	10	2.1	16	2.0	1	0.8	4	1.4	17	1.8	3
Caucasian	295	63.7	309	65.6	527	65.2	77	61.1	176	60.5	604	64.7	190
Unknown	75	16.2	37	7.9	105	13.0	7	5.6	50	17.2	112	12.0	2
Total	463	49.6	471	50.4	808	86.5	126	13.5	291	31.2	934		248

Tuition and Fees

	Resident	Nonresident
Full-time	$28,920	$28,920
Part-time	$20,450	$20,450

Living Expenses

Estimated living expenses for singles

Living on campus	Living off campus	Living at home
N/A	$16,904	$10,154

California Western School of Law

ABA Approved Since 1962

GPA and LSAT Scores

	Total	Full-time	Part-time
# of apps	4,304	4,031	273
# of admits	1,224	1,156	68
# of matrics	330	306	24
75% GPA	3.47	3.47	3.26
25% GPA	2.94	2.95	2.86
75% LSAT	157	157	156
25% LSAT	152	152	151

Grants and Scholarships (from prior year)

	Total		Full-time		Part-time	
	#	%	#	%	#	%
Total # of students	955		831		124	
Total # receiving grants	318	33.3	282	33.9	36	29.0
Less than 1/2 tuition	118	12.4	105	12.6	13	10.5
Half to full tuition	108	11.3	96	11.6	12	9.7
Full tuition	60	6.3	49	5.9	11	8.9
More than full tuition	32	3.4	32	3.9	0	0.0
Median grant amount			$13,100		$9,250	

Informational and Library Resources

# of volumes and volume equivalents	313,598
# of titles	136,453
# of active serial subscriptions	3,955
Study seating capacity inside the library	626
# of professional librarians	9
Hours per week library is open	110
# of open, wired connections available to students	515
# of networked computers available for use by students	80
# of simultaneous wireless users	400
Require computer?	N

JD Attrition (from prior year)

	Academic	Other	Total	
	#	#	#	%
1st year	35	63	98	28.4%
2nd year	0	10	10	2.6%
3rd year	0	0	0	0.0%
4th year	0	0	0	0.0%

Employment

	Total	Percentage
Employment status known	221	93.6
Employment status unknown	15	6.4
Employed	192	86.9
Pursuing graduate degrees	2	0.9
Unemployed seeking employment	22	10.0
Unemployed not seeking employment	5	2.3

Type of Employment

# employed in law firms	126	65.6
# employed in business and industry	18	9.4
# employed in government	19	9.9
# employed in public interest	6	3.1
# employed as judicial clerks	10	5.2
# employed in academia	2	1.0

Geographic Location

# employed in state	132	68.7
# employed in foreign countries	4	2.1
# of states where employed		20

Bar Passage Rates

Jurisdiction	California		
Exam	Sum 03	Win 04	Total
# from school taking bar for the first time	82	80	162
School's pass rate for all first-time takers	62%	61%	62%
State's pass rate for all first-time takers	63%	47%	60%

California Western School of Law

225 Cedar Street
San Diego, CA 92101
Phone: 800.255.4252 ext. 1401; Bulletin requests: 619.525.7083; Fax: 619.615.1401
E-mail: admissions@cwsl.edu; Website: www.californiawestern.edu

■ Introduction

Chartered in 1924, California Western School of Law is an independent, not-for-profit institution accredited by the ABA (1962) and is a member of the AALS (1967). The downtown San Diego law school complements the traditional curriculum with innovative programs that advance a student's educational experience and capacity to enter the legal profession with superior training.

■ Library and Physical Facilities

The new, award-winning, four-story, 50,000-square-foot law library was dedicated September 11, 2000. The law library is wired with high-speed digital lines for fast network communications. There are 250 data ports for laptop computers in the building. Recently completed extensive renovation of the historic classroom building provides a 74-seat lecture hall, office space for 30 on-campus student organizations, an 1,840-square-foot student lounge, individual study rooms, and a computer lab. Students enjoy additional access to the student network and Internet via campus-wide wireless technology.

■ Curriculum

The trimester academic calendar allows students to study law year-round to complete their legal education in two years. California Western offers a part-time day program. The curriculum offers a broad and diverse selection that includes such contemporary fields as entertainment and sports law, biotechnology law, and environmental law.

Areas of concentration, with curriculum requirements for upper-level students, provide an overview of international law; labor and employment law; child, family, and elder law; criminal prosecution and defense; creative problem-solving; and intellectual property, telecommunications, and technology-regulations law.

■ Dual-Degree Program

Students interested in business, social work, history, or political science can apply to the dual-degree program, which permits students to study two disciplines concurrently at California Western and San Diego State University (JD/MBA and JD/MSW) and the University of California, San Diego (JD/PhD in political science or history).

■ University of California, San Diego Affiliation

California Western and the University of California, San Diego, have an Agreement of Association that will provide broad interdisciplinary opportunities for the faculty and students of both institutions. Plans include provisions for new academic programs, joint research efforts, sharing of facilities and involvement of faculty and board members in each other's academic bodies and community outreach programs. Planned programs in law and medicine draw on the expertise of both institutions.

■ Study Abroad

Students have the opportunity to study abroad and intern at British legal offices. Law in London is a summer program that provides students with a chance to study English and European Union Law and Practice. The program is offered in conjunction with The College of Law of England and Wales–Europe's largest provider of legal training. Students may also spend a summer abroad in Galway, Ireland, in Prague, Czech Republic, or at the University of Malta, studying international law. Semester abroad opportunities are available at Victoria University of Wellington in New Zealand and at Leiden University School of Law in The Netherlands.

■ Special Programs

The McGill Center for Creative Problem Solving is a training institute at California Western that provides the community with collaborative approaches to communication, conflict resolution, and problem solving.

Through the California Innocence Project, which is part of the Institute for Criminal Defense Advocacy, law students work alongside practicing criminal defense lawyers to seek the release of wrongfully convicted prisoners. Law students assist in the investigation, write briefs, and advocate for the release of clients. The school also offers an LLM program for foreign law graduates and an LLM in trial advocacy.

■ Clinical Internship Program

California Western's Clinical Internship Program provides opportunities for students to gain practical lawyering experience in law offices, agencies, and courts. Nearly 80 percent of California Western students participate in this popular program. Students have the opportunity to intern in almost any area of law. Some out-of-town internships are available for situations where a similar experience is not available in San Diego. Students have arranged internships at the United Nations, Paramount Studios, the Federal Communications Commission, and abroad, such as in Brazil, Poland, Singapore, Jamaica, and Liechtenstein.

■ Student Activities

The *Law Review* and the *International Law Journal* publish articles by experts in particular fields of work and study as well as by California Western students. Students edit and manage the publications under supervision from faculty advisors. Nearly 30 student organizations reflect a broad range of interest and diversity. Students also participate in advocacy and trial competitions.

■ Career Services

Career Services offers individualized, professional advice to students about their personal career goals and tailors strategies to assist students in reaching those goals. The department coordinates the On-Campus Recruitment program, practice area panel discussions, a national alumni mentor network, the Pro Bono Honors program, and access to technological resources for career development.

■ Alumni

More than 6,000 California Western alumni work in large firms, domestic and foreign governments, large corporations, private practice, the judiciary, and academia. The law school's Alumni Admissions Recruiter program matches alumni with prospective students in the area in which they reside. The Admissions Office can provide prospective students with a list of alumni in their area who are available to talk with them.

■ Diversity

California Western's belief is that a richly diversified student body enhances the academic and interpersonal experiences of the law school. More than half of the student body is female and approximately one-third is ethnic minority. California Western does not discriminate on the basis of race, color, creed, religion, sex, national origin, disability, sexual orientation, or veteran status.

■ Admission

Admission decisions are made on a rolling basis. Applicants are admitted based on an evaluation of the LSAT score, undergraduate academic record, personal statement, letters of recommendation, and other criteria, including work experience, campus and community activities, life/personal experiences, and evidence of leadership promise. Students are admitted to California Western both in August and January. Bachelor's degree and registration with LSDAS are required. Application deadlines: Fall—April 1; Spring—November 1.

■ Financial Aid and Scholarships

More than 85 percent of California Western's students are assisted with their legal education by financial aid programs. Need-based financial aid includes loans, grants, and work study. Numerous scholarships are awarded based on academic criteria and LSAT scores. Scholarships include the prestigious Kennedy Scholarship, which, among other benefits, provides full tuition for three years. Other merit-based full and partial scholarships are awarded to incoming students, including diversity, career transition, and creative problem-solving scholarships. Academic achievement scholarships are available to continuing students.

Applicant Profile

California Western School of Law

LSAT	3.75 +		3.50 - 3.74		3.25 - 3.49		3.00 - 3.24		2.75 - 2.99		2.50 - 2.74		Below 2.50		No GPA		Total	
Score	Apps	Adm	Apps	Adm	Apps	Adm	Apps	Adm	Apps	Adm	Apps	Adm	Apps	Adm	Apps	Adm	Apps	Adm
170-180	1	1	1	1	1	1	1	1	1	1	0	0	1	1	0	0	6	6
165-169	5	5	2	2	7	7	7	6	3	3	5	5	6	6	1	0	36	34
160-164	18	17	18	17	24	23	31	31	33	32	14	14	18	14	1	1	157	149
155-159	39	39	68	67	110	104	112	102	103	81	68	40	65	27	5	4	570	464
150-154	48	37	158	110	237	129	261	82	206	39	147	13	94	5	10	4	1161	419
145-149	42	7	148	13	213	10	283	8	218	4	142	0	107	1	14	1	1167	44
140-144	19	0	57	2	94	0	143	0	112	0	86	0	75	0	9	0	595	2
Below 140	7	0	20	0	23	0	46	0	56	0	48	0	43	0	4	0	247	0
Total	179	106	472	212	709	274	884	230	732	160	510	72	409	54	44	10	3939	1118

Apps = Number of Applicants
Adm = Number Admitted
Applicants with 120-180 LSAT scores earned under standard administrations
Miscellaneous applicants with no LSAT (i.e., MCL/LLM program) and nonstandard administration (not in grid)

Campbell University, Norman Adrian Wiggins School of Law

PO Box 158, 113 Main Street
Buies Creek, NC 27506
Phone: 800.334.4111, ext. 1754; Fax: 910.893.1780
E-mail: admissions@law.campbell.edu; Website: www.law.campbell.edu

ABA Approved Since 1979

The Basics

Type of school	Private
Term	Semester
Application deadline	3/31
Application fee	$50
Financial aid deadline	3/15
Can first year start other than fall?	No
Student to faculty ratio (fall)	19.2 to 1
Does the university offer:	
housing restricted to law students?	No
graduate housing for which law students are eligible?	Yes

Faculty and Administrators

	Total		Men		Women		Minorities	
	Fall	Spr	Fall	Spr	Fall	Spr	Fall	Spr
Full-time	16	15	14	13	2	2	2	1
Other Full-time	1	1	1	1	0	0	0	0
Deans, librarians, & others who teach	5	5	3	3	2	2	0	0
Part-time	12	15	9	11	3	4	0	0
Total	34	36	27	28	7	8	2	1

Curriculum

	Full-time	Part-time
Typical first-year section size	98	0
Is there typically a "small section" of the first-year class, other than Legal Writing, taught by full-time faculty	Yes	No
If yes, typical size offered last year	49	0
# of classroom course titles beyond 1st year curriculum	79	
# of upper division courses, excluding seminars with an enrollment: Under 25	36	
25-49	34	
50-74	7	
75-99	5	
100+	2	
# of seminars	12	
# of seminar positions available	273	
# of seminar positions filled	234	0
# of positions available in simulation courses	115	
# of simulation positions filled	115	0
# of positions available in faculty supervised clinical courses	0	
# of faculty supervised clinical positions filled	0	0
# involved in field placements	25	0
# involved in law journals	33	0
# involved in moot court or trial competitions	55	0
# of credit hours required to graduate	90	

JD Enrollment and Ethnicity

	Men #	Men %	Women #	Women %	Full-time #	Full-time %	Part-time #	Part-time %	1st-year #	1st-year %	Total #	Total %	JD Degs. Awd.
African Amer.	5	2.5	11	6.4	16	4.3	0	0.0	11	7.5	16	4.3	2
Amer. Indian	2	1.0	2	1.2	4	1.1	0	0.0	4	2.7	4	1.1	1
Asian Amer.	3	1.5	4	2.3	7	1.9	0	0.0	5	3.4	7	1.9	0
Mex. Amer.	0	0.0	1	0.6	1	0.3	0	0.0	0	0.0	1	0.3	0
Puerto Rican	1	0.5	2	1.2	3	0.8	0	0.0	3	2.0	3	0.8	1
Hispanic	3	1.5	4	2.3	7	1.9	0	0.0	0	0.0	7	1.9	0
Total Minority	14	7.1	24	14.0	38	10.3	0	0.0	23	15.6	38	10.3	4
For. Nation.	0	0.0	3	1.7	3	0.8	0	0.0	0	0.0	3	0.8	0
Caucasian	183	92.9	145	84.3	328	88.9	0	0.0	124	84.4	328	88.9	92
Unknown	0	0.0	0	0.0	0	0.0	0	0.0	0	0.0	0	0.0	1
Total	197	53.4	172	46.6	369	100.0	0	0.0	147	39.8	369		97

Tuition and Fees

	Resident	Nonresident
Full-time	$22,252	$22,252
Part-time	$0	$0

Living Expenses

Estimated living expenses for singles

Living on campus	Living off campus	Living at home
$10,120	$12,718	N/A

Campbell University, Norman Adrian Wiggins School of Law

ABA
Approved
Since
1979

GPA and LSAT Scores

	Total	Full-time	Part-time
# of apps	1,194	1,194	0
# of admits	249	249	0
# of matrics	143	143	0
75% GPA	0.00	3.50	0.00
25% GPA	0.00	3.01	0.00
75% LSAT	0	157	0
25% LSAT	0	152	0

Grants and Scholarships (from prior year)

	Total		Full-time		Part-time	
	#	%	#	%	#	%
Total # of students	337		337		0	
Total # receiving grants	136	40.4	136	40.4	0	0.0
Less than 1/2 tuition	117	34.7	117	34.7	0	0.0
Half to full tuition	14	4.2	14	4.2	0	0.0
Full tuition	5	1.5	5	1.5	0	0.0
More than full tuition	0	0.0	0	0.0	0	0.0
Median grant amount			$3,000		$0	

Informational and Library Resources

# of volumes and volume equivalents	186,913
# of titles	22,048
# of active serial subscriptions	2,584
Study seating capacity inside the library	411
# of professional librarians	4
Hours per week library is open	103
# of open, wired connections available to students	165
# of networked computers available for use by students	53
# of simultaneous wireless users	350
Require computer?	N

JD Attrition (from prior year)

	Academic	Other	Total	
	#	#	#	%
1st year	14	12	26	21.8%
2nd year	4	1	5	4.3%
3rd year	0	0	0	0.0%
4th year	0	0	0	0.0%

Employment

	Total	Percentage
Employment status known	93	95.9
Employment status unknown	4	4.1
Employed	91	97.8
Pursuing graduate degrees	1	1.1
Unemployed seeking employment	1	1.1
Unemployed not seeking employment	0	0.0

Type of Employment

# employed in law firms	68	74.7
# employed in business and industry	1	1.1
# employed in government	13	14.3
# employed in public interest	1	1.1
# employed as judicial clerks	7	7.7
# employed in academia	1	1.1

Geographic Location

# employed in state	85	93.4
# employed in foreign countries	1	1.1
# of states where employed	5	

Bar Passage Rates

Jurisdiction	North Carolina		
Exam	Sum 03	Win 04	Total
# from school taking bar for the first time	87	3	90
School's pass rate for all first-time takers	92%	33%	90%
State's pass rate for all first-time takers	78%	64%	76%

Campbell University, Norman Adrian Wiggins School of Law

PO Box 158, 113 Main Street
Buies Creek, NC 27506
Phone: 800.334.4111, ext. 1754; Fax: 910.893.1780
E-mail: admissions@law.campbell.edu; Website: www.law.campbell.edu

■ Introduction

The School of Law admitted its charter class in August 1976 and was accredited by the American Bar Association in 1979. The School of Law enjoys a heritage derived from three distinct but interrelated traditions: the noble tradition of the legal profession, the Judeo-Christian tradition, and the finer traditions of the new rural South.

Campbell University occupies a spacious 875-acre campus in the rural village of Buies Creek, located approximately 30 miles from Raleigh, Fayetteville, and the Research Triangle Park, one of the nation's leading technological and research centers. The location combines the advantages of accessible urban convenience with the friendly atmosphere of the rural university village.

Established in 1887 as Buies Creek Academy, Campbell University offers numerous undergraduate degrees and graduate instruction in law, business, education, divinity, and pharmacy. Campbell University is the second-largest Baptist-affiliated university in the United States and the second-largest private university in North Carolina.

■ Library and Physical Facilities

The School of Law is housed in historic Kivett Hall, which was renovated in 1992, and Wiggins Hall, completed that same year. The buildings contain the law library; classrooms featuring the latest in electronic instructional equipment; two courtrooms featuring state-of-the-art video, audio, and computer equipment; faculty and administrative offices; a student commons and lounge area; and offices for various student organizations.

The library contains individual study carrels, traditional reading tables, casual seating, conference rooms, and computer labs that provide students with a variety of study and research options. Students may access the university network and Internet through computers in the computer labs, through Ethernet connections in the library study carrels, and through wireless connectivity in the library and throughout the law school.

■ Curriculum

The School of Law's curriculum has been carefully planned to coalesce the practical and theoretical. Each Campbell student has at least two courtroom experiences: an appellate argument and a mock trial. In 1986, Campbell received the American College of Trial Lawyers' Emil Gumpert Award as the outstanding trial advocacy program in the nation.

Because there are certain courses that the School of Law believes are essential to a practicing lawyer, a majority of the total hours of study consists of required courses. Courses considered electives at other schools, such as wills and trusts, evidence, and commercial law, are required at Campbell. By taking these essential courses during law school, students are well prepared for the bar examination and the practice of law.

The curriculum is designed to produce well-rounded attorneys. Over 20 percent of the required courses are devoted to business topics. Campbell is one of the few schools in the nation to provide a law office management course. The school offers a broad range of electives, many in the form of seminars of 10 or fewer students. Students may choose to pursue elective tracks in trial and appellate advocacy or business transactions.

In 2003, Campbell's Professionalism Development Program received the ABA's E. Smythe Gambrell Professionalism Award.

■ Special Programs

Through a cooperative agreement between the School of Law and the university's Lundy-Fetterman School of Business, students may pursue the JD and MBA degrees concurrently. The law school is also engaged in a cooperative program with the Handong International Law School, which allows Campbell students to attend summer school in South Korea. In addition, the law school offers a juvenile justice mediation project, which instructs students in mediation techniques and allows them to participate in mediations in the juvenile justice arena.

Teams compete annually in trial advocacy, appellate advocacy, client counseling, and arbitration competitions. These teams often win regional competitions and finish in the top 10 in national competitions.

■ Student Publications and Organizations

Campbell's size allows its students outstanding opportunities for participation in cocurricular activities. Each year, approximately 70 students serve as editors and writers for the *Campbell Law Observer*, a legal newspaper distributed to lawyers in North Carolina. Approximately 35 students serve as editors and staff members of the *Campbell Law Review*. About 25 percent of the class represents the law school in regional and national advocacy competitions.

Each student is a member of the Student Bar Association. Students are also active in a variety of other organizations, including the ABA—Law Student Division, the Black Law Students Association, the Christian Legal Society, Women in Law, and two legal fraternities.

■ Faculty

The faculty consists of noted experts and authors in various areas of law. The primary mission and greatest accomplishment of Campbell's faculty is that it is a

Campbell University, Norman Adrian Wiggins School of Law

teaching faculty. The faculty prides itself on its accessibility and observes an open-door policy.

■ Admission

Admission decisions are made on a rolling basis, and the priority deadline is March 31. Admission is granted on the basis of the faculty Admission Committee's evaluation of the applicant's probable contributions to the law school, the legal profession, and society. Each applicant's file is fully reviewed. Factors considered include the applicant's GPA; LSAT score; work experience; participation and leadership in cocurricular, civic, or volunteer activities; character; work ethic; and maturity.

A personal interview, held upon invitation of the Admissions Committee, is a prerequisite for admission. Because of the large number of applications received, the committee extends invitations for interviews to approximately half of the applicants. During their visits, applicants receive a student-guided tour of the facilities.

■ Summer Performance-Based Admission Program

Select students who are not offered regular admission in the fall class may be invited to participate in the Summer Performance-Based Admission Program. Each summer, between 50 and 75 applicants are admitted to this program and attend a seven-week session. Law school credit is not granted for these courses. Admission is offered to students who perform satisfactorily in both

courses. Historically, 20–30 percent of the applicants participating in the program have gained admission.

■ Expenses and Financial Aid

The cost of living is low by national standards. Approximately 35 percent of students receive scholarship assistance. Approximately 95 percent of the students receive financial aid. The priority deadline for financial aid applications is April 15; however, financial aid applications received after this date will be processed.

■ Housing and Recreational Facilities

Dormitory housing and apartments are available, and private housing is available in Buies Creek and the surrounding towns.

Law students receive discounted rates at Keith Hills Golf Course. Also available are the university tennis center, weight training facilities, natatorium, and cross-country course.

■ Career Services

The Career Services Office provides individualized attention to students seeking summer and permanent positions. Over the past five years, the placement rate has consistently exceeded 95 percent within six months of graduation. Graduates practice law in large and small firms, government agencies, and corporations across the nation.

Applicant Profile

Campbell University, Norman Adrian Wiggins School of Law
This grid includes only applicants who earned 120-180 LSAT scores under standard administrations.

LSAT	3.75 +		3.50 - 3.74		3.25 - 3.49		3.00 - 3.24		2.75 - 2.99		2.50 - 2.74		2.25 - 2.49		2.00 - 2.24		Below 2.00		No GPA		Total	
Score	Apps	Adm	Apps	Adm	Apps	Adm	Apps	Adm	Apps	Adm	Apps	Adm	Apps	Adm	Apps	Adm	Apps	Adm	Apps	Adm	Apps	Adm
175-180	0	0	0	0	0	0	0	0	0	0	0	0	0	0	0	0	0	0	0	0	0	0
170-174	0	0	0	0	0	0	0	0	0	0	1	0	0	0	1	0	0	0	0	0	2	0
165-169	0	0	3	1	3	2	2	2	1	1	2	1	0	0	0	0	0	0	0	0	11	7
160-164	5	4	10	6	13	7	12	7	8	3	6	3	1	1	1	0	0	0	0	0	56	31
155-159	24	10	31	20	46	20	50	23	26	14	16	5	17	2	4	0	0	0	0	0	214	94
150-154	26	9	42	19	80	29	59	10	57	7	28	5	17	3	11	0	1	0	1	0	322	82
145-149	14	3	32	4	51	6	56	8	43	4	32	1	18	0	10	1	2	0	4	0	262	27
140-144	8	0	21	0	22	0	34	1	32	0	23	1	11	0	5	0	3	0	1	0	160	2
135-139	0	0	6	0	10	0	9	0	12	0	5	0	3	0	5	0	2	0	1	0	53	0
130-134	3	0	2	0	3	0	4	0	5	0	4	1	5	0	3	0	1	0	1	0	31	1
125-129	0	0	0	0	0	0	3	0	1	0	0	0	1	0	1	0	0	0	1	0	7	0
120-124	0	0	0	0	0	0	0	0	1	0	0	0	0	0	0	0	0	0	0	0	1	0
Total	80	26	147	50	228	64	229	51	186	29	117	17	73	6	41	1	9	0	9	0	1119	244

Apps = Number of Applicants   Adm = Number Offered Admission   Reflects approximately 99% of the total applicant pool.

Note: The admissions in the grid above include individuals who gain admission through the summer PBAP program.

Capital University Law School

303 E Broad Street
Columbus, OH 43215-3200
Phone: 614.236.6310; Fax: 614.236.6972
E-mail: admissions@law.capital.edu; Website: www.law.capital.edu

The Basics

Type of school	Private
Term	Semester
Application deadline	5/1
Application fee	$35
Financial aid deadline	4/1
Can first year start other than fall?	No
Student to faculty ratio (fall)	18.3 to 1
Does the university offer:	
housing restricted to law students?	No
graduate housing for which law students are eligible?	No

Faculty and Administrators

	Total		Men		Women		Minorities	
	Fall	Spr	Fall	Spr	Fall	Spr	Fall	Spr
Full-time	31	30	19	18	12	12	3	3
Other Full-time	5	4	1	0	4	4	1	1
Deans, librarians, & others who teach	6	6	4	4	2	2	1	1
Part-time	35	36	31	33	4	3	0	4
Total	77	76	55	55	22	21	5	9

Curriculum

		Full-time	Part-time
Typical first-year section size		80	90
Is there typically a "small section" of the first-year class, other than Legal Writing, taught by full-time faculty		Yes	Yes
If yes, typical size offered last year		40	45
# of classroom course titles beyond 1st year curriculum		114	
# of upper division courses, excluding seminars with an enrollment:	Under 25	98	
	25-49	37	
	50-74	15	
	75-99	21	
	100+	0	
# of seminars		6	
# of seminar positions available		90	
# of seminar positions filled	53	24	
# of positions available in simulation courses		582	
# of simulation positions filled	294	157	
# of positions available in faculty supervised clinical courses		64	
# of faculty supervised clinical positions filled	57	12	
# involved in field placements	105	29	
# involved in law journals	33	12	
# involved in moot court or trial competitions	14	5	
# of credit hours required to graduate		86	

JD Enrollment and Ethnicity

	Men		Women		Full-time		Part-time		1st-year		Total		JD Degs. Awd.
	#	%	#	%	#	%	#	%	#	%	#	%	
African Amer.	23	5.7	39	10.2	26	5.5	36	11.5	23	8.2	62	7.9	10
Amer. Indian	1	0.2	0	0.0	1	0.2	0	0.0	1	0.4	1	0.1	1
Asian Amer.	3	0.7	10	2.6	10	2.1	3	1.0	4	1.4	13	1.7	2
Mex. Amer.	0	0.0	0	0.0	0	0.0	0	0.0	0	0.0	0	0.0	0
Puerto Rican	0	0.0	0	0.0	0	0.0	0	0.0	0	0.0	0	0.0	0
Hispanic	8	2.0	5	1.3	9	1.9	4	1.3	4	1.4	13	1.7	4
Total Minority	35	8.7	54	14.1	46	9.7	43	13.7	32	11.5	89	11.3	17
For. Nation.	2	0.5	2	0.5	3	0.6	1	0.3	2	0.7	4	0.5	0
Caucasian	342	84.7	312	81.5	396	83.5	258	82.4	225	80.6	654	83.1	170
Unknown	25	6.2	15	3.9	29	6.1	11	3.5	20	7.2	40	5.1	4
Total	404	51.3	383	48.7	474	60.2	313	39.8	279	35.5	787		191

Tuition and Fees

	Resident	Nonresident
Full-time	$22,540	$22,540
Part-time	$16,100	$16,100

Living Expenses

Estimated living expenses for singles

Living on campus	Living off campus	Living at home
N/A	$10,358	$10,358

Capital University Law School

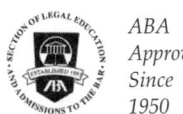

*ABA
Approved
Since
1950*

GPA and LSAT Scores

	Total	Full-time	Part-time
# of apps	1,391	1,094	297
# of admits	621	485	136
# of matrics	280	188	92
75% GPA	3.56	3.61	3.51
25% GPA	3.02	3.02	2.93
75% LSAT	156	156	156
25% LSAT	150	150	150

Grants and Scholarships (from prior year)

	Total		Full-time		Part-time	
	#	%	#	%	#	%
Total # of students	763		458		305	
Total # receiving grants	365	47.8	278	60.7	87	28.5
Less than 1/2 tuition	335	43.9	252	55.0	83	27.2
Half to full tuition	30	3.9	26	5.7	4	1.3
Full tuition	0	0.0	0	0.0	0	0.0
More than full tuition	0	0.0	0	0.0	0	0.0
Median grant amount			$7,000		$3,000	

Informational and Library Resources

# of volumes and volume equivalents	262,420
# of titles	47,241
# of active serial subscriptions	2,477
Study seating capacity inside the library	460
# of professional librarians	5
Hours per week library is open	94
# of open, wired connections available to students	706
# of networked computers available for use by students	75
# of simultaneous wireless users	70
Require computer?	N

JD Attrition (from prior year)

	Academic	Other	Total	
	#	#	#	%
1st year	9	43	52	20.7%
2nd year	9	7	16	6.8%
3rd year	3	2	5	2.3%
4th year	0	0	0	0.0%

Employment

	Total	Percentage
Employment status known	209	98.1
Employment status unknown	4	1.9
Employed	187	89.5
Pursuing graduate degrees	5	2.4
Unemployed seeking employment	9	4.3
Unemployed not seeking employment	8	3.8

Type of Employment

# employed in law firms	90	48.1
# employed in business and industry	44	23.5
# employed in government	36	19.3
# employed in public interest	5	2.7
# employed as judicial clerks	7	3.7
# employed in academia	5	2.7

Geographic Location

# employed in state	160	85.6
# employed in foreign countries	0	0.0
# of states where employed		14

Bar Passage Rates

Jurisdiction		Ohio	
Exam	Sum 03	Win 04	Total
# from school taking bar for the first time	156	29	185
School's pass rate for all first-time takers	62%	48%	59%
State's pass rate for all first-time takers	81%	72%	79%

Capital University Law School

303 E Broad Street
Columbus, OH 43215-3200
Phone: 614.236.6310; Fax: 614.236.6972
E-mail: admissions@law.capital.edu; Website: www.law.capital.edu

■ Introduction

Capital University Law School, located in downtown Columbus, is in the heart of Ohio's legal community. Columbus is home to the Ohio Supreme Court, the state legislature, and numerous state agencies, including the Ohio Attorney General's Office. In addition, a Federal District Court, the Ohio Court of Appeals, and various trial courts are within a short walk of the Law School. Our location provides a wealth of learning opportunities through clinical and externship programs, and our facility affords Capital University law students a state-of-the-art law school that is second to none.

For more than a century, Capital University Law School has produced some of the region's finest lawyers, judges, and business professionals. We invite you to take a closer look at the factors that distinguish this law school: an excellent teaching faculty, an ideal location, high placement rates, innovative institutes and programs, distinguished alumni, and reasonable tuition.

■ Curriculum

The school's primary mission is to provide both day- and evening-division students with an excellent educational experience that combines competency-based legal education with a commitment to service and leadership. Capital combines a theoretical education with a program that emphasizes the skills and values necessary to practice in the twenty-first century and combines the best of a traditional legal education with innovative programs. Our professors are accomplished scholars whose first and foremost duty is teaching. For further details and specific course offerings, visit our website at *www.law.capital.edu*.

■ Multicultural Affairs

Capital's students come from every walk of life: from small towns to large metropolitan cities, from small private colleges to large state universities. Students come to Capital with diverse educational, cultural, and professional backgrounds. Capital's students bring valid and valuable life experiences to the classroom from which each student is subsequently enriched.

Capital University Law School is committed to racial and cultural diversity. The Law School actively recruits African American, Asian, Hispanic, and Native American students. Capital has many programs to aid in the retention of minority students, including the presence of minority faculty, a director of multicultural affairs, availability of financial aid, academic as well as nonacademic support, and participation in the Columbus Bar Association minority clerkship program.

■ Special Programs

Diversity of opportunity is a trademark of Capital University Law. Capital offers certificate programs to students who wish to develop their skills and knowledge in an area of particular interest.

Capital's **Governmental Affairs** concentration allows students to participate in externships with local, state, and federal courts and governmental agencies, and to conduct extensive research in the area of governmental affairs.

The **Labor and Employment Law** concentration is designed for law students who have an interest in studying laws and regulations governing the workplace.

The **Small Business Entities and Publicly Held Companies** concentrations give interested students an opportunity to focus part of their legal education on exploring the many legal issues and policies affecting business entities.

The **Dispute Resolution** concentration prepares students to understand the full spectrum of settlement processes. Capital's concentration in **Environmental Law** prepares students for employment in the field of environmental law and policy.

The **Children and Family Law** concentration provides students an in-depth understanding of the legal rights and obligations of parents, children, and family units. Innovative programs give students an opportunity to explore various specialties within the legal profession, to improve their skills, and to provide a valuable service to the community.

The Institute for International Education has made Capital the scene of a variety of projects, conferences, and ongoing activities related to international comparative law. Capital has sister-institutional agreements and international connections with the Centre for International and European Economic Law in Greece, Demokritus University of Thrace, University of Saskatchewan, University of Glasgow, and University of Passau. Capital Law students also have the opportunity to participate in Summer International Law Study Programs in Germany or Greece.

The Center for Dispute Resolution is a multifaceted resource for the teaching, development, and implementation of various dispute resolution methods.

The National Center for Adoption Law and Policy at Capital, the first resource of its kind in the nation, creates programs and promotes activities focusing on all aspects of family law dealing with adoption.

The Family Advocacy Clinic provides students with the opportunity to represent victims of domestic violence in court.

Capital offers the following joint-degree programs: **JD/Master of Sports Administration, JD/Master of Business Administration, JD/Master of Science in**

Nursing Degree, **JD/LLM in Taxation**, **JD/LLM in Business**, and **JD/Masters in Theological Studies**. Participation in these dual-degree programs allows students to earn both degrees in less time than pursuing them separately.

Admission

The Law School seeks applicants who rank in the upper half of their undergraduate class and achieve an LSAT score above the 50th percentile. Other factors used in evaluation include the competitiveness and difficulty of the candidate's undergraduate school and course of study, any graduate coursework, employment history, writing ability, leadership experience, and general background.

Student Activities

Student organizations at Capital Law School offer many opportunities for leadership development. Capital's Black Law Students Association won the 2002–2003 National Chapter of the Year Award.

The Capital University Law Review provides the legal community with scholarly analysis of contemporary legal issues. Our student newspaper, *Res Ipsa Loquitur*, is published for the Law School community.

Associations for black; Hispanic; Asian; Jewish; Christian; women; and gay, lesbian, and bisexual students bring together individuals with similar backgrounds and interests. There are organizations for those interested in

specific areas of practice such as sports and entertainment law, environmental law, corporate law, intellectual property, and public interest. Students also have the opportunity to be involved in one of three legal fraternities at Capital. Those wishing to hone their skills and test them in competition will want to investigate Capital's highly successful moot court teams.

Career Services

Capital Law's Career Services Office provides counseling and information so individuals can explore legal career options. It also serves as a resource to help students assess their skills and plan a productive job search strategy. The office is responsible for developing an on-campus interview program that last year brought over 60 firms, companies, and organizations from different geographical locations to campus to interview for internships, clerkships, and full-time positions. Capital graduates have had great success seeking employment after graduation. Typically, over 90 percent of each graduating class has been employed within six months of graduation.

Capital Law School graduates are employed in a variety of different fields of law. Private practice is the largest of these areas, with approximately 42 percent of the graduating class entering this field. Many Capital graduates also enter the corporate sector (22 percent) or government work (26 percent). Other fields that graduates have entered are judicial clerkships, public interest, and academia.

Applicant Profile

Capital University Law School

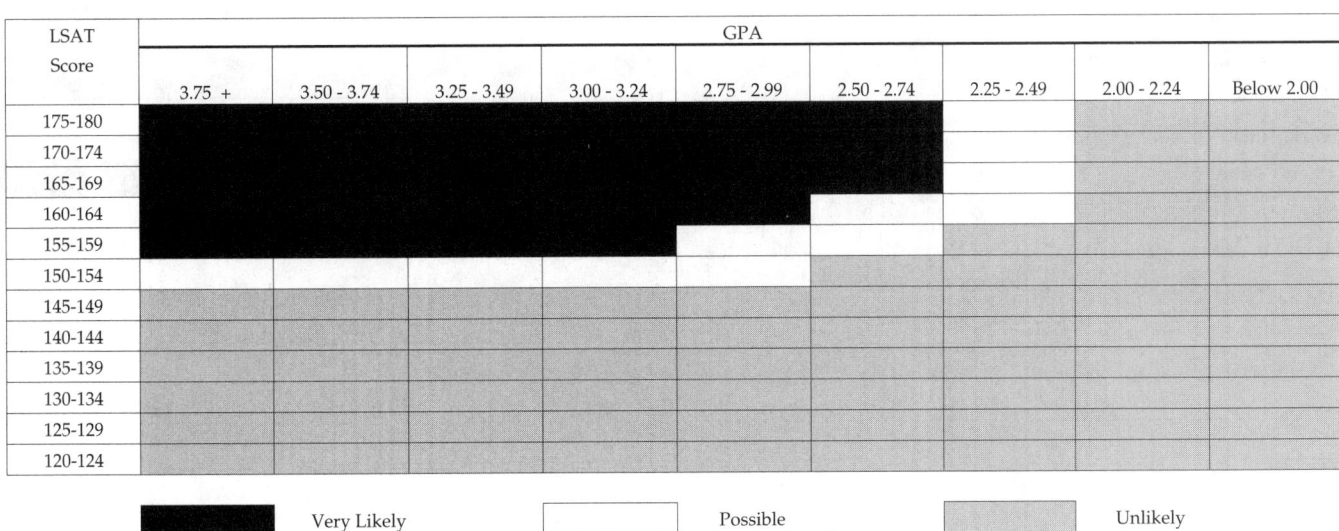

Benjamin N. Cardozo School of Law, Yeshiva University

55 Fifth Avenue
New York, NY 10003
Phone: 212.790.0274; Fax: 212.790.0482
E-mail: lawinfo@yu.edu; Website: www.cardozo.yu.edu/

ABA Approved Since 1978

The Basics

Type of school	Private
Term	Semester
Application deadline	4/1 12/1
Application fee	$65
Financial aid deadline	4/15
Can first year start other than fall?	Yes
Student to faculty ratio (fall)	16.5 to 1
Does the university offer:	
housing restricted to law students?	Yes
graduate housing for which law students are eligible?	No

Faculty and Administrators

	Total Fall	Total Spr	Men Fall	Men Spr	Women Fall	Women Spr	Minorities Fall	Minorities Spr
Full-time	51	50	39	36	12	14	2	4
Other Full-time	2	3	2	3	0	0	0	0
Deans, librarians, & others who teach	4	4	1	1	3	3	0	0
Part-time	66	72	51	56	15	16	1	2
Total	123	129	93	96	30	33	3	6

Curriculum

	Full-time	Part-time
Typical first-year section size	50	0
Is there typically a "small section" of the first-year class, other than Legal Writing, taught by full-time faculty	No	No
If yes, typical size offered last year	0	0
# of classroom course titles beyond 1st year curriculum	150	
# of upper division courses, excluding seminars with an enrollment: Under 25	55	
25-49	37	
50-74	12	
75-99	7	
100+	21	
# of seminars	57	
# of seminar positions available	751	
# of seminar positions filled	625	0
# of positions available in simulation courses	617	
# of simulation positions filled	485	0
# of positions available in faculty supervised clinical courses	136	
# of faculty supervised clinical positions filled	105	0
# involved in field placements	178	0
# involved in law journals	336	0
# involved in moot court or trial competitions	78	0
# of credit hours required to graduate	84	

JD Enrollment and Ethnicity

	Men #	Men %	Women #	Women %	Full-time #	Full-time %	Part-time #	Part-time %	1st-year #	1st-year %	Total #	Total %	JD Degs. Awd.
African Amer.	11	2.0	32	6.4	37	3.8	6	8.1	16	5.2	43	4.1	12
Amer. Indian	1	0.2	1	0.2	2	0.2	0	0.0	0	0.0	2	0.2	2
Asian Amer.	48	8.9	58	11.7	95	9.9	11	14.9	34	11.0	106	10.2	31
Mex. Amer.	0	0.0	0	0.0	0	0.0	0	0.0	0	0.0	0	0.0	0
Puerto Rican	6	1.1	5	1.0	11	1.1	0	0.0	0	0.0	11	1.1	0
Hispanic	23	4.3	30	6.0	49	5.1	4	5.4	17	5.5	53	5.1	18
Total Minority	89	16.5	126	25.4	194	20.1	21	28.4	67	21.6	215	20.7	63
For. Nation.	10	1.9	10	2.0	20	2.1	0	0.0	5	1.6	20	1.9	0
Caucasian	441	81.7	361	72.6	749	77.8	53	71.6	238	76.8	802	77.3	227
Unknown	0	0.0	0	0.0	0	0.0	0	0.0	0	0.0	0	0.0	44
Total	540	52.1	497	47.9	963	92.9	74	7.1	310	29.9	1037		334

Tuition and Fees

	Resident	Nonresident
Full-time	$32,950	$32,950
Part-time	$32,950	$32,950

Living Expenses

Estimated living expenses for singles

Living on campus	Living off campus	Living at home
$25,120	$25,120	$10,592

Benjamin N. Cardozo School of Law, Yeshiva University

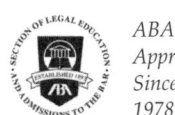

ABA
Approved
Since
1978

GPA and LSAT Scores

	Total	Full-time	Part-time
# of apps	5,171	4,815	356
# of admits	1,185	1,060	125
# of matrics	349	275	74
75% GPA	3.64	3.64	3.62
25% GPA	3.14	3.14	3.19
75% LSAT	165	166	161
25% LSAT	159	161	157

Grants and Scholarships (from prior year)

	Total		Full-time		Part-time	
	#	%	#	%	#	%
Total # of students	1,041		993		48	
Total # receiving grants	602	57.8	600	60.4	2	4.2
Less than 1/2 tuition	493	47.4	492	49.5	1	2.1
Half to full tuition	104	10.0	103	10.4	1	2.1
Full tuition	5	0.5	5	0.5	0	0.0
More than full tuition	0	0.0	0	0.0	0	0.0
Median grant amount			$8,000		$0	

Informational and Library Resources

# of volumes and volume equivalents	501,276
# of titles	93,246
# of active serial subscriptions	6,492
Study seating capacity inside the library	483
# of professional librarians	8
Hours per week library is open	88
# of open, wired connections available to students	104
# of networked computers available for use by students	136
# of simultaneous wireless users	652
Require computer?	N

JD Attrition (from prior year)

	Academic	Other	Total	
	#	#	#	%
1st year	3	15	18	5.4%
2nd year	2	0	2	0.5%
3rd year	1	0	1	0.3%
4th year	0	0	0	0.0%

Employment

	Total	Percentage
Employment status known	301	99.3
Employment status unknown	2	0.7
Employed	256	85.0
Pursuing graduate degrees	13	4.3
Unemployed seeking employment	17	5.6
Unemployed not seeking employment	15	5.0

Type of Employment

	Total	Percentage
# employed in law firms	171	66.8
# employed in business and industry	32	12.5
# employed in government	30	11.7
# employed in public interest	5	2.0
# employed as judicial clerks	15	5.9
# employed in academia	3	1.2

Geographic Location

	Total	Percentage
# employed in state	208	81.2
# employed in foreign countries	8	3.1
# of states where employed	13	

Bar Passage Rates

Jurisdiction	New York		
Exam	Sum 03	Win 04	Total
# from school taking bar for the first time	253	28	281
School's pass rate for all first-time takers	88%	64%	86%
State's pass rate for all first-time takers	78%	58%	75%

Benjamin N. Cardozo School of Law, Yeshiva University

55 Fifth Avenue
New York, NY 10003
Phone: 212.790.0274; Fax: 212.790.0482
E-mail: lawinfo@yu.edu; Website: www.cardozo.yu.edu/

■ Introduction

Benjamin N. Cardozo School of Law offers students a stimulating and supportive educational experience. Its curriculum combines practical training in basic skills and legal doctrine, sophisticated study of recent developments in legal theory, and interdisciplinary approaches to the study of law. Courses provide depth and breadth in all the standard subjects of legal study, as well as many more specialized ones, including intellectual property law and alternative dispute resolution. Extensive clinical and externship opportunities allow students to gain practical lawyering experiences while performing important community service. A Cardozo education emphasizes ethics and the pursuit of intellectual excellence.

■ Faculty

Professors at Cardozo are vibrant, intellectually curious, accessible to students, and committed to the twin goals of teaching and scholarship. They are an interdisciplinary faculty, curious and serious about how the law relates to other expressions of the human spirit such as philosophy, literature, economics, politics, and history. More than half hold advanced degrees in addition to a law degree, about a dozen hold PhDs as well. The faculty is prolific, writing on both visionary and practical subjects, with many of their publications required reading in law schools across the nation.

■ A Campus in New York City

Cardozo is in an elegant residential neighborhood in the heart of Greenwich Village. It is easily accessible to all points in New York City, including the courts, Wall Street, Midtown, and the art and music centers on the East and West Sides. In 2003, the school completed a $40 million renovation and expansion of its facilities, including a new moot courtroom, additional library space, new lobby and student offices, and refurbished classrooms.

The Cardozo residence hall is located on a residential, tree-lined street just one block south of the main building. A limited number of studio and one-bedroom apartments—all of which are air-conditioned, attractively furnished, and have a full kitchen—are available for incoming students.

■ Career Services

Cardozo prides itself on a sophisticated and professionally staffed career office that offers individual assistance with interviewing techniques, résumé writing, and job search strategies as well as panels and other opportunities for learning about a variety of legal careers. An impressive 94.3 percent of those reporting from the class of 2003 were employed within several months of graduation. Sixty-seven percent of these graduates went into private practice at an average starting salary of $101,023; the average overall starting salary was $87,835. Additionally, at 88 percent, Cardozo graduates taking the July 2003 New York Bar Examination had the third highest passage rate among New York City law schools.

■ Curriculum

Cardozo offers a rich curriculum that has been especially recognized for its offerings in Intellectual Property Law (students may receive both the JD and LLM degrees in seven semesters), Alternative Dispute Resolution, Criminal Law, Corporate Law, and International Law. Upper-level courses are elective except for a course in Professional Responsibility, completion of Advanced Legal Research, an upper-level writing requirement, and fulfillment of minimal distribution requirements.

Cardozo offers LLM degrees in Intellectual Property Law, Comparative Legal Thought, and in General Studies. A joint-degree program between Cardozo and the Wurzweiler School of Social Work allows students to earn the JD and MSW in four years of study.

■ Clinical Opportunities/Special Programs

Cardozo offers 20 different clinical and externship programs. In the **Holocaust Claims Restitution Practicum**, students pursue claims made by Holocaust survivors and their heirs; students in the **Criminal Defense Clinic** represent defendants in the Manhattan Criminal Court; the **Innocence Project** represents prisoners whose innocence may be proved through DNA testing; in the **Prosecutor Practicum**, students work in the Manhattan District Attorney's Office; the **Bet Tzedek Legal Services Clinic** provides legal assistance to the elderly and disabled; the **Mediation Clinic** provides training in alternative dispute resolution; the **Human Rights and Genocide Prevention Clinic** provides students with the opportunity to design and implement creative solutions to improve the lives of victims of human rights abuses throughout the world; and Cardozo's simulation-based **Intensive Trial Advocacy Program** sharpens student's trial skills. Other clinics include the **Family Court Clinic, Tax Clinic,** and **Immigration Law Clinic**.

Externships: The **Intellectual Property Law Program** combines a specialized curriculum with related externships in this burgeoning area of practice; the **Summer Institute for Career Development** offers seminars linked to field placements in specialty areas such as entertainment law, dispute resolution processes, and civil and criminal litigation; the **Alexander Judicial**

Benjamin N. Cardozo School of Law, Yeshiva University

Fellows Program places outstanding third-year students in clerkships with prominent federal judges; and the **Labor and Employment Law Externship** places students in law firms, government agencies, and unions.

Public Service: Cardozo's **Center for Public Service** emphasizes the law school's commitment to serving the greater public good and helping students find meaningful ways to engage in public service. In 2004, through the **Public Service Summer Stipend Program**, 71 students received $3,500 stipends while working with such underrepresented groups as the elderly, the homeless, recent immigrants, and juveniles. A **Public Service Scholars Program** awards scholarships to students who demonstrate an interest in public service through their application for admission.

Panels/Symposia: Intellectual life at Cardozo extends beyond the classroom. The school sponsors numerous conferences, panels, and symposia that provoke dialogue and critical thought on wide-ranging topics such as communications law and policy, human rights, corporate governance, and legal ethics.

■ Students/Student Activities

The student body at Cardozo is a diverse and impressive group. A typical entering class includes graduates from well over 100 colleges, and from over 35 states and several foreign countries. Twenty-two percent of the class are members of minority groups and about the same percentage is returning to school after spending time in the working world.

More than half of the second- and third-year students participate on one of six student-edited journals or in the Moot Court Honor Society. Journals include the *Cardozo Law Review*, *Cardozo Arts and Entertainment Law Journal*, *Cardozo Journal of International and Comparative Law*, *Cardozo Women's Law Journal*, *Cardozo Journal of Conflict Resolution*, and *Cardozo Public Law, Policy, and Ethics Journal*.

■ Admission/Alternative Entry/Financial Aid

Students may enter Cardozo in September, January, or May. Those entering in January and May complete six semesters of law school in two-and-one-half years. This can be particularly appealing to midyear graduates, juniors in college who wish to jumpstart their graduate education, and returning students.

Both need- and merit-based scholarships are available. Approximately 60 percent of the students receive scholarship aid. Instructions on applying for aid can be found at *www.cardozo.yu.edu/admissions/tuition/how_to/guides.html*.

Applicant Profile

Benjamin N. Cardozo School of Law, Yeshiva University
This grid includes only applicants who earned 120-180 LSAT scores under standard administrations.

LSAT Score	3.75 + Apps	3.75 + Adm	3.50 - 3.74 Apps	3.50 - 3.74 Adm	3.25 - 3.49 Apps	3.25 - 3.49 Adm	3.00 - 3.24 Apps	3.00 - 3.24 Adm	2.75 - 2.99 Apps	2.75 - 2.99 Adm	2.50 - 2.74 Apps	2.50 - 2.74 Adm	2.25 - 2.49 Apps	2.25 - 2.49 Adm	2.00 - 2.24 Apps	2.00 - 2.24 Adm	Below 2.00 Apps	Below 2.00 Adm	No GPA Apps	No GPA Adm	Total Apps	Total Adm
175-180	4	4	5	5	2	2	2	2	2	2	0	0	0	0	1	1	0	0	0	0	16	16
170-174	22	22	21	20	29	29	14	10	3	3	6	5	1	1	1	0	0	0	1	1	98	91
165-169	77	70	97	93	93	83	75	63	28	19	22	10	14	3	4	3	0	0	6	5	416	349
160-164	147	114	277	159	242	93	169	37	79	14	51	3	20	1	5	2	2	0	11	2	1003	425
155-159	161	25	289	33	301	12	228	12	118	6	52	4	28	1	10	0	0	0	18	1	1205	94
150-154	90	7	166	5	178	8	178	8	103	1	50	0	20	0	7	0	1	0	14	2	807	31
145-149	26	0	67	1	76	1	82	0	52	0	39	0	23	0	7	0	0	0	11	0	383	2
140-144	14	0	19	0	39	0	51	0	37	0	34	0	13	0	3	0	0	0	4	0	214	0
135-139	3	0	9	0	10	0	13	0	12	0	18	0	9	0	2	0	4	0	2	0	82	0
130-134	0	0	1	0	2	0	6	0	7	0	2	0	3	0	4	0	1	0	3	0	29	0
125-129	0	0	0	0	1	0	0	0	1	0	3	0	1	0	0	0	0	0	1	0	7	0
120-124	0	0	0	0	0	0	0	0	0	0	0	0	1	0	1	0	0	0	0	0	2	0
Total	544	242	951	316	973	228	818	132	442	45	277	22	133	6	45	6	8	0	71	11	4262	1008

Apps = Number of Applicants
Adm = Number Admitted
Reflects 99% of the fall applicant pool.

Case Western Reserve University School of Law

11075 East Boulevard
Cleveland, OH 44122
Phone: 216.368.3600, 800.756.0036; Fax: 216.368.1042
E-mail: lawadmissions@case.edu, lawmoney@case.edu; Website: www.law.case.edu

ABA Approved Since 1923

The Basics

Type of school	Private
Term	Semester
Application deadline	11/15 2/2 4/1
Application fee	$40
Financial aid deadline	5/1
Can first year start other than fall?	No
Student to faculty ratio (fall)	14.2 to 1
Does the university offer:	
housing restricted to law students?	No
graduate housing for which law students are eligible?	No

Faculty and Administrators

	Total		Men		Women		Minorities	
	Fall	Spr	Fall	Spr	Fall	Spr	Fall	Spr
Full-time	41	38	28	26	13	12	6	5
Other Full-time	10	10	6	6	4	4	3	3
Deans, librarians, & others who teach	4	4	2	2	2	2	0	0
Part-time	71	96	47	63	24	33	40	49
Total	126	148	83	97	43	51	49	57

Curriculum

	Full-time	Part-time
Typical first-year section size	76	0
Is there typically a "small section" of the first-year class, other than Legal Writing, taught by full-time faculty	No	No
If yes, typical size offered last year	0	0
# of classroom course titles beyond 1st year curriculum	114	
# of upper division courses, excluding seminars with an enrollment: Under 25	64	
25-49	22	
50-74	4	
75-99	5	
100+	0	
# of seminars	24	
# of seminar positions available	281	
# of seminar positions filled	166	0
# of positions available in simulation courses	397	
# of simulation positions filled	374	0
# of positions available in faculty supervised clinical courses	90	
# of faculty supervised clinical positions filled	62	0
# involved in field placements	0	0
# involved in law journals	68	0
# involved in moot court or trial competitions	25	0
# of credit hours required to graduate	88	

JD Enrollment and Ethnicity

	Men #	Men %	Women #	Women %	Full-time #	Full-time %	Part-time #	Part-time %	1st-year #	1st-year %	Total #	Total %	JD Degs. Awd.
African Amer.	14	3.3	13	4.6	27	3.9	0	0.0	7	3.0	27	3.8	9
Amer. Indian	2	0.5	1	0.4	2	0.3	1	5.3	2	0.9	3	0.4	0
Asian Amer.	34	8.0	29	10.2	62	9.0	1	5.3	23	9.9	63	8.9	13
Mex. Amer.	1	0.2	0	0.0	1	0.1	0	0.0	1	0.4	1	0.1	0
Puerto Rican	1	0.2	0	0.0	1	0.1	0	0.0	0	0.0	1	0.1	0
Hispanic	7	1.6	2	0.7	8	1.2	1	5.3	2	0.9	9	1.3	3
Total Minority	59	13.9	45	15.9	101	14.7	3	15.8	35	15.0	104	14.7	25
For. Nation.	6	1.4	8	2.8	14	2.0	0	0.0	3	1.3	14	2.0	0
Caucasian	353	83.1	227	80.2	566	82.1	14	73.7	192	82.4	580	81.9	188
Unknown	7	1.6	3	1.1	8	1.2	2	10.5	3	1.3	10	1.4	3
Total	425	60.0	283	40.0	689	97.3	19	2.7	233	32.9	708		216

Tuition and Fees

	Resident	Nonresident
Full-time	$28,276	$28,276
Part-time	$11,826	$11,826

Living Expenses

Estimated living expenses for singles

Living on campus	Living off campus	Living at home
$43,500	$43,500	$36,000

Case Western Reserve University School of Law

ABA Approved Since 1923

GPA and LSAT Scores

	Total	Full-time	Part-time
# of apps	2,851	2,851	0
# of admits	808	808	0
# of matrics	228	209	19
75% GPA	3.52	3.53	3.50
25% GPA	3.04	3.04	2.96
75% LSAT	161	161	157
25% LSAT	157	157	156

Grants and Scholarships (from prior year)

	Total #	Total %	Full-time #	Full-time %	Part-time #	Part-time %
Total # of students	704		701		3	
Total # receiving grants	366	52.0	366	52.2	0	0.0
Less than 1/2 tuition	226	32.1	226	32.2	0	0.0
Half to full tuition	122	17.3	122	17.4	0	0.0
Full tuition	18	2.6	18	2.6	0	0.0
More than full tuition	0	0.0	0	0.0	0	0.0
Median grant amount			$12,600		$0	

Informational and Library Resources

# of volumes and volume equivalents	395,973
# of titles	104,648
# of active serial subscriptions	5,243
Study seating capacity inside the library	353
# of professional librarians	10
Hours per week library is open	108
# of open, wired connections available to students	30
# of networked computers available for use by students	81
# of simultaneous wireless users	400
Require computer?	N

J.D. Attrition (from prior year)

	Academic #	Other #	Total #	Total %
1st year	0	0	0	0.0%
2nd year	1	30	31	13.2%
3rd year	0	0	0	0.0%
4th year	0	0	0	0.0%

Employment

	Total	Percentage
Employment status known	194	98.5
Employment status unknown	3	1.5
Employed	184	94.8
Pursuing graduate degrees	7	3.6
Unemployed seeking employment	0	0.0
Unemployed not seeking employment	3	1.5

Type of Employment

# employed in law firms	106	57.6
# employed in business and industry	21	11.4
# employed in government	21	11.4
# employed in public interest	9	4.9
# employed as judicial clerks	10	5.4
# employed in academia	8	4.3

Geographic Location

# employed in state	110	59.8
# employed in foreign countries	3	1.6
# of states where employed	19	

Bar Passage Rates

Jurisdiction		Ohio	
Exam	Sum 03	Win 04	Total
# from school taking bar for the first time	111	10	121
School's pass rate for all first-time takers	85%	70%	83%
State's pass rate for all first-time takers	81%	72%	79%

Case Western Reserve University School of Law

11075 East Boulevard
Cleveland, OH 44122
Phone: 216.368.3600, 800.756.0036; Fax: 216.368.1042
E-mail: lawadmissions@case.edu, lawmoney@case.edu; Website: www.law.case.edu

■ Welcome

Over the past seven years, Case School of Law has responded to the growing complexities of the ever-changing legal, social, and economic environments by implementing major reforms in our curriculum and educational program. The result is an innovative academic program that provides our students with an enhanced classical legal education, an extensive and unique array of hands-on learning (close to 400 spaces in skills courses alone), opportunities for in-depth study in key fields, extensive coursework in emerging and leading-edge areas of the law, an understanding of the context in which legal matters and disputes take place, knowledge of other disciplines that can be used to solve legal problems, and unique methods of instruction.

■ The Curriculum and Concentrations

More than ever, lawyers must act as counselors and partners to their clients to achieve the clients' strategic goals and take an even greater leadership role in providing service to their communities and addressing key societal issues. We offer specialized courses to encourage learning, teamwork, and interaction with key fields with which lawyers will work. The centerpiece of our curriculum is the Case*Arc* Integrated Lawyering Skills Program, which coordinates over four semesters experientially based instruction in fundamental lawyering skills with traditional classroom methods for teaching legal analysis.

Concentrations: Our optional concentration program provides students with in-depth learning in their area of interest and value to employers seeking increased contributions from new lawyers in the current competitive environment. Concentration options: Law, Technology, and the Arts (Law and Technology or Law and the Arts); Criminal Law; Business Organizations; Litigation; Health Law; International Law; and Public Law (Rights and Social Reform or Public and Regulatory Institutions).

Dual-Degree Programs: JD/MBA (Management); JD/MA (Bioethics); JD/MSSA (Social Work); JD/MS (Biochemistry); JD/MD (Medicine); JD/MNO (Nonprofit Management); JD/CNM (Certificate of Nonprofit Management); JD/MPH (Public Health); and JD/MA (Legal History).

■ Centers of Excellence

Center for Law, Technology, and the Arts. Focuses on teaching, research, and programs on intellectual property, technology development and transfer, the intersection of science and the legal system, legal issues concerning biotechnology and computer technologies, and the law of the creative arts.

Law-Medicine Center. The oldest of its kind in the nation, the center offers courses and programs that prepare our students to confront the challenges that lie at the intersection of law and medicine, including health care regulation, health care finance, and bioethics.

Frederick K. Cox International Law Center. Prepares our students for contemporary and future international legal challenges and opportunities and advances knowledge on the substance and process of international legal reform. Sponsors a stipend program for student international internships and foreign study.

Milton A. Kramer Law Clinic Center. Provides students with the opportunity to represent actual clients, in real legal matters, under the close supervision of the clinical faculty. Sixty students a year provide legal services to over 250 clients in one of our clinics.

Center for Business Law and Regulation. Prepares future leaders with a better understanding of business issues facing entrepreneurs, business entities, and other clients.

■ The University and Cleveland

Case law school stands among the nation's foremost independent research institutions. It is 12th among private universities in federal research and development awards and is one of only 20 in the world with an endowment greater than $1 billion. The law school is located on the university's campus, right in the heart of University Circle.

The nation's 14th largest metropolitan area, Cleveland ranks among the nation's premier legal, corporate, and health care centers, providing students with a wealth of local job opportunities and externships and bringing them into direct contact with distinguished members of the legal community. Cleveland is also extremely affordable. We assist students in finding housing close to the law school; a large two-bedroom apartment typically rents for approximately $750 per month.

■ Our Career Services Office

The Career Services Office (CSO) has developed and implemented an ambitious program that delivers to our students real job opportunities with leading employers coast to coast and helps our students achieve their career goals. Our program complements our mission of preparing leaders in the practice of law, public and community service, and commerce. Statistics for our law school's class of 2003 showed 98.4 percent employed or in full-time post-JD degree programs, while the national average for law schools that year was 91.6 percent. The median salary for our law school's class of 2003 was $82,000, compared to the national figure of $55,000. Fifty-nine percent of our students obtained employment through a CSO-sponsored interview program or job posting, compared to a national figure of 42 percent. And over 40 percent of our 2003 graduates took positions outside Ohio, compared with a national figure of 31.9 percent taking positions outside of the state in which their law school is located. Over 350 employers participate in our fall recruitment programs, which include opportunities for students to interview with employers on campus as well as in New York; Chicago; Los Angeles; and Washington, DC.

■ Student Activities and Leadership

There are over 40 professional, social, and academic student organizations supported by the Student Bar Association, reflecting the wide range of interest of our students. The school also sponsors three student-edited scholarly journals: the *Case Western Reserve Law Review,* the *Journal of International Law,* and *Health Matrix: Journal of Law-Medicine.*

■ Admission and Financial Aid

The Admission Process—Our admission process is selective, with each applicant receiving full-file review. We weigh not only GPA and LSAT scores, but also nonquantitative factors. Candidates who apply under our Early Decision Process are notified by December 20. File review through the regular admission process begins in December and concludes by May 15, at which time a summer wait list is established. The application

fee for candidates who apply through the LSA*CD* or on our website is waived.

Financial Aid and Scholarships—We benefit from one of the largest endowments of any law school, enabling us to provide significant scholarship support to approximately one-third of each entering class. Each year, we offer Academic Scholarships ranging from $5,000 to $28,000; Leadership Grants, awarded to students with unique backgrounds whose records demonstrate leadership qualities and who will enrich the diversity of the student body; Law-Medicine Scholarships; and up to two Law-Medicine Fellowships, which provide a combination of scholarship aid and summer research fellowship.

Loan Repayment Assistance Program—Each year we provide financial assistance for selected graduates who use their legal training to provide services that are in the public interest.

■ Graduate Law Study

Our **LLM in US and Global Legal Studies** provides graduates from foreign law schools the opportunity to study the US legal system and institutions.

■ Visiting the Case School of Law

We offer many opportunities for prospective students to visit the law school. Just check our website to take our "Virtual Tour" or to check the schedule for the visitation day, daily "Taste of Case," individual visit, or Super Saturday that is most convenient for you.

Applicant Profile

Case Western Reserve University School of Law
This grid includes only applicants who earned 120-180 LSAT scores.

LSAT Score	GPA						
	3.75 +	3.50 - 3.74	3.25 - 3.49	3.00 - 3.24	2.75 - 2.99	2.50 - 2.74	Below 2.50
165-180	■	■	■	■	■	▨	▨
163-164	■	■	■	■	■	▨	▨
161-162	■	■	■	■	▨	▨	
159-160	■	■	■	■	▨		
157-158	■	■	▨	▨			
154-156	■	▨					
150-153							
Below 150							

■	Good Possibility	▨	Possibility	☐	Slight Possibility

The Catholic University of America, Columbus School of Law

Cardinal Station
Washington, DC 20064
Phone: 202.319.5151; Fax: 202.319.6285
E-mail: admissions@law.edu; Website: www.law.edu

ABA
Approved
Since
1925

The Basics

Type of school	Private
Term	Semester
Application deadline	3/1
Application fee	$60
Financial aid deadline	5/1
Can first year start other than fall?	No
Student to faculty ratio (fall)	17.4 to 1
Does the university offer:	
housing restricted to law students?	No
graduate housing for which law students are eligible?	Yes

Faculty and Administrators

	Total		Men		Women		Minorities	
	Fall	Spr	Fall	Spr	Fall	Spr	Fall	Spr
Full-time	41	42	25	28	16	14	8	7
Other Full-time	8	8	4	4	4	4	1	1
Deans, librarians, & others who teach	4	4	2	2	2	2	0	0
Part-time	53	66	43	55	10	11	4	7
Total	106	120	74	89	32	31	13	15

Curriculum

	Full-time	Part-time
Typical first-year section size	80	80
Is there typically a "small section" of the first-year class, other than Legal Writing, taught by full-time faculty	Yes	Yes
If yes, typical size offered last year	40	40
# of classroom course titles beyond 1st year curriculum	141	
# of upper division courses, excluding seminars with an enrollment: Under 25	145	
25-49	38	
50-74	22	
75-99	2	
100+	0	
# of seminars	27	
# of seminar positions available	640	
# of seminar positions filled	275	134
# of positions available in simulation courses	407	
# of simulation positions filled	188	92
# of positions available in faculty supervised clinical courses	126	
# of faculty supervised clinical positions filled	79	17
# involved in field placements	149	37
# involved in law journals	94	31
# involved in moot court or trial competitions	33	11
# of credit hours required to graduate	84	

JD Enrollment and Ethnicity

	Men		Women		Full-time		Part-time		1st-year		Total		JD Degs. Awd.
	#	%	#	%	#	%	#	%	#	%	#	%	
African Amer.	14	3.0	29	6.1	20	3.0	23	8.1	13	4.3	43	4.5	24
Amer. Indian	2	0.4	2	0.4	4	0.6	0	0.0	1	0.3	4	0.4	0
Asian Amer.	27	5.7	51	10.7	53	7.9	25	8.8	21	7.0	78	8.2	16
Mex. Amer.	5	1.1	1	0.2	4	0.6	2	0.7	0	0.0	6	0.6	2
Puerto Rican	5	1.1	4	0.8	4	0.6	5	1.8	3	1.0	9	0.9	1
Hispanic	16	3.4	20	4.2	25	3.7	11	3.9	15	5.0	36	3.8	9
Total Minority	69	14.6	107	22.4	110	16.5	66	23.2	53	17.5	176	18.5	52
For. Nation.	3	0.6	4	0.8	3	0.4	4	1.4	1	0.3	7	0.7	4
Caucasian	317	66.9	260	54.5	399	59.8	178	62.7	176	58.3	577	60.7	234
Unknown	85	17.9	106	22.2	155	23.2	36	12.7	71	23.5	191	20.1	0
Total	474	49.8	477	50.2	667	70.1	284	29.9	301	31.8	951		290

Tuition and Fees

	Resident	Nonresident
Full-time	$30,185	$0
Part-time	$21,820	$0

Living Expenses

Estimated living expenses for singles

Living on campus	Living off campus	Living at home
$20,250	$20,250	$20,250

The Catholic University of America, Columbus School of Law

*ABA
Approved
Since
1925*

GPA and LSAT Scores

	Total	Full-time	Part-time
# of apps	3,503	2,745	758
# of admits	949	763	186
# of matrics	310	233	77
75% GPA	3.49	3.52	3.39
25% GPA	3.01	3.05	2.88
75% LSAT	159	160	158
25% LSAT	155	156	152

Grants and Scholarships (from prior year)

	Total		Full-time		Part-time	
	#	%	#	%	#	%
Total # of students	980		681		299	
Total # receiving grants	295	30.1	235	34.5	60	20.1
Less than 1/2 tuition	270	27.6	212	31.1	58	19.4
Half to full tuition	24	2.4	22	3.2	2	0.7
Full tuition	1	0.1	1	0.1	0	0.0
More than full tuition	0	0.0	0	0.0	0	0.0
Median grant amount			$10,000		$5,000	

Informational and Library Resources

# of volumes and volume equivalents	397,117
# of titles	120,973
# of active serial subscriptions	5,139
Study seating capacity inside the library	502
# of professional librarians	10
Hours per week library is open	115
# of open, wired connections available to students	432
# of networked computers available for use by students	112
# of simultaneous wireless users	500
Require computer?	N

JD Attrition (from prior year)

	Academic	Other	Total	
	#	#	#	%
1st year	6	19	25	7.8%
2nd year	1	2	3	1.1%
3rd year	1	2	3	0.9%
4th year	0	0	0	0.0%

Employment

	Total	Percentage
Employment status known	291	99.7
Employment status unknown	1	0.3
Employed	257	88.3
Pursuing graduate degrees	3	1.0
Unemployed seeking employment	22	7.6
Unemployed not seeking employment	9	3.1

Type of Employment

	Total	Percentage
# employed in law firms	97	37.7
# employed in business and industry	49	19.1
# employed in government	59	23.0
# employed in public interest	8	3.1
# employed as judicial clerks	39	15.2
# employed in academia	5	1.9

Geographic Location

	Total	Percentage
# employed in state	123	47.9
# employed in foreign countries	0	0.0
# of states where employed	21	

Bar Passage Rates

Jurisdiction	Maryland		
Exam	Sum 03	Win 04	Total
# from school taking bar for the first time	101	23	124
School's pass rate for all first-time takers	67%	52%	65%
State's pass rate for all first-time takers	73%	62%	71%

The Catholic University of America, Columbus School of Law

Cardinal Station
Washington, DC 20064
Phone: 202.319.5151; Fax: 202.319.6285
E-mail: admissions@law.edu; Website: www.law.edu

■ Introduction

Founded in 1897, The Catholic University of America, Columbus School of Law is located on the 193-acre campus of the university. Students and faculty have easy access to nearly limitless legal resources: the Supreme Court, Congress, the United States and District of Columbia courts, and other federal, executive, and administrative agencies and branches of government. For a campus so close to a center of world power, it is peaceful, pleasant, and scenic, offering a sense of neighborhood and community. Classes are small and personal.

The law school is proud of its vibrant intellectual tradition and extends it to exploring new intersections of issues of law and morality. Students are trained and encouraged to use their hearts and minds, in concert with their skills, to practice effectively in the complex world of the twenty-first century. The school welcomes students of all religious, racial, and ethnic backgrounds to a program that is renowned for its consistently high number of graduates entering public and community service. The Columbus School of Law has been a member of the AALS since 1921 and approved by the ABA since 1925.

■ Enrollment/Student Body

Total enrollment is typically more than 900 students, making the School of Law the 33rd largest in the US. Law students come from nearly every state and a dozen foreign countries. Approximately one-third of the school's enrollment is part-time, making its evening program one of the most flexible and accommodating available anywhere. First-year classes typically have 32–70 students. Upperclass courses range from 10 to 70 students. Faculty members keep posted office hours and are accessible for informal sessions, making for a more personal education.

■ Faculty

The 49-member full-time faculty brings a wealth of experience and expertise to the classroom. The majority have private-sector practice in their backgrounds. Adjunct faculty members are primarily active legal practitioners and complement the "real world" flavor of course offerings. Classroom instruction is supplemented by many distinguished guest speakers, such as federal appellate judges, justices of the US Supreme Court, and leading academicians and theologians from around the world.

■ Library and Physical Facilities

The Library of Congress and specialized law collections throughout the city complement the law school's legal collections of over 370,000 titles. The law school facility, completed in 1994, houses all components of the law school. Law students have full access to other campus facilities, including a 40-acre athletic complex.

■ Curriculum

The prescribed first-year curriculum and method of teaching are designed to develop the analytical skills that characterize the able lawyer and to give the student familiarity with the major substantive areas of law, as well as an introduction to jurisprudence and the Catholic intellectual tradition as it relates to the larger questions of social justice. While lawyers traditionally have been heavily involved with the commercial interests of private or corporate clients, law is becoming increasingly responsive to problems that affect the public interest. The CUA law school curriculum is designed to provide students with the basic knowledge to become effective lawyers in a changing legal environment.

■ Special Programs

CUA law school's institutes and special programs offer certification of a student's developed expertise in his or her chosen legal specialty. Each program provides invaluable externship opportunities, offering for-credit placements available nowhere else but in Washington, DC.

The Institute for Communications Law Studies is nearly 25 years old and offers unique specialized training in communications law, ranging from First Amendment law to FCC practices and procedures.

The Comparative and International Law Institute provides superb background training to students who intend to specialize in international law. The institute offers a six-week summer abroad program at the Jagiellonian University in Krakow, Poland.

The Law and Public Policy Program combines classroom study in legislative and administrative processes with externships in government agencies and advocacy organizations that affect national public policy.

The Corporate and Securities Law Program offers a broad concentration of securities and corporate law courses and related externships. Many of its course offerings are taught by senior staff from the Securities and Exchange Commission and the National Association of Securities Dealers, in addition to faculty members.

The Interdisciplinary Program in Law and Religion was created to provide a forum for study, research, and public discussion of the issues that arise from the nexus of law and religion. These include questions of separation of church and state, public and private morality, and the concerns of the institutional church regarding established legal norms.

Clinical Programs

The law school offers seven clinical programs, including five that emphasize client representation, case planning, and trial and administrative advocacy. A group of nine simulation courses are also offered that closely approximate real-life lawyering through courtroom experiences and simulated trials and procedures. The two other clinical offerings are the SEC Observer Program and the Legal Externship Program.

Admission

While considerable weight is given to an applicant's grade-point average and LSAT score, admission decisions are also influenced by such factors as leadership qualities, rank in class, improving performance, potential for contributing to diversity, and relevant work experience. Close attention is also paid to a candidate's personal statement and reasons for wanting to study at CUA.

The Preface Program summer introductory course is offered to entering students whose credentials suggest that a brief preparatory program would be especially beneficial.

Student Activities

The *Catholic University Law Review*, the *Journal of Contemporary Health Law and Policy*, and *CommLaw Conspectus: Journal of Communications Law and Policy* are scholarly law journals staffed and published by outstanding students.

The Moot Court Board, in addition to facilitating at least eight intraschool competitions each year, also hosts two major contests at CUA: the National Telecommunications Competition and the Sutherland Cup. There are upwards of 30 voluntary student organizations at the Columbus School of Law, encompassing a broad range of professional interests, ethnic and racial affiliations, political and religious outlooks, and recreational activities.

Expenses and Financial Aid

Financial aid decisions are made beginning in March.

Career Services

The Office of Legal Career Services actively supports students and graduates in their search for employment by providing counseling as well as workshops, panel discussions, and access to a national alumni network. On-campus interviews are provided. The school's small size permits individual counseling for each student desiring assistance. Our admission brochure lists employment statistics.

Housing

The availability of graduate housing varies each year. It is advisable to contact the office of campus housing as early as possible. Housing that is on or near campus is convenient to public transportation, including the Metrorail system.

Applicant Profile

The Catholic University of America, Columbus School of Law
This grid includes only applicants who earned 120-180 LSAT scores under standard administrations.

LSAT Score	3.75 +		3.50 - 3.74		3.25 - 3.49		3.00 - 3.24		2.75 - 2.99		2.50 - 2.74		2.25 - 2.49		2.00 - 2.24		Below 2.00		No GPA		Total	
	Apps	Adm	Apps	Adm	Apps	Adm	Apps	Adm	Apps	Adm	Apps	Adm	Apps	Adm	Apps	Adm	Apps	Adm	Apps	Adm	Apps	Adm
175-180	0	0	0	0	0	0	0	0	0	0	1	1	0	0	0	0	0	0	0	0	1	1
170-174	0	0	1	1	1	1	3	3	0	0	0	0	2	2	0	0	0	0	0	0	7	7
165-169	4	3	9	9	8	7	15	13	8	7	5	3	7	2	4	1	0	0	0	0	60	45
160-164	44	39	61	50	75	64	74	66	48	33	35	20	21	9	4	2	1	0	2	1	365	284
155-159	72	58	181	109	240	127	201	109	127	35	68	11	44	5	10	0	2	0	4	1	949	455
150-154	81	22	200	36	258	33	245	19	152	6	97	4	37	1	21	2	2	0	13	3	1106	126
145-149	30	2	78	7	147	2	138	5	99	3	78	1	44	1	10	0	1	0	9	0	634	21
140-144	8	0	25	0	45	0	56	0	64	2	34	0	24	1	10	0	4	0	8	0	278	3
135-139	1	0	6	0	17	0	18	0	26	0	18	0	12	0	7	0	6	0	6	0	117	0
130-134	0	0	0	0	3	0	4	0	7	0	6	0	5	0	5	0	0	0	1	0	31	0
125-129	0	0	0	0	1	0	3	0	2	0	0	0	2	0	1	0	0	0	1	0	10	0
120-124	0	0	0	0	0	0	0	0	1	0	0	0	0	0	0	0	0	0	0	0	1	0
Total	240	124	561	212	795	234	757	215	534	86	342	40	198	21	72	5	16	0	44	5	3559	942

Apps = Number of Applicants   Adm = Number Admitted   Reflects 99% of the total applicant pool.

This grid should be used only as a general guide, as many nonnumerical factors are considered in admission decisions.

Chapman University School of Law

One University Drive
Orange, CA 92866
Phone: 877.CHAPLAW or 714.628.2500; Fax: 714.628.2501
E-mail: lawadm@chapman.edu; Website: www.chapman.edu/law

ABA
Approved
Since
1998

The Basics

Type of school	Private
Term	Semester
Application deadline	6/1
Application fee	$60
Financial aid deadline	3/2
Can first year start other than fall?	No
Student to faculty ratio (fall)	18.9 to 1
Does the university offer:	
housing restricted to law students?	No
graduate housing for which law students are eligible?	No

Faculty and Administrators

	Total		Men		Women		Minorities	
	Fall	Spr	Fall	Spr	Fall	Spr	Fall	Spr
Full-time	22	22	14	14	8	8	3	3
Other Full-time	0	0	0	0	0	0	0	0
Deans, librarians, & others who teach	6	6	3	3	3	3	0	0
Part-time	35	40	25	29	10	11	3	6
Total	63	68	42	46	21	22	6	9

Curriculum

		Full-time	Part-time
Typical first-year section size		62	0
Is there typically a "small section" of the first-year class, other than Legal Writing, taught by full-time faculty		No	No
If yes, typical size offered last year		0	0
# of classroom course titles beyond 1st year curriculum		80	
# of upper division courses, excluding seminars with an enrollment:	Under 25	62	
	25-49	22	
	50-74	7	
	75-99	1	
	100+	0	
# of seminars		9	
# of seminar positions available		136	
# of seminar positions filled		92	25
# of positions available in simulation courses		142	
# of simulation positions filled		44	73
# of positions available in faculty supervised clinical courses		62	
# of faculty supervised clinical positions filled	33		0
# involved in field placements	70		0
# involved in law journals	112		28
# involved in moot court or trial competitions	39		23
# of credit hours required to graduate		88	

J.D. Enrollment and Ethnicity

	Men		Women		Full-time		Part-time		1st-year		Total		JD Degs. Awd.
	#	%	#	%	#	%	#	%	#	%	#	%	
African Amer.	2	0.8	3	1.1	4	0.9	1	1.5	0	0.0	5	1.0	1
Amer. Indian	1	0.4	3	1.1	3	0.7	1	1.5	1	0.6	4	0.8	0
Asian Amer.	43	16.6	54	20.6	87	19.2	10	14.7	38	21.0	97	18.6	16
Mex. Amer.	9	3.5	7	2.7	10	2.2	6	8.8	2	1.1	16	3.1	8
Puerto Rican	0	0.0	1	0.4	1	0.2	0	0.0	0	0.0	1	0.2	0
Hispanic	7	2.7	8	3.1	12	2.6	3	4.4	6	3.3	15	2.9	5
Total Minority	62	23.9	76	29.0	117	25.8	21	30.9	47	26.0	138	26.5	30
For. Nation.	0	0.0	0	0.0	0	0.0	0	0.0	0	0.0	0	0.0	0
Caucasian	127	49.0	131	50.0	230	50.8	28	41.2	94	51.9	258	49.5	68
Unknown	70	27.0	55	21.0	106	23.4	19	27.9	40	22.1	125	24.0	0
Total	259	49.7	262	50.3	453	86.9	68	13.1	181	34.7	521		98

Tuition and Fees

	Resident	Nonresident
Full-time	$27,941	$27,941
Part-time	$19,217	$19,217

Living Expenses

Estimated living expenses for singles

Living on campus	Living off campus	Living at home
N/A	$15,400	$7,460

Chapman University School of Law

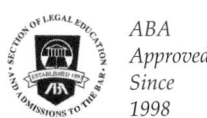

*ABA
Approved
Since
1998*

GPA and LSAT Scores

	Total	Full-time	Part-time
# of apps	2,333	2,333	0
# of admits	595	595	0
# of matrics	181	181	0
75% GPA	3.47	3.47	0.00
25% GPA	3.00	3.00	0.00
75% LSAT	158	158	0
25% LSAT	154	154	0

Grants and Scholarships (from prior year)

	Total		Full-time		Part-time	
	#	%	#	%	#	%
Total # of students	449		352		97	
Total # receiving grants	231	51.4	206	58.5	25	25.8
Less than 1/2 tuition	86	19.2	71	20.2	15	15.5
Half to full tuition	107	23.8	99	28.1	8	8.2
Full tuition	35	7.8	33	9.4	2	2.1
More than full tuition	3	0.7	3	0.9	0	0.0
Median grant amount			$15,210		$5,226	

Informational and Library Resources

# of volumes and volume equivalents	273,687
# of titles	156,362
# of active serial subscriptions	3,141
Study seating capacity inside the library	322
# of professional librarians	4
Hours per week library is open	100
# of open, wired connections available to students	577
# of networked computers available for use by students	40
# of simultaneous wireless users	500
Require computer?	N

JD Attrition (from prior year)

	Academic	Other	Total	
	#	#	#	%
1st year	11	6	17	9.2%
2nd year	1	12	13	9.4%
3rd year	1	2	3	2.9%
4th year	0	1	1	4.5%

Employment

	Total	Percentage
Employment status known	94	97.9
Employment status unknown	2	2.1
Employed	85	90.4
Pursuing graduate degrees	2	2.1
Unemployed seeking employment	5	5.3
Unemployed not seeking employment	2	2.1

Type of Employment

	Total	Percentage
# employed in law firms	35	41.2
# employed in business and industry	31	36.5
# employed in government	5	5.9
# employed in public interest	2	2.4
# employed as judicial clerks	6	7.1
# employed in academia	4	4.7

Geographic Location

	Total	Percentage
# employed in state	77	90.6
# employed in foreign countries	1	1.2
# of states where employed	6	

Bar Passage Rates

Jurisdiction	California		
Exam	Sum 03	Win 04	Total
# from school taking bar for the first time	74	21	95
School's pass rate for all first-time takers	57%	43%	54%
State's pass rate for all first-time takers	63%	47%	60%

Chapman University School of Law

One University Drive
Orange, CA 92866
Phone: 877.CHAPLAW or 714.628.2500; Fax: 714.628.2501
E-mail: lawadm@chapman.edu; Website: www.chapman.edu/law

■ Introduction

Chapman University School of Law is located in the Historic Old Towne District of Orange, California, and shares the campus with the university, a 144-year-old institution. The law school, established in 1995, received full approval by the ABA in 2002.

In nine short years, the law school is rapidly gaining a national reputation for its high quality of faculty, students, and facilities. Offering a curriculum strong in business and corporate law, the law school also has focus areas in taxation, environmental/real estate/land use and advocacy, and dispute resolution, a joint JD/MBA degree, and an LLM degree in Taxation. The law school's successes have been aided by its location in vibrant and dynamic Orange County.

Affiliation with a well-established university allows for cross-disciplinary engagement, joint degrees, and a lively and engaging intellectual environment beyond the classroom. Chapman University offers an impressive selection of artistic and cultural opportunities for its students.

■ Enrollment/Student Body

Chapman Law has committed itself to building a small, talented, and diverse student body. Total student enrollment in 2004–2005 was 529 law students.

The 2004 entering class consisted of 181 law students. The students were divided into three small first-year sections. The Legal Research and Writing course has approximately 12 to 15 students in each of the 15 sections. Currently, about 10 percent of the entering class comes from outside California; that number is expected to increase over the next few years as Chapman's reputation reaches a more national audience. The minority enrollment has been 33 to 34 percent for the past three consecutive years.

Competition for seats is keen. Only 26 percent of applicants in the 2004 entering class were admitted.

■ Faculty

Chapman has assembled an impressive law faculty (including two former US Supreme Court clerks) who are excellent teachers, accomplished scholars, and outstanding mentors. Chapman Law's environment is conducive to learning. Students have access to the faculty and frequent opportunities to engage them in both formal and informal settings.

■ Library and Physical Facilities

The stately and beautifully appointed $30 million Donald P. Kennedy Hall opened in 1999, with state-of-the-art learning facilities in its classrooms, law library, and trial and appellate courtrooms.

Library holdings now exceed 276,000 volumes and volume equivalents, and the collection is expected to continue its rapid growth. The collection is fully accessible to students both in hard copy and through the computer network.

Library carrels and desktops are generous in number, and many are wired for Internet access. Several private study rooms are available for student use and extended research.

Two state-of-the-art courtrooms provide computers, cameras, and electronic blackboards for trial advocacy exercises, competitions, and formal hearings by visiting courts.

Student relaxation lounges, locker areas, and office space are located throughout the building.

■ Special Programs/Clinics/Externships

The law school offers the JD/MBA program, affording students the opportunity to earn the equivalent of two accredited professional degrees in four instead of the typical five years. Chapman's George L. Argyros School of Business and Economics is AACSB accredited.

About 10 percent of the students choose to focus their electives in one of three certificate areas: taxation, environmental/real estate/land use, or advocacy and dispute resolution. The Tax Program affords students the opportunity to represent claimants against the IRS in the US Tax Court Clinic. The Center for Land Resources allows students to network with practicing professionals. In the Externship Program, students receive placements in the offices of appellate justices, trial judges, district attorneys, and public defenders where they gain hands-on experience and academic credit.

Clinic offerings include those in Elder Law, Constitutional Litigation, Tax Law, and Appellate Practice. Nearly all clinics allow students additional opportunities to represent actual clients in an array of legal settings.

■ Admission

The School of Law seeks to admit stellar students who are passionately interested in a legal education that will challenge them to grow intellectually, ethically, and professionally. The law school seeks a diverse student body that will make a meaningful contribution to the legal profession. Many variables enter into the decision-making process. The applicant's entire file is considered and each application is individually reviewed. The Admission Committee reviews the traditional numbers—your academic record and LSAT—but also considers additional indicators of potential success in law school. Such indicators include the nature and rigor of the undergraduate discipline, an upward trend in academic performance, coursework, writing ability, employment history, graduate-level courses taken and degrees earned, scholarly achievement, community and volunteer service, research projects, demonstrated leadership ability, fluency in foreign languages, personal background, including a history of overcoming adversity, and unusual contributions or other maturing experiences. Two letters of recommendation are required; these should be submitted directly to the LSDAS. A personal statement and résumé are also required, and they should be submitted with your application. Early application is encouraged as the entering class is filled on a rolling basis and scholarship funds may be exhausted early in the admission cycle. There is a priority consideration deadline of April 1, 2005, for merit-based scholarships.

Student Curricular and Cocurricular Activities

The law school offers many activities that enrich the academic program and provide important training in leadership. Two journals offer valuable experience in research, writing, and editing. The Student Bar Association administers a full range of programs. Other organizations include the Minority Law Students Association, LaRaza, Asian Pacific American Law Student Association, the Public Interest Law Foundation, the Federalist Society, and the student-run Honor Council.

Chapman offers a range of advocacy experiences, including participation in mock trial, moot court, client counseling, international law, and negotiation competitions. Chapman teams have won regional competitions and have performed competitively in national and international tournaments. The Moot Court Board and the Mock Trial Board administer their programs and provide excellent practical training.

Scholarships and Financial Aid

Chapman Law offers a generous merit- and need-based scholarship program. For the 2004 entering class, more than 61 percent of new students received scholarships. After the first year, law students are eligible to compete for merit scholarships provided they rank within the top 30 percent of their class. For 2004, over $2.8 million in scholarship funds were distributed among a student body of approximately 529.

Chapman also offers a full range of loan programs to complement students' financial needs, including Stafford loans, Perkins loans, and private loans. All students receiving scholarship funds and/or loans should plan to file the FAFSA and a preliminary financial aid application. International students are eligible for merit scholarships.

Career Services

Chapman Law has established an enviable network of relationships in Orange County to assist students in their job-search efforts. A student/attorney mentor program places students in a direct mentoring relationship with many of the area's outstanding practitioners.

An active Career Services Office provides on-campus interviews, workshops, panels, and guest speakers to help educate students about the many possible areas of practice and how to secure employment.

Applicant Profile

Chapman University School of Law

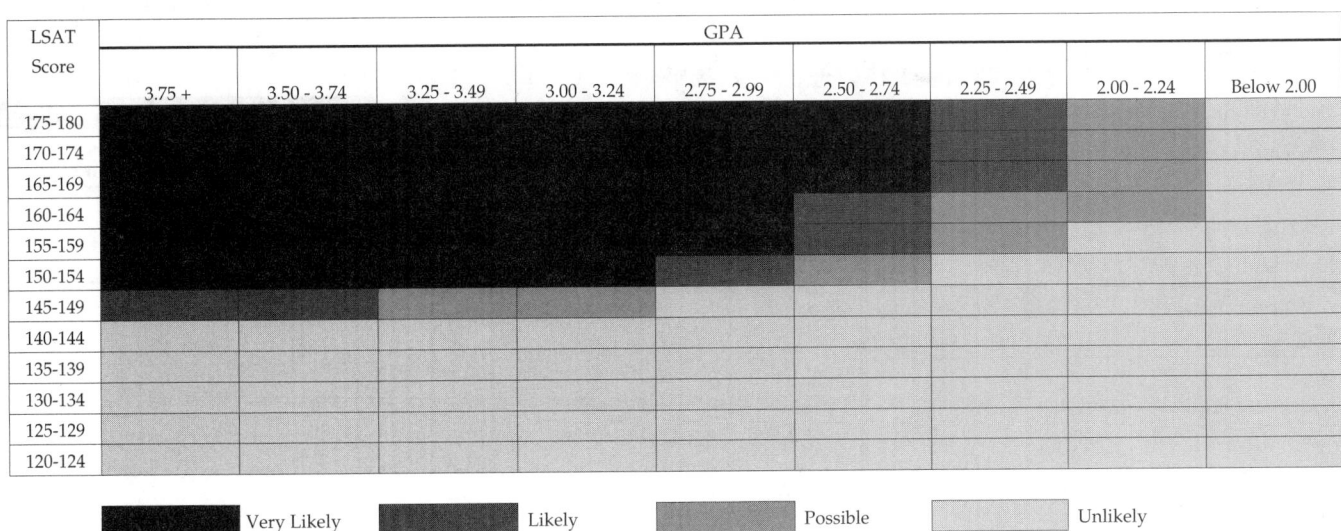

The University of Chicago Law School

1111 E 60th Street
Chicago, IL 60637
Phone: 773.702.9494; Fax: 773.834.0942
E-mail: admissions@law.uchicago.edu; Website: www.law.uchicago.edu

ABA Approved Since 1923

The Basics

Type of school	Private
Term	Quarter
Application deadline	2/1
Application fee	$65
Financial aid deadline	3/1
Can first year start other than fall?	No
Student to faculty ratio (fall)	9.9 to 1
Does the university offer:	
housing restricted to law students?	No
graduate housing for which law students are eligible?	Yes

Curriculum

		Full-time	Part-time
Typical first-year section size		98	0
Is there typically a "small section" of the first-year class, other than Legal Writing, taught by full-time faculty		No	No
If yes, typical size offered last year		0	0
# of classroom course titles beyond 1st year curriculum		99	
# of upper division courses, excluding seminars with an enrollment:	Under 25	36	
	25-49	30	
	50-74	16	
	75-99	9	
	100+	8	
# of seminars		75	
# of seminar positions available		1,319	
# of seminar positions filled		1,319	0
# of positions available in simulation courses		440	
# of simulation positions filled		440	0
# of positions available in faculty supervised clinical courses		69	
# of faculty supervised clinical positions filled		69	0
# involved in field placements		28	0
# involved in law journals		80	0
# involved in moot court or trial competitions		50	0
# of credit hours required to graduate		105	

Faculty and Administrators

	Total		Men		Women		Minorities	
	Fall	Spr	Fall	Spr	Fall	Spr	Fall	Spr
Full-time	50	47	41	38	9	9	3	5
Other Full-time	11	11	4	4	7	7	1	1
Deans, librarians, & others who teach	2	2	1	1	1	1	0	0
Part-time	18	57	14	47	4	10	1	3
Total	81	117	60	90	21	27	5	9

JD Enrollment and Ethnicity

	Men		Women		Full-time		Part-time		1st-year		Total		JD Degs. Awd.
	#	%	#	%	#	%	#	%	#	%	#	%	
African Amer.	15	4.5	26	9.8	41	6.9	0	0.0	15	7.8	41	6.9	10
Amer. Indian	1	0.3	2	0.8	3	0.5	0	0.0	1	0.5	3	0.5	4
Asian Amer.	42	12.7	49	18.5	91	15.3	0	0.0	26	13.5	91	15.3	22
Mex. Amer.	6	1.8	10	3.8	16	2.7	0	0.0	8	4.2	16	2.7	2
Puerto Rican	1	0.3	4	1.5	5	0.8	0	0.0	2	1.0	5	0.8	12
Hispanic	13	3.9	19	7.2	32	5.4	0	0.0	13	6.8	32	5.4	0
Total Minority	78	23.6	110	41.5	188	31.5	0	0.0	65	33.9	188	31.5	50
For. Nation.	5	1.5	4	1.5	9	1.5	0	0.0	1	0.5	9	1.5	0
Caucasian	199	60.1	132	49.8	331	55.5	0	0.0	100	52.1	331	55.5	122
Unknown	49	14.8	19	7.2	68	11.4	0	0.0	26	13.5	68	11.4	19
Total	331	55.5	265	44.5	596	100.0	0	0.0	192	32.2	596		191

Tuition and Fees

	Resident	Nonresident
Full-time	$34,419	$34,419
Part-time	$0	$0

Living Expenses

Estimated living expenses for singles

Living on campus	Living off campus	Living at home
$20,304	$20,304	$20,304

The University of Chicago Law School

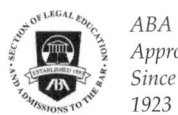

ABA
Approved
Since
1923

GPA and LSAT Scores

	Total	Full-time	Part-time
# of apps	4,737	4,737	0
# of admits	750	750	0
# of matrics	192	192	0
75% GPA	0.00	3.78	0.00
25% GPA	0.00	3.47	0.00
75% LSAT	0	171	0
25% LSAT	0	167	0

Grants and Scholarships (from prior year)

	Total #	Total %	Full-time #	Full-time %	Part-time #	Part-time %
Total # of students	589		589		0	
Total # receiving grants	306	52.0	306	52.0	0	0.0
Less than 1/2 tuition	226	38.4	226	38.4	0	0.0
Half to full tuition	80	13.6	80	13.6	0	0.0
Full tuition	0	0.0	0	0.0	0	0.0
More than full tuition	0	0.0	0	0.0	0	0.0
Median grant amount			$11,000		$0	

Informational and Library Resources

# of volumes and volume equivalents	703,843
# of titles	285,875
# of active serial subscriptions	8,855
Study seating capacity inside the library	450
# of professional librarians	10
Hours per week library is open	90
# of open, wired connections available to students	1,038
# of networked computers available for use by students	32
# of simultaneous wireless users	220
Require computer?	Y

JD Attrition (from prior year)

	Academic #	Other #	Total #	Total %
1st year	0	8	8	4.1%
2nd year	0	0	0	0.0%
3rd year	1	0	1	0.5%
4th year	0	0	0	0.0%

Employment

	Total	Percentage
Employment status known	211	100.0
Employment status unknown	0	0.0
Employed	203	96.2
Pursuing graduate degrees	0	0.0
Unemployed seeking employment	3	1.4
Unemployed not seeking employment	5	2.4

Type of Employment

# employed in law firms	151	74.4
# employed in business and industry	3	1.5
# employed in government	7	3.4
# employed in public interest	6	3.0
# employed as judicial clerks	33	16.3
# employed in academia	3	1.5

Geographic Location

# employed in state	82	40.4
# employed in foreign countries	1	0.5
# of states where employed	28	

Bar Passage Rates

Jurisdiction	Illinois			New York		
Exam	Sum 03	Win 04	Total	Sum 03	Win 04	Total
# from school taking bar for the first time	92	7	99	47	6	53
School's pass rate for all first-time takers	97%	100%	97%	91%	100%	92%
State's pass rate for all first-time takers	86%	78%	84%	78%	58%	75%

The University of Chicago Law School

1111 E 60th Street
Chicago, IL 60637
Phone: 773.702.9494; Fax: 773.834.0942
E-mail: admissions@law.uchicago.edu; Website: www.law.uchicago.edu

■ Introduction

Chicago graduates lead and innovate in government, public causes, academia, and business, as well as law. For this reason, Chicago aims not to certify lawyers, but to train well-rounded, critical, and socially conscious thinkers and doers. Three cornerstones provide the foundation for Chicago's educational mission: the life of the mind, participatory learning, and interdisciplinary inquiry.

■ Enrollment/Student Body

Our students' chief passion is intellectual rigor. They have shown this passion through their academic success, and they exhibit signs of great professional promise. About 5,000 applicants seek approximately 190–195 seats in each incoming class. Chicago students come from more than 100 undergraduate institutions with degrees in nearly every discipline, and one in ten have graduate degrees. Many of our students have also had interesting and successful careers before law school.

■ Faculty

What distinguishes Chicago faculty is their devotion to both teaching and scholarship. This might seem a contradiction at first, but at Chicago, teaching and scholarship complement each other. Chicago professors blaze trails in legal thought, and their revolutionary ideas infuse classroom discussion with immediacy and excitement. Our professors write the books, draft the statutes, and decide the cases that students read at law schools across America. During the 2004–2005 academic year, our faculty will teach more than 170 courses and seminars at the Law School.

■ Curriculum

As a first-year student, you will take a core sequence covering five principal areas of the law: contracts, torts, property, criminal law, and civil procedure; a required interdisciplinary course—Elements of the Law; an elective; as well as a year-long course on research and writing. This curriculum familiarizes you with the basic principles of Anglo-American law, cultivates legal reasoning, develops writing ability, and introduces students to interdisciplinary approaches to the law.

In the second and third years, you can choose courses from the full range of Chicago's more than 170 classes. Generally, classes are small; more than 60 percent have fewer than 25 students in them. Additionally, in an average year, about one-third of the second- and third-year students take classes in other divisions of the university.

■ Special Programs

Students may also pursue joint degrees with any other division of the university. Popular programs include business, public policy, international affairs, history, and economics. Students must apply separately to the other program they want to pursue, and they can apply for the other program either before they start law school or during their first year of law school.

■ Clinical Opportunities

Housed in the Arthur Kane Center, our clinics involve more than 100 students each year in representing clients with real-world problems. The Mandel Legal Aid Clinic handles matters involving appellate advocacy, criminal and juvenile justice, employment discrimination, civil rights, housing, and mental health. The MacArthur Justice Center litigates a wide range of matters with constitutional significance to the criminal justice system. The Institute for Justice Clinic on Entrepreneurship assists aspiring entry-level entrepreneurs from low- and moderate-income neighborhoods. The Law School also partners with outside agencies to provide additional clinical opportunities to our students.

■ Student Activities

About 40 percent of upper-class students serve on one of the three student-edited journals, the newest of which is *The Chicago Journal of International Law*. The Hinton Moot Court Board conducts a program in appellate advocacy for upper-class students, and first-year students participate in a moot court as part of the writing and research program. More than 40 student organizations provide opportunities for the exploration of legal specialties, affiliation with like-minded students, or networking within identity groups.

■ Career Services

Our career services office assists students with permanent and summer employment. Four professional career advisors counsel students in one-on-one planning sessions. Programs on types of practices and nontraditional careers are organized throughout the year for students. Graduates of the Class of 2004 took jobs in these areas: 69 percent joined law firms, 21 percent are clerking for judges, 7 percent are in government/public service, 2 percent are in business, and 1 percent are continuing their education. During the 2004–2005 term, seven graduates clerked for the US Supreme Court. The top four destinations for our graduates are Chicago, Los Angeles, New York, and Washington DC.

The University of Chicago Law School

■ Location

Hyde Park provides Chicago students with the best of all possible worlds: a campus with a college-town atmosphere just a few miles from the downtown of a vibrant city. Hyde Park is a dynamic community complete with parks, museums, and multiple bookstores. The Law School is located at the southern end of campus, facing an expansive "front lawn" known as the Midway Plaisance. Surrounding the Law School are a tree-lined, diverse residential neighborhood, a sandy Lake Michigan beach, and two sprawling parks. The campus itself is a Gothic masterpiece whose limestone buildings, built around tree-shaded quadrangles, sport gargoyles, ivy, and turrets. The Law School's modern building promotes interaction among faculty and students, while the recently remodeled classroom wing enhances the learning experience.

■ Housing

A graduate residence hall, located two blocks from the Law School, is available to law students. Most rooms are singles with private baths. In addition, the university has plenty of single and married students neighborhood housing available. Many upper-class students choose to rent housing from private landlords. Buses run frequently throughout the surrounding neighborhood, providing transportation to and from residences and the Law School. Public transportation is easily accessible to other neighborhoods in Chicago.

■ Admission

Each year we seek to create a community from among the best and brightest law school applicants. We want students who are intellectually curious, lively, collegial, and rigorous in their academic approach. We want students who will take their legal education seriously but not take themselves too seriously. And because we are preparing students to enter a multifaceted profession, we want multidimensional students with a wide range of talents, backgrounds, experiences, and accomplishments. We do not use indices, formulas, or cutoffs.

■ Financial Aid

Your Chicago legal education is an investment in your future. Because many students will not have sufficient personal resources to make this investment, Chicago provides generous financial aid. Approximately 50 percent of the students receive scholarships and most of these are supplemented if the student engages in public interest work during the summer after second year. In addition to scholarships, over 75 percent of students receive government-backed and private loans. Also, the Law School provides financial assistance to graduates who enter careers in public interest legal work through our generous Hormel Public Interest Program.

Applicant Profile

We seek to create a community from among the best, the brightest, and the most interesting law school applicants. We do not believe that the LSAT and GPA alone provide us with sufficient information to evaluate an applicant's likely contributions to our community; therefore, we do not use any formulas, indices, or numerical cutoffs. We do not provide an applicant profile here, because it would be based solely on the LSAT and GPA.

Chicago-Kent College of Law, Illinois Institute of Technology

565 West Adams Street
Chicago, IL 60661
Phone: 312.906.5020; Fax: 312.906.5274
E-mail: admit@kentlaw.edu; Website: www.kentlaw.edu

*ABA
Approved
Since
1936*

The Basics

Type of school	Private
Term	Semester
Application deadline	3/1
Application fee	$60
Financial aid deadline	4/15
Can first year start other than fall?	No
Student to faculty ratio (fall)	12.5 to 1
Does the university offer:	
housing restricted to law students?	No
graduate housing for which law students are eligible?	Yes

Faculty and Administrators

	Total		Men		Women		Minorities	
	Fall	Spr	Fall	Spr	Fall	Spr	Fall	Spr
Full-time	65	66	42	43	23	23	3	3
Other Full-time	1	1	0	0	1	1	0	0
Deans, librarians, & others who teach	4	4	2	2	2	2	1	1
Part-time	79	97	58	72	21	25	7	8
Total	**149**	**168**	**102**	**117**	**47**	**51**	**11**	**12**

Curriculum

	Full-time	Part-time
Typical first-year section size	54	48
Is there typically a "small section" of the first-year class, other than Legal Writing, taught by full-time faculty	No	No
If yes, typical size offered last year	0	0
# of classroom course titles beyond 1st year curriculum	139	

# of upper division courses, excluding seminars with an enrollment:		
Under 25	197	
25-49	44	
50-74	17	
75-99	10	
100+	3	

# of seminars	30	
# of seminar positions available	465	
# of seminar positions filled	227	51
# of positions available in simulation courses	653	
# of simulation positions filled	211	291
# of positions available in faculty supervised clinical courses	218	
# of faculty supervised clinical positions filled	192	18
# involved in field placements	133	8
# involved in law journals	51	10
# involved in moot court or trial competitions	57	4
# of credit hours required to graduate	87	

J.D. Enrollment and Ethnicity

	Men		Women		Full-time		Part-time		1st-year		Total		JD Degs. Awd.
	#	%	#	%	#	%	#	%	#	%	#	%	
African Amer.	25	4.3	31	6.2	38	4.7	18	6.7	23	5.8	56	5.2	14
Amer. Indian	2	0.3	3	0.6	4	0.5	1	0.4	1	0.3	5	0.5	0
Asian Amer.	53	9.2	38	7.6	71	8.8	20	7.5	36	9.5	91	8.5	7
Mex. Amer.	9	1.6	9	1.8	12	1.5	6	2.2	6	1.6	18	1.7	3
Puerto Rican	5	0.9	0	0.0	4	0.5	1	0.4	1	0.3	5	0.5	0
Hispanic	11	1.9	13	2.6	18	2.2	6	2.2	13	3.4	24	2.2	3
Total Minority	105	18.2	94	18.9	147	18.3	52	19.4	80	20.8	199	18.5	27
For. Nation.	4	0.7	6	1.2	5	0.6	5	1.9	0	0.0	10	0.9	3
Caucasian	427	74.1	366	73.6	600	74.6	193	72.0	274	72.1	793	74.0	227
Unknown	40	6.9	31	6.2	53	6.6	18	6.7	27	7.1	71	6.6	23
Total	576	53.7	497	46.4	805	75.0	268	25.0	381	35.4	1073		280

Tuition and Fees

	Resident	Nonresident
Full-time	$27,696	$27,696
Part-time	$20,240	$20,240

Living Expenses

Estimated living expenses for singles

Living on campus	Living off campus	Living at home
$14,506	$19,700	$11,150

Chicago-Kent College of Law, Illinois Institute of Technology

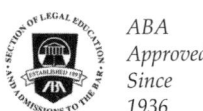

*ABA
Approved
Since
1936*

GPA and LSAT Scores

	Total	Full-time	Part-time
# of apps	3,827	3,178	649
# of admits	1,211	987	224
# of matrics	381	280	101
75% GPA	3.59	3.64	3.41
25% GPA	3.08	3.14	2.94
75% LSAT	161	162	158
25% LSAT	156	157	154

Grants and Scholarships (from prior year)

	Total		Full-time		Part-time	
	#	%	#	%	#	%
Total # of students	992		746		246	
Total # receiving grants	482	48.6	374	50.1	108	43.9
Less than 1/2 tuition	355	35.8	256	34.3	99	40.2
Half to full tuition	97	9.8	89	11.9	8	3.3
Full tuition	10	1.0	9	1.2	1	0.4
More than full tuition	20	2.0	20	2.7	0	0.0
Median grant amount			$7,000		$4,000	

Informational and Library Resources

# of volumes and volume equivalents	585,763
# of titles	146,352
# of active serial subscriptions	9,399
Study seating capacity inside the library	602
# of professional librarians	11
Hours per week library is open	96
# of open, wired connections available to students	1,819
# of networked computers available for use by students	76
# of simultaneous wireless users	125
Require computer?	N

JD Attrition (from prior year)

	Academic	Other	Total	
	#	#	#	%
1st year	14	20	34	10.6%
2nd year	6	4	10	3.0%
3rd year	0	0	0	0.0%
4th year	0	0	0	0.0%

Employment

	Total	Percentage
Employment status known	272	98.9
Employment status unknown	3	1.1
Employed	243	89.3
Pursuing graduate degrees	5	1.8
Unemployed seeking employment	7	2.6
Unemployed not seeking employment	17	6.3

Type of Employment

	Total	Percentage
# employed in law firms	160	65.8
# employed in business and industry	29	11.9
# employed in government	41	16.9
# employed in public interest	1	0.4
# employed as judicial clerks	7	2.9
# employed in academia	5	2.1

Geographic Location

	Total	Percentage
# employed in state	212	87.2
# employed in foreign countries	0	0.0
# of states where employed	21	

Bar Passage Rates

Jurisdiction		Illinois		
Exam	Sum 03	Win 04	Total	
# from school taking bar for the first time	205	42	247	
School's pass rate for all first-time takers	89%	83%	88%	
State's pass rate for all first-time takers	86%	78%	84%	

Chicago-Kent College of Law, Illinois Institute of Technology

Office of Admissions, 565 West Adams Street
Chicago, IL 60661
Phone: 312.906.5020; Fax: 312.906.5274
E-mail: admit@kentlaw.edu; Website: www.kentlaw.edu

■ Introduction

Chicago-Kent College of Law, Illinois Institute of Technology, is a national leader in legal education, recognized for the strength of its faculty and for its innovative approaches to traditional legal education.
The second oldest law school in Illinois, Chicago-Kent was founded in 1888 by two judges who believed that legal education should be available to working men and women. In 1895, Chicago-Kent graduated its first female and minority students. Today, Chicago-Kent students come from 37 states and several foreign countries, and from more than 260 colleges and universities.

Drawing on its distinctive affiliation with Illinois Institute of Technology, Chicago-Kent is at the vanguard of exploring new frontiers in the law raised by biotechnology, cyberspace, environmental regulation, intellectual property, international criminal law enforcement, and much more. Chicago-Kent is located in downtown Chicago, the heart of the city's commercial and legal communities. The law school is fully accredited by the ABA and the AALS, and is a member of the Order of the Coif.

■ Faculty

The foundation for academic excellence at Chicago-Kent derives from its faculty, which engages in broad-ranging legal scholarship and research. Chicago-Kent's faculty is among the nation's most productive law faculties based on the number of scholarly books and articles they have published in leading academic presses, law reviews, and journals. As advisors frequently approached for their expertise, they help shape policy and thinking on a variety of issues, and make it a point to involve students in their particular areas of influence.

■ Library and Physical Facilities

Chicago-Kent's modern, 10-story building features a three-story atrium, five-level library, technologically advanced courtroom, auditorium, computer labs, student lounges, and cafeteria. Chicago-Kent's library is one of the 30 largest law school libraries in the country. The collection includes the Library of International Relations, one of the largest and most comprehensive international law collections, and a wealth of material on environmental and energy law, intellectual property law, international trade law, and labor law.

The law school houses a sophisticated computer network with more than 1,900 network connections located throughout the building and library, and at each seat in the majority of classrooms. Wireless service is available in the courtroom, front lobby, cafeteria, student lounge, and select classrooms.

Affordable housing is available in nearby urban and suburban neighborhoods. On-campus housing is available on the university's main campus, approximately five miles south of the law school. A free shuttle runs between the two campuses. The law school is close to all public transportation downtown.

■ Curriculum

Both full-time and part-time programs are available. Full-time students usually complete the JD degree in three years. Part-time students usually finish in four years. Students may apply to transfer between divisions after completing the required courses in the division in which they originally enrolled. First-year class sizes range from 30 to 90 students.

Degrees available include JD; JD/MBA; JD/MPA; JD/MPH; JD/LLM in Taxation; JD/LLM in Financial Services Law; JD/MS in Financial Markets and Trading; JD/MS in Environmental Management; LLM in Taxation; LLM in Financial Services Law; LLM in International Intellectual Property Law; and LLM in International and Comparative Law.

■ Special Programs

Legal Research and Writing—Chicago-Kent's acclaimed legal research and writing program is one of the most comprehensive in the nation. The three-year, five-course curriculum teaches students to analyze a wide range of legal problems and to write about them persuasively.

Clinical Education—The Law Offices of Chicago-Kent, one of the largest in-house clinical education programs in the country, offers 10 clinical programs and externships with government agencies and federal judges.

Trial Skills/Litigation and Alternative Dispute Resolution—The law school offers a two-semester sequence in trial advocacy and an intensive course taught by veteran judges and experienced practitioners. Students in the Litigation and Alternative Dispute Resolution program receive training in case analysis as well as exposure to the theoretical and ethical foundations of the law to develop their skills in using litigation and alternative methods to resolve disputes.

Environmental and Energy Law—The program's interdisciplinary approach to the problems of environmental regulation and natural resources allocation prepares students for practice through a series of courses in law, economic and public policy analysis, and in the scientific aspects of environmental problems.

International and Comparative Law—The program encompasses study in international business and trade, international and comparative law, and international human rights. The Library of International Relations, an

Chicago-Kent College of Law, Illinois Institute of Technology

official depository for documents of the United Nations and the European Union, is one of the largest public research collections of this material in the Midwest.

Intellectual Property Law—The program focuses on issues relating to patent, trademark, copyright, trade secrets, and unfair competition, both in the US and abroad.

Labor and Employment Law—The program provides students with theoretical and practical training in the law governing the workplace.

Institutional Initiatives—Global Law and Policy Initiative; the Institute for Law and the Humanities; the Institute for Law and the Workplace; the Institute for Science, Law, and Technology; and the Institute on Biotechnology and the Human Future.

■ Admission

Admission is highly selective. Each application is individually reviewed and decisions are based on a range of factors, including quantitative and qualitative criteria. Although the GPA and LSAT are important criteria, consideration also is given to nonnumerical factors such as the nature and rigor of the undergraduate curriculum, writing ability, graduate work and professional experience, extracurricular activities, diversity, and the personal statement. The admission requirements for the full- and part-time divisions are the same. Entering classes begin only in the fall. The law school is committed to attracting and retaining students from a variety of racial, ethnic, economic, geographic, and educational backgrounds.

■ Student Activities

Student editors and staff, in association with a faculty editor, publish the *Chicago-Kent Law Review* in symposium format. Moot Court and Trial Advocacy teams successfully compete in local, regional, and national competitions each year providing numerous opportunities to develop litigation expertise. Diverse student interests are represented in a wide variety of social, political, and professional student groups.

■ Scholarship Support

Substantial scholarship assistance is offered to entering and continuing students based on factors which include merit, financial need, and contribution to the law school community. The Honors Scholars Program provides renewable scholarships of full-tuition and living expenses, research assistantships, and special seminars to a select group of students who demonstrate exceptional academic and leadership ability.

■ Career Services

The Office of Career Services, with six full-time staff, offers individual counseling on résumé-writing, interview techniques, and job-search strategies and sponsors both on- and off-campus interview programs. Typically, 96 percent of recent graduates find professional employment within nine months of graduation.

Applicant Profile

Chicago-Kent College of Law, Illinois Institute of Technology

LSAT	GPA																				
	3.75 +		3.50 - 3.74		3.25 - 3.49		3.00 - 3.24		2.75 - 2.99		2.50 - 2.74		2.25 - 2.49		2.00 - 2.24		Below 2.00		No GPA		Total
Score	Apps	Adm	Apps	Adm	Apps	Adm	Apps	Adm	Apps	Adm	Apps	Adm	Apps	Adm	Apps	Adm	Apps	Adm	Apps	Adm	Apps	Adm
170-180	12	4	22	13	20	7	10	2	8	5	2	2	4	3	1	1	0	0	1	0	80	37
165-169	67	29	74	25	77	28	46	24	24	17	10	8	4	4	0	0	0	0	4	1	306	136
160-164	69	51	99	74	147	120	121	106	62	47	33	22	11	3	6	3	0	0	4	4	552	430
155-159	106	75	215	115	281	159	201	87	152	37	83	12	40	3	13	0	1	0	11	0	1103	488
150-154	85	13	184	23	278	17	235	24	175	10	91	3	37	2	16	0	0	0	16	2	1117	94
145-149	28	1	68	5	106	2	118	4	116	3	58	1	41	0	19	0	4	0	17	0	575	16
140-144	7	0	26	0	31	0	65	0	50	0	48	0	34	0	16	0	3	0	12	0	292	0
Below 140	6	0	12	0	10	0	19	0	23	0	25	0	27	0	10	0	5	0	9	0	146	0
Total	380	173	700	255	950	333	815	247	610	119	350	48	198	15	81	4	13	0	74	7	4171	1201

Apps= Number of Applicants   Adm= Number Admitted   Reflects 99% of the total applicant pool.

This grid represents admission data for applicants to both the full- and part-time programs. The information in this grid is to be used only as an approximate gauge of the likelihood of admission and not as a guarantee. Individual accomplishments and other nonnumerical factors are also of importance to the Admissions Committee.

University of Cincinnati College of Law

PO Box 210040
Cincinnati, OH 45221-0040
Phone: 513.556.6805; Fax: 513.556.2391
E-mail: admissions@law.uc.edu; Website: www.law.uc.edu

The Basics

Type of school	Public
Term	Semester
Application deadline	4/1
Application fee	$35
Financial aid deadline	4/1
Can first year start other than fall?	No
Student to faculty ratio (fall)	12.7 to 1
Does the university offer:	
housing restricted to law students?	No
graduate housing for which law students are eligible?	Yes

Faculty and Administrators

	Total		Men		Women		Minorities	
	Fall	Spr	Fall	Spr	Fall	Spr	Fall	Spr
Full-time	25	22	15	13	10	9	5	5
Other Full-time	3	3	0	0	3	3	0	0
Deans, librarians, & others who teach	4	4	1	1	3	3	1	1
Part-time	29	42	25	33	4	9	1	6
Total	**61**	**71**	**41**	**47**	**20**	**24**	**7**	**12**

Curriculum

	Full-time	Part-time
Typical first-year section size	21	0
Is there typically a "small section" of the first-year class, other than Legal Writing, taught by full-time faculty	Yes	No
If yes, typical size offered last year	22	0
# of classroom course titles beyond 1st year curriculum	101	
# of upper division courses, excluding seminars with an enrollment: Under 25	59	
25-49	14	
50-74	10	
75-99	1	
100+	0	
# of seminars	21	
# of seminar positions available	311	
# of seminar positions filled	193	0
# of positions available in simulation courses	273	
# of simulation positions filled	182	0
# of positions available in faculty supervised clinical courses	6	
# of faculty supervised clinical positions filled	4	0
# involved in field placements	89	0
# involved in law journals	120	0
# involved in moot court or trial competitions	34	0
# of credit hours required to graduate	90	

JD Enrollment and Ethnicity

	Men		Women		Full-time		Part-time		1st-year		Total		JD Degs. Awd.
	#	%	#	%	#	%	#	%	#	%	#	%	
African Amer.	9	4.6	23	12.4	32	8.4	0	0.0	10	7.8	32	8.4	6
Amer. Indian	1	0.5	1	0.5	2	0.5	0	0.0	1	0.8	2	0.5	0
Asian Amer.	14	7.1	11	5.9	25	6.5	0	0.0	7	5.5	25	6.5	6
Mex. Amer.	0	0.0	0	0.0	0	0.0	0	0.0	0	0.0	0	0.0	2
Puerto Rican	1	0.5	1	0.5	2	0.5	0	0.0	2	1.6	2	0.5	0
Hispanic	1	0.5	2	1.1	3	0.8	0	0.0	1	0.8	3	0.8	3
Total Minority	26	13.2	38	20.5	64	16.8	0	0.0	21	16.4	64	16.8	17
For. Nation.	0	0.0	1	0.5	1	0.3	0	0.0	0	0.0	1	0.3	0
Caucasian	171	86.8	146	78.9	317	83.0	0	0.0	107	83.6	317	83.0	81
Unknown	0	0.0	0	0.0	0	0.0	0	0.0	0	0.0	0	0.0	0
Total	197	51.6	185	48.4	382	100.0	0	0.0	128	33.5	382		98

Tuition and Fees

	Resident	Nonresident
Full-time	$14,084	$26,190
Part-time	$0	$0

Living Expenses

Estimated living expenses for singles

Living on campus	Living off campus	Living at home
$12,521	$12,521	$12,521

University of Cincinnati College of Law

*ABA
Approved
Since
1923*

GPA and LSAT Scores

	Total	Full-time	Part-time
# of apps	1,157	1,157	0
# of admits	416	416	0
# of matrics	129	129	0
75% GPA	3.80	3.80	0.00
25% GPA	3.24	3.24	0.00
75% LSAT	162	162	0
25% LSAT	157	157	0

Grants and Scholarships (from prior year)

	Total		Full-time		Part-time	
	#	%	#	%	#	%
Total # of students	365		365		0	
Total # receiving grants	239	65.5	239	65.5	0	0.0
Less than 1/2 tuition	144	39.5	144	39.5	0	0.0
Half to full tuition	74	20.3	74	20.3	0	0.0
Full tuition	20	5.5	20	5.5	0	0.0
More than full tuition	1	0.3	1	0.3	0	0.0
Median grant amount			$5,500		$0	

Informational and Library Resources

# of volumes and volume equivalents	415,266
# of titles	192,722
# of active serial subscriptions	8,367
Study seating capacity inside the library	332
# of professional librarians	7
Hours per week library is open	95
# of open, wired connections available to students	6
# of networked computers available for use by students	71
# of simultaneous wireless users	220
Require computer?	N

JD Attrition (from prior year)

	Academic	Other	Total	
	#	#	#	%
1st year	0	9	9	6.7%
2nd year	0	0	0	0.0%
3rd year	0	0	0	0.0%
4th year	0	0	0	0.0%

Employment

	Total	Percentage
Employment status known	134	99.3
Employment status unknown	1	0.7
Employed	126	94.0
Pursuing graduate degrees	6	4.5
Unemployed seeking employment	2	1.5
Unemployed not seeking employment	0	0.0

Type of Employment

# employed in law firms	68	54.0
# employed in business and industry	17	13.5
# employed in government	16	12.7
# employed in public interest	9	7.1
# employed as judicial clerks	10	7.9
# employed in academia	4	3.2

Geographic Location

# employed in state	90	71.4
# employed in foreign countries	0	0.0
# of states where employed		17

Bar Passage Rates

Jurisdiction	Ohio		
Exam	Sum 03	Win 04	Total
# from school taking bar for the first time	95	4	99
School's pass rate for all first-time takers	87%	75%	87%
State's pass rate for all first-time takers	81%	72%	79%

University of Cincinnati College of Law

PO Box 210040, Office of Admission and Financial Aid
Cincinnati, OH 45221-0040
Phone: 513.556.6805; Fax: 513.556.2391
E-mail: admissions@law.uc.edu; Website: www.law.uc.edu

■ Introduction

The College of Law was established in 1833. America's fourth-oldest law school, the College of Law limits enrollment to 135 students per class. The small size of the school allows for a selective admission process, small classes, and a high degree of faculty and student interaction. The law school is located on UC's recently renovated main campus in Clifton, approximately 10 minutes north of the city's central business district. This provides easy access to state, county, and federal courts, including the US Court of Appeals for the Sixth Circuit. A charter member of the AALS, UC was one of the first law schools to have a chapter of the Order of the Coif and to be approved by the ABA.

■ Student Body

Enrollment is limited to approximately 385 students—about 135 per class. Students come from a wide variety of backgrounds, experiences, and perspectives. For the class enrolled for fall 2004 over 1,100 applications were received. The 75th/25th LSAT and UGPA percentiles for this class were 162/157 and 3.80/3.24. The applicant pool is evenly divided between residents and nonresident applicants. The College of Law is committed to enrolling a diverse class. For the 2004–2005 academic year 18 percent of our students are from minority backgrounds, 50 percent are female, and 33 percent enrolled from states other than Ohio. The average age each year is 25.

■ Faculty

The college employs a full-time faculty of 26 who pride themselves on their teaching, scholarship, and accessibility to students. As the core of the academic program, faculty members bring areas of expertise into the classroom that add depth, perspective, and professionalism to the law students' studies. The student to faculty ratio of under 12.7:1 provides ample opportunities for individual discussions with faculty or in-depth research in areas of interest.

■ Library and Physical Facilities

The Robert S. Marx Law Library has the capacity to seat the entire student body. Two computer labs offer an excellent array of digital research resources and tools plus free networked printing. The law library staff is well regarded by students and faculty for their dedication to assisting patrons with law library resources. The law library collections are carefully maintained to support faculty and student research and the college curriculum. Library staff maintains the college website, which serves as a gateway to news, announcements, student services, and other resources.

■ Curriculum

First-year students have the unusual advantage of very small first-year sections (typically no larger than 25) that allow further inquiry beyond the typical first-year curriculum. First-year students take three courses in small sections with opportunities to study with all members of their class over the entire year. The upper level is well balanced between theory and skills-related courses. Institutes and research centers exist in the areas of International Human Rights, Law and Justice/Ohio Innocence Project, Corporate Law, Center for Practice in Negotiation and Problem Solving (ADR), and Law and Psychiatry. The college also offers joint programs with Women's Studies, Business, Community Planning, and Social Work.

■ Special Programs

The College of Law recognizes that a lawyer needs both a firm grasp of subject matter and expertise in professional skills. The college has therefore developed an extensive legal research and writing program that not only encompasses the first year, but upper-level courses as well. The Center for Professional Development provides students with extern experiences, opportunities to work with practicing attorneys and with public agencies. The Rosenthal Justice Center has also been recently endowed to ensure popular programs like the Ohio Innocence Project are available to students now and in the future. Each institute and research center offers a fellowship program, research opportunities, and in-depth study in their respective areas. The college was the first to offer a joint degree in law and Women's Studies and has the oldest endowed international human rights program at an American law school, the Urban Morgan Institute for Human Rights.

■ Admission Standards

Admission to the college is based upon a selective review of each candidate's file. Although the admission committee relies on the grade-point average and LSAT score to determine the applicant's academic potential, other non-quantitative factors believed to be relevant to success in law school are considered; that is, the quality of the applicant's education, participation in community service, employment experience, graduate work, and letters of recommendation. The educational philosophy of the college reflects a belief that a quality legal education is enhanced by having a heterogeneous student body. The committee, therefore, also considers race, cultural background, unusual personal circumstances, and age. Admission decisions are made on a rolling basis. The college is committed to enrolling a diverse and engaging class each year. Particular effort is made to provide adequate financial assistance for all students admitted.

■ Student Activities

The College of Law offers numerous opportunities for students to sharpen their legal writing, advocacy, and leadership skills. *The University of Cincinnati Law Review* was founded in 1927 and was the first law review published by an Ohio law school. Edited quarterly by student editors, members of the *Law Review* are selected on a combination of first-year grade-point average and a writing competition. The Urban Morgan Institute for Human Rights edits the *Human Rights Quarterly*, the leading international human rights journal in the world. *The Immigration and Nationality Law Review* is an annual publication of papers on the subjects of immigration and citizenship. Also published annually is the *Freedom Center Journal of Law and History*, a collaborative project with the National Underground Railroad and Freedom Center located in Cincinnati. The College of Law also offers a very well-respected Moot Court program. Teams participate in all national competitions, and the college annually hosts the National Product Liability Competition each April. The Student Bar Association and Student Legal Education Committee are active participants in the committee form of governance within the college.

■ Expenses and Financial Aid

For the 2004–2005 academic year, resident and non-resident tuition and fees figures are $14,084 and $26,190, respectively. Nonresidents can reclassify as state residents after one year if they are independent and self-sustaining. Cincinnati is a cosmopolitan yet affordable city to reside in with rent in the university area of Clifton about $450 per month. Living expenses are estimated at $12,521 for the nine-month academic year. Scholarships are awarded in order to attract an academically talented and diverse student body. Priority deadline for receipt of the Scholarship Information forms is April 1. The FAFSA should be filed by March 1 as a priority deadline. The average law school debt load for a 2004 graduate was $47,391. A large percentage of second- and third-year students work with law firms and agencies in the Greater Cincinnati area.

■ Placement

The college maintains an active Center for Professional Development with a staff of three attorneys. This JD staff member to law student ratio is one of the best in the country. Each year over 100 employers seek our students for postgraduate, summer, and part-time employment. In recent years, at least 94 percent of each graduating class has accepted employment within six months of graduation. In the most recent survey of graduates, the average starting salary for our graduates was almost $10,000 higher than the national average. Graduates are most commonly employed in the Midwest but can be found throughout the US and overseas.

Applicant Profile

University of Cincinnati College of Law
This grid includes only applicants who earned 120-180 LSAT scores under standard administrations.

LSAT Score	3.75 +		3.50 - 3.74		3.25 - 3.49		3.00 - 3.24		2.75 - 2.99		2.50 - 2.74		2.25 - 2.49		2.00 - 2.24		Below 2.00		No GPA		Total	
	Apps	Adm	Apps	Adm	Apps	Adm	Apps	Adm	Apps	Adm	Apps	Adm	Apps	Adm	Apps	Adm	Apps	Adm	Apps	Adm	Apps	Adm
175-180	0	0	0	0	1	1	0	0	1	1	0	0	0	0	0	0	0	0	0	0	2	2
170-174	2	2	1	1	1	1	1	1	1	1	0	0	0	0	1	0	0	0	0	0	7	6
165-169	17	17	21	21	10	10	5	5	3	3	2	2	1	1	0	0	0	0	0	0	59	59
160-164	49	49	52	50	36	36	19	18	14	12	10	9	6	5	0	0	1	0	2	1	189	180
155-159	67	48	86	39	80	18	48	6	19	3	17	4	7	0	4	0	0	0	3	1	331	119
150-154	47	17	49	7	66	8	61	4	22	1	18	1	6	1	1	0	2	0	3	0	275	39
145-149	17	6	37	2	44	1	24	0	24	0	14	0	6	0	4	0	0	0	1	0	171	9
140-144	7	1	11	0	8	0	17	0	8	0	8	0	6	0	2	0	0	0	4	0	71	1
135-139	0	0	4	0	5	0	7	0	6	0	6	0	3	0	3	0	0	0	1	0	35	0
130-134	0	0	0	0	1	0	1	0	1	0	0	0	1	0	2	0	0	0	0	0	6	0
125-129	0	0	0	0	0	0	1	0	0	0	0	0	0	0	0	0	0	0	0	0	1	0
120-124	0	0	0	0	0	0	0	0	0	0	0	0	0	0	0	0	0	0	0	0	0	0
Total	206	140	261	120	252	75	184	34	99	21	75	16	36	7	17	0	3	0	14	2	1147	415

Apps = Number of Applicants   Adm = Number Admitted   Reflects 99% of the total applicant pool.

City University of New York School of Law at Queens College

65-21 Main Street
Flushing, NY 11367-1300
Phone: 718.340.4210; Fax: 718.340.4435
E-mail: admissions@mail.law.cuny.edu; Website: www.law.cuny.edu

ABA
Approved
Since
1985

The Basics

Type of school	Public
Term	Semester
Application deadline	3/15
Application fee	$50
Financial aid deadline	5/1
Can first year start other than fall?	No
Student to faculty ratio (fall)	12.3 to 1
Does the university offer:	
housing restricted to law students?	No
graduate housing for which law students are eligible?	No

Faculty and Administrators

	Total		Men		Women		Minorities	
	Fall	Spr	Fall	Spr	Fall	Spr	Fall	Spr
Full-time	30	30	14	14	16	16	13	12
Other Full-time	4	4	1	1	3	3	2	2
Deans, librarians, & others who teach	6	6	2	2	4	4	0	0
Part-time	13	14	7	5	6	8	8	8
Total	53	54	24	22	29	31	23	22

Curriculum

	Full-time	Part-time
Typical first-year section size	80	0
Is there typically a "small section" of the first-year class, other than Legal Writing, taught by full-time faculty	Yes	No
If yes, typical size offered last year	20	0
# of classroom course titles beyond 1st year curriculum	47	
# of upper division courses, excluding seminars with an enrollment: Under 25	32	
25-49	21	
50-74	10	
75-99	1	
100+	3	
# of seminars	17	
# of seminar positions available	385	
# of seminar positions filled	218	0
# of positions available in simulation courses	225	
# of simulation positions filled	197	0
# of positions available in faculty supervised clinical courses	148	
# of faculty supervised clinical positions filled	134	0
# involved in field placements	74	0
# involved in law journals	39	0
# involved in moot court or trial competitions	31	0
# of credit hours required to graduate	91	

J.D. Enrollment and Ethnicity

	Men		Women		Full-time		Part-time		1st-year		Total		JD Degs. Awd.
	#	%	#	%	#	%	#	%	#	%	#	%	
African Amer.	15	10.1	36	12.0	50	11.4	1	12.5	17	10.9	51	11.4	15
Amer. Indian	2	1.4	0	0.0	2	0.5	0	0.0	0	0.0	2	0.4	1
Asian Amer.	21	14.2	31	10.4	51	11.6	1	12.5	26	16.7	52	11.6	17
Mex. Amer.	0	0.0	5	1.7	5	1.1	0	0.0	1	0.6	5	1.1	2
Puerto Rican	5	3.4	8	2.7	12	2.7	1	12.5	2	1.3	13	2.9	9
Hispanic	12	8.1	19	6.4	31	7.1	0	0.0	13	8.3	31	6.9	14
Total Minority	55	37.2	99	33.1	151	34.4	3	37.5	59	37.8	154	34.5	58
For. Nation.	7	4.7	9	3.0	16	3.6	0	0.0	9	5.8	16	3.6	3
Caucasian	78	52.7	168	56.2	241	54.9	5	62.5	77	49.4	246	55.0	73
Unknown	8	5.4	23	7.7	31	7.1	0	0.0	11	7.1	31	6.9	6
Total	148	33.1	299	66.9	439	98.2	8	1.8	156	34.9	447		140

Tuition and Fees

	Resident	Nonresident
Full-time	$8,731	$13,481
Part-time	$0	$0

Living Expenses

Estimated living expenses for singles

Living on campus	Living off campus	Living at home
N/A	$11,340	$7,409

City University of New York School of Law at Queens College

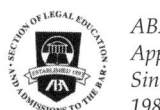

*ABA
Approved
Since
1985*

GPA and LSAT Scores

	Total	Full-time	Part-time
# of apps	2,318	2,318	0
# of admits	474	474	0
# of matrics	153	153	0
75% GPA	3.56	3.56	0.00
25% GPA	2.95	2.95	0.00
75% LSAT	154	154	0
25% LSAT	148	148	0

Grants and Scholarships (from prior year)

	Total #	Total %	Full-time #	Full-time %	Part-time #	Part-time %
Total # of students	468		467		1	
Total # receiving grants	83	17.7	83	17.8	0	0.0
Less than 1/2 tuition	83	17.7	83	17.8	0	0.0
Half to full tuition	0	0.0	0	0.0	0	0.0
Full tuition	0	0.0	0	0.0	0	0.0
More than full tuition	0	0.0	0	0.0	0	0.0
Median grant amount			$294		$0	

Informational and Library Resources

# of volumes and volume equivalents	275,207
# of titles	34,905
# of active serial subscriptions	3,070
Study seating capacity inside the library	267
# of professional librarians	9
Hours per week library is open	61
# of open, wired connections available to students	62
# of networked computers available for use by students	99
# of simultaneous wireless users	300
Require computer?	N

JD Attrition (from prior year)

	Academic #	Other #	Total #	Total %
1st year	5	20	25	14.7%
2nd year	8	4	12	7.6%
3rd year	2	0	2	1.3%
4th year	0	0	0	0.0%

Employment

	Total	Percentage
Employment status known	96	74.4
Employment status unknown	33	25.6
Employed	80	83.3
Pursuing graduate degrees	1	1.0
Unemployed seeking employment	6	6.2
Unemployed not seeking employment	9	9.4

Type of Employment

# employed in law firms	19	23.7
# employed in business and industry	14	17.5
# employed in government	16	20.0
# employed in public interest	25	31.2
# employed as judicial clerks	3	3.7
# employed in academia	2	2.5

Geographic Location

# employed in state	57	71.2
# employed in foreign countries	1	1.2
# of states where employed	8	

Bar Passage Rates

Jurisdiction	New York		
Exam	Sum 03	Win 04	Total
# from school taking bar for the first time	100	10	110
School's pass rate for all first-time takers	56%	40%	55%
State's pass rate for all first-time takers	78%	58%	75%

City University of New York School of Law at Queens College

65-21 Main Street
Flushing, NY 11367-1300
Phone: 718.340.4210; Fax: 718.340.4435
E-mail: admissions@mail.law.cuny.edu; Website: www.law.cuny.edu

■ Mission

Following its motto of "Law in the Service of Human Needs," the mission of the City University of New York (CUNY) School of Law is to train excellent public interest lawyers through curriculum that integrates doctrine, legal theory, clinical education, and professional responsibility.

■ Academic Program

Our innovative educational program, leading to the Juris Doctor (JD) degree, honors students' aspirations toward a legal career built on a commitment to justice, fairness, and equality. The law school's commitment to professional education and training reflecting these values pervades the core doctrinal classes and comes to life in our program of experiential learning, which is comprehensively integrated throughout the course of study. All first-year students take a required two-semester Lawyering Seminar where they focus on the fundamental skills of legal analysis and legal writing and engage in simulations requiring a wide range of lawyering tasks: They draft documents, interview and counsel clients, engage in negotiations, and make arguments before trial and appellate courts. Faculty guidance, supervision, and feedback permeate the process. In the second year, each student elects a four-credit Lawyering Seminar focused on developing more advanced lawyering skills in a subject matter area of her/his choice, including trial practice, mediation, labor, and appellate advocacy. The Law School's Workfare Advocacy Project, which is a second-year lawyering seminar, received the New York State Bar Association's 2002 President's Pro Bono Service Award.

Excellent and comprehensive academic support is provided by the Irene Diamond Professional Skills Center.

■ Clinical Programs

Each third-year student devotes 12 to 16 credits to participation in CUNY's nationally recognized clinical program, either in a concentration of Equality or Health Law or in one of the following clinics: Battered Women's Rights, Defender, Immigrant and Refugee Rights, International Women's Human Rights, Elder Law, Juvenile Defender, and Mediation. The clinics are organized under the umbrella of Main Street Legal Services, Inc., an in-house law firm that provides information, counseling, or representation to more than 1,000 clients yearly, as well as preparing students for a seamless transition into practice. Students' work in clinics often has enormous impact; for example, students and faculty in the International Women's Human Rights Clinic drafted an amicus brief to the International Criminal Tribunal for Rwanda that was instrumental in the tribunal's decision, for the first time in international law, to include systematic rape as a crime of genocide.

■ Diversity

The diversity of the City of New York is reflected in our dynamic student body and faculty. Women constitute 68 percent of the student body; minorities, 42 percent. Faculty percentages are similar: 46 percent are women and 36 percent are people of color. The concern for diversity is also threaded through the curriculum; for example, a required course for all first-year students is Liberty, Equality, and Due Process, which examines issues of racial and gender equality and sexual orientation in the context of legal and historical analysis.

■ Student Life

Despite the relatively small size of the law school, numerous student organizations thrive on campus. Students also have a major role in the law school's governance, recognizing and preparing them for their future as professionals and community leaders. One exemplary student program is the Mississippi Project, which, since 1992, has sent a delegation of law students to Mississippi over midyear break to work with lawyers in civil rights organizations across the state. CUNY students work and learn together in an exceptionally collaborative, noncompetitive atmosphere and interact on a first-name basis with the faculty. The student experience is further enriched by New York City's cultural offerings and by the exceptional resources of the third-largest university system in the country, CUNY.

■ Faculty

Most of the faculty have themselves been public interest practitioners, with experience in a wide area of issues, including employment discrimination, immigration, racial justice, environmental law, women's rights, labor, and international law. They have worked in China, Haiti, South Africa, Mongolia, Costa Rica, the Middle East, Russia, Papua New Guinea, Australia, the Philippines, and many other countries. Their prestigious awards include Fulbright, Ford, MacArthur, Revson, Rockefeller, and National Endowment for the Humanities fellowships; and their scholarship reflects their interest in, among other areas, international human rights and access to justice for underserved communities.

■ Career Opportunities

CUNY law graduates are employed in the full range of public interest jobs—legal services and public defender

City University of New York School of Law at Queens College

organizations, government agencies, international human rights organizations, not-for-profits, and the judiciary. Almost 85 percent of alumni/ae secure positions within eight months of graduation. Historically, 60–65 percent of graduates enter the public interest/public service profession each year, while 25–30 percent are employed at private firms from large to small and solo community-based practices. CUNY law graduates are consistently awarded prestigious public interest postgraduate fellowships that include the National Association for Public Interest Law, Skadden Arps, Soros, Echoing Green, New Voices, and the Yale Public Interest Fellowships. Although the vast majority are employed in the mid-Atlantic states, CUNY graduates can be found throughout the United States and abroad where they are engaged in international human rights work.

■ Child Care

The law school offers an on-site Children's Center, which provides high-quality, reasonably priced all-day care for children of students from 2 1/2 to 6 years of age. One of only two on-site day care centers in American law schools, the center enables parents to pursue their education while fulfilling their responsibility to their children.

■ Special Opportunities

The law school offers a number of unique programs and initiatives that enrich the experience of students and provide continuing support for graduates. The Haywood Burns Chair in Civil Rights is a visiting faculty position, which allows distinguished practitioners and jurists—this year, Commissioner of the New Jersey State Department of Personnel, and former Chair of the US Equal Employment Opportunity Commission, Ida Castro—to share their experience and knowledge of civil and human rights. The Community Legal Resource Network provides resources and supports graduates working in solo or small-firm practices in underserved communities. Students in CUNY Immigrant Initiatives expand their knowledge of issues facing immigrant communities and provide direct service in a variety of areas. A new curricular initiative, the Worker, Employment, Labor Program, is designed to develop legal skills in representing workers in diverse settings. Finally, the law school is part of a rich university, the City University of New York, and law students may take some interdisciplinary graduate courses with the approval of the Academic Dean.

■ Nontraditional Students

The law school's student profile includes many individuals returning to school after careers, and many possess advanced degrees. The average age of the student body is 28; some students enter directly from undergraduate school while others are older, making the law school a comfortable environment.

■ Affordable Tuition

CUNY offers an excellent legal education at substantially less than half the cost of most private law schools.

Applicant Profile

City University of New York School of Law at Queens College
This grid includes only applicants who earned 120-180 LSAT scores under standard administrations.

LSAT Score	3.75 +		3.50 - 3.74		3.25 - 3.49		3.00 - 3.24		2.75 - 2.99		2.50 - 2.74		2.25 - 2.49		2.00 - 2.24		Below 2.00		No GPA		Total	
	Apps	Adm	Apps	Adm	Apps	Adm	Apps	Adm	Apps	Adm	Apps	Adm	Apps	Adm	Apps	Adm	Apps	Adm	Apps	Adm	Apps	Adm
175-180	1	1	0	0	0	0	1	1	0	0	0	0	0	0	0	0	0	0	0	0	2	2
170-174	1	1	0	0	4	4	2	1	1	0	0	0	0	0	0	0	1	1	0	0	9	7
165-169	7	7	2	2	2	2	2	1	2	1	4	0	1	1	0	0	0	0	1	1	21	15
160-164	8	5	9	7	25	18	16	8	14	4	8	1	6	1	4	1	0	0	2	1	92	46
155-159	23	19	29	19	43	25	53	23	34	8	26	9	27	1	14	2	1	0	6	2	256	108
150-154	30	19	68	36	82	34	116	44	97	25	74	16	29	6	22	1	4	0	13	7	535	188
145-149	19	8	75	22	123	21	138	24	134	13	91	6	51	1	17	0	4	1	19	2	671	98
140-144	13	0	54	2	90	1	103	4	95	0	74	0	47	0	21	0	3	0	25	0	525	7
135-139	3	0	14	0	24	0	42	0	46	0	47	0	34	0	9	0	4	0	9	0	232	0
130-134	1	0	3	0	6	0	11	0	11	0	12	0	9	0	7	0	2	0	5	0	67	0
125-129	0	0	0	0	1	0	0	0	2	0	6	0	2	0	3	0	1	0	3	0	18	0
120-124	0	0	0	0	0	0	0	0	0	0	0	0	0	0	0	0	0	0	1	0	1	0
Total	106	60	254	88	400	105	484	106	436	51	342	32	206	10	97	4	20	2	84	13	2429	471

Apps = Number of Applicants   Adm = Number Admitted   Reflects 99% of the total applicant pool.

Cleveland State University—Cleveland-Marshall College of Law

2121 Euclid Avenue - LB 138
Cleveland, OH 44115-2214
Phone: 216.687.2304, 866.687.2304; Fax: 216.687.6881
E-mail: admissions@law.csuohio.edu; Website: www.law.csuohio.edu

ABA
Approved
Since
1957

The Basics

Type of school	Public
Term	Semester
Application deadline	4/15
Application fee	$35
Financial aid deadline	4/15
Can first year start other than fall?	No
Student to faculty ratio (fall)	13.3 to 1
Does the university offer:	
housing restricted to law students?	No
graduate housing for which law students are eligible?	Yes

Faculty and Administrators

	Total		Men		Women		Minorities	
	Fall	Spr	Fall	Spr	Fall	Spr	Fall	Spr
Full-time	42	39	23	23	19	16	3	3
Other Full-time	0	0	0	0	0	0	0	0
Deans, librarians, & others who teach	5	5	3	3	2	2	1	1
Part-time	26	31	19	28	7	3	0	0
Total	73	75	45	54	28	21	4	4

Curriculum

	Full-time	Part-time
Typical first-year section size	68	58
Is there typically a "small section" of the first-year class, other than Legal Writing, taught by full-time faculty	No	No
If yes, typical size offered last year	0	0
# of classroom course titles beyond 1st year curriculum	91	
# of upper division courses, excluding seminars with an enrollement: Under 25	112	
25-49	39	
50-74	29	
75-99	0	
100+	0	
# of seminars	9	
# of seminar positions available	180	
# of seminar positions filled	107	11
# of positions available in simulation courses	238	
# of simulation positions filled	113	96
# of positions available in faculty supervised clinical courses	96	
# of faculty supervised clinical positions filled	43	10
# involved in field placements	48	6
# involved in law journals	75	31
# involved in moot court or trial competitions	20	7
# of credit hours required to graduate	90	

JD Enrollment and Ethnicity

	Men		Women		Full-time		Part-time		1st-year		Total		JD Degs. Awd.
	#	%	#	%	#	%	#	%	#	%	#	%	
African Amer.	18	4.4	32	9.4	29	5.9	21	8.3	19	7.8	50	6.7	8
Amer. Indian	1	0.2	0	0.0	1	0.2	0	0.0	0	0.0	1	0.1	0
Asian Amer.	14	3.4	16	4.7	19	3.8	11	4.3	14	5.8	30	4.0	4
Mex. Amer.	0	0.0	0	0.0	0	0.0	0	0.0	0	0.0	0	0.0	0
Puerto Rican	0	0.0	0	0.0	0	0.0	0	0.0	0	0.0	0	0.0	0
Hispanic	15	3.7	8	2.4	13	2.6	10	4.0	8	3.3	23	3.1	3
Total Minority	48	11.8	56	16.5	62	12.6	42	16.6	41	16.9	104	13.9	15
For. Nation.	4	1.0	4	1.2	6	1.2	2	0.8	2	0.8	8	1.1	0
Caucasian	346	85.0	269	79.1	409	82.8	206	81.4	187	77.0	615	82.3	227
Unknown	9	2.2	11	3.2	17	3.4	3	1.2	13	5.3	20	2.7	4
Total	407	54.5	340	45.5	494	66.1	253	33.9	243	32.5	747		246

Tuition and Fees

	Resident	Nonresident
Full-time	$13,052	$17,969
Part-time	$10,040	$13,822

Living Expenses

Estimated living expenses for singles

Living on campus	Living off campus	Living at home
$11,050	$11,050	$11,050

Cleveland State University—Cleveland-Marshall College of Law

*ABA
Approved
Since
1957*

GPA and LSAT Scores

	Total	Full-time	Part-time
# of apps	1,814	1,468	346
# of admits	562	460	102
# of matrics	247	173	74
75% GPA	3.60	3.61	3.54
25% GPA	3.02	3.13	2.88
75% LSAT	156	156	155
25% LSAT	151	152	149

Grants and Scholarships (from prior year)

	Total		Full-time		Part-time	
	#	%	#	%	#	%
Total # of students	818		544		274	
Total # receiving grants	208	25.4	164	30.1	44	16.1
Less than 1/2 tuition	149	18.2	109	20.0	40	14.6
Half to full tuition	23	2.8	23	4.2	0	0.0
Full tuition	36	4.4	32	5.9	4	1.5
More than full tuition	0	0.0	0	0.0	0	0.0
Median grant amount			$2,500		$2,000	

Informational and Library Resources

# of volumes and volume equivalents	515,164
# of titles	148,063
# of active serial subscriptions	3,281
Study seating capacity inside the library	412
# of professional librarians	10
Hours per week library is open	97
# of open, wired connections available to students	148
# of networked computers available for use by students	105
# of simultaneous wireless users	1,000
Require computer?	N

JD Attrition (from prior year)

	Academic	Other	Total	
	#	#	#	%
1st year	27	16	43	16.3%
2nd year	1	2	3	1.4%
3rd year	3	1	4	1.5%
4th year	0	1	1	1.3%

Employment

	Total	Percentage
Employment status known	220	96.9
Employment status unknown	7	3.1
Employed	202	91.8
Pursuing graduate degrees	3	1.4
Unemployed seeking employment	13	5.9
Unemployed not seeking employment	2	0.9

Type of Employment

	Total	Percentage
# employed in law firms	112	55.4
# employed in business and industry	42	20.8
# employed in government	25	12.4
# employed in public interest	4	2.0
# employed as judicial clerks	15	7.4
# employed in academia	4	2.0

Geographic Location

	Total	Percentage
# employed in state	182	90.1
# employed in foreign countries	0	0.0
# of states where employed	13	

Bar Passage Rates

Jurisdiction		Ohio		
Exam	Sum 03	Win 04	Total	
# from school taking bar for the first time	150	43	193	
School's pass rate for all first-time takers	75%	58%	71%	
State's pass rate for all first-time takers	81%	72%	79%	

Cleveland State University—Cleveland-Marshall College of Law

Office of Law Admissions, 2121 Euclid Avenue - LB 138
Cleveland, OH 44115-2214
Phone: 216.687.2304, 866.687.2304; Fax: 216.687.6881
E-mail: admissions@law.csuohio.edu; Website: www.law.csuohio.edu

■ Introduction

Founded in 1897, Cleveland-Marshall College of Law was the first law school in Ohio to admit women and one of the first to admit minorities. Becoming part of Cleveland State University in 1969, the law school has maintained its long-standing reputation for educating some of the region's outstanding leaders of the bench and bar, heads of law firms and corporations, and distinguished public servants.

Cleveland-Marshall continues to enhance its national reputation and influence with its law lecture series and visiting scholars program, through outreach efforts with its National Advisory Council and through the law school's recruiting activities. The College of Law receives applications of prospective students from over 450 different colleges and universities. Tuition for non-Ohio residents is among the most reasonable of any law school in the country.

The college offers a full-time day, a part-time day, and a part-time evening program. After completing the program selected for the first year of law school, a student may switch programs according to his or her scheduling needs. The student body is diverse in many ways. Approximately half of the students are female, roughly 15 to 20 percent of each entering class is likely to be over the age of 30, and many students have had careers in other fields and/or earned advanced degrees before beginning the study of law. The college's pro bono, extracurricular, and cocurricular activities help to round out the richness of experience gained by studying law at Cleveland-Marshall.

■ Location

The College of Law is located on the university's urban campus in downtown Cleveland on Lake Erie. With downtown Cleveland becoming a fast growing housing market, students at Cleveland-Marshall enjoy all that the city has to offer, including the Cleveland Museum of Art; Severance Hall, home of the world-renowned Cleveland Orchestra; the Museum of Contemporary Art; the Botanical Garden; Playhouse Square; the House of Blues; and major professional sports teams. On the North Coast Harbor sit the Great Lakes Science Center and the Rock and Roll Hall of Fame and Museum. The law school is in close proximity to the federal, state, and county courthouses. Cleveland is also a major industrial center and headquarters for many large corporations and law firms.

■ Library and Physical Facilities

In 1997, the College of Law dedicated its new law library. This research facility is one of the 15 largest academic law libraries in the country, with 85,000 net square feet, housing more than 500,000 volumes. At Cleveland-Marshall students have access to online research services, a 50-seat computer lab, group study rooms, a bibliographic instruction room, and a media center. And they can study and research in the four-story light-filled atrium where there are 206 student carrels with built-in power and network ports for portable computers. A wireless network allows use of personal computers throughout the campus.

■ The Curriculum

The urban setting of the college brings challenging legal experiences to students. Clinical programs and externships include (1) the employment law, community advocacy, fair housing, and environmental law clinics that offer students academic credit for serving clients in a variety of areas; (2) the Judicial Externship Program in which students work with state appellate and federal court judges; and (3) the Public Interest Externship Program designed to offer experiences in settings such as the County Prosecutor's Office, the County Public Defender's Office, local health care institutions, and the Cleveland chapter of the American Civil Liberties Union. Students may undertake a concentration in five areas: Business Law, Civil Litigation and Dispute Resolution, Criminal Law, Employment and Labor Law, and Tax Law by completing core and elective courses in their chosen area.

■ Joint-Degree Programs and Graduate Program

Four joint-degree programs are offered: the JD/MPA (Master of Public Administration); the JD/MUPDD (Master of Urban Planning, Design, and Development); the JD/MBA (Master of Business Administration); and the JD/MAES (Master of Arts in Environmental Science). The law school also offers a graduate LLM degree.

■ Pro Bono Program

The Pro Bono Program at Cleveland-Marshall offers a variety of community service opportunities. Some of these experiences include building homes with Habitat for Humanity and planting gardens in the city of Cleveland. Popular placements include teaching practical law in public high schools, assisting with the legal needs of women recently released from incarceration, or addressing the concerns of the poor by delivering legal assistance in cooperation with local attorneys and community agencies.

■ Admission

Applicants are admitted by the dean upon the recommendation of an admission committee composed of faculty, professional staff, and students. Criteria for admission are identical for the full-time and part-time programs. Each

Cleveland State University—Cleveland-Marshall College of Law

applicant must have received a bachelor's degree from an accredited college or university by the time law classes begin. Undergraduate academic performance and LSAT scores are generally the most reliable measures for predicting success in law school. However, an applicant's personal statement, letters of recommendation, and overall strength of the file are factors also strongly considered in the admission process.

■ The Legal Career Opportunities Program

The Legal Career Opportunities Program (LCOP) is an admission program for applicants who have encountered adversity in their lives that negatively affected their traditional academic indicators (i.e., LSAT score and/or undergraduate grades), but whose employment history or life experiences may indicate stronger candidacy for success in law school than traditional indicators. In most cases, applicants to this program have academic indicators that are generally a bit lower than those of regularly admitted applicants. The Legal Career Opportunities Program is not a provisional program. Being admitted through the program is acceptance to law school. Students admitted through the program are required to enroll in a course during the summer prior to the beginning of their first year.

■ Career Services

There are more than 300 law firms in the Cleveland area providing an array of clerking opportunities. Cleveland-Marshall provides a wide range of services, including résumé and cover letter review, a fall interview program,

and career planning workshops. While many graduates choose to remain in Ohio, many also return to their home states or venture to other regions across the country and abroad. This year, with the assistance of our Career Planning Office, students obtained clerkships and permanent positions in various legal fields.

■ Housing

The majority of Cleveland-Marshall students live in a wide range of convenient and affordable housing throughout the city and surrounding suburbs. There is on-campus housing offered through the university. Double and single rooms are available and several meal plans are offered. Additional on-campus housing information can be obtained from the Cleveland State University Department of Residence Life at 216.687.5196 or at *www.csuohio.edu/reslife/*. The law school's Office of Admissions provides admitted students with information to assist with locating housing off campus.

■ Expenses, Financial Aid, and Scholarships

Tuition and Fees—Ohio resident, $6,526/semester ($502/credit hour); nonresident, $8,983/semester ($691/credit hour). FAFSA is due April 1. The financial aid program utilizes combinations of tuition scholarships, work-study employment, and loans. Scholarship awards are distributed on the basis of merit or need. In 2004–2005, 37 percent of first-year students received scholarship awards. Applicants are considered for scholarships when their files are reviewed. There is no separate application process.

Applicant Profile

Cleveland State University—Cleveland-Marshall College of Law

LSAT Score	GPA								Below 2.00	No GPA
	3.75 +	3.50 - 3.74	3.25 - 3.49	3.00 - 3.24	2.75 - 2.99	2.50 - 2.74	2.25 - 2.49	2.00 - 2.24		
175-180										
170-174										
165-169										
160-164										
155-159										
150-154										
145-149										
140-144										
135-139										
130-134										
125-129										
120-124										

■ Very Likely   ■ Likely   ■ Possible   □ Unlikely

University of Colorado School of Law

UCB 403
Boulder, CO 80309-0403
Phone: 303.492.7203
E-mail: lawadmin@colorado.edu; Website: www.colorado.edu/law

ABA
Approved
Since
1923

The Basics

Type of school	Public
Term	Semester
Application deadline	2/15
Application fee	$65
Financial aid deadline	3/1
Can first year start other than fall?	No
Student to faculty ratio (fall)	16.7 to 1
Does the university offer:	
housing restricted to law students?	No
graduate housing for which law students are eligible?	Yes

Faculty and Administrators

	Total		Men		Women		Minorities	
	Fall	Spr	Fall	Spr	Fall	Spr	Fall	Spr
Full-time	25	25	15	15	10	10	7	6
Other Full-time	0	0	0	0	0	0	0	0
Deans, librarians, & others who teach	15	14	10	9	5	5	2	2
Part-time	19	19	13	17	6	2	0	0
Total	59	58	38	41	21	17	9	8

Curriculum

	Full-time	Part-time
Typical first-year section size	86	0
Is there typically a "small section" of the first-year class, other than Legal Writing, taught by full-time faculty	Yes	No
If yes, typical size offered last year	35	0
# of classroom course titles beyond 1st year curriculum	92	

# of upper division courses, excluding seminars with an enrollment:		
Under 25	45	
25-49	24	
50-74	13	
75-99	6	
100+	0	

# of seminars	26	
# of seminar positions available	312	
# of seminar positions filled	287	0
# of positions available in simulation courses	270	
# of simulation positions filled	217	0
# of positions available in faculty supervised clinical courses	196	
# of faculty supervised clinical positions filled	129	0
# involved in field placements	194	0
# involved in law journals	288	0
# involved in moot court or trial competitions	76	0
# of credit hours required to graduate	89	

J.D. Enrollment and Ethnicity

	Men #	Men %	Women #	Women %	Full-time #	Full-time %	Part-time #	Part-time %	1st-year #	1st-year %	Total #	Total %	JD Degs. Awd.
African Amer.	9	3.7	11	4.2	20	4.0	0	0.0	6	3.7	20	4.0	5
Amer. Indian	7	2.9	8	3.1	15	3.0	0	0.0	8	4.9	15	3.0	3
Asian Amer.	10	4.1	26	10.0	36	7.2	0	0.0	18	11.0	36	7.2	4
Mex. Amer.	10	4.1	10	3.9	20	4.0	0	0.0	2	1.2	20	4.0	6
Puerto Rican	0	0.0	2	0.8	2	0.4	0	0.0	1	0.6	2	0.4	0
Hispanic	5	2.1	3	1.2	8	1.6	0	0.0	6	3.7	8	1.6	5
Total Minority	41	16.9	60	23.2	101	20.1	0	0.0	41	25.0	101	20.1	23
For. Nation.	0	0.0	0	0.0	0	0.0	0	0.0	0	0.0	0	0.0	0
Caucasian	202	83.1	199	76.8	401	79.9	0	0.0	123	75.0	401	79.9	134
Unknown	0	0.0	0	0.0	0	0.0	0	0.0	0	0.0	0	0.0	0
Total	243	48.4	259	51.6	502	100.0	0	0.0	164	32.7	502		157

Tuition and Fees

	Resident	Nonresident
Full-time	$10,737	$26,329
Part-time	$0	$0

Living Expenses

Estimated living expenses for singles

Living on campus	Living off campus	Living at home
$12,063	$11,735	$8,198

University of Colorado School of Law

ABA
Approved
Since
1923

GPA and LSAT Scores

	Total	Full-time	Part-time
# of apps	2,899	2,899	0
# of admits	679	679	0
# of matrics	166	166	0
75% GPA	3.84	3.84	0.00
25% GPA	3.45	3.45	0.00
75% LSAT	164	164	0
25% LSAT	159	159	0

Grants and Scholarships (from prior year)

	Total #	Total %	Full-time #	Full-time %	Part-time #	Part-time %
Total # of students	486		485		1	
Total # receiving grants	255	52.5	255	52.6	0	0.0
Less than 1/2 tuition	206	42.4	206	42.5	0	0.0
Half to full tuition	41	8.4	41	8.5	0	0.0
Full tuition	1	0.2	1	0.2	0	0.0
More than full tuition	7	1.4	7	1.4	0	0.0
Median grant amount			$2,125		$0	

Informational and Library Resources

# of volumes and volume equivalents	506,344
# of titles	165,804
# of active serial subscriptions	4,168
Study seating capacity inside the library	341
# of professional librarians	8
Hours per week library is open	108
# of open, wired connections available to students	0
# of networked computers available for use by students	70
# of simultaneous wireless users	0
Require computer?	N

JD Attrition (from prior year)

	Academic #	Other #	Total #	Total %
1st year	0	2	2	1.2%
2nd year	0	10	10	6.1%
3rd year	0	1	1	0.6%
4th year	0	0	0	0.0%

Employment

	Total	Percentage
Employment status known	144	97.3
Employment status unknown	4	2.7
Employed	130	90.3
Pursuing graduate degrees	1	0.7
Unemployed seeking employment	8	5.6
Unemployed not seeking employment	5	3.5

Type of Employment

# employed in law firms	54	41.5
# employed in business and industry	13	10.0
# employed in government	21	16.2
# employed in public interest	7	5.4
# employed as judicial clerks	31	23.8
# employed in academia	4	3.1

Geographic Location

# employed in state	91	70.0
# employed in foreign countries	1	0.8
# of states where employed		25

Bar Passage Rates

Jurisdiction	Colorado		
Exam	Sum 03	Win 04	Total
# from school taking bar for the first time	105	13	118
School's pass rate for all first-time takers	88%	77%	86%
State's pass rate for all first-time takers	75%	73%	75%

University of Colorado School of Law

Office of Admissions, UCB 403
Boulder, CO 80309-0403
Phone: 303.492.7203
E-mail: lawadmin@colorado.edu; Website: www.colorado.edu/law

■ Introduction

The School of Law, established in 1892, is located on the Boulder campus of the University of Colorado and lies at the foot of the Rocky Mountains. High admission standards, a relatively small student body, and a favorable faculty-to-student ratio assure a stimulating and challenging academic environment that encourages class participation and interactions with faculty. The school is a charter member of the AALS and is ABA approved.

■ Faculty

The faculty has a demonstrated record of excellence in teaching, research, and public service. Particular areas of strength include natural resources and constitutional law, but the faculty also includes some of the nation's leading scholars on criminal law, dispute resolution, evidence, health law, international law, labor and employment, securities, tax, and telecommunications law.

■ Physical Facilities and Library

The new Wolf Law Building is under construction and is expected to open in 2006.

The Law Library consists of over 506,000 volumes and microform equivalents, including a comprehensive collection of case law from all jurisdictions, statutes of all the states, and the major digests, encyclopedias, and texts dealing with American law. English, Canadian, and other Commonwealth materials are almost as complete. German and French material and other foreign and international law holdings provide a basis for comparative law studies. Access to material in the library's collection is available through the online Public Access Catalog, which also provides access to full text e-journals, online databases, and other library holdings. A PC-based computer lab and wireless LAN are available.

■ Special Programs

The Natural Resources Law Center has three major areas of activity: research and publication, legal education, and the distinguished visitors and fellows program. The National Wildlife Federation's Natural Resources Litigation Clinic involves students in complex environmental litigation, much of which reaches the state supreme court or federal appellate court level.

The Legal Aid and Defender Program allows students to represent low-income clients in civil and criminal cases in Colorado courts under supervision of full-time faculty who are experienced trial attorneys. The Indian Law Clinic provides students the opportunity to work with Native Americans on their unique legal problems.

The Appellate Advocacy Clinic alternates annually between attorneys from the Public Defender's office and the Attorney General's office. Each student, under direct supervision of an instructor, is responsible for completing an appellate brief and attending the oral argument in the Colorado Supreme Court or the Colorado Court of Appeals.

The Wrongful Convictions Clinic allows students to work with attorneys representing Colorado inmates whose traditional appellate remedies have been exhausted. Students focus on legal and factual issues commonly arising in wrongful conviction cases.

The Byron R. White Center for the Study of American Constitutional Law furthers the study, teaching, and publication of Constitutional law. The White Center hosts the annual Ira C. Rothgerber Constitutional Law Conference, which exposes students to analysis and debate of contemporary constitutional issues.

The Entrepreneurial Law Center's mission is to connect the law school, faculty, and students with the flourishing Colorado entrepreneurial community. It plans to be a hub of high-tech start-ups and emerging growth companies by conducting educational, research, and service activities on legal matters relevant to entrepreneurs, venture capitalists, and the lawyers who serve them. The center also conducts a clinic.

The Silicon Flatirons Telecommunications Program's mission is to create an environment for analyzing the dynamic changes in the telecommunications marketplace and regulatory environment. The program supports the academic community by fostering relationships between students and telecommunications professionals through its mentor and internship opportunities.

■ Curriculum

First semester runs from late August to mid-December, and second semester from mid-January to mid-May. Three summer sessions from three to five weeks each begin in May for students enrolled at any accredited law school. With a limited number of additional hours, a certificate in tax or environmental policy is attainable. The first-year curriculum is required of all students. During the second and third years, students may emphasize such areas of the law as natural resources, environment, crime, business, constitution, taxation, public interest, American Indians, litigation, intellectual property, and jurisprudence. Established joint-degree programs are the JD/MBA, JD/MPA, JD/MST, and JD/MSES. Others can be arranged.

■ Admission

A bachelor's degree from an institution that is accredited by an agency recognized by the Department of Education is required. The application deadline is February 15. The LSAT and registration with the LSDAS are required. Offers of admission are based on GPA and LSAT, but these scores are considered in the context of the entire application. Substantial weight is accorded to special qualities such as motivation, undergraduate program, diversity, unusual employment or other experience, leadership, and perseverance in overcoming personal handicaps or disadvantages. The school seeks to increase ethnic, cultural, and other diversity of its student body. The earliest admission letters go out about November 1, and the class is filled in May or June. Admission thereafter is from a waitlist.

Several positions are offered each year to transfer and visiting students. Admission criteria for these students include law school performance.

Housing

For information about the university's family housing, call 303.492.6384, and 303.492.7053 for off-campus housing. Call 303.492.8491 about dormitories.

Student Activities

Over 20 student organizations invite participation in projects, programs, and social activities.

Students participate in the Rothgerber Moot Court Competition, the Jessup International Law Moot Court Competition, the Saul Lefkowitz Trademark Moot Court Competition, National Trial Competition, and other national moot court competitions. CU teams have won regional, national, and international recognition in these events.

The *University of Colorado Law Review, Journal on Telecommunications and High Technology Law*, and *Colorado Journal of International Environmental Law and Policy* are professional journals edited entirely by students.

Financial Aid

Limited state and privately funded scholarships are available. Scholarships are based on merit, financial need, and diversity. State grants, available to eligible resident students, are awarded on the basis of need. Nonresident students qualify for lower resident tuition rates by maintaining domicile in Colorado for 12 consecutive months. Students may not be employed during their first year, but limited outside employment is compatible with second- and third-year schedules. Students applying for financial aid must file the FAFSA as soon as possible after January 1.

Career Services

Career Services provides counseling to students and alumni on career options, including legal positions and alternative career paths. The office solicits employers nationwide for on-campus interviews and to hire students through off-campus programs as well. The office also sponsors and coordinates numerous information sessions and career development programs throughout the academic year. The office helped develop the Colorado Pledge to Diversity Law Firms 1L Summer Clerkship Program.

Applicant Profile

University of Colorado School of Law
This grid includes only applicants who earned 120-180 LSAT scores under standard administrations.

LSAT Score	3.75 +		3.50 - 3.74		3.25 - 3.49		3.00 - 3.24		2.75 - 2.99		2.50 - 2.74		2.25 - 2.49		2.00 - 2.24		Below 2.00		No GPA		Total	
	Apps	Adm	Apps	Adm	Apps	Adm	Apps	Adm	Apps	Adm	Apps	Adm	Apps	Adm	Apps	Adm	Apps	Adm	Apps	Adm	Apps	Adm
175-180	2	2	3	3	1	1	2	1	0	0	0	0	0	0	0	0	0	0	0	0	8	7
170-174	6	6	12	10	15	13	8	4	2	0	1	0	1	0	0	0	0	0	2	2	47	35
165-169	53	52	52	49	59	41	39	14	21	6	9	5	3	1	0	0	0	0	0	0	236	168
160-164	132	120	214	158	180	53	116	17	63	5	22	1	10	3	3	0	0	0	2	2	742	359
155-159	145	20	228	36	210	11	142	3	75	4	38	1	13	0	4	0	1	0	2	0	858	75
150-154	72	6	137	10	134	7	103	2	62	2	28	1	9	0	4	0	0	0	4	0	553	28
145-149	26	0	48	2	53	0	44	0	35	0	20	0	15	0	6	0	0	0	5	0	252	2
140-144	4	0	13	0	16	0	21	0	20	0	17	0	4	0	3	0	1	0	3	0	102	0
135-139	0	0	3	0	5	0	2	0	4	0	3	0	3	0	3	0	0	0	2	0	25	0
130-134	0	0	1	0	1	0	1	0	0	0	2	0	2	0	2	0	1	0	1	0	11	0
125-129	0	0	0	0	0	0	0	0	0	0	0	0	0	0	0	0	0	0	2	0	2	0
120-124	0	0	0	0	0	0	0	0	0	0	0	0	1	0	0	0	0	0	0	0	1	0
Total	440	206	711	268	674	126	478	41	282	17	140	8	61	4	25	0	3	0	23	4	2837	674

Apps = Number of Applicants   Adm = Number Admitted   Reflects 100% of the total applicant pool.

Columbia University School of Law

435 West 116th Street
New York, NY 10027
Phone: 212.854.2670; Fax: 212.854.1109
E-mail: admissions@law.columbia.edu; Website: www.law.columbia.edu

ABA
Approved
Since
1923

The Basics

Type of school	Private
Term	Semester
Application deadline	2/15
Application fee	$70
Financial aid deadline	3/1
Can first year start other than fall?	No
Student to faculty ratio (fall)	11.2 to 1
Does the university offer:	
housing restricted to law students?	Yes
graduate housing for which law students are eligible?	Yes

Faculty and Administrators

	Total		Men		Women		Minorities	
	Fall	Spr	Fall	Spr	Fall	Spr	Fall	Spr
Full-time	94	62	63	42	31	20	12	7
Other Full-time	3	3	3	3	0	0	1	1
Deans, librarians, & others who teach	4	4	2	2	2	2	0	0
Part-time	62	94	47	68	15	26	5	9
Total	163	163	115	115	48	48	18	17

Curriculum

	Full-time	Part-time
Typical first-year section size	110	0
Is there typically a "small section" of the first-year class, other than Legal Writing, taught by full-time faculty	Yes	No
If yes, typical size offered last year	34	0
# of classroom course titles beyond 1st year curriculum		202

# of upper division courses, excluding seminars with an enrollment:		
	Under 25	67
	25-49	33
	50-74	14
	75-99	9
	100+	18

# of seminars		111
# of seminar positions available		2,135
# of seminar positions filled	1,637	0
# of positions available in simulation courses		766
# of simulation positions filled	749	0
# of positions available in faculty supervised clinical courses		170
# of faculty supervised clinical positions filled	170	0
# involved in field placements	276	0
# involved in law journals	597	0
# involved in moot court or trial competitions	125	0
# of credit hours required to graduate		83

JD Enrollment and Ethnicity

	Men		Women		Full-time		Part-time		1st-year		Total		JD Degs. Awd.
	#	%	#	%	#	%	#	%	#	%	#	%	
African Amer.	39	5.7	72	13.0	111	9.0	0	0.0	31	8.3	111	9.0	30
Amer. Indian	4	0.6	4	0.7	8	0.6	0	0.0	5	1.3	8	0.6	1
Asian Amer.	78	11.4	82	14.8	160	12.9	0	0.0	45	12.0	160	12.9	46
Mex. Amer.	23	3.4	20	3.6	43	3.5	0	0.0	18	4.8	43	3.5	13
Puerto Rican	3	0.4	10	1.8	13	1.0	0	0.0	2	0.5	13	1.0	9
Hispanic	16	2.3	9	1.6	25	2.0	0	0.0	9	2.4	25	2.0	19
Total Minority	163	23.8	197	35.6	360	29.1	0	0.0	110	29.4	360	29.1	118
For. Nation.	74	10.8	50	9.0	124	10.0	0	0.0	25	6.7	124	10.0	39
Caucasian	444	64.8	305	55.1	749	60.5	0	0.0	235	62.8	749	60.5	240
Unknown	4	0.6	2	0.4	6	0.5	0	0.0	4	1.1	6	0.5	0
Total	685	55.3	554	44.7	1239	100.0	0	0.0	374	30.2	1239		397

Tuition and Fees

	Resident	Nonresident
Full-time	$37,256	$37,256
Part-time	$0	$0

Living Expenses

Estimated living expenses for singles

Living on campus	Living off campus	Living at home
$17,305	$17,305	$4,705

Columbia University School of Law

ABA Approved Since 1923

GPA and LSAT Scores

	Total	Full-time	Part-time
# of apps	8,355	8,355	0
# of admits	1,187	1,187	0
# of matrics	374	374	0
75% GPA	3.83	3.83	0.00
25% GPA	3.50	3.50	0.00
75% LSAT	173	173	0
25% LSAT	167	167	0

Grants and Scholarships (from prior year)

	Total #	Total %	Full-time #	Full-time %	Part-time #	Part-time %
Total # of students	1,225		1,225		0	
Total # receiving grants	615	50.2	615	50.2	0	0.0
Less than 1/2 tuition	520	42.4	520	42.4	0	0.0
Half to full tuition	47	3.8	47	3.8	0	0.0
Full tuition	48	3.9	48	3.9	0	0.0
More than full tuition	0	0.0	0	0.0	0	0.0
Median grant amount			$13,400		$0	

Informational and Library Resources

# of volumes and volume equivalents	1,076,939
# of titles	371,442
# of active serial subscriptions	6,802
Study seating capacity inside the library	342
# of professional librarians	21
Hours per week library is open	102
# of open, wired connections available to students	3,132
# of networked computers available for use by students	116
# of simultaneous wireless users	2,944
Require computer?	N

JD Attrition (from prior year)

	Academic #	Other #	Total #	Total %
1st year	0	0	0	0.0%
2nd year	0	2	2	0.5%
3rd year	1	2	3	0.7%
4th year	0	0	0	0.0%

Employment

	Total	Percentage
Employment status known	410	100.0
Employment status unknown	0	0.0
Employed	398	97.1
Pursuing graduate degrees	0	0.0
Unemployed seeking employment	9	2.2
Unemployed not seeking employment	3	0.7

Type of Employment

# employed in law firms	319	80.2
# employed in business and industry	6	1.5
# employed in government	7	1.8
# employed in public interest	13	3.3
# employed as judicial clerks	52	13.1
# employed in academia	1	0.3

Geographic Location

# employed in state	284	71.4
# employed in foreign countries	9	2.3
# of states where employed		24

Bar Passage Rates

Jurisdiction	New York		
Exam	Sum 03	Win 04	Total
# from school taking bar for the first time	303	21	324
School's pass rate for all first-time takers	96%	95%	96%
State's pass rate for all first-time takers	78%	58%	75%

Columbia University School of Law

435 West 116th Street
New York, NY 10027
Phone: 212.854.2670; Fax: 212.854.1109
E-mail: admissions@law.columbia.edu; Website: www.law.columbia.edu

■ Introduction

Columbia law school is distinguished, perhaps uniquely among leading American law schools, as an international center of legal education that stimulates its students to consider the full dimensions of the possibility of the law—as an intellectual pursuit, as a career, and as an instrument of human progress. The character of academic and social life at Columbia is fiercely democratic, dynamic, creative, and innovative. The law school is especially committed to educating students of differing perspectives, from diverse backgrounds, and with varied life experiences.

Professional prospects for Columbia law graduates are quite extraordinary. Our graduates proceed to productive careers in every conceivable arena of private practice. But, it should be emphasized that while Columbia-trained attorneys are especially well-regarded for their work in corporate law and finance, an unusually high number also serve as state and federal judges, prosecutors, civil and human rights advocates, legal scholars, public defenders, entrepreneurs, business executives, elected government officials, and national and international leaders. Many Columbia law alumni/ae contribute significantly to the shaping of American culture at large. Currently our graduates serve in leadership roles across the fields of art, music, film, publishing, science, professional athletics, philanthropy, and higher education.

With an exceptionally talented student body and faculty, and a strong tradition of encouraging students with specialized interests to develop those interests in depth, Columbia law school provides a legal education that gives our students a singular capacity for imagination, originality, and high responsibility in their professional lives.

■ JD Student Body Profile

Columbia continues to place among the handful of the most highly selective JD programs in our nation—as evaluated by the principal criteria used to measure admissions selectivity (application volume, acceptance rates, LSAT scores, and academic performance). Indeed, in recent years, the demand for a Columbia legal education has never been greater, and the academic credentials of our entering classes are stronger than ever. Columbia's JD student body is further distinguished by standing as one of the most culturally diverse among America's leading law schools. Men and women choosing to study law at Columbia hail from the small towns, farms, and suburbs of the West, Midwest, and South; the industrial corridors and ivy halls of the Northeast; the inner cities of every major American metropolis; and the international centers of Europe, Asia, Africa, and Latin America.

Each entering class reflects the broad range of economic, ethnic, and cultural backgrounds found in America. And

from around the world, we welcome students who will enrich learning at Columbia and thereafter advance the developing legal cultures of their homelands.

With the largest percentage of international students in its JD program of any leading law school; with one of the very highest percentages of students of color; with its students hailing from 48 states, 49 foreign countries, and 246 different colleges and universities; with 14 percent of its JD students having earned at least one graduate or professional degree before studying law, Columbia's student body abounds with a diversity of life experiences, cultural backgrounds, and intellectual perspectives.

■ The Law School Campus

Columbia law school recently completed a $133 million physical expansion and renewal project, ensuring that our facilities are among the finest of any law school in the country. Our main building, Greene Hall, has undergone significant expansion and improvements, devoted primarily to our students—a spacious new entrance and foyer, library renovations, and the creation of a student commons that includes a student lounge and café. New seminar rooms and state-of-the-art multimedia classrooms have also been designed to provide students with full Internet and other legal research access. Across the street from Greene Hall is William C. Warren Hall, home to the *Columbia Law Review*, Morningside Heights Legal Services (a law school clinic serving our community), and the Center for Public Interest Law.

William and June Warren Hall, opened in 1999, includes amphitheater-style classrooms equipped with modern teaching resources, a center for the law school's international programs, and conference facilities. It is also home for the center for student services, which includes the Offices of Admissions, Financial Aid, Registration Services, and the Dean of Students Office. And Lenfest Hall, a gracious apartment complex for law students, opened in August 2003.

The renovation and expansion of the law school's facilities have greatly enhanced the quality of life and learning at Columbia. Students have a superb learning environment that is conducive to community-building and social and intellectual engagement, and reflects the changing nature of legal education in the twenty-first century.

■ Library Resources and Research Facilities

One of the largest and most comprehensive law collections in the world, Columbia's library is especially rich in American law and legal history, international law, comparative law, Roman law, and the legal literature of the major European countries, China, and Japan. Access to the Internet and CD-ROMs provide additional resources with materials from Germany, South Africa, and a wide range of international organizations. In addition, the many libraries of the university, containing more than seven million volumes, are available to law students.

The law library's online catalog provides complete access to the collection and acts as an index to the major legal serials, as well as providing access to the online catalogs of other major law school libraries. Columbia provides its law students with some of the most sophisticated technologies of any law school in the nation.

■ Curriculum

The foundation of the JD program consists of legal methods, contracts, torts, constitutional law, civil procedure, property, criminal law, and one elective focusing on the law's engagement with public policy, the intellectual and historical foundations of the rule of law, and law's transnational and comparative expression.

Columbia has a special commitment to clinical education, which places the student in the role of a lawyer doing a lawyer's actual work under intensive faculty supervision. Some examples of clinical opportunities are Lawyering in the Digital Age, Law and the Arts, Non-Profit Organizations, Prisoners and Families, Child Advocacy, Mediation, Environmental Law, and Human Rights. Unique to Columbia is a summer program which places 60–70 students in civil rights and human rights internships in law firms and organizations throughout this country and around the world. Especially

distinguished are Columbia's offerings in international, foreign, and comparative law; constitutional law and theory; corporate and securities law; intellectual property; critical race theory; and human rights.

■ Research Centers and Special Programs

Research centers and special programs include Kernochan Center for Law, Media, and the Arts; Silver Program in Law, Science, and Technology; Center for Law and Philosophy; Center for Law and Economic Studies; Center for the Study of Law and Culture; Rubin Program for Liberty and Equality through Law; Center for Public Interest Law; Public Interest Law Initiative in Transitional Societies; Human Rights Institute; Parker School of Foreign and Comparative Law; Center for Chinese Legal Studies; Center for Japanese Legal Studies; Center for Korean Legal Studies; European Legal Studies Center; the Legislative Drafting Research Fund; and programs in alternative dispute resolution and in law and history.

■ Admission

All first-year students enter in mid-August. Candidates applying for regular admission should apply after September 1 of the year preceding their desired matriculation, but before February 15, the application deadline. Early Decision candidates must complete their applications by November 15 and are notified in late December.

Applicant Profile

Columbia has chosen not to provide prospective students with an admission selectivity profile based on LSAT scores and undergraduate GPA because we believe it does not accurately portray our selection process. Ours is a comprehensive, multivariate evaluation of academic performance and professional promise. Columbia evaluates every application individually—while carefully considering the candidate's background, interests, accomplishments, and goals. We are proud that Columbia is among the handful of the most highly selective law schools in the country, as measured by LSAT and UGPA statistics and other selectivity measures. But we wish to emphasize, by not reducing our selection process to a two-dimensional grid, that the recognized excellence of our student body and distinction of our alumni/ae are rooted not only in their intellectual power and outstanding academic records, but also in their personal strengths, professional skills, and diverse backgrounds.

University of Connecticut School of Law

45 Elizabeth Street
Hartford, CT 06105
Phone: 860.570.5100; Fax: 860.570.5153
E-mail: admit@law.uconn.edu; Website: www.law.uconn.edu

ABA Approved Since 1933

The Basics

Type of school	Public
Term	Semester
Application deadline	3/1
Application fee	$30
Financial aid deadline	3/1
Can first year start other than fall?	No
Student to faculty ratio (fall)	12.3 to 1
Does the university offer:	
housing restricted to law students?	No
graduate housing for which law students are eligible?	No

Faculty and Administrators

	Total Fall	Total Spr	Men Fall	Men Spr	Women Fall	Women Spr	Minorities Fall	Minorities Spr
Full-time	42	36	30	25	12	11	3	2
Other Full-time	4	3	1	1	3	2	1	1
Deans, librarians, & others who teach	2	2	1	1	1	1	0	0
Part-time	34	50	26	37	8	13	3	2
Total	82	91	58	64	24	27	7	5

Curriculum

	Full-time	Part-time
Typical first-year section size	68	68
Is there typically a "small section" of the first-year class, other than Legal Writing, taught by full-time faculty	Yes	Yes
If yes, typical size offered last year	23	23
# of classroom course titles beyond 1st year curriculum	138	
# of upper division courses, excluding seminars with an enrollment: Under 25	68	
25-49	17	
50-74	8	
75-99	0	
100+	0	
# of seminars	48	
# of seminar positions available	898	
# of seminar positions filled	469	218
# of positions available in simulation courses	512	
# of simulation positions filled	289	172
# of positions available in faculty supervised clinical courses	155	
# of faculty supervised clinical positions filled	146	9
# involved in field placements	46	36
# involved in law journals	206	4
# involved in moot court or trial competitions	7	1
# of credit hours required to graduate	86	

J.D. Enrollment and Ethnicity

	Men #	Men %	Women #	Women %	Full-time #	Full-time %	Part-time #	Part-time %	1st-year #	1st-year %	Total #	Total %	JD Degs. Awd.
African Amer.	14	4.1	26	7.6	29	5.5	11	7.1	12	6.2	40	5.8	5
Amer. Indian	3	0.9	1	0.3	2	0.4	2	1.3	1	0.5	4	0.6	4
Asian Amer.	12	3.5	32	9.4	33	6.2	11	7.1	13	6.7	44	6.4	8
Mex. Amer.	2	0.6	3	0.9	5	0.9	0	0.0	1	0.5	5	0.7	0
Puerto Rican	6	1.7	11	3.2	15	2.8	2	1.3	6	3.1	17	2.5	0
Hispanic	19	5.5	17	5.0	31	5.8	5	3.2	11	5.7	36	5.2	3
Total Minority	56	16.2	90	26.3	115	21.7	31	19.9	44	22.7	146	21.3	20
For. Nation.	0	0.0	0	0.0	0	0.0	0	0.0	0	0.0	0	0.0	0
Caucasian	273	79.1	243	71.1	400	75.3	116	74.4	128	66.0	516	75.1	152
Unknown	16	4.6	9	2.6	16	3.0	9	5.8	23	11.9	25	3.6	0
Total	345	50.2	342	49.8	531	77.3	156	22.7	194	28.2	687		172

Tuition and Fees

	Resident	Nonresident
Full-time	$15,388	$31,780
Part-time	$10,774	$22,214

Living Expenses

Estimated living expenses for singles

Living on campus	Living off campus	Living at home
N/A	$13,550	$6,290

University of Connecticut School of Law

ABA
Approved
Since
1933

GPA and LSAT Scores

	Total	Full-time	Part-time
# of apps	2,965	2,229	736
# of admits	622	461	161
# of matrics	190	126	64
75% GPA	3.58	3.58	3.61
25% GPA	3.13	3.13	3.15
75% LSAT	162	164	160
25% LSAT	156	160	156

Grants and Scholarships (from prior year)

	Total		Full-time		Part-time	
	#	%	#	%	#	%
Total # of students	683		518		165	
Total # receiving grants	389	57.0	380	73.4	9	5.5
Less than 1/2 tuition	340	49.8	331	63.9	9	5.5
Half to full tuition	32	4.7	32	6.2	0	0.0
Full tuition	0	0.0	0	0.0	0	0.0
More than full tuition	17	2.5	17	3.3	0	0.0
Median grant amount			$6,300		$1,253	

Informational and Library Resources

# of volumes and volume equivalents	517,142
# of titles	153,554
# of active serial subscriptions	5,381
Study seating capacity inside the library	637
# of professional librarians	13
Hours per week library is open	87
# of open, wired connections available to students	781
# of networked computers available for use by students	127
# of simultaneous wireless users	0
Require computer?	N

JD Attrition (from prior year)

	Academic	Other	Total	
	#	#	#	%
1st year	0	12	12	1.8%
2nd year	1	2	3	0.4%
3rd year	0	0	0	0.0%
4th year	0	0	0	0.0%

Employment

	Total	Percentage
Employment status known	166	97.6
Employment status unknown	4	2.4
Employed	159	95.8
Pursuing graduate degrees	1	0.6
Unemployed seeking employment	5	3.0
Unemployed not seeking employment	1	0.6

Type of Employment

# employed in law firms	78	49.1
# employed in business and industry	25	15.7
# employed in government	18	11.3
# employed in public interest	6	3.8
# employed as judicial clerks	30	18.9
# employed in academia	2	1.3

Geographic Location

# employed in state	103	64.8
# employed in foreign countries	0	0.0
# of states where employed	17	

Bar Passage Rates

Jurisdiction	Connecticut		
Exam	Sum 03	Win 04	Total
# from school taking bar for the first time	106	22	128
School's pass rate for all first-time takers	89%	82%	88%
State's pass rate for all first-time takers	82%	78%	81%

University of Connecticut School of Law

45 Elizabeth Street
Hartford, CT 06105
Phone: 860.570.5100; Fax: 860.570.5153
E-mail: admit@law.uconn.edu; Website: www.law.uconn.edu

■ Introduction

Through several decades of sustained intellectual growth, the University of Connecticut School of Law has emerged as one of the leading public law schools in the United States. Because of Connecticut's extraordinary ratio of full-time students to full-time faculty, 40 percent of the first-year curriculum is offered in seminar format and 70 percent of the advanced courses have 20 or fewer students. An outstanding and accessible faculty, an intensive first-year skills program, a rich and varied curriculum, four student-edited journals, student organizations active across the spectrum of legal and social concerns, a regular flow of visiting lecturers, and a committed body of graduates all combine to make the University of Connecticut a law school of exceptional strength.

■ Library and Physical Facilities

The campus, listed on the National Register of Historic Sites, is probably the most beautiful in the United States. The library, completed in 1996, is one of the largest legal research and technology centers in the world, with more than 500,000 volumes housed in the 120,000-square-foot facility.

With its immediate neighbors—the Hartford Seminary, the Hartford College for Women, the Connecticut Historical Society, and the Connecticut Attorney General's Office—the school is part of an academic enclave in a turn-of-the-century residential neighborhood.

■ Dual-Degree Programs

The law school offers seven interdisciplinary programs: JD/LLM in Insurance Law, JD/Master of Business Administration, JD/Master of Library Science (with Southern Connecticut State University), JD/Master of Public Administration, JD/Master of Public Health, JD/Master of Public Policy (with Trinity College), and JD/Master of Social Work.

■ International Study Programs

The economic and political realities of globalization place new demands on the graduates of the law school. International law occupies an increasingly prominent place in the curriculum, reinforced by the student-edited *Connecticut Journal of International Law*. The law school has formal and informal study-abroad programs with universities in Aix-Marseille, Berlin, Dublin, Exeter, Leiden, London, Mannheim, San Juan, Sienna, and Tilburg. These relationships bring a wealth of international visitors to the school. Legal scholars have visited and lectured from Albania, Bosnia, Bulgaria, China, France, Germany, Great Britain, Hungary, Israel, Japan, Korea, Latvia, The Netherlands, Poland, Russia, South Africa, Taiwan, and Ukraine.

The LLM in United States Legal Studies for graduates of foreign law schools provides further opportunity for our students to learn from and study with peers trained in different legal systems.

■ Special Programs

Connecticut was a pioneer in clinical legal education, and our clinics continue to be a distinguishing strength of the school. If you are interested in the way law intersects with other disciplines or with such varied topics as critical identity theory, intellectual property, or European Community law, you will find courses and specialists to meet your needs. Extensive offerings in environmental law are supplemented by a semester-exchange program with the University of London and another with the Environmental Law Center at Vermont Law School.

The **Center for Children's Advocacy, Inc.**, a nonprofit corporation housed at the law school, works on behalf of the legal rights of underprivileged children. The **Connecticut Urban Legal Initiative, Inc.**, another nonprofit corporation housed at the law school, involves law students and the bar in identifying neighborhood problems that typify urban blight and devising strategies to address them. The **Insurance Law Center** offers a specialized insurance curriculum with its LLM program, innovative research initiatives on the role of insurance in law and society, conferences and workshops, and the student-edited *Connecticut Insurance Law Journal*.

The **Intellectual Property Certificate Program**, for students with a special interest in IP law, exposes participants to a broad curriculum of courses—from classes on patent, trademark, and copyright law to specialized seminars, including those in art law, cyberlaw, and European Union IP law. The **Tax Certificate Program** affords an opportunity to participate in a supervised writing project, externship, or clinic in the area of tax law. Participants in the Certificate Program may begin their tax studies in Federal Income Taxation in their first year and continue the study of taxation in a variety of courses during the last four semesters of law school.

■ Student Activities

Selected students may participate in four student-edited journals: the *Connecticut Law Review*, the *Connecticut Journal of International Law*, the *Connecticut Insurance Law Journal*, and the *Public Interest Law Journal*.

The **Connecticut Moot Court Board** provides students with the opportunity to practice oral advocacy in intramural and interscholastic competitions. Participants have placed extremely well in regional, national, and international competitions.

The **Student Bar Association** is the representative student government of the school. It manages an annual budget consisting of funds derived from the student activities fee and university tuition to support the various student organizations and to enhance generally the quality of student life. Under the governance of the Student Bar, a large number of student-run organizations, reflecting the diversity of our students, have active chapters on campus.

■ Career Services

Connecticut operates a comprehensive career services office for the benefit of students and alumni/ae. The school offers a large and geographically diverse on-campus interviewing program (*www.law.uconn.edu/careersvcs/employer-list.htm*), extensive individual and group counseling, a resource library, job listings, mentor programs, employment

information sessions, newsletters, and job bulletins. The school also participates in several off-site job fairs.

Within six months of graduation, 95.8 percent of the class of 2003 was employed, 18.9 percent were in judicial clerkships, and .6 percent of the same class were pursuing advanced degrees.

■ Services for Students with Disabilities

The Assistant to the Dean for Student Services at the School of Law works with students with disabilities in the development and implementation of reasonable accommodations to allow access to both its physical facilities and its educational and extracurricular programs. Dr. Jane Thierfeld Brown serves in this capacity.

Students with disabilities who are considering applying or who have been admitted to the School of Law are invited to tour the campus. Students may contact the dean's office for discussion of accommodations.

Applicant Profile

University of Connecticut School of Law

	GPA																			
LSAT Score	3.75 +		3.50 - 3.74		3.25 - 3.49		3.00 - 3.24		2.75 - 2.99		2.50 - 2.74		2.25 - 2.49		2.00 - 2.24		Below 2.00		No GPA		Total
	Apps	Adm	Apps	Adm	Apps	Adm	Apps	Adm	Apps	Adm	Apps	Adm	Apps	Adm	Apps	Adm	Apps	Adm	Apps	Adm	Apps	Adm
175-180	0	0	0	0	1	0	0	0	0	0	0	0	0	0	0	0	0	0	0	0	1	0
170-174	1	1	5	3	7	5	2	1	3	0	2	0	0	0	0	0	0	0	0	0	20	10
165-169	23	11	30	17	38	22	32	21	12	8	4	3	2	1	1	0	0	0	0	0	142	83
160-164	76	33	142	72	133	68	122	54	48	13	30	6	6	0	2	0	0	0	4	1	563	247
155-159	103	17	191	29	227	32	151	18	50	3	25	2	12	0	0	0	0	0	9	0	768	101
150-154	57	5	106	6	115	9	103	7	65	4	37	2	15	1	4	0	0	0	2	0	504	34
145-149	17	3	47	3	76	5	49	3	41	1	22	0	12	0	4	0	0	0	5	0	273	15
140-144	11	0	15	2	34	0	31	0	21	1	17	0	10	0	5	0	0	0	2	0	146	3
135-139	1	0	9	0	9	0	14	0	8	0	8	0	8	0	4	0	2	0	3	0	66	0
130-134	0	0	1	0	3	0	2	0	3	0	3	0	2	0	0	0	1	0	2	0	17	0
125-129	0	0	0	0	0	0	1	0	0	0	2	0	0	0	1	0	0	0	2	0	6	0
120-124	0	0	0	0	0	0	0	0	0	0	1	0	0	0	0	0	0	0	0	0	1	0
Total	289	70	546	132	643	141	507	104	251	30	151	13	67	2	21	0	3	0	29	1	2507	493

Apps = Number of Applicants
Adm = Number Admitted

This grid includes only full-time applicants with LSAT scores earned under standard administrations (99% of all full-time applicants).

Cornell Law School

Myron Taylor Hall
Ithaca, NY 14853-4901
Phone: 607.255.5141
E-mail: lawadmit@postoffice.law.cornell.edu; Website: www.lawschool.cornell.edu

ABA Approved Since 1923

The Basics

Type of school	Private
Term	Semester
Application deadline	2/1
Application fee	$70
Financial aid deadline	3/15
Can first year start other than fall?	No
Student to faculty ratio (fall)	10.8 to 1
Does the university offer:	
housing restricted to law students?	Yes
graduate housing for which law students are eligible?	Yes

Faculty and Administrators

	Total Fall	Total Spr	Men Fall	Men Spr	Women Fall	Women Spr	Minorities Fall	Minorities Spr
Full-time	46	48	29	30	17	18	3	3
Other Full-time	0	0	0	0	0	0	0	0
Deans, librarians, & others who teach	10	10	6	6	4	4	0	0
Part-time	14	22	9	14	5	8	0	2
Total	70	80	44	50	26	30	3	5

Curriculum

	Full-time	Part-time
Typical first-year section size	98	0
Is there typically a "small section" of the first-year class, other than Legal Writing, taught by full-time faculty	Yes	No
If yes, typical size offered last year	32	0
# of classroom course titles beyond 1st year curriculum	99	

# of upper division courses, excluding seminars with an enrollment:		
	Under 25	28
	25-49	18
	50-74	10
	75-99	4
	100+	8

# of seminars	31	
# of seminar positions available	480	
# of seminar positions filled	436	0
# of positions available in simulation courses	311	
# of simulation positions filled	290	0
# of positions available in faculty supervised clinical courses	77	
# of faculty supervised clinical positions filled	68	0
# involved in field placements	34	0
# involved in law journals	244	0
# involved in moot court or trial competitions	75	0
# of credit hours required to graduate	84	

JD Enrollment and Ethnicity

	Men #	Men %	Women #	Women %	Full-time #	Full-time %	Part-time #	Part-time %	1st-year #	1st-year %	Total #	Total %	JD Degs. Awd.
African Amer.	10	3.2	35	12.3	45	7.6	0	0.0	16	8.4	45	7.6	11
Amer. Indian	1	0.3	1	0.4	2	0.3	0	0.0	1	0.5	2	0.3	2
Asian Amer.	49	15.9	64	22.5	113	19.1	0	0.0	48	25.1	113	19.1	16
Mex. Amer.	6	1.9	7	2.5	13	2.2	0	0.0	5	2.6	13	2.2	4
Puerto Rican	4	1.3	4	1.4	8	1.3	0	0.0	5	2.6	8	1.3	5
Hispanic	4	1.3	4	1.4	8	1.3	0	0.0	3	1.6	8	1.3	0
Total Minority	74	24.0	115	40.4	189	31.9	0	0.0	78	40.8	189	31.9	38
For. Nation.	18	5.8	17	6.0	35	5.9	0	0.0	7	3.7	35	5.9	7
Caucasian	216	70.1	153	53.7	369	62.2	0	0.0	106	55.5	369	62.2	141
Unknown	0	0.0	0	0.0	0	0.0	0	0.0	0	0.0	0	0.0	0
Total	308	51.9	285	48.1	593	100.0	0	0.0	191	32.2	593		186

Tuition and Fees

	Resident	Nonresident
Full-time	$35,342	$35,342
Part-time	$0	$0

Living Expenses

Estimated living expenses for singles

Living on campus	Living off campus	Living at home
$15,960	$15,960	$15,960

Cornell Law School

*ABA
Approved
Since
1923*

GPA and LSAT Scores

	Total	Full-time	Part-time
# of apps	4,583	4,583	0
# of admits	879	879	0
# of matrics	191	191	0
75% GPA	3.76	3.76	0.00
25% GPA	3.43	3.43	0.00
75% LSAT	168	168	0
25% LSAT	164	164	0

Grants and Scholarships (from prior year)

	Total		Full-time		Part-time	
	#	%	#	%	#	%
Total # of students	585		585		0	
Total # receiving grants	280	47.9	280	47.9	0	0.0
Less than 1/2 tuition	200	34.2	200	34.2	0	0.0
Half to full tuition	76	13.0	76	13.0	0	0.0
Full tuition	4	0.7	4	0.7	0	0.0
More than full tuition	0	0.0	0	0.0	0	0.0
Median grant amount			$11,950		$0	

Informational and Library Resources

# of volumes and volume equivalents	689,856
# of titles	211,590
# of active serial subscriptions	6,570
Study seating capacity inside the library	425
# of professional librarians	10
Hours per week library is open	80
# of open, wired connections available to students	40
# of networked computers available for use by students	63
# of simultaneous wireless users	350
Require computer?	N

JD Attrition (from prior year)

	Academic	Other	Total	
	#	#	#	%
1st year	0	9	9	4.7%
2nd year	0	1	1	0.5%
3rd year	0	0	0	0.0%
4th year	0	0	0	0.0%

Employment

	Total	Percentage
Employment status known	177	100.0
Employment status unknown	0	0.0
Employed	173	97.7
Pursuing graduate degrees	1	0.6
Unemployed seeking employment	3	1.7
Unemployed not seeking employment	0	0.0

Type of Employment

# employed in law firms	131	75.7
# employed in business and industry	3	1.7
# employed in government	6	3.5
# employed in public interest	3	1.7
# employed as judicial clerks	21	12.1
# employed in academia	4	2.3

Geographic Location

# employed in state	104	60.1
# employed in foreign countries	1	0.6
# of states where employed		21

Bar Passage Rates

Jurisdiction	New York		
Exam	Sum 03	Win 04	Total
# from school taking bar for the first time	130	4	134
School's pass rate for all first-time takers	94%	50%	93%
State's pass rate for all first-time takers	78%	58%	75%

Cornell Law School

Myron Taylor Hall
Ithaca, NY 14853-4901
Phone: 607.255.5141
E-mail: lawadmit@postoffice.law.cornell.edu; Website: www.lawschool.cornell.edu

■ Introduction

Cornell is a national center of learning located in Ithaca, New York, the heart of the Finger Lakes region of New York State. The Law School's small classes, broad curriculum, and distinguished faculty, combined with the advantages of being part of one of the world's leading research universities, make it ideal for those who value both depth and breadth in their legal studies. Students find Ithaca to be a safe and nonstressful, yet culturally rich, environment in which to pursue legal studies.

■ Enrollment/Student Body

Sixty percent of Cornell's entering students have taken one or more years between completion of their undergraduate degree and enrollment in law school. Selective admission standards, combined with an emphasis on applicants' unique records and achievements, ensure that the student body is made up of people with wide-ranging interests, skills, concerns, and backgrounds.

■ Faculty

Cornell's faculty are known not only as prolific scholars but also as great teachers. Tenured and tenure-track faculty teach and produce scholarship in their area of law; clinical faculty run client-focused and simulation courses centered around legal aid and several specialty clinics; and a large number of visitors, associated faculty from other university divisions, and adjunct faculty teach at the school each year. Many of the latter group are legal scholars and professors from other countries who teach in the law school's significant international program.

■ Library, Physical Facilities, and Computing

The Law School is located in the renovated and expanded Myron Taylor Hall, at the heart of the scenic 740-acre Cornell University campus. Hughes Hall, the Law School dormitory, is adjacent to the main Law School building and contains single rooms for about 48 students and a dining facility.

Cornell is one of the nation's leaders in the development and support of electronic legal research. It combines outstanding collections with professional expertise and access to worldwide electronic information sources, for Anglo-American, as well as foreign and international law. Students have access to the full array of Internet services. The Law School's multiple-node network, wireless network, and computer terminals are available to students for word processing, legal research, statistical analysis, and database management. Students also have access to the many satellite computer clusters and mainframe facilities located on the university campus.

■ Curriculum/Clinical Studies

Cornell offers a national law curriculum leading to the JD degree. First-year students take a group of required courses and an intensive lawyering course stressing a variety of legal research, writing, and advocacy techniques. After the first year, students may choose from a wide range of elective courses, including many seminars and problem courses.

The Cornell Legal Aid Clinic, offering legal services to individuals financially unable to employ an attorney, provides students with the chance to engage in the supervised practice of law under the direction of experienced attorneys. Clinical faculty also conduct a variety of other specialized clinics and skills courses within the regular curriculum.

■ International Legal Studies

The Berger International Legal Studies Program is one of the country's oldest and most distinguished programs in international legal education. Cornell's comprehensive program features a unique JD specialization opportunity, a three-year JD/LLM degree in International and Comparative Law, a four-year JD/Maîtrise en Droit (French law degree) program, a four-year JD/MLLP (German law degree) program, a three-year JD/DESS in Global Business Law, a Paris summer institute with the University of Paris I (Panthéon-Sorbonne), a comprehensive speaker series, a large number of visiting foreign professors and scholars, a weekly luncheon discussion series, and a leading journal of international and comparative law edited by students.

In addition, the Clarke Center for International and Comparative Legal Studies brings scholars, students, philosophers, and experts to support the study of law in Asia and the Middle East.

■ Programs and Projects

Cornell Law School is the home for several unique programs and projects of interest to students. These programs and projects include the following: Cornell Death Penalty Project (clinics and symposia related to capital punishment); Clarke Women in Law Fund (visiting scholars) Feminism and Legal Theory Project (workshops and conferences attended by scholars and practitioners from around the world; director on leave calendar year 2004); Gender, Sexuality, and Family Project (international exchange and enrichment program); *Journal of Empirical Legal Studies* (only legal journal dedicated exclusively to empirical legal scholarship); Clarke Program in East Asian Law and Culture (broad interdisciplinary and humanistic focus to the study of law in East Asia); John Olin Program in Law and Economics (visiting fellows); Legal Information Institute (world's leading investigator of new ways to do electronic legal research); and Empirical Studies Project (empirical study of court cases).

■ Student Activities

Student-edited law journals include the *Cornell Law Review* (published continuously since 1916), the *Cornell International Law Journal* (established in 1967), and the *Cornell Journal of Law and Public Policy*. Student organizations and activities include American Constitution Society; Amicus; Asian Pacific American Law Students Association; Black Law Students Association; Brehon Law Society; Briggs Society of International Law; Christian Legal Society; Bioethics and Law Society; Cornell Sports & Entertainment Law Consortium; Cornell European Law Student Association; Cornell Law Student Association; Cornell Law Democrats; Law, Economics and Business Society; Cornell Law Republicans; Discourses; *The Tower*; Environmental Law Society; Federalist Society; Intellectual Property Student Organization; J. Reuben Clark Law Society; Jewish Law Student Association; *Juris Diction*; Lambda Law Students; Latino American Law Students Association; LLM Association; Moot Court Board; National Lawyer's Guild; Native American Law Students Association; Phi Alpha Delta;

Phi Delta Phi; Public Interest Law Union; the Society of Law and the Arts; the Veteran's Society; and the Women's Law Coalition.

■ Expenses and Financial Aid

Cornell offers both need- and merit-based financial aid programs. About 40 percent of students receive scholarship aid, with a higher percentage receiving government-backed loans. Minority or economically disadvantaged students are eligible for enhanced scholarship awards.

Our Public Interest Low Income Protection Plan, one of the most generous of such programs, assists those choosing qualifying public interest law jobs through the use of a moderated loan repayment plan and loan forgiveness.

■ Career Services

Cornell's students continue to be among the most recruited in the country. Every fall, hundreds of employers from across the country visit the Law School and conduct employment interviews. Employers also participate in law school-sponsored job fairs in locations such as Boston, Chicago, Texas, Los Angeles, New York, Bay Area, Miami, Atlanta, New Hampshire, and Washington, DC. A professionally staffed Career Office provides employment counseling to students and serves as a liaison with legal employers, both public and private. In addition, Cornell has a full-time professional staff member dedicated to public interest job opportunities and counseling.

Applicant Profile

Admission to Cornell Law is very competitive. Members of the most recent entering class had an aggregate 3.6 undergraduate grade-point average and median LSAT scores that placed them in the 96th percentile nationwide (167).

But Cornell Law does not evaluate candidates by the numbers alone. The admission committee carefully considers such nonquantifiable factors as extracurricular and community activities, life experience and work background, and recommendations. Cornell Law

subscribes to the university's 130-year tradition of affirmative action, and members of traditionally underrepresented minority groups are encouraged to mention their status where they think it is relevant.

The decision to offer admission ultimately rests on whether the committee is convinced that the applicant will be an energetic, productive, and successful member of the Cornell Law community and eventually, the legal profession.

Creighton University School of Law

2500 California Plaza
Omaha, NE 68178
Phone: 402.280.2872; Fax: 402.280.3161
E-mail: lawadmit@creighton.edu; Website: http://culaw2.creighton.edu

ABA Approved Since 1924

The Basics

Type of school	Private
Term	Semester
Application deadline	5/1
Application fee	$45
Financial aid deadline	7/1
Can first year start other than fall?	No
Student to faculty ratio (fall)	16.3 to 1
Does the university offer:	
housing restricted to law students?	No
graduate housing for which law students are eligible?	Yes

Faculty and Administrators

	Total		Men		Women		Minorities	
	Fall	Spr	Fall	Spr	Fall	Spr	Fall	Spr
Full-time	24	23	17	16	7	7	3	3
Other Full-time	1	1	0	0	1	1	0	0
Deans, librarians, & others who teach	6	6	5	5	1	1	0	0
Part-time	18	26	11	19	4	5	1	1
Total	49	56	33	40	13	14	4	4

Curriculum

	Full-time	Part-time
Typical first-year section size	80	0
Is there typically a "small section" of the first-year class, other than Legal Writing, taught by full-time faculty	No	No
If yes, typical size offered last year	0	0
# of classroom course titles beyond 1st year curriculum	80	

# of upper division courses, excluding seminars with an enrollment:		
	Under 25	115
	25-49	27
	50-74	8
	75-99	7
	100+	1

# of seminars	6	
# of seminar positions available	131	
# of seminar positions filled	109	0
# of positions available in simulation courses	440	
# of simulation positions filled	394	0
# of positions available in faculty supervised clinical courses	18	
# of faculty supervised clinical positions filled	18	0
# involved in field placements	55	0
# involved in law journals	45	0
# involved in moot court or trial competitions	185	0
# of credit hours required to graduate	94	

J.D. Enrollment and Ethnicity

	Men #	Men %	Women #	Women %	Full-time #	Full-time %	Part-time #	Part-time %	1st-year #	1st-year %	Total #	Total %	JD Degs. Awd.
African Amer.	7	2.6	3	1.4	9	2.0	1	4.3	5	2.9	10	2.1	7
Amer. Indian	1	0.4	2	0.9	3	0.7	0	0.0	2	1.2	3	0.6	2
Asian Amer.	6	2.3	4	1.9	10	2.2	0	0.0	2	1.2	10	2.1	5
Mex. Amer.	5	1.9	6	2.8	11	2.4	0	0.0	6	3.5	11	2.3	2
Puerto Rican	0	0.0	0	0.0	0	0.0	0	0.0	0	0.0	0	0.0	1
Hispanic	4	1.5	3	1.4	7	1.5	0	0.0	3	1.7	7	1.5	4
Total Minority	23	8.6	18	8.5	40	8.8	1	4.3	18	10.4	41	8.6	21
For. Nation.	1	0.4	0	0.0	1	0.2	0	0.0	0	0.0	1	0.2	0
Caucasian	242	91.0	194	91.5	414	91.0	22	95.7	155	89.6	436	91.2	148
Unknown	0	0.0	0	0.0	0	0.0	0	0.0	0	0.0	0	0.0	0
Total	266	55.6	212	44.4	455	95.2	23	4.8	173	36.2	478		169

Tuition and Fees

	Resident	Nonresident
Full-time	$22,312	$22,312
Part-time	$14,448	$14,448

Living Expenses

Estimated living expenses for singles

Living on campus	Living off campus	Living at home
$16,020	$16,020	$16,020

Creighton University School of Law

ABA
Approved
Since
1924

GPA and LSAT Scores

	Total	Full-time	Part-time
# of apps	1,319	1,282	37
# of admits	512	501	11
# of matrics	168	162	6
75% GPA	3.71	3.72	3.56
25% GPA	3.19	3.20	2.64
75% LSAT	156	156	153
25% LSAT	151	151	145

Grants and Scholarships (from prior year)

	Total		Full-time		Part-time	
	#	%	#	%	#	%
Total # of students	497		471		26	
Total # receiving grants	197	39.6	195	41.4	2	7.7
Less than 1/2 tuition	126	25.4	124	26.3	2	7.7
Half to full tuition	52	10.5	52	11.0	0	0.0
Full tuition	18	3.6	18	3.8	0	0.0
More than full tuition	1	0.2	1	0.2	0	0.0
Median grant amount			$6,000		$3,250	

Informational and Library Resources

# of volumes and volume equivalents	331,170
# of titles	81,442
# of active serial subscriptions	4,583
Study seating capacity inside the library	418
# of professional librarians	7
Hours per week library is open	104
# of open, wired connections available to students	226
# of networked computers available for use by students	69
# of simultaneous wireless users	219
Require computer?	N

JD Attrition (from prior year)

	Academic	Other	Total	
	#	#	#	%
1st year	6	11	17	10.2%
2nd year	0	0	0	0.0%
3rd year	0	1	1	0.6%
4th year	0	0	0	0.0%

Employment

	Total	Percentage
Employment status known	148	100.0
Employment status unknown	0	0.0
Employed	135	91.2
Pursuing graduate degrees	5	3.4
Unemployed seeking employment	4	2.7
Unemployed not seeking employment	4	2.7

Type of Employment

	Total	Percentage
# employed in law firms	77	57.0
# employed in business and industry	27	20.0
# employed in government	15	11.1
# employed in public interest	1	0.7
# employed as judicial clerks	9	6.7
# employed in academia	5	3.7

Geographic Location

	Total	Percentage
# employed in state	72	53.3
# employed in foreign countries	0	0.0
# of states where employed		20

Bar Passage Rates

Jurisdiction	Nebraska			Iowa		
Exam	Sum 03	Win 04	Total	Sum 03	Win 04	Total
# from school taking bar for the first time	55	2	57	23	8	31
School's pass rate for all first-time takers	75%	50%	74%	87%	88%	87%
State's pass rate for all first-time takers	84%	55%	82%	84%	90%	86%

Creighton University School of Law

2500 California Plaza
Omaha, NE 68178
Phone: 402.280.2872; Fax: 402.280.3161
E-mail: lawadmit@creighton.edu; Website: http://culaw2.creighton.edu

■ The School of Law

The School of Law, established in 1904, has been a member of the AALS since 1907 and approved by the ABA for more than 75 years. Alumni from the law school are practicing in all 50 states and in more than 5 foreign countries. The law school's current enrollment is 478. Students come from 41 states and 163 undergraduate institutions.

■ Introduction

Creighton University, a privately endowed and supported Jesuit university, was founded in 1878. Creighton is the most diverse educational institution of its size in the nation. In addition to the School of Law, Creighton has a Medical School, Dental School, School of Pharmacy and Health Professions, School of Nursing, School of Business Administration, College of Arts and Sciences, and a Graduate School, making it the center of professional education in the Midwest. The university is located just blocks from downtown Omaha, a metropolitan area with a population of more than 750,000. Known as the River City, Omaha is the heart of the Midlands and the largest metroplex between Chicago and Denver.

■ Faculty

The faculty is composed of 28 full-time professors and a group of part-time specialists chosen from the bench and bar. Creighton's full-time faculty members have earned reputations as outstanding classroom teachers. In addition, faculty scholarship brings to the classroom insights gained through the publication of leading texts and thought-provoking articles. A distinguished adjunct faculty of judges and practicing attorneys teaches courses in specialty areas. Faculty offices surround the Law School Commons making them easily accessible to students. Faculty members maintain an open-door policy that encourages students to drop in to discuss the latest case, current events, or the newest restaurant in town.

■ Library and Physical Facilities

The School of Law is entirely contained in the Ahmanson Law Center built in 1974. The Klutznik Law Library/McGrath North Legal Research Center houses one of the Midwest's finest legal collections. Students have the option to access the law school computer network via a wireless connection. Wireless access is available in the Klutznik Law Library, the Law School Commons, and other classroom areas.

■ Curriculum and Areas of Concentration

The first-year curriculum, required of all students, consists of Civil Procedure, Constitutional Law, Contracts, Legal Research, Legal Writing, Property, and Torts. Second-year required courses include Business Associations, Criminal Procedure, Evidence, Legal Writing, Professional Responsibility, Secured Transactions in Personal Property, and Trusts and Estates. Beyond the required courses, students design their own program of studies from the numerous electives and seminars offered. Students may earn a certificate indicating that they focused their studies in a particular area of concentration. Areas of concentration are (a) Business, Taxation, and Commercial Transactions; (b) Criminal Law and Procedure; and (c) Dispute Resolution. The curriculum prepares students for the practice of law in any state.

■ Combined-Degree Programs

Creighton's School of Law and College of Business Administration offer two coordinating programs to their students. Combined-degree programs leading to the separate conferral of both the JD and MBA and the JD and Master of Science in Information Technology Management (MS–ITM) degrees are offered. The School of Law and the Graduate School offer a coordinate program leading to the separate conferral of both the JD and Master of Arts in International Relations degrees. These innovative programs allow students to obtain both degrees at a lower cost and in less time than would be required if each degree was earned separately. Students may complete both degrees in three years, especially if the foundation coursework has been completed. The School of Law and the Graduate School have coordinated a new program to allow law students interested in health care law and related practice areas to obtain a certificate in Health Services Administration in connection with their JD degree.

■ Clinic and Internships

Students may participate in a broad variety of internships with city, county, and federal legal offices in the Omaha area. Third-year students also have the opportunity to work and study in the Milton R. Abrahams Legal Clinic located in the law school. The clinic offers free legal assistance on civil matters to low-income residents of Douglas County, Nebraska. Creighton's legal clinic not only provides a much-needed service to the community but also provides a hands-on learning environment for Creighton students.

■ Student Activities

The Student Bar Association is the student government of the law school. The purposes of the organization are to make law students aware of the obligations and opportunities existing for lawyers through SBA activities, promote a consciousness of professional responsibility, and provide a forum for student activities. The *Creighton Law Review*, edited and managed by students, is a scholarly legal journal that is circulated nationally and internationally. The school has chapters of Phi Alpha Delta and Phi Delta Phi legal fraternities. Other student groups include the Black Law Students Association, Environmental Law Society, International Law Society, Latino Law Students Association, Law Ambassadors, Law Partners, Law School Democrats, Law School Republicans, Public Interest Law Forum, Sports and Entertainment Law Society, St. Thomas More Society, and the Women's Law Student Association.

Financial Aid and Scholarships

Creighton University School of Law offers three types of financial aid: merit-based scholarships, government loans, and private loans. Students seeking financial aid and scholarships must complete the Free Application for Federal Student Aid (FAFSA). The loan program consists of the Federal Stafford Loan program and private loan programs. All first-year scholarships have merit requirements, including, but not limited to, LSAT score and undergraduate GPA. Admitted applicants with an LSAT score and undergraduate grade-point average above Creighton's medians for the previous year will receive strong consideration for scholarship assistance. In 2004,

over one-third of all students received scholarship assistance with an average award of over $8,500. Applicants who qualify for a Dean's Merit Scholarship will be notified at the time of acceptance. The Frances M. Ryan Diversity Scholarship and the A.A. and Ethel Yossem Scholarship (for students of Jewish faith) are also available for first-year students. Applicants must request consideration in their Application for Admission if they are eligible for either of these scholarships.

■ Frances M. Ryan Diversity Scholarship Program

The School of Law actively recruits minority students and has a substantial diversity scholarship program. For the 2004–2005 academic year, 29 students have minority scholarships ranging from one-quarter to full tuition.

■ Career Services

The Career Services Office provides a full array of services to Creighton Law students, including individual career counseling, a law alumni network stretching from coast-to-coast, and a dynamic website that allows students to explore thousands of career opportunities throughout the world. Creighton's 2003 graduating class had a 97 percent employment rate nine months after graduation. Graduates of 2003 are working in the areas of academics, business, government, private practice, public interest, and as judicial clerks in 21 states.

Applicant Profile

Creighton University School of Law
This grid includes only applicants who earned 120-180 LSAT scores under standard administration.

LSAT Score	3.75 +		3.50 - 3.74		3.25 - 3.49		3.00 - 3.24		2.75 - 2.99		2.50 - 2.74		2.25 - 2.49		2.00 - 2.24		Below 2.00		No GPA		Total	
	Apps	Adm	Apps	Adm	Apps	Adm	Apps	Adm	Apps	Adm	Apps	Adm	Apps	Adm	Apps	Adm	Apps	Adm	Apps	Adm	Apps	Adm
175-180	0	0	0	0	0	0	0	0	0	0	0	0	0	0	0	0	0	0	0	0	0	0
170-174	0	0	0	0	0	0	0	0	0	0	0	0	0	0	0	0	0	0	0	0	0	0
165-169	6	6	1	1	2	2	1	1	4	4	2	2	0	0	0	0	0	0	0	0	16	16
160-164	17	17	21	21	8	8	5	5	5	5	4	3	2	1	1	0	1	1	0	0	64	61
155-159	37	36	38	37	22	20	31	29	26	17	18	13	7	3	2	0	1	0	0	0	182	155
150-154	56	52	67	57	97	63	103	38	56	9	25	7	22	1	5	0	1	0	0	0	432	227
145-149	37	19	83	15	95	6	93	4	62	1	32	3	20	0	3	0	1	0	6	1	432	49
140-144	5	0	13	0	27	0	31	1	19	1	15	0	12	0	4	0	0	0	4	0	130	2
135-139	2	0	5	0	7	0	9	1	8	0	5	0	2	0	3	0	1	0	3	0	45	1
130-134	0	0	1	0	2	0	1	0	2	0	1	0	2	0	1	0	0	0	0	0	10	0
125-129	0	0	0	0	0	0	0	0	1	0	0	0	0	0	0	0	1	0	2	0	4	0
120-124	0	0	0	0	0	0	0	0	0	0	0	0	0	0	0	0	0	0	0	0	0	0
Total	160	130	229	131	260	99	274	79	183	37	102	28	67	5	19	0	6	1	15	1	1315	511

Apps = Number of Applicants   Adm = Number Admitted   Reflects 100% of the total applicant pool.

University of Dayton School of Law

300 College Park, 112 Keller Hall
Dayton, OH 45469-2760
Phone: 937.229.3555; Fax: 937.229.4194
E-mail: lawinfo@notes.udayton.edu; Website: www.law.udayton.edu

ABA Approved Since 1975

The Basics

Type of school	Private
Term	Semester
Application deadline	5/1
Application fee	
Financial aid deadline	3/1
Can first year start other than fall?	No
Student to faculty ratio (fall)	17.4 to 1
Does the university offer:	
housing restricted to law students?	Yes
graduate housing for which law students are eligible?	Yes

Faculty and Administrators

	Total		Men		Women		Minorities	
	Fall	Spr	Fall	Spr	Fall	Spr	Fall	Spr
Full-time	26	25	19	17	7	8	4	4
Other Full-time	0	0	0	0	0	0	0	0
Deans, librarians, & others who teach	3	3	1	1	2	2	0	0
Part-time	23	22	11	17	12	5	1	1
Total	52	50	31	35	21	15	5	5

Curriculum

	Full-time	Part-time
Typical first-year section size	90	0
Is there typically a "small section" of the first-year class, other than Legal Writing, taught by full-time faculty	No	No
If yes, typical size offered last year	0	0
# of classroom course titles beyond 1st year curriculum	64	
# of upper division courses, excluding seminars with an enrollment: Under 25	69	
25-49	21	
50-74	12	
75-99	10	
100+	0	
# of seminars	11	
# of seminar positions available	220	
# of seminar positions filled	144	0
# of positions available in simulation courses	398	
# of simulation positions filled	350	0
# of positions available in faculty supervised clinical courses	54	
# of faculty supervised clinical positions filled	43	0
# involved in field placements	25	0
# involved in law journals	58	0
# involved in moot court or trial competitions	30	0
# of credit hours required to graduate	87	

JD Enrollment and Ethnicity

	Men		Women		Full-time		Part-time		1st-year		Total		JD Degs. Awd.
	#	%	#	%	#	%	#	%	#	%	#	%	
African Amer.	10	3.3	13	5.5	23	4.2	0	0.0	10	4.6	23	4.2	4
Amer. Indian	1	0.3	3	1.3	4	0.7	0	0.0	3	1.4	4	0.7	0
Asian Amer.	12	3.9	15	6.3	27	5.0	0	0.0	6	2.8	27	5.0	5
Mex. Amer.	3	1.0	2	0.8	5	0.9	0	0.0	2	0.9	5	0.9	5
Puerto Rican	1	0.3	0	0.0	1	0.2	0	0.0	1	0.5	1	0.2	0
Hispanic	6	2.0	4	1.7	10	1.8	0	0.0	6	2.8	10	1.8	3
Total Minority	33	10.8	37	15.5	70	12.9	0	0.0	28	12.9	70	12.9	17
For. Nation.	0	0.0	2	0.8	2	0.4	0	0.0	0	0.0	2	0.4	0
Caucasian	273	89.2	199	83.6	471	86.7	1	100.0	189	87.1	472	86.8	115
Unknown	0	0.0	0	0.0	0	0.0	0	0.0	0	0.0	0	0.0	0
Total	306	56.3	238	43.8	543	99.8	1	0.2	217	39.9	544		132

Tuition and Fees

	Resident	Nonresident
Full-time	$24,174	$24,174
Part-time	$0	$0

Living Expenses

Estimated living expenses for singles

Living on campus	Living off campus	Living at home
$10,355	$10,355	$5,855

University of Dayton School of Law

*ABA
Approved
Since
1975*

GPA and LSAT Scores

	Total	Full-time	Part-time
# of apps	1,861	1,861	0
# of admits	730	730	0
# of matrics	219	219	0
75% GPA	3.45	3.45	0.00
25% GPA	2.89	2.89	0.00
75% LSAT	154	154	0
25% LSAT	150	150	0

Grants and Scholarships (from prior year)

	Total		Full-time		Part-time	
	#	%	#	%	#	%
Total # of students	482		481		1	
Total # receiving grants	240	49.8	240	49.9	0	0.0
Less than 1/2 tuition	215	44.6	215	44.7	0	0.0
Half to full tuition	25	5.2	25	5.2	0	0.0
Full tuition	0	0.0	0	0.0	0	0.0
More than full tuition	0	0.0	0	0.0	0	0.0
Median grant amount			$8,500		$0	

Informational and Library Resources

# of volumes and volume equivalents	301,170
# of titles	41,181
# of active serial subscriptions	4,678
Study seating capacity inside the library	501
# of professional librarians	5
Hours per week library is open	102
# of open, wired connections available to students	1,530
# of networked computers available for use by students	81
# of simultaneous wireless users	1,200
Require computer?	N

JD Attrition (from prior year)

	Academic	Other	Total	
	#	#	#	%
1st year	7	13	20	10.9%
2nd year	1	2	3	1.8%
3rd year	0	0	0	0.0%
4th year	0	0	0	0.0%

Employment

	Total	Percentage
Employment status known	112	93.3
Employment status unknown	8	6.7
Employed	105	93.7
Pursuing graduate degrees	0	0.0
Unemployed seeking employment	6	5.4
Unemployed not seeking employment	1	0.9

Type of Employment

# employed in law firms	65	61.9
# employed in business and industry	18	17.1
# employed in government	12	11.4
# employed in public interest	1	1.0
# employed as judicial clerks	7	6.7
# employed in academia	1	1.0

Geographic Location

# employed in state	71	67.6
# employed in foreign countries	1	1.0
# of states where employed		18

Bar Passage Rates

Jurisdiction		Ohio	
Exam	Sum 03	Win 04	Total
# from school taking bar for the first time	64	13	77
School's pass rate for all first-time takers	86%	69%	83%
State's pass rate for all first-time takers	81%	72%	79%

University of Dayton School of Law

300 College Park, 112 Keller Hall
Dayton, OH 45469-2760
Phone: 937.229.3555; Fax: 937.229.4194
E-mail: lawinfo@notes.udayton.edu; Website: www.law.udayton.edu

■ Introduction and Mission

The mission of the School of Law is to enroll a diverse group of intellectually curious, self-disciplined, and well-motivated men and women, and to educate them in the substantive and procedural principles of public and private law. We seek to graduate highly qualified attorneys who will uphold the highest professional standards and recognize that service to others is the chief measure of professional competence.

We are a full-time JD program, providing a distinguished tradition of concern for the individual student in a supportive and professional environment. Our curriculum gives students a foundation in traditional courses but also helps them develop their skills with innovative programs such as our Legal Professions Program, our Program in Law and Technology, and our Academic Excellence Program. Our diverse student body of 522 promotes ample opportunity for one-on-one interaction with faculty, staff, and fellow students, creating an atmosphere of collegiality and active involvement in a myriad of law school organizations. The University of Dayton School of Law is accredited by the ABA and a member of the AALS.

■ Keller Hall, the University, and Dayton

Joseph E. Keller Hall is a 122,500-square-foot complex featuring a dramatic atrium, a variety of classroom space, and a spacious law library with technology integrated throughout the building. Ready access is provided by 1,400 data and power outlets and wireless capability to the law school network from virtually any location in the law building. Every seat in the 270,000 volume **Zimmerman Law Library** has a data and power outlet and contains a computer training center where students learn to conduct online and computer-based research. Group study rooms allow students to meet in groups of up to 25.

Founded in 1850, the **University of Dayton** enrolls more than 10,000 undergraduate and graduate students in a campus setting. Located minutes from the city's center, the campus contains a physical activities center and provides student services, on-campus housing, child care, meal plans, and banking. On-campus housing is available for half of the entering law students within three blocks of the law school.

The Dayton metropolitan area, population 950,000, is home to a sizable judicial and legal community where law students find full- and part-time employment with the area's law firms and companies. As the birthplace of the Wright Brothers, the city offers a variety of flight-related museums and events, as well as a variety of other cultural and recreational activities. Students may also explore Cincinnati and Columbus, each of which are located within an hour of Dayton.

■ Curriculum and Programs

Five- or Six-Semester Study Options—Our calendar allows you to complete your studies in either five semesters (accelerated) or six semesters (traditional). Either option allows you at least one summer off, during which you can participate in valuable clerkship opportunities.

Fall or Summer Start Options—Our calendar is designed so that you may choose between a fall or summer start. The five-semester study option combined with the summer start option allows you to earn your JD in only 24 calendar months.

Curricular Tracks—The three different curricular tracks, advocacy and dispute resolution, general practice, and law and technology, provide you with an in-depth knowledge of a particular area of law.

Capstone Courses—To bring closure to the track you choose, these courses encourage you to take the knowledge you have gained from your track courses and apply it to real-world experience.

Intra-session Courses—These one-week courses are taught during the middle week of each semester and are offered in a variety of topics of most interest to you. Completing these courses gives you more breadth in your legal knowledge.

Externships—These semester-long positions of legal work under the supervision of a licensed attorney allow you to experience a legal career firsthand and gain some real-world experience in the field.

■ Faculty

Students consistently praise our faculty, not only for their outstanding teaching skills, but also for their constant involvement in, concern for, and support of students' lives inside and outside of the classroom. They are also interesting individuals with diverse backgrounds and a variety of experiences.

■ Student Life

Collegiality, support, and a positive atmosphere distinguish our student body, which benefits from the diversity of their classmates in race, age, gender, and background. Students may participate in organizations that help develop writing, research, and oral advocacy skills; those which speak to their mutual professional interests; or those that provide support of a student's personal and biographical background and interests. Our Student Bar Association is made up of officers and representatives from each class who oversee all student organizations and is the voice of student governance at the law school.

University of Dayton School of Law

Career Services and Alumni

Our Career Services Dean and his staff are committed to assisting students with identifying and securing positions commensurate with each individual's interests and career goals. Thanks to our curriculum and Road to Bar Passage Program, our graduates have been highly successful in passing the Ohio and other state's bar examinations. As alumni, they take an active interest in the life of the law school, participating in panel discussions, mentor programs, and alumni events, as well as contributing their time and resources to various scholarship and fundraising activities.

Admission and Financial Aid

The Admissions Committee looks for a well-rounded and diverse group of students. Undergraduate GPA and LSAT score are highly considered, but commitment, motivation, leadership, and a breadth and depth of experiences are also a large part of the applicant review. Scholarships are given to approximately half of the entering class, with academic performance a requirement for retention. For consideration for scholarships, application is encouraged before March 1. Federal and private loans are available pending a student's citizenship status and credit rating.

Prospective Students

Prospective students are encouraged to contact the School of Law Office of Admissions to schedule informational visits or obtain assistance with questions or concerns. The office holds open houses during the year, and staff participate in many events off-campus so that students may easily acquire more information. Office hours are 8:30 AM to 4:30 PM, Monday through Friday.

Applicant Profile

University of Dayton School of Law
This grid includes all full-time applicants who earned LSAT scores on the 120-180 scale under standard test administrations and whose submission files were complete and reviewed by the faculty admission committee.

LSAT Score	GPA								
	3.75 +	3.50 - 3.74	3.25 - 3.49	3.00 - 3.24	2.75 - 2.99	2.50 - 2.74	2.25 - 2.49	2.00 - 2.24	Below 2.00
175-180									
170-174									
165-169									
160-164									
155-159									
150-154									
145-149									
140-144									
135-139									
130-134									
125-129									
120-124									

■ Good Possibility   ■ Possible   □ Unlikely

This chart is to be used as a general guide only. Nonnumerical factors are considered for all applicants.

University of Denver Sturm College of Law

2255 E Evans Avenue
Denver, CO 80208
Phone: 303.871.6135; Fax: 303.871.6992
E-mail: admissions@law.du.edu; Website: www.law.du.edu

ABA
Approved
Since
1923

The Basics

Type of school	Private
Term	Semester
Application deadline	
Application fee	$60
Financial aid deadline	
Can first year start other than fall?	Yes
Student to faculty ratio (fall)	14.2 to 1
Does the university offer:	
housing restricted to law students?	No
graduate housing for which law students are eligible?	Yes

Faculty and Administrators

	Total		Men		Women		Minorities	
	Fall	Spr	Fall	Spr	Fall	Spr	Fall	Spr
Full-time	62	58	32	28	30	30	13	12
Other Full-time	1	1	1	1	0	0	0	0
Deans, librarians, & others who teach	7	7	3	3	4	4	2	2
Part-time	71	77	53	60	17	17	5	8
Total	141	143	89	92	51	51	20	22

Curriculum

		Full-time	Part-time
Typical first-year section size		84	104
Is there typically a "small section" of the first-year class, other than Legal Writing, taught by full-time faculty		Yes	No
If yes, typical size offered last year		45	0
# of classroom course titles beyond 1st year curriculum		152	
# of upper division courses, excluding seminars with an enrollment:	Under 25	172	
	25-49	83	
	50-74	41	
	75-99	8	
	100+	2	
# of seminars		19	
# of seminar positions available		317	
# of seminar positions filled		95	66
# of positions available in simulation courses		466	
# of simulation positions filled		174	131
# of positions available in faculty supervised clinical courses		95	
# of faculty supervised clinical positions filled	95	0
# involved in field placements	326	0
# involved in law journals	249	0
# involved in moot court or trial competitions	48	0
# of credit hours required to graduate		90	

JD Enrollment and Ethnicity

	Men		Women		Full-time		Part-time		1st-year		Total		JD Degs. Awd.
	#	%	#	%	#	%	#	%	#	%	#	%	
African Amer.	24	4.1	42	7.3	37	4.3	29	9.4	16	4.8	66	5.7	10
Amer. Indian	26	4.4	30	5.2	43	5.0	13	4.2	20	6.0	56	4.8	7
Asian Amer.	37	6.3	28	4.9	53	6.2	12	3.9	18	5.4	65	5.6	16
Mex. Amer.	30	5.1	34	5.9	50	5.9	14	4.5	15	4.5	64	5.5	34
Puerto Rican	0	0.0	0	0.0	0	0.0	0	0.0	0	0.0	0	0.0	0
Hispanic	0	0.0	0	0.0	0	0.0	0	0.0	0	0.0	0	0.0	0
Total Minority	117	20.0	134	23.3	183	21.5	68	21.9	69	20.5	251	21.6	67
For. Nation.	10	1.7	11	1.9	17	2.0	4	1.3	7	2.1	21	1.8	7
Caucasian	459	78.3	431	74.8	652	76.5	238	76.8	260	77.4	890	76.6	289
Unknown	0	0.0	0	0.0	0	0.0	0	0.0	0	0.0	0	0.0	0
Total	586	50.4	576	49.6	852	73.3	310	26.7	336	28.9	1162		363

Tuition and Fees

	Resident	Nonresident
Full-time	$23,308	$23,308
Part-time	$16,640	$16,640

Living Expenses

Estimated living expenses for singles

Living on campus	Living off campus	Living at home
$13,455	$13,455	$13,455

University of Denver Sturm College of Law

*ABA
Approved
Since
1923*

GPA and LSAT Scores

	Total	Full-time	Part-time
# of apps	3,769	3,355	414
# of admits	836	714	122
# of matrics	342	251	91
75% GPA	3.46	3.46	3.48
25% GPA	2.83	2.81	2.86
75% LSAT	161	162	158
25% LSAT	150	153	148

Grants and Scholarships (from prior year)

	Total #	Total %	Full-time #	Full-time %	Part-time #	Part-time %
Total # of students	1,192		872		320	
Total # receiving grants	313	26.3	289	33.1	24	7.5
Less than 1/2 tuition	238	20.0	221	25.3	17	5.3
Half to full tuition	55	4.6	52	6.0	3	0.9
Full tuition	20	1.7	16	1.8	4	1.3
More than full tuition	0	0.0	0	0.0	0	0.0
Median grant amount			$10,000		$5,550	

Informational and Library Resources

# of volumes and volume equivalents	349,715
# of titles	159,568
# of active serial subscriptions	5,370
Study seating capacity inside the library	333
# of professional librarians	13
Hours per week library is open	106
# of open, wired connections available to students	1,535
# of networked computers available for use by students	135
# of simultaneous wireless users	1,000
Require computer?	Y

JD Attrition (from prior year)

	Academic #	Other #	Total #	Total %
1st year	5	16	21	5.8%
2nd year	0	3	3	0.7%
3rd year	0	0	0	0.0%
4th year	0	0	0	0.0%

Employment

	Total	Percentage
Employment status known	393	99.7
Employment status unknown	1	0.3
Employed	363	92.4
Pursuing graduate degrees	25	6.4
Unemployed seeking employment	2	0.5
Unemployed not seeking employment	3	0.8

Type of Employment

# employed in law firms	185	51.0
# employed in business and industry	77	21.2
# employed in government	45	12.4
# employed in public interest	8	2.2
# employed as judicial clerks	34	9.4
# employed in academia	4	1.1

Geographic Location

# employed in state	292	80.4
# employed in foreign countries	1	0.3
# of states where employed	30	

Bar Passage Rates

Jurisdiction	Colorado		
Exam	Sum 03	Win 04	Total
# from school taking bar for the first time	262	58	320
School's pass rate for all first-time takers	69%	67%	69%
State's pass rate for all first-time takers	75%	73%	75%

University of Denver Sturm College of Law

2255 E Evans Avenue
Denver, CO 80208
Phone: 303.871.6135; Fax: 303.871.6992
E-mail: admissions@law.du.edu; Website: www.law.du.edu

■ Introduction

The Sturm College of Law relocated to a brand-new, state-of-the-art facility on University Park campus in August 2003. The 210,000-square-foot structure is the first in the nation to conform to the US Green Building Council's Leadership in Energy and Environmental Design certification system. University Park campus is just eight miles from downtown Denver and 15 miles from the mountains.

■ Curriculum

Lawyering Process Course—The first-year curriculum includes an innovative Lawyering Process Course which offers students, in small group settings, experience with the standard operations and skills of the lawyer's craft. The small groups replicate law firms and reinforce cooperative work.

■ Special Programs

Drawing upon its location in one of the nation's natural resource and energy capitals, the University of Denver Sturm College of Law offers a rich program in natural resources and environmental law. Students can choose from a variety of courses. There are also abundant opportunities for independent research and internships in the local energy, environment, and natural resource community.

The International Legal Studies program is designed for students interested in international comparative law, international organizations, or transnational business. Students in the program may work on the *Denver Journal of International Law and Policy* as staff members and editors. The International Law Society sponsors a rich schedule of outside speakers and an annual conference with invited guests from many organizations.

The Business and Commercial Law program not only trains students to work with business entities but also prepares them for the specific needs of the corporate attorney. The program culminates in specialized seminars in business and commercial law. Corporate internships, highly prized one-semester assignments with large local corporations, are a valuable supplement to the coursework.

The University of Denver has a number of other unique programs. Practicing Law in Spanish is one of the few programs in the United States that involve teaching substantive law and skills courses in Spanish. The Sports and Entertainment Law program includes a comprehensive cluster of classes designed to prepare students to practice in those areas. The Law and Technology program looks at the interrelationship between law and technology in the areas of litigation, privacy, and intellectual property.

Courses in the regular curriculum are supplemented by the practical experience gained through legal work in the Student Law Office or through internships or externships. The capstone of the program is the Student Law Office (Civil Representation Clinic, Criminal Representation Clinic, Mediation/Arbitration Clinic, Low-Income Taxpayer Representation Clinic, and Domestic Violence Civil Justice Project), where students represent needy clients at all levels of the dispute resolution process. If the case reaches the litigation phase, the student handles all aspects of pretrial, trial preparation, and the trial itself under faculty supervision. Focusing on one-to-one teaching and student responsibility, the program offers a rare opportunity to acquire lawyering skills.

■ Admission

All applications should be submitted online and reach the Sturm College of Law between November and February to receive maximum consideration for admission the following August. Students may begin law study only in August. Applicants must take the LSAT and register for the LSDAS. LSAT scores and records of academic performances are individually evaluated in the admission process. Of equal importance, however, are the applicant's work experience, significant personal accomplishments, interests, goals, and reasons for seeking admission to law school.

■ Student Activities

The University of Denver's Moot Court program is designed to promote the necessary development of students' oral and written skills. DU's law students have the opportunity to participate in six different Moot Court competitions. The Moot Court Board is composed of students who have demonstrated merit in DU's Moot Court program and have displayed a commitment to improving the oral and written skills of the student body. With faculty integrated support, the Moot Court Board organizes and runs DU's Moot Court program.

Five scholarly journals are edited at the Sturm College of Law, allowing students to participate in scholarly research in varied fields. Academic credit is awarded for work on the *Denver University Law Review, Denver Journal of International Law and Policy, Transportation Law Journal*, the *Preventative Law Reporter*, and the *Water Law Review*.

Many special interest organizations on campus are officially recognized by the Student Bar Association. Among those groups are the Animal Legal Defense Fund, Asian American Law Students Association, the

Black Law Students Association, the Business Law Society, the Christian Legal Society, the Federalist Society, International Law Society, Intellectual Property Law Student, Natural Resources and Environmental Law Society, Jewish Law Students Association, Latino Law Students Association, Native American Law Students Association, Phi Alpha Delta, Phi Delta Phi, Public Interest Law Group, and Sports and Entertainment Law Society.

■ Expenses and Financial Aid

The Chancellor's Scholarship Program provides 12 full-tuition scholarships to entering first-year students for commitment to public service through law. The annual scholarships are renewed for successive years based on satisfactory academic performance and full participation in all the activities of the program.

■ Housing

Residence halls are available on campus. Both traditional dorm-style living and unfurnished apartments are available.

■ Career Services

The law school maintains a Career Services Office staffed by six professionals who aid both students and alumni in securing employment. The Career Services Office offers direct referral to part-time, full-time, summer, and career positions; arrangement of on-campus interviews each fall for second- and third-year students with law firms, governmental agencies, and corporations; and career counseling.

Applicant Profile

University of Denver Sturm College of Law
This grid includes only applicants who earned 120-180 LSAT scores under standard administrations.

LSAT Score	3.75 +		3.50 - 3.74		3.25 - 3.49		3.00 - 3.24		2.75 - 2.99		2.50 - 2.74		2.25 - 2.49		2.00 - 2.24		Below 2.00		No GPA		Total	
	Apps	Adm	Apps	Adm	Apps	Adm	Apps	Adm	Apps	Adm	Apps	Adm	Apps	Adm	Apps	Adm	Apps	Adm	Apps	Adm	Apps	Adm
175-180	0	0	0	0	0	0	0	0	0	0	0	0	0	0	0	0	0	0	0	0	0	0
170-174	4	4	3	3	0	0	3	3	2	1	1	1	1	1	1	0	0	0	0	0	15	13
165-169	14	12	14	14	11	9	22	19	8	8	7	7	4	2	2	2	0	0	2	1	84	74
160-164	48	41	61	56	76	63	65	59	59	50	36	30	14	14	5	3	0	0	1	1	365	317
155-159	106	29	183	40	182	27	200	38	134	23	70	8	34	5	12	3	3	0	4	1	928	174
150-154	116	18	173	11	252	22	234	18	179	16	95	8	42	6	13	2	3	1	8	1	1115	103
145-149	36	2	101	11	122	15	154	14	113	10	65	3	48	4	17	2	2	1	16	3	674	65
140-144	8	1	26	4	39	3	63	7	59	4	55	7	30	5	6	0	0	0	11	2	297	33
135-139	3	1	10	0	10	1	24	0	19	0	22	1	9	0	8	0	2	0	8	0	115	3
130-134	0	0	1	0	3	0	1	0	1	0	6	0	2	0	7	0	1	0	9	0	31	0
125-129	0	0	0	0	0	0	1	0	1	0	0	0	1	0	0	0	1	0	1	0	5	0
120-124	0	0	0	0	0	0	0	0	0	0	0	0	0	0	0	0	0	0	0	0	0	0
Total	335	108	572	139	695	140	767	158	575	112	357	65	185	37	71	12	12	2	60	9	3629	782

Apps = Number of Applicants
Adm = Number Admitted
Reflects 99% of the total applicant pool.

DePaul University College of Law

25 East Jackson Boulevard
Chicago, IL 60604-2219
Phone: 312.362.6831 or 800.428.7453; Fax: 312.362.5280
E-mail: lawinfo@depaul.edu; Website: www.law.depaul.edu

ABA
Approved
Since
1925

The Basics

Type of school	Private
Term	Semester
Application deadline	3/1
Application fee	$60
Financial aid deadline	3/1
Can first year start other than fall?	No
Student to faculty ratio (fall)	17.0 to 1
Does the university offer:	
housing restricted to law students?	Yes
graduate housing for which law students are eligible?	No

Faculty and Administrators

	Total		Men		Women		Minorities	
	Fall	Spr	Fall	Spr	Fall	Spr	Fall	Spr
Full-time	49	51	28	31	21	20	8	7
Other Full-time	3	3	1	1	2	2	1	1
Deans, librarians, & others who teach	7	7	4	4	3	3	0	0
Part-time	41	46	27	27	14	18	4	1
Total	100	107	60	63	40	43	13	9

Curriculum

	Full-time	Part-time
Typical first-year section size	82	92
Is there typically a "small section" of the first-year class, other than Legal Writing, taught by full-time faculty	No	No
If yes, typical size offered last year	0	0
# of classroom course titles beyond 1st year curriculum	142	
# of upper division courses, excluding seminars with an enrollment: Under 25	125	
25-49	35	
50-74	18	
75-99	11	
100+	1	
# of seminars	16	
# of seminar positions available	288	
# of seminar positions filled	158	99
# of positions available in simulation courses	512	
# of simulation positions filled	35	310
# of positions available in faculty supervised clinical courses	133	
# of faculty supervised clinical positions filled	114	0
# involved in field placements	181	0
# involved in law journals	63	0
# involved in moot court or trial competitions	51	0
# of credit hours required to graduate	86	

JD Enrollment and Ethnicity

	Men		Women		Full-time		Part-time		1st-year		Total		JD Degs. Awd.
	#	%	#	%	#	%	#	%	#	%	#	%	
African Amer.	23	4.3	43	7.5	45	5.8	21	6.3	29	8.0	66	5.9	17
Amer. Indian	4	0.7	0	0.0	3	0.4	1	0.3	3	0.8	4	0.4	1
Asian Amer.	36	6.7	36	6.3	54	7.0	18	5.4	25	6.9	72	6.5	26
Mex. Amer.	0	0.0	0	0.0	0	0.0	0	0.0	0	0.0	0	0.0	0
Puerto Rican	0	0.0	0	0.0	0	0.0	0	0.0	0	0.0	0	0.0	0
Hispanic	36	6.7	40	7.0	56	7.2	20	6.0	34	9.3	76	6.8	18
Total Minority	99	18.3	119	20.8	158	20.4	60	17.9	91	25.0	218	19.6	62
For. Nation.	2	0.4	3	0.5	4	0.5	1	0.3	3	0.8	5	0.5	1
Caucasian	379	70.2	403	70.6	533	68.7	249	74.3	242	66.5	782	70.4	206
Unknown	60	11.1	46	8.1	81	10.4	25	7.5	28	7.7	106	9.5	19
Total	540	48.6	571	51.4	776	69.8	335	30.2	364	32.8	1111		288

Tuition and Fees

	Resident	Nonresident
Full-time	$27,710	$27,710
Part-time	$18,000	$18,000

Living Expenses

Estimated living expenses for singles

Living on campus	Living off campus	Living at home
$18,114	$18,114	$18,114

DePaul University College of Law

*ABA
Approved
Since
1925*

GPA and LSAT Scores

	Total	Full-time	Part-time
# of apps	4,814	4,036	778
# of admits	1,444	1,132	312
# of matrics	364	262	102
75% GPA	3.50	3.54	3.41
25% GPA	2.98	2.97	3.01
75% LSAT	160	161	156
25% LSAT	154	156	153

Grants and Scholarships (from prior year)

	Total		Full-time		Part-time	
	#	%	#	%	#	%
Total # of students	1,114		810		304	
Total # receiving grants	471	42.3	423	52.2	48	15.8
Less than 1/2 tuition	401	36.0	355	43.8	46	15.1
Half to full tuition	70	6.3	68	8.4	2	0.7
Full tuition	0	0.0	0	0.0	0	0.0
More than full tuition	0	0.0	0	0.0	0	0.0
Median grant amount			$5,000		$2,500	

Informational and Library Resources

# of volumes and volume equivalents	377,004
# of titles	75,221
# of active serial subscriptions	5,256
Study seating capacity inside the library	465
# of professional librarians	7
Hours per week library is open	94
# of open, wired connections available to students	82
# of networked computers available for use by students	125
# of simultaneous wireless users	400
Require computer?	N

JD Attrition (from prior year)

	Academic	Other	Total	
	#	#	#	%
1st year	15	9	24	5.8%
2nd year	0	1	1	0.3%
3rd year	2	0	2	0.7%
4th year	0	0	0	0.0%

Employment

	Total	Percentage
Employment status known	284	99.3
Employment status unknown	2	0.7
Employed	236	83.1
Pursuing graduate degrees	6	2.1
Unemployed seeking employment	32	11.3
Unemployed not seeking employment	10	3.5

Type of Employment

# employed in law firms	139	58.9
# employed in business and industry	37	15.7
# employed in government	39	16.5
# employed in public interest	6	2.5
# employed as judicial clerks	3	1.3
# employed in academia	7	3.0

Geographic Location

# employed in state	206	87.3
# employed in foreign countries	2	0.8
# of states where employed	18	

Bar Passage Rates

Jurisdiction	Illinois		
Exam	Sum 03	Win 04	Total
# from school taking bar for the first time	221	43	264
School's pass rate for all first-time takers	75%	63%	73%
State's pass rate for all first-time takers	86%	78%	84%

DePaul University College of Law

25 East Jackson Boulevard
Chicago, IL 60604-2219
Phone: 312.362.6831 or 800.428.7453; Fax: 312.362.5280
E-mail: lawinfo@depaul.edu; Website: www.law.depaul.edu

■ Introduction

DePaul University is the largest private university in Illinois and enjoys the advantages of its vibrant urban setting. Its strong reputation for academic excellence is distinguished by its dedicated faculty, unrivaled professional skills training, and its genuine sense of community.

Located in the heart of Chicago's business and legal communities, the College of Law affords extensive contact with Chicago's legal community. It is within walking distance of the state and federal courts, government offices, and many law firms. DePaul law alumni include the mayor of Chicago, numerous state and federal judges, and managing partners of Chicago law firms. The college offers full-time, part-time, and summer programs. DePaul is fully accredited by the ABA, and is a member of AALS and Order of the Coif.

■ Students

Founded in 1898 by Vincentian Fathers as a school for children of immigrants, DePaul University students represent a rich diversity in age, ethnicity, education, and career experiences. Because of the broad diversity of backgrounds and experiences of its law students, there is a connectedness within the institution that creates a genuine sense of community. Approximately 50 percent of full-time students in the entering class of 2004 were women, while 27 percent were minorities. Approximately one-half of the 2004 entering full-time class were from out of state. The average age of full-time students is 24, while the average age of part-time students is 26.

■ Faculty

DePaul faculty members, including many who have earned advanced degrees, are recognized scholars who represent a variety of professional backgrounds and interests. Consistent with the university's Vincentian mission of service to the community, faculty members work tirelessly in service to the profession and to the community, and they have achieved national recognition in teaching, research, scholarly activities, and professional service. The faculty is extremely accessible, approachable, and deeply committed to its students.

■ Library, Research Centers, and Institutes

The three-story law library offers extensive resources for study and research. Its staff includes 8 professional librarians and 11 full-time support staff.

The College of Law also maintains nine research centers and institutes:

- Health Law Institute;
- International Aviation Law Institute;
- International Human Rights Law Institute;
- Schiller, DuCanto and Fleck Family Law Center;
- Center for Intellectual Property Law and Information Technology;
- Center for Justice in Capital Cases;
- Center for Law and Science;
- Center for Rural and Urban Community Development; and
- Center for the Study of Race and Bioethics.

■ Special Programs

Academic Support Program: DePaul is committed to ensuring that all students have the tools they need to attain academic success. Toward that end, DePaul has one of the premier academic support programs in the nation.

Legal Clinic: Students gain valuable hands-on experience in six clinical concentrations: asylum/immigration, community development, criminal appeals, death penalty, disability rights, and technology/intellectual property.

Field Placement Program: Providing students with academic credit through supervised field work, externships are offered by federal and state judges, various municipal agencies, and a number of not-for-profit organizations.

Mediation Program: Students learn essential client counseling skills by working with mediators on cases referred by the County Domestic Relations Courts.

Skills Competitions: As a leader in the field of professional skills, DePaul has enjoyed considerable success in skills competitions. DePaul student teams regularly place among the top teams in both regional and national moot court competitions.

Certificate Programs: DePaul offers 10 comprehensive certificate programs, including criminal law, family law, health law, international and comparative law, public interest law, tax law, and four in intellectual property law (general, arts and museum, information technology, and patents).

University College Dublin (UCD) Student Exchange Program: DePaul and UCD have a student-exchange program in which second-year students undertake legal studies abroad during their spring semester.

Asian Legal Studies Institute: Students receive academic credit for summer courses taken at Beijing Foreign Studies University in China. Students focus on legal principles and planning related to international transactions in the Pacific-East Asia areas. Lectures are presented by professors from DePaul and major Chinese law schools.

Joint-Degree and Master of Laws (LLM) Programs: DePaul offers five joint-degree and three master of laws programs:

DePaul University College of Law

- JD/MBA in coordination with DePaul's nationally recognized Kellstadt Graduate School of Business.
- JD/MS in Public Service Management promotes effective management of government and nonprofit organizations.
- JD/MA in International Studies offers concentrations in political economy and global culture and complements DePaul's strong international law offerings.
- JD/MA and JD/MS in Computer Science explore the intersections of law, computer science, telecommunications, and information systems.
- DePaul's Master of Laws (LLM) Programs include health law, intellectual property law, and taxation.

Special First-Year Legal Writing Sections: Students may apply for a seat in one of three special sections of Legal Analysis, Research and Communications, focusing on family law, health law, and intellectual property law.

■ Housing

Located in Chicago's Loop just two blocks south of the law school, the University Center of Chicago (UCC) is a new residence hall offering furnished apartments and suites. Amenities include a rooftop garden, multimedia rooms, a fitness center, food court, laundry facilities, shops on the lower level, 24-hour security, and keycard access to the building and elevators.

■ Admission

DePaul adheres to a policy of nondiscrimination and encourages applications from traditionally underrepresented minority groups. Admission decisions are based on a variety of factors and each file is reviewed thoroughly. Undergraduate GPA and LSAT scores are significant admission criteria. For the 2004–2005 academic year, 4,052 candidates applied for admission to the full-time division, while 792 applied to the part-time division. Admitted students are automatically considered for available merit- and need-based scholarships.

■ Career Services

Alumni, faculty, and students contribute to an active and aggressive career services network. The teaching and publishing reputations of the faculty, as well as the largest alumni bench and bar network in the Chicago area, complement three full-time DePaul law career services officers.

Applicant Profile

DePaul University College of Law

LSAT Score	GPA																				
	3.75 +		3.50 - 3.74		3.25 - 3.49		3.00 - 3.24		2.75 - 2.99		2.50 - 2.74		2.25 - 2.49		2.00 - 2.24		Below 2.00		No GPA		Total	
	Apps	Adm	Apps	Adm	Apps	Adm	Apps	Adm	Apps	Adm	Apps	Adm	Apps	Adm	Apps	Adm	Apps	Adm	Apps	Adm	Apps	Adm
175-180	0	0	1	1	0	0	0	0	0	0	0	0	0	0	0	0	0	0	0	0	1	1
170-174	1	1	4	3	3	3	5	5	5	5	1	1	1	1	2	2	0	0	0	0	22	21
165-169	12	12	16	15	17	17	26	26	14	12	8	8	4	4	1	1	0	0	0	0	98	95
160-164	57	52	97	93	126	120	119	114	79	76	32	31	10	9	7	5	0	0	4	2	531	502
155-159	116	87	240	142	296	147	229	105	150	59	82	23	49	9	15	1	1	0	8	2	1186	575
150-154	142	23	269	43	361	52	344	43	227	22	111	6	55	3	22	0	2	0	10	1	1543	193
145-149	42	2	121	13	175	15	200	12	179	5	90	0	67	1	26	0	6	0	18	0	924	48
120-144	17	0	58	1	77	0	120	0	122	0	87	0	68	0	29	0	10	0	25	0	613	1
Total	387	177	806	311	1055	354	1043	305	776	179	411	69	254	27	102	9	19	0	65	5	4918	1436

Apps = Number of Applicants
Adm = Number Admitted
Reflects 99% of the total applicant pool.

The information in this grid represents admission data for applicants to both the full-time and part-time programs and should be used only as a gauge of the likelihood of admission and not as a guarantee.

DePaul University College of Law 245

University of Detroit Mercy School of Law

Admissions Office, 651 East Jefferson Avenue
Detroit, MI 48226
Phone: 313.596.0264
E-mail: udmlawao@udmercy.edu; Website: www.law.udmercy.edu

ABA Approved Since 1933

The Basics

Type of school	Private
Term	Semester
Application deadline	4/15
Application fee	$50
Financial aid deadline	4/1
Can first year start other than fall?	No
Student to faculty ratio (fall)	17.9 to 1
Does the university offer:	
housing restricted to law students?	No
graduate housing for which law students are eligible?	No

Faculty and Administrators

	Total		Men		Women		Minorities	
	Fall	Spr	Fall	Spr	Fall	Spr	Fall	Spr
Full-time	25	23	15	12	10	11	3	3
Other Full-time	0	0	0	0	0	0	0	0
Deans, librarians, & others who teach	5	5	4	4	1	1	0	0
Part-time	23	22	17	14	6	8	1	1
Total	53	50	36	30	17	20	4	4

Curriculum

		Full-time	Part-time
Typical first-year section size		64	63
Is there typically a "small section" of the first-year class, other than Legal Writing, taught by full-time faculty		No	No
If yes, typical size offered last year		0	0
# of classroom course titles beyond 1st year curriculum		93	
# of upper division courses, excluding seminars with an enrollment:	Under 25	6	
	25-49	1	
	50-74	21	
	75-99	9	
	100+	0	
# of seminars		13	
# of seminar positions available		208	
# of seminar positions filled		81	39
# of positions available in simulation courses		289	
# of simulation positions filled		148	54
# of positions available in faculty supervised clinical courses		48	
# of faculty supervised clinical positions filled	17	3	
# involved in field placements	17	6	
# involved in law journals	68	13	
# involved in moot court or trial competitions	67	4	
# of credit hours required to graduate		90	

JD Enrollment and Ethnicity

	Men		Women		Full-time		Part-time		1st-year		Total		JD Degs. Awd.
	#	%	#	%	#	%	#	%	#	%	#	%	
African Amer.	7	2.2	21	7.4	7	1.7	21	10.7	6	2.6	28	4.6	9
Amer. Indian	0	0.0	0	0.0	0	0.0	0	0.0	0	0.0	0	0.0	1
Asian Amer.	1	0.3	4	1.4	3	0.7	2	1.0	2	0.9	5	0.8	2
Mex. Amer.	0	0.0	0	0.0	0	0.0	0	0.0	0	0.0	0	0.0	0
Puerto Rican	0	0.0	0	0.0	0	0.0	0	0.0	0	0.0	0	0.0	0
Hispanic	3	0.9	8	2.8	5	1.2	6	3.0	4	1.7	11	1.8	5
Total Minority	11	3.4	33	11.6	15	3.7	29	14.7	12	5.2	44	7.3	17
For. Nation.	38	11.9	39	13.7	75	18.4	2	1.0	28	12.2	77	12.7	22
Caucasian	198	61.9	153	53.9	219	53.8	132	67.0	103	45.0	351	58.1	82
Unknown	73	22.8	59	20.8	98	24.1	34	17.3	86	37.6	132	21.9	0
Total	320	53.0	284	47.0	407	67.4	197	32.6	229	37.9	604		121

Tuition and Fees

	Resident	Nonresident
Full-time	$12,828	$12,828
Part-time	$8,838	$8,838

Living Expenses

Estimated living expenses for singles

Living on campus	Living off campus	Living at home
N/A	$16,236	$10,174

University of Detroit Mercy School of Law

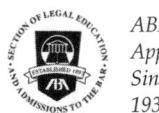

*ABA
Approved
Since
1933*

GPA and LSAT Scores

	Total	Full-time	Part-time
# of apps	1,500	1,238	262
# of admits	599	461	138
# of matrics	232	162	70
75% GPA	3.45	3.47	3.48
25% GPA	2.72	2.90	3.01
75% LSAT	152	152	152
25% LSAT	147	147	148

Grants and Scholarships (from prior year)

	Total #	Total %	Full-time #	Full-time %	Part-time #	Part-time %
Total # of students	542		353		189	
Total # receiving grants	89	16.4	71	20.1	18	9.5
Less than 1/2 tuition	22	4.1	19	5.4	3	1.6
Half to full tuition	60	11.1	45	12.7	15	7.9
Full tuition	3	0.6	3	0.8	0	0.0
More than full tuition	4	0.7	4	1.1	0	0.0
Median grant amount			$12,667		$10,735	

Informational and Library Resources

# of volumes and volume equivalents	346,972
# of titles	151,364
# of active serial subscriptions	3,012
Study seating capacity inside the library	299
# of professional librarians	5
Hours per week library is open	91
# of open, wired connections available to students	39
# of networked computers available for use by students	41
# of simultaneous wireless users	400
Require computer?	N

JD Attrition (from prior year)

	Academic #	Other #	Total #	Total %
1st year	14	26	40	17.5%
2nd year	3	0	3	2.0%
3rd year	0	0	0	0.0%
4th year	0	0	0	0.0%

Employment

	Total	Percentage
Employment status known	84	90.3
Employment status unknown	9	9.7
Employed	72	85.7
Pursuing graduate degrees	3	3.6
Unemployed seeking employment	7	8.3
Unemployed not seeking employment	2	2.4

Type of Employment

# employed in law firms	45	62.5
# employed in business and industry	10	13.9
# employed in government	7	9.7
# employed in public interest	2	2.8
# employed as judicial clerks	3	4.2
# employed in academia	5	6.9

Geographic Location

# employed in state	69	95.8
# employed in foreign countries	2	2.8
# of states where employed		2

Bar Passage Rates

Jurisdiction		Michigan	
Exam	Sum 03	Win 04	Total
# from school taking bar for the first time	70	28	98
School's pass rate for all first-time takers	66%	79%	69%
State's pass rate for all first-time takers	77%	71%	75%

University of Detroit Mercy School of Law

Admissions Office, 651 East Jefferson Avenue
Detroit, MI 48226
Phone: 313.596.0264
E-mail: udmlawao@udmercy.edu; Website: www.law.udmercy.edu

■ Introduction

Founded in 1912, the University of Detroit Mercy School of Law is a well-established Catholic law school in downtown Detroit sponsored by the Society of Jesus (Jesuits) and the Sisters of Mercy of the Americas. Located opposite the General Motors headquarters in the Renaissance Center, the School of Law is within walking distance of federal and state courts, downtown law firms, and Detroit's municipal centers. Windsor, Ontario, Canada, is a five-minute drive by tunnel or bridge across the Detroit River. Metropolitan Detroit not only offers renowned cultural institutions like the Detroit Institute of Art, the Detroit Symphony, and the Detroit Opera House, but also provides a distinctive setting for the study of contemporary legal issues, including urban redevelopment, corporate entity formation, immigration, international trade, and many more.

The School of Law offers a comprehensive legal education through day and evening programs that incorporate a broad array of required and elective courses. The school is approved by the ABA and is a member of the AALS.

■ The Kresge Law Library and Law School Facilities

The School of Law's Kresge Law Library is situated within the School of Law and contains comfortable individual and group study, reading, and computer areas. The library houses more than 340,000 volumes and serves as a federal depository. Faculty offices, classrooms, and common areas with wireless access, administrative and student services offices, a bookstore, cafeteria, and student organization offices are all located within the law school complex.

■ Curriculum

The School of Law offers a three-year full-time day program, four-year part-time day and evening programs, and a five-year part-time evening program, all leading to the JD degree. Required courses include Contracts, Property, Torts, Civil Procedure, Applied Legal Theory and Analysis, Criminal Law, Constitutional Law, Evidence, Professional Responsibility, Taxation, and a senior seminar. Students complete the 90 credits required with elective courses. Courses after the first year integrate legal writing and document drafting as well as ethical and professional responsibility issues with the theoretical study of the law.

The School of Law's commitment to excellence in legal education includes numerous clinical opportunities: the Urban Law Clinic, the Immigration Law Clinic, our new mobile law office, mediation training, an Appellate Advocacy course, and a wide array of externships. With faculty supervision, students in these externships and clinical programs represent clients with a variety of legal problems, including landlord-tenant conflicts, immigration issues, elder law cases, and others.

All students in the School of Law are assigned a faculty advisor to assist them in the development of a course of study. The school's full-time director of academic support also provides individual and group counseling specific to the study of law.

■ Special Programs

- **Joint JD/MBA**—The School of Law and the College of Business Administration collaborate to offer an integrated degree program leading to the JD and MBA degrees. Students enrolled in the joint-degree program can earn both degrees in significantly less time than would be required for degrees pursued independently. Students are first admitted to and attend law school. At the end of the first year of law school, students apply to the joint-degree program.

- **JD/LLB**—The School of Law and the University of Windsor Faculty of Law offer a unique JD/LLB program designed to educate students to understand the legal doctrines and cultures of the United States and Canada. A student completes 60 credit hours of coursework at UDM and 44 credit hours of coursework at the University of Windsor. Most required courses taken at both law schools cover US and Canadian law relevant to the subject areas. The program enables the successful student to obtain an American Bar Association-approved Juris Doctor (JD) from the University of Detroit Mercy and the Bachelor of Laws (LLB) degree from the University of Windsor.

- **Intellectual Property Law Institute**—Through a consortium with other law schools, the School of Law offers a wide variety of courses in intellectual property such as Copyright Law, Patent Law, Computer Law, Entertainment Law, and others.

- **The McElroy Chair in Law and Religion**—The school's McElroy Chair in Law and Religion hosts an annual lecture and special colloquia on issues related to law and religion. Recent speakers have included John T. Noonan Jr., Martha Minow, and many others.

- **French Scholar Program**—The School of Law participates in a professional exchange program with the University of Clermont-Ferrand. French scholars visiting the law school each spring teach a comparative law course in English while UDM scholars teach at Clermont-Ferrand.

- **Special Summer Program (SSP)**—The School of Law offers this program for applicants who do not meet the minimum standards for admission, but who show potential for the study of law. This seven-week program, beginning in late May, requires students to demonstrate ability in the study of substantive law and in legal writing and research in order to gain admission as a regular student in the fall semester.

■ Student Organizations and Activities

The School of Law's students edit and publish the *Law Review*, a quarterly publication of scholarly articles.

A student **Moot Court Board of Advocacy** administers the School of Law's Gallagher and Professional Responsibility competitions; participates in state, regional, and national competitions in First Amendment Law, Ethics, and other areas; and helps to administer the G. Mennen Williams mandatory moot court competition for first-year students.

The **Student Bar Association (SBA)**, affiliated with the Law Student Division of the American Bar Association, plays a significant role in student affairs. As the student government of the school, the SBA authorizes other student organizations, including the Black Law Student Alliance, the Environmental Law Society, Phi Alpha Delta, St. Thomas More Society, the Women's Law Caucus, the Arab and Chaldean Law Student Society, the Sports and Entertainment Law Society, and many others. Students also regularly publish a student newsletter, *In Brief.*

■ Career Services

The school's Career Services Office provides students with a wide range of opportunities through which they may explore career paths in law. The office sponsors a Preparing to Practice series for upper-class students that introduces a variety of practice areas and issues. The assistant dean for career services and the national employment counselor provide career counseling services, including résumé and cover letter review. The office administers the school's annual on-campus interview programs, maintains a job information hotline and newsletter, sponsors a mock interview program for first-year students, and hosts special events to acquaint students with practitioners.

■ Admission

The School of Law encourages applicants to submit an application for admission by April 15. The Admission Committee considers all elements of an application, including undergraduate grade-point average, Law School Admission Test scores, writing skills, leadership and maturity as evidenced by work and service experiences, graduate work, letters of recommendation, and the personal statement. The committee reviews applications as they become complete on a continuous basis and communicates decisions as early as possible. An applicant may accept an offer of admission by submitting the required nonrefundable deposits, which are credited toward tuition. The university and the School of Law adhere to nondiscrimination policies.

Applicant Profile

University of Detroit Mercy School of Law
This grid includes only applicants who earned 120-180 LSAT scores under standard administrations.

LSAT Score	3.75 +		3.50 - 3.74		3.25 - 3.49		3.00 - 3.24		2.75 - 2.99		2.50 - 2.74		2.25 - 2.49		2.00 - 2.24		Below 2.00		No GPA		Total	
	Apps	Adm	Apps	Adm	Apps	Adm	Apps	Adm	Apps	Adm	Apps	Adm	Apps	Adm	Apps	Adm	Apps	Adm	Apps	Adm	Apps	Adm
175-180	0	0	0	0	0	0	0	0	0	0	0	0	0	0	0	0	0	0	0	0	0	0
170-174	0	0	0	0	0	0	0	0	0	0	0	0	0	0	0	0	0	0	0	0	0	0
165-169	2	2	2	2	0	0	0	0	2	2	0	0	0	0	0	0	0	0	1	1	7	7
160-164	6	6	7	6	7	7	3	3	9	8	3	2	1	1	1	1	0	0	2	2	39	36
155-159	12	12	10	10	20	20	19	19	8	8	16	13	5	1	3	3	0	0	6	6	99	92
150-154	19	19	36	34	37	34	56	50	41	34	25	19	14	7	4	0	2	1	11	10	245	208
145-149	11	9	39	35	52	43	70	50	65	31	44	7	25	5	11	0	1	0	9	4	327	184
140-144	4	1	23	13	52	10	61	5	47	0	26	0	23	0	5	0	3	0	4	0	248	29
135-139	1	0	9	0	16	0	25	0	20	0	19	0	11	0	5	0	1	0	4	0	111	0
130-134	0	0	1	0	4	0	5	0	6	0	8	0	5	0	6	0	2	0	4	0	41	0
125-129	0	0	1	0	0	0	2	0	2	0	2	0	2	0	1	0	1	0	3	0	14	0
120-124	0	0	0	0	0	0	0	0	0	0	0	0	0	0	0	0	0	0	0	0	0	0
Total	55	49	128	100	188	114	241	127	200	83	143	41	86	14	36	4	10	1	44	23	1131	556

Apps = Number of Applicants   Adm = Number Admitted   Reflects 98% of the total applicant pool.

University of The District of Columbia—The David A. Clarke School of Law

4200 Connecticut Avenue, NW
Washington, DC 20008
Phone: 202.274.7341; Fax: 202.274.5583
E-mail: lawadmission@udc.edu; Website: www.law.udc.edu

ABA Approved Since 1991

The Basics

Type of school	Public
Term	Semester
Application deadline	3/15
Application fee	$35
Financial aid deadline	3/31
Can first year start other than fall?	No
Student to faculty ratio (fall)	12.2 to 1
Does the university offer:	
housing restricted to law students?	No
graduate housing for which law students are eligible?	No

Faculty and Administrators

	Total Fall	Total Spr	Men Fall	Men Spr	Women Fall	Women Spr	Minorities Fall	Minorities Spr
Full-time	15	16	8	9	7	7	7	7
Other Full-time	0	0	0	0	0	0	0	0
Deans, librarians, & others who teach	3	3	1	1	2	2	0	0
Part-time	19	15	12	9	7	6	10	10
Total	37	34	21	19	16	15	17	17

Curriculum

		Full-time	Part-time
Typical first-year section size		89	0
Is there typically a "small section" of the first-year class, other than Legal Writing, taught by full-time faculty		Yes	No
If yes, typical size offered last year		45	0
# of classroom course titles beyond 1st year curriculum		50	
# of upper division courses, excluding seminars with an enrollement:	Under 25	41	
	25-49	7	
	50-74	4	
	75-99	0	
	100+	0	
# of seminars		4	
# of seminar positions available		40	
# of seminar positions filled		20	0
# of positions available in simulation courses		82	
# of simulation positions filled		61	0
# of positions available in faculty supervised clinical courses		88	
# of faculty supervised clinical positions filled	86		0
# involved in field placements		6	0
# involved in law journals		22	0
# involved in moot court or trial competitions	4		0
# of credit hours required to graduate		90	

JD Enrollment and Ethnicity

	Men #	Men %	Women #	Women %	Full-time #	Full-time %	Part-time #	Part-time %	1st-year #	1st-year %	Total #	Total %	JD Degs. Awd.
African Amer.	25	29.1	46	34.3	71	32.3	0	0.0	23	28.4	71	32.3	13
Amer. Indian	0	0.0	1	0.7	1	0.5	0	0.0	1	1.2	1	0.5	0
Asian Amer.	3	3.5	11	8.2	14	6.4	0	0.0	7	8.6	14	6.4	0
Mex. Amer.	0	0.0	0	0.0	0	0.0	0	0.0	0	0.0	0	0.0	0
Puerto Rican	1	1.2	1	0.7	2	0.9	0	0.0	0	0.0	2	0.9	1
Hispanic	2	2.3	12	9.0	14	6.4	0	0.0	5	6.2	14	6.4	1
Total Minority	31	36.0	71	53.0	102	46.4	0	0.0	36	44.4	102	46.4	15
For. Nation.	6	7.0	8	6.0	14	6.4	0	0.0	7	8.6	14	6.4	0
Caucasian	49	57.0	55	41.0	104	47.3	0	0.0	38	46.9	104	47.3	10
Unknown	0	0.0	0	0.0	0	0.0	0	0.0	0	0.0	0	0.0	0
Total	86	39.1	134	60.9	220	100.0	0	0.0	81	36.8	220		25

Tuition and Fees

	Resident	Nonresident
Full-time	$7,135	$14,135
Part-time	$0	$0

Living Expenses

Estimated living expenses for singles

Living on campus	Living off campus	Living at home
N/A	$23,300	$1,340

University of The District of Columbia—The David A. Clarke School of Law

ABA Approved Since 1991

GPA and LSAT Scores

	Total	Full-time	Part-time
# of apps	1,172	1,172	0
# of admits	248	248	0
# of matrics	81	81	0
75% GPA	0.00	3.41	0.00
25% GPA	0.00	2.82	0.00
75% LSAT	0	154	0
25% LSAT	0	148	0

Grants and Scholarships (from prior year)

	Total #	Total %	Full-time #	Full-time %	Part-time #	Part-time %
Total # of students	183		183		0	
Total # receiving grants	142	77.6	142	77.6	0	0.0
Less than 1/2 tuition	82	44.8	82	44.8	0	0.0
Half to full tuition	55	30.1	55	30.1	0	0.0
Full tuition	3	1.6	3	1.6	0	0.0
More than full tuition	2	1.1	2	1.1	0	0.0
Median grant amount			$4,500		$0	

Informational and Library Resources

# of volumes and volume equivalents	259,690
# of titles	131,815
# of active serial subscriptions	1,585
Study seating capacity inside the library	230
# of professional librarians	7
Hours per week library is open	101
# of open, wired connections available to students	16
# of networked computers available for use by students	16
# of simultaneous wireless users	762
Require computer?	Y

JD Attrition (from prior year)

	Academic #	Other #	Total #	Total %
1st year	2	13	15	16.9%
2nd year	0	4	4	6.7%
3rd year	0	0	0	0.0%
4th year	0	0	0	0.0%

Employment

	Total	Percentage
Employment status known	32	94.1
Employment status unknown	2	5.9
Employed	27	84.4
Pursuing graduate degrees	3	9.4
Unemployed seeking employment	0	0.0
Unemployed not seeking employment	2	6.2

Type of Employment

	Total	Percentage
# employed in law firms	10	37.0
# employed in business and industry	5	18.5
# employed in government	3	11.1
# employed in public interest	6	22.2
# employed as judicial clerks	2	7.4
# employed in academia	1	3.7

Geographic Location

	Total	Percentage
# employed in state	12	44.4
# employed in foreign countries	0	0.0
# of states where employed		11

Bar Passage Rates

Jurisdiction	Maryland		
Exam	Sum 03	Win 04	Total
# from school taking bar for the first time	16	1	17
School's pass rate for all first-time takers	38%	0%	35%
State's pass rate for all first-time takers	73%	62%	71%

University of The District of Columbia—The David A. Clarke School of Law

4200 Connecticut Avenue, NW
Washington, DC 20008
Phone: 202.274.7341; Fax: 202.274.5583
E-mail: lawadmission@udc.edu; Website: www.law.udc.edu

■ Introduction

In 1986, the City Council of the District of Columbia authorized the establishment of the District of Columbia School of Law. The council created a dual mission for the School of Law and charged its Board of Governors with a mandate to recruit and enroll, to the degree feasible, students from ethnic, racial, or other population groups that in the past have been underrepresented among persons admitted to the bar. It also charged the board with representing the legal needs of low-income persons, particularly those who reside in the District of Columbia.

The DC School of Law, the only publicly funded law school in Washington, DC, formally merged with the University of the District of Columbia (UDC) in 1996 and became the University of the District of Columbia School of Law. In April 1998, the UDC School of Law was named the UDC David A. Clarke School of Law (UDC-DCSL). The law school operates a full-time day program.

■ Library and Physical Facilities

The School of Law is located on the University of the District of Columbia's Van Ness campus in the upper northwest section of Washington, DC, a neighborhood known for its harmonious blend of residential and business communities.

The law library is a teaching-, research-, and practice-oriented library. It contains more than 265,000 volumes and volume equivalents. The law library expands its collection on an ongoing basis, with an emphasis on reference and scholarly materials. The library's online catalog is available at *http://catalog.law.udc.edu/search*.

In May 2004, the law library completed a major expansion and renovation project. The new *Charlie and Hilda H. M. Mason Library* is a beautiful and modern facility that provides the traditional and high-tech resources required for today's study of the law. Power is available at every seat. In addition, the Internet/Portal is accessible via the law library's wireless LAN throughout the law library.

The UDC campus is conveniently located on the Metro's Red Line at the UDC/Van Ness subway stop.

■ Curriculum

Consistent with UDC School of Law's mission, the basic program is designed to provide a well-rounded theoretical and practical legal education that will enable students to be effective and ethical advocates, and to represent the legal needs of low-income residents through the school's legal clinics.

First-year students participate in a two-week orientation program that introduces them to the study of law and the School of Law community. During orientation, students take the course Law and Justice, which introduces legal, political, social, and philosophical aspects of poverty and inequality in American society. They also take the course Lawyering Process I. Students participate in the Dean's Reception and in other events planned by student organizations and the Office of Admission. First-year students are also required to perform 40 hours of community service.

In the first year, students take a prescribed program consisting of required courses and one elective course. After the first year, students must also take courses in Evidence, Constitutional Law I and II, Professional Responsibility, and Moot Court. Each UDC-DCSL student is required to produce significant pieces of writing each of the three years of study. The School of Law offers a limited number of summer courses, including an internship program; however, it does not allow early graduation.

While the emphasis of the school is on public interest law, public policy, and public service, the overall curriculum—clinic and classroom—provides the skills necessary to pursue any field of law.

■ Clinical Program

Students must complete two seven-credit clinics during their second and third years. The clinics offered in the 2003–2004 academic year are Housing and Consumer, HIV/AIDS, Juvenile and Special Education, Legislation, Government Accountability Project, and Community Development and Small Business Law Center. Students may do an internship or work-study in the school's Immigration Law Project.

■ Academic Support and Summer Program

UDC-DCSL considers academic support to be an integral part of its course of study. Students in academic difficulty at the end of their first semester may apply to the enhanced program, which may involve adjusting course loads, taking a legal reasoning course, counseling, and group and individual tutoring. In addition, faculty members hold extra review sessions during the semester in required courses and provide sample examination questions with model answers.

The School of Law offers the Mason Enhancement Program for Academic Success, a four-week conditional-admission summer program, to selected entering students.

■ Internship Program

Students in the second and third year may elect to do internships in which they work in federal or local

University of The District of Columbia—The David A. Clarke School of Law

government agencies; judicial, legislative, or congressional offices; or in public interest legal organizations. Students are required to attend a weekly internship seminar at the school. The School of Law emphasizes the importance of supervision, educational merit, and public service in each internship.

■ Admission

Admission is based upon academic and nonacademic achievements and professional promise. UDC-DCSL looks at an applicant's LSAT and grades in tandem with other criteria that it believes may provide a more accurate measure of a candidate's determination, commitment, and potential for success in the study of law. The Admission Committee considers all submitted application materials, e.g., personal statement and essays, recommendations, community service, and employment experience. Applicants are encouraged to contact the Admission Office or to visit the website for information about visiting the School of Law, sitting in on a class, and attending one of the law day programs.

■ Financial Assistance and Scholarships

The financial aid policy provides students with financial assistance to support full-time study for three years. This is usually accomplished through a combination of scholarships, grants, and loans. These include merit

scholarships, need-based scholarships, the Federal Stafford loan program, and federal and other work-study employment. About 60 percent of UDC-DCSL students receive scholarship assistance, and 98 percent receive some form of financial aid. Detailed information about financial aid application policies and procedures is available on the website—*www.law.udc.edu*.

■ Student Activities

The first issue of the annual *The District of Columbia Law Review* was published in 1992. Active student groups include the Student Bar Association, BLSA, International Law Society, Voces Juridicas, OUTLAW, Women's Law Society, Sports and Entertainment Law Society, Phi Alpha Delta, and the National Lawyer's Guild.

■ Career Services

The Career Services Office provides employment information, individual career counseling, and résumé assistance to the School of Law's student body and graduates. The office maintains listings of permanent job openings, fellowships, summer clerkships, and part-time opportunities. The office also coordinates potential internship sites and invites employers to conduct on-campus interviews. The office provides resources for career planning, counseling sessions to assist students in developing their career goals, résumé workshops, and other relevant seminars.

Applicant Profile

The David A. Clarke School of Law prides itself on its admission philosophy, competitive and comprehensive admission process, and student diversity. While the applicant profile grids can be helpful to students, they may also discourage some students whose numerical profiles may be slightly below our school's LSAT and GPA medians, but whose life experiences may be compelling. Numbers do not always provide an accurate picture of an applicant's potential for law study or motivation to succeed. The School of Law, therefore, does not provide an applicant profile grid, but rather a brief description of its student body.

The student body is a diverse and accomplished group. The age range of students is 21 to 62 years. The average age is 28 years. Students of color comprise over half of the students. More than 25 states are represented in our student body and over 85 undergraduate schools. About 100 students a year are admitted. Smaller class sizes provide students with an ideal student-faculty ratio and with a rich theoretical and practical learning environment. The LSAT range of the fall 2004 entering class was 144–172, with a 150 median and a 151 mean. The GPA range was 2.33–3.91, with a median of 3.12 and a mean of 3.08. The student body represents strong competency and contribution potential.

Drake University Law School

2507 University Avenue
Des Moines, IA 50311-4505
Phone: 800.44.DRAKE, ext. 2782 or 515.271.2782; Fax: 515.271.1990
E-mail: lawadmit@drake.edu; Website: www.law.drake.edu

ABA
Approved
Since
1923

The Basics

Type of school	Private
Term	Semester
Application deadline	4/1
Application fee	$40
Financial aid deadline	3/1
Can first year start other than fall?	Yes
Student to faculty ratio (fall)	18.5 to 1
Does the university offer:	
housing restricted to law students?	No
graduate housing for which law students are eligible?	Yes

Faculty and Administrators

	Total		Men		Women		Minorities	
	Fall	Spr	Fall	Spr	Fall	Spr	Fall	Spr
Full-time	21	20	13	11	8	9	1	1
Other Full-time	2	2	2	2	0	0	1	1
Deans, librarians, & others who teach	4	4	3	3	1	1	0	0
Part-time	17	13	11	9	6	4	1	3
Total	44	39	29	25	15	14	3	5

Curriculum

		Full-time	Part-time
Typical first-year section size		86	0
Is there typically a "small section" of the first-year class, other than Legal Writing, taught by full-time faculty		No	No
If yes, typical size offered last year		0	0
# of classroom course titles beyond 1st year curriculum		111	
# of upper division courses, excluding seminars with an enrollment:	Under 25	154	
	25-49	22	
	50-74	6	
	75-99	6	
	100+	0	
# of seminars		7	
# of seminar positions available		175	
# of seminar positions filled		80	0
# of positions available in simulation courses		350	
# of simulation positions filled		227	0
# of positions available in faculty supervised clinical courses		77	
# of faculty supervised clinical positions filled		67	0
# involved in field placements		148	0
# involved in law journals		174	0
# involved in moot court or trial competitions		80	0
# of credit hours required to graduate		90	

JD Enrollment and Ethnicity

	Men #	Men %	Women #	Women %	Full-time #	Full-time %	Part-time #	Part-time %	1st-year #	1st-year %	Total #	Total %	JD Degs. Awd.
African Amer.	4	1.7	16	6.8	19	4.2	1	5.3	9	5.1	20	4.2	7
Amer. Indian	0	0.0	1	0.4	1	0.2	0	0.0	1	0.6	1	0.2	0
Asian Amer.	5	2.1	10	4.2	14	3.1	1	5.3	5	2.8	15	3.2	4
Mex. Amer.	4	1.7	3	1.3	7	1.5	0	0.0	4	2.3	7	1.5	1
Puerto Rican	0	0.0	0	0.0	0	0.0	0	0.0	0	0.0	0	0.0	0
Hispanic	0	0.0	0	0.0	0	0.0	0	0.0	0	0.0	0	0.0	1
Total Minority	13	5.5	30	12.7	41	9.0	2	10.5	19	10.8	43	9.1	13
For. Nation.	1	0.4	2	0.8	3	0.7	0	0.0	1	0.6	3	0.6	4
Caucasian	202	85.2	199	84.3	386	85.0	15	78.9	141	80.1	401	84.8	115
Unknown	21	8.9	5	2.1	24	5.3	2	10.5	15	8.5	26	5.5	0
Total	237	50.1	236	49.9	454	96.0	19	4.0	176	37.2	473		132

Tuition and Fees

	Resident	Nonresident
Full-time	$22,550	$22,550
Part-time	$0	$0

Living Expenses

Estimated living expenses for singles

Living on campus	Living off campus	Living at home
N/A	$11,525	$5,450

Drake University Law School

*ABA
Approved
Since
1923*

GPA and LSAT Scores

	Total	Full-time	Part-time
# of apps	1,130	1,101	29
# of admits	484	481	3
# of matrics	171	168	3
75% GPA	3.67	3.67	0.00
25% GPA	3.15	3.12	0.00
75% LSAT	157	157	0
25% LSAT	153	153	0

Grants and Scholarships (from prior year)

	Total		Full-time		Part-time	
	#	%	#	%	#	%
Total # of students	446		432		14	
Total # receiving grants	210	47.1	210	48.6	0	0.0
Less than 1/2 tuition	147	33.0	147	34.0	0	0.0
Half to full tuition	32	7.2	32	7.4	0	0.0
Full tuition	31	7.0	31	7.2	0	0.0
More than full tuition	0	0.0	0	0.0	0	0.0
Median grant amount			$7,500		$0	

Informational and Library Resources

# of volumes and volume equivalents	315,316
# of titles	42,908
# of active serial subscriptions	3,217
Study seating capacity inside the library	705
# of professional librarians	7
Hours per week library is open	109
# of open, wired connections available to students	160
# of networked computers available for use by students	123
# of simultaneous wireless users	520
Require computer?	N

JD Attrition (from prior year)

	Academic	Other	Total	
	#	#	#	%
1st year	4	6	10	5.9%
2nd year	0	10	10	7.2%
3rd year	0	0	0	0.0%
4th year	0	0	0	0.0%

Employment

	Total	Percentage
Employment status known	119	87.5
Employment status unknown	17	12.5
Employed	112	94.1
Pursuing graduate degrees	3	2.5
Unemployed seeking employment	4	3.4
Unemployed not seeking employment	0	0.0

Type of Employment

# employed in law firms	66	58.9
# employed in business and industry	18	16.1
# employed in government	13	11.6
# employed in public interest	2	1.8
# employed as judicial clerks	8	7.1
# employed in academia	1	0.9

Geographic Location

# employed in state	72	64.3
# employed in foreign countries	1	0.9
# of states where employed	15	

Bar Passage Rates

Jurisdiction		Iowa	
Exam	Sum 03	Win 04	Total
# from school taking bar for the first time	70	17	87
School's pass rate for all first-time takers	79%	88%	80%
State's pass rate for all first-time takers	84%	90%	86%

Drake University Law School

2507 University Avenue
Des Moines, IA 50311-4505
Phone: 800.44.DRAKE, ext. 2782 or 515.271.2782; Fax: 515.271.1990
E-mail: lawadmit@drake.edu; Website: www.law.drake.edu

■ Introduction

Drake University Law School can trace its history back to 1865, making it one of the nation's 25 oldest law schools. Accredited by the ABA, the Law School provides a personal education with a low student-to-faculty ratio. Our commitment to an education that balances theory and practice has earned a reputation of training proven practitioners.

Drake Law School is located in Iowa's capital, Des Moines, providing law students the opportunity to get hands-on experience with the executive, judicial, and legislative branches of state government; the federal courts; federal and state administrative agencies; and a wide array of law firms and businesses.

■ Legal Clinic

Drake had one of the first clinics in the country and has built on that tradition. The Neal and Bea Smith Law Center, built in 1987, houses the Drake Law School Legal Clinic. The center is a state-of-the-art law office that enables Drake students to represent real clients out of their own fully computerized offices. The center was selected as the national training and resource institute for public service attorneys. The $1.75 million addition, built in 1994, includes a technologically enhanced courtroom and training facilities. In fall 2001, the clinic added the Joan and Lyle Middleton Center for Children's Rights to its operations.

■ First-Year Trial Practicum

The only program of its kind in the country, the trial practicum adds an important experiential learning dimension to the first-year curriculum. During the spring semester, first-year students observe a real trial—from jury selection to verdict—in the courtroom of the Neal and Bea Smith Law Center. Break-out discussion groups and posttrial debriefings of the attorneys, judges, and jurors poignantly illustrate how law on the books becomes law in action.

■ Centers of Excellence

Constitutional Law Center—Drake is one of only four schools selected to receive a congressional endowment for the establishment of a Constitutional Law Resource Center. The center sponsors a lecture series and annual symposia featuring nationally recognized constitutional scholars. The nationally renowned Dwight D. Opperman Lecture in Constitutional Law has been delivered by eight current and former justices of the US Supreme Court; one justice has twice returned for a week-long residency to teach a course to Drake law students.

The center also conducts the Summer Institute in Constitutional Law, a program designed for first-year students interested in getting their law school career off to an early start. During the six-week session, students enroll in three courses that examine different aspects of constitutional law combined with a writing component to help establish the critical thinking, research, writing, and study skills needed for law school success.

Agricultural Law Center—Our internationally recognized agricultural law program addresses the important issues in American and international law and policy regarding food production. Students conduct research, publish an agricultural law journal, and write articles on a wide range of topics. Lecturers from France, the United Kingdom, Canada, Italy, and China have visited the center in recent years to share their knowledge and expertise on topics such as farmland preservation, legal issues in biotechnology, and tax planning for agricultural businesses. The center also offers a series of one-week courses for students and attorneys in the Summer Agricultural Law Institute. In fall 2002, the center began offering a Food and Agricultural Law Certificate program, the first of its kind at an American law school.

Center for Legislative Practice—Drake is one of a few schools in the country that offers a certificate program in legislative law. The two-year schedule of classroom study and a wide range of internships expose students to the underpinnings of legislative and rule-making processes. Students who complete the program are uniquely prepared for careers in administrative or government agencies, public interest groups, trade associations, unions, and private law firms that do governmental work.

■ Litigation and Dispute Resolution Certificate Program

Beginning in spring 2003, the Law School instituted a Litigation Certificate program to capitalize on the school's traditional strengths in advocacy and dispute resolution.

■ Summer in France

You can add an international element to your legal education by participating in our summer program at the University of Nantes Law School in France. Classes in comparative and international law and on-site visits to European legal institutions allow you to absorb and experience another country's legal system and be better prepared to practice law in a global society.

Drake University Law School

Joint-Degree Programs

If you are interested in combining your legal studies with other academic disciplines, you can do so in one of several joint-degree programs that will broaden your skills and increase your career options. Students may combine their Juris Doctor degree with the following: Master of Business Administration, Master of Public Administration, Doctor of Pharmacy, Master of Arts in Political Science (in cooperation with Iowa State University), Master of Science in Agricultural Economics (in cooperation with Iowa State University), and Master of Social Work (in cooperation with the University of Iowa).

Student Activities

Law students participate in many student organizations and cocurricular activities. The *Drake Law Review*, a student-edited journal, is published quarterly. Drake moot court teams consistently win regional competitions and finish strong in national competitions. Drake's National Moot Court team won the 2001 national championship. The Student Bar Association, Legal Research Service, and honorary societies provide students with leadership, public service, and learning opportunities. Drake students have also formed a variety of organizations around their special interests, including the Drake Law Women, Black Law Students Association, International Law Society, Christian Legal Society, Environmental Law Society, Federalist Society, National Lawyers Guild, Intellectual Property Law Society, Agricultural Law Society, Alternative Dispute Resolution Society, and an organization for students with alternative sexual orientation.

Networking

Drake Law School alumni practice in all 50 states and several foreign countries. Many law alumni participate in our Volunteers in Placement (VIP) mentoring program and are available to offer career advice or simply encouragement and support. You can request a VIP in a particular geographic location or certain area of law to find out about the employment climate and job opportunities. Through the VIP program, you can form a national networking system right from the start of your legal education.

Career Services

The Career Services Office offers career planning and counseling services, assistance with résumés and cover letter preparation, salary and geographical employment statistics, nationwide job postings, and state bar examination information. The office also arranges interviews—both on and off campus—and exchanges job listings with 90 other law schools around the country. To expand opportunities for students, the Law School participates in several special recruiting conferences in the Midwest and in Washington, DC. The job placement rate for Drake Law School graduates is consistently above the national average.

Applicant Profile

Drake University Law School
This grid includes only applicants who earned 120-180 LSAT scores under standard administrations.

LSAT Score	3.75 +		3.50 - 3.74		3.25 - 3.49		3.00 - 3.24		2.75 - 2.99		2.50 - 2.74		2.25 - 2.49		2.00 - 2.24		Below 2.00		No GPA		Total	
	Apps	Adm	Apps	Adm	Apps	Adm	Apps	Adm	Apps	Adm	Apps	Adm	Apps	Adm	Apps	Adm	Apps	Adm	Apps	Adm	Apps	Adm
175-180	0	0	0	0	0	0	0	0	0	0	0	0	0	0	0	0	0	0	0	0	0	0
170-174	0	0	0	0	0	0	0	0	0	0	0	0	0	0	0	0	0	0	0	0	0	0
165-169	6	6	2	2	1	1	1	1	2	2	1	1	0	0	1	1	0	0	0	0	14	14
160-164	17	17	14	14	16	15	9	9	6	6	2	2	3	3	1	1	0	0	1	1	69	68
155-159	42	42	47	47	40	40	41	39	19	18	10	8	7	6	4	1	0	0	0	0	210	201
150-154	46	35	61	46	78	45	69	21	37	12	24	3	16	0	4	0	1	0	2	0	338	162
145-149	17	4	55	8	57	5	45	4	41	3	25	2	11	0	2	0	1	0	3	0	257	26
140-144	4	0	14	2	17	0	24	2	16	1	10	0	16	0	6	0	1	0	1	0	109	5
135-139	3	1	3	0	6	0	9	0	10	1	3	0	7	0	6	0	1	0	3	0	51	2
130-134	1	0	0	0	1	0	1	0	2	0	1	0	5	0	3	0	0	0	0	0	15	0
125-129	0	0	0	0	1	0	0	0	1	0	0	0	2	0	0	0	0	0	1	0	5	0
120-124	0	0	0	0	0	0	0	0	0	0	0	0	0	0	0	0	0	0	0	0	0	0
Total	136	105	196	119	217	106	199	76	134	43	76	16	67	9	27	3	4	0	12	1	1068	478

Apps = Number of Applicants
Adm = Number Admitted
Reflects 99% of the total applicant pool.

Duke University School of Law

Science Drive & Towerview Road, Box 90393
Durham, NC 27708-0393
Phone: 919.613.7020; Fax: 919.613.7257
E-mail: admissions@law.duke.edu; Website: admissions.law.duke.edu

ABA
Approved
Since
1931

The Basics

Type of school	Private
Term	Semester
Application deadline	1/1
Application fee	$70
Financial aid deadline	3/15
Can first year start other than fall?	Yes
Student to faculty ratio (fall)	11.7 to 1
Does the university offer:	
housing restricted to law students?	No
graduate housing for which law students are eligible?	No

Faculty and Administrators

	Total		Men		Women		Minorities	
	Fall	Spr	Fall	Spr	Fall	Spr	Fall	Spr
Full-time	45	41	34	33	11	8	3	3
Other Full-time	4	4	0	0	4	4	1	1
Deans, librarians, & others who teach	11	11	3	3	8	8	2	2
Part-time	30	34	16	20	14	14	4	2
Total	90	90	53	56	37	34	10	8

Curriculum

	Full-time	Part-time
Typical first-year section size	87	0
Is there typically a "small section" of the first-year class, other than Legal Writing, taught by full-time faculty	Yes	No
If yes, typical size offered last year	35	0
# of classroom course titles beyond 1st year curriculum	151	

# of upper division courses, excluding seminars with an enrollment:		
Under 25	62	
25-49	28	
50-74	16	
75-99	1	
100+	6	

# of seminars	47	
# of seminar positions available	742	
# of seminar positions filled	611	0
# of positions available in simulation courses	348	
# of simulation positions filled	327	0
# of positions available in faculty supervised clinical courses	89	
# of faculty supervised clinical positions filled	82	0
# involved in field placements	2	0
# involved in law journals	261	0
# involved in moot court or trial competitions	77	0
# of credit hours required to graduate	84	

JD Enrollment and Ethnicity

	Men		Women		Full-time		Part-time		1st-year		Total		JD Degs. Awd.
	#	%	#	%	#	%	#	%	#	%	#	%	
African Amer.	25	7.1	41	14.2	61	10.0	5	16.7	30	14.0	66	10.3	20
Amer. Indian	3	0.9	1	0.3	4	0.7	0	0.0	0	0.0	4	0.6	3
Asian Amer.	29	8.3	27	9.3	51	8.4	5	16.7	23	10.7	56	8.8	19
Mex. Amer.	0	0.0	0	0.0	0	0.0	0	0.0	0	0.0	0	0.0	0
Puerto Rican	0	0.0	0	0.0	0	0.0	0	0.0	0	0.0	0	0.0	0
Hispanic	11	3.1	9	3.1	18	3.0	2	6.7	6	2.8	20	3.1	13
Total Minority	68	19.4	78	27.0	134	22.0	12	40.0	59	27.4	146	22.8	55
For. Nation.	1	0.3	5	1.7	6	1.0	0	0.0	0	0.0	6	0.9	0
Caucasian	233	66.4	180	62.3	399	65.4	14	46.7	122	56.7	413	64.5	160
Unknown	49	14.0	26	9.0	71	11.6	4	13.3	34	15.8	75	11.7	22
Total	351	54.8	289	45.2	610	95.3	30	4.7	215	33.6	640		237

Tuition and Fees

	Resident	Nonresident
Full-time	$34,574	$0
Part-time	$0	$0

Living Expenses

Estimated living expenses for singles

Living on campus	Living off campus	Living at home
$15,230	$15,230	$15,230

Duke University School of Law

*ABA
Approved
Since
1931*

GPA and LSAT Scores

	Total	Full-time	Part-time
# of apps	4,099	4,099	0
# of admits	869	869	0
# of matrics	219	219	0
75% GPA	0.00	3.83	0.00
25% GPA	0.00	3.38	0.00
75% LSAT	0	169	0
25% LSAT	0	162	0

Grants and Scholarships (from prior year)

	Total #	Total %	Full-time #	Full-time %	Part-time #	Part-time %
Total # of students	654		654		0	
Total # receiving grants	446	68.2	446	68.2	0	0.0
Less than 1/2 tuition	391	59.8	391	59.8	0	0.0
Half to full tuition	45	6.9	45	6.9	0	0.0
Full tuition	9	1.4	9	1.4	0	0.0
More than full tuition	1	0.2	1	0.2	0	0.0
Median grant amount			$8,000		$0	

Informational and Library Resources

# of volumes and volume equivalents	606,017
# of titles	212,267
# of active serial subscriptions	6,867
Study seating capacity inside the library	450
# of professional librarians	9
Hours per week library is open	104
# of open, wired connections available to students	787
# of networked computers available for use by students	152
# of simultaneous wireless users	400
Require computer?	Y

JD Attrition (from prior year)

	Academic #	Other #	Total #	Total %
1st year	0	2	2	1.0%
2nd year	0	5	5	2.3%
3rd year	0	2	2	0.9%
4th year	0	0	0	0.0%

Employment

	Total	Percentage
Employment status known	191	100.0
Employment status unknown	0	0.0
Employed	188	98.4
Pursuing graduate degrees	2	1.0
Unemployed seeking employment	0	0.0
Unemployed not seeking employment	1	0.5

Type of Employment

	Total	Percentage
# employed in law firms	136	72.3
# employed in business and industry	4	2.1
# employed in government	10	5.3
# employed in public interest	1	0.5
# employed as judicial clerks	35	18.6
# employed in academia	2	1.1

Geographic Location

	Total	Percentage
# employed in state	21	11.2
# employed in foreign countries	2	1.1
# of states where employed	27	

Bar Passage Rates

Jurisdiction	New York		
Exam	Sum 03	Win 04	Total
# from school taking bar for the first time	66	5	71
School's pass rate for all first-time takers	98%	100%	99%
State's pass rate for all first-time takers	78%	58%	75%

Duke University School of Law

Science Drive & Towerview Road, Box 90393
Durham, NC 27708-0393
Phone: 919.613.7020; Fax: 919.613.7257
E-mail: admissions@law.duke.edu; Website: admissions.law.duke.edu

■ Introduction

Located in North Carolina's technology-focused
Research Triangle area, Duke law school has established
itself as one of the leading law schools in the nation.
Students come to Duke Law from every state and, as
alumni, are dispersed throughout the country and
around the world.

One of the reasons students choose Duke Law is its
collaborative environment, where growth is encouraged
not only through rigorous scholarship, but also through
cooperation and support. Within this close academic
community, students discover a rare level of interaction
with faculty and fellow students.

Duke law school's faculty members have
long-established reputations for being not only insightful
and engaging in their teaching, but also accessible and
responsive to students. The open-door policy practiced
by faculty encourages students to ask questions,
continue discussions, and seek advice on specialized
interests. Faculty-student interaction extends beyond the
classroom to committee work, pro bono opportunities,
career counseling, and mentoring. Ultimately, students
experience a nurturing environment where the focus is
on training and developing the whole person in a diverse
atmosphere that values different perspectives,
backgrounds, and orientations.

■ Enrollment/Student Body

Duke Law admits a select group of students with diverse
backgrounds who have in common a record of academic
excellence. In 2004, JD students came to Duke from 38
states and 5 foreign countries. These students represented 102 different undergraduate institutions and had
a wealth of different experiences. Approximately 40 percent of the students entering Duke Law in 2004 came
directly from college, while the other 60 percent entered
law school after gaining experience for a year or more in
another profession or graduate school.

■ Faculty

Central to Duke Law's success is its faculty. Well-respected
in the legal field, Duke Law professors are known for
groundbreaking legal scholarship and the practice of law
in both the public and private sectors in the United States
and abroad. Their backgrounds are as varied as they are
distinguished; they are former Fulbright Scholars, Rhodes
Scholars, and Marshall Scholars. A number of faculty
members have served as Supreme Court clerks, and one
was the chief judge for the US Court of Military Appeals.
Faculty members hold joint appointments in departments
throughout the university and have obtained PhDs in a
wide variety of disciplines. Several visiting professors from
abroad teach at Duke Law each year, and many full-time
faculty members have extensive international connections.

■ Joint Degrees

The Duke Law faculty believes that society is best served
by lawyers with diverse education and training. The law
school jointly sponsors numerous academic and professional programs, including 21 joint-degree programs in
conjunction with other schools or departments at
Duke University.

The law school and the graduate school jointly sponsor
programs of study in law and several other disciplines
including, at the master's level, cultural anthropology, East
Asian studies, economics, electrical and computer
engineering, English, environmental science and policy,
history, humanities, mechanical engineering, philosophy,
political science, psychology, public policy studies, religion,
and Romance studies. The only additional time necessary to
obtain both degrees is the summer prior to the first year of
school. At the doctoral level, joint programs in philosophy
and political science are available.

The law school offers joint professional degrees with
the Fuqua School of Business, the Divinity School, the
Nicholas School of the Environment, the Medical School,
and the Sanford Institute of Public Policy. Specific
information about applying to the joint professional
degree programs and time requirements for these
programs is available on the Duke Law website.

Duke Law students may also earn graduate certificates
in Slavic, Eurasian, and East European Legal Studies;
Health Care Policy; Health System Management; or
Women's Studies.

■ Special Programs

- **JD/LLM in International and Comparative Law**—
  Duke Law has pioneered a unique joint-degree program that makes it possible for students to earn a JD
  and a Master of Laws in International and Comparative Law concurrently in three years. The only
  additional time needed to complete both degrees is
  the summer prior to the first year of law school and
  the first half of the following summer, during which
  students attend one of Duke's Institutes of Transnational Law, either in Switzerland or Asia.
- **International Study Abroad and Externships**—Duke
  law school has arrangements at 19 top foreign universities, which give all interested Duke students an
  opportunity to study abroad. Programs are arranged
  on an individual basis and are supervised by Duke
  and the host institution. Duke Law also offers international externship opportunities in legal internships for

one semester's credit at public sector institutions that engage in international work. Duke has preapproved externships with certain agencies, but students are also encouraged to submit their own proposals if they are interested in working with other groups.

■ Admission

Admission to Duke law school is highly competitive. In addition to the academic criteria, other factors may help to distinguish some applicants. These include capacity for leadership, dedication to community service, excellence in a particular field, motivation, graduate study, work experience, extracurricular activities, and character.

Duke Law tries to achieve broad diversity in terms of general background, geography, and undergraduate institutions represented. Students are chosen not only for their potential for academic success but also because of qualities that will enhance the overall character of the class. Duke takes special care in evaluating applications from minorities who traditionally have not been well represented in the legal profession.

Duke Law offers a nonbinding early-action option. To be eligible for early action, the LSAT must be taken no later than June, and the application, along with all supporting material, must be received in the Office of Admission no later than November 1. Early action applications are judged by a higher than normal standard since we must make decisions before the size and quality of the rest of the pool of applications is known. Early action applicants who are admitted will be notified by January 1. All other candidates will be considered in comparison to the rest of the pool.

■ Cocurricular Activities

Scholarship in the classroom is reinforced through a variety of opportunities for hands-on leadership training and professional experience. These begin soon after students arrive and continue throughout their tenure at Duke Law. Through pro bono work, legal clinics, public interest projects, moot court, and opportunities for scholarly writing and editing on seven different legal journals, Duke prepares students for the real-world practice of law.

Applicant Profile

Duke University School of Law
This grid includes only applicants who earned 120-180 LSAT scores under standard administrations.

LSAT Score	3.75 +		3.50 - 3.74		3.25 - 3.49		3.00 - 3.24		2.75 - 2.99		2.50 - 2.74		2.25 - 2.49		2.00 - 2.24		Below 2.00		No GPA		Total	
	Apps	Adm	Apps	Adm	Apps	Adm	Apps	Adm	Apps	Adm	Apps	Adm	Apps	Adm	Apps	Adm	Apps	Adm	Apps	Adm	Apps	Adm
175-180	15	14	24	23	14	12	8	2	0	0	1	0	0	0	0	0	0	0	0	0	62	51
170-174	122	116	94	86	86	66	35	18	10	1	9	0	3	1	1	0	0	0	5	3	365	291
165-169	319	155	374	120	257	51	115	17	32	3	10	0	4	0	1	0	1	0	16	3	1129	349
160-164	346	52	445	22	254	10	147	6	33	1	15	0	8	1	3	0	0	0	24	0	1275	92
155-159	134	14	174	15	161	8	77	5	27	0	13	0	5	0	0	0	0	0	10	0	601	42
150-154	57	6	83	1	83	3	49	1	20	0	18	1	5	0	2	0	2	0	10	0	329	12
145-149	27	0	33	1	33	1	34	0	21	0	4	0	7	0	1	0	0	0	5	0	165	2
140-144	4	0	6	0	15	0	23	0	11	0	11	0	5	0	3	0	0	0	5	0	83	0
135-139	0	0	1	0	3	0	4	0	7	0	4	0	2	0	4	0	0	0	0	0	25	0
130-134	1	0	0	0	0	0	1	0	2	0	2	0	2	0	1	0	1	0	0	0	10	0
125-129	0	0	0	0	0	0	0	0	2	0	0	0	0	0	0	0	0	0	1	0	3	0
120-124	0	0	0	0	0	0	0	0	0	0	0	0	0	0	0	0	0	0	0	0	0	0
Total	1025	357	1234	268	906	151	493	49	165	5	87	1	41	2	16	0	4	0	76	6	4047	839

Apps = Number of Applicants
Adm = Number Admitted
Reflects 99% of the total applicant pool.

Duquesne University School of Law

201 Edward J. Hanley Hall, 900 Locust Street
Pittsburgh, PA 15282-0700
Phone: 412.396.6296; Fax: 412.396.1073
E-mail: campion@duq.edu; Website: www.law.duq.edu

*ABA
Approved
Since
1960*

The Basics

Type of school	Private
Term	Semester
Application deadline	4/1 5/1
Application fee	$50
Financial aid deadline	5/31
Can first year start other than fall?	No
Student to faculty ratio (fall)	18.8 to 1
Does the university offer:	
housing restricted to law students?	No
graduate housing for which law students are eligible?	Yes

Faculty and Administrators

	Total		Men		Women		Minorities	
	Fall	Spr	Fall	Spr	Fall	Spr	Fall	Spr
Full-time	24	24	19	19	5	5	3	3
Other Full-time	3	3	1	1	2	2	0	0
Deans, librarians, & others who teach	2	2	1	1	1	1	0	0
Part-time	25	33	17	25	8	8	1	0
Total	54	62	38	46	16	16	4	3

Curriculum

	Full-time	Part-time
Typical first-year section size	79	43
Is there typically a "small section" of the first-year class, other than Legal Writing, taught by full-time faculty	Yes	No
If yes, typical size offered last year	51	0
# of classroom course titles beyond 1st year curriculum	106	
# of upper division courses, excluding seminars with an enrollment: Under 25	56	
25-49	25	
50-74	28	
75-99	5	
100+	0	
# of seminars	16	
# of seminar positions available	281	
# of seminar positions filled	146	47
# of positions available in simulation courses	413	
# of simulation positions filled	185	130
# of positions available in faculty supervised clinical courses	55	
# of faculty supervised clinical positions filled	36	8
# involved in field placements	73	10
# involved in law journals	81	41
# involved in moot court or trial competitions	24	4
# of credit hours required to graduate	86	

JD Enrollment and Ethnicity

	Men		Women		Full-time		Part-time		1st-year		Total		JD Degs. Awd.
	#	%	#	%	#	%	#	%	#	%	#	%	
African Amer.	4	1.2	12	4.2	6	1.5	10	4.9	2	1.0	16	2.6	4
Amer. Indian	0	0.0	0	0.0	0	0.0	0	0.0	0	0.0	0	0.0	0
Asian Amer.	3	0.9	7	2.4	4	1.0	6	2.9	5	2.6	10	1.6	3
Mex. Amer.	0	0.0	0	0.0	0	0.0	0	0.0	0	0.0	0	0.0	0
Puerto Rican	0	0.0	0	0.0	0	0.0	0	0.0	0	0.0	0	0.0	0
Hispanic	3	0.9	1	0.3	2	0.5	2	1.0	0	0.0	4	0.7	2
Total Minority	10	3.1	20	6.9	12	3.0	18	8.8	7	3.6	30	4.9	9
For. Nation.	2	0.6	1	0.3	2	0.5	1	0.5	2	1.0	3	0.5	0
Caucasian	310	96.3	268	92.7	392	96.6	186	90.7	185	95.4	578	94.6	169
Unknown	0	0.0	0	0.0	0	0.0	0	0.0	0	0.0	0	0.0	0
Total	322	52.7	289	47.3	406	66.4	205	33.6	194	31.8	611		178

Tuition and Fees

	Resident	Nonresident
Full-time	$22,865	$22,865
Part-time	$17,724	$17,724

Living Expenses

Estimated living expenses for singles

Living on campus	Living off campus	Living at home
$10,280	$10,280	$3,400

Duquesne University School of Law

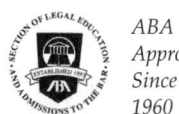

ABA
Approved
Since
1960

GPA and LSAT Scores

	Total	Full-time	Part-time
# of apps	1,026	851	175
# of admits	378	319	59
# of matrics	201	166	35
75% GPA	3.64	3.61	3.68
25% GPA	3.24	3.20	3.28
75% LSAT	157	157	157
25% LSAT	153	153	154

Grants and Scholarships (from prior year)

	Total		Full-time		Part-time	
	#	%	#	%	#	%
Total # of students	630		397		233	
Total # receiving grants	138	21.9	123	31.0	15	6.4
Less than 1/2 tuition	84	13.3	76	19.1	8	3.4
Half to full tuition	13	2.1	6	1.5	7	3.0
Full tuition	41	6.5	41	10.3	0	0.0
More than full tuition	0	0.0	0	0.0	0	0.0
Median grant amount			$5,534		$5,218	

Informational and Library Resources

# of volumes and volume equivalents	289,519
# of titles	79,038
# of active serial subscriptions	3,822
Study seating capacity inside the library	358
# of professional librarians	10
Hours per week library is open	102
# of open, wired connections available to students	70
# of networked computers available for use by students	92
# of simultaneous wireless users	325
Require computer?	N

JD Attrition (from prior year)

	Academic	Other	Total	
	#	#	#	%
1st year	19	14	33	16.3%
2nd year	5	0	5	2.9%
3rd year	0	1	1	0.5%
4th year	0	0	0	0.0%

Employment

	Total	Percentage
Employment status known	182	97.8
Employment status unknown	4	2.2
Employed	173	95.1
Pursuing graduate degrees	3	1.6
Unemployed seeking employment	4	2.2
Unemployed not seeking employment	2	1.1

Type of Employment

	Total	Percentage
# employed in law firms	96	55.5
# employed in business and industry	34	19.7
# employed in government	16	9.2
# employed in public interest	5	2.9
# employed as judicial clerks	22	12.7
# employed in academia	0	0.0

Geographic Location

	Total	Percentage
# employed in state	152	87.9
# employed in foreign countries	0	0.0
# of states where employed	9	

Bar Passage Rates

Jurisdiction	Pennsylvania		
Exam	Sum 03	Win 04	Total
# from school taking bar for the first time	156	9	165
School's pass rate for all first-time takers	71%	56%	70%
State's pass rate for all first-time takers	78%	66%	76%

Duquesne University School of Law

201 Edward J. Hanley Hall, 900 Locust Street
Pittsburgh, PA 15282-0700
Phone: 412.396.6296; Fax: 412.396.1073
E-mail: campion@duq.edu; Website: www.law.duq.edu

■ Introduction

The Duquesne University School of Law is a Catholic
law school that has been in existence since 1911 and is
the only multiple-division law school in western
Pennsylvania. Admission requirements, instruction,
and the nature and scope of the work required of
students are identical for both the full-time day division
and the part-time evening and part-time day divisions.
The School of Law is approved by the ABA and is a
member of the AALS.

Situated on the attractive 43-acre Duquesne University
campus, the law school is within walking distance to the
vibrant Pittsburgh downtown legal, corporate, and
government communities.

Recognized as one of the best cities in which to practice
law and a center for corporate and legal headquarters,
Pittsburgh is a leading metropolis for high technology
ventures and a thriving arts and cultural community,
with major-league sports entertainment.

■ Library and Physical Facilities

Duquesne's proximity to the Pittsburgh region's legal
center makes the law school library a major source for
legal research and information services. The Duquesne
law library has assumed management responsibility of
the Allegheny County Law Library, resulting in one of
the largest collections of legal materials in Pennsylvania.

The law school recently completed a $12 million
renovation and expansion, adding 33,000 square feet to
Hanley Hall. The four new floors of space include a
state-of-the-art moot courtroom (giving us three); three new
technology-aided classrooms with ports and power sources
at every seat; an upgraded lounge area with a cafeteria;
new faculty and administrative offices; student locker areas;
a conference room; and a wireless computer lab.

■ Curriculum

The course of study offered at the School of Law is sufficiently broad to prepare students for practice in all states.
Three years are required for completion of the course of
study in the day division, four years in the evening
division as well as the part-time day division. Eighty-six
credits are required for graduation.

While emphasis is placed upon skills such as legal
research and writing and trial advocacy, the required
courses are sufficiently broad to provide all students
with the requisite skills to become competent lawyers in
any field of practice. A wide selection of elective courses,
seminars, and student in-house and internal clinics
allows students to focus on specialized legal fields and
explore the contemporary problems of law and society.

■ Admission

*Bachelor's degree required; Application deadlines: day, April 1;
evening, May 1; part-time day, June 1; rolling admission;
LSAT, LSDAS required.*

All candidates for admission must take the LSAT,
register for the LSDAS, and be graduates of an accredited
college or university before enrolling in the law school.
Personal interviews are not granted, but applicants are
encouraged to schedule an appointment to visit the
school for an information session or a tour of
the facilities.

The admission process is selective. Most applicants
apply well in advance of the deadlines. Students are
admitted only for the fall semester.

In evaluating applications, the complete academic
record is reviewed with consideration given to the
competitiveness of the undergraduate institution, the
college major, rank in class, and the overall academic
performance. The LSAT is considered an important
factor. Graduate study, extracurricular activities, and
recommendations also contribute to the committee's
assessment. Work experience is considered when an
applicant has been employed full time for a significant
length of time.

■ Joint-Degree Programs

The School of Law offers the following joint-degree
programs: JD/MBA, JD/MS Environmental Science and
Management, JD/MS Taxation, and JD/MDiv.

■ Clinical Opportunities

The School of Law operates five in-house live client clinics.

The **Economic and Community Development Law
Clinic** is a unique nationally recognized clinic. Students
represent nonprofit organizations that provide a vast
array of greatly needed services to the community.
Through the **Civil and Family Justice Clinic** students
represent indigent individuals who would not otherwise
find assistance through the civil justice system. The
Criminal Advocacy Clinic is operated in cooperation
with the Allegheny County District Attorney's and
Public Defender's offices. Through the **Federal
Low-Income Tax Practicum** students learn litigation
skills as they represent clients in appeals conferences,
settlement negotiations, and before the US Tax Court.
The **Securities Arbitration Practicum** created with
the support of the Securities and Exchange Commission
is designed to enable law students to represent
small investors through the NASD Dispute
Resolution process.

Duquesne University School of Law

■ International Programs

The law school has established a summer program and faculty exchange with the Chinese University of Political Science and Law (CUPL). Located in Beijing, CUPL, with official ties to China's Ministry of Justice, is the most prestigious center for legal study in all of China. Duquesne has an outstanding ABA-approved summer program of study on Comparative Law and the European Union at the American College, Dublin. The Duquesne law school has recently established an ABA-approved program for law students in Vatican City focusing on subjects relating to Canon Law and Roman Law. Duquesne is the only law school offering a program for law students within Vatican City.

■ Student Activities

The Student Bar Association maintains a liaison between students and faculty and sponsors social and professional activities for the student body.

Membership in the *Duquesne Law Review* is based on the demonstrated academic ability of the student as well as his or her interest in becoming active in this publication. *Juris*, the law school news magazine, is an ABA award-winning publication containing articles of current interest to the entire legal community. Students also publish the *Duquesne Business Law Journal*.

■ Financial Aid

Duquesne consistently strives to ensure that the outstanding private legal education provided by the law school is within the reach of all qualified students. Merit scholarships are awarded to outstanding day-division applicants; grants-in-aid are awarded primarily on the basis of need; and state and federal government-sponsored loans are available.

■ Housing

Law students have access to an array of housing options throughout the neighborhoods of Pittsburgh and the surrounding communities. The Office of Commuter Affairs will assist law students in their search for housing by providing a list of available locations. For further information, please write to the Office of Commuter Affairs, Duquesne University, Pittsburgh, PA 15282 or call 412.396.6660.

■ Career Services

The Career Services Office staff offers assistance to students and alumni who are interested in obtaining full-time, part-time, and summer employment. The office offers a fall and spring on-campus interview program in which law firms, government agencies, corporations, and accounting firms conduct individual interviews.

The School of Law is a member of the National Association for Law Placement, the National Association for Public Interest Law Publication Network, and the Allegheny County Bar Association Minority Job Fair.

Graduates have consistently been placed at a rate at or above 90 percent within six months of graduation. The law school has nearly 5,000 alumni throughout the United States and in several foreign countries.

Applicant Profile

The law school recognizes the different strengths presented by our day division, evening division, and part-time day students and acknowledges that the diversity in the groups cannot be accurately or completely represented in a single grid of average and undergraduate GPA and LSAT scores. Graduate degrees, personal and professional accomplishments, and extensive employment experience predominate in the evening division, part-time, and day divisions.

These factors are considered crucial to an individual assessment of admissibility. Applications are reviewed individually, and factors such as leadership experience, community service, and other nonacademic experiences are considered. Applicants should contact the Admissions Office for specific information on the current year's class; phone: 412.396.6296. Applicants are encouraged to visit the law school.

Emory University School of Law

Gambrell Hall, 1301 Clifton Road
Atlanta, GA 30322-2770
Phone: 404.727.6802; Fax: 404.727.2477
E-mail: lawinfo@law.emory.edu; Website: www.law.emory.edu

*ABA
Approved
Since
1923*

The Basics

Type of school	Private
Term	Semester
Application deadline	3/1
Application fee	$70
Financial aid deadline	2/15
Can first year start other than fall?	No
Student to faculty ratio (fall)	14.2 to 1
Does the university offer:	
housing restricted to law students?	No
graduate housing for which law students are eligible?	Yes

Faculty and Administrators

	Total		Men		Women		Minorities	
	Fall	Spr	Fall	Spr	Fall	Spr	Fall	Spr
Full-time	40	41	28	27	12	14	4	5
Other Full-time	7	8	1	2	6	6	0	0
Deans, librarians, & others who teach	4	4	2	2	2	2	1	1
Part-time	21	21	15	17	6	4	3	0
Total	72	74	46	48	26	26	8	6

Curriculum

		Full-time	Part-time
Typical first-year section size		75	0
Is there typically a "small section" of the first-year class, other than Legal Writing, taught by full-time faculty		Yes	No
If yes, typical size offered last year		37	0
# of classroom course titles beyond 1st year curriculum		116	
# of upper division courses, excluding seminars with an enrollment:	Under 25	72	
	25-49	25	
	50-74	21	
	75-99	5	
	100+	1	
# of seminars		16	
# of seminar positions available		228	
# of seminar positions filled		199	0
# of positions available in simulation courses		492	
# of simulation positions filled		474	0
# of positions available in faculty supervised clinical courses		32	
# of faculty supervised clinical positions filled	7		0
# involved in field placements		176	0
# involved in law journals		135	0
# involved in moot court or trial competitions	102		0
# of credit hours required to graduate		90	

JD Enrollment and Ethnicity

	Men		Women		Full-time		Part-time		1st-year		Total		JD Degs. Awd.
	#	%	#	%	#	%	#	%	#	%	#	%	
African Amer.	16	4.8	43	12.3	59	8.6	0	0.0	21	9.7	59	8.6	20
Amer. Indian	0	0.0	0	0.0	0	0.0	0	0.0	0	0.0	0	0.0	0
Asian Amer.	29	8.6	28	8.0	57	8.3	0	0.0	23	10.6	57	8.3	15
Mex. Amer.	0	0.0	0	0.0	0	0.0	0	0.0	0	0.0	0	0.0	0
Puerto Rican	0	0.0	0	0.0	0	0.0	0	0.0	0	0.0	0	0.0	0
Hispanic	14	4.2	22	6.3	36	5.3	0	0.0	16	7.4	36	5.3	5
Total Minority	59	17.6	93	26.6	152	22.2	0	0.0	60	27.8	152	22.2	40
For. Nation.	7	2.1	10	2.9	17	2.5	0	0.0	8	3.7	17	2.5	2
Caucasian	263	78.3	242	69.3	505	73.7	0	0.0	141	65.3	505	73.7	174
Unknown	7	2.1	4	1.1	11	1.6	0	0.0	7	3.2	11	1.6	1
Total	336	49.1	349	50.9	685	100.0	0	0.0	216	31.5	685		217

Tuition and Fees

	Resident	Nonresident
Full-time	$32,772	$32,772
Part-time	$0	$0

Living Expenses

Estimated living expenses for singles

Living on campus	Living off campus	Living at home
$12,600	$12,600	$12,600

Emory University School of Law

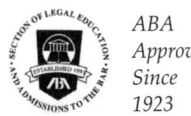

*ABA
Approved
Since
1923*

GPA and LSAT Scores

	Total	Full-time	Part-time
# of apps	3,852	3,852	0
# of admits	1,016	1,016	0
# of matrics	215	215	0
75% GPA	3.62	3.62	0.00
25% GPA	3.27	3.27	0.00
75% LSAT	165	165	0
25% LSAT	161	161	0

Grants and Scholarships (from prior year)

	Total		Full-time		Part-time	
	#	%	#	%	#	%
Total # of students	697		697		0	
Total # receiving grants	216	31.0	216	31.0	0	0.0
Less than 1/2 tuition	70	10.0	70	10.0	0	0.0
Half to full tuition	74	10.6	74	10.6	0	0.0
Full tuition	59	8.5	59	8.5	0	0.0
More than full tuition	13	1.9	13	1.9	0	0.0
Median grant amount			$19,739		$0	

Informational and Library Resources

# of volumes and volume equivalents	395,752
# of titles	143,477
# of active serial subscriptions	4,119
Study seating capacity inside the library	487
# of professional librarians	6
Hours per week library is open	113
# of open, wired connections available to students	241
# of networked computers available for use by students	78
# of simultaneous wireless users	0
Require computer?	N

JD Attrition (from prior year)

	Academic	Other	Total	
	#	#	#	%
1st year	0	4	4	1.8%
2nd year	0	11	11	4.3%
3rd year	0	1	1	0.5%
4th year	0	0	0	0.0%

Employment

	Total	Percentage
Employment status known	216	100.0
Employment status unknown	0	0.0
Employed	195	90.3
Pursuing graduate degrees	5	2.3
Unemployed seeking employment	10	4.6
Unemployed not seeking employment	6	2.8

Type of Employment

# employed in law firms	119	61.0
# employed in business and industry	15	7.7
# employed in government	28	14.4
# employed in public interest	2	1.0
# employed as judicial clerks	20	10.3
# employed in academia	2	1.0

Geographic Location

# employed in state	80	41.0
# employed in foreign countries	0	0.0
# of states where employed		28

Bar Passage Rates

Jurisdiction	Georgia		
Exam	Sum 03	Win 04	Total
# from school taking bar for the first time	102	9	111
School's pass rate for all first-time takers	94%	78%	93%
State's pass rate for all first-time takers	86%	75%	83%

Emory University School of Law

Gambrell Hall, 1301 Clifton Road
Atlanta, GA 30322-2770
Phone: 404.727.6802; Fax: 404.727.2477
E-mail: lawinfo@law.emory.edu; Website: www.law.emory.edu

■ Introduction

Emory's location in Atlanta, a national business and legal center, gives Emory law students the opportunity to take advanced classes from, and work with, some of the leading judges and lawyers in the United States. Atlanta also is one of America's most beautiful and most livable cities.

The law school also benefits from being located on the campus of Emory University, which was founded in 1836. Emory University School of Law is accredited by the American Bar Association, is a member of the Association of American Law Schools, and has a chapter of the Order of the Coif.

■ Library and Physical Facilities

The Emory School of Law is located in Gambrell Hall, a part of Emory's 630-acre campus in Druid Hills, six miles southeast of downtown Atlanta.

Gambrell Hall contains classrooms, faculty offices, administrative offices, student-organization offices, and a 320-seat auditorium. Gambrell Hall also houses a state-of-the-art courtroom with computer connections for judge, counsel, and jury; a document camera; DVD; videoconferencing; and four-camera operation with feeds to remote locations.

The Hugh F. McMillan Law Library sits adjacent to Gambrell Hall and is designed for easy student access. Students are trained on LexisNexis and Westlaw terminals and learn both the techniques of computer-assisted legal research and traditional research methods. Students also may use the library's computer labs that offer MacIntosh and IBM-compatible computers.

■ Curriculum

The basic program of study involves three years of full-time study leading to the JD degree. The fall semester runs from late August to mid-December; the spring semester begins in early January and ends in mid-May.

The program of courses for the first year is prescribed. The program of courses for the second and third years is primarily elective. Students can sample a broad spectrum of courses or concentrate on a particular area of law.

All first-year courses and the basic second- and third-year courses are taught by full-time faculty members. A distinguished group of judges and practicing attorneys offer specialized courses.

■ Special Programs

Emory offers a variety of unique special programs. It's Trial Techniques Program is consistently ranked among the best in the nation. Students are exposed to the challenges of conducting direct and cross-examination, developing a case theory and approach, and conducting opening and closing arguments. More than half of the students participate in Emory's field placement program, where students may earn academic credit doing things like clerking for a federal judge, researching intellectual property issues for corporations such as Coca-Cola and Delta Air Lines, and representing clients on behalf of Atlanta Legal Aid. Students also may gain practical experience in intellectual property and corporate/commercial law by participating in TI:GER (Technological Innovation: Generating Economic Results), a program of technology law and business law cosponsored by Emory's School of Law and Economics Department and Georgia Tech's Dupree School of Management. Students may participate in three of Emory's own clinics: the Barton Clinic, working to promote and protect the well-being of neglected and abused children; the Southern Juvenile Defender Center, providing real-world experiences in helping attorneys defend children accused of crimes; and the Turner Environmental Law Clinic, offering a practical clinical education to the aspiring environmental attorney. Emory offers a comprehensive international law program. Emory Law also capitalizes on the presence of other strong campus programs by combining coursework and programs to create unique, synergistic international programs of study. The law school offers joint-degree programs with Emory's School of Business Administration, School of Theology, School of Public Health, and the Graduate School of Arts and Sciences.

■ Admission

The law school accepts beginning students for the fall term only. Prior to enrollment, a student must have earned a bachelor's degree from an approved institution.

Applications for admission must be received by Emory no later than March 1. Early applications are encouraged.

Many factors are considered in making admission decisions. Of particular importance are academic accomplishments and LSAT scores. Extracurricular activities, work experience, level of quality and difficulty of undergraduate courses, performance in graduate school, and letters of recommendation also are considered. We encourage applications from members of under-represented groups, and such applicants should provide the Dean of Admission with specific information about their background or accomplishments that would be of particular interest.

Applicants are encouraged to visit the law school. Upon acceptance, applicants are required to submit a nonrefundable $750 tuition deposit to reserve a space in the entering class.

■ Student Activities

A wide variety of organizations and activities are available to students. There are three law reviews at Emory—*Emory Law Journal*, *Emory Bankruptcy Developments Journal*, and *Emory International Law Review*; more than 30 percent of the second- and third-year students are involved in law review research, writing, and editing. Candidates for the reviews are selected from second- and third-year classes by the student editorial boards on the basis of scholarship and writing ability.

Students also participate in moot court. Each first-year student prepares a brief and presents an oral argument. In addition, many second- and third-year students compete in intramural and national moot court competitions.

There are numerous special interest and social groups and a very active Student Bar Association.

■ Career Services

The law school regards career services as a matter of highest priority. A full-time career services office assists students in obtaining permanent, summer, and part-time employment. It arranges interviews with employers from many parts of the country and maintains extensive files on a wide variety of professional opportunities all over the United States. The great majority of Emory graduates join private law firms after graduation. Others work as judicial clerks, enter government service, or work for banks, corporations, or legal aid agencies. The career services office provides extensive training on résumés, interview skills, and job-search techniques, as well as numerous opportunities to network with attorneys in a variety of practice areas and settings.

Emory School of Law provides a full range of career planning and placement services. The class of 2003 reported approximately 95 percent full- and part-time employment within nine months after graduation in the following fields: 61 percent in the private sector, 14 percent in government, 10 percent in judicial clerkships, and 15 percent in business and industry, public interest, academic, and other fields. The majority of Emory's students stay in the Southeast. Approximately 21 percent work in the Northeast and Mid-Atlantic. Smaller percentages work in the Midwest, Southwest, and West. The class of 2003 found employment in 28 states and the District of Columbia.

Applicant Profile

Emory University School of Law

LSAT Score	GPA								
	3.75 +	3.50 - 3.74	3.25 - 3.49	3.00 - 3.24	2.75 - 2.99	2.50 - 2.74	2.25 - 2.49	2.00 - 2.24	Below 2.00
175-180									
170-174									
165-169									
160-164									
155-159									
150-154									
145-149									
140-144									
135-139									
130-134									
125-129									
120-124									

■ Good Possibility   □ Possible   ▨ Unlikely

Note: This graph reflects admission decisions as of 6/1/04 and is to be used as a general guide to determining chances for admittance. It does not reflect actual decisions but should serve as a guideline.

University of Florida, Fredric G. Levin College of Law

PO Box 117635, 141 BGH
Gainesville, FL 32611-7635
Phone: 352.392.2087, Toll-free: 877.429.1297; Fax: 352.392.4087
E-mail: admissions@law.ufl.edu; Website: www.law.ufl.edu

*ABA
Approved
Since
1925*

The Basics

Type of school	Public
Term	Semester
Application deadline	1/15
Application fee	$30
Financial aid deadline	3/15
Can first year start other than fall?	Yes
Student to faculty ratio (fall)	15.9 to 1
Does the university offer:	
housing restricted to law students?	No
graduate housing for which law students are eligible?	Yes

Faculty and Administrators

	Total		Men		Women		Minorities	
	Fall	Spr	Fall	Spr	Fall	Spr	Fall	Spr
Full-time	60	66	32	33	28	33	8	7
Other Full-time	7	7	3	3	4	4	0	0
Deans, librarians, & others who teach	10	10	8	8	2	2	0	0
Part-time	34	35	27	28	7	7	5	3
Total	111	118	70	72	41	46	13	10

Curriculum

		Full-time	Part-time
Typical first-year section size		100	0
Is there typically a "small section" of the first-year class, other than Legal Writing, taught by full-time faculty		No	No
If yes, typical size offered last year		0	0
# of classroom course titles beyond 1st year curriculum		128	
# of upper division	Under 25	48	
courses, excluding	25-49	52	
seminars with	50-74	73	
an enrollment:	75-99	32	
	100+	4	
# of seminars		42	
# of seminar positions available		630	
# of seminar positions filled		630	0
# of positions available in simulation courses		468	
# of simulation positions filled		458	0
# of positions available in faculty supervised clinical courses		126	
# of faculty supervised clinical positions filled	122		0
# involved in field placements		213	0
# involved in law journals		186	0
# involved in moot court or trial competitions	152		0
# of credit hours required to graduate		88	

JD Enrollment and Ethnicity

	Men		Women		Full-time		Part-time		1st-year		Total		JD Degs. Awd.
	#	%	#	%	#	%	#	%	#	%	#	%	
African Amer.	30	5.0	56	10.2	86	7.5	0	0.0	27	7.9	86	7.5	40
Amer. Indian	1	0.2	3	0.5	4	0.3	0	0.0	2	0.6	4	0.3	3
Asian Amer.	25	4.1	36	6.5	61	5.3	0	0.0	19	5.6	61	5.3	16
Mex. Amer.	0	0.0	0	0.0	0	0.0	0	0.0	0	0.0	0	0.0	0
Puerto Rican	0	0.0	0	0.0	0	0.0	0	0.0	0	0.0	0	0.0	0
Hispanic	62	10.3	50	9.1	112	9.7	0	0.0	33	9.7	112	9.7	48
Total Minority	118	19.6	145	26.4	263	22.8	0	0.0	81	23.8	263	22.8	107
For. Nation.	3	0.5	0	0.0	3	0.3	0	0.0	0	0.0	3	0.3	0
Caucasian	462	76.6	381	69.3	843	73.1	0	0.0	255	74.8	843	73.1	294
Unknown	20	3.3	24	4.4	44	3.8	0	0.0	5	1.5	44	3.8	7
Total	603	52.3	550	47.7	1153	100.0	0	0.0	341	29.6	1153		408

Tuition and Fees

	Resident	Nonresident
Full-time	$7,168	$26,475
Part-time	$0	$0

Living Expenses

Estimated living expenses for singles

Living on campus	Living off campus	Living at home
$11,300	$11,560	$5,960

*As of 2006, the law school's spring admissions will cease. Toward that end, 200 students will be enrolled for both fall 2004 and spring 2005. For fall 2005, 200 students will be enrolled; spring 2006, 100 enrolled from fall 2005 pool. For fall 2006, 400 enrolled.

University of Florida, Fredric G. Levin College of Law

*ABA
Approved
Since
1925*

GPA and LSAT Scores

	Total	Full-time	Part-time
# of apps	3,729	3,729	0
# of admits	813	813	0
# of matrics	418	418	0
75% GPA	3.81	3.81	0.00
25% GPA	3.35	3.35	0.00
75% LSAT	161	161	0
25% LSAT	155	155	0

Grants and Scholarships (from prior year)

	Total		Full-time		Part-time	
	#	%	#	%	#	%
Total # of students	1,139		1,139		0	
Total # receiving grants	251	22.0	251	22.0	0	0.0
Less than 1/2 tuition	112	9.8	112	9.8	0	0.0
Half to full tuition	110	9.7	110	9.7	0	0.0
Full tuition	19	1.7	19	1.7	0	0.0
More than full tuition	10	0.9	10	0.9	0	0.0
Median grant amount			$2,500		$0	

Informational and Library Resources

# of volumes and volume equivalents	608,612
# of titles	179,714
# of active serial subscriptions	7,669
Study seating capacity inside the library	215
# of professional librarians	10
Hours per week library is open	99
# of open, wired connections available to students	75
# of networked computers available for use by students	39
# of simultaneous wireless users	300
Require computer?	Y

JD Attrition (from prior year)

	Academic	Other	Total	
	#	#	#	%
1st year	0	14	14	3.7%
2nd year	0	0	0	0.0%
3rd year	0	0	0	0.0%
4th year	0	0	0	0.0%

Employment

	Total	Percentage
Employment status known	432	99.8
Employment status unknown	1	0.2
Employed	382	88.4
Pursuing graduate degrees	26	6.0
Unemployed seeking employment	17	3.9
Unemployed not seeking employment	7	1.6

Type of Employment

	Total	Percentage
# employed in law firms	213	55.8
# employed in business and industry	26	6.8
# employed in government	85	22.3
# employed in public interest	6	1.6
# employed as judicial clerks	18	4.7
# employed in academia	6	1.6

Geographic Location

	Total	Percentage
# employed in state	303	79.3
# employed in foreign countries	1	0.3
# of states where employed	19	

Bar Passage Rates

Jurisdiction	Florida		
Exam	Sum 03	Win 04	Total
# from school taking bar for the first time	289	224	513
School's pass rate for all first-time takers	76%	81%	79%
State's pass rate for all first-time takers	76%	75%	76%

University of Florida, Fredric G. Levin College of Law

Assistant Dean for Admissions, PO Box 117635, 141 BGH
Gainesville, FL 32611-7635
Phone: 352.392.2087, Toll-free: 877.429.1297; Fax: 352.392.4087
E-mail: admissions@law.ufl.edu; Website: www.law.ufl.edu

■ Introduction

The University of Florida Levin College of Law was founded in 1909, has been a member of the AALS since 1920, and was approved by the ABA in 1925. It offers a three-year post-baccalaureate curriculum leading to the JD, close to 30 joint-degree programs, post-JD programs for Master of Laws and Doctor of Laws in Taxation, and Master of Laws in Comparative Law for foreign lawyers.

The college's faculty and alumni are recognized at national and international levels, and its student body is consistently among the nation's finest. It is known for graduating state and national legal, political, business, government, and educational leaders. UF law graduates include 4 of the last 30 ABA presidents, numerous federal and state judges, partners in major national and international law firms, members of Congress and the Cabinet, governors, and state legislators.

Alumni support has built the endowment into the sixth largest in the country for public law schools. This, combined with the state's financial assistance, allows the College of Law to remain affordable while its academic quality rivals many of the best-known private colleges.

The University of Florida is a member of the prestigious Association of American Universities and is recognized as one of the nation's leading research universities by the Carnegie Commission on Higher Education. UF occupies 2,000 acres, mostly within Gainesville's 111,228 population urban area. The area is consistently ranked among the best places to live in America, with extensive educational, cultural, and recreational offerings.

■ Programs and Curriculum

The College of Law offers students personalized courses of study and innovative interdisciplinary programs not available at other institutions. The diverse activities and scholarship of approximately 100 full-time and many adjunct/visiting faculty allow for interesting programs and curricular concentrations. More than 100 courses and 30 seminars are offered, including traditional courses on law and legal analysis, skills training, international law, and seminars on contemporary legal issues. Semesters start in August and January, and the summer term begins in May. Students are required to complete the first-year curriculum in sequence. All students must complete a major senior-year research and writing project.

Students may specialize and earn a certificate in Estates and Trusts Practice, Intellectual Property Law, Environmental and Land Use Law, Family Law, or International and Comparative Law. The Levin College of Law also offers one of the most extensive joint-degree programs of any US law school. Among the more popular joint-degree tracks are Business Administration, Public Health, Accounting, and Health Administration.

■ Special Programs

The college's nationally acclaimed Graduate Tax Program leads to LLM and SJD degrees in Taxation, and a LLM in International Tax is under development. The college's innovative centers and institutes include the Center for Estate and Elder Law Planning, Center for Children and Families, Institute for Dispute Resolution, Center for the Study of Race and Race Relations, and Center for Governmental Responsibility.

UF is a major hub for international legal programs and has decades of experience and relationships in Latin America, Asia, and Europe. Students can take advantage of a number of study abroad opportunities. Externships, pro bono, and clinical programs provide students with hands-on experience in litigation, negotiation, mediation, client relations, and government service at the highest levels—including the Florida Supreme Court and US president-appointed posts.

■ Student/Extracurricular Activities

Student activities include *Florida Law Review, Florida Journal of International Law, Florida Journal of Law and Public Policy, Florida Tax Review,* and nationally honored US and international moot courts and trial teams. More than 35 extracurricular organizations provide additional opportunities for student involvement.

■ Library and Facilities

Following completion of a major expansion and renovation project in summer 2005, the Lawton Chiles Legal Information Center (LIC) will be one of the largest academic law libraries in the Southeast and among the top 20 in the nation in terms of space. The expanded LIC will offer additional study areas, reading rooms, computer training labs, multimedia workstations, and conference rooms for use by students and faculty. Two new three-story classroom towers were completed in fall 2004 and feature spacious, state-of-the-art teaching and study space, desktop outlets for laptop use, wireless Internet access, and "smart podia."

■ Career Services

The college's Center for Career Services assists students in finding summer internships/externships or clerkships and permanent postgraduation employment. More than 200 employers recruit on-campus each year. The college's recent employment rate at graduation matched or exceeded other top law schools.

University of Florida, Fredric G. Levin College of Law

■ Admission

Students must have earned a bachelor's degree from an accredited college or university and apply for fall 2006 by January 15 (rolling admission, early application preferred). LSAT and LSDAS are required. Only full-time students are enrolled.

Applicants must provide a personal statement and résumé, and up to four evaluation letters are accepted. Early completion of applications is strongly recommended (but not more than one year in advance). Applicants must take the LSAT prior to application deadline (December). To arrange a meeting or tour the law school, contact the Admissions Office.

Students may transfer in August, January, or May from ABA-approved law schools, but only applicants who have completed the required first-year full-time curriculum before enrolling at UF and who are in the upper one-third of their class will be considered. A letter of good standing from the dean is required and no more than 29 semester hours will be transferred.

The admission staff and the faculty admission committee base their selection on the applicant's academic credentials, including LSAT score, UGPA, level of writing skills, breadth of studies, and on other criteria including but not limited to the applicant's work and other life experience, leadership experience, depth of particular interest, and any other aspect of an applicant's background suggesting a suitability for the study and practice of law.

■ Expenses and Financial Aid

The 2004–2005 semester credit-hour fees were $256 for Florida residents and $946 for nonresidents. Additional expenses are around $10,800 for room, board, and books. Merit-/need-based scholarships and grants are available, and FAFSA is **required**. The college provides short and long-term loans to qualified students.

To qualify for merit-/need-based scholarships, an applicant must show high achievement, return the Application for Need-Based Scholarships and Need-Based Grants after they have received their acceptance letter, and have the electronic FAFSA results on file with the Levin College of Law by March 15 for fall entrants and July 1 for spring entrants. If needed the application can be downloaded online, but is sent out by the admission office following acceptance.

The college actively recruits minority students. Address inquiries to: Office of Admissions, University of Florida Levin College of Law, PO Box 117622, Gainesville, FL 32611-7622, *admissions@law.ufl.edu*.

■ Housing

Housing is available for single students in dormitories and for families in university apartments. Off-campus housing is available. New and current UF law students also may access the UF College of Law Roommate Referral System online.

Applicant Profile

University of Florida, Fredric G. Levin College of Law
This grid includes only applicants who earned 120-180 LSAT scores under standard administrations. Data reflects 99% of the fall candidate pool. See prior two pages of ABA data for credentials of the spring candidate pool.

LSAT Score	3.75 +		3.50 - 3.74		3.25 - 3.49		3.00 - 3.24		2.75 - 2.99		2.50 - 2.74		2.25 - 2.49		2.00 - 2.24		Below 2.00		No GPA		Total	
	Apps	Adm	Apps	Adm	Apps	Adm	Apps	Adm	Apps	Adm	Apps	Adm	Apps	Adm	Apps	Adm	Apps	Adm	Apps	Adm	Apps	Adm
175-180	1	1	0	0	1	1	1	1	0	0	0	0	0	0	0	0	0	0	0	0	3	3
170-174	9	9	4	3	8	8	7	7	2	2	0	0	0	0	0	0	0	0	0	0	30	29
165-169	42	40	33	30	36	26	27	14	13	4	4	2	3	0	0	0	1	0	1	1	160	117
160-164	113	95	116	60	118	32	74	18	44	3	17	4	5	0	0	0	0	0	4	2	491	214
155-159	153	48	214	32	243	19	164	11	82	2	29	0	16	0	3	1	0	0	7	0	911	113
150-154	121	28	196	10	214	9	147	8	122	4	40	0	12	1	6	0	4	1	8	2	870	63
145-149	39	2	88	4	118	4	96	5	54	1	43	0	14	1	6	0	2	0	8	1	468	18
140-144	6	0	30	5	34	1	54	0	31	0	16	0	11	0	4	0	0	0	8	1	194	7
135-139	1	0	8	0	18	0	20	0	6	0	8	0	8	0	2	0	1	0	2	0	74	0
130-134	0	0	0	0	3	0	5	0	3	0	3	0	3	0	2	0	0	0	2	0	21	0
125-129	0	0	0	0	0	0	1	0	1	0	1	0	1	0	1	0	0	0	1	0	6	0
120-124	0	0	0	0	0	0	0	0	0	0	0	0	0	0	0	0	0	0	0	0	0	0
Total	485	223	689	144	793	100	596	64	358	16	161	6	73	2	24	1	8	1	41	7	3228	564

Apps = Number of Applicants   Adm = Number Admitted

Florida Agricultural and Mechanical University, College of Law

PO Box 3113
Orlando, FL 32802-3113
Phone: 407.254.3268; Fax: 407.254.3213
E-mail: famulaw.admissions@famu.edu; Website: www.famu.edu/law

Provisional

ABA
Approved
Since
2004

The Basics

Type of school	Public
Term	Semester
Application deadline	5/1
Application fee	$20
Financial aid deadline	4/1
Can first year start other than fall?	No
Student to faculty ratio (fall)	13.5 to 1
Does the university offer:	
housing restricted to law students?	No
graduate housing for which law students are eligible?	No

Faculty and Administrators

	Total		Men		Women		Minorities	
	Fall	Spr	Fall	Spr	Fall	Spr	Fall	Spr
Full-time	16	16	9	9	7	7	12	12
Other Full-time	4	4	2	2	2	2	2	2
Deans, librarians, & others who teach	3	3	2	2	1	1	3	3
Part-time	0	0	0	0	0	0	0	0
Total	23	23	13	13	10	10	17	17

Curriculum

	Full-time	Part-time
Typical first-year section size	35	35
Is there typically a "small section" of the first-year class, other than Legal Writing, taught by full-time faculty	No	No
If yes, typical size offered last year	0	0
# of classroom course titles beyond 1st year curriculum	29	
# of upper division courses, excluding seminars with an enrollment: Under 25	17	
25-49	6	
50-74	5	
75-99	0	
100+	0	
# of seminars	7	
# of seminar positions available	126	
# of seminar positions filled	81	4
# of positions available in simulation courses	138	
# of simulation positions filled	98	38
# of positions available in faculty supervised clinical courses	0	
# of faculty supervised clinical positions filled	0	0
# involved in field placements	0	0
# involved in law journals	0	0
# involved in moot court or trial competitions	0	0
# of credit hours required to graduate	90	

JD Enrollment and Ethnicity

	Men		Women		Full-time		Part-time		1st-year		Total		JD Degs. Awd.
	#	%	#	%	#	%	#	%	#	%	#	%	
African Amer.	37	32.2	72	41.4	90	44.3	19	22.1	42	36.8	109	37.7	0
Amer. Indian	0	0.0	2	1.1	1	0.5	1	1.2	1	0.9	2	0.7	0
Asian Amer.	3	2.6	3	1.7	3	1.5	3	3.5	2	1.8	6	2.1	0
Mex. Amer.	0	0.0	0	0.0	0	0.0	0	0.0	0	0.0	0	0.0	0
Puerto Rican	0	0.0	0	0.0	0	0.0	0	0.0	0	0.0	0	0.0	0
Hispanic	18	15.7	19	10.9	26	12.8	11	12.8	18	15.8	37	12.8	0
Total Minority	58	50.4	96	55.2	120	59.1	34	39.5	63	55.3	154	53.3	0
For. Nation.	0	0.0	0	0.0	0	0.0	0	0.0	0	0.0	0	0.0	0
Caucasian	52	45.2	77	44.3	79	38.9	50	58.1	51	44.7	129	44.6	0
Unknown	5	4.3	1	0.6	4	2.0	2	2.3	0	0.0	6	2.1	0
Total	115	39.8	174	60.2	203	70.2	86	29.8	114	39.4	289		

Tuition and Fees

	Resident	Nonresident
Full-time	$7,274	$26,696
Part-time	$5,365	$19,608

Living Expenses

Estimated living expenses for singles

Living on campus	Living off campus	Living at home
N/A	$14,974	$7,630

Florida Agricultural and Mechanical University, College of Law

ABA Approved Since 2004

GPA and LSAT Scores

	Total	Full-time	Part-time
# of apps	597	407	190
# of admits	194	143	51
# of matrics	120	87	33
75% GPA	3.36	3.33	3.37
25% GPA	2.74	2.77	2.67
75% LSAT	151	150	151
25% LSAT	143	143	146

Grants and Scholarships (from prior year)

	Total		Full-time		Part-time	
	#	%	#	%	#	%
Total # of students	192		131		61	
Total # receiving grants	27	14.1	20	15.3	7	11.5
Less than 1/2 tuition	27	14.1	20	15.3	7	11.5
Half to full tuition	0	0.0	0	0.0	0	0.0
Full tuition	0	0.0	0	0.0	0	0.0
More than full tuition	0	0.0	0	0.0	0	0.0
Median grant amount			$0		$0	

Informational and Library Resources

# of volumes and volume equivalents	290,520
# of titles	9,591
# of active serial subscriptions	584
Study seating capacity inside the library	174
# of professional librarians	6
Hours per week library is open	100
# of open, wired connections available to students	0
# of networked computers available for use by students	87
# of simultaneous wireless users	250
Require computer?	N

JD Attrition (from prior year)

	Academic	Other	Total	
	#	#	#	%
1st year	2	15	17	15.0%
2nd year	1	0	1	1.3%
3rd year	0	0	0	0.0%
4th year	0	0	0	0.0%

Employment

	Total	Percentage
Employment status known	0	0.0
Employment status unknown	0	0.0
Employed	0	0.0
Pursuing graduate degrees	0	0.0
Unemployed seeking employment	0	0.0
Unemployed not seeking employment	0	0.0

Type of Employment

# employed in law firms	0	0.0
# employed in business and industry	0	0.0
# employed in government	0	0.0
# employed in public interest	0	0.0
# employed as judicial clerks	0	0.0
# employed in academia	0	0.0

Geographic Location

# employed in state	0	0.0
# employed in foreign countries	0	0.0
# of states where employed	0	

Bar Passage Rates

Jurisdiction

Exam	Sum 03	Win 04	Total
# from school taking bar for the first time	0	0	0
School's pass rate for all first-time takers			
State's pass rate for all first-time takers			

The information on these pages was provided by the law school

Florida Agricultural and Mechanical University, College of Law

PO Box 3113
Orlando, FL 32802-3113
Phone: 407.254.3268; Fax: 407.254.3213
E-mail: famulaw.admissions@famu.edu; Website: www.famu.edu/law

■ Introduction

Established in 1887, Florida A&M University is a comprehensive, public, coeducational, and fully accredited land-grant university offering a broad range of instruction, research, and service programs at the undergraduate, graduate, and professional levels. The main campus occupies over 419 acres located in the capital city of Tallahassee. The College of Law's rich tradition of excellence dates back to its original founding in 1949. From 1949 to 1968, the College of Law graduated 57 students. In 2002, the FAMU College of Law reopened in downtown Orlando, Florida.

■ Location and Physical Facilities

Considered one of the fastest growing metropolitan areas in Florida and the nation, the city of Orlando is a racially and culturally diverse community ideal for a progressive law school. Located in downtown Orlando, the College of Law is within walking distance to the courts, county library, government buildings, and a wide variety of cultural, educational, and recreational opportunities. The 10-story building temporarily housing the law school includes the law library, classrooms, administrative offices, and faculty offices. The permanent campus, which is scheduled to open in the fall of 2005, will be a new state-of-the-art, four-story, 112,000-square-foot building conveniently located accessible from Interstate 4. The facility will house a law library, classrooms, faculty and administrative offices, and an area dealing with student affairs, including admission, financial aid, the registrar, alumni affairs, and career planning and placement. The new facility will also house a moot courtroom, space for student organizations and meetings, and space allocated for students to participate in the hands-on clinical program.

■ Enrollment and Student Body

Since opening in the fall of 2002, the Florida A&M University College of Law has admitted three entering classes and has a current student enrollment of 293 students. The student body is composed of 204 full-time day students and 89 part-time evening students. With 60 percent women and 53 percent minority students, the FAMU College of Law is one of the most diverse law schools in the state of Florida. The College of Law is committed to helping its students further develop their talents, professional skills, and goals. To that end, we offer cocurricular and extracurricular activities, including the Academic Success Program and the Law in America lecture series. These programs enhance not only the study of the law, but students' leadership and

professional abilities, and oral and written communication skills. FAMU College of Law students are very active within the law school and in the Central Florida community. As students at a recently reestablished law school, they have taken on the challenge of establishing organizations that will serve current and future students for years to come. The FAMU College of Law Student Bar Association supports and governs all student activities and organizations at the College of Law. In three short years, students have founded the following student organizations: the Jesse J. McCrary Jr. Chapter of the National Black Law Students Association; the Association of Trial Lawyers of America; the Women's Law Caucus; the Entertainment, Arts, & Sports Law Society; and the Hispanic Law Students Association. Over the next several years, the law school will continue to support students in their efforts to establish additional organizations and interest groups.

■ Programs of Study

The FAMU College of Law offers both a full-time day program and a part-time evening program of study. Full-time day program students must successfully complete six semesters or three academic years for their degree requirements. Enrollment in the day program represents a commitment to the full-time study of law. Part-time evening program students must successfully complete their degree requirements in four years, consisting of eight semesters and three summers. Part-time evening classes meet Monday, Tuesday, and Thursday evenings from 6:30 to 10:00 pm. The part-time evening program is designed for particularly well-qualified and dedicated students who are unable to attend on a full-time basis and want to earn a law degree while working full-time. Courses in both programs demand the same standards of performance by students and are taught by full-time faculty members who are assisted by adjunct faculty.

■ Curriculum

The law school offers a rigorous traditional curriculum of required and elective courses that are complemented by extensive skills training which includes an intensive three-year writing program and a strong clinical program. The College of Law's curriculum is designed to provide students with both the intellectual and practical skills necessary to meet the demands of the modern practice of law by combining theoretical coursework with clinical and practical experiences. Through the use of elective courses and leading practitioners as adjunct faculty, students are introduced to emerging trends and developments in the law.

Florida Agricultural and Mechanical University, College of Law

■ Expenses and Financial Aid

Tuition rates and fees are set annually by the Florida Legislature and the Florida A&M University Board of Trustees and may be changed at any time without advance notice. For the 2004–2005 academic year, tuition for law students is $238.60 per credit hour for Florida residents and $886 per credit hour for non-Florida residents. In addition, Florida A&M University imposes additional fees on all graduate and professional students. Approximately 90 percent of law students are receiving some form of financial aid, including federal loans, law loans, need-based stipends, and merit-based scholarships. Need-based stipends and merit-based scholarships are awarded to a select number of entering full-time and part-time students who have excelled academically and who possess other outstanding qualifications for the study of law. All admitted students are automatically considered for these awards. Scholarships are not automatically renewable and may vary in the amount awarded. The average scholarship award in 2004–2005 was $1,500.

■ Admission

Admission to the College of Law is highly competitive. The law school seeks diligent, hardworking students with a broad array of talents and experiences who demonstrate both an exceptional aptitude for the study of law and a strong history of, or commitment to, public service. Selection for admission is based on a thorough evaluation of all factors in an applicant's file. While an applicant's academic record and LSAT performance are weighted heavily in the evaluative process, the Admissions Committee considers other factors, including writing ability as evidenced by the LSAT writing sample and the personal statement; community and public service; academic honors and awards; work experience; leadership ability; extracurricular activities; letters of recommendation; and character and motivation. The standards for admission in the full-time day and part-time evening programs are not the same. Greater demands of work and study for evening students necessitate a different emphasis on admission criteria than in the day program. While the entire application file is reviewed, the evening program admission standards place a greater emphasis on the objective indicators of LSAT scores and undergraduate grade-point average than the day program.

Advanced Standing—the College of Law admits students for first-year status only. Current law students from other ABA-approved law schools seeking admission to the College of Law will be considered for first-year status only. In addition, graduates of foreign law schools will also be considered for first-year status only. The College of Law does not accept transferred credits to our program.

Applicant Profile

FAMU College of Law does not provide a profile chart because while an applicant's undergraduate record and LSAT are important, they are not the sole determinants for admission to law school. No index or cut-off is used in reviewing applications. There are no combination of grades or scores that assure admission or denial.

An applicant's transcripts are analyzed for breadth and depth of coursework, trend in grades, and rank; the competitiveness of the school and major are taken into consideration, as are special honors, awards, and activities. Other aspects of the application significantly influence the decision such as work experience and evidence of a commitment or interest in public service.

In making its decision, the committee aims to enroll an entering class of students with the strongest combination of qualifications and the greatest potential to contribute to FAMU College of Law and to the legal profession.

Florida Coastal School of Law

7555 Beach Boulevard
Jacksonville, FL 32216
Phone: 877.210.2591 (toll free) or 904.680.7700; Fax: 904.680.7777
E-mail: admissions@fcsl.edu; Website: www.fcsl.edu

ABA Approved Since 2002

The Basics

Type of school	Private
Term	Semester
Application deadline	7/31
Application fee	$50
Financial aid deadline	
Can first year start other than fall?	Yes
Student to faculty ratio (fall)	18.9 to 1
Does the university offer:	
housing restricted to law students?	No
graduate housing for which law students are eligible?	No

Faculty and Administrators

	Total		Men		Women		Minorities	
	Fall	Spr	Fall	Spr	Fall	Spr	Fall	Spr
Full-time	36	36	15	15	21	21	5	5
Other Full-time	0	0	0	0	0	0	0	0
Deans, librarians, & others who teach	4	4	3	3	1	1	1	1
Part-time	29	43	17	28	12	15	2	2
Total	69	83	35	46	34	37	8	8

Curriculum

	Full-time	Part-time
Typical first-year section size	78	76
Is there typically a "small section" of the first-year class, other than Legal Writing, taught by full-time faculty	No	No
If yes, typical size offered last year	0	0
# of classroom course titles beyond 1st year curriculum	92	
# of upper division courses, excluding seminars with an enrollment: Under 25	46	
25-49	31	
50-74	12	
75-99	3	
100+	0	
# of seminars	8	
# of seminar positions available	92	
# of seminar positions filled	65	27
# of positions available in simulation courses	265	
# of simulation positions filled	186	79
# of positions available in faculty supervised clinical courses	111	
# of faculty supervised clinical positions filled	82	29
# involved in field placements	8	3
# involved in law journals	28	11
# involved in moot court or trial competitions	38	15
# of credit hours required to graduate	87	

JD Enrollment and Ethnicity

	Men #	Men %	Women #	Women %	Full-time #	Full-time %	Part-time #	Part-time %	1st-year #	1st-year %	Total #	Total %	JD Degs. Awd.
African Amer.	29	6.0	48	11.4	40	6.2	37	14.4	40	8.1	77	8.5	13
Amer. Indian	5	1.0	7	1.7	10	1.5	2	0.8	6	1.2	12	1.3	0
Asian Amer.	8	1.7	8	1.9	11	1.7	5	1.9	6	1.2	16	1.8	10
Mex. Amer.	0	0.0	2	0.5	2	0.3	0	0.0	1	0.2	2	0.2	2
Puerto Rican	2	0.4	0	0.0	1	0.2	1	0.4	1	0.2	2	0.2	1
Hispanic	8	1.7	20	4.8	22	3.4	6	2.3	19	3.8	28	3.1	4
Total Minority	52	10.7	85	20.2	86	13.3	51	19.8	73	14.8	137	15.2	30
For. Nation.	7	1.4	5	1.2	12	1.9	0	0.0	10	2.0	12	1.3	0
Caucasian	283	58.5	241	57.4	381	58.9	143	55.6	284	57.5	524	58.0	81
Unknown	142	29.3	89	21.2	168	26.0	63	24.5	127	25.7	231	25.6	44
Total	484	53.5	420	46.5	647	71.6	257	28.4	494	54.6	904		155

Tuition and Fees

	Resident	Nonresident
Full-time	$23,410	$23,410
Part-time	$18,920	$18,920

Living Expenses

Estimated living expenses for singles

Living on campus	Living off campus	Living at home
N/A	$16,580	$16,580

Florida Coastal School of Law

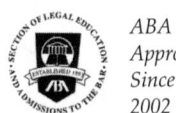

*ABA
Approved
Since
2002*

GPA and LSAT Scores

	Total	Full-time	Part-time
# of apps	5,536	5,186	350
# of admits	1,973	1,722	251
# of matrics	433	347	86
75% GPA	3.36	3.38	3.32
25% GPA	2.73	2.71	2.85
75% LSAT	153	153	152
25% LSAT	149	149	147

Grants and Scholarships (from prior year)

	Total		Full-time		Part-time	
	#	%	#	%	#	%
Total # of students	685		411		274	
Total # receiving grants	307	44.8	242	58.9	65	23.7
Less than 1/2 tuition	301	43.9	241	58.6	60	21.9
Half to full tuition	6	0.9	1	0.2	5	1.8
Full tuition	0	0.0	0	0.0	0	0.0
More than full tuition	0	0.0	0	0.0	0	0.0
Median grant amount			$5,000		$4,000	

Informational and Library Resources

# of volumes and volume equivalents	216,901
# of titles	102,097
# of active serial subscriptions	3,139
Study seating capacity inside the library	426
# of professional librarians	5
Hours per week library is open	91
# of open, wired connections available to students	151
# of networked computers available for use by students	83
# of simultaneous wireless users	500
Require computer?	N

JD Attrition (from prior year)

	Academic	Other	Total	
	#	#	#	%
1st year	23	39	62	14.7%
2nd year	5	4	9	8.6%
3rd year	0	0	0	0.0%
4th year	0	0	0	0.0%

Employment

	Total	Percentage
Employment status known	125	100.0
Employment status unknown	0	0.0
Employed	117	93.6
Pursuing graduate degrees	1	0.8
Unemployed seeking employment	5	4.0
Unemployed not seeking employment	2	1.6

Type of Employment

# employed in law firms	63	53.8
# employed in business and industry	25	21.4
# employed in government	22	18.8
# employed in public interest	4	3.4
# employed as judicial clerks	2	1.7
# employed in academia	1	0.9

Geographic Location

# employed in state	95	81.2
# employed in foreign countries	0	0.0
# of states where employed	14	

Bar Passage Rates

Jurisdiction	Florida		
Exam	Sum 03	Win 04	Total
# from school taking bar for the first time	62	48	110
School's pass rate for all first-time takers	76%	79%	77%
State's pass rate for all first-time takers	76%	75%	76%

Florida Coastal School of Law

7555 Beach Boulevard
Jacksonville, FL 32216
Phone: 877.210.2591 (toll free) or 904.680.7700; Fax: 904.680.7777
E-mail: admissions@fcsl.edu; Website: www.fcsl.edu

■ Introduction

Florida Coastal School of Law (FCSL) was founded upon and is dedicated to the proposition that your future is our first and foremost priority. The student-centered ethos that defines and permeates our institution responds to the reality that today's law school graduates confront a world of unprecedented challenge and change. Professional success in the twenty-first century hinges not only upon academic achievement, but also upon accelerated development of practical skills and effective appreciation of the imperatives of technology, globalization, and multiculturalism.

Until recently, law school graduates could enter the legal profession with the luxury of growing and polishing practical skills during their early years of practice. Today's market realities, however, demand immediate productivity and performance. Knowing that traditional indicators of and grounds for academic excellence no longer accurately predict professional success, we offer a learning partnership that aims to develop the broad spectrum competencies you must have to succeed.

At the core of our program is a course of study designed to help you effectively reach your career goals after graduation. Formal instruction is delivered by a faculty composed of individuals with records of professional achievement and a sincere interest in sharing their expertise with you. Consistent with the reality that today's law students require more attention to, support for, and facilitation of their interests, faculty responsibilities do not end with the traditional functions of classroom instruction and scholarship. Each faculty member has mentoring responsibilities that include seeking out opportunities for personal interaction and impact.

At Florida Coastal School of Law, student-centeredness is not empty rhetoric. It is at the core of our philosophy, the basis for our founding, and the predicate for our program, policies, and daily interactions.

We invite you to visit our campus and speak with any member of the law school community, particularly our students, and learn firsthand about the nature of our commitment to your future.

■ Our Students

Student-centeredness, multiculturalism as a norm, and a partnered learning experience that effectively prepares you to meet the challenges of an increasingly competitive world are the cornerstones of your educational experience here. Teaching, mentoring, networking, and getting to know you personally and professionally are responsibilities we take seriously. Multiculturalism as a norm means that diversity is not just our future, it is now. Par-ticularly against the backdrop of modern societal and global realities, multicultural functionality cannot be a mere aspiration. Effective interaction with and appreciation of diverse experiences and lives are essential prerequisites for high achievement both personally and professionally.

■ FCSL's Learning Partnership

A learning partnership means working closely inside and outside the classroom with faculty members who are committed to sharing their expertise, experience, and networks; are eager to learn from your life experience; and aim to develop synergies on the basis of shared opportunity and mutual respect. These qualities are among those that have distinguished FCSL as a law school that takes your aspirations seriously. We believe that our supportive learning environment makes a difference in your educational experience, personal growth, and professional functioning. Our students, more than anyone, can attest to the fact that our words and promises are not empty rhetoric. We urge you not to take our representations at face value, but to call or visit us, meet with our students, and learn firsthand of their experience and enthusiasm.

■ Faculty

The faculty includes not only outstanding legal scholars, but also former judges, trial attorneys, government officials, and corporate leaders who interact with students on a daily basis and bring a practical perspective to the learning process. The vast majority of the faculty at FCSL have at least a decade of practical experience in their respective fields of expertise. We consider this an essential factor in developing well-rounded graduates capable of meeting the challenges of the twenty-first century.

■ Curriculum

The Infusion Curriculum is a program that brings professional responsibility, ethics, values, skills training, multiculturalism, and internationalism into all first-year and some advanced courses as a part of the pedagogical process. Through the use of role-playing, simulations, special problems, and multidiscipline presentations, students directly experience the lawyering process, observe the interaction of law with other disciplines, and acquire an appreciation for the relationship of law to the client, the court, and the community.

■ Closing Invitation from the Dean

Florida Coastal School of Law has been described as "the most exciting experiment in American legal education."

This description reflects a growing sense of enthusiasm within legal education and the legal profession for our institution's unique attributes. Foremost among these is the proposition that students are our overarching priority.

Florida Coastal School of Law was founded upon and is defined by the premise that students are the axis upon which our school turns. This originating premise differentiates us from institutions where other priorities make faculty remote from and inaccessible or even indifferent to students. FCSL has its share of distinguished and prolific scholars. The entire faculty is composed, however, of persons with extensive experience in the real world of lawyering who consciously have rejected an ivory-tower existence. They have a common commitment and the know-how to provide a legal education that enables you to hit the ground running as a lawyer when you graduate.

Every law school has a mission and underlying value system that define it programmatically and culturally. Ours are rooted in the premise of student-centeredness. The result is a supportive learning environment where students are seen, heard, listened and responded to, and

the administration's, faculty's, and staff's commitment to them and their future is pervasive. Student-centeredness is why FCSL is dedicated to staying small, pursuing its leapfrog strategy that will secure the institution's prominence and increase the value of your degree, maintaining an environment in which multiculturalism is a norm rather than aspiration, infusing practical skills and international perspective into its program of study, and offering a faculty of teachers and mentors who engage you in a learning partnership that graduates lawyers rather than law students.

To appreciate the difference that these student-centered qualities can make for your future, I encourage you to contact any member of our law school community. I urge you to meet with our graduates or current students, particularly those who have transferred from other law schools. You will be impressed by what they will confirm as the value of learning in an environment that is actively, sincerely, and sharply focused upon your life and aspirations. I welcome the opportunity to meet and discuss our interest in and commitment to your future.

Applicant Profile

Florida Coastal School of Law

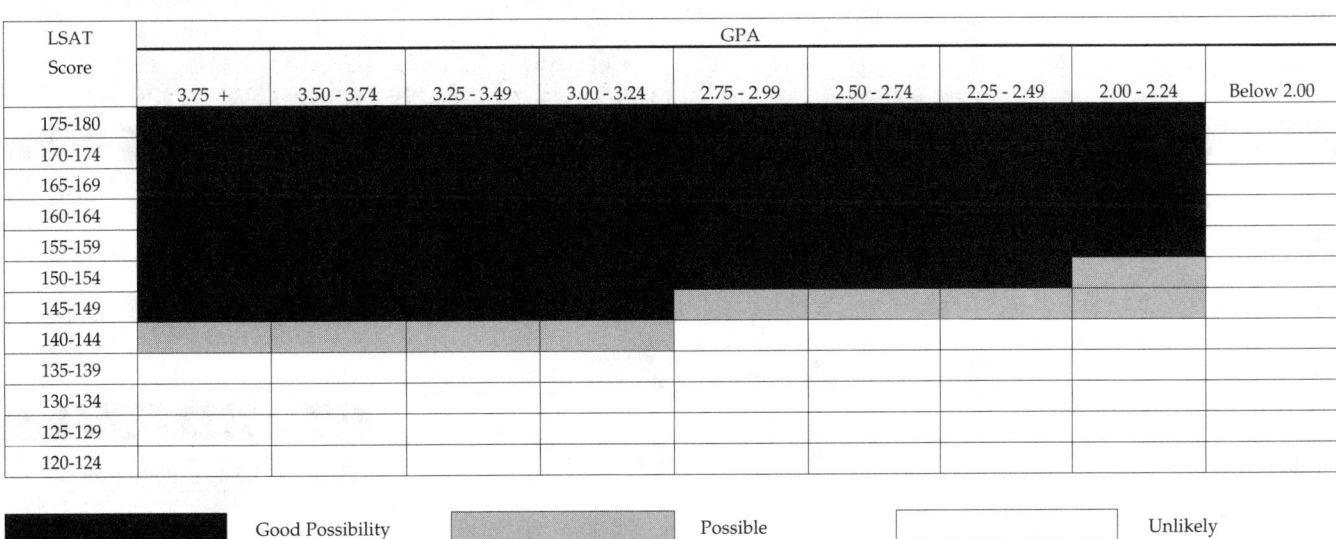

LSAT Score	GPA								
	3.75 +	3.50 - 3.74	3.25 - 3.49	3.00 - 3.24	2.75 - 2.99	2.50 - 2.74	2.25 - 2.49	2.00 - 2.24	Below 2.00
175-180									
170-174									
165-169									
160-164									
155-159									
150-154									
145-149									
140-144									
135-139									
130-134									
125-129									
120-124									

Good Possibility   Possible   Unlikely

Florida International University, College of Law

GL 475
Miami, FL 33186
Phone: 305.348.8006; Fax: 305.348.2965
E-mail: lawadmit@fiu.edu; Website: http://law.fiu.edu/

Provisional　　*ABA Approved Since 2004*

The Basics

Type of school	Public
Term	Semester
Application deadline	6/1
Application fee	$20
Financial aid deadline	3/1
Can first year start other than fall?	No
Student to faculty ratio (fall)	14.7 to 1
Does the university offer:	
housing restricted to law students?	No
graduate housing for which law students are eligible?	Yes

Faculty and Administrators

	Total		Men		Women		Minorities	
	Fall	Spr	Fall	Spr	Fall	Spr	Fall	Spr
Full-time	14	14	10	10	4	4	7	7
Other Full-time	6	8	2	3	4	5	4	4
Deans, librarians, & others who teach	6	6	4	4	2	2	1	1
Part-time	8	8	7	8	1	0	2	4
Total	34	36	23	25	11	11	14	16

Curriculum

	Full-time	Part-time
Typical first-year section size	62	44
Is there typically a "small section" of the first-year class, other than Legal Writing, taught by full-time faculty	No	No
If yes, typical size offered last year	0	0
# of classroom course titles beyond 1st year curriculum	21	
# of upper division courses, excluding seminars with an enrollement: Under 25	24	
25-49	10	
50-74	0	
75-99	0	
100+	0	
# of seminars	1	
# of seminar positions available	15	
# of seminar positions filled	7	0
# of positions available in simulation courses	40	
# of simulation positions filled	37	0
# of positions available in faculty supervised clinical courses	0	
# of faculty supervised clinical positions filled	0	0
# involved in field placements	1	0
# involved in law journals	10	0
# involved in moot court or trial competitions	24	0
# of credit hours required to graduate	90	

JD Enrollment and Ethnicity

	Men		Women		Full-time		Part-time		1st-year		Total		JD Degs. Awd.
	#	%	#	%	#	%	#	%	#	%	#	%	
African Amer.	12	7.5	18	14.5	14	8.0	16	14.5	16	15.1	30	10.6	0
Amer. Indian	0	0.0	1	0.8	0	0.0	1	0.9	0	0.0	1	0.4	0
Asian Amer.	5	3.1	4	3.2	6	3.4	3	2.7	3	2.8	9	3.2	0
Mex. Amer.	0	0.0	0	0.0	0	0.0	0	0.0	0	0.0	0	0.0	0
Puerto Rican	0	0.0	0	0.0	0	0.0	0	0.0	0	0.0	0	0.0	0
Hispanic	65	40.6	55	44.4	70	40.2	50	45.5	43	40.6	120	42.3	0
Total Minority	82	51.3	78	62.9	90	51.7	70	63.6	62	58.5	160	56.3	0
For. Nation.	0	0.0	0	0.0	0	0.0	0	0.0	0	0.0	0	0.0	0
Caucasian	74	46.3	37	29.8	72	41.4	39	35.5	38	35.8	111	39.1	0
Unknown	4	2.5	9	7.3	12	6.9	1	0.9	6	5.7	13	4.6	0
Total	160	56.3	124	43.7	174	61.3	110	38.7	106	37.3	284		0

Tuition and Fees

	Resident	Nonresident
Full-time	$7,129	$25,751
Part-time	$5,092	$18,395

Living Expenses

Estimated living expenses for singles

Living on campus	Living off campus	Living at home
$14,134	$14,690	$7,776

Florida International University, College of Law

*ABA
Approved
Since
2004*

GPA and LSAT Scores

	Total	Full-time	Part-time
# of apps	1,091	752	339
# of admits	203	139	64
# of matrics	112	65	47
75% GPA	3.47	3.51	3.46
25% GPA	2.86	2.88	2.83
75% LSAT	156	156	156
25% LSAT	151	152	151

Grants and Scholarships (from prior year)

	Total		Full-time		Part-time	
	#	%	#	%	#	%
Total # of students	194		114		80	
Total # receiving grants	88	45.4	72	63.2	16	20.0
Less than 1/2 tuition	34	17.5	31	27.2	3	3.8
Half to full tuition	43	22.2	30	26.3	13	16.3
Full tuition	5	2.6	5	4.4	0	0.0
More than full tuition	6	3.1	6	5.3	0	0.0
Median grant amount			$3,502		$2,500	

Informational and Library Resources

# of volumes and volume equivalents	187,210
# of titles	87,180
# of active serial subscriptions	1,868
Study seating capacity inside the library	196
# of professional librarians	4
Hours per week library is open	112
# of open, wired connections available to students	2
# of networked computers available for use by students	51
# of simultaneous wireless users	1,000
Require computer?	N

JD Attrition (from prior year)

	Academic	Other	Total	
	#	#	#	%
1st year	15	9	24	22.6%
2nd year	1	0	1	1.1%
3rd year	0	0	0	0.0%
4th year	0	0	0	0.0%

Employment

	Total	Percentage
Employment status known	0	0.0
Employment status unknown	0	0.0
Employed	0	0.0
Pursuing graduate degrees	0	0.0
Unemployed seeking employment	0	0.0
Unemployed not seeking employment	0	0.0

Type of Employment

# employed in law firms	0	0.0
# employed in business and industry	0	0.0
# employed in government	0	0.0
# employed in public interest	0	0.0
# employed as judicial clerks	0	0.0
# employed in academia	0	0.0

Geographic Location

# employed in state	0	0.0
# employed in foreign countries	0	0.0
# of states where employed	0	

Bar Passage Rates

Jurisdiction

Exam	Sum 03	Win 04	Total
# from school taking bar for the first time	0	0	0
School's pass rate for all first-time takers			
State's pass rate for all first-time takers			

Florida International University, College of Law

GL 475
Miami, FL 33186
Phone: 305.348.8006; Fax: 305.348.2965
E-mail: lawadmit@fiu.edu; Website: http://law.fiu.edu/

■ Introduction

The Florida International University, College of Law was established by an act of the Florida legislature in June 2000. Its first class was admitted in the fall of 2002. In August 2004, the College of Law was awarded provisional accreditation by the American Bar Association, assuring that its graduates would be eligible to apply for admission to the practice of law in all 50 states and the District of Columbia. The law school plans to apply for full ABA approval in the fall of 2006 and hopes to achieve such approval in 2007, the earliest time it will be eligible for such consideration.

Florida International University is a public research university which enrolls approximately 35,000 students, most on its beautiful University Park campus where the College of Law is located. This campus will be the site of a new law building designed by nationally and internationally renowned architect Robert A.M. Stern; the anticipated occupancy date is the summer of 2006. The campus enjoys nearby access to South Florida's beaches, Everglades National Park, and the Florida Keys.

The College of Law reflects the diverse character and the international perspective of the city of Miami. The curriculum incorporates important developments in the globalization of both public and private law. The academic program takes a pervasive approach to both international and comparative law, incorporating their perspectives into all domestic law classes.

■ Curriculum and Special Programs

The FIU College of Law's academic program emphasizes international and comparative law. The required curriculum includes a three-hour first-year course entitled Introduction to International and Comparative Law. Further, all domestic law courses include an international or comparative law dimension. This pervasive approach to international and comparative law encourages students to analyze legal systemic, political, economic, social, and other cultural differences that may contribute to different legal treatment of comparable problems in different countries. Beginning in the summer of 2005, the College of Law will offer a foreign summer program in Sevilla, Spain.

The curriculum also emphasizes instruction in the legal skills and values of the profession. The Legal Skills and Values Program combines demanding traditional instruction in legal research and writing with an introduction to other lawyering skills, like interviewing and counseling, and to issues of professionalism.

The Clinical Program advances the law school's goals of educating lawyers for the ethical and effective practice of law and of promoting community service through the representation of real clients. The first clinics at the College of Law are an Immigration/Human Rights Clinic and a Criminal Law Clinic.

As a public, urban law school, the College of Law is committed to serving the community of which it is a part by educating future lawyers who will understand the value—to the community and to them personally— of helping those in need. In recognition of this important mission, students must satisfy a community service requirement.

As the state of Florida's public research university in South Florida, FIU offers a broad range of high quality graduate-level degree programs. Law students interested in interdisciplinary study may take advantage of these curricula through one of the following joint-degree programs: JD/Master of Business Administration, JD/Master of International Business, JD/Master of Latin American and Caribbean Studies, JD/Master of Public Administration, JD/MS in Psychology, JD/Master of Social Work, JD/MS in Criminal Justice.

■ Admission

The FIU College of Law offers both a full-time day and part-time evening program. The review of applications is done on a rolling basis. An LSDAS report, three letters of recommendation, and a personal statement are required. Transfer students from other ABA-approved law schools may apply if they are in the good standing at their current institutions. Visit our website at *http://law.fiu.edu* for additional information.

■ Financial Aid

The primary financial aid resources available to students are loans and need- or merit-based scholarships. Students must apply for financial aid (FAFSA) to be considered for any type of loan or need-based scholarships. Financial aid is granted on an annual basis and awards are subject to student eligibility and availability of funds. Tuition is comparable to other Florida state-supported law schools at $254 per credit for Florida residents and $920 per credit for nonresidents. An additional $14,500 (approximate) can be expected to cover room and board, books, transportation, and personal expenses. Please call 305.348.8006 for further information.

■ Library

The Law Library supports the law school curriculum and research of its students and faculty. It contains approximately 185,000 volumes in book and microform format. The Law Library also provides law students with a full range of electronic legal information, including Westlaw, LexisNexis, and an extensive array of web-based resources. When doing other research, law students may also use the FIU Green Library's 1.5 million volumes and extensive electronic resources.

■ Career Planning and Placement

The Office of Career Planning and Placement provides individual assistance to students that enables them to establish their personal career goals and tailors strategies that assists students in reaching those goals. The Office facilitates both on- and off-campus recruitment for summer and permanent legal positions as well as an active internship program. Other services include individual career counseling sessions; workshops and handbooks regarding résumé preparation, interview skills and techniques, and job searches; and mock-interviews with local attorneys.

■ Student Activities

Success in law school involves more than just intellectual curiosity and a sense of purpose. It involves the refining of time management skills, handling stress proactively, and forging relationships with faculty and peers. It also involves making the best possible use of available services and opportunities. Students bring a wealth of distinctive educational and professional experiences to the College of Law. However, they all share a common interest and goal-service to the law school, the local community, and the profession. Together with the support of the faculty and the administration, students have created a number of organizations and cocurricular activities reflective of this commitment. In its brief but productive history, the College of Law has established a student-edited law review; an award winning Moot Court Program, competing locally and nationally against teams throughout the country; and 16 student organizations, including the Student Bar Association.

Applicant Profile

The Florida International University College of Law Admissions Committee seeks to enroll a diverse group of students who have demonstrated academic and personal achievement. While a prospective student's academic record and LSAT performance are weighted heavily in the evaluative process, the Admissions Committee considers other factors, including leadership ability, commitment to public service, command of global issues, work history, military service, any history of criminality or academic misconduct, and evidence of obstacles that an applicant may have overcome (for example, English is not the applicant's native language, discrimination, economic or family hardship, severe medical condition, disability, etc.)

The Florida State University College of Law

425 West Jefferson Street
Tallahassee, FL 32306-1601
Phone: 850.644.3787; Fax: 850.644.5487
E-mail: admissions@law.fsu.edu; Website: www.law.fsu.edu

ABA Approved Since 1968

The Basics

Type of school	Public
Term	Semester
Application deadline	2/15
Application fee	$20
Financial aid deadline	2/15
Can first year start other than fall?	No
Student to faculty ratio (fall)	13.9 to 1
Does the university offer:	
housing restricted to law students?	No
graduate housing for which law students are eligible?	Yes

Faculty and Administrators

	Total		Men		Women		Minorities	
	Fall	Spr	Fall	Spr	Fall	Spr	Fall	Spr
Full-time	46	45	27	26	19	19	6	5
Other Full-time	0	0	0	0	0	0	0	0
Deans, librarians, & others who teach	7	7	2	2	5	5	1	1
Part-time	30	15	21	9	9	6	3	1
Total	83	67	50	37	33	30	10	7

Curriculum

	Full-time	Part-time
Typical first-year section size	80	0
Is there typically a "small section" of the first-year class, other than Legal Writing, taught by full-time faculty	No	No
If yes, typical size offered last year	0	0
# of classroom course titles beyond 1st year curriculum	102	

# of upper division courses, excluding seminars with an enrollment:		
	Under 25	62
	25-49	29
	50-74	13
	75-99	6
	100+	7

# of seminars	23	
# of seminar positions available	475	
# of seminar positions filled	344	0
# of positions available in simulation courses	460	
# of simulation positions filled	353	0
# of positions available in faculty supervised clinical courses	55	
# of faculty supervised clinical positions filled	54	0
# involved in field placements	105	0
# involved in law journals	166	0
# involved in moot court or trial competitions	63	0
# of credit hours required to graduate	88	

J.D. Enrollment and Ethnicity

	Men		Women		Full-time		Part-time		1st-year		Total		JD Degs. Awd.
	#	%	#	%	#	%	#	%	#	%	#	%	
African Amer.	13	3.3	37	10.5	50	6.7	0	0.0	14	6.4	50	6.7	21
Amer. Indian	7	1.8	0	0.0	7	0.9	0	0.0	3	1.4	7	0.9	2
Asian Amer.	15	3.8	18	5.1	33	4.4	0	0.0	12	5.5	33	4.4	4
Mex. Amer.	0	0.0	0	0.0	0	0.0	0	0.0	0	0.0	0	0.0	0
Puerto Rican	0	0.0	3	0.9	3	0.4	0	0.0	3	1.4	3	0.4	0
Hispanic	23	5.8	40	11.4	63	8.4	0	0.0	19	8.7	63	8.4	23
Total Minority	58	14.6	98	27.9	156	20.9	0	0.0	51	23.4	156	20.9	50
For. Nation.	1	0.3	0	0.0	1	0.1	0	0.0	0	0.0	1	0.1	0
Caucasian	329	82.9	247	70.4	576	77.0	0	0.0	161	73.9	576	77.0	155
Unknown	9	2.3	6	1.7	15	2.0	0	0.0	6	2.8	15	2.0	0
Total	397	53.1	351	46.9	748	100.0	0	0.0	218	29.1	748		205

Tuition and Fees

	Resident	Nonresident
Full-time	$7,504	$27,517
Part-time	$0	$0

Living Expenses

Estimated living expenses for singles

Living on campus	Living off campus	Living at home
$14,510	$14,510	$14,510

The Florida State University College of Law

*ABA
Approved
Since
1968*

GPA and LSAT Scores

	Total	Full-time	Part-time
# of apps	4,225	4,225	0
# of admits	828	828	0
# of matrics	243	243	0
75% GPA	3.65	3.65	0.00
25% GPA	3.29	3.29	0.00
75% LSAT	161	161	0
25% LSAT	156	156	0

Grants and Scholarships (from prior year)

	Total		Full-time		Part-time	
	#	%	#	%	#	%
Total # of students	742		742		0	
Total # receiving grants	226	30.5	226	30.5	0	0.0
Less than 1/2 tuition	208	28.0	208	28.0	0	0.0
Half to full tuition	12	1.6	12	1.6	0	0.0
Full tuition	2	0.3	2	0.3	0	0.0
More than full tuition	4	0.5	4	0.5	0	0.0
Median grant amount			$1,000		$0	

Informational and Library Resources

# of volumes and volume equivalents	454,319
# of titles	163,293
# of active serial subscriptions	3,803
Study seating capacity inside the library	410
# of professional librarians	10
Hours per week library is open	168
# of open, wired connections available to students	0
# of networked computers available for use by students	40
# of simultaneous wireless users	2,700
Require computer?	Y

JD Attrition (from prior year)

	Academic	Other	Total	
	#	#	#	%
1st year	3	5	8	3.3%
2nd year	0	1	1	0.4%
3rd year	1	0	1	0.5%
4th year	0	0	0	0.0%

Employment

	Total	Percentage
Employment status known	245	98.0
Employment status unknown	5	2.0
Employed	220	89.8
Pursuing graduate degrees	13	5.3
Unemployed seeking employment	1	0.4
Unemployed not seeking employment	11	4.5

Type of Employment

# employed in law firms	100	45.5
# employed in business and industry	12	5.5
# employed in government	77	35.0
# employed in public interest	7	3.2
# employed as judicial clerks	11	5.0
# employed in academia	1	0.5

Geographic Location

# employed in state	194	88.2
# employed in foreign countries	3	1.4
# of states where employed	11	

Bar Passage Rates

Jurisdiction	Florida		
Exam	Sum 03	Win 04	Total
# from school taking bar for the first time	178	49	227
School's pass rate for all first-time takers	85%	67%	81%
State's pass rate for all first-time takers	76%	75%	76%

The Florida State University College of Law

425 West Jefferson Street
Tallahassee, FL 32306-1601
Phone: 850.644.3787; Fax: 850.644.5487
E-mail: admissions@law.fsu.edu; Website: www.law.fsu.edu

■ Introduction

The Florida State University College of Law is widely recognized for both its commitment to teaching and its cutting-edge scholarship. The college subscribes to the idea that the best legal education is the result of a lively dialogue in an intimate learning environment. The law school's distinguished faculty is highly accessible to students and strives to provide a legal education with a personal touch.

The curriculum at the College of Law is continuously evolving to reflect the changes in the practice of law. Environmental and land use law, international law, and business law and economics are among the areas that have received increased emphasis in the curriculum in recent years. Students with an interest in these areas have opportunities to take a rich curriculum with inter-disciplinary opportunities, work on student-run legal journals, and participate in extracurricular activities that help hone practical skills.

Tallahassee is also a wonderful community in which to study law. The college is situated blocks from the Florida Capitol, the First District Court of Appeal, the Florida Supreme Court, the United States District Court, and other centers for judicial and administrative activity. All branches of state government are headquartered in Florida's capital city, which is also home to local offices of top law firms from throughout Florida and the nation.

■ Enrollment/Student Body

More than 4,200 applications are received for approximately 220 places in the entering class. The current student body represents 37 states and 208 undergraduate institutions. The student body is diverse and gifted, and the racial and ethnical mix represents society as a whole. The college prides itself on having a warm and collegial student body, which is also extremely competitive in state and national trial and appellate advocacy competitions.

■ Curriculum

The College of Law's three-year curriculum provides students a foundational first-year program and a rich and varied offering of upper-level courses, seminars, clinics, and cocurricular opportunities. The curriculum is designed to prepare graduates for the basic demands of legal practice through a broad "liberal arts" approach to curricular offerings supplemented with a wide variety of specialized courses emphasizing the college's strengths in environmental and land use law and international law.

■ Special Programs

The College of Law offers seven joint-degree programs, two certificate programs, and an LLM program for foreign lawyers. The following joint degrees are available: JD/MBA, JD/MPA, JD/MSW, JD/MIS, JD/Master in International Affairs, JD/Master in Urban and Regional Planning, and JD/MS in Library Information Systems. The college offers certificate programs in Environmental, Natural Resources, and Land Use Law, and in International Law. The certificate programs are rigorous, focused courses of study that, when coupled with experience gained through externships and other opportunities, are designed to prepare graduates to work in highly specialized areas of the law. The college also offers an LLM program for foreign lawyers, which provides foreign graduate students trained in law the opportunity to develop an understanding of the American legal system and the role of law in the United States.

The college offers one of the most extensive clinical externship programs in the United States. Judicial externships are available with state trial and appellate courts, including the Florida Supreme Court and the federal courts. Externship opportunities with government agencies and commissions, the state attorney, the public defender, and legal services offices are also provided, as well as opportunities abroad with the International Bar Association in London. The college's Children Advocacy Center, an in-house legal clinic, offers law students an opportunity to represent children in a variety of legal areas under the supervision of clinical faculty.

The college also sponsors a summer program at Oxford University in England. As the oldest on-going program in Oxford sponsored by a US law school, it provides students with a unique opportunity to study comparative law and the history of the common law and its institutions in their original setting.

■ Library and Physical Facilities

The College of Law has a wireless Ethernet network that extends throughout the facilities. This provides Internet access to all wireless-capable laptops within range of the college at a speed of 11 megabits (over 100 times the speed of a conventional modem).

The physical facilities of the College of Law consist of B.K. Roberts Hall, opened in 1971; a separate, connected law library, opened in 1983; and the Village Green, completed in 1988.

Roberts Hall houses faculty, staff and student offices, lounges, classrooms, seminar rooms, and a practice courtroom making extensive use of video technology. Both Roberts Hall and the law library comply with all architectural regulations facilitating use for students with disabilities.

The law library's volumes and microform volume equivalents are all catalogued in the Florida State University libraries' online database, accessible through computer terminals located throughout the library and also available for remote access using computers with modems. The law library's collections match the most significant law collections in the southeast. Individual and group study, video viewing, microform reading, and computer use and instruction are accommodated within the law library.

■ Student Activities

One of the most attractive aspects of the College of Law's academic climate is the wide variety of educational and professional opportunities available outside the traditional classroom. The College of Law sponsors *Law Review*, the *Journal of Land Use & Environmental Law*, the *Journal of Transnational Law & Policy*, a nationally recognized moot court and trial advocacy program, and a variety of social and professional organizations. Some of the active student organizations include ACLU; Public Interest Law Students; Women's Law Society; Black Law Students Association; Christian Legal Society; Entertainment, Arts, and Sports Law Society; Federalist Society; International Law Society; Dispute Resolution Society; Environmental Law Society; Spanish-American Law Students Association; Asian Law

Students Association; and Law Partners, a law students' spouse and significant others support group. Both Phi Delta Phi and Phi Alpha Delta legal honoraries maintain a chapter on campus. The College of Law was granted a chapter of Order of the Coif in 1979. The Student Bar Association serves an active student government role and coordinates many law school-sponsored social activities and community projects and programs.

■ Career Services

The College of Law's Placement Office takes pride in helping students acquire the tools needed to successfully launch legal careers. The office offers individualized career planning, on-campus and off-campus interview programs, job search assistance, an alumni mentorship program, and skills workshops and seminars on topics ranging from effective résumé writing to interviewing techniques.

The college's most recent placement statistics show that approximately 99 percent of its graduates reported that they were either employed, seeking another graduate degree, or not seeking employment nine months after graduation. The college's graduates work in 47 states and in major markets, including Atlanta, Chicago, New York, and Washington, DC. Graduates are prominent in all Florida cities.

Applicant Profile

The Florida State University College of Law
This grid includes only applicants who earned 120-180 LSAT scores under standard administrations.

LSAT Score	3.75 + Apps	3.75 + Adm	3.50 - 3.74 Apps	3.50 - 3.74 Adm	3.25 - 3.49 Apps	3.25 - 3.49 Adm	3.00 - 3.24 Apps	3.00 - 3.24 Adm	2.75 - 2.99 Apps	2.75 - 2.99 Adm	2.50 - 2.74 Apps	2.50 - 2.74 Adm	2.25 - 2.49 Apps	2.25 - 2.49 Adm	2.00 - 2.24 Apps	2.00 - 2.24 Adm	Below 2.00 Apps	Below 2.00 Adm	No GPA Apps	No GPA Adm	Total Apps	Total Adm
175-180	0	0	0	0	0	0	2	2	0	0	0	0	0	0	0	0	0	0	0	0	2	2
170-174	1	1	0	0	3	3	2	2	3	3	0	0	2	1	0	0	0	0	0	0	11	10
165-169	7	7	15	15	15	12	17	15	8	7	6	3	4	2	0	0	0	0	0	0	72	61
160-164	53	52	58	55	73	69	65	48	53	12	24	4	16	1	1	0	0	0	2	2	345	243
155-159	142	106	198	106	264	102	195	22	141	5	47	1	28	2	9	0	1	0	4	0	1029	344
150-154	147	17	255	12	323	18	242	12	183	1	74	4	33	2	15	0	2	0	5	0	1279	66
145-149	54	4	127	1	197	4	151	3	117	1	64	0	40	0	6	0	9	0	6	0	771	13
140-144	15	1	45	0	59	0	86	0	75	0	33	0	29	0	6	0	1	0	6	0	355	1
135-139	3	0	14	0	26	0	31	0	31	0	24	0	16	0	3	0	0	0	4	0	152	0
130-134	1	0	1	0	3	0	6	0	3	0	8	0	6	0	6	0	2	0	1	0	37	0
125-129	0	0	0	0	1	0	2	0	2	0	1	0	2	0	2	0	0	0	0	0	10	0
120-124	0	0	0	0	0	0	0	0	0	0	0	0	0	0	0	0	0	0	0	0	0	0
Total	423	188	713	189	964	208	799	104	616	29	281	12	176	8	48	0	15	0	28	2	4063	740

Apps = Number of Applicants
Adm = Number Admitted
Reflects 99% of the total applicant pool.

Fordham University School of Law

140 West 62nd Street
New York, NY 10023
Phone: 212.636.6810; Fax: 212.636.7984
E-mail: lawadmissions@law.fordham.edu; Website: law.fordham.edu

*ABA
Approved
Since
1936*

The Basics

Type of school	Private
Term	Semester
Application deadline	3/1
Application fee	$65
Financial aid deadline	3/1
Can first year start other than fall?	No
Student to faculty ratio (fall)	16.4 to 1
Does the university offer:	
housing restricted to law students?	No
graduate housing for which law students are eligible?	Yes

Faculty and Administrators

	Total		Men		Women		Minorities	
	Fall	Spr	Fall	Spr	Fall	Spr	Fall	Spr
Full-time	71	68	45	41	26	27	13	15
Other Full-time	4	4	1	1	3	3	0	0
Deans, librarians, & others who teach	9	9	6	6	3	3	1	1
Part-time	126	153	87	98	39	55	13	14
Total	210	234	139	146	71	88	27	30

Curriculum

		Full-time	Part-time
Typical first-year section size		80	80
Is there typically a "small section" of the first-year class, other than Legal Writing, taught by full-time faculty		Yes	Yes
If yes, typical size offered last year		40	40
# of classroom course titles beyond 1st year curriculum		193	
# of upper division courses, excluding seminars with an enrollment:	Under 25	142	
	25-49	57	
	50-74	27	
	75-99	13	
	100+	9	
# of seminars		93	
# of seminar positions available		2,077	
# of seminar positions filled		993	657
# of positions available in simulation courses		904	
# of simulation positions filled		344	456
# of positions available in faculty supervised clinical courses		516	
# of faculty supervised clinical positions filled	318		76
# involved in field placements		181	126
# involved in law journals		479	38
# involved in moot court or trial competitions		183	40
# of credit hours required to graduate		83	

JD Enrollment and Ethnicity

	Men		Women		Full-time		Part-time		1st-year		Total		JD Degs. Awd.
	#	%	#	%	#	%	#	%	#	%	#	%	
African Amer.	35	4.3	55	7.7	63	5.4	27	7.5	21	4.4	90	5.9	44
Amer. Indian	3	0.4	3	0.4	5	0.4	1	0.3	3	0.6	6	0.4	0
Asian Amer.	76	9.4	89	12.5	115	9.9	50	14.0	48	10.1	165	10.8	36
Mex. Amer.	5	0.6	1	0.1	3	0.3	3	0.8	2	0.4	6	0.4	2
Puerto Rican	11	1.4	11	1.5	19	1.6	3	0.8	4	0.8	22	1.4	15
Hispanic	43	5.3	50	7.0	70	6.0	23	6.4	39	8.2	93	6.1	28
Total Minority	173	21.4	209	29.3	275	23.6	107	29.9	117	24.6	382	25.1	125
For. Nation.	0	0.0	0	0.0	0	0.0	0	0.0	0	0.0	0	0.0	0
Caucasian	520	64.4	435	60.9	749	64.3	206	57.5	284	59.8	955	62.7	344
Unknown	115	14.2	70	9.8	140	12.0	45	12.6	74	15.6	185	12.2	23
Total	808	53.1	714	46.9	1164	76.5	358	23.5	475	31.2	1522		492

Tuition and Fees

	Resident	Nonresident
Full-time	$33,216	$33,216
Part-time	$24,963	$24,963

Living Expenses

Estimated living expenses for singles

Living on campus	Living off campus	Living at home
$19,729	$19,729	$19,729

Fordham University School of Law

ABA
Approved
Since
1936

GPA and LSAT Scores

	Total	Full-time	Part-time
# of apps	7,598	6,449	1,149
# of admits	1,467	1,222	245
# of matrics	479	316	163
75% GPA	3.76	3.78	3.66
25% GPA	3.31	3.37	3.21
75% LSAT	166	167	163
25% LSAT	161	163	160

Grants and Scholarships (from prior year)

	Total		Full-time		Part-time	
	#	%	#	%	#	%
Total # of students	1,546		1,184		362	
Total # receiving grants	458	29.6	378	31.9	80	22.1
Less than 1/2 tuition	421	27.2	347	29.3	74	20.4
Half to full tuition	25	1.6	24	2.0	1	0.3
Full tuition	8	0.5	4	0.3	4	1.1
More than full tuition	4	0.3	3	0.3	1	0.3
Median grant amount			$6,900		$4,000	

Informational and Library Resources

# of volumes and volume equivalents	613,199
# of titles	198,140
# of active serial subscriptions	7,693
Study seating capacity inside the library	473
# of professional librarians	14
Hours per week library is open	119
# of open, wired connections available to students	448
# of networked computers available for use by students	220
# of simultaneous wireless users	400
Require computer?	N

JD Attrition (from prior year)

	Academic	Other	Total	
	#	#	#	%
1st year	1	10	11	2.3%
2nd year	1	18	19	3.8%
3rd year	0	0	0	0.0%
4th year	0	0	0	0.0%

Employment

	Total	Percentage
Employment status known	424	98.4
Employment status unknown	7	1.6
Employed	417	98.3
Pursuing graduate degrees	2	0.5
Unemployed seeking employment	0	0.0
Unemployed not seeking employment	5	1.2

Type of Employment

	Total	Percentage
# employed in law firms	319	76.5
# employed in business and industry	43	10.3
# employed in government	21	5.0
# employed in public interest	6	1.4
# employed as judicial clerks	18	4.3
# employed in academia	2	0.5

Geographic Location

	Total	Percentage
# employed in state	342	82.0
# employed in foreign countries	4	1.0
# of states where employed	17	

Bar Passage Rates

Jurisdiction	New York		
Exam	Sum 03	Win 04	Total
# from school taking bar for the first time	397	24	421
School's pass rate for all first-time takers	86%	63%	85%
State's pass rate for all first-time takers	78%	58%	75%

Fordham University School of Law

140 West 62nd Street
New York, NY 10023
Phone: 212.636.6810; Fax: 212.636.7984
E-mail: lawadmissions@law.fordham.edu; Website: law.fordham.edu

■ Introduction

Fordham law school is an extraordinary place, where a nationally recognized faculty of scholar-teachers and a deep commitment to social justice create an atmosphere in which students feel appreciated and valued as they prepare to become part of the next generation of leaders. For nearly 100 years, Fordham has trained attorneys who have made their mark throughout society. Today, our graduates practice in 49 states, in the District of Columbia, and in dozens of nations around the world. Among our 15,000 living alumni are partners and associates of leading law firms, CEOs of major corporations, members of academia, and a legion of individuals engaged in numerous areas of public service.

Fordham's central Manhattan location provides instant access to all New York City has to offer, enabling students to begin their careers at the center of the world's legal, financial, and entertainment capital. Such proximity puts students close to a broad range of professional opportunities at some of the largest law firms in the world, the busiest federal and state courts, the US and New York State Attorney General's Office, a myriad of state and federal agencies, and Wall Street.

Also within easy reach are New York's equally famous diversions. The campus is just two blocks away from Central Park. Lincoln Center for the Performing Arts—home to the world-renowned Metropolitan Opera, New York Philharmonic, and the Julliard School of Music—is right across the street.

■ Curriculum

Fordham's faculty prides itself on being teachers as well as scholars. As teachers they recognize the importance of welcoming students, being accessible to them, and encouraging them. The large faculty enables Fordham to offer 200 courses that reinforce its traditional strengths in contracts, commercial law, corporate law, evidence, and international law, as well as enhance its significant scholarship in the fields of constitutional law and jurisprudence, international human rights, legal ethics, legal history, intellectual property, and clinical legal education.

Fordham also promotes the art and science of legal analysis and the cultivation of a vigorous ongoing dialogue between students and professor through the following nationally renowned academic centers.

Brendan Moore Advocacy Center fosters the teaching and study of lawyers as advocates, with special emphasis on client representation at the trial level.

Center for Corporate, Securities, and Financial Law serves as the focal point for the school's business law programs and includes roundtable discussions with business leaders, corporate law practitioners, and state and federal regulators.

Joseph R. Crowley Program in International Human Rights is one of the nation's premier academic organizations dealing with the rights of individuals throughout the world and whose annual fact-finding human rights mission to a designated host country is unprecedented in American legal education.

Louis Stein Center for Law and Ethics promotes the integration of ethical perspectives in legal practice, legal institutions, and the development of the law generally. The center also oversees the Stein Scholars Program, a three-year program for specially selected first-year law students who demonstrate commitment to public service and who undertake specialized academic work in legal ethics.

■ Cocurricular Activities

There are six student-edited law journals at Fordham, as well as two intramural moot court competitions.

The school also participates in the interschool competitions, fielding six award-winning appellate moot court teams, a trial advocacy team, and several alternative dispute resolution teams every year.

■ Worldwide Significance

Long before "globalism" was mainstream, Fordham was devoting resources to programs that, today, are internationally known, including:

- the nation's preeminent Center on European Union Law;
- the school's Stein Center for Law and Ethics (see above);
- an International Antitrust Law and Policy Conference, now in its 31st year;
- an annual International Intellectual Property Law Conference;
- the Joseph R. Crowley Program in International Human Rights (see above);
- a Belfast/Dublin summer program, which offers two weeks of study in each country with a special emphasis on international alternative dispute resolution; and
- two graduate degree programs—the LLM in International Business and Trade Law and the LLM in Banking, Corporate, and Finance Law—that have created a network of Fordham alumni in 70 countries.

■ Experiential Programs

Fordham's clinical program affords opportunities for students to integrate legal analysis with lawyering theory and skills by assuming lawyering roles or performing lawyering functions in problem-solving settings. With 17 full-time faculty, three part-time professors, one adjunct, and one full-time social worker, Fordham Law's clinical program—one of the largest in the nation—engages more than 300 students in live-client clinics and simulation courses in 13 practice areas, including an innovative interdisciplinary Child and Family Litigation Clinic, where students are placed on teams supervised by law, social work, and psychology faculty. Fordham also offers one of the widest ranges of externship placements in American legal education—more than 250 opportunities at nonprofit and nongovernmental organizations and in state and federal courts.

■ Career Services and Placement

Fordham offers a fully staffed career services office to assist students and alumni in planning their careers. For the past several years, between 97 and 100 percent of our graduates obtained employment within nine months of graduation. The program features:
- an on-campus interview program that brings nearly 300 potential employers to campus to conduct more than 5,000 individual student interviews;
- a searchable, proprietary, online database of job listings;
- individualized student counseling, mock videotaped interviews with optional critiques, seminars on interviewing skills and networking, and assistance with résumé preparation, including 24-hour turnaround time for edits.

■ Public Service

Fordham believes that the development of a lifelong commitment to public service is an integral part of a legal education. Last year, Fordham law students volunteered 62,000 hours of their time to some form of pro bono work through the school's nationally recognized Public Interest Resource Center. The PIRC's 14 student-run organizations address issues concerning the environment, housing for the poor, domestic violence, unemployment, police brutality, the death penalty, immigration, and community service. Fordham also has created a Loan Forgiveness Program as well as a Loan Repayment Assistance Program (LRAP) to assist those who pursue public service careers. Today, Fordham continues to set the standard for law schools nationwide by assisting and inspiring those students who, regardless of their ultimate career choice, are committed to the spirit of *pro bono publico*—work for the public good.

■ Living at Lincoln Center

Approximately 120 spaces are set aside for entering students in McMahon Hall, the university's Lincoln Center residence. Students live in two- or three-bedroom apartments, each of which contains private bedrooms, a living room, full kitchen, and bath. Preference is given to those students who live beyond a commutable distance from the law school. Inquiries regarding housing should be directed to the law school admission office.

Applicant Profile

Fordham Law School's Admissions Committee—composed of full-time faculty members and assistant deans evaluates each completed application received. While the best available evidence suggests that the LSAT score and GPA should be accorded significant weight in evaluating most applicants, the Admissions Committee believes that securing the most diverse, interesting, and able entering class involves the consideration of qualitative factors—including prior employment, student activities, community service, leadership ability, propensity for public service, and communication skills—which also suggest an applicant's potential to make extraordinary contributions to the success of the entering class and the legal profession.

Applicants who have been educationally, socially, and economically disadvantaged, and who have had to overcome significant obstacles in their lives are afforded a particularly careful review. Finally, efforts are made to ensure that the entire selection process is fair, and the committee goes to great lengths to ensure that all applicants are accorded equal treatment, respect, and consideration.

Notwithstanding the close attention Fordham gives to each application and its unique characteristics, entering students exhibit incredibly consistent and closely clustered numeric indicators. For example, the LSAT and GPA distribution of the full-time class entering in fall 2004 was 167 and 3.78 in the 75th percentile and 163 and 3.37 in the 25th percentile.

Franklin Pierce Law Center

2 White Street
Concord, NH 03301
Phone: 603.228.9217; Fax: 603.224.4661
E-mail: admissions@piercelaw.edu; Website: www.piercelaw.edu

ABA
Approved
Since
1974

The Basics

Type of school	Private
Term	Semester
Application deadline	4/1
Application fee	$55
Financial aid deadline	
Can first year start other than fall?	No
Student to faculty ratio (fall)	17.8 to 1
Does the university offer:	
housing restricted to law students?	No
graduate housing for which law students are eligible?	Yes

Faculty and Administrators

	Total		Men		Women		Minorities	
	Fall	Spr	Fall	Spr	Fall	Spr	Fall	Spr
Full-time	20	20	14	14	6	6	1	1
Other Full-time	2	2	2	2	0	0	0	0
Deans, librarians, & others who teach	5	5	3	3	2	2	0	0
Part-time	37	33	29	20	8	13	0	1
Total	64	60	48	39	16	21	1	2

Curriculum

	Full-time	Part-time
Typical first-year section size	83	0
Is there typically a "small section" of the first-year class, other than Legal Writing, taught by full-time faculty	Yes	No
If yes, typical size offered last year	20	0
# of classroom course titles beyond 1st year curriculum	91	

# of upper division courses, excluding seminars with an enrollment:		
Under 25	72	
25-49	26	
50-74	16	
75-99	2	
100+	0	

# of seminars	18	
# of seminar positions available	371	
# of seminar positions filled	235	0
# of positions available in simulation courses	358	
# of simulation positions filled	261	0
# of positions available in faculty supervised clinical courses	123	
# of faculty supervised clinical positions filled	95	0
# involved in field placements	65	0
# involved in law journals	41	0
# involved in moot court or trial competitions	15	0
# of credit hours required to graduate	84	

JD Enrollment and Ethnicity

	Men		Women		Full-time		Part-time		1st-year		Total		JD Degs. Awd.
	#	%	#	%	#	%	#	%	#	%	#	%	
African Amer.	7	2.8	8	4.4	15	3.6	0	0.0	10	6.4	15	3.5	1
Amer. Indian	0	0.0	0	0.0	0	0.0	0	0.0	0	0.0	0	0.0	0
Asian Amer.	31	12.5	16	8.9	47	11.1	0	0.0	17	10.8	47	11.0	4
Mex. Amer.	2	0.8	0	0.0	2	0.5	0	0.0	2	1.3	2	0.5	0
Puerto Rican	0	0.0	0	0.0	0	0.0	0	0.0	0	0.0	0	0.0	0
Hispanic	9	3.6	2	1.1	11	2.6	0	0.0	4	2.5	11	2.6	2
Total Minority	49	19.8	26	14.4	75	17.8	0	0.0	33	21.0	75	17.5	7
For. Nation.	9	3.6	7	3.9	13	3.1	3	50.0	6	3.8	16	3.7	12
Caucasian	167	67.3	124	68.9	290	68.7	1	16.7	103	64.3	291	68.0	81
Unknown	23	9.3	23	12.8	44	10.4	2	33.3	17	10.8	46	10.7	10
Total	248	57.9	180	42.1	422	98.6	6	1.4	159	36.7	428		110

Tuition and Fees

	Resident	Nonresident
Full-time	$25,274	$25,274
Part-time	$0	$0

Living Expenses

Estimated living expenses for singles

Living on campus	Living off campus	Living at home
$14,419	$14,419	$14,419

Franklin Pierce Law Center

ABA Approved Since 1974

GPA and LSAT Scores

	Total	Full-time	Part-time
# of apps	1,473	1,473	0
# of admits	570	570	0
# of matrics	159	159	0
75% GPA	3.50	3.50	0.00
25% GPA	3.00	3.00	0.00
75% LSAT	156	156	0
25% LSAT	150	150	0

Grants and Scholarships (from prior year)

	Total		Full-time		Part-time	
	#	%	#	%	#	%
Total # of students	393		386		7	
Total # receiving grants	226	57.5	225	58.3	1	14.3
Less than 1/2 tuition	220	56.0	219	56.7	1	14.3
Half to full tuition	4	1.0	4	1.0	0	0.0
Full tuition	0	0.0	0	0.0	0	0.0
More than full tuition	2	0.5	2	0.5	0	0.0
Median grant amount			$3,000		$2,250	

Informational and Library Resources

# of volumes and volume equivalents	247,306
# of titles	65,683
# of active serial subscriptions	2,536
Study seating capacity inside the library	235
# of professional librarians	6
Hours per week library is open	105
# of open, wired connections available to students	338
# of networked computers available for use by students	58
# of simultaneous wireless users	540
Require computer?	N

JD Attrition (from prior year)

	Academic	Other	Total	
	#	#	#	%
1st year	2	10	12	7.3%
2nd year	0	2	2	1.8%
3rd year	0	0	0	0.0%
4th year	0	0	0	0.0%

Employment

	Total	Percentage
Employment status known	131	98.5
Employment status unknown	2	1.5
Employed	108	82.4
Pursuing graduate degrees	7	5.3
Unemployed seeking employment	3	2.3
Unemployed not seeking employment	13	9.9

Type of Employment

# employed in law firms	58	53.7
# employed in business and industry	12	11.1
# employed in government	9	8.3
# employed in public interest	4	3.7
# employed as judicial clerks	9	8.3
# employed in academia	3	2.8

Geographic Location

# employed in state	31	28.7
# employed in foreign countries	6	5.6
# of states where employed	22	

Bar Passage Rates

Jurisdiction	New Hampshire		
Exam	Sum 03	Win 04	Total
# from school taking bar for the first time	33	2	35
School's pass rate for all first-time takers	55%	100%	57%
State's pass rate for all first-time takers	64%	58%	63%

Franklin Pierce Law Center

Admissions Office, 2 White Street
Concord, NH 03301
Phone: 603.228.9217; Fax: 603.224.4661
E-mail: admissions@piercelaw.edu; Website: www.piercelaw.edu

■ Introduction

Franklin Pierce Law Center is known throughout the world as an innovative leader in legal education, providing its students with the skills to lead and serve, and to meet the emerging needs of a global society. Established in 1973, Pierce Law emphasizes individually tailored legal programs a broad range of learning settings, including lectures and seminars, real-client clinics, independent study, and externships in law firms, courts, and in private and public agencies. In addition, we promote a community spirit of caring and compassion, with a close working relationship between students and faculty. Self-reliant students who know their own strengths and objectives thrive at Pierce Law and find the focus on personal pride and responsibility more motivating than fear, competition, or class rank.

Pierce Law is one of the smallest private law schools in the United States. Each entering class numbers approximately 150 students, allowing for a 13.5 to 1 student-teacher ratio. Classes are small, especially after the first year. Seventy-five of the 109 elective courses enroll 35 or fewer students.

Located in New Hampshire's capital city of Concord (45,000 population), Pierce Law is ideally situated one hour from Boston, the Atlantic seacoast, the state's Lakes Region, and the White Mountains.

■ Special Programs

- **Intellectual Property**—The internationally recognized intellectual and industrial property specialization (patents, licensing, technology transfer, trade secrets, trademarks, cyberlaw, and copyrights) is supported by 12 full-time faculty members, all intellectual property lawyers. Training includes learning to advise clients regarding intellectual property protection, infringement, and technology transfer. Students with technical backgrounds may focus on patent law, many passing the patent bar prior to graduation. Other intellectual property areas do not require a technical background.
- **Commerce and Technology Law**—The business curriculum prepares students for traditional types of practice and brings new opportunities for students choosing to confront the legal issues involving electronic commerce. The business and e-commerce curriculum also integrates well with the intellectual property curriculum, particularly for students interested in business and legal innovations associated with the Internet.
- **Social Justice Institute**—This hands-on professional training program prepares students for public interest law in private practice, governmental service, social policy advocacy, and criminal practice. Civil Practice Clinic students provide legal assistance to clients in

cases involving divorce; neglect and abuse of children; juvenile issues; social security; personal bankruptcy; consumer issues; and housing problems. In addition, students have the opportunity to assist in projects with the Institute for Health, Law, and Ethics.

- **Criminal Law**—As part of our Social Justice Institute, our Criminal Law curriculum offers courses, individual mentoring, clinics, and externships to prepare students for careers in prosecution or defense. Criminal Practice Clinic students represent clients charged with misdemeanor and juvenile offenses at the district court level. In the Appellate Defender Program, students prepare briefs for the New Hampshire Supreme Court in criminal cases. Externship opportunities are available in prosecutorial positions at the local, state, and federal level and in defense positions with law firms and governmental agencies.
- **Education Law**—This unique program recognizes the increasingly important role law plays in educational institutions from K-12 to universities. Courses and externship opportunities with government agencies, university counsel, school attorneys, and child advocates prepare students for this growing area of legal practice.
- **Health Law**—The Pierce Law Institute for Health, Law, and Ethics collaborates with faculty members of Dartmouth Medical School and the University of New Hampshire to provide ongoing programs to encourage understanding and cooperation among the separate disciplines. In addition, students may participate in institute projects such as developing a plan for quality, cost-effective elder care and representation of persons with disabilities.

■ Technology

Our commitment to training lawyers with the skills to practice in the information age is evident in our new facilities, including our smart classroom and high-technology courtroom. Through a variety of courses held in the courtroom, students significantly deepen their understanding of file and case management, particularly in complex cases, and expand their knowledge of visual persuasion beyond the traditional bounds of demonstrative evidence.

■ Joint-Degree Programs and LLM

Pierce Law offers two joint-degree programs: JD/Master of Education Law and the JD/Master of Intellectual Property, Commerce, and Technology. Summer programs enable students to earn additional credits needed to complete joint-degree programs in three years. The Master of Laws (LLM) in Intellectual Property, Commerce, and Technology is designed for law graduates who wish to examine the legally sophisticated intellectual property issues that often arise in policymaking and teaching.

■ Student Activities

Students prepare notes and comments for *IDEA: The Journal of Law and Technology; Pierce Law Review*; and *Annual Survey of New Hampshire Law*, an annual publication consisting of six articles focusing on recent New Hampshire Supreme Court opinions. Articles are written by second-year students and edited by third-year students. Students organize and participate in a wide variety of formal organizations and informal activities and events throughout the year.

■ Career Services

The Career Services Office works with students and alumni to find the best match to meet their skills and interests in changing legal markets. The office provides extensive individual counseling and guidance; brings attorneys to campus to provide first-hand information about the practice of law; advises students of all resources through weekly publications and job boards; coordinates the efforts of faculty, staff, and student groups to provide information about opportunities to gain experience; and conducts outreach to employers.

More than 75 percent of our graduates secure positions outside New Hampshire. Over 90 percent of our graduates are employed within six months after graduation.

■ Clinics

- Intellectual Property and Business Transaction
- Administrative Advocacy
- Family and Housing Law
- Consumer and Commercial Law
- Criminal Practice
- Mediation
- Appellate Defender Program

■ Admission

While LSAT scores and grade-point average are factors that must be considered in the decision-making process, neither alone is determinative. Every application receives a thorough and thoughtful review. The candidate's personal statement, letters of recommendation, and résumé are evaluated along with the numbers. Community service, employment during college, and other nonacademic accomplishments are given weight to the extent that they reflect initiative, social responsibility, maturity, and other qualities.

Applicant Profile

Franklin Pierce Law Center

LSAT Score	GPA								
	3.75 +	3.50 - 3.74	3.25 - 3.49	3.00 - 3.24	2.75 - 2.99	2.50 - 2.74	2.25 - 2.49	2.00 - 2.24	Below 2.00
175-180									
170-174									
165-169									
160-164									
155-159									
150-154									
145-149									
140-144									
135-139									
130-134									
125-129									
120-124									

Good Possibility   Possible   Unlikely

Note: This chart is to be used as a general guide in determining the chances for admittance. Nonnumerical factors are strongly considered for applicants.

George Mason University School of Law

3301 Fairfax Drive
Arlington, VA 22201
Phone: 703.993.8010; Fax: 703.993.8088
E-mail: arichar5@gmu.edu; Website: www.law.gmu.edu

*ABA
Approved
Since
1980*

The Basics

Type of school	Public
Term	Semester
Application deadline	3/15
Application fee	$35
Financial aid deadline	3/1
Can first year start other than fall?	No
Student to faculty ratio (fall)	14.6 to 1
Does the university offer:	
housing restricted to law students?	No
graduate housing for which law students are eligible?	No

Faculty and Administrators

	Total		Men		Women		Minorities	
	Fall	Spr	Fall	Spr	Fall	Spr	Fall	Spr
Full-time	35	28	34	25	1	3	1	1
Other Full-time	0	0	0	0	0	0	0	0
Deans, librarians, & others who teach	3	3	2	2	1	1	0	0
Part-time	79	61	56	52	23	9	4	4
Total	117	92	92	79	25	13	5	5

Curriculum

	Full-time	Part-time
Typical first-year section size	71	91
Is there typically a "small section" of the first-year class, other than Legal Writing, taught by full-time faculty	Yes	No
If yes, typical size offered last year	51	0
# of classroom course titles beyond 1st year curriculum	159	
# of upper division courses, excluding seminars with an enrollment: Under 25	129	
25-49	31	
50-74	17	
75-99	3	
100+	3	
# of seminars	42	
# of seminar positions available	609	
# of seminar positions filled	229	184
# of positions available in simulation courses	211	
# of simulation positions filled	139	61
# of positions available in faculty supervised clinical courses	105	
# of faculty supervised clinical positions filled	29	14
# involved in field placements	34	3
# involved in law journals	65	17
# involved in moot court or trial competitions	18	2
# of credit hours required to graduate	84	

JD Enrollment and Ethnicity

	Men		Women		Full-time		Part-time		1st-year		Total		JD Degs. Awd.
	#	%	#	%	#	%	#	%	#	%	#	%	
African Amer.	13	2.9	11	4.1	9	2.3	15	4.6	11	5.1	24	3.3	3
Amer. Indian	3	0.7	2	0.7	2	0.5	3	0.9	2	0.9	5	0.7	0
Asian Amer.	31	6.8	28	10.5	26	6.6	33	10.1	16	7.4	59	8.2	11
Mex. Amer.	0	0.0	0	0.0	0	0.0	0	0.0	0	0.0	0	0.0	0
Puerto Rican	0	0.0	0	0.0	0	0.0	0	0.0	0	0.0	0	0.0	0
Hispanic	20	4.4	3	1.1	11	2.8	12	3.7	12	5.6	23	3.2	3
Total Minority	67	14.7	44	16.5	48	12.1	63	19.3	41	19.0	111	15.4	17
For. Nation.	8	1.8	12	4.5	6	1.5	14	4.3	1	0.5	20	2.8	0
Caucasian	381	83.6	211	79.0	342	86.4	250	76.5	174	80.6	592	81.9	217
Unknown	0	0.0	0	0.0	0	0.0	0	0.0	0	0.0	0	0.0	0
Total	456	63.1	267	36.9	396	54.8	327	45.2	216	29.9	723		234

Tuition and Fees

	Resident	Nonresident
Full-time	$10,906	$21,532
Part-time	$7,790	$15,380

Living Expenses

Estimated living expenses for singles

Living on campus	Living off campus	Living at home
$12,522	$15,604	$8,802

George Mason University School of Law

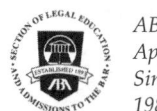

*ABA
Approved
Since
1980*

GPA and LSAT Scores

	Total	Full-time	Part-time
# of apps	5,039	4,353	686
# of admits	758	617	141
# of matrics	209	138	71
75% GPA	3.82	3.80	3.85
25% GPA	3.01	3.01	3.00
75% LSAT	166	166	165
25% LSAT	158	159	157

Grants and Scholarships (from prior year)

	Total #	Total %	Full-time #	Full-time %	Part-time #	Part-time %
Total # of students	737		390		347	
Total # receiving grants	74	10.0	62	15.9	12	3.5
Less than 1/2 tuition	60	8.1	56	14.4	4	1.2
Half to full tuition	7	0.9	2	0.5	5	1.4
Full tuition	0	0.0	0	0.0	0	0.0
More than full tuition	7	0.9	4	1.0	3	0.9
Median grant amount			$3,000		$3,250	

Informational and Library Resources

# of volumes and volume equivalents	432,475
# of titles	163,034
# of active serial subscriptions	5,559
Study seating capacity inside the library	316
# of professional librarians	7
Hours per week library is open	96
# of open, wired connections available to students	836
# of networked computers available for use by students	85
# of simultaneous wireless users	400
Require computer?	N

JD Attrition (from prior year)

	Academic #	Other #	Total #	Total %
1st year	6	11	17	10.1%
2nd year	1	1	2	0.9%
3rd year	0	0	0	0.0%
4th year	0	0	0	0.0%

Employment

	Total	Percentage
Employment status known	182	100.0
Employment status unknown	0	0.0
Employed	171	94.0
Pursuing graduate degrees	4	2.2
Unemployed seeking employment	1	0.5
Unemployed not seeking employment	6	3.3

Type of Employment

# employed in law firms	83	48.5
# employed in business and industry	25	14.6
# employed in government	30	17.5
# employed in public interest	8	4.7
# employed as judicial clerks	17	9.9
# employed in academia	8	4.7

Geographic Location

# employed in state	89	52.0
# employed in foreign countries	3	1.8
# of states where employed	14	

Bar Passage Rates

Jurisdiction	Virginia		
Exam	Sum 03	Win 04	Total
# from school taking bar for the first time	120	19	139
School's pass rate for all first-time takers	73%	63%	72%
State's pass rate for all first-time takers	75%	60%	72%

George Mason University School of Law

3301 Fairfax Drive
Arlington, VA 22201
Phone: 703.993.8010; Fax: 703.993.8088
E-mail: arichar5@gmu.edu; Website: www.law.gmu.edu

■ Introduction

George Mason University School of Law sits on the doorstep of the nation's capital. One of three public law schools in Virginia, it was established by authority of the Virginia General Assembly in 1979.

■ Enrollment/Student Body

George Mason University is an equal opportunity/ affirmative action institution.

■ Library and Physical Facilities

In January 1999, the law school relocated to a new, state-of-the-art facility equipped with electrical and data connections at every classroom and library seat, and two ultramodern moot courtrooms.

The school is a member of the library network of the Consortium for Continuing Higher Education in Northern Virginia, affording access to general university and public library collections.

■ Curriculum

George Mason University offers both full- and part-time divisions. The full-time division operates during the day and takes three years to complete. Students who elect the part-time division study at night and take four years to complete the requirements for the juris doctor degree.

A grounding in economics and basic mathematical and financial skills is important to a sophisticated legal education and to the development of a competent attorney. To ensure that George Mason graduates have this grounding, all students take a first-year course in Economic Foundations.

George Mason law students complete a three-year legal writing program, which emphasizes the use of technology and continual practice of skills in the development of actual transactions and cases. A separate writing grade-point average further underscores the importance of good writing at George Mason.

The curriculum begins with exposure to the courses fundamental to a well-rounded legal education. Students at George Mason can also elect one of our specialty programs, thus demonstrating depth as well as breadth in their training. All specialties are offered in both the full-time and part-time divisions.

George Mason has a number of clinical program offerings: the Immigration Law Clinic, the Legal Clinic, the Public Interest Law Clinic, the Domestic Relations Legal Clinic, the Telemedicine Law Clinic, the Law and Mental Illness Clinic, and the Clinic for Legal Assistance to Service Members. George Mason is a leader in

technology and law and is the headquarters for the Tech Center (National Center for Technology and Law), which brings together academics, high-tech industry leaders, and policy makers to debate and formulate national policy to keep pace with technological advances. George Mason, in conjunction with James Madison University, is also home to the Critical Infrastructure Protection (CIP) Project, a program that fully integrates the disciplines of law, policy, and technology for enhancing the security of cyber networks and economic processes supporting the nation's critical infrastructure.

■ Special Programs

- **Corporate and Securities Law**—prepares students to work in a variety of fields related to corporate law and financial markets. By developing a thorough understanding of both law and underlying theory, students are prepared to deal with rapidly changing business and legal environments.
- **Regulatory Law**—prepares students for practice in and before the numerous agencies that regulate business and other activities. Students are taught economics, the economic analysis of law, administrative law, legislation, lobbying, and negotiation, as well as several substantive areas of regulatory law.
- **International Business**—prepares students for practice in the rapidly changing global business community and provides them with a well-rounded legal education emphasizing analytical and writing skills.
- **Litigation Law**—provides an academic program for students interested in litigation and other dispute resolution processes. This is not a clinical training program. The track courses focus on the processes of dispute resolution and lawyers' roles from an analytical perspective.
- **Intellectual Property Law**—is designed for students having a degree in engineering or one of the physical or biological sciences who intend to practice within the field of intellectual property.
- **Technology Law Program**—combines coursework in the fields of technology law, intellectual property law, and business law. The program prepares students for work in law firms that serve high-technology clients, as in-house counsel for Internet start-up companies, and as attorneys for state and federal regulatory agencies with jurisdiction over technology industries.
- **LLM Programs**—for students wishing to pursue specialized study beyond the JD, George Mason offers two LLM programs: (1) the **LLM in Law and Economics;** and (2) the **LLM in Intellectual Property Law**. Detailed information about these programs is available at *www.law.gmu.edu/academics/llm.html.*

Admission

Two of the primary factors considered in the admission process are performance on the LSAT and undergraduate grade-point average. Other factors that are considered include difficulty of undergraduate major, undergraduate institution attended, possession of advanced degrees, writing ability, recommendations, extracurricular activities, employment experience, demonstrated commitment to public and community service, leadership skills and experience, history of overcoming personal or professional challenges, and other academic, personal, and professional achievements.

Student Activities

George Mason University provides many services to enhance the law school experience and enable students to take full advantage of the university's educational and personal enrichment opportunities.

Student activities include the *George Mason University Law Review*, *Civil Rights Law Journal*, *Federal Circuit Bar Journal*, a newspaper, and numerous law-related organizations. Students have an unparalleled opportunity to gain experience in such varied settings as the Office of the US Attorney for both the District of Columbia and the Eastern District of Virginia, as well as federal courts and agencies, local governments, and private firms.

Minority Student Services, Disability Support Services, and the Office of Veterans Services provide specialized assistance, as does the Counseling Center, where a staff of professionals helps students to reach personal, social, and academic goals.

Expenses and Financial Aid

George Mason University participates in the Direct Lending Program. There is no deadline for applying for financial aid, but applicants should complete the FAFSA as soon as possible in order to assure the timely award of aid.

In addition to loans available through the Direct Lending Program, George Mason students are eligible for a number of merit-based fellowships.

Career Services

The Office of Career Services aids students and alumni in finding permanent, part-time, and summer jobs by serving as a clearinghouse for information on available positions. It also advises on résumé and interview preparation and coordinates on-campus interviews. More than 150 firms, businesses, and government agencies recruit on campus each year. Graduates find employment in the legal profession throughout the country.

Applicant Profile

George Mason University School of Law
This grid includes only applicants who earned 120-180 LSAT scores under standard administrations.

LSAT Score	3.75 +		3.50 - 3.74		3.25 - 3.49		3.00 - 3.24		2.75 - 2.99		2.50 - 2.74		2.25 - 2.49		2.00 - 2.24		Below 2.00		No GPA		Total	
	Apps	Adm	Apps	Adm	Apps	Adm	Apps	Adm	Apps	Adm	Apps	Adm	Apps	Adm	Apps	Adm	Apps	Adm	Apps	Adm	Apps	Adm
175-180	1	1	2	2	0	0	1	1	0	0	2	2	0	0	0	0	0	0	0	0	6	6
170-174	13	13	15	15	14	14	10	9	13	11	2	1	4	2	2	2	0	0	0	0	73	67
165-169	61	59	84	72	72	63	59	47	47	27	26	18	14	8	6	0	1	0	5	4	375	298
160-164	154	98	243	51	223	17	194	22	125	17	66	6	26	6	12	1	2	0	11	3	1056	221
155-159	196	56	302	19	339	4	268	4	134	2	62	1	43	0	8	0	2	0	16	1	1370	87
150-154	121	18	176	11	256	4	242	3	134	0	87	0	32	0	12	1	3	0	19	1	1082	38
145-149	49	5	99	7	127	0	142	0	126	0	80	0	44	0	21	0	2	0	12	0	702	12
140-144	9	0	27	0	40	0	50	0	48	0	43	0	23	0	12	0	3	0	9	0	264	0
135-139	4	0	11	0	11	0	17	0	18	0	18	0	16	0	8	0	4	0	10	0	117	0
130-134	0	0	0	0	5	0	12	0	7	0	8	0	9	0	5	0	0	0	2	0	48	0
125-129	1	0	0	0	2	0	1	0	0	0	1	0	1	0	2	0	0	0	2	0	10	0
120-124	0	0	0	0	0	0	0	0	1	0	1	0	1	0	0	0	0	0	0	0	3	0
Total	609	250	959	177	1089	102	996	86	653	57	396	28	213	16	88	4	17	0	86	9	5106	729

Apps = Number of Applicants   Adm = Number Admitted   Reflects 99% of the total applicant pool.

This chart is to be used as a general guide only. Every application is reviewed and evaluated in its entirety.

The George Washington University Law School

2000 H Street, NW
Washington, DC 20052
Phone: 202.994.6288; Fax: 202.994.3597
E-mail: jdadmit@law.gwu.edu; Website: www.law.gwu.edu

ABA Approved Since 1923

The Basics

Type of school	Private
Term	Semester
Application deadline	3/1
Application fee	$70
Financial aid deadline	
Can first year start other than fall?	No
Student to faculty ratio (fall)	14.6 to 1
Does the university offer:	
housing restricted to law students?	Yes
graduate housing for which law students are eligible?	No

Faculty and Administrators

	Total Fall	Total Spr	Men Fall	Men Spr	Women Fall	Women Spr	Minorities Fall	Minorities Spr
Full-time	85	87	56	57	29	30	12	13
Other Full-time	8	8	6	6	2	2	1	1
Deans, librarians, & others who teach	4	4	4	4	0	0	0	0
Part-time	181	213	126	143	55	70	26	24
Total	278	312	192	210	86	102	39	38

Curriculum

	Full-time	Part-time
Typical first-year section size	103	131
Is there typically a "small section" of the first-year class, other than Legal Writing, taught by full-time faculty	Yes	No
If yes, typical size offered last year	36	0
# of classroom course titles beyond 1st year curriculum	197	
# of upper division courses, excluding seminars with an enrollment: Under 25	225	
25-49	74	
50-74	37	
75-99	14	
100+	15	
# of seminars	25	
# of seminar positions available	400	
# of seminar positions filled	178	153
# of positions available in simulation courses	879	
# of simulation positions filled	305	522
# of positions available in faculty supervised clinical courses	128	
# of faculty supervised clinical positions filled	120	8
# involved in field placements	212	22
# involved in law journals	308	23
# involved in moot court or trial competitions	207	27
# of credit hours required to graduate	84	

JD Enrollment and Ethnicity

	Men #	Men %	Women #	Women %	Full-time #	Full-time %	Part-time #	Part-time %	1st-year #	1st-year %	Total #	Total %	JD Degs. Awd.
African Amer.	48	5.7	95	13.0	131	10.0	12	4.5	47	9.1	143	9.1	61
Amer. Indian	4	0.5	4	0.5	5	0.4	3	1.1	1	0.2	8	0.5	1
Asian Amer.	68	8.0	100	13.7	136	10.4	32	12.0	47	9.1	168	10.6	38
Mex. Amer.	0	0.0	0	0.0	0	0.0	0	0.0	0	0.0	0	0.0	0
Puerto Rican	0	0.0	0	0.0	0	0.0	0	0.0	0	0.0	0	0.0	0
Hispanic	78	9.2	59	8.1	126	9.6	11	4.1	40	7.8	137	8.7	36
Total Minority	198	23.3	258	35.3	398	30.4	58	21.7	135	26.2	456	28.9	136
For. Nation.	3	0.4	4	0.5	7	0.5	0	0.0	0	0.0	7	0.4	6
Caucasian	559	65.9	418	57.3	797	60.8	180	67.4	325	63.0	977	61.9	293
Unknown	88	10.4	50	6.8	109	8.3	29	10.9	56	10.9	138	8.7	31
Total	848	53.7	730	46.3	1311	83.1	267	16.9	516	32.7	1578		466

Tuition and Fees

	Resident	Nonresident
Full-time	$32,620	$32,620
Part-time	$22,940	$22,940

Living Expenses

Estimated living expenses for singles

Living on campus	Living off campus	Living at home
$16,340	$16,340	$16,340

The George Washington University Law School

*ABA
Approved
Since
1923*

GPA and LSAT Scores

	Total	Full-time	Part-time
# of apps	11,171	N/A	N/A
# of admits	2,066	N/A	N/A
# of matrics	512	393	119
75% GPA	3.76	3.78	3.65
25% GPA	3.39	3.45	3.22
75% LSAT	166	166	164
25% LSAT	161	162	160

Grants and Scholarships (from prior year)

	Total		Full-time		Part-time	
	#	%	#	%	#	%
Total # of students	1,555		1,264		291	
Total # receiving grants	615	39.5	573	45.3	42	14.4
Less than 1/2 tuition	528	34.0	495	39.2	33	11.3
Half to full tuition	84	5.4	75	5.9	9	3.1
Full tuition	3	0.2	3	0.2	0	0.0
More than full tuition	0	0.0	0	0.0	0	0.0
Median grant amount			$10,000		$7,000	

Informational and Library Resources

# of volumes and volume equivalents	580,994
# of titles	134,500
# of active serial subscriptions	4,588
Study seating capacity inside the library	643
# of professional librarians	20
Hours per week library is open	110
# of open, wired connections available to students	54
# of networked computers available for use by students	113
# of simultaneous wireless users	2,000
Require computer?	Y

JD Attrition (from prior year)

	Academic	Other	Total	
	#	#	#	%
1st year	0	29	29	5.4%
2nd year	0	3	3	0.6%
3rd year	0	1	1	0.2%
4th year	0	0	0	0.0%

Employment

	Total	Percentage
Employment status known	436	100.0
Employment status unknown	0	0.0
Employed	421	96.6
Pursuing graduate degrees	2	0.5
Unemployed seeking employment	11	2.5
Unemployed not seeking employment	2	0.5

Type of Employment

# employed in law firms	238	56.5
# employed in business and industry	31	7.4
# employed in government	73	17.3
# employed in public interest	11	2.6
# employed as judicial clerks	52	12.4
# employed in academia	2	0.5

Geographic Location

# employed in state	197	46.8
# employed in foreign countries	2	0.5
# of states where employed	34	

Bar Passage Rates

Jurisdiction	Maryland			New York		
Exam	Sum 03	Win 04	Total	Sum 03	Win 04	Total
# from school taking bar for the first time	105	6	111	93	11	104
School's pass rate for all first-time takers	82%	50%	80%	86%	64%	84%
State's pass rate for all first-time takers	73%	62%	71%	78%	58%	75%

The George Washington University Law School

2000 H Street, NW
Washington, DC 20052
Phone: 202.994.6288; Fax: 202.994.3597
E-mail: jdadmit@law.gwu.edu; Website: www.law.gwu.edu

■ Introduction

Established in 1865, The George Washington University Law School is the oldest law school in the District of Columbia. Just four blocks from the White House and minutes away from Congress, the US Supreme Court, and various federal departments and agencies, GW offers its students special opportunities to study and observe lawmaking at its source.

The Law School is located on the main campus of The George Washington University, a private nonsectarian institution established in 1821.

■ Library and Physical Facilities

The collection of the Jacob Burns Law Library numbers more than 500,000 volumes and volume equivalents. It contains a comprehensive research library of Anglo-American law, including the annotated statutes of the federal government, the 50 states, the territories, and other common-law countries as well as the reported decisions of these jurisdictions, in many editions and often in multiple copies. The library is especially strong in administrative and regulatory material and congressional coverage. The extensive treatise collection covers not only the field of law, but also a wide range of law-related disciplines. A portion of the holdings of the former Library of the Carnegie Endowment of International Peace, acquired by the university in 1950, has been incorporated into the library. Especially strong collections are maintained for tax, labor, intellectual property, and international law.

A staff of 35 permanent and numerous part-time employees offer information, instruction, and other research support services, and the library offers extensive hours to meet the needs of both full- and part-time students. Computing facilities for student use are located throughout the library. A computer lab with Windows-based computers offers word processing, spreadsheet, and presentation software. These and other dedicated workstations provide access to the Internet, e-mail, and online research databases. Students using properly equipped laptops may connect to the Internet and selected research databases via numerous network outlets.

The Law School occupies seven buildings. Four of the buildings adjoin one another, have internal passageways on most floors, and largely function as one consolidated complex that comprises the library, classrooms, student lounges, and administrative, faculty, and student group offices. Three additional buildings located directly across from the main complex house the Community Legal Clinics and student publication offices. Since 2000, significant interior renovations have been made throughout the Law School, increasing its aesthetic appeal, ergonomics, instructional capabilities, and

student space. All of the Law School's classrooms are equipped with advanced sound systems, multimedia presentation capabilities, and laptop outlets at each student space. In 2002, the Law School redesigned its main moot courtroom in cooperation with the National Center for State Courts as a model for how technology can be used to enhance litigation practice.

■ Curriculum

One of the Law School's greatest strengths is the richness of its curriculum. With over 250 courses and more than 200 electives offered each year, students have an opportunity to sample a broad array of legal subjects and to design a program of study that fits their individual interests and career plans. In addition to introductory and more advanced courses in a variety of fields, there are many highly specialized courses that allow students to develop expertise in a field, including environmental law, international law, intellectual property law, government regulation, and constitutional law.

■ Clinical Programs

The Law School's extensive clinical programs provide critically needed services to the community while giving motivated students the opportunity to experience the practical application of law and to develop skills as negotiators, advocates, and litigators. Clinical programs are offered in the areas of civil litigation, consumer mediation, federal and criminal appeals, environmental law, health rights law, immigration, international human rights, older prisoners, public justice advocacy, small business/community development, and vaccine injury. In addition, a wide variety of externship opportunities are available with more than 200 government agencies, the judiciary, and nonprofit organizations.

■ Special Programs

For JD students, the following joint-degree programs are offered: JD/MBA; JD/MPA; JD/MPH; JD/MPP; and JD/MA (in international affairs, history, or women's studies).

The Master of Laws (LLM) degree is offered in the areas of environmental law, international law, intellectual property law, government procurement law, and litigation and dispute resolution.

Summer study abroad opportunities include the Oxford–GW Program in International Human Rights Law, the GW–Munich Intellectual Property Law Program, and the GW–Augsburg (Germany) Student Exchange Program. GW is also a member of the North American Consortium on Legal Education, which allows

The George Washington University Law School

students to study at member Canadian and Mexican law schools.

■ Student Activities

Membership is available on four publications—the *Law Review, International Law Review, Public Contract Law Journal* (cosponsored by ABA sections), and the *American Intellectual Property Law Association Quarterly Journal*, which is published by AIPLA and housed at the Law School. Three skills boards—the Moot Court Board, Trial Court Board, and Alternative Dispute Resolution Board—provide opportunities for participation in a number of inter- and intrascholastic competitions. In addition, over 20 student groups are active at the Law School each year, sponsoring social, educational, career, and public interest-related programs and events. Each year the Enrichment Program brings a number of distinguished speakers to the Law School. Recent speakers have included Supreme Court justices, legal scholars, authors, and leaders from government and public interest organizations.

■ Career Development

The Career Development Office (CDO) provides a full range of services to support the career decision-making process of students and alumni and to serve prospective employers. Because the Law School does not emphasize any geographic region in its instruction, graduates are prepared to meet the needs of society in many fields of law and in any part of the country or abroad.

■ Housing and Fitness Facilities

The Law School offers its students assistance in securing housing in two nearby apartment buildings by reserving units exclusively for GW Law student use and negotiating special lease terms and a waiver of minimum income requirements. These privately owned buildings are within short walking distance from the Law School complex and in close proximity to public transportation, shopping, entertainment, and other amenities. For recreation and sports, students have full use of the university's Lerner Health and Wellness Center, multistory, state-of-the-art complex featuring a wide range of fitness facilities and classes.

Applicant Profile

The George Washington University Law School
This grid includes only applicants who earned 120-180 LSAT scores under standard administrations.

LSAT Score	3.75 +		3.50 - 3.74		3.25 - 3.49		3.00 - 3.24		2.75 - 2.99		2.50 - 2.74		2.25 - 2.49		2.00 - 2.24		Below 2.00		No GPA		Total	
	Apps	Adm	Apps	Adm	Apps	Adm	Apps	Adm	Apps	Adm	Apps	Adm	Apps	Adm	Apps	Adm	Apps	Adm	Apps	Adm	Apps	Adm
175-180	13	13	10	10	12	10	8	5	3	2	2	0	1	0	1	0	0	0	0	0	50	40
170-174	63	62	87	85	81	67	49	20	21	0	13	2	7	0	1	0	0	0	4	1	326	237
165-169	331	319	475	433	381	201	224	33	107	7	36	2	14	0	3	0	1	0	17	8	1589	1003
160-164	635	223	1069	171	816	98	497	43	197	10	73	2	26	0	12	0	2	0	40	6	3367	553
155-159	441	37	721	49	727	30	482	31	193	2	86	0	40	0	9	0	3	0	36	0	2738	149
150-154	167	16	355	24	407	25	310	12	155	0	86	0	28	0	9	0	3	0	34	0	1554	77
145-149	43	0	111	0	157	0	137	0	106	0	62	0	32	0	14	0	3	0	14	0	679	0
140-144	14	0	40	0	49	0	63	0	64	0	30	0	13	0	10	0	4	0	8	0	295	0
135-139	1	0	10	0	20	0	12	0	23	0	14	0	8	0	9	0	2	0	6	0	105	0
130-134	0	0	0	0	2	0	5	0	6	0	4	0	5	0	3	0	0	0	1	0	26	0
125-129	0	0	0	0	1	0	2	0	1	0	2	0	1	0	0	0	0	0	1	0	8	0
120-124	0	0	0	0	0	0	0	0	0	0	1	0	0	0	0	0	0	0	0	0	1	0
Total	1708	670	2878	772	2653	431	1789	144	876	21	409	6	175	0	71	0	18	0	161	15	10738	2059

Apps = Number of Applicants
Adm = Number Admitted
Reflects 99% of the total applicant pool.

Georgetown University Law Center

600 New Jersey Avenue, NW, Room 589
Washington, DC 20001
Phone: 202.662.9010; Fax: 202.662.9439
E-mail: admis@law.georgetown.edu; Website: www.law.georgetown.edu

ABA
Approved
Since
1924

The Basics

Type of school	Private
Term	Semester
Application deadline	11/1 2/1 3/1
Application fee	$70
Financial aid deadline	3/1
Can first year start other than fall?	No
Student to faculty ratio (fall)	14.8 to 1
Does the university offer: housing restricted to law students?	Yes
graduate housing for which law students are eligible?	No

Faculty and Administrators

	Total Fall	Total Spr	Men Fall	Men Spr	Women Fall	Women Spr	Minorities Fall	Minorities Spr
Full-time	102	102	69	67	33	35	13	14
Other Full-time	3	3	2	2	1	1	1	1
Deans, librarians, & others who teach	12	11	9	8	3	3	1	1
Part-time	105	122	88	91	17	31	8	3
Total	**222**	**238**	**168**	**168**	**54**	**70**	**23**	**19**

Curriculum

	Full-time	Part-time
Typical first-year section size	112	125
Is there typically a "small section" of the first-year class, other than Legal Writing, taught by full-time faculty	Yes	Yes
If yes, typical size offered last year	26	32
# of classroom course titles beyond 1st year curriculum	275	
# of upper division courses, excluding seminars with an enrollment: Under 25	150	
25-49	53	
50-74	30	
75-99	17	
100+	18	
# of seminars	158	
# of seminar positions available	2,649	
# of seminar positions filled	1,071	911
# of positions available in simulation courses	1,043	
# of simulation positions filled	463	392
# of positions available in faculty supervised clinical courses	339	
# of faculty supervised clinical positions filled	309	12
# involved in field placements	26	3
# involved in law journals	719	62
# involved in moot court or trial competitions	421	139
# of credit hours required to graduate	83	

JD Enrollment and Ethnicity

	Men #	Men %	Women #	Women %	Full-time #	Full-time %	Part-time #	Part-time %	1st-year #	1st-year %	Total #	Total %	JD Degs. Awd.
African Amer.	58	5.5	121	13.6	144	9.3	35	9.1	61	10.5	179	9.2	95
Amer. Indian	3	0.3	1	0.1	1	0.1	3	0.8	3	0.5	4	0.2	3
Asian Amer.	101	9.6	86	9.7	148	9.5	39	10.1	43	7.4	187	9.7	59
Mex. Amer.	8	0.8	3	0.3	9	0.6	2	0.5	3	0.5	11	0.6	0
Puerto Rican	1	0.1	5	0.6	3	0.2	3	0.8	3	0.5	6	0.3	1
Hispanic	40	3.8	30	3.4	56	3.6	14	3.6	24	4.1	70	3.6	34
Total Minority	211	20.1	246	27.7	361	23.3	96	24.9	137	23.5	457	23.6	192
For. Nation.	30	2.9	32	3.6	47	3.0	15	3.9	20	3.4	62	3.2	17
Caucasian	806	76.8	606	68.3	1140	73.5	272	70.6	423	72.7	1412	72.9	478
Unknown	2	0.2	3	0.3	3	0.2	2	0.5	2	0.3	5	0.3	0
Total	1049	54.2	887	45.8	1551	80.1	385	19.9	582	30.1	1936		687

Tuition and Fees

	Resident	Nonresident
Full-time	$33,055	$33,055
Part-time	$24,200	$24,200

Living Expenses

Estimated living expenses for singles

Living on campus	Living off campus	Living at home
$18,095	$18,095	$13,320

Georgetown University Law Center

*ABA
Approved
Since
1924*

GPA and LSAT Scores

	Total	Full-time	Part-time
# of apps	12,498	11,620	878
# of admits	2,333	2,143	190
# of matrics	583	453	130
75% GPA	3.78	3.80	3.71
25% GPA	3.27	3.43	3.18
75% LSAT	170	170	166
25% LSAT	164	166	160

Grants and Scholarships (from prior year)

	Total		Full-time		Part-time	
	#	%	#	%	#	%
Total # of students	1,993		1,601		392	
Total # receiving grants	469	23.5	461	28.8	8	2.0
Less than 1/2 tuition	344	17.3	336	21.0	8	2.0
Half to full tuition	93	4.7	93	5.8	0	0.0
Full tuition	32	1.6	32	2.0	0	0.0
More than full tuition	0	0.0	0	0.0	0	0.0
Median grant amount			$11,350		$3,500	

Informational and Library Resources

# of volumes and volume equivalents	1,104,965
# of titles	349,097
# of active serial subscriptions	9,920
Study seating capacity inside the library	1,265
# of professional librarians	23
Hours per week library is open	107
# of open, wired connections available to students	1,278
# of networked computers available for use by students	319
# of simultaneous wireless users	3,000
Require computer?	N

JD Attrition (from prior year)

	Academic	Other	Total	
	#	#	#	%
1st year	0	9	9	1.6%
2nd year	0	10	10	1.6%
3rd year	0	4	4	0.6%
4th year	2	0	2	2.3%

Employment

	Total	Percentage
Employment status known	653	97.8
Employment status unknown	15	2.2
Employed	590	90.4
Pursuing graduate degrees	2	0.3
Unemployed seeking employment	10	1.5
Unemployed not seeking employment	51	7.8

Type of Employment

# employed in law firms	371	62.9
# employed in business and industry	13	2.2
# employed in government	58	9.8
# employed in public interest	20	3.4
# employed as judicial clerks	62	10.5
# employed in academia	4	0.7

Geographic Location

# employed in state	202	34.2
# employed in foreign countries	9	1.5
# of states where employed	33	

Bar Passage Rates

Jurisdiction	New York			Maryland		
Exam	Sum 03	Win 04	Total	Sum 03	Win 04	Total
# from school taking bar for the first time	221	16	237	91	19	110
School's pass rate for all first-time takers	92%	88%	92%	91%	89%	91%
State's pass rate for all first-time takers	78%	58%	75%	73%	62%	71%

Georgetown University Law Center

600 New Jersey Avenue, NW, Room 589
Washington, DC 20001
Phone: 202.662.9010; Fax: 202.662.9439
E-mail: admis@law.georgetown.edu; Website: www.law.georgetown.edu

■ Introduction

Georgetown University Law Center, founded in 1870, is a dynamic and diverse intellectual community in which to study law. Its curriculum includes more courses and seminars than any other law school. Its distinguished full-time faculty is the nation's largest and is augmented by the experience and perspective of outstanding members of the bench and bar. The goal is education in its fullest sense—not only mastery of law—but a sense of the philosophical, political, and ethical dimensions of law. Preeminent in the fields of constitutional, international, and tax law, as well as clinical legal education, the Georgetown faculty is also known for its expertise in civil rights, corporate law, environmental law, family law, feminist jurisprudence, health law, immigration and refugee law, intellectual property law, legal history, and securities law. The Supreme Court, the Congress of the United States, and the Library of Congress are within walking distance of the campus, forming a unique environment for creative legal thought and learning.

■ Student Body

The student body, one of the most diverse in the nation, is recruited from more than 250 undergraduate colleges and universities and 17 foreign nations. The school actively recruits women and men from diverse ethnic, racial, economic, and educational backgrounds.

■ The Law Center Campus

Georgetown Law Center's campus completion project, finished in the fall of 2004, added two new buildings to the Law Center campus, the Eric E. Hotung International Law Center Building, and the Sport and Fitness Center. The construction project was the culmination of a goal set more than two decades ago: to create a campus that would nurture students in mind, body, and spirit. The Hotung building brings all the major components of Georgetown's international programs under one roof, and includes the new John Wolff International and Comparative Law Library. The Sport and Fitness Center features a four-lane lap pool and basketball and racquetball courts, as well as a café and lounge with wireless network connectivity.

The Law Center's Edward Bennett Williams Law Library houses the third largest academic law library collection in the nation. The library also provides students access to many web-based services to ensure they have the most advanced research support available.

Georgetown's McDonough Hall, with its lecture halls, seminar rooms, faculty offices, bookstore, student dining area, and lounges is the academic center of the campus.

Housing for approximately 300 students is available in the Gewirz Student Center. It offers a variety of apartment styles with one, two, and three bedrooms. Apartments designed for students with disabilities are also available.

■ Curriculum

The Law Center offers day and evening programs leading to the JD degree. Entry to both programs is in the fall. First year students choose either the A or B curriculum. Students in the A curriculum begin their studies with eight courses, including one elective course in the spring semester. The B curriculum includes courses that emphasize the sources of law in history, philosophy, political theory, and economics. It also seeks to reflect the increasingly public nature of contemporary law. A residency of six semesters is required for full-time students, eight semesters for part-time students.

■ Joint Degrees

Georgetown has established 11 joint-degree programs: JD/Master of Public Policy, JD/Master of Foreign Service, JD/Master of Arts in Arab Studies, JD/Master of Arts in German and European Studies, JD/Master of Arts in Latin American Studies, JD/Master of Arts in Eurasian, Russian and East European Studies, JD/Master of Arts in Security Studies, JD/Master of Business Administration, JD/Master of Public Health (with Johns Hopkins School of Public Health), JD/Master or Doctorate in Philosophy, and the JD/Doctorate in Government.

■ International and Comparative Law Programs

The Law Center has many highly regarded programs dealing with different aspects of international law.

The Global Law Scholars Program provides a special opportunity for a limited number of full-time JD students to prepare for a law practice in which they regularly encounter problems involving more than one legal system. The program aims to combine language skills and cultural familiarity with rigorous and directed legal training to produce lawyers who are ready to practice in the global legal environment of the twenty-first century.

The Law Center's Institute of International Economic Law offers the opportunity for students to obtain a certificate testifying to special competence in World Trade Organization (WTO) understanding. In addition, the Law Center's International Summer Internship Program offers students opportunities to work abroad with practicing lawyers in law firms, corporations, and government organizations. Georgetown also offers the opportunity to study law during the summer in London with distinguished professors from Europe and the US.

■ Clinical Programs and Public Interest Law

Georgetown Law Center, a pioneer in clinical legal education, offers an unmatched clinical program. Clinical programs are divided into two categories: (1) programs that permit students to represent clients in court or in administrative hearings and (2) programs that enable students to participate in a nontrial context in federal and local agencies, schools, and other institutions.

The Public Interest Law Scholars Program gives special encouragement, in the form of enriched educational opportunities, career counseling, financial support of up to one-third tuition, and a limited number of summer employment stipends, to eight students per class who are committed to practice law in the public interest.

The Office of Public Interest and Community Service promotes community service projects, provides academic counseling, conducts career-related programs and workshops, and maintains public interest job listings for all students and graduates interested in pursuing public interest employment.

■ Admission

The Law Center evaluates candidates on two scales: academic or objective criteria and personal or subjective criteria. Academic information includes undergraduate records and LSAT scores. Personal factors include extra-curricular activities, recommendations, work experience, and diversity of background. Georgetown does not use numerical cutoffs. Early application is encouraged since Georgetown employs a rolling admission process.

■ Student Activities

Students edit and publish 10 scholarly journals. The *Law Weekly*, the school newspaper, is printed under student direction. The Barristers Council is responsible for the many appellate advocacy and mock trial programs. Students participate in the decision processes of the Law Center through the Student Bar Association and student/faculty committees. Over 70 law student organizations support personal, social, and professional interests.

■ Financial Aid

Georgetown offers need-based, three-year financial aid grants to approximately one-third of the entering full-time class. Federal and commercial loans with preferred terms, along with on- and off-campus work-study opportunities, are available. Approximately 85 percent of Georgetown's JD students obtain financial aid.

Recently acknowledged as one of the nation's top programs by Equal Justice Works, Georgetown's Loan Repayment Assistance Program enables JD graduates to pursue careers in public service.

■ Career Services

The Office of Career Services offers a wide range of career counseling and job-related programming. First-year students are assigned a section advisor who works individually with them throughout law school. The on-campus interview program is one of the largest in the country. The office also coordinates the Judicial Clerkship program.

Applicant Profile

Since the Georgetown Admissions Committee takes into consideration a number of factors in evaluating whether a candidate would be suitable for admission, we cannot provide an applicant profile based solely on GPA and LSAT scores. In making such determinations, the committee focuses on various aspects of a candidate's background and experience which, in combination with GPA and LSAT scores, gives insight into a candidate's suitability for admission.

University of Georgia School of Law

Harold Hirsch Hall, 225 Herty Drive
Athens, GA 30602-6012
Phone: 706.542.7060; Fax: 706.542.5556
E-mail: ugajd@uga.edu; Website: www.law.uga.edu

ABA Approved Since 1930

The Basics

Type of school	Public
Term	Semester
Application deadline	2/1
Application fee	$30
Financial aid deadline	2/1
Can first year start other than fall?	No
Student to faculty ratio (fall)	17.4 to 1
Does the university offer:	
housing restricted to law students?	No
graduate housing for which law students are eligible?	Yes

Faculty and Administrators

	Total		Men		Women		Minorities	
	Fall	Spr	Fall	Spr	Fall	Spr	Fall	Spr
Full-time	33	31	25	23	8	8	2	2
Other Full-time	8	8	3	3	5	5	0	0
Deans, librarians, & others who teach	7	7	3	3	4	4	0	0
Part-time	13	20	11	14	2	6	1	1
Total	**61**	**66**	**42**	**43**	**19**	**23**	**3**	**3**

Curriculum

		Full-time	Part-time
Typical first-year section size		79	0
Is there typically a "small section" of the first-year class, other than Legal Writing, taught by full-time faculty		No	No
If yes, typical size offered last year		0	0
# of classroom course titles beyond 1st year curriculum		119	
# of upper division courses, excluding seminars with an enrollment:	Under 25	83	
	25-49	38	
	50-74	12	
	75-99	8	
	100+	8	
# of seminars		23	
# of seminar positions available		433	
# of seminar positions filled		299	0
# of positions available in simulation courses		322	
# of simulation positions filled		258	0
# of positions available in faculty supervised clinical courses		387	
# of faculty supervised clinical positions filled		347	0
# involved in field placements		134	0
# involved in law journals		193	0
# involved in moot court or trial competitions		337	0
# of credit hours required to graduate		88	

JD Enrollment and Ethnicity

	Men #	Men %	Women #	Women %	Full-time #	Full-time %	Part-time #	Part-time %	1st-year #	1st-year %	Total #	Total %	JD Degs. Awd.
African Amer.	30	8.8	56	16.0	86	12.5	0	0.0	32	13.7	86	12.5	28
Amer. Indian	1	0.3	1	0.3	2	0.3	0	0.0	1	0.4	2	0.3	0
Asian Amer.	10	2.9	14	4.0	24	3.5	0	0.0	3	1.3	24	3.5	2
Mex. Amer.	0	0.0	0	0.0	0	0.0	0	0.0	0	0.0	0	0.0	0
Puerto Rican	0	0.0	0	0.0	0	0.0	0	0.0	0	0.0	0	0.0	0
Hispanic	5	1.5	7	2.0	12	1.7	0	0.0	5	2.1	12	1.7	2
Total Minority	46	13.5	78	22.3	124	18.0	0	0.0	41	17.6	124	18.0	32
For. Nation.	0	0.0	1	0.3	1	0.1	0	0.0	1	0.4	1	0.1	0
Caucasian	270	79.2	252	72.2	522	75.7	0	0.0	161	69.1	522	75.7	180
Unknown	25	7.3	18	5.2	43	6.2	0	0.0	30	12.9	43	6.2	11
Total	341	49.4	349	50.6	690	100.0	0	0.0	233	33.8	690		223

Tuition and Fees

	Resident	Nonresident
Full-time	$7,978	$25,084
Part-time	$0	$0

Living Expenses

Estimated living expenses for singles

Living on campus	Living off campus	Living at home
$8,746	$10,188	$6,328

University of Georgia School of Law

ABA
Approved
Since
1930

GPA and LSAT Scores

	Total	Full-time	Part-time
# of apps	2,870	2,870	0
# of admits	580	580	0
# of matrics	235	235	0
75% GPA	0.00	3.82	0.00
25% GPA	0.00	3.35	0.00
75% LSAT	0	164	0
25% LSAT	0	157	0

Grants and Scholarships (from prior year)

	Total		Full-time		Part-time	
	#	%	#	%	#	%
Total # of students	692		692		0	
Total # receiving grants	215	31.1	215	31.1	0	0.0
Less than 1/2 tuition	148	21.4	148	21.4	0	0.0
Half to full tuition	9	1.3	9	1.3	0	0.0
Full tuition	42	6.1	42	6.1	0	0.0
More than full tuition	16	2.3	16	2.3	0	0.0
Median grant amount			$2,000		$0	

Informational and Library Resources

# of volumes and volume equivalents	505,957
# of titles	131,729
# of active serial subscriptions	7,046
Study seating capacity inside the library	403
# of professional librarians	12
Hours per week library is open	103
# of open, wired connections available to students	0
# of networked computers available for use by students	54
# of simultaneous wireless users	400
Require computer?	N

JD Attrition (from prior year)

	Academic	Other	Total	
	#	#	#	%
1st year	0	5	5	1.9%
2nd year	0	1	1	0.5%
3rd year	0	0	0	0.0%
4th year	0	0	0	0.0%

Employment

	Total	Percentage
Employment status known	201	98.0
Employment status unknown	4	2.0
Employed	189	94.0
Pursuing graduate degrees	7	3.5
Unemployed seeking employment	4	2.0
Unemployed not seeking employment	1	0.5

Type of Employment

	Total	Percentage
# employed in law firms	115	60.8
# employed in business and industry	12	6.3
# employed in government	19	10.1
# employed in public interest	7	3.7
# employed as judicial clerks	31	16.4
# employed in academia	4	2.1

Geographic Location

	Total	Percentage
# employed in state	159	84.1
# employed in foreign countries	0	0.0
# of states where employed		15

Bar Passage Rates

Jurisdiction	Georgia		
Exam	Sum 03	Win 04	Total
# from school taking bar for the first time	154	10	164
School's pass rate for all first-time takers	92%	70%	90%
State's pass rate for all first-time takers	86%	75%	83%

University of Georgia School of Law

Harold Hirsch Hall, 225 Herty Drive
Athens, GA 30602-6012
Phone: 706.542.7060; Fax: 706.542.5556
E-mail: ugajd@uga.edu; Website: www.law.uga.edu

■ Introduction

The University of Georgia School of Law, founded in 1859, is on the campus of the University of Georgia in Athens, Georgia. The university provides an excellent setting for the study of law with superb libraries and outstanding academic, cultural, recreational, and social opportunities. Athens, a town of 91,000, is the commercial and legal center for northeast Georgia and is less than an hour from downtown Atlanta. Athens also features a cultural richness ranging from antebellum homes to the latest in the alternative music scene.

The School of Law is approved by the American Bar Association, is a member of the Association of American Law Schools, and has a chapter of the Order of the Coif.

■ The Student Body

The law school student body shares a strong sense of community, and the school prides itself on the collegiality among students, faculty, and staff. The entering class usually numbers around 200, and the entire student body, including LLM students, averages 640 students. The law school is also a vital part of the university community, which supports a cosmopolitan mix of over 30,000 undergraduate, graduate, and professional students. Many law students take advantage of these assets by taking courses in other schools and colleges of the university, and by participating in the intellectual and social life of the campus.

■ Curriculum

The law curriculum is rich and diverse. The first year of study consists of required core courses, but, after its completion, students may choose from a wealth of classes, seminars, and clinical programs to suit their interests.

Clinical program opportunities, both criminal and civil, abound. Clinical education expands upon the classroom knowledge by providing essential experiential learning. Students interested in criminal law can participate in the Prosecutorial Clinic or the Legal Aid and Defender Clinic. Students interested in environmental law, family law, public interest law, and any of a number of other areas of study will find the Civil Externship Clinic, Family Violence Clinic, and the Environmental Law Practicum add to their understanding and preparedness.

■ Faculty

While some law schools choose to emphasize either scholarship or teaching, the University of Georgia seeks a balance of the two, firmly believing that classroom teaching is enhanced by scholarly expertise. The college town setting fosters student-faculty interaction by increasing faculty availability and promoting a conducive atmosphere for dialogue.

The ranks of the faculty include a Pulitzer Prize winner, former law clerks for the US Supreme Court and appellate courts, recipients of the university's highest honor for teaching excellence, and Fulbright Scholars. Most bring practical experience to the classroom as well; they have been trial and corporate attorneys, and many continue to accept pro bono cases or serve as legal consultants.

Faculty expertise is expanded by the addition of outstanding adjuncts, including leading members of the state and federal judiciary, corporate attorneys from the region's most powerful firms, international attorneys, government leaders, and prominent attorneys in the fields of public interest and environmental law. In addition, the law school's Dean Rusk Center—International, Comparative, and Graduate Legal Studies—annually is host to several international scholars who may teach mini-courses in their areas of interest. Recent courses include European Union banking law, international sales law, law of Mexico, and international investment law of Japan.

■ Educational Enrichment Programs

University of Georgia law students have several opportunities to expand their educational horizons. First, joint programs with other schools and colleges in the university enable students to complete two degrees in less time than it would take to pursue them separately. Existing joint programs include JD/MBA (business administration), JD/MPA (public administration), JD/MHP (historic preservation), JD/MSW (social work), and JD/MEd in Sports Studies.

Students may also take graduate coursework in other schools and colleges of the university and have it count as elective credit toward the 88 semester hours required for graduation. For example, students interested in tax law might take courses in the school of accounting, and students interested in public policy might take courses in the department of political science. Finally, for those who are not interested in the joint-degree programs but want more coursework than can be satisfied by elective credit, it is possible to be concurrently enrolled; that is, students may pursue other advanced degrees in the university at the same time they are fulfilling the requirements for the law degree.

■ Study Abroad

Law students may participate in the law school's study-abroad program in London or in programs offered around the globe by other ABA-approved schools. The London Law Consortium takes place in the spring semester and features a variety of courses. Students from the eight consortium-member law schools can participate.

■ Library and Physical Facilities

The law library's vast collection makes it one of the largest in legal education. While it has extensive holdings in international law, it focuses on being a functional library serving the needs of students. The university's main library is adjacent to the law school and is one of the 20 largest research libraries in the nation.

The law school is headquartered in Hirsch Hall on the northern edge of the campus, the most scenic and historic section of the University of Georgia. Dean Rusk Hall is adjacent to Hirsch Hall and provides additional office space and classrooms. The majority of clinical settings are just a short walk from Hirsch Hall in the downtown area.

■ Career Services

The law school offers a fully staffed career services office that assists law students and graduates. Placement rates are among the highest in the nation, and a very high percentage of students do clerkships around the country prior to beginning the second and third years of studies. The career services website is a comprehensive source of information and answers many questions.

Applicant Profile

University of Georgia School of Law
This grid includes only applicants who earned 120-180 LSAT scores under standard administrations.

LSAT Score	3.75 +		3.50 - 3.74		3.25 - 3.49		3.00 - 3.24		2.75 - 2.99		2.50 - 2.74		2.25 - 2.49		2.00 - 2.24		Below 2.00		No GPA		Total	
	Apps	Adm	Apps	Adm	Apps	Adm	Apps	Adm	Apps	Adm	Apps	Adm	Apps	Adm	Apps	Adm	Apps	Adm	Apps	Adm	Apps	Adm
175-180	2	2	1	1	0	0	2	2	0	0	0	0	0	0	0	0	0	0	0	0	5	5
170-174	9	8	7	7	10	10	4	2	2	0	3	0	0	0	1	0	0	0	1	0	37	27
165-169	46	44	35	34	42	38	27	24	8	2	10	1	7	1	1	1	1	0	0	0	177	145
160-164	124	95	176	61	156	45	105	33	51	8	18	1	13	0	2	0	0	0	2	0	647	243
155-159	148	39	216	19	179	7	125	5	60	1	31	0	18	0	2	0	1	0	10	2	790	73
150-154	78	18	124	7	149	14	103	8	74	2	35	0	12	0	8	0	0	0	1	0	584	49
145-149	38	9	58	3	64	1	62	1	38	0	23	0	19	0	3	0	5	0	8	1	318	15
140-144	6	0	25	0	31	0	34	0	36	0	11	0	13	0	2	0	1	0	5	0	164	0
135-139	2	0	9	0	14	0	17	0	18	0	11	0	10	0	2	0	2	0	3	0	88	0
130-134	1	0	2	0	2	0	3	0	5	0	2	0	2	0	1	0	1	0	3	0	22	0
125-129	0	0	0	0	1	0	0	0	1	0	0	0	1	0	0	0	0	0	1	0	4	0
120-124	0	0	0	0	0	0	0	0	0	0	0	0	0	0	0	0	0	0	0	0	0	0
Total	454	215	653	132	648	115	482	75	293	13	144	2	95	1	22	1	11	0	34	3	2836	557

Apps = Number of Applicants
Adm = Number Admitted
Reflects 99% of the total applicant pool.

Georgia State University College of Law

PO Box 4037
Atlanta, GA 30302-4037
Phone: 404.651.2048; Fax: 404.651.1244
E-mail: admissions@gsulaw.gsu.edu; Website: law.gsu.edu

ABA
Approved
Since
1984

The Basics

Type of school	Public
Term	Semester
Application deadline	3/15
Application fee	$50
Financial aid deadline	4/1
Can first year start other than fall?	No
Student to faculty ratio (fall)	15.6 to 1
Does the university offer:	
housing restricted to law students?	No
graduate housing for which law students are eligible?	Yes

Faculty and Administrators

	Total		Men		Women		Minorities	
	Fall	Spr	Fall	Spr	Fall	Spr	Fall	Spr
Full-time	33	34	22	22	11	12	4	3
Other Full-time	3	4	0	0	3	4	0	1
Deans, librarians, & others who teach	9	9	2	2	7	7	2	2
Part-time	15	36	11	24	4	12	3	6
Total	60	83	35	48	25	35	9	12

Curriculum

		Full-time	Part-time
Typical first-year section size		65	65
Is there typically a "small section" of the first-year class, other than Legal Writing, taught by full-time faculty		No	No
If yes, typical size offered last year		0	0
# of classroom course titles beyond 1st year curriculum		94	
# of upper division courses, excluding seminars with an enrollment:	Under 25	64	
	25-49	32	
	50-74	18	
	75-99	6	
	100+	0	
# of seminars		26	
# of seminar positions available		343	
# of seminar positions filled		274	0
# of positions available in simulation courses		282	
# of simulation positions filled		275	0
# of positions available in faculty supervised clinical courses		200	
# of faculty supervised clinical positions filled		50	0
# involved in field placements		171	0
# involved in law journals		62	0
# involved in moot court or trial competitions		24	0
# of credit hours required to graduate		90	

JD Enrollment and Ethnicity

	Men		Women		Full-time		Part-time		1st-year		Total		JD Degs. Awd.
	#	%	#	%	#	%	#	%	#	%	#	%	
African Amer.	18	5.2	48	14.2	51	10.2	15	8.2	26	11.3	66	9.7	22
Amer. Indian	1	0.3	3	0.9	3	0.6	1	0.5	0	0.0	4	0.6	1
Asian Amer.	12	3.5	23	6.8	31	6.2	4	2.2	14	6.1	35	5.1	5
Mex. Amer.	0	0.0	0	0.0	0	0.0	0	0.0	0	0.0	0	0.0	0
Puerto Rican	0	0.0	0	0.0	0	0.0	0	0.0	0	0.0	0	0.0	0
Hispanic	9	2.6	6	1.8	13	2.6	2	1.1	7	3.0	15	2.2	5
Total Minority	40	11.7	80	23.7	98	19.7	22	12.0	47	20.4	120	17.6	33
For. Nation.	0	0.0	0	0.0	0	0.0	0	0.0	0	0.0	0	0.0	0
Caucasian	252	73.5	221	65.4	339	68.1	134	73.2	152	66.1	473	69.5	159
Unknown	51	14.9	37	10.9	61	12.2	27	14.8	31	13.5	88	12.9	20
Total	343	50.4	338	49.6	498	73.1	183	26.9	230	33.8	681		212

Tuition and Fees

	Resident	Nonresident
Full-time	$6,112	$20,306
Part-time	$5,696	$18,698

Living Expenses

Estimated living expenses for singles

Living on campus	Living off campus	Living at home
$14,974	$14,974	$7,900

Georgia State University College of Law

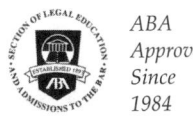

ABA
Approved
Since
1984

GPA and LSAT Scores

	Total	Full-time	Part-time
# of apps	3,273	2,793	480
# of admits	577	506	71
# of matrics	230	183	47
75% GPA	3.62	3.62	3.68
25% GPA	3.08	3.08	3.00
75% LSAT	160	160	163
25% LSAT	157	156	157

Grants and Scholarships (from prior year)

	Total		Full-time		Part-time	
	#	%	#	%	#	%
Total # of students	683		484		199	
Total # receiving grants	28	4.1	18	3.7	10	5.0
Less than 1/2 tuition	0	0.0	0	0.0	0	0.0
Half to full tuition	2	0.3	1	0.2	1	0.5
Full tuition	25	3.7	16	3.3	9	4.5
More than full tuition	1	0.1	1	0.2	0	0.0
Median grant amount			$6,551		$4,824	

Informational and Library Resources

# of volumes and volume equivalents	329,472
# of titles	63,907
# of active serial subscriptions	2,379
Study seating capacity inside the library	354
# of professional librarians	7
Hours per week library is open	105
# of open, wired connections available to students	541
# of networked computers available for use by students	54
# of simultaneous wireless users	210
Require computer?	N

JD Attrition (from prior year)

	Academic	Other	Total	
	#	#	#	%
1st year	5	32	37	17.6%
2nd year	0	7	7	3.3%
3rd year	0	2	2	1.0%
4th year	0	1	1	1.9%

Employment

	Total	Percentage
Employment status known	164	98.2
Employment status unknown	3	1.8
Employed	146	89.0
Pursuing graduate degrees	4	2.4
Unemployed seeking employment	9	5.5
Unemployed not seeking employment	5	3.0

Type of Employment

# employed in law firms	92	63.0
# employed in business and industry	15	10.3
# employed in government	23	15.8
# employed in public interest	1	0.7
# employed as judicial clerks	12	8.2
# employed in academia	3	2.1

Geographic Location

# employed in state	132	90.4
# employed in foreign countries	0	0.0
# of states where employed	11	

Bar Passage Rates

Jurisdiction	Georgia		
Exam	Sum 03	Win 04	Total
# from school taking bar for the first time	123	33	156
School's pass rate for all first-time takers	93%	85%	91%
State's pass rate for all first-time takers	86%	75%	83%

Georgia State University College of Law

PO Box 4037
Atlanta, GA 30302-4037
Phone: 404.651.2048; Fax: 404.651.1244
E-mail: admissions@gsulaw.gsu.edu; Website: law.gsu.edu

■ Introduction

Georgia State University College of Law is located in downtown Atlanta, the center of legal, financial, and governmental activities in the Southeast. This location provides easy access to federal, state, and local courts and agencies, the state capitol, legislature, corporations, major law firms in the metropolitan area, and the library and other facilities of Georgia State University.

The College of Law began operation in 1982. The College of Law is accredited by the ABA and is a member of the AALS.

■ Library and Physical Facilities

The College of Law library is designed and equipped to meet the demanding research needs of today's students, faculty members, staff, and members of the legal community. With a collection of more than 278,500 volumes, the library provides research materials in American, British, Canadian, and international law. Students find a host of computer applications available in the law library computer lab, which is staffed by computer consultants. The college dedicates state-of-the-art computer equipment for training purposes only in our computer training room. The classrooms and study carrels accommodate laptop computers.

The College of Law is one of the leading law schools in the Southeast. Located on a 25-acre campus in the heart of downtown Atlanta, the building houses a moot courtroom equipped with state-of-the-art video technology and provides activities directed toward trial and appellate advocacy. Students have access to many other campus facilities including the athletic complex, which offers a variety of individual fitness opportunities and team sports.

■ Curriculum

The college offers students the opportunity to study full or part time and provides a traditional yet innovative curriculum. It offers extensive coverage of the foundational areas of the law to first-year students while providing an array of elective opportunities in public and private law. Opportunities range from the study of legal philosophy and jurisprudence to vital skills training through courses in litigation, counseling, negotiation, legal drafting, and alternative dispute resolution.

The growth of technology in our lives is reflected in courses in Intellectual Property and Computers and the Law, in our innovative course Law and the Internet, and in the increasing use of computer programs and online discussion groups. Opportunities exist for in-depth study in international and comparative law, environmental law, health law, tax law, employment law, commercial law, and bankruptcy.

■ Admission

The College of Law actively seeks to enroll a student body with diversity in educational, cultural, and racial backgrounds that will enrich the educational experience of the entire group.

Applicants are encouraged to visit. Please make arrangements through the Admissions Office to tour the campus; talk with students, faculty, and admission staff; or attend a class.

■ Special Programs

Joint-Degree Programs—Six joint JD and master's degree programs are available with the J. Mack Robinson College of Business, the Andrew Young School of Policy Studies, the Department of Philosophy in the College of Arts and Sciences, and the College of Architecture at the Georgia Institute of Technology.

International Programs—Students have the opportunity to participate in two summer abroad programs. The Transnational Comparative Dispute Resolution Program in Europe and the Urban Environment and Health: Law, Policy, and Culture in Brazil.

Clinics—The Criminal Justice Clinic and Tax Clinic provide a live-client component to the college's Lawyer Skill Development Program. Both clinics give students hands-on real-life experience in client representation and handling cases. In the Criminal Justice Clinic, students have the primary responsibility for cases assigned to them and practice law pursuant to Georgia's Third-Year Practice Rule. Students in the clinic are likely to be lead counsel in pretrial hearings and participate as active cocounsel in the conduct of trials. Work in the Tax Clinic teaches case management, evidence gathering, document preparation, interviewing, counseling, and effective negotiation.

Externships—Externships are designed to tie theoretical knowledge to a practical base of experience in the profession. Externships involve actual participation in rendering legal services. Students interested in the externship program should contact the Lawyer Skills Development Office.

Trial Advocacy—The College of Law offers students an extensive variety of opportunities in the area of trial advocacy. Our Litigation Workshop, offered each spring semester, offers second-year students an intensive skills training experience. Working in small seminar groups, students are asked to conduct drafting and simulation exercises on all phases of the pretrial and trial process, including a full jury trial. In addition to the workshop, the college offers several advanced litigation courses in which students can further enhance their advocacy skills in civil and criminal areas.

Moot Court—Each year, students compete in several of the most challenging and prestigious moot court competitions throughout the country. The Moot Court program has achieved substantial renown and success in its 20-year history. The National Moot Court Competition, sponsored by the Association of the Bar of the City of New York, is the oldest and most recognized national competition, and in 1988 the College of Law became the first law school in Georgia to place first in that competition. Teams from the college have since won numerous other competitions.

Centers—The College of Law has three centers. The Capitol City Center for State Law, Legislation, and Policy; Center for Law, Health, and Society; and Center for the Comparative Study of Metropolitan Growth. The Capitol City Center for State Law, Legislation, and Policy allows students to observe the legislative process, assist legislators, and watch how the topics they analyzed emerge into law. The Center for Law, Health, and Society promotes the integration of health law and ethics into health policy and research, the health science, the provision of health services, and the interdisciplinary education of law students. The Center for Comparative Metropolitan Growth Research produces research, teaching, and academic exchange on the range of issues relating to metropolitan growth.

■ Student Activities

The *Georgia State University Law Review* is published four times a year by students who have demonstrated outstanding writing and academic skills.

The college also boasts a nationally renowned student mock trial program in which our students compete annually in numerous mock trial competitions held at locations throughout the country. Our student teams have amassed an incredible record of success at the national, regional, and state levels. The College of Law has won three national championships, competed in four national finals, and won eight regional championships and several state championships.

The College of Law regards student organizations as an important part of a legal education experience and encourages participation in our wide variety of organizations, some traditionally found in law schools, some less common. The college recognizes 25 organizations, most of which are affiliated with national professional associations. We are proud of the accomplishments of these groups.

■ Career Services

The Career Planning Office offers a broad range of services. Students may begin using the office in November of the first year of law school and may continue utilizing career planning services throughout their careers. Specific programs geared toward minority students are the Atlanta Bar Association Minority Clerkship Program and the Southeastern Minority Job Fair. Typically, over 90 percent of each graduating class accept employment within six months of graduation.

Applicant Profile

Georgia State University College of Law
This grid includes only applicants who earned 120-180 LSAT scores under standard administrations.

LSAT Score	3.75 +		3.50 - 3.74		3.25 - 3.49		3.00 - 3.24		2.75 - 2.99		2.50 - 2.74		2.25 - 2.49		2.00 - 2.24		Below 2.00		No GPA		Total	
	Apps	Adm	Apps	Adm	Apps	Adm	Apps	Adm	Apps	Adm	Apps	Adm	Apps	Adm	Apps	Adm	Apps	Adm	Apps	Adm	Apps	Adm
175-180	0	0	0	0	0	0	1	1	0	0	0	0	0	0	0	0	0	0	0	0	1	1
170-174	2	2	1	1	4	4	0	0	0	0	1	1	0	0	1	0	0	0	1	1	10	9
165-169	11	11	9	8	9	8	11	10	6	4	7	4	4	1	2	0	1	1	0	0	60	47
160-164	33	29	57	53	59	52	63	49	45	19	14	7	19	1	10	1	1	0	4	3	305	214
155-159	75	35	160	70	168	55	185	51	111	15	55	11	33	3	9	0	1	0	3	1	800	241
150-154	71	8	164	9	205	13	202	17	143	6	93	2	33	1	30	0	3	0	10	0	954	56
145-149	37	0	88	0	142	1	134	0	105	0	67	0	34	0	18	0	6	0	12	0	643	1
140-144	14	0	42	0	82	0	94	0	81	0	46	0	42	0	20	0	0	0	16	0	437	0
135-139	2	0	8	0	30	0	42	0	40	0	26	0	35	0	11	0	6	0	15	0	215	0
130-134	0	0	5	0	7	0	13	0	16	0	18	0	8	0	6	0	1	0	13	0	87	0
125-129	0	0	0	0	2	0	2	0	3	0	1	0	5	0	2	0	0	0	3	0	18	0
120-124	0	0	0	0	0	0	0	0	0	0	0	0	1	0	0	0	0	0	0	0	1	0
Total	245	85	534	141	708	133	747	128	550	44	328	25	214	6	109	1	19	1	77	5	3531	569

Apps = Number of Applicants   Adm = Number Admitted   Reflects 99% of the total applicant pool.

Golden Gate University School of Law

536 Mission Street
San Francisco, CA 94105-2968
Phone: 415.442.6630 or 800.GGU.4YOU; Fax: 415.442.6631
E-mail: lawadmit@ggu.edu; Website: www.ggu.edu/law

ABA
Approved
Since
1956

The Basics

Type of school	Private	
Term	Semester	
Application deadline	4/1	6/1
Application fee	$60	
Financial aid deadline	3/1	
Can first year start other than fall?	Yes	
Student to faculty ratio (fall)	21.2 to 1	
Does the university offer:		
housing restricted to law students?		No
graduate housing for which law students are eligible?		No

Faculty and Administrators

	Total		Men		Women		Minorities	
	Fall	Spr	Fall	Spr	Fall	Spr	Fall	Spr
Full-time	31	29	18	17	13	12	9	9
Other Full-time	7	7	4	4	3	3	1	1
Deans, librarians, & others who teach	11	11	5	5	6	6	1	1
Part-time	68	42	37	19	31	23	13	11
Total	117	89	64	45	53	44	24	22

Curriculum

	Full-time	Part-time
Typical first-year section size	72	72
Is there typically a "small section" of the first-year class, other than Legal Writing, taught by full-time faculty	Yes	No
If yes, typical size offered last year	40	0
# of classroom course titles beyond 1st year curriculum	137	

# of upper division courses, excluding seminars with an enrollment:		
	Under 25	171
	25-49	42
	50-74	9
	75-99	7
	100+	0

# of seminars		18
# of seminar positions available		270
# of seminar positions filled	130	50
# of positions available in simulation courses		372
# of simulation positions filled	189	113
# of positions available in faculty supervised clinical courses		277
# of faculty supervised clinical positions filled	152	23
# involved in field placements	97	23
# involved in law journals	41	10
# involved in moot court or trial competitions	40	8
# of credit hours required to graduate		88

JD Enrollment and Ethnicity

	Men		Women		Full-time		Part-time		1st-year		Total		JD Degs. Awd.
	#	%	#	%	#	%	#	%	#	%	#	%	
African Amer.	13	3.6	23	4.7	18	2.7	18	9.7	10	2.7	36	4.2	11
Amer. Indian	3	0.8	0	0.0	2	0.3	1	0.5	1	0.3	3	0.4	1
Asian Amer.	59	16.3	92	18.8	120	18.0	31	16.7	83	22.3	151	17.7	27
Mex. Amer.	8	2.2	11	2.2	17	2.5	2	1.1	10	2.7	19	2.2	1
Puerto Rican	0	0.0	0	0.0	0	0.0	0	0.0	0	0.0	0	0.0	0
Hispanic	15	4.1	20	4.1	24	3.6	11	5.9	11	2.9	35	4.1	9
Total Minority	98	27.0	146	29.8	181	27.1	63	33.9	115	30.8	244	28.6	49
For. Nation.	2	0.6	3	0.6	3	0.4	2	1.1	0	0.0	5	0.6	4
Caucasian	204	56.2	287	58.6	394	59.1	97	52.2	212	56.8	491	57.6	88
Unknown	59	16.3	54	11.0	89	13.3	24	12.9	46	12.3	113	13.2	27
Total	363	42.6	490	57.4	667	78.2	186	21.8	373	43.7	853		168

Tuition and Fees

	Resident	Nonresident
Full-time	$26,000	$26,000
Part-time	$18,640	$18,640

Living Expenses

Estimated living expenses for singles

Living on campus	Living off campus	Living at home
N/A	$18,100	N/A

Golden Gate University School of Law

ABA
Approved
Since
1956

GPA and LSAT Scores

	Total	Full-time	Part-time
# of apps	3,341	2,961	380
# of admits	1,267	1,145	122
# of matrics	357	298	59
75% GPA	3.41	3.43	3.22
25% GPA	2.87	2.92	2.64
75% LSAT	155	155	156
25% LSAT	151	151	150

Grants and Scholarships (from prior year)

	Total		Full-time		Part-time	
	#	%	#	%	#	%
Total # of students	808		612		196	
Total # receiving grants	341	42.2	269	44.0	72	36.7
Less than 1/2 tuition	273	33.8	226	36.9	47	24.0
Half to full tuition	53	6.6	32	5.2	21	10.7
Full tuition	8	1.0	7	1.1	1	0.5
More than full tuition	7	0.9	4	0.7	3	1.5
Median grant amount			$8,000		$7,500	

Informational and Library Resources

# of volumes and volume equivalents	327,474
# of titles	40,259
# of active serial subscriptions	3,829
Study seating capacity inside the library	358
# of professional librarians	8
Hours per week library is open	95
# of open, wired connections available to students	583
# of networked computers available for use by students	138
# of simultaneous wireless users	300
Require computer?	N

JD Attrition (from prior year)

	Academic	Other	Total	
	#	#	#	%
1st year	65	72	137	34.9%
2nd year	6	9	15	6.8%
3rd year	5	1	6	3.6%
4th year	0	0	0	0.0%

Employment

	Total	Percentage
Employment status known	120	91.6
Employment status unknown	11	8.4
Employed	75	62.5
Pursuing graduate degrees	3	2.5
Unemployed seeking employment	3	2.5
Unemployed not seeking employment	39	32.5

Type of Employment

# employed in law firms	45	60.0
# employed in business and industry	9	12.0
# employed in government	8	10.7
# employed in public interest	4	5.3
# employed as judicial clerks	4	5.3
# employed in academia	5	6.7

Geographic Location

# employed in state	66	88.0
# employed in foreign countries	0	0.0
# of states where employed	7	

Bar Passage Rates

Jurisdiction	California		
Exam	Sum 03	Win 04	Total
# from school taking bar for the first time	70	30	100
School's pass rate for all first-time takers	31%	23%	29%
State's pass rate for all first-time takers	63%	47%	60%

Golden Gate University School of Law

536 Mission Street
San Francisco, CA 94105-2968
Phone: 415.442.6630 or 800.GGU.4YOU; Fax: 415.442.6631
E-mail: lawadmit@ggu.edu; Website: www.ggu.edu/law

■ Introduction

Founded in 1901, Golden Gate University School of Law is located in the heart of San Francisco's legal and financial district. The law school is noted for integrating practical skills training with legal theory. Golden Gate has a distinguished faculty who share a strong commitment to both excellence in teaching and accessibility to students. The school is accredited by the ABA and is a member of the AALS.

The curriculum at Golden Gate University School of Law is designed to lay the foundations of modern legal theory but also to foster those practical skills necessary to be a successful lawyer. Because writing is the lawyer's basic tool, the school trains students to master the skills to draft a wide array of legal documents. The law school's Academic Support Program provides all students with additional instruction in legal analysis and exam-writing skills.

■ Program Options

The law school offers both full-time day and part-time evening programs. The full-time program normally involves three years of study; the part-time program takes four years. Golden Gate also offers midyear admission, allowing students to begin law school in January (full-time program only).

■ Honors Lawyering Program

In addition to the standard law school curriculum, Golden Gate offers the Honors Lawyering Program. Honors Lawyering students spend two semesters working as apprentices in law offices. They attend two intensive summer programs in simulated law firm settings to learn substantive law and prepare themselves for their apprenticeships. In this way, the program integrates classroom theory, skills, values, and practice. Honors Lawyering students still complete law school in three years, pay the same tuition, and take the same number of units as students in the standard curriculum.

■ Public Interest Law

At Golden Gate, the law curriculum and programs integrate public interest law and service to the community. Students may earn a public interest law certificate by completing 14 credits of approved elective courses, a 150-hour public interest practicum, and 25 hours of work for a campus or community organization. Some students are selected to be part of the Public Interest Law Scholars Program, which provides students with scholarships, a summer employment stipend, and mentoring.

■ Joint Degrees and Certificates of Specialization

Students may earn the following joint degrees: JD/MBA and JD/PhD in Clinical Psychology.

Golden Gate offers JD students the opportunity to earn specialization certificates in Business Law, Criminal Law, Environmental Law, Intellectual Property Law, International Law, Labor and Employment Law, Litigation, Public Interest Law, Real Estate Law, and Taxation. Requirements for the areas of specialization vary, but students generally complete coursework and clinical practice to earn a certificate.

■ Clinical Programs

Golden Gate University has one of the most extensive clinical programs in the country, offering students opportunities to earn academic credit while working closely with practicing attorneys.

The law school has three in-house clinics. In the Women's Employment Rights Clinic, students represent low-income women with employment-related problems. Through the Environmental Law and Justice Clinic, students assist northern California communities in protecting their environmental interests. In the Northern California Innocence Project at Golden Gate University, students investigate and litigate prisoners' claims of innocence.

In field-placement clinics, students work under the supervision of faculty and outside judges and attorneys in government agencies, law offices, and judges' chambers. These off-site clinics include Civil Practice Clinic, Criminal Litigation Clinic, Environmental Law Clinic, Family Law Clinic, Immigration and Refugee Policy Clinic, Judicial Externships, Landlord-Tenant Law Clinic, Public Interest/Government Counsel Clinic, Real Estate Clinic, and Tax-Aid Clinic.

■ Summer Programs

In addition to an on-campus summer session, Golden Gate University School of Law offers summer abroad programs in Bangkok, Thailand and in Paris, France.

■ Graduate Programs

Golden Gate University School of Law offers five LLM programs: Environmental Law, Intellectual Property Law, International Legal Studies, Taxation, and US Legal Studies. It also offers an SJD program in International Legal Studies.

Golden Gate University School of Law

■ Law Library

The law library houses the largest law collection in the San Francisco financial district—more than 300,000 volumes. Its holdings include a comprehensive series of case law reporters, statutes, digests, encyclopedias, periodicals, and treatises dealing with American law; a strong tax collection; a microforms collection; and a growing body of work in environmental law, law and literature, and international law. International law holdings target selected Pacific Rim countries and English, Canadian, and commonwealth materials.

■ Career Services and Placement

The Law Career Services (LCS) Office helps students prepare for a successful legal career by providing many services throughout law school and beyond. LCS helps students to research the legal market, develop contacts, and build skills through jobs and internships. For first-year students, LCS provides a free *Job Search Guide*, a one-on-one orientation session, and a special workshop on résumés and cover letters. For continuing students, LCS offers print and online job listings, talks by graduates about their career experiences, individual and small-group career counseling, job search skills workshops, panels, and events highlighting the career paths of Golden Gate alumni and other attorneys, special recruitment programs, and more. Many of these services continue beyond graduation.

■ Student Activities and Scholarship

The law school has more than 15 student organizations ranging from groups representing minority students to groups focusing on specific areas of the law. A student editorial board publishes three issues annually of the *Golden Gate University Law Review*. The law school also publishes the *Annual Survey of International and Comparative Law*.

■ Admission

The Admissions Committee considers each applicant's undergraduate GPA, LSAT score, and information contained in his or her personal statement. The committee also weighs such factors as graduate work, social and economic background, and personal and employment accomplishments. People who are underrepresented in the legal community are encouraged to apply.

Applicant Profile

Golden Gate University School of Law
This grid includes only applicants who earned 120-180 LSAT scores under standard administrations.

LSAT Score	3.75 +		3.50 - 3.74		3.25 - 3.49		3.00 - 3.24		2.75 - 2.99		2.50 - 2.74		2.25 - 2.49		2.00 - 2.24		Below 2.00		No GPA		Total	
	Apps	Adm	Apps	Adm	Apps	Adm	Apps	Adm	Apps	Adm	Apps	Adm	Apps	Adm	Apps	Adm	Apps	Adm	Apps	Adm	Apps	Adm
175-180	0	0	0	0	0	0	0	0	0	0	0	0	0	0	0	0	0	0	0	0	0	0
170-174	0	0	0	0	1	1	1	1	0	0	0	0	0	0	0	0	0	0	0	0	2	2
165-169	6	6	2	2	15	13	8	5	2	1	4	2	1	1	2	2	0	0	1	1	41	33
160-164	21	18	30	26	35	30	29	24	22	21	14	12	10	9	6	6	0	0	6	4	173	150
155-159	38	32	83	70	93	77	87	78	63	51	50	36	32	15	10	1	2	2	8	5	466	367
150-154	46	41	116	94	190	137	219	144	138	51	108	29	44	5	22	5	2	0	15	10	900	516
145-149	22	5	74	9	127	6	200	7	166	8	116	3	63	0	29	0	6	0	20	1	823	39
140-144	14	2	36	0	66	0	109	1	101	0	71	0	48	0	10	0	3	0	16	0	474	3
135-139	7	0	22	0	24	0	30	0	40	0	43	0	9	0	8	0	2	0	11	0	196	0
130-134	0	0	3	0	2	0	2	0	12	0	10	0	5	0	6	0	2	0	5	0	47	0
125-129	0	0	0	0	0	0	2	0	4	0	2	0	4	0	1	0	1	0	1	0	15	0
120-124	0	0	0	0	0	0	0	0	1	0	1	0	0	0	0	0	0	0	0	0	2	0
Total	154	104	366	201	553	264	687	260	549	132	419	82	216	30	94	14	18	2	83	21	3139	1110

Apps = Number of Applicants
Adm = Number Admitted
Reflects 99% of the total applicant pool.

This chart is a general guide only. Nonnumerical factors are strongly considered for all applicants. "No GPA" includes applicants who received their undergraduate degrees from foreign institutions and/or US institutions in which letter grades are not utilized or calculated.

Gonzaga University School of Law

PO Box 3528
Spokane, WA 99220-3528
Phone: 800.793.1710 or 509.323.5532
E-mail: admissions@lawschool.gonzaga.edu; Website: www.law.gonzaga.edu

ABA
Approved
Since
1951

The Basics

Type of school	Private
Term	Semester
Application deadline	2/1
Application fee	$50
Financial aid deadline	2/1
Can first year start other than fall?	Yes
Student to faculty ratio (fall)	19.1 to 1
Does the university offer:	
housing restricted to law students?	No
graduate housing for which law students are eligible?	No

Faculty and Administrators

	Total Fall	Total Spr	Men Fall	Men Spr	Women Fall	Women Spr	Minorities Fall	Minorities Spr
Full-time	27	27	14	15	13	12	2	3
Other Full-time	0	0	0	0	0	0	0	0
Deans, librarians, & others who teach	6	6	2	2	4	4	0	0
Part-time	23	29	17	20	6	9	0	0
Total	56	62	33	37	23	25	2	3

Curriculum

	Full-time	Part-time
Typical first-year section size	85	0
Is there typically a "small section" of the first-year class, other than Legal Writing, taught by full-time faculty	No	No
If yes, typical size offered last year	0	0
# of classroom course titles beyond 1st year curriculum	94	
# of upper division courses, excluding seminars with an enrollment: Under 25	44	
25-49	23	
50-74	21	
75-99	3	
100+	3	
# of seminars	8	
# of seminar positions available	160	
# of seminar positions filled	106	0
# of positions available in simulation courses	330	
# of simulation positions filled	249	0
# of positions available in faculty supervised clinical courses	125	
# of faculty supervised clinical positions filled	125	0
# involved in field placements	43	0
# involved in law journals	47	0
# involved in moot court or trial competitions	42	0
# of credit hours required to graduate	90	

JD Enrollment and Ethnicity

	Men #	Men %	Women #	Women %	Full-time #	Full-time %	Part-time #	Part-time %	1st-year #	1st-year %	Total #	Total %	JD Degs. Awd.
African Amer.	0	0.0	3	1.0	3	0.5	0	0.0	0	0.0	3	0.5	1
Amer. Indian	4	1.2	3	1.0	7	1.2	0	0.0	4	1.8	7	1.1	2
Asian Amer.	21	6.2	21	7.2	42	7.0	0	0.0	15	6.8	42	6.7	8
Mex. Amer.	10	3.0	14	4.8	22	3.6	2	8.3	9	4.1	24	3.8	10
Puerto Rican	0	0.0	0	0.0	0	0.0	0	0.0	0	0.0	0	0.0	0
Hispanic	0	0.0	0	0.0	0	0.0	0	0.0	0	0.0	0	0.0	0
Total Minority	35	10.4	41	14.1	74	12.3	2	8.3	28	12.6	76	12.1	21
For. Nation.	2	0.6	0	0.0	2	0.3	0	0.0	0	0.0	2	0.3	1
Caucasian	300	89.0	250	85.9	528	87.4	22	91.7	194	87.4	550	87.6	163
Unknown	0	0.0	0	0.0	0	0.0	0	0.0	0	0.0	0	0.0	0
Total	337	53.7	291	46.3	604	96.2	24	3.8	222	35.4	628		185

Tuition and Fees

	Resident	Nonresident
Full-time	$24,678	$24,678
Part-time	$14,832	$14,832

Living Expenses

Estimated living expenses for singles

Living on campus	Living off campus	Living at home
N/A	$13,615	$13,615

Gonzaga University School of Law

*ABA
Approved
Since
1951*

GPA and LSAT Scores

	Total	Full-time	Part-time
# of apps	1,742	1,742	0
# of admits	574	574	0
# of matrics	222	222	0
75% GPA	3.57	3.57	0.00
25% GPA	3.19	3.19	0.00
75% LSAT	156	156	0
25% LSAT	150	150	0

Grants and Scholarships (from prior year)

	Total #	Total %	Full-time #	Full-time %	Part-time #	Part-time %
Total # of students	626		609		17	
Total # receiving grants	464	74.1	464	76.2	0	0.0
Less than 1/2 tuition	337	53.8	337	55.3	0	0.0
Half to full tuition	111	17.7	111	18.2	0	0.0
Full tuition	16	2.6	16	2.6	0	0.0
More than full tuition	0	0.0	0	0.0	0	0.0
Median grant amount			$10,000		$0	

Informational and Library Resources

# of volumes and volume equivalents	270,316
# of titles	59,079
# of active serial subscriptions	2,585
Study seating capacity inside the library	452
# of professional librarians	6
Hours per week library is open	110
# of open, wired connections available to students	140
# of networked computers available for use by students	83
# of simultaneous wireless users	800
Require computer?	N

JD Attrition (from prior year)

	Academic #	Other #	Total #	Total %
1st year	15	18	33	14.2%
2nd year	2	0	2	1.0%
3rd year	0	0	0	0.0%
4th year	0	0	0	0.0%

Employment

	Total	Percentage
Employment status known	143	100.0
Employment status unknown	0	0.0
Employed	110	76.9
Pursuing graduate degrees	12	8.4
Unemployed seeking employment	7	4.9
Unemployed not seeking employment	14	9.8

Type of Employment

# employed in law firms	46	41.8
# employed in business and industry	21	19.1
# employed in government	24	21.8
# employed in public interest	4	3.6
# employed as judicial clerks	13	11.8
# employed in academia	2	1.8

Geographic Location

# employed in state	55	50.0
# employed in foreign countries	1	0.9
# of states where employed		20

Bar Passage Rates

Jurisdiction	Washington		
Exam	Sum 03	Win 04	Total
# from school taking bar for the first time	74	17	91
School's pass rate for all first-time takers	74%	71%	74%
State's pass rate for all first-time takers	71%	79%	74%

Gonzaga University School of Law

PO Box 3528
Spokane, WA 99220-3528
Phone: 800.793.1710 or 509.323.5532
E-mail: admissions@lawschool.gonzaga.edu; Website: www.law.gonzaga.edu

■ Introduction

Gonzaga University School of Law belongs to a long and distinguished tradition of humanistic, Catholic, and Jesuit education. Founded in 1887, Gonzaga continues to maintain the tradition of academic excellence in education that is at the heart of the mission of the 450-year-old Jesuit order. The School of Law, established in 1912, is a member of the AALS and is approved by the ABA. The campus is located in Spokane, Washington, a four-season city with the Spokane River flowing through its center. The metropolitan area of approximately 400,000 serves as the regional hub of the Inland Northwest, a large area running from the Cascade Mountains in the west to the Rockies in the east. Canada is a mere 100 miles to the north.

Spokane is not only an economic hub for manufacturing, agriculture, and light industry, but is also a recreational sports area abundant with lakes, mountains, and forest. In minutes you can get away from the city's robust, rapidly growing business community to the surrounding pine-covered hills.

■ Physical Facilities and Library

Rising from the banks of the beautiful Spokane River, the Gonzaga Law Center, which opened in May 2000, provides a stunning setting for research and learning. The law center offers a variety of classroom and library environments that support today's interactive teaching methods. Features throughout the building encourage students to greet each other and linger to talk and debate ideas in beautiful outdoor spaces, roof plazas and balconies, and comfortable lounges. Miles of state of the art voice, data, and video cable provide the highway for audiovisual, computer, and telecommunications technology throughout the building. The mix of classrooms, rooms for simulations of various sizes, and clinical teaching spaces provides flexibility to preserve the best of traditional law teaching while introducing new methods. The law library, designed to accommodate more than 250,000 volumes, reflects the changing patterns of legal research in a warm and inviting environment filled with natural light. Gonzaga's fine tradition of advocacy training and moot court competitions are promoted in the elegant Barbieri Courtroom.

■ Curriculum and Faculty

There is a deliberate and delicate balance to legal education at Gonzaga. The rigorous curriculum focuses on legal analysis, problem solving, values, and ethics. Equally as important is the emphasis on practical experience to develop real-world lawyering skills. As a capstone to its innovative approach to legal education, the School of Law offers Juris Doctor degrees with special concentrations in public interest law, environmental/natural resource law, and business law (including tax law).

The term "teaching faculty" applies in a very special way to the School of Law faculty. The Jesuit tradition demands a high degree of student-professor interaction inside and outside the classroom, and this emphasis attracts exceptional faculty. Gonzaga's focus on the individual student, a favorable student-to-faculty ratio, and the promotion of positive rather than negative competition provides an atmosphere of success in which to study.

■ Special Programs

The first year of coursework is devoted to building a strong legal foundation for upper-division study. In order to ease the transition to the rigorous demands of law school, entering students may take advantage of the support offered through orientation, student and attorney mentor programs, academic resource programs, academic advisors, and special tutorials. Entering students also have the option of enrolling in the summer through the Early Start Program.

Joint programs leading to the JD/MBA and the JD/MAcc degree are offered to prepare students who anticipate careers in fields that require thorough knowledge of business, accountancy, and the law.

In 2005–2006, the law school will offer a new dual degree program combining the Juris Doctor and Master of Social Work degrees. The JD/MSW program is designed to allow students to complete the requirements of both degrees in four years or less.

An added dimension to the legal education for many law students is the opportunity to practice law while in school through Gonzaga's Center for Law and Justice, the award-winning clinical law program.

■ Admission

The School of Law endeavors to attract students with ambitious minds, professional motivation, and commitment to the highest ethics and values of the legal profession and to public service. Consideration of applicants is not restricted to impersonal statistics but includes recognition and review of the enriching qualities of applicants reflected in their personal statement and letters of recommendation. Gonzaga seeks to enroll an ethnically and geographically diverse student body.

The School of Law offers acceptance to a Summer Academic Resource Program to a limited number of applicants who do not meet regular admission requirements, but whose application file suggests there may be potential for success beyond what the statistics would normally predict. There is no special application procedure for this program, and applicants will be considered automatically.

■ Student Activities

Students find it easy to become involved in a broad range of activities at the School of Law. Gonzaga is a major player in moot court competition through five moot court teams. The student-run *Gonzaga Law Review* is circulated throughout the country, and *Across Borders*, the online international law journal, receives submissions from around the world. The Student Bar Association is a strong, active organization that encourages student involvement, and there is also opportunity to participate in intraschool moot court competition, legal fraternities, and other numerous organizations and activities. Law students, representing many cultural heritages, join together in the Multi-Cultural Law Caucus to provide a support network on campus and in the Spokane community for students of diverse backgrounds.

■ Housing

The Gonzaga campus is in a residential area within close proximity to downtown Spokane. Housing is available within walking distance to the law center and rental rates are reasonably priced compared to most large population centers.

■ Financial Aid

Law school is a career investment. For students who need financial assistance to help fund this investment, Gonzaga University will assist in identifying and obtaining financial aid packages. Approximately half of the entering students receive scholarship awards.

■ Career Services

Gonzaga's active Career Services Office successfully assists law students and alumni in planning their careers and seeking employment throughout law school and in the course of their professional careers. The size of the student body allows the director the opportunity to work individually with students and alumni in their job searches across the country. Gonzaga law students may apply for a limited license to practice in Washington state, participate in federal and state work-study programs, and intern at one of the more than 200 Spokane law firms and numerous government agencies.

Applicant Profile

Gonzaga University School of Law
This grid includes only applicants who earned 120-180 LSAT scores under standard administrations.

LSAT Score	3.75 +		3.50 - 3.74		3.25 - 3.49		3.00 - 3.24		2.75 - 2.99		2.50 - 2.74		2.25 - 2.49		2.00 - 2.24		Below 2.00		No GPA		Total	
	Apps	Adm	Apps	Adm	Apps	Adm	Apps	Adm	Apps	Adm	Apps	Adm	Apps	Adm	Apps	Adm	Apps	Adm	Apps	Adm	Apps	Adm
175-180	0	0	0	0	0	0	0	0	0	0	0	0	0	0	0	0	0	0	0	0	0	0
170-174	0	0	0	0	0	0	1	1	0	0	0	0	0	0	1	0	0	0	0	0	2	1
165-169	2	2	5	5	6	6	2	1	1	1	3	1	0	0	1	0	0	0	0	0	20	16
160-164	8	8	14	11	15	13	12	8	10	6	12	3	6	2	1	0	1	0	0	0	79	51
155-159	21	18	48	43	48	41	59	50	33	14	26	11	6	0	2	0	4	0	0	0	247	177
150-154	37	27	95	66	121	68	118	48	84	15	68	10	31	2	10	0	2	0	1	0	567	236
145-149	20	14	72	29	118	27	129	15	84	4	48	0	31	0	9	0	2	0	6	0	519	89
140-144	8	1	20	1	31	0	55	0	42	1	31	0	17	0	7	0	1	0	3	0	215	3
135-139	2	0	7	0	11	0	18	0	9	0	9	0	5	0	0	0	1	0	2	0	64	0
130-134	0	0	0	0	0	0	4	0	4	0	3	0	0	0	1	0	1	0	0	0	13	0
125-129	0	0	0	0	0	0	1	0	0	0	1	0	0	0	0	0	0	0	1	0	3	0
120-124	0	0	1	0	0	0	0	0	0	0	0	0	0	0	0	0	0	0	0	0	1	0
Total	98	70	262	155	350	155	399	123	267	41	201	25	96	4	32	0	12	0	13	0	1730	573

Apps = Number of Applicants
Adm = Number Admitted
Reflects 99% of the total applicant pool.

Hamline University School of Law

1536 Hewitt Avenue
St. Paul, MN 55104
Phone: 651.523.2461, 800.388.3688; Fax: 651.523.3064
E-mail: lawadm@hamline.edu; Website: www.hamline.edu/law

ABA Approved Since 1975

The Basics

Type of school	Private
Term	Semester
Application deadline	4/1
Application fee	$40
Financial aid deadline	5/1
Can first year start other than fall?	No
Student to faculty ratio (fall)	17.4 to 1
Does the university offer:	
housing restricted to law students?	Yes
graduate housing for which law students are eligible?	Yes

Faculty and Administrators

	Total		Men		Women		Minorities	
	Fall	Spr	Fall	Spr	Fall	Spr	Fall	Spr
Full-time	31	29	18	16	13	13	5	5
Other Full-time	3	3	1	1	2	2	0	0
Deans, librarians, & others who teach	5	5	2	2	3	3	0	0
Part-time	44	44	30	31	14	13	3	3
Total	83	81	51	50	32	31	8	8

Curriculum

		Full-time	Part-time
Typical first-year section size		66	50
Is there typically a "small section" of the first-year class, other than Legal Writing, taught by full-time faculty		No	No
If yes, typical size offered last year		0	0
# of classroom course titles beyond 1st year curriculum		151	
# of upper division courses, excluding seminars with an enrollment:	Under 25	84	
	25-49	37	
	50-74	15	
	75-99	5	
	100+	0	
# of seminars		15	
# of seminar positions available		240	
# of seminar positions filled		151	36
# of positions available in simulation courses		728	
# of simulation positions filled		386	120
# of positions available in faculty supervised clinical courses		114	
# of faculty supervised clinical positions filled		82	6
# involved in field placements		90	8
# involved in law journals		223	0
# involved in moot court or trial competitions		62	0
# of credit hours required to graduate		88	

JD Enrollment and Ethnicity

	Men		Women		Full-time		Part-time		1st-year		Total		JD Degs. Awd.
	#	%	#	%	#	%	#	%	#	%	#	%	
African Amer.	15	4.8	16	4.0	20	3.9	11	5.5	13	5.1	31	4.3	2
Amer. Indian	2	0.6	3	0.7	1	0.2	4	2.0	1	0.4	5	0.7	1
Asian Amer.	10	3.2	23	5.7	26	5.0	7	3.5	10	3.9	33	4.6	8
Mex. Amer.	0	0.0	0	0.0	0	0.0	0	0.0	0	0.0	0	0.0	1
Puerto Rican	0	0.0	0	0.0	0	0.0	0	0.0	0	0.0	0	0.0	0
Hispanic	12	3.9	15	3.7	20	3.9	7	3.5	6	2.3	27	3.8	3
Total Minority	39	12.6	57	14.1	67	13.0	29	14.6	30	11.7	96	13.4	15
For. Nation.	1	0.3	6	1.5	7	1.4	0	0.0	3	1.2	7	1.0	2
Caucasian	266	85.8	336	83.2	434	84.3	168	84.4	220	85.6	602	84.3	145
Unknown	4	1.3	5	1.2	7	1.4	2	1.0	4	1.6	9	1.3	2
Total	310	43.4	404	56.6	515	72.1	199	27.9	257	36.0	714		164

Tuition and Fees

	Resident	Nonresident
Full-time	$23,858	$23,858
Part-time	$17,190	$17,190

Living Expenses

Estimated living expenses for singles

Living on campus	Living off campus	Living at home
$9,740	$13,500	$13,500

Hamline University School of Law

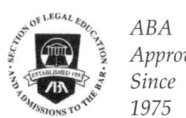

*ABA
Approved
Since
1975*

GPA and LSAT Scores

	Total	Full-time	Part-time
# of apps	1,306	1,066	240
# of admits	568	435	133
# of matrics	233	159	74
75% GPA	3.59	3.63	3.56
25% GPA	3.07	3.14	3.00
75% LSAT	158	158	155
25% LSAT	150	152	147

Grants and Scholarships (from prior year)

	Total		Full-time		Part-time	
	#	%	#	%	#	%
Total # of students	667		512		155	
Total # receiving grants	290	43.5	244	47.7	46	29.7
Less than 1/2 tuition	105	15.7	81	15.8	24	15.5
Half to full tuition	139	20.8	120	23.4	19	12.3
Full tuition	45	6.7	42	8.2	3	1.9
More than full tuition	1	0.1	1	0.2	0	0.0
Median grant amount			$12,248		$7,920	

Informational and Library Resources

# of volumes and volume equivalents	261,883
# of titles	131,509
# of active serial subscriptions	2,749
Study seating capacity inside the library	354
# of professional librarians	6
Hours per week library is open	110
# of open, wired connections available to students	319
# of networked computers available for use by students	36
# of simultaneous wireless users	0
Require computer?	Y

JD Attrition (from prior year)

	Academic	Other	Total	
	#	#	#	%
1st year	0	20	20	6.8%
2nd year	0	0	0	0.0%
3rd year	0	1	1	0.6%
4th year	0	0	0	0.0%

Employment

	Total	Percentage
Employment status known	144	92.9
Employment status unknown	11	7.1
Employed	118	81.9
Pursuing graduate degrees	4	2.8
Unemployed seeking employment	12	8.3
Unemployed not seeking employment	10	6.9

Type of Employment

# employed in law firms	53	44.9
# employed in business and industry	30	25.4
# employed in government	13	11.0
# employed in public interest	6	5.1
# employed as judicial clerks	14	11.9
# employed in academia	0	0.0

Geographic Location

# employed in state	91	77.1
# employed in foreign countries	0	0.0
# of states where employed		20

Bar Passage Rates

Jurisdiction	Minnesota		
Exam	Sum 03	Win 04	Total
# from school taking bar for the first time	104	15	119
School's pass rate for all first-time takers	88%	40%	82%
State's pass rate for all first-time takers	92%	75%	89%

Hamline University School of Law

1536 Hewitt Avenue
St. Paul, MN 55104
Phone: 651.523.2461, 800.388.3688; Fax: 651.523.3064
E-mail: lawadm@hamline.edu; Website: www.hamline.edu/law

■ Introduction

Hamline University School of Law combines theoretical exploration with hands-on experience to create the ideal education for lawyers and leaders in every profession. Nine clinical offerings and comprehensive practical externships build upon an in-depth grounding in the legal fundamentals to create a rich, rewarding law school experience. One essential mission of Hamline is to integrate the values of social commitment throughout the law school. Hamline fulfills that mission through its course offerings and extracurricular programs.

Hamline offers this dynamic approach to law school in an ideal learning environment. Located in the vibrant urban centers of Minneapolis/St. Paul, the law school sits among 55 acres of wooded campus, creating a blend of culture, ideas, perspectives, and people. The result is a passionate, highly engaged community, which works collaboratively on education, scholarship, and public policy—the ideal environment to become a lawyer. The nationally recognized Dispute Resolution Institute, newly founded Hamline Health Law Center, unique international programs, and interdisciplinary degree options round out the exceptional learning opportunities provided in a small, close-knit law school community.

■ Library and Physical Facilities

Hamline's law library provides modern collections of print, electronic, and microform resources to accomplish student's research and writing. In addition to the library's holdings of over 270,000 volumes and numerous electronic databases, students have access to the libraries of seven other colleges and universities through a consortium arrangement. The library has a computer lab with 30 personal computers, wireless access, and network ports throughout the library. An experienced staff is available to assist students and to teach research techniques using both print and on-line resources. Through the library's extensive website, students have access to many electronic resources from home.

The law building's architectural design encourages easy access to faculty and administrative offices, and the extensive use of glass creates a feeling of spaciousness. Classrooms range in size from small seminar rooms to 100 seat, fully-wired lecture halls. The school's newly renovated moot courtroom is a technological showplace.

■ Curriculum

Excellent Academic Foundation: Hamline law school's core curriculum provides the analytical grounding necessary for success as a law student and as a law graduate. Taught by highly respected faculty, the student-centered

academic program is both rigorous and cooperative. The offerings reflect considerable breadth, enabling students to concentrate their studies in a variety of substantive areas, including business representation, children and the law, civil dispute resolution, commercial law, criminal law, government and regulatory affairs, health law, intellectual property, international law, labor and employment law, and social justice. Given Hamline's expertise in Alternative Dispute Resolution, the school provides a full range of ADR-related programming, including a summer institute, January term courses, certificate programs, and a biannual symposium.

Scheduling Options: Meeting the diverse needs of its student body, Hamline flexibly provides a full-time, three-year program and a part-time, four-year weekend program. Students may select electives from weekday and weekend opportunities.

Skills Courses: Students can experience meaningful real world client contact through Hamline's Clinics and Practicum Program of externships. The law school runs law clinics in the areas of immigration law, small business planning, criminal law, child advocacy, alternative dispute resolution, education law, and trial practice. Each clinic operates as a small law office with students handling their own caseload and representing clients. In the Practicum Program students learn law and lawyering skills outside the traditional law school setting. Placed in varied externships in private law firms, public agencies, courts, corporations, and legislative offices, students work directly with mentor-attorneys and judges.

International Studies: Being a Hamline law student extends beyond national borders. Select Hamline students participate in an international exchange with Hamline's European law school partners. Others compete in the Vienna International Moot Court competition. In addition, the law school regularly offers unique study abroad opportunities in the following locations: Bergen, Norway; Rome, Italy; Paris, France; Budapest, Hungary; Jerusalem, Israel; and London, England.

Interdisciplinary Opportunities: The law school offers dual degree and course exchange options that give students the chance to combine their legal education with a second disciplinary focus. Dual degrees are available in Public Administration, Management, Nonprofit Management, Organizational Leadership, and Library and Information Science.

■ Faculty

In the past three years, Hamline has invested heavily in expanding its faculty, increasing the size by one-third with nationally recognized experts in bioethics, intellectual property, international trade, corporate law, and critical race theory. These faculty members join a faculty nationally

Hamline University School of Law

recognized for scholarship and academic leadership in dispute resolution, commercial law, state constitutional law, and many other fields. All Hamline faculty are committed to an "open door" policy to help students learn and enjoy the law. The Constance Bakken Fellows program provides funding for collaborative research between faculty and students. An emphasis on seminars allows students to learn in small classes, make presentations, and create original research on topics of their interest, ensuring that students work closely with Hamline's dedicated faculty throughout their law school experience.

■ Student Activities

Hamline law students staff the *Hamline Law Review* and the *Hamline Journal of Public Law and Policy*, and provide editorial assistance for the *Journal of Law and Religion*. Hamline also offers students the opportunity to participate in over 10 moot court teams. Hamline has student organizations to fit every interest, ranging from political activism, to pro bono service, to an ice hockey team. The Student Bar Association is the school's student government.

■ Admission and Financial Aid

Admission: The School of Law strives to maintain a selection process that emphasizes a rigorous but fair examination of each person as an individual, not merely as a set of credentials. In addition to the LSAT and

undergraduate GPA, the admission committee gives significant weight to motivation, personal experiences, employment history, graduate education, maturity, letters of recommendation, and the ability to articulate one's interest in and suitability for the study of law. Our admission policy is designed to enhance the academic rigor, professional dedication, social concern, and diversity of the student body, including cultural, economic, racial, and ethnic composition.

Financial Aid: Prospective law students are understandably concerned about how to meet the substantial expense of law school. Hamline responds to that concern by providing a comprehensive financial aid program. At Hamline, 95 percent of law school students qualify for need-based loans.

Scholarships: Hamline offers numerous merit-based scholarships, diversity scholarships, and endowed scholarships made possible by generous donors.

■ Career Services

The Career Services Office assists all students in their job searches and career planning. It provides informational programs, mock interviews, one-on-one counseling, networking opportunities, and an online job bank. It also hosts on-campus interviews for interested employers and works extensively with employers to market Hamline law students and to solicit postings and information. The office maintains a large library of resources for students engaged in job searches.

Applicant Profile

Hamline University School of Law
This grid includes only applicants with 120-180 LSAT scores earned under standard administrations.

LSAT Score	3.75 +		3.50 - 3.74		3.25 - 3.49		3.00 - 3.24		2.75 - 2.99		2.50 - 2.74		2.25 - 2.49		2.00 - 2.24		Below 2.00		No GPA		Totals	
	Apps	Adm	Apps	Adm	Apps	Adm	Apps	Adm	Apps	Adm	Apps	Adm	Apps	Adm	Apps	Adm	Apps	Adm	Apps	Adm	Apps	Adm
175-180	0	0	0	0	0	0	0	0	0	0	0	0	0	0	0	0	0	0	0	0	0	0
170-174	1	1	1	1	1	1	0	0	0	0	0	0	1	1	0	0	0	0	0	0	4	4
165-169	4	4	3	3	2	2	1	1	3	3	1	0	1	0	0	0	0	0	0	0	15	13
160-164	13	13	10	10	26	26	11	11	10	8	6	5	2	1	2	0	1	0	1	0	82	74
155-159	21	20	52	50	36	35	38	34	23	20	15	7	10	4	3	0	0	0	0	0	198	170
150-154	35	33	51	43	79	57	68	43	43	15	30	9	13	2	6	1	2	0	2	1	329	204
145-149	23	9	53	24	77	20	71	12	51	14	38	5	18	0	5	0	1	0	1	0	338	84
140-144	9	4	20	1	30	3	45	3	36	4	35	0	12	1	7	0	1	0	3	0	198	16
135-139	3	0	6	0	11	1	17	1	14	0	10	0	8	0	4	0	3	0	3	0	79	2
130-134	0	0	0	0	0	0	4	0	5	0	4	0	3	0	5	0	4	0	4	0	29	0
125-129	0	0	0	0	2	0	1	0	0	0	0	0	0	0	0	0	0	0	1	0	4	0
120-124	0	0	0	0	0	0	0	0	0	0	0	0	0	0	0	0	0	0	0	0	0	0
Total	109	84	196	132	264	145	256	105	185	64	139	26	68	9	32	1	12	0	15	1	1276	567

Apps = Number of Applicants   Adm = Number Admitted   Reflects 98% of the total applicant pool.

This chart is to be used as a general guide only. Nonnumerical factors are strongly considered for all applicants.

Harvard Law School

1563 Massachusetts Avenue
Cambridge, MA 02138
Phone: 617.495.3109
E-mail: jdadmiss@law.harvard.edu; Website: www.law.harvard.edu

ABA
Approved
Since
1923

The Basics

Type of school	Private
Term	Semester
Application deadline	2/1
Application fee	$75
Financial aid deadline	3/1
Can first year start other than fall?	No
Student to faculty ratio (fall)	11.3 to 1
Does the university offer:	
housing restricted to law students?	Yes
graduate housing for which law students are eligible?	Yes

Faculty and Administrators

	Total		Men		Women		Minorities	
	Fall	Spr	Fall	Spr	Fall	Spr	Fall	Spr
Full-time	127	114	93	78	34	36	17	16
Other Full-time	19	28	13	21	6	7	2	2
Deans, librarians, & others who teach	5	5	2	2	3	3	1	1
Part-time	32	34	22	21	10	13	1	1
Total	183	181	130	122	53	59	21	20

Curriculum

		Full-time	Part-time
Typical first-year section size		79	0
Is there typically a "small section" of the first-year class, other than Legal Writing, taught by full-time faculty		No	No
If yes, typical size offered last year		0	0
# of classroom course titles beyond 1st year curriculum		194	
# of upper division courses, excluding seminars with an enrollment:	Under 25	67	
	25-49	59	
	50-74	34	
	75-99	12	
	100+	22	
# of seminars		69	
# of seminar positions available		1,518	
# of seminar positions filled		881	0
# of positions available in simulation courses		240	
# of simulation positions filled		159	0
# of positions available in faculty supervised clinical courses		309	
# of faculty supervised clinical positions filled	223		0
# involved in field placements		142	0
# involved in law journals		882	0
# involved in moot court or trial competitions	557		0
# of credit hours required to graduate		80	

JD Enrollment and Ethnicity

	Men		Women		Full-time		Part-time		1st-year		Total		JD Degs. Awd.
	#	%	#	%	#	%	#	%	#	%	#	%	
African Amer.	68	7.2	105	14.1	173	10.2	0	0.0	57	10.2	173	10.2	43
Amer. Indian	7	0.7	4	0.5	11	0.6	0	0.0	5	0.9	11	0.6	0
Asian Amer.	92	9.7	111	14.9	203	12.0	0	0.0	73	13.1	203	12.0	61
Mex. Amer.	24	2.5	11	1.5	35	2.1	0	0.0	12	2.2	35	2.1	8
Puerto Rican	5	0.5	4	0.5	9	0.5	0	0.0	3	0.5	9	0.5	3
Hispanic	20	2.1	25	3.4	45	2.7	0	0.0	20	3.6	45	2.7	8
Total Minority	216	22.8	260	34.9	476	28.1	0	0.0	170	30.5	476	28.1	123
For. Nation.	27	2.8	25	3.4	52	3.1	0	0.0	17	3.0	52	3.1	22
Caucasian	559	58.9	361	48.5	920	54.3	0	0.0	292	52.3	920	54.3	311
Unknown	147	15.5	99	13.3	246	14.5	0	0.0	79	14.2	246	14.5	95
Total	949	56.0	745	44.0	1694	100.0	0	0.0	558	32.9	1694		551

Tuition and Fees

	Resident	Nonresident
Full-time	$34,568	$0
Part-time	$0	$0

Living Expenses

Estimated living expenses for singles

Living on campus	Living off campus	Living at home
$17,890	$17,890	$17,890

Harvard Law School

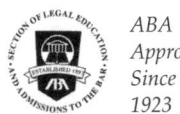

*ABA
Approved
Since
1923*

GPA and LSAT Scores

	Total	Full-time	Part-time
# of apps	7,391	7,391	0
# of admits	834	834	0
# of matrics	554	554	0
75% GPA	3.94	3.94	0.00
25% GPA	3.73	3.73	0.00
75% LSAT	175	175	0
25% LSAT	169	169	0

Grants and Scholarships (from prior year)

	Total		Full-time		Part-time	
	#	%	#	%	#	%
Total # of students	1,654		1,654		0	
Total # receiving grants	616	37.2	616	37.2	0	0.0
Less than 1/2 tuition	365	22.1	365	22.1	0	0.0
Half to full tuition	233	14.1	233	14.1	0	0.0
Full tuition	18	1.1	18	1.1	0	0.0
More than full tuition	0	0.0	0	0.0	0	0.0
Median grant amount			$13,683		$0	

Informational and Library Resources

# of volumes and volume equivalents	2,158,660
# of titles	815,222
# of active serial subscriptions	15,802
Study seating capacity inside the library	761
# of professional librarians	46
Hours per week library is open	99
# of open, wired connections available to students	2,750
# of networked computers available for use by students	207
# of simultaneous wireless users	1,800
Require computer?	N

JD Attrition (from prior year)

	Academic	Other	Total	
	#	#	#	%
1st year	0	0	0	0.0%
2nd year	0	5	5	0.9%
3rd year	0	3	3	0.6%
4th year	0	0	0	0.0%

Employment

	Total	Percentage
Employment status known	573	99.5
Employment status unknown	3	0.5
Employed	560	97.7
Pursuing graduate degrees	11	1.9
Unemployed seeking employment	1	0.2
Unemployed not seeking employment	1	0.2

Type of Employment

# employed in law firms	375	67.0
# employed in business and industry	17	3.0
# employed in government	15	2.7
# employed in public interest	23	4.1
# employed as judicial clerks	125	22.3
# employed in academia	5	0.9

Geographic Location

# employed in state	61	10.9
# employed in foreign countries	19	3.4
# of states where employed	37	

Bar Passage Rates

Jurisdiction	New York			Massachusetts		
Exam	Sum 03	Win 04	Total	Sum 03	Win 04	Total
# from school taking bar for the first time	227	0	227	73	3	76
School's pass rate for all first-time takers	96%		96%	99%	100%	99%
State's pass rate for all first-time takers	78%	58%	75%	82%	82%	82%

Harvard Law School

1563 Massachusetts Avenue
Cambridge, MA 02138
Phone: 617.495.3109
E-mail: jdadmiss@law.harvard.edu; Website: www.law.harvard.edu

■ A Legal Metropolis

Harvard Law School combines the resources of the world's premier center for legal education and research with educational settings scaled to enrich individual and interactive learning. The result is a uniquely vibrant and collaborative environment. Harvard's scope generates enormous vitality—an unparalleled breadth and depth of academic options, a wide array of research programs, a diverse student body drawn from across the nation and around the world, and a global network of distinguished alumni. Within this dynamic environment, law students have broad opportunities for intellectual engagement with faculty and classmates: first-year sections have fewer than 80 students; 110 courses have enrollments of 25 or fewer; and opportunities to work directly with faculty members abound. First-year students may join in intimate, faculty-led reading groups on topics ranging from cyberlaw to terrorism. Harvard's extensive resources and collaborative approach create unmatched opportunities to prepare for leadership in public service, private practice, the judiciary, academia, business, or government.

■ Public Service

HLS strongly promotes public service. The school guarantees funding for summer public interest work, and 350 JD students received funds to work in 31 states and 31 countries in 2004. The Office of Public Interest Advising provides comprehensive services to students pursuing public service careers. The Low Income Protection Plan allows graduates substantial financial flexibility to pursue lower-paying employment, and a variety of fellowship programs provide additional support to graduates entering public service. Reflecting its public service commitment, HLS has a 40-hour minimum pro bono work requirement, with students actually completing over 300 hours of pro bono work during law school on average.

■ Faculty

The centerpiece of the HLS experience is working directly with teachers who shape the landscape of American and international law. The faculty includes leading scholars and specialists in every subject area. Beyond the classroom, students provide critical support to faculty producing cutting-edge research and influencing law's development around the world. The student/faculty ratio has fallen dramatically in recent years, and Harvard Law School's commitment to hire more core faculty means that this trend is likely to continue.

■ Student Life

Drawn from 50 states, dozens of countries, and hundreds of colleges and graduate schools, students have remarkably varied perspectives and aspirations. HLS is a global community that includes foreign attorneys pursuing advanced degrees (LLM, SJD) who study alongside upper-level JD students. Reflecting the diversity of students' interests, more than 80 student organizations and student journals complement the classroom experience.

HLS recently renovated its physical space to meet the standard of its iconic Langdell Library. Along with state-of-the-art classrooms, there is now a stylish student center with dining facilities and lounge areas that are centers of activity. Renovation of the gymnasium will be completed over the summer of 2005. A constant stream of outside speakers—from Supreme Court Justices to community organizers to renowned academics—adds to the bustle. A variety of student groups plan off- and on-campus social events, from watching the Red Sox to organizing charity drives.

■ Curriculum

With fewer than 80 students, first-year sections ensure multiple perspectives yet facilitate participation. The First-Year Lawyering Program provides training in legal research and writing in small groups. During the spring, first-year students take an upper-level elective and participate in the Ames competition (moot court). Second- and third-year students tailor Harvard's extensive educational opportunities to their individual interests with more than 230 courses and seminars in the upper-level curriculum, one of the most extensive clinical programs in the nation, independent study, and cross-registration beyond the Law School. A major writing project is required for graduation, and opportunities for individual writing projects abound.

■ Preparing Future Law Teachers

HLS has trained more of today's American law professors than any other law school. HLS builds on that tradition with expanded opportunities to publish, to work one-on-one with faculty, and to develop an independent scholarly agenda. Students can present their work in scholarly settings, participate in faculty seminars, and prepare for a life in academe. The unparalleled reach of the curriculum permits students to make new connections within legal scholarship, while the opportunity for outside study supports an interdisciplinary approach that is unmatched anywhere.

Research Centers

Students can affiliate with any of the Law School's 18 research centers that cover human rights, East Asian legal studies, Islamic law, law and economics, Internet law, negotiation, and other fields.

Joint Degrees and Study Abroad

Students can combine legal studies with advanced training in other fields through joint-degree programs in business, government, and public health or by designing concurrent degree programs with other graduate schools at Harvard, MIT, or the Fletcher School at Tufts University. Law students may propose a one-semester course of study at a foreign institution, and HLS offers a JD/LLM with the University of Cambridge, England.

Library, Campus, and Location

With over 2.1 million volumes, the library is the largest law school library in the world. Recently renovated, the library provides a modern and accessible facility for research and study. There are 20 buildings on the Law School campus, including eight dormitories, a newly renovated student center, offices for student groups, and space for an array of programs. The vibrant cities of Cambridge and Boston offer an exciting array of professional, cultural, and recreational opportunities.

Admission

A team of faculty members and admission officers reviews applications, and decisions are based on experi-enced judgment applied to individual cases. There are no shortcuts to assessing scholarship, service, and excellence in prospective law students, and applicants are encouraged to provide any information about their achievements in school, at work, and in the world that informs these assessments. A student body that is richly diverse in experiences, interests, and backgrounds helps to create the best teaching and learning environment imaginable. The Law School encourages all who would like to study law at Harvard to apply for admission.

Financial Assistance for Law School and Beyond

HLS provides need-based student aid and loan-repayment assistance, ensuring that students can cover their educational expenses during law school and repay their educational loans after graduation. The Law School's Low Income Protection Plan helps maximize career options by providing sufficient financial flexibility to pursue a wide variety of career paths. Graduates working full-time in government, nonprofits, academia, or law-related private sector jobs may receive LIPP assistance.

Career Services

HLS graduates choose many career paths within and beyond the legal profession. The Career Services Office and the Office of Public Interest Advising provide a full range of services to help students choose their direction. Each year, more than 700 employers interview HLS students in Cambridge. About 65 percent of the graduating class enters private practice, and about 135 graduates enter judicial clerkships. The remainder enters public service, business and industry, academia, or other pursuits.

Applicant Profile

HLS does not provide a profile chart because it would be based solely upon undergraduate GPA and LSAT scores. Admission decisions are based on many factors beyond GPA and LSAT. Each application is read in its entirety by at least two members of a team of faculty members and admission officers. Although most admitted candidates graduated near the top of their college classes and presented LSAT scores in the top few percentiles, a significant proportion of candidates who meet these characterizations may not be offered admission. At the same time, some admitted candidates do not have as high college or LSAT standings but present combined academic and other achievements that are comparable nonetheless. Candidates with higher grades and scores tend to be admitted at higher rates than candidates with lower grades and scores, but at no point on the GPA or LSAT scales are the chances for admission to Harvard Law School zero or 100 percent.

University of Hawai'i at Mānoa—William S. Richardson School of Law

2515 Dole Street
Honolulu, HI 96822
Phone: 808.956.7966; Fax: 808.956.3813
E-mail: lawadm@hawaii.edu; Website: www.hawaii.edu/law

*ABA
Approved
Since
1974*

The Basics

Type of school	Public
Term	Semester
Application deadline	3/1
Application fee	$60
Financial aid deadline	3/1
Can first year start other than fall?	No
Student to faculty ratio (fall)	15.9 to 1
Does the university offer:	
housing restricted to law students?	No
graduate housing for which law students are eligible?	Yes

Faculty and Administrators

	Total		Men		Women		Minorities	
	Fall	Spr	Fall	Spr	Fall	Spr	Fall	Spr
Full-time	17	21	11	13	6	8	5	6
Other Full-time	1	4	0	4	1	0	1	2
Deans, librarians, & others who teach	7	7	2	2	5	5	4	4
Part-time	21	23	13	16	8	7	9	10
Total	46	55	26	35	20	20	19	22

Curriculum

	Full-time	Part-time
Typical first-year section size	108	0
Is there typically a "small section" of the first-year class, other than Legal Writing, taught by full-time faculty	Yes	No
If yes, typical size offered last year	17	0
# of classroom course titles beyond 1st year curriculum	63	

# of upper division courses, excluding seminars with an enrollment:		
	Under 25	42
	25-49	12
	50-74	5
	75-99	4
	100+	1

# of seminars	28	
# of seminar positions available	312	
# of seminar positions filled	312	0
# of positions available in simulation courses	161	
# of simulation positions filled	149	0
# of positions available in faculty supervised clinical courses	8	
# of faculty supervised clinical positions filled	8	0
# involved in field placements	132	0
# involved in law journals	61	0
# involved in moot court or trial competitions	39	0
# of credit hours required to graduate	89	

JD Enrollment and Ethnicity

	Men		Women		Full-time		Part-time		1st-year		Total		JD Degs. Awd.
	#	%	#	%	#	%	#	%	#	%	#	%	
African Amer.	5	3.4	1	0.6	6	1.9	0	0.0	1	0.9	6	1.9	0
Amer. Indian	4	2.7	4	2.2	8	2.5	0	0.0	3	2.7	8	2.5	1
Asian Amer.	73	50.0	105	59.0	178	54.9	0	0.0	64	58.2	178	54.9	51
Mex. Amer.	0	0.0	1	0.6	1	0.3	0	0.0	0	0.0	1	0.3	1
Puerto Rican	0	0.0	2	1.1	2	0.6	0	0.0	0	0.0	2	0.6	2
Hispanic	1	0.7	1	0.6	2	0.6	0	0.0	0	0.0	2	0.6	2
Total Minority	83	56.8	114	64.0	197	60.8	0	0.0	68	61.8	197	60.8	57
For. Nation.	2	1.4	3	1.7	5	1.5	0	0.0	2	1.8	5	1.5	0
Caucasian	30	20.5	31	17.4	61	18.8	0	0.0	19	17.3	61	18.8	19
Unknown	31	21.2	30	16.9	61	18.8	0	0.0	21	19.1	61	18.8	2
Total	146	45.1	178	54.9	324	100.0	0	0.0	110	34.0	324		78

Tuition and Fees

	Resident	Nonresident
Full-time	$11,529	$19,689
Part-time	$0	$0

Living Expenses

Estimated living expenses for singles

Living on campus	Living off campus	Living at home
$9,437	$11,955	$5,185

University of Hawai'i at Mānoa—William S. Richardson School of Law

ABA
Approved
Since
1974

GPA and LSAT Scores

	Total	Full-time	Part-time
# of apps	1,080	1,080	0
# of admits	230	230	0
# of matrics	100	100	0
75% GPA	3.64	3.64	0.00
25% GPA	3.08	3.08	0.00
75% LSAT	160	160	0
25% LSAT	154	154	0

Grants and Scholarships (from prior year)

	Total		Full-time		Part-time	
	#	%	#	%	#	%
Total # of students	310		301		9	
Total # receiving grants	106	34.2	106	35.2	0	0.0
Less than 1/2 tuition	17	5.5	17	5.6	0	0.0
Half to full tuition	83	26.8	83	27.6	0	0.0
Full tuition	6	1.9	6	2.0	0	0.0
More than full tuition	0	0.0	0	0.0	0	0.0
Median grant amount			$5,400		$0	

Informational and Library Resources

# of volumes and volume equivalents	334,239
# of titles	40,932
# of active serial subscriptions	4,090
Study seating capacity inside the library	415
# of professional librarians	5
Hours per week library is open	94
# of open, wired connections available to students	244
# of networked computers available for use by students	53
# of simultaneous wireless users	500
Require computer?	Y

JD Attrition (from prior year)

	Academic	Other	Total	
	#	#	#	%
1st year	1	0	1	0.9%
2nd year	0	5	5	5.0%
3rd year	0	0	0	0.0%
4th year	0	0	0	0.0%

Employment

	Total	Percentage
Employment status known	72	98.6
Employment status unknown	1	1.4
Employed	65	90.3
Pursuing graduate degrees	5	6.9
Unemployed seeking employment	1	1.4
Unemployed not seeking employment	1	1.4

Type of Employment

# employed in law firms	19	29.2
# employed in business and industry	7	10.8
# employed in government	10	15.4
# employed in public interest	1	1.5
# employed as judicial clerks	26	40.0
# employed in academia	1	1.5

Geographic Location

# employed in state	56	86.2
# employed in foreign countries	1	1.5
# of states where employed	5	

Bar Passage Rates

Jurisdiction	Hawaii		
Exam	Sum 03	Win 04	Total
# from school taking bar for the first time	49	9	58
School's pass rate for all first-time takers	96%	67%	91%
State's pass rate for all first-time takers	90%	78%	86%

The information on these pages was provided by the law school

University of Hawai'i at Mānoa—William S. Richardson School of Law

2515 Dole Street
Honolulu, HI 96822
Phone: 808.956.7966; Fax: 808.956.3813
E-mail: lawadm@hawaii.edu; Website: www.hawaii.edu/law

■ Introduction

The William S. Richardson School of Law at the University of Hawai'i is located at the foot of beautiful Mānoa valley, minutes from sandy beaches and lush rain forests, as well as from the economic and legal center of urban Honolulu. The School of Law offers an excellent academic program with professors committed to scholarship and research who have a national reputation for teaching excellence. The school is noted for its friendly and collegial student body, its accessible faculty, and its rich cultural and ethnic diversity.

Placement after graduation is consistently very high. The school's distinguished alumni serve as leaders in Hawai'i as well as in national and international arenas. The University of Hawai'i is recognized as a center for environmental law study and international law with an Asian and Pacific focus. The William S. Richardson School of Law is fully accredited by the American Bar Association and is a member of the American Association of Law Schools.

■ Curriculum

The JD program is a three-year program of full-time day study. Full-time registration is defined as enrollment for a minimum of 12 credits each semester. First-year students begin with a three-day orientation; the first-year curriculum is entirely prescribed. All students must complete 60 hours of pro bono law-related community service in order to graduate.

■ Library and Physical Facilities

The library contains a study carrel with wired and wireless Internet access for most students and seminar/discussion rooms for study groups. The air-conditioned classroom building features a moot courtroom with video technology for support of clinical education programs. Law students have full access to all facilities of the university, including the health, counseling, and computing centers, and extensive athletic facilities. The classroom building has wireless Internet access for students, faculty, and staff.

■ Pacific-Asian Legal Studies

Enhanced by Hawai'i's location, population, culture, and economic relationships, the law school offers a program in Pacific-Asian Legal Studies (PALS). The program has the twofold purpose of conducting new research and enriching the JD curriculum. A number of faculty have expertise in Pacific/Asian research, teaching, and law reform. Recent course offerings in PALS have included

Chinese Business Law, Chinese Law and Society, Pacific Island Legal Systems, Korean Law, Philippine Law, Japanese Law and Society, and US-Japan Business Transactions. The Certificate in Pacific-Asian Legal Studies allows students to focus their coursework and to earn the certificate in addition to the JD.

Selected students may do a full semester externship for academic credit with the court systems in certain Pacific Island nations or, with approval, in agencies or entities in Asia. Students may also arrange a semester of study with law faculties in Asia with prior approval.

■ Environmental/Ocean Law Programs

Students may focus their elective courses in the area of environmental law and can earn a Certificate in Environmental Law along with the JD degree. Emphasis is on freshwater resources, oceans, coastal waters, and land use —all areas of special interest to Hawai'i and the Pacific.

The University of Hawai'i also has extensive programs in different types of marine research, and the law faculty is particularly interested in ocean law and policy. Law students may elect to combine their JD studies with a university certificate program in Ocean Policy. The university also offers a certificate in Resource Management.

■ Admission

Admission is determined by an applicant's academic achievement, aptitude for the study of law, and professional promise. Preference is given to residents of Hawai'i and to nonresidents with strong ties to or special interest in Hawai'i, the Asia/Pacific region, or other programs in the law school. Approximately 30 percent of the student body may be nonresidents.

Besides LSAT and undergraduate GPA and major, other factors considered include academic work beyond the bachelor's degree, work experience, writing ability, community service, diversity, overcoming hardship, and unusual accomplishments.

Applications from students wishing to transfer, or from those wishing to visit for a semester or two, are considered for both August and January admission.

■ Student Activities

Student editorial boards publish the *University of Hawai'i Law Review* and the online *Asian and Pacific Law and Policy Journal*. Students also regularly organize and participate in the moot court program, including national moot court competitions in international and environmental law. The 1993 Jessup International Moot Court Team placed first in the nation and second in international competition. The 1994 and 1996 Jessup teams again won

University of Hawai'i at Mānoa—William S. Richardson School of Law

the Northwest region and finished among the top teams in the national rounds while the 1995 Jessup team captured the Pacific Regional championship and won first place honors for best memorial in the international competition. The 1999 Environmental Moot Court Team won the National Environmental Moot Court Competition. The 1996 Client Counseling Team placed second in the national competition, and placed first in regional competitions in 1996, 1998, 1999, 2000, and 2001. In 1999, 2000, 2001, and 2002 the Native American Moot Court Team captured the national championship at the Annual National Native American Law Students Moot Court Competitions.

Many students are active in a variety of organizations within the school and the Honolulu community including, for example, Advocates for Public Interest Law (APIL); student divisions of the American Bar Association, National Lawyers Guild, and American Trial Lawyers Association; American Inns of Court; Student Bar Association; Phi Delta Phi and Delta Theta Phi International Legal Fraternities; the Pacific Islands and Pacific-Asian Legal Studies Organizations; Association of Women Law Students; and Environmental Law Society. Student affinity groups include the Filipino Law Students Association and the 'Ahahui 'O Hawai'i, an organization of native Hawaiian law students.

■ Career Services

Career counseling and services assist students and alumni in obtaining part-time, summer clerk, or associate positions in both the public and private sectors. Placement emphasis is on Hawai'i and the Asia/Pacific region, and about 85 percent of our graduates remain here immediately upon graduation. On-campus facilities are available for interviews. All large firms in Honolulu and many medium and small firms participate in the fall on-campus interview season for second- and third-year students. Our students are highly successful in obtaining much sought after judicial clerkships upon graduation. Most recent graduating classes have had a greater than 90 percent employment rate six months after graduation.

Applicant Profile

University of Hawai'i at Mānoa—William S. Richardson School of Law
This grid includes only applicants who earned 120-180 LSAT scores under standard administrations.

LSAT Score	3.75 +		3.50 - 3.74		3.25 - 3.49		3.00 - 3.24		2.75 - 2.99		2.50 - 2.74		2.25 - 2.49		2.00 - 2.24		Below 2.00		No GPA		Totals	
	Apps	Adm	Apps	Adm	Apps	Adm	Apps	Adm	Apps	Adm	Apps	Adm	Apps	Adm	Apps	Adm	Apps	Adm	Apps	Adm	Apps	Adm
175-180	0	0	0	0	0	0	0	0	1	1	0	0	0	0	0	0	0	0	0	0	1	1
170-174	1	1	2	2	1	0	1	1	0	0	1	0	0	0	1	0	0	0	0	0	7	4
165-169	4	4	9	8	10	10	3	2	6	2	2	0	2	1	0	0	0	0	0	0	36	27
160-164	20	18	38	30	31	20	28	8	26	6	12	3	4	1	2	0	0	0	2	2	163	88
155-159	24	14	49	16	66	20	49	18	29	3	19	1	12	1	5	0	2	0	5	2	260	75
150-154	28	5	33	7	69	3	77	5	43	1	23	1	6	0	3	0	0	0	9	1	291	23
145-149	7	0	22	0	31	0	41	0	23	0	20	0	10	0	4	0	0	0	2	0	160	0
140-144	4	0	7	0	19	0	15	0	23	0	14	0	8	0	1	0	0	0	4	0	95	0
135-139	0	0	6	0	8	0	4	0	7	0	7	0	3	0	3	0	1	0	1	0	40	0
130-134	0	0	2	0	1	0	3	0	3	0	3	0	1	0	3	0	0	0	0	0	16	0
125-129	0	0	0	0	0	0	0	0	1	0	3	0	0	0	0	0	0	0	2	0	6	0
120-124	0	0	0	0	0	0	0	0	0	0	0	0	0	0	0	0	0	0	0	0	0	0
Total	88	42	168	63	236	53	221	34	162	13	104	5	46	3	22	0	3	0	25	5	1075	218

Apps = Number of Applicants
Adm = Number Admitted
Reflects 100% of the total applicant pool.

Hofstra University School of Law

121 Hofstra University
Hempstead, NY 11549
Phone: 516.463.5916; Fax: 516.463.6264
E-mail: lawadmissions@hofstra.edu; Website: www.hofstra.edu/law

ABA
Approved
Since
1971

The Basics

Type of school	Private
Term	Semester
Application deadline	4/15
Application fee	$60
Financial aid deadline	6/1
Can first year start other than fall?	No
Student to faculty ratio (fall)	18.5 to 1
Does the university offer:	
housing restricted to law students?	No
graduate housing for which law students are eligible?	Yes

Faculty and Administrators

	Total		Men		Women		Minorities	
	Fall	Spr	Fall	Spr	Fall	Spr	Fall	Spr
Full-time	44	44	30	29	14	15	6	5
Other Full-time	0	0	0	0	0	0	0	0
Deans, librarians, & others who teach	6	5	2	2	4	3	1	1
Part-time	30	47	27	39	3	8	0	2
Total	80	96	59	70	21	26	7	8

Curriculum

		Full-time	Part-time
Typical first-year section size		116	0
Is there typically a "small section" of the first-year class, other than Legal Writing, taught by full-time faculty		Yes	No
If yes, typical size offered last year		30	0
# of classroom course titles beyond 1st year curriculum		123	
# of upper division courses, excluding seminars with an enrollment:	Under 25	64	
	25-49	36	
	50-74	8	
	75-99	10	
	100+	17	
# of seminars		50	
# of seminar positions available		909	
# of seminar positions filled		630	29
# of positions available in simulation courses		841	
# of simulation positions filled		759	24
# of positions available in faculty supervised clinical courses		94	
# of faculty supervised clinical positions filled	92	2
# involved in field placements		66	7
# involved in law journals		150	0
# involved in moot court or trial competitions	24	0
# of credit hours required to graduate		87	

JD Enrollment and Ethnicity

	Men		Women		Full-time		Part-time		1st-year		Total		JD Degs. Awd.
	#	%	#	%	#	%	#	%	#	%	#	%	
African Amer.	14	2.6	47	9.8	54	6.2	7	4.8	21	5.7	61	6.0	11
Amer. Indian	3	0.6	1	0.2	3	0.3	1	0.7	1	0.3	4	0.4	0
Asian Amer.	30	5.6	31	6.5	49	5.6	12	8.2	34	9.2	61	6.0	5
Mex. Amer.	0	0.0	0	0.0	0	0.0	0	0.0	0	0.0	0	0.0	0
Puerto Rican	0	0.0	0	0.0	0	0.0	0	0.0	0	0.0	0	0.0	0
Hispanic	18	3.3	39	8.2	52	6.0	5	3.4	18	4.9	57	5.6	10
Total Minority	65	12.0	118	24.7	158	18.1	25	17.1	74	19.9	183	18.0	26
For. Nation.	14	2.6	9	1.9	20	2.3	3	2.1	15	4.0	23	2.3	2
Caucasian	306	56.7	242	50.6	464	53.2	84	57.5	246	66.3	548	53.8	50
Unknown	155	28.7	109	22.8	230	26.4	34	23.3	36	9.7	264	25.9	205
Total	540	53.0	478	47.0	872	85.7	146	14.3	371	36.4	1018		283

Tuition and Fees

	Resident	Nonresident
Full-time	$31,440	$31,440
Part-time	$22,408	$22,408

Living Expenses

Estimated living expenses for singles

Living on campus	Living off campus	Living at home
$13,552	$17,222	$7,528

Hofstra University School of Law

ABA
Approved
Since
1971

GPA and LSAT Scores

	Total	Full-time	Part-time
# of apps	5,539	4,579	960
# of admits	1,458	1,233	225
# of matrics	381	268	113
75% GPA	3.64	3.68	3.51
25% GPA	3.00	3.06	2.87
75% LSAT	159	159	156
25% LSAT	153	155	151

Grants and Scholarships (from prior year)

	Total		Full-time		Part-time	
	#	%	#	%	#	%
Total # of students	923		872		51	
Total # receiving grants	458	49.6	445	51.0	13	25.5
Less than 1/2 tuition	359	38.9	346	39.7	13	25.5
Half to full tuition	62	6.7	62	7.1	0	0.0
Full tuition	30	3.3	30	3.4	0	0.0
More than full tuition	7	0.8	7	0.8	0	0.0
Median grant amount			$6,000		$3,750	

Informational and Library Resources

# of volumes and volume equivalents	541,948
# of titles	138,985
# of active serial subscriptions	5,929
Study seating capacity inside the library	630
# of professional librarians	9
Hours per week library is open	99
# of open, wired connections available to students	166
# of networked computers available for use by students	115
# of simultaneous wireless users	1,000
Require computer?	N

JD Attrition (from prior year)

	Academic	Other	Total	
	#	#	#	%
1st year	2	14	16	5.6%
2nd year	0	2	2	0.6%
3rd year	1	1	2	0.7%
4th year	0	0	0	0.0%

Employment

	Total	Percentage
Employment status known	236	93.7
Employment status unknown	16	6.3
Employed	203	86.0
Pursuing graduate degrees	14	5.9
Unemployed seeking employment	5	2.1
Unemployed not seeking employment	14	5.9

Type of Employment

# employed in law firms	133	65.5
# employed in business and industry	25	12.3
# employed in government	26	12.8
# employed in public interest	2	1.0
# employed as judicial clerks	12	5.9
# employed in academia	3	1.5

Geographic Location

# employed in state	169	83.3
# employed in foreign countries	1	0.5
# of states where employed	10	

Bar Passage Rates

Jurisdiction	New York		
Exam	Sum 03	Win 04	Total
# from school taking bar for the first time	231	14	245
School's pass rate for all first-time takers	66%	36%	64%
State's pass rate for all first-time takers	78%	58%	75%

Hofstra University School of Law

121 Hofstra University
Hempstead, NY 11549
Phone: 516.463.5916; Fax: 516.463.6264
E-mail: lawadmissions@hofstra.edu; Website: www.hofstra.edu/law

■ Introduction

Hofstra University School of Law offers both full- and part-time JD programs as well as Master of Law programs in International Law and the American Legal System. Hofstra's curriculum teaches the craft of lawyering while preparing for practice in any jurisdiction. We focus on imparting knowledge, developing analytical abilities, and training law students in the professional skills needed to excel. Located in suburban Long Island, the law school is housed on the university campus, a recognized member of the Association of Botanical Gardens and Arboreta. The law school is ABA accredited and is a member of the AALS.

■ Faculty

Hofstra faculty are nationally and internationally recognized authorities in diverse fields. Faculty members have clerked for justices of the US Supreme Court, chaired major ABA and law reform committees, won awards for scholarship and leadership in legal education, and are recognized as leaders in skills training. Faculty's open-door policy creates an accessible and collegial environment.

■ Special Programs

Entering students are placed in a small section in a substantive course. This small section experience enables a close relationship to develop between students and faculty. The law school prides itself on an extensive array of courses designed to develop lawyering skills. Each January, students are able to select a unique three-credit course on trial techniques that is patterned on the programs offered by the National Institute for Trial Advocacy. A carefully orchestrated sequence of exercises builds students' abilities so that they are able to conduct a full jury trial at the end of the course. This popular course has recently been joined by a second intersession course, offering intensive training in mediation. The law school offers two joint-degree programs in conjunction with the business school, a JD/MBA program and a combined JD/MS in Taxation.

■ Advocacy for the Equality of Lesbian, Gay, Bisexual, and Transgendered People

Each year, Hofstra selects up to three entering students to receive fellowships based on their demonstrated commitment to advocacy on behalf of the LGBT community. These students receive tuition assistance, gain valuable internship experience, and pursue an interdisciplinary course of study that provides knowledge and skills needed to use the law to advocate effectively for the interests of the LGBT community. The fellowship is open to persons of all sexual identities, not only to recognize the diversity of individuals who may ally themselves with sexual equality but also to underscore the importance of alliances between the LGBT community and the public needed to guarantee full civil rights for all.

■ Child and Family Advocacy Fellowship

Each year, Hofstra, in conjunction with the Center for Children, Families, and the Law, selects up to six fellows. Fellows receive scholarship assistance and internship experience, and pursue an interdisciplinary course of study that provides the knowledge and skills needed to advocate effectively for the interests of children and families.

■ Center for Children, Families, and the Law

The center is devoted to education, research, and public service focused on children and families involved in the legal system. This center provides interdisciplinary legal and mental health care training for students and practitioners, as well as community outreach.

■ Externship Programs

The Civil Externship Program provides students with opportunities to learn lawyering skills through placements in a variety of nonprofit organizations or government agencies. The Criminal Externship Program provides experience in criminal law practice through placements in agencies. The Judicial Externship Program places students with state and federal judges for a semester, performing research, writing memoranda, observing court proceedings, and discussing cases with their judge.

■ Clinics

The law school has substantially expanded its clinical offerings and now offers five clinics in different areas of practice, permitting students to work in litigation contexts, collaborate with medical and social work experts in children's rights cases, or develop counseling and mediation skills. In the **Child Advocacy Clinic**, students represent children in abuse, neglect, custody, and order of protection cases. The **Criminal Justice Clinic** allows students to represent criminal defendants in pretrial conferences, witness interviewing, motion and brief writing, case investigations, and trials. Students in the **Housing Rights Clinic** handle a wide variety of housing cases for low-income clients, including defenses of eviction cases; actions against landlords challenging substandard conditions; fair housing and exclusionary zoning cases; public utility shut-off cases; and work on behalf of housing rehabilitation. In our **Mediation Clinic**, students facilitate the negotiations of parties involved in a conflict and help them make decisions about the outcome. Students counsel parties on mediation and help draft settlement agreements. Weekly training on mediation theory and practice, field observation, and simulated mediation exercises prepare students to become professional mediators. The **Political Asylum (Immigration) Clinic** allows students to represent clients who are fleeing from other countries because of persecution. Students represent their clients in hearings before asylum officers, Immigration Court proceedings, and appeals to the US Court of Appeals for the Second Circuit. These cases require extensive investigation, tracking down key witnesses, and trial preparation.

■ Pro Bono Student Lawyers Project

The Pro Bono Student Lawyers Project places students with a variety of agencies, service organizations, law firms, and private practitioners. Students volunteer their time without compensation or credit to work on cases.

■ Unemployment Action Center

The Unemployment Action Center (UAC) is a nonprofit, student-run corporation that offers free advice and representation to persons denied unemployment benefits. The UAC is a past recipient of the New York State Bar Association Law Student Pro Bono Award.

■ Study Abroad

Four study abroad programs are offered each year. Three are summer abroad programs that focus on international and comparative law, in France, Italy, and Australia. A winter abroad program (during winter break) is offered in Curacao, The Netherlands Antilles. Classes are conducted in English and there are many opportunities for cross-cultural experiences.

■ Student Activities

Hofstra students publish four journals: *The Hofstra Law Review,* the *Labor and Employment Law Journal,* the *Family Court Review,* and the *Journal of International Business and Law.* Other student organizations include Asian Pacific American Law Students Association; Black Law Students Association; *Conscience* (student newspaper); Corporate Law Society; Cyberlaw Forum; Democratic Law Students Association; Environmental Law Society; Federalist Society; Gaelic Law Students Society; Hofstra Law Women; Intellectual Property Association; Italian Law Students Association; International Law Society; Jewish Law Students Association; Latino American Law Students Association; OWLS (Older and Wiser Law Students); Phi Alpha Delta; *Pocket Part* (yearbook); People Responding to Issues of Sexual Minorities; Public Justice Foundation; Research, Education and Advocacy to Combat Homelessness; Trial Advocacy Club; and the Unemployment Action Center.

■ Career Services

The Office of Career Services provides a wide range of services to facilitate job placement. An ongoing series of guest lectures and informational panels help to educate students about various career opportunities. OCS has a record of success, with 94 percent of our recent graduates obtaining employment within nine months of graduation.

Applicant Profile Not Available

University of Houston Law Center

100 Law Center
Houston, TX 77204-6060
Phone: 713.743.2280; Fax: 713.743.2194
E-mail: lawadmissions@uh.edu; Website: www.law.uh.edu

ABA
Approved
Since
1950

The Basics

Type of school	Public
Term	Semester
Application deadline	11/1 2/1 2/15
Application fee	$70
Financial aid deadline	4/1
Can first year start other than fall?	Yes
Student to faculty ratio (fall)	23.3 to 1
Does the university offer:	
housing restricted to law students?	No
graduate housing for which law students are eligible?	Yes

Curriculum

	Full-time	Part-time
Typical first-year section size	80	60
Is there typically a "small section" of the first-year class, other than Legal Writing, taught by full-time faculty	Yes	Yes
If yes, typical size offered last year	0	0
# of classroom course titles beyond 1st year curriculum	204	

# of upper division courses, excluding seminars with an enrollment:		
Under 25	124	
25-49	50	
50-74	36	
75-99	11	
100+	3	

# of seminars	30	
# of seminar positions available	453	
# of seminar positions filled	372	0
# of positions available in simulation courses	677	
# of simulation positions filled	513	0
# of positions available in faculty supervised clinical courses	436	
# of faculty supervised clinical positions filled	313	0
# involved in field placements	140	0
# involved in law journals	764	0
# involved in moot court or trial competitions	120	0
# of credit hours required to graduate	90	

Faculty and Administrators

	Total		Men		Women		Minorities	
	Fall	Spr	Fall	Spr	Fall	Spr	Fall	Spr
Full-time	37	34	30	24	7	10	5	4
Other Full-time	19	18	8	8	11	10	3	3
Deans, librarians, & others who teach	4	4	2	2	2	2	0	0
Part-time	52	54	40	46	12	8	2	0
Total	112	110	80	80	32	30	10	7

JD Enrollment and Ethnicity

	Men		Women		Full-time		Part-time		1st-year		Total		JD Degs. Awd.
	#	%	#	%	#	%	#	%	#	%	#	%	
African Amer.	10	1.8	23	4.2	23	2.5	10	5.1	6	1.9	33	3.0	6
Amer. Indian	4	0.7	5	0.9	7	0.8	2	1.0	1	0.3	9	0.8	1
Asian Amer.	55	9.8	61	11.3	101	11.1	15	7.6	37	11.5	116	10.5	27
Mex. Amer.	14	2.5	27	5.0	37	4.1	4	2.0	15	4.7	41	3.7	16
Puerto Rican	0	0.0	0	0.0	0	0.0	0	0.0	0	0.0	0	0.0	0
Hispanic	22	3.9	18	3.3	29	3.2	11	5.6	16	5.0	40	3.6	5
Total Minority	105	18.7	134	24.7	197	21.7	42	21.3	75	23.4	239	21.7	55
For. Nation.	1	0.2	0	0.0	1	0.1	0	0.0	0	0.0	1	0.1	1
Caucasian	441	78.6	394	72.7	685	75.6	150	76.1	236	73.5	835	75.7	237
Unknown	14	2.5	14	2.6	23	2.5	5	2.5	10	3.1	28	2.5	0
Total	561	50.9	542	49.1	906	82.1	197	17.9	321	29.1	1103		293

Tuition and Fees

	Resident	Nonresident
Full-time	$13,313	$20,093
Part-time	$7,229	$9,941

*Full-time (15 hours); part-time (7 hours)

Living Expenses

Estimated living expenses for singles

Living on campus	Living off campus	Living at home
$10,612	$13,850	$8,310

University of Houston Law Center

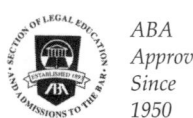

ABA
Approved
Since
1950

GPA and LSAT Scores

	Total	Full-time	Part-time
# of apps	4,024	3,576	448
# of admits	880	810	70
# of matrics	325	271	54
75% GPA	3.70	3.70	3.71
25% GPA	3.25	3.30	3.01
75% LSAT	161	161	161
25% LSAT	157	158	157

Grants and Scholarships (from prior year)

	Total		Full-time		Part-time	
	#	%	#	%	#	%
Total # of students	1,094		901		193	
Total # receiving grants	522	47.7	522	57.9	0	0.0
Less than 1/2 tuition	487	44.5	487	54.1	0	0.0
Half to full tuition	32	2.9	32	3.6	0	0.0
Full tuition	0	0.0	0	0.0	0	0.0
More than full tuition	3	0.3	3	0.3	0	0.0
Median grant amount			$6,014		$0	

Informational and Library Resources

# of volumes and volume equivalents	435,277
# of titles	67,916
# of active serial subscriptions	3,693
Study seating capacity inside the library	566
# of professional librarians	10
Hours per week library is open	107
# of open, wired connections available to students	27
# of networked computers available for use by students	80
# of simultaneous wireless users	3,600
Require computer?	Y

JD Attrition (from prior year)

	Academic	Other	Total	
	#	#	#	%
1st year	0	4	4	1.2%
2nd year	0	8	8	2.0%
3rd year	0	2	2	0.6%
4th year	0	0	0	0.0%

Employment

	Total	Percentage
Employment status known	271	100.0
Employment status unknown	0	0.0
Employed	243	89.7
Pursuing graduate degrees	5	1.8
Unemployed seeking employment	15	5.5
Unemployed not seeking employment	8	3.0

Type of Employment

	Total	Percentage
# employed in law firms	171	70.4
# employed in business and industry	39	16.0
# employed in government	8	3.3
# employed in public interest	8	3.3
# employed as judicial clerks	11	4.5
# employed in academia	6	2.5

Geographic Location

	Total	Percentage
# employed in state	234	96.3
# employed in foreign countries	0	0.0
# of states where employed	5	

Bar Passage Rates

Jurisdiction	Texas		
Exam	Sum 03	Win 04	Total
# from school taking bar for the first time	213	55	268
School's pass rate for all first-time takers	89%	82%	88%
State's pass rate for all first-time takers	83%	69%	80%

University of Houston Law Center

100 Law Center
Houston, TX 77204-6060
Phone: 713.743.2280; Fax: 713.743.2194
E-mail: lawadmissions@uh.edu; Website: www.law.uh.edu

■ Introduction

The University of Houston Law Center is located at the University of Houston, three miles south of downtown. The state-assisted Law Center, located in one of the nation's top 10 largest legal markets, is noted throughout the South and Southwest not only for its excellence, but also for its progressive and innovative approach to the teaching of law. The College of Law, the academic branch of the Law Center, is fully accredited by the American Bar Association and the American Association of Law Schools and has a chapter of the Order of the Coif, the national legal honorary scholastic society. The Law Center confers a JD degree as a first degree in law and a Master of Laws (LLM) degree to students pursuing work beyond the JD degree.

■ Curriculum/Basic Program of Study

The first-year curriculum at the Law Center is prescribed. Students are also required to complete a course in professional responsibility and one major piece of legal research and writing before graduation. Emphasis is placed on legal theory and the varying approaches to the law.

■ Special Programs

The University of Houston Law Center emphasizes current legal and administrative problems confronting the region and nation, including intellectual property law, environmental law, energy law, tax law, health law, and international law. The Law Center is home to the Health Law and Policy Institute, a research and instruction center on interdisciplinary issues. The Law Center is also host to the Institute for Intellectual Property, Information Law, and the Blakely Advocacy Institute.

■ Clinical Programs and Trial Advocacy

The Law Center offers a wide variety of clinical courses. Students can choose among different areas of concentration such as agency or judicial internships; health or environmental law; and criminal prosecution or defense. The Law Center houses the Legal Aid Clinic, which gives students clinic opportunities in providing legal services to the indigent in the areas of family law, bankruptcy, or immigration law.

Practice skills courses coordinated through the Blakely Advocacy Institute are an integral part of the curriculum. Students can enhance their skills in trial, negotiation, pretrial, and appellate work through hands-on courses that simulate real-life situations. Several levels of courses are offered in civil and criminal advocacy. Intramural mock trial and moot court competitions are sponsored by

the Advocates, an affiliated student organization. The institute also sponsors teams for criminal and civil interscholastic moot court and mock trial competitions, with UH Law Center students earning top honors in both throughout the nation.

■ Activities

Extracurricular activities give voice to the diversity of the campus. Student groups represent special interests and provide important avenues to help law students succeed. Many arrange mentoring programs and match first-year students with second- or third-year students or working professionals. Others coordinate résumé-writing workshops, guest-speaker forums, preregistration discussions of specific course offerings, or law-related charitable efforts that benefit the community.

The Student Bar Association has input into every facet of student life at the Law Center. The SBA participates in the first-year orientation, organizes the annual charity Fun-Run, aids in the selection of student representatives to sit on various faculty committees, and presents student attitudes and views both within and outside the Law Center.

Students are encouraged to become involved in one or more student organizations, to participate in the scholarly *Houston Law Review*, *Houston Journal of International Law*, *Houston Journal of Health Law and Policy*, *Houston Business and Tax Law Journal*, and the *Texas Consumer Law Journal*; and to compete in tournaments ranging from moot court to mock trial, from mediation to negotiation.

Other student organizations include the Association of Women in Law, Black Law Students Association, Hispanic Law Students Association, Asian Law Students Association, Mandamus (Gay and Lesbian Student Organization), Lex Judaica (Jewish students), Public Interest Law Organization, Health Law Organization, Intellectual Property Student Organization, Environmental Law Society, Phi Delta Phi, Phi Alpha Delta, Computer Law Society, and Senior Partners.

■ Career Development

The Career Development Office strives for a creative approach in its job-search partnership with students. The First Year Initiative exposes first-year students to a comprehensive career education series that surveys dozens of career opportunities. Students in small groups actively gather the information they need to make informed decisions on their career plans.

The Career Development Office also presents a variety of panel discussions, receptions, and seminars with members of the Houston legal community to assist students in understanding law career options. Topics covered include duties and responsibilities of a law clerk, judicial clerkship opportunities, solo practice, and nontraditional uses of a law degree.

The office provides individual assistance in résumé preparation and interviewing techniques for all students and alumni. The annual On-Campus Interview program for second- and third-year students seeking summer clerkships and permanent positions to commence upon graduation attracts approximately 130 prospective employers to the campus.

■ Admission

The Law Center enrolls first-year, full-time students beginning in the fall semester, which starts in August.

First-year, part-time students who will attend evening classes enroll in the summer semester, which starts in May. There are no spring admissions.

Demonstrated academic ability and strong LSAT scores are not the only criteria for admission. Consideration is also given to background, achievements, honors, extracurricular activities, service to others, unique abilities, hardships overcome, advanced degrees, employment, and leadership. The UH Law Center is also committed to diversity, and the UH System Board of Regents recognizes and endorses the benefits of diversity in the university setting. The Admissions Committee will consider the following additional factors: cultural history, ethnic origin, and race. These and other elements may be addressed in a personal statement of up to three pages, double-spaced.

Applicant Profile

University of Houston Law Center
This grid includes only applicants who earned 120-180 LSAT scores under standard administrations.

LSAT Score	3.75 +		3.50 - 3.74		3.25 - 3.49		3.00 - 3.24		2.75 - 2.99		2.50 - 2.74		2.25 - 2.49		2.00 - 2.24		Below 2.00		No GPA		Total	
	Apps	Adm	Apps	Adm	Apps	Adm	Apps	Adm	Apps	Adm	Apps	Adm	Apps	Adm	Apps	Adm	Apps	Adm	Apps	Adm	Apps	Adm
175-180	0	0	2	2	0	0	0	0	2	2	0	0	0	0	1	1	0	0	0	0	5	5
170-174	0	0	6	6	4	4	4	4	1	1	0	0	1	0	0	0	0	0	0	0	16	15
165-169	20	20	29	29	28	28	23	23	14	12	14	6	6	0	1	0	0	0	0	0	135	118
160-164	80	78	110	108	123	113	82	47	68	18	42	10	17	2	3	0	0	0	6	3	531	379
155-159	130	104	207	100	213	46	206	18	129	12	64	2	33	1	8	0	2	0	9	5	1001	288
150-154	108	22	218	18	229	8	220	3	130	2	91	0	35	1	9	0	3	0	17	3	1060	57
145-149	44	3	106	2	119	2	146	5	93	0	65	0	26	0	19	0	2	0	17	0	637	12
140-144	21	0	42	0	63	0	86	0	68	0	55	0	36	0	15	0	3	0	14	1	403	1
135-139	4	0	8	0	15	0	26	0	28	0	28	0	18	0	12	0	3	0	2	0	144	0
130-134	0	0	3	0	3	0	8	0	4	0	8	0	6	0	7	0	2	0	6	0	47	0
125-129	0	0	0	0	0	0	4	0	0	0	1	0	2	0	1	0	0	0	5	0	13	0
120-124	0	0	0	0	0	0	0	0	1	0	0	0	0	0	0	0	0	0	1	0	2	0
Total	407	227	731	265	797	201	805	100	538	47	368	18	180	4	76	1	15	0	77	12	3994	875

Apps = Number of Applicants
Adm = Number Admitted
Reflects 99% of the total applicant pool.

Howard University School of Law

2900 Van Ness Street, NW
Washington, DC 20008
Phone: 202.806.8008/8009; Fax: 202.806.8162
E-mail: admissions@law.howard.edu; Website: www.law.howard.edu

ABA
Approved
Since
1931

The Basics

Type of school	Private
Term	Semester
Application deadline	3/31
Application fee	$60
Financial aid deadline	2/15
Can first year start other than fall?	No
Student to faculty ratio (fall)	18.8 to 1
Does the university offer:	
housing restricted to law students?	No
graduate housing for which law students are eligible?	Yes

Faculty and Administrators

	Total		Men		Women		Minorities	
	Fall	Spr	Fall	Spr	Fall	Spr	Fall	Spr
Full-time	23	22	14	14	9	8	19	18
Other Full-time	2	2	0	0	2	2	1	1
Deans, librarians, & others who teach	5	6	2	2	3	4	4	5
Part-time	16	23	7	14	9	8	14	20
Total	46	53	23	30	23	22	38	44

Curriculum

		Full-time	Part-time
Typical first-year section size		50	0
Is there typically a "small section" of the first-year class, other than Legal Writing, taught by full-time faculty		No	No
If yes, typical size offered last year		0	0
# of classroom course titles beyond 1st year curriculum		64	
# of upper division courses, excluding seminars with an enrollment:	Under 25	37	
	25-49	21	
	50-74	10	
	75-99	2	
	100+	0	
# of seminars		16	
# of seminar positions available		275	
# of seminar positions filled		275	0
# of positions available in simulation courses		214	
# of simulation positions filled		0	0
# of positions available in faculty supervised clinical courses		0	
# of faculty supervised clinical positions filled		0	0
# involved in field placements		0	0
# involved in law journals		0	0
# involved in moot court or trial competitions		0	0
# of credit hours required to graduate		88	

JD Enrollment and Ethnicity

	Men		Women		Full-time		Part-time		1st-year		Total		JD Degs. Awd.
	#	%	#	%	#	%	#	%	#	%	#	%	
African Amer.	147	81.7	294	87.0	440	85.1	1	100.0	134	84.3	441	85.1	124
Amer. Indian	0	0.0	2	0.6	2	0.4	0	0.0	0	0.0	2	0.4	0
Asian Amer.	10	5.6	8	2.4	18	3.5	0	0.0	12	7.5	18	3.5	4
Mex. Amer.	0	0.0	0	0.0	0	0.0	0	0.0	0	0.0	0	0.0	0
Puerto Rican	0	0.0	0	0.0	0	0.0	0	0.0	0	0.0	0	0.0	0
Hispanic	5	2.8	11	3.3	16	3.1	0	0.0	4	2.5	16	3.1	2
Total Minority	162	90.0	315	93.2	476	92.1	1	100.0	150	94.3	477	92.1	130
For. Nation.	4	2.2	5	1.5	9	1.7	0	0.0	2	1.3	9	1.7	7
Caucasian	8	4.4	14	4.1	22	4.3	0	0.0	5	3.1	22	4.2	6
Unknown	6	3.3	4	1.2	10	1.9	0	0.0	2	1.3	10	1.9	0
Total	180	34.7	338	65.3	517	99.8	1	0.2	159	30.7	518		143

Tuition and Fees

	Resident	Nonresident
Full-time	$16,895	$16,895
Part-time	$0	$0

Living Expenses

Estimated living expenses for singles

Living on campus	Living off campus	Living at home
$15,614	$15,614	$15,614

Howard University School of Law

ABA
Approved
Since
1931

GPA and LSAT Scores

	Total	Full-time	Part-time
# of apps	2,352	2,352	0
# of admits	488	488	0
# of matrics	158	158	0
75% GPA	3.49	3.49	0.00
25% GPA	2.86	2.86	0.00
75% LSAT	156	156	0
25% LSAT	148	148	0

Grants and Scholarships (from prior year)

	Total #	Total %	Full-time #	Full-time %	Part-time #	Part-time %
Total # of students	520		520		0	
Total # receiving grants	255	49.0	255	49.0	0	0.0
Less than 1/2 tuition	95	18.3	95	18.3	0	0.0
Half to full tuition	142	27.3	142	27.3	0	0.0
Full tuition	0	0.0	0	0.0	0	0.0
More than full tuition	18	3.5	18	3.5	0	0.0
Median grant amount			$7,500		$0	

Informational and Library Resources

# of volumes and volume equivalents	704,446
# of titles	30,196
# of active serial subscriptions	1,150
Study seating capacity inside the library	374
# of professional librarians	9
Hours per week library is open	105
# of open, wired connections available to students	1,013
# of networked computers available for use by students	143
# of simultaneous wireless users	400
Require computer?	N

JD Attrition (from prior year)

	Academic #	Other #	Total #	Total %
1st year	6	4	10	6.5%
2nd year	9	3	12	5.4%
3rd year	5	0	5	3.5%
4th year	0	0	0	0.0%

Employment

	Total	Percentage
Employment status known	113	96.6
Employment status unknown	4	3.4
Employed	108	95.6
Pursuing graduate degrees	2	1.8
Unemployed seeking employment	3	2.7
Unemployed not seeking employment	0	0.0

Type of Employment

	Total	Percentage
# employed in law firms	50	46.3
# employed in business and industry	23	21.3
# employed in government	21	19.4
# employed in public interest	6	5.6
# employed as judicial clerks	6	5.6
# employed in academia	2	1.9

Geographic Location

	Total	Percentage
# employed in state	45	41.7
# employed in foreign countries	0	0.0
# of states where employed	25	

Bar Passage Rates

Jurisdiction	Maryland			New York		
Exam	Sum 03	Win 04	Total	Sum 03	Win 04	Total
# from school taking bar for the first time	35	0	35	21	3	24
School's pass rate for all first-time takers	54%		54%	76%	67%	75%
State's pass rate for all first-time takers	73%	62%	71%	78%	58%	75%

Howard University School of Law

Office of Admissions, 2900 Van Ness Street, NW
Washington, DC 20008
Phone: 202.806.8008/8009; Fax: 202.806.8162
E-mail: admissions@law.howard.edu; Website: www.law.howard.edu

■ Introduction

Howard University, a coeducational, private institution in Washington, DC, was chartered by the US Congress in 1867. Howard is a historically black institution that offers an educational experience of exceptional quality and value to students with high academic potential. Particular emphasis is placed on providing educational opportunities for promising African Americans and other persons of color who have been underrepresented in the legal profession, and nonminority persons with a strong interest in civil and human rights, as well as public service. The main campus of Howard is located in northwest Washington.

The School of Law opened its doors in 1869. There was a great need to train lawyers with a strong commitment to helping black Americans secure and protect their newly established rights. In those days, the law school did not have classrooms, at least not the way we know them today. The students (there were six in the first class) met at night in the homes and offices of the faculty, all of whom were part-time.

In time, the law school grew. The law school has a diverse student body and faculty. The law school is located on a separate 22-acre campus, also in northwest Washington, approximately three miles from the main campus. Howard University School of Law is fully accredited by the American Bar Association and the Association of American Law Schools, and certifies its graduates for bar examination in all jurisdictions of the United States.

■ Degree Programs

The School of Law offers programs leading to the Juris Doctor (JD); Master of Laws (LLM) for foreign law graduates; and Juris Doctor/Master in Business Administration (JD/MBA) degrees.

An applicant applying to the JD program must have a baccalaureate degree from an accredited college or university before enrolling in the Howard University School of Law. Competitive numerical predictors for admission to Howard University include a Law School Admission Test (LSAT) score of 153 and above and an undergraduate grade-point average of 3.4. In addition to the LSAT score and UGPA, we consider the rigor of an applicant's undergraduate course of study, letters of recommendation (particularly from faculty members who have taught the applicant), any graduate study, employment, extracurricular activities, and other indicators of potential for success in law school and excellence in the profession.

Applicants applying to the JD/MBA program must apply and meet the independent admission requirements of both schools, including completion of the GMAT.

The LLM program offers foreign law graduates an opportunity to further their legal studies through advanced study and research. To be admitted as a candidate for the Master of Laws degree, applicants must be in high academic standing and must have a degree in law from an accredited foreign university or its equivalent (as determined by the faculty of law) and some experience in the judiciary, administrative establishment, bar, or law faculty.

■ Special Programs

The School of Law has a strong commitment to public service and to human and civil rights. Many programs and activities of the school reflect that fact. The school also provides an opportunity for clinical experience in civil and criminal litigation. Howard law school also offers a summer study-abroad program in comparative and international law at the University of Western Cape in South Africa. The six-week program is approved by the ABA and offers constitutional, business, and trade law courses for credit. A student-exchange program has been established with Vermont Law School and Brigham Young University. Through the exchange program, a limited number of third-year JD students may spend a semester at one of these law schools to take advantage of curricular offerings that may be of specific interest to students.

■ Curriculum

The curriculum leading to the first degree in law covers three academic years of two semesters each. During the first two years, emphasis is on the fundamental analytical concepts and skills of the law and the system by which it is administered—the functions required of a lawyer within a legal system based upon the common law. The curriculum in the third year provides diversified experience and a solid foundation of whatever specialization is desired.

■ Research Facilities

In May 2001, Howard University School of Law moved into a new, state-of-the-art law library. This four-story, 76,000-square-foot building provides for a book collection of up to 215,000 volumes; seating for over 295 students (more than 70 percent of the student population), including 90 open carrels, with all locations wired for computer use; enlarged microfilm and audiovisual facilities; and distinctive rooms of wood and brick for special collections, newspaper and periodical reading, and the rare book collection.

The Law Library is both a working collection for law students and lawyers and a research institution for legal scholars. The civil rights archive contains briefs, working papers, and materials of the NAACP and other civil rights organizations. The library has a collection that emphasizes civil and political rights and literature to support study of the legal problems of the poor. Its collection has been expanded to also include considerable CD-ROM resources. The Law Library has an online catalogue system, e-mail capabilities, and Internet access.

■ Student Activities

The *Howard Law Journal* publishes legal materials for scholarly and professional interest. The national and international moot court teams, which sponsor intramural competition and participate in competitions nationwide, have won numerous honors. The Student Bar Association is the general student government organization. The *Barrister*, the student newspaper, publishes several issues a year. Other organizations represent students from diverse ethnic backgrounds, including African Americans, Latinos, Africans, Caribbean Islanders, and Asian Pacific Islanders.

■ Career Services

The Career Services Office is an integral part of the law school. To assist students, the office offers workshops on job-search techniques and résumé writing and seminars on career development and practice specialties. The office also maintains an extensive resource library with online employer research systems, newsletters, and updated listings of career opportunities. Each year, the Career Services Office sponsors two on-campus interview programs, and more than 250 recruiters from law firms, government agencies, and corporations visit the law school with offers of employment for promising students and graduates. Approximately 1,900 interviews are scheduled annually. Graduates receive highly competitive and prestigious judicial clerkships and work for large and small private firms; federal, state, and local government agencies; public interest organizations; and public and private corporations throughout the United States.

Applicant Profile

Howard University School of Law

LSAT Score	3.75 +		3.50 - 3.74		3.25 - 3.49		3.00 - 3.24		2.75 - 2.99		2.50 - 2.74		2.25 - 2.49		2.00 - 2.24		Below 2.00		No GPA		Totals	
	Apps	Adm	Apps	Adm	Apps	Adm	Apps	Adm	Apps	Adm	Apps	Adm	Apps	Adm	Apps	Adm	Apps	Adm	Apps	Adm	Apps	Adm
175-180	0	0	0	0	0	0	0	0	0	0	0	0	0	0	0	0	0	0	0	0	0	0
170-174	0	0	0	0	1	1	0	0	0	0	0	0	0	0	0	0	0	0	0	0	1	1
165-169	1	1	5	4	4	4	0	0	1	1	0	0	0	0	0	0	0	0	0	0	11	10
160-164	3	2	6	5	9	8	10	10	6	4	7	6	4	3	0	0	0	0	1	1	46	39
155-159	11	10	24	21	29	25	27	24	31	26	16	12	19	5	1	1	2	0	0	0	160	124
150-154	34	26	64	35	103	51	108	39	84	25	72	18	40	5	23	1	2	0	1	0	531	200
145-149	32	24	65	24	117	16	160	14	140	10	79	6	43	1	23	0	4	0	9	0	672	95
140-144	16	5	59	2	102	2	119	3	153	0	74	0	66	0	33	0	4	0	9	0	635	12
135-139	9	1	27	0	37	1	56	0	75	1	53	1	33	0	18	0	6	0	8	0	322	4
130-134	0	0	4	0	8	0	17	0	21	0	23	0	14	0	7	0	2	0	2	0	98	0
125-129	1	0	0	0	4	0	5	0	5	0	3	0	11	0	3	0	2	0	5	0	39	0
120-124	0	0	0	0	0	0	1	0	0	0	2	0	1	0	0	0	0	0	0	0	4	0
Total	107	69	254	91	414	108	503	90	516	67	329	43	231	14	108	2	22	0	35	1	2519	485

Apps = Number of Applicants
Adm = Number Admitted
Reflects 99% of the total applicant pool.

University of Idaho College of Law

PO Box 442321
Moscow, ID 83844-2321
Phone: 208.885.2300; Fax: 208.885.5709
E-mail: lawadmit@uidaho.edu; Website: www.law.uidaho.edu

ABA Approved Since 1925

The Basics

Type of school	Public
Term	Semester
Application deadline	2/15
Application fee	$50
Financial aid deadline	2/15
Can first year start other than fall?	No
Student to faculty ratio (fall)	14.8 to 1
Does the university offer:	
housing restricted to law students?	No
graduate housing for which law students are eligible?	Yes

Curriculum

		Full-time	Part-time
Typical first-year section size		56	0
Is there typically a "small section" of the first-year class, other than Legal Writing, taught by full-time faculty		No	No
If yes, typical size offered last year		0	0
# of classroom course titles beyond 1st year curriculum		59	
# of upper division courses, excluding seminars with an enrollment:	Under 25	43	
	25-49	13	
	50-74	7	
	75-99	9	
	100+	0	
# of seminars		19	
# of seminar positions available		310	
# of seminar positions filled	192	0	
# of positions available in simulation courses		300	
# of simulation positions filled	229	0	
# of positions available in faculty supervised clinical courses		158	
# of faculty supervised clinical positions filled	91	0	
# involved in field placements	25	0	
# involved in law journals	28	0	
# involved in moot court or trial competitions	46	0	
# of credit hours required to graduate		88	

Faculty and Administrators

	Total		Men		Women		Minorities	
	Fall	Spr	Fall	Spr	Fall	Spr	Fall	Spr
Full-time	17	18	10	11	7	7	2	2
Other Full-time	1	1	1	1	0	0	0	0
Deans, librarians, & others who teach	7	7	5	5	2	2	1	1
Part-time	5	5	4	4	1	1	0	0
Total	30	31	20	21	10	10	3	3

JD Enrollment and Ethnicity

	Men		Women		Full-time		Part-time		1st-year		Total		JD Degs. Awd.
	#	%	#	%	#	%	#	%	#	%	#	%	
African Amer.	1	0.6	3	2.4	4	1.3	0	0.0	3	2.7	4	1.3	1
Amer. Indian	1	0.6	2	1.6	3	1.0	0	0.0	0	0.0	3	1.0	0
Asian Amer.	10	5.7	6	4.8	16	5.3	0	0.0	10	8.8	16	5.3	1
Mex. Amer.	2	1.1	2	1.6	4	1.3	0	0.0	2	1.8	4	1.3	3
Puerto Rican	0	0.0	0	0.0	0	0.0	0	0.0	0	0.0	0	0.0	0
Hispanic	0	0.0	1	0.8	1	0.3	0	0.0	1	0.9	1	0.3	0
Total Minority	14	8.0	14	11.2	28	9.3	0	0.0	16	14.2	28	9.3	5
For. Nation.	0	0.0	0	0.0	0	0.0	0	0.0	0	0.0	0	0.0	0
Caucasian	147	83.5	108	86.4	255	84.7	0	0.0	90	79.6	255	84.7	99
Unknown	15	8.5	3	2.4	18	6.0	0	0.0	7	6.2	18	6.0	2
Total	176	58.5	125	41.5	301	100.0	0	0.0	113	37.5	301		106

Tuition and Fees

	Resident	Nonresident
Full-time	$7,572	$15,592
Part-time	$0	$0

Living Expenses

Estimated living expenses for singles

Living on campus	Living off campus	Living at home
$12,528	$12,528	$6,698

University of Idaho College of Law

ABA Approved Since 1925

GPA and LSAT Scores

	Total	Full-time	Part-time
# of apps	946	946	0
# of admits	270	270	0
# of matrics	113	113	0
75% GPA	3.68	3.68	0.00
25% GPA	3.06	3.06	0.00
75% LSAT	158	158	0
25% LSAT	153	153	0

Grants and Scholarships (from prior year)

	Total		Full-time		Part-time	
	#	%	#	%	#	%
Total # of students	308		308		0	
Total # receiving grants	102	33.1	102	33.1	0	0.0
Less than 1/2 tuition	44	14.3	44	14.3	0	0.0
Half to full tuition	42	13.6	42	13.6	0	0.0
Full tuition	12	3.9	12	3.9	0	0.0
More than full tuition	4	1.3	4	1.3	0	0.0
Median grant amount			$3,786		$0	

Informational and Library Resources

# of volumes and volume equivalents	204,375
# of titles	34,287
# of active serial subscriptions	4,087
Study seating capacity inside the library	360
# of professional librarians	4
Hours per week library is open	86
# of open, wired connections available to students	302
# of networked computers available for use by students	29
# of simultaneous wireless users	720
Require computer?	N

JD Attrition (from prior year)

	Academic	Other	Total	
	#	#	#	%
1st year	5	7	12	12.0%
2nd year	1	2	3	3.0%
3rd year	0	0	0	0.0%
4th year	0	0	0	0.0%

Employment

	Total	Percentage
Employment status known	95	100.0
Employment status unknown	0	0.0
Employed	81	85.3
Pursuing graduate degrees	6	6.3
Unemployed seeking employment	7	7.4
Unemployed not seeking employment	1	1.1

Type of Employment

	Total	Percentage
# employed in law firms	33	40.7
# employed in business and industry	4	4.9
# employed in government	17	21.0
# employed in public interest	1	1.2
# employed as judicial clerks	21	25.9
# employed in academia	5	6.2

Geographic Location

	Total	Percentage
# employed in state	53	65.4
# employed in foreign countries	0	0.0
# of states where employed	11	

Bar Passage Rates

Jurisdiction	Idaho			Washington		
Exam	Sum 03	Win 04	Total	Sum 03	Win 04	Total
# from school taking bar for the first time	54	8	62	14	1	15
School's pass rate for all first-time takers	76%	75%	76%	86%	100%	87%
State's pass rate for all first-time takers	79%	80%	80%	71%	79%	74%

University of Idaho College of Law

PO Box 442321
Moscow, ID 83844-2321
Phone: 208.885.2300; Fax: 208.885.5709
E-mail: lawadmit@uidaho.edu; Website: www.law.uidaho.edu

■ Introduction

Emphasizing quality over quantity, the College of Law offers a distinctive legal education founded on collegiality and a dedication to the highest ideals of a noble profession. Each student is assured individual attention. The college's strategic directions include emphases on natural resources and environmental law, business law and entrepreneurship, and advocacy coupled with mediation and dispute resolution. These are subject areas of growing importance to law and public policy in the US. Students may combine study in a small residential environment with an opportunity to spend a semester in Boise, Idaho, one of America's fastest growing metropolitan areas.

The College of Law is located on the main campus of the University of Idaho, about 90 miles southeast of Spokane, Washington, and about 8 miles east of Pullman, Washington. The Moscow-Pullman community is the cultural center of a vast inland area of the Northwest covering parts of Idaho, Washington, and Oregon. This area is renowned for outstanding opportunities for outdoor sports and activities. Washington State University and the University of Idaho are only eight miles apart, and the two universities make their resources jointly available in many fields, including the concurrent JD/MBA program. The College of Law was established in 1909. It has been a member of the AALS since 1915 and has been on the approved list of the ABA since 1925.

■ Enrollment/Student Body

Students from Idaho constitute approximately 60 percent of the student body; the others come from all regions of the US. Although the total enrollment of the College of Law is relatively small (approximately 300), students typically represent over 70 different colleges and universities. The college promotes diversity in the student body. Because the learning environment is positive, and because admission is highly selective, the academic attrition recently has been less than 5 percent.

■ Library and Physical Facilities

The College of Law occupies a building designed for, and dedicated to, its use. The law library houses a collection of more than 200,000 volumes and volume-equivalents and more than 4,000 serial titles. This is combined with two computer labs, wireless Internet access throughout the building, and LexisNexis, Westlaw/Dialog, and Hein-On-Line services. The law library is located across the street from the general library.

The law library subscribes to CD-ROM libraries. Membership in the Western Library Network and the Inland Northwest Library Automation Network allows users to access holdings of libraries across the nation.

Law students have access to the other libraries of the University of Idaho and those at Washington State University.

■ Curriculum

The first day of law school focuses on professionalism, featuring small-group discussions with distinguished lawyers and judges. The college combines a traditional first year of study with opportunities to pursue specialized interests in the second and third years. Students may focus on the strategic directions mentioned above: natural resources/environmental law, business law/entrepreneurism, and advocacy/dispute resolution. The curriculum also provides enrichments in international law, technology and the law, and ethics and civic leadership. Real-world exposure is provided through a semester in practice program in the Boise metropolitan area, and through externships.

The school operates on a semester basis with 88 semester credit-hours required for the JD degree. Graduates of the college are educated and prepared for careers throughout the nation.

■ Special Programs

The College of Law operates a variety of clinical programs. Law students in their third year may qualify as interns under the laws of Idaho and work in the live client clinic. Interns are eligible to present cases in court under appropriate supervision. The live client clinic includes a general practice clinic, an appellate clinic in which students practice in federal and state appellate courts, a tribal/immigration law clinic in which students serve as public defenders in the Nez Perce Tribal Court and represent clients in federal immigration matters, and a tax clinic. The clinical program also sponsors a special trial advocacy course and is home to the Northwest Institute for Dispute Resolution.

Externships are available with the Supreme Court and Court of Appeals of Idaho, the United States Court of Appeals for the Ninth Circuit, the United States District Court for the District of Idaho, the Attorney General of Idaho, the United States Attorney for the District of Idaho, and various county prosecutor and public defender offices. Eligible third-year students may participate in a full semester in practice away in Boise.

A concurrent JD/MS (Environmental Science) degree in cooperation with the University of Idaho College of Graduate Studies Environmental Science Program is available. Students may be able to obtain both degrees in four years rather than the five years it normally would take to earn them separately.

University of Idaho College of Law

A concurrent JD/MBA degree in cooperation with the Washington State University Graduate School of Business and Economics is offered in which students may obtain both degrees in as few as seven semesters rather than the normal eight semesters.

A concurrent JD/Master of Accounting degree in cooperation with the University of Idaho College of Business and Economics is available. The program allows students to obtain both degrees in as few as seven semesters rather than the normal eight semesters.

■ Admission

Applications are accepted beginning in September preceding the year in which enrollment is desired. Entering students are admitted only for the fall semester. Applicants must submit LSAT scores and college transcripts for evaluation through LSDAS. Late fall application is recommended as completed applications will be reviewed as early as December; applications completed after March 1 will still be reviewed, but the earlier applications will receive priority consideration. The Admission Committee looks at all information presented by an applicant, including the LSAT, the college record, work experience, references, and the personal statement.

■ Student Activities

Students publish the *Idaho Law Review*, which covers topics ranging from state and regional problems to national and international issues. Students currently assist in publication of the *German Law Journal*, a widely read journal of German and international public law. A Board of Student Advocates and the Law Students for Appropriate Dispute Resolution coordinate intramural competitions and provide opportunities for students to participate in national competitions that build professional skills. Student successes have included the 2001 National Bankruptcy Moot Court Championship. The Student Bar Association represents student interests, both educational and social. From its ranks come elected student members who sit on various faculty/student committees. There are chapters of the Phi Alpha Delta, Delta Theta Phi, and Phi Delta Phi legal fraternities. The College of Law has other student organizations. Please visit our website at *www.law.uidaho.edu* for more information regarding these groups.

■ Career Services

The college features a career services office staffed full-time by a licensed attorney. The office sponsors a variety of activities designed to facilitate students' career planning and assist in their employment search as summer clerks or for permanent positions. Facilities are available for on-campus interviews, and the school works with employers who cannot visit the school but have indicated a desire to recruit by mail. Historically, 90–95 percent of graduates find employment within six months of graduation or go on to advanced graduate study. A majority of students find employment in Idaho, although Utah, Washington, and Oregon continue to be popular locations. Graduates are employed throughout the US and several foreign countries.

Applicant Profile

University of Idaho College of Law
This grid includes only applicants who earned 120-180 LSAT scores under standard administrations.

LSAT Score	3.75 +		3.50 - 3.74		3.25 - 3.49		3.00 - 3.24		2.75 - 2.99		2.50 - 2.74		2.25 - 2.49		2.00 - 2.24		Below 2.00		No GPA		Total	
	Apps	Adm	Apps	Adm	Apps	Adm	Apps	Adm	Apps	Adm	Apps	Adm	Apps	Adm	Apps	Adm	Apps	Adm	Apps	Adm	Apps	Adm
175-180	0	0	0	0	0	0	0	0	0	0	0	0	0	0	0	0	0	0	0	0	0	0
170-174	1	1	0	0	0	0	0	0	0	0	0	0	0	0	0	0	0	0	0	0	1	1
165-169	2	2	3	3	2	2	3	3	2	2	2	2	0	0	0	0	0	0	0	0	14	14
160-164	6	5	12	11	11	9	1	1	9	6	2	2	3	1	0	0	1	0	0	0	45	35
155-159	25	24	45	41	32	21	31	19	23	11	14	3	5	4	3	0	0	0	0	0	178	123
150-154	32	19	58	23	52	10	68	12	48	3	22	2	7	1	4	0	2	0	0	0	293	70
145-149	17	4	35	3	65	7	51	5	41	2	15	0	12	0	4	0	1	0	0	0	241	21
140-144	9	1	16	0	22	0	20	3	20	0	18	0	4	0	4	0	0	0	5	0	118	4
135-139	1	0	8	0	6	0	5	0	7	1	7	0	4	0	1	0	1	0	2	0	42	1
130-134	0	0	1	0	0	0	3	0	0	0	1	0	0	0	0	0	0	0	0	0	5	0
125-129	0	0	0	0	0	0	0	0	0	0	0	0	0	0	0	0	1	0	0	0	1	0
120-124	0	0	0	0	0	0	0	0	0	0	0	0	0	0	0	0	0	0	0	0	0	0
Total	93	56	178	81	190	49	182	43	150	25	81	9	35	6	16	0	6	0	7	0	938	269

Apps = Number of Applicants   Adm = Number Admitted   Reflects 99% of the total applicant pool.

University of Illinois, College of Law

504 East Pennsylvania Avenue
Champaign, IL 61820
Phone: 217.244.6415
E-mail: admissions@law.uiuc.edu; Website: www.law.uiuc.edu

ABA
Approved
Since
1923

The Basics

Type of school	Public
Term	Semester
Application deadline	3/15
Application fee	$40
Financial aid deadline	3/15
Can first year start other than fall?	No
Student to faculty ratio (fall)	14.4 to 1
Does the university offer:	
housing restricted to law students?	No
graduate housing for which law students are eligible?	Yes

Faculty and Administrators

	Total		Men		Women		Minorities	
	Fall	Spr	Fall	Spr	Fall	Spr	Fall	Spr
Full-time	39	39	28	27	11	12	4	5
Other Full-time	7	9	4	6	3	3	0	1
Deans, librarians, & others who teach	3	3	1	1	2	2	0	0
Part-time	25	27	19	17	6	10	4	3
Total	74	78	52	51	22	27	8	9

Curriculum

		Full-time	Part-time
Typical first-year section size		76	0
Is there typically a "small section" of the first-year class, other than Legal Writing, taught by full-time faculty		Yes	No
If yes, typical size offered last year		0	0
# of classroom course titles beyond 1st year curriculum		113	
# of upper division courses, excluding seminars with an enrollment:	Under 25	109	
	25-49	45	
	50-74	18	
	75-99	5	
	100+	5	
# of seminars		21	
# of seminar positions available		376	
# of seminar positions filled		267	0
# of positions available in simulation courses		1,159	
# of simulation positions filled		957	0
# of positions available in faculty supervised clinical courses		200	
# of faculty supervised clinical positions filled	105		0
# involved in field placements		156	0
# involved in law journals		155	0
# involved in moot court or trial competitions	103		0
# of credit hours required to graduate		90	

JD Enrollment and Ethnicity

	Men		Women		Full-time		Part-time		1st-year		Total		JD Degs. Awd.
	#	%	#	%	#	%	#	%	#	%	#	%	
African Amer.	24	6.1	27	9.5	51	7.5	0	0.0	13	5.7	51	7.5	21
Amer. Indian	3	0.8	1	0.4	4	0.6	0	0.0	2	0.9	4	0.6	0
Asian Amer.	60	15.2	54	19.0	114	16.8	0	0.0	51	22.4	114	16.8	25
Mex. Amer.	0	0.0	0	0.0	0	0.0	0	0.0	0	0.0	0	0.0	0
Puerto Rican	0	0.0	0	0.0	0	0.0	0	0.0	0	0.0	0	0.0	0
Hispanic	21	5.3	29	10.2	50	7.4	0	0.0	19	8.3	50	7.4	15
Total Minority	108	27.3	111	39.1	219	32.3	0	0.0	85	37.3	219	32.3	61
For. Nation.	6	1.5	5	1.8	11	1.6	0	0.0	6	2.6	11	1.6	0
Caucasian	250	63.3	149	52.5	399	58.8	0	0.0	116	50.9	399	58.8	141
Unknown	31	7.8	19	6.7	50	7.4	0	0.0	21	9.2	50	7.4	12
Total	395	58.2	284	41.8	679	100.0	0	0.0	228	33.6	679		214

Tuition and Fees

	Resident	Nonresident
Full-time	$15,888	$28,224
Part-time	$0	$0

Living Expenses

Estimated living expenses for singles

Living on campus	Living off campus	Living at home
$12,190	$12,190	$12,190

University of Illinois, College of Law

ABA
Approved
Since
1923

GPA and LSAT Scores

	Total	Full-time	Part-time
# of apps	2,930	2,930	0
# of admits	676	676	0
# of matrics	228	228	0
75% GPA	3.64	3.64	0.00
25% GPA	3.12	3.12	0.00
75% LSAT	165	165	0
25% LSAT	160	160	0

Grants and Scholarships (from prior year)

	Total		Full-time		Part-time	
	#	%	#	%	#	%
Total # of students	681		681		0	
Total # receiving grants	392	57.6	392	57.6	0	0.0
Less than 1/2 tuition	341	50.1	341	50.1	0	0.0
Half to full tuition	24	3.5	24	3.5	0	0.0
Full tuition	27	4.0	27	4.0	0	0.0
More than full tuition	0	0.0	0	0.0	0	0.0
Median grant amount			$4,000		$0	

Informational and Library Resources

# of volumes and volume equivalents	745,593
# of titles	264,140
# of active serial subscriptions	8,992
Study seating capacity inside the library	398
# of professional librarians	5.5
Hours per week library is open	102
# of open, wired connections available to students	720
# of networked computers available for use by students	39
# of simultaneous wireless users	500
Require computer?	Y

JD Attrition (from prior year)

	Academic	Other	Total	
	#	#	#	%
1st year	0	0	0	0.0%
2nd year	0	11	11	4.7%
3rd year	1	0	1	0.4%
4th year	0	0	0	0.0%

Employment

	Total	Percentage
Employment status known	203	100.0
Employment status unknown	0	0.0
Employed	192	94.6
Pursuing graduate degrees	3	1.5
Unemployed seeking employment	3	1.5
Unemployed not seeking employment	5	2.5

Type of Employment

# employed in law firms	129	67.2
# employed in business and industry	16	8.3
# employed in government	19	9.9
# employed in public interest	3	1.6
# employed as judicial clerks	21	10.9
# employed in academia	4	2.1

Geographic Location

# employed in state	138	71.9
# employed in foreign countries	4	2.1
# of states where employed	21	

Bar Passage Rates

Jurisdiction	Illinois		
Exam	Sum 03	Win 04	Total
# from school taking bar for the first time	148	2	150
School's pass rate for all first-time takers	97%	100%	97%
State's pass rate for all first-time takers	86%	78%	84%

University of Illinois, College of Law

504 East Pennsylvania Avenue
Champaign, IL 61820
Phone: 217.244.6415
E-mail: admissions@law.uiuc.edu; Website: www.law.uiuc.edu

■ Introduction

Established over a century ago, the University of Illinois College of Law fosters excellence in legal education through a close community of faculty members and students, where teaching goes hand-in-hand with scholarship. The resources—intellectual, cultural, and recreational—of one of the world's largest and best universities are readily available to our law students, as is the appealing ambience of a university community. The college's comparatively low tuition cost makes the program an outstanding value.

■ Library and Physical Facilities

A hallmark of the University of Illinois is its library system, the world's largest university collection and the nation's first major research library with an online catalogue. The University of Illinois College of Law library is, itself, one of the largest in the country. The collection includes more than 730,000 volumes, ranking 12th nationally in the number of titles held. It is designated as a federal depository library, with extensive holdings of federal, legislative, and administrative materials. The library also has a substantial international collection and is one of the few American law libraries designated as a depository by the European Economic Community.

Directly across the street from the law school is one of the country's largest physical education buildings, with indoor and outdoor swimming pools, tennis courts, four gyms, weight and exercise equipment, archery, and ball courts of all kinds. The facility is free for students.

■ Joint-Degree Programs

The College of Law administers 11 formal joint JD and master's or doctoral degree programs. The combined degrees available are JD/MBA; JD/MD; JD/DVM; JD/MHRIR in Human Resources and Industrial Relations; JD/MA in Urban Planning; JD/Master of Education; JD/Doctor of Education; JD/MA in Journalism; JD/MS in Chemistry; JD/MS in Natural Resources and Environmental Sciences; and JD/MCS in Computer Science.

■ Special Programs

Environmental Law—The college has an active program of environmental and planning studies. Beyond the first-year course in property, the college offers courses in environmental law, natural resources, and land-use planning.

Intellectual Property—The College of Law boasts a strong intellectual property curriculum and offers a rich array of courses taught by nationally known faculty and experienced practitioners. Students choose from a variety of offerings ranging from core patent, copyright, and trademark courses to cutting-edge classes like Law and Regulation of Cyberspace, Internet and Web Law, International Copyright Principles, and International IP Transfers. Beyond its own curriculum, the College of Law's intellectual property faculty capitalizes upon the university's top-ranked academic programs in science and engineering, as well as its National Center for Supercomputing Applications, recognized as the world's leader in computer design applications. The College of Law is currently collaborating with these premier university departments to develop joint-degree programs in the rapidly changing intellectual property arena.

Interdisciplinary Study—While the College of Law course offerings are so varied that it would take a student 12 years to sample all of them, students interested in related subjects outside the law school may receive up to 12 hours of credit for study in another discipline. This flexibility allows students to complement their legal education with advanced coursework in a top-ranked university.

International Legal Studies—Students pursuing international legal studies can choose from 15 international and comparative law courses. Faculty members have long-standing international connections, and some collaborate with international scholars and legal experts to teach these courses.

Public Interest Law and Public Policy—As one of the premier public law schools, the College of Law plays a special role in educating students to serve both the public interest and formulate public policy. The college's commitment to public interest law is demonstrated by the pro bono notation placed on diplomas of graduates who have performed at least 60 hours of unpaid legal work. In addition, students may choose from a variety of timely courses addressing public interest and policy issues.

Skills Training—The college offers four live-client clinics: Civil Litigation Clinic, International Human Rights Clinic, Transactional and Community Economic Development Clinic, and Employees Justice Clinic, as well as classes in legal drafting, business planning, advanced bankruptcy, environmental management, estate planning, and tax practice; all challenge students to solve concrete problems and draft legal documents in a variety of fields. Courses on computer applications in the law and quantitative methods in legal decision making familiarize students with sophisticated techniques necessary in today's law practice; these include computerized methods of document preparation and information retrieval, statistical analysis, the use of computer simulations in litigation, and the calculation of damage awards.

Offerings on alternative dispute resolution, the lawyer as negotiator, and collective bargaining and labor arbitration engage students in mock negotiations, arbitrations, and alternatives to traditional trials.

Taxation—Illinois offers one of the strongest tax curricula in the country, with core courses that address all aspects of tax practice and advanced offerings that integrate tax problems with other fields of law.

Trial Advocacy Program—The college's trial advocacy program is especially popular, enrolling about three-quarters of the third-year class. The year-long program teaches the art of courtroom litigation and concludes with students conducting a day-long mock trial.

■ Housing

College of Law students live both off-campus and in graduate- or married-student campus housing. For information concerning campus housing, contact the Graduate and Family Housing Department at 217.333.5656.

In addition, the Urbana-Champaign area has ample private rental opportunities available at relatively low cost. Most current College of Law students choose to live in private, off-campus housing due to its low cost and easy access to the award-winning Urbana-Champaign Mass Transit system, which is free for all University of Illinois students.

■ Student Activities

College of Law students write for the highly regarded *University of Illinois Law Review* and *The Elder Law Journal*, the only journal in the country to focus exclusively on issues affecting the nation's aging population. Students can also write for *The University of Illinois Journal of Law, Technology & Policy*, which is a joint venture among the College of Law, National Center for Supercomputing Applications, and the Institute for Government and Public Affairs. Students have additional opportunities for publication by writing for the *Recent Development Section of the Illinois Bar Journal*, the monthly periodical published by the Illinois State Bar Association.

Students interested in appellate advocacy can compete in any number of moot court competitions and can gain practical experience through the client counseling and negotiation competitions and the live-client clinics.

The small size of the college allows students to become actively involved in nearly 40 organizations.

■ Scholarships

The College of Law offers a number of scholarships ranging from $1,000 to full tuition, and they are awarded to students who show the greatest promise in the study of law. Previous academic success is a primary consideration; the committee also considers other relevant factors.

■ Career Services

The Office of Career Services works individually with students to assist with career planning and locating summer and permanent positions. Students participate in an active on-campus interviewing program and respond to requests for résumés from hundreds of employers nationwide. On average, over the last five years, approximately 95 percent of our graduates known to be seeking employment accepted positions within six months of completing the JD.

Applicant Profile

Our admission process takes into consideration many factors beyond the undergraduate GPA and the LSAT score. A statistical grid, as is typically provided here, only takes into consideration these two factors. Admission decisions at the University of Illinois College of Law are based on the Admission Committee's experienced judgment applied to individual cases. Consequently, we have chosen not to provide applicants with a grid that does not accurately portray our admission process.

Indiana University School of Law—Bloomington

211 S Indiana Avenue, Law Building, Room 230
Bloomington, IN 47405-7001
Phone: 812.855.4765; Fax: 812.855.0555
E-mail: lawadmis@indiana.edu; Website: www.law.indiana.edu

ABA
Approved
Since
1937

The Basics

Type of school	Public
Term	Semester
Application deadline	3/1
Application fee	$35
Financial aid deadline	3/1
Can first year start other than fall?	Yes
Student to faculty ratio (fall)	13.9 to 1
Does the university offer:	
housing restricted to law students?	No
graduate housing for which law students are eligible?	Yes

Faculty and Administrators

	Total		Men		Women		Minorities	
	Fall	Spr	Fall	Spr	Fall	Spr	Fall	Spr
Full-time	38	40	28	27	10	13	3	4
Other Full-time	0	0	0	0	0	0	0	0
Deans, librarians, & others who teach	15	15	8	8	7	7	2	2
Part-time	9	20	6	13	3	7	0	0
Total	62	75	42	48	20	27	5	6

Curriculum

	Full-time	Part-time
Typical first-year section size	79	0
Is there typically a "small section" of the first-year class, other than Legal Writing, taught by full-time faculty	No	No
If yes, typical size offered last year	0	0
# of classroom course titles beyond 1st year curriculum	118	

# of upper division courses, excluding seminars with an enrollment:		
Under 25	76	
25-49	28	
50-74	8	
75-99	7	
100+	5	

# of seminars	24	
# of seminar positions available	283	
# of seminar positions filled	255	0
# of positions available in simulation courses	231	
# of simulation positions filled	185	0
# of positions available in faculty supervised clinical courses	97	
# of faculty supervised clinical positions filled	97	0
# involved in field placements	135	0
# involved in law journals	148	0
# involved in moot court or trial competitions	50	0
# of credit hours required to graduate	88	

JD Enrollment and Ethnicity

	Men		Women		Full-time		Part-time		1st-year		Total		JD Degs. Awd.
	#	%	#	%	#	%	#	%	#	%	#	%	
African Amer.	17	4.6	21	7.9	38	6.0	0	0.0	11	5.5	38	6.0	16
Amer. Indian	0	0.0	1	0.4	1	0.2	0	0.0	1	0.5	1	0.2	0
Asian Amer.	22	5.9	16	6.0	38	6.0	0	0.0	13	6.5	38	6.0	7
Mex. Amer.	10	2.7	16	6.0	26	4.1	0	0.0	9	4.5	26	4.1	11
Puerto Rican	0	0.0	0	0.0	0	0.0	0	0.0	0	0.0	0	0.0	0
Hispanic	0	0.0	0	0.0	0	0.0	0	0.0	0	0.0	0	0.0	0
Total Minority	49	13.2	54	20.4	103	16.2	0	0.0	34	16.9	103	16.2	34
For. Nation.	2	0.5	1	0.4	3	0.5	0	0.0	0	0.0	3	0.5	5
Caucasian	302	81.2	205	77.4	505	79.5	2	100.0	159	79.1	507	79.6	165
Unknown	19	5.1	5	1.9	24	3.8	0	0.0	8	4.0	24	3.8	4
Total	372	58.4	265	41.6	635	99.7	2	0.3	201	31.6	637		208

Tuition and Fees

	Resident	Nonresident
Full-time	$13,045	$25,875
Part-time	$0	$0

Living Expenses

Estimated living expenses for singles

Living on campus	Living off campus	Living at home
$18,380	$18,380	$8,576

Indiana University School of Law—Bloomington

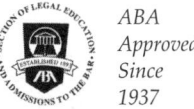

ABA
Approved
Since
1937

GPA and LSAT Scores

	Total	Full-time	Part-time
# of apps	2,724	2,724	0
# of admits	952	952	0
# of matrics	202	202	0
75% GPA	3.74	3.74	0.00
25% GPA	2.97	2.97	0.00
75% LSAT	164	164	0
25% LSAT	158	158	0

Grants and Scholarships (from prior year)

	Total		Full-time		Part-time	
	#	%	#	%	#	%
Total # of students	655		653		2	
Total # receiving grants	451	68.9	451	69.1	0	0.0
Less than 1/2 tuition	352	53.7	352	53.9	0	0.0
Half to full tuition	62	9.5	62	9.5	0	0.0
Full tuition	9	1.4	9	1.4	0	0.0
More than full tuition	28	4.3	28	4.3	0	0.0
Median grant amount			$5,000		$0	

Informational and Library Resources

# of volumes and volume equivalents	732,792
# of titles	234,351
# of active serial subscriptions	9,051
Study seating capacity inside the library	681
# of professional librarians	11
Hours per week library is open	115
# of open, wired connections available to students	300
# of networked computers available for use by students	80
# of simultaneous wireless users	900
Require computer?	Y

JD Attrition (from prior year)

	Academic	Other	Total	
	#	#	#	%
1st year	0	1	1	0.5%
2nd year	0	3	3	1.4%
3rd year	0	0	0	0.0%
4th year	0	0	0	0.0%

Employment

	Total	Percentage
Employment status known	212	99.5
Employment status unknown	1	0.5
Employed	173	81.6
Pursuing graduate degrees	10	4.7
Unemployed seeking employment	3	1.4
Unemployed not seeking employment	26	12.3

Type of Employment

# employed in law firms	95	54.9
# employed in business and industry	15	8.7
# employed in government	25	14.5
# employed in public interest	5	2.9
# employed as judicial clerks	17	9.8
# employed in academia	10	5.8

Geographic Location

# employed in state	89	51.4
# employed in foreign countries	0	0.0
# of states where employed		21

Bar Passage Rates

Jurisdiction	Indiana		
Exam	Sum 03	Win 04	Total
# from school taking bar for the first time	87	18	105
School's pass rate for all first-time takers	89%	72%	86%
State's pass rate for all first-time takers	79%	76%	79%

Indiana University School of Law—Bloomington

211 S Indiana Avenue, Law Building, Room 230
Bloomington, IN 47405-7001
Phone: 812.855.4765; Fax: 812.855.0555
E-mail: lawadmis@indiana.edu; Website: www.law.indiana.edu

■ Introduction

The Indiana University School of Law—Bloomington provides the highest quality legal education in a relaxed, collegial setting. Founded in 1842, the law school is located on the beautifully wooded campus of one of the nation's largest teaching and research universities. The presence of the university, including its world famous School of Music, offers students cultural opportunities available in few urban areas, while retaining the advantages of a small university town. With over 650 students, drawn from more than 200 undergraduate schools in the United States and abroad, the law school is small enough to retain its distinctive sense of community and collegiality, while large enough to facilitate a stimulating, cosmopolitan environment. The school is a charter member of the AALS and is approved by the ABA.

■ Library and Physical Facilities

With nearly 750,000 volumes, the law library is one of the 16 largest law libraries in the US, the largest in the state of Indiana, and was recently named best law school library in the nation by a national law school magazine. Law-trained librarians give instruction in research techniques and provide reference assistance. While continuing its commitment to a high quality print collection, the library is a national leader in computer applications in legal education. Through Internet access students can utilize systems specific to law, such as LexisNexis and Westlaw, or access the rapidly expanding national and international networks. Students can bring their own laptop computers to the library and connect to the university's network at study carrels, in library conference rooms, in the laptop room, or through the law school's wireless Internet system. Law students can also access many of these resources from home.

■ Curriculum

The curriculum offers traditional courses as well as specialized courses such as intellectual property, communications and Internet law, law and biomedical advances, immigration law, international business transactions, and environmental law. The school offers intensive training in litigation and dispute resolution. Students may participate in clinics that enable them to deal with client problems and, in some cases, represent clients in local courts, all under close faculty supervision. The law school divides first-year law students into small, informal groups of five to seven, which are mentored by second- and/or third-year students. These groups are supervised by faculty and provide both academic and peer support.

■ Joint-Degree Programs

Formal joint-degree programs combine a law program with programs from the Kelley School of Business, the School of Public and Environmental Affairs, School of Journalism, Department of Telecommunications, School of Library and Information Science, or the University Graduate School, enabling a student to earn a JD and a master's degree or PhD in another academic discipline. Joint-degree programs with other disciplines may be designed to meet the student's learning and career goals.

■ Opportunities to Study Abroad

The School of Law provides students a wide variety of opportunities to study abroad. A limited number of second- and third-year students can take advantage of the unique opportunity to study in and immerse themselves in the legal education system and culture of another country. Semester-long opportunities are available through the London Law Consortium and exchange programs with Université Panthéon-Assas (Paris II) Law School; ESADE Law School in Barcelona, Spain; Bucerius Law School in Hamburg, Germany; China University of Political Science and Law in Beijing (CUPL); and the Law School at the University of Hong Kong (HKU). All classes, with the exception of those taken at Bucerius and HKU, are taught in the schools' respective native language. Finally, the law school offers all students the opportunity to participate in summer-study abroad programs hosted by the Institute on International and Comparative Law in England, France, Ireland, Italy, Russia, and Spain. All courses are taught in English.

■ Early-Start Program

An early-start program is offered for students who wish to begin their legal studies in the summer session. This program allows students to take one 4- or 5-credit-hour class in the summer in a small, intimate environment as they make the transition into the law school.

■ Admission

Generally, the quality and size of the applicant pool forces the Admissions Committee to rely heavily on the undergraduate grade-point average and the LSAT score. However, numerical indicators are not the only considerations used in evaluating applications. The committee considers the quality of the applicant's undergraduate institution, level and rigor of coursework, letters of recommendation (particularly those from faculty), graduate work, employment during and after college, extracurricular activities, potential for service to the profession, educational/geographic/socioeconomic diversity, and the applicant's personal statement. Applicants are encouraged to explain matters that may have adversely affected their undergraduate performance. Applicants who feel they have been disadvantaged because of economic, educational, racial, or cultural factors are urged to bring this to the attention of the Admissions Committee. An application for admission may be obtained from *www.law.indiana.edu*, by contacting the Admissions Office, or by using the *LSACD* or LSACD on the Web.

■ Housing

The Bloomington area offers a variety of housing options for students. There are numerous apartments and houses available as off-campus rentals as well as on-campus housing. The university has campus housing facilities for both married and single students. For information concerning on-campus housing, contact Indiana University Halls of Residence, 801 N. Jordan Avenue, Bloomington, IN 47405-2107 or *www.rps.indiana.edu*. Information on off-campus housing options is available on the law school's website *www.law.indiana.edu* or can be obtained by contacting the Admissions Office.

■ Student Activities

A variety of student organizations present opportunities for involvement in groups focused on specialized areas of the law and public service. Some of the most active

groups include the Black Law Student Association, Women's Law Caucus, Public Interest Law Foundation, Hispanic Law Student Association, and the Environmental Law Society. Students may also obtain practical experience in a number of clinical opportunities, including the Child Advocacy Clinic, Mental Health and Disability Law Clinic, Federal Courts Clinic, Entrepreneurship Clinic, and Protective Order Project. Second- and third-year students are offered the opportunity to gain valuable writing, editing, and advocacy skills through participation in the Moot Court Competition and/or one of our three journals. The *Indiana Law Journal* publishes articles by legal scholars, practitioners, jurists, and IU law students. The *Federal Communications Law Journal* is the nation's oldest and largest circulation communications law journal. The *Indiana Journal of Global Legal Studies* is a multidisciplinary journal that specializes in international and comparative law articles.

■ Career Services

The Career Services Office actively provides career planning and employment assistance to law students. Both on- and off-campus interviews are coordinated to facilitate contact between students and employers. In recent years, more than 97 percent of the graduates have secured employment within the first nine months after graduation. Approximately one-half locate outside the state of Indiana. Graduates are found in all 50 states and 31 foreign countries.

Applicant Profile

Indiana University School of Law—Bloomington
This grid includes only applicants who earned 120-180 LSAT scores under standard administrations.

LSAT Score	GPA															
	3.75 +		3.50 - 3.74		3.25 - 3.49		3.00 - 3.24		2.75 - 2.99		2.50 - 2.74		Below 2.50		No GPA		Total	
	Apps	Adm	Apps	Adm	Apps	Adm	Apps	Adm	Apps	Adm	Apps	Adm	Apps	Adm	Apps	Adm	Apps	Adm
175-180	2	2	6	6	1	1	0	0	0	0	0	0	1	1	0	0	10	10
170-174	26	26	26	26	9	9	12	12	5	5	3	3	3	3	0	0	84	84
165-169	63	63	68	68	51	51	31	30	28	28	18	18	17	16	3	1	279	275
160-164	136	116	164	115	155	73	116	60	55	29	33	14	21	8	5	2	685	417
155-159	111	35	159	22	168	14	127	8	55	2	31	0	11	0	13	1	675	82
150-154	88	20	95	16	145	17	130	10	47	2	18	1	10	0	4	0	537	66
145-149	26	3	35	5	57	5	59	0	30	0	23	0	12	0	10	0	252	13
140-144	4	1	16	0	13	0	26	0	17	0	16	0	18	0	6	0	116	1
Below 140	5	0	4	0	5	0	9	0	7	0	13	0	18	0	4	0	65	0
Total	461	266	573	258	604	170	510	120	244	66	155	36	111	28	45	4	2703	948

Apps = Number of Applicants
Adm = Number Admitted
Reflects 99% of the total applicant pool.

Indiana University School of Law—Indianapolis

530 West New York Street
Indianapolis, IN 46202-3225
Phone: 317.274.2459; Fax: 317.278.4780
E-mail: lawadmit@iupui.edu; Website: www.indylaw.indiana.edu

ABA Approved Since 1944

The Basics

Type of school	Public
Term	Semester
Application deadline	2/1 3/1
Application fee	$45
Financial aid deadline	3/1
Can first year start other than fall?	Yes
Student to faculty ratio (fall)	14.2 to 1
Does the university offer:	
housing restricted to law students?	No
graduate housing for which law students are eligible?	Yes

Faculty and Administrators

	Total		Men		Women		Minorities	
	Fall	Spr	Fall	Spr	Fall	Spr	Fall	Spr
Full-time	47	43	28	26	19	17	5	5
Other Full-time	4	4	1	1	3	3	0	0
Deans, librarians, & others who teach	9	9	7	7	2	2	0	0
Part-time	33	41	22	28	11	13	3	2
Total	93	97	58	62	35	35	8	7

Curriculum

	Full-time	Part-time
Typical first-year section size	95	70
Is there typically a "small section" of the first-year class, other than Legal Writing, taught by full-time faculty	Yes	No
If yes, typical size offered last year	50	0
# of classroom course titles beyond 1st year curriculum	106	
# of upper division courses, excluding seminars with an enrollment: Under 25	48	
25-49	48	
50-74	21	
75-99	13	
100+	2	
# of seminars	13	
# of seminar positions available	260	
# of seminar positions filled	122	50
# of positions available in simulation courses	426	
# of simulation positions filled	264	122
# of positions available in faculty supervised clinical courses	74	
# of faculty supervised clinical positions filled	53	16
# involved in field placements	91	14
# involved in law journals	112	25
# involved in moot court or trial competitions	150	46
# of credit hours required to graduate	90	

JD Enrollment and Ethnicity

	Men		Women		Full-time		Part-time		1st-year		Total		JD Degs. Awd.
	#	%	#	%	#	%	#	%	#	%	#	%	
African Amer.	16	3.4	44	10.4	39	6.3	21	7.8	25	7.0	60	6.7	27
Amer. Indian	1	0.2	0	0.0	1	0.2	0	0.0	0	0.0	1	0.1	1
Asian Amer.	16	3.4	16	3.8	23	3.7	9	3.3	14	3.9	32	3.6	8
Mex. Amer.	11	2.3	6	1.4	12	1.9	5	1.9	7	2.0	17	1.9	0
Puerto Rican	4	0.8	5	1.2	7	1.1	2	0.7	4	1.1	9	1.0	1
Hispanic	7	1.5	8	1.9	10	1.6	5	1.9	11	3.1	15	1.7	2
Total Minority	55	11.7	79	18.7	92	14.8	42	15.6	61	17.1	134	15.0	39
For. Nation.	11	2.3	5	1.2	15	2.4	1	0.4	9	2.5	16	1.8	1
Caucasian	405	86.0	338	80.1	516	82.8	227	84.1	286	80.3	743	83.2	207
Unknown	0	0.0	0	0.0	0	0.0	0	0.0	0	0.0	0	0.0	0
Total	471	52.7	422	47.3	623	69.8	270	30.2	356	39.9	893		247

Tuition and Fees

	Resident	Nonresident
Full-time	$11,661	$24,472
Part-time	$7,402	$15,667

Living Expenses

Estimated living expenses for singles

Living on campus	Living off campus	Living at home
$13,232	$14,144	$9,406

Indiana University School of Law—Indianapolis

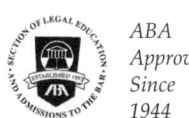

*ABA
Approved
Since
1944*

GPA and LSAT Scores

	Total	Full-time	Part-time
# of apps	1,820	1,438	382
# of admits	474	368	106
# of matrics	286	201	85
75% GPA	3.66	3.70	3.52
25% GPA	3.09	3.14	2.88
75% LSAT	158	158	158
25% LSAT	151	152	150

Grants and Scholarships (from prior year)

	Total		Full-time		Part-time	
	#	%	#	%	#	%
Total # of students	857		586		271	
Total # receiving grants	149	17.4	117	20.0	32	11.8
Less than 1/2 tuition	98	11.4	86	14.7	12	4.4
Half to full tuition	24	2.8	18	3.1	6	2.2
Full tuition	0	0.0	0	0.0	0	0.0
More than full tuition	27	3.2	13	2.2	14	5.2
Median grant amount			$3,550		$2,000	

Informational and Library Resources

# of volumes and volume equivalents	580,361
# of titles	189,679
# of active serial subscriptions	2,466
Study seating capacity inside the library	493
# of professional librarians	10
Hours per week library is open	99
# of open, wired connections available to students	1,140
# of networked computers available for use by students	155
# of simultaneous wireless users	1,500
Require computer?	N

JD Attrition (from prior year)

	Academic	Other	Total	
	#	#	#	%
1st year	2	16	18	5.3%
2nd year	5	6	11	4.1%
3rd year	0	1	1	0.4%
4th year	0	0	0	0.0%

Employment

	Total	Percentage
Employment status known	245	100.0
Employment status unknown	0	0.0
Employed	217	88.6
Pursuing graduate degrees	4	1.6
Unemployed seeking employment	24	9.8
Unemployed not seeking employment	0	0.0

Type of Employment

# employed in law firms	111	51.2
# employed in business and industry	42	19.4
# employed in government	38	17.5
# employed in public interest	9	4.1
# employed as judicial clerks	6	2.8
# employed in academia	6	2.8

Geographic Location

# employed in state	183	84.3
# employed in foreign countries	2	0.9
# of states where employed	15	

Bar Passage Rates

Jurisdiction	Indiana		
Exam	Sum 03	Win 04	Total
# from school taking bar for the first time	174	46	220
School's pass rate for all first-time takers	79%	76%	79%
State's pass rate for all first-time takers	79%	76%	79%

Indiana University School of Law—Indianapolis

530 West New York Street
Indianapolis, IN 46202-3225
Phone: 317.274.2459; Fax: 317.278.4780
E-mail: lawadmit@iupui.edu; Website: www.indylaw.indiana.edu

■ Introduction

Founded in 1894 as the Indiana Law School, the IU School of Law—Indianapolis has emerged as a premier educational institution, located in the dynamic heart of Indiana on the Indianapolis campus of Indiana University and Purdue University. This campus is also home to the Schools of Medicine, Dentistry, Nursing, and Social Work. The law school building, Lawrence W. Inlow Hall, is a state-of-the-art facility, enabling the faculty to employ the latest technology and teaching methods. The building houses modern classrooms, private study areas, and an unparalleled law library. The school is just minutes away from the state's courts, the legislature, and major law firms, giving students opportunities to observe the legal process in action and to participate in that process as law clerks, judicial interns, and legislative staff assistants. The school is the largest in the state of Indiana and one of the few Big Ten law schools to offer the cultural, recreational, and professional advantages of an urban educational environment.

■ Clinical Experiences

The law school offers several clinical programs: The Civil Practice Clinic allows students the opportunity to represent clients in a variety of cases, including housing, divorce, child support, consumer, and administrative matters. In the Civil Practice Disability Clinic, students represent school-age children with special needs, as well as persons who are afflicted with the HIV virus, Alzheimer's disease, and AIDS. In the Criminal Defense Clinic, students represent clients in criminal cases involving a variety of misdemeanor or class D felony charges.

■ Internships and Special Programs

The school's research centers and programs make significant contributions to the profession, both locally and nationally. The William S. and Christine S. Hall Center for Law and Health is considered one of the top health law programs in the nation. The center serves as a preeminent information resource on health law issues for the bar, government, and health care community. Through the center, students may pursue a concentration in Law and Health and participate in the *Indiana Health Law Review*.

The Program on Law and State Government enriches the dialogue between the academic legal community and state government policymakers. The program offers internships with nearly 40 government offices and also sponsors a mediation course that qualifies students to become registered civil mediators.

The Court Internship Program provides internships with federal, state, and local courts. Interns work closely with judges and law clerks, learning about the legal process by experiencing it firsthand.

The newly established Center for Intellectual Property Law and Innovation allows students to pursue in-depth study of intellectual property issues and provides an important resource to the legal community.

■ International Law Program

Because the school recognizes that international considerations touch all areas of the law—from human rights to economic issues, it established the Center for International and Comparative Law. A wide variety of international courses, combined with opportunities for overseas experiences, demonstrate our commitment to a legal education with a world view. Our program in International Human Rights Law has placed students in internships in locations from Argentina to Zimbabwe.

The study of European law takes place each summer in Strasbourg, France, at the Robert Schuman University. Strasbourg not only boasts one of France's preeminent universities, but is also the seat of the Parliament of the European Union and the European Court of Human Rights. It is the perfect starting point for educational field trips and excursions to Paris, London, Luxembourg, and Brussels. The law school also sponsors a summer program in cooperation with the University of Zagreb School of Law in the ancient Croatian city of Dubrovnik.

Established in 1987, the Chinese Law Summer Program is hosted by Renmin (People's) University of China School of Law and introduces students to the Chinese legal system, its dispute resolution mechanisms, Chinese constitutional law, and the lawyering system of China.

Students can also travel to Argentina and other Latin American countries to study the legal system of Latin America through the Latin America Law Program offered in cooperation with the Universidad Nacional de La Plata.

In addition to offering several courses and seminars in the area of international law, the school sponsors the *Indiana International and Comparative Law Review* and a student organization, the International Law Society. It is also home to the editorial offices of the *European Journal of Law Reform*.

■ Academic Support Programs

Students are offered assistance through the Dean's Tutorial Society and the Tutorial Study Group. Supervised by a tenured faculty member, the tutorial society is staffed by academically distinguished students who offer individual tutoring as well as assistance in case briefing and exam preparation. The Tutorial Study Group meets weekly under the direction of a faculty member and assists students with their legal writing and analytical skills.

Indiana University School of Law—Indianapolis

Special Summer Program

Summer admission is offered to a select group of applicants who can benefit from a class emphasizing writing and analytical skills. Applicants who have either an LSAT score or GPA that is outside of the median range of accepted students, persons who are returning to school after several years outside of the classroom, and students for whom English is a second language may be considered for the summer program. Summer admittees earn two credits toward their JD degree and continuation in the fall is not contingent upon performance in the summer program. There is no special application procedure. Applicants who are not presumptively admitted and whose files are completed by February 1 may be considered for this program.

Additionally, the school strongly supports the Indiana Council on Legal Education Opportunity program, which provides those who are currently underrepresented in the legal profession or underrepresented in practice areas with assistance in preparing for law school through a six-week summer institute.

Admission

LSAT and LSDAS are required.

The law school seeks to attain a culturally rich and diverse student body. To this end, admission decisions are based on a variety of factors in addition to the LSAT and undergraduate GPA.

Joint-Degree Programs

The school offers six joint-degree options in cooperation with IU's School of Business, School of Public and Environmental Affairs, School of Medicine, School of Library and Information Science, and School of Liberal Arts. Available degrees are the Doctor of Jurisprudence and Master of Business Administration (JD/MBA), Master of Health Administration (JD/MHA), Master of Public Affairs (JD/MPA), Master of Public Health (JD/MPH), Master of Library Science (JD/MLS), and Master of Arts in Philosophy (JD/MPhil).

Student Activities

Students can participate in any of 30 different interest groups and organizations, ranging from the Equal Justice Works to the Law and Technology Society. The school also offers an extensive moot court program, a client counseling program, and three law reviews.

Office for Professional Development

The Office for Professional Development provides career counseling and job search assistance to students and alumni. Services include an on-campus interview program, a résumé review service, a mock interview program, and a variety of workshops and seminars.

Applicant Profile

Indiana University School of Law—Indianapolis
This grid includes only applicants who earned 120-180 LSAT scores under standard administrations.

LSAT Score	GPA 3.75 +		3.50 - 3.74		3.25 - 3.49		3.00 - 3.24		2.75 - 2.99		2.50 - 2.74		2.25 - 2.49		2.00 - 2.24		Below 2.00		No GPA		Total	
	Apps	Adm	Apps	Adm	Apps	Adm	Apps	Adm	Apps	Adm	Apps	Adm	Apps	Adm	Apps	Adm	Apps	Adm	Apps	Adm	Apps	Adm
175-180	0	0	0	0	0	0	0	0	0	0	0	0	0	0	0	0	0	0	0	0	0	0
170-174	0	0	0	0	3	2	2	2	0	0	1	1	1	1	0	0	0	0	0	0	7	6
165-169	8	8	6	6	4	4	5	5	2	2	1	1	2	1	0	0	0	0	0	0	28	27
160-164	15	15	27	25	25	24	20	17	14	10	8	2	5	3	1	0	0	0	2	1	117	97
155-159	43	38	64	53	74	44	72	26	49	14	25	3	8	2	2	0	1	1	8	3	346	184
150-154	57	25	102	20	112	19	130	14	78	8	33	3	32	3	3	0	2	0	12	1	561	93
145-149	27	7	61	5	86	10	101	12	59	2	32	0	18	1	13	0	4	0	11	2	412	39
140-144	7	0	23	2	31	6	39	6	38	4	26	0	28	1	11	0	1	0	12	2	216	21
135-139	7	2	3	1	7	1	22	1	12	0	10	0	11	0	2	0	1	0	5	2	80	7
130-134	1	0	1	0	2	0	5	0	6	0	5	0	6	0	7	0	1	0	3	0	37	0
125-129	0	0	0	0	0	0	0	0	1	0	1	0	2	0	0	0	1	0	1	0	6	0
120-124	0	0	0	0	0	0	0	0	0	0	0	0	0	0	0	0	1	0	0	0	1	0

Apps = Number of Applicants   Adm = Number Admitted   Reflects 99% of the total applicant pool.

Inter American University School of Law

PO Box 70351
San Juan, PR 00936-8351
Phone: 787.751.1912, exts. 2013, 2012
Website: www.derecho.inter.edu

ABA Approved Since 1969

The Basics

Type of school	Private
Term	Semester
Application deadline	3/31
Application fee	$63
Financial aid deadline	10/15
Can first year start other than fall?	No
Student to faculty ratio (fall)	24.7 to 1
Does the university offer:	
housing restricted to law students?	No
graduate housing for which law students are eligible?	No

Faculty and Administrators

	Total		Men		Women		Minorities	
	Fall	Spr	Fall	Spr	Fall	Spr	Fall	Spr
Full-time	22	23	14	14	8	9	22	23
Other Full-time	3	3	0	0	3	3	3	3
Deans, librarians, & others who teach	4	4	3	3	1	1	4	4
Part-time	39	31	25	22	12	7	38	30
Total	68	61	42	39	24	20	67	60

Curriculum

	Full-time	Part-time
Typical first-year section size	60	45
Is there typically a "small section" of the first-year class, other than Legal Writing, taught by full-time faculty	No	No
If yes, typical size offered last year	0	0
# of classroom course titles beyond 1st year curriculum		33
# of upper division courses, excluding seminars with an enrollement: Under 25		25
25-49		28
50-74		28
75-99		0
100+		0
# of seminars		7
# of seminar positions available		20
# of seminar positions filled	20	20
# of positions available in simulation courses		6
# of simulation positions filled	4	2
# of positions available in faculty supervised clinical courses		10
# of faculty supervised clinical positions filled	6	4
# involved in field placements	0	0
# involved in law journals	0	0
# involved in moot court or trial competitions	0	0
# of credit hours required to graduate		92

JD Enrollment and Ethnicity

	Men		Women		Full-time		Part-time		1st-year		Total		JD Degs. Awd.
	#	%	#	%	#	%	#	%	#	%	#	%	
African Amer.	0	0.0	0	0.0	0	0.0	0	0.0	0	0.0	0	0.0	0
Amer. Indian	0	0.0	0	0.0	0	0.0	0	0.0	0	0.0	0	0.0	0
Asian Amer.	0	0.0	0	0.0	0	0.0	0	0.0	0	0.0	0	0.0	0
Mex. Amer.	0	0.0	0	0.0	0	0.0	0	0.0	0	0.0	0	0.0	0
Puerto Rican	360	99.4	395	99.7	445	100.0	310	99.0	245	98.8	755	99.6	219
Hispanic	0	0.0	1	0.3	0	0.0	1	0.3	1	0.4	1	0.1	0
Total Minority	360	99.4	396	100.0	445	100.0	311	99.4	246	99.2	756	99.7	219
For. Nation.	0	0.0	0	0.0	0	0.0	0	0.0	0	0.0	0	0.0	0
Caucasian	2	0.6	0	0.0	0	0.0	2	0.6	2	0.8	2	0.3	0
Unknown	0	0.0	0	0.0	0	0.0	0	0.0	0	0.0	0	0.0	0
Total	362	47.8	396	52.2	445	58.7	313	41.3	248	32.7	758		219

Tuition and Fees

	Resident	Nonresident
Full-time	$13,227	$13,227
Part-time	$10,767	$10,767

Living Expenses

Estimated living expenses for singles

Living on campus	Living off campus	Living at home
N/A	$9,594	$6,094

Inter American University School of Law

ABA
Approved
Since
1969

GPA and LSAT Scores

	Total	Full-time	Part-time
# of apps	973	514	459
# of admits	386	206	180
# of matrics	248	146	102
75% GPA	3.46	3.27	3.13
25% GPA	2.48	3.70	3.53
75% LSAT	142	139	136
25% LSAT	146	144	142

Grants and Scholarships (from prior year)

	Total		Full-time		Part-time	
	#	%	#	%	#	%
Total # of students	770		439		331	
Total # receiving grants	121	15.7	72	16.4	49	14.8
Less than 1/2 tuition	0	0.0	0	0.0	0	0.0
Half to full tuition	12	1.6	4	0.9	8	2.4
Full tuition	109	14.2	68	15.5	41	12.4
More than full tuition	0	0.0	0	0.0	0	0.0
Median grant amount			$4,627		$4,241	

Informational and Library Resources

# of volumes and volume equivalents	181,610
# of titles	25,976
# of active serial subscriptions	152
Study seating capacity inside the library	307
# of professional librarians	8
Hours per week library is open	102
# of open, wired connections available to students	17
# of networked computers available for use by students	55
# of simultaneous wireless users	0
Require computer?	N

JD Attrition (from prior year)

	Academic	Other	Total	
	#	#	#	%
1st year	2	20	22	9.1%
2nd year	6	12	18	6.4%
3rd year	3	4	7	3.7%
4th year	0	0	0	0.0%

Employment

	Total	Percentage
Employment status known	182	95.8
Employment status unknown	8	4.2
Employed	171	94.0
Pursuing graduate degrees	5	2.7
Unemployed seeking employment	5	2.7
Unemployed not seeking employment	1	0.5

Type of Employment

# employed in law firms	85	49.7
# employed in business and industry	12	7.0
# employed in government	32	18.7
# employed in public interest	6	3.5
# employed as judicial clerks	15	8.8
# employed in academia	3	1.8

Geographic Location

# employed in state	170	99.4
# employed in foreign countries	0	0.0
# of states where employed	2	

Bar Passage Rates

Jurisdiction	Puerto Rico		
Exam	Sum 03	Win 04	Total
# from school taking bar for the first time	171	40	211
School's pass rate for all first-time takers	44%	40%	44%
State's pass rate for all first-time takers	57%	38%	54%

Inter American University School of Law

PO Box 70351
San Juan, PR 00936-8351
Phone: 787.751.1912, exts. 2013, 2012
Website: www.derecho.inter.edu

■ Introduction

The Inter American University School of Law is one of
the 11 units of the Inter American University of Puerto
Rico, a private nonprofit educational corporation
accredited by the Middle States Association of Colleges
and Secondary Schools, the Puerto Rico Council of
Higher Education, and the Commonwealth of Puerto
Rico Department of Education. The School of Law is
approved by the ABA and is located in San Juan, the
capital city of Puerto Rico. Since its founding, the
School of Law has succeeded in meeting the needs of
the legal profession, in particular, and Puerto Rico's
society in general.

■ Enrollment/Student Body

The incoming class for academic year 2002–2003 was
comprised of 219 students. The student body comes
mainly from Puerto Rico, although applicants from the
mainland are encouraged to apply.

■ Library and Physical Facilities

The law school has developed its library into a center
of access to traditional library services as well as
computerized legal-research services.

The school was relocated to a new building in 1993,
which includes seven classrooms equipped with air
conditioning, accessibility to students with disabilities,
state-of-the-art audiovisual equipment, seminar rooms,
library, legal clinic, faculty offices, conference room,
lounge, Continuing Legal Education Program office, Law
Review offices, student organization offices,
administrative offices, chapel, student center, cafeteria,
bookstore, auditorium with a capacity of 310 seats,
parking, and more. The site has been landscaped to
achieve a sense of serenity and beauty compatible with
the building's functions.

In January 1990, the library signed a collaboration
agreement to establish a consortium with the law school
library of the Catholic University of Puerto Rico and the
library of the Supreme Court of Puerto Rico, with the
purpose of coordinating collection development
and sharing its resources through an automated
bibliographic network, interlibrary loans, and
telecommunication services.

■ Curriculum

The JD program covers three years in the day division
and four years in the evening division. Candidates must
complete a minimum of 92 credit hours with a GPA of
not less than 2.5 to qualify for graduation.

Inter American University School of Law offers a
three-week preparation course to be taken during the
summer on a compulsory basis by students admitted to
the school.

Students who enter law school must be willing to make
a heavy commitment of time and energy. For its part,
Inter American University is willing to provide the best
possible professional educational experience through the
careful recruitment of a first-rate faculty, the
development of a progressive curriculum, and a
willingness to create new and exciting programs of
clinical studies and research.

■ Admission

Proficiency in Spanish is essential in the program.
Applicants must have a minimum grade index of 2.5,
a medical certificate for students 21 years or younger,
a police department certificate of good conduct, and
appear for a personal interview, if required.

Candidates are required to take the Prueba de
Admision para Estudios Graduados (PAEG), the
Aptitude Test for Graduate Education, and the Law
School Admission Test (LSAT). Students should attain
a 575 minimum score on the PAEG and a minimum
score of 130 on the LSAT. Application forms and other
relevant information concerning the PAEG may be
obtained from Educational Testing Service, GPO Box
1271, San Juan, PR 00936.

■ Housing

The university does not provide housing for law students. However, the areas surrounding the School of Law
contain many private houses, apartments, and condominiums for rent.

■ Student Activities

Student organizations include the student council, an
organization that represents the student body and
participates in matters of administrative policy related
to students' interests. Council representatives serve on
various faculty committees as well as the university
senate and the board of trustees.

Other student organizations are the Law Student
Division of the American Bar Association, Phi Alpha
Delta legal fraternity (comprised not only of law
students but also of distinguished honorary members
who are Supreme Court justices, federal district court
judges, and other prominent attorneys), the National
Association of Law Students, Women Law Students
Association, United Students Forging an Environmental
Consciousness, Law Student Division of the

Inter-American Federation of Lawyers, the Student's Cooperative Bookstore, and class officers.

The *Inter American School of Law Review* is the official publication of the School of Law. Its members work under the supervision of an editorial board of four students chosen on the basis of merit and dedication to the *Review* and an academic advisor who is a faculty member appointed by the dean.

■ Clinical Programs

The general university fee is $20 per semester. Students pay $125 to reserve a place in the class (after admission approval), $5 for the *Law Review,* and $10 per semester for student activities. There is a deferred-payment plan, and financial aid options include Federal Guaranteed Loan Program, Perkins Loan, Stafford, LAL, the Commonwealth Education Fund, the Students Incentive Grant program, and the College Work-Study Program. The university also has an Honor Scholarship program for law students based on academic accomplishment and financial need.

■ Career Services

The mission of the Career Placement Office is to prepare students and alumni for the legal job market by encouraging them to conduct self-assessment in an effort to focus their job search and to educate them on their legal and nonlegal options in today's competitive legal market. This is accomplished through a variety of services including, but not limited to, individual counseling, group seminars, self-assessment materials, interviewing programs, a career resource library, and the alumni network.

■ Continuing Legal Education Program

The Continuing Legal Education Program offers advanced courses and seminars concerning different fields of the law of interest to practicing lawyers as well as to the community in general.

The CLE Program enjoys a good reputation and has been able to develop a consistent course offering, primarily in the following categories: courses designed for specialists; refresher courses for experienced lawyers; courses designed to provide information in nontraditional areas or stimulated by recent legislation, decisions, or agency rulings; and courses designed to develop lawyering skills.

Applicant Profile Not Available

University of Iowa College of Law

276 Boyd Law Building, Melrose at Byington Streets
Iowa City, IA 52242
Phone: 800.553.IOWA, ext. 9095; 319.335.9095; Fax: 319.335.9019
E-mail: law-admissions@uiowa.edu; Website: www.law.uiowa.edu

ABA
Approved
Since
1923

The Basics

Type of school	Public
Term	Semester
Application deadline	2/15
Application fee	$50
Financial aid deadline	1/1
Can first year start other than fall?	Yes
Student to faculty ratio (fall)	13.5 to 1
Does the university offer:	
housing restricted to law students?	No
graduate housing for which law students are eligible?	Yes

Faculty and Administrators

	Total		Men		Women		Minorities	
	Fall	Spr	Fall	Spr	Fall	Spr	Fall	Spr
Full-time	44	44	29	30	15	14	5	5
Other Full-time	3	6	2	4	1	2	0	1
Deans, librarians, & others who teach	13	11	5	5	8	6	1	0
Part-time	14	20	10	12	4	8	0	0
Total	74	81	46	51	28	30	6	6

Curriculum

	Full-time	Part-time
Typical first-year section size	75	0
Is there typically a "small section" of the first-year class, other than Legal Writing, taught by full-time faculty	Yes	No
If yes, typical size offered last year	25	0
# of classroom course titles beyond 1st year curriculum	85	
# of upper division courses, excluding seminars with an enrollment: Under 25	56	
25-49	36	
50-74	16	
75-99	8	
100+	1	
# of seminars	32	
# of seminar positions available	384	
# of seminar positions filled	381	0
# of positions available in simulation courses	158	
# of simulation positions filled	155	0
# of positions available in faculty supervised clinical courses	83	
# of faculty supervised clinical positions filled	83	0
# involved in field placements	46	0
# involved in law journals	188	0
# involved in moot court or trial competitions	439	0
# of credit hours required to graduate	90	

JD Enrollment and Ethnicity

	Men		Women		Full-time		Part-time		1st-year		Total		JD Degs. Awd.
	#	%	#	%	#	%	#	%	#	%	#	%	
African Amer.	13	3.5	19	5.6	32	4.5	0	0.0	12	4.9	32	4.5	9
Amer. Indian	5	1.3	4	1.2	9	1.3	0	0.0	2	0.8	9	1.3	3
Asian Amer.	19	5.1	19	5.6	38	5.3	0	0.0	13	5.3	38	5.3	11
Mex. Amer.	19	5.1	19	5.6	38	5.3	0	0.0	12	4.9	38	5.3	4
Puerto Rican	0	0.0	0	0.0	0	0.0	0	0.0	0	0.0	0	0.0	0
Hispanic	0	0.0	0	0.0	0	0.0	0	0.0	0	0.0	0	0.0	0
Total Minority	56	15.0	61	18.0	117	16.4	0	0.0	39	15.9	117	16.4	27
For. Nation.	4	1.1	2	0.6	6	0.8	0	0.0	4	1.6	6	0.8	2
Caucasian	289	77.5	252	74.3	541	76.0	0	0.0	178	72.7	541	76.0	201
Unknown	24	6.4	24	7.1	48	6.7	0	0.0	24	9.8	48	6.7	0
Total	373	52.4	339	47.6	712	100.0	0	0.0	245	34.4	712		230

Tuition and Fees

	Resident	Nonresident
Full-time	$12,348	$26,556
Part-time	$0	$0

Living Expenses

Estimated living expenses for singles

Living on campus	Living off campus	Living at home
$11,690	$11,690	$6,800

University of Iowa College of Law

*ABA
Approved
Since
1923*

GPA and LSAT Scores

	Total	Full-time	Part-time
# of apps	1,601	1,601	0
# of admits	494	494	0
# of matrics	248	248	0
75% GPA	3.82	3.82	0.00
25% GPA	3.32	3.32	0.00
75% LSAT	163	163	0
25% LSAT	156	156	0

Grants and Scholarships (from prior year)

	Total		Full-time		Part-time	
	#	%	#	%	#	%
Total # of students	725		725		0	
Total # receiving grants	232	32.0	232	32.0	0	0.0
Less than 1/2 tuition	81	11.2	81	11.2	0	0.0
Half to full tuition	23	3.2	23	3.2	0	0.0
Full tuition	124	17.1	124	17.1	0	0.0
More than full tuition	4	0.6	4	0.6	0	0.0
Median grant amount			$10,810		$0	

Informational and Library Resources

# of volumes and volume equivalents	1,099,823
# of titles	404,138
# of active serial subscriptions	9,836
Study seating capacity inside the library	673
# of professional librarians	15
Hours per week library is open	106
# of open, wired connections available to students	548
# of networked computers available for use by students	111
# of simultaneous wireless users	500
Require computer?	N

JD Attrition (from prior year)

	Academic	Other	Total	
	#	#	#	%
1st year	0	5	5	2.3%
2nd year	0	8	8	2.9%
3rd year	0	0	0	0.0%
4th year	0	0	0	0.0%

Employment

	Total	Percentage
Employment status known	231	100.0
Employment status unknown	0	0.0
Employed	216	93.5
Pursuing graduate degrees	13	5.6
Unemployed seeking employment	2	0.9
Unemployed not seeking employment	0	0.0

Type of Employment

# employed in law firms	118	54.6
# employed in business and industry	20	9.3
# employed in government	31	14.4
# employed in public interest	10	4.6
# employed as judicial clerks	28	13.0
# employed in academia	3	1.4

Geographic Location

# employed in state	64	29.6
# employed in foreign countries	2	0.9
# of states where employed		29

Bar Passage Rates

Jurisdiction	Iowa		
Exam	Sum 03	Win 04	Total
# from school taking bar for the first time	69	23	92
School's pass rate for all first-time takers	93%	96%	93%
State's pass rate for all first-time takers	84%	90%	86%

University of Iowa College of Law

276 Boyd Law Building, Melrose at Byington Streets
Iowa City, IA 52242
Phone: 800.553.IOWA, ext. 9095; 319.335.9095; Fax: 319.335.9019
E-mail: law-admissions@uiowa.edu; Website: www.law.uiowa.edu

■ Introduction

The University of Iowa College of Law, founded in 1865, is the oldest law school in continuous operation west of the Mississippi River. Iowa enjoys a top national reputation and its faculty is renowned for its outstanding scholarship and teaching.

The college is located in Iowa City, a cosmopolitan college town that is home to a dynamic teaching and research university and approximately 60,000 people. Students from all 50 states and roughly 100 countries attend the university. Iowa City offers a rich cultural life, Big Ten athletic events, and the world-famous Iowa Writer's Workshop.

The Boyd Law Building's central campus location on a bluff overlooking the Iowa River provides a professional enclave well suited to the college's intensive style of education and easy access to the academic, cultural, social, and recreational resources of a major research university.

■ Curriculum

Iowa's greatest academic strengths lie in its program-wide recognition of students as individual learners, its continuous emphasis on writing skills, its international and comparative orientation, and its longstanding commitment to diversity.

Iowa is a leader among the nation's law schools in the development of a modern curriculum in which individual instruction in basic lawyering skills is integrated with the exploration of conceptual and institutional issues central to the legal process. The centerpiece of this progressive curriculum is an ambitious writing program in which faculty-supervised writing opportunities are provided individually or in small classes in every semester of a student's educational program.

■ Iowa Law Library

The Iowa law library is one of the major repositories of legal materials in the United States. According to the latest annual law school data report published by the ABA, Iowa's collection currently is first among all public US law school libraries in the number of volumes and volume equivalents. Westlaw/Dialog and LexisNexis are available for training and research activities through 64 public work stations and over 400 data ports located in student study carrels.

■ Special Programs

Iowa's unique Writing Resource Center is dedicated to furthering the college's aim of strengthening law students' command of the writing skills central to the study and practice of law. It serves as an extension of the classroom and supplements the college's small-section writing program and upper-level writing requirements.

The Academic Achievement Program (AAP) helps students achieve their full academic potential as they move from successful undergraduate careers to face the new challenges of law study. AAP presents a variety of programs, including a first-semester lecture series for new students. Individual study-skills counseling is also available for all students.

■ Legal Clinic

The Clinical Law Program gives students opportunities to gain experience in many different areas of substantive law, including civil rights, disability rights, employment law, immigration, criminal defense, consumer law, domestic violence, nonprofit organizations, and bankruptcy. Through the representation of real clients, students are able to develop and hone a diverse complement of lawyering skills from interviewing, counseling, and drafting court papers to trial practice, appellate advocacy, legislative lobbying, and policy development.

■ International Law

Iowa offers one of the nation's strongest programs for the study of international and comparative law. Over 40 percent of the faculty regularly teach or conduct research on international and comparative law subjects. Iowa offers three study-abroad programs. Iowa is the stateside home of the London Law Consortium through which seven US law schools conduct a study-abroad program for a spring semester in London. The Iowa/Bordeaux Summer Program offers one month of intensive coursework in Arcachon, France. Students also have the opportunity to participate in an exchange program with Bucerius Law School in Germany. In addition, students may receive credit for participating in other study-abroad programs offered by ABA-approved law schools.

■ Accelerated/Summer Program

Iowa offers two starting dates for entering students: May and August. These are separate applicant pools. Admission to the May entering class does not guarantee admission to the fall, or vice versa. Students who elect to enter law school in the fall also may attend summer school at any point during their academic career.

Students entering in May complete nearly a full semester of work in the first summer term, which consists of 2 five-and-a-half week sessions. A May entrant who completes at least one additional summer session, (five-and-a-half weeks) in the following two years may graduate in two-and-a-half years. Thus, a student who begins law school in May 2005 may graduate in December of 2007.

■ Admission

Iowa strives to enroll a student body that reflects the academic quality and diversity expected of a leading national law school. The college's numbers-plus policy, which looks beyond numerical indicators, utilizes a full file review to evaluate an applicant's potential contribution to enhancing classroom discussion through consideration of factors such as maturity, work experience, ability to overcome adversity, and cultural background.

■ Student Activities

Alianza (formerly known as the Chicano Hispanic Association of Legal Education); American Constitution Society; Amnesty International; Asian American Law Students Association; Association of Trial Lawyers of America; Black Law Students Association; Client Counseling; Environmental Law Society; Equal Justice Foundation; Federalist Society; Intellectual Property Law Society; *Iowa Journal of Gender, Race, and Justice*; *Iowa Law Review*; International Law Society; Iowa Student Bar Association; J. Reuben Clark Law Society; *Journal of Corporation Law*; *Journal of Transnational Law and Contemporary Problems*; Moot Court; Native American Law Students Association; National Lawyers Guild; Order of the Coif; Organization for Women Law Students and Staff; the Outlaws (formerly known as the National Lesbian and Gay Law Association); People Accompanying Law Students (PALS); Parents/Partners Weekend; Phi Alpha Delta; Pro Bono Society; Students Animal Legal Defense Fund; Stephenson Competition; Supreme Court Day; Trial Advocacy.

■ Expenses and Financial Aid

All admitted students are automatically considered for merit scholarships and fellowships based on their academic achievement. A separate application is not required. The Law Merit Fellowship funds a limited number of three-year tuition grants and research assistant positions for students with outstanding academic credentials. The Law Opportunity Fellowship Program funds a limited number of three-year tuition grant and research assistant positions for members of traditionally underrepresented groups and others. Eligibility for financial aid based on need is established by completion of the FAFSA, available at *www.fafsa.ed.gov*.

■ Career Services

Each year the Career Services Office provides students with access to numerous job fairs, posts openings for over 2,500 employers interested in Iowa students, and hosts a substantial number of employers for its on-campus interview program. Over the past five years, more than 1,000 employers have visited the campus to recruit students for positions in private firms, corporations, and government as well as for judicial clerkships. Additionally, over the past five years, we have had between 97 and 100 percent of our students employed within nine months of graduation. The Career Services Office strives to work with all students throughout their law school careers to help them seek and find summer employment as well as permanent employment. Be it private practice, in-house corporate, government, or academics to name a few, our alumni excel in their legal professions.

Applicant Profile Not Available

The John Marshall Law School

315 South Plymouth Court
Chicago, IL 60604
Phone: 800.537.4280; 312.987.1406; Fax: 312.427.5136
E-mail: admission@jmls.edu; Website: www.jmls.edu

*ABA
Approved
Since
1951*

The Basics

Type of school	Private
Term	Semester
Application deadline	3/1 10/15
Application fee	$50
Financial aid deadline	6/1
Can first year start other than fall?	Yes
Student to faculty ratio (fall)	19.5 to 1
Does the university offer:	
housing restricted to law students?	No
graduate housing for which law students are eligible?	No

Faculty and Administrators

	Total		Men		Women		Minorities	
	Fall	Spr	Fall	Spr	Fall	Spr	Fall	Spr
Full-time	55	54	39	38	16	16	7	8
Other Full-time	1	1	0	0	1	1	0	0
Deans, librarians, & others who teach	12	12	5	5	7	7	3	3
Part-time	109	110	83	79	26	31	15	17
Total	177	177	127	122	50	55	25	28

Curriculum

	Full-time	Part-time
Typical first-year section size	85	60
Is there typically a "small section" of the first-year class, other than Legal Writing, taught by full-time faculty	No	No
If yes, typical size offered last year	0	0
# of classroom course titles beyond 1st year curriculum	186	

# of upper division courses, excluding seminars with an enrollment:		
Under 25	149	
25-49	42	
50-74	40	
75-99	19	
100+	2	

# of seminars	100	
# of seminar positions available	1,520	
# of seminar positions filled	474	560
# of positions available in simulation courses	1,096	
# of simulation positions filled	305	581
# of positions available in faculty supervised clinical courses	178	
# of faculty supervised clinical positions filled	97	40
# involved in field placements	107	22
# involved in law journals	126	27
# involved in moot court or trial competitions	88	11
# of credit hours required to graduate	90	

JD Enrollment and Ethnicity

	Men		Women		Full-time		Part-time		1st-year		Total		JD Degs. Awd.
	#	%	#	%	#	%	#	%	#	%	#	%	
African Amer.	26	3.2	40	6.9	37	3.5	29	8.0	17	3.4	66	4.7	27
Amer. Indian	2	0.2	4	0.7	4	0.4	2	0.6	0	0.0	6	0.4	2
Asian Amer.	40	4.8	39	6.7	56	5.4	23	6.4	34	6.8	79	5.6	11
Mex. Amer.	15	1.8	12	2.1	23	2.2	4	1.1	13	2.6	27	1.9	2
Puerto Rican	0	0.0	2	0.3	0	0.0	2	0.6	0	0.0	2	0.1	1
Hispanic	19	2.3	14	2.4	23	2.2	10	2.8	7	1.4	33	2.3	2
Total Minority	102	12.4	111	19.1	143	13.7	70	19.4	71	14.3	213	15.1	45
For. Nation.	10	1.2	5	0.9	13	1.2	2	0.6	7	1.4	15	1.1	13
Caucasian	694	84.1	449	77.1	858	82.0	285	78.9	410	82.5	1143	81.2	317
Unknown	19	2.3	17	2.9	32	3.1	4	1.1	9	1.8	36	2.6	1
Total	825	58.6	582	41.4	1046	74.3	361	25.7	497	35.3	1407		376

Tuition and Fees

	Resident	Nonresident
Full-time	$26,756	$26,756
Part-time	$19,140	$19,140

Living Expenses

Estimated living expenses for singles

Living on campus	Living off campus	Living at home
$19,579	$19,579	$19,579

The John Marshall Law School

ABA Approved Since 1951

GPA and LSAT Scores

	Total	Full-time	Part-time
# of apps	3,684	3,043	641
# of admits	1,317	1,073	244
# of matrics	522	392	130
75% GPA	3.34	3.35	3.30
25% GPA	2.71	2.74	1.30
75% LSAT	156	156	155
25% LSAT	151	152	151

Grants and Scholarships (from prior year)

	Total		Full-time		Part-time	
	#	%	#	%	#	%
Total # of students	1,329		957		372	
Total # receiving grants	438	33.0	343	35.8	95	25.5
Less than 1/2 tuition	370	27.8	300	31.3	70	18.8
Half to full tuition	46	3.5	29	3.0	17	4.6
Full tuition	6	0.5	2	0.2	4	1.1
More than full tuition	16	1.2	12	1.3	4	1.1
Median grant amount			$6,000		$4,500	

Informational and Library Resources

# of volumes and volume equivalents	381,666
# of titles	92,681
# of active serial subscriptions	5,468
Study seating capacity inside the library	624
# of professional librarians	9
Hours per week library is open	100
# of open, wired connections available to students	28
# of networked computers available for use by students	100
# of simultaneous wireless users	1,200
Require computer?	N

JD Attrition (from prior year)

	Academic	Other	Total	
	#	#	#	%
1st year	39	45	84	18.3%
2nd year	15	31	46	11.6%
3rd year	3	10	13	3.5%
4th year	0	0	0	0.0%

Employment

	Total	Percentage
Employment status known	313	98.4
Employment status unknown	5	1.6
Employed	258	82.4
Pursuing graduate degrees	8	2.6
Unemployed seeking employment	45	14.4
Unemployed not seeking employment	2	0.6

Type of Employment

# employed in law firms	150	58.1
# employed in business and industry	32	12.4
# employed in government	49	19.0
# employed in public interest	9	3.5
# employed as judicial clerks	10	3.9
# employed in academia	4	1.6

Geographic Location

# employed in state	227	88.0
# employed in foreign countries	0	0.0
# of states where employed		16

Bar Passage Rates

Jurisdiction	Illinois		
Exam	Sum 03	Win 04	Total
# from school taking bar for the first time	200	109	309
School's pass rate for all first-time takers	73%	61%	69%
State's pass rate for all first-time takers	86%	78%	84%

The John Marshall Law School

315 South Plymouth Court
Chicago, IL 60604
Phone: 800.537.4280; 312.987.1406; Fax: 312.427.5136
E-mail: admission@jmls.edu; Website: www.jmls.edu

■ Introduction

John Marshall is an independent law school, well known for consistently training attorneys who are ready to step directly into integral firm, corporate, and public service roles. John Marshall graduates enter the legal profession with confidence, secure in the practical benefits gained from rigorous classes and through clinical and externship experiences.

An innovator in offering legal education to women, minorities, and students needing to work while attending law school, John Marshall today remains true to the guiding ideals it has espoused for more than a century. Our legacy of opportunity includes maintaining diversity in our academic programs, student body, and faculty, and providing a harmonious blend of the theory and practice of law.

John Marshall's location in the heart of Chicago's legal, financial, and commercial districts offers students a vibrant, cosmopolitan setting for legal study. The federal courthouse is across the street, and the nation's largest circuit court—Cook County—is just a few blocks away, as are many government offices. This proximity offers John Marshall students enhanced learning experiences.

The John Marshall Law School is also renowned for its outstanding specialty programs: Nationally renowned in both trial advocacy and intellectual property, John Marshall also offers the nation's only graduate program in employee benefits, one of the first ever in information technology and privacy law, and one of only two in the nation in real estate law.

■ Curriculum

John Marshall has day and evening divisions, with identical instruction, course content, and scholastic requirements. Lawyering skills courses, which focus on writing, research, and oral argument, are an integral part of the core curriculum. These courses are taught in small groups to maximize the individual attention given to each student. A student may specialize in a certain area of the law and receive a certificate or focus more emphatically and earn a joint degree (JD/LLM).

■ Clinics, Externships, and Special Programs

Practical legal experience plays a vital role in education at The John Marshall Law School. John Marshall is the only law school in the nation with a training program in fair housing law and enforcement. Meanwhile, the Patent Clinic provides valuable training for future attorneys who want to practice in the area of intellectual property. The John Marshall Law School also offers several programs that enable students to learn important lawyering skills while working as externs with various members of the bench and bar.

The John Marshall Law School offers seven Master of Laws (LLM) programs for attorneys seeking specialized education in legal issues and for current JD students who would like the maximum concentration in particular areas of the law. As the largest graduate law school in the Midwest, John Marshall offers a comprehensive curriculum in the following areas: employee benefits law, information technology and privacy law, intellectual property law, international business and trade law, real estate law, and tax law. John Marshall also offers Master of Science (MS) degrees for nonlawyers in information technology, employee benefits, tax, and real estate.

■ Library

The Louis L. Biro Law Library collection includes more than 380,000 volumes and 2,500 audiovisual tapes and also serves as the library resource for the Chicago Bar Association, whose headquarters building is next door. The John Marshall Law School was the first law school in Chicago to teach legal research on computers. The library has more than 75 IBM-compatible computers available for student use. John Marshall has a school-wide computer network with a backbone of high-speed, digital fiber-optic cabling that allows students, faculty, and staff access to word processing software, LexisNexis, Westlaw, CALI, and the Internet. In addition, a wireless network has been added to the backbone, allowing laptop users anywhere in the school to connect to the Internet without being tethered by cords. Computerized research and reference resources are available to students through the Law School's website *www.jmls.edu*.

■ Admission

Students are admitted in August and January. Applications for August entrance may be filed between October 1 and March 1; for January entrance, between May 1 and October 15. The LSAT score is evaluated together with the cumulative grade point average and other relevant factors, including difficulty of undergraduate program, postgraduate experience, leadership potential, business and professional background, and letters of recommendation. Applicants from minority and other disadvantaged groups will be given special consideration in cases where their overall records are competitive with other applicants. Minority representation in the class enrolled in 2004 was 20 percent. Applicants with a B average overall and an LSAT score in the 60th percentile may be presumed to be within the range for favorable consideration.

Student Activities

The student community at The John Marshall Law School includes over 40 student organizations engaging in social awareness, community service, legal discussions, and social activities. There are five honors programs, including the *John Marshall Law Review*, the *Journal of Computer and Information Law*, the *Review of Intellectual Property Law* (an online journal), the Moot Court Honors Program, and Advocacy and Dispute Resolution Honors Program. Every student group at John Marshall reflects the diversity, highlights the talents, and enhances the opportunities of our entire student body.

Career Opportunities

The Career Services Office (CSO) offers personal assistance to help students assess and refine their career goals. The CSO sponsors more than 60 career-related programs each year, many featuring alumni as panelists and speakers, and also implements a robust Alumni Mentor Program, where mentors meet with students one-on-one to provide real-world advice on practice areas, law school courses, and the day-to-day practice of law. The CSO also aggressively promotes John Marshall students to employers. John Marshall graduates are employed at 33 of Chicago's 35 largest firms. Public service is another favored career path, with graduates serving as attorneys in the courts and government. Nearly one-fifth of all Illinois judges are John Marshall alumni (circuit, appellate, and state supreme court).

Correspondence

We encourage you to visit our website, *www.jmls.edu*, and to come see us in person. Visit a class and talk with our faculty and our students. Find out for yourself what it's like to learn, in an intimate classroom environment, from a top-notch faculty that consistently imparts an understanding of both the theory and the practice of law.

Visit with our personable admission and financial aid staff. Then, if you feel drawn to become a member of the John Marshall community—if the excellence and diversity we represent resonate with your desires for your own legal education—we would be pleased to receive your application.

Applicant Profile

The John Marshall Law School
This grid includes only applicants who earned 120-180 LSAT scores under standard administrations.

LSAT Score	GPA						
	3.75 +	3.50 - 3.74	3.25 - 3.49	3.00 - 3.24	2.75 - 2.99	2.50 - 2.74	Below 2.50
175-180							
170-174							
165-169							
160-164							
155-159							
150-154							
145-149							
140-144							
135-139							
130-134							
125-129							
120-124							

Likely · Possible · Unlikely

The University of Kansas School of Law

1535 West 15th Street
Lawrence, KS 66045-7577
Phone: 866.220.3654 (toll free), 785.864.4378; Fax: 785.864.5054
E-mail: admitlaw@ku.edu; Website: www.law.ku.edu

ABA Approved Since 1923

The Basics

Type of school	Public
Term	Semester
Application deadline	3/15
Application fee	$50
Financial aid deadline	3/1
Can first year start other than fall?	Yes
Student to faculty ratio (fall)	15.6 to 1
Does the university offer:	
housing restricted to law students?	No
graduate housing for which law students are eligible?	Yes

Faculty and Administrators

	Total Fall	Total Spr	Men Fall	Men Spr	Women Fall	Women Spr	Minorities Fall	Minorities Spr
Full-time	28	31	18	21	10	10	4	4
Other Full-time	3	3	0	0	3	3	0	0
Deans, librarians, & others who teach	6	6	4	4	2	2	1	1
Part-time	20	19	14	13	6	6	1	1
Total	57	59	36	38	21	21	6	6

Curriculum

	Full-time	Part-time
Typical first-year section size	55	0
Is there typically a "small section" of the first-year class, other than Legal Writing, taught by full-time faculty	Yes	No
If yes, typical size offered last year	17	0
# of classroom course titles beyond 1st year curriculum	86	
# of upper division courses, excluding seminars with an enrollment: Under 25	74	
25-49	33	
50-74	10	
75-99	4	
100+	4	
# of seminars	11	
# of seminar positions available	221	
# of seminar positions filled	164	0
# of positions available in simulation courses	330	
# of simulation positions filled	282	0
# of positions available in faculty supervised clinical courses	101	
# of faculty supervised clinical positions filled	86	0
# involved in field placements	54	0
# involved in law journals	75	0
# involved in moot court or trial competitions	48	0
# of credit hours required to graduate	90	

JD Enrollment and Ethnicity

	Men #	Men %	Women #	Women %	Full-time #	Full-time %	Part-time #	Part-time %	1st-year #	1st-year %	Total #	Total %	JD Degs. Awd.
African Amer.	12	4.1	10	4.3	22	4.2	0	0.0	3	1.8	22	4.2	5
Amer. Indian	6	2.1	6	2.6	12	2.3	0	0.0	2	1.2	12	2.3	4
Asian Amer.	17	5.8	19	8.2	36	6.9	0	0.0	14	8.4	36	6.9	10
Mex. Amer.	0	0.0	0	0.0	0	0.0	0	0.0	0	0.0	0	0.0	0
Puerto Rican	0	0.0	0	0.0	0	0.0	0	0.0	0	0.0	0	0.0	0
Hispanic	27	9.2	15	6.5	42	8.0	0	0.0	12	7.2	42	8.0	9
Total Minority	62	21.2	50	21.6	112	21.4	0	0.0	31	18.7	112	21.4	28
For. Nation.	0	0.0	0	0.0	0	0.0	0	0.0	0	0.0	0	0.0	0
Caucasian	214	73.3	174	75.0	388	74.0	0	0.0	126	75.9	388	74.0	166
Unknown	16	5.5	8	3.4	24	4.6	0	0.0	9	5.4	24	4.6	3
Total	292	55.7	232	44.3	524	100.0	0	0.0	166	31.7	524		197

Tuition and Fees

	Resident	Nonresident
Full-time	$8,725	$16,573
Part-time	$0	$0

Living Expenses

Estimated living expenses for singles

Living on campus	Living off campus	Living at home
$12,130	$12,130	$12,130

The University of Kansas School of Law

*ABA
Approved
Since
1923*

GPA and LSAT Scores

	Total	Full-time	Part-time
# of apps	1,238	1,238	0
# of admits	313	313	0
# of matrics	167	167	0
75% GPA	3.80	3.80	0.00
25% GPA	3.28	3.28	0.00
75% LSAT	160	160	0
25% LSAT	153	153	0

Grants and Scholarships (from prior year)

	Total #	Total %	Full-time #	Full-time %	Part-time #	Part-time %
Total # of students	550		550		0	
Total # receiving grants	319	58.0	319	58.0	0	0.0
Less than 1/2 tuition	253	46.0	253	46.0	0	0.0
Half to full tuition	44	8.0	44	8.0	0	0.0
Full tuition	0	0.0	0	0.0	0	0.0
More than full tuition	22	4.0	22	4.0	0	0.0
Median grant amount			$3,336		$0	

Informational and Library Resources

# of volumes and volume equivalents	392,225
# of titles	131,275
# of active serial subscriptions	5,273
Study seating capacity inside the library	385
# of professional librarians	7
Hours per week library is open	105
# of open, wired connections available to students	115
# of networked computers available for use by students	48
# of simultaneous wireless users	245
Require computer?	N

JD Attrition (from prior year)

	Academic #	Other #	Total #	Total %
1st year	0	7	7	4.3%
2nd year	0	0	0	0.0%
3rd year	0	0	0	0.0%
4th year	0	0	0	0.0%

Employment

	Total	Percentage
Employment status known	146	95.4
Employment status unknown	7	4.6
Employed	124	84.9
Pursuing graduate degrees	0	0.0
Unemployed seeking employment	20	13.7
Unemployed not seeking employment	2	1.4

Type of Employment

	Total	Percentage
# employed in law firms	60	48.4
# employed in business and industry	23	18.5
# employed in government	23	18.5
# employed in public interest	4	3.2
# employed as judicial clerks	9	7.3
# employed in academia	3	2.4

Geographic Location

	Total	Percentage
# employed in state	48	38.7
# employed in foreign countries	2	1.6
# of states where employed	23	

Bar Passage Rates

Jurisdiction	Kansas Sum 03	Kansas Win 04	Kansas Total	Missouri Sum 03	Missouri Win 04	Missouri Total
# from school taking bar for the first time	64	49	113	37	35	72
School's pass rate for all first-time takers	83%	86%	84%	95%	94%	94%
State's pass rate for all first-time takers	81%	85%	83%	83%	87%	84%

The University of Kansas School of Law

1535 West 15th Street
Lawrence, KS 66045-7577
Phone: 866.220.3654 (toll free), 785.864.4378; Fax: 785.864.5054
E-mail: admitlaw@ku.edu; Website: www.law.ku.edu

■ Introduction

The University of Kansas School of Law is an excellent place to begin a legal career. It has a venerable history and a commitment to educating for the future. Legal education at KU began in 1878, and the school was a charter member of the Association of American Law Schools. It has had a chapter of Order of the Coif, a national law school honor society with chapters at leading law schools throughout the country, since 1924. The law school is fully accredited by the American Bar Association.

The law school is on KU's main campus—one of the most beautiful in the country. It occupies Green Hall, named in honor of James Woods Green, first dean of the school. Green Hall is a modern, five-story building with extensive clinical facilities, spacious and attractive classrooms, seminar rooms, a formal courtroom, and common areas. The school is equipped with a state-of-the-art wireless network, allowing students to access the Internet and e-mail from anywhere in the law school.

The school's primary mission is to prepare its students to be outstanding members of the legal profession, well educated in the law, with a commitment to professional achievement and public service. The school educates students in both general principles of law and the skills needed for practice in a changing legal environment. Students develop technical competence, pride in legal craftsmanship, a sound sense of ethics and professionalism, and an appreciation for the role of law and the practice of law in society.

■ Faculty

Law faculty care about teaching. They are committed to excellence in the classroom and to serving as mentors for law students. This is the KU law tradition. Students are encouraged to consult regularly with their teachers about their progress in the study of law as well as about career plans, job opportunities, and the professional responsibilities of lawyers. Law faculty offices are scattered throughout Green Hall, and doors are open to students.

Faculty members enrich their teaching by researching and writing about the areas of law they teach. They regularly participate in symposia, publish widely in legal journals, and enjoy national and international recognition for the quality of their work. Many have written important treatises and casebooks used at law schools around the country.

■ Learning the Law

Entering students take basic courses that provide a solid foundation for upper-level classes and for the practice of law. The lawyering course focuses on the skills and values of the profession. Taught by faculty members with extensive practice experience, the course introduces students to the tools all lawyers use and brings them to an understanding of the legal system and legal institutions, case law and statutes, legal research and writing, and advocacy. First-year students take one of their other required courses in a small section of approximately 20 students providing an informal learning atmosphere and encouraging in-depth discussions and critical analysis.

More than 100 courses are available to upper-level students covering a broad range of practice areas from agricultural law to the law of cyberspace. Nine clinical programs permit students, acting under faculty supervision, to develop legal skills and learn professional values in actual practice settings: Criminal Justice Clinic, Paul E. Wilson Defender Project, Elder Law Clinic, Judicial Clerkship Clinic, Legal Aid Clinic, Legislative Clinic, Media Law Clinic, Public Policy Clinic, and Tribal Judicial Support Clinic. The large number of clinical placements available means that every student can take at least one clinic and many take more than one.

The school's setting at the heart of a major university makes possible the eight joint-degree programs open to law students. The most popular joint-degree programs are business, health policy and administration, and social welfare, but joint degrees are also available in economics, philosophy, public administration, urban planning, and indigenous nations studies. In addition, the school offers six certification programs: Elder Law; Media, Law, and Policy; Tax Law; Environmental and Natural Resources Law; Tribal Lawyering; and International Trade and Finance.

■ Accelerated/Summer Program

The law school's unique summer school program is fully integrated with the curriculum of the fall and spring semesters. Students who begin law school in May and attend summer school each of the following two summers may complete degree requirements in just 27 months.

■ Student Life

Because the school seeks students with strong personal qualities in addition to high academic credentials, students learn law with classmates who have the interpersonal skills, maturity, judgment, and ambition to succeed. The law school values diversity, and students have a wide range of education and work experience, enriching classroom discussions and student life.

KU law students develop friendships that last a lifetime. They find as many opportunities for collaboration as for competition. They socialize and develop leadership skills and an appreciation for community service through membership in the many student organizations. They hone research and writing and editing skills through work on two student-edited publications: the *Kansas Law Review* and the *Kansas Journal of Law and Public Policy*. They participate regularly and successfully in moot court, mock trial, and client counseling competitions. Study abroad is available through the London Consortium, the school's Limerick and Istanbul Programs, and other programs approved by the American Bar Association.

■ Career Services and Alumni

The school's Office of Career Services helps students define career goals and find employment that matches their interests. The office coordinates an extensive on-campus interviewing program, sponsors workshops exploring career options, and helps students develop job-seeking skills.

KU law students and graduates are highly sought after by employers throughout the state, region, and nation. Most recent graduates chose employment in private law firms, but many chose government service, including work as prosecutors, public interest work, the military, graduate study, and nontraditional careers. A considerable number of graduates accept judicial clerkships. Recent graduates have been law clerks at all levels, including the Supreme Court of the United States.

KU graduates have been highly successful in passing Kansas and Missouri bar examinations and have performed extremely well on examinations in other states. The Office of Career Services provides up-to-date information on bar requirements for all states.

The school's 6,000+ alumni live in all 50 states, the District of Columbia, Puerto Rico, and 11 foreign countries. Many participate in the law school's mentor program for first-year law students or in the Career Services Alumni Network, serving as sources of information about practice specialties and practice opportunities.

Applicant Profile

The University of Kansas School of Law
This grid includes applicants who earned 120-180 LSAT scores under standard administrations.

LSAT Score	3.75 +		3.50 - 3.74		3.25 - 3.49		3.00 - 3.24		2.75 - 2.99		2.50 - 2.74		Below 2.50		No GPA		Total	
	Apps	Adm	Apps	Adm	Apps	Adm	Apps	Adm	Apps	Adm	Apps	Adm	Apps	Adm	Apps	Adm	Apps	Adm
170-180	6	5	3	3	2	1	1	0	1	1	0	0	0	0	0	0	13	10
165-169	10	9	5	1	8	7	3	1	7	3	1	0	3	0	1	0	38	21
160-164	36	26	23	17	33	22	21	6	16	5	2	0	6	0	2	0	139	76
155-159	60	43	60	30	72	27	49	10	39	6	14	3	12	0	0	0	306	119
150-154	50	28	80	20	86	7	81	6	45	6	13	0	6	0	6	0	367	67
145-149	26	2	40	6	35	4	38	4	26	2	18	2	13	0	0	0	196	20
140-144	3	0	12	0	21	0	33	1	15	1	12	1	11	0	4	1	111	4
Below 140	1	0	4	1	3	0	7	0	6	0	12	0	16	0	4	0	53	1
Total	192	113	227	78	260	68	233	28	155	24	72	6	67	0	17	1	1223	318

Apps = Number of Applicants
Adm = Number Admitted

University of Kentucky College of Law

209 Law Building, South Limestone St.
Lexington, KY 40506-0048
Phone: 859.257.1678; Fax: 859.323.1061
E-mail: dbakert@uky.edu; Website: www.uky.edu/Law

ABA Approved Since 1925

The Basics

Type of school	Public
Term	Semester
Application deadline	3/1
Application fee	$50
Financial aid deadline	4/1
Can first year start other than fall?	No
Student to faculty ratio (fall)	16.7 to 1
Does the university offer:	
housing restricted to law students?	No
graduate housing for which law students are eligible?	Yes

Faculty and Administrators

	Total		Men		Women		Minorities	
	Fall	Spr	Fall	Spr	Fall	Spr	Fall	Spr
Full-time	21	21	15	15	6	6	1	0
Other Full-time	0	0	0	0	0	0	0	0
Deans, librarians, & others who teach	6	6	4	4	2	2	0	0
Part-time	17	18	12	12	5	6	0	0
Total	44	45	31	31	13	14	1	0

Curriculum

	Full-time	Part-time
Typical first-year section size	70	0
Is there typically a "small section" of the first-year class, other than Legal Writing, taught by full-time faculty	Yes	No
If yes, typical size offered last year	40	0
# of classroom course titles beyond 1st year curriculum		61
# of upper division courses, excluding seminars with an enrollement: Under 25		58
25-49		31
50-74		11
75-99		0
100+		0
# of seminars		9
# of seminar positions available		144
# of seminar positions filled	125	0
# of positions available in simulation courses	116	
# of simulation positions filled	108	0
# of positions available in faculty supervised clinical courses		28
# of faculty supervised clinical positions filled	28	0
# involved in field placements	69	0
# involved in law journals	54	0
# involved in moot court or trial competitions	53	0
# of credit hours required to graduate		90

JD Enrollment and Ethnicity

	Men		Women		Full-time		Part-time		1st-year		Total		JD Degs. Awd.
	#	%	#	%	#	%	#	%	#	%	#	%	
African Amer.	6	2.5	16	8.7	22	5.2	0	0.0	7	4.9	22	5.2	6
Amer. Indian	1	0.4	0	0.0	1	0.2	0	0.0	1	0.7	1	0.2	0
Asian Amer.	2	0.8	0	0.0	2	0.5	0	0.0	2	1.4	2	0.5	1
Mex. Amer.	0	0.0	0	0.0	0	0.0	0	0.0	0	0.0	0	0.0	0
Puerto Rican	0	0.0	0	0.0	0	0.0	0	0.0	0	0.0	0	0.0	0
Hispanic	0	0.0	1	0.5	1	0.2	0	0.0	1	0.7	1	0.2	2
Total Minority	9	3.8	17	9.2	26	6.2	0	0.0	11	7.6	26	6.2	9
For. Nation.	1	0.4	2	1.1	3	0.7	0	0.0	3	2.1	3	0.7	0
Caucasian	218	92.4	162	88.0	380	90.5	0	0.0	119	82.6	380	90.5	116
Unknown	8	3.4	3	1.6	11	2.6	0	0.0	11	7.6	11	2.6	2
Total	236	56.2	184	43.8	420	100.0	0	0.0	144	34.3	420		127

Tuition and Fees

	Resident	Nonresident
Full-time	$10,268	$19,868
Part-time	$0	$0

Living Expenses

Estimated living expenses for singles

Living on campus	Living off campus	Living at home
$12,422	$12,422	$5,032

University of Kentucky College of Law

ABA
Approved
Since
1925

GPA and LSAT Scores

	Total	Full-time	Part-time
# of apps	1,273	1,273	0
# of admits	397	397	0
# of matrics	144	144	0
75% GPA	3.81	3.81	0.00
25% GPA	3.33	3.33	0.00
75% LSAT	162	162	0
25% LSAT	156	156	0

Grants and Scholarships (from prior year)

	Total		Full-time		Part-time	
	#	%	#	%	#	%
Total # of students	413		413		0	
Total # receiving grants	227	55.0	227	55.0	0	0.0
Less than 1/2 tuition	121	29.3	121	29.3	0	0.0
Half to full tuition	58	14.0	58	14.0	0	0.0
Full tuition	28	6.8	28	6.8	0	0.0
More than full tuition	20	4.8	20	4.8	0	0.0
Median grant amount			$4,000		$0	

Informational and Library Resources

# of volumes and volume equivalents	464,984
# of titles	69,810
# of active serial subscriptions	3,854
Study seating capacity inside the library	345
# of professional librarians	6
Hours per week library is open	100
# of open, wired connections available to students	48
# of networked computers available for use by students	59
# of simultaneous wireless users	60
Require computer?	N

JD Attrition (from prior year)

	Academic	Other	Total	
	#	#	#	%
1st year	4	7	11	7.5%
2nd year	0	0	0	0.0%
3rd year	0	0	0	0.0%
4th year	0	0	0	0.0%

Employment

	Total	Percentage
Employment status known	126	100.0
Employment status unknown	0	0.0
Employed	121	96.0
Pursuing graduate degrees	5	4.0
Unemployed seeking employment	0	0.0
Unemployed not seeking employment	0	0.0

Type of Employment

# employed in law firms	72	59.5
# employed in business and industry	8	6.6
# employed in government	14	11.6
# employed in public interest	4	3.3
# employed as judicial clerks	22	18.2
# employed in academia	1	0.8

Geographic Location

# employed in state	95	78.5
# employed in foreign countries	1	0.8
# of states where employed		16

Bar Passage Rates

Jurisdiction	Kentucky		
Exam	Sum 03	Win 04	Total
# from school taking bar for the first time	101	10	111
School's pass rate for all first-time takers	86%	90%	86%
State's pass rate for all first-time takers	77%	84%	79%

University of Kentucky College of Law

209 Law Building, South Limestone St.
Lexington, KY 40506-0048
Phone: 859.257.1678; Fax: 859.323.1061
E-mail: dbakert@uky.edu; Website: www.uky.edu/Law

■ Introduction

The University of Kentucky College of Law is a small, state-supported law school on the main campus of the university in scenic Lexington, Kentucky, a city of approximately 250,000 in the center of the Bluegrass horse farm region. Founded in 1908, the college has been a member of the AALS since 1912 and has been accredited by the ABA since 1925. The faculty has wide experience in law practice and government service, as well as teaching and research. UK Law has a strong tradition of faculty concern about their students' progress and success. The curriculum offers broad training in the law and legal methods, drawing upon sources from all jurisdictions. Accordingly, UK Law graduates are prepared to practice in any of the 50 states.

■ Library and Physical Facilities

The college is self-contained in a contemporary building that provides all facilities for a complete program of legal education. Classrooms provide for student use of laptop computers with wired and wireless Internet access. The law library includes two large study areas and a number of study carrels that are wired for laptop access, and laptops are available for you to check out and use in the library.

■ Curriculum

UK Law offers a full-time program only, designed to be completed over three academic years or two and one-half years if you take classes during both summer sessions. The first-year program is prescribed. As an upper-level student, you can select from a full range of elective courses in both traditional and newly developing legal fields. After the first year, the only specific requirements are that you take a course in professional ethics and complete a seminar that involves substantial writing.

■ Legal Clinic

UK Law's Legal Clinic is located in its own building near the college. As a third-year student in the clinic course, you would represent low-income clients in a variety of civil legal matters: The clinic is supervised by a faculty member who was a very successful trial attorney for ten years.

■ Externships

UK Law offers four externships for course credit in which you can obtain experience in applied research, fact gathering, interviewing, counseling, negotiation, and trial advocacy.

The judicial clerkship externship enables you to serve as a law clerk for a local state or federal judge. The participating judges see that you are exposed to every aspect of motion and litigation practice.

In your third year you can be placed in the Fayette Commonwealth Attorney's Office, where you will gain criminal trial experience and participate in court proceedings under the close supervision of an attorney.

A unique program at the Federal Correctional Institute—Lexington, permits you to counsel inmates in civil and criminal matters.

In the externship with the Kentucky Innocence Project, you work with the Kentucky Department of Public Advocacy on selected criminal appeals where a claim of factual innocence is made.

■ Joint Degrees

The **JD/MBA** joint degree can be obtained in as little time as four years. You must apply and be admitted to both UK's College of Law and its Carol Martin Gatton College of Business and Economics.

If you are interested in a career in public administration, public service, or politics, you should consider the four-year **JD/MPA** joint-degree program with UK's Martin School of Public Policy. You must apply and be admitted to both programs.

If you are interested in a career in international law, public or private, in international business, or in government service in the international sector, you should consider the four-year **JD/MA** dual-degree program with UK's Patterson School of Diplomacy and International Commerce. You must apply and be admitted to both programs.

■ Student Activities

There are a variety of cocurricular activities in which you may earn course credit. The *Kentucky Law Journal* is the tenth oldest American law review and is edited entirely by students, as is the *Journal of Natural Resources and Environmental Law*. The college fields several moot court teams that participate in both national and international competitions. UK Law's Trial Advocacy teams advanced to national title competitions in five of the last six years.

UK Law's Student Bar Association serves as the law student governing body and student activities board. The SBA publishes a weekly student newspaper and sponsors regular student social events and community service activities. UK's SBA was recognized by the ABA as the best SBA in the nation in 2002.

The Student Public Interest Law Foundation, through grants and fundraising, sponsors 15–20 summer internships with public interest and public service organizations selected by the students who apply. Other active student groups include the Black Law Students

Association, the Women's Law Caucus, the International Law Society, the Environmental Law Society, the Equine Law Society, the Federalist Society, and the Intellectual Property Law Society.

■ Admission

Admission is considered and granted by the faculty Admissions Committee. Each file is reviewed completely and is voted on by the full committee. While your undergraduate record and LSAT score are the primary indicators of potential for success in law school, all other factors you present will be considered. You are urged to read the full description of the admission process contained in the UK Law Bulletin and to provide full information about your intellectual and nonacademic achievements. The February LSAT is the last examination accepted by the Admissions Committee for that year. Admission as a first-year student is for the fall term only.

■ Scholarships and Financial Aid

Scholarships for the first year of study are merit based and usually awarded to students whose credentials are exceptional. The largest and most prestigious scholarships are the Bert Combs Scholars, two of whom are chosen each year by an application and interview process, and the Ashland Inc. Legal Scholars, one of whom is chosen each year from among Kentucky residents by an application and interview process.

For all other first-year student scholarship awards, including the nonresident three-year tuition reduction scholarships, no application is necessary. All admitted students are considered automatically based upon their admission files. Fifty percent of the 2004 entering class received some form of scholarship award.

UK Law students are eligible for loan assistance through the Federal Direct Student Loan Program, as well as three national private loan programs. Admitted candidates are mailed the FAFSA form and complete information on financial aid. To receive forms and information prior to admission, contact UK's Student Financial Aid Office, 128 Funkhouser Building, University of Kentucky, Lexington, KY 40506-0054.

■ Career Services

UK Law students have the benefit of a large on-campus job interview program for regional employers, as well as national placement through the college's participation in off-campus interviewing conferences in Atlanta, Chicago, New York, and Washington, DC. The Career Services Office uses alumni contacts and a computerized service to connect students with employers.

UK Law's job placement rate is very good. For the 2003 graduating class, 100 percent were employed or in advanced-degree programs within nine months after graduation. A majority of UK Law graduates choose private practice, with 15–20 percent of each graduating class selected for prestigious state and federal judicial clerkships.

Applicant Profile

University of Kentucky College of Law
Probability of admission to the University of Kentucky College of Law, based on admission decisions for the 2003 entering class.

LSAT Score	3.75 - 4.00	3.50 - 3.74	3.25 - 3.49	3.00 - 3.24	2.75 - 2.99	2.50 - 2.74	2.25 - 2.49	Below 2.25	GPA not scaled
165 & Above									
160-164									
157-159									
155-156									
153-154									
150-152									
145-149									
Below 145									

Probable   Very Competitive   Somewhat Competitive   Possible   Unlikely

Lewis & Clark Law School

10015 SW Terwilliger Blvd.
Portland, OR 97219-7799
Phone: 800.303.4860 or 503.768.6613; Fax: 503.768.6793
E-mail: lawadmss@lclark.edu; Website: law.lclark.edu

ABA Approved Since 1970

The Basics

Type of school	Private
Term	Semester
Application deadline	3/1
Application fee	$50
Financial aid deadline	3/1
Can first year start other than fall?	No
Student to faculty ratio (fall)	13.6 to 1
Does the university offer:	
housing restricted to law students?	Yes
graduate housing for which law students are eligible?	No

Faculty and Administrators

	Total		Men		Women		Minorities	
	Fall	Spr	Fall	Spr	Fall	Spr	Fall	Spr
Full-time	41	42	26	27	15	15	2	2
Other Full-time	5	3	2	1	3	2	1	1
Deans, librarians, & others who teach	10	10	4	4	6	6	0	0
Part-time	29	34	17	22	12	11	1	0
Total	85	89	49	54	36	34	4	3

Curriculum

	Full-time	Part-time
Typical first-year section size	77	71
Is there typically a "small section" of the first-year class, other than Legal Writing, taught by full-time faculty	Yes	Yes
If yes, typical size offered last year	39	35
# of classroom course titles beyond 1st year curriculum		117
# of upper division courses, excluding seminars with an enrollment: Under 25		74
25-49		38
50-74		15
75-99		6
100+		0
# of seminars		31
# of seminar positions available		587
# of seminar positions filled	296	98
# of positions available in simulation courses		277
# of simulation positions filled	163	47
# of positions available in faculty supervised clinical courses		152
# of faculty supervised clinical positions filled	108	30
# involved in field placements	60	8
# involved in law journals	99	14
# involved in moot court or trial competitions	93	27
# of credit hours required to graduate		86

JD Enrollment and Ethnicity

	Men #	Men %	Women #	Women %	Full-time #	Full-time %	Part-time #	Part-time %	1st-year #	1st-year %	Total #	Total %	JD Degs. Awd.
African Amer.	8	2.1	10	2.8	10	1.9	8	3.8	5	2.2	18	2.4	6
Amer. Indian	7	1.8	7	1.9	8	1.5	6	2.9	5	2.2	14	1.9	6
Asian Amer.	27	7.1	41	11.3	47	8.8	21	10.0	29	12.5	68	9.2	17
Mex. Amer.	9	2.4	11	3.0	11	2.1	9	4.3	4	1.7	20	2.7	3
Puerto Rican	3	0.8	2	0.6	5	0.9	0	0.0	3	1.3	5	0.7	0
Hispanic	10	2.6	8	2.2	10	1.9	8	3.8	4	1.7	18	2.4	4
Total Minority	64	16.8	79	21.8	91	17.1	52	24.9	50	21.6	143	19.3	36
For. Nation.	5	1.3	7	1.9	5	0.9	7	3.3	6	2.6	12	1.6	7
Caucasian	272	71.6	245	67.7	387	72.6	130	62.2	160	69.0	517	69.7	139
Unknown	39	10.3	31	8.6	50	9.4	20	9.6	16	6.9	70	9.4	23
Total	380	51.2	362	48.8	533	71.8	209	28.2	232	31.3	742		205

Tuition and Fees

	Resident	Nonresident
Full-time	$25,334	$25,334
Part-time	$19,004	$19,004

Living Expenses

Estimated living expenses for singles

Living on campus	Living off campus	Living at home
N/A	$13,999	N/A

Lewis & Clark Law School

ABA Approved Since 1970

GPA and LSAT Scores

	Total	Full-time	Part-time
# of apps	2,479	2,294	185
# of admits	903	836	67
# of matrics	236	197	39
75% GPA	3.54	3.51	3.61
25% GPA	3.00	2.99	3.08
75% LSAT	164	164	164
25% LSAT	158	158	155

Grants and Scholarships (from prior year)

	Total		Full-time		Part-time	
	#	%	#	%	#	%
Total # of students	712		530		182	
Total # receiving grants	260	36.5	225	42.5	35	19.2
Less than 1/2 tuition	174	24.4	153	28.9	21	11.5
Half to full tuition	72	10.1	59	11.1	13	7.1
Full tuition	14	2.0	13	2.5	1	0.5
More than full tuition	0	0.0	0	0.0	0	0.0
Median grant amount			$10,000		$7,500	

Informational and Library Resources

# of volumes and volume equivalents	491,510
# of titles	91,593
# of active serial subscriptions	4,110
Study seating capacity inside the library	385
# of professional librarians	8
Hours per week library is open	113
# of open, wired connections available to students	948
# of networked computers available for use by students	95
# of simultaneous wireless users	500
Require computer?	N

JD Attrition (from prior year)

	Academic	Other	Total	
	#	#	#	%
1st year	1	10	11	4.7%
2nd year	0	6	6	2.7%
3rd year	4	1	5	2.2%
4th year	0	1	1	3.3%

Employment

	Total	Percentage
Employment status known	189	95.9
Employment status unknown	8	4.1
Employed	173	91.5
Pursuing graduate degrees	5	2.6
Unemployed seeking employment	4	2.1
Unemployed not seeking employment	7	3.7

Type of Employment

	Total	
# employed in law firms	83	48.0
# employed in business and industry	25	14.5
# employed in government	33	19.1
# employed in public interest	19	11.0
# employed as judicial clerks	11	6.4
# employed in academia	2	1.2

Geographic Location

# employed in state	116	67.1
# employed in foreign countries	0	0.0
# of states where employed	19	

Bar Passage Rates

Jurisdiction	Oregon		
Exam	Sum 03	Win 04	Total
# from school taking bar for the first time	125	26	151
School's pass rate for all first-time takers	78%	77%	77%
State's pass rate for all first-time takers	78%	76%	78%

Lewis & Clark Law School

10015 SW Terwilliger Blvd.
Portland, OR 97219-7799
Phone: 800.303.4860 or 503.768.6613; Fax: 503.768.6793
E-mail: lawadmss@lclark.edu; Website: law.lclark.edu

■ Introduction

Lewis & Clark Law School believes in a balanced approach to legal education that assures a solid theoretical foundation along with hands-on experience in practice. The campus is one of the most beautiful in the nation. Situated next to a state park, students are only a moment away from an extensive trail system used by joggers, walkers, and bicyclists.

■ Enrollment/Student Body

The approximately 700 students attending the Law School represent a spectrum of ages, experiences, and priorities. Business executives, scientists, students of politics, musicians, and school teachers—people from almost all of the analytical disciplines meet at the Law School in a common pursuit. The atmosphere is one of mutual support during a time of academic challenge. Students and faculty can often be found discussing questions long after class has ended.

■ Faculty

The full-time faculty were educated at the nation's most distinguished law schools. The faculty reflect a breadth of experience and interests that give depth and creative energy to their teaching. A number of faculty members have spent sabbaticals in recent years teaching in other countries; several have been Fulbright professors in such places as China, Greece, Germany, and Venezuela.

■ Library and Physical Facilities

The resources and staff of the Paul Boley Law Library, the largest law library in the state, and the second largest in the northwest, well exceed the standards set by the Association of American Law Schools.

Our collection includes extensive materials in Environmental Law, Federal Legislative History, Tax, Commercial Law, Intellectual Property, and Legal History. It is also the only academic law library in the country to be a Patent and Trademark Depository Library. Supporting our collection is a sophisticated computer infrastructure of instruction labs and local area networks.

In January 2002, the Law School completed a major expansion project, which consisted of remodeling the existing library and adding 40,000 square feet of exquisite study space, state-of-the-art classrooms, and computer labs equipped with the latest technology. The campus was also updated to accommodate wireless technology.

Framed by majestic fir trees, the campus is composed of contemporary buildings with both classrooms and a large state park within a moment's walk from the library.

Traditional student needs and those of individuals with disabilities are met through a variety of facilities.

■ Curriculum

The Law School confers both the JD degree and a specialized LLM in Environmental and Natural Resources Law. To earn a JD, a student must take a prescribed first-year set of courses. In the upper division, students must take a seminar, Constitutional Law II, and Professionalism, and fulfill two writing requirements. Students choose between a three-year day program and a four-year evening program. Admission criteria, faculty, academic opportunities, and graduation requirements are the same for each.

Because the Law School offers both a full-time and a part-time program, students have great flexibility in scheduling courses and in determining the pace at which they want to pursue law school. Classes are offered both during the day and in the evening. Many students transfer between divisions and use the summer school program to accelerate progress toward graduation. Regardless of the division in which a student is enrolled, students may select courses from either the day or evening schedule as they find appropriate.

■ Specific Special Programs

Certificates: By taking a group of upper-division courses approved by the faculty, and by maintaining a superior grade-point average in those courses, a student may earn a certificate showing a concentration in environmental and natural resources law, business law, tax law, intellectual property law, or criminal law.

The Law School has a nationally recognized natural resources and environmental law program. The school is also home to a strong business and commercial law program. The intellectual property law program is particularly dynamic. All the traditional areas of legal study are fully covered. Students who do not wish to pursue a certificate may choose to study another area of particular interest.

Clinical Opportunities, Externships, and Simulations: A student may create a schedule with precisely the mix of practical skills courses that fit that student's interests and needs. Students may choose among live client clinical experience, externships and internships, or simulation courses. The legal clinic located in downtown Portland offers students the opportunity to interview and counsel real clients, prepare documents, conduct trials, negotiate settlements, and prepare appeals. Externships place a student in full-time work for a semester or for a summer and require a substantial research paper and attendance at a special seminar. Externs are placed throughout the

United States and in foreign countries. Clinical internship seminars and environmental clinic are similar to externships but the student works only part-time, attending other classes during the semester. Clinical internship seminars include placements with in-house counsel, government agencies, law firms, and public interest, nonprofit organizations. Other courses such as moot courts, advanced advocacy, trial advocacy, criminal law seminar, estate planning seminar, corporate transactions seminar, and family mediation seminar involve extensive simulations.

■ Admission

Lewis & Clark affirmatively seeks a diverse student body. The Admission Committee makes a serious effort to consider each applicant as an individual. Factors such as college, program, length of time since the degree was obtained, experience, writing ability, and community activities are taken into consideration. Only those candidates with excellent professional promise are admitted. Academic attrition is low, averaging 2 to 4 percent.

■ Student Activities

Activities include two law reviews, *Environmental Law* and *Lewis & Clark Law Review*; the journal, *Animal Law*; numerous speakers on campus; programs that bring outstanding legal scholars to campus for lectures and seminars; and many student organizations reflecting the diverse make-up of the student body.

■ Expenses and Financial Aid

Approximately 40 percent of the students at Lewis & Clark receive some scholarship support during their law school career. The school annually awards Dean's Scholarships, Natural Resources Law Scholarships, Business Law Scholarships, Tax Law Scholarships, and Public Interest Law Scholarships. In addition, loan money and work-study funds are available. There is no separate application procedure for scholarship funds. Scholarship consideration is part of the admission process. Students are reviewed on the basis of undergraduate record, LSAT score, writing ability, and activities.

Students interested in loans need to apply for financial aid as early as possible and should not wait for an admission decision to begin the financial aid application. Applicants should submit the FAFSA (Free Application for Federal Student Aid) at *www.fafsa.ed.gov*.

■ Career Services

The Career Services Office maintains and runs an extraordinary number and variety of programs. In addition to posting clerk positions for law students and running the on-campus interviews, the office maintains an extensive mentoring program, runs dozens of panels each year on various areas of practice, and counsels individual students from the first year onward.

Applicant Profile

Lewis & Clark Law School

LSAT Score	GPA															
	3.75 +		3.50 - 3.74		3.25 - 3.49		3.00 - 3.24		2.75 - 2.99		2.50 - 2.74		Below 2.50		No GPA		Total	
	Apps	Adm	Apps	Adm	Apps	Adm	Apps	Adm	Apps	Adm	Apps	Adm	Apps	Adm	Apps	Adm	Apps	Adm
170-180	3	3	11	11	14	13	2	2	5	5	5	3	3	2	1	1	44	40
165-169	33	31	43	43	36	35	31	28	16	15	13	11	7	7	1	1	180	171
160-164	81	74	132	114	109	98	97	73	72	48	27	21	23	13	9	9	550	450
155-159	83	33	163	49	168	34	127	20	93	18	44	5	20	2	12	7	710	168
150-154	57	6	116	11	117	14	109	5	78	8	43	3	28	0	11	4	559	51
145-149	15	1	40	1	56	6	64	5	33	0	27	1	17	0	3	0	255	14
140-144	2	0	10	1	25	1	19	2	27	0	11	0	17	0	5	0	116	4
Below 140	1	0	4	0	7	0	7	0	5	0	6	0	10	0	6	0	46	0
Total	275	148	519	230	532	201	456	135	329	94	176	44	125	24	48	22	2460	898

Apps = Number of Applicants
Adm = Number Admitted
Reflects 99% of the total applicant pool.

This chart is to be used as a guide only. Nonnumerical factors are strongly considered for all applicants.

Louis D. Brandeis School of Law at the University of Louisville

University of Louisville
Louisville, KY 40292
Phone: 502.852.6364; Fax: 502.852.0862
E-mail: lawadmissions@louisville.edu; Website: www.louisville.edu/brandeislaw/

ABA Approved Since 1931

The Basics

Type of school	Public
Term	Semester
Application deadline	3/1 5/15
Application fee	$45
Financial aid deadline	4/15
Can first year start other than fall?	No
Student to faculty ratio (fall)	14.0 to 1
Does the university offer:	
housing restricted to law students?	No
graduate housing for which law students are eligible?	Yes

Faculty and Administrators

	Total		Men		Women		Minorities	
	Fall	Spr	Fall	Spr	Fall	Spr	Fall	Spr
Full-time	21	21	12	12	9	9	2	2
Other Full-time	0	0	0	0	0	0	0	0
Deans, librarians, & others who teach	7	7	5	5	2	2	1	1
Part-time	11	11	9	10	2	1	1	3
Total	**39**	**39**	**26**	**27**	**13**	**12**	**4**	**6**

Curriculum

	Full-time	Part-time
Typical first-year section size	49	42
Is there typically a "small section" of the first-year class, other than Legal Writing, taught by full-time faculty	No	No
If yes, typical size offered last year	0	0
# of classroom course titles beyond 1st year curriculum	58	

# of upper division courses, excluding seminars with an enrollment:	Under 25	28
	25-49	19
	50-74	12
	75-99	1
	100+	0

# of seminars	23	
# of seminar positions available	414	
# of seminar positions filled	215	93
# of positions available in simulation courses	581	
# of simulation positions filled	148	142
# of positions available in faculty supervised clinical courses	0	
# of faculty supervised clinical positions filled	0	0
# involved in field placements	102	25
# involved in law journals	53	7
# involved in moot court or trial competitions	41	6
# of credit hours required to graduate	90	

JD Enrollment and Ethnicity

	Men		Women		Full-time		Part-time		1st-year		Total		JD Degs. Awd.
	#	%	#	%	#	%	#	%	#	%	#	%	
African Amer.	5	2.8	7	3.4	8	2.7	4	4.3	3	2.2	12	3.1	7
Amer. Indian	1	0.6	0	0.0	1	0.3	0	0.0	1	0.7	1	0.3	0
Asian Amer.	2	1.1	10	4.9	10	3.4	2	2.1	3	2.2	12	3.1	0
Mex. Amer.	0	0.0	2	1.0	2	0.7	0	0.0	0	0.0	2	0.5	0
Puerto Rican	0	0.0	0	0.0	0	0.0	0	0.0	0	0.0	0	0.0	0
Hispanic	1	0.6	3	1.5	3	1.0	1	1.1	3	2.2	4	1.0	2
Total Minority	9	5.0	22	10.7	24	8.2	7	7.4	10	7.2	31	8.1	9
For. Nation.	0	0.0	1	0.5	1	0.3	0	0.0	0	0.0	1	0.3	2
Caucasian	169	93.9	177	86.3	259	89.0	87	92.6	126	90.6	346	89.9	109
Unknown	2	1.1	5	2.4	7	2.4	0	0.0	3	2.2	7	1.8	0
Total	180	46.8	205	53.2	291	75.6	94	24.4	139	36.1	385		120

Tuition and Fees

	Resident	Nonresident
Full-time	$9,200	$20,760
Part-time	$7,680	$17,300

Living Expenses

Estimated living expenses for singles

Living on campus	Living off campus	Living at home
$14,386	$14,386	$14,386

Louis D. Brandeis School of Law at the University of Louisville

*ABA
Approved
Since
1931*

GPA and LSAT Scores

	Total	Full-time	Part-time
# of apps	1,198	1,011	187
# of admits	296	229	67
# of matrics	134	97	37
75% GPA	3.75	3.79	3.70
25% GPA	3.06	3.12	2.94
75% LSAT	159	159	158
25% LSAT	153	154	149

Grants and Scholarships (from prior year)

	Total		Full-time		Part-time	
	#	%	#	%	#	%
Total # of students	390		297		93	
Total # receiving grants	158	40.5	141	47.5	17	18.3
Less than 1/2 tuition	111	28.5	103	34.7	8	8.6
Half to full tuition	44	11.3	35	11.8	9	9.7
Full tuition	2	0.5	2	0.7	0	0.0
More than full tuition	1	0.3	1	0.3	0	0.0
Median grant amount			$4,000		$5,000	

Informational and Library Resources

# of volumes and volume equivalents	425,516
# of titles	75,944
# of active serial subscriptions	5,408
Study seating capacity inside the library	441
# of professional librarians	5
Hours per week library is open	89
# of open, wired connections available to students	6
# of networked computers available for use by students	27
# of simultaneous wireless users	99
Require computer?	N

JD Attrition (from prior year)

	Academic	Other	Total	
	#	#	#	%
1st year	12	4	16	11.2%
2nd year	2	3	5	4.0%
3rd year	0	0	0	0.0%
4th year	0	0	0	0.0%

Employment

	Total	Percentage
Employment status known	113	100.0
Employment status unknown	0	0.0
Employed	107	94.7
Pursuing graduate degrees	3	2.7
Unemployed seeking employment	3	2.7
Unemployed not seeking employment	0	0.0

Type of Employment

# employed in law firms	60	56.1
# employed in business and industry	15	14.0
# employed in government	24	22.4
# employed in public interest	2	1.9
# employed as judicial clerks	4	3.7
# employed in academia	2	1.9

Geographic Location

# employed in state	84	78.5
# employed in foreign countries	1	0.9
# of states where employed	11	

Bar Passage Rates

Jurisdiction	Kentucky		
Exam	Sum 03	Win 04	Total
# from school taking bar for the first time	83	18	101
School's pass rate for all first-time takers	76%	83%	77%
State's pass rate for all first-time takers	77%	84%	79%

Louis D. Brandeis School of Law at the University of Louisville

University of Louisville
Louisville, KY 40292
Phone: 502.852.6364; Fax: 502.852.0862
E-mail: lawadmissions@louisville.edu; Website: www.louisville.edu/brandeislaw/

■ Introduction

Founded in 1846, the Louis D. Brandeis School of Law at the University of Louisville is Kentucky's oldest law school and America's fifth oldest in continuous operation. Heir to the legacy of Justice Louis D. Brandeis, the school is distinguished by a rich history, national outreach, and profound dedication to public service. It is an integral part of the University of Louisville, a public institution and major research center founded in 1798. The metropolitan area, with a population of approximately one million, combines a gracious ambience of southern hospitality with cultural, aesthetic, and recreational attractions (including historic Churchill Downs, Actors' Theatre of Louisville, and the J.B. Speed Art Museum).

■ Enrollment/Student Body

The Brandeis School of Law enrolls first-year students beginning in the fall semester, which starts in August. Candidates may apply for admission to either the full-time (three-year) division or the part-time (four-year) division. Part-time students take their first-year courses Monday through Thursday evenings and generally continue to take evening courses throughout their program.

Candidates must have completed a bachelor's degree at an accredited college or university prior to enrollment. All undergraduate majors are acceptable, with courses that emphasize critical reasoning, writing, and communication skills recognized as good preparation for the study of law.

With the entering class numbering about 135 each fall, first-year class size seldom exceeds 50. Basic Legal Skills (the first-year writing course) has classes that are only half that size.

The entire student body (composed of almost as many women as men) numbers about 400, enabling every student to be a name, not just a number, and presenting the opportunity to develop close relationships with their professors.

■ Faculty

With 33 full-time faculty members (12 women and 4 faculty of color) and numerous part-time or adjunct teachers, the faculty/student ratio is one of the best in the country at 1 to 14.

The faculty gives a high priority to excellence in teaching and accessibility to students. They are also a community of active scholars.

■ Library and Physical Facilities

The law school is housed in Wilson W. Wyatt Hall, a gracious colonial-style building overlooking the formal entrance to the University of Louisville Belknap campus —a traditional college campus located in an urban setting. The University of Louisville also includes two other campuses: the Health Sciences Center (housing the Medical and Dental schools) and the Shelby Campus, which offers continuing education classes.

The school's law library houses a collection of more than 300,000 volumes and microform volume equivalents, carefully selected to aid student instruction and promote research. The library also has wireless service.

The library still receives original briefs of the US Supreme Court—a rare distinction for a law school and a practice originated by Justice Brandeis that continues today.

Students have access to Westlaw, LexisNexis, the Internet, and word processing programs through two computer laboratories and via their home computers. Interactive video workstations allow students to learn legal concepts by viewing and participating in real-time situations.

■ Curriculum

The law school full-time day division and part-time evening division share the same curriculum, faculty, and academic standards. After basic courses in the first year, students take core courses in doctrinal subjects, advanced research and writing, and professional responsibility. Students also may choose from among a rich variety of specialized and interdisciplinary electives. The Brandeis School of Law conducts a summer enrichment program for a limited number of newly admitted students.

A highly successful academic support program provides tutoring groups in all first-year courses and guidance in study and test-taking skills, as well as individual advising and counseling.

■ Samuel L. Greenebaum Public Service Program

Reflecting the spirit of Justice Louis D. Brandeis, the School of Law was one of America's first five law schools to adopt public service as part of the prescribed course of study. Through this public service work, students develop lawyering skills, serve their communities, and establish professional values.

■ Special Programs

The Brandeis School of Law offers several dual-degree programs designed to enhance the student's understanding, skills, and career opportunities in both areas of study. Each requires application and admission to both participating schools: Master of Business Administration/Juris Doctor (MBA/JD); Master of Science in Social Work/Juris Doctor (MSSW/JD); Juris Doctor/Master of Arts in Humanities (JD/MA); Juris Doctor/Master of

Louis D. Brandeis School of Law at the University of Louisville

Divinity—at the Louisville Presbyterian Theological Seminary (JD/MDiv); and Juris Doctor/Master of Arts in Political Science (JD/MAPS).

The school also operates clinical externship programs in which upper-class students, with supervision, represent clients and appear in court. A third-year student may receive credit by working in the criminal arena (DA or PD), in tax (IRS), in the judicial branch (various judges), in family law (Center for Women and Families or Legal Aid Society), or in technology (University of Louisville Office of Technology Transfer).

International experience is another unique opportunity. The Brandeis School offers faculty or student exchanges with law schools in France, England, Germany, Finland, Australia, and South Africa.

■ Practical Success

Participating annually in about a dozen moot court and skills competitions, the law school has won several regional and national championships.

Students are also actively involved in writing for and publishing the *Brandeis Law Journal* and the *Journal of Law and Education*. Graduates of the Brandeis School of Law consistently achieve high employment rates.

■ Admission

Applicants are urged to apply beginning **October 1** and before **March 1** of the year they intend to enter law school. However, applications received prior to **May 15** will be given consideration on a space-available basis. Both full-time and part-time first-year students must start classes in the fall semester.

For the best chance of consideration, it is recommended that the LSAT be taken no later than February. LSAT scores taken in June, prior to the first semester of enrollment, will be considered only under extraordinary circumstances.

Applicant Profile

Louis D. Brandeis School of Law at the University of Louisville
This grid includes only applicants who earned 120-180 LSAT scores under standard administrations.

LSAT Score	3.75 +		3.50 - 3.74		3.25 - 3.49		3.00 - 3.24		2.75 - 2.99		2.50 - 2.74		2.25 - 2.49		2.00 - 2.24		Below 2.00		No GPA		Total	
	Apps	Adm	Apps	Adm	Apps	Adm	Apps	Adm	Apps	Adm	Apps	Adm	Apps	Adm	Apps	Adm	Apps	Adm	Apps	Adm	Apps	Adm
175-180	0	0	0	0	0	0	0	0	0	0	0	0	0	0	0	0	0	0	0	0	0	0
170-174	0	0	0	0	0	0	0	0	0	0	0	0	0	0	0	0	0	0	0	0	0	0
165-169	4	2	5	4	5	3	1	1	2	1	2	1	1	0	0	0	0	0	0	0	20	12
160-164	20	19	15	13	4	2	16	14	14	8	9	3	6	1	3	1	0	0	0	0	87	61
155-159	41	33	58	46	52	33	57	28	31	9	20	7	11	1	7	0	1	0	0	0	278	157
150-154	61	16	68	5	82	7	83	4	51	1	31	3	12	0	7	0	0	0	1	0	396	36
145-149	23	4	38	2	44	1	45	3	36	2	24	0	10	0	4	0	1	0	8	0	233	12
140-144	7	0	15	2	18	0	20	0	15	0	15	0	12	0	4	0	1	0	1	0	108	2
120-139	4	0	7	0	5	0	7	0	7	0	15	0	9	0	6	0	1	0	4	0	65	0
Total	160	74	206	72	210	46	229	50	156	21	116	14	61	2	31	1	4	0	14	0	1187	280

Apps = Number of Applicants
Adm = Number Admitted
Reflects 99% of the total applicant pool.

The faculty admission committee reads all files very carefully. Beyond numerical indicators (LSAT scores and grade-point averages), the committee looks for individuals with unique attributes who will bring diversity to the entering class and good character to the legal profession. Numerical quantifiers are not automatic grounds for admission or denial.

Louisiana State University, Paul M. Hebert Law Center

202 Law Center
Baton Rouge, LA 70803
Phone: 225.578.8646; Fax: 225.578.8647
E-mail: admissions@law.lsu.edu; Website: www.law.lsu.edu

ABA Approved Since 1926

The Basics

Type of school	Public
Term	Semester
Application deadline	2/1
Application fee	$25
Financial aid deadline	4/1
Can first year start other than fall?	No
Student to faculty ratio (fall)	16.4 to 1
Does the university offer:	
housing restricted to law students?	No
graduate housing for which law students are eligible?	No

Faculty and Administrators

	Total		Men		Women		Minorities	
	Fall	Spr	Fall	Spr	Fall	Spr	Fall	Spr
Full-time	33	33	26	27	7	6	4	4
Other Full-time	9	10	5	6	4	4	0	4
Deans, librarians, & others who teach	5	5	5	5	0	0	0	0
Part-time	28	31	23	28	4	3	2	3
Total	75	79	59	66	15	13	6	11

Curriculum

	Full-time	Part-time
Typical first-year section size	71	0
Is there typically a "small section" of the first-year class, other than Legal Writing, taught by full-time faculty	Yes	No
If yes, typical size offered last year	40	0
# of classroom course titles beyond 1st year curriculum	74	

# of upper division courses, excluding seminars with an enrollment:		
Under 25	43	
25-49	46	
50-74	5	
75-99	13	
100+	1	

# of seminars	12	
# of seminar positions available	220	
# of seminar positions filled	148	0
# of positions available in simulation courses	572	
# of simulation positions filled	487	0
# of positions available in faculty supervised clinical courses	0	
# of faculty supervised clinical positions filled	0	0
# involved in field placements	25	0
# involved in law journals	53	0
# involved in moot court or trial competitions	125	0
# of credit hours required to graduate	97	

JD Enrollment and Ethnicity

	Men		Women		Full-time		Part-time		1st-year		Total		JD Degs. Awd.
	#	%	#	%	#	%	#	%	#	%	#	%	
African Amer.	20	6.3	41	12.1	57	8.9	4	23.5	27	12.8	61	9.3	29
Amer. Indian	1	0.3	1	0.3	2	0.3	0	0.0	1	0.5	2	0.3	2
Asian Amer.	6	1.9	4	1.2	9	1.4	1	5.9	4	1.9	10	1.5	1
Mex. Amer.	0	0.0	0	0.0	0	0.0	0	0.0	0	0.0	0	0.0	0
Puerto Rican	0	0.0	0	0.0	0	0.0	0	0.0	0	0.0	0	0.0	0
Hispanic	3	0.9	6	1.8	9	1.4	0	0.0	3	1.4	9	1.4	1
Total Minority	30	9.5	52	15.3	77	12.1	5	29.4	35	16.6	82	12.5	33
For. Nation.	0	0.0	0	0.0	0	0.0	0	0.0	0	0.0	0	0.0	0
Caucasian	254	80.1	268	79.1	517	80.9	5	29.4	152	72.0	522	79.6	186
Unknown	33	10.4	19	5.6	45	7.0	7	41.2	24	11.4	52	7.9	3
Total	317	48.3	339	51.7	639	97.4	17	2.6	211	32.2	656		222

Tuition and Fees

	Resident	Nonresident
Full-time	$11,650	$20,746
Part-time	$0	$0

Living Expenses

Estimated living expenses for singles

Living on campus	Living off campus	Living at home
$10,450	$12,128	$6,917

Louisiana State University, Paul M. Hebert Law Center

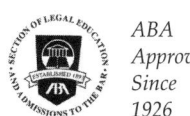

*ABA
Approved
Since
1926*

GPA and LSAT Scores

	Total	Full-time	Part-time
# of apps	1,846	1,846	0
# of admits	473	473	0
# of matrics	213	213	0
75% GPA	0.00	3.76	0.00
25% GPA	0.00	3.25	0.00
75% LSAT	0	158	0
25% LSAT	0	151	0

Grants and Scholarships (from prior year)

	Total		Full-time		Part-time	
	#	%	#	%	#	%
Total # of students	681		669		12	
Total # receiving grants	257	37.7	257	38.4	0	0.0
Less than 1/2 tuition	168	24.7	168	25.1	0	0.0
Half to full tuition	70	10.3	70	10.5	0	0.0
Full tuition	0	0.0	0	0.0	0	0.0
More than full tuition	19	2.8	19	2.8	0	0.0
Median grant amount			$2,739		$0	

Informational and Library Resources

# of volumes and volume equivalents	826,519
# of titles	192,619
# of active serial subscriptions	12,229
Study seating capacity inside the library	461
# of professional librarians	9
Hours per week library is open	101
# of open, wired connections available to students	61
# of networked computers available for use by students	58
# of simultaneous wireless users	160
Require computer?	N

JD Attrition (from prior year)

	Academic	Other	Total	
	#	#	#	%
1st year	7	5	12	4.7%
2nd year	0	2	2	1.0%
3rd year	0	1	1	0.4%
4th year	0	0	0	0.0%

Employment

	Total	Percentage
Employment status known	176	95.1
Employment status unknown	9	4.9
Employed	153	86.9
Pursuing graduate degrees	7	4.0
Unemployed seeking employment	15	8.5
Unemployed not seeking employment	1	0.6

Type of Employment

	Total	Percentage
# employed in law firms	99	64.7
# employed in business and industry	6	3.9
# employed in government	11	7.2
# employed in public interest	0	0.0
# employed as judicial clerks	37	24.2
# employed in academia	0	0.0

Geographic Location

	Total	Percentage
# employed in state	127	83.0
# employed in foreign countries	0	0.0
# of states where employed	13	

Bar Passage Rates

Jurisdiction	Louisiana		
Exam	Sum 03	Win 04	Total
# from school taking bar for the first time	167	5	172
School's pass rate for all first-time takers	74%	40%	73%
State's pass rate for all first-time takers	62%	60%	61%

Louisiana State University, Paul M. Hebert Law Center

202 Law Center
Baton Rouge, LA 70803
Phone: 225.578.8646; Fax: 225.578.8647
E-mail: admissions@law.lsu.edu; Website: www.law.lsu.edu

■ Introduction

The Louisiana State University Law Center was originally established as the Louisiana State University Law School in 1906, pursuant to an authorization contained in the university charter. In 1979, the Law Center was renamed the Paul M. Hebert Law Center of Louisiana State University. The Law Center holds membership in the AALS and is on the approved list of the ABA.

■ Library and Physical Facilities

The Law Center, completed in October 1969, added extensive facilities to the original Law Center building, dedicated in 1938. This complex provides classroom areas, seminar and discussion rooms, and meeting areas as well as a courtroom. Separate offices for student research and student activities such as the *Louisiana Law Review*, Moot Court Board, and Student Bar Association are included in the facility. The law library, housed in the complex, pro-vides one of the most complete collections of Roman and modern civil law reports and materials in the country. Library resources include reading and discussion rooms, study carrels, computer labs, and audiovisual facilities. Students also have access to other campus facilities, including the Student Health Center, residential housing, and the Sports Recreational Complex.

■ Curriculum

The LSU Law Center established a joint JD/BCL program through which its graduates will receive the JD (Juris Doctor) degree and a BCL (Bachelor of Civil Law) degree. First-year students follow a prescribed curriculum and, thereafter, students will choose a wide variety of courses to complete their degrees. An orientation program and library tour introduces the first-year class to the study of law. The Law Center's dedication to the study of both the civil and the common law prepares its graduates to practice in any state and in many foreign countries. Seven semesters of resident study are required for the degree. In addition to its full-time law faculty, each semester the LSU Law Center invites a number of distinguished lecturers, including practicing attorneys and legal scholars, to teach courses in their areas of specialty. A number of faculty members have law degrees from foreign countries.

■ Summer Session Abroad

The Law Center conducts a six-week summer program in France. All classes are conducted in English and are designed to meet the requirements of the ABA and AALS.

■ Special Programs

A wide variety of courses affords each student the opportunity to participate in the preparation and trial of mock cases, both civil and criminal, and also to develop skill in legal negotiation and counseling. LSU sponsors and encourages student participation in national trial and appellate competitions throughout the school year.

In cooperation with the Center for Continuing Professional Development, the Law Center presents seminars, institutes, and conferences for practicing lawyers.

The LSU Law Center admits candidates for the degrees of Master of Laws (LLM) and Master of Civil Law (MCL). The program is highly selective and admits students with exceptional ability.

■ Admission

The Admissions Committee considers many factors in reaching admission decisions. An admission index is cal-culated for each applicant. The index is equal to 10 times the applicant's undergraduate grade-point average, added to the applicant's average LSAT score ((10xUGPA) + LSAT). Although the index is the most important factor in the admission decision, the Admissions Committee also considers other factors, including the ability to analyze and write well, as demonstrated by the personal statement and the written portion of the LSAT; two letters of recommenda-tion from teachers and others who can express an opinion on the applicant's aptitude for the study of law; the rigor of the undergraduate program of study and grade trends; extracurricular activities; work experience or military service; social and economic background; and other evidence of an applicant's aptitude for the study of law and likely contribution to academic and community life. A baccalaureate degree from an accredited college or university is required for admission.

Applicants are advised to take the LSAT in October, and not later than December, prior to the year in which they seek admission to the Law Center. The Law Center admits students only in the fall and only for full-time study. There are no night courses offered. Transfer applications are considered.

Louisiana State University assures equal opportunity for all qualified persons without regard to race, color, religion, sexual orientation, national origin, age, disability, marital status, or veteran's status in the admission to, participation in, or employment in the programs and activities that the university operates.

■ Joint Programs

The LSU Law Center offers the JD/BCL-MPA and the JD/BCL-MBA joint-degree programs. Admission

Louisiana State University, Paul M. Hebert Law Center

requirements for each program are listed in the LSU Graduate School Catalog and the Law Center Catalog. Students must apply separately for each program.

■ Student Activities

The *Louisiana Law Review* was established to encourage high-quality legal scholarship in the student body, to contribute to the development of the law by scholarly criticism and analysis, and to serve the bar of Louisiana by comments and discussion of current cases and legal problems. It is edited by a board of student editors with faculty cooperation.

The Louisiana Chapter of the Order of the Coif, a national honorary law fraternity, was established in the Law Center in 1942. Election to the Order of the Coif is recognized as the highest honor a law student may receive.

Since a large number of graduates of the Law Center go directly into practice, the LSU Law Center has an extensive Trial Advocacy Program in which moot court training is offered both for trial work and in appellate argument.

All students in the Law Center are members of the Student Bar Association. This association promotes and coordinates student activities within the Law Center and serves as an instructional medium for postgraduate bar association activities.

■ Expenses and Financial Aid

A number of loan funds are available to help deserving students who need financial assistance to continue their education. All such funds are subject to the policies and regulations authorized by the LSU Student Loan Fund Committee. Detailed information on all loan funds may be secured by contacting the Student Loan Section, LSU Office of Financial Aid and Scholarships, 202 Himes Hall, Baton Rouge, LA 70803.

■ Career Services

The Career Services Office of the Law Center is dedicated to enhancing the personal growth and professional opportunities for LSU law students and alumni. The office offers a series of workshops and individual counseling sessions to assist students as they search for summer and permanent employment opportunities. More than 165 legal employers visit the school each year to recruit our students.

Applicant Profile

Louisiana State University, Paul M. Hebert Law Center
This grid includes only applicants who earned 120-180 LSAT scores under standard administrations.

LSAT Score	3.75 +		3.50 - 3.74		3.25 - 3.49		3.00 - 3.24		2.75 - 2.99		2.50 - 2.74		2.25 - 2.49		2.00 - 2.24		Below 2.00		No GPA		Total	
	Apps	Adm	Apps	Adm	Apps	Adm	Apps	Adm	Apps	Adm	Apps	Adm	Apps	Adm	Apps	Adm	Apps	Adm	Apps	Adm	Apps	Adm
175-180	0	0	0	0	0	0	0	0	0	0	0	0	0	0	0	0	0	0	0	0	0	0
170-174	0	0	1	1	0	0	0	0	0	0	0	0	0	0	0	0	0	0	0	0	1	1
165-169	7	7	0	0	3	2	2	1	0	0	3	3	1	0	0	0	0	0	0	0	16	13
160-164	26	24	18	17	17	15	10	10	16	10	13	4	4	0	2	0	0	0	2	1	108	81
155-159	41	40	61	56	66	43	66	23	49	9	21	4	13	1	2	0	2	0	2	0	323	176
150-154	59	39	118	43	146	33	123	21	78	5	45	5	18	1	8	0	1	0	3	0	599	147
145-149	38	14	76	9	113	7	119	7	66	2	51	3	27	0	6	0	1	0	8	2	505	44
140-144	23	6	15	1	29	2	47	1	31	0	27	0	14	0	6	0	3	0	3	0	198	10
135-139	1	0	6	0	12	0	10	0	13	0	6	0	5	0	2	0	1	0	2	0	58	0
130-134	1	0	0	0	3	0	3	0	2	0	2	0	2	0	1	0	0	0	2	0	16	0
125-129	0	0	0	0	0	0	0	0	0	0	0	0	2	0	1	0	0	0	1	0	4	0
120-124	0	0	0	0	0	0	0	0	0	0	0	0	0	0	0	0	0	0	0	0	0	0
Total	196	130	295	127	389	102	380	63	255	26	168	19	86	2	28	0	8	0	23	3	1828	472

Apps = Number of Applicants
Adm = Number Admitted
Reflects 99% of the total applicant pool.

Loyola Law School, Loyola Marymount University

919 Albany Street
Los Angeles, CA 90015
Phone: 213.736.1074; Fax: 213.736.6523
E-mail: admissions@lls.edu; Website: www.lls.edu

ABA
Approved
Since
1935

The Basics

Type of school	Private
Term	Semester
Application deadline	2/2 4/15
Application fee	$50
Financial aid deadline	3/2
Can first year start other than fall?	No
Student to faculty ratio (fall)	16.4 to 1
Does the university offer:	
housing restricted to law students?	No
graduate housing for which law students are eligible?	No

Faculty and Administrators

	Total		Men		Women		Minorities	
	Fall	Spr	Fall	Spr	Fall	Spr	Fall	Spr
Full-time	62	63	34	34	28	29	14	14
Other Full-time	2	2	1	1	1	1	1	1
Deans, librarians, & others who teach	7	7	6	6	1	1	1	1
Part-time	55	54	40	43	15	11	5	8
Total	126	126	81	84	45	42	21	24

Curriculum

		Full-time	Part-time
Typical first-year section size		85	86
Is there typically a "small section" of the first-year class, other than Legal Writing, taught by full-time faculty		No	No
If yes, typical size offered last year		0	0
# of classroom course titles beyond 1st year curriculum		153	
# of upper division courses, excluding seminars with an enrollment:	Under 25	144	
	25-49	50	
	50-74	14	
	75-99	13	
	100+	9	
# of seminars		23	
# of seminar positions available		508	
# of seminar positions filled		200	139
# of positions available in simulation courses		736	
# of simulation positions filled		450	178
# of positions available in faculty supervised clinical courses		150	
# of faculty supervised clinical positions filled		104	32
# involved in field placements		225	54
# involved in law journals		177	24
# involved in moot court or trial competitions		126	15
# of credit hours required to graduate		87	

JD Enrollment and Ethnicity

	Men		Women		Full-time		Part-time		1st-year		Total		JD Degs. Awd.
	#	%	#	%	#	%	#	%	#	%	#	%	
African Amer.	27	3.8	34	5.5	43	4.3	18	5.4	22	5.2	61	4.6	14
Amer. Indian	4	0.6	5	0.8	5	0.5	4	1.2	1	0.2	9	0.7	2
Asian Amer.	137	19.2	164	26.5	230	23.0	71	21.5	93	21.9	301	22.6	86
Mex. Amer.	43	6.0	42	6.8	65	6.5	20	6.0	23	5.4	85	6.4	32
Puerto Rican	0	0.0	3	0.5	3	0.3	0	0.0	1	0.2	3	0.2	1
Hispanic	29	4.1	24	3.9	40	4.0	13	3.9	27	6.4	53	4.0	12
Total Minority	240	33.7	272	44.0	386	38.6	126	38.1	167	39.3	512	38.5	147
For. Nation.	4	0.6	3	0.5	6	0.6	1	0.3	4	0.9	7	0.5	4
Caucasian	423	59.3	316	51.1	550	55.0	189	57.1	244	57.4	739	55.5	218
Unknown	46	6.5	27	4.4	58	5.8	15	4.5	10	2.4	73	5.5	32
Total	713	53.6	618	46.4	1000	75.1	331	24.9	425	31.9	1331		401

Tuition and Fees

	Resident	Nonresident
Full-time	$29,828	$29,828
Part-time	$20,022	$20,022

Living Expenses

Estimated living expenses for singles

Living on campus	Living off campus	Living at home
N/A	$17,772	$9,934

Loyola Law School, Loyola Marymount University

*ABA
Approved
Since
1935*

GPA and LSAT Scores

	Total	Full-time	Part-time
# of apps	5,219	4,582	637
# of admits	1,052	932	120
# of matrics	422	343	79
75% GPA	3.58	3.58	3.55
25% GPA	3.10	3.14	2.94
75% LSAT	164	164	162
25% LSAT	159	159	155

Grants and Scholarships (from prior year)

	Total #	Total %	Full-time #	Full-time %	Part-time #	Part-time %
Total # of students	1,313		967		346	
Total # receiving grants	165	12.6	134	13.9	31	9.0
Less than 1/2 tuition	23	1.8	19	2.0	4	1.2
Half to full tuition	61	4.6	42	4.3	19	5.5
Full tuition	27	2.1	26	2.7	1	0.3
More than full tuition	54	4.1	47	4.9	7	2.0
Median grant amount			$28,074		$15,000	

Informational and Library Resources

# of volumes and volume equivalents	558,721
# of titles	247,559
# of active serial subscriptions	7,307
Study seating capacity inside the library	549
# of professional librarians	10
Hours per week library is open	108
# of open, wired connections available to students	852
# of networked computers available for use by students	157
# of simultaneous wireless users	600
Require computer?	N

JD Attrition (from prior year)

	Academic #	Other #	Total #	Total %
1st year	11	15	26	6.4%
2nd year	3	19	22	5.2%
3rd year	5	3	8	2.1%
4th year	1	3	4	4.2%

Employment

	Total	Percentage
Employment status known	405	100.0
Employment status unknown	0	0.0
Employed	383	94.6
Pursuing graduate degrees	2	0.5
Unemployed seeking employment	14	3.5
Unemployed not seeking employment	6	1.5

Type of Employment

# employed in law firms	259	67.6
# employed in business and industry	62	16.2
# employed in government	22	5.7
# employed in public interest	23	6.0
# employed as judicial clerks	4	1.0
# employed in academia	8	2.1

Geographic Location

# employed in state	362	94.5
# employed in foreign countries	0	0.0
# of states where employed	13	

Bar Passage Rates

Jurisdiction	California		
Exam	Sum 03	Win 04	Total
# from school taking bar for the first time	361	35	396
School's pass rate for all first-time takers	70%	57%	68%
State's pass rate for all first-time takers	63%	47%	60%

Loyola Law School, Loyola Marymount University

919 Albany Street
Los Angeles, CA 90015
Phone: 213.736.1074; Fax: 213.736.6523
E-mail: admissions@lls.edu; Website: www.lls.edu

■ Law School and Campus

Loyola Law School was founded in 1920 and is California's largest law school. Having graduated more than 12,000 men and women, Loyola has had a profound effect on the legal profession and American history. Known best for producing many of our nation's most exciting and influential attorneys, Loyola instills in its graduates a deep commitment to public service and ethical practice while emphasizing the philosophical, analytical, and professional skills essential to the lawyering process.

The Law School, a division of Loyola Marymount University (LMU), includes 1,350 full-time day and part-time evening students, nearly 140 full-time and adjunct faculty, and 110 administrative and technical staff. Housed on a modern, innovative campus, including eight buildings, a spacious parking facility, green lawns, and athletic courts, Loyola encompasses an entire city block in downtown Los Angeles. The campus, designed by architect Frank Gehry, is both unique and inviting.

The William M. Rains Law Library is one of the largest private law libraries in the western United States, providing extensive research capabilities with a collection of over 500,000 volumes and the latest advances in information technology.

■ Juris Doctor

The Juris Doctor prepares students to be effective lawyers and judges in any jurisdiction in the United States. Loyola recognizes that a quality education must do more than simply prepare a student to file a lawsuit or draft a contract. The program is designed to teach students to think and reason critically. The faculty strives to instill in students a respect and appreciation for the law and a desire to improve the society in which we live. The Juris Doctor is offered in both a full-time, three-year day division and a part-time, four-year evening division.

■ Master of Laws

Loyola also offers two Master of Laws (LLM) degrees—one in Taxation and another in American Law and International Legal Practice. The LLM in Taxation degree distinguishes tax specialists by its advanced legal theory, tax policy, and scholarship. Law students can take advanced tax courses for double credit—counting toward both the Juris Doctor and the Tax LLM. The Master of Laws program in American Law and International Legal Practice provides American and international law school graduates the unique opportunity to earn an American LLM from Loyola while attending the University of Bologna, a premiere European university.

■ JD/ MBA and International JD/MBA

Loyola Law School and the Graduate Program of the College of Business Administration of Loyola Marymount University offer a dual-degree program in law and business. Graduates of the program receive the Juris Doctor degree (JD) and the Master of Business Administration (MBA). The International Master of Business Administration program may also be completed concurrently with the Law School curriculum. A Graduate Certificate in International Business will be awarded with the MBA.

The dual-degree program provides for the achievement of both degrees in four years instead of the five normally required to complete the degree programs separately. The program is only open to full-time day students. Students may receive up to 12 units of business classes toward the 87 units required to earn a JD and may be allowed to count up to 12 units of law classes toward the 54 units required to earn an MBA.

Applicants must apply and be accepted separately to the Law School and the MBA program. Applicants must also apply and be accepted to the JD/MBA program. Applications for the MBA and JD/MBA program may be submitted in the same year as the Law School application or during the first year of Law School. Interested applicants should contact the LMU College of Business Administration to request an application for the MBA program and Law School Admissions Office to request an application for the JD/MBA program.

■ Faculty

The faculty is composed of scholars who publish innovative theories, influencing the development and direction of the legal profession. They draft hundreds of scholarly articles and books, advise law firms and agencies on recent developments, and lecture at universities around the world. They also include seasoned attorneys with extensive and varied practice experience as Supreme Court clerks, public interest lawyers, agency chiefs, and law firm partners. But most importantly, the Loyola faculty are exceptional teachers who maintain an open door to encourage free and continuous interaction with their students.

■ Curriculum

The curriculum is designed to provide the knowledge and skills that will enable students to become excellent practicing lawyers. The curriculum integrates traditional instruction in legal doctrine and theory with a special commitment to the development of legal skills.

The Law School has a wide variety of course offerings and seminars in business/corporate law, commercial law, constitutional and civil rights law, criminal law, environmental law, cyberlaw/entertainment/sports law, international law, jurisprudence, law and social policy, litigation and legal skills, personal injury law, property law, public law, and taxation law.

■ Innovative Programs

Loyola demonstrates its commitment to public service by requiring all students to donate 40 hours to working in the **public interest** sector. The **Entertainment Law Practicum** provides students with an opportunity to get hands-on experience through field placements at television networks, major movie studios, record companies, talent agencies, and entertainment law firms. **International Programs** allow upper-division students to study abroad in Costa Rica, China, and Italy. The **Public Interest Law Department** coordinates public interest activities, counsels students about law practice and fellowships, and administers the five public service programs. The **Center for Ethical Lawyering** is one of Loyola's greatest strengths, featuring specialized training courses and externships designed to prepare students for the courtroom. Loyola students have won

numerous international and national moot court competitions in recent years.

■ Career Services

The Office of Career Services offers a wealth of services, programs, and resources to students and alumni. A large professional staff counsels and assists students and graduates in the job development process. Hundreds of national, international, and regional employers recruit from Loyola annually. Graduates are employed by the nation's most prestigious private and public legal organizations.

■ Admission/Financial Aid/Scholarships

Applications for admission are accepted on a rolling basis. Deadlines are February 2 for the day program and April 15 for the evening program. Early applicants have greater prospects for gaining admission and receiving scholarship awards. Three different types of scholarships are awarded: merit, diversity/merit, and public interest/merit. Financial aid to cover education and personal expenses is available to all qualifying applicants.

Applicant Profile

Loyola Law School, Loyola Marymount University
This grid includes only applicants who earned 120-180 LSAT scores under standard administrations.

LSAT Score	3.75 + Apps	Adm	3.50 - 3.74 Apps	Adm	3.25 - 3.49 Apps	Adm	3.00 - 3.24 Apps	Adm	2.75 - 2.99 Apps	Adm	2.50 - 2.74 Apps	Adm	2.25 - 2.49 Apps	Adm	2.00 - 2.24 Apps	Adm	Below 2.00 Apps	Adm	No GPA Apps	Adm	Total Apps	Adm
175-180	1	0	1	1	1	0	2	2	0	0	0	0	0	0	0	0	0	0	0	0	5	3
170-174	6	3	3	3	10	7	10	7	2	2	2	0	2	1	1	0	0	0	1	1	37	24
165-169	34	26	44	35	54	43	37	28	26	13	9	6	6	5	5	1	0	0	3	2	218	159
160-164	108	93	219	171	248	181	168	106	101	39	43	13	19	4	10	1	0	0	8	3	924	611
155-159	136	36	308	63	376	30	320	29	174	9	72	5	28	1	12	0	2	0	24	2	1452	175
150-154	97	13	234	19	307	16	285	8	170	5	93	1	47	0	12	0	2	0	16	0	1263	62
145-149	34	0	90	3	133	3	168	1	130	0	73	0	44	0	13	0	6	0	19	0	710	7
140-144	11	0	23	1	53	0	65	0	72	0	56	0	35	0	19	0	3	0	8	0	345	1
135-139	1	0	11	0	9	0	28	0	28	0	24	0	11	0	5	0	2	0	8	0	127	0
130-134	0	0	2	0	4	0	8	0	4	0	6	0	6	0	5	0	1	0	9	0	45	0
125-129	0	0	0	0	0	0	0	0	0	0	3	0	4	0	1	0	1	0	2	0	11	0
120-124	0	0	0	0	0	0	0	0	1	0	0	0	0	0	0	0	1	0	1	0	3	0
Total	428	171	935	296	1195	280	1091	181	708	68	381	25	202	11	83	2	18	0	99	8	5140	1042

Apps = Number of Applicants (Grid represents 99% of applicant pool)
Adm = Number Admitted

Loyola University Chicago School of Law

25 East Pearson Street
Chicago, IL 60611
Phone: 312.915.7170, 800.545.5744; Fax: 312.915.7906
E-mail: law-admissions@luc.edu; Website: www.luc.edu/law

ABA
Approved
Since
1925

The Basics

Type of school	Private
Term	Semester
Application deadline	4/1
Application fee	$50
Financial aid deadline	3/1
Can first year start other than fall?	No
Student to faculty ratio (fall)	17.2 to 1
Does the university offer:	
housing restricted to law students?	No
graduate housing for which law students are eligible?	No

Faculty and Administrators

	Total		Men		Women		Minorities	
	Fall	Spr	Fall	Spr	Fall	Spr	Fall	Spr
Full-time	37	35	22	21	15	14	4	3
Other Full-time	0	0	0	0	0	0	0	0
Deans, librarians, & others who teach	7	7	3	3	4	4	0	0
Part-time	104	65	55	39	49	26	12	7
Total	148	107	80	63	68	44	16	10

Curriculum

		Full-time	Part-time
Typical first-year section size		62	66
Is there typically a "small section" of the first-year class, other than Legal Writing, taught by full-time faculty		No	No
If yes, typical size offered last year		0	0
# of classroom course titles beyond 1st year curriculum		122	
# of upper division courses, excluding seminars with an enrollment:	Under 25	61	
	25-49	43	
	50-74	22	
	75-99	2	
	100+	0	
# of seminars		49	
# of seminar positions available		747	
# of seminar positions filled		493	114
# of positions available in simulation courses		600	
# of simulation positions filled		314	83
# of positions available in faculty supervised clinical courses		160	
# of faculty supervised clinical positions filled	100		20
# involved in field placements		127	20
# involved in law journals		196	49
# involved in moot court or trial competitions		58	10
# of credit hours required to graduate		86	

JD Enrollment and Ethnicity

	Men		Women		Full-time		Part-time		1st-year		Total		JD Degs. Awd.
	#	%	#	%	#	%	#	%	#	%	#	%	
African Amer.	15	3.9	29	6.3	29	4.8	15	6.2	9	3.6	44	5.2	8
Amer. Indian	1	0.3	1	0.2	0	0.0	2	0.8	1	0.4	2	0.2	2
Asian Amer.	29	7.5	40	8.7	45	7.5	24	9.9	21	8.4	69	8.1	27
Mex. Amer.	8	2.1	3	0.7	6	1.0	5	2.1	2	0.8	11	1.3	6
Puerto Rican	0	0.0	1	0.2	1	0.2	0	0.0	0	0.0	1	0.1	3
Hispanic	4	1.0	15	3.3	16	2.6	3	1.2	7	2.8	19	2.2	4
Total Minority	57	14.8	89	19.3	97	16.1	49	20.2	40	15.9	146	17.2	50
For. Nation.	8	2.1	5	1.1	8	1.3	5	2.1	5	2.0	13	1.5	2
Caucasian	288	74.6	326	70.7	441	73.0	173	71.2	180	71.7	614	72.5	189
Unknown	33	8.5	41	8.9	58	9.6	16	6.6	26	10.4	74	8.7	3
Total	386	45.6	461	54.4	604	71.3	243	28.7	251	29.6	847		244

Tuition and Fees

	Resident	Nonresident
Full-time	$28,440	$28,440
Part-time	$21,390	$21,390

Living Expenses

Estimated living expenses for singles

Living on campus	Living off campus	Living at home
$18,880	$18,880	$18,880

Loyola University Chicago School of Law

*ABA
Approved
Since
1925*

GPA and LSAT Scores

	Total	Full-time	Part-time
# of apps	2,845	2,458	387
# of admits	696	565	131
# of matrics	249	174	75
75% GPA	3.56	3.58	3.45
25% GPA	3.11	3.17	2.85
75% LSAT	162	162	159
25% LSAT	156	159	153

Grants and Scholarships (from prior year)

	Total		Full-time		Part-time	
	#	%	#	%	#	%
Total # of students	859		602		257	
Total # receiving grants	494	57.5	411	68.3	83	32.3
Less than 1/2 tuition	454	52.9	378	62.8	76	29.6
Half to full tuition	39	4.5	32	5.3	7	2.7
Full tuition	1	0.1	1	0.2	0	0.0
More than full tuition	0	0.0	0	0.0	0	0.0
Median grant amount			$6,200		$4,000	

Informational and Library Resources

# of volumes and volume equivalents	403,338
# of titles	62,101
# of active serial subscriptions	4,736
Study seating capacity inside the library	380
# of professional librarians	7
Hours per week library is open	99
# of open, wired connections available to students	408
# of networked computers available for use by students	65
# of simultaneous wireless users	0
Require computer?	N

JD Attrition (from prior year)

	Academic	Other	Total	
	#	#	#	%
1st year	0	0	0	0.0%
2nd year	0	10	10	3.4%
3rd year	0	0	0	0.0%
4th year	0	0	0	0.0%

Employment

	Total	Percentage
Employment status known	212	99.1
Employment status unknown	2	0.9
Employed	195	92.0
Pursuing graduate degrees	5	2.4
Unemployed seeking employment	3	1.4
Unemployed not seeking employment	9	4.2

Type of Employment

# employed in law firms	109	55.9
# employed in business and industry	28	14.4
# employed in government	40	20.5
# employed in public interest	3	1.5
# employed as judicial clerks	15	7.7
# employed in academia	0	0.0

Geographic Location

# employed in state	170	87.2
# employed in foreign countries	1	0.5
# of states where employed	14	

Bar Passage Rates

Jurisdiction	Illinois		
Exam	Sum 03	Win 04	Total
# from school taking bar for the first time	165	21	186
School's pass rate for all first-time takers	90%	76%	88%
State's pass rate for all first-time takers	86%	78%	84%

Loyola University Chicago School of Law

25 East Pearson Street
Chicago, IL 60611
Phone: 312.915.7170, 800.545.5744; Fax: 312.915.7906
E-mail: law-admissions@luc.edu; Website: www.luc.edu/law

■ Introduction

Loyola University Chicago School of Law is located on the Water Tower campus of the university, a few blocks north of the Chicago Loop. This campus adjoins Michigan Avenue at the historical Water Tower, a Chicago landmark, in approximately the center of the renowned Magnificent Mile, a commercial center over which the John Hancock Center towers. This location provides ready access to the state and federal courts and to the offices of most other institutions of federal, state, and local government, as well as the cultural centers of Chicago. The school is a member of the AALS and is approved by the ABA.

■ Library and Physical Facilities

The School of Law library is a laboratory dedicated to the study of law and fills 43,900 square feet. More than 380,000 volumes enhance Loyola's broad-based law curriculum and support the varied research needs of students and faculty. Offering custom-designed furnishings and private study carrels, this facility creates a comfortable and accommodating atmosphere for users. The library is open 100 hours each week, with expanded hours during examination periods. A professional staff of lawyer-librarians and reference personnel is available nearly all the time the library is open.

■ Foreign Study Programs

Since 1983, the School of Law has offered a program of international and comparative law courses at the Rome Center for Liberal Arts, the university's campus in Rome, Italy. Each summer, for approximately five weeks, law students from the United States and elsewhere can take one or more of the courses offered in Rome by members of the full-time Loyola law faculty.

In 1997, the law school added a program in Strasbourg, France, at the European Court of Human Rights in the Council of Europe and at NATO and the European Union in Brussels, Belgium. Coursework is completed through Loyola's summer program in Nottingham, England.

In 1989, Loyola inaugurated its London Comparative Advocacy Program in which students travel to London for approximately 15 days to become immersed in the world of the British barrister.

In spring 2003, Loyola inaugurated an immersion program at Universidad Alberto Hurtado, a Jesuit law school in Santiago, Chile.

■ Special Opportunities

The School of Law has dual-degree programs with the School of Social Work's graduate program of the Department of Political Science, and the Graduate School of Business. Automatic acceptance is granted to the MA in Political Science for candidates admitted to the law school. Provisional admission to the MBA program is granted based upon LSAT score and law school grades. The multidegree programs are structured to allow completion after four years. Loyola offers accelerated LLM programs in health law, child and family law, and taxation to JD students who fulfill program requirements.

■ Child and Family Law Center

The Loyola ChildLaw Center was created in 1993 to prepare law students to represent abused and neglected children. The center is the first of its kind at any American law school; was the recipient of the National Association of Counsel for Children 1996 Outstanding Legal Advocacy Award; and draws on the full resources of Loyola University, including the schools of medicine, social work, and education. The program includes an LLM degree and a master's degree program for nonlawyers.

The law school and Teach for America have entered into a partnership. TFA corps members who are interested in using their legal education to advocate for children's legal interests and well-being will receive an application fee waiver and matching Americorps Awards. One fellowship is reserved for a TFA corps member.

Annually, eight fellows are selected from the entering law class. Each fellow receives financial support. At the conclusion of the three-year JD program, students are trained thoroughly to serve as skilled litigators and advocates for children.

■ Institute for Health Law

The Institute for Health Law was created in 1984 in recognition of the need for an academic forum to study the field of health law and to act as a vehicle to foster dialogue between the law and the health sciences. Through the institute, the law school offers an SJD in Health Law and Policy and an LLM in Health Law. In addition, it offers the first Master of Jurisprudence (MJ) in Health Law and Doctor of Law (DLaw) in Health Law and Policy, providing health care professionals with an intensive overview in health law. More than two dozen health law classes are offered in the law school.

■ Business Law Center

The Business Law Center was created in 1996 to further enhance Loyola's corporate law curriculum by offering more specialized and practical skills classes to its students. The center offers corporate externships for law students, sponsors continuing education programs for both corporate attorneys and employees, and includes a legal clinic for small business.

■ Institute for Consumer Antitrust Studies

The Institute for Consumer Antitrust Studies is an independent, academically based institute designed to explore the impact of antitrust and consumer law enforcement on the individual consumer and the general public. The institute was founded by a grant from the US District Court for the Northern District of Illinois and is supported by Loyola and private donors.

■ Advocacy

Loyola prepares its students for careers of leadership at the bar and on the bench. We number among our alumni some of the most prominent trial lawyers and judges in the country. The advocacy program comprises a second-year required course in advocacy; courses in beginning and advanced trial advocacy; numerous moot court competitions; the Corboy Fellowship Program in Trial Advocacy for mock trial competitions; and a wide variety of litigation-related courses. A certificate in advocacy is available for students who complete a menu of advocacy courses.

Symbolic of our advocacy success is our selection by the National Institute for Trial Advocacy as the site for two of its largest advocacy training programs, the Midwest Regional Trial Advocacy Program and the Midwest Regional Deposition Training Program.

■ Admission

Factors other than LSAT scores and college grades are considered. Such factors include work experience, personal goals, specialized education, and other evidence of ability to contribute invaluable insight to law classes.

■ Career Services

The Career Resources Office assists students and alumni with career planning and employment selection.

A year-round, on-campus employer interview and recruitment program provides employment opportunities.

Seminars by practicing attorneys and alumni, résumé preparation, interviewing techniques, individual counseling, and job-search strategies are just some of the many programs administered by the Career Resources Office.

The School of Law is a member of NALP.

■ Cocurricular Activities

Students are encouraged to participate in cocurricular activities. There are nine student- and faculty-edited publications. The *Loyola Law Journal* is a quarterly professional journal edited by students who are selected on a competitive basis. The *Loyola Consumer Law Review* is devoted to legal analyses of current issues affecting consumers. Students compete in moot court and mock trial competitions. All students are members of the Loyola Student Bar Association, the principal instrument of student government. There are over 25 student organizations and groups devoted to legal practice, ethnic groups, or law student chapters of professional bar associations.

Applicant Profile

Loyola University Chicago School of Law
This grid includes only applicants who earned 120-180 LSAT scores under standard administrations.

LSAT Score	GPA																	
	3.75 +		3.50 - 3.74		3.25 - 3.49		3.00 - 3.24		2.50 - 2.99		2.00 - 2.49		Below 2.00		No GPA		Total	
	Apps	Adm	Apps	Adm	Apps	Adm	Apps	Adm	Apps	Adm	Apps	Adm	Apps	Adm	Apps	Adm	Apps	Adm
165-180	27	25	22	15	21	15	15	13	21	9	4	1	1	0	0	0	111	78
160-164	61	56	101	86	127	102	101	70	64	21	8	4	0	0	1	1	463	340
155-159	103	35	214	44	234	56	158	24	137	24	26	6	0	0	5	1	877	190
145-154	102	9	205	15	263	20	224	16	232	20	61	3	2	0	13	1	1102	84
120-144	8	0	21	0	40	0	63	0	84	0	47	0	6	0	15	0	284	0
Total	301	125	563	160	685	193	561	123	538	74	146	14	9	0	34	3	2837	692

Apps = Number of Applicants
Adm = Number Admitted
Reflects 99% of the total applicant pool.

Loyola University New Orleans School of Law

7214 St. Charles Avenue, Box 904
New Orleans, LA 70118
Phone: 504.861.5575; Fax: 504.861.5772
E-mail: ladmit@loyno.edu; Website: law.loyno.edu

ABA Approved Since 1931

The Basics

Type of school	Private
Term	Semester
Application deadline	
Application fee	$40
Financial aid deadline	
Can first year start other than fall?	No
Student to faculty ratio (fall)	17.6 to 1
Does the university offer:	
housing restricted to law students?	No
graduate housing for which law students are eligible?	No

Curriculum

	Full-time	Part-time
Typical first-year section size	83	73
Is there typically a "small section" of the first-year class, other than Legal Writing, taught by full-time faculty	No	No
If yes, typical size offered last year	0	0
# of classroom course titles beyond 1st year curriculum	96	
# of upper division courses, excluding seminars with an enrollment: Under 25	25	
25-49	35	
50-74	19	
75-99	9	
100+	2	
# of seminars	15	
# of seminar positions available	345	
# of seminar positions filled	232	80
# of positions available in simulation courses	94	
# of simulation positions filled	62	22
# of positions available in faculty supervised clinical courses	4	
# of faculty supervised clinical positions filled	94	0
# involved in field placements	26	4
# involved in law journals	107	16
# involved in moot court or trial competitions	31	2
# of credit hours required to graduate	90	

Faculty and Administrators

	Total		Men		Women		Minorities	
	Fall	Spr	Fall	Spr	Fall	Spr	Fall	Spr
Full-time	37	39	26	27	11	12	9	10
Other Full-time	0	0	0	0	0	0	0	0
Deans, librarians, & others who teach	4	4	4	4	0	0	0	0
Part-time	17	28	15	21	2	7	0	2
Total	58	71	45	52	13	19	9	12

JD Enrollment and Ethnicity

	Men		Women		Full-time		Part-time		1st-year		Total		JD Degs. Awd.
	#	%	#	%	#	%	#	%	#	%	#	%	
African Amer.	20	5.2	58	13.8	56	8.8	22	12.9	19	7.0	78	9.7	29
Amer. Indian	2	0.5	3	0.7	3	0.5	2	1.2	3	1.1	5	0.6	2
Asian Amer.	10	2.6	16	3.8	25	3.9	1	0.6	10	3.7	26	3.2	4
Mex. Amer.	0	0.0	0	0.0	0	0.0	0	0.0	0	0.0	0	0.0	2
Puerto Rican	14	3.6	25	6.0	30	4.7	9	5.3	0	0.0	39	4.9	21
Hispanic	4	1.0	11	2.6	11	1.7	4	2.4	15	5.5	15	1.9	0
Total Minority	50	13.0	113	27.0	125	19.7	38	22.4	47	17.3	163	20.3	58
For. Nation.	1	0.3	1	0.2	2	0.3	0	0.0	2	0.7	2	0.2	0
Caucasian	302	78.6	279	66.6	460	72.7	121	71.2	190	69.9	581	72.4	206
Unknown	31	8.1	26	6.2	46	7.3	11	6.5	33	12.1	57	7.1	11
Total	384	47.8	419	52.2	633	78.8	170	21.2	272	33.9	803		275

Tuition and Fees

	Resident	Nonresident
Full-time	$27,746	$27,746
Part-time	$18,716	$18,716

Living Expenses

Estimated living expenses for singles

Living on campus	Living off campus	Living at home
$14,865	$14,865	$12,365

Loyola University New Orleans School of Law

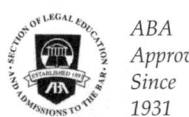

*ABA
Approved
Since
1931*

GPA and LSAT Scores

	Total	Full-time	Part-time
# of apps	1,955	1,746	209
# of admits	680	593	87
# of matrics	272	215	57
75% GPA	3.66	3.63	3.53
25% GPA	3.10	3.16	3.00
75% LSAT	156	156	154
25% LSAT	150	151	147

Grants and Scholarships (from prior year)

	Total		Full-time		Part-time	
	#	%	#	%	#	%
Total # of students	849		661		188	
Total # receiving grants	322	37.9	271	41.0	51	27.1
Less than 1/2 tuition	223	26.3	189	28.6	34	18.1
Half to full tuition	96	11.3	81	12.3	15	8.0
Full tuition	0	0.0	0	0.0	0	0.0
More than full tuition	3	0.4	1	0.2	2	1.1
Median grant amount			$10,938		$10,938	

Informational and Library Resources

# of volumes and volume equivalents	338,150
# of titles	113,890
# of active serial subscriptions	3,806
Study seating capacity inside the library	448
# of professional librarians	8
Hours per week library is open	107
# of open, wired connections available to students	142
# of networked computers available for use by students	83
# of simultaneous wireless users	200
Require computer?	N

JD Attrition (from prior year)

	Academic	Other	Total	
	#	#	#	%
1st year	14	25	39	15.1%
2nd year	1	7	8	2.9%
3rd year	0	1	1	0.4%
4th year	0	0	0	0.0%

Employment

	Total	Percentage
Employment status known	224	100.0
Employment status unknown	0	0.0
Employed	189	84.4
Pursuing graduate degrees	16	7.1
Unemployed seeking employment	3	1.3
Unemployed not seeking employment	16	7.1

Type of Employment

# employed in law firms	95	50.3
# employed in business and industry	40	21.2
# employed in government	18	9.5
# employed in public interest	4	2.1
# employed as judicial clerks	31	16.4
# employed in academia	1	0.5

Geographic Location

# employed in state	126	66.7
# employed in foreign countries	1	0.5
# of states where employed	19	

Bar Passage Rates

Jurisdiction	Louisiana		
Exam	Sum 03	Win 04	Total
# from school taking bar for the first time	123	25	148
School's pass rate for all first-time takers	60%	60%	60%
State's pass rate for all first-time takers	62%	60%	61%

Loyola University New Orleans School of Law

7214 St. Charles Avenue, Box 904
New Orleans, LA 70118
Phone: 504.861.5575; Fax: 504.861.5772
E-mail: ladmit@loyno.edu; Website: law.loyno.edu

■ Introduction

Loyola University New Orleans is a Catholic institution of higher learning in the Jesuit tradition. The School of Law was established in 1914, approved by the ABA in 1931, and has been a member of the AALS since 1934. The School of Law is committed to excellence in legal education in the tradition of its spiritual heritage, with our goal being wisdom, not mere technical competence. We welcome all persons who strive for the truth and are prepared to challenge all assumptions in light of this commitment.

■ Physical Facilities and Library

Loyola University has two campuses, both located approximately five miles from the historic French Quarter. The 20-acre main campus, in the heart of the uptown residential community, faces the nationally recognized Audubon Park and Zoo. The 4.2-acre Broadway campus is the home of the School of Law.

The law library's collection of 335,000 volumes and microform equivalents supports the curriculum and research needs. In addition to conventional resources, the library has extensive computer facilities in place to access information outside the confines of the library. The Online Catalog Library Center service permits the library to access a national bibliographic database of over 10 million publications. The law library houses remote-controlled viewing/listening rooms, a computerized legal research room, and two computer labs equipped with 59 personal computers on a network and access to the Internet, LexisNexis, Westlaw, e-mail, and other computer resources.

■ Curriculum and Special Programs

The curricula of Loyola New Orleans have been shaped by Louisiana's unique role as the only state in the union that has a legal system based on significant elements of both the civil law and common law traditions. The civil law was imported into Louisiana during the eighteenth century, when it was first a colony of France, and later, of Spain. As a result of Louisiana's unique legal heritage, Loyola New Orleans has developed three separate curricula: two full-time divisions, civil law and common law; and one part-time division, which is civil law. It is important to note that the JD degree offered by Loyola New Orleans will allow a student to sit for the bar in any of the 50 states, without regard for the curriculum chosen. Loyola offers a Certificate in Common Law Studies and a Certificate in Civil Law Studies for students who wish to acquire a foundation in both disciplines. Full-time students are required to be in residence for a minimum of

six full semesters. The normal time frame for part-time students is eight semesters and one summer session.

Practical Lawyering Skills Program—In 1985 the faculty adopted one of the most unique and far-reaching Professional Lawyering Skills Programs in the country. Recognizing hands-on, learn-by-doing opportunities to develop the future practitioner's skills to be as important as the traditional academic studies, the curriculum developed specialized courses and sought the expertise of attorneys and judges. Currently, over 100 members of the bench and bar teach in the skills curriculum. Each student must accumulate a number of lawyering-skills points in order to graduate.

International Law Specialty—Loyola has founded summer sessions in four continents and six countries, established ties with a number of important foreign law schools, and sent its professors to teach or lecture at law schools in more than a dozen foreign countries. Courses are taught in special five-week summer-abroad sessions in Cuernavaca, Mexico, and Eastern Europe. There are also three- and two-week sessions offered each summer in Brazil or Costa Rica. Additionally, students may obtain a Certificate in International Legal Studies.

Other Specialties at Loyola—In addition to our International Law specialty, Loyola's other major area of specialization is Public Interest Law. Other areas of significant emphasis are Corporate, Maritime, and Tax law. Environmental Law is an emerging specialty. Loyola recently was awarded the first $2 million endowed professorship in the state. This grant will address legal issues relative to economic development, protection of the environment, and the public's role in environmental policy issues through law school classes and other activities at the law school.

Clinical Education—The Law Clinic is a vital component to the law school. Students chosen to participate in the senior year program will be assigned cases, civil and criminal, and will be expected to prepare them for trial. Thereafter, they will actually participate in the trial process. Upper-division students also have an opportunity to serve as judicial clerks in the federal extern program sponsored in conjunction with the US District Court for the Eastern District of Louisiana.

The Public Law Center represents a new departure in American legal education by taking legislative initiatives from the conceptual stage through research and drafting into the actual legislative process, then beyond into administrative rulemaking following the enactment of new statutes.

■ Scholarly Publications and Student Activities

The *Loyola Law Review* is published by a student editorial board and includes student work and articles written by specialists from the practicing bar and academic community. Staff membership is based on scholarship and interest in legal writing.

The *Law Journal of Public Interest Law* is devoted to issues faced by the poor, children, the elderly, and all others who are unable to afford legal representation.

The *Loyola Intellectual Property and High Technology Law Annual* is a scholarly publication focusing on current legal issues in patents, copyrights, trademarks, and technology law.

The *Loyola Maritime Law Journal* provides an avenue for research and writing in the field of maritime law. Staff membership is based on scholarship.

The Moot Court Board, selected from prior years' competitions, is responsible for the Moot Court Program. Teams are entered each year in competitions. Loyola teams have an impressive winning record in a wide variety of competitions both nationally and internationally.

There are a number of student organizations, including three legal fraternities. Other organizations include Environmental Law Society, Sports and Entertainment Law Society, St. Thomas More Law Club, and the Association of Trial Lawyers of America.

■ Admission

The law school begins processing applications for admission on September 1 each year. The first decision letters are generally released in December. The admission decision is based on an initial evaluation of a combination of the LSAT score and the undergraduate cumulative grade-point average. Additionally, the undergraduate institution attended, the undergraduate major, and any grade trends will be taken into consideration. Also included in the evaluation will be letters of recommendation, résumés, and a personal statement from the applicant; all of which may present a more illuminating portrait of the applicant's skills and accomplishments. Competition for acceptance to the law school is high, thus all information provided is used to make the final admission decision.

■ Career Services

The School of Law Career Services Office offers a variety of services to both students and alumni. The office maintains and operates a career-planning center, assists students in preparing résumés, videotapes mock interviews, and conducts seminars on career planning, employment opportunities, and interviewing techniques. The office actively solicits job opportunities for summer and school-term clerkships, as well as employment options for each year's graduating class.

Applicant Profile

Loyola University New Orleans School of Law
This grid includes only applicants who earned 120-180 LSAT scores under standard administrations.

LSAT Score	GPA								
	3.75 +	3.50 - 3.74	3.25 - 3.49	3.00 - 3.24	2.75 - 2.99	2.50 - 2.74	2.25 - 2.49	2.00 - 2.24	Below 2.00
175-180									
170-174									
165-169									
160-164									
155-159									
150-154									
145-149									
140-144									
135-139									
130-134									
125-129									
120-124									

Excellent   Possible   Unlikely

The School of Law considers many factors beyond LSAT score and GPA. This chart should be used only as a general guide.

University of Maine School of Law

246 Deering Avenue
Portland, ME 04102
Phone: 207.780.4355
E-mail: mainelaw@usm.maine.edu; Website: mainelaw.maine.edu

ABA
Approved
Since
1962

The Basics

Type of school	Public
Term	Semester
Application deadline	3/1
Application fee	$50
Financial aid deadline	1/31
Can first year start other than fall?	No
Student to faculty ratio (fall)	19.1 to 1
Does the university offer:	
housing restricted to law students?	No
graduate housing for which law students are eligible?	Yes

Faculty and Administrators

	Total		Men		Women		Minorities	
	Fall	Spr	Fall	Spr	Fall	Spr	Fall	Spr
Full-time	12	10	8	7	4	3	0	0
Other Full-time	4	4	1	1	3	3	0	0
Deans, librarians, & others who teach	4	4	1	1	3	3	0	0
Part-time	10	12	8	6	2	6	0	0
Total	30	30	18	15	12	15	0	0

Curriculum

	Full-time	Part-time
Typical first-year section size	91	0
Is there typically a "small section" of the first-year class, other than Legal Writing, taught by full-time faculty	Yes	No
If yes, typical size offered last year	46	0
# of classroom course titles beyond 1st year curriculum		48

# of upper division courses, excluding seminars with an enrollment:		
	Under 25	41
	25-49	13
	50-74	3
	75-99	3
	100+	0

# of seminars		6
# of seminar positions available		99
# of seminar positions filled	95	0
# of positions available in simulation courses		114
# of simulation positions filled	111	0
# of positions available in faculty supervised clinical courses		48
# of faculty supervised clinical positions filled	48	0
# involved in field placements	14	0
# involved in law journals	43	0
# involved in moot court or trial competitions	22	0
# of credit hours required to graduate		90

JD Enrollment and Ethnicity

	Men		Women		Full-time		Part-time		1st-year		Total		JD Degs. Awd.
	#	%	#	%	#	%	#	%	#	%	#	%	
African Amer.	2	1.6	3	1.9	5	1.8	0	0.0	1	1.2	5	1.8	1
Amer. Indian	1	0.8	0	0.0	1	0.4	0	0.0	0	0.0	1	0.4	1
Asian Amer.	4	3.2	3	1.9	7	2.6	0	0.0	1	1.2	7	2.5	1
Mex. Amer.	0	0.0	0	0.0	0	0.0	0	0.0	0	0.0	0	0.0	0
Puerto Rican	1	0.8	0	0.0	1	0.4	0	0.0	1	1.2	1	0.4	0
Hispanic	1	0.8	1	0.6	2	0.7	0	0.0	0	0.0	2	0.7	2
Total Minority	9	7.3	7	4.5	16	5.9	0	0.0	3	3.6	16	5.8	5
For. Nation.	1	0.8	1	0.6	2	0.7	0	0.0	1	1.2	2	0.7	0
Caucasian	97	78.2	139	90.3	229	84.5	7	100.0	69	82.1	236	84.9	75
Unknown	17	13.7	7	4.5	24	8.9	0	0.0	11	13.1	24	8.6	2
Total	124	44.6	154	55.4	271	97.5	7	2.5	84	30.2	278		82

Tuition and Fees

	Resident	Nonresident
Full-time	$14,114	$22,514
Part-time	$9,470	$15,070

Living Expenses

Estimated living expenses for singles

Living on campus	Living off campus	Living at home
$10,401	$10,401	$5,861

University of Maine School of Law

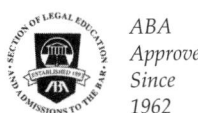

*ABA
Approved
Since
1962*

GPA and LSAT Scores

	Total	Full-time	Part-time
# of apps	765	765	0
# of admits	271	271	0
# of matrics	85	85	0
75% GPA	3.54	3.54	0.00
25% GPA	3.15	3.15	0.00
75% LSAT	158	158	0
25% LSAT	153	153	0

Grants and Scholarships (from prior year)

	Total		Full-time		Part-time	
	#	%	#	%	#	%
Total # of students	278		266		12	
Total # receiving grants	88	31.7	88	33.1	0	0.0
Less than 1/2 tuition	76	27.3	76	28.6	0	0.0
Half to full tuition	4	1.4	4	1.5	0	0.0
Full tuition	8	2.9	8	3.0	0	0.0
More than full tuition	0	0.0	0	0.0	0	0.0
Median grant amount			$3,500		$0	

Informational and Library Resources

# of volumes and volume equivalents	347,986
# of titles	70,099
# of active serial subscriptions	3,186
Study seating capacity inside the library	216
# of professional librarians	6
Hours per week library is open	97
# of open, wired connections available to students	9
# of networked computers available for use by students	21
# of simultaneous wireless users	200
Require computer?	N

JD Attrition (from prior year)

	Academic	Other	Total	
	#	#	#	%
1st year	2	1	3	3.3%
2nd year	1	1	2	2.0%
3rd year	0	1	1	1.2%
4th year	0	0	0	0.0%

Employment

	Total	Percentage
Employment status known	61	100.0
Employment status unknown	0	0.0
Employed	53	86.9
Pursuing graduate degrees	3	4.9
Unemployed seeking employment	4	6.6
Unemployed not seeking employment	1	1.6

Type of Employment

# employed in law firms	23	43.4
# employed in business and industry	7	13.2
# employed in government	5	9.4
# employed in public interest	2	3.8
# employed as judicial clerks	13	24.5
# employed in academia	1	1.9

Geographic Location

# employed in state	35	66.0
# employed in foreign countries	1	1.9
# of states where employed		14

Bar Passage Rates

Jurisdiction	Maine		
Exam	Sum 03	Win 04	Total
# from school taking bar for the first time	39	6	45
School's pass rate for all first-time takers	69%	33%	64%
State's pass rate for all first-time takers	73%	68%	71%

University of Maine School of Law

246 Deering Avenue
Portland, ME 04102
Phone: 207.780.4355
E-mail: mainelaw@usm.maine.edu; Website: mainelaw.maine.edu

■ Introduction

The University of Maine School of Law is a wonderful, distinctive place to study law. Students have the opportunity to study law in a humane and personalized environment, and to be prepared for success in today's global economy.

Maine Law, the state's only law school, is distinguished by the excellence of its students, faculty, and graduates. One of the smallest law schools in the country, Maine Law fosters educational excellence, professionalism, and public service through a close community of faculty members and students. Our location in Portland, Maine—the largest city in the state and our proximity to the greater New England region generally—allows students to benefit from a multitude of hands-on training opportunities offered through clinical programs, externships, community service projects, and employment. Maine Law is an administrative unit of the University of Southern Maine and the law school of the University of Maine System.

■ Faculty

Maine Law faculty members are well regarded for their commitment to teaching and for their accessibility to students. They come from a variety of backgrounds and have extensive experience in private practice and government service. They make significant contributions to legislative, judicial and professional bodies, community organizations, and in the courtroom. Their research spans matters of state, national, and international interest and examines topics as varied as international treaty practice, Maine tort law, coastal zone management, federal tax elections, constitutional controls over the military, intellectual property, and commercial practice.

■ Curriculum

Maine Law offers a broad based curriculum preparing students for practice in all states. The law school's strengths are in business and commercial law, environmental and marine law, international law, clinical training, and trial advocacy. Ninety credit hours are required for graduation.

The first-year curriculum is a prescribed program of courses. Students develop legal analytical skills and the ability to read and understand cases and statutory material. The program provides the foundation course in legal research and writing, including a moot court experience. Most courses after the first year are elective. However, all students are required to complete Professional Responsibility, Constitutional Law II, and one of the courses designated by the faculty as a perspective course—one that places the law in a broader philosophical, historical, or comparative context. Each student must fulfill the

Independent Writing Requirement through a substantial research paper under the direction of a member of the faculty, or through membership on the *Maine Law Review* or *Ocean and Coastal Law Journal*. Maine Law has a practical skills program that includes courses in trial practice, negotiation, and alternative dispute resolution. The course in advanced trial advocacy has fielded award-winning teams.

■ Special Programs

- *Cumberland Legal Aid Clinic*—Through Maine's Integrated Clinical Education Program, third-year law students represent clients under faculty supervision in this approved legal assistance office. Students work on family law and domestic matters, criminal, consumer, housing, employment, and probate issues at both the trial and appellate levels. A Prisoner Assistance Clinic provides representation for prisoners in a variety of civil matters. All clinical courses coordinate with the state's domestic violence project.

- *Environmental Law Clinic*—The Environmental Law Clinic pairs students with government agencies, environmental advocacy groups, or private firms with environmental practices, to assist with current problems in environmental, marine, and natural resources issues, under faculty supervision.

- *Externships*—Six-credit externships allow third-year students to gain legal experience and receive feedback from seasoned professionals with support from a faculty member. Placements are available at Pine Tree Legal Assistance, the Maine Attorney General's Office, the United States Attorney, the Maine Patent Program, Immigrant Legal Advocacy, and Legal Services for the Elderly.

- *Marine Law Institute, Ocean and Coastal Law Program*—The MLI conducts research on laws and policies affecting ocean and coastal resources under grants and contracts from federal and state agencies and private foundations. Much of the institute's work is directed toward understanding the intergovernmental problems associated with management of marine resources and the relationship between legal and scientific principles in the implementation of marine policies. Maine Law's Ocean and Coastal Law Program also supports a student-edited journal and offers courses in coastal zone law, marine resources law, and a law of the sea seminar.

- *Technology Law Center*—The Technology Law Center provides Maine law students with courses, conferences, and hands-on work experiences to enhance their understanding of the role of law in the development of technological progress and innovation. Through the center, courses are offered in intellectual property and Internet law, as well as special summer session technology law courses that bring distinguished scholars and practitioners to the school. Students can enroll in an externship with the Maine Patent Program, a unique service program established by the Maine legislature to provide education and legal assistance regarding the patent process to Maine inventors, entrepreneurs, and businesses.

- *Pro Bono Program*—The faculty has established a voluntary standard of 80 hours of pro bono legal service for each student during the three years of law school and has instituted means of providing encouragement for students to fulfill the standard and recognition for those who do so.
- *Joint-Degree Programs*—Maine Law and the University of Southern Maine's Edmund S. Muskie School of Public Service offer the following joint degrees that combine legal education with graduate public policy education: JD/MCP in Community Planning and Development, JD/MS in Health Policy and Management; and JD/MA in Public Policy and Management. A joint JD/MBA program begins fall 2005.
- *International Exchange Programs*—The law school is engaged in exchange programs with Dalhousie University Faculty of Law (Halifax, Nova Scotia), University of New Brunswick Faculty of Law (Fredericton, New Brunswick), National University of Ireland (Galway), Universite du Maine (LeMans, France), and University of Buckingham (England).

■ Student Activities

The Student Bar Association performs the varied functions of student government and acts as an umbrella organization of other student organizations, including American Constitution Society, Animal Legal Defense Fund, Black Law Students Association, Business Law Association, Environmental Law Society, Federalist Society, Health Law Association, International Law Society, Latino/a Law Students Association, Lesbian/Gay/Bisexual Law Caucus, Maine Association for Public Interest Law, Maine Law and Technology Association, National Lawyers Guilds, Native American Law Association, Prisoner Justice Project, Sports and Entertainment Law Society, and the Women's Law Association.

■ Career Services

The Career Services Office provides a full range of services, including counseling; career resource materials; specific summer, full-time, part-time, and work/study job listings; and extensive on-campus recruiting. The small size of the law school ensures services tailored to meet the specific needs of students. A number of workshops, speakers, and panel discussions throughout the year assist students in learning about the diverse opportunities available to them.

Applicant Profile

University of Maine School of Law
This grid includes only applicants who earned 120-180 LSAT scores under standard administrations.

LSAT Score	GPA																		
	3.75 +		3.50 - 3.74		3.25 - 3.49		3.00 - 3.24		2.75 - 2.99		2.50 - 2.74		2.25 - 2.49		2.00 - 2.24		Below 2.00		No GPA		Total	
	Apps	Adm	Apps	Adm	Apps	Adm	Apps	Adm	Apps	Adm	Apps	Adm	Apps	Adm	Apps	Adm	Apps	Adm	Apps	Adm	Apps	Adm
175-180	0	0	0	0	0	0	0	0	0	0	0	0	0	0	0	0	0	0	0	0	0	0
170-174	1	1	0	0	1	1	0	0	0	0	0	0	0	0	0	0	0	0	0	0	2	2
165-169	2	2	2	2	7	7	6	4	2	2	2	1	3	2	0	0	0	0	0	0	24	20
160-164	5	5	10	10	15	15	8	8	7	6	5	0	1	0	3	1	0	0	1	1	55	46
155-159	17	17	26	26	43	37	42	34	26	11	14	1	7	2	3	0	0	0	4	2	182	130
150-154	13	12	31	23	55	33	49	12	37	3	26	0	6	0	1	0	4	0	4	1	226	84
145-149	10	3	21	3	46	2	29	0	18	1	19	0	10	0	4	0	1	0	3	1	161	10
140-144	4	0	8	0	16	1	18	0	19	0	6	0	7	0	1	0	0	0	0	0	79	1
135-139	2	0	2	0	3	0	8	0	4	0	2	0	3	0	0	0	1	0	0	0	25	0
130-134	0	0	0	0	1	0	0	0	1	0	1	0	1	0	2	0	0	0	3	0	9	0
125-129	0	0	0	0	0	0	0	0	0	0	0	0	0	0	0	0	1	0	0	0	1	0
120-124	0	0	0	0	0	0	0	0	0	0	0	0	0	0	0	0	0	0	0	0	0	0
Total	54	40	100	64	187	96	160	58	114	23	75	2	38	4	14	1	7	0	15	5	764	293

Apps = Number of Applicants   Adm = Number Admitted   Reflects 99% of the total applicant pool.

This chart is to be used as a general guide only. Nonnumerical factors are strongly considered for all applicants.

Marquette University Law School

Sensenbrenner Hall, 1103 W Wisconsin Ave., PO Box 1881
Milwaukee, WI 53201-1881
Phone: 414.288.6767; Fax: 414.288.0676
E-mail: law.admission@marquette.edu; Website: http://law.marquette.edu

ABA Approved Since 1925

The Basics

Type of school	Private
Term	Semester
Application deadline	4/1 6/1
Application fee	$50
Financial aid deadline	3/1
Can first year start other than fall?	No
Student to faculty ratio (fall)	17.4 to 1
Does the university offer:	
housing restricted to law students?	No
graduate housing for which law students are eligible?	Yes

Faculty and Administrators

	Total		Men		Women		Minorities	
	Fall	Spr	Fall	Spr	Fall	Spr	Fall	Spr
Full-time	32	29	16	15	16	14	3	2
Other Full-time	1	1	0	0	1	1	0	0
Deans, librarians, & others who teach	9	9	6	6	3	3	0	0
Part-time	27	45	23	32	4	13	1	3
Total	69	84	45	53	24	31	4	5

Curriculum

	Full-time	Part-time
Typical first-year section size	80	80
Is there typically a "small section" of the first-year class, other than Legal Writing, taught by full-time faculty	Yes	Yes
If yes, typical size offered last year	52	38
# of classroom course titles beyond 1st year curriculum	110	
# of upper division courses, excluding seminars with an enrollment: Under 25	67	
25-49	34	
50-74	10	
75-99	3	
100+	0	
# of seminars	20	
# of seminar positions available	300	
# of seminar positions filled	255	255
# of positions available in simulation courses	496	
# of simulation positions filled	472	472
# of positions available in faculty supervised clinical courses	0	
# of faculty supervised clinical positions filled	0	0
# involved in field placements	193	193
# involved in law journals	113	113
# involved in moot court or trial competitions	75	75
# of credit hours required to graduate	90	

JD Enrollment and Ethnicity

	Men		Women		Full-time		Part-time		1st-year		Total		JD Degs. Awd.
	#	%	#	%	#	%	#	%	#	%	#	%	
African Amer.	12	3.0	11	3.5	22	3.9	1	0.6	9	4.0	23	3.2	7
Amer. Indian	2	0.5	1	0.3	3	0.5	0	0.0	0	0.0	3	0.4	1
Asian Amer.	11	2.7	10	3.2	14	2.5	7	4.4	10	4.5	21	2.9	5
Mex. Amer.	0	0.0	1	0.3	0	0.0	1	0.6	0	0.0	1	0.1	0
Puerto Rican	0	0.0	0	0.0	0	0.0	0	0.0	0	0.0	0	0.0	0
Hispanic	4	1.0	3	0.9	7	1.2	0	0.0	3	1.3	7	1.0	0
Total Minority	29	7.2	26	8.2	46	8.2	9	5.7	22	9.8	55	7.6	13
For. Nation.	2	0.5	2	0.6	0	0.0	4	2.5	1	0.4	4	0.6	1
Caucasian	373	92.3	289	91.2	517	91.8	145	91.8	208	92.9	662	91.8	154
Unknown	0	0.0	0	0.0	0	0.0	0	0.0	0	0.0	0	0.0	0
Total	404	56.0	317	44.0	563	78.1	158	21.9	224	31.1	721		168

Tuition and Fees

	Resident	Nonresident
Full-time	$24,930	$24,930
Part-time	$14,925	$14,925

Living Expenses

Estimated living expenses for singles

Living on campus	Living off campus	Living at home
$15,176	$15,176	$15,176

Marquette University Law School

ABA
Approved
Since
1925

GPA and LSAT Scores

	Total	Full-time	Part-time
# of apps	1,802	1,595	207
# of admits	611	538	73
# of matrics	224	168	56
75% GPA	3.59	3.58	3.60
25% GPA	3.10	3.15	3.05
75% LSAT	159	159	158
25% LSAT	154	155	152

Grants and Scholarships (from prior year)

	Total #	Total %	Full-time #	Full-time %	Part-time #	Part-time %
Total # of students	681		543		138	
Total # receiving grants	248	36.4	173	31.9	75	54.3
Less than 1/2 tuition	159	23.3	108	19.9	51	37.0
Half to full tuition	52	7.6	37	6.8	15	10.9
Full tuition	27	4.0	27	5.0	0	0.0
More than full tuition	10	1.5	1	0.2	9	6.5
Median grant amount			$10,000		$3,500	

Informational and Library Resources

# of volumes and volume equivalents	316,942
# of titles	154,358
# of active serial subscriptions	2,857
Study seating capacity inside the library	371
# of professional librarians	9
Hours per week library is open	106
# of open, wired connections available to students	154
# of networked computers available for use by students	39
# of simultaneous wireless users	540
Require computer?	N

JD Attrition (from prior year)

	Academic #	Other #	Total #	Total %
1st year	0	8	8	3.1%
2nd year	0	9	9	4.3%
3rd year	0	0	0	0.0%
4th year	0	0	0	0.0%

Employment

	Total	Percentage
Employment status known	187	91.7
Employment status unknown	17	8.3
Employed	178	95.2
Pursuing graduate degrees	1	0.5
Unemployed seeking employment	7	3.7
Unemployed not seeking employment	1	0.5

Type of Employment

# employed in law firms	126	70.8
# employed in business and industry	22	12.4
# employed in government	11	6.2
# employed in public interest	4	2.2
# employed as judicial clerks	11	6.2
# employed in academia	4	2.2

Geographic Location

# employed in state	139	78.1
# employed in foreign countries	2	1.1
# of states where employed	17	

Bar Passage Rates

Jurisdiction	Wisconsin		
Exam	Sum 03	Win 04	Total
# from school taking bar for the first time	179	22	201
School's pass rate for all first-time takers	100%	100%	100%
State's pass rate for all first-time takers	82%	69%	79%

All graduates were admitted to the Wisconsin bar via the diploma privilege.

Marquette University Law School

Office of Admissions, Sensenbrenner Hall, 1103 W Wisconsin Ave., PO Box 1881
Milwaukee, WI 53201-1881
Phone: 414.288.6767; Fax: 414.288.0676
E-mail: law.admission@marquette.edu; Website: http://law.marquette.edu

■ Introduction

For more than a century, Marquette University Law School has been committed to training men and women to serve the public interest by becoming highly skilled, ethical, and moral attorneys. Traditionally, the curriculum emphasized the practical aspects of legal practice. In recent years that emphasis has expanded to include particular excellence in the areas of intellectual property, alternative dispute resolution, sports law, international law, business law, criminal law and procedure, children and the law, and litigation-related courses. The National Sports Law Institute, the premiere sports law program in the US, is part of the Law School. Our 5,500 alumni/ae serve in a broad range of legal, public, and corporate positions throughout the US.

The Law School is located on the university campus—two blocks from the state courthouse and a short walk to the federal courthouse and downtown Milwaukee. Marquette is the only law school in southeast Wisconsin. Marquette—a Catholic, Jesuit, and urban university—is the largest private university in Wisconsin. The Catholic and Jesuit nature of the institution translates into a specific concern for the well-being of each individual, whether he or she is a law student, a legal client, or the victim of a crime. Persons of all religious backgrounds attend Marquette, serve on our faculty, and are valued in our law school community. The Law School is committed to academic freedom, the broadest possible scope of inquiry, and the examination of any subject.

Milwaukee is a lively city on Lake Michigan, 90 miles north of Chicago. It is Wisconsin's largest city, with a population of 600,000, but it retains the appeal of a small town. Clean and well-run, it is known for its many ethnic festivals and the variety of cuisine.

■ Enrollment/Student Body

In the Marquette Law family, people know and care about one another. Our students come together from over 180 colleges and universities. Students come from over 34 states and Canada, Ghana, and the UK. Our faculty includes 35 full-time professors and prominent practicing attorneys and judges who serve as adjunct professors.

Law students at Marquette represent a broad range of backgrounds, beliefs, and life experiences. Students of color comprise about 10 percent of the student body. We respect our different traditions and believe diversity enriches the legal education we offer.

■ Library and Physical Facilities

The Law School is located in Sensenbrenner Hall, an attractive, comfortable, four-story, air-conditioned building that houses faculty offices, classrooms, a courtroom, and administrative offices. The law library, a modern, four-level facility, is connected to the Law School. The law library has two computer labs and provides students access to computer-assisted legal research systems and computer-assisted legal instruction exercises. The law library is a federal document depository and is the largest legal research facility in southeastern Wisconsin. Law students have access to all Marquette University campus facilities, including the university computer center. Wireless capability exists throughout Sensenbrenner Hall, including the law library.

■ Curriculum

The Law School curriculum is designed to prepare students to practice law in the twenty-first century, with an explicit emphasis on a strong core curriculum that includes consideration of the theoretical underpinnings of the law as well as the practical application of substantive legal concepts. The Law School's curriculum is national in focus and scope and emphasizes the skills and values necessary to be a competent and ethical lawyer, as well as a contributing citizen and community leader. The Law School takes advantage of its location to include on its adjunct faculty many of the state's outstanding practitioners who supplement required and core courses with a broad range of elective and specialty courses. In everything you take as a 1L, you will work on developing your communication skills and the ability to think on your feet. With frequent practice in a supportive atmosphere, you will become increasingly self-confident and articulate.

■ Joint-Degree Programs

Students may earn a **JD/MBA** through the Law School and the College of Business Administration, including the new JD/MBA program with a specialization in **sports business**. Our joint programs with the Graduate School allow students to earn a **JD/MA** in **international affairs**, the **history of philosophy**, **social and applied philosophy**, or **political science**. In conjunction with the Medical College of Wisconsin, we offer the **JD/MA** in **bioethics**. Each joint-degree program requires meeting all requirements of both the Law School and the other degree-granting institution; each can be completed in four years. As an alternative to a joint degree, law students may take up to six hours of coursework in a related graduate program at Marquette, such as public policy, criminology, philosophy, or history.

■ Special Programs

Our comprehensive trial-practice courses provide an exceptional opportunity for students to develop trial skills. Distinctive clinics include the Prosecutor and Defender Clinics, Judicial Internships, and numerous supervised field work opportunities.

The Law School and the University of Queensland, Australia, jointly sponsor a program in international, foreign, and comparative law.

■ Admission

Review of completed applications begins after October 1 and continues through the spring. Although the applicant's LSAT score and academic record are important considerations in the selection process, the Admission Committee also considers qualitative factors, such as letters of recommendation, essays, work experience, extracurricular activities, and personal accomplishments and characteristics that contribute to the diversity of the school, the legal community, and the profession. Admitted applicants are required to submit nonrefundable tuition deposits in April and June. These deposits are applied to the student's fall semester tuition. Interviews are not part of the application process.

■ Diploma Privilege

Since 1933, graduates of the Law School who qualify have been admitted to the practice of law in Wisconsin without having to take the Wisconsin Bar Examination. Marquette graduates are entitled to sit for bar examinations in any American jurisdiction.

■ Student Activities

The Law School publishes the *Marquette Law Review*, the *Marquette Sports Law Review*, the *Marquette Intellectual Property Law Review*, and the *Elder Law Journal*. All students may develop advocacy skills in moot court competitions. Marquette moot court teams have won regional titles and championships in National Moot Court and National Labor Law competitions. A wide variety of student organizations are active at the Law School.

■ Career Services

The Career Planning Center processes hundreds of listings of employment opportunities, coordinates campus interviews, and provides counseling assistance to students. In recent years, over 95 percent of our graduates had secured employment within nine months of graduation. Our on-campus interview program includes a broad range of legal employers from both coasts and major cities. The office will help students network with Marquette alumni and other potential resource persons. Our goal is to keep our placement rate high and to ensure a good fit and job satisfaction for all our graduates.

■ Housing

There are many university and campus area apartments within six blocks of the Law School. Ample, affordable housing is also available throughout Milwaukee and its suburbs. Applications for university housing may be obtained from the Office of Residence Life, Marquette University, Room 203 Tower Hall, 716 North 11th Street, Milwaukee, WI 53233 (phone: 414.288.7208).

Applicant Profile

Marquette University Law School
This grid includes only applicants who earned 120-180 LSAT scores under standard administrations.

LSAT Score	3.75 + Apps	Adm	3.50 - 3.74 Apps	Adm	3.25 - 3.49 Apps	Adm	3.00 - 3.24 Apps	Adm	2.75 - 2.99 Apps	Adm	2.50 - 2.74 Apps	Adm	2.25 - 2.49 Apps	Adm	2.00 - 2.24 Apps	Adm	Below 2.00 Apps	Adm	No GPA Apps	Adm	Total Apps	Adm
175-180	1	1	0	0	0	0	0	0	0	0	0	0	0	0	0	0	0	0	0	0	1	1
170-174	0	0	0	0	1	1	2	2	1	1	0	0	1	1	1	0	0	0	0	0	6	5
165-169	6	6	1	1	7	7	5	5	2	2	4	3	2	1	0	0	0	0	0	0	27	25
160-164	19	18	28	28	28	28	37	36	25	23	10	8	7	4	1	0	2	0	0	0	157	145
155-159	55	52	94	83	125	93	90	60	51	20	28	6	13	5	3	0	0	0	1	1	460	320
150-154	86	23	127	26	131	16	127	16	81	8	35	3	17	1	7	1	1	0	5	2	617	96
145-149	16	1	60	1	64	4	79	4	49	1	31	1	16	2	7	0	1	0	3	0	326	14
Below 145	7	0	14	0	46	0	42	0	45	0	30	0	22	0	11	0	4	0	4	0	225	0
Total	190	101	324	139	402	149	382	123	254	55	138	21	78	14	30	1	8	0	13	3	1819	606

Apps = Number of Applicants   Adm = Number Admitted   Reflects 99% of the total applicant pool.

University of Maryland School of Law

500 West Baltimore Street
Baltimore, MD 21201
Phone: 410.706.3492; Fax: 410.706.1793
E-mail: admissions@law.umaryland.edu; Website: www.law.umaryland.edu

ABA
Approved
Since
1930

The Basics

Type of school	Public
Term	Semester
Application deadline	3/1
Application fee	$60
Financial aid deadline	3/1
Can first year start other than fall?	No
Student to faculty ratio (fall)	11.1 to 1
Does the university offer:	
housing restricted to law students?	No
graduate housing for which law students are eligible?	Yes

Faculty and Administrators

	Total		Men		Women		Minorities	
	Fall	Spr	Fall	Spr	Fall	Spr	Fall	Spr
Full-time	54	50	33	31	21	19	11	10
Other Full-time	0	0	0	0	0	0	0	0
Deans, librarians, & others who teach	12	12	2	2	10	10	0	0
Part-time	56	49	39	33	17	16	6	4
Total	122	111	74	66	48	45	17	14

Curriculum

	Full-time	Part-time
Typical first-year section size	61	30
Is there typically a "small section" of the first-year class, other than Legal Writing, taught by full-time faculty	Yes	Yes
If yes, typical size offered last year	26	28
# of classroom course titles beyond 1st year curriculum	145	

# of upper division courses, excluding seminars with an enrollment:		
	Under 25	138
	25-49	27
	50-74	14
	75-99	4
	100+	3

# of seminars	60	
# of seminar positions available	865	
# of seminar positions filled	421	190
# of positions available in simulation courses	1,104	
# of simulation positions filled	531	376
# of positions available in faculty supervised clinical courses	412	
# of faculty supervised clinical positions filled	281	52
# involved in field placements	117	19
# involved in law journals	165	11
# involved in moot court or trial competitions	55	4
# of credit hours required to graduate	85	

JD Enrollment and Ethnicity

	Men		Women		Full-time		Part-time		1st-year		Total		JD Degs. Awd.
	#	%	#	%	#	%	#	%	#	%	#	%	
African Amer.	24	7.0	82	19.2	63	10.4	43	26.1	47	18.2	106	13.7	35
Amer. Indian	0	0.0	2	0.5	2	0.3	0	0.0	1	0.4	2	0.3	1
Asian Amer.	36	10.5	36	8.4	63	10.4	9	5.5	20	7.8	72	9.3	23
Mex. Amer.	1	0.3	1	0.2	1	0.2	1	0.6	0	0.0	2	0.3	0
Puerto Rican	0	0.0	3	0.7	3	0.5	0	0.0	0	0.0	3	0.4	1
Hispanic	5	1.5	17	4.0	20	3.3	2	1.2	11	4.3	22	2.8	8
Total Minority	66	19.2	141	32.9	152	25.0	55	33.3	79	30.6	207	26.8	68
For. Nation.	1	0.3	7	1.6	8	1.3	0	0.0	2	0.8	8	1.0	7
Caucasian	266	77.3	268	62.6	432	71.2	102	61.8	165	64.0	534	69.2	263
Unknown	11	3.2	12	2.8	15	2.5	8	4.8	12	4.7	23	3.0	2
Total	344	44.6	428	55.4	607	78.6	165	21.4	258	33.4	772		340

Tuition and Fees

	Resident	Nonresident
Full-time	$16,253	$27,532
Part-time	$12,311	$20,771

Living Expenses

Estimated living expenses for singles

Living on campus	Living off campus	Living at home
$16,413	$20,351	$10,968

University of Maryland School of Law

ABA
Approved
Since
1930

GPA and LSAT Scores

	Total	Full-time	Part-time
# of apps	4,303	3,782	521
# of admits	486	438	48
# of matrics	255	221	34
75% GPA	3.70	3.75	3.54
25% GPA	3.29	3.31	3.02
75% LSAT	162	162	161
25% LSAT	156	155	150

Grants and Scholarships (from prior year)

	Total #	Total %	Full-time #	Full-time %	Part-time #	Part-time %
Total # of students	862		674		188	
Total # receiving grants	416	48.3	379	56.2	37	19.7
Less than 1/2 tuition	368	42.7	336	49.9	32	17.0
Half to full tuition	44	5.1	39	5.8	5	2.7
Full tuition	4	0.5	4	0.6	0	0.0
More than full tuition	0	0.0	0	0.0	0	0.0
Median grant amount			$4,800		$3,000	

Informational and Library Resources

# of volumes and volume equivalents	456,529
# of titles	107,848
# of active serial subscriptions	3,997
Study seating capacity inside the library	522
# of professional librarians	11
Hours per week library is open	96
# of open, wired connections available to students	1,208
# of networked computers available for use by students	205
# of simultaneous wireless users	20
Require computer?	N

JD Attrition (from prior year)

	Academic #	Other #	Total #	Total %
1st year	1	15	16	6.7%
2nd year	0	8	8	3.4%
3rd year	0	1	1	0.3%
4th year	0	0	0	0.0%

Employment

	Total	Percentage
Employment status known	252	98.8
Employment status unknown	3	1.2
Employed	211	83.7
Pursuing graduate degrees	18	7.1
Unemployed seeking employment	4	1.6
Unemployed not seeking employment	19	7.5

Type of Employment

# employed in law firms	76	36.0
# employed in business and industry	33	15.6
# employed in government	38	18.0
# employed in public interest	6	2.8
# employed as judicial clerks	52	24.6
# employed in academia	6	2.8

Geographic Location

# employed in state	140	66.4
# employed in foreign countries	2	0.9
# of states where employed	18	

Bar Passage Rates

Jurisdiction	Maryland		
Exam	Sum 03	Win 04	Total
# from school taking bar for the first time	171	35	206
School's pass rate for all first-time takers	80%	69%	78%
State's pass rate for all first-time takers	73%	62%	71%

University of Maryland School of Law

500 West Baltimore Street
Baltimore, MD 21201
Phone: 410.706.3492; Fax: 410.706.1793
E-mail: admissions@law.umaryland.edu; Website: www.law.umaryland.edu

■ Introduction

The University of Maryland School of Law provides students with the knowledge, experience, and expertise to prepare them for professional leadership as lawyers, business executives, legislators, public policy makers, community advocates, and other agents of social, political, and economic progress. Its favorable tuition structure makes it a superb value in American legal education.

The law school is an integral part of the Baltimore/Washington/Annapolis legal-business community. Located in downtown Baltimore, just a few blocks from the Inner Harbor's tourist attractions, the school's location affords opportunities for extensive interaction with local, state, and national governments, as well as many law firms, public-interest institutions, agencies, and other organizations of prominence.

Founded in 1816, the School of Law is fully accredited by the ABA and is a member of the AALS. The Juris Doctor curriculum is available in a three-year day or four-year evening program.

■ Community of Students, Faculty, and Alumni

Entering students quickly become part of our supportive community. We are a diverse group (age, gender, race, academic background, and prior employment), and this diversity is reflected in our students and in our faculty and deans. The faculty/student ratio of 1:11.1 provides opportunity for close working relationships in a profes- sional yet collegial setting. Many resources are available to students to ease the transition to law school, including upper-class peer advisors, skills enhancement sessions, and one-on-one academic counseling. Students also directly benefit from a wide network of involved alumni who occupy positions of professional leadership throughout the state, region, and nation.

■ Law School Complex and Library

The School of Law and the Thurgood Marshall Law Library occupy a state-of-the-art complex supportive of the school's programs integrating classroom and experiential learning.

The Thurgood Marshall Law Library houses a collection of approximately 456,000 volumes and equivalents accessible through the online catalog. A staff of 23, including 10 librarians, provides customized reference and consulting services to faculty and students.

■ Curriculum

The required curriculum includes civil, constitutional, criminal, contract, property, and tort law, as well as a three-semester course focusing on legal skills of analysis, research, writing, and oral argument. More than 150 electives include a wide range of courses, seminars, independent studies, simulations, clinics, and externships. Each student must produce at least one substantial paper based on extensive research.

Maryland's strong academic programs in business/corporation/commercial law; criminal law; environmental law; family law/child advocacy; general practice; health law; intellectual property and technology transfer; international/comparative law; jurisprudence/legal history; labor/employment/ administrative law; litigation/advocacy; legislation/ politics/public policy; property/real estate/decedent's estates law; public interest law/community development; and tax law enable students to develop expertise and experience in fields of critical importance to the future.

■ Clinical Law Program

The clinical training program, among the best in the country, offers students real-life court appearances on behalf of a wide range of clients. In addition to this variety of in-house clinical student practice settings, students may gain hands-on experience in public and private nonprofit externships in the Baltimore/ Washington region.

■ Dual Degrees and Interdisciplinary Study

Maryland's interdisciplinary programs, including environment, healthcare, and technology-transfer law offer students the opportunity to work with lawyers and other professionals toward the resolution of problems that transcend traditional disciplinary boundaries. Dual-degree programs include Business Administration, Community Planning, Criminal Justice, Liberal Educa- tion, Pharmacy, Policy Sciences, Public Health, Public Management, Risk and Environmental Assessment, and Social Work. Students are encouraged to enroll in as many as nine credits in related graduate-level programs.

■ Admission

Maryland's law faculty believes the quality of legal education is directly affected by the diversity of our students. The admission committee selects applicants with the greatest potential for law school studies and whose background, character, and experience contribute to the diversity we believe is important to the law school learning experience and to the future benefit of the community. Factors considered in this selection process include geographical origin; cultural and language background; racial, social, disability, or economic barriers overcome; interpersonal skills as demonstrated by extracurricular pursuits, work or service experience, leadership activities, and social experience; potential for intellectual and social growth, as demonstrated by talents, skills, maturity, and compassion; and other special circumstances and characteristics that, when combined with academic skills needed for sound legal education, hold promise as qualities that will be valuable to the school community. The personal statement and letters of recommendation are the primary means for candidates to convey this information and these characteristics to the admission and scholarship committees.

First-year students are admitted only for the fall. The School of Law uses a "rolling" admission process, reviewing applications in the order in which files are completed. Applicants should file applications as early as possible after September 1 of the year preceding enrollment and prior to March 1. Applicants are encouraged to complete the application early; applications completed later may be at a competitive disadvantage. Multiple LSAT scores normally are averaged. Residency may be a factor in close cases. Applicants are encouraged to visit the school, but interviews are not part of the admission process.

■ Student Activities

Maryland law students participate in a variety of activities. The law school is home to over 30 active and diverse student-run organizations.

More than half of our students participate in inter- and intrascholastic advocacy competitions. Students also have the opportunity to participate in four student-edited publications.

■ Scholarships and Need-Based Financial Assistance

The School of Law offers a number of scholarships as well as a traditional need-based financial aid program. Scholarships are awarded on the basis of grades, test score(s), and other evidence of potential for unusual contributions to the academic, cocurricular, and student affairs programs. Such potential should be clearly described in the personal statement included with the application for admission. All admitted applicants are automatically considered for law school scholarship awards. Applications for financial aid (FAFSA) should be submitted as soon after January 1 as possible.

■ Career Development

Maryland law students benefit from extensive connections to the bar, judiciary, business and industry, government, and community organizations within the state of Maryland; Washington, DC; and beyond.

The Career Development Office assists law students and graduates in developing effective job-search strategies to secure legal employment and experience. Ninety-eight percent of the 255 graduates in the class of 2003 reported employment in the following categories: 36 percent in private practice, 24.6 percent in judicial clerkships, 18 percent in government and other public service, 15.6 percent in business and industry, 2.9 percent in public interest organizations, and 2.9 percent in academia.

Applicant Profile

University of Maryland School of Law

| | LSAT Score | | | | | | | | | |
| | 149 & Below | | 150 - 154 | | 155 - 159 | | 160 - 164 | | 165 & Above | |
GPA	Apps	Adm	Apps	Adm	Apps	Adm	Apps	Adm	Apps	Adm
3.75-4.00	76	7	87	23	114	63	55	37	30	25
3.50-3.74	195	9	222	31	234	87	99	76	27	19
3.25-3.49	285	9	288	16	280	44	128	64	45	28
3.00-3.24	316	2	297	14	252	24	108	45	26	12
2.99 & Below	623	1	363	5	263	1	130	8	44	12
Total	1495	28	1257	89	1143	219	520	230	172	96

Apps = Number of Applicants
Adm = Number Admitted

The University of Memphis—Cecil C. Humphreys School of Law

207 Humphreys Law School
Memphis, TN 38152-3140
Phone: 901.678.5403; Fax: 901.678.5210
E-mail: lawadmissions@mail.law.memphis.edu; Website: www.law.memphis.edu

ABA
Approved
Since
1965

The Basics

Type of school	Public
Term	Semester
Application deadline	2/15
Application fee	$25
Financial aid deadline	4/1
Can first year start other than fall?	No
Student to faculty ratio (fall)	16.5 to 1
Does the university offer:	
housing restricted to law students?	No
graduate housing for which law students are eligible?	Yes

Faculty and Administrators

	Total		Men		Women		Minorities	
	Fall	Spr	Fall	Spr	Fall	Spr	Fall	Spr
Full-time	22	21	14	14	8	7	2	1
Other Full-time	0	0	0	0	0	0	0	0
Deans, librarians, & others who teach	5	5	4	4	1	1	0	0
Part-time	17	22	11	13	6	9	1	2
Total	44	48	29	31	15	17	3	3

Curriculum

	Full-time	Part-time
Typical first-year section size	70	0
Is there typically a "small section" of the first-year class, other than Legal Writing, taught by full-time faculty	No	No
If yes, typical size offered last year	0	0
# of classroom course titles beyond 1st year curriculum	67	
# of upper division courses, excluding seminars with an enrollment: Under 25	40	
25-49	15	
50-74	12	
75-99	15	
100+	0	
# of seminars	12	
# of seminar positions available	144	
# of seminar positions filled	125	0
# of positions available in simulation courses	140	
# of simulation positions filled	126	0
# of positions available in faculty supervised clinical courses	88	
# of faculty supervised clinical positions filled	62	0
# involved in field placements	21	0
# involved in law journals	96	0
# involved in moot court or trial competitions	28	0
# of credit hours required to graduate	90	

JD Enrollment and Ethnicity

	Men		Women		Full-time		Part-time		1st-year		Total		JD Degs. Awd.
	#	%	#	%	#	%	#	%	#	%	#	%	
African Amer.	17	6.7	26	13.7	25	5.9	18	81.8	22	16.2	43	9.7	15
Amer. Indian	1	0.4	0	0.0	1	0.2	0	0.0	0	0.0	1	0.2	2
Asian Amer.	2	0.8	4	2.1	6	1.4	0	0.0	2	1.5	6	1.4	2
Mex. Amer.	0	0.0	0	0.0	0	0.0	0	0.0	0	0.0	0	0.0	0
Puerto Rican	0	0.0	0	0.0	0	0.0	0	0.0	0	0.0	0	0.0	0
Hispanic	0	0.0	0	0.0	0	0.0	0	0.0	0	0.0	0	0.0	1
Total Minority	20	7.9	30	15.8	32	7.6	18	81.8	24	17.6	50	11.3	20
For. Nation.	1	0.4	0	0.0	1	0.2	0	0.0	0	0.0	1	0.2	1
Caucasian	232	91.7	160	84.2	388	92.2	4	18.2	112	82.4	392	88.5	111
Unknown	0	0.0	0	0.0	0	0.0	0	0.0	0	0.0	0	0.0	0
Total	253	57.1	190	42.9	421	95.0	22	5.0	136	30.7	443		132

Tuition and Fees

	Resident	Nonresident
Full-time	$8,286	$23,046
Part-time	$7,850	$21,270

Living Expenses

Estimated living expenses for singles

Living on campus	Living off campus	Living at home
$11,903	$11,903	$7,833

The University of Memphis—Cecil C. Humphreys School of Law

*ABA
Approved
Since
1965*

GPA and LSAT Scores

	Total	Full-time	Part-time
# of apps	1,200	1,163	37
# of admits	137	123	14
# of matrics	134	121	13
75% GPA	3.26	3.61	3.64
25% GPA	2.57	3.00	3.05
75% LSAT	150	158	158
25% LSAT	142	154	154

Grants and Scholarships (from prior year)

	Total		Full-time		Part-time	
	#	%	#	%	#	%
Total # of students	466		448		18	
Total # receiving grants	112	24.0	99	22.1	13	72.2
Less than 1/2 tuition	29	6.2	29	6.5	0	0.0
Half to full tuition	65	13.9	52	11.6	13	72.2
Full tuition	13	2.8	13	2.9	0	0.0
More than full tuition	5	1.1	5	1.1	0	0.0
Median grant amount			$5,000		$3,500	

Informational and Library Resources

# of volumes and volume equivalents	265,403
# of titles	46,273
# of active serial subscriptions	2,494
Study seating capacity inside the library	291
# of professional librarians	4
Hours per week library is open	105
# of open, wired connections available to students	314
# of networked computers available for use by students	2
# of simultaneous wireless users	1,250
Require computer?	N

JD Attrition (from prior year)

	Academic	Other	Total	
	#	#	#	%
1st year	9	9	18	12.5%
2nd year	3	1	4	2.4%
3rd year	2	0	2	1.4%
4th year	0	0	0	0.0%

Employment

	Total	Percentage
Employment status known	132	99.2
Employment status unknown	1	0.8
Employed	127	96.2
Pursuing graduate degrees	3	2.3
Unemployed seeking employment	1	0.8
Unemployed not seeking employment	1	0.8

Type of Employment

# employed in law firms	97	76.4
# employed in business and industry	9	7.1
# employed in government	9	7.1
# employed in public interest	1	0.8
# employed as judicial clerks	11	8.7
# employed in academia	0	0.0

Geographic Location

# employed in state	115	90.6
# employed in foreign countries	0	0.0
# of states where employed	9	

Bar Passage Rates

Jurisdiction	Tennessee		
Exam	Sum 03	Win 04	Total
# from school taking bar for the first time	110	19	129
School's pass rate for all first-time takers	90%	74%	88%
State's pass rate for all first-time takers	81%	79%	81%

The University of Memphis—Cecil C. Humphreys School of Law

207 Humphreys Law School
Memphis, TN 38152-3140
Phone: 901.678.5403; Fax: 901.678.5210
E-mail: lawadmissions@mail.law.memphis.edu; Website: www.law.memphis.edu

■ History of the School of Law

The University of Memphis School of Law was founded in 1962 and was fully accredited by the ABA in 1965, when it graduated its first class. The School of Law is an active member of the AALS. Since its inception, the School of Law has graduated over 5,000 students and continues its tradition of preparing competent, ethical attorneys to enter the practice of law, the federal and state judiciary, corporate boardrooms, and service to the community and government.

■ Memphis and the School of Law

Memphis is one of the south's largest and most beautiful and diverse cities. Memphis has one of the lowest cost-of-living rates of any major US city, and its temperate climate provides ample opportunity for year-round activities. The downtown area of Memphis has a distinctive sense of place and a unique skyline.

The School of Law brings together unique individuals with a wide variety of cultural, geographical, employment, and academic backgrounds. Many of its students come to law school immediately after finishing their undergraduate education; however, a significant number enroll after having been in the workforce or after completing advanced degrees. Its entering class usually has students that represent a variety of backgrounds.

The diversity within the student body enriches the classroom experience for all students and enhances the overall quality of the educational experience.

■ The University of Memphis

The University of Memphis serves as a regional center for education, service, and research. It is a comprehensive urban university that enrolls over 20,000 students and is accredited by the Commission on Colleges of the Southern Association of Colleges and Schools.

The University of Memphis is linked historically, intellectually, and emotionally with its community. The university is situated in the pleasant surroundings of residential neighborhoods away from the hustle of the city.

■ Curriculum

The law school offers a full-time day program. A part-time day program is also available for a limited number of students whose other responsibilities make full-time study difficult. The curriculum is designed to challenge its students and prepare them for the modern practice of law. The curriculum reflects a commitment to traditional legal education, and academic emphasis is placed on fundamental lawyering skills and areas of knowledge.

■ Lawyering Skills and Legal Clinics

The School of Law provides the opportunity to take advanced courses in lawyering skills. These include trial advocacy, mediation, and alternative dispute resolution. Several externships are available for students to work under the supervision of a faculty instructor or field supervisor in administrative agencies in the court system and in the criminal justice field. Students can choose from one of three legal clinics operated by the School of Law: a General Litigation Clinic, an Elder Law Clinic, and a Child Advocacy Clinic. Students enrolled in the legal clinic courses work with indigent and elderly clients through the Memphis Area Legal Services and with children in delinquency and dependency proceedings.

■ Joint-Degree Programs

The School of Law and the Fogelman College of Business and Economics offer a coordinated degree program leading to both the JD and MBA degrees. The purpose of this program is to allow students to study both modern business management and law. The JD/MBA program enables the student to complete both the JD and MBA in considerably less time than would be required to complete each degree separately.

■ Library and Information Technology

The University of Memphis law library is enhancing the School of Law's reputation as an information technology center for the Mid-South, assisting students and the legal community with legal research and the efficient delivery of legal services. The law school's wireless network can accommodate more than 1,250 simultaneous users. The Ned R. McWherter Library, the main campus library, features state-of-the-art information technology and is a regional federal depository library as well as a depository for Tennessee state publications.

■ Student Programs and Activities

The law school has two scholarly publications, edited and staffed entirely by students, that are an integral part of the law school experience: *The University of Memphis Law Review* and *Tennessee Journal of Practice & Procedure*. The Moot Court Board (MCB) is composed of 20 third-year students, who are dedicated to the development of advocacy skills. Members of the MCB plan, organize, and oversee three intraschool competitions. The law school also fields several moot court teams in national moot court and mock trial competitions. The Student Bar Association (SBA) is the student government of the law school. The SBA coordinates a wide variety of

The University of Memphis—Cecil C. Humphreys School of Law

extracurricular activities, ranging from informal weekly gatherings with faculty members to formal lectures and philanthropic opportunities in and around the Memphis community. Students can also choose from approximately 20 other organizations, ranging from legal fraternities to special interest organizations.

■ Admission

The majority of applicants are admitted based on a weighted combination of the LSAT score and the cumulative undergraduate GPA. Some applicants are selected by the Faculty Admission Committee through the qualifiable admission process. Other factors, such as quality of the applicant's undergraduate institution, level and rigor of coursework, letters of recommendation, graduate work, employment during and after college, extracurricular activities, educational diversity, and state of residence are considered in this process. In an attempt to attract a diverse student population, the School of Law has developed a selection process that provides a full review of qualified applicants but assures that admission is on the merits of each applicant.

■ Career Services

The Career Services Office actively assists students and alumni by developing their interest in specific areas of the law, enhancing their professional skills, and providing information about opportunities for part-time and full-time employment in their law careers. A comprehensive national Internet job bank as well as a network of alumni mentors is available to help students who are interested in law careers outside the Memphis area.

In addition to hosting a large number of firms, corporations, and public interest/governmental employers for fall and spring on-campus interviewing and seminars, the School of Law is a member of several organizations that conduct annual recruiting conferences that provide second- and third-year law students and judicial law clerks with the opportunity to interview with law firms, government agencies, and corporations throughout the nation.

Employment statistics for Memphis law graduates have remained consistently high during the last decade, and according to the National Association for Law Placement, the 2003 class of Memphis graduates reported a 98.5 percent employment rate within nine months of graduation. Memphis has graduates practicing in all 50 states and in several foreign countries.

■ Tennessee Institute for Pre-Law

The Tennessee Institute for Pre-Law facilitates admission of African American students who are Tennessee residents, to the two state-supported law schools in Tennessee. The program is an eight-week session offered each summer. Participants who successfully complete the senior-partner level of the program and who meet specified requirements for admission will be guaranteed admission to one or both of the state-supported law schools.

Applicant Profile

The University of Memphis—Cecil C. Humphreys School of Law
This grid includes only applicants who earned 120-180 LSAT scores under standard administrations.

LSAT Score	GPA																				
	3.75 +		3.50 - 3.74		3.25 - 3.49		3.00 - 3.24		2.75 - 2.99		2.50 - 2.74		2.25 - 2.49		2.00 - 2.24		Below 2.00		No GPA		Total	
	Apps	Adm	Apps	Adm	Apps	Adm	Apps	Adm	Apps	Adm	Apps	Adm	Apps	Adm	Apps	Adm	Apps	Adm	Apps	Adm	Apps	Adm
175-180	0	0	0	0	0	0	0	0	0	0	0	0	0	0	0	0	0	0	0	0	0	0
170-174	0	0	1	0	1	1	0	0	0	0	1	1	0	0	0	0	0	0	0	0	3	2
165-169	5	5	2	2	2	2	3	3	1	1	2	2	1	1	1	1	0	0	0	0	17	17
160-164	5	5	12	12	10	10	7	6	8	8	4	4	8	7	1	0	1	1	1	0	57	53
155-159	21	20	35	33	45	40	40	32	40	28	11	8	7	4	3	1	1	0	1	0	204	166
150-154	36	14	66	18	66	6	66	10	60	7	30	2	12	2	8	0	2	0	4	0	350	59
145-149	19	0	31	1	54	3	59	2	42	3	38	4	18	2	9	1	3	0	5	0	278	16
140-144	5	0	19	1	26	3	33	2	27	1	21	1	21	0	4	0	2	0	10	0	168	8
135-139	5	0	3	0	7	0	12	1	12	0	14	0	10	0	4	0	3	0	3	0	73	1
130-134	1	0	1	1	2	0	5	0	3	0	2	0	4	0	5	0	2	0	3	0	28	1
125-129	0	0	0	0	0	0	0	0	1	0	1	0	0	0	3	0	0	0	6	0	11	0
120-124	0	0	1	0	0	0	0	0	0	0	0	0	0	0	1	0	0	0	1	0	3	0
Total	97	44	171	68	213	65	225	56	194	48	124	22	81	16	39	3	14	1	34	0	1192	323

Apps = Number of Applicants   Adm = Number Admitted   Reflects 98% of the total applicant pool.

Mercer University—Walter F. George School of Law

1021 Georgia Avenue
Macon, GA 31207
Phone: 478.301.2605; Fax: 478.301.2989
E-mail: martin_sv@mercer.edu; Website: www.law.mercer.edu

ABA
Approved
Since
1925

The Basics

Type of school	Private
Term	Semester
Application deadline	3/15
Application fee	$50
Financial aid deadline	4/1
Can first year start other than fall?	No
Student to faculty ratio (fall)	14.4 to 1
Does the university offer:	
housing restricted to law students?	No
graduate housing for which law students are eligible?	Yes

Faculty and Administrators

	Total		Men		Women		Minorities	
	Fall	Spr	Fall	Spr	Fall	Spr	Fall	Spr
Full-time	25	26	16	18	9	8	3	3
Other Full-time	0	0	0	0	0	0	0	0
Deans, librarians, & others who teach	9	9	4	4	5	5	0	0
Part-time	9	25	8	21	1	4	2	2
Total	**43**	**60**	**28**	**43**	**15**	**17**	**5**	**5**

Curriculum

	Full-time	Part-time
Typical first-year section size	72	0
Is there typically a "small section" of the first-year class, other than Legal Writing, taught by full-time faculty	Yes	No
If yes, typical size offered last year	23	0
# of classroom course titles beyond 1st year curriculum		89
# of upper division courses, excluding seminars with an enrollment: Under 25		85
25-49		22
50-74		9
75-99		4
100+		0
# of seminars		17
# of seminar positions available		255
# of seminar positions filled	162	0
# of positions available in simulation courses		844
# of simulation positions filled	718	0
# of positions available in faculty supervised clinical courses		0
# of faculty supervised clinical positions filled	0	0
# involved in field placements	77	0
# involved in law journals	47	0
# involved in moot court or trial competitions	51	0
# of credit hours required to graduate		91

JD Enrollment and Ethnicity

	Men		Women		Full-time		Part-time		1st-year		Total		JD Degs. Awd.
	#	%	#	%	#	%	#	%	#	%	#	%	
African Amer.	11	4.8	25	12.9	36	8.5	0	0.0	14	9.9	36	8.5	9
Amer. Indian	2	0.9	2	1.0	4	0.9	0	0.0	1	0.7	4	0.9	1
Asian Amer.	4	1.7	9	4.6	13	3.1	0	0.0	6	4.2	13	3.1	1
Mex. Amer.	1	0.4	0	0.0	1	0.2	0	0.0	1	0.7	1	0.2	0
Puerto Rican	1	0.4	1	0.5	2	0.5	0	0.0	0	0.0	2	0.5	1
Hispanic	0	0.0	1	0.5	1	0.2	0	0.0	1	0.7	1	0.2	2
Total Minority	19	8.3	38	19.6	57	13.5	0	0.0	23	16.2	57	13.4	14
For. Nation.	0	0.0	2	1.0	2	0.5	0	0.0	1	0.7	2	0.5	0
Caucasian	187	81.7	138	71.6	325	77.0	2	100.0	106	74.6	327	77.1	110
Unknown	23	10.0	15	7.7	38	9.0	0	0.0	12	8.5	38	9.0	5
Total	229	54.2	193	45.8	422	99.5	2	0.5	142	33.5	424		129

Tuition and Fees

	Resident	Nonresident
Full-time	$25,450	$25,450
Part-time	$0	$0

Living Expenses

Estimated living expenses for singles

Living on campus	Living off campus	Living at home
$13,000	$13,000	$13,000

Mercer University—Walter F. George School of Law

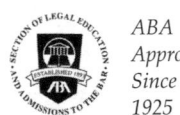

ABA
Approved
Since
1925

GPA and LSAT Scores

	Total	Full-time	Part-time
# of apps	1,694	1,694	0
# of admits	375	375	0
# of matrics	143	143	0
75% GPA	3.63	3.63	0.00
25% GPA	3.05	3.05	0.00
75% LSAT	158	158	0
25% LSAT	154	154	0

Grants and Scholarships (from prior year)

	Total		Full-time		Part-time	
	#	%	#	%	#	%
Total # of students	421		419		2	
Total # receiving grants	147	34.9	147	35.1	0	0.0
Less than 1/2 tuition	67	15.9	67	16.0	0	0.0
Half to full tuition	15	3.6	15	3.6	0	0.0
Full tuition	30	7.1	30	7.2	0	0.0
More than full tuition	35	8.3	35	8.4	0	0.0
Median grant amount			$12,595		$0	

Informational and Library Resources

# of volumes and volume equivalents	327,654
# of titles	41,243
# of active serial subscriptions	3,319
Study seating capacity inside the library	388
# of professional librarians	5
Hours per week library is open	68
# of open, wired connections available to students	673
# of networked computers available for use by students	69
# of simultaneous wireless users	80
Require computer?	Y

JD Attrition (from prior year)

	Academic	Other	Total	
	#	#	#	%
1st year	4	8	12	8.6%
2nd year	0	5	5	3.4%
3rd year	0	0	0	0.0%
4th year	0	0	0	0.0%

Employment

	Total	Percentage
Employment status known	147	98.7
Employment status unknown	2	1.3
Employed	137	93.2
Pursuing graduate degrees	7	4.8
Unemployed seeking employment	3	2.0
Unemployed not seeking employment	0	0.0

Type of Employment

# employed in law firms	99	72.3
# employed in business and industry	8	5.8
# employed in government	17	12.4
# employed in public interest	1	0.7
# employed as judicial clerks	10	7.3
# employed in academia	1	0.7

Geographic Location

# employed in state	108	78.8
# employed in foreign countries	1	0.7
# of states where employed	9	

Bar Passage Rates

Jurisdiction	Georgia		
Exam	Sum 03	Win 04	Total
# from school taking bar for the first time	110	7	117
School's pass rate for all first-time takers	85%	71%	84%
State's pass rate for all first-time takers	86%	75%	83%

Mercer University—Walter F. George School of Law

Office of Admissions, 1021 Georgia Avenue
Macon, GA 31207
Phone: 478.301.2605; Fax: 478.301.2989
E-mail: martin_sv@mercer.edu; Website: www.law.mercer.edu

■ Introduction

The Walter F. George School of Law of Mercer University is located in Macon, Georgia, about 80 miles south of Atlanta. Founded in 1873, it is one of the oldest private law schools in the nation. Named for a distinguished alumnus who served as a United States senator for 36 years, the school became a member of AALS in 1923 and has been ABA-approved since 1925. In 1987, George Woodruff bequeathed the school $15 million. Two major initiatives were pursued as a result of Mr. Woodruff's beneficence: Enrollment was reduced to approximately 400 students and a new curriculum was put in place. The new curriculum emphasizes small classes, an innovative progression in the course of study, and a unique sixth semester designed to facilitate the transition from student to lawyer.

■ Admission

Mercer University's Walter F. George School of Law accepts applications between September 1 and March 15 from prospective students wishing to begin their studies in the fall semester. The requirements for application are straight-forward. Applicants must have completed a bachelor's degree prior to law school enrollment. They must register with LSDAS and take the LSAT, preferably in the summer or fall before application is made. Applicants must submit two letters of recommendation, an application fee, and a personal statement candidly discussing their strengths and weaknesses as prospective law students.

LSAT performance and undergraduate grades are very important in determining admission to the Mercer law school, but other factors will be considered to arrive at a fair evaluation of an applicant's potential to become a competent and ethical attorney. Postgraduate work, employment, community and military service, leadership ability, personal circumstances, and other relevant background information will be evaluated.

■ Library Facilities

The Furman Smith Law Library is the primary resource center of the law school. The law library and computing facilities are accessible to students 24 hours a day. The library's over 325,000 volume collection is enhanced by a wide array of online services that support the curricular and research needs of the law school community. Students are able to access network resources from any of the more than 69 computers and 753 network access points throughout the law school. The law library staff of 15 includes 7 professional law librarians who teach legal research courses and provide superior service to students and the legal community.

■ Curriculum

Mercer's Woodruff Curriculum and the atmosphere of the law school work together to provide students with the four Measures of Mercer: a thorough intellectual foundation, strong practical skills, professional relationships, and a commitment to ethical behavior. The combination of these measures offers the strongest possible foundation for success in the practice of law. Mercer is one of a few select schools in the country to receive the prestigious Gambrell Professionalism Award from the American Bar Association. The award cites the depth and excellence of the Woodruff Curriculum and its obvious commitment to professionalism.

Implemented in 1990, the practice-oriented Woodruff Curriculum helps ensure that Mercer graduates develop problem-solving, counseling, and trial and appellate advocacy skills, and acquire the legal knowledge to become exceptional practicing attorneys. Each year begins with an introductory week-long course exploring one role of the practicing lawyer.

One pervasive skill needed for law practice is the ability to write clearly and convincingly. All students take research and writing courses during at least four semesters of law study, and many take one every term. Mercer is the first law school in the nation to offer a Certificate in Advanced Legal Writing, Research, and Drafting. Students are selected into the certificate program through a lottery system and those who complete the Certificate Program will have earned the equivalent of 18 credit hours in research and writing—by far the most intense and thorough training in legal writing anywhere. In 2003, in recognition of Mercer's nationally known Legal Writing Program, the Legal Writing Institute selected Mercer as its host school. The Legal Writing Institute is the world's largest organization of lawyers and law professors interested in improving legal writing.

The last semester of study is the most distinctive component of the Woodruff Curriculum as it offers students a unique opportunity to make the transition from law school to law practice. An intensive session features advanced courses in a variety of practical lawyering skills such as Advanced Counseling, Pretrial Practice, and Advanced Trial Practice.

■ Joint JD/MBA Program

Mercer's School of Law and Mercer's School of Business and Economics offer a four-year program leading to both the Juris Doctor and Master of Business Administration degrees. Applicants to this program must file separate and complete applications with both schools and obtain admission to both schools.

Mercer University—Walter F. George School of Law

■ Special Programs

The Woodruff Curriculum is one of the most innovative and exciting education programs available, and it is offered to every Mercer student. A more complete description of the program is listed under the heading, "Curriculum."

Since 1985, the National Criminal Defense College (NCDC) has held its Summer Trial Practice Institute every year on the Mercer law school campus. NCDC conducts 2 two-week-long trial skills sessions for nearly 200 public defenders and criminal defense attorneys.

■ Student Activities

In Mercer's moot court program, students improve their written and oral advocacy, negotiation, and client counseling skills. The team members' commitment and superior preparation are evident in our moot court competition victories.

The Mercer Law Review (the oldest continually published law review in Georgia) has been edited and published quarterly by law students since 1949.

Students may also gain editorial experience in connection with the *Journal of Southern Legal History*, which is published by the law school.

■ Financial Aid

Mercer awards over $2 million in scholarship aid every year to students whose academic records, LSAT scores, and personal achievements demonstrate the potential for outstanding performance in the study of law. Two of our most prestigious scholarships are the George W. Woodruff Scholarship (full-tuition plus a $5,000 stipend) and the Walter F. George Foundation Public Service Scholarship (full-tuition plus a $3,500 summer community service grant). In order to be considered for these scholarships, you must have your admission application and scholarship application completed and received in our office no later than February 1. A complete list of scholarships is available on our website at *www.law.mercer.edu* under Prospective Students. In addition to scholarship aid, students may qualify for student loans, and work-study is available after the first year of law school.

■ Career Services

Mercer law school has an active career services office. Alumni and faculty members support students in their efforts to find satisfying employment. The office assists students in obtaining permanent, summer, and part-time employment.

Services of the office include arranging on-campus interviews with employers, career planning seminars, and off-campus interviewing consortia. Individual career counseling and résumé and cover-letter writing workshops also comprise much of the work of the office. An extensive library of career resources is available for student use.

The Office of Career Services reports that 98 percent of the Class of 2003 was employed or pursuing LLM degrees within six to nine months after graduation.

Applicant Profile

Mercer University—Walter F. George School of Law
This grid includes only applicants who earned 120-180 LSAT scores under standard administrations.

LSAT Score	3.75 +		3.50 - 3.74		3.25 - 3.49		3.00 - 3.24		2.75 - 2.99		2.50 - 2.74		2.25 - 2.49		2.00 - 2.24		Below 2.00		No GPA		Total	
	Apps	Adm	Apps	Adm	Apps	Adm	Apps	Adm	Apps	Adm	Apps	Adm	Apps	Adm	Apps	Adm	Apps	Adm	Apps	Adm	Apps	Adm
175-180	0	0	0	0	0	0	0	0	0	0	0	0	0	0	0	0	0	0	0	0	0	0
170-174	0	0	0	0	0	0	1	1	0	0	1	1	0	0	0	0	0	0	0	0	2	2
165-169	1	1	2	2	0	0	2	2	2	2	3	3	2	2	1	0	0	0	0	0	13	12
160-164	10	9	15	15	8	8	12	11	7	5	10	8	6	4	3	3	0	0	1	1	72	64
155-159	29	27	51	47	63	50	76	29	51	15	31	13	16	4	3	1	1	0	1	1	322	187
150-154	42	24	107	34	121	14	125	9	98	5	46	4	19	2	16	0	1	0	3	1	578	93
145-149	31	4	65	4	65	2	81	3	63	1	34	1	27	0	9	1	3	0	6	0	384	16
140-144	8	0	20	0	35	0	60	0	46	0	20	0	22	0	4	0	2	0	4	0	221	0
135-139	1	0	2	0	11	0	14	0	18	0	14	0	6	0	4	0	1	0	5	0	76	0
130-134	0	0	2	0	1	0	4	0	5	0	5	0	3	0	1	0	1	0	1	0	23	0
125-129	0	0	0	0	1	0	1	0	1	0	0	0	0	0	1	0	0	0	1	0	5	0
120-124	0	0	0	0	0	0	0	0	0	0	0	0	0	0	1	0	0	0	0	0	1	0
Total	122	65	264	102	305	74	376	55	291	28	164	30	101	12	43	5	9	0	22	3	1697	374

Apps = Number of Applicants   Adm = Number Admitted   Reflects 99% of the total applicant pool.
This chart is to be used as a general guide only. Nonnumerical factors are strongly considered for all applicants.

University of Miami School of Law

PO Box 248087
Coral Gables, FL 33124-8087
Phone: 305.284.2523; Fax: 305.284.3084
E-mail: admissions@law.miami.edu; Website: www.law.miami.edu

ABA
Approved
Since
1941

The Basics

Type of school	Private
Term	Semester
Application deadline	7/31
Application fee	$50
Financial aid deadline	3/1
Can first year start other than fall?	No
Student to faculty ratio (fall)	20.0 to 1
Does the university offer:	
housing restricted to law students?	No
graduate housing for which law students are eligible?	No

Faculty and Administrators

	Total		Men		Women		Minorities	
	Fall	Spr	Fall	Spr	Fall	Spr	Fall	Spr
Full-time	49	46	32	31	17	15	7	7
Other Full-time	8	10	4	6	4	4	3	4
Deans, librarians, & others who teach	9	9	5	5	4	4	2	2
Part-time	100	113	72	79	28	34	17	20
Total	166	178	113	121	53	57	29	33

Curriculum

	Full-time	Part-time
Typical first-year section size	100	0
Is there typically a "small section" of the first-year class, other than Legal Writing, taught by full-time faculty	Yes	No
If yes, typical size offered last year	50	0
# of classroom course titles beyond 1st year curriculum	179	
# of upper division courses, excluding seminars with an enrollment: Under 25	34	
25-49	38	
50-74	21	
75-99	5	
100+	15	
# of seminars	40	
# of seminar positions available	600	
# of seminar positions filled	405	0
# of positions available in simulation courses	971	
# of simulation positions filled	751	0
# of positions available in faculty supervised clinical courses	59	
# of faculty supervised clinical positions filled	59	0
# involved in field placements	147	0
# involved in law journals	140	0
# involved in moot court or trial competitions	70	0
# of credit hours required to graduate	88	

JD Enrollment and Ethnicity

	Men		Women		Full-time		Part-time		1st-year		Total		JD Degs. Awd.
	#	%	#	%	#	%	#	%	#	%	#	%	
African Amer.	32	5.1	47	8.5	76	6.6	3	10.3	28	6.6	79	6.7	29
Amer. Indian	3	0.5	1	0.2	4	0.3	0	0.0	1	0.2	4	0.3	1
Asian Amer.	16	2.5	21	3.8	36	3.1	1	3.4	13	3.1	37	3.1	18
Mex. Amer.	0	0.0	0	0.0	0	0.0	0	0.0	0	0.0	0	0.0	0
Puerto Rican	0	0.0	0	0.0	0	0.0	0	0.0	0	0.0	0	0.0	0
Hispanic	52	8.2	87	15.7	131	11.3	8	27.6	39	9.2	139	11.7	60
Total Minority	103	16.3	156	28.2	247	21.3	12	41.4	81	19.2	259	21.8	108
For. Nation.	27	4.3	34	6.1	56	4.8	5	17.2	15	3.6	61	5.1	24
Caucasian	468	74.1	340	61.4	796	68.8	12	41.4	292	69.2	808	68.1	245
Unknown	34	5.4	24	4.3	58	5.0	0	0.0	34	8.1	58	4.9	4
Total	632	53.3	554	46.7	1157	97.6	29	2.4	422	35.6	1186		381

Tuition and Fees

	Resident	Nonresident
Full-time	$29,458	$29,458
Part-time	$21,812	$21,812

Living Expenses

Estimated living expenses for singles

Living on campus	Living off campus	Living at home
N/A	$16,917	$9,469

University of Miami School of Law

*ABA
Approved
Since
1941*

GPA and LSAT Scores

	Total	Full-time	Part-time
# of apps	5,131	4,986	145
# of admits	1,768	1,754	14
# of matrics	429	426	3
75% GPA	3.59	3.59	3.51
25% GPA	3.16	3.16	3.20
75% LSAT	160	160	166
25% LSAT	155	155	161

Grants and Scholarships (from prior year)

	Total		Full-time		Part-time	
	#	%	#	%	#	%
Total # of students	1,181		1,140		41	
Total # receiving grants	305	25.8	305	26.8	0	0.0
Less than 1/2 tuition	132	11.2	132	11.6	0	0.0
Half to full tuition	153	13.0	153	13.4	0	0.0
Full tuition	9	0.8	9	0.8	0	0.0
More than full tuition	11	0.9	11	1.0	0	0.0
Median grant amount			$15,309		$0	

Informational and Library Resources

# of volumes and volume equivalents	582,243
# of titles	90,833
# of active serial subscriptions	6,961
Study seating capacity inside the library	769
# of professional librarians	11
Hours per week library is open	111
# of open, wired connections available to students	87
# of networked computers available for use by students	157
# of simultaneous wireless users	1,400
Require computer?	N

JD Attrition (from prior year)

	Academic	Other	Total	
	#	#	#	%
1st year	7	40	47	11.8%
2nd year	1	0	1	0.3%
3rd year	0	0	0	0.0%
4th year	0	0	0	0.0%

Employment

	Total	Percentage
Employment status known	320	91.4
Employment status unknown	30	8.6
Employed	297	92.8
Pursuing graduate degrees	12	3.7
Unemployed seeking employment	7	2.2
Unemployed not seeking employment	4	1.2

Type of Employment

# employed in law firms	195	65.7
# employed in business and industry	27	9.1
# employed in government	48	16.2
# employed in public interest	9	3.0
# employed as judicial clerks	12	4.0
# employed in academia	1	0.3

Geographic Location

# employed in state	239	80.5
# employed in foreign countries	1	0.3
# of states where employed	19	

Bar Passage Rates

Jurisdiction	Florida		
Exam	Sum 03	Win 04	Total
# from school taking bar for the first time	239	59	298
School's pass rate for all first-time takers	83%	66%	80%
State's pass rate for all first-time takers	76%	75%	76%

University of Miami School of Law

PO Box 248087
Coral Gables, FL 33124-8087
Phone: 305.284.2523; Fax: 305.284.3084
E-mail: admissions@law.miami.edu; Website: www.law.miami.edu

■ Introduction

Established in 1926 in Coral Gables, Florida, the University of Miami School of Law is part of one of the largest private research universities in the United States. The school's location on the main campus enables students to attend law school in a tranquil subtropical setting while taking advantage of the opportunities available in one of the most dynamic and rapidly expanding legal communities in the country. Miami is accredited by the ABA, is a member of the AALS, and has a chapter of the prestigious scholastic society, the Order of the Coif.

■ Faculty

The faculty of the University of Miami have exceptional credentials—including education at the world's top universities and law schools; significant prior work experience in private practice, government, and prestigious judicial clerkships; and extensive research, writing, and pro bono activities. Their expertise is especially strong in international and foreign law (with half of them having written or taught in those fields); taxation and estate planning; the interaction of legal doctrine with contemporary social issues, such as immigration, crime, the Internet, and intellectual property; legal ethics; and other fields.

■ Library

With approximately 600,000 volumes in print and microform, the Law Library is one of the largest in the Southeast. The library has liberal hours, a superb student/staff ratio, computer labs, and ample seating for individual study and group study rooms. Carrels throughout the library contain computers or ports for easy access to electronic resources. The campus is wireless.

■ Curriculum

The school provides a solid foundation in all the traditional subjects basic to understanding and practicing the law throughout the nation. It also offers ambitious programs designed to teach students the craft as well as the theory of the law, to develop the research and writing skills critical to the legal profession, and to expose students to other skills necessary for effective professional service.

Choosing from more than 160 courses, workshops, and seminars, students ordinarily complete the JD degree in three academic years of full-time study. A part-time day program and summer sessions are available. Miami's course offerings in inter-American, international, and comparative law are outstanding. Several international

and comparative law courses are taught in Spanish, giving Spanish-speaking students the opportunity to learn foreign law in the original language. Joint JD/Masters programs are offered in business administration, public health, and marine affairs, and a JD/LLM in taxation.

Master of Laws (LLM) programs include inter-American law, international law, ocean and coastal law, taxation, estate planning, real property development, and comparative law. A JD degree (or equivalent degree from a foreign law school) is required for entrance into an LLM program.

■ Special Programs

The school offers one of the most comprehensive and sophisticated skills training programs in the nation, integrating trial, pre-trial, and clinical experiences into one program. Directed by a full-time faculty member, distinguished trial attorneys and judges from both state and federal courts assist with the trial and pretrial courses and help supervise the clinical placements. Additional skills training is available in transactional skills, alternative dispute resolution, mediation, and domestic and international legal research.

The school runs one of the nation's largest mock trial competitions and is distinguished by winning state, regional, and national competitions in moot court, mock trial, negotiation, and client counseling.

The Center for Ethics and Public Service is an interdisciplinary project teaching the values of ethical judgment, professional responsibility, and public service.

The Children & Youth Law Clinic provides representation to abused and neglected children and youth in the foster care system.

H.O.P.E. (Helping Others Through Pro Bono Efforts) is the law school's community outreach and advocacy project, offering a myriad of service opportunities for the law school community.

The James Weldon Johnson/Robert H. Waters Summer Institute acquaints selected incoming students with the tools necessary to succeed in law school.

Study abroad options consist of five summer integrated module programs that are held in England, Spain, and the Mediterranean, as well as a semester in Barcelona option.

■ Admission

Admission is competitive. LSAT scores and undergraduate averages are used in the selection process, and letters of recommendation are required. Also considered are the applicant's work and extracurricular history, special skills, and background. Entering students are admitted only in the fall semester. Applicants are urged to apply for admission as early as possible after September 1. Applications received after February 3 will be considered on a space-available basis.

■ The Student Body and Student Life

Miami's student body is highly talented and exceptionally diverse, enriching students' educational experience by exposing them to a wide variety of viewpoints and life experiences. The school consistently ranks among the leaders in numbers of Hispanics, African Americans, and foreign students graduated from its JD program. The school's many student activities include an active Student Bar Association, Honor Council, and more than 30 diverse student organizations. Students regularly take part in a wide range of pro bono activities. Miami's law journals include *The University of Miami Law Review*; the *University of Miami Inter-American Law Review*; the *University of Miami International and Comparative Law Review*; the *Business Law Review*; and *Psychology, Public Policy, and Law*.

■ Expenses and Financial Aid

Scholarship aid available through the school normally does not exceed the cost of tuition. Most scholarships are merit based, although need is sometimes considered.

Admitted applicants are automatically considered for most scholarship awards. Applicants who wish to be considered for a merit scholarship should complete their files prior to January 5. Most scholarships are awarded on a rolling basis. Those admitted by February 1 are considered for the prestigious Harvey T. Reid and Soia Mentschikoff scholarships. In addition, admitted students are eligible to apply for the public-interest related Miami Scholars Program which requires a separate application with a deadline of March 15. The law school assists students in applying for public and private loans.

Federal loans may be applied for by filing the FAFSA online at *www.fafsa.ed.gov*. Our Federal School Code is E00532. Private loans may also be applied for online, and this information is sent to students upon admission.

■ Career Services

The Career Planning Center (CPC) provides career counseling and resources to law students and alumni. The center's On-Campus Interviewing Program attracts national and local employers, providing interview opportunities with law firms, government agencies, public service organizations, corporate counsel, and the judiciary. CPC offers a wide range of job-related seminars and job fairs and also provides access to a career resource library, computer research terminals, and job postings via the Internet.

Applicant Profile

University of Miami School of Law
This grid includes only applicants who earned 120-180 LSAT scores under standard administrations.

LSAT Score	3.75 +	3.50 - 3.74	3.25 - 3.49	3.00 - 3.24	2.75 - 2.99	2.50 - 2.74	2.25 - 2.49	2.00 - 2.24	Below 2.00	No GPA
175-180										
170-174										
165-169										
160-164										
155-159										
150-154										
145-149										
140-144										
135-139										
130-134										
125-129										
120-124										

■ Good Possibility   □ Possible   ▨ Unlikely

When reviewing the grid, it is important to note that admission to the school is based upon all aspects of an applicant's background, and not limited to the LSAT and undergraduate grade-point average.

The University of Michigan Law School

Hutchins Hall, 625 South State Street
Ann Arbor, MI 48109-1215
Phone: 734.764.1358
E-mail: law.jd.admissions@umich.edu; Website: www.law.umich.edu

ABA
Approved
Since
1923

The Basics

Type of school	Public
Term	Semester
Application deadline	11/15 2/15
Application fee	$60
Financial aid deadline	
Can first year start other than fall?	Yes
Student to faculty ratio (fall)	16.0 to 1
Does the university offer:	
housing restricted to law students?	Yes
graduate housing for which law students are eligible?	Yes

Faculty and Administrators

	Total		Men		Women		Minorities	
	Fall	Spr	Fall	Spr	Fall	Spr	Fall	Spr
Full-time	61	46	40	31	21	15	6	5
Other Full-time	8	9	5	5	3	4	0	0
Deans, librarians, & others who teach	5	5	3	3	2	2	0	0
Part-time	23	21	15	13	8	8	1	1
Total	97	81	63	52	34	29	7	6

Curriculum

	Full-time	Part-time
Typical first-year section size	100	0
Is there typically a "small section" of the first-year class, other than Legal Writing, taught by full-time faculty	Yes	No
If yes, typical size offered last year	50	0
# of classroom course titles beyond 1st year curriculum	182	
# of upper division courses, excluding seminars with an enrollment: Under 25	67	
25-49	36	
50-74	18	
75-99	18	
100+	9	
# of seminars	62	
# of seminar positions available	1,077	
# of seminar positions filled	722	0
# of positions available in simulation courses	358	
# of simulation positions filled	176	0
# of positions available in faculty supervised clinical courses	226	
# of faculty supervised clinical positions filled	204	0
# involved in field placements	14	0
# involved in law journals	377	0
# involved in moot court or trial competitions	110	0
# of credit hours required to graduate	80	

JD Enrollment and Ethnicity

	Men		Women		Full-time		Part-time		1st-year		Total		JD Degs. Awd.
	#	%	#	%	#	%	#	%	#	%	#	%	
African Amer.	28	4.2	44	8.4	72	6.1	0	0.0	26	6.8	72	6.1	31
Amer. Indian	15	2.3	14	2.7	29	2.5	0	0.0	8	2.1	29	2.5	3
Asian Amer.	55	8.3	69	13.2	124	10.5	0	0.0	44	11.5	124	10.5	41
Mex. Amer.	0	0.0	0	0.0	0	0.0	0	0.0	0	0.0	0	0.0	0
Puerto Rican	0	0.0	0	0.0	0	0.0	0	0.0	0	0.0	0	0.0	0
Hispanic	42	6.4	33	6.3	75	6.3	0	0.0	23	6.0	75	6.3	17
Total Minority	140	21.2	160	30.7	300	25.4	0	0.0	101	26.4	300	25.4	92
For. Nation.	12	1.8	10	1.9	22	1.9	0	0.0	8	2.1	22	1.9	3
Caucasian	439	66.4	309	59.3	748	63.3	0	0.0	222	58.1	748	63.3	278
Unknown	70	10.6	42	8.1	112	9.5	0	0.0	51	13.4	112	9.5	14
Total	661	55.9	521	44.1	1182	100.0	0	0.0	382	32.3	1182		387

Tuition and Fees

	Resident	Nonresident
Full-time	$29,358	$34,358
Part-time	$0	$0

Living Expenses

Estimated living expenses for singles

Living on campus	Living off campus	Living at home
$14,815	$14,815	$5,400

The University of Michigan Law School

ABA
Approved
Since
1923

GPA and LSAT Scores

	Total	Full-time	Part-time
# of apps	5,523	5,523	0
# of admits	1,098	1,098	0
# of matrics	381	381	0
75% GPA	3.77	3.77	0.00
25% GPA	3.44	3.44	0.00
75% LSAT	169	169	0
25% LSAT	164	164	0

Grants and Scholarships (from prior year)

	Total		Full-time		Part-time	
	#	%	#	%	#	%
Total # of students	1,149		1,149		0	
Total # receiving grants	452	39.3	452	39.3	0	0.0
Less than 1/2 tuition	388	33.8	388	33.8	0	0.0
Half to full tuition	35	3.0	35	3.0	0	0.0
Full tuition	0	0.0	0	0.0	0	0.0
More than full tuition	29	2.5	29	2.5	0	0.0
Median grant amount			$8,595		$0	

Informational and Library Resources

# of volumes and volume equivalents	952,277
# of titles	309,071
# of active serial subscriptions	9,772
Study seating capacity inside the library	855
# of professional librarians	13
Hours per week library is open	112
# of open, wired connections available to students	357
# of networked computers available for use by students	189
# of simultaneous wireless users	1,200
Require computer?	N

JD Attrition (from prior year)

	Academic	Other	Total	
	#	#	#	%
1st year	0	8	8	2.0%
2nd year	0	0	0	0.0%
3rd year	6	0	6	1.6%
4th year	0	0	0	0.0%

Employment

	Total	Percentage
Employment status known	359	99.7
Employment status unknown	1	0.3
Employed	333	92.8
Pursuing graduate degrees	11	3.1
Unemployed seeking employment	4	1.1
Unemployed not seeking employment	11	3.1

Type of Employment

# employed in law firms	204	61.3
# employed in business and industry	14	4.2
# employed in government	18	5.4
# employed in public interest	19	5.7
# employed as judicial clerks	74	22.2
# employed in academia	4	1.2

Geographic Location

# employed in state	47	14.1
# employed in foreign countries	3	0.9
# of states where employed		36

Bar Passage Rates

Jurisdiction	New York			Illinois		
Exam	Sum 03	Win 04	Total	Sum 03	Win 04	Total
# from school taking bar for the first time	74	31	105	65	21	86
School's pass rate for all first-time takers	96%	94%	95%	95%	100%	97%
State's pass rate for all first-time takers	78%	58%	75%	86%	78%	84%

The University of Michigan Law School

Hutchins Hall, 625 South State Street
Ann Arbor, MI 48109-1215
Phone: 734.764.1358
E-mail: law.jd.admissions@umich.edu; Website: www.law.umich.edu

■ Introduction

The University of Michigan Law School, founded in 1859, is one of the nation's finest institutions of legal education. The school is home to a distinguished and diverse faculty, many of its scholars preeminent in their fields. Our students come from around the globe to contribute their remarkable talents and accomplishments to make the Law School a community that exudes a sense of serious purpose, high academic achievement, and social commitment. Our graduates serve with distinction in all sectors of law, business, and government.

■ Faculty

Michigan has over 70 full-time faculty members; many distinguished visiting scholars and practitioners further enhance course offerings. While maintaining a long tradition of eminence in constitutional, criminal, international, and comparative law, the faculty has expanded legal scholarship with insights into such fields as classics, economics, English, feminist theory, history, life sciences, philosophy, political theory, psychology, public policy, and sociology.

■ Physical Facilities and Library

The location of residential and academic buildings within the strikingly beautiful Gothic architecture of the William W. Cook Law Quadrangle fosters the integration of activities for both students and faculty.

With over 952,290 volumes, the law library has one of the world's premier collections. Law students also have access to other university libraries. Wireless access technology allows law students network access throughout the law library, classrooms, the Quadrangle, and beyond.

■ Curriculum

Recognized as a leader in interdisciplinary legal studies, the insights and methods of other fields are apparent throughout Michigan's broad curriculum. Formal joint programs are available in 13 disciplines, and students may count nine credits of other graduate-level work toward their JD.

A key component of the first year is the Legal Practice Program. A leader among the top law schools, Michigan's program provides individualized instruction in legal writing, research, and oral advocacy taught by full-time faculty to first-year students, as well as upper-level corporate drafting instruction.

Renowned for international scholarship, Michigan requires all students to complete Transnational Law.

Externships, such as the South African Program, provide students with advanced training in their areas of interest. Internships are generally also available through such initiatives as the Program for Cambodian Law and Development.

■ Clinical Opportunities

For over 30 years, the Law School has provided a clinical practice program. Students represent clients selected from a rich pool of cases, and the nature of local court dockets allows students to handle many cases from beginning to end. Offerings include a general clinic, in which students may be involved in civil and/or criminal trial work; a Child Advocacy Law Clinic; a Criminal Appellate Defense Clinic; the transactional Legal Assistance for Urban Communities Clinic; a mediation clinic; and the medico-legal Pediatric Advocacy Clinic. Students can also enroll in a practicum in environmental law or asylum and refugee law, or participate in the Family Law Project, a student-run advocacy program for victims of domestic violence.

■ Admission and Student Body

The quality of the applicant's educational experience and LSAT scores are important in the admission process, but extracurricular and work experience, the personal statement, and letters of recommendation are also relied on heavily. Refer to Applicant Profile for more information.

■ Student Activities

Nearly 380 students participate in six journals: the *Michigan Law Review*, the *Journal of Law Reform*, the *Michigan Journal of International Law*, the *Michigan Journal of Gender and Law*, the *Michigan Telecommunication and Technology Law Review*, and the *Michigan Journal of Race and Law*. Students interested in honing oral advocacy and legal writing skills may choose to enter numerous moot court competitions. The Law School Student Senate funds approximately 50 student organizations, and students also participate in groups throughout the larger university community.

■ Expenses and Financial Aid

The Financial Aid Program is substantial, drawing on a variety of scholarship and loan funds. While the Law School emphasizes financial need in dispensing grants and loans, merit aid is also awarded annually to outstanding candidates remarkable for their anticipated contribution to the Law School and the legal profession. The Law School endeavors to provide financial assistance to all full-time students who would be unable to meet the costs of their law school education if relying only on savings and family support.

Michigan's Debt Management Program is the most progressive of its kind. It provides graduates with the flexibility to choose jobs from a wide range of law-related opportunities, including lower-paying public interest positions, while still maintaining a reasonable lifestyle and remaining current on outstanding loan obligations.

■ Career Services/Public Service

Our graduates consistently enjoy a 98–99 percent employment rate. Every student is individually assigned an attorney-counselor to provide assistance throughout his or her law school career and after graduation. Michigan's On-Campus Interviewing Program (which includes an Early Interview Week in late August) regularly brings more than 750 employers from all over the country and abroad to the Law School. An additional 1,300 employers contact the Law School to solicit applications from students. Nearly all the *American Lawyer* Top 100 firms, Global 100 firms, and Best Places to Work firms visit or request résumés, putting Michigan among the top five schools for placement in elite firms. The largest number of our graduates go to New York City and Chicago, followed closely by California; Washington, DC; and Detroit.

The Law School has a long-standing commitment to public service, and the Office of Public Service provides career counseling to assist students interested in employment in public interest organizations and government. OPS is dedicated to connecting students with mentors, volunteer opportunities, and stimulating jobs. The staff acts as a link between Michigan law students and the hundreds of Michigan graduates doing public service work throughout the world.

Career counselors and Law School faculty advise and support students seeking judicial clerkships. Approximately 20 percent of Michigan graduates each year accept prestigious clerkships with federal, state, and international courts.

■ Housing

Ann Arbor combines ease of living with superb cultural, athletic, and entertainment offerings. High-quality off-campus housing is available in a wide variety of choices and neighborhoods. Family housing, which is relatively economical, is available to married students, domestic partners, and single parents with custody of their children. Approximately half of entering first-year students reside in the Lawyers Club, enjoying the easy access and camaraderie of on-campus life. Nearly 95 percent of all Lawyers Club spaces provide for a private bedroom.

Applicant Profile

We choose not to provide an applicant profile because we do not believe a grid based on undergraduate GPA and LSAT scores can accurately reflect our comprehensive admission process, which focuses on many elements in an application in order to determine an applicant's particular intellectual strengths, nonacademic achievements, and unique personal circumstances. We view our student body as one of our greatest assets, and our goal is to admit a group of students who, individually and collectively, are among the best applying to American law schools in a given year. We seek a mix of students with varying backgrounds and experiences who will respect and learn from each other. Our most general measures are an applicant's LSAT score and undergraduate GPA and, as measured by those statistics, Michigan is among the handful of the most selective law schools in the country. However, each of these measures is far from perfect. Even the highest possible scores will not guarantee admission, and low scores will, likewise, not automatically result in a denial, as both circumstances may have significant offsetting considerations.

Michigan State University College of Law

230 Law College Building
East Lansing, MI 48824-1300
Phone: 800.844.9352, 517.432.0222; Fax: 517.432.0098
E-mail: law@law.msu.edu; Website: www.law.msu.edu

ABA
Approved
Since
1941

The Basics

Type of school	Private
Term	Semester
Application deadline	4/15
Application fee	$50
Financial aid deadline	4/15
Can first year start other than fall?	No
Student to faculty ratio (fall)	22.8 to 1
Does the university offer:	
housing restricted to law students?	No
graduate housing for which law students are eligible?	Yes

Faculty and Administrators

	Total		Men		Women		Minorities	
	Fall	Spr	Fall	Spr	Fall	Spr	Fall	Spr
Full-time	38	37	24	23	14	14	5	5
Other Full-time	1	1	1	1	0	0	0	0
Deans, librarians, & others who teach	11	11	5	5	6	6	1	1
Part-time	45	47	35	35	10	12	1	0
Total	95	96	65	64	30	32	7	6

Curriculum

		Full-time	Part-time
Typical first-year section size		81	87
Is there typically a "small section" of the first-year class, other than Legal Writing, taught by full-time faculty		No	No
If yes, typical size offered last year		0	0
# of classroom course titles beyond 1st year curriculum		136	
# of upper division courses, excluding seminars with an enrollment:	Under 25	88	
	25-49	36	
	50-74	11	
	75-99	8	
	100+	7	
# of seminars		65	
# of seminar positions available		1,224	
# of seminar positions filled		309	587
# of positions available in simulation courses		822	
# of simulation positions filled		268	373
# of positions available in faculty supervised clinical courses		108	
# of faculty supervised clinical positions filled		61	5
# involved in field placements		93	32
# involved in law journals		74	7
# involved in moot court or trial competitions		31	2
# of credit hours required to graduate		88	

JD Enrollment and Ethnicity

	Men		Women		Full-time		Part-time		1st-year		Total		JD Degs. Awd.
	#	%	#	%	#	%	#	%	#	%	#	%	
African Amer.	18	2.9	39	7.9	40	4.5	17	7.6	11	3.3	57	5.1	14
Amer. Indian	4	0.6	1	0.2	4	0.4	1	0.4	3	0.9	5	0.4	2
Asian Amer.	24	3.8	20	4.1	32	3.6	12	5.4	15	4.5	44	3.9	11
Mex. Amer.	10	1.6	4	0.8	12	1.3	2	0.9	6	1.8	14	1.3	3
Puerto Rican	0	0.0	0	0.0	0	0.0	0	0.0	0	0.0	0	0.0	0
Hispanic	2	0.3	0	0.0	0	0.0	2	0.9	1	0.3	2	0.2	0
Total Minority	58	9.3	64	13.0	88	9.8	34	15.2	36	10.8	122	10.9	30
For. Nation.	35	5.6	27	5.5	61	6.8	1	0.4	10	3.0	62	5.6	0
Caucasian	518	83.0	398	80.7	729	81.5	187	83.9	281	84.6	916	82.0	193
Unknown	13	2.1	4	0.8	16	1.8	1	0.4	5	1.5	17	1.5	0
Total	624	55.9	493	44.1	894	80.0	223	20.0	332	29.7	1117		223

Tuition and Fees

	Resident	Nonresident
Full-time	$23,156	$23,156
Part-time	$16,540	$16,540

Living Expenses

Estimated living expenses for singles

Living on campus	Living off campus	Living at home
$12,306	$12,306	$12,306

Michigan State University College of Law

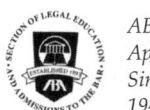

*ABA
Approved
Since
1941*

GPA and LSAT Scores

	Total	Full-time	Part-time
# of apps	2,397	2,150	247
# of admits	897	755	142
# of matrics	323	234	89
75% GPA	3.57	3.58	3.54
25% GPA	3.01	3.08	2.95
75% LSAT	159	159	155
25% LSAT	152	154	149

Grants and Scholarships (from prior year)

	Total		Full-time		Part-time	
	#	%	#	%	#	%
Total # of students	1,008		798		210	
Total # receiving grants	237	23.5	217	27.2	20	9.5
Less than 1/2 tuition	30	3.0	29	3.6	1	0.5
Half to full tuition	53	5.3	46	5.8	7	3.3
Full tuition	154	15.3	142	17.8	12	5.7
More than full tuition	0	0.0	0	0.0	0	0.0
Median grant amount			$22,148		$18,194	

Informational and Library Resources

# of volumes and volume equivalents	262,857
# of titles	133,882
# of active serial subscriptions	4,460
Study seating capacity inside the library	455
# of professional librarians	7
Hours per week library is open	109
# of open, wired connections available to students	1,219
# of networked computers available for use by students	52
# of simultaneous wireless users	5,865
Require computer?	N

JD Attrition (from prior year)

	Academic	Other	Total	
	#	#	#	%
1st year	9	20	29	7.8%
2nd year	4	1	5	1.3%
3rd year	0	0	0	0.0%
4th year	0	0	0	0.0%

Employment

	Total	Percentage
Employment status known	199	95.7
Employment status unknown	9	4.3
Employed	178	89.4
Pursuing graduate degrees	8	4.0
Unemployed seeking employment	8	4.0
Unemployed not seeking employment	5	2.5

Type of Employment

# employed in law firms	99	55.6
# employed in business and industry	26	14.6
# employed in government	31	17.4
# employed in public interest	3	1.7
# employed as judicial clerks	11	6.2
# employed in academia	3	1.7

Geographic Location

# employed in state	118	66.3
# employed in foreign countries	0	0.0
# of states where employed		22

Bar Passage Rates

Jurisdiction		Michigan	
Exam	Sum 03	Win 04	Total
# from school taking bar for the first time	126	23	149
School's pass rate for all first-time takers	87%	70%	85%
State's pass rate for all first-time takers	77%	71%	75%

Michigan State University College of Law

Office of Admissions & Financial Aid, 230 Law College Building
East Lansing, MI 48824-1300
Phone: 800.844.9352, 517.432.0222; Fax: 517.432.0098
E-mail: law@law.msu.edu; Website: www.law.msu.edu

■ Introduction

MSU College of Law is fully integrated with Michigan State University, a Big Ten school and one of the top research universities in the world. While we remain a private, financially independent law school, MSU Law is a constituent college within MSU and is located in a state-of-the-art facility in the center of MSU's East Lansing campus. Our association with a major university means that you will benefit from distinctive inter-disciplinary programs. MSU Law is fully accredited by the ABA and is a member of the AALS.

■ Enrollment/Student Body

The students of MSU Law represent a diversity of educational backgrounds, experiences, and national origins. MSU College of Law students receive a legal education in the theory and purpose of the law, along with its practical application, thus equipping them to fulfill unique and complicated demands in legal and nonlegal careers.

■ Faculty

The faculty is composed of resident professors who are devoted to the teaching of law, legal research instructors, and a cadre of adjunct faculty members and practicing attorneys who are specialists with extensive experience in the field of law they teach.

■ Library and Physical Facilities

This major research collection includes the statutes of the 50 states, the United States, and Canada, as well as collections of numerous decisions, legal periodicals, and treatises. The computer lab is equipped with 40 networked computers. Students have access to word processing, CALI tutorials, Westlaw, LexisNexis, individual e-mail accounts, and the Internet. Most classrooms, the library, and some study areas are fully wired, and students are encouraged to use their laptops during class. The law college also offers a complete wireless network throughout the building. In fall 2004, MSU Law completed $600,000 in renovations to its moot courtroom, making it one of the most technologically advanced teaching courtrooms in the nation.

■ Special Programs

One of the nation's most prominent practicing trial lawyers—MSU Law alum Geoffrey N. Fieger, 1979—has partnered with the law college to establish the first trial practice institute at a law school designed specifically to train law students as successful trial lawyers. The institute offers:

- a rigorous, comprehensive two-year certificate program designed in collaboration with practicing trial lawyers and judges
- a selective admission process that admits students based on their potential for successful trial advocacy
- a scholarship program
- an annual lecture series that showcases nationally known trial lawyers
- hands-on learning experiences through clinics, externships, field placements, and simulations
- the law college's moot courtroom, one of the most technologically advanced teaching courtrooms in the nation
- national and international trial advocacy and moot court competition teams
- interdisciplinary learning opportunities, which include collaborations with the MSU theatre department to teach courtroom communication and the study of forensic science

MSU Law Concentrations include corporate law, criminal law, environmental and natural resource law, family law, health law, intellectual property and communications law, international and comparative law, and taxation. The concentrations allow students to use a portion of their elective credits to develop expertise in a particular practice area.

Certificate Programs—In addition to the trial practice certificate program, MSU Law offers a Child and Family Advocacy certificate program in cooperation with the MSU School of Social Work.

Dual Degrees—MSU Law's affiliation with MSU—and its relationship with Grand Valley State University in Grand Rapids—make it possible for law students to pursue both a JD and another advanced degree at the same time. You can choose from 15 dual-degree programs in the following areas: accounting; business; bioethics, humanities, and society; English; fisheries and wildlife; forestry; labor relations and human resources; park, recreation, and tourism resources; taxation; or urban and regional planning. It is possible to earn a law degree and a master's degree in just four years. A joint LLB/JD degree program is available in conjunction with the University of Ottawa Faculty of Law.

Study-Abroad Programs—The MSU Law Canadian Summer Externship Program and Canadian Study Abroad Program provide students with the opportunity to study US-Canadian and international law and gain legal work experience in Ottawa. The Study Abroad in Mexico Program gives students international law experience during one-, two-, or three-week summer programs in Guadalajara.

Dean Charles H. King Scholarship Program is designed to enhance educational opportunities for high achievers by offering selected candidates a substantial scholarship to study law at MSU Law. King Scholars receive merit-based scholarships that cover 100 percent of tuition. First-year students must have a minimum 161 LSAT score and 3.5 undergraduate grade-point average to be considered for the King Scholarship.

A Master of Laws (LLM) program in the American Legal System, requiring one full year of study, is offered for foreign lawyers. An LLM/MJ (Master of Jurisprudence) is offered in Intellectual Property and Communications Law.

■ Admission

MSU Law is committed to a broad inquiry into the role and function of law in society and seeks a diverse student body as an integral part of its educational program. The primary considerations for admission are the applicant's undergraduate grade-point average and LSAT score.

■ Curricular Activities

MSU Law Clinics—MSU Law operates six law clinics to benefit low-income citizens and give law students an opportunity to put their legal knowledge into practice. Second- and third-year law students can provide legal counsel under the supervision of clinic faculty who are members of the State Bar of Michigan. The clinics include Rental Housing, Tax, Small Business/Nonprofit Law, Chance at Childhood Law and Social Work, Indigenous Law, and Midwest Student Press Clinic.

Externships—The MSU Law externship programs are classified under three broad categories: judicial, legal

aid, and government attorney externships. There is a Washington, DC, federal externship program in addition to an innovative environmental law externship. Students may propose externships as well.

The Law Review, Journal of International Law, and Moot Court and Trial Advocacy Board each provide students with opportunities to excel academically and practice their lawyering, legal research, and writing skills.

■ Student Activities

ABA/Law Student Division, ACLU of MSU Law, Amnesty International, Asian Pacific American Association, Association of Trial Lawyers of America, Business Law Society, Canadian Student Legal Association, Chinese Legal Society, Christian Legal Society, Delta Theta Phi, Entertainment and Sports Law Society, Environmental Law Society, Family Law Society, Federalist Society, Intellectual Property Law Society, International Law Society, Jewish Legal Organization of MSU Law, Jewish Legal Society, *Journal of International Law, Journal of Medicine and Law*, Labor and Employment Law Society, *Michigan State Intellectual Property Review, Michigan State Law Review*, Medical Legal Society, Military Law Society, Moot Court and Advocacy Board, MSU Law Basketball Association, MSU Law Ice Hockey Club, MSU Law Rugby, Phi Alpha Delta, Phi Delta Phi, Public Interest Law Society, St. Thomas More Society, Student Animal Legal Defense Fund, Student Bar Association, Tax and Estate Planning Society, Triangle Bar Association, Wolverine Student Bar Association, and Women's Law Caucus.

Applicant Profile

Michigan State University College of Law
This grid includes only applicants who earned 120-180 LSAT scores under standard administrations.

LSAT Score	3.75 +		3.50 - 3.74		3.25 - 3.49		3.00 - 3.24		2.75 - 2.99		2.50 - 2.74		2.25 - 2.49		2.00 - 2.24		Below 2.00		No GPA		Total	
	Apps	Adm	Apps	Adm	Apps	Adm	Apps	Adm	Apps	Adm	Apps	Adm	Apps	Adm	Apps	Adm	Apps	Adm	Apps	Adm	Apps	Adm
175-180	0	0	0	0	0	0	0	0	0	0	0	0	0	0	0	0	0	0	0	0	0	0
170-174	0	0	1	1	1	1	0	0	1	1	0	0	0	0	1	1	1	0	0	0	5	4
165-169	5	5	3	3	4	4	10	9	4	4	2	2	1	1	0	0	0	0	0	0	29	28
160-164	21	21	29	29	30	30	32	32	24	23	8	8	3	3	3	3	1	0	2	2	153	151
155-159	29	29	67	67	84	84	76	73	55	48	30	21	17	5	8	4	1	0	4	4	371	335
150-154	52	40	102	65	143	85	169	81	132	37	69	16	37	6	12	0	3	0	7	3	726	333
145-149	27	11	80	15	128	29	133	12	107	9	69	2	38	2	10	1	3	0	11	0	606	81
140-144	6	0	29	0	56	0	57	1	54	2	43	1	32	0	6	0	5	0	8	1	296	5
135-139	0	0	11	0	19	0	30	0	30	0	17	0	15	0	5	0	3	0	7	0	137	0
130-134	0	0	1	0	5	0	6	0	6	0	7	0	2	0	3	0	2	0	2	0	34	0
125-129	0	0	0	0	1	0	0	0	2	0	5	0	4	0	1	0	1	0	1	0	15	0
120-124	0	0	0	0	0	0	0	0	0	0	0	0	0	0	0	0	0	0	0	0	0	0
Total	140	106	323	180	471	233	513	208	415	124	250	50	149	17	49	9	20	0	42	10	2372	937

Apps = Number of Applicants   Adm = Number Admitted   Reflects 98% of the total applicant pool.

University of Minnesota Law School

Walter F. Mondale Hall, 229 19th Avenue South
Minneapolis, MN 55455
Phone: 612.625.3487; Fax: 612.626.1874
E-mail: umnlsadm@umn.edu; Website: www.law.umn.edu

ABA
Approved
Since
1923

The Basics

Type of school	Public
Term	Semester
Application deadline	3/1
Application fee	$60
Financial aid deadline	3/1
Can first year start other than fall?	No
Student to faculty ratio (fall)	14.5 to 1
Does the university offer:	
housing restricted to law students?	No
graduate housing for which law students are eligible?	No

Faculty and Administrators

	Total		Men		Women		Minorities	
	Fall	Spr	Fall	Spr	Fall	Spr	Fall	Spr
Full-time	47	45	33	29	14	16	8	7
Other Full-time	1	2	1	2	0	0	0	0
Deans, librarians, & others who teach	10	10	3	3	7	7	3	3
Part-time	66	103	36	60	30	43	3	5
Total	124	160	73	94	51	66	14	15

Curriculum

		Full-time	Part-time
Typical first-year section size		112	0
Is there typically a "small section" of the first-year class, other than Legal Writing, taught by full-time faculty		Yes	No
If yes, typical size offered last year		56	0
# of classroom course titles beyond 1st year curriculum		189	
# of upper division courses, excluding seminars with an enrollment:	Under 25	86	
	25-49	24	
	50-74	13	
	75-99	13	
	100+	2	
# of seminars		51	
# of seminar positions available		816	
# of seminar positions filled	627		0
# of positions available in simulation courses		302	
# of simulation positions filled	271		0
# of positions available in faculty supervised clinical courses		265	
# of faculty supervised clinical positions filled	248		0
# involved in field placements	119		0
# involved in law journals	192		0
# involved in moot court or trial competitions	190		0
# of credit hours required to graduate		88	

JD Enrollment and Ethnicity

	Men		Women		Full-time		Part-time		1st-year		Total		JD Degs. Awd.
	#	%	#	%	#	%	#	%	#	%	#	%	
African Amer.	12	2.6	6	1.6	18	2.2	0	0.0	4	1.5	18	2.2	6
Amer. Indian	4	0.9	3	0.8	7	0.9	0	0.0	4	1.5	7	0.9	4
Asian Amer.	31	6.8	46	12.6	77	9.4	0	0.0	30	11.1	77	9.4	24
Mex. Amer.	1	0.2	1	0.3	2	0.2	0	0.0	2	0.7	2	0.2	0
Puerto Rican	1	0.2	0	0.0	1	0.1	0	0.0	1	0.4	1	0.1	1
Hispanic	14	3.1	12	3.3	26	3.2	0	0.0	7	2.6	26	3.2	6
Total Minority	63	13.9	68	18.7	131	16.0	0	0.0	48	17.7	131	16.0	41
For. Nation.	12	2.6	8	2.2	20	2.4	0	0.0	2	0.7	20	2.4	5
Caucasian	365	80.6	273	75.0	638	78.1	0	0.0	206	76.0	638	78.1	182
Unknown	13	2.9	15	4.1	28	3.4	0	0.0	15	5.5	28	3.4	1
Total	453	55.4	364	44.6	817	100.0	0	0.0	271	33.2	817		229

Tuition and Fees

	Resident	Nonresident
Full-time	$17,948	$28,042
Part-time	$0	$0

Living Expenses

Estimated living expenses for singles

Living on campus	Living off campus	Living at home
$12,930	$12,930	$5,972

University of Minnesota Law School

ABA
Approved
Since
1923

GPA and LSAT Scores

	Total	Full-time	Part-time
# of apps	2,509	2,509	0
# of admits	716	716	0
# of matrics	270	270	0
75% GPA	3.81	3.81	0.00
25% GPA	3.48	3.48	0.00
75% LSAT	166	166	0
25% LSAT	160	160	0

Grants and Scholarships (from prior year)

	Total		Full-time		Part-time	
	#	%	#	%	#	%
Total # of students	787		787		0	
Total # receiving grants	443	56.3	443	56.3	0	0.0
Less than 1/2 tuition	234	29.7	234	29.7	0	0.0
Half to full tuition	174	22.1	174	22.1	0	0.0
Full tuition	35	4.4	35	4.4	0	0.0
More than full tuition	0	0.0	0	0.0	0	0.0
Median grant amount			$7,500		$0	

Informational and Library Resources

# of volumes and volume equivalents	1,003,529
# of titles	279,981
# of active serial subscriptions	10,486
Study seating capacity inside the library	942
# of professional librarians	14
Hours per week library is open	81
# of open, wired connections available to students	86
# of networked computers available for use by students	86
# of simultaneous wireless users	1,600
Require computer?	Y

JD Attrition (from prior year)

	Academic	Other	Total	
	#	#	#	%
1st year	0	4	4	1.4%
2nd year	0	9	9	3.3%
3rd year	0	0	0	0.0%
4th year	0	0	0	0.0%

Employment

	Total	Percentage
Employment status known	246	99.6
Employment status unknown	1	0.4
Employed	240	97.6
Pursuing graduate degrees	4	1.6
Unemployed seeking employment	0	0.0
Unemployed not seeking employment	2	0.8

Type of Employment

# employed in law firms	125	52.1
# employed in business and industry	30	12.5
# employed in government	24	10.0
# employed in public interest	16	6.7
# employed as judicial clerks	37	15.4
# employed in academia	0	0.0

Geographic Location

# employed in state	149	62.1
# employed in foreign countries	4	1.7
# of states where employed	27	

Bar Passage Rates

Jurisdiction	Minnesota		
Exam	Sum 03	Win 04	Total
# from school taking bar for the first time	155	6	161
School's pass rate for all first-time takers	98%	83%	98%
State's pass rate for all first-time takers	92%	75%	89%

University of Minnesota Law School

Walter F. Mondale Hall, 229 19th Avenue South
Minneapolis, MN 55455
Phone: 612.625.3487; Fax: 612.626.1874
E-mail: umnlsadm@umn.edu; Website: www.law.umn.edu

■ Introduction

The University of Minnesota Law School, founded in 1888, is one of the country's premier law schools. The quality of Minnesota's faculty, the academic credentials of its students, and the caliber of its library and physical facilities are the strongest in the history of the school. This vitality is the result of thoughtful and forward-looking development of the school's century-old tradition of excellence and innovation in legal education. In keeping with its midwest traditions, the Law School provides a personal, collegial environment for the study of law. At the same time, the school's location in the midst of a thriving, cosmopolitan area provides a variety of academic, work, cultural, and recreational benefits. Students have easy access to the resources of a world-class research university and to the Twin Cities of Minneapolis and St. Paul, one of the most progressive and livable metropolitan communities in the country.

■ Faculty

The faculty's wide-ranging expertise allows students to choose from an academically rich and innovative curriculum that integrates theory and doctrine with skills, ethics, and practice.

Faculty members are prolific and influential scholars, having published over 160 books and 1,400 articles. Forty-eight percent of the tenured faculty are invited members of the prestigious American Law Institute, and 87 percent of them have been honored with chair-level appointments. Members of the faculty include a recent Chair of the United Nations Sub-Commission on the Promotion and Protection of Human Rights (the first US citizen to chair the commission since Eleanor Roosevelt), a member of the American Academy of Arts and Sciences, and a former Counselor on International Law for the US Department of State.

But while the faculty's scholarship has earned them national acclaim, their equally energetic passion for teaching and mentoring, along with a 15.1:1 student-faculty ratio, have earned them the respect and appreciation of their students.

■ Student Body/Admission

With 260 students in the entering class, the student body is large enough to enjoy the benefits of diverse back-grounds, perspectives, and interests, while remaining small enough to foster the kind of collegial and support-ive community that is a hallmark of Minnesota life.

Although the atmosphere and camaraderie reflect distinctly Minnesotan values, 42 states, 7 countries, and 209 undergraduate institutions are represented in the current JD student body. The admission committee looks beyond a simple evaluation of LSAT and undergraduate GPA to compose a class that will produce leaders in the legal profession. Many students have advanced degrees and/or prior work experience.

■ Library and Physical Facilities

The award-winning Walter F. Mondale Hall was substan-tially expanded in 2001. The building houses all faculty offices, five law school research institutes, model class-rooms in varying sizes, a beautiful auditorium, the law clinic, a cafeteria, the law school bookstore, student lockers, offices for student organizations and publica-tions, a variety of lounge areas, and a computer lab. Students can access the Internet using wireless technology in all student areas of the building.

Mondale Hall also houses the law library, which is the eighth largest in the US. The library offers students 24-hour access. The professional staff takes pride in the outstanding collection of materials and in the individualized service they provide to students and faculty.

■ Curriculum

Hallmarks of the Minnesota curriculum include an unusually strong public law selection. Minnesota also is one of only a handful of schools with three years of writing requirements and enjoys one of the smallest first-year writing section sizes, with only 12–14 students per section. The upper-level curriculum is broad and rich, and includes a remarkably diverse selection of clinical and simulation courses.

Drawing on the strength of our world-class university, qualified students may pursue dual or joint degrees with a myriad of nationally ranked graduate and professional schools. Especially noteworthy is Minnesota's unique joint-degree program in law, health, and the life sciences.

■ Clinical Programs

With 16 separate clinics, Minnesota has one of the country's largest and most active clinical programs. Through the clinics, students represent real clients under the close tutelage of the clinic faculty. Over 55 percent of the student body participates in a live-client clinic prior to graduation, providing more than 18,000 hours of pro bono legal work for the Twin Cities community each year.

■ Special Programs

Minnesota hosts **international exchange programs** in the following countries: France, Germany, Ireland, the Netherlands, Spain, and Sweden. These programs enable interested students to study abroad and allow our students to benefit from the international perspectives students from these countries bring to our classrooms.

Through the **Law School Public Service Program**, students are asked to perform 50 hours of pro bono legal service for low-income and disadvantaged Minnesotans. Those who complete at least 50 hours of service are recognized for their dedication with a notation on their transcript and at the graduation ceremony.

Five major **research institutes** are housed in the law school: Human Rights Center; Institute on Race and Poverty; Kommerstad Center for Business Law and Entrepreneurship; Consortium on Law and Values in Health, Environment and the Life Sciences; and Minnesota Center for Legal Studies. These institutes enrich the school's intellectual life, contribute to policy debate and formation, and provide research and employment opportunities for selected law students.

■ Student Activities

Minnesota hosts four student-edited journals: *Minnesota Law Review*; *Law and Inequality: A Journal of Theory and Practice*; *Minnesota Journal of Global Trade*; and *Minnesota Intellectual Property Review*. Students receive academic credit for their journal work.

Students also receive credit for moot court participation. The breadth of Minnesota's moot court program is unusual, with eight programs spanning a wide variety of subject areas: Civil Rights Moot Court, Intellectual Property Moot Court, Jessup International Law Moot Court, Environmental Law Moot Court, Wagner Labor Law Moot Court, National Moot Court, ABA Moot Court, and Maynard Pirsig Moot Court.

Student extracurricular activities include 37 separate student organizations.

■ Expenses and Financial Aid

In recent years, approximately 85 percent of the student body has received financial aid, primarily loans, but also including a substantial number of scholarships. Second- and third-year students also may apply for research assistantships.

■ Career Services

With alumni in all 50 states and over 260 federal and state court judges nationwide, our graduates are leaders in the judiciary, government, law practice, business, and academics. Employers interview on campus, at regional interview programs sponsored by the Career Services Office, and at job fairs for nearly 700 offices, including law firms, corporations, and governmental agencies from around the US. Employers nationwide regularly solicit résumés from our students for job postings. Each year, 24–27 percent of our graduates accept prestigious judicial clerkships, and 99 percent are employed within six months of graduation.

Applicant Profile

University of Minnesota Law School

LSAT Score	GPA 3.75 +		3.50 - 3.74		3.25 - 3.49		3.00 - 3.24		2.75 - 2.99		2.50 - 2.74		2.25 - 2.49		2.00 - 2.24		Below 2.00		No GPA		Total	
	Apps	Adm	Apps	Adm	Apps	Adm	Apps	Adm	Apps	Adm	Apps	Adm	Apps	Adm	Apps	Adm	Apps	Adm	Apps	Adm	Apps	Adm
175-180	4	4	3	2	2	1	0	0	2	1	0	0	0	0	0	0	0	0	0	0	11	8
170-174	17	16	14	11	15	12	11	7	8	5	4	0	2	1	0	0	0	0	0	0	71	52
165-169	82	72	81	69	71	54	38	15	23	4	8	1	6	0	1	0	1	0	2	1	313	216
160-164	167	144	256	135	209	44	115	5	46	3	18	1	7	0	2	0	0	0	10	4	830	336
155-159	144	57	185	18	145	3	86	7	34	0	12	0	5	0	1	0	0	0	11	0	623	85
150-154	65	5	90	7	88	3	64	0	27	1	9	0	5	0	2	0	0	0	5	0	355	16
145-149	15	0	37	0	40	1	35	0	23	0	9	0	7	0	1	0	1	0	7	0	175	1
140-144	3	0	8	0	10	0	21	0	9	0	12	0	4	0	4	0	0	0	3	0	74	0
135-139	1	0	1	0	4	0	4	0	8	0	5	0	4	0	0	0	0	0	2	0	29	0
130-134	0	0	1	0	0	0	0	0	2	0	3	0	2	0	0	0	1	0	1	0	11	0
125-129	0	0	0	0	0	0	0	0	0	0	0	0	0	0	0	0	0	0	1	0	1	0
120-124	0	0	0	0	0	0	0	0	0	0	0	0	0	0	0	0	0	0	0	0	0	0
Total	498	298	676	242	584	118	374	34	182	14	80	2	42	1	12	0	3	0	42	5	2493	714

Apps = Number of Applicants   Adm = Number Admitted   Reflects 99% of the total applicant pool.

This grid includes all applicants who earned 120-180 LSAT scores.
This chart is to be used as a general guide only. Nonnumerical factors are strongly considered for all applicants.

The University of Mississippi School of Law

Lamar Law Center, Post Office Box 1848
University, MS 38677
Phone: Admission: 662.915.6910, Main: 662.915.7361; Fax: 662.915.1289
E-mail: lawmiss@olemiss.edu; Website: www.olemiss.edu/depts/law_school

ABA Approved Since 1930

The Basics

Type of school	Public
Term	Semester
Application deadline	3/1
Application fee	$40
Financial aid deadline	3/15
Can first year start other than fall?	Yes
Student to faculty ratio (fall)	22.0 to 1
Does the university offer:	
housing restricted to law students?	No
graduate housing for which law students are eligible?	Yes

Faculty and Administrators

	Total		Men		Women		Minorities	
	Fall	Spr	Fall	Spr	Fall	Spr	Fall	Spr
Full-time	22	22	16	16	6	6	4	4
Other Full-time	9	9	5	5	4	4	1	1
Deans, librarians, & others who teach	7	7	5	5	2	2	0	0
Part-time	7	8	6	7	1	1	0	0
Total	45	46	32	33	13	13	5	5

Curriculum

		Full-time	Part-time
Typical first-year section size		57	0
Is there typically a "small section" of the first-year class, other than Legal Writing, taught by full-time faculty		No	No
If yes, typical size offered last year		0	0
# of classroom course titles beyond 1st year curriculum		69	
# of upper division courses, excluding seminars with an enrollment:	Under 25	35	
	25-49	18	
	50-74	12	
	75-99	5	
	100+	5	
# of seminars		17	
# of seminar positions available		336	
# of seminar positions filled		257	0
# of positions available in simulation courses		274	
# of simulation positions filled		261	0
# of positions available in faculty supervised clinical courses		47	
# of faculty supervised clinical positions filled		38	0
# involved in field placements		52	0
# involved in law journals		73	0
# involved in moot court or trial competitions		45	0
# of credit hours required to graduate		90	

JD Enrollment and Ethnicity

	Men		Women		Full-time		Part-time		1st-year		Total		JD Degs. Awd.
	#	%	#	%	#	%	#	%	#	%	#	%	
African Amer.	13	4.0	35	13.8	48	8.3	0	0.0	12	7.1	48	8.3	15
Amer. Indian	3	0.9	0	0.0	3	0.5	0	0.0	0	0.0	3	0.5	1
Asian Amer.	0	0.0	3	1.2	3	0.5	0	0.0	3	1.8	3	0.5	0
Mex. Amer.	0	0.0	0	0.0	0	0.0	0	0.0	0	0.0	0	0.0	0
Puerto Rican	0	0.0	0	0.0	0	0.0	0	0.0	0	0.0	0	0.0	0
Hispanic	2	0.6	0	0.0	2	0.3	0	0.0	1	0.6	2	0.3	1
Total Minority	18	5.5	38	15.0	56	9.6	0	0.0	16	9.4	56	9.6	17
For. Nation.	0	0.0	2	0.8	2	0.3	0	0.0	2	1.2	2	0.3	0
Caucasian	310	94.5	213	84.2	523	90.0	0	0.0	152	89.4	523	90.0	128
Unknown	0	0.0	0	0.0	0	0.0	0	0.0	0	0.0	0	0.0	0
Total	328	56.5	253	43.5	581	100.0	0	0.0	170	29.3	581		145

Tuition and Fees

	Resident	Nonresident
Full-time	$7,210	$13,380
Part-time	$360	$669

Living Expenses

Estimated living expenses for singles

Living on campus	Living off campus	Living at home
$17,844	$17,844	$17,844

The University of Mississippi School of Law

ABA
Approved
Since
1930

GPA and LSAT Scores

	Total	Full-time	Part-time
# of apps	1,942	1,942	0
# of admits	387	387	0
# of matrics	170	170	0
75% GPA	0.00	3.79	0.00
25% GPA	0.00	3.30	0.00
75% LSAT	0	159	0
25% LSAT	0	153	0

Grants and Scholarships (from prior year)

	Total		Full-time		Part-time	
	#	%	#	%	#	%
Total # of students	576		576		0	
Total # receiving grants	173	30.0	173	30.0	0	0.0
Less than 1/2 tuition	85	14.8	85	14.8	0	0.0
Half to full tuition	51	8.9	51	8.9	0	0.0
Full tuition	5	0.9	5	0.9	0	0.0
More than full tuition	32	5.6	32	5.6	0	0.0
Median grant amount			$6,072		$0	

Informational and Library Resources

# of volumes and volume equivalents	326,212
# of titles	72,405
# of active serial subscriptions	2,144
Study seating capacity inside the library	336
# of professional librarians	7
Hours per week library is open	102
# of open, wired connections available to students	715
# of networked computers available for use by students	61
# of simultaneous wireless users	200
Require computer?	N

JD Attrition (from prior year)

	Academic	Other	Total	
	#	#	#	%
1st year	7	8	15	6.7%
2nd year	0	0	0	0.0%
3rd year	0	0	0	0.0%
4th year	0	0	0	0.0%

Employment

	Total	Percentage
Employment status known	158	100.0
Employment status unknown	0	0.0
Employed	145	91.8
Pursuing graduate degrees	9	5.7
Unemployed seeking employment	3	1.9
Unemployed not seeking employment	1	0.6

Type of Employment

	Total	Percentage
# employed in law firms	105	72.4
# employed in business and industry	4	2.8
# employed in government	11	7.6
# employed in public interest	1	0.7
# employed as judicial clerks	20	13.8
# employed in academia	4	2.8

Geographic Location

	Total	Percentage
# employed in state	101	69.7
# employed in foreign countries	0	0.0
# of states where employed	14	

Bar Passage Rates

Jurisdiction	Mississippi		
Exam	Sum 03	Win 04	Total
# from school taking bar for the first time	106	30	136
School's pass rate for all first-time takers	95%	77%	91%
State's pass rate for all first-time takers	92%	91%	92%

The University of Mississippi School of Law

Lamar Law Center, Post Office Box 1848
University, MS 38677
Phone: Admission: 662.915.6910, Main: 662.915.7361; Fax: 662.915.1289
E-mail: lawmiss@olemiss.edu; Website: www.olemiss.edu/depts/law_school

■ Introduction

Recognizing the need for formal law instruction in the state of Mississippi, the legislature, in 1854, established the Department of Law at The University of Mississippi. Over the years, the law department has evolved into today's modern law center. Located in Oxford, on the main campus of The University of Mississippi, the law center is housed in Lamar Hall, named in honor of the late Mississippian, L.Q.C. Lamar, former Associate Justice of the United States Supreme Court and one of the first law professors at the university. Oxford, a small town of approximately 10,000 people, lies nestled in the quiet hills of North Mississippi, just 75 miles southeast of bustling Memphis, Tennessee, and 180 miles north of the state capital of Jackson.

The University of Mississippi is the fourth oldest state-supported law school in the nation. The School of Law is fully approved by the American Bar Association and is a long-standing member of the Association of American Law Schools.

■ Library and Physical Facilities

The library houses one of the most extensive federal, state, and international law collections in the southeast. The library's experienced, service-oriented staff is available to assist patrons with these materials and to provide training in all aspects of traditional and computer-assisted legal research. Other library features include open stacks, an online catalog, two state-of-the-art computer labs, and private study rooms and carrels that may be reserved. The library has a strong commitment to new information technologies and has recently added additional multi-media support, along with enhanced wired and wireless network access for patrons.

■ Admission

Admission to law school is gained by committee approval based upon an applicant's credentials. These credentials include a satisfactory LSAT score and an acceptable academic record at the undergraduate level. A bachelor's degree from an accredited school is required before an applicant can register for law school.

There are no prelaw requisites. Every applicant must take the LSAT and register for the LSDAS. An LSAT score obtained more than three years before application is not valid, and the applicant will be required to retake the test. Applications are available the September preceding admission, with the application completion deadline for both summer and fall enrollment being March 1. However, early application is encouraged. Applicants who file late risk being placed on a waiting list.

Although the LSAT and GPA are obviously the most important factors in the admission process, other considerations are (1) grade patterns and progression; (2) quality of undergraduate institution; (3) difficulty of major field of study; (4) number of years since bachelor's degree was earned; (5) job experience; (6) social, personal, or economic circumstances that may have affected college grades or performance on the LSAT or academic record; (7) nonacademic achievements; (8) letters of recommendation; and (9) residency.

■ Entrance Dates

Students are given the option to enter in the summer or fall of each admission year. Because summer and fall enrollees are considered as one class, the same standards are applied in the decision-making process.

■ Curriculum

First-year students complete a predetermined curriculum that focuses on the development of analytical skills and a foundation of substantive knowledge. Largely, second- and third-year students are free to select their own courses of study and emphasis, although a number of courses are recommended to ensure a broad-based substantive and procedural background. Students may select from a large number of elective courses, including seminars, clinical, and trial advocacy courses. The elective curriculum offers generous opportunities for students to pursue special interests such as constitutional and individual rights, business and commercial transactions, federal taxation, international law, and environmental law.

■ Clinical Programs

Civil Law Clinic—Under the supervision of the director of the clinic, students provide legal counseling for indigent clients on civil matters.

Criminal Appeals Clinic—The Criminal Appeals Clinic was established by the National Center for Justice and the Rule of Law. The course of study is designed to give students practical experience representing clients in criminal appellate cases and includes direct student participation in the pro bono representation of indigent persons in their cases on appeal.

Prosecutorial Externship Program—The Prosecutorial Clinic was established by the National Center for Justice and the Rule of Law. It is designed to prepare law students for careers in criminal law by combining academic training with placements as externs in local, state, and federal prosecutor offices.

The University of Mississippi School of Law

Student Activities

The Mississippi Law Journal, edited and published by law students three times each year, includes articles by distinguished professors, judges, and practitioners.

The **Moot Court Board** oversees the administration of moot court trial and appellate cases, as well as several moot court competitions.

Summer Abroad Programs

The School of Law offers an opportunity to earn up to six semester credit hours in its summer sessions held annually in England at Downing College, Cambridge University, and at the University of Hawaii School of Law. Classes offered in both programs are for full academic credit and subject to the same academic standards maintained in the domestic program.

Special Programs

One of the most active organizations is the **Public Interest Law Foundation**. The student-run organization focuses its efforts on community groups that need legal assistance— victims of domestic violence, children, and defendants who cannot afford an attorney. The organization raises money to support students working in public interest jobs.

The **National Center for Justice and the Rule of Law** is a new component of the law center funded by a multimillion dollar grant from the Department of Justice. The center works cooperatively with agencies in sponsoring research, hosting international and national conferences, and presenting educational programs on issues related to criminal justice, such as international and domestic terrorism, drug-trafficking, and the role of the proposed International Criminal Court.

The **National Remote Sensing and Space Law Center** is funded by a multiyear, multimillion dollar grant from NASA. The only center of its kind in the United States, it will serve as a research, advisory, and training resource for the emerging commercial geospatial industry, the international legal community, and related user groups.

Housing

On-campus housing is available, and students who are interested in living on campus should make early application to the Housing Office. The majority of law students live off campus in rental units.

Career Services

A full-time director of career services assists students in finding employment. Seventy-five to 100 law firms and other prospective employers interview at the law school each year. Approximately 60 percent of graduating seniors are employed prior to graduation, with the remaining number being placed within six months of graduation. The law school is an active member of NALP and annually participates in the Atlanta Legal Hiring Conference, the Equal Justice Works Public Interest Career Fair, the Patent Law Career Fair, and the Southeastern Minority Job Fair.

Applicant Profile

The University of Mississippi School of Law
This grid includes only applicants who earned 120-180 LSAT scores under standard administrations.

LSAT Score	3.75 + Apps	Adm	3.50 - 3.74 Apps	Adm	3.25 - 3.49 Apps	Adm	3.00 - 3.24 Apps	Adm	2.75 - 2.99 Apps	Adm	2.50 - 2.74 Apps	Adm	2.25 - 2.49 Apps	Adm	2.00 - 2.24 Apps	Adm	Below 2.00 Apps	Adm	No GPA Apps	Adm	Total Apps	Adm
175-180	0	0	0	0	0	0	0	0	0	0	0	0	0	0	0	0	0	0	0	0	0	0
170-174	0	0	1	1	1	1	0	0	0	0	0	0	0	0	0	0	0	0	0	0	2	2
165-169	6	6	3	3	2	2	2	2	2	1	3	0	2	0	1	0	0	0	0	0	21	14
160-164	20	19	23	22	25	18	27	24	26	11	13	2	8	0	4	0	0	0	2	1	148	97
155-159	58	56	60	47	86	47	81	18	66	10	26	1	7	0	6	0	2	0	3	1	395	180
150-154	69	23	130	22	147	17	137	10	107	0	46	0	9	0	11	0	2	0	6	0	664	72
145-149	31	8	62	6	93	0	82	3	62	1	35	0	19	0	6	0	2	0	6	0	398	18
140-144	10	0	23	0	33	0	32	1	21	0	16	0	19	0	4	0	1	0	3	0	162	1
135-139	4	0	8	0	9	0	22	0	13	0	12	0	5	0	1	0	1	0	6	0	81	0
130-134	1	0	1	0	3	0	5	0	6	0	3	0	2	0	3	0	0	0	3	0	27	0
125-129	0	0	0	0	0	0	1	0	0	0	0	0	2	0	0	0	0	0	1	0	4	0
120-124	0	0	0	0	0	0	0	0	0	0	0	0	0	0	0	0	0	0	0	0	0	0
Total	199	112	311	101	399	85	389	58	303	23	154	3	73	0	36	0	8	0	30	2	1902	384

Apps = Number of Applicants   Adm = Number Admitted   Reflects 98% of the total applicant pool.

Mississippi College School of Law

151 E Griffith Street
Jackson, MS 39201
Phone: 800.738.1236 or 601.925.7150
E-mail: law-admissions@mc.edu; Website: law.mc.edu

ABA Approved Since 1980

The Basics

Type of school	Private
Term	Semester
Application deadline	5/1
Application fee	$50
Financial aid deadline	6/1
Can first year start other than fall?	No
Student to faculty ratio (fall)	22.3 to 1
Does the university offer:	
housing restricted to law students?	No
graduate housing for which law students are eligible?	No

Faculty and Administrators

	Total Fall	Total Spr	Men Fall	Men Spr	Women Fall	Women Spr	Minorities Fall	Minorities Spr
Full-time	17	17	11	11	6	6	2	2
Other Full-time	0	0	0	0	0	0	0	0
Deans, librarians, & others who teach	3	3	1	1	2	2	0	0
Part-time	23	15	17	14	6	1	0	1
Total	43	35	29	26	14	9	2	3

Curriculum

	Full-time	Part-time
Typical first-year section size	55	0
Is there typically a "small section" of the first-year class, other than Legal Writing, taught by full-time faculty	No	No
If yes, typical size offered last year	0	0
# of classroom course titles beyond 1st year curriculum	54	

# of upper division courses, excluding seminars with an enrollment:		
Under 25	45	
25-49	26	
50-74	14	
75-99	1	
100+	0	

# of seminars	4	
# of seminar positions available	60	
# of seminar positions filled	57	0
# of positions available in simulation courses	465	
# of simulation positions filled	396	0
# of positions available in faculty supervised clinical courses	36	
# of faculty supervised clinical positions filled	24	0
# involved in field placements	29	0
# involved in law journals	44	0
# involved in moot court or trial competitions	7	0
# of credit hours required to graduate	90	

JD Enrollment and Ethnicity

	Men #	Men %	Women #	Women %	Full-time #	Full-time %	Part-time #	Part-time %	1st-year #	1st-year %	Total #	Total %	JD Degs. Awd.
African Amer.	12	4.1	24	15.1	36	7.9	0	0.0	8	4.4	36	7.9	10
Amer. Indian	1	0.3	0	0.0	1	0.2	0	0.0	1	0.5	1	0.2	0
Asian Amer.	0	0.0	0	0.0	0	0.0	0	0.0	0	0.0	0	0.0	0
Mex. Amer.	0	0.0	0	0.0	0	0.0	0	0.0	0	0.0	0	0.0	0
Puerto Rican	0	0.0	0	0.0	0	0.0	0	0.0	0	0.0	0	0.0	0
Hispanic	1	0.3	2	1.3	3	0.7	0	0.0	2	1.1	3	0.7	2
Total Minority	14	4.7	26	16.4	40	8.8	0	0.0	11	6.0	40	8.8	12
For. Nation.	0	0.0	0	0.0	0	0.0	0	0.0	0	0.0	0	0.0	0
Caucasian	278	94.2	132	83.0	410	90.3	0	0.0	168	91.8	410	90.3	109
Unknown	3	1.0	1	0.6	4	0.9	0	0.0	4	2.2	4	0.9	0
Total	295	65.0	159	35.0	454	100.0	0	0.0	183	40.3	454		121

Tuition and Fees

	Resident	Nonresident
Full-time	$17,672	$17,672
Part-time	$0	$0

Living Expenses

Estimated living expenses for singles

Living on campus	Living off campus	Living at home
$17,273	$17,273	$17,273

Mississippi College School of Law

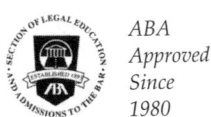

*ABA
Approved
Since
1980*

GPA and LSAT Scores

	Total	Full-time	Part-time
# of apps	1,136	1,136	0
# of admits	401	401	0
# of matrics	183	183	0
75% GPA	0.00	3.48	0.00
25% GPA	0.00	2.99	0.00
75% LSAT	0	154	0
25% LSAT	0	149	0

Grants and Scholarships (from prior year)

	Total #	Total %	Full-time #	Full-time %	Part-time #	Part-time %
Total # of students	426		426		0	
Total # receiving grants	75	17.6	75	17.6	0	0.0
Less than 1/2 tuition	21	4.9	21	4.9	0	0.0
Half to full tuition	17	4.0	17	4.0	0	0.0
Full tuition	35	8.2	35	8.2	0	0.0
More than full tuition	2	0.5	2	0.5	0	0.0
Median grant amount			$9,098		$0	

Informational and Library Resources

# of volumes and volume equivalents	323,278
# of titles	170,988
# of active serial subscriptions	3,486
Study seating capacity inside the library	396
# of professional librarians	4
Hours per week library is open	103
# of open, wired connections available to students	96
# of networked computers available for use by students	33
# of simultaneous wireless users	0
Require computer?	N

JD Attrition (from prior year)

	Academic #	Other #	Total #	Total %
1st year	10	23	33	20.0%
2nd year	1	1	2	1.5%
3rd year	0	0	0	0.0%
4th year	0	0	0	0.0%

Employment

	Total	Percentage
Employment status known	123	100.0
Employment status unknown	0	0.0
Employed	121	98.4
Pursuing graduate degrees	1	0.8
Unemployed seeking employment	1	0.8
Unemployed not seeking employment	0	0.0

Type of Employment

# employed in law firms	86	71.1
# employed in business and industry	4	3.3
# employed in government	9	7.4
# employed in public interest	1	0.8
# employed as judicial clerks	21	17.4
# employed in academia	0	0.0

Geographic Location

# employed in state	98	81.0
# employed in foreign countries	0	0.0
# of states where employed	4	

Bar Passage Rates

Jurisdiction	Mississippi		
Exam	Sum 03	Win 04	Total
# from school taking bar for the first time	81	14	95
School's pass rate for all first-time takers	86%	93%	87%
State's pass rate for all first-time takers	92%	91%	92%

Mississippi College School of Law

151 E Griffith Street
Jackson, MS 39201
Phone: 800.738.1236 or 601.925.7150
E-mail: law-admissions@mc.edu; Website: law.mc.edu

■ Introduction

Mississippi College School of Law is conveniently located in downtown Jackson, the state's capital and largest city. Jackson, with a metropolitan population of nearly 400,000, is the legal, cultural, and commercial center of Mississippi. In addition to the current five-story building, an expansion of the law school campus this fall provided a newly constructed 18,000-square-foot spacious facility that houses high-tech classrooms, a multipurpose courtroom and lecture hall, seminar rooms, a jury room, judges' chambers, and teaching centers. Within walking distance of our school lies a vibrant, thriving legal community, as well as the legislature, federal, and state administrative agencies and courts. The law school is fully accredited by the American Bar Association and is a member of the Association of American Law Schools. The main campus of Mississippi College, with an enrollment of more than 3,000 students, is located in Clinton, a suburb 12 miles west of Jackson.

■ Admission

The law school has rolling admission, and the admission standards are set annually by the faculty. The standards are based on the college undergraduate grade-point average, the LSAT score, and personal or academic achievements or honors. A degree from an accredited four-year college or university is a prerequisite to admission. Every applicant must take the LSAT and register for the LSDAS prior to being considered for admission. The school makes admission decisions without discrimination against any person on the basis of race, religion, sex, or national origin. The application deadline is May 1, and a $50 fee must accompany the application. When an applicant is accepted, a deposit of $100 is required to reserve a seat in the entering class. A second deposit of $200 must be received by June 1. Upon enrollment, these nonrefundable payments are credited to the applicant's tuition.

■ Learning Environment

Our students receive one-on-one attention, and the school is dedicated to maintaining an environment in which they come first. Classes are small, and professors will encourage the students to excel and challenge them to perform.

■ Curriculum

Mississippi College School of Law is an institution that provides superior academic instruction with a curriculum that is national in focus. Recognizing the importance of developing lawyering skills, the curriculum includes instruction in both theoretical and practice skills. In order to assist students in choosing elective courses after the first year, four areas of concentration have been developed. These areas consist of general practice, commercial and corporate practice, government-related practice, and litigation practice. These groupings, however, are not intended to provide specialization during a student's first degree in law. The school is operated on a semester basis, and a beginning student must enter in the fall semester. A summer term is available to second- and third-year students who wish to accelerate or enrich their studies.

■ Externship Program

At MCSOL, classroom theory and practical application go hand-in-hand. In addition to courses in legal doctrine, a wide range of instruction in the skills of modern practice is offered. Student externs work alongside practicing attorneys in government offices and public interest organizations. Depending on the particular externship, students present cases in court, interview witnesses, prepare pleadings and other legal documents, take depositions, negotiate with opposing parties, research legal issues, and draft court opinions. This program allows students to practice in the real world what they have learned in more traditional law school classes.

■ Student Activities

The *Mississippi College Law Review* is a legal journal edited and published by law students who are selected on the basis of scholarship and the ability to do creative, scholarly research, and writing. The students write comments and notes on legal developments and significant cases and edit lead articles and book reviews written by professors, lawyers, judges, legislators, and other scholars. Membership on the *Law Review* staff is recognized as both an honor and a unique educational experience. The law school also provides an appellate advocacy program administered by the Moot Court Board, composed of second- and third-year students. This required program provides students with instruction and practice in both brief writing and oral argument. The Law Student Bar Association is the organized student government of the law school. All students are members and are eligible to hold office in the association. Other student activities include three national legal fraternity chapters, Phi Alpha Delta, Delta Theta Phi, and Phi Delta Phi; a student chapter of the Mississippi Trial Lawyers Association; the Women's Student Bar; Christian Legal Society; Black Law Students Association; Federalist Society; and the Environmental Law Club.

Mississippi College School of Law

■ Career Services

The Career Services Office assists in placement activities. In addition to the traditional on-campus interviews, the law school participates in regional interviews and a clerkship interaction program to help students find employment prior to graduation. Graduates are locating employment with major law firms, corporations, and government agencies throughout the United States, with a primary focus in the Southeast. Students have received clerkships with the United States Circuit Court of Appeals, United States District Courts, and the Supreme Courts of various states.

■ Minority Program

The law school offers a variety of programs to assist minority students: dedicated scholarships/stipends and an Academic Support Program. Minority students are strongly encouraged to apply, and each applicant's entire record will be carefully considered.

■ Library and Physical Facilities

The law library is housed on the first, second, and third floors of the facility in an attractive space that makes generous use of natural light and affords pleasing views of the park-like law school grounds. The library has separate rooms for individual and group study, audiovisual equipment, and photocopying. A chief feature is the computer lab that provides computer-assisted legal instruction and word processing. The library is a government depository and serves bench and bar, along with its students, by providing access to primary and secondary authority for legal research in federal and state law, in addition to selective foreign and international materials.

Applicant Profile

Mississippi College School of Law
This grid includes only applicants with 120-180 LSAT scores earned under standard administrations.

LSAT Score	3.75 + Apps	Adm	3.50-3.74 Apps	Adm	3.25-3.49 Apps	Adm	3.00-3.24 Apps	Adm	2.75-2.99 Apps	Adm	2.50-2.74 Apps	Adm	2.25-2.49 Apps	Adm	2.00-2.24 Apps	Adm	Below 2.00 Apps	Adm	No GPA Apps	Adm	Total Apps	Adm
175-180	0	0	0	0	0	0	0	0	0	0	0	0	0	0	0	0	0	0	0	0	0	0
170-174	0	0	0	0	0	0	0	0	0	0	0	0	0	0	0	0	0	0	0	0	0	0
165-169	1	1	1	1	1	1	0	0	0	0	0	0	1	1	0	0	0	0	0	0	4	4
160-164	2	2	4	3	4	3	3	2	3	2	2	1	3	2	0	0	0	0	0	0	21	15
155-159	13	12	10	7	8	7	15	13	17	14	9	8	7	3	4	2	0	0	0	0	83	66
150-154	21	19	34	30	49	32	55	37	45	27	32	18	14	2	11	2	3	0	2	0	266	167
145-149	25	17	39	22	79	44	93	37	78	9	41	3	26	1	10	0	5	0	2	0	398	133
140-144	10	3	18	0	33	2	56	4	39	1	33	1	24	0	7	0	2	0	7	0	229	11
135-139	5	0	13	0	11	0	25	0	14	0	15	0	9	0	5	0	2	0	2	0	101	0
130-134	1	0	0	0	1	0	8	0	4	0	4	0	2	0	3	0	2	0	2	0	27	0
125-129	0	0	0	0	0	0	0	0	0	0	0	0	0	0	1	0	0	0	3	0	4	0
120-124	0	0	0	0	0	0	0	0	0	0	0	0	0	0	0	0	0	0	0	0	0	0
Total	78	54	119	63	186	89	255	93	200	53	136	31	86	9	41	4	14	0	18	0	1133	396

Apps = Number of Applicants
Adm = Number Admitted
Reflects 99% of the total applicant pool.

University of Missouri—Columbia School of Law

103 Hulston Hall
Columbia, MO 65211
Phone: 573.882.6042, toll-free: 888.MULaw4u; Fax: 573.882.9625
E-mail: UMCLawAdmissions@Missouri.edu; Website: www.Law.Missouri.edu

ABA Approved Since 1923

The Basics

Type of school	Public
Term	Semester
Application deadline	3/1
Application fee	$50
Financial aid deadline	3/1
Can first year start other than fall?	No
Student to faculty ratio (fall)	15.2 to 1
Does the university offer:	
housing restricted to law students?	No
graduate housing for which law students are eligible?	Yes

Curriculum

	Full-time	Part-time
Typical first-year section size	75	0
Is there typically a "small section" of the first-year class, other than Legal Writing, taught by full-time faculty	Yes	No
If yes, typical size offered last year	28	0
# of classroom course titles beyond 1st year curriculum	91	
# of upper division courses, excluding seminars with an enrollment: Under 25	54	
25-49	25	
50-74	12	
75-99	7	
100+	0	
# of seminars	8	
# of seminar positions available	168	
# of seminar positions filled	110	0
# of positions available in simulation courses	396	
# of simulation positions filled	365	0
# of positions available in faculty supervised clinical courses	100	
# of faculty supervised clinical positions filled	77	0
# involved in field placements	62	0
# involved in law journals	85	0
# involved in moot court or trial competitions	250	0
# of credit hours required to graduate	89	

Faculty and Administrators

	Total		Men		Women		Minorities	
	Fall	Spr	Fall	Spr	Fall	Spr	Fall	Spr
Full-time	24	25	15	15	9	10	2	3
Other Full-time	1	1	0	0	1	1	0	0
Deans, librarians, & others who teach	12	12	8	8	4	4	0	0
Part-time	7	12	5	10	2	2	0	1
Total	44	50	28	33	16	17	2	4

JD Enrollment and Ethnicity

	Men		Women		Full-time		Part-time		1st-year		Total		JD Degs. Awd.
	#	%	#	%	#	%	#	%	#	%	#	%	
African Amer.	12	4.5	12	7.0	23	5.3	1	50.0	11	7.6	24	5.5	9
Amer. Indian	4	1.5	0	0.0	4	0.9	0	0.0	0	0.0	4	0.9	1
Asian Amer.	6	2.3	5	2.9	10	2.3	1	50.0	3	2.1	11	2.5	4
Mex. Amer.	0	0.0	0	0.0	0	0.0	0	0.0	0	0.0	0	0.0	0
Puerto Rican	0	0.0	0	0.0	0	0.0	0	0.0	0	0.0	0	0.0	0
Hispanic	3	1.1	1	0.6	4	0.9	0	0.0	1	0.7	4	0.9	1
Total Minority	25	9.4	18	10.5	41	9.4	2	100.0	15	10.3	43	9.8	15
For. Nation.	0	0.0	0	0.0	0	0.0	0	0.0	0	0.0	0	0.0	0
Caucasian	225	84.9	152	88.4	377	86.7	0	0.0	124	85.5	377	86.3	161
Unknown	15	5.7	2	1.2	17	3.9	0	0.0	6	4.1	17	3.9	5
Total	265	60.6	172	39.4	435	99.5	2	0.5	145	33.2	437		181

Tuition and Fees

	Resident	Nonresident
Full-time	$12,117	$23,073
Part-time	$8,788	$16,614

Living Expenses

Estimated living expenses for singles

Living on campus	Living off campus	Living at home
$13,640	$13,640	$13,640

University of Missouri—Columbia School of Law

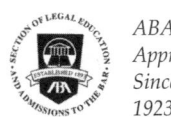

*ABA
Approved
Since
1923*

GPA and LSAT Scores

	Total	Full-time	Part-time
# of apps	1,058	1,058	0
# of admits	319	319	0
# of matrics	145	145	0
75% GPA	3.72	3.72	0.00
25% GPA	3.22	3.22	0.00
75% LSAT	161	161	0
25% LSAT	157	157	0

Grants and Scholarships (from prior year)

	Total		Full-time		Part-time	
	#	%	#	%	#	%
Total # of students	488		488		0	
Total # receiving grants	214	43.9	214	43.9	0	0.0
Less than 1/2 tuition	196	40.2	196	40.2	0	0.0
Half to full tuition	10	2.0	10	2.0	0	0.0
Full tuition	0	0.0	0	0.0	0	0.0
More than full tuition	8	1.6	8	1.6	0	0
Median grant amount			$4,000		$0	

Informational and Library Resources

# of volumes and volume equivalents	353,357
# of titles	184,252
# of active serial subscriptions	2,113
Study seating capacity inside the library	481
# of professional librarians	8
Hours per week library is open	73
# of open, wired connections available to students	0
# of networked computers available for use by students	45
# of simultaneous wireless users	768
Require computer?	N

JD Attrition (from prior year)

	Academic	Other	Total	
	#	#	#	%
1st year	4	6	10	6.4%
2nd year	0	9	9	6.2%
3rd year	0	1	1	0.5%
4th year	0	0	0	0.0%

Employment

	Total	Percentage
Employment status known	177	100.0
Employment status unknown	0	0.0
Employed	163	92.1
Pursuing graduate degrees	5	2.8
Unemployed seeking employment	6	3.4
Unemployed not seeking employment	3	1.7

Type of Employment

# employed in law firms	92	56.4
# employed in business and industry	13	8.0
# employed in government	42	25.8
# employed in public interest	1	0.6
# employed as judicial clerks	8	4.9
# employed in academia	2	1.2

Geographic Location

# employed in state	137	84.0
# employed in foreign countries	0	0.0
# of states where employed	12	

Bar Passage Rates

Jurisdiction	Missouri		
Exam	Sum 03	Win 04	Total
# from school taking bar for the first time	149	10	159
School's pass rate for all first-time takers	85%	70%	84%
State's pass rate for all first-time takers	83%	87%	84%

University of Missouri—Columbia School of Law

Office of Admissions, 103 Hulston Hall
Columbia, MO 65211
Phone: 573.882.6042, toll-free: 888.MULaw4u; Fax: 573.882.9625
E-mail: UMCLawAdmissions@Missouri.edu; Website: www.Law.Missouri.edu

■ Introduction

The University of Missouri—Columbia is a dynamic and collegial community. Founded in 1839, MU is the first state university west of the Mississippi. The School of Law was established in 1872 and has had an enviable history of service to the state and nation. Graduates include judges, governors, attorneys general, and legislators who serve nationwide. The law school is a charter member of the AALS and is fully accredited.

Located in Columbia, MU is 35 miles from Jefferson City, the state capital. Our location provides students with easy access to the legislature, the Supreme Court, and various offices of state. In addition to living and studying in one of America's most livable cities, students are within two hours of the cultural, athletic, and entertainment centers of St. Louis and Kansas City.

■ Enrollment/Student Body

The student body of the law school is composed of students from numerous states and several foreign countries. This diverse group provides a wealth of experiences and fosters a stimulating learning environment.

■ Faculty

The faculty at MU is strong and vibrant. MU is among the top 10 percent of law schools in American Law Institute membership. Four members of the faculty serve as commissioners to the National Conference of Commissioners on Uniform State Laws and four serve as reporters. The Executive Director of the National Conference is an emeritus professor. A recent president of the AALS is also on the faculty. The faculty focus is on teaching, research, and service. Faculty maintain an open-door policy for students.

■ Library and Physical Facilities

John K. Hulston Hall is dominated by open spaces, sky-lights, and windows. It is a magnificent, state-of-the-art laboratory in which to study law. The law school is part of the campus wireless network. Students can access the Internet and computer-assisted legal services anywhere on campus or in the law building.

The law library houses an extensive collection of legal volumes and reference materials and a rare book collection. It employs a large staff of specialized librarians, researchers, and computer support personnel. Faculty and students have 24-hour access to the law library.

■ Curriculum

The academic program leading to the JD degree traditionally consists of six semesters of study. One seven-week semester is offered each summer. The first-year curriculum is proscribed, as is a substantial portion of the second-year curriculum.

To graduate, students must complete 89 semester hours, including a writing requirement, with a minimum average of 70 on a scale of 55 to 100.

■ Special Programs: Alternative Dispute Resolution

The Center for the Study of Dispute Resolution is a unique feature of the law school and provides national leadership in this rapidly developing area of the law. First-year students are exposed to dispute resolution processes. MU also offers a variety of dispute resolution courses and opportunities for second- and third-year students.

The center also houses a Master of Laws in Dispute Resolution degree program, one of the first programs of its kind in the country.

■ Dual-Degree Programs

The School of Law has dual-degree programs with the graduate schools of Business Administration (JD/MBA), Public Administration (JD/MPA), Health Administration (JD/MHA), Library Science (JD/MLS), and Journalism (JD/MA and JD/PhD) The law school will consider establishing other dual-degree programs to meet individual interests. Traditionally, dual-degree students spend their first year in the school of law. (Students must fulfill the entrance requirements of both schools.)

■ Certificate Programs

The law school offers a certificate in Alternative Dispute Resolution. Students can complete this certificate by concentrating their elective hours in this area of the law.

In addition, a certificate in Journalism, the Digital Globe, or the European Union is available to law students through the Graduate School.

MU is one of 10 European Union (EU) centers in the United States working to develop a better understanding of the transatlantic agenda between the EU and the United States that is shaping our relations.

■ Study Abroad

The School of Law offers second- and third-year students three opportunities to study abroad. An exchange program at Bucerius University in Hamburg, Germany, offers a fall semester abroad. Courses are taught in

English by German faculty. Students proficient in German have additional course opportunities. The London Law Consortium provides a winter semester in London. A summer program in Capetown, South Africa, is available for all students.

■ Clinics and Externships

MU provides students practical experience to enhance lawyering skills and to promote awareness of ethical issues. An active externship and judicial clerkship program and five clinical programs—the Child Advocacy Clinic, Criminal Prosecution Clinic, Family Violence Clinic, Legislative Clinic, and Mediation Clinic—have been developed to address these needs.

■ Student Activities

Students are eligible to participate on the *Missouri Law Review*, the *Journal of Dispute Resolution*, or the *Missouri Environmental Law and Policy Review*. The Board of Advocates sponsors a wide variety of advocacy competitions. The school has chapters of the Order of the Coif, the Order of Barristers, Student Bar Association, and two legal fraternities. Other student organizations, encompassing almost every aspect of social and academic life, are offered.

■ Admission

A faculty committee reviews all applications. In many cases, factors other than the GPA or LSAT score have proven to be determinative. If the LSAT is repeated, the school uses an average of the scores for its evaluation. Applications from disadvantaged students are especially encouraged.

Students are encouraged to apply early and to visit the law school. The Admissions Office can arrange for students to meet with an admission counselor, attend a class, and tour the facility.

■ Expenses and Financial Aid

Law school is a career investment. MU offers an outstanding value for the cost. In addition, the cost of housing, utilities, and related expenses in Columbia are low when compared to urban standards.

Financial assistance is available to students.

■ Career Services

The Career Development Office serves as a liaison between students or alumni and prospective employers. Workshops, seminars, and individual counseling are offered to help students develop career goals and sharpen their job-search skills. Typically, over 90 percent of each graduating class accepts employment within nine months of graduation. The majority of graduates practice in Missouri, however, graduates find employment throughout the world.

Applicant Profile

University of Missouri—Columbia School of Law
This grid includes only applicants who earned 120-180 LSAT scores under standard administrations.

LSAT Score	GPA								
	3.75 +	3.50 - 3.74	3.25 - 3.49	3.00 - 3.24	2.75 - 2.99	2.50 - 2.74	2.25 - 2.49	2.00 - 2.24	Below 2.00
175-180									
170-174									
165-169									
160-164									
155-159									
150-154									
145-149									
140-144									
135-139									
130-134									
125-129									
120-124									

Good Possibility   Possible   Unlikely

This chart is to be used as a general guide only. Nonnumerical factors are strongly considered for all applicants.

University of Missouri—Kansas City School of Law

5100 Rockhill Road
Kansas City, MO 64110
Phone: 816.235.1644; Fax: 816.235.5276
E-mail: law@umkc.edu; Website: www.law.umkc.edu

ABA
Approved
Since
1936

The Basics

Type of school	Public
Term	Semester
Application deadline	
Application fee	$50
Financial aid deadline	
Can first year start other than fall?	No
Student to faculty ratio (fall)	18.6 to 1
Does the university offer:	
housing restricted to law students?	No
graduate housing for which law students are eligible?	Yes

Faculty and Administrators

	Total		Men		Women		Minorities	
	Fall	Spr	Fall	Spr	Fall	Spr	Fall	Spr
Full-time	23	23	17	17	6	6	1	1
Other Full-time	2	2	0	0	2	2	0	0
Deans, librarians, & others who teach	5	5	3	3	2	2	0	0
Part-time	32	46	22	35	10	11	1	1
Total	**62**	**76**	**42**	**55**	**20**	**21**	**2**	**2**

Curriculum

		Full-time	Part-time
Typical first-year section size		56	0
Is there typically a "small section" of the first-year class, other than Legal Writing, taught by full-time faculty		No	No
If yes, typical size offered last year		0	0
# of classroom course titles beyond 1st year curriculum		99	
# of upper division courses, excluding seminars with an enrollment:	Under 25	69	
	25-49	18	
	50-74	15	
	75-99	8	
	100+	0	
# of seminars		15	
# of seminar positions available		279	
# of seminar positions filled		221	0
# of positions available in simulation courses		404	
# of simulation positions filled		335	0
# of positions available in faculty supervised clinical courses		73	
# of faculty supervised clinical positions filled		59	0
# involved in field placements		54	0
# involved in law journals		104	0
# involved in moot court or trial competitions		167	0
# of credit hours required to graduate		91	

JD Enrollment and Ethnicity

	Men		Women		Full-time		Part-time		1st-year		Total		JD Degs. Awd.
	#	%	#	%	#	%	#	%	#	%	#	%	
African Amer.	4	1.4	13	5.2	17	3.5	0	0.0	5	2.4	17	3.2	1
Amer. Indian	2	0.7	4	1.6	6	1.2	0	0.0	0	0.0	6	1.1	1
Asian Amer.	9	3.2	6	2.4	15	3.1	0	0.0	5	2.4	15	2.8	2
Mex. Amer.	2	0.7	2	0.8	4	0.8	0	0.0	3	1.4	4	0.8	0
Puerto Rican	0	0.0	0	0.0	0	0.0	0	0.0	0	0.0	0	0.0	0
Hispanic	2	0.7	3	1.2	5	1.0	0	0.0	2	0.9	5	0.9	3
Total Minority	19	6.9	28	11.2	47	9.7	0	0.0	15	7.1	47	8.9	7
For. Nation.	1	0.4	0	0.0	1	0.2	0	0.0	1	0.5	1	0.2	1
Caucasian	257	92.8	223	88.8	439	90.1	41	100.0	195	92.4	480	90.9	154
Unknown	0	0.0	0	0.0	0	0.0	0	0.0	0	0.0	0	0.0	0
Total	277	52.5	251	47.5	487	92.2	41	7.8	211	40.0	528		162

Tuition and Fees

	Resident	Nonresident
Full-time	$13,342	$25,456
Part-time	$9,033	$17,109

Living Expenses

Estimated living expenses for singles

Living on campus	Living off campus	Living at home
$21,240	$23,100	$14,830

University of Missouri—Kansas City School of Law

*ABA
Approved
Since
1936*

GPA and LSAT Scores

	Total	Full-time	Part-time
# of apps	1,021	971	50
# of admits	466	447	19
# of matrics	211	197	14
75% GPA	3.62	3.63	3.62
25% GPA	3.15	3.14	3.25
75% LSAT	156	156	156
25% LSAT	151	151	150

Grants and Scholarships (from prior year)

	Total #	Total %	Full-time #	Full-time %	Part-time #	Part-time %
Total # of students	498		464		34	
Total # receiving grants	162	32.5	162	34.9	0	0.0
Less than 1/2 tuition	69	13.9	69	14.9	0	0.0
Half to full tuition	68	13.7	68	14.7	0	0.0
Full tuition	17	3.4	17	3.7	0	0.0
More than full tuition	8	1.6	8	1.7	0	0.0
Median grant amount			$8,904		$0	

Informational and Library Resources

# of volumes and volume equivalents	325,941
# of titles	69,242
# of active serial subscriptions	1,816
Study seating capacity inside the library	475
# of professional librarians	7
Hours per week library is open	100
# of open, wired connections available to students	18
# of networked computers available for use by students	63
# of simultaneous wireless users	2,530
Require computer?	N

JD Attrition (from prior year)

	Academic #	Other #	Total #	Total %
1st year	16	6	22	13.9%
2nd year	0	2	2	1.1%
3rd year	0	0	0	0.0%
4th year	0	0	0	0.0%

Employment

	Total	Percentage
Employment status known	133	100.0
Employment status unknown	0	0.0
Employed	112	84.2
Pursuing graduate degrees	6	4.5
Unemployed seeking employment	15	11.3
Unemployed not seeking employment	0	0.0

Type of Employment

	Total	Percentage
# employed in law firms	77	68.7
# employed in business and industry	11	9.8
# employed in government	22	19.6
# employed in public interest	0	0.0
# employed as judicial clerks	2	1.8
# employed in academia	0	0.0

Geographic Location

	Total	Percentage
# employed in state	85	75.9
# employed in foreign countries	1	0.9
# of states where employed	9	

Bar Passage Rates

Jurisdiction	Missouri		
Exam	Sum 03	Win 04	Total
# from school taking bar for the first time	101	53	154
School's pass rate for all first-time takers	88%	87%	88%
State's pass rate for all first-time takers	83%	87%	84%

University of Missouri—Kansas City School of Law

5100 Rockhill Road
Kansas City, MO 64110
Phone: 816.235.1644; Fax: 816.235.5276
E-mail: law@umkc.edu; Website: www.law.umkc.edu

■ Introduction

Located in the midst of a beautiful college campus, UMKC takes pride in being the urban public law school with a small liberal arts feel. From this unique vantage point, UMKC serves and collaborates with the legal communities in two major metropolitan areas of the states of Missouri and Kansas. Students, faculty, and alumni actively lead and participate in professional activities with area bar associations, lawyers, and law firms, as well as government agencies and the judiciary. A variety of community-based projects benefit from this involvement.

UMKC law school graduates hold important responsibilities in legal arenas across the country, distinguishing themselves in private practice, government service, academia, and corporate roles. Notable UMKC alumni include a president of the United States, a justice of the US Supreme Court, and a director of the FBI. Many other UMKC alumni currently serve as judges at the federal, state, and local levels—an unmistakable sign of community respect for the school and its graduates.

The law school enjoys support from its alumni, a number of whom participate in the Inns of UMKC, a program designed to help students achieve academic success, improve their preparation for the bar exam, and better prepare them for life as practicing attorneys. Modeled after the English Inns of Court system of training young lawyers (barristers), each Inn is led by prominent members of the local bar—attorneys and a judge—as well as two law school faculty. Inns meet on a regular basis throughout the year, and each student meets with his or her faculty advisor for individual advising on a prescribed schedule.

Founded in 1895, the school is accredited by the ABA and is a member of the AALS.

■ Library and Physical Facilities

Office suites shared by faculty and students are designed to foster the exchange of ideas and to promote collegiality between faculty and students. The school has over 121,000 square feet of modern, usable space, which includes wireless computer access throughout the building, a recently renovated student lounge and computer bar, an outdoor courtyard, four lecture halls with state-of-the-art projection equipment, student offices, and a courtroom.

The Leon E. Bloch Law Library is a modern facility that combines the traditions of print media with electronic media in preparing the lawyer of the future and supporting the legal community.

■ Curriculum

UMKC School of Law is a community of learners bridging the gap between theory and practice. Courses are taught in a variety of formats, but all have high-quality teaching and student-faculty interaction. Many of the substantive courses include problem solving, service learning, and the development of skills components essential to the practice of law.

The first-year JD program is prescribed, with classes that average fewer than 60 students each. A year-long intensive course in Introduction to Law and Lawyering Processes provides instruction in legal analysis, research, writing, and advocacy. The upper-level program includes a combination of required courses, as well as a broad selection of elective courses, including approved non-law courses in other UMKC divisions. No class offered is larger than 80 students and most are significantly smaller.

The school is committed to the success of its students. Academic enrichment opportunities in the form of supervised, structured study groups, lecture series, and weekly workshops are offered. Additional opportunities include a weeklong summer program available on a limited basis.

While the school's innovative new Solo & Small Firm Initiative prepares students for general practice, those seeking more focused study can pursue one of our four emphasis areas: Litigation; Business & Entrepreneurial Law; Urban, Land Use and Environmental Law; and Law in Service to Children and Families. These emphases build on our long-standing tradition of excellence in these areas and prepare students to enter the job market with specialized knowledge and skills. In addition, the School of Law has established dual-degree programs with the Henry W. Bloch School of Business and Public Administration. The program allows students to earn a JD degree and a Master of Business Administration or Master of Public Administration degree on an accelerated basis through cross-acceptance of some credit hours. Applicants must satisfy the admission requirements of each school. Students also have the opportunity to participate in one of two annual study abroad programs that visit China and Ireland.

A part-time day program is available for those students with family or career responsibilities who are unable to enroll on a full-time basis. Students may graduate in two-and-one-half years by attending two summer sessions.

■ JD/LLM and Combined-Degree Programs

The School of Law has adopted combined-degree programs that allow qualified JD students to apply up to 12 credit hours (with the permission of the Graduate Studies Committee) of UMKC tax or estate planning courses approved for this purpose toward an LLM on an accelerated basis, generally requiring only one additional semester (or two summer sessions) beyond that required for the JD degree.

University of Missouri—Kansas City School of Law

■ Student Activities

The law school's location in a metropolitan area provides many opportunities for students to engage in real-life representation of clients (under faculty supervision) in clinical programs that include UMKC's Child and Family Services Clinic, Tax Clinic, Entrepreneurial Law and Practice Clinic, and Wrongful Convictions (the school's "Innocence Project"). The school also offers a number of field placements, including judicial clerkships with federal and state judges, and internships with prosecutors, public defenders, Legal Aid, the Department of Labor, the EPA, and the US Attorney's Office.

Students write and edit a substantial portion of the *UMKC Law Review*, a scholarly legal journal, and also serve as assistant editors of the *Urban Lawyer*, published by the ABA Section of Local Government Law, and the national and international *Journal of the American Academy of Matrimonial Lawyers*.

Students obtain advanced skills development in trial and appellate advocacy through sequenced upper-level courses and competition participation. Students also participate in client counseling and negotiation competitions. UMKC teams frequently win regional and national honors in these competitions.

UMKC benefits from an active Student Bar Association, which represents students at faculty and committee meetings and plays an important role in establishing school policy. Three national legal fraternities have chapters at the school, as do the following law student associations: Black Law Students, Hispanic Law Students, Jewish Law Students, Asian Pacific Islander Students, Women Law Students, and Non-traditional Law Students. Additional student organizations specialize in

Environmental Law, Public Interest Law, Intellectual Property Law, International Law, and other areas of interest, comprising over 30 student organizations.

■ Admission

While some students are admitted primarily on undergraduate GPA and LSAT scores, most applications are considered by a committee that examines applicants' complete files to ensure that the entering class contains persons of diverse backgrounds and interests whose achievements qualify them for law study.

Students may be admitted with a bachelor's degree from an approved institution or, in appropriate cases, with 90 hours of acceptable academic work. A $200 seat deposit is payable by April 1, or within 20 days of admission, whichever comes later and a second $100.00 seat deposit is due June 15th. Applicants are strongly encouraged to visit the school. Arrangements can be made to meet with students and faculty, visit a class, or tour the law school.

■ Career Services

The Office of Career Services assists law students in exploring and defining career options. It also provides advice and assistance in résumé preparation and interviewing skills. The office sponsors a series of programs to introduce students to a variety of career opportunities. Participants in the school's Judicial Clerkship Initiative have enjoyed a high placement rate in pursuing clerkships with state and federal judges.

Applicant Profile

University of Missouri—Kansas City School of Law

LSAT Score	3.75 +		3.50 - 3.74		3.25 - 3.49		3.00 - 3.24		2.75 - 2.99		2.50 - 2.74		2.25 - 2.49		2.00 - 2.24		Below 2.00		No GPA		Total	
	Apps	Adm	Apps	Adm	Apps	Adm	Apps	Adm	Apps	Adm	Apps	Adm	Apps	Adm	Apps	Adm	Apps	Adm	Apps	Adm	Apps	Adm
165 +	5	5	1	1	3	3	1	0	2	2	2	0	0	0	0	0	0	0	0	0	14	11
160-164	8	7	5	5	16	16	12	11	6	2	3	2	3	1	1	0	0	0	1	0	55	44
155-159	31	30	32	31	37	36	29	27	25	12	7	3	5	1	1	0	1	0	2	1	170	141
150-154	46	43	68	63	73	60	66	57	41	17	22	2	14	0	6	0	1	0	5	2	342	244
145-149	16	3	42	9	53	8	58	3	37	1	20	1	12	1	4	0	0	0	2	0	244	26
140-144	8	0	16	0	18	1	32	0	18	0	14	0	13	1	2	0	1	0	4	0	126	2
Below 140	0	0	5	0	5	0	14	0	8	0	8	0	7	0	3	0	5	0	5	0	60	0
Total	114	88	169	109	205	124	212	98	137	34	76	8	54	4	17	0	8	0	19	3	1011	468

Apps = Number of Applicants   Adm = Number Admitted   Reflects 99% of the total applicant pool.

The School of Law considers many factors beyond LSAT scrore and GPA. This chart should be used only as a general guide.

University of Montana School of Law

32 Campus Drive
Missoula, MT 59812
Phone: 406.243.4311
E-mail: lawadmis@umontana.edu; Website: www.umt.edu/law

The Basics

Type of school	Public
Term	Semester
Application deadline	3/1
Application fee	$60
Financial aid deadline	3/1
Can first year start other than fall?	No
Student to faculty ratio (fall)	13.4 to 1
Does the university offer:	
housing restricted to law students?	No
graduate housing for which law students are eligible?	No

Faculty and Administrators

	Total		Men		Women		Minorities	
	Fall	Spr	Fall	Spr	Fall	Spr	Fall	Spr
Full-time	15	14	10	9	5	5	2	2
Other Full-time	1	1	1	1	0	0	0	0
Deans, librarians, & others who teach	2	2	1	1	1	1	0	0
Part-time	9	20	7	16	2	4	0	0
Total	27	37	19	27	8	10	2	2

Curriculum

	Full-time	Part-time
Typical first-year section size	42	0
Is there typically a "small section" of the first-year class, other than Legal Writing, taught by full-time faculty	No	No
If yes, typical size offered last year	0	0
# of classroom course titles beyond 1st year curriculum	65	

# of upper division courses, excluding seminars with an enrollment:		
	Under 25	8
	25-49	6
	50-74	2
	75-99	0
	100+	0

	Full-time	Part-time
# of seminars	24	
# of seminar positions available	448	
# of seminar positions filled	448	0
# of positions available in simulation courses	257	
# of simulation positions filled	257	0
# of positions available in faculty supervised clinical courses	80	
# of faculty supervised clinical positions filled	75	0
# involved in field placements	45	0
# involved in law journals	31	0
# involved in moot court or trial competitions	21	0
# of credit hours required to graduate	90	

JD Enrollment and Ethnicity

	Men		Women		Full-time		Part-time		1st-year		Total		JD Degs. Awd.
	#	%	#	%	#	%	#	%	#	%	#	%	
African Amer.	1	0.8	0	0.0	1	0.4	0	0.0	1	1.2	1	0.4	0
Amer. Indian	5	3.9	6	5.4	11	4.6	0	0.0	8	9.6	11	4.6	2
Asian Amer.	0	0.0	2	1.8	2	0.8	0	0.0	1	1.2	2	0.8	0
Mex. Amer.	0	0.0	0	0.0	0	0.0	0	0.0	0	0.0	0	0.0	0
Puerto Rican	0	0.0	1	0.9	1	0.4	0	0.0	1	1.2	1	0.4	0
Hispanic	0	0.0	0	0.0	0	0.0	0	0.0	0	0.0	0	0.0	0
Total Minority	6	4.7	9	8.0	15	6.2	0	0.0	11	13.3	15	6.2	2
For. Nation.	0	0.0	0	0.0	0	0.0	0	0.0	0	0.0	0	0.0	0
Caucasian	123	95.3	103	92.0	226	93.8	0	0.0	72	86.7	226	93.8	75
Unknown	0	0.0	0	0.0	0	0.0	0	0.0	0	0.0	0	0.0	0
Total	129	53.5	112	46.5	241	100.0	0	0.0	83	34.4	241		77

Tuition and Fees

	Resident	Nonresident
Full-time	$8,710	$17,415
Part-time	$0	$0

Living Expenses

Estimated living expenses for singles

Living on campus	Living off campus	Living at home
$9,300	$9,300	$6,900

University of Montana School of Law

*ABA
Approved
Since
1923*

GPA and LSAT Scores

	Total	Full-time	Part-time
# of apps	543	543	0
# of admits	188	188	0
# of matrics	83	83	0
75% GPA	3.68	3.68	0.00
25% GPA	3.18	3.18	0.00
75% LSAT	158	158	0
25% LSAT	151	151	0

Grants and Scholarships (from prior year)

	Total		Full-time		Part-time	
	#	%	#	%	#	%
Total # of students	241		241		0	
Total # receiving grants	107	44.4	107	44.4	0	0.0
Less than 1/2 tuition	104	43.2	104	43.2	0	0.0
Half to full tuition	3	1.2	3	1.2	0	0.0
Full tuition	0	0.0	0	0.0	0	0.0
More than full tuition	0	0.0	0	0.0	0	0.0
Median grant amount			$1,250		$0	

Informational and Library Resources

# of volumes and volume equivalents	118,813
# of titles	21,855
# of active serial subscriptions	1,737
Study seating capacity inside the library	364
# of professional librarians	3
Hours per week library is open	106
# of open, wired connections available to students	112
# of networked computers available for use by students	48
# of simultaneous wireless users	180
Require computer?	N

JD Attrition (from prior year)

	Academic	Other	Total	
	#	#	#	%
1st year	0	10	10	12.2%
2nd year	0	0	0	0.0%
3rd year	0	0	0	0.0%
4th year	0	0	0	0.0%

Employment

	Total	Percentage
Employment status known	82	98.8
Employment status unknown	1	1.2
Employed	65	79.3
Pursuing graduate degrees	9	11.0
Unemployed seeking employment	7	8.5
Unemployed not seeking employment	1	1.2

Type of Employment

	Total	Percentage
# employed in law firms	29	44.6
# employed in business and industry	5	7.7
# employed in government	10	15.4
# employed in public interest	1	1.5
# employed as judicial clerks	19	29.2
# employed in academia	0	0.0

Geographic Location

	Total	Percentage
# employed in state	41	63.1
# employed in foreign countries	0	0.0
# of states where employed		16

Bar Passage Rates

Jurisdiction	Montana		
Exam	Sum 03	Win 04	Total
# from school taking bar for the first time	47	8	55
School's pass rate for all first-time takers	79%	63%	76%
State's pass rate for all first-time takers	79%	89%	82%

University of Montana School of Law

32 Campus Drive
Missoula, MT 59812
Phone: 406.243.4311
E-mail: lawadmis@umontana.edu; Website: www.umt.edu/law

■ Introduction

The University of Montana is located in Missoula on the west slopes of the Rocky Mountains. Missoula is situated halfway between Yellowstone and Glacier National Parks and is surrounded by several of the largest designated wilderness areas in the continental United States. The city is known for its outdoor opportunities and quality of life.

The University of Montana School of Law was established in 1911 and serves as a legal center for the state. It has been accredited by the AALS since 1914 and by the ABA since 1923. As one of the smallest law schools in the nation, students enjoy a congenial academic, intellectual, and social environment.

■ UM's Program

The University of Montana School of Law integrates theory and practice throughout its curriculum to instill entry-level practice and competence in its graduates. The School of Law's curriculum, teaching methodology, and assessment techniques are designed to address the following components of a lawyer's work: (1) knowledge of the law, (2) ability to apply legal rules to solve problems, (3) ability to use lawyering skills (e.g., negotiation and client counseling), (4) perspective on the societal role and responsibility of lawyers, and (5) sensitivity to the dynamics of social and interpersonal interaction.

The school has created three distinctive programs to acquaint first-year students with the ways lawyers think and work: (1) the Introductory Program, (2) the Lawyer Skills Program, and (3) the Law Firm Program. In the Introductory Program, students are initiated into the legal culture by surveying legal history, the American legal system, the litigation process, legal writing, and legal analysis and jurisprudence. The School of Law is one of the few to introduce first-year students to the skills involved in dispute resolution, including client counseling, legal document drafting, and oral argument. Our program encourages students to cooperate and collaborate rather than compete as they begin to think and work as lawyers. Entering students belong to "law firms," groups of six students (called associates) directed by upper-class students.

The school has long emphasized performance in its curriculum. The school's legal writing and dispute-resolution programs represent a coherent and comprehensive approach to lawyer skills. Students master specific transactional skills such as planning an estate, drafting a contract, and creating a small business.

The upper-division clinical training program provides students with a wide range of opportunities to earn required academic credit by working on actual cases

under the supervision of faculty and practicing attorneys in Missoula. The clinical offerings include the Natural Resource Clinic, Indian Law Clinic, Montana Legal Services Association Clinic, Prosecutory clinics (federal, state, county, and municipal), University of Montana Legal Counsel Clinic, and the Disability Law Clinic.

■ Special Programs

Because of Montana's natural setting, many students enroll in the natural resource and environmental law courses. Montana offers a certificate program in environmental and natural resources law, natural resource clinics, and the opportunity to participate on the *Public Land and Resources Law Review.*

The School of Law also offers concentrations in the areas of trial advocacy and dispute resolution, Indian law, and business and tax law. Montana is home to seven Indian reservations. The School of Law's Indian Law courses, Indian Law Clinic, and Native American Law Student Association provide opportunities for students to learn about and participate in the administration of justice for Montana's Native Americans.

The School of Law offers three joint-degree programs. Students can combine their law degrees with a Master of Science in Environmental Studies, a Master of Business Administration, or a Master of Public Administration. These programs can lead to completion of joint degrees in as little as four years.

■ Admission

A committee of law faculty reviews applications. Candidates must be of good moral character, have intellectual promise, and have a baccalaureate degree from an approved college or university prior to matriculation. Applicants are considered in two distinct pools: resident and nonresident. The School of Law seeks a diverse student body and welcomes applications from members of groups historically underrepresented in the legal profession.

The School of Law recommends you submit your application as soon as possible. We begin reviewing completed applications after January 1. Applications are not considered complete until all application materials, including the LSDAS report, are received. If your file is completed by February 15, you will be notified of a decision (admit, deny, or retain for further review) by March 15. If your file is completed by March 15, you will be notified of a decision by April 15. Files completed after March 15 may be considered on a space-available basis.

The most important admission criteria are the cumulative undergraduate GPA and the LSAT score. If the LSAT is repeated, all scores will be used in evaluating the applicant. The admission committee weighs such factors as writing ability; college attended; trend in grades; quality of work in difficult courses; experience prior to application to law school, including graduate study; ability to overcome economic or other disadvantage; and change in performance after an absence from school.

The school recognizes a commitment to provide full opportunities for the study of law and entry into the legal profession of qualified members of groups (notably racial and ethnic minorities) who have been victims of discrimination.

■ Student Activities

All students are members of the Student Bar Association. Its programs contribute to the professional development and the social life of the student body. Clayberg Inn of Phi Delta Phi national law fraternity encourages scholarship, promotes fellowship, and fosters the ideals of the profession. Other organizations include student chapters of the American Trial Lawyers Association—Montana Trial Lawyers Association and the Montana Defense Trial Lawyers Association, the Women's Law Caucus, the Environmental Law Group, the Native American Law Student Association, the Federalist Society, and the University of Montana Public Interest Law Coalition. The *Montana Law Review* and the *Public Land and Resources Law Review* afford supplementary training in analyzing legal problems precisely and presenting legal issues cogently.

The University of Montana School of Law is proud of its performance in interscholastic competitions. Nearly every year the School of Law fields teams that compete at the national level. Most recently, UM won the 2000 National Moot Court Championship. UM won the ATLA trial competition national championship in 1992 and the national ABA client-counseling championship in 1990.

Applicant Profile

University of Montana School of Law
This grid includes only applicants who earned 120-180 LSAT scores under standard administrations.

LSAT Score	3.75 +		3.50 - 3.74		3.25 - 3.49		3.00 - 3.24		2.75 - 2.99		2.50 - 2.74		2.25 - 2.49		2.00 - 2.24		Below 2.00		No GPA		Total	
	Apps	Adm	Apps	Adm	Apps	Adm	Apps	Adm	Apps	Adm	Apps	Adm	Apps	Adm	Apps	Adm	Apps	Adm	Apps	Adm	Apps	Adm
175-180	0	0	0	0	0	0	0	0	0	0	0	0	0	0	0	0	0	0	0	0	0	0
170-174	0	0	1	1	0	0	0	0	0	0	1	0	0	0	0	0	0	0	0	0	2	1
165-169	5	5	2	1	4	4	0	0	1	1	0	0	0	0	0	0	0	0	0	0	12	11
160-164	7	7	12	11	17	14	3	2	10	7	4	0	1	0	0	0	0	0	0	0	54	41
155-159	15	14	24	24	14	6	31	11	21	5	9	3	6	1	1	0	1	0	0	0	122	64
150-154	11	7	29	12	36	15	34	8	28	3	17	3	4	2	1	0	2	0	0	0	162	50
145-149	7	2	20	4	35	5	27	3	23	1	5	0	7	3	1	0	0	0	0	0	125	18
140-144	0	0	5	0	9	1	11	1	8	0	9	0	2	0	4	0	0	0	2	0	50	2
135-139	2	0	0	0	1	0	1	0	3	0	4	0	2	0	1	0	0	0	0	0	14	0
130-134	0	0	1	0	0	0	1	0	0	0	0	0	0	0	0	0	1	0	1	0	4	0
125-129	0	0	0	0	0	0	1	0	1	0	0	0	0	0	0	0	0	0	0	0	2	0
120-124	0	0	0	0	0	0	0	0	0	0	0	0	0	0	0	0	0	0	0	0	0	0
Total	47	35	94	53	116	45	109	25	95	17	49	6	22	6	8	0	4	0	3	0	547	187

Apps = Number of Applicants
Adm = Number Admitted
Reflects 99% of the total applicant pool.

University of Nebraska College of Law

PO Box 830902
Lincoln, NE 68583-0902
Phone: 402.472.2161; Fax: 402.472.5185
E-mail: lawadm@unl.edu; Website: law.unl.edu

ABA
Approved
Since
1923

The Basics

Type of school	Public
Term	Semester
Application deadline	3/1
Application fee	$25
Financial aid deadline	5/1
Can first year start other than fall?	No
Student to faculty ratio (fall)	14.8 to 1
Does the university offer:	
housing restricted to law students?	No
graduate housing for which law students are eligible?	Yes

Faculty and Administrators

	Total		Men		Women		Minorities	
	Fall	Spr	Fall	Spr	Fall	Spr	Fall	Spr
Full-time	23	22	16	15	7	7	2	2
Other Full-time	0	0	0	0	0	0	0	0
Deans, librarians, & others who teach	8	8	5	5	3	3	0	0
Part-time	20	20	14	15	6	5	0	0
Total	51	50	35	35	16	15	2	2

Curriculum

		Full-time	Part-time
Typical first-year section size		70	0
Is there typically a "small section" of the first-year class, other than Legal Writing, taught by full-time faculty		Yes	No
If yes, typical size offered last year		23	0
# of classroom course titles beyond 1st year curriculum		67	
# of upper division courses, excluding seminars with an enrollment:	Under 25	32	
	25-49	29	
	50-74	10	
	75-99	3	
	100+	0	
# of seminars		11	
# of seminar positions available		135	
# of seminar positions filled		135	0
# of positions available in simulation courses		358	
# of simulation positions filled		358	0
# of positions available in faculty supervised clinical courses		58	
# of faculty supervised clinical positions filled		58	0
# involved in field placements		13	0
# involved in law journals		31	0
# involved in moot court or trial competitions		48	0
# of credit hours required to graduate		96	

JD Enrollment and Ethnicity

	Men		Women		Full-time		Part-time		1st-year		Total		JD Degs. Awd.
	#	%	#	%	#	%	#	%	#	%	#	%	
African Amer.	6	2.7	6	3.2	12	3.0	0	0.0	8	6.0	12	2.9	1
Amer. Indian	0	0.0	3	1.6	3	0.7	0	0.0	0	0.0	3	0.7	0
Asian Amer.	3	1.3	7	3.8	9	2.2	1	33.3	3	2.2	10	2.5	5
Mex. Amer.	4	1.8	6	3.2	10	2.5	0	0.0	4	3.0	10	2.5	2
Puerto Rican	0	0.0	0	0.0	0	0.0	0	0.0	0	0.0	0	0.0	0
Hispanic	0	0.0	0	0.0	0	0.0	0	0.0	0	0.0	0	0.0	5
Total Minority	13	5.8	22	11.9	34	8.4	1	33.3	15	11.2	35	8.6	13
For. Nation.	4	1.8	0	0.0	4	1.0	0	0.0	0	0.0	4	1.0	2
Caucasian	206	92.4	163	88.1	367	90.6	2	66.7	119	88.8	369	90.4	117
Unknown	0	0.0	0	0.0	0	0.0	0	0.0	0	0.0	0	0.0	0
Total	223	54.7	185	45.3	405	99.3	3	0.7	134	32.8	408		132

Tuition and Fees

	Resident	Nonresident
Full-time	$8,998	$20,612
Part-time	$0	$0

Living Expenses

Estimated living expenses for singles

Living on campus	Living off campus	Living at home
$10,576	$11,068	$6,818

University of Nebraska College of Law

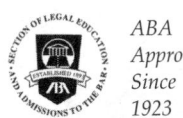

ABA
Approved
Since
1923

GPA and LSAT Scores

	Total	Full-time	Part-time
# of apps	829	828	1
# of admits	346	346	0
# of matrics	131	130	1
75% GPA	3.83	3.83	0.00
25% GPA	3.43	3.43	0.00
75% LSAT	159	159	0
25% LSAT	152	152	0

Grants and Scholarships (from prior year)

	Total		Full-time		Part-time	
	#	%	#	%	#	%
Total # of students	420		420		0	
Total # receiving grants	155	36.9	155	36.9	0	0.0
Less than 1/2 tuition	31	7.4	31	7.4	0	0.0
Half to full tuition	36	8.6	36	8.6	0	0.0
Full tuition	33	7.9	33	7.9	0	0.0
More than full tuition	55	13.1	55	13.1	0	0.0
Median grant amount			$7,246		$0	

Informational and Library Resources

# of volumes and volume equivalents	394,714
# of titles	57,286
# of active serial subscriptions	2,722
Study seating capacity inside the library	372
# of professional librarians	4
Hours per week library is open	109
# of open, wired connections available to students	36
# of networked computers available for use by students	26
# of simultaneous wireless users	256
Require computer?	N

JD Attrition (from prior year)

	Academic	Other	Total	
	#	#	#	%
1st year	7	3	10	7.1%
2nd year	0	6	6	4.3%
3rd year	0	0	0	0.0%
4th year	0	0	0	0.0%

Employment

	Total	Percentage
Employment status known	120	98.4
Employment status unknown	2	1.6
Employed	101	84.2
Pursuing graduate degrees	5	4.2
Unemployed seeking employment	7	5.8
Unemployed not seeking employment	7	5.8

Type of Employment

	Total	Percentage
# employed in law firms	45	44.6
# employed in business and industry	16	15.8
# employed in government	22	21.8
# employed in public interest	7	6.9
# employed as judicial clerks	6	5.9
# employed in academia	5	5.0

Geographic Location

	Total	Percentage
# employed in state	69	68.3
# employed in foreign countries	1	1.0
# of states where employed	19	

Bar Passage Rates

Jurisdiction	Nebraska			Missouri		
Exam	Sum 03	Win 04	Total	Sum 03	Win 04	Total
# from school taking bar for the first time	63	3	66	6	0	6
School's pass rate for all first-time takers	95%	100%	95%	100%		100%
State's pass rate for all first-time takers	84%	55%	82%	83%	87%	84%

University of Nebraska College of Law

PO Box 830902
Lincoln, NE 68583-0902
Phone: 402.472.2161; Fax: 402.472.5185
E-mail: lawadm@unl.edu; Website: law.unl.edu

■ Introduction

Founded in 1888, the University of Nebraska College of Law offers an excellent legal education at a reasonable cost. It is large enough to provide students with a diverse curriculum, yet small enough to ensure that students are not lost in a faceless crowd. The College of Law is a charter member of the AALS and is accredited by the ABA. The University of Nebraska College of Law is located on the East Campus of the University of Nebraska in Lincoln, a city of approximately 225,000 and the state capital.

■ Curriculum

The College of Law's academic year runs from late August to early May. A two-day orientation before the beginning of the fall semester introduces first-year students to the law school. Each incoming student is assigned a faculty advisor who can answer questions about law school, course selections, and career goals. The first-year curriculum is 18 hours per semester and includes civil procedure, contracts, criminal law, legal process, legal writing, property, and torts. Courses in the second and third years are elective, with the exception of required courses in constitutional law, professional responsibility, and a research seminar. The curriculum encompasses a broad range of areas. The curriculum offers particular depth in the areas of litigation, taxation, environmental, employment, and corporate and commercial law. Students who wish to focus on a particular area of the law may develop an individualized program of concentrated study.

The College of Law provides an Academic Resource Program for first-year students to assist them in developing and improving fundamental skills such as note-taking, briefing cases, legal analysis, outlining, and writing examinations. The program provides weekly skills classes as well as a series of lectures and individual academic counseling.

Although completing the requirements for a JD degree normally takes three years, it is possible to graduate in two and one-half years by attending summer school during two summers. The college offers no night classes and only rarely accepts part-time students. Students receiving the JD degree are qualified to practice in any state upon passage of that state's bar examination.

■ Skills and Clinical Education

The College of Law recognizes that becoming a lawyer involves more than learning legal theory. Students need to be able to develop practical skills to effectively represent clients and function as lawyers. The College of Law has offered courses which emphasize "learning by doing" since the early 1970s. The college offers professional skills courses in pretrial litigation, trial advocacy, appellate advocacy, mediation, negotiations, alternative dispute resolution, client interviewing and counseling, business planning, civil clinic, and criminal clinic. These classes allow second- and third-year students to develop lawyering skills in simulated settings or in the handling of real cases for actual clients. In civil clinic, third-year students represent clients in and out of court in a wide range of matters, including bankruptcy, domestic relations, immigration, and landlord-tenant disputes. Students in criminal clinic prosecute misdemeanor cases in Lancaster County.

■ Joint-Degree Programs

The college's interdisciplinary program in Law and Psychology is recognized as one of the finest in the nation. The college also participates in seven other joint-degree programs and will work with students to individually design programs in disciplines not covered by a formal program. In each program, students will earn two degrees with fewer credit-hours and in less time than if the degrees were pursued separately. The formal joint-degree programs include JD/MBA (Business), JD/MPA (Accounting), JD/PhD (Psychology), JD/MA (Political Science), JD/MA or MS (Economics), JD/MCRP (Community and Regional Planning), JD/PhD (Educational Administration), and JD/MA (International Affairs with the University of Denver).

■ Library and Physical Facilities

The newly remodeled and expanded Schmid Law Library boasts a collection of about 395,000 volumes and a full complement of the latest developments in information technology. The "new" library boasts seating for 335 students and has 14 group study rooms, each with full access to power and fast data connections, both wired and wireless, for the best access to the Internet from any place in the library. The five professional librarians and their staff strive to create a service-oriented environment for legal research and scholarship. All these attributes combine to make the Schmid Law Library not only the largest, but the most effective, efficient, and friendliest law library in the region.

■ Student Activities

The *Nebraska Law Review*, published by a student editorial board, publishes leading articles from well-known authorities in their fields, as well as student notes and comments. Other extracurricular academic programs include the National Moot Court Competition, Client Counseling Competition, and National Trial Competition.

Students can become involved in over 20 activities and organizations, including the Student Bar Association, Women's Law Caucus, Black Law Students Association, Equal Justice Foundation, Federalist Society, Multicultural Legal Society, and two national legal fraternities.

■ Career Services

The College of Law operates its own career services office for students seeking full-time employment or summer clerkships. The office provides students with a variety of placement-related services and also organizes on-campus interviews by private law firms, governmental agencies, corporations, and other potential employers. As of December 2003, approximately 94 percent of the members of the class of 2003 were employed or were enrolled in advanced-degree programs.

■ Admission

The College of Law starts reviewing applications in early January, and the application deadline is March 1. Admission decisions are made on a rolling basis. Students are required to have a bachelor's degree from an accredited institution, take the LSAT, and register for the LSDAS. In making its decisions, the Admissions Committee seeks to identify those individuals who have the ability to compete successfully in a rigorous academic environment. The major factors that the committee considers are the applicant's LSAT score and the applicant's undergraduate grade-point average. However, admission decisions are not simply a function of the numbers. The committee also takes into account any upward (or downward) trend in the applicant's academic performance over time, quality of the applicant's undergraduate institution, course of study, personal statement, work experience, graduate study, extracurricular activities, letters of recommendation, and other information supplied by the applicant.

The college takes special care in evaluating applications from members of minority groups that have been underrepresented in the legal profession.

The College of Law will waive the application fee upon demonstration of financial need. To visit a law class, meet with admission personnel, or tour the law college, contact the Admissions Office.

Applicant Profile

University of Nebraska College of Law
This grid includes only applicants who earned 120-180 LSAT scores under standard administrations.

LSAT Score	3.75 +		3.50 - 3.74		3.25 - 3.49		3.00 - 3.24		2.75 - 2.99		2.50 - 2.74		2.25 - 2.49		2.00 - 2.24		Below 2.00		No GPA		Total	
	Apps	Adm	Apps	Adm	Apps	Adm	Apps	Adm	Apps	Adm	Apps	Adm	Apps	Adm	Apps	Adm	Apps	Adm	Apps	Adm	Apps	Adm
175-180	0	0	0	0	0	0	0	0	0	0	0	0	0	0	0	0	0	0	0	0	0	0
170-174	2	2	1	1	0	0	0	0	0	0	0	0	0	0	0	0	0	0	0	0	3	3
165-169	7	7	5	5	2	2	0	0	4	3	0	0	0	0	0	0	0	0	0	0	18	17
160-164	20	20	16	15	10	10	9	6	9	4	5	2	0	0	1	0	1	0	0	0	71	57
155-159	52	52	49	45	36	26	24	11	13	2	10	1	3	1	2	0	0	0	2	0	191	138
150-154	58	45	58	29	70	15	50	6	20	1	10	0	4	0	1	0	0	0	3	0	274	96
145-149	22	6	37	3	21	5	37	0	14	0	15	3	4	0	2	0	2	0	1	0	155	17
140-144	6	0	11	0	13	0	13	1	11	0	6	0	8	0	3	0	2	0	4	0	77	1
135-139	2	0	2	0	7	0	3	1	6	0	0	0	4	0	0	0	0	0	1	0	25	1
130-134	1	0	0	0	1	0	1	0	2	0	0	0	2	0	1	0	0	0	1	0	9	0
125-129	0	0	0	0	0	0	0	0	0	0	1	0	0	0	0	0	0	0	0	0	1	0
120-124	0	0	0	0	0	0	0	0	0	0	0	0	0	0	0	0	0	0	0	0	0	0
Total	170	132	179	98	160	58	137	25	79	10	47	6	25	1	10	0	5	0	12	0	824	330

Apps = Number of Applicants
Adm = Number Admitted
Reflects 99% of the total applicant pool.

Official ABA Data

University of Nevada, Las Vegas, William S. Boyd School of Law

4505 Maryland Parkway, Box 451003
Las Vegas, NV 89154-1003
Phone: 702.895.2440; Fax: 702.895.2414
E-mail: request@law.unlv.edu; Website: www.law.unlv.edu

ABA
Approved
Since
2000

The Basics

Type of school	Public
Term	Semester
Application deadline	3/15
Application fee	$40
Financial aid deadline	2/1
Can first year start other than fall?	No
Student to faculty ratio (fall)	13.2 to 1
Does the university offer:	
housing restricted to law students?	No
graduate housing for which law students are eligible?	No

Faculty and Administrators

	Total		Men		Women		Minorities	
	Fall	Spr	Fall	Spr	Fall	Spr	Fall	Spr
Full-time	26	26	14	14	12	12	7	7
Other Full-time	3	3	2	2	1	1	0	0
Deans, librarians, & others who teach	7	8	2	3	5	5	0	0
Part-time	7	15	7	12	0	3	1	1
Total	43	52	25	31	18	21	8	8

Curriculum

	Full-time	Part-time
Typical first-year section size	55	43
Is there typically a "small section" of the first-year class, other than Legal Writing, taught by full-time faculty	No	No
If yes, typical size offered last year	0	0
# of classroom course titles beyond 1st year curriculum	76	
# of upper division courses, excluding seminars with an enrollment: Under 25	91	
25-49	32	
50-74	4	
75-99	0	
100+	0	
# of seminars	8	
# of seminar positions available	117	
# of seminar positions filled	46	23
# of positions available in simulation courses	96	
# of simulation positions filled	65	11
# of positions available in faculty supervised clinical courses	59	
# of faculty supervised clinical positions filled	47	23
# involved in field placements	81	27
# involved in law journals	38	11
# involved in moot court or trial competitions	22	2
# of credit hours required to graduate	86	

JD Enrollment and Ethnicity

	Men #	Men %	Women #	Women %	Full-time #	Full-time %	Part-time #	Part-time %	1st-year #	1st-year %	Total #	Total %	JD Degs. Awd.
African Amer.	4	1.6	10	4.6	8	2.6	6	3.7	8	5.5	14	3.0	2
Amer. Indian	1	0.4	1	0.5	1	0.3	1	0.6	1	0.7	2	0.4	2
Asian Amer.	18	7.3	31	14.2	33	10.9	16	9.8	19	13.0	49	10.5	5
Mex. Amer.	12	4.8	7	3.2	11	3.6	8	4.9	2	1.4	19	4.1	4
Puerto Rican	0	0.0	0	0.0	0	0.0	0	0.0	0	0.0	0	0.0	1
Hispanic	9	3.6	7	3.2	13	4.3	3	1.8	8	5.5	16	3.4	5
Total Minority	44	17.7	56	25.6	66	21.7	34	20.9	38	26.0	100	21.4	19
For. Nation.	0	0.0	0	0.0	0	0.0	0	0.0	0	0.0	0	0.0	0
Caucasian	184	74.2	144	65.8	210	69.1	118	72.4	99	67.8	328	70.2	99
Unknown	20	8.1	19	8.7	28	9.2	11	6.7	9	6.2	39	8.4	4
Total	248	53.1	219	46.9	304	65.1	163	34.9	146	31.3	467		122

Tuition and Fees

	Resident	Nonresident
Full-time	$7,833	$15,078
Part-time	$5,716	$10,916

Living Expenses

Estimated living expenses for singles

Living on campus	Living off campus	Living at home
$12,630	$12,410	$8,120

University of Nevada, Las Vegas, William S. Boyd School of Law

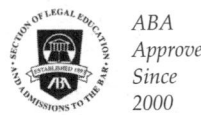

*ABA
Approved
Since
2000*

GPA and LSAT Scores

	Total	Full-time	Part-time
# of apps	2,146	1,852	294
# of admits	265	215	50
# of matrics	150	105	45
75% GPA	3.71	3.73	3.68
25% GPA	3.14	3.28	2.94
75% LSAT	160	160	160
25% LSAT	153	154	152

Grants and Scholarships (from prior year)

	Total		Full-time		Part-time	
	#	%	#	%	#	%
Total # of students	469		300		169	
Total # receiving grants	161	34.3	148	49.3	13	7.7
Less than 1/2 tuition	81	17.3	80	26.7	1	0.6
Half to full tuition	24	5.1	18	6.0	6	3.6
Full tuition	56	11.9	50	16.7	6	3.6
More than full tuition	0	0.0	0	0.0	0	0.0
Median grant amount			$3,623		$2,580	

Informational and Library Resources

# of volumes and volume equivalents	264,670
# of titles	31,179
# of active serial subscriptions	3,912
Study seating capacity inside the library	313
# of professional librarians	6
Hours per week library is open	105
# of open, wired connections available to students	1,004
# of networked computers available for use by students	78
# of simultaneous wireless users	100
Require computer?	N

JD Attrition (from prior year)

	Academic	Other	Total	
	#	#	#	%
1st year	2	17	19	12.1%
2nd year	3	5	8	5.8%
3rd year	0	1	1	0.7%
4th year	1	0	1	2.6%

Employment

	Total	Percentage
Employment status known	132	100.0
Employment status unknown	0	0.0
Employed	104	78.8
Pursuing graduate degrees	1	0.8
Unemployed seeking employment	17	12.9
Unemployed not seeking employment	10	7.6

Type of Employment

	Total	Percentage
# employed in law firms	41	39.4
# employed in business and industry	18	17.3
# employed in government	22	21.2
# employed in public interest	3	2.9
# employed as judicial clerks	18	17.3
# employed in academia	1	1.0

Geographic Location

	Total	Percentage
# employed in state	95	91.3
# employed in foreign countries	0	0.0
# of states where employed	5	

Bar Passage Rates

Jurisdiction	Nevada		
Exam	Sum 03	Win 04	Total
# from school taking bar for the first time	113	15	128
School's pass rate for all first-time takers	59%	40%	57%
State's pass rate for all first-time takers	65%	0%	65%

University of Nevada, Las Vegas, William S. Boyd School of Law

4505 Maryland Parkway, Box 451003
Las Vegas, NV 89154-1003
Phone: 702.895.2440; Fax: 702.895.2414
E-mail: request@law.unlv.edu; Website: www.law.unlv.edu

■ Introduction

The William S. Boyd School of Law is a relatively new, state-supported law school, the first in Nevada's history. Located at the University of Nevada, Las Vegas, in a desert mountain setting, and in one of the fastest grow-ing cities in the country, the law school commenced classes in August 1998. The Boyd School of Law is fully accredited by the American Bar Association and is a member of the Association of American Law Schools.

■ Faculty

The Boyd School of Law has assembled a faculty of more than 40 experienced, accomplished, and well-respected legal educators who view teaching and mentoring students as their first priority and who are eager to serve their community through scholarship and outreach programs.

■ Curriculum

The Boyd School of Law offers, and encourages its students to undertake, a generalist curriculum. Specific course offerings are constantly reviewed and revised as societal needs change. The curriculum generally empha-sizes the responsibilities, skills, and values required of members of the legal profession. This emphasis comes to the fore in Lawyering Process, a three-semester required course that offers students the opportunity to examine the relationship between legal analysis and other legal skills such as research, writing, oral advocacy, and client interviewing and counseling, with significant emphasis on professionalism and ethics.

■ Programs of Study

The Boyd School of Law offers a traditional three-year, full-time JD program, as well as a four-year, part-time JD program during evening hours and a four-year, part-time JD program during day hours. Each part-time program requires the completion of summer course work. The Boyd School of Law and the UNLV College of Business offer a dual Juris Doctor/Master of Business Administra-tion degree program that allows students to pursue the two degrees concurrently.

■ Community Service

The law school requires first-year students to participate in a community service program. Working with Clark County Legal Services and Nevada Legal Services, teams of students prepare and conduct weekly workshops for unrepresented people on basic procedures in family or small claims court and on paternity, custody, guardianship,

and bankruptcy matters. This program, by offering students the chance to educate groups of people in a general way without giving specific legal advice, reinforces students' commitment to community service and acquaints them with the large unmet need for legal services.

■ Hands-on Experience

The Thomas & Mack Legal Clinic houses the school's "law firm" and offers an integrated academic and practice-based educational experience that teaches students to be reflective practitioners and community-oriented professionals. The clinic provides service to communities in need of legal assistance and seeks to improve the quality of, and access to, legal systems that affect those communities. The clinic currently focuses on four specific areas: child welfare, juve-nile justice, capital defense, and immigration. Additionally, the law school has made a significant commitment to provide an extensive externship program. Working closely with the legal community, the externship director has estab-lished a year-round program to provide opportunities for approximately 100 students with the federal and state judiciary, government and public service agencies, and Nevada and US legislatures.

■ Saltman Center for Conflict Resolution

The Saltman Center for Conflict Resolution was estab-lished in 2003 to provide a venue for advanced study of the nature of conflict and the methods through which conflicts may be resolved. The work of the center encom-passes conflicts arising out of regional, national, and international concerns, and involving both the public and private sectors. Recognizing that a sophisticated understanding of conflict necessarily requires insights derived from disciplines other than law, the center places particular emphasis on interdisciplinary approaches to understanding and resolving disputes.

■ Student Activities

The *Nevada Law Journal* presents scholarly research to the national and state legal communities.

The Society of Advocates is the school's appellate and trial forensic program. The society consists of an executive board and team members who participate in interscholastic competitions. Teams compete in mock trial, client counseling, negotiation, mediation, and alternative dispute resolution competitions, as well as traditional appellate advocacy.

Among the student organizations established at the Boyd School of Law are the Student Bar Association, Environmental Law Society, Minority Law Students Association, Criminal Law Society, Gaming Law Student

University of Nevada, Las Vegas, William S. Boyd School of Law

Association, Sports and Entertainment Law Association, Federalist Society, Public Interest Law Association, Sexual and Gender Equality, American Constitution Society, Vegas Immigration Student Association, and Phi Alpha Delta.

■ Career Services

The Department of Career Services offers personalized career counseling, employment workshops, a job opportunity board, on-campus interviewing programs, and a state-of-the-art online job-search program to assist students.

■ Academic Success Program

The objective of the Boyd School of Law Academic Success Program is to provide a comprehensive network of presentations, activities, tutorials, and workshops designed to stimulate learning and to amplify the classroom experience. The program supplements the curriculum with opportunities to enhance learning skills and develop more efficient, effective methods of studying, comprehending, and writing. The Academic Success Program supervises a student-operated mentoring, advising, and tutoring program.

■ Facility

The Boyd School of Law facility, comprising William S. Boyd Hall and the James E. Rogers Center for Administration and Justice, was dedicated in September 2002. Classrooms include the technology necessary for presentations using Power Point, video, and document cameras. The largest classroom and trial courtroom are equipped to facilitate videoconferencing and distance learning. Lounge and study space offer students indoor and outdoor seating areas where they can make productive use of their time between classes.

■ Library

The Wiener-Rogers Law Library holds the most substantial collection of legal materials in the state of Nevada. The library is staffed by excellent, service-oriented librarians who have come from major libraries across the country. Patrons and students have access to a core collection of important materials in printed and micro formats. The library houses two computer labs and provides numerous carrels for individual study, as well as group study rooms. The growing library collection now exceeds 275,000 volumes and microform volume equivalents.

■ Admission

The Boyd School of Law seeks to enroll an accomplished and diverse group of women and men who will enrich the educational program, the community, and the legal profession. The school seeks students who have demonstrated significant accomplishments in their lives by achieving distinguished academic records, by succeeding in important and challenging careers, by providing community service, or by meeting challenges associated with their race, ethnicity, gender, economic status, or disability. Students with diverse backgrounds, attitudes, and interests contribute to the breadth and quality of the classroom and out-of-classroom dialogue that is a critical element of legal education.

Applicant Profile

The Boyd School of Law has elected not to publish an admission profile based on LSAT scores and undergraduate GPA. Those two factors, while certainly important, are not the only factors taken into consideration. The Boyd School of Law uses no form of indexing system in reaching its admissions decisions. Each completed application file is reviewed by the admissions committee.

New England School of Law

154 Stuart Street
Boston, MA 02116
Phone: 617.422.7210; Fax: 617.457.3033
E-mail: admit@admin.nesl.edu; Website: www.nesl.edu

The Basics

Type of school	Private
Term	Semester
Application deadline	3/15
Application fee	$50
Financial aid deadline	4/20
Can first year start other than fall?	No
Student to faculty ratio (fall)	28.0 to 1
Does the university offer:	
housing restricted to law students?	No
graduate housing for which law students are eligible?	No

Faculty and Administrators

	Total		Men		Women		Minorities	
	Fall	Spr	Fall	Spr	Fall	Spr	Fall	Spr
Full-time	29	29	17	18	12	11	3	4
Other Full-time	0	0	0	0	0	0	0	0
Deans, librarians, & others who teach	4	4	4	4	0	0	1	1
Part-time	72	64	41	43	31	21	4	1
Total	105	97	62	65	43	32	8	6

Curriculum

	Full-time	Part-time
Typical first-year section size	145	130
Is there typically a "small section" of the first-year class, other than Legal Writing, taught by full-time faculty	No	No
If yes, typical size offered last year	0	0
# of classroom course titles beyond 1st year curriculum	100	
# of upper division courses, excluding seminars with an enrollment: Under 25	59	
25-49	30	
50-74	19	
75-99	14	
100+	1	
# of seminars	30	
# of seminar positions available	800	
# of seminar positions filled	223	164
# of positions available in simulation courses	713	
# of simulation positions filled	209	365
# of positions available in faculty supervised clinical courses	58	
# of faculty supervised clinical positions filled	31	7
# involved in field placements	197	39
# involved in law journals	75	8
# involved in moot court or trial competitions	7	8
# of credit hours required to graduate	84	

JD Enrollment and Ethnicity

	Men #	Men %	Women #	Women %	Full-time #	Full-time %	Part-time #	Part-time %	1st-year #	1st-year %	Total #	Total %	JD Degs. Awd.
African Amer.	16	3.2	23	3.8	22	3.0	17	4.7	14	3.6	39	3.5	7
Amer. Indian	0	0.0	1	0.2	0	0.0	1	0.3	0	0.0	1	0.1	0
Asian Amer.	28	5.6	35	5.8	47	6.4	16	4.4	26	6.8	63	5.7	14
Mex. Amer.	5	1.0	3	0.5	4	0.5	4	1.1	2	0.5	8	0.7	0
Puerto Rican	3	0.6	6	1.0	7	0.9	2	0.6	3	0.8	9	0.8	5
Hispanic	3	0.6	19	3.2	15	2.0	7	1.9	8	2.1	22	2.0	5
Total Minority	55	11.0	87	14.5	95	12.9	47	12.9	53	13.8	142	12.9	31
For. Nation.	0	0.0	0	0.0	0	0.0	0	0.0	0	0.0	0	0.0	0
Caucasian	399	79.8	454	75.5	576	78.0	277	76.3	256	66.5	853	77.5	229
Unknown	46	9.2	60	10.0	67	9.1	39	10.7	76	19.7	106	9.6	5
Total	500	45.4	601	54.6	738	67.0	363	33.0	385	35.0	1101		265

Tuition and Fees

	Resident	Nonresident
Full-time	$22,475	$0
Part-time	$16,875	$0

Living Expenses

Estimated living expenses for singles

Living on campus	Living off campus	Living at home
N/A	$13,500	$8,730

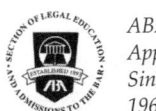

*ABA
Approved
Since
1969*

GPA and LSAT Scores

	Total	Full-time	Part-time
# of apps	3,467	2,922	545
# of admits	1,317	1,074	243
# of matrics	394	256	138
75% GPA	3.42	3.45	3.38
25% GPA	2.84	2.91	2.77
75% LSAT	153	154	152
25% LSAT	149	150	147

Grants and Scholarships (from prior year)

	Total		Full-time		Part-time	
	#	%	#	%	#	%
Total # of students	1,040		693		347	
Total # receiving grants	439	42.2	339	48.9	100	28.8
Less than 1/2 tuition	306	29.4	240	34.6	66	19.0
Half to full tuition	34	3.3	22	3.2	12	3.5
Full tuition	99	9.5	77	11.1	22	6.3
More than full tuition	0	0.0	0	0.0	0	0.0
Median grant amount			$4,000		$4,000	

Informational and Library Resources

# of volumes and volume equivalents	344,380
# of titles	53,814
# of active serial subscriptions	5,065
Study seating capacity inside the library	374
# of professional librarians	8
Hours per week library is open	104
# of open, wired connections available to students	300
# of networked computers available for use by students	320
# of simultaneous wireless users	600
Require computer?	N

JD Attrition (from prior year)

	Academic	Other	Total	
	#	#	#	%
1st year	17	39	56	14.7%
2nd year	2	4	6	1.8%
3rd year	0	0	0	0.0%
4th year	0	0	0	0.0%

Employment

	Total	Percentage
Employment status known	229	93.1
Employment status unknown	17	6.9
Employed	191	83.4
Pursuing graduate degrees	9	3.9
Unemployed seeking employment	27	11.8
Unemployed not seeking employment	2	0.9

Type of Employment

	Total	Percentage
# employed in law firms	92	48.2
# employed in business and industry	32	16.8
# employed in government	39	20.4
# employed in public interest	9	4.7
# employed as judicial clerks	11	5.8
# employed in academia	4	2.1

Geographic Location

	Total	Percentage
# employed in state	120	62.8
# employed in foreign countries	2	1.0
# of states where employed	24	

Bar Passage Rates

Jurisdiction	Massachusetts		
Exam	Sum 03	Win 04	Total
# from school taking bar for the first time	159	19	178
School's pass rate for all first-time takers	70%	74%	70%
State's pass rate for all first-time takers	82%	82%	82%

New England School of Law

154 Stuart Street
Boston, MA 02116
Phone: 617.422.7210; Fax: 617.457.3033
E-mail: admit@admin.nesl.edu; Website: www.nesl.edu

■ Introduction

New England School of Law was founded in 1908 as Portia Law School, the only law school in the nation exclusively for women. Coeducational since 1938, the law school is accredited by the American Bar Association and is a member of the Association of American Law Schools. It is an independent institution, not affiliated with a university, and, as a result, is able to make its own decisions on how to develop and improve its educational program.

■ Location

Situated in the heart of Boston's theater district and a block from the famous Public Garden, New England School of Law is within walking distance of prominent law firms, courthouses, and government agencies. This central location opens extensive possibilities for clinical placements, clerkships, and part-time employment.

Relying on a good public transportation system, residents can take advantage of the city's lively and varied neighborhoods, historic sights, fine cultural institutions, and professional sports teams. With nearly three dozen colleges, universities, and professional schools in the city, Boston has a large population of students and young professionals.

■ Curriculum and Academic Activities

The curriculum at New England School of Law prepares students to practice in any jurisdiction in the United States. In addition to required courses, students can choose from among approximately 150 electives. Courses and cocurricular activities can be combined to focus on areas such as tax, international, business, public interest, criminal, family, and environmental law. New England School of Law also has an extensive clinical program that allows students to combine fieldwork with classroom study in 18 subject areas. About 60 percent of the students take a clinical course while they are in law school.

The law school is a pioneer in incorporating relevant international law into domestic law courses throughout the curriculum. Students in Business Organizations, Contracts, Criminal Law, Family Law, Tax Law, and other classes learn about applicable international law, laws of other nations that impact Americans, and American laws that affect foreign nationals.

The law school has three nationally distributed scholarly journals, the *New England Law Review*, the *New England Journal on Criminal and Civil Confinement*, and the *New England International and Comparative Law Journal*. The *Journal on Criminal and Civil Confinement* is the only publication produced by law students that is devoted solely to prison and incarceration issues.

The required Legal Research and Writing Program includes a moot court component in the first semester of the second year. The law school also sponsors six cocurricular advocacy teams. Competition teams have reached advanced rounds and won brief or oralist awards in recent years. The Phillip C. Jessup International Law Moot Court Team advanced to the international competition in 2001 and received the best brief award.

Three programs provide various types of judicial clerkship opportunities. The school's Academic Skills Program offers optional academic support and supervised skills practice for first-year students.

■ Study Options

Students may enroll in the full-time day division, the part-time day or evening divisions, or the Special Part-time Program, a unique arrangement for parents with primary childrearing responsibilities.

New England School of Law accepts foreign lawyers in an advanced placement JD program or an LLM in Advanced Legal Studies.

■ Academic Centers

New England School of Law is home to the Center for International Law and Policy, which sponsors an annual conference on a current issue in international law, other programs on international law, and the International War Crimes Prosecution Project, through which students provide research and analysis to the prosecutors of the International Criminal Tribunals for the Former Yugoslavia and Rwanda.

The Center for Law and Social Responsibility, also located at the law school, supports a variety of projects through which faculty and students engage in legal work that focuses on social problems. The center includes the following programs: criminal justice, domestic violence, environmental justice, law and science, and public service.

The Center for Business Law, the law school's newest center, builds on the law school's offerings in various areas of business law and serves as a forum for faculty and students to integrate coursework with policy research. Activities focus on the areas of intellectual property law, tax law, and corporate governance and ethics.

■ Study Abroad

Students may study in the law school's summer abroad programs in Galway, Ireland; London; Malta; or Prague or in semester abroad programs in The Netherlands or Denmark. Students may also participate in an exchange program for a semester at the University of Paris X-Nanterre.

■ Faculty

Full-time faculty members are dedicated teachers, accessible to students, and maintain a high level of scholarly publication. Nearly all have practiced in their fields of law. The full-time faculty is supplemented by an outstanding adjunct faculty of practicing attorneys and judges.

■ Technology

Wireless technology throughout the law school allows Internet access from anywhere in the building. Several classrooms and portions of the library are hardwired for Internet access. The Computer and Media Center houses viewing equipment for audiovisual materials and reader/printers for microform materials. It maintains PC labs and provides laptops for check out.

The law school's award-winning website includes a web board that faculty use to post materials and answer student questions, student-run online discussions on class topics, and extensive links to legal research sites.

■ Financial Aid

Financial aid consists of a combination of federal loan programs, private loans, and institutional grants and scholarships. Most grants are need-based; however, the law school awards several academic and merit scholarships. Federal work-study grants are also available.

■ Student Activities

New England School of Law has a Student Bar Association, which oversees more than two dozen student groups. Many of those organizations sponsor speakers, social events, and volunteer activities during the year. Student representatives sit on most faculty committees.

■ Career Services

The Career Services Office provides students with individual counseling, networking information, and programs on job-related issues. The office maintains an extensive resource library of directories of lawyers and legal organizations, books on practice areas, and periodicals. The career services site on the web page features a searchable job-posting database, more than 3,200 career-related links, online recruitment, and an e-mail service that communicates job postings to students. The office also organizes an alumni networking and mentoring program, which is accessible online. As a member of the Massachusetts Law School Consortium, New England School of Law participates in recruitment programs with the state's six other ABA-accredited law schools. The school is also a member of the Northeast Law School Consortium and participates in recruitment programs with eight ABA-accredited law schools in the region. The office also offers virtual recruitment using teleconferencing technology.

Most students take the Massachusetts bar exam, while many take exams in New York, the District of Columbia, Florida, New Hampshire, and New Jersey.

Applicant Profile

New England School of Law
This grid includes only applicants who earned 120-180 LSAT scores under standard administrations.

LSAT Score	GPA 3.75 + Apps	Adm	3.50 - 3.74 Apps	Adm	3.25 - 3.49 Apps	Adm	3.00 - 3.24 Apps	Adm	2.75 - 2.99 Apps	Adm	2.50 - 2.74 Apps	Adm	2.25 - 2.49 Apps	Adm	2.00 - 2.24 Apps	Adm	Below 2.00 Apps	Adm	No GPA Apps	Adm	Total Apps	Adm
175-180	0	0	0	0	0	0	1	1	0	0	0	0	0	0	0	0	0	0	0	0	1	1
170-174	1	1	0	0	1	1	0	0	0	0	1	1	0	0	0	0	0	0	0	0	3	3
165-169	0	0	5	3	5	4	4	4	4	3	2	2	2	1	0	0	1	0	0	0	23	17
160-164	10	9	21	20	26	23	22	21	20	17	9	7	6	2	1	0	1	0	0	0	116	99
155-159	23	22	46	45	61	56	87	81	63	57	39	30	25	6	11	2	4	0	4	1	363	300
150-154	48	43	128	113	197	163	195	156	190	133	105	58	57	8	18	0	2	0	9	4	949	678
145-149	36	18	148	51	194	34	256	30	217	26	146	11	80	3	29	0	5	0	17	5	1128	178
140-144	16	1	62	5	128	5	148	3	124	1	109	3	45	1	19	0	3	0	22	1	676	20
135-139	7	0	13	0	31	0	47	1	36	0	32	0	25	0	14	0	2	0	6	0	213	1
130-134	0	0	2	0	7	0	8	0	11	0	11	0	5	0	4	0	1	0	7	0	56	0
125-129	0	0	0	0	1	0	3	0	3	0	2	0	2	0	1	0	0	0	4	0	16	0
120-124	0	0	0	0	0	0	0	0	0	0	1	0	1	0	0	0	0	0	1	0	3	0
Total	141	94	425	237	651	286	771	297	668	237	457	112	248	21	97	2	19	0	70	11	3547	1297

Apps = Number of Applicants   Adm = Number Admitted   Reflects 99% of the total applicant pool.

The University of New Mexico School of Law

MSC11 6070, 1 University of New Mexico
Albuquerque, NM 87131-0001
Phone: 505.277.2146
E-mail: admissions@law.unm.edu; Website: lawschool.unm.edu

ABA Approved Since 1948

The Basics

Type of school	Public
Term	Semester
Application deadline	2/15
Application fee	$40
Financial aid deadline	2/15
Can first year start other than fall?	No
Student to faculty ratio (fall)	10.6 to 1
Does the university offer:	
housing restricted to law students?	No
graduate housing for which law students are eligible?	No

Faculty and Administrators

	Total Fall	Total Spr	Men Fall	Men Spr	Women Fall	Women Spr	Minorities Fall	Minorities Spr
Full-time	27	25	16	14	11	11	11	11
Other Full-time	4	4	1	1	3	3	0	0
Deans, librarians, & others who teach	13	13	4	4	9	9	4	4
Part-time	11	18	10	11	1	7	2	3
Total	55	60	31	30	24	30	17	18

Curriculum

	Full-time	Part-time
Typical first-year section size	56	0
Is there typically a "small section" of the first-year class, other than Legal Writing, taught by full-time faculty	Yes	No
If yes, typical size offered last year	38	0
# of classroom course titles beyond 1st year curriculum	88	
# of upper division courses, excluding seminars with an enrollement: Under 25	36	
25-49	13	
50-74	4	
75-99	0	
100+	0	
# of seminars	27	
# of seminar positions available	373	
# of seminar positions filled	289	0
# of positions available in simulation courses	193	
# of simulation positions filled	143	0
# of positions available in faculty supervised clinical courses	96	
# of faculty supervised clinical positions filled	83	0
# involved in field placements	35	0
# involved in law journals	104	0
# involved in moot court or trial competitions	20	0
# of credit hours required to graduate	86	

JD Enrollment and Ethnicity

	Men #	Men %	Women #	Women %	Full-time #	Full-time %	Part-time #	Part-time %	1st-year #	1st-year %	Total #	Total %	JD Degs. Awd.
African Amer.	8	5.2	4	2.1	12	3.5	0	0.0	4	3.5	12	3.5	2
Amer. Indian	14	9.2	19	10.1	33	9.6	0	0.0	14	12.2	33	9.6	8
Asian Amer.	1	0.7	5	2.6	6	1.8	0	0.0	4	3.5	6	1.8	1
Mex. Amer.	39	25.5	39	20.6	78	22.8	0	0.0	25	21.7	78	22.8	22
Puerto Rican	0	0.0	0	0.0	0	0.0	0	0.0	0	0.0	0	0.0	0
Hispanic	0	0.0	0	0.0	0	0.0	0	0.0	0	0.0	0	0.0	0
Total Minority	62	40.5	67	35.4	129	37.7	0	0.0	47	40.9	129	37.7	33
For. Nation.	0	0.0	0	0.0	0	0.0	0	0.0	0	0.0	0	0.0	0
Caucasian	80	52.3	105	55.6	185	54.1	0	0.0	58	50.4	185	54.1	51
Unknown	11	7.2	17	9.0	28	8.2	0	0.0	10	8.7	28	8.2	8
Total	153	44.7	189	55.3	342	100.0	0	0.0	115	33.6	342		92

Tuition and Fees

	Resident	Nonresident
Full-time	$7,567	$19,901
Part-time	$0	$0

Living Expenses

Estimated living expenses for singles

Living on campus	Living off campus	Living at home
$10,228	$11,676	$7,128

The University of New Mexico School of Law

*ABA
Approved
Since
1948*

GPA and LSAT Scores

	Total	Full-time	Part-time
# of apps	1,044	1,044	0
# of admits	243	243	0
# of matrics	120	120	0
75% GPA	3.68	3.68	0.00
25% GPA	3.09	3.09	0.00
75% LSAT	159	159	0
25% LSAT	150	150	0

Grants and Scholarships (from prior year)

	Total #	Total %	Full-time #	Full-time %	Part-time #	Part-time %
Total # of students	316		316		0	
Total # receiving grants	68	21.5	68	21.5	0	0.0
Less than 1/2 tuition	11	3.5	11	3.5	0	0.0
Half to full tuition	11	3.5	11	3.5	0	0.0
Full tuition	32	10.1	32	10.1	0	0.0
More than full tuition	14	4.4	14	4.4	0	0.0
Median grant amount			$6,708		$0	

Informational and Library Resources

# of volumes and volume equivalents	417,052
# of titles	104,048
# of active serial subscriptions	3,249
Study seating capacity inside the library	434
# of professional librarians	9
Hours per week library is open	96
# of open, wired connections available to students	309
# of networked computers available for use by students	123
# of simultaneous wireless users	0
Require computer?	N

JD Attrition (from prior year)

	Academic #	Other #	Total #	Total %
1st year	0	0	0	0.0%
2nd year	0	4	4	3.8%
3rd year	1	2	3	3.0%
4th year	0	0	0	0.0%

Employment

	Total	Percentage
Employment status known	103	99.0
Employment status unknown	1	1.0
Employed	95	92.2
Pursuing graduate degrees	2	1.9
Unemployed seeking employment	4	3.9
Unemployed not seeking employment	2	1.9

Type of Employment

# employed in law firms	47	49.5
# employed in business and industry	5	5.3
# employed in government	28	29.5
# employed in public interest	2	2.1
# employed as judicial clerks	10	10.5
# employed in academia	2	2.1

Geographic Location

# employed in state	76	80.0
# employed in foreign countries	2	2.1
# of states where employed		14

Bar Passage Rates

Jurisdiction	New Mexico		
Exam	Sum 03	Win 04	Total
# from school taking bar for the first time	77	14	91
School's pass rate for all first-time takers	87%	93%	88%
State's pass rate for all first-time takers	85%	86%	86%

The University of New Mexico School of Law

MSC11 6070, 1 University of New Mexico
Albuquerque, NM 87131-0001
Phone: 505.277.2146
E-mail: admissions@law.unm.edu; Website: lawschool.unm.edu

■ Introduction

Located in Albuquerque, the School of Law is known for its small classes, easy student-faculty interaction, and special programs in clinical law, natural resources law, and Indian law. The 10:1 student-faculty ratio, one of the best in the country, facilitates a sense of community in the educational experience. It also allows the school to offer more courses with smaller enrollments. The school is a member of the AALS and is approved by the ABA. The University of New Mexico is the state's flagship institution with nearly 31,000 students on its main and branch campuses.

■ Curriculum

The Juris Doctor program is a full-time day curriculum. Students normally complete the required 86 hours of law credit for the JD degree in three academic years (six semesters). First-year students must take a full first-year curriculum, including basic courses in torts, contracts, civil procedure, property, and criminal law. Emphasis is also placed on the skills of advocacy: legal writing, oral argument, litigation, counseling, and negotiation. First-year classes range in size from approximately 13 to 60 students. Second- and third-year courses are elective except for Ethics, Introduction to Constitutional Law, and a clinical program. Typically, one-half of the electives have fewer than 15 students. Every student must complete the advanced writing requirement.

■ Special Programs

Clinical Law. UNM's program in Clinical Law is regarded as one of the finest practical-lawyering programs in the country and includes the Law Practice Clinic, a Criminal Law clinic, a Business Law clinic, the Community Lawyering Clinic, and the Southwest Indian Law Clinic. Students may also participate in the extern placement program and elect assignment to a judge's office, the Public Defender's Office, federal and state administrative offices, and private practitioners. Unlike most other law schools, UNM requires six credit hours of clinical work for graduation. In 1970, the New Mexico Supreme Court adopted a rule permitting students to practice before state courts.

Indian Law. UNM has long been a leader in Indian Law and has developed one of the most comprehensive programs in the country. The school offers students the Southwest Indian Law Clinic, the *Tribal Law Journal*, the Certificate in Indian Law (ILC), scholarly research, guest lectures, seminars, and social activities. An ILC student completes the JD while enrolling in 21 hours of required and elective Indian law courses.

Natural Resources Law. The UNM School of Law is widely known for its strength in the areas of natural resources and environmental law and offers a number of electives in these subjects. Students who want to gain a more comprehensive understanding of resource problems may participate in the Natural Resources Law Certificate Program, which includes work on the *Natural Resources Journal*, an internationally recognized quarterly.

International Law. The school has developed a variety of programs and courses that provide opportunities for students interested in International Law. Students may expand their experience through coursework at the law school and through the study-abroad and exchange programs.

- Guanajuato Summer Law Institute. The School of Law, in conjunction with the Universidad de Guanajuato, Southwestern University, and Texas Tech University, offers six weeks of summer law study in Guanajuato, Mexico. The institute features an introduction to Mexican Law and international law subjects related to Latin America. The institute is ABA-approved.
- North American Exchange Program. Students can participate in a semester exchange with a Canadian or Mexican law school. Students may visit for a semester in the second or third years and receive up to 12 credits.
- Tasmania. Students have the opportunity to study for one semester at the University of Tasmania School of Law and receive up to 12 credits.

■ Dual-Degree Program

Three formal dual JD and master's degree programs are offered: the JD and MA in Public Administration, the JD and MBA, and the JD and MA in Latin American Studies. Students can also earn the JD degree and an MA, MS, or PhD in other academic fields. Students must satisfy the admission and academic requirements of both the School of Law and the Graduate School.

■ Facilities

The School of Law, a state-of-the-art facility, is located on the northern edge of the UNM campus. A two-story atrium connects the Frederick M. Hart Wing to Bratton Hall. The law school includes classroom and seminar rooms, all faculty offices, student organization and publication offices, two computer labs, the Clinical Program, and the law library. Internet access is available to students throughout the building via network connections. The law school is also home to the American Indian Law Center, Inc. Adjacent to the law school is the New Mexico Law Center in which the Institute of Public Law and the Albuquerque branch of the New Mexico Court of Appeals are located.

The University of New Mexico School of Law

Law Library. The UNM Law Library is the largest legal research facility in New Mexico. The library offers a wide variety of electronic products, and its book and microform collection of 417,052 includes special collections in American Indian law, Mexican and Latin American law, land grant law, and natural resources law. The library's 32,443 square feet of space provides 434 seats, pocket lounges and browsing areas, audiovisual carrels, group study rooms, a photocopy facility, and the school's second computer lab for student use.

Career and Student Services. The school's smaller size allows for individualized attention in all aspects of career development and job search methodology. Regular workshops are provided on résumé and cover letter writing, interviewing, and job search strategies. In addition, the law school sponsors on-campus interviews, a career fair, a mock interview program, and presentations on various practice opportunities. Career counseling for students and graduates is provided by two full-time attorney counselors.

■ Student Activities

Extracurricular activities include the *Natural Resources Journal*, the *New Mexico Law Review*, the *Tribal Law Journal*, the *US-Mexico Law Journal*, and several moot court and mock trial competitions. All law students are members of the university's Graduate/Professional Student Association and the Student Bar Association. Students may participate in 30 law-student organizations.

■ Admission and Financial Aid

Applicants must take the LSAT, register for the LSDAS, and have a bachelor's degree from an accredited university or college before registration in the fall. A five-member committee reviews applications. Substantial weight is given to the applicant's personal statement, prior work experience, extracurricular activities, letters of recommendation, and other information supplied by the applicant. Applications from New Mexico residents are given a preference. Students apply for financial aid by filing the FAFSA; no additional loan application is necessary. Types of financial aid include loans, grants, and work-study. The school awards grants to students based on the Access Group's Need Access application.

■ Albuquerque

From golf to mountain climbing, students have access to outdoor New Mexico. In addition, students also have the opportunity to visit museums and art galleries or take in theater or musical events. The combination of multiple cultures reflected in food, music, art, architecture, and local customs heightens Albuquerque's appeal.

Applicant Profile

The University of New Mexico School of Law
This grid includes only applicants who earned 120-180 LSAT scores under standard administrations.

LSAT Score	3.75 +		3.50 - 3.74		3.25 - 3.49		3.00 - 3.24		2.75 - 2.99		2.50 - 2.74		2.25 - 2.49		2.00 - 2.24		Below 2.00		No GPA		Total	
	Apps	Adm	Apps	Adm	Apps	Adm	Apps	Adm	Apps	Adm	Apps	Adm	Apps	Adm	Apps	Adm	Apps	Adm	Apps	Adm	Apps	Adm
175-180	0	0	0	0	0	0	0	0	0	0	0	0	0	0	0	0	0	0	0	0	0	0
170-174	0	0	1	1	3	3	1	1	1	1	1	1	0	0	0	0	0	0	0	0	7	7
165-169	4	3	3	3	6	5	2	2	4	2	1	1	3	1	1	0	0	0	0	0	24	17
160-164	18	15	13	11	26	16	15	7	10	3	8	1	2	1	3	0	0	0	1	0	96	54
155-159	34	18	42	14	41	17	42	14	31	5	20	3	8	0	2	1	2	0	4	2	226	74
150-154	30	14	53	14	50	5	83	8	40	6	22	0	8	1	4	0	2	0	0	0	292	48
145-149	14	1	33	8	44	6	53	4	26	3	27	0	13	3	1	0	1	0	1	0	213	25
140-144	4	0	7	1	22	2	24	7	22	2	13	2	11	2	1	0	1	0	3	0	108	16
135-139	3	0	4	0	5	1	5	0	8	0	10	0	8	0	5	0	0	0	3	0	51	1
130-134	0	0	1	0	1	0	1	0	3	0	2	0	2	0	3	0	1	0	2	0	16	0
125-129	0	0	0	0	0	0	1	0	0	0	0	0	1	0	1	0	0	0	2	0	5	0
120-124	0	0	0	0	0	0	0	0	0	0	0	0	0	0	0	0	0	0	1	0	1	0
Total	107	51	157	52	198	55	227	43	145	22	104	8	56	8	21	1	7	0	17	2	1039	242

Apps = Number of Applicants
Adm = Number Admitted
Reflects 99% of the total applicant pool.

New York Law School

57 Worth Street
New York, NY 10013
Phone: 212.431.2888; Fax: 212.966.1522
E-mail: admissions@nyls.edu; Website: www.nyls.edu

ABA Approved Since 1954

The Basics

Type of school	Private
Term	Semester
Application deadline	4/1
Application fee	$60
Financial aid deadline	4/1
Can first year start other than fall?	No
Student to faculty ratio (fall)	22.7 to 1
Does the university offer:	
housing restricted to law students?	No
graduate housing for which law students are eligible?	Yes

Faculty and Administrators

	Total		Men		Women		Minorities	
	Fall	Spr	Fall	Spr	Fall	Spr	Fall	Spr
Full-time	52	51	31	32	21	19	7	6
Other Full-time	4	4	2	2	2	2	1	1
Deans, librarians, & others who teach	12	12	7	7	5	5	0	0
Part-time	92	80	56	50	35	30	3	3
Total	160	147	96	91	63	56	11	10

Curriculum

	Full-time	Part-time
Typical first-year section size	123	123
Is there typically a "small section" of the first-year class, other than Legal Writing, taught by full-time faculty	Yes	Yes
If yes, typical size offered last year	41	41
# of classroom course titles beyond 1st year curriculum	170	
# of upper division courses, excluding seminars with an enrollment: Under 25	90	
25-49	57	
50-74	22	
75-99	16	
100+	16	
# of seminars	69	
# of seminar positions available	1,140	
# of seminar positions filled	687	220
# of positions available in simulation courses	138	
# of simulation positions filled	106	27
# of positions available in faculty supervised clinical courses	56	
# of faculty supervised clinical positions filled	56	0
# involved in field placements	157	10
# involved in law journals	91	16
# involved in moot court or trial competitions	46	1
# of credit hours required to graduate	86	

JD Enrollment and Ethnicity

	Men #	Men %	Women #	Women %	Full-time #	Full-time %	Part-time #	Part-time %	1st-year #	1st-year %	Total #	Total %	JD Degs. Awd.
African Amer.	25	3.4	69	8.5	48	4.1	46	12.7	29	5.8	94	6.1	29
Amer. Indian	1	0.1	4	0.5	5	0.4	0	0.0	1	0.2	5	0.3	3
Asian Amer.	42	5.7	70	8.7	82	6.9	30	8.3	34	6.9	112	7.3	28
Mex. Amer.	2	0.3	4	0.5	6	0.5	0	0.0	2	0.4	6	0.4	2
Puerto Rican	8	1.1	5	0.6	7	0.6	6	1.7	3	0.6	13	0.8	7
Hispanic	22	3.0	31	3.8	36	3.1	17	4.7	20	4.0	53	3.4	21
Total Minority	100	13.6	183	22.6	184	15.6	99	27.3	89	17.9	283	18.4	90
For. Nation.	7	1.0	11	1.4	18	1.5	0	0.0	9	1.8	18	1.2	1
Caucasian	598	81.6	574	71.0	926	78.5	246	68.0	370	74.6	1172	76.0	301
Unknown	28	3.8	41	5.1	52	4.4	17	4.7	28	5.6	69	4.5	15
Total	733	47.5	809	52.5	1180	76.5	362	23.5	496	32.2	1542		407

Tuition and Fees

	Resident	Nonresident
Full-time	$36,480	$36,480
Part-time	$28,050	$28,050

Living Expenses

Estimated living expenses for singles

Living on campus	Living off campus	Living at home
$18,535	$18,535	$8,330

New York Law School

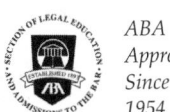

*ABA
Approved
Since
1954*

GPA and LSAT Scores

	Total	Full-time	Part-time
# of apps	6,349	5,271	1,078
# of admits	2,057	1,752	305
# of matrics	496	362	134
75% GPA	3.55	3.54	3.46
25% GPA	3.10	3.06	2.90
75% LSAT	157	157	155
25% LSAT	154	154	151

Grants and Scholarships (from prior year)

	Total		Full-time		Part-time	
	#	%	#	%	#	%
Total # of students	1,551		1,201		350	
Total # receiving grants	824	53.1	701	58.4	123	35.1
Less than 1/2 tuition	820	52.9	698	58.1	122	34.9
Half to full tuition	4	0.3	3	0.2	1	0.3
Full tuition	0	0.0	0	0.0	0	0.0
More than full tuition	0	0.0	0	0.0	0	0.0
Median grant amount			$6,500		$3,750	

Informational and Library Resources

# of volumes and volume equivalents	510,041
# of titles	251,899
# of active serial subscriptions	5,479
Study seating capacity inside the library	616
# of professional librarians	15
Hours per week library is open	98
# of open, wired connections available to students	360
# of networked computers available for use by students	118
# of simultaneous wireless users	1,024
Require computer?	N

JD Attrition (from prior year)

	Academic	Other	Total	
	#	#	#	%
1st year	32	43	75	13.7%
2nd year	0	10	10	1.8%
3rd year	1	0	1	0.3%
4th year	0	0	0	0.0%

Employment

	Total	Percentage
Employment status known	351	93.1
Employment status unknown	26	6.9
Employed	323	92.0
Pursuing graduate degrees	3	0.9
Unemployed seeking employment	17	4.8
Unemployed not seeking employment	8	2.3

Type of Employment

	Total	Percentage
# employed in law firms	162	50.2
# employed in business and industry	43	13.3
# employed in government	36	11.1
# employed in public interest	11	3.4
# employed as judicial clerks	21	6.5
# employed in academia	3	0.9

Geographic Location

	Total	Percentage
# employed in state	222	68.7
# employed in foreign countries	1	0.3
# of states where employed	14	

Bar Passage Rates

Jurisdiction	New York		
Exam	Sum 03	Win 04	Total
# from school taking bar for the first time	310	36	346
School's pass rate for all first-time takers	71%	67%	71%
State's pass rate for all first-time takers	78%	58%	75%

New York Law School

57 Worth Street
New York, NY 10013
Phone: 212.431.2888; Fax: 212.966.1522
E-mail: admissions@nyls.edu; Website: www.nyls.edu

■ Introduction

New York Law School has developed a unique approach to legal education that it calls *The Right Program for Each Student*. At its core is an acknowledgment that different practice settings require different levels of training. For example, students working in larger organizations with extensive in-house training programs have less need for hands-on training than those who will open a solo practice. Those in larger organizations may need training in a specialized area, while those in general practice may need more breadth and less specialized expertise. The following components of *The Right Program for Each Student* are described on our website: Harlan Scholars Program, Individual Program, Comprehensive Curriculum, and the Professional Development Project.

Founded in 1891, New York Law School is one of the oldest independent law schools in the country. The school is fully accredited by the American Bar Association and is a member of the Association of American Law Schools.

■ Location/Physical Facilities/Library

New York Law School is located in Manhattan's historic district, TriBeCa, in Lower Manhattan. It is an extraordinary setting for the study of law and one of the city's most colorful and dynamic neighborhoods. Lower Manhattan is the site of New York's largest concentration of government agencies, courts, law firms, banks, corporate headquarters, and securities exchanges. Federal Courts, New York State Civil and Criminal Courts, Family Court, and the Court of International Trade are within a four-block radius of the Law School. The Law School's four connected buildings are located on a single block in the heart of TriBeCa, with easy access to major public transportation systems.

The Mendik Law Library, with its staff of 15 professional law librarians, includes nearly 500,000 volumes and a variety of computer-assisted research services. Its collection features concentrations in constitutional law, communications, labor law, and international and comparative law. The library also is a partial depository of state and federal documents.

■ Student Life

We are committed to giving students a first-rate law school experience—in and out of the classroom. In return, we demand of them the seriousness of purpose necessary to become ethical professionals—the kind of lawyers sought by clients, law firms, government agencies, advocacy groups, and corporations.

New York Law School has a long-standing and continuing interest in enrolling students from varied backgrounds, including older students, minority students, women, career-changers, and public servants. Students range in age from 21 to 65, with the average age 26.

■ Faculty

The Law School's distinguished full-time faculty is composed of productive scholars who are dedicated educators and who share a strong commitment to the school's vision and philosophy embodied in its core values: embracing innovation, fostering integrity and professionalism, and advancing justice for a diverse society. A national survey of law faculty scholarship includes them among the 50 most prolific law faculties in the country and notes the significant number of their books published by university presses. Leading jurists and attorneys who work in nearby offices are members of the adjunct faculty.

■ Curriculum and Special Programs

The required curriculum, comprising the entire first year and part of the second year, provides a foundation in legal reasoning and in areas of law that are considered indispensable building blocks of a legal education. In the second year and thereafter, students may design their programs with elective courses chosen from an extraordinarily rich array.

Elements such as legal analysis and legal writing, counseling, interviewing, negotiating, advocacy, planning, and strategizing form the core subject areas of the school's Lawyering Skills Program. The Civil and Human Rights Clinic offers students the opportunity to represent real clients.

Externship and judicial internship programs permit students to do actual lawyering work in law offices.

■ Admission

In the admission process, a number of factors are taken into account, including the applicant's academic record and LSAT scores. The admission committee also looks for those applicants who have demonstrated leadership ability, motivation, and a sense of service and responsibility to society. Excellence in a particular field of study, progression of grades, strength of undergraduate curriculum, work and community service experience, graduate study in other disciplines, and extracurricular activities all are considered as well. Writing ability receives particular attention and the admission committee strongly urges applicants to submit the optional writing sample.

The school seeks to enroll students who, through their diversity of backgrounds, experiences, perspectives, and ambitions, promise to enrich the law school community and, ultimately, the larger society.

Under a special admission option, the Wallace Stevens Scholars Program, a small group of professionals with postgraduate degrees and significant work experience will be admitted without having taken the LSAT, but who will be required to take the LSAT after admission to the Law School.

■ Academic Centers

The Institute for Information Law and Policy is the home for the study of technology, intellectual property, and information law. It includes our Media Law Center.

The Center for New York City Law focuses on governmental and legal processes in the urban setting.

The Center for International Law focuses on legal issues relating to international trade and finance.

The Justice Action Center seeks to develop students' expertise in civil rights and civil liberties law and international human rights.

The Center for Professional Values serves as a vehicle through which to examine the role of the legal profession and alternative approaches to the practice of law.

■ Moot Court/Law Journals/Student Organizations

New York Law School students exhibit well-honed courtroom skills, in recent years winning outright three national moot court competitions and earning awards in many others. The school's annual Robert F. Wagner Sr. Labor and Employment Law Competition is one of the nation's largest student-run moot court competitions.

The Law School currently has three scholarly publications, edited and staffed by students, that are an integral part of the Law School's program: *Law Review, Journal of International and Comparative Law,* and *Journal of Human Rights.*

Students have established some 32 interest organizations as well.

■ Expenses and Financial Aid

New York Law School has established a program of financial aid to assist students in meeting the costs of a legal education through grants, scholarships, work-study awards, and loans. Scholarships are awarded on the basis of academic merit and financial need.

■ Office of Professional Development

The Office of Professional Development brings together three key student services: Student Life, Career Services, and Public Interest and Community Service. This innovative structure allows us to offer students personal attention from their first day of study to help them pursue their professional goals. The Career Services Office offers a wide array of services, including individual career counseling, on-campus interview programs, career panels and workshops, alumni network and mentoring programs, online employer databases, and information on summer, full-time, and part-time positions and alternative career opportunities.

Applicant Profile

New York Law School
This grid includes only applicants who earned 120-180 LSAT scores under standard administrations.

LSAT Score	3.50 +		3.25 - 3.49		3.00 - 3.24		2.75 - 2.99		2.50 - 2.74		2.00 - 2.49		Below 2.00		No GPA		Total	
	Apps	Adm	Apps	Adm	Apps	Adm	Apps	Adm	Apps	Adm	Apps	Adm	Apps	Adm	Apps	Adm	Apps	Adm
165-180	31	28	14	13	18	17	8	8	9	7	11	7	0	0	3	3	94	83
155-164	372	360	344	329	337	316	199	169	127	74	102	26	4	1	25	20	1510	1295
145-154	691	273	692	153	778	130	605	69	367	20	245	11	11	1	51	13	3440	670
Below 145	127	1	183	0	249	2	239	1	211	0	173	0	16	0	48	1	1246	5
Total	1221	662	1233	495	1382	465	1051	247	714	101	531	44	31	2	127	37	6290	2053

Apps = Number of Applicants
Adm = Number Admitted
Reflects 98% of the total applicant pool.

New York University School of Law

40 Washington Square South
New York, NY 10012
Phone: 212.998.6060; Fax: 212.995.4527
E-mail: law.moreinfo@nyu.edu; Website: www.law.nyu.edu

ABA
Approved
Since
1930

The Basics

Type of school	Private
Term	Semester
Application deadline	2/1
Application fee	$75
Financial aid deadline	4/15
Can first year start other than fall?	No
Student to faculty ratio (fall)	11.2 to 1
Does the university offer:	
housing restricted to law students?	Yes
graduate housing for which law students are eligible?	No

Faculty and Administrators

	Total		Men		Women		Minorities	
	Fall	Spr	Fall	Spr	Fall	Spr	Fall	Spr
Full-time	101	102	71	70	30	32	12	10
Other Full-time	23	23	13	13	10	10	5	5
Deans, librarians, & others who teach	7	7	3	3	4	4	1	1
Part-time	56	74	42	50	14	24	8	7
Total	187	206	129	136	58	70	26	23

Curriculum

	Full-time	Part-time
Typical first-year section size	107	0
Is there typically a "small section" of the first-year class, other than Legal Writing, taught by full-time faculty	Yes	No
If yes, typical size offered last year	53	0
# of classroom course titles beyond 1st year curriculum	242	

# of upper division courses, excluding seminars with an enrollment:		
	Under 25	77
	25-49	53
	50-74	30
	75-99	22
	100+	20

# of seminars	126	
# of seminar positions available	2,396	
# of seminar positions filled	2,002	0
# of positions available in simulation courses	380	
# of simulation positions filled	348	0
# of positions available in faculty supervised clinical courses	328	
# of faculty supervised clinical positions filled	277	0
# involved in field placements	0	0
# involved in law journals	492	0
# involved in moot court or trial competitions	164	0
# of credit hours required to graduate	82	

JD Enrollment and Ethnicity

	Men		Women		Full-time		Part-time		1st-year		Total		JD Degs. Awd.
	#	%	#	%	#	%	#	%	#	%	#	%	
African Amer.	45	6.2	74	11.6	119	8.8	0	0.0	49	11.3	119	8.8	32
Amer. Indian	0	0.0	0	0.0	0	0.0	0	0.0	0	0.0	0	0.0	0
Asian Amer.	62	8.6	71	11.2	133	9.8	0	0.0	49	11.3	133	9.8	44
Mex. Amer.	7	1.0	2	0.3	9	0.7	0	0.0	2	0.5	9	0.7	0
Puerto Rican	1	0.1	8	1.3	9	0.7	0	0.0	2	0.5	9	0.7	4
Hispanic	34	4.7	29	4.6	63	4.6	0	0.0	28	6.4	63	4.6	14
Total Minority	149	20.6	184	28.9	333	24.5	0	0.0	130	29.9	333	24.5	94
For. Nation.	22	3.0	20	3.1	42	3.1	0	0.0	18	4.1	42	3.1	5
Caucasian	311	43.0	238	37.4	549	40.4	0	0.0	182	41.8	549	40.4	150
Unknown	242	33.4	194	30.5	436	32.1	0	0.0	105	24.1	436	32.1	190
Total	724	53.2	636	46.8	1360	100.0	0	0.0	435	32.0	1360		439

Tuition and Fees

	Resident	Nonresident
Full-time	$36,768	$36,768
Part-time	$0	$0

Living Expenses

Estimated living expenses for singles

Living on campus	Living off campus	Living at home
$20,299	$20,299	$20,299

New York University School of Law

*ABA
Approved
Since
1930*

GPA and LSAT Scores

	Total	Full-time	Part-time
# of apps	8,220	8,220	0
# of admits	1,628	1,628	0
# of matrics	441	441	0
75% GPA	3.85	3.85	0.00
25% GPA	3.57	3.57	0.00
75% LSAT	172	172	0
25% LSAT	167	167	0

Grants and Scholarships (from prior year)

	Total #	Total %	Full-time #	Full-time %	Part-time #	Part-time %
Total # of students	1,346		1,346		0	
Total # receiving grants	410	30.5	410	30.5	0	0.0
Less than 1/2 tuition	234	17.4	234	17.4	0	0.0
Half to full tuition	75	5.6	75	5.6	0	0.0
Full tuition	101	7.5	101	7.5	0	0.0
More than full tuition	0	0.0	0	0.0	0	0.0
Median grant amount		$15,150			$0	

Informational and Library Resources

# of volumes and volume equivalents	1,064,532
# of titles	291,194
# of active serial subscriptions	7,150
Study seating capacity inside the library	849
# of professional librarians	11
Hours per week library is open	108
# of open, wired connections available to students	1,785
# of networked computers available for use by students	260
# of simultaneous wireless users	1,200
Require computer?	Y

JD Attrition (from prior year)

	Academic #	Other #	Total #	Total %
1st year	0	5	5	1.2%
2nd year	0	5	5	1.1%
3rd year	0	3	3	0.6%
4th year	0	0	0	0.0%

Employment

	Total	Percentage
Employment status known	450	100.0
Employment status unknown	0	0.0
Employed	437	97.1
Pursuing graduate degrees	3	0.7
Unemployed seeking employment	3	0.7
Unemployed not seeking employment	7	1.6

Type of Employment

# employed in law firms	306	70.0
# employed in business and industry	11	2.5
# employed in government	12	2.7
# employed in public interest	43	9.8
# employed as judicial clerks	63	14.4
# employed in academia	2	0.5

Geographic Location

# employed in state	290	66.4
# employed in foreign countries	11	2.5
# of states where employed		30

Bar Passage Rates

Jurisdiction	New York		
Exam	Sum 03	Win 04	Total
# from school taking bar for the first time	333	13	346
School's pass rate for all first-time takers	97%	100%	97%
State's pass rate for all first-time takers	78%	58%	75%

New York University School of Law

40 Washington Square South
New York, NY 10012
Phone: 212.998.6060; Fax: 212.995.4527
E-mail: law.moreinfo@nyu.edu; Website: www.law.nyu.edu

■ Introduction

Founded in 1835, New York University School of Law has a record of academic excellence and national scholarly influence extending back into the nineteenth century. More than 100 years ago, it became one of the first law schools to routinely admit women and those from groups discriminated against by many other institutions.

NYU School of Law has been a pioneer in such widely diverse programs as clinical education, law and business, public service, interdisciplinary colloquia, and global studies.

These traditions remain vibrant today as the School of Law, located on the university's campus in Greenwich Village, continues to use its position in New York City to create a twenty-first century legal education in global justice, grounded in solid sociological and jurisprudential training and reflected in sensitive professional service to the world's peoples.

■ Library and Physical Facilities

One of the largest academic law libraries in the world, NYU School of Law's collection boasts widely recognized strengths in tax, legal history, intellectual property, constitutional law, and the law of democratic institutions. The extensive public law collection is complemented by primary law materials for over 20 non-US jurisdictions. The library's award-winning home page is a gateway to specialized legal research guides, e-journals, annotated foreign and international law sites, and commercial databases.

In 2004 the School of Law opened Furman Hall, its first new academic building in 50 years. Furman Hall is adjacent to newly renovated Vanderbilt Hall and connects underground via the law library. The law school also owns two apartment buildings which provide housing for more than 800 law students, many with spouses, partners, and children.

■ Curriculum

NYU School of Law's curriculum is distinguished by its strength in traditional areas of legal study, interdisciplinary study, and clinical education, and has long been committed to educating lawyers who will use their degrees to serve the public. Students enjoy the intellectual and pedagogical diversity of the law school by mixing traditional courses with colloquia, global courses, clinics, independent research, journal work, study abroad, fellowships, and more.

The JD program is enriched by the graduate program, which offers advanced degrees in corporation law, general studies, international legal studies, international taxation, labor and employment law, public service law, taxation, and trade regulation.

■ Institutes and Centers

The curriculum is complemented by 17 institutes and centers which represent the law school's extraordinary commitment of resources and energy to the collegial study of law at the most advanced level. These include the Brennan Center for Justice, the Hauser Global Law School Program, the Institute for International Law and Justice, the Center for Environmental and Land Use Law, and the Center for Law and Business.

■ Admission

The admission process is highly selective and seeks to enroll men and women of exceptional ability. The Committee on Admissions makes decisions after considering all the information in an application. It reviews the undergraduate transcript closely, with attention to factors such as trends in the applicant's grades, class rank, the ratio of pass/fail to graded courses, the diversity and depth of coursework, and the length of time since graduation. Factors other than undergraduate grades and LSAT scores may be particularly significant for applicants who have experienced educational or socioeconomic disadvantage. In all cases, however, other aspects of the application significantly influence the decision. The committee evaluates work experience and extracurricular and community activities for evidence of advancement, leadership, and capacity for assuming responsibility. A recommendation letter is particularly valuable when the writer provides substantive information about the applicant's abilities, activities, and personal qualities. The personal statement provides an opportunity for the applicant to supplement the information supplied in the application.

The committee seeks to enroll an entering class of students with diverse experience, backgrounds, and points of view. Applicants are encouraged to provide information to help the committee reach thoughtful, informed decisions on their applications.

■ Student Activities

Student-edited publications are *New York University Law Review, Annual Survey of American Law, Environmental Law Journal, Journal of International Law and Politics, Journal of Legislation and Public Policy, Review of Law and Social Change,* and *Tax Law Review. The Commentator* is the law school newspaper. There are more than 45 student organizations.

■ Financial Aid

NYU School of Law will award a number of Root-Tilden-Kern Scholarships to entering students chosen for their intellectual potential, capacity for, and demonstrated commitment to, public service through law. A limited number of awards will also be made on the basis of outstanding intellectual potential or substantial records indicating that the student will enrich the educational experience at the law school. The An-Bryce Scholarship will be awarded to a small number of outstanding students who are the first in their immediate family to pursue a graduate degree. The Furman Academic Scholarship will be awarded to a small number of students who show promise in becoming legal academics. Students may also apply for scholarships in the areas of business law, criminal law, environmental law, intellectual property, and law and economics. Federal and private loans provide the majority of funding. Graduates who pursue careers in public service or other low-paying sectors of the legal profession may be eligible for postgraduation benefits through the School of Law's Loan Repayment Assistance Program.

■ Career Services

NYU School of Law has an extensive career services program. Career planning for first-year students includes personal career counseling, workshops on all aspects of the job search, specialty panels featuring speakers from all areas of practice, and a videotape mock interview program. In 2004, more than 540 private law firms, public interest organizations, government agencies, corporations, and public accounting firms visited the law school to interview students. Sixty-eight percent of these employers were from outside New York.

The focal point of the law school's public service activities is the Public Interest Law Center, which provides students interested in public service with comprehensive support, including advice on courses and career opportunities. The Public Interest Summer Scholarship Program guarantees funding to all first- and second-year students who want to work in public interest positions. The Public Interest Law Center, with area law schools, also annually sponsors a public interest legal career symposium.

Applicant Profile

NYU School of Law does not provide a profile chart because while an applicant's undergraduate record and LSAT are important, they are not the sole determinants for admission to the law school. No index or cutoff is used in reviewing applications. There is no combination of grades or scores, therefore, that assure admission or denial.

An applicant's transcripts are analyzed for breadth and depth of coursework, trend in grades, and rank; the competitiveness of the school and major are taken into consideration, as are special honors, awards, and activities. Other aspects of the application significantly influence the decision, such as letters of recommendation, activities, and work experience.

In making its decision, the committee aims to enroll an entering class of students with the strongest combination of qualifications and the greatest potential to contribute to NYU School of Law and to the legal profession.

University of North Carolina School of Law

Campus Box 3380, 5026 Van Hecke-Wettach Hall
Chapel Hill, NC 27599-3380
Phone: 919.962.5109; Fax: 919.843.7939
E-mail: law_admissions@unc.edu; Website: www.law.unc.edu

 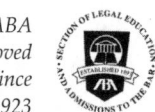

ABA Approved Since 1923

The Basics

Type of school	Public
Term	Semester
Application deadline	2/1
Application fee	$65
Financial aid deadline	3/1
Can first year start other than fall?	No
Student to faculty ratio (fall)	16.4 to 1
Does the university offer:	
housing restricted to law students?	No
graduate housing for which law students are eligible?	Yes

Faculty and Administrators

	Total		Men		Women		Minorities	
	Fall	Spr	Fall	Spr	Fall	Spr	Fall	Spr
Full-time	36	36	25	25	11	11	6	6
Other Full-time	1	1	1	0	0	1	0	0
Deans, librarians, & others who teach	15	14	5	5	10	9	0	0
Part-time	28	48	22	32	6	16	5	9
Total	**80**	**99**	**53**	**62**	**27**	**37**	**11**	**15**

Curriculum

	Full-time	Part-time
Typical first-year section size	76	0
Is there typically a "small section" of the first-year class, other than Legal Writing, taught by full-time faculty	Yes	No
If yes, typical size offered last year	28	0
# of classroom course titles beyond 1st year curriculum	113	
# of upper division courses, excluding seminars with an enrollment: Under 25	51	
25-49	29	
50-74	12	
75-99	2	
100+	5	
# of seminars	34	
# of seminar positions available	510	
# of seminar positions filled	485	0
# of positions available in simulation courses	978	
# of simulation positions filled	794	0
# of positions available in faculty supervised clinical courses	58	
# of faculty supervised clinical positions filled	37	0
# involved in field placements	100	0
# involved in law journals	174	0
# involved in moot court or trial competitions	49	0
# of credit hours required to graduate	86	

JD Enrollment and Ethnicity

	Men		Women		Full-time		Part-time		1st-year		Total		JD Degs. Awd.
	#	%	#	%	#	%	#	%	#	%	#	%	
African Amer.	36	10.4	57	15.7	93	13.1	0	0.0	22	9.3	93	13.1	24
Amer. Indian	7	2.0	5	1.4	12	1.7	0	0.0	6	2.5	12	1.7	4
Asian Amer.	18	5.2	21	5.8	39	5.5	0	0.0	12	5.1	39	5.5	13
Mex. Amer.	0	0.0	0	0.0	0	0.0	0	0.0	0	0.0	0	0.0	0
Puerto Rican	0	0.0	0	0.0	0	0.0	0	0.0	0	0.0	0	0.0	0
Hispanic	17	4.9	6	1.7	23	3.2	0	0.0	9	3.8	23	3.2	6
Total Minority	78	22.5	89	24.5	167	23.5	0	0.0	49	20.7	167	23.5	47
For. Nation.	0	0.0	0	0.0	0	0.0	0	0.0	0	0.0	0	0.0	0
Caucasian	264	76.1	268	73.8	532	74.9	0	0.0	181	76.4	532	74.9	182
Unknown	5	1.4	6	1.7	11	1.5	0	0.0	7	3.0	11	1.5	0
Total	347	48.9	363	51.1	710	100.0	0	0.0	237	33.4	710		229

Tuition and Fees

	Resident	Nonresident
Full-time	$11,118	$23,036
Part-time	$0	$0

Living Expenses

Estimated living expenses for singles

Living on campus	Living off campus	Living at home
$15,438	$15,438	$6,400

University of North Carolina School of Law

*ABA
Approved
Since
1923*

GPA and LSAT Scores

	Total	Full-time	Part-time
# of apps	3,835	3,835	0
# of admits	613	613	0
# of matrics	239	239	0
75% GPA	3.79	3.79	0.00
25% GPA	3.40	3.40	0.00
75% LSAT	164	164	0
25% LSAT	157	157	0

Grants and Scholarships (from prior year)

	Total #	Total %	Full-time #	Full-time %	Part-time #	Part-time %
Total # of students	707		707		0	
Total # receiving grants	450	63.6	450	63.6	0	0.0
Less than 1/2 tuition	394	55.7	394	55.7	0	0.0
Half to full tuition	42	5.9	42	5.9	0	0.0
Full tuition	0	0.0	0	0.0	0	0.0
More than full tuition	14	2.0	14	2.0	0	0.0
Median grant amount			$2,900		$0	

Informational and Library Resources

# of volumes and volume equivalents	509,552
# of titles	102,891
# of active serial subscriptions	6,301
Study seating capacity inside the library	481
# of professional librarians	12
Hours per week library is open	109
# of open, wired connections available to students	597
# of networked computers available for use by students	118
# of simultaneous wireless users	220
Require computer?	N

JD Attrition (from prior year)

	Academic #	Other #	Total #	Total %
1st year	0	10	10	4.2%
2nd year	0	3	3	1.2%
3rd year	0	0	0	0.0%
4th year	0	0	0	0.0%

Employment

	Total	Percentage
Employment status known	314	99.4
Employment status unknown	2	0.6
Employed	286	91.1
Pursuing graduate degrees	11	3.5
Unemployed seeking employment	8	2.5
Unemployed not seeking employment	9	2.9

Type of Employment

	Total	Percentage
# employed in law firms	175	61.2
# employed in business and industry	20	7.0
# employed in government	30	10.5
# employed in public interest	13	4.5
# employed as judicial clerks	45	15.7
# employed in academia	3	1.0

Geographic Location

	Total	Percentage
# employed in state	150	52.4
# employed in foreign countries	1	0.3
# of states where employed	24	

Bar Passage Rates

Jurisdiction	North Carolina			New York		
Exam	Sum 03	Win 04	Total	Sum 03	Win 04	Total
# from school taking bar for the first time	166	15	181	20	2	22
School's pass rate for all first-time takers	87%	60%	85%	90%	100%	91%
State's pass rate for all first-time takers	78%	64%	76%	78%	58%	75%

University of North Carolina School of Law

Campus Box 3380, 5026 Van Hecke-Wettach Hall
Chapel Hill, NC 27599-3380
Phone: 919.962.5109; Fax: 919.843.7939
E-mail: law_admissions@unc.edu; Website: www.law.unc.edu

■ Introduction

The University of North Carolina, the first state university chartered in the United States, has offered degrees in law since 1845. The School of Law has been a member of the American Association of Law Schools since 1920 and has been an approved school since the American Bar Association began its accreditation activities in 1923. The School of Law is one of the outstanding institutions in the United States, and the University of North Carolina is recognized as being among the nation's leaders in graduate and professional education. The programs at the School of Law reflect a powerful, active commitment to the goals of teaching, scholarship, and public service. The town of Chapel Hill, a university community, is close to the Research Triangle Park, the metropolitan and industrial centers of Greensboro and Durham, and the state capital, Raleigh. The immediate area offers an attractive blend of a strong academic atmosphere in a multicultural, cosmopolitan setting.

■ Library and Physical Facilities

Housed on five floors within the law school, the library provides critical support to the school's academic program and to lawyers and members of the public throughout the state. Its collection, which totals over 488,000 volumes, includes court reports for American and English appellate courts, current codes and session laws for all states, and other primary legal materials. Within the library, a university computer lab provides Internet access, electronic mail, and word processing capabilities and is easily accessible to law students. Additionally, students can bring their own laptop computers and connect to the university's network in many of the high technology classrooms, library study carrels, and other areas in the building.

The School of Law aims to provide a quality legal education that will prepare students to practice successfully in any jurisdiction. The three-year Juris Doctor program begins with a first-year core curriculum designed to provide a theoretical and analytical foundation for law students. The second-year curriculum provides an important bridge between the core instruction of the first year and the culminating electives, seminars, and skills-oriented instruction of the third year. Finally in the third year, the curriculum is designed to provide a capstone for students' legal education and begins the transition into practice.

■ Joint-Degree Programs/Certificate Programs

Nine formal joint JD and master's degree programs are available: JD/MAPPS (in conjunction with Duke University); JD/MBA; JD/MPA; JD/MPH; JD/MRP; JD/MSW; JD/MASA; JD/MSLS; or MSIS.

The Nonprofit Leadership Certificate Program prepares graduate students for leadership roles in North Carolina's rapidly growing nonprofit sector. The program provides an in-depth examination of leadership issues within human services, education, the arts, and other nonprofit organizations.

■ International Study Opportunities

In addition to the regularly taught courses in international business and human rights and the *International Law Journal*, students interested in international law can enhance their legal experience further with foreign study during the spring semester in France, The Netherlands, Mexico, England, and Scotland. Additionally, after the first year, students may also participate in the school's Summer Law Programs in Sydney, Australia; Augsburg, Germany; or Nice, France.

■ Centers and Initiatives

Carolina boasts nationally recognized centers in banking and financial services law, civil rights, and entrepreneurial law—all key areas tied to our history and the unique opportunities unfolding in North Carolina and the South. These centers and initiatives expand and enliven our curriculum, push the frontiers of teaching and research, and open new channels of scholarship for students.

■ Student Activities

Out of the classroom, student organizations provide a forum for the enormous talent and energy characteristic of Carolina Law students. Students can write for five prominent student publications—the *North Carolina Law Review*, the *North Carolina Journal of International Law and Commercial Regulation*, the *North Carolina Banking Journal*, the *North Carolina First Amendment Law Review*, and the *Journal of Law and Technology*. The Student Bar Association sponsors a full range of professional, athletic, and social events; a speakers program; minority recruitment events; a legal research service for practicing lawyers; and participation in school governance. The Moot Court Program is student operated and fields a number of successful teams in regional, national, and international competitions. Over 40 student organizations are active in the School of Law, including the Black Law Students Association, Child Action, the Federalist Society, the Hispanic and Latino Law Students Association, the Native American Law Students Association, Second Careers in Law, Women in Law, and our nationally recognized Pro Bono Program.

■ Expenses and Financial Aid

Full-time tuition and fees—North Carolina resident, $11,118; nonresident, $23,036. Estimated additional expenses—$15,438. Chancellors' Scholars Program scholarships available, as well as other merit-based scholarships. Need-based assistance is awarded on the basis of FAFSA information. Students must submit parental information to FAFSA to be considered for need-based grants.

Admitted applicants are automatically considered for merit-based scholarships. Awards range from $1,000 to $10,000. Scholarship offers are made beginning in February.

■ Housing

There are graduate dormitories near the law school for single students. University student family housing and private apartments are available. Information may be obtained from the University Housing Office, Carr Building CB 5500, Chapel Hill, North Carolina 27399-5580; 919.962.5401.

■ Career Services Office

The Career Services Office staff assists students and alumni with summer and permanent positions. Each year, approximately 200 employers from across the nation interview at the School of Law. Of those 2003 graduates reporting to the Career Services Office, 97 percent had accepted employment or were in graduate school within nine months of graduation. Of those 2003 graduates who entered into the practice arena, 61 percent entered private practice; 31 percent entered public sector work, including public interest; 16 percent accepted judicial clerkships; approximately 11 percent entered government practice (district attorneys'/public defenders' offices, government, and military); 4 percent entered legal services/nonprofit; 7 percent entered business/corporate related practice; and 1 percent entered academia.

Applicant Profile

University of North Carolina School of Law
This grid includes only applicants who earned 120-180 LSAT scores under standard administrations.

LSAT Score	3.75 + Apps	Adm	3.50 - 3.74 Apps	Adm	3.25 - 3.49 Apps	Adm	3.00 - 3.24 Apps	Adm	2.75 - 2.99 Apps	Adm	2.50 -2.74 Apps	Adm	2.25 - 2.49 Apps	Adm	2.00 - 2.24 Apps	Adm	Below 2.00 Apps	Adm	No GPA Apps	Adm	Total Apps	Adm
175-180	4	4	2	2	2	1	0	0	0	0	1	0	0	0	0	0	0	0	0	0	9	7
170-174	19	19	16	13	20	10	11	3	8	0	0	0	0	0	0	0	0	0	1	0	75	45
165-169	74	60	94	58	88	25	43	4	20	4	7	1	3	0	1	0	0	0	3	1	333	153
160-164	213	115	312	75	250	28	155	10	62	2	27	1	10	0	1	1	0	0	7	1	1037	233
155-159	239	44	282	22	286	19	198	17	83	3	29	2	19	0	4	0	0	0	16	0	1156	107
150-154	102	10	153	19	170	17	114	8	60	2	32	0	18	1	11	0	3	0	5	0	668	57
145-149	31	0	61	2	67	2	63	1	36	0	23	0	16	0	6	0	1	0	3	1	307	6
140-144	14	1	28	0	39	0	32	0	26	1	24	0	8	0	4	0	0	0	1	0	176	2
135-139	3	0	11	0	9	0	12	0	12	0	5	0	3	0	4	0	1	0	5	0	65	0
130-134	3	0	1	0	4	0	4	0	5	0	1	0	1	0	5	0	3	0	0	0	27	0
125-129	0	0	0	0	0	0	0	0	2	0	0	0	0	0	1	0	0	0	2	0	5	0
120-124	0	0	0	0	0	0	0	0	0	0	0	0	1	0	0	0	0	0	0	0	1	0
Total	702	253	960	191	935	102	632	43	314	12	149	4	79	1	37	1	8	0	43	3	3859	610

Apps = Number of Applicants
Adm = Number Admitted
Reflects 99% of the total applicant pool.

North Carolina Central University School of Law

1512 South Alston Avenue
Durham, NC 27707
Phone: 919.530.6333; Fax: 919.530.6339
E-mail: kalston@wpo.nccu.edu; Website: www.nccu.edu/law

ABA
Approved
Since
1950

The Basics

Type of school	Public
Term	Semester
Application deadline	4/15
Application fee	$40
Financial aid deadline	
Can first year start other than fall?	No
Student to faculty ratio (fall)	19.8 to 1
Does the university offer:	
housing restricted to law students?	No
graduate housing for which law students are eligible?	Yes

Faculty and Administrators

	Total		Men		Women		Minorities	
	Fall	Spr	Fall	Spr	Fall	Spr	Fall	Spr
Full-time	17	17	9	9	8	8	10	10
Other Full-time	1	2	1	1	0	1	1	1
Deans, librarians, & others who teach	8	8	0	0	8	8	4	4
Part-time	11	13	6	7	5	6	6	6
Total	37	40	16	17	21	23	21	21

Curriculum

	Full-time	Part-time
Typical first-year section size	68	35
Is there typically a "small section" of the first-year class, other than Legal Writing, taught by full-time faculty	No	No
If yes, typical size offered last year	0	0
# of classroom course titles beyond 1st year curriculum	61	

# of upper division courses, excluding seminars with an enrollment:	Under 25	54
	25-49	15
	50-74	19
	75-99	15
	100+	4

# of seminars	2	
# of seminar positions available	40	
# of seminar positions filled	17	0
# of positions available in simulation courses	336	
# of simulation positions filled	198	24
# of positions available in faculty supervised clinical courses	149	
# of faculty supervised clinical positions filled	65	4
# involved in field placements	33	6
# involved in law journals	35	5
# involved in moot court or trial competitions	25	4
# of credit hours required to graduate	88	

JD Enrollment and Ethnicity

	Men		Women		Full-time		Part-time		1st-year		Total		JD Degs. Awd.
	#	%	#	%	#	%	#	%	#	%	#	%	
African Amer.	65	36.5	132	51.0	176	52.1	21	21.2	97	59.5	197	45.1	43
Amer. Indian	6	3.4	8	3.1	11	3.3	3	3.0	3	1.8	14	3.2	2
Asian Amer.	2	1.1	3	1.2	2	0.6	3	3.0	1	0.6	5	1.1	2
Mex. Amer.	0	0.0	0	0.0	0	0.0	0	0.0	0	0.0	0	0.0	0
Puerto Rican	0	0.0	2	0.8	0	0.0	2	2.0	2	1.2	2	0.5	0
Hispanic	1	0.6	1	0.4	2	0.6	0	0.0	1	0.6	2	0.5	2
Total Minority	74	41.6	146	56.4	191	56.5	29	29.3	104	63.8	220	50.3	49
For. Nation.	0	0.0	0	0.0	0	0.0	0	0.0	0	0.0	0	0.0	0
Caucasian	97	54.5	105	40.5	135	39.9	67	67.7	50	30.7	202	46.2	30
Unknown	7	3.9	8	3.1	12	3.6	3	3.0	9	5.5	15	3.4	13
Total	178	40.7	259	59.3	338	77.3	99	22.7	163	37.3	437		92

Tuition and Fees

	Resident	Nonresident
Full-time	$3,891	$15,751
Part-time	$3,891	$15,751

Living Expenses

Estimated living expenses for singles

Living on campus	Living off campus	Living at home
$6,950	$10,450	$3,150

North Carolina Central University School of Law

*ABA
Approved
Since
1950*

GPA and LSAT Scores

	Total	Full-time	Part-time
# of apps	2,253	1,571	682
# of admits	304	263	41
# of matrics	172	138	34
75% GPA	3.63	3.46	3.63
25% GPA	2.99	2.93	3.17
75% LSAT	151	150	157
25% LSAT	144	143	150

Grants and Scholarships (from prior year)

	Total		Full-time		Part-time	
	#	%	#	%	#	%
Total # of students	412		319		93	
Total # receiving grants	122	29.6	122	38.2	0	0.0
Less than 1/2 tuition	51	12.4	51	16.0	0	0.0
Half to full tuition	16	3.9	16	5.0	0	0.0
Full tuition	30	7.3	30	9.4	0	0.0
More than full tuition	25	6.1	25	7.8	0	0.0
Median grant amount			$3,193		$0	

Informational and Library Resources

# of volumes and volume equivalents	330,134
# of titles	63,927
# of active serial subscriptions	4,250
Study seating capacity inside the library	51
# of professional librarians	5
Hours per week library is open	100
# of open, wired connections available to students	38
# of networked computers available for use by students	39
# of simultaneous wireless users	200
Require computer?	N

JD Attrition (from prior year)

	Academic	Other	Total	
	#	#	#	%
1st year	34	4	38	22.1%
2nd year	1	8	9	7.7%
3rd year	1	0	1	1.0%
4th year	0	0	0	0.0%

Employment

	Total	Percentage
Employment status known	76	88.4
Employment status unknown	10	11.6
Employed	69	90.8
Pursuing graduate degrees	1	1.3
Unemployed seeking employment	5	6.6
Unemployed not seeking employment	1	1.3

Type of Employment

	Total	Percentage
# employed in law firms	42	60.9
# employed in business and industry	7	10.1
# employed in government	8	11.6
# employed in public interest	11	15.9
# employed as judicial clerks	1	1.4
# employed in academia	0	0.0

Geographic Location

	Total	Percentage
# employed in state	60	87.0
# employed in foreign countries	0	0.0
# of states where employed	5	

Bar Passage Rates

Jurisdiction	North Carolina		
Exam	Sum 03	Win 04	Total
# from school taking bar for the first time	69	7	76
School's pass rate for all first-time takers	68%	86%	70%
State's pass rate for all first-time takers	78%	64%	76%

North Carolina Central University School of Law

1512 South Alston Avenue
Durham, NC 27707
Phone: 919.530.6333; Fax: 919.530.6339
E-mail: kalston@wpo.nccu.edu; Website: www.nccu.edu/law

■ Introduction

The North Carolina Central University School of Law was established in 1939. The School of Law is located in Durham, North Carolina. Durham, Raleigh, and Chapel Hill form the world's largest university-related research park and the vast region known as the Research Triangle. Durham is in the northeast corner of North Carolina's central piedmont, a geographic foothills region lying between the mountains and the coastal plains.

The School of Law has been accredited by the North Carolina State Bar Council and the ABA since 1950. Today, the School of Law is one of the most affordable and diverse in the country. The School of Law offers two programs leading to the Juris Doctor degree: a full-time day program and the only part-time evening program between Atlanta, Georgia, and Washington, DC. The School of Law participates in an interinstitutional agreement with Duke University and the University of North Carolina at Chapel Hill that permits students to enroll in electives at any member school with no increase in tuition.

North Carolina Central University was chartered in 1909 as a private institution and first opened to students in July 1910. In 1923, the institution became the first state-supported liberal arts college for African Americans in the United States. In July 1972, North Carolina Central University became one of the 16 constituent institutions of the University of North Carolina system.

■ Library and Physical Facilities

From January 2004 until July 2005, the Albert L. Turner Law Building will undergo complete renovation and expansion. During that time, the law school has been temporarily relocated to two floors of the historic North Carolina Mutual Life Insurance Building near downtown. These temporary quarters, with beautiful views of the City of Durham, contain a library, four classrooms, a model law office, offices for faculty and administration, including career services, information technology support, academic support, and admission, and offices for student organizations.

■ Special Academic Programs

- **Joint-Degree Options**—There are two joint-degree programs available to day-program students. Day-program students, in these programs, must successfully complete all their required first-year studies in the School of Law. JD/MBA Program—The joint-degree JD/MBA program allows students interested in a career in law and business to receive both degrees in four years instead of the traditional five years. Students must apply and be accepted to both the School of Law and School of Business.

JD/MLS Program—The joint-degree JD/MLS program allows students who are interested in a career in law librarianship to simultaneously pursue both degrees. Students must apply and be accepted to both the School of Law and School of Library and Information Sciences.

- **Evening Program**—The Evening Program is a four-year, year-round program that offers a unique opportunity for motivated professionals to pursue a legal education while maintaining their current daytime work commitments. Evening Program admission standards place a greater emphasis on the objective indicators of LSAT scores and undergraduate grade-point average.
- **Academic Support Program**—The Academic Support Program is available to assist students with the rigors of law school. The support program consists of a first-year, noncredit writing lab; tutorials; academic success workshops; and individual counseling and guidance sessions.
- **Faculty Advising Program**—Each student is assigned a faculty advisor who is available to discuss questions or problems related to the School of Law experience, career choices, and personal problems that might affect academic performance.
- **Clinical Program**—The Clinical Program operates year-round out of a state-of-the-art model law office. The clinical experiences currently offered at the School of Law are Civil Litigation, Criminal Litigation, Alternative Dispute Resolution, Family Law, Small Business Planning and Development, Domestic Violence, and Juvenile Justice. Under the supervision of a licensed attorney, clinical students represent real clients with real legal issues.
- **Pro Bono Program**—The Pro Bono Program provides opportunities for law students to volunteer with nonprofit organizations, government agencies; and private attorneys on supervised projects that include the Teen Court Program; NCCU Law School Innocence Project; NC Fair Housing Center; Volunteer Income Tax Assistance; Center for Death Penalty Litigation; Carolina Dispute Settlement Services, Inc.; Guardian *Ad Litem* Program; NC Association of Black Lawyers Land Loss Prevention Project; Prisoner Legal Services, Inc.; American Civil Liberties Union; NC Coalition against Domestic Violence; Carolina Legal Assistance Mental Disability Law Project; NC Association of Community Development Corporations; NC Attorney General's Office; Legal Aid of North Carolina; Center for Child and Family Health Legal Project; Child Advocacy Commission of Durham; Durham County Attorney's Office; and NC Volunteer Lawyers for the Arts.

■ Admission

Applicants selected for admission bring excellent intellectual abilities, strong academic credentials, and diverse talents and experiences. The School of Law does not prescribe or endorse any particular prelaw course of study. Admission is competitive. Selection for admission is based upon a thorough evaluation of all factors in an applicant's file, including but not limited to LSAT scores, undergraduate grades, and recommendations. Careful consideration is given to professional experience, volunteer or community service, unusual achievements, special circumstances, honors, economic hardship, undergraduate degree and college, graduate degree and school, and grade trends. Applicants may apply to either the day, evening, or both programs. Visit our website for more information.

■ Performance-Based Admission Program (PBAP)

The PBAP is a conditional admission program for approximately 30 applicants whose credentials do not qualify them for unconditional admission, but whose records nonetheless show promise of success. Participants are selected by the Admission Committee from those applicants to the Day Program.

■ Student Activities

The *North Carolina Central Law Journal* is devoted to a broad range of legal topics submitted by diverse authors, including legal scholars, attorneys, and law students. Students are selected for membership based on their GPA and their performance in the annual Law Journal Writing Competition.

The Moot Court Board consists of third-year students who have demonstrated exceptional ability in appellate skills.

The Trial Advocacy Board consists of student teams who participate in mock jury trial competitions. The board has gained regional and national recognition for its excellence in trial advocacy.

Other student organizations are ABA/Law Student Division; ACLU; Black Law Students Association; Christian Legal Society; Future Attorneys Challenging Elementary Students; Intellectual Property Society and Trademark Moot Court; Sports and Entertainment Law Society; Women's Caucus; and chapters of the legal fraternities of Phi Alpha Delta, Delta Theta Phi, and Phi Delta Phi.

■ Expenses and Financial Aid

Write the Office of Scholarships and Student Aid, North Carolina Central University, PO Box 19496, Shepard Station, Durham, NC 27707 and visit our website for more information.

■ Housing

Limited on-campus housing is available for single law students. Write the University Housing Director, North Carolina Central University, PO Box 19382, Durham, NC 27707, or call 919.530.6227.

■ Career Services

The Office of Career Services offers a range of career planning and placement services, including career counseling, interview preparation, résumé writing workshops, firm and résumé referral banks, a placement information booklet and resource library, and an on-campus interview program. Graduates find employment in law firms, corporations, state and federal government agencies, public interest organizations, the judiciary, and the military.

Please note: **Prospective applicants should contact the Office of Recruitment at 919.530.6333** or *kalston@nccu.edu* for information. **For applicant status contact the Office of Admissions at 919.530.5243.**

Applicant Profile Not Available

University of North Dakota School of Law

PO Box 9003
Grand Forks, ND 58202
Phone: 701.777.2104; Fax: 701.777.2217
E-mail: myszkowski@law.und.edu; Website: www.law.und.nodak.edu

ABA Approved Since 1923

The Basics

Type of school	Public
Term	Semester
Application deadline	4/1
Application fee	$35
Financial aid deadline	4/15
Can first year start other than fall?	No
Student to faculty ratio (fall)	21.2 to 1
Does the university offer:	
housing restricted to law students?	No
graduate housing for which law students are eligible?	Yes

Faculty and Administrators

	Total Fall	Total Spr	Men Fall	Men Spr	Women Fall	Women Spr	Minorities Fall	Minorities Spr
Full-time	8	7	5	5	3	2	0	0
Other Full-time	2	2	0	0	2	2	1	1
Deans, librarians, & others who teach	8	8	4	4	4	4	1	1
Part-time	7	9	5	5	2	4	0	0
Total	25	26	14	14	11	12	2	2

Curriculum

		Full-time	Part-time
Typical first-year section size		75	0
Is there typically a "small section" of the first-year class, other than Legal Writing, taught by full-time faculty		No	No
If yes, typical size offered last year		0	0
# of classroom course titles beyond 1st year curriculum		47	
# of upper division courses, excluding seminars with an enrollment:	Under 25	31	
	25-49	14	
	50-74	4	
	75-99	2	
	100+	0	
# of seminars		3	
# of seminar positions available		34	
# of seminar positions filled	34	0	
# of positions available in simulation courses		66	
# of simulation positions filled	56	0	
# of positions available in faculty supervised clinical courses		29	
# of faculty supervised clinical positions filled	29	0	
# involved in field placements	22	0	
# involved in law journals	38	0	
# involved in moot court or trial competitions	43	0	
# of credit hours required to graduate		90	

JD Enrollment and Ethnicity

	Men #	Men %	Women #	Women %	Full-time #	Full-time %	Part-time #	Part-time %	1st-year #	1st-year %	Total #	Total %	JD Degs. Awd.
African Amer.	2	1.9	1	1.0	3	1.5	0	0.0	2	2.7	3	1.5	1
Amer. Indian	3	2.9	1	1.0	4	2.0	0	0.0	1	1.3	4	2.0	6
Asian Amer.	1	1.0	0	0.0	1	0.5	0	0.0	0	0.0	1	0.5	0
Mex. Amer.	3	2.9	1	1.0	4	2.0	0	0.0	0	0.0	4	2.0	0
Puerto Rican	0	0.0	0	0.0	0	0.0	0	0.0	0	0.0	0	0.0	0
Hispanic	0	0.0	0	0.0	0	0.0	0	0.0	0	0.0	0	0.0	0
Total Minority	9	8.7	3	3.0	12	5.9	0	0.0	3	4.0	12	5.9	7
For. Nation.	2	1.9	5	5.1	7	3.4	0	0.0	4	5.3	7	3.4	2
Caucasian	82	78.8	81	81.8	163	80.3	0	0.0	57	76.0	163	80.3	42
Unknown	11	10.6	10	10.1	21	10.3	0	0.0	11	14.7	21	10.3	11
Total	104	51.2	99	48.8	203	100.0	0	0.0	75	36.9	203		62

Tuition and Fees

	Resident	Nonresident
Full-time	$7,032	$14,900
Part-time	$0	$0

Living Expenses

Estimated living expenses for singles

Living on campus	Living off campus	Living at home
$13,500	$13,500	$13,500

University of North Dakota School of Law

*ABA
Approved
Since
1923*

GPA and LSAT Scores

	Total	Full-time	Part-time
# of apps	360	360	0
# of admits	167	167	0
# of matrics	74	74	0
75% GPA	3.62	3.62	0.00
25% GPA	3.21	3.21	0.00
75% LSAT	154	154	0
25% LSAT	148	148	0

Grants and Scholarships (from prior year)

	Total		Full-time		Part-time	
	#	%	#	%	#	%
Total # of students	200		200		0	
Total # receiving grants	112	56.0	112	56.0	0	0.0
Less than 1/2 tuition	74	37.0	74	37.0	0	0.0
Half to full tuition	18	9.0	18	9.0	0	0.0
Full tuition	4	2.0	4	2.0	0	0.0
More than full tuition	16	8.0	16	8.0	0	0.0
Median grant amount			$952		$0	

Informational and Library Resources

# of volumes and volume equivalents	312,313
# of titles	118,713
# of active serial subscriptions	2,221
Study seating capacity inside the library	227
# of professional librarians	6
Hours per week library is open	100
# of open, wired connections available to students	145
# of networked computers available for use by students	52
# of simultaneous wireless users	1,400
Require computer?	N

JD Attrition (from prior year)

	Academic	Other	Total	
	#	#	#	%
1st year	3	7	10	14.5%
2nd year	1	0	1	1.4%
3rd year	0	0	0	0.0%
4th year	0	0	0	0.0%

Employment

	Total	Percentage
Employment status known	64	98.5
Employment status unknown	1	1.5
Employed	59	92.2
Pursuing graduate degrees	1	1.6
Unemployed seeking employment	2	3.1
Unemployed not seeking employment	2	3.1

Type of Employment

# employed in law firms	31	52.5
# employed in business and industry	4	6.8
# employed in government	10	16.9
# employed in public interest	5	8.5
# employed as judicial clerks	9	15.3
# employed in academia	0	0.0

Geographic Location

# employed in state	26	44.1
# employed in foreign countries	2	3.4
# of states where employed		8

Bar Passage Rates

Jurisdiction	North Dakota		
Exam	Sum 03	Win 04	Total
# from school taking bar for the first time	32	0	32
School's pass rate for all first-time takers	75%		75%
State's pass rate for all first-time takers	78%	0%	78%

University of North Dakota School of Law

Office of the Dean, PO Box 9003
Grand Forks, ND 58202
Phone: 701.777.2104; Fax: 701.777.2217
E-mail: myszkowski@law.und.edu; Website: www.law.und.nodak.edu

■ Introduction

The University of North Dakota School of Law was established in 1899 and has been a member of the AALS since 1910. In 1923, it was approved by the ABA; it is a fully accredited graduate professional school awarding the JD degree. The School of Law is located on the main campus in Grand Forks, a city of approximately 50,000, in the northeastern part of the state. The third largest city in the state, Grand Forks is a center of commerce for the Upper Great Plains, as well as a large legal community, including county, state, and federal trial courts.

■ Library and Physical Facilities

The Thormodsgard Law Library offers generous seating and study space on its four levels. The Baker Moot Court Room provides facilities for trial and appellate arguments and is occasionally used by the North Dakota Supreme Court, United States Court of Appeals for the Eighth Circuit, United States District Court for the District of North Dakota, and other state and federal courts.

■ Curriculum

The curriculum of the School of Law covers a period of three full academic years. All the work of the first year is prescribed. Courses in the second and third years are elective, except for the course in Professional Responsibility.

■ Special Programs

The size of the student body is ideally suited for close professional contact with the faculty. Students are given ample opportunity to participate in the governance of the school. Elected members of the Student Bar Association attend regularly scheduled faculty meetings and are active voting participants in most law school committees.

The School of Law is committed to the principle that all students should have an opportunity to elect, as a portion of their educational development, clinical legal education. This is not intended to diminish the law school's responsibility for education in legal analysis and legal principles, but adds an additional responsibility, providing experience in the application of analysis and theory.

The clinical program provides training in practical skills through simulation training and client representation. Under supervision, law students work with clients in cases, as permitted under the rule of the North Dakota Supreme Court. Training is received in such skills as interviewing, counseling, negotiating, fact gathering, and advocacy.

The school has an extensive Trial Advocacy Program in which students learn trial skills in a simulated advocacy setting under the close supervision of experienced trial lawyers. Each student in this course is responsible, with one student advocate cocounsel, for the trial of at least one full civil or criminal case during the semester.

The School of Law, in consultation with area tribes and Indian leaders, has established the Northern Plains Indian Law Center. The center's purposes are to assist tribal governments in addressing legal issues affecting tribal lands and members and to promote diversity within the legal profession by increasing recruitment and retention of American Indian law students.

The center is a clearinghouse for American Indian legal materials and provides a forum for discussing and resolving legal issues confronting Indian tribes, the states, and the federal government. It will also support tribal advocacy training programs. Among the center's programs are the Northern Plains Tribal Judicial Training Institute, the Tribal Environmental Law Project, and the Tribal Gaming Law and Policy Institute.

During sessions of the state legislature, selected students serve as legislative interns at the state capital in Bismarck.

Central Legal Research, directed by an attorney under the supervision of the dean, is the research arm for the criminal justice system of the state of North Dakota. Competitively hired students perform original legal research, upon request, for judges, prosecutors, court-appointed defense counsel, police, and others.

In 1982 the law school initiated a foreign exchange program, the UND–University of Oslo Program. The Norwegian program provides for exchange of students and faculty between these two fine law schools.

■ Admission

The School of Law has no specific undergraduate course prerequisites and agrees with the observations in the introduction to this guide. The school admits students only in August and only for full-time study. Applications are available upon request. The policy of the faculty of the School of Law is to admit those applicants who, in the determination of the faculty, will be able to satisfactorily complete the law school program. The admission committee utilizes the following criteria to achieve this goal: (1) LSAT score; (2) undergraduate GPA; (3) past performance in an academic environment; (4) past performance in activities that would tend to predict the applicant's ability to complete successfully the law school program; and (5) other evidence relevant to predicted success and prospective professional responsibility. The total number of students admitted is, of course, limited by considerations involving space and faculty courseload.

The law school does not have a nonresident quota; however, preference is given to residents.

Students who have begun the study of law in other accredited law schools may be admitted in exceptional circumstances to advanced standing, provided they have fulfilled the requirements for admission to the University of North Dakota School of Law. Ordinarily, no transfer credit will be allowed for more than two semesters of work completed elsewhere, nor will transfer credit be given for any courses in which an unsatisfactory or failing grade has been received. Moreover, admission may be conditioned upon meeting such additional requirements as the faculty may prescribe. No student will be admitted as a transfer student with advanced standing who is not eligible to continue as a student at his or her present law school.

■ Student Activities

The *North Dakota Law Review* provides research and writing opportunities. Students also participate in various moot court activities. Student organizations include the Environmental Law Society, Federalist Society, Law Women's Caucus, Native American Law Students Association, Public Interest Law Students Association, Student Trial Lawyers Association, *Rhadamanthus* (newsletter), and an active Student Bar Association. The School of Law also has chapters of the Order of the Coif and legal fraternities.

■ Expenses and Financial Aid

Tuition and fees per semester for academic year 2004–2005 were $3,516/resident and $7,450/nonresident. The semester fees include student activity and university fees totaling $410 per semester and a $750 per semester professional fee. The student activity and university fees cover payment for health services, the university center, campus publications, and drama and athletic events. The professional fee is assessed by the School of Law and is used to support and improve the law school program. Fees are subject to change without notice. Loan funds for all qualified students are available through the university Student Financial Aid Office, Post Office Box 8371, Grand Forks, ND 58202.

■ Housing

The university's family housing facilities are open to law students. University residence halls are open to single law students. Inquiries should be directed to the Housing Office, Post Office Box 9029, Grand Forks, ND 58202.

■ Career Services

The Career Services Office serves students and alumni by assisting with the job-search process and employment information, and provides job seekers with information about types of employment, specific employers, positions available, and wage and salary information. The office also assists in job-search strategies and skills such as résumé writing, interviewing techniques, and electronic job-search strategies. Over 90 percent of graduates find employment within six months of graduation. While a majority choose employment in North Dakota and Minnesota, graduates are employed nationally and internationally.

Applicant Profile

University of North Dakota School of Law
This grid includes only applicants who earned 120-180 LSAT scores under standard administrations.

LSAT Score	3.75 +		3.50 - 3.74		3.25 - 3.49		3.00 - 3.24		2.75 - 2.99		2.50 - 2.74		2.25 - 2.49		2.00 - 2.24		Below 2.00		No GPA		Total	
	Apps	Adm	Apps	Adm	Apps	Adm	Apps	Adm	Apps	Adm	Apps	Adm	Apps	Adm	Apps	Adm	Apps	Adm	Apps	Adm	Apps	Adm
175-180	0	0	0	0	0	0	0	0	0	0	0	0	0	0	0	0	0	0	0	0	0	0
170-174	0	0	0	0	0	0	0	0	0	0	0	0	0	0	0	0	0	0	0	0	0	0
165-169	1	1	2	2	1	1	0	0	0	0	1	0	0	0	0	0	0	0	0	0	5	4
160-164	3	3	2	2	5	5	1	1	3	3	1	0	2	1	1	0	0	0	0	0	18	15
155-159	3	3	12	11	8	7	6	5	4	3	1	1	0	0	1	0	0	0	0	0	35	30
150-154	12	12	12	12	20	20	22	15	12	1	8	2	4	2	0	0	1	0	1	0	92	64
145-149	5	5	20	14	29	15	16	4	13	0	10	0	8	0	2	0	0	0	3	0	106	38
140-144	5	3	7	3	9	0	15	1	11	0	10	2	8	1	1	0	2	0	1	0	69	10
135-139	1	0	3	0	7	0	13	1	3	0	4	1	6	1	1	1	1	0	2	1	41	4
130-134	0	0	2	0	1	0	0	0	1	0	2	0	0	0	0	0	1	0	0	0	7	0
125-129	0	0	0	0	0	0	0	0	0	0	1	0	0	0	0	0	0	0	0	0	1	0
120-124	0	0	0	0	0	0	0	0	0	0	0	0	0	0	0	0	0	0	0	0	0	0
Total	30	27	60	44	80	48	73	27	47	7	38	6	28	5	6	0	5	0	7	1	374	165

Apps = Number of Applicants   Adm = Number Admitted   Reflects 99% of the total applicant pool.

Northeastern University School of Law

PO Box 728, Boston, MA 02117-0728
400 Huntington Avenue, Boston, MA 02115
Phone: 617.373.2395; Fax: 617.373.8865
E-mail: lawadmissions@neu.edu; Website: www.slaw.neu.edu

*ABA
Approved
Since
1969*

The Basics

Type of school	Private
Term	Quarter
Application deadline	11/15 3/1
Application fee	$65
Financial aid deadline	2/15
Can first year start other than fall?	No
Student to faculty ratio (fall)	19.1 to 1
Does the university offer:	
housing restricted to law students?	No
graduate housing for which law students are eligible?	Yes

Faculty and Administrators

	Total		Men		Women		Minorities	
	Fall	Spr	Fall	Spr	Fall	Spr	Fall	Spr
Full-time	27	28	12	14	15	14	8	7
Other Full-time	0	0	0	0	0	0	0	0
Deans, librarians, & others who teach	5	5	2	2	3	3	0	0
Part-time	28	27	19	12	9	15	3	3
Total	60	60	33	28	27	32	11	10

Curriculum

		Full-time	Part-time
Typical first-year section size		73	0
Is there typically a "small section" of the first-year class, other than Legal Writing, taught by full-time faculty		No	No
If yes, typical size offered last year		0	0
# of classroom course titles beyond 1st year curriculum		51	
# of upper division courses, excluding seminars with an enrollment:	Under 25	41	
	25-49	32	
	50-74	12	
	75-99	1	
	100+	0	
# of seminars		10	
# of seminar positions available		176	
# of seminar positions filled		166	0
# of positions available in simulation courses		304	
# of simulation positions filled		263	0
# of positions available in faculty supervised clinical courses		124	
# of faculty supervised clinical positions filled	114		0
# involved in field placements		400	0
# involved in law journals		0	0
# involved in moot court or trial competitions	23		0
# of credit hours required to graduate		103	

JD Enrollment and Ethnicity

	Men		Women		Full-time		Part-time		1st-year		Total		JD Degs. Awd.
	#	%	#	%	#	%	#	%	#	%	#	%	
African Amer.	12	5.0	33	8.7	45	7.3	0	0.0	15	6.7	45	7.3	13
Amer. Indian	3	1.3	4	1.1	7	1.1	0	0.0	2	0.9	7	1.1	1
Asian Amer.	25	10.4	46	12.1	71	11.5	0	0.0	29	13.0	71	11.5	11
Mex. Amer.	0	0.0	0	0.0	0	0.0	0	0.0	0	0.0	0	0.0	1
Puerto Rican	1	0.4	1	0.3	2	0.3	0	0.0	0	0.0	2	0.3	0
Hispanic	18	7.5	23	6.1	41	6.6	0	0.0	17	7.6	41	6.6	12
Total Minority	59	24.6	107	28.2	166	26.8	0	0.0	63	28.3	166	26.8	38
For. Nation.	1	0.4	2	0.5	3	0.5	0	0.0	0	0.0	3	0.5	3
Caucasian	166	69.2	257	67.8	423	68.3	0	0.0	133	59.6	423	68.3	150
Unknown	14	5.8	13	3.4	27	4.4	0	0.0	27	12.1	27	4.4	0
Total	240	38.8	379	61.2	619	100.0	0	0.0	223	36.0	619		191

Tuition and Fees

	Resident	Nonresident
Full-time	$31,281	$31,281
Part-time	$0	$0

Living Expenses

Estimated living expenses for singles

Living on campus	Living off campus	Living at home
$15,798	$15,798	$7,698

Northeastern University School of Law

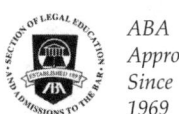

*ABA
Approved
Since
1969*

GPA and LSAT Scores

	Total	Full-time	Part-time
# of apps	3,845	3,845	0
# of admits	921	921	0
# of matrics	223	223	0
75% GPA	0.00	3.62	0.00
25% GPA	0.00	3.19	0.00
75% LSAT	0	162	0
25% LSAT	0	157	0

Grants and Scholarships (from prior year)

	Total #	Total %	Full-time #	Full-time %	Part-time #	Part-time %
Total # of students	590		590		0	
Total # receiving grants	412	69.8	412	69.8	0	0.0
Less than 1/2 tuition	357	60.5	357	60.5	0	0.0
Half to full tuition	55	9.3	55	9.3	0	0.0
Full tuition	0	0.0	0	0.0	0	0.0
More than full tuition	0	0.0	0	0.0	0	0.0
Median grant amount			$7,195		$0	

Informational and Library Resources

# of volumes and volume equivalents	269,732
# of titles	41,389
# of active serial subscriptions	3,059
Study seating capacity inside the library	399
# of professional librarians	4
Hours per week library is open	95
# of open, wired connections available to students	60
# of networked computers available for use by students	60
# of simultaneous wireless users	60
Require computer?	N

JD Attrition (from prior year)

	Academic #	Other #	Total #	Total %
1st year	0	6	6	3.0%
2nd year	2	4	6	3.0%
3rd year	0	0	0	0.0%
4th year	0	0	0	0.0%

Employment

	Total	Percentage
Employment status known	183	100.0
Employment status unknown	0	0.0
Employed	165	90.2
Pursuing graduate degrees	3	1.6
Unemployed seeking employment	13	7.1
Unemployed not seeking employment	2	1.1

Type of Employment

# employed in law firms	66	40.0
# employed in business and industry	31	18.8
# employed in government	11	6.7
# employed in public interest	27	16.4
# employed as judicial clerks	27	16.4
# employed in academia	3	1.8

Geographic Location

# employed in state	108	65.5
# employed in foreign countries	1	0.6
# of states where employed	18	

Bar Passage Rates

Jurisdiction	Massachusetts		
Exam	Sum 03	Win 04	Total
# from school taking bar for the first time	120	10	130
School's pass rate for all first-time takers	88%	90%	88%
State's pass rate for all first-time takers	82%	82%	82%

Northeastern University School of Law

PO Box 728, Boston, MA 02117-0728
400 Huntington Avenue, Boston, MA 02115
Phone: 617.373.2395; Fax: 617.373.8865
E-mail: lawadmissions@neu.edu; Website: www.slaw.neu.edu

■ Introduction

Northeastern University School of Law, located in Boston, offers the nation's only Cooperative Legal Education Program. Combining classroom theory with practical work, Northeastern law students receive their JD degree in the same three-year time period as students at other law schools but graduate with one full year of hands-on legal employment gained in law offices around the world.

Northeastern provides a supportive, student-centered learning environment. The curriculum is rigorous, with students receiving detailed narrative evaluations of their work in each academic course in lieu of alphabetic or numeric grades. In addition, co-op employers submit written appraisals of each student's professional performance. These academic and professional evaluations comprise the student's permanent record, clearly indicating the quality of a student's performance. Without grades and class ranking, there is a culture of cooperation based on constructive relationships and mutual respect, avoiding the adversarial attitude that often characterizes legal education.

■ Cooperative Legal Education

Northeastern's unique Cooperative Legal Education Program alternates periods of academic study with equal periods of workplace experience during the second and third years of law school. During the first year of law school, students follow a traditional, full-time academic schedule. At the end of the first year, half of the class begins the first academic quarter of their second year during the summer, while the other half starts their first co-op. For the remaining two years, students alternate every three months between working full time as legal interns and attending classes. By participating in four, 11-week co-op placements with four different legal employers, students are provided with an extraordinary opportunity to experience the actual practice of law and to determine their career paths based on practical training.

More than 700 employers nationwide currently participate in the Co-op Program, representing virtually every practice area, including law firms of all sizes, trial and appellate judges in federal and state courts, public defender and legal services organizations, government agencies, corporate and union legal departments, and a variety of advocacy groups.

While many co-op placements are in the Greater Boston area, students work with employers in more than 40 states and countries in any given quarter. In recent years, students have increasingly developed their own co-ops both in the United States and abroad. All students

are required to successfully complete four full-time legal internships in order to graduate.

While the Co-op Program is not intended as a financial aid program, earnings from co-op employment may somewhat reduce the net cost of attending law school during the second and third years. Salaries range from nominal amounts for public interest jobs to $2,500 per week in major law firms. To assist students in low-paying co-ops in the public interest area and the judiciary, the school provides approximately $500,000 in stipends each year.

■ Clinics and Institutes

Nationally recognized for its clinical education program, Northeastern offers students the opportunity to engage in advocacy on behalf of individuals and community organizations too often unacknowledged or underrepresented by the justice system. Students can participate with faculty and staff in the work of five outstanding research and service centers: the Domestic Violence Institute, the Urban Law and Public Policy Institute, the Tobacco Control Resource Center, the Public Health Advocacy Institute, and the Partnering for Prevention and Community Safety Initiative. Together, the clinics and institutes reflect and fulfill a commitment to social and economic justice that distinguishes Northeastern as the nation's foremost public interest law school.

Northeastern offers five clinics: Criminal Advocacy, Domestic Violence, Poverty Law and Practice, Prisoners' Rights, and Tobacco Control. The clinics differ from one another by substantive legal focus, advocacy experience, and the primary skills each seeks to impart. Students engage in challenging legal practice, with the support of clinical faculty who provide the requisite training, close supervision, and opportunity for reflection.

■ Dual-Degree Programs

Four dual-degree programs are offered. In cooperation with Tufts University School of Medicine, students may pursue both the JD and the Master of Public Health degrees. With a specialized curriculum, the two institutions enhance the training of law students who seek to understand the role advocacy and public action can play in reducing risk and ameliorating conditions that threaten community health. Completion of the dual-degree program takes three and one-half years, rather than the average five years if the degrees were obtained sequentially.

Concurrent degrees are also available from other schools and colleges at Northeastern University. A four-year program coordinates the academic and cooperative features of the School of Law and the

Graduate School of Business Administration at the university, enabling students to earn both the JD and the MBA degrees in 45 months rather than the 54 months required if undertaken sequentially.

Law students with nonaccounting undergraduate degrees are eligible for admission to a program leading to a concurrent JD/MS/MBA. The program enables students to earn these degrees in 45 months rather than the 48 months required if undertaken sequentially.

The Law, Policy, and Society JD/MS/PhD interdisciplinary graduate program is designed to offer students in the School of Law the opportunity to study policy, social issues, and the law in pursuit of an MS or PhD in Law, Policy, and Society. The program is based in the Graduate School of Arts and Sciences and is affiliated with graduate schools throughout the university.

■ Student Life

The student body is diverse and active. More than 60 percent of the students are women, and approximately 25 percent are people of color. Students are active participants in the law school community, serving on all of the school's standing committees, including the Admissions Committee. Students also run a wide variety of organizations.

■ Career Services

The Office of Career Services actively assists students and graduates in their pursuit of professionally rewarding careers. In recent years, approximately 93 percent of each class has obtained employment within six months of graduation. Students also generally find their postgraduate prospects substantially enhanced through the Co-op Program; on average, 40 percent accept postgraduate employment with one of their former co-op employers. Northeastern graduates are employed throughout the world in every practice area. They may be found teaching at distinguished law schools, sitting on the bench at both the state and federal levels, practicing as partners in prominent law firms, and serving as directors of legal aid and public defender programs throughout the nation. The school is also well known for its emphasis on public service. Graduates of Northeastern enter public service careers at a rate that is five times the national average. In addition, graduates have been consistently awarded prestigious postgraduate fellowships, including those granted by Equal Justice Works, Echoing Green, Georgetown, and Soros.

Applicant Profile

Northeastern University School of Law
This grid includes only applicants who earned 120-180 LSAT scores under standard administrations.

LSAT Score	3.75 +		3.50 - 3.74		3.25 - 3.49		3.00 - 3.24		2.75 - 2.99		2.50 -2.74		2.25 - 2.49		2.00 - 2.24		Below 2.00		No GPA		Total	
	Apps	Adm	Apps	Adm	Apps	Adm	Apps	Adm	Apps	Adm	Apps	Adm	Apps	Adm	Apps	Adm	Apps	Adm	Apps	Adm	Apps	Adm
175-180	0	0	0	0	2	2	2	1	0	0	0	0	1	0	0	0	0	0	0	0	5	3
170-174	1	1	12	12	7	7	2	2	4	1	2	0	0	0	0	0	0	0	0	0	28	23
165-169	31	30	37	35	36	35	34	30	12	5	11	3	6	1	0	0	0	0	1	0	168	139
160-164	79	74	172	162	147	136	117	93	54	6	28	3	12	0	4	0	0	0	5	2	618	476
155-159	129	36	269	58	309	47	250	19	113	3	56	0	20	1	3	0	0	0	11	2	1160	166
150-154	92	10	211	28	256	27	222	13	150	2	52	0	23	1	9	0	2	0	10	0	1027	81
145-149	20	3	69	2	112	7	122	3	85	1	42	0	22	0	6	0	4	1	9	0	491	17
140-144	8	0	22	0	31	0	39	0	35	0	24	0	11	0	4	0	1	0	8	0	183	0
135-139	2	0	9	0	12	0	10	0	10	0	8	0	7	0	7	0	2	0	0	0	67	0
130-134	0	0	1	0	2	0	3	0	3	0	4	0	3	0	3	0	1	0	2	0	22	0
125-129	0	0	0	0	0	0	2	0	0	0	0	0	0	0	0	0	0	0	1	0	3	0
120-124	0	0	0	0	0	0	0	0	0	0	0	0	0	0	0	0	1	0	1	0	2	0
Total	362	154	802	297	914	261	803	161	466	18	227	6	105	3	36	0	11	1	48	4	3774	905

Apps = Number of Applicants
Adm = Number Admitted
Reflects 99% of the total applicant pool.

Northern Illinois University College of Law

Swen Parson Hall, Room 276
DeKalb, IL 60115-2890
Phone: 800.892.3050 or 815.753.9485; Fax: 815.753.4501
E-mail: lawadm@niu.edu; Website: law.niu.edu

ABA Approved Since 1978

The Basics

Type of school	Public
Term	Semester
Application deadline	5/15
Application fee	$50
Financial aid deadline	3/1
Can first year start other than fall?	No
Student to faculty ratio (fall)	17.7 to 1
Does the university offer:	
housing restricted to law students?	Yes
graduate housing for which law students are eligible?	No

Faculty and Administrators

	Total		Men		Women		Minorities	
	Fall	Spr	Fall	Spr	Fall	Spr	Fall	Spr
Full-time	15	15	9	9	6	6	6	7
Other Full-time	3	3	0	0	3	3	0	0
Deans, librarians, & others who teach	7	7	5	5	2	2	1	1
Part-time	8	8	8	7	0	1	1	0
Total	33	33	22	21	11	12	8	8

Curriculum

		Full-time	Part-time
Typical first-year section size		62	0
Is there typically a "small section" of the first-year class, other than Legal Writing, taught by full-time faculty		No	No
If yes, typical size offered last year		0	0
# of classroom course titles beyond 1st year curriculum		61	
# of upper division courses, excluding seminars with an enrollment:	Under 25	34	
	25-49	21	
	50-74	7	
	75-99	5	
	100+	0	
# of seminars		9	
# of seminar positions available		108	
# of seminar positions filled		101	0
# of positions available in simulation courses		136	
# of simulation positions filled		128	0
# of positions available in faculty supervised clinical courses		40	
# of faculty supervised clinical positions filled	36	0
# involved in field placements	15	0
# involved in law journals	38	0
# involved in moot court or trial competitions	60	0
# of credit hours required to graduate		90	

JD Enrollment and Ethnicity

	Men		Women		Full-time		Part-time		1st-year		Total		JD Degs. Awd.
	#	%	#	%	#	%	#	%	#	%	#	%	
African Amer.	12	8.0	24	13.8	35	11.2	1	9.1	13	12.1	36	11.1	7
Amer. Indian	0	0.0	2	1.1	1	0.3	1	9.1	0	0.0	2	0.6	0
Asian Amer.	12	8.0	15	8.6	27	8.6	0	0.0	11	10.3	27	8.3	4
Mex. Amer.	17	11.3	11	6.3	26	8.3	2	18.2	8	7.5	28	8.6	5
Puerto Rican	0	0.0	0	0.0	0	0.0	0	0.0	0	0.0	0	0.0	0
Hispanic	0	0.0	0	0.0	0	0.0	0	0.0	0	0.0	0	0.0	0
Total Minority	41	27.3	52	29.9	89	28.4	4	36.4	32	29.9	93	28.7	16
For. Nation.	0	0.0	0	0.0	0	0.0	0	0.0	0	0.0	0	0.0	0
Caucasian	109	72.7	122	70.1	224	71.6	7	63.6	75	70.1	231	71.3	80
Unknown	0	0.0	0	0.0	0	0.0	0	0.0	0	0.0	0	0.0	0
Total	150	46.3	174	53.7	313	96.6	11	3.4	107	33.0	324		96

Tuition and Fees

	Resident	Nonresident
Full-time	$10,504	$18,850
Part-time	$0	$0

Living Expenses

Estimated living expenses for singles

Living on campus	Living off campus	Living at home
$10,504	$11,404	$11,404

Northern Illinois University College of Law

*ABA
Approved
Since
1978*

GPA and LSAT Scores

	Total	Full-time	Part-time
# of apps	1,504	1,472	32
# of admits	396	391	5
# of matrics	105	102	3
75% GPA	3.61	3.59	3.77
25% GPA	2.95	2.94	2.69
75% LSAT`	158	158	151
25% LSAT	153	153	146

Grants and Scholarships (from prior year)

	Total		Full-time		Part-time	
	#	%	#	%	#	%
Total # of students	333		318		15	
Total # receiving grants	69	20.7	69	21.7	0	0.0
Less than 1/2 tuition	9	2.7	9	2.8	0	0.0
Half to full tuition	17	5.1	17	5.3	0	0.0
Full tuition	40	12.0	40	12.6	0	0.0
More than full tuition	3	0.9	3	0.9	0	0.0
Median grant amount			$7,747		$0	

Informational and Library Resources

# of volumes and volume equivalents	238,509
# of titles	39,052
# of active serial subscriptions	3,256
Study seating capacity inside the library	209
# of professional librarians	5
Hours per week library is open	99
# of open, wired connections available to students	16
# of networked computers available for use by students	25
# of simultaneous wireless users	100
Require computer?	N

JD Attrition (from prior year)

	Academic	Other	Total	
	#	#	#	%
1st year	6	10	16	12.9%
2nd year	0	8	8	7.4%
3rd year	0	1	1	1.0%
4th year	0	0	0	0.0%

Employment

	Total	Percentage
Employment status known	96	99.0
Employment status unknown	1	1.0
Employed	90	93.7
Pursuing graduate degrees	1	1.0
Unemployed seeking employment	5	5.2
Unemployed not seeking employment	0	0.0

Type of Employment

# employed in law firms	44	48.9
# employed in business and industry	12	13.3
# employed in government	21	23.3
# employed in public interest	3	3.3
# employed as judicial clerks	2	2.2
# employed in academia	1	1.1

Geographic Location

# employed in state	71	78.9
# employed in foreign countries	0	0.0
# of states where employed		10

Bar Passage Rates

Jurisdiction	Illinois		
Exam	Sum 03	Win 04	Total
# from school taking bar for the first time	82	7	89
School's pass rate for all first-time takers	85%	57%	83%
State's pass rate for all first-time takers	86%	78%	84%

Northern Illinois University College of Law

Swen Parson Hall, Room 276
DeKalb, IL 60115-2890
Phone: 800.892.3050 or 815.753.9485; Fax: 815.753.4501
E-mail: lawadm@niu.edu; Website: law.niu.edu

■ Introduction

Northern Illinois University was founded in 1895, and the College of Law was established in 1978. The College of Law seeks to prepare its graduates not only for the traditional role of lawyers, but also for the tasks we can now only speculate will be assumed by the law-trained. The school has a diverse and professionally distinguished faculty dedicated to teaching and scholarship.

■ Our Campus

The College of Law is located in DeKalb, a community conveniently located approximately 65 miles west of Chicago and 25 miles from the suburban area on the Ronald Reagan Memorial Tollway (I-88). DeKalb is close enough to the Chicago metropolitan area to draw on its many resources, yet retains its own college town flavor—a safe and affordable environment with a high quality of life.

Northern's main campus is set on 756 acres of rolling country land. The lush campus features two lagoons, museums, and a vast variety of cultural opportunities. It ultimately provides an excellent environment for quiet contemplation.

Though on a relatively large campus with all of the associated activities and opportunities, the College of Law is a small oasis at its center. For an online tour go to our website at *law.niu.edu*.

■ Libraries

The David C. Shapiro Memorial Law Library provides one of the best ratios of library resources to students. It has rapidly expanding holdings of nearly 238,500 volumes. The Founders Memorial Library, located adjacent to the law school, contains more than two million volumes and an additional one million federal, state, and international governmental documents.

The law library houses a wireless communications node covering a substantial part of the building and allows laptop users high speed access to the Internet. The computer lab is equipped with access to LexisNexis, Westlaw, and a wide range of web-based legal resources. There are also study carrels equipped with power strips for laptop computer users.

■ Enrollment/Student Body

Northern's student body represents universities from coast to coast and reflects a broad spectrum of ethnic, cultural, and geographic diversity. Our low student-faculty ratio, which is normally 14 to 1, facilitates a supportive environment with a lively exchange of ideas. The school has a diverse and professionally distinguished faculty dedicated to teaching and scholarship. The law school provides an atmosphere of shared goals and achievement and a genuine sense of community.

■ Curriculum and Clinical Experience Opportunities

The College of Law provides its students with a curriculum that will make them well-rounded legal professionals. The first-year program consists of the traditional ABA-required courses. After the first year the only required courses are Constitutional Law II and Professional Responsibility, the remaining 90 hours are from a wide range of electives. Northern offers an Academic Support Program during the first-year of classes. The ultimate goal is to help students succeed in law school.

During the summer, electives are offered on the main campus. Also during the summer, NIU offers an international law program in France. During this program, students receive six hours of credit in international and comparative law.

The clinical lawyering skills programs offer students the opportunity to acquire essential techniques needed in pretrial and trial work through structured simulations and experiences in an array of legal settings. The externship program provides students with sound experience under the supervision of a highly qualified practicing attorney or the opportunity to be a law clerk for a state or federal judge. The Zeke Giorgi Legal Clinic in Rockford gives students the opportunity to apply legal theory by representing clients and resolving disputes in a real-world setting.

■ Admission

Considering Northern's small entering class size of between 105 to 115 out of an applicant pool ranging from 1,200 to 1,600, we are a relatively selective institution. The College of Law grants admission strictly on a competitive basis through an evaluation of an applicant's aptitude and professional promise. Factors of most importance to the admission committee are the applicant's undergraduate record, LSAT score, reasons for seeking admission, school or community activities and accomplishments, employment background, and ability to add diversity to the law school community and the legal community.

Applicants may submit their application either online or by paper form. In addition to the application, prospective students need to submit a personal statement and application fee directly to the Office of Admission and Financial Aid. Northern requires applicants to use the LSDAS (international students should refer to *law.niu.edu* for instructions on this subject). In order for Northern to receive LSAT scores, applicants need to submit official undergraduate and graduate transcripts as well as two letters of recommendation to LSAC. To be considered for the part-time option, an additional application, also available online, is required. Applicants are encouraged to submit their application early, even if the LSAT has not yet been taken, due to the limited number of seats in each entering class. Prospective students are encouraged to visit the College of Law.

■ Student Activities

Students are offered a wide variety of educational and professionally oriented activities. Among these are the *Law Review*, a forum for the expression of serious legal scholarship (and *The Advocate*, a newspaper published by law students). Students compete in a wide selection of moot court and client counseling competitions. Organizations range from BLSA to the Women's Law Caucus.

■ Expenses and Financial Aid

Northern offers its students small class sizes and a quality legal education all at an affordable cost. For the 2004–2005 academic year, in-state tuition is $8,346 and out-of-state is $16,692. Out-of-state residents can also qualify for in-state tuition in six months, which is why so few students after the first year are classified as out-of-state.

Scholarships and grants are available for students from a variety of sources. After the first year, students may qualify for research assistantships.

Scholarship, grant, and loan information is on our website at *law.niu.edu/go.cfm?do=Page.View&ID=31*. The priority deadline for the FAFSA form is March 1.

■ Career Opportunities

The Career Opportunities Office has a strong track record in assisting and preparing our graduates for rewarding careers through references to prospective employers and on-campus interviews. The office assists current students in obtaining enriching summer legal employment. Due to Northern's small class size, personalized counseling, normally not available at larger law schools, is offered.

■ Housing

Affordable housing is available both on and off campus. University Apartments ($5,950) offer unfurnished efficiencies or one bedroom units, as well as options for living in the University Residence Halls. Married and handicap accessible housing is also available on campus. For information about on-campus housing you may telephone 815.753.5125, or visit our website at *www.shds.niu.edu/*.

Many moderately priced apartments are available close to the university. You may contact off-campus housing at 815.753.5105 or visit our website at *www.niu.edu/housing/och/och.shtml*.

■ Correspondence

We encourage you to visit our campus and our website. Check our calendar on our website at *law.niu.edu* for activities, or call us toll free. Once you visit us, we are confident that you will agree that Northern is the law school for you.

Applicant Profile

Northern Illinois University College of Law
This grid includes only applicants who earned 120-180 LSAT scores under standard administrations.

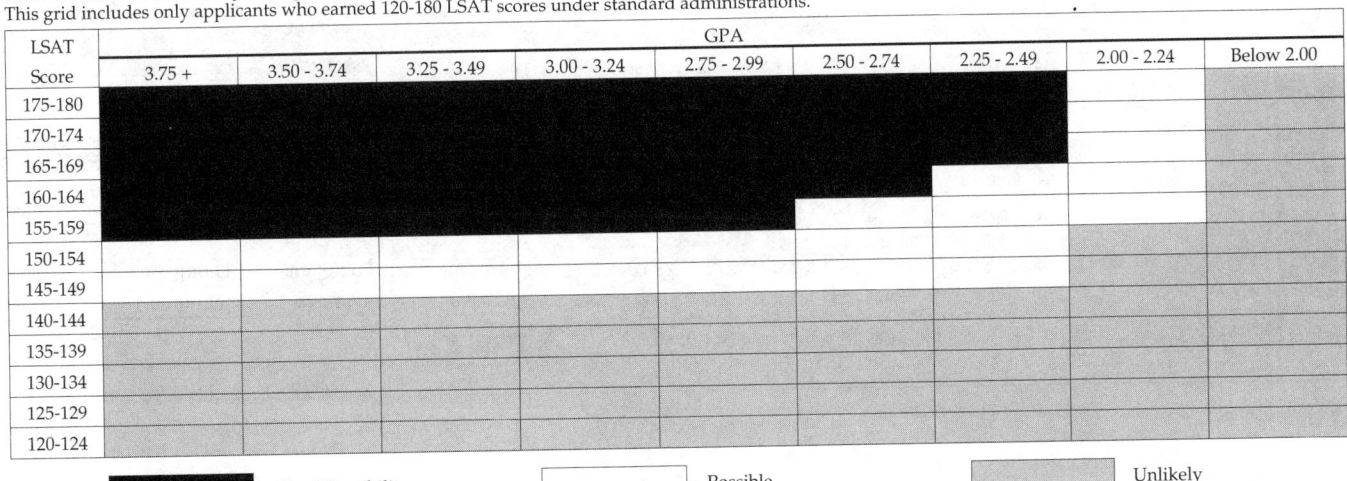

LSAT Score	3.75 +	3.50 - 3.74	3.25 - 3.49	3.00 - 3.24	2.75 - 2.99	2.50 - 2.74	2.25 - 2.49	2.00 - 2.24	Below 2.00
175-180									
170-174									
165-169									
160-164									
155-159									
150-154									
145-149									
140-144									
135-139									
130-134									
125-129									
120-124									

■ Good Possibility   □ Possible   ▨ Unlikely

Note: This chart is to be used as a general guide in determining the chances for admittance.

Northern Kentucky University—Salmon P. Chase College of Law

Nunn Hall
Highland Heights, KY 41099
Phone: 859.572.6476; Fax: 859.572.6081
E-mail: beersk@nku.edu; Website: www.nku.edu/~chase

ABA Approved Since 1954

The Basics

Type of school	Public
Term	Semester
Application deadline	3/1
Application fee	$30
Financial aid deadline	3/1
Can first year start other than fall?	No
Student to faculty ratio (fall)	17.6 to 1
Does the university offer:	
housing restricted to law students?	No
graduate housing for which law students are eligible?	Yes

Curriculum

	Full-time	Part-time
Typical first-year section size	120	75
Is there typically a "small section" of the first-year class, other than Legal Writing, taught by full-time faculty	Yes	Yes
If yes, typical size offered last year	63	40
# of classroom course titles beyond 1st year curriculum		62
# of upper division courses, excluding seminars with an enrollment: Under 25		53
25-49		26
50-74		12
75-99		3
100+		2
# of seminars		17
# of seminar positions available		425
# of seminar positions filled	128	45
# of positions available in simulation courses		210
# of simulation positions filled	123	56
# of positions available in faculty supervised clinical courses		15
# of faculty supervised clinical positions filled	0	2
# involved in field placements	37	0
# involved in law journals	17	0
# involved in moot court or trial competitions	44	15
# of credit hours required to graduate		90

Faculty and Administrators

	Total		Men		Women		Minorities	
	Fall	Spr	Fall	Spr	Fall	Spr	Fall	Spr
Full-time	23	22	17	17	6	5	3	3
Other Full-time	1	1	0	0	1	1	0	0
Deans, librarians, & others who teach	11	12	4	5	7	7	0	0
Part-time	17	13	10	7	7	6	0	1
Total	52	48	31	29	21	19	3	4

JD Enrollment and Ethnicity

	Men		Women		Full-time		Part-time		1st-year		Total		JD Degs. Awd.
	#	%	#	%	#	%	#	%	#	%	#	%	
African Amer.	5	1.5	17	6.7	9	3.0	13	4.7	7	3.1	22	3.8	2
Amer. Indian	4	1.2	1	0.4	3	1.0	2	0.7	3	1.3	5	0.9	0
Asian Amer.	3	0.9	2	0.8	0	0.0	5	1.8	2	0.9	5	0.9	3
Mex. Amer.	0	0.0	0	0.0	0	0.0	0	0.0	0	0.0	0	0.0	0
Puerto Rican	0	0.0	0	0.0	0	0.0	0	0.0	0	0.0	0	0.0	0
Hispanic	5	1.5	4	1.6	6	2.0	3	1.1	2	0.9	9	1.6	2
Total Minority	17	5.2	24	9.4	18	6.0	23	8.3	14	6.2	41	7.1	7
For. Nation.	0	0.0	0	0.0	0	0.0	0	0.0	0	0.0	0	0.0	0
Caucasian	309	94.8	230	90.6	284	94.0	255	91.7	213	93.8	539	92.9	98
Unknown	0	0.0	0	0.0	0	0.0	0	0.0	0	0.0	0	0.0	0
Total	326	56.2	254	43.8	302	52.1	278	47.9	227	39.1	580		105

Tuition and Fees

	Resident	Nonresident
Full-time	$9,240	$20,184
Part-time	$7,700	$16,820

Living Expenses

Estimated living expenses for singles

Living on campus	Living off campus	Living at home
$8,348	$13,670	$5,670

Official ABA Data

Northern Kentucky University—Salmon P. Chase College of Law

ABA Approved Since 1954

GPA and LSAT Scores

	Total	Full-time	Part-time
# of apps	956	681	275
# of admits	433	252	181
# of matrics	224	104	120
75% GPA	3.56	3.57	3.50
25% GPA	2.90	3.09	2.85
75% LSAT	155	157	154
25% LSAT	150	152	149

Grants and Scholarships (from prior year)

	Total #	Total %	Full-time #	Full-time %	Part-time #	Part-time %
Total # of students	522		288		234	
Total # receiving grants	148	28.4	107	37.2	41	17.5
Less than 1/2 tuition	62	11.9	44	15.3	18	7.7
Half to full tuition	26	5.0	15	5.2	11	4.7
Full tuition	60	11.5	48	16.7	12	5.1
More than full tuition	0	0.0	0	0.0	0	0.0
Median grant amount			$8,193		$3,861	

Informational and Library Resources

# of volumes and volume equivalents	313,792
# of titles	57,859
# of active serial subscriptions	2,128
Study seating capacity inside the library	224
# of professional librarians	5
Hours per week library is open	80
# of open, wired connections available to students	23
# of networked computers available for use by students	60
# of simultaneous wireless users	550
Require computer?	N

JD Attrition (from prior year)

	Academic #	Other #	Total #	Total %
1st year	25	21	46	23.6%
2nd year	10	4	14	8.0%
3rd year	0	1	1	0.9%
4th year	0	0	0	0.0%

Employment

	Total	Percentage
Employment status known	97	97.0
Employment status unknown	3	3.0
Employed	94	96.9
Pursuing graduate degrees	0	0.0
Unemployed seeking employment	3	3.1
Unemployed not seeking employment	0	0.0

Type of Employment

	Total	Percentage
# employed in law firms	45	47.9
# employed in business and industry	22	23.4
# employed in government	12	12.8
# employed in public interest	1	1.1
# employed as judicial clerks	12	12.8
# employed in academia	2	2.1

Geographic Location

	Total	Percentage
# employed in state	50	53.2
# employed in foreign countries	0	0.0
# of states where employed	6	

Bar Passage Rates

Jurisdiction	Kentucky			Ohio		
Exam	Sum 03	Win 04	Total	Sum 03	Win 04	Total
# from school taking bar for the first time	51	20	71	44	12	56
School's pass rate for all first-time takers	71%	95%	77%	84%	83%	84%
State's pass rate for all first-time takers	77%	84%	79%	81%	72%	79%

The information on these pages was provided by the law school

Northern Kentucky University—Salmon P. Chase College of Law

Nunn Hall
Highland Heights, KY 41099
Phone: 859.572.6476; Fax: 859.572.6081
E-mail: beersk@nku.edu; Website: www.nku.edu/~chase

■ Introduction

The Salmon P. Chase College of Law, founded in 1893, is now located in Nunn Hall on the main campus of Northern Kentucky University, a learner-centered metropolitan university in a thriving legal and business community just seven miles south of Cincinnati, Ohio. Accredited by the American Bar Association and a member of the Association of American Law Schools, Chase offers full-time and part-time, day and evening programs.

■ Library and Learning Environment

Chase students have access to the law library 24 hours a day, 7 days a week. Students may access the library's electronic resources in the legal information technology lab or throughout the building via the library's wireless network. The library provides access to a wide range of online resources including Hein Online, LexisNexis, Westlaw, e-mail, CALI exercises, and many other web-based products.

Nunn Hall's two courtrooms are equipped with state-of-the-art video and computer technology. Numerous classrooms are also technologically enhanced.

■ Curriculum

The curriculum consists of required courses, core courses, and elective courses. Ninety credit hours are required to graduate. Fifty-two hours are in required courses. Full-time students may complete the program in three years, while part-time students generally complete the program in four years. A five-year part-time option has recently been added. Chase has a number of academic support and development programs designed to enhance the law school experience.

■ Joint-Degree Program

Chase offers a Juris Doctor/Master of Business Administration (JD/MBA) degree program. This program is an attractive alternative for individuals who wish to practice law and/or business in an increasingly complex environment. Courses in the College of Law serve as electives for the MBA degree, and specific MBA courses serve as electives for the law degree. Thus, the number of hours required to obtain both degrees through the combined program is less than the number of hours required to complete each degree separately.

■ Special Programs

The **Clinical Extern Program** aids law students in the development of practical legal skills through work experience in supervised governmental and nonprofit organization legal settings. Opportunities include placements with state and federal judges, prosecutors, public defenders, legal aid programs, and various governmental agencies. Students also participate in a weekly roundtable discussion and classroom component.

Through the **Federal Trial Practice Seminar**, students serve as law clerks for a United States District Court judge or magistrate. Students conduct legal research and prepare bench memoranda on legal issues pending before the court. Students participate in weekly discussions with the judges or magistrates regarding issues before the court.

IOLTA Public Interest Fellowships enable a number of students each year to serve in paid fellowships with local public interest organizations, Northern Kentucky Legal Aid, and the Children's Law Center.

The **IRS Chief Counsel Externships and Chase Tax Clinic** are excellent opportunities for students interested in practicing in the area of taxation.

Working on the **Kentucky Innocence Project**, students assist the Kentucky Department of Public Advocacy (DPA) by investigating and possibly litigating claims of innocence from state and federal prisoners. The clinic focuses on the discovery and analysis of new evidence, especially DNA evidence. Participants are placed in the field and work directly under the supervision of DPA attorneys.

The **Local Government Law Center** externships provide a unique clinical opportunity in which students handle actual cases in government and nonprofit agencies throughout Kentucky. Externships are individually tailored to meet each student's background, experience, and career interest. Past placements include the Kentucky Governor's Office, the Kentucky Attorney General's Office, the Kentucky Supreme Court, prosecutors, public defenders, legal aid societies, and state judges throughout Kentucky; Tri-County Economic Development Corporation; and the Kentucky General Assembly. Students participate in a weekly roundtable discussion and lecture series.

The **Summer Program for Legal Analysis** is a noncredit, voluntary workshop for entering Chase students devoted to helping students develop the skills necessary for success in law school. Participants receive intensive instruction in reading cases and analyzing legal materials.

Through the **Volunteer Income Tax Assistance Program** students assist low income, elderly, and disabled taxpayers in filing state and federal tax returns under the direction of a full-time faculty member specializing in the area of taxation.

■ Admission

Chase seeks to admit those applicants who have the best prospect of high-quality academic work; thus, the

Northern Kentucky University—Salmon P. Chase College of Law

Admission Committee relies heavily on the applicant's undergraduate grades and performance on the LSAT during the application review process. Additional factors considered include upward trend of undergraduate grades; time between college graduation and application to Chase; college grading and course selection patterns; outside work while in college; letters of recommendation; graduate study; cultural, educational, or sociological deprivation; employment background; leadership ability; speaking or linguistic ability; and demonstrated competence in another profession or vocation. Chase seeks diversity in the student body by considering, in no particular order, sex, age, cultural or geographic background, and minority status. First-year students enter in the fall semester.

■ Student Activities

The *Northern Kentucky Law Review* is published by Chase students and includes scholarly legal writings by law professors, practitioners, jurists, and students. Chase has a prestigious moot court program, with teams competing successfully in national and other competitions. Chase's National Trial Advocacy Team competes in state and national mock trial competitions. The Student Bar Association sponsors professional, social, and community service events, and selects students to participate on several faculty committees. Chase has chapters of the American Constitution Society, the American Trial Lawyers Association, the Black American Law Students Association, Delta Theta Phi, the Federalist Society, the Law Student Division of the American Bar Association, and Phi Alpha Delta. Other groups include the Salmon P. Chase Inn of Court, the Chase Public Interest Group, the Appalachian Law Society, the Christian Legal Society, the International Law Society, and the Women's Law Caucus.

■ Career Development

The Career Development Office assists students in career planning and in the development of employment seeking skills. The office schedules fall and spring on-campus interviews, posts job notices weekly, and holds seminars to prepare students for the job market. The Alumni Career Options Days, held annually in conjunction with the Chase Alumni Association, enable Chase students to network with alumni representing a wide variety of legal specialties.

Applicant Profile

Northern Kentucky University—Salmon P. Chase College of Law
This grid includes only applicants who earned 120-180 LSAT scores under standard administrations.

LSAT Score	GPA 3.75 +		3.50 - 3.74		3.25 - 3.49		3.00 - 3.24		2.75 - 2.99		2.50 - 2.74		2.25 - 2.49		2.00 - 2.24		Below 2.00		No GPA		Total	
	Apps	Adm	Apps	Adm	Apps	Adm	Apps	Adm	Apps	Adm	Apps	Adm	Apps	Adm	Apps	Adm	Apps	Adm	Apps	Adm	Apps	Adm
175-180	0	0	0	0	0	0	0	0	0	0	0	0	0	0	0	0	0	0	0	0	0	0
170-174	0	0	0	0	0	0	0	0	0	0	0	0	0	0	0	0	0	0	0	0	0	0
165-169	3	2	0	0	0	0	2	2	0	0	0	0	0	0	0	0	0	0	0	0	5	4
160-164	5	4	10	9	4	4	2	2	9	7	4	4	2	1	1	1	0	0	1	0	38	32
155-159	14	12	28	27	25	25	32	24	18	12	20	11	9	8	4	3	0	0	3	1	151	122
150-154	44	32	49	38	54	36	71	50	35	19	28	17	16	7	3	1	2	0	5	0	305	201
145-149	18	7	37	14	54	11	64	10	48	8	27	3	14	3	4	0	0	0	5	0	272	56
140-144	6	0	14	1	16	0	15	3	15	0	16	0	14	0	6	0	0	0	4	0	106	4
135-139	4	0	8	0	3	1	11	0	11	0	6	0	6	0	3	0	0	0	0	0	52	1
130-134	0	0	0	0	0	0	2	0	3	0	2	0	5	0	2	0	2	0	0	0	16	0
125-129	0	0	0	0	1	0	0	0	1	0	1	0	0	0	1	0	0	0	1	0	5	0
120-124	0	0	0	0	0	0	0	0	0	0	0	0	0	0	0	0	0	0	0	0	0	0
Total	94	57	146	89	157	77	199	91	140	46	104	35	66	19	24	5	5	0	15	1	950	420

Apps = Number of Applicants
Adm = Number Admitted
Reflects 99% of the total applicant pool.

Northwestern University School of Law

357 East Chicago Avenue
Chicago, IL 60611-3069
Phone: 312.503.3100; Fax: 312.503.0178
E-mail: nulawadm@law.northwestern.edu; Website: www.law.northwestern.edu

The Basics

Type of school	Private
Term	Semester
Application deadline	12/1 2/15
Application fee	$80
Financial aid deadline	2/15
Can first year start other than fall?	No
Student to faculty ratio (fall)	12.5 to 1
Does the university offer:	
housing restricted to law students?	No
graduate housing for which law students are eligible?	Yes

Faculty and Administrators

	Total		Men		Women		Minorities	
	Fall	Spr	Fall	Spr	Fall	Spr	Fall	Spr
Full-time	52	52	38	38	14	14	4	4
Other Full-time	39	40	5	6	34	34	5	5
Deans, librarians, & others who teach	9	9	6	6	3	3	1	1
Part-time	54	66	45	47	9	19	2	11
Total	154	167	94	97	60	70	12	21

Curriculum

	Full-time	Part-time
Typical first-year section size	65	0
Is there typically a "small section" of the first-year class, other than Legal Writing, taught by full-time faculty	No	No
If yes, typical size offered last year	0	0
# of classroom course titles beyond 1st year curriculum	200	

# of upper division courses, excluding seminars with an enrollment:		
Under 25	67	
25-49	55	
50-74	10	
75-99	12	
100+	1	

# of seminars	61	
# of seminar positions available	1,494	
# of seminar positions filled	1,039	0
# of positions available in simulation courses	456	
# of simulation positions filled	397	0
# of positions available in faculty supervised clinical courses	201	
# of faculty supervised clinical positions filled	195	0
# involved in field placements	166	0
# involved in law journals	216	0
# involved in moot court or trial competitions	82	0
# of credit hours required to graduate	86	

JD Enrollment and Ethnicity

	Men		Women		Full-time		Part-time		1st-year		Total		JD Degs. Awd.
	#	%	#	%	#	%	#	%	#	%	#	%	
African Amer.	18	4.5	34	9.0	52	6.7	0	0.0	20	8.2	52	6.7	17
Amer. Indian	1	0.2	2	0.5	3	0.4	0	0.0	2	0.8	3	0.4	2
Asian Amer.	43	10.7	70	18.6	113	14.5	0	0.0	37	15.1	113	14.5	24
Mex. Amer.	31	7.7	25	6.6	56	7.2	0	0.0	16	6.5	56	7.2	15
Puerto Rican	1	0.2	0	0.0	1	0.1	0	0.0	1	0.4	1	0.1	0
Hispanic	0	0.0	0	0.0	0	0.0	0	0.0	0	0.0	0	0.0	0
Total Minority	94	23.3	131	34.7	225	28.8	0	0.0	76	31.0	225	28.8	58
For. Nation.	10	2.5	18	4.8	28	3.6	0	0.0	7	2.9	28	3.6	0
Caucasian	240	59.6	184	48.8	424	54.4	0	0.0	133	54.3	424	54.4	64
Unknown	59	14.6	44	11.7	103	13.2	0	0.0	29	11.8	103	13.2	102
Total	403	51.7	377	48.3	780	100.0	0	0.0	245	31.4	780		224

Tuition and Fees

	Resident	Nonresident
Full-time	$35,896	$35,896
Part-time	$0	$0

Living Expenses

Estimated living expenses for singles

Living on campus	Living off campus	Living at home
$23,076	$23,076	$23,076

Northwestern University School of Law

*ABA
Approved
Since
1923*

GPA and LSAT Scores

	Total	Full-time	Part-time
# of apps	4,802	4,802	0
# of admits	774	774	0
# of matrics	245	245	0
75% GPA	3.78	3.78	0.00
25% GPA	3.47	3.47	0.00
75% LSAT	170	170	0
25% LSAT	166	166	0

Grants and Scholarships (from prior year)

	Total		Full-time		Part-time	
	#	%	#	%	#	%
Total # of students	732		732		0	
Total # receiving grants	300	41.0	300	41.0	0	0.0
Less than 1/2 tuition	193	26.4	193	26.4	0	0.0
Half to full tuition	107	14.6	107	14.6	0	0.0
Full tuition	0	0.0	0	0.0	0	0.0
More than full tuition	0	0.0	0	0.0	0	0.0
Median grant amount			$15,000		$0	

Informational and Library Resources

# of volumes and volume equivalents	734,669
# of titles	304,825
# of active serial subscriptions	5,371
Study seating capacity inside the library	644
# of professional librarians	9
Hours per week library is open	105
# of open, wired connections available to students	211
# of networked computers available for use by students	100
# of simultaneous wireless users	650
Require computer?	Y

JD Attrition (from prior year)

	Academic	Other	Total	
	#	#	#	%
1st year	0	3	3	1.2%
2nd year	0	5	5	1.9%
3rd year	0	0	0	0.0%
4th year	0	0	0	0.0%

Employment

	Total	Percentage
Employment status known	228	100.0
Employment status unknown	0	0.0
Employed	217	95.0
Pursuing graduate degrees	2	0.9
Unemployed seeking employment	1	0.0
Unemployed not seeking employment	8	3.5

Type of Employment

# employed in law firms	158	73.1
# employed in business and industry	11	5.1
# employed in government	7	3.2
# employed in public interest	4	1.9
# employed as judicial clerks	35	16.2
# employed in academia	1	0.5

Geographic Location

# employed in state	95	44.0
# employed in foreign countries	5	2.3
# of states where employed		24

Bar Passage Rates

Jurisdiction		Illinois		
Exam		Sum 03	Win 04	Total
# from school taking bar for the first time		117	8	125
School's pass rate for all first-time takers		97%	100%	98%
State's pass rate for all first-time takers		86%	78%	84%

Northwestern University School of Law

357 East Chicago Avenue
Chicago, IL 60611-3069
Phone: 312.503.3100; Fax: 312.503.0178
E-mail: nulawadm@law.northwestern.edu; Website: www.law.northwestern.edu

■ Introduction

Northwestern University School of Law, founded in 1859, advances the understanding of law and produces graduates prepared to excel in a rapidly changing world. Northwestern uniquely blends a rigorous intellectual environment within a collegial and supportive community. With one of the lowest student-faculty ratios in the country, students have unusually close contact with full-time professors who are noted scholars.

The law school's lakefront location in the heart of downtown Chicago provides a wealth of part-time employment options for students while in school and a spectacular setting in which to study law. Northwestern's proximity to courts, commerce, and public interest activities enables students to experience the practice of law as well as its theory.

■ Enrollment and Admission

By limiting the total JD enrollment, the law school maintains a close-knit and supportive community that fosters friendships among students and faculty. Northwestern seeks students diverse in experience, background, and perspective. The Admissions Committee considers many factors beyond test scores and GPAs when evaluating applicants. More than 90 percent enter with at least one year of full-time work experience. Through its unique interviewing program, the law school is able to attract not only students with strong academic credentials but also those with the interpersonal skills and maturity needed to thrive in Northwestern's community.

■ Faculty

The faculty is composed of nationally recognized scholars, diverse in background and perspective, whose research and writing make major contributions to important academic and public policy debates. Northwestern professors have a passion for teaching and for engaging students in theoretical and practical legal applications.

The faculty includes scholars with advanced degrees in economics, history, philosophy, and political science as well as law. It includes a former chairman of the Securities and Exchange Commission; a leading expert on race, gender, and the law; the first American attorney to argue before the European Court of Human Rights; and the senior author of the most widely used casebook on American legal history. The full-time faculty is supplemented by a distinguished group of adjunct professors who teach a wide variety of specialized courses.

■ Curriculum

In the rigorous first year of study, Northwestern provides a superior foundation in legal reasoning, analysis, and writing as well as a thorough understanding of the structures and policies of the law. Communication, collaborative learning, teamwork, and cross-training in business are also hallmarks of Northwestern.

The law school's size enables students to have one-on-one relationships with professors. Required first-year courses are taught in sections of approximately 60 students. The JD program requires 86 semester hours of credit and can ordinarily be completed in three years, although permission can be given for a four-year program.

The broad and flexible curriculum gives upper-level students the opportunity to specialize in particular areas and to pursue advanced research in legal theory or to pursue a range of hands-on simulation and live-client opportunities. The Owen L. Coon/James A. Rahl Senior Research Program enables third-year students to do individual research under the supervision of a professor, using library, field, and interdisciplinary research methods.

■ Special Degree Programs

A combined program in law and business is offered with Northwestern's Kellogg School of Management in which students earn both a JD from the law school and an MBA degree from Kellogg after only three years of study. Students may also enroll in a joint JD/PhD program with the law school and one of the social sciences departments. In a joint program with Northwestern's Medill School of Journalism, non-JD students interested in reporting about the law and legal institutions can earn both a master of science in journalism (MSJ) degree and a master of studies in law (MSL) degree.

Students who wish to specialize in the study of tax law can earn an LLM in Taxation. Students educated outside the United States can earn an LLM through a nine-month program of advanced study or an LLM degree and a certificate in business administration from Kellogg through a 12-month program in law and business. Legal and business professionals in Korea can earn an LLM degree from Northwestern through an Executive LLM Program that commences each March in Seoul, Korea.

■ Legal Clinics

In Northwestern's comprehensive clinical program, students learn strong litigation and negotiation skills and gain direct experience with representing clients and reforming laws.

The innovative simulation-based curriculum, including the **Program on Advocacy and Professionalism** and the **Program on Negotiation and Mediation**, gives students the skills they need to negotiate and communicate effectively, solve problems, prepare briefs, examine witnesses, present evidence, and argue cases.

Students represent impoverished clients as well as challenge the fairness of our legal institutions and propose solutions for reform. Working in teams, they prepare cases in juvenile justice, immigration and asylum, and criminal matters. In addition to fine-tuning their skills as advocates, they often effect change in the law and legal institutions. **Bluhm Legal Clinic** centers—**Bartlit Center for Trial Strategy, Children and Family Justice Center, Small Business Opportunity Center, Center for International Human Rights, Center on Wrongful Convictions**—are nationally recognized for their direct involvement in legal reform.

■ Library and Physical Facilities

With more than a half million volumes and access to a wide range of electronic resources, the Pritzker Legal Research Center is one of the country's largest law libraries.

Wireless technology and Ethernet connections are available throughout the law school. Most large classrooms are equipped with smart podiums including video projection and Internet connections. The law school's three interconnected buildings along Chicago's lakefront also house the national headquarters of the American Bar Foundation.

■ Student Activities

Northwestern students take an intense and energetic interest in their community and education. Five scholarly journals are available for research, writing, and editing. Students automatically belong to the Student Bar Association, which gives them a voice in curriculum and administration, and they have an opportunity to participate in more than 30 student organizations. Students also enjoy the benefits of living, studying, and working in one of the most vibrant legal and business communities in the world.

■ Expenses and Financial Aid

The law school annually awards $4.5 million in grants and scholarships in addition to long-term, low-interest institutional loans. These resources enable the law school to cover 100 percent of a student's calculated financial need. Approximately 85 percent of the students currently enrolled are receiving financial aid.

■ Career Services

The Center for Career Strategy and Advancement staff aggressively cultivates relationships with potential employers while assisting students in focusing their goals and developing short- and long-term career strategies. In the fall of 2004, more than 700 national employers recruited our students. In recent years, approximately 75 percent of the recruiters were based in regions outside the Midwest. In 2003, about half of our students chose to remain in the Midwest.

Applicant Profile

At Northwestern, emphasis on teamwork, communication, and interpersonal skills begins during the admission process in which every applicant is urged to interview. Currently about 70 percent of applicants are interviewed and college seniors must be interviewed. We also place a heavy emphasis on work experience, which contributes to an environment where students learn a great deal from not only faculty but also each other.

Notre Dame Law School

112 Law School
Notre Dame, IN 46556-0959
Phone: 574.631.6626; Fax: 574.631.5474
E-mail: lawadmit@nd.edu; Website: www.lawadmissions.nd.edu

ABA
Approved
Since
1925

The Basics

Type of school	Private
Term	Semester
Application deadline	11/1 1/15 3/1
Application fee	$55
Financial aid deadline	1/15
Can first year start other than fall?	No
Student to faculty ratio (fall)	15.6 to 1
Does the university offer:	
housing restricted to law students?	No
graduate housing for which law students are eligible?	Yes

Faculty and Administrators

	Total		Men		Women		Minorities	
	Fall	Spr	Fall	Spr	Fall	Spr	Fall	Spr
Full-time	28	30	21	20	7	10	3	2
Other Full-time	1	1	0	0	1	1	0	0
Deans, librarians, & others who teach	16	16	10	10	6	6	1	1
Part-time	33	36	22	20	11	16	2	1
Total	78	83	53	50	25	33	6	4

Curriculum

	Full-time	Part-time
Typical first-year section size	91	0
Is there typically a "small section" of the first-year class, other than Legal Writing, taught by full-time faculty	No	No
If yes, typical size offered last year	0	0
# of classroom course titles beyond 1st year curriculum	116	

# of upper division courses, excluding seminars with an enrollment:		
	Under 25	73
	25-49	33
	50-74	13
	75-99	8
	100+	1

# of seminars	22	
# of seminar positions available	361	
# of seminar positions filled	277	0
# of positions available in simulation courses	224	
# of simulation positions filled	201	0
# of positions available in faculty supervised clinical courses	89	
# of faculty supervised clinical positions filled	80	0
# involved in field placements	26	0
# involved in law journals	143	0
# involved in moot court or trial competitions	78	0
# of credit hours required to graduate	90	

JD Enrollment and Ethnicity

	Men		Women		Full-time		Part-time		1st-year		Total		JD Degs. Awd.
	#	%	#	%	#	%	#	%	#	%	#	%	
African Amer.	14	4.5	18	7.4	32	5.8	0	0.0	12	6.7	32	5.8	4
Amer. Indian	1	0.3	3	1.2	4	0.7	0	0.0	2	1.1	4	0.7	1
Asian Amer.	18	5.8	20	8.2	38	6.9	0	0.0	13	7.3	38	6.9	10
Mex. Amer.	6	1.9	2	0.8	8	1.4	0	0.0	3	1.7	8	1.4	2
Puerto Rican	4	1.3	2	0.8	6	1.1	0	0.0	3	1.7	6	1.1	1
Hispanic	15	4.9	11	4.5	26	4.7	0	0.0	8	4.5	26	4.7	10
Total Minority	58	18.8	56	23.0	114	20.6	0	0.0	41	23.0	114	20.6	28
For. Nation.	1	0.3	6	2.5	7	1.3	0	0.0	1	0.6	7	1.3	2
Caucasian	242	78.3	175	71.7	417	75.4	0	0.0	121	68.0	417	75.4	136
Unknown	8	2.6	7	2.9	15	2.7	0	0.0	15	8.4	15	2.7	0
Total	309	55.9	244	44.1	553	100.0	0	0.0	178	32.2	553		166

Tuition and Fees

	Resident	Nonresident
Full-time	$30,140	$30,140
Part-time	$0	$0

Living Expenses

Estimated living expenses for singles

Living on campus	Living off campus	Living at home
$11,800	$11,800	$11,800

Notre Dame Law School

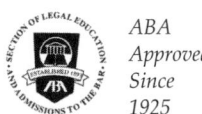

*ABA
Approved
Since
1925*

GPA and LSAT Scores

	Total	Full-time	Part-time
# of apps	3,773	3,773	0
# of admits	516	516	0
# of matrics	178	178	0
75% GPA	3.77	3.77	0.00
25% GPA	3.26	3.26	0.00
75% LSAT	167	167	0
25% LSAT	162	162	0

Grants and Scholarships (from prior year)

	Total		Full-time		Part-time	
	#	%	#	%	#	%
Total # of students	552		552		0	
Total # receiving grants	349	63.2	349	63.2	0	0.0
Less than 1/2 tuition	219	39.7	219	39.7	0	0.0
Half to full tuition	110	19.9	110	19.9	0	0.0
Full tuition	17	3.1	17	3.1	0	0.0
More than full tuition	3	0.5	3	0.5	0	0.0
Median grant amount			$11,250		$0	

Informational and Library Resources

# of volumes and volume equivalents	619,347
# of titles	197,502
# of active serial subscriptions	6,742
Study seating capacity inside the library	416
# of professional librarians	9
Hours per week library is open	95
# of open, wired connections available to students	116
# of networked computers available for use by students	88
# of simultaneous wireless users	570
Require computer?	N

JD Attrition (from prior year)

	Academic	Other	Total	
	#	#	#	%
1st year	0	8	8	4.4%
2nd year	1	2	3	1.5%
3rd year	1	0	1	0.6%
4th year	0	0	0	0.0%

Employment

	Total	Percentage
Employment status known	173	97.7
Employment status unknown	4	2.3
Employed	166	96.0
Pursuing graduate degrees	4	2.3
Unemployed seeking employment	3	1.7
Unemployed not seeking employment	0	0.0

Type of Employment

# employed in law firms	114	68.7
# employed in business and industry	7	4.2
# employed in government	15	9.0
# employed in public interest	3	1.8
# employed as judicial clerks	25	15.1
# employed in academia	2	1.2

Geographic Location

# employed in state	19	11.4
# employed in foreign countries	3	1.8
# of states where employed	34	

Bar Passage Rates

Jurisdiction	Illinois			Indiana		
Exam	Sum 03	Win 04	Total	Sum 03	Win 04	Total
# from school taking bar for the first time	32	6	38	19	4	23
School's pass rate for all first-time takers	97%	100%	97%	95%	100%	96%
State's pass rate for all first-time takers	86%	78%	84%	79%	76%	79%

Notre Dame Law School

Admissions Office, 112 Law School
Notre Dame, IN 46556-0959
Phone: 574.631.6626; Fax: 574.631.5474
E-mail: lawadmit@nd.edu; Website: www.lawadmissions.nd.edu

■ Introduction

With a rich history that dates to its founding in 1869, Notre Dame Law School today enjoys a national and international reputation for preparing consummate professionals—men and women who are extraordinarily competent in their professional endeavors and who commit themselves to serve their clients and the profession effectively and honorably. Distinctive among nationally regarded law schools as a result of the school's and the university's Catholic heritage and tradition, faith and values, and community spirit, the Law School inspires students to examine their practice of law within the context of their responsibilities as members of the bar, as leaders within their respective fields, and as citizens of the world community.

Graduates of the Law School enjoy an impressive career-placement record and achieve success in a variety of challenging and rewarding careers. In recent years, six alumni have clerked for justices of the United States Supreme Court. The typical class graduating from Notre Dame is employed in 30–35 states in positions ranging from public interest law to practice in the nation's most prominent law firms.

■ Enrollment/Student Body

The student body represents the national stature and international nature of the programs of the Law School and the university. Our student body of approximately 575 students represent all states and a number of foreign countries. The small size of the student body fosters a sense of community and allows significant interaction between faculty and students.

■ Faculty

Faculty members come to the Notre Dame Law School with extensive experience in private practice and government service, and represent a wide range of undergraduate institutions, law schools, and state bars. Members of the faculty are well regarded for their commitment to teaching and their accessibility to students outside of the classroom. Notre Dame law faculty support students' professional development through active counseling, mentoring, and advising.

■ Library and Physical Facilities

The Kresge Law Library is among the top tier of American law school research libraries. The library is considered a national leader in legal research techniques using automated technology. The Law School provides significant computing support for students and other members of the Law School community. A staff of five, full-time professionals offers assistance with both hardware and software, in addition to other computing and technology needs.

■ Curriculum

The JD curriculum provides a strong foundation in those areas that have proven to be fundamental to the actual practice of law in every American jurisdiction, while giving students the opportunity to tailor coursework to particular career aspirations. Required courses, those that are critical to a mastery of specialized areas of the law, total 42 of the 90 credit hours needed for graduation. In addition to the JD degree, the Law School confers three graduate law degrees: an LLM in International and Comparative Law, an LLM in International Human Rights, and a JSD (also in International Human Rights). The LLM in International and Comparative Law is offered exclusively at the Law School's London Law Centre.

■ London Programs

Notre Dame Law School recognizes that today's legal practice increasingly involves matters of international law.

JD candidates may augment their legal education by participating in one of two programs offered by the Law School through its London Law Centre. Second-year students who wish to immerse themselves in comparative and international law, as well as in the traditions of the American and British common-law systems, can study in the only year-long overseas program offered by an American law school. Students who desire a shorter international-study experience and who have completed their first year of law school can spend six weeks in London during Notre Dame's summer program.

■ Admission

Notre Dame offers both an Early Decision and a Regular Decision Program. The Early Decision Program is designed for those candidates who have researched other law schools and who are committed to enrolling at Notre Dame if admitted. The application deadline for applying via Early Decision is November 1. Early decision applicants will be notified of an admission decision by December 15. The Regular Decision Program follows a "rolling admissions" process. Regular decision applicants are encouraged to apply at the earliest possible date. Candidates who apply January 15 or earlier are charged a reduced application fee of $55. Candidates whose applications are postmarked January 16 or later must pay a $70 application fee. March 1 is the deadline for submitting an application.

Student Life

The sense of community and the quality of student life at Notre Dame have developed out of long-standing traditions that make the Notre Dame Law School experience different: admission policies that emphasize the importance of qualitative factors such as service to others; a mission that focuses on teaching, scholarship, and service in the legal and Judeo-Christian traditions; and an emphasis on forming and nurturing collegial relationships among and between students and faculty. The Law School building is centrally located on the Notre Dame campus and law students fully participate in athletic, cultural, religious, and social events on the campus. Law students also manage to find a comfortable balance between their studies and involvement in the Law School's four law journals and any of 25 organizations that reflect and respond to the professional and personal interests of the student body.

Expenses and Financial Aid

Notre Dame is committed to providing a legal education of the highest quality at a tuition structure that compares favorably to other nationally regarded private law schools. Additionally, law students benefit from the low cost of living in northern Indiana.

Fellowship assistance is provided annually to 90–95 entering students on the basis of merit, commitment to the Law School's mission, and financial need.

Fellowships range from $5,000 to $25,000 and are renewable for all three years of legal study.

Housing

Many single law students choose to live on campus in graduate-student housing. Married students with children can live in the unfurnished University Village apartments. Students who wish to live off campus can find reasonably priced accommodations near the campus and can secure on-campus parking for a nominal additional charge.

Career Services

Graduates of Notre Dame Law School find success in identifying and obtaining a spectrum of rewarding and satisfying careers in all areas of the nation and abroad. For recent graduating classes, the employment rate has ranged between 96 and 100 percent within six months of graduation. Each year, approximately 250 employers visit campus to interview Notre Dame law students. These employers, and others, are interested in interviewing Notre Dame law students because of the law school's reputation for preparing extraordinarily competent lawyers.

A national network of over 7,900 law school alumni and friends assist students and graduates in finding employment opportunities across the country.

Applicant Profile

We do not provide a profile chart of applicants considered and admitted because admission decisions are made based on the whole-person concept. Academic ability reflected in LSAT scores and grade-point averages is, of course, important. However, it is recognized that the real meaning of a GPA will vary with the quality of the institution attended, rigor of courses selected, and degree of grade inflation. The committee considers a broad array of elements in addition to the essential factors of LSAT and GPA with a view toward assembling a diverse class while at the same time arriving at a fair appraisal of the individual applicant.

Notre Dame Law School officials involved in the admission process are mindful of the school's objective to produce lawyers who are both competent and compassionate. Admission decisions are inevitably the result of selecting a relatively small class from a large number of highly qualified applicants.

Nova Southeastern University—Shepard Broad Law Center

3305 College Avenue
Fort Lauderdale, FL 33314-7721
Phone: 954.262.6117; Fax: 954.262.3844
E-mail: admission@nsu.law.nova.edu; Website: www.nsulaw.nova.edu

ABA
Approved
Since
1975

The Basics

Type of school	Private
Term	Semester
Application deadline	3/1
Application fee	$50
Financial aid deadline	4/1
Can first year start other than fall?	No
Student to faculty ratio (fall)	15.3 to 1
Does the university offer:	
housing restricted to law students?	No
graduate housing for which law students are eligible?	Yes

Faculty and Administrators

	Total		Men		Women		Minorities	
	Fall	Spr	Fall	Spr	Fall	Spr	Fall	Spr
Full-time	49	51	24	26	25	25	8	8
Other Full-time	5	5	0	0	5	5	3	3
Deans, librarians, & others who teach	6	6	3	3	3	3	2	2
Part-time	56	44	41	34	15	10	6	7
Total	116	106	68	63	48	43	19	20

Curriculum

	Full-time	Part-time
Typical first-year section size	54	62
Is there typically a "small section" of the first-year class, other than Legal Writing, taught by full-time faculty	No	No
If yes, typical size offered last year	0	0
# of classroom course titles beyond 1st year curriculum	131	
# of upper division courses, excluding seminars with an enrollment: Under 25	161	
25-49	39	
50-74	23	
75-99	7	
100+	3	
# of seminars	19	
# of seminar positions available	380	
# of seminar positions filled	196	45
# of positions available in simulation courses	1,659	
# of simulation positions filled	1,100	222
# of positions available in faculty supervised clinical courses	180	
# of faculty supervised clinical positions filled	50	29
# involved in field placements	200	15
# involved in law journals	123	21
# involved in moot court or trial competitions	76	16
# of credit hours required to graduate	90	

JD Enrollment and Ethnicity

	Men		Women		Full-time		Part-time		1st-year		Total		JD Degs. Awd.
	#	%	#	%	#	%	#	%	#	%	#	%	
African Amer.	13	2.7	55	11.5	46	6.0	22	11.4	19	5.4	68	7.1	27
Amer. Indian	0	0.0	2	0.4	2	0.3	0	0.0	1	0.3	2	0.2	1
Asian Amer.	13	2.7	16	3.3	26	3.4	3	1.6	6	1.7	29	3.0	9
Mex. Amer.	2	0.4	5	1.0	7	0.9	0	0.0	2	0.6	7	0.7	2
Puerto Rican	6	1.2	12	2.5	14	1.8	4	2.1	2	0.6	18	1.9	14
Hispanic	71	14.7	97	20.3	116	15.1	52	26.9	61	17.2	168	17.4	64
Total Minority	105	21.7	187	39.0	211	27.4	81	42.0	91	25.7	292	30.3	117
For. Nation.	5	1.0	6	1.3	9	1.2	2	1.0	1	0.3	11	1.1	5
Caucasian	358	74.0	277	57.8	530	68.8	105	54.4	249	70.3	635	65.9	206
Unknown	16	3.3	9	1.9	20	2.6	5	2.6	13	3.7	25	2.6	3
Total	484	50.3	479	49.7	770	80.0	193	20.0	354	36.8	963		331

Tuition and Fees

	Resident	Nonresident
Full-time	$23,873	$23,873
Part-time	$17,905	$17,905

Living Expenses

Estimated living expenses for singles

Living on campus	Living off campus	Living at home
$11,588	$14,771	$6,719

Nova Southeastern University—Shepard Broad Law Center

ABA Approved Since 1975

GPA and LSAT Scores

	Total	Full-time	Part-time
# of apps	2,908	0	0
# of admits	746	0	0
# of matrics	359	299	60
75% GPA	3.29	3.32	3.17
25% GPA	2.79	2.79	2.72
75% LSAT	152	152	153
25% LSAT	147	148	146

Grants and Scholarships (from prior year)

	Total #	Total %	Full-time #	Full-time %	Part-time #	Part-time %
Total # of students	998		791		207	
Total # receiving grants	176	17.6	128	16.2	48	23.2
Less than 1/2 tuition	110	11.0	69	8.7	41	19.8
Half to full tuition	3	0.3	1	0.1	2	1.0
Full tuition	56	5.6	53	6.7	3	1.4
More than full tuition	7	0.7	5	0.6	2	1.0
Median grant amount			$10,000		$5,000	

Informational and Library Resources

# of volumes and volume equivalents	354,205
# of titles	146,268
# of active serial subscriptions	5,554
Study seating capacity inside the library	535
# of professional librarians	9
Hours per week library is open	104
# of open, wired connections available to students	170
# of networked computers available for use by students	37
# of simultaneous wireless users	1,200
Require computer?	Y

JD Attrition (from prior year)

	Academic #	Other #	Total #	Total %
1st year	23	27	50	14.9%
2nd year	8	6	14	4.7%
3rd year	0	0	0	0.0%
4th year	0	0	0	0.0%

Employment

	Total	Percentage
Employment status known	252	82.6
Employment status unknown	53	17.4
Employed	211	83.7
Pursuing graduate degrees	6	2.4
Unemployed seeking employment	33	13.1
Unemployed not seeking employment	2	0.8

Type of Employment

# employed in law firms	122	57.8
# employed in business and industry	32	15.2
# employed in government	37	17.5
# employed in public interest	2	0.9
# employed as judicial clerks	5	2.4
# employed in academia	2	0.9

Geographic Location

# employed in state	184	87.2
# employed in foreign countries	1	0.5
# of states where employed	9	

Bar Passage Rates

Jurisdiction	Florida		
Exam	Sum 03	Win 04	Total
# from school taking bar for the first time	191	88	279
School's pass rate for all first-time takers	60%	55%	58%
State's pass rate for all first-time takers	76%	75%	76%

The information on these pages was provided by the law school

Nova Southeastern University—Shepard Broad Law Center

3305 College Avenue
Fort Lauderdale, FL 33314-7721
Phone: 954.262.6117; Fax: 954.262.3844
E-mail: admission@nsu.law.nova.edu; Website: www.nsulaw.nova.edu

■ Introduction

NSU Law Center is one of 20 graduate and professional schools of Nova Southeastern University, the largest private independent university in Florida and the 10th largest in the US. NSU Law is accredited by the ABA and is a member of the AALS. The Law Center is located in the suburbs of Fort Lauderdale, in the heart of South Florida's fast-growing Broward, Miami-Dade, Palm Beach area. We encourage applicants to tour the campus and speak with the staff of the Admission Office.

■ Two Admission Programs

The Law Center's Admissions Committee oversees two separate programs. The Regular Admission Program combines each applicant's undergraduate grades and LSAT score according to a weighted formula based on the academic success of NSU Law students. The committee also values the applicant's personal statement, writing sample, work experience, and letters of recommendation. While no single factor is determinative, if the LSAT/UGPA combination does not demonstrate the promise of academic achievement, an applicant is unlikely to be offered regular admission.

Selected applicants who are denied regular admission will be offered the opportunity to earn admission to the Law Center by successful performance in NSU Law's unique Alternative Admission Model Program for Legal Education (AAMPLE®). In 25 years of AAMPLE's operation, more than 1,000 students have qualified for admission. AAMPLE students who enroll in an eight-week summer session and earn a C+ average in the two courses are offered admission to the Law Center. AAMPLE is presented in two formats, the traditional on-campus program and a new and innovative online model.

Approximately one-third of our applicants are offered seats through the Regular Admission Program. Another 15 percent are invited to the AAMPLE Program. Traditionally, about half of the AAMPLE students who complete the program qualify for admission. Applicants are encouraged to review the charts that follow this narrative to evaluate the likelihood of being admitted to the Law Center via the Regular Admission or the AAMPLE Program. NSU Law's two admission programs produce a diverse student body. Recent classes are about evenly divided between men and women, with approximately one-third of the class members of minority groups. The average age of first-year day students is 24; of evening students, 29.

The Admissions Committee awards full tuition scholarships to approximately 10 percent of students admitted through the Regular Admission Program on the basis of academic merit.

■ Faculty

NSU Law professors have a long tradition of teaching excellence. The faculty's open-door policy is enhanced by our sophisticated electronic communications system, accessible all through NSU Law's pioneering wireless and laptop program. Limits on the size of first-year sections results in more individualized feedback. The faculty's expertise is reflected in rich classroom discussion and a wide range of scholarly publications and professional service activities.

■ Curriculum and Special Academic-Professional Programs

The Law Center offers a rigorous traditional academic program in three-year day and four-year evening versions. NSU Law prides itself on preparing graduates to make a smooth transition from the classroom to the courtroom or boardroom.

Lawyering Skills and Values (LSV)—Every student completes a five-semester LSV sequence that combines traditional legal reasoning, writing, and research with an introduction to lawyer interviewing, counseling, negotiating, mediating, advocating, and other critical skills in a simulated law firm experience.

Guaranteed Clinical Semester—NSU students are *guaranteed* a full-semester clinic in their final year. In seven clinical programs, students are introduced to a practice specialty under the guidance of a seasoned mentor. Each clinical semester begins with three weeks of intensive classes that focus on advanced substantive law and lawyering skills in the clinic specialty plus an interdisciplinary workshop. For the rest of the term, students are placed in practice settings where faculty supervise their representation of clients. Students are placed in Law Center Clinics or in public and private law offices throughout Florida, across the country, or around the world.

Dual Law Degree Opportunities—NSU Law students can earn a civil law degree from the University of Barcelona in accelerated study programs. NSU students who complete the University of Barcelona program can qualify to practice in the US and Spain.

Joint Degrees—NSU Law offers students opportunities to earn a second graduate degree in a complementary discipline and in a compressed time frame.

Internship—In addition to an award-winning pro bono service program, the Law Center operates judicial internship, mediation, street law, and Guardian Ad Litem programs that provide valuable real-world experiences.

Nova Southeastern University—Shepard Broad Law Center

■ Library and Physical Facilities

The Law Center's spacious, modern building includes state-of-the-art information technology. The first law school facility with a wireless technology system and an early advocate of mandatory laptops for all students, NSU Law leads the way in the use of computers in legal education. While most classrooms have power at each desk, the latest long-life batteries permit all students to connect with classmates, professors, the library, and the Internet from any point in the building.

The Law Library's extensive holdings include special collections in tax, criminal law, law and popular culture, admiralty, and international law. The library is a depository for state, federal, and United Nations documents.

Goodwin Hall, the Law Center's building, has two courtrooms used by students in our trial advocacy and moot court program, by National Institute for Trial Advocacy, and by state appellate court judges.

■ Student Activities

The Law Center is home to four significant publications: the *Nova Law Review*; the *Journal of International and Comparative Law*; the *International Travel Law Journal*; and the *International Citator and Research Guide*.

The Moot Court Society sponsors a national invitational as well as intramural competitions. Members of the society compete in major national events. ATLA and other student advocacy groups field teams in competitions around the country.

Students shape the life of the Law Center by their involvement in a wide range of service organizations and social clubs. Groups such as APALSA, BLSA, JLSA, HLSA, Lambda, Student Bar Association, Florida Association for Women Lawyers, National Association for Public Interest Law, International Law Society, and a variety of practice specialty and sports clubs are extremely active. Students also guide chapters of national legal fraternities, participate with lawyers and judges in the Inns of Court, and serve on faculty committees.

■ Career Services

Our Career Development Office assists students and alumni with career counseling and the employment process. In addition to facilitating on-campus interviews and résumé distributions, the director coordinates career-option seminars and interviewing workshops. The office also sponsors skill courses and assists students in finding pro bono experiences with law firms and legal agencies throughout the country.

Applicant Profile

Nova Southeastern University—Shepard Broad Law Center

LSAT Score	GPA								
	3.75 +	3.50 - 3.74	3.25 - 3.49	3.00 - 3.24	2.75 - 2.99	2.50 - 2.74	2.25 - 2.49	2.00 - 2.24	Below 2.00
165-180									
160-164									
155-159									
150-154									
145-149									
140-144									
135-139									
130-134									
Below 130									

Good Possibility   Possible   Unlikely

Please use this chart as a general guide in determining admission chances for the Regular Admission Program. Nonnumerical factors are also considered during the file-evaluation process.

AAMPLE®

Enrolled/Successful

LSAT Score	GPA								
	3.75 +	3.50 - 3.74	3.25 - 3.49	3.00 - 3.24	2.75 - 2.99	2.50 - 2.74	2.25 - 2.49	2.00 - 2.24	Below 2.00
150-154							1/1	1/1	1/0
145-149	2/0	9/7	7/5	20/9	16/7	8/4	12/3	2/0	
140-144	1/0	8/2	13/4	21/4	17/5	16/4	6/0	1/0	
135-139		2/1	3/2	1/0	1/0	4/1			
130-134					1/0				

Please use this chart to determine the possibility of being admitted through AAMPLE® (Alternative Admission Model Program for Legal Education). The chart reflects admission data for the summer 2004 on-campus AAMPLE class and a portion of the online AAMPLE class. The traditional indicators (LSAT and GPA) are not identified for the online AAMPLE students who were referred to NSU Law by the LSAC. Overall, there were 118 students enrolled online and 17 were successful in 2004.

Ohio Northern University—Claude W. Pettit College of Law

525 South Main Street
Ada, OH 45810
Phone: 877.452.9668, 419.772.2211; Fax: 419.772.3042
E-mail: law-admissions@onu.edu; Website: www.law.onu.edu

*ABA
Approved
Since
1948*

The Basics

Type of school	Private
Term	Semester
Application deadline	
Application fee	$40
Financial aid deadline	6/1
Can first year start other than fall?	No
Student to faculty ratio (fall)	14.0 to 1
Does the university offer:	
housing restricted to law students?	Yes
graduate housing for which law students are eligible?	Yes

Faculty and Administrators

	Total		Men		Women		Minorities	
	Fall	Spr	Fall	Spr	Fall	Spr	Fall	Spr
Full-time	19	18	13	12	6	6	1	1
Other Full-time	0	0	0	0	0	0	0	0
Deans, librarians, & others who teach	6	6	4	4	2	2	0	0
Part-time	7	6	5	3	2	3	0	0
Total	32	30	22	19	10	11	1	1

Curriculum

	Full-time	Part-time
Typical first-year section size	65	0
Is there typically a "small section" of the first-year class, other than Legal Writing, taught by full-time faculty	No	No
If yes, typical size offered last year	0	0
# of classroom course titles beyond 1st year curriculum	52	
# of upper division courses, excluding seminars with an enrollement: Under 25	69	
25-49	16	
50-74	7	
75-99	0	
100+	0	
# of seminars	8	
# of seminar positions available	96	
# of seminar positions filled	75	0
# of positions available in simulation courses	88	
# of simulation positions filled	82	0
# of positions available in faculty supervised clinical courses	60	
# of faculty supervised clinical positions filled	57	0
# involved in field placements	22	0
# involved in law journals	21	0
# involved in moot court or trial competitions	30	0
# of credit hours required to graduate	87	

JD Enrollment and Ethnicity

	Men		Women		Full-time		Part-time		1st-year		Total		JD Degs. Awd.
	#	%	#	%	#	%	#	%	#	%	#	%	
African Amer.	7	4.4	12	7.6	19	6.0	0	0.0	5	4.2	19	6.0	4
Amer. Indian	0	0.0	1	0.6	1	0.3	0	0.0	0	0.0	1	0.3	0
Asian Amer.	1	0.6	4	2.5	5	1.6	0	0.0	2	1.7	5	1.6	0
Mex. Amer.	0	0.0	0	0.0	0	0.0	0	0.0	0	0.0	0	0.0	0
Puerto Rican	0	0.0	0	0.0	0	0.0	0	0.0	0	0.0	0	0.0	0
Hispanic	2	1.3	2	1.3	4	1.3	0	0.0	0	0.0	4	1.3	1
Total Minority	10	6.3	19	12.0	29	9.1	0	0.0	7	5.9	29	9.1	5
For. Nation.	0	0.0	0	0.0	0	0.0	0	0.0	0	0.0	0	0.0	1
Caucasian	149	93.1	139	88.0	288	90.6	0	0.0	111	94.1	288	90.6	75
Unknown	1	0.6	0	0.0	1	0.3	0	0.0	0	0.0	1	0.3	0
Total	160	50.3	158	49.7	318	100.0	0	0.0	118	37.1	318		81

Tuition and Fees

	Resident	Nonresident
Full-time	$22,790	$0
Part-time	$0	$0

Living Expenses

Estimated living expenses for singles

Living on campus	Living off campus	Living at home
$10,300	$11,340	$6,690

Ohio Northern University—Claude W. Pettit College of Law

*ABA
Approved
Since
1948*

GPA and LSAT Scores

	Total	Full-time	Part-time
# of apps	1,540	1,540	0
# of admits	424	424	0
# of matrics	120	120	0
75% GPA	3.62	3.62	0.00
25% GPA	3.02	3.02	0.00
75% LSAT	156	156	0
25% LSAT	149	149	0

Grants and Scholarships (from prior year)

	Total		Full-time		Part-time	
	#	%	#	%	#	%
Total # of students	294		294		0	
Total # receiving grants	138	46.9	138	46.9	0	0.0
Less than 1/2 tuition	62	21.1	62	21.1	0	0.0
Half to full tuition	70	23.8	70	23.8	0	0.0
Full tuition	6	2.0	6	2.0	0	0.0
More than full tuition	0	0.0	0	0.0	0	0.0
Median grant amount			$12,000		$0	

Informational and Library Resources

# of volumes and volume equivalents	352,995
# of titles	88,523
# of active serial subscriptions	2,226
Study seating capacity inside the library	319
# of professional librarians	4
Hours per week library is open	113
# of open, wired connections available to students	230
# of networked computers available for use by students	53
# of simultaneous wireless users	800
Require computer?	N

JD Attrition (from prior year)

	Academic	Other	Total	
	#	#	#	%
1st year	7	10	17	13.3%
2nd year	0	0	0	0.0%
3rd year	0	0	0	0.0%
4th year	0	0	0	0.0%

Employment

	Total	Percentage
Employment status known	70	97.2
Employment status unknown	2	2.8
Employed	66	94.3
Pursuing graduate degrees	2	2.9
Unemployed seeking employment	2	2.9
Unemployed not seeking employment	0	0.0

Type of Employment

# employed in law firms	40	60.6
# employed in business and industry	6	9.1
# employed in government	9	13.6
# employed in public interest	1	1.5
# employed as judicial clerks	6	9.1
# employed in academia	2	3.0

Geographic Location

# employed in state	23	34.8
# employed in foreign countries	0	0.0
# of states where employed		22

Bar Passage Rates

Jurisdiction		Ohio		
Exam		Sum 03	Win 04	Total
# from school taking bar for the first time		26	2	28
School's pass rate for all first-time takers		73%	100%	75%
State's pass rate for all first-time takers		81%	72%	79%

Ohio Northern University—Claude W. Pettit College of Law

525 South Main Street
Ada, OH 45810
Phone: 877.452.9668, 419.772.2211; Fax: 419.772.3042
E-mail: law-admissions@onu.edu; Website: www.law.onu.edu

■ Introduction

Men and women have been studying law at Ohio Northern University for well over a century. Since 1885, generations of law students have found the Claude W. Pettit College of Law the ideal place to begin remarkable careers in private practice, public service, business, and industry.

Located in the heart of Ohio, the college sits on a beautiful campus with facilities that reflect well over a century of investment. The college offers its students opportunities to study law in small classes, seminars, clinical programs, law offices, and judges' chambers.

■ The College and University

The Claude W. Pettit College of Law is accredited by the American Bar Association and is a member of the Association of American Law Schools. The college is centered in newly renovated Tilton Hall, a modern building that houses all law classes and the Taggart Law Library. Recent additions to this building include a second trial courtroom, a state-of-the-art computer lab, sky-lit student lounges, and a faculty office wing where students are always welcome.

The Taggart Law Library, a federal government depository, is devoted to the research needs of the students and faculty of the law college. The current collection numbers 352,995 volumes. The library has computer and communication facilities that are second to none and an extensive collection of books and periodicals acquired over decades. The reading rooms of the library offer ideal locations for both quiet and group study.

The College of Law lies at the center of the tree-lined campus. The university's facilities are readily available to all law students and are located only steps away from the law building. These facilities include hiking and biking trails, a sports center, and the Freed Center for the Performing Arts. Law students may bowl, swim, and play handball, racquet sports, and basketball all year round in indoor and outdoor facilities. The Sports Center houses a wide variety of modern fitness machines and one of the best indoor tracks in the Midwest. The Freed Center brings the very best in the performing arts to the campus.

■ Faculty and Students

The faculty of the College of Law strives for excellence in both teaching and scholarship. All faculty members have practiced law, bringing a wealth of practical experience gained from law firms, corporate law departments, and government to the classroom. The faculty also maintains a high level of scholarly productivity and professional service.

Small classes and personalized attention are the hallmarks of the college. First-year classes are generally limited to 60 or fewer students. Enrollment in upper-division classes and seminars is often even smaller. The faculty prides itself on offering a student-centered education. Members of the faculty meet regularly with students outside the classroom.

The students of the college bring remarkably diverse backgrounds and interests to the study of law. The college draws students from across the nation and the world. Students from virtually every state in the union have entered the college. The law students currently enrolled in the college have degrees from more than 200 undergraduate colleges and universities.

■ The Curriculum and Special Programs

Students may choose from more than 67 elective courses, including advanced courses and seminars. In addition, the College of Law offers many opportunities for experiential learning through its clinical education program. The clinical experiences available to Ohio Northern students include externships in environmental law, bankruptcy, and government. Students can also counsel nonprofit corporations in the Transactional Clinic. Legal Aid Clinics that focus on the concerns of the economically disadvantaged and elderly are offered at offices in nearby Lima and Findlay. Finally, students can also participate in Criminal and Judicial Externships with judges, legal aid societies, public defenders' offices, and prosecutors' offices.

The College of Law shares a student exchange program with the law school at the University of Iceland. Participating students travel to Iceland to experience its culture and legal system.

The College of Law has an academic support program to assist all students in attaining their full academic potential.

Throughout the academic year, the college hosts speakers and symposia on contemporary legal issues. Topics treated recently include capital punishment, affirmative action, and the revolution in federal and state relations.

The College of Law offers a Summer Starter program for a small number of selected students. These individuals begin taking first-year law courses the summer prior to the regular school year and receive academic support on a weekly basis. In the fall, summer starters take the remaining first-year courses not completed during the summer.

■ Student Activities

Students can choose from a variety of extracurricular activities. The College of Law publishes the *Ohio Northern University Law Review*, a student-edited commentary on legal issues whose excellence has been recognized by the Ohio Supreme Court.

Intraschool, regional, and national moot court competitions are open to all students. Ohio Northern students participate in at least 10 national and regional moot court competitions each year.

Through the Student Bar Association, students participate in a variety of extracurricular activities such as the environmental law and international law societies. Students volunteer their services through the Street Law and Volunteer Income Tax Assistance Programs.

■ Admission and Financial Aid

While Ohio Northern gives significant weight to the LSAT and undergraduate GPA, the Admissions Committee may consider other factors such as candidates' undergraduate programs, grade trends, completion of other graduate degrees, professional accomplishments, and socioeconomic or cultural barriers faced by the applicant. Although letters of recommendation are not required, letters from persons who have a basis to assess the candidate's intellectual ability and potential for success in law school, such as former professors or employers, are strongly recommended.

Ohio Northern University is committed to a culturally and socially diverse student body. Applications from women and minorities are strongly encouraged. In order to foster diversity in the student body and the legal profession, the university awards grants-in-aid to eligible students.

The College of Law also provides scholarship awards for students whose undergraduate records demonstrate academic excellence. The scholarship amounts range from $5,000 to $22,000 and are renewable provided the student remains in good academic standing. Additionally, substantial scholarships are awarded to students who excel in their first year of law school.

The facilities of the College of Law are accessible to physically disabled students.

■ Student Services and Housing

The staff of the College of Law takes pride in the quality of its student services. The size of the college permits these services to be tailored to the individual needs of each student. Through individualized counseling, students and graduates obtain valuable guidance in obtaining summer jobs and permanent positions. The Office of Career Strategies assists in the application and interviewing processes; provides current listings of positions in law firms, governmental agencies, and corporations; and hosts on-campus interviews.

Housing is generally available to law students in the university's apartments. Most law students live off-campus. Listings of available apartments can be obtained from the admission office. Visit the Pettit College of Law website at *www.law.onu.edu*. Better still, call the admission office to arrange a campus tour at 877.452.9668.

Applicant Profile

Ohio Northern University—Claude W. Pettit College of Law
This grid includes only applicants who earned 120-180 LSAT scores under standard administrations.

LSAT Score	GPA								
	3.75 +	3.50 - 3.74	3.25 - 3.49	3.00 - 3.24	2.75 - 2.99	2.50 - 2.74	2.25 - 2.49	2.00 - 2.24	Below 2.00
175-180									
170-174									
165-169									
160-164									
155-159									
150-154									
145-149									
140-144									
135-139									
130-134									
125-129									
120-124									

■ Very Likely　　□ Possible　　▨ Unlikely

The Ohio State University Moritz College of Law

John Deaver Drinko Hall, 55 West 12th Avenue
Columbus, OH 43210-1391
Phone: 614.292.8810; Fax: 614.292.1492
E-mail: lawadmit@osu.edu; Website: www.moritzlaw.osu.edu

ABA Approved Since 1923

The Basics

Type of school	Public
Term	Semester
Application deadline	3/1
Application fee	$40
Financial aid deadline	3/1
Can first year start other than fall?	No
Student to faculty ratio (fall)	15.2 to 1
Does the university offer: housing restricted to law students?	No
graduate housing for which law students are eligible?	Yes

Faculty and Administrators

	Total Fall	Total Spr	Men Fall	Men Spr	Women Fall	Women Spr	Minorities Fall	Minorities Spr
Full-time	41	42	29	28	12	14	8	8
Other Full-time	4	4	3	3	1	1	0	0
Deans, librarians, & others who teach	13	12	4	3	9	9	4	4
Part-time	15	18	11	12	4	6	0	2
Total	**73**	**76**	**47**	**46**	**26**	**30**	**12**	**14**

Curriculum

	Full-time	Part-time
Typical first-year section size	70	0
Is there typically a "small section" of the first-year class, other than Legal Writing, taught by full-time faculty	Yes	No
If yes, typical size offered last year	40	0
# of classroom course titles beyond 1st year curriculum	130	
# of upper division courses, excluding seminars with an enrollment: Under 25	30	
25-49	38	
50-74	17	
75-99	6	
100+	6	
# of seminars	23	
# of seminar positions available	460	
# of seminar positions filled	334	0
# of positions available in simulation courses	124	
# of simulation positions filled	98	0
# of positions available in faculty supervised clinical courses	176	
# of faculty supervised clinical positions filled	153	0
# involved in field placements	72	0
# involved in law journals	169	0
# involved in moot court or trial competitions	122	0
# of credit hours required to graduate	88	

JD Enrollment and Ethnicity

	Men #	Men %	Women #	Women %	Full-time #	Full-time %	Part-time #	Part-time %	1st-year #	1st-year %	Total #	Total %	JD Degs. Awd.
African Amer.	17	4.3	37	10.6	54	7.2	0	0.0	20	8.4	54	7.2	14
Amer. Indian	2	0.5	0	0.0	2	0.3	0	0.0	0	0.0	2	0.3	0
Asian Amer.	29	7.3	37	10.6	66	8.8	0	0.0	29	12.2	66	8.8	10
Mex. Amer.	7	1.8	2	0.6	9	1.2	0	0.0	5	2.1	9	1.2	0
Puerto Rican	0	0.0	2	0.6	2	0.3	0	0.0	0	0.0	2	0.3	0
Hispanic	13	3.3	9	2.6	22	2.9	0	0.0	8	3.4	22	2.9	7
Total Minority	68	17.0	87	25.0	155	20.7	0	0.0	62	26.2	155	20.7	31
For. Nation.	6	1.5	8	2.3	14	1.9	0	0.0	4	1.7	14	1.9	0
Caucasian	316	79.2	243	69.8	559	74.8	0	0.0	152	64.1	559	74.8	178
Unknown	9	2.3	10	2.9	19	2.5	0	0.0	19	8.0	19	2.5	0
Total	399	53.4	348	46.6	747	100.0	0	0.0	237	31.7	747		209

Tuition and Fees

	Resident	Nonresident
Full-time	$14,405	$27,237
Part-time	$0	$0

Living Expenses

Estimated living expenses for singles

Living on campus	Living off campus	Living at home
$13,856	$13,856	$13,856

The Ohio State University Moritz College of Law

*ABA
Approved
Since
1923*

GPA and LSAT Scores

	Total	Full-time	Part-time
# of apps	2,268	2,268	0
# of admits	634	634	0
# of matrics	237	237	0
75% GPA	3.77	3.77	0.00
25% GPA	3.32	3.32	0.00
75% LSAT	162	162	0
25% LSAT	156	156	0

Grants and Scholarships (from prior year)

	Total		Full-time		Part-time	
	#	%	#	%	#	%
Total # of students	727		727		0	
Total # receiving grants	560	77.0	560	77.0	0	0.0
Less than 1/2 tuition	442	60.8	442	60.8	0	0.0
Half to full tuition	76	10.5	76	10.5	0	0.0
Full tuition	6	0.8	6	0.8	0	0.0
More than full tuition	36	5.0	36	5.0	0	0.0
Median grant amount			$6,500		$0	

Informational and Library Resources

# of volumes and volume equivalents	776,639
# of titles	174,521
# of active serial subscriptions	8,263
Study seating capacity inside the library	689
# of professional librarians	9
Hours per week library is open	107
# of open, wired connections available to students	0
# of networked computers available for use by students	62
# of simultaneous wireless users	1,240
Require computer?	N

JD Attrition (from prior year)

	Academic	Other	Total	
	#	#	#	%
1st year	0	7	7	2.6%
2nd year	0	0	0	0.0%
3rd year	0	2	2	0.9%
4th year	0	0	0	0.0%

Employment

	Total	Percentage
Employment status known	211	96.3
Employment status unknown	8	3.7
Employed	193	91.5
Pursuing graduate degrees	11	5.2
Unemployed seeking employment	5	2.4
Unemployed not seeking employment	2	0.9

Type of Employment

# employed in law firms	114	59.1
# employed in business and industry	21	10.9
# employed in government	31	16.1
# employed in public interest	5	2.6
# employed as judicial clerks	19	9.8
# employed in academia	3	1.6

Geographic Location

# employed in state	134	69.4
# employed in foreign countries	4	2.1
# of states where employed	20	

Bar Passage Rates

Jurisdiction		Ohio	
Exam	Sum 03	Win 04	Total
# from school taking bar for the first time	160	10	170
School's pass rate for all first-time takers	92%	80%	91%
State's pass rate for all first-time takers	81%	72%	79%

The Ohio State University Moritz College of Law

John Deaver Drinko Hall, 55 West 12th Avenue
Columbus, OH 43210-1391
Phone: 614.292.8810; Fax: 614.292.1492
E-mail: lawadmit@osu.edu; Website: www.moritzlaw.osu.edu

■ Introduction

Founded in 1891, the Ohio State University Moritz College of Law has played a leading role in the legal profession through countless contributions made by graduates and faculty. The administration of the College of Law is committed to advancing the quality and reputation of the college through ongoing improvements to the academic program and student services, thereby creating a learning environment second to none.

Ohio State's 8,500 law alumni are central to the college's national reputation. Graduates of the college include justices of the Ohio Supreme Court, current and former US Senators and Representatives, managing partners in law firms, chief executive officers, professors, and attorneys with nonprofit organizations and public interest law firms.

The comprehensive scope of the university and its location in the state capital provide law students with access to a wealth of educational, professional, cultural, and recreational resources and opportunities. Law students are able to pursue joint degrees with one of the university's more than 100 graduate programs and also may extern with federal and state judges or find employment with one of the more than 500 law firms located in central Ohio.

■ Academic Program

With approximately 135 classes offered annually, Ohio State students have a rich array of courses from which to choose. The curriculum is designed to provide a strong theoretical and analytical foundation, as well as multiple opportunities for developing and honing lawyering skills.

Alternative Dispute Resolution—The College of Law is widely regarded as having one of the nation's finest programs in the area of Alternative Dispute Resolution. The program emphasizes training in an array of dispute resolution methods beyond litigation, including negotiation, mediation, and arbitration. Students with an especially strong interest may want to serve as a member or editor of the *Ohio State Journal on Dispute Resolution* or pursue a certificate in Dispute Resolution.

Clinical Opportunities—The College of Law offers an extensive selection of clinics in civil, criminal, children's issues, housing, mediation, and legislation. Students enrolled in a clinic course receive the benefit of working with real clients, the court, or other parties while receiving intensive feedback and supervision from one of the college's 15 clinical faculty. The fieldwork component of each clinic course is augmented by a classroom component in which topics such as lawyering skills, legal doctrine, and ethical and strategic issues are addressed.

Judicial Externship Program—Ohio State law students have the opportunity to gain first-hand insight into the judicial system through the college's Judicial Externship Program. As externs, students earn academic credit for conducting legal research and drafting legal documents for justices of the Ohio Supreme Court and for judges at the federal and county levels.

A Global Perspective on the Law—Students with an interest in international law may select from a menu of approximately 16 courses that have an international law or comparative law focus, including a summer study-abroad program in Oxford, England. The College of Law awards a Certificate in International Trade and Development to students who combine their law coursework with select courses in international economics, politics, history, culture, and foreign language.

■ Faculty

One of the most frequently cited strengths of the College of Law is the quality of the faculty. Faculty members consistently are recognized for the experiences they bring to the classroom, for the clarity of their teaching, and for their accessibility to students outside of the classroom. As a group, they are highly regarded for being committed teachers who care about students. Members of the Ohio State law faculty also have earned a reputation within the profession for their expertise in specific areas of the law. Faculty are regularly cited in court and in the national media; they serve on legal reform commissions, help draft model statutes, and provide testimony before Congress.

■ Moritz Law Library

The Moritz Law Library provides Ohio State law students with the 14th largest collection among law school libraries in the nation and access to a vast array of electronic databases. Law students with a laptop and network card can tap into online resources from virtually any point within the Moritz Law Library or the law building. All classrooms are wired for use of laptop computers.

■ Extracurricular Opportunities

Learning Outside of the Classroom—Recognizing that a student's legal education rests upon what occurs in the classroom as well as the intellectual interchange and professional development outside of the classroom, the College of Law strives to provide an environment that is rich with extracurricular and cocurricular opportunities. Each year, the college brings to campus more than 100 speakers to address students, law faculty, and members of the bar.

Ohio State law students have the opportunity to refine their legal writing skills through participation in one of the college's three highly regarded law journals, the *Ohio State Law Journal*, the *Ohio State Journal on Dispute Resolution*, and the *Ohio State Journal of Criminal Law*. Students are able to refine their skills in the areas of oral advocacy and legal writing through a variety of intramural and interscholastic competitions. In recent years, Ohio State law students have competed in the National Moot Court Competition, the Jessup International Law Competition, the Frederick Douglass Moot Court Competition, the National Health Law Competition, the National Environmental Law Competition, and the National Tax Competition.

Service to the Public—The College of Law enjoys a strong reputation for its commitment to public service as part of the educational mission of the college. Ohio State law students are encouraged to become involved in one or more of the college's many public interest initiatives, such as the ProBono Research Group. To encourage Ohio State law students to accept low-paying or volunteer positions with public interest organizations during the summer, the college and the Public Interest Law Foundation annually offers several student-funded fellowships.

■ Placement Opportunities

Moritz College of Law students and graduates are provided an array of career and professional development services by a staff of six full- and part-time professionals, three of whom have a JD. Students and alumni have access to an Internet-based online job posting system and a wide variety of programs, workshops, and events. All programming and counseling services are designed to teach skills and to provide a foundation for gaining legal and professional career experience. The on-campus

recruiting program, which brings over 120 employers to campus to interview students annually, is conducted through a state-of-the-art web-based recruiting system that allows students access at all hours. Alumni and practitioners interact with students through many avenues, including a practice interview program and a mentoring database. Each year, students find employment across the country. Cutting-edge technology, current resources, talented staff, and creative initiatives give College of Law students a sound professional development foundation.

■ Admission and Financial Aid

The Moritz College of Law is committed to enrolling highly motivated men and women who have excelled academically and who bring to the College of Law a diversity of personal and professional backgrounds. In selecting members of each entering class, the Admissions Committee seeks to enroll men and women who represent all segments of society, as well as those who, as attorneys, will respect the profession's public service obligations.

An Ohio State legal education is among the best values among nationally regarded law schools. The annual cost of tuition for residents of Ohio is below half the tuition charged by comparably ranked private law schools. Nonresidents of Ohio who relocate to the state may be reclassified as Ohio residents after residing in the state for 12 months. Each year, the College of Law awards more than $1.7 million in need-based and merit-based financial aid to members of the student body.

Applicant Profile

The Ohio State University Moritz College of Law
This grid includes only applicants who earned 120-180 LSAT scores under standard administrations.

LSAT Score	GPA 3.75 +		3.50 - 3.74		3.25 - 3.49		3.00 - 3.24		2.75 - 2.99		2.50 - 2.74		2.25 - 2.49		2.00 - 2.24		Below 2.00		No GPA		Total	
	Apps	Adm	Apps	Adm	Apps	Adm	Apps	Adm	Apps	Adm	Apps	Adm	Apps	Adm	Apps	Adm	Apps	Adm	Apps	Adm	Apps	Adm
175-180	1	1	0	0	3	3	1	1	1	1	0	0	0	0	0	0	0	0	0	0	6	6
170-174	8	8	4	4	1	1	2	2	1	1	1	0	2	1	0	0	0	0	0	0	19	17
165-169	47	47	30	29	17	17	16	12	12	8	6	2	1	1	0	0	0	0	0	0	129	116
160-164	83	80	107	94	90	67	55	29	33	10	12	1	2	0	1	0	0	0	2	1	385	282
155-159	126	47	202	33	183	25	92	10	51	3	30	2	10	0	1	0	0	0	8	2	703	122
150-154	101	16	97	7	127	9	88	9	44	3	20	1	14	0	3	0	1	0	4	1	499	46
145-149	26	5	53	4	69	9	54	4	32	4	19	0	8	0	5	0	2	0	2	0	270	26
140-144	16	2	19	5	21	1	25	2	24	0	14	0	11	0	1	0	0	0	4	0	135	10
135-139	3	0	5	0	8	0	15	0	13	0	7	0	5	0	1	0	0	0	3	0	60	0
130-134	1	0	0	0	3	0	2	0	2	0	5	0	2	0	0	0	0	0	2	0	17	0
125-129	0	0	0	0	0	0	0	0	0	0	0	0	1	0	0	0	0	0	2	0	3	0
120-124	0	0	0	0	0	0	0	0	0	0	0	0	0	0	0	0	0	0	0	0	0	0
Total	412	206	517	176	522	132	350	69	213	30	114	6	56	2	12	0	3	0	27	4	2226	625

Apps = Number of Applicants   Adm = Number Admitted   Reflects 99% of total applicant pool.

University of Oklahoma College of Law

Andrew M. Coats Hall, 300 Timberdell Road
Norman, OK 73019
Phone: 405.325.4726; Fax: 405.325.0502
E-mail: law-admissions@ou.edu; Website: www.law.ou.edu

ABA Approved Since 1923

The Basics

Type of school	Public
Term	Semester
Application deadline	3/15 3/15
Application fee	$50
Financial aid deadline	3/1
Can first year start other than fall?	No
Student to faculty ratio (fall)	16.0 to 1
Does the university offer:	
housing restricted to law students?	No
graduate housing for which law students are eligible?	Yes

Faculty and Administrators

	Total		Men		Women		Minorities	
	Fall	Spr	Fall	Spr	Fall	Spr	Fall	Spr
Full-time	27	28	22	22	5	6	4	4
Other Full-time	7	7	2	2	5	5	0	0
Deans, librarians, & others who teach	5	5	3	3	2	2	1	1
Part-time	12	18	10	12	2	6	0	0
Total	51	58	37	39	14	19	5	5

Curriculum

		Full-time	Part-time
Typical first-year section size		43	0
Is there typically a "small section" of the first-year class, other than Legal Writing, taught by full-time faculty		No	No
If yes, typical size offered last year		0	0
# of classroom course titles beyond 1st year curriculum		119	
# of upper division courses, excluding seminars with an enrollment:	Under 25	55	
	25-49	32	
	50-74	14	
	75-99	4	
	100+	1	
# of seminars		13	
# of seminar positions available		222	
# of seminar positions filled		212	0
# of positions available in simulation courses		337	
# of simulation positions filled		328	0
# of positions available in faculty supervised clinical courses		57	
# of faculty supervised clinical positions filled	46		0
# involved in field placements		7	0
# involved in law journals		103	0
# involved in moot court or trial competitions	34		0
# of credit hours required to graduate		90	

JD Enrollment and Ethnicity

	Men		Women		Full-time		Part-time		1st-year		Total		JD Degs. Awd.
	#	%	#	%	#	%	#	%	#	%	#	%	
African Amer.	12	4.5	14	5.6	26	5.0	0	0.0	12	7.0	26	5.0	4
Amer. Indian	14	5.2	30	12.0	44	8.5	0	0.0	18	10.5	44	8.5	13
Asian Amer.	9	3.4	7	2.8	16	3.1	0	0.0	8	4.7	16	3.1	1
Mex. Amer.	4	1.5	6	2.4	10	1.9	0	0.0	5	2.9	10	1.9	3
Puerto Rican	0	0.0	0	0.0	0	0.0	0	0.0	0	0.0	0	0.0	0
Hispanic	1	0.4	0	0.0	1	0.2	0	0.0	1	0.6	1	0.2	0
Total Minority	40	14.9	57	22.7	97	18.7	0	0.0	44	25.7	97	18.7	21
For. Nation.	0	0.0	1	0.4	1	0.2	0	0.0	0	0.0	1	0.2	0
Caucasian	214	79.9	182	72.5	396	76.3	0	0.0	119	69.6	396	76.3	144
Unknown	14	5.2	11	4.4	25	4.8	0	0.0	8	4.7	25	4.8	6
Total	268	51.6	251	48.4	519	100.0	0	0.0	171	32.9	519		171

Tuition and Fees

	Resident	Nonresident
Full-time	$9,386	$18,652
Part-time	$0	$0

Living Expenses

Estimated living expenses for singles

Living on campus	Living off campus	Living at home
$13,091	$14,360	$9,639

University of Oklahoma College of Law

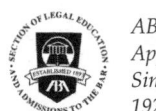

*ABA
Approved
Since
1923*

GPA and LSAT Scores

	Total	Full-time	Part-time
# of apps	1,307	1,307	0
# of admits	321	321	0
# of matrics	172	172	0
75% GPA	3.84	3.84	0.00
25% GPA	3.37	3.37	0.00
75% LSAT	160	160	0
25% LSAT	153	153	0

Grants and Scholarships (from prior year)

	Total		Full-time		Part-time	
	#	%	#	%	#	%
Total # of students	523		523		0	
Total # receiving grants	278	53.2	278	53.2	0	0.0
Less than 1/2 tuition	179	34.2	179	34.2	0	0.0
Half to full tuition	25	4.8	25	4.8	0	0.0
Full tuition	0	0.0	0	0.0	0	0.0
More than full tuition	74	14.1	74	14.1	0	0.0
Median grant amount			$1,938		$0	

Informational and Library Resources

# of volumes and volume equivalents	343,322
# of titles	138,168
# of active serial subscriptions	4,330
Study seating capacity inside the library	408
# of professional librarians	6
Hours per week library is open	96
# of open, wired connections available to students	111
# of networked computers available for use by students	102
# of simultaneous wireless users	512
Require computer?	N

JD Attrition (from prior year)

	Academic	Other	Total	
	#	#	#	%
1st year	2	12	14	8.1%
2nd year	0	2	2	1.2%
3rd year	0	1	1	0.6%
4th year	0	0	0	0.0%

Employment

	Total	Percentage
Employment status known	147	89.6
Employment status unknown	17	10.4
Employed	125	85.0
Pursuing graduate degrees	3	2.0
Unemployed seeking employment	15	10.2
Unemployed not seeking employment	4	2.7

Type of Employment

	Total	Percentage
# employed in law firms	77	61.6
# employed in business and industry	5	4.0
# employed in government	28	22.4
# employed in public interest	6	4.8
# employed as judicial clerks	5	4.0
# employed in academia	4	3.2

Geographic Location

	Total	Percentage
# employed in state	91	72.8
# employed in foreign countries	0	0.0
# of states where employed	11	

Bar Passage Rates

Jurisdiction	Oklahoma		
Exam	Sum 03	Win 04	Total
# from school taking bar for the first time	107	10	117
School's pass rate for all first-time takers	90%	100%	91%
State's pass rate for all first-time takers	82%	83%	82%

University of Oklahoma College of Law

Andrew M. Coats Hall, 300 Timberdell Road
Norman, OK 73019
Phone: 405.325.4726; Fax: 405.325.0502
E-mail: law-admissions@ou.edu; Website: www.law.ou.edu

■ Introduction

The University of Oklahoma College of Law is located on the main campus of the university in Norman, a city of approximately 100,000 adjacent to the Oklahoma City metropolitan area. The college was founded in 1909 and joined the membership of the Association of American Law Schools in 1911. The law school has been accredited by the American Bar Association's Section on Legal Education since that list was first published in 1923.

The College of Law is housed in beautiful Andrew M. Coats Hall, located on the south part of the university campus. A substantial addition to the existing building was completed in 2002. It has the largest law library in Oklahoma and houses three courtrooms for training prospective lawyers. The entering classes are limited to 175 students so that the first-year sections consist of not more that 45 students. Admission is very competitive. More than 90 percent of the students admitted will graduate. More than 90 percent will pass the bar exam on their first try, and more than 90 percent will have employment using their legal skills within three months of graduation.

The College of Law benefits from being part of a strong university community. The University of Oklahoma, the state's flagship university, is a major doctoral degree-granting research university. Founded in 1890, the university has 18 colleges.

■ Admission

The College of Law utilizes a rolling admission process. A faculty committee meets regularly throughout the academic year to review applications. Admission to the College of Law is highly competitive, and many factors are considered in the selection process. Although considerable weight is given to undergraduate grade-point average and performance on the LSAT, thoughtful attention is also given to an applicant's extracurricular activities, employment experience, graduate studies, military service, adjustments to personal difficulties, and other relevant factors.

In addition to the regular fall entering class, the College of Law conducts a special Early Admission Program each summer. Admission is offered to a select group of approximately 20 students whose statistical scores may not meet the current standards for regular admission but who have demonstrated a probable capacity for success in the study and practice of law. Students in the program receive six hours of credit for the summer study and then join the fall class.

■ International Programs

For the 31st year, the College of Law will conduct a summer program at Oxford University for American law students. The program affords students an opportunity to live and study in stimulating and beautiful surroundings under the guidance of American and English legal educators. Other opportunities exist for foreign study abroad in almost any country in which a student wishes to study.

■ Library and Physical Facilities

Andrew M. Coats Hall provides 170,000 square feet of instructional space for its programs. The modern facility contains Internet access and multimedia technology in classrooms, the library, and student areas. The building features three courtrooms, one of which has seating for 250 persons and is equipped with the latest in technological innovations. The library offers access to electronic web-based services and maintains over 350,000 volumes and equivalents and also contains one of the nation's largest Native People's collection.

■ Student Activities

The College of Law sponsors three major student-directed journals, the *Oklahoma Law Review*, the *American Indian Law Review*, and the newly created *Journal of Law and Technology*, which will focus on intellectual property law. Since 1948, the *Oklahoma Law Review* has been published quarterly to give expression to legal scholarship nationally and to serve the profession and the public with timely discussion of important legal issues.

The *American Indian Law Review*, published biannually, serves as a nationwide scholarly forum for the presentation of important developments in Indian law and affairs. The *Review* offers in-depth articles written by nationally recognized experts on a wide range of issues in the rapidly expanding field of Indian law.

The *Oklahoma Journal of Law and Technology* is a web based collection of important articles on the various aspects of intellectual property. The student board of editors continually monitors and updates the articles and other materials on the website.

The College of Law recently substantially expanded the opportunities for students to participate in a wide range of extracurricular interscholastic appellate moot court, counseling and interviewing, negotiation, and trial advocacy competitions. The student Board of Advocates works closely with the students to facilitate participation in those competitions and provide intramural competitions for 1L and upper-level students.

All students at the College of Law may join a wide variety of organizations and participate in many kinds of extracurricular activities. The law school has an active Student Bar Association, affiliated with the Law Student Division of the American Bar Association. The student elected Board of Governors supervise student activities and work with the faculty and administration of the law school.

■ Career Services

The College of Law's Career Services Office provides comprehensive professional planning and placement services to all students. The Director and the Assistant Dean for External Affairs work personally with students on the entire range of career development, including offering workshops on interviewing and résumé and cover letter writing; using web-based resources; on campus interview scheduling; and individual counseling.

The office works closely with law firms, government agencies, judges, and alumni around the country to expand employment opportunities for graduates.

Employment opportunities have continually expanded for University of Oklahoma law graduates, and the market placement has been very strong. In recent years, over 95 percent of graduates consistently are employed within nine months of graduation, ranking the College of Law among the upper echelon of schools nationally. Approximately two-thirds of the college's graduates practice in Oklahoma. The other one-third are found in all 50 states and 14 foreign countries, with concentrations in Texas, Washington, DC, and California. In addition to traditional legal careers as attorneys, prosecutors, and judges, University of Oklahoma law graduates work in areas such as corporate management, banking, journalism, public service, government, entrepreneurial enterprises, teaching, and academia.

Applicant Profile

University of Oklahoma College of Law
This grid includes only applicants who earned 120-180 LSAT scores under standard administrations.

LSAT Score	3.75 +		3.50 - 3.74		3.25 - 3.49		3.00 - 3.24		2.75 - 2.99		2.50 - 2.74		2.25 - 2.49		2.00 - 2.24		Below 2.00		No GPA		Total	
	Apps	Adm	Apps	Adm	Apps	Adm	Apps	Adm	Apps	Adm	Apps	Adm	Apps	Adm	Apps	Adm	Apps	Adm	Apps	Adm	Apps	Adm
175-180	0	0	1	1	0	0	0	0	1	1	0	0	0	0	1	0	0	0	0	0	3	2
170-174	3	3	2	1	4	3	0	0	1	1	0	0	0	0	0	0	0	0	0	0	10	8
165-169	17	17	9	9	4	3	4	1	2	0	0	0	1	0	0	0	0	0	1	0	38	30
160-164	38	34	23	20	26	19	10	2	18	4	11	1	6	0	0	0	0	0	0	0	132	80
155-159	49	37	72	39	65	18	60	9	28	1	19	4	6	0	0	0	0	0	1	0	300	108
150-154	58	25	95	19	97	13	84	8	56	0	23	0	7	0	1	0	0	0	4	0	425	65
145-149	23	4	46	8	60	4	44	0	26	0	23	0	15	0	4	0	1	0	2	0	244	16
140-144	8	1	6	0	23	1	21	0	20	0	15	0	2	0	2	0	3	0	7	0	107	2
135-139	1	0	4	0	6	0	7	0	9	0	5	0	4	0	3	0	1	0	2	0	42	0
130-134	0	0	1	0	3	0	2	0	1	0	2	0	2	0	2	0	0	0	1	0	14	0
125-129	1	0	0	0	0	0	0	0	0	0	2	0	0	0	0	0	0	0	2	0	5	0
120-124	0	0	0	0	0	0	0	0	0	0	0	0	0	0	0	0	0	0	0	0	0	0
Total	198	121	259	97	288	61	232	20	162	7	100	5	43	0	13	0	5	0	20	0	1320	311

Apps = Number of Applicants
Adm = Number Admitted
Reflects 99% of the total applicant pool.

Oklahoma City University School of Law

2501 North Blackwelder Avenue
Oklahoma City, OK 73106-1493
Phone: 800.633.7242 or 405.208.5354
E-mail: lawadmit@okcu.edu; Website: www.okcu.edu/law

ABA
Approved
Since
1960

The Basics

Type of school	Private
Term	Semester
Application deadline	8/1
Application fee	$50
Financial aid deadline	3/1
Can first year start other than fall?	No
Student to faculty ratio (fall)	21.5 to 1
Does the university offer:	
housing restricted to law students?	No
graduate housing for which law students are eligible?	Yes

Faculty and Administrators

	Total		Men		Women		Minorities	
	Fall	Spr	Fall	Spr	Fall	Spr	Fall	Spr
Full-time	24	23	18	17	6	6	3	3
Other Full-time	4	4	0	0	4	4	0	0
Deans, librarians, & others who teach	6	6	3	3	3	3	1	1
Part-time	18	29	13	20	5	9	1	2
Total	52	62	34	40	18	22	5	6

Curriculum

	Full-time	Part-time
Typical first-year section size	80	80
Is there typically a "small section" of the first-year class, other than Legal Writing, taught by full-time faculty	Yes	Yes
If yes, typical size offered last year	53	40
# of classroom course titles beyond 1st year curriculum	92	

# of upper division courses, excluding seminars with an enrollment:		
	Under 25	113
	25-49	21
	50-74	16
	75-99	9
	100+	0

# of seminars	9	
# of seminar positions available	152	
# of seminar positions filled	87	25
# of positions available in simulation courses	137	
# of simulation positions filled	105	16
# of positions available in faculty supervised clinical courses	87	
# of faculty supervised clinical positions filled	9	5
# involved in field placements	64	19
# involved in law journals	15	5
# involved in moot court or trial competitions	13	4
# of credit hours required to graduate	90	

JD Enrollment and Ethnicity

	Men		Women		Full-time		Part-time		1st-year		Total		JD Degs. Awd.
	#	%	#	%	#	%	#	%	#	%	#	%	
African Amer.	9	2.3	20	7.0	17	3.5	12	6.2	4	1.6	29	4.2	8
Amer. Indian	24	6.0	15	5.2	22	4.5	17	8.8	14	5.7	39	5.7	6
Asian Amer.	16	4.0	9	3.1	22	4.5	3	1.5	13	5.3	25	3.7	8
Mex. Amer.	16	4.0	16	5.6	21	4.3	11	5.7	9	3.7	32	4.7	0
Puerto Rican	0	0.0	0	0.0	0	0.0	0	0.0	0	0.0	0	0.0	0
Hispanic	0	0.0	0	0.0	0	0.0	0	0.0	0	0.0	0	0.0	3
Total Minority	65	16.4	60	20.9	82	16.7	43	22.2	40	16.3	125	18.3	25
For. Nation.	2	0.5	2	0.7	3	0.6	1	0.5	3	1.2	4	0.6	0
Caucasian	327	82.4	222	77.4	403	82.2	146	75.3	196	80.0	549	80.3	121
Unknown	3	0.8	3	1.0	2	0.4	4	2.1	6	2.4	6	0.9	0
Total	397	58.0	287	42.0	490	71.6	194	28.4	245	35.8	684		146

Tuition and Fees

	Resident	Nonresident
Full-time	$24,230	$24,230
Part-time	$16,400	$16,400

Living Expenses

Estimated living expenses for singles

Living on campus	Living off campus	Living at home
$12,540	$14,540	$14,540

Oklahoma City University School of Law

*ABA
Approved
Since
1960*

GPA and LSAT Scores

	Total	Full-time	Part-time
# of apps	1,587	1,389	198
# of admits	765	645	120
# of matrics	246	169	77
75% GPA	3.41	3.50	3.22
25% GPA	2.71	2.72	2.68
75% LSAT	153	154	152
25% LSAT	148	148	146

Grants and Scholarships (from prior year)

	Total		Full-time		Part-time	
	#	%	#	%	#	%
Total # of students	632		474		158	
Total # receiving grants	149	23.6	112	23.6	37	23.4
Less than 1/2 tuition	104	16.5	71	15.0	33	20.9
Half to full tuition	28	4.4	25	5.3	3	1.9
Full tuition	0	0.0	0	0.0	0	0.0
More than full tuition	17	2.7	16	3.4	1	0.6
Median grant amount			$8,252		$3,500	

Informational and Library Resources

# of volumes and volume equivalents	306,888
# of titles	88,537
# of active serial subscriptions	3,867
Study seating capacity inside the library	381
# of professional librarians	7
Hours per week library is open	102
# of open, wired connections available to students	206
# of networked computers available for use by students	81
# of simultaneous wireless users	350
Require computer?	N

JD Attrition (from prior year)

	Academic	Other	Total	
	#	#	#	%
1st year	9	23	32	12.9%
2nd year	4	5	9	4.6%
3rd year	1	0	1	0.6%
4th year	0	0	0	0.0%

Employment

	Total	Percentage
Employment status known	127	100.0
Employment status unknown	0	0.0
Employed	101	79.5
Pursuing graduate degrees	1	0.8
Unemployed seeking employment	23	18.1
Unemployed not seeking employment	2	1.6

Type of Employment

# employed in law firms	60	59.4
# employed in business and industry	12	11.9
# employed in government	21	20.8
# employed in public interest	0	0.0
# employed as judicial clerks	0	0.0
# employed in academia	2	2.0

Geographic Location

# employed in state	71	70.3
# employed in foreign countries	0	0.0
# of states where employed		10

Bar Passage Rates

Jurisdiction	Oklahoma		
Exam	Sum 03	Win 04	Total
# from school taking bar for the first time	71	29	100
School's pass rate for all first-time takers	62%	72%	65%
State's pass rate for all first-time takers	82%	83%	82%

Oklahoma City University School of Law

2501 North Blackwelder Avenue
Oklahoma City, OK 73106-1493
Phone: 800.633.7242 or 405.208.5354
E-mail: lawadmit@okcu.edu; Website: www.okcu.edu/law

■ Introduction

Oklahoma City University School of Law (OCULAW) is located within a metropolitan area of over 1,000,000 people and only minutes from some of Oklahoma's largest law firms, corporations, banks, city and state government agencies, the state capitol, and state and federal courts.

The School of Law is fully accredited by the ABA and is a member of the AALS.

■ Faculty

The faculty at OCU LAW includes professionals assembled from throughout the United States with law degrees from a variety of law schools, including the nation's most prestigious. Many faculty members also hold advanced degrees in law and other fields of study.

■ Library and Physical Facilities

The School of Law sits on an attractive quadrangle of the OCU campus comprising Sarkeys Law Center, the Gold Star Memorial Building (law library), and two residence halls that are open to law students living on campus. The Sarkeys Law Center houses the school's classrooms, administrative offices, student organizations, the student lounge, and the Homsey Family Moot Courtroom. The law library holds over 304,000 volumes and volume equivalents and features computer labs with access to all online research databases as well as to each student's personal e-mail account. A wireless network is available in the law library and Sarkeys Law Center.

■ Curriculum

The School of Law offers a full-time JD program during the day and a part-time evening program. Both require the completion of 90 semester hours. In conjunction with OCU's Meinders School of Business, a student may also attain a joint JD/MBA. The School of Law also offers specialized certificate programs in business law (with a concentration in e-commerce or financial services and commercial law) and public law.

The school operates two 16-week semesters and one 8-week summer term. Full-time students may complete their degree requirements in as little as two-and-a-half years, and part-time students in three-and-a-half years by attending summer sessions.

The required curriculum lays a thorough foundation for the continuing study of law. These foundation courses include Legal Analysis and two semesters of Legal Research and Writing (LR&W), two of the most important skills needed in any practice area. The School

of Law's LR&W program is staffed with four full-time professors and a director.

The remaining upper-division course hours may be selected from a wide range of electives and seminars. All upper-division students are required to complete a substantial written product.

■ Special Programs

In Oklahoma, students who have completed just 50 course hours are eligible for a limited license, and those who qualify may appear in court under certain circumstances. As a companion to this state licensing policy, OCULAW has created a range of externship opportunities where academic credit can be earned in approximately 40 practice placement sites with field supervisors, operating under the guidance of a full-time director of externship programs.

OCU School of Law operates three legal centers for its students and the legal community. The Center on Alternative Dispute Resolution provides mediation services in courts, to Indian tribes, and government agencies, and provides training for students to represent clients in mediation, arbitration, and negotiation. The Native American Legal Resource Center focuses on Native American law and provides legal services to tribes and tribal courts, frequently through federal grants. The Center for the Study of State Constitutional Law and Government promotes scholarship and discussion on important issues relating to state government.

Three times each year, the student-edited *Law Review* is published. Student moot court teams participate in numerous national interscholastic competitions.

OCULAW cosponsors (with Stetson University) summer international programs in Buenos Aires, Argentina; Granada, Spain; Tallinn, Estonia, and Freiberg, Germany. OCULAW also participates in a student exchange program with Bucerius Law School in Hamburg, Germany.

■ Admission

Admission decisions are determined by a faculty committee. Many factors are considered, including academic performance, undergraduate curriculum, advanced degrees, work experiences, background, activities, recommendations, and LSAT scores.

Beginning students are admitted only in the fall term. Transcript evaluations by LSDAS are required, as are two letters of recommendation.

The Alternate Summer Admission Program offers applicants who do not meet traditional admission requirements an opportunity to demonstrate their capacity for law study and to earn admission for the fall.

Although priority consideration is given to applications received by April 1, the law school will accept applications until August 1 if space remains available.

■ Student Activities

There are approximately 30 active student organizations at the law school, led by an award-winning ABA Law Student Division Chapter. These organizations are available to meet the social and service needs of the entire student body.

■ Expenses, Scholarships, and Financial Aid

In addition to the nonrefundable $50 application fee, when an applicant is accepted, he or she is required to pay a $250 nonrefundable tuition deposit that is credited toward the first semester's tuition. The School of Law also offers a number of merit scholarships each year,

including some full-tuition awards. Additional assistance is available to upper-division students based on a variety of factors, including academic performance. Each year, the Hatton W. Sumners Foundation provides up to five scholarships to incoming law students on the basis of academic and leadership potential. These awards include full tuition plus a book and living expenses stipend. Candidates for the Hatton W. Sumners scholarship must submit a separate application and participate in an interview process.

■ Career Services

The Office of Law Career Services assists students, beginning in the first year of law school, in seeking employment or legal internship positions, as well as graduates seeking career opportunities. Details of services provided are available on the career services section of the law school's website.

Applicant Profile

Oklahoma City University School of Law
This grid includes only applicants who earned 120-180 LSAT scores under standard administrations.

LSAT Score	3.75 +		3.50 - 3.74		3.25 - 3.49		3.00 - 3.24		2.75 - 2.99		2.50 - 2.74		2.25 - 2.49		2.00 - 2.24		Below 2.00		No GPA		Total	
	Apps	Adm	Apps	Adm	Apps	Adm	Apps	Adm	Apps	Adm	Apps	Adm	Apps	Adm	Apps	Adm	Apps	Adm	Apps	Adm	Apps	Adm
175-180	0	0	0	0	0	0	0	0	0	0	0	0	0	0	0	0	0	0	0	0	0	0
170-174	0	0	0	0	0	0	0	0	0	0	0	0	0	0	0	0	0	0	0	0	0	0
165-169	2	2	1	1	1	1	3	3	0	0	0	0	0	0	0	0	0	0	0	0	7	7
160-164	14	13	11	10	14	14	2	2	10	10	4	2	2	2	0	0	0	0	0	0	57	53
155-159	29	28	49	49	26	22	24	23	13	11	10	10	6	6	0	0	2	1	0	0	159	150
150-154	36	33	48	44	55	46	60	54	60	55	42	37	20	15	10	7	2	1	0	0	333	292
145-149	30	16	55	33	89	58	116	59	84	37	68	27	43	10	13	3	3	2	7	1	508	246
140-144	16	2	27	1	47	2	77	3	56	3	48	3	33	0	11	0	5	0	9	0	329	14
135-139	2	0	20	1	15	0	32	0	29	1	18	0	12	0	14	0	2	0	5	0	149	2
130-134	1	0	2	0	0	0	4	0	7	0	6	0	3	0	1	0	2	0	4	0	30	0
125-129	0	0	0	0	0	0	1	0	2	0	2	0	1	0	1	0	0	0	1	0	8	0
120-124	0	0	1	0	0	0	0	0	0	0	0	0	0	0	0	0	0	0	0	0	1	0
Total	130	94	214	139	247	143	319	144	261	117	198	79	120	33	50	10	16	4	26	1	1581	764

Apps = Number of Applicants
Adm = Number Admitted
Reflects 99% of the total applicant pool.

University of Oregon School of Law

1221 University of Oregon
Eugene, OR 97403-1221
Phone: 541.346.3846
E-mail: admissions@law.uoregon.edu; Website: www.law.uoregon.edu

ABA
Approved
Since
1923

The Basics

Type of school	Public
Term	Semester
Application deadline	3/1
Application fee	$50
Financial aid deadline	3/1
Can first year start other than fall?	No
Student to faculty ratio (fall)	20.9 to 1
Does the university offer:	
housing restricted to law students?	No
graduate housing for which law students are eligible?	Yes

Faculty and Administrators

	Total		Men		Women		Minorities	
	Fall	Spr	Fall	Spr	Fall	Spr	Fall	Spr
Full-time	21	21	15	15	6	6	3	4
Other Full-time	3	4	0	0	3	4	1	1
Deans, librarians, & others who teach	7	7	2	2	5	5	0	0
Part-time	19	25	13	20	6	5	1	1
Total	50	57	30	37	20	20	5	6

Curriculum

	Full-time	Part-time
Typical first-year section size	65	0
Is there typically a "small section" of the first-year class, other than Legal Writing, taught by full-time faculty	No	No
If yes, typical size offered last year	0	0
# of classroom course titles beyond 1st year curriculum	91	
# of upper division courses, excluding seminars with an enrollment: Under 25	26	
25-49	19	
50-74	10	
75-99	4	
100+	1	
# of seminars	30	
# of seminar positions available	625	
# of seminar positions filled	438	0
# of positions available in simulation courses	234	
# of simulation positions filled	180	0
# of positions available in faculty supervised clinical courses	150	
# of faculty supervised clinical positions filled	118	0
# involved in field placements	16	0
# involved in law journals	112	0
# involved in moot court or trial competitions	132	0
# of credit hours required to graduate	85	

JD Enrollment and Ethnicity

	Men		Women		Full-time		Part-time		1st-year		Total		JD Degs. Awd.
	#	%	#	%	#	%	#	%	#	%	#	%	
African Amer.	6	1.9	8	3.7	14	2.6	0	0.0	11	5.9	14	2.6	3
Amer. Indian	2	0.6	4	1.9	6	1.1	0	0.0	3	1.6	6	1.1	4
Asian Amer.	21	6.7	11	5.1	32	6.0	0	0.0	10	5.4	32	6.0	11
Mex. Amer.	8	2.6	4	1.9	12	2.3	0	0.0	8	4.3	12	2.3	3
Puerto Rican	1	0.3	0	0.0	1	0.2	0	0.0	0	0.0	1	0.2	0
Hispanic	10	3.2	10	4.6	20	3.8	0	0.0	4	2.2	20	3.8	0
Total Minority	48	15.3	37	17.1	85	16.1	0	0.0	36	19.5	85	16.1	21
For. Nation.	3	1.0	6	2.8	9	1.7	0	0.0	4	2.2	9	1.7	3
Caucasian	262	83.7	173	80.1	435	82.2	0	0.0	145	78.4	435	82.2	138
Unknown	0	0.0	0	0.0	0	0.0	0	0.0	0	0.0	0	0.0	0
Total	313	59.2	216	40.8	529	100.0	0	0.0	185	35.0	529		162

Tuition and Fees

	Resident	Nonresident
Full-time	$16,156	$20,458
Part-time	$0	$0

Living Expenses

Estimated living expenses for singles

Living on campus	Living off campus	Living at home
$10,490	$10,490	$5,948

University of Oregon School of Law

ABA
Approved
Since
1923

GPA and LSAT Scores

	Total	Full-time	Part-time
# of apps	1,869	1,869	0
# of admits	650	650	0
# of matrics	184	184	0
75% GPA	3.64	3.64	0.00
25% GPA	3.27	3.27	0.00
75% LSAT	160	160	0
25% LSAT	155	155	0

Grants and Scholarships (from prior year)

	Total		Full-time		Part-time	
	#	%	#	%	#	%
Total # of students	514		514		0	
Total # receiving grants	264	51.4	264	51.4	0	0.0
Less than 1/2 tuition	231	44.9	231	44.9	0	0.0
Half to full tuition	22	4.3	22	4.3	0	0.0
Full tuition	3	0.6	3	0.6	0	0.0
More than full tuition	8	1.6	8	1.6	0	0.0
Median grant amount			$3,200		$0	

Informational and Library Resources

# of volumes and volume equivalents	392,135
# of titles	55,876
# of active serial subscriptions	2,939
Study seating capacity inside the library	306
# of professional librarians	6
Hours per week library is open	109
# of open, wired connections available to students	1,388
# of networked computers available for use by students	37
# of simultaneous wireless users	3,200
Require computer?	Y

JD Attrition (from prior year)

	Academic	Other	Total	
	#	#	#	%
1st year	0	21	21	11.4%
2nd year	0	0	0	0.0%
3rd year	0	0	0	0.0%
4th year	0	0	0	0.0%

Employment

	Total	Percentage
Employment status known	161	95.8
Employment status unknown	7	4.2
Employed	138	85.7
Pursuing graduate degrees	14	8.7
Unemployed seeking employment	7	4.3
Unemployed not seeking employment	2	1.2

Type of Employment

	Total	Percentage
# employed in law firms	61	44.2
# employed in business and industry	16	11.6
# employed in government	16	11.6
# employed in public interest	6	4.3
# employed as judicial clerks	27	19.6
# employed in academia	12	8.7

Geographic Location

	Total	Percentage
# employed in state	79	57.2
# employed in foreign countries	0	0.0
# of states where employed	18	

Bar Passage Rates

Jurisdiction	Oregon		
Exam	Sum 03	Win 04	Total
# from school taking bar for the first time	89	7	96
School's pass rate for all first-time takers	79%	57%	77%
State's pass rate for all first-time takers	78%	76%	78%

University of Oregon School of Law

1221 University of Oregon
Eugene, OR 97403-1221
Phone: 541.346.3846
E-mail: admissions@law.uoregon.edu; Website: www.law.uoregon.edu

■ Introduction

Founded in 1884, the University of Oregon School of Law enjoys the distinction of being one of the oldest law schools in the west, was one of the first law schools approved by the ABA, and was one of the early members of the AALS. Oregon's faculty is comprised of exceptionally talented women and men whose scholarship has brought national recognition to the law school's many programs. The University of Oregon School of Law remains the only law school in Oregon to enjoy membership in Order of the Coif, confirming the reputation of its faculty as distinguished contributors to legal scholarship.

The University of Oregon School of Law is the smallest public law school on the West Coast. A state supported institution, the law school attracts a national student body. The Class of 2004 passed the most recent Oregon bar examination at 81 percent, significantly above the state's average of 72 percent for first-time test takers.

■ Environs

The University of Oregon is situated in Eugene, Oregon, a progressive city of 142,000 residents. Home to a federal courthouse and the Hult Center for the Performing Arts, residents enjoy debating politics and celebrating the arts. Eugene is also informal and affordable. Outdoor enthusiasts value our setting at the Willamette and McKenzie Rivers and the pleasure of being at the ocean or in the mountains in an hour. Salem, the capital, is also about one hour away; Portland, two.

Dedicated in 1999, the University of Oregon School of Law William W. Knight Law Center features a technological infrastructure that will ensure its state-of-the-art status. Students have access to a wireless network and have wired access from every seat in every classroom and the courtroom. The 389,000 volume collection of the John E. Jaqua Law Library is enhanced by a partnership with Orbis Cascade Alliance, a Northwest library consortium. The Knight Center also includes the computer lab, café, east plaza and lawn, and a half-court basketball court.

■ Curriculum

A broad base of common understanding is established in the first year followed by opportunities for developing areas of special interest. More than 140 courses are offered beyond the first-year curriculum. The core curriculum emphasizes traditional legal subjects. The elective curriculum allows students to concentrate their studies in areas for which the School of Law is recognized, such as environmental and natural resources law; business, financial, and corporate law; public interest and public service law; and appropriate dispute resolution.

■ Centers and Programs

Endowed centers and special programs enrich the curriculum. They include Appropriate Dispute Resolution, Environmental and Natural Resources Law, Law and Entrepreneurship, Ocean and Coastal Law, Portland Program (in downtown Portland), Public Interest-Public Service, the Wayne Morse Center for Law and Politics (which offers fellowships), and the Legal Research and Writing Program. Other opportunities include:

Concurrent Degrees: In one additional year, a concurrent master's degree can be earned by a student pursuing the JD. The concurrent degree programs are in business administration (JD/MBA), environmental studies (JD/MS), international studies (JD/MA), and conflict and dispute resolution (JD/MA or JD/MS). Students must apply separately to these masters' programs.

Certificates of Completion: Students can earn a certificate of completion in business law, law and entrepreneurship, criminal practice, environmental and natural resources law, estate planning, tax law, intellectual property, public interest and public service law, international law, or ocean and coastal law.

Clinics: The school also offers live-client clinic opportunities in business law, criminal prosecution, criminal defense, civil practice, environmental law, domestic violence, and mediation. An intensive year-long research and writing program is required. Students present final oral arguments in a courtroom setting.

Appropriate Dispute Resolution: The law school is keenly aware of the extent to which appropriate methods of dispute resolution (ADR) are now a staple of legal practice. The ADR program provides extensive integration of ADR into the traditional curriculum, and specialized training in the skills of mediation, counseling, and negotiation, and opportunities to practice those skills.

International Summer Program: Students are provided the opportunity to study in Australia at the University of Adelaide School of Law.

■ Admission

Almost 1,900 applications were received for the 180 seats in the fall 2004 first-year class. The candidate's full range of accomplishments is considered; qualitative factors such as GPA and performance on the LSAT also are important. For the Class of 2007, the 75th, median, and 25th percentile cumulative undergraduate GPAs were 3.64, 3.51, and 3.27. The 75th, median, and 25th percentile LSAT scores were 161, 159, and 156. The mission of the law school places diversity as an important goal. Women comprised 43 percent of the latest entering class and students of color comprised 22 percent. Almost 100

University of Oregon School of Law

undergraduate institutions were represented in the class. Historically, about 40 percent of the first-year class are Oregon residents.

■ Student Activities

The University of Oregon School of Law enjoys a well deserved reputation as an active, committed, and energetic place. Most students have had significant public interest, public policy, or international experience prior to law school. It is not uncommon for the typical student to contribute knowledge and time to a range of initiatives in the law school, the university, and city and state. Since 2001, University of Oregon School of Law students have contributed the most pro bono hours of any law school in Oregon. Within the walls of the Knight law center exists a lively place. There are three student-run law journals: *Oregon Law Review, Journal of Environmental Law and Litigation*, and *Oregon Review of International Law*. Annually, the Moot Court Board sponsors five in-house school competitions. Students serve on all faculty committees and the SBA sponsors numerous activities which are designed to enrich the intellectual life and professional experiences of the students, as well as encourage camaraderie. There are more than 35 diverse student organizations, including: American Constitution Society, Beeristers, Christian Legal Society, Family Law in

Practice, Federalist Society, International Law Students Association, Jewish Law Students, Land Air Water, Lesbian and Gay Law Student Association, Middle Eastern Law Students Association, Oregon Innocence Network, Pacific Wine Law Society, Peer Advising Group, Public Interest Service Program, Run Club, Sports Entertainment Law Forum, Streetlaw, Women's Law Forum, and several ethnic student organizations.

■ Career Services

Employment statistics are impressive. Nine months after graduation, 94 percent of the class reports employment, primarily in full-time law jobs. The Career Services Office provides comprehensive career counseling, which includes assistance with job-search strategy, interviewing skills, and résumé development. It maintains a close relationship with a strong, devoted network of more than 5,500 alumni. Each fall, Career Services oversees an on-campus interview program which brings prominent law firms, corporations, government organizations, and public interest agencies to recruit at Oregon. A popular Portland Interview Program complements Eugene-based programs. Oregon graduates work on Wall Street, in Washington DC, and throughout the west. Alumni have risen to prominent positions, particularly in Portland and Seattle and in federal and state courts.

Applicant Profile

University of Oregon School of Law

LSAT Score	GPA								
	3.75 +	3.50 - 3.74	3.25 - 3.49	3.00 - 3.24	2.75 - 2.99	2.50 - 2.74	2.25 - 2.49	2.00 - 2.24	Below 2.00
175-180									
170-174									
165-169									
160-164									
155-159									
150-154									
145-149									
140-144									
135-139									
130-134									
125-129									
120-124									

■ Good Possibility   □ Possible   ▨ Unlikely

Pace University School of Law

78 North Broadway
White Plains, NY 10603
Phone: 914.422.4210; Fax: 914.989.8714
E-mail: admissions@law.pace.edu; Website: www.law.pace.edu

ABA Approved Since 1978

The Basics

Type of school	Private
Term	Semester
Application deadline	11/5 3/1
Application fee	$65
Financial aid deadline	2/1
Can first year start other than fall?	No
Student to faculty ratio (fall)	16.0 to 1
Does the university offer:	
housing restricted to law students?	No
graduate housing for which law students are eligible?	Yes

Faculty and Administrators

	Total		Men		Women		Minorities	
	Fall	Spr	Fall	Spr	Fall	Spr	Fall	Spr
Full-time	36	35	23	23	13	12	4	4
Other Full-time	1	1	0	0	1	1	0	0
Deans, librarians, & others who teach	4	4	0	0	4	4	0	0
Part-time	31	36	16	21	15	15	1	2
Total	72	76	39	44	33	32	5	6

Curriculum

	Full-time	Part-time
Typical first-year section size	66	54
Is there typically a "small section" of the first-year class, other than Legal Writing, taught by full-time faculty	Yes	Yes
If yes, typical size offered last year	23	22
# of classroom course titles beyond 1st year curriculum	126	

# of upper division courses, excluding seminars with an enrollment:		
	Under 25	120
	25-49	25
	50-74	13
	75-99	10
	100+	0

# of seminars	21	
# of seminar positions available	420	
# of seminar positions filled	139	144
# of positions available in simulation courses	370	
# of simulation positions filled	145	128
# of positions available in faculty supervised clinical courses	100	
# of faculty supervised clinical positions filled	44	23
# involved in field placements	107	18
# involved in law journals	62	18
# involved in moot court or trial competitions	28	5
# of credit hours required to graduate	84	

JD Enrollment and Ethnicity

	Men		Women		Full-time		Part-time		1st-year		Total		JD Degs. Awd.
	#	%	#	%	#	%	#	%	#	%	#	%	
African Amer.	6	1.9	20	4.3	11	2.1	15	6.1	7	2.8	26	3.4	10
Amer. Indian	0	0.0	0	0.0	0	0.0	0	0.0	0	0.0	0	0.0	0
Asian Amer.	14	4.5	41	8.8	40	7.6	15	6.1	17	6.7	55	7.1	8
Mex. Amer.	1	0.3	3	0.6	3	0.6	1	0.4	1	0.4	4	0.5	0
Puerto Rican	4	1.3	5	1.1	6	1.1	3	1.2	2	0.8	9	1.2	4
Hispanic	7	2.3	16	3.4	14	2.6	9	3.7	6	2.4	23	3.0	11
Total Minority	32	10.3	85	18.3	74	14.0	43	17.6	33	13.1	117	15.1	33
For. Nation.	5	1.6	9	1.9	14	2.6	0	0.0	8	3.2	14	1.8	4
Caucasian	219	70.6	306	65.9	356	67.3	169	69.0	163	64.7	525	67.8	149
Unknown	54	17.4	64	13.8	85	16.1	33	13.5	48	19.0	118	15.2	5
Total	310	40.1	464	59.9	529	68.3	245	31.7	252	32.6	774		191

Tuition and Fees

	Resident	Nonresident
Full-time	$31,224	$31,224
Part-time	$23,457	$23,457

Living Expenses

Estimated living expenses for singles

Living on campus	Living off campus	Living at home
$14,820	$16,790	$6,530

Pace University School of Law

ABA
Approved
Since
1978

GPA and LSAT Scores

	Total	Full-time	Part-time
# of apps	3,128	2,626	502
# of admits	882	723	159
# of matrics	256	179	77
75% GPA	3.52	3.56	3.38
25% GPA	3.06	3.11	2.91
75% LSAT	157	157	155
25% LSAT	152	154	151

Grants and Scholarships (from prior year)

	Total		Full-time		Part-time	
	#	%	#	%	#	%
Total # of students	742		488		254	
Total # receiving grants	375	50.5	296	60.7	79	31.1
Less than 1/2 tuition	287	38.7	214	43.9	73	28.7
Half to full tuition	87	11.7	81	16.6	6	2.4
Full tuition	1	0.1	1	0.2	0	0.0
More than full tuition	0	0.0	0	0.0	0	0.0
Median grant amount			$9,000		$4,000	

Informational and Library Resources

# of volumes and volume equivalents	374,044
# of titles	128,065
# of active serial subscriptions	3,957
Study seating capacity inside the library	346
# of professional librarians	9
Hours per week library is open	102
# of open, wired connections available to students	278
# of networked computers available for use by students	75
# of simultaneous wireless users	5,632
Require computer?	N

JD Attrition (from prior year)

	Academic	Other	Total	
	#	#	#	%
1st year	7	25	32	12.5%
2nd year	3	4	7	3.0%
3rd year	0	1	1	0.5%
4th year	0	0	0	0.0%

Employment

	Total	Percentage
Employment status known	195	96.5
Employment status unknown	7	3.5
Employed	169	86.7
Pursuing graduate degrees	2	1.0
Unemployed seeking employment	17	8.7
Unemployed not seeking employment	7	3.6

Type of Employment

# employed in law firms	79	46.7
# employed in business and industry	37	21.9
# employed in government	25	14.8
# employed in public interest	4	2.4
# employed as judicial clerks	9	5.3
# employed in academia	3	1.8

Geographic Location

# employed in state	131	77.5
# employed in foreign countries	0	0.0
# of states where employed		6

Bar Passage Rates

Jurisdiction	New York		
Exam	Sum 03	Win 04	Total
# from school taking bar for the first time	159	29	188
School's pass rate for all first-time takers	74%	55%	71%
State's pass rate for all first-time takers	78%	58%	75%

Pace University School of Law

78 North Broadway
White Plains, NY 10603
Phone: 914.422.4210; Fax: 914.989.8714
E-mail: admissions@law.pace.edu; Website: www.law.pace.edu

■ Introduction

Located on a sprawling 12-acre campus just 20 miles from New York City, Pace University School of Law combines the beauty of open spaces and classic buildings with the convenience of technology and the amenities of a small, vibrant urban community. Law firms are abundant in White Plains, the federal and district courthouses are close by, and the new City Center has just been built.

The law school is home to the New York State Judicial Institute, an innovative center for judicial education and the only center of its kind in the United States. Students working with the institute through the Center for Judicial Studies will pursue a rigorous course of study leading to enhanced opportunities for judicial fellowships and clerkships.

Students are attracted nationally and from abroad for our congenial atmosphere, diverse population, and our award-winning centers. Extensive opportunities exist through our clinics, externships, and internships for students to learn practical lawyering skills and to become litigators.

Pace law school has a history of student-centered growth and innovation built on a foundation of deep mutual respect between faculty and students. Students from diverse backgrounds come together to learn lawyering skills, gain vital professional experience, and contribute to the creation of a more just society.

■ Curriculum

The JD program provides students with the fundamental skills necessary to the practice of law nationally, and the flexibility to shape their elective coursework based on particular career goals. The curriculum is based on the concept that rigorous standards and high-quality teaching can coexist with an atmosphere congenial to learning and enjoyment. Students can obtain certificates in Environmental Law and in International Law by completing a sequence of courses with a specified GPA in the applicable area. Pace offers the opportunity to pursue joint degrees in the JD/MBA and JD/MPA with Pace University, as well as the JD/MEM with Yale University School of Forestry, JD/MS in Environmental Policy with Bard College, JD/MA in Women's History with Sarah Lawrence College, and a JD/MPH with New York Medical College. These programs can be completed on a full-time or part-time basis. Graduate law degrees, LLM in Comparative Legal Studies or Environmental Law and an SJD in Environmental Law, attract attorneys from around the world.

The majority of classes have less than 25 students, which enables close faculty-student relationships. The range of scholarship reflects a faculty of diverse interests, and the curriculum offers courses in traditional areas of legal study, legal theory, and specialized studies. Curricular concentrations include civil litigation, constitutional law, commercial law, corporate law, criminal law and criminal procedure, evidence, family law, real estate, women's justice, and land use law. Faculty scholarship also covers such specialized areas as the Americans with Disabilities Act, children's legal representation, environmental and toxic torts, equal pay, hazardous waste, health care fraud, international commercial law, land use, admiralty law, legal and ethical issues in health care, nonprofit organizations, prosecutorial and judicial ethics, racially motivated violence, securities fraud, and white collar crime.

■ Advocacy and Skills Training

The Women's Justice Center is a training, resource, and direct legal services center that trains thousands of judges, attorneys, and others who work to eradicate injustice to women. Pace law students participate in all aspects of the program, including direct representation of clients in family court.

Pace law school has one of the top environmental programs in the country. The program offers over 20 classes in environmental law, opportunities to conduct research in energy and land use law, externships in Washington, DC and New York, and international environmental law classes taught in Brazil.

The Land Use Law Center teaches students to understand how best to develop and conserve the land through research and publications, outreach and community service, and project management and technology.

The Federal Judicial Extern Honors Program allows students to hone their writing skills in a mentoring program with a faculty member, and as judicial externs in a United States district or circuit judge's chambers.

Direct representation clinics enable students to take their extensive classroom training and make the transition to representing clients or prosecuting charges. Students take full responsibility for their own caseloads under close supervision of a full-time faculty member. Externship programs are also available and are clinical courses in which fieldwork is conducted under the supervision of practicing attorneys who are not full-time members of the faculty. Simulation courses give students the opportunity to learn specific components of lawyering work such as written and oral advocacy, interviewing and counseling clients, negotiation, analyzing a trial record, developing strategy, opening and closing arguments, selecting a jury and drafting jury instructions, and witness preparation and examination.

Pace University School of Law

Library and Physical Facilities

The Pace law library is housed in an airy, modern facility, the Glass Law Center. The law library contains an extensive collection of law and law-related publications, provides access to materials in other libraries in metropolitan New York and throughout the United States, and subscribes to national online research systems such as LexisNexis, Westlaw, and Dialog. Pace law students have free access to these databases from computer terminals distributed throughout the law library, in the student lounge, and from their home computers. A wireless network is available in the law library, classroom buildings, and throughout the campus.

Financial Aid

A comprehensive aid program has been developed to include scholarships, need-based grants, employment, loans, and a loan forgiveness program for graduates who choose a public interest career. Over 1.8 million dollars have been allocated for first-year students in 2005. These funds may be available on the basis of financial need, academic merit, education costs, or credit considerations.

Career Services

The Center for Career Development actively solicits job listings for part-time, summer, and permanent postgraduate positions as well as full-time jobs for evening students through various outreach activities. In addition to regularly contacting legal employers regarding hiring needs, visits with law firms and other organizations are scheduled throughout the year. Respondents to the 2003 class survey reported 87 percent employment within the nine months following graduation.

Student Activities

Pace Law School publishes three law reviews, the *Pace Law Review*, the *Pace Environmental Law Review*, and the *Pace International Law Review*. Students compete in interscholastic moot court competitions and host the largest environmental moot court competition in the country. The school offers more than 26 organizations in which students can participate. Available activities include professional organizations, minority student groups, issue-centered organizations, political groups, social action groups, religious groups, a student bar association, and a student newspaper.

Interviews/Visits to Campus

Pace seeks students with demonstrated potential to meaningfully contribute to the diversity of the law school community and the legal profession. Pace offers a unique opportunity for candidates to participate in a formal interview as part of their application process.

The law school hosts several open house programs which include tours; discussions with faculty, administrators, and students; and information regarding the admission process, financial aid, placement, and life at Pace Law. For a complete list of our on-campus events, visit our website at *www.law.pace.edu*.

Applicant Profile

Pace University School of Law
This grid includes only applicants who earned 120-180 LSAT scores under standard administrations.

LSAT Score	3.75 + Apps	Adm	3.50 - 3.74 Apps	Adm	3.25 - 3.49 Apps	Adm	3.00 - 3.24 Apps	Adm	2.75 - 2.99 Apps	Adm	2.50 - 2.74 Apps	Adm	2.25 - 2.49 Apps	Adm	2.00 - 2.24 Apps	Adm	Below 2.00 Apps	Adm	No GPA Apps	Adm	Total Apps	Adm
175-180	0	0	0	0	0	0	0	0	0	0	0	0	0	0	0	0	0	0	0	0	0	0
170-174	0	0	0	0	1	1	1	1	1	1	0	0	0	0	0	0	0	0	0	0	3	3
165-169	9	5	3	2	3	3	6	4	2	2	1	0	2	0	1	0	0	0	0	0	27	16
160-164	12	10	35	32	44	34	34	20	22	8	18	6	6	0	3	0	0	0	3	3	177	113
155-159	44	42	88	77	136	121	119	94	74	36	47	15	35	6	12	0	1	1	6	4	562	396
150-154	57	27	174	62	197	68	213	71	167	42	89	12	42	1	16	0	4	0	13	4	972	287
145-149	43	7	114	9	161	4	163	11	132	3	85	1	36	0	16	0	1	0	15	3	766	38
140-144	12	0	29	0	70	1	93	1	70	0	68	0	35	0	18	0	1	0	7	0	403	2
135-139	4	0	14	0	24	0	37	0	32	0	37	0	15	0	8	0	2	0	6	0	179	0
130-134	1	0	3	0	5	0	9	0	14	0	11	0	2	0	3	0	4	0	4	0	56	0
125-129	0	0	0	0	0	0	1	0	3	0	4	0	3	0	1	0	1	0	1	0	14	0
120-124	0	0	0	0	0	0	0	0	0	0	0	0	0	0	1	0	0	0	0	0	1	0
Total	182	91	460	182	641	232	676	202	517	92	360	34	176	7	79	0	14	1	55	14	3160	855

Apps = Number of Applicants   Adm = Number Admitted   Reflects 99% of the total applicant pool.

University of the Pacific, McGeorge School of Law

3200 Fifth Avenue
Sacramento, CA 95817
Phone: 916.739.7105; Fax: 916.739.7134
E-mail: admissionsmcgeorge@pacific.edu; Website: www.mcgeorge.edu

The Basics

Type of school	Private
Term	Semester
Application deadline	5/1
Application fee	$50
Financial aid deadline	
Can first year start other than fall?	No
Student to faculty ratio (fall)	8.8 to 1
Does the university offer:	
housing restricted to law students?	Yes
graduate housing for which law students are eligible?	Yes

Faculty and Administrators

	Total		Men		Women		Minorities	
	Fall	Spr	Fall	Spr	Fall	Spr	Fall	Spr
Full-time	92	92	58	58	34	34	12	11
Other Full-time	3	3	2	2	1	1	0	0
Deans, librarians, & others who teach	12	11	7	7	5	4	1	1
Part-time	58	85	44	65	13	20	3	4
Total	165	191	111	132	53	59	16	16

Curriculum

		Full-time	Part-time
Typical first-year section size		85	110
Is there typically a "small section" of the first-year class, other than Legal Writing, taught by full-time faculty		Yes	No
If yes, typical size offered last year		48	0
# of classroom course titles beyond 1st year curriculum		133	
# of upper division courses, excluding seminars with an enrollment:	Under 25	68	
	25-49	41	
	50-74	16	
	75-99	16	
	100+	4	
# of seminars		21	
# of seminar positions available		471	
# of seminar positions filled		269	62
# of positions available in simulation courses		731	
# of simulation positions filled		326	158
# of positions available in faculty supervised clinical courses		123	
# of faculty supervised clinical positions filled		83	14
# involved in field placements		127	27
# involved in law journals		71	15
# involved in moot court or trial competitions		39	14
# of credit hours required to graduate		88	

JD Enrollment and Ethnicity

	Men		Women		Full-time		Part-time		1st-year		Total		JD Degs. Awd.
	#	%	#	%	#	%	#	%	#	%	#	%	
African Amer.	9	1.6	12	2.3	6	0.8	15	3.9	11	3.1	21	1.9	4
Amer. Indian	7	1.2	3	0.6	7	1.0	3	0.8	2	0.6	10	0.9	6
Asian Amer.	60	10.5	69	12.9	88	12.2	41	10.7	44	12.2	129	11.7	33
Mex. Amer.	9	1.6	9	1.7	6	0.8	12	3.1	7	1.9	18	1.6	9
Puerto Rican	2	0.4	1	0.2	2	0.3	1	0.3	1	0.3	3	0.3	0
Hispanic	17	3.0	23	4.3	17	2.4	23	6.0	6	1.7	40	3.6	5
Total Minority	104	18.2	117	22.0	126	17.5	95	24.8	71	19.7	221	20.0	57
For. Nation.	3	0.5	1	0.2	2	0.3	2	0.5	3	0.8	4	0.4	0
Caucasian	464	81.3	415	77.9	593	82.2	286	74.7	286	79.4	879	79.6	199
Unknown	0	0.0	0	0.0	0	0.0	0	0.0	0	0.0	0	0.0	0
Total	571	51.7	533	48.3	721	65.3	383	34.7	360	32.6	1104		256

Tuition and Fees

	Resident	Nonresident
Full-time	$29,275	$29,275
Part-time	$19,481	$19,481

Living Expenses

Estimated living expenses for singles

Living on campus	Living off campus	Living at home
$18,368	$18,368	$8,418

University of the Pacific, McGeorge School of Law

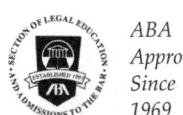

ABA
Approved
Since
1969

GPA and LSAT Scores

	Total	Full-time	Part-time
# of apps	3,489	3,078	411
# of admits	1,043	865	178
# of matrics	361	255	106
75% GPA	3.46	3.46	3.45
25% GPA	2.88	2.88	2.86
75% LSAT	159	160	156
25% LSAT	155	156	152

Grants and Scholarships (from prior year)

	Total #	Total %	Full-time #	Full-time %	Part-time #	Part-time %
Total # of students	1,104		749		355	
Total # receiving grants	607	55.0	450	60.1	157	44.2
Less than 1/2 tuition	506	45.8	363	48.5	143	40.3
Half to full tuition	81	7.3	69	9.2	12	3.4
Full tuition	13	1.2	12	1.6	1	0.3
More than full tuition	7	0.6	6	0.8	1	0.3
Median grant amount			$8,160		$5,000	

Informational and Library Resources

# of volumes and volume equivalents	462,967
# of titles	114,703
# of active serial subscriptions	3,099
Study seating capacity inside the library	466
# of professional librarians	14
Hours per week library is open	105
# of open, wired connections available to students	65
# of networked computers available for use by students	62
# of simultaneous wireless users	450
Require computer?	N

JD Attrition (from prior year)

	Academic #	Other #	Total #	Total %
1st year	33	32	65	15.8%
2nd year	4	30	34	9.9%
3rd year	0	9	9	3.2%
4th year	0	2	2	3.1%

Employment

	Total	Percentage
Employment status known	233	100.0
Employment status unknown	0	0.0
Employed	221	94.8
Pursuing graduate degrees	2	0.9
Unemployed seeking employment	2	0.9
Unemployed not seeking employment	8	3.4

Type of Employment

# employed in law firms	119	53.8
# employed in business and industry	34	15.4
# employed in government	48	21.7
# employed in public interest	6	2.7
# employed as judicial clerks	7	3.2
# employed in academia	4	1.8

Geographic Location

# employed in state	191	86.4
# employed in foreign countries	0	0.0
# of states where employed	15	

Bar Passage Rates

Jurisdiction	California		
Exam	Sum 03	Win 04	Total
# from school taking bar for the first time	189	23	212
School's pass rate for all first-time takers	70%	57%	68%
State's pass rate for all first-time takers	63%	47%	60%

University of the Pacific, McGeorge School of Law

3200 Fifth Avenue
Sacramento, CA 95817
Phone: 916.739.7105; Fax: 916.739.7134
E-mail: admissionsmcgeorge@pacific.edu; Website: www.mcgeorge.edu

■ Overview

The University of the Pacific, McGeorge School of Law is in Sacramento, California, capital of the nation's most populous state with one of the world's leading economies. The school is a member of the AALS, is accredited by the ABA, and has a chapter of the Order of the Coif.

Day and evening division programs provide flexibility to earn a JD degree in three, four, or five years of study. Approximately 1,000 students pursue a JD or LLM on Pacific/McGeorge's unique 13-acre law-school-only campus. The school's reputation for educating well-prepared, practice-ready lawyers grows from the vitality of students and faculty working together. The diversity of the student body is reflected in the 150 or more colleges and universities students attended as undergraduates, the 50 or more major fields, the range in years of age from 20 to over 60, and the gender and ethnic diversity represented each year by the growing number of students from a wide range of ethnic and cultural heritages.

■ Library and Physical Facilities

Pacific/McGeorge's students study on a campus designed exclusively for legal education that includes class and seminar rooms; a student center; technologically equipped trial courtroom; lecture hall; clinical legal education center; law library and computer center; administrative, faculty, and student services offices; recreational facilities; and student apartments.

■ Curriculum

Pacific/McGeorge offers more than 100 advanced elective offerings, ranging from comprehensive courses in traditional areas such as business, constitutional law, criminal justice, and family and juvenile law to a wide variety of courses in specialty areas such as environmental (both US and international), entertainment, labor, intellectual property, mass media, banking, and elder law. Certificate and concentration curricula are offered for those with specific career interests.

Clinical Experience: Pacific/McGeorge believes that clinical education—working in a practice setting while guided by a faculty mentor—is a key part of the law school experience. On-campus clinics include Community Legal Services, Business and Community Development, Administrative Adjudication, Parole Representation, Bankruptcy, Immigration, and Legislative Process. Off-campus, the internship program makes available more than 125 placements.

■ Governmental Affairs Program

Pacific/McGeorge's Governmental Affairs Program prepares students for private practice or public service and policy-making careers in governmental positions. Significant opportunities are offered for hands-on work and networking contacts with governmental entities. Graduates of the program are practicing in law firms whose clients are involved with governmental regulatory matters as consultants, lobbyists, or in-house counsel with business and nonprofit organizations, and in staff and policy positions with legislative branches, executive departments, or administrative agencies at all levels of government. A one- or two-year LLM program in Government and Public Policy is available.

■ International Legal Studies

Law and accounting firms, government agencies, and corporations require lawyers who better understand international law. Pacific/McGeorge offers international law certificate and concentration programs. Students can also study in an international setting at the Center for International Legal Studies in Salzburg, Austria. The Summer Institute offers international and comparative law courses in Austria and China. Pacific/McGeorge also offers an LLM in International Water Law and International Business and a JSD in International Water Law.

■ Trial and Appellate Advocacy

In its broadest sense, advocacy is an integral part of any legal career, whether representing clients in civil and criminal litigation or at administrative hearings, negotiating business agreements, resolving disputes through alternative dispute-resolution mechanisms, or advising on legal matters to avoid litigation. Pacific/McGeorge's curriculum offers the opportunity for all students to gain advanced advocacy skills. For those especially attracted to courtroom advocacy, Pacific/McGeorge's concentration equips future litigators for success.

■ Intellectual Property Law

Intellectual property is one of the fastest growing practice areas. Pacific/McGeorge graduates are practicing in diverse settings and areas of intellectual property law that include the entertainment industry; music and theater law; intellectual property litigation; sports, trademark, and domain-name law; patent and biotechnology law; and the rapidly emerging areas of computer and Internet law.

University of the Pacific, McGeorge School of Law

■ Taxation

Pacific/McGeorge has responded to the need for tax expertise in a booming economy by creating a tax concentration within its JD program that provides students with the needed foundation to enter business or estate-planning practice.

■ Criminal Justice

Pacific/McGeorge's criminal justice curriculum includes advanced electives in a wide range of subjects, including sentencing and post-conviction remedies, white-collar crime, capital punishment, criminal pretrial litigation, specialized evidence courses, juvenile law, family violence, and problems in criminal justice. Hands-on training is available through a rich program of internship opportunities. A concentration curriculum is structured for those who wish to specialize.

■ Student Activities

Over 30 professional, social, and academic student organizations at Pacific/McGeorge represent the breadth of interests and diversity of the student community. Student staffs manage, edit, and write for the *Pacific/McGeorge Law Review* and *The Transnational Lawyer Journal*. Pacific/McGeorge competition teams compete with notable success in a wide range of trial, appellate, counseling, and dispute-resolution competitions on the regional and national levels as well as at the Vis International Commercial Arbitration Moot Competition in Vienna, Austria.

■ Admission and Financial Aid

Admission is competitive. Prelegal education includes at least a bachelor's degree or senior standing from an accredited college or university. An applicant's undergraduate record and LSAT results are important factors in the decision process. When there are multiple LSAT scores, the highest may be accorded significant weight. Other factors considered are grade patterns or trends, employment and career accomplishments, graduate work, and extracurricular or community activities. Ethnic, cultural, and experiential backgrounds that contribute to student-body diversity are valued. Strong merit- and need-based financial aid programs provide scholarship awards and grants to entering and advanced students. A knowledgeable financial aid staff provides counseling to assist students in minimizing student loan indebtedness.

■ Housing

Pacific/McGeorge has 157 on-campus apartments, furnished and unfurnished, including one- and two-bedroom units, studios, and townhouses. Early application is advised. The school's full-time housing coordinator also assists in locating off-campus accommodations that are readily available in Sacramento.

■ Career Services

The well-staffed Career Development Office offers a full range of counseling and resource services for students and alumni. Workshops and individual counseling about career paths are provided by the CDO.

Applicant Profile

University of the Pacific, McGeorge School of Law
This grid includes only applicants who earned 120-180 LSAT scores under standard administrations.

LSAT Score	3.75 +		3.50 - 3.74		3.25 - 3.49		3.00 - 3.24		2.75 - 2.99		2.50 - 2.74		2.25 - 2.49		2.00 - 2.24		Below 2.00		No GPA		Total	
	Apps	Adm	Apps	Adm	Apps	Adm	Apps	Adm	Apps	Adm	Apps	Adm	Apps	Adm	Apps	Adm	Apps	Adm	Apps	Adm	Apps	Adm
165-180	9	8	15	13	18	17	5	4	13	13	7	6	4	3	3	3	0	0	2	2	76	69
160-164	35	33	52	50	42	41	51	49	42	40	29	27	6	6	5	1	0	0	7	5	269	252
155-159	71	63	135	123	159	136	130	107	114	85	64	44	26	14	13	2	2	0	9	4	723	578
150-154	58	11	132	13	184	24	244	27	156	17	106	9	42	0	16	1	6	0	18	1	962	103
145-149	28	1	87	3	135	2	177	1	148	2	97	0	46	0	25	0	6	0	16	1	765	10
120-144	13	0	57	0	86	0	116	0	126	1	98	0	64	0	25	0	13	0	36	0	634	1
Total	214	116	478	202	624	220	723	188	599	158	401	86	188	23	87	7	27	0	88	13	3429	1013

Apps = Number of Applicants
Adm = Number Admitted
Reflects 98% of the total applicant pool.

Penn State University, The Dickinson School of Law

150 South College Street
Carlisle, PA 17013
Phone: 800.840.1122; 717.240.5207; Fax: 717.241.3503
E-mail: dsladmit@psu.edu; Website: www.dsl.psu.edu

ABA
Approved
Since
1931

The Basics

Type of school	Public
Term	Semester
Application deadline	3/1
Application fee	$60
Financial aid deadline	3/1
Can first year start other than fall?	No
Student to faculty ratio (fall)	17.3 to 1
Does the university offer:	
housing restricted to law students?	Yes
graduate housing for which law students are eligible?	No

Faculty and Administrators

	Total		Men		Women		Minorities	
	Fall	Spr	Fall	Spr	Fall	Spr	Fall	Spr
Full-time	30	28	21	19	9	9	5	5
Other Full-time	8	8	1	1	7	7	0	0
Deans, librarians, & others who teach	7	7	4	4	3	3	0	0
Part-time	44	25	33	21	11	4	2	1
Total	89	68	59	45	30	23	7	6

Curriculum

	Full-time	Part-time
Typical first-year section size	80	0
Is there typically a "small section" of the first-year class, other than Legal Writing, taught by full-time faculty	No	No
If yes, typical size offered last year	0	0
# of classroom course titles beyond 1st year curriculum	122	
# of upper division courses, excluding seminars with an enrollment: Under 25	92	
25-49	28	
50-74	25	
75-99	9	
100+	0	
# of seminars	23	
# of seminar positions available	448	
# of seminar positions filled	299	0
# of positions available in simulation courses	717	
# of simulation positions filled	586	0
# of positions available in faculty supervised clinical courses	44	
# of faculty supervised clinical positions filled	37	0
# involved in field placements	116	0
# involved in law journals	100	0
# involved in moot court or trial competitions	33	0
# of credit hours required to graduate	88	

JD Enrollment and Ethnicity

	Men		Women		Full-time		Part-time		1st-year		Total		JD Degs. Awd.
	#	%	#	%	#	%	#	%	#	%	#	%	
African Amer.	12	3.6	29	10.1	41	6.6	0	0.0	17	9.7	41	6.6	1
Amer. Indian	1	0.3	0	0.0	1	0.2	0	0.0	0	0.0	1	0.2	2
Asian Amer.	18	5.4	19	6.6	37	5.9	0	0.0	11	6.3	37	5.9	11
Mex. Amer.	0	0.0	0	0.0	0	0.0	0	0.0	0	0.0	0	0.0	0
Puerto Rican	14	4.2	12	4.2	26	4.2	0	0.0	9	5.1	26	4.2	0
Hispanic	6	1.8	4	1.4	10	1.6	0	0.0	8	4.5	10	1.6	8
Total Minority	51	15.2	64	22.3	115	18.5	0	0.0	45	25.6	115	18.5	22
For. Nation.	1	0.3	0	0.0	1	0.2	0	0.0	0	0.0	1	0.2	0
Caucasian	283	84.5	223	77.7	506	81.4	0	0.0	131	74.4	506	81.4	154
Unknown	0	0.0	0	0.0	0	0.0	0	0.0	0	0.0	0	0.0	0
Total	335	53.9	287	46.1	622	100.0	0	0.0	176	28.3	622		176

Tuition and Fees

	Resident	Nonresident
Full-time	$25,650	$25,650
Part-time	$0	$0

Living Expenses

Estimated living expenses for singles

Living on campus	Living off campus	Living at home
$11,947	$13,646	$13,646

Penn State University, The Dickinson School of Law

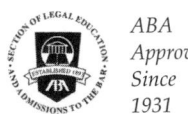

ABA Approved Since 1931

GPA and LSAT Scores

	Total	Full-time	Part-time
# of apps	2,561	2,561	0
# of admits	699	699	0
# of matrics	176	176	0
75% GPA	3.50	3.50	0.00
25% GPA	3.08	3.08	0.00
75% LSAT	157	157	0
25% LSAT	154	154	0

Grants and Scholarships (from prior year)

	Total		Full-time		Part-time	
	#	%	#	%	#	%
Total # of students	639		638		1	
Total # receiving grants	312	48.8	312	48.9	0	0.0
Less than 1/2 tuition	158	24.7	158	24.8	0	0.0
Half to full tuition	63	9.9	63	9.9	0	0.0
Full tuition	86	13.5	86	13.5	0	0.0
More than full tuition	5	0.8	5	0.8	0	0.0
Median grant amount			$12,000		$0	

Informational and Library Resources

# of volumes and volume equivalents	497,356
# of titles	81,841
# of active serial subscriptions	4,111
Study seating capacity inside the library	425
# of professional librarians	7
Hours per week library is open	168
# of open, wired connections available to students	37
# of networked computers available for use by students	138
# of simultaneous wireless users	480
Require computer?	N

JD Attrition (from prior year)

	Academic	Other	Total	
	#	#	#	%
1st year	4	18	22	9.9%
2nd year	0	1	1	0.4%
3rd year	0	0	0	0.0%
4th year	0	0	0	0.0%

Employment

	Total	Percentage
Employment status known	163	98.8
Employment status unknown	2	1.2
Employed	147	90.2
Pursuing graduate degrees	3	1.8
Unemployed seeking employment	4	2.5
Unemployed not seeking employment	9	5.5

Type of Employment

# employed in law firms	78	53.1
# employed in business and industry	13	8.8
# employed in government	20	13.6
# employed in public interest	7	4.8
# employed as judicial clerks	25	17.0
# employed in academia	0	0.0

Geographic Location

# employed in state	94	63.9
# employed in foreign countries	0	0.0
# of states where employed	16	

Bar Passage Rates

Jurisdiction	Pennsylvania		
Exam	Sum 03	Win 04	Total
# from school taking bar for the first time	115	2	117
School's pass rate for all first-time takers	87%	100%	87%
State's pass rate for all first-time takers	78%	66%	76%

Penn State University, The Dickinson School of Law

150 South College Street
Carlisle, PA 17013
Phone: 800.840.1122; 717.240.5207; Fax: 717.241.3503
E-mail: dsladmit@psu.edu; Website: www.dsl.psu.edu

■ Introduction and Mission

The Dickinson School of Law has a long tradition of training remarkably distinguished graduates. Governors; US senators; federal, state, and county judges; and prominent lawyers and civic leaders proudly list Dickinson as their legal alma mater. With the merger of The Dickinson School of Law and Penn State University in 2000, the law school embarked on a new chapter in its history. While we still produce exemplary legal practitioners with a high bar passage rate and the ability to self-confidently take up the reins of legal practice, we have added the global and technological perspectives of a major research university. Penn State Dickinson embraces the twenty-first century by preparing students in the new frontiers of law, such as intellectual property and international law, and by offering interdisciplinary programs that combine law with business, public policy, engineering, medicine, and environmental studies.

■ Faculty

Our faculty is composed of distinguished scholars and practitioners deeply committed to preparing students for success. They incorporate real-life experiences into classroom instruction, supplement standard teaching methods with the latest modes of instruction, and encourage open communication.

You will have the opportunity to take courses with faculty such as the former legal advisor to the United Nations High Commissioner for Human Rights; a leading scholar of international and domestic arbitration; the former legal director of Amnesty International; one of the nation's most important emerging scholars of gay rights; a tax law scholar who has achieved national recognition for her research combining classical history with modern day tax law; the current legal counsel to the September 11 Commission; the chair of an EPA advisory committee; and scholars and experts in emerging areas of the law.

■ Curriculum

The Penn State Dickinson curriculum is organized into integrated sequences of required and elective courses designed to develop analytical skills and teach the fundamental body of knowledge required by beginning lawyers while building competence in the skills needed for professional success.

The law school's depth in fields such as business and corporate law; international law; health, science, natural resources, and agricultural law; public interest; and trial advocacy and dispute resolution gives Penn State Dickinson graduates the edge when embarking on challenging legal careers.

We offer an inclusive academic program that can help you achieve excellence in a variety of legal specialties in addition to those previously mentioned. By choosing complementary elective courses and pursuing related practical experiences, you can follow a concentrated course of study tailored to the areas of legal practice that interest you most.

The first-year curriculum and certain second-year courses are required. Students may then choose from nearly 100 elective courses available to both JD and master of laws (LLM) candidates.

■ Academic Programs and Activities

Penn State Dickinson provides students with essential programs and activities that enhance the overall academic experience. Students can conduct research and publish articles through the Agricultural Law Resource and Reference Center, earn certificates in dispute resolution and international and comparative law, participate in one of our award-winning moot court teams, provide pro bono representation to clients through the Miller Center for Public Interest Advocacy, or engage in the representation of clients through our in-house disability, elder, family, and arts, sports, and entertainment law clinics.

In addition, students edit and publish four journals: the *Penn State Law Review*, the *Penn State Environmental Law Review*, the *Penn State International Law Review*, and *The Journal of American Arbitration*.

Our status as a unit of a world-class research university also enables us to offer a variety of joint-degree programs with Penn State, including but not limited to a JD/MBA, JD/MPA, JD/MSIS, JD/MEPC, JD/MEng, and JD/MSEPC. If you have an interest in pursuing a joint degree in a particular field, we can work with you to create a program that meets your aspirations.

■ International Programs

We are one of the few American law schools to offer a semester-long overseas program in partnership with a European law school. In conjunction with the prestigious Institute of Advanced Legal Studies at the University of London, we provide students a full semester of credits in courses taught by professors from Penn State, the University of London, the University of Cambridge, and the University of Southampton.

Penn State Dickinson also operates three summer abroad programs: the Florence, Rome, and Siena, Italy, programs; the Capitals of Europe program, which travels to The Hague, The Netherlands; Brussels, Belgium; Strasbourg, France; and Vienna, Austria; and the Summer Program at McGill University in Montreal, Quebec, Canada.

Library and Technology Resources

The library's collection of more than 440,000 volumes supports the research and study activities of students, faculty, and members of the bar. The library is accessible to students at all times.

Technology resources include five technologically equipped classrooms and three 24-hour computer labs. Wireless networking is also available throughout the school.

Student Body

Our students are vibrant, motivated, and intelligent individuals who actively engage in the Penn State Dickinson academic experience. Their diversity, varying perspectives, and enthusiasm for the law create a stimulating environment in which to learn and discuss the dynamics of the law.

An extensive assortment of approximately 40 student groups, along with student-sponsored activities and events, give students the opportunities to not only enhance their overall learning experience but also to participate in the life of the law school. Many individuals and groups are also active outside the law school and provide valuable services to the local community.

Career Services

The Career Services Office provides a range of services to ensure that students are able to realize their professional ambitions. The office maintains contacts with employers across the nation and sponsors two on-campus interview programs. The office annually posts more than 1,100 legal positions from employers in more than 40 states. Each year, more than 90 percent of Penn State Dickinson graduates are successfully employed or pursuing graduate degrees in the year after graduation. Graduates find employment nationwide, in major metropolitan areas and smaller communities.

Admission and Financial Aid

You can apply online at *www.dsl.psu.edu/apply/*. All applicants for the JD program must hold a bachelor's degree from a regionally accredited institution and are required to take the Law School Admission Test (LSAT). Students are admitted and matriculate for first-year classes in the fall semester only. The Admissions Committee begins to review completed files in mid-December and may admit highly qualified candidates at that time. The majority of our decisions will be made during February and March.

Admission is based on a review of the applicant's entire file and there are no formulas used in the admission process. Applicants are encouraged to visit the law school for a student-led tour, to observe a first-year class, and to meet with faculty, staff, and students. Applicants should arrange their visit through the Admission Office.

The Financial Aid Office works with accepted students to obtain the funding necessary to finance their education. All admitted students are considered for scholarship opportunities.

Applicant Profile

Penn State University, The Dickinson School of Law
This grid includes only applicants who earned 120-180 LSAT scores under standard administrations.

LSAT Score	3.75 +		3.50 - 3.74		3.25 - 3.49		3.00 - 3.24		2.75 - 2.99		2.50 -2.74		2.25 - 2.49		2.00 - 2.24		Below 2.00		No GPA		Total	
	Apps	Adm	Apps	Adm	Apps	Adm	Apps	Adm	Apps	Adm	Apps	Adm	Apps	Adm	Apps	Adm	Apps	Adm	Apps	Adm	Apps	Adm
175-180	0	0	0	0	0	0	0	0	0	0	0	0	0	0	0	0	0	0	0	0	0	0
170-174	0	0	2	1	1	1	0	0	0	0	0	0	0	0	0	0	0	0	0	0	3	2
165-169	7	3	5	4	6	6	4	3	2	1	1	1	0	0	1	0	0	0	0	0	26	18
160-164	22	19	13	13	27	22	18	12	13	9	8	6	6	1	1	1	0	0	2	1	110	84
155-159	66	60	90	78	142	124	108	81	70	28	32	15	25	7	7	1	1	0	8	3	549	397
150-154	110	27	162	28	210	26	209	28	101	8	56	4	30	0	13	1	1	0	5	0	897	122
145-149	47	10	101	7	124	18	129	12	106	5	42	1	37	0	11	0	2	0	10	0	609	53
140-144	8	0	15	0	50	1	59	0	45	0	26	0	15	0	9	0	2	0	5	0	234	1
135-139	1	0	5	0	11	0	17	0	20	0	6	0	6	0	5	0	0	0	3	0	74	0
130-134	0	0	4	0	4	0	7	0	4	0	6	0	2	0	2	0	0	0	4	0	33	0
125-129	0	0	0	0	0	0	0	0	1	0	1	0	1	0	0	0	1	0	2	0	6	0
120-124	0	0	1	0	0	0	0	0	0	0	0	0	1	0	0	0	0	0	1	0	3	0
Total	261	119	398	131	575	198	551	136	362	51	178	27	123	8	49	3	7	0	40	4	2544	677

Apps = Number of Applicants   Adm = Number Admitted   Reflects 99% of the total applicant pool.

University of Pennsylvania Law School

3400 Chestnut Street
Philadelphia, PA 19104-6204
Phone: 215.898.7400; Fax: 215.573.2025
E-mail: admissions@law.upenn.edu; Website: www.law.upenn.edu

ABA
Approved
Since
1923

The Basics

Type of school	Private
Term	Semester
Application deadline	2/15
Application fee	$70
Financial aid deadline	3/1
Can first year start other than fall?	No
Student to faculty ratio (fall)	13.1 to 1
Does the university offer:	
housing restricted to law students?	No
graduate housing for which law students are eligible?	Yes

Faculty and Administrators

	Total		Men		Women		Minorities	
	Fall	Spr	Fall	Spr	Fall	Spr	Fall	Spr
Full-time	53	55	43	46	10	9	4	4
Other Full-time	3	3	1	1	2	2	1	1
Deans, librarians, & others who teach	7	7	5	5	2	2	0	0
Part-time	60	53	36	30	24	23	8	10
Total	123	118	85	82	38	36	13	15

Curriculum

	Full-time	Part-time
Typical first-year section size	76	0
Is there typically a "small section" of the first-year class, other than Legal Writing, taught by full-time faculty	No	No
If yes, typical size offered last year	0	0
# of classroom course titles beyond 1st year curriculum	96	
# of upper division courses, excluding seminars with an enrollment: Under 25	38	
25-49	42	
50-74	20	
75-99	10	
100+	8	
# of seminars	50	
# of seminar positions available	700	
# of seminar positions filled	658	0
# of positions available in simulation courses	246	
# of simulation positions filled	233	0
# of positions available in faculty supervised clinical courses	120	
# of faculty supervised clinical positions filled	117	0
# involved in field placements	19	0
# involved in law journals	346	0
# involved in moot court or trial competitions	122	0
# of credit hours required to graduate	89	

JD Enrollment and Ethnicity

	Men		Women		Full-time		Part-time		1st-year		Total		JD Degs. Awd.
	#	%	#	%	#	%	#	%	#	%	#	%	
African Amer.	23	5.0	38	10.1	61	7.3	0	0.0	24	9.4	61	7.3	23
Amer. Indian	3	0.7	3	0.8	6	0.7	0	0.0	2	0.8	6	0.7	1
Asian Amer.	37	8.1	52	13.9	89	10.7	0	0.0	33	12.9	89	10.7	25
Mex. Amer.	2	0.4	5	1.3	7	0.8	0	0.0	3	1.2	7	0.8	5
Puerto Rican	4	0.9	4	1.1	8	1.0	0	0.0	2	0.8	8	1.0	2
Hispanic	23	5.0	28	7.5	51	6.1	0	0.0	16	6.3	51	6.1	14
Total Minority	92	20.1	130	34.7	222	26.7	0	0.0	80	31.4	222	26.7	70
For. Nation.	20	4.4	15	4.0	35	4.2	0	0.0	14	5.5	35	4.2	11
Caucasian	346	75.5	230	61.3	576	69.1	0	0.0	161	63.1	576	69.1	168
Unknown	0	0.0	0	0.0	0	0.0	0	0.0	0	0.0	0	0.0	0
Total	458	55.0	375	45.0	833	100.0	0	0.0	255	30.6	833		249

Tuition and Fees

	Resident	Nonresident
Full-time	$34,988	$34,988
Part-time	$0	$0

Living Expenses

Estimated living expenses for singles

Living on campus	Living off campus	Living at home
$15,492	$15,492	$8,541

University of Pennsylvania Law School

ABA
Approved
Since
1923

GPA and LSAT Scores

	Total	Full-time	Part-time
# of apps	5,189	5,189	0
# of admits	826	826	0
# of matrics	257	257	0
75% GPA	3.81	3.81	0.00
25% GPA	3.45	3.45	0.00
75% LSAT	171	171	0
25% LSAT	166	166	0

Grants and Scholarships (from prior year)

	Total		Full-time		Part-time	
	#	%	#	%	#	%
Total # of students	827		826		1	
Total # receiving grants	275	33.3	275	33.3	0	0.0
Less than 1/2 tuition	201	24.3	201	24.3	0	0.0
Half to full tuition	49	5.9	49	5.9	0	0.0
Full tuition	24	2.9	24	2.9	0	0.0
More than full tuition	1	0.1	1	0.1	0	0.0
Median grant amount			$11,750		$0	

Informational and Library Resources

# of volumes and volume equivalents	808,017
# of titles	327,648
# of active serial subscriptions	7,737
Study seating capacity inside the library	512
# of professional librarians	16
Hours per week library is open	110
# of open, wired connections available to students	255
# of networked computers available for use by students	178
# of simultaneous wireless users	2,160
Require computer?	N

JD Attrition (from prior year)

	Academic	Other	Total	
	#	#	#	%
1st year	0	7	7	2.7%
2nd year	0	0	0	0.0%
3rd year	0	0	0	0.0%
4th year	0	0	0	0.0%

Employment

	Total	Percentage
Employment status known	245	100.0
Employment status unknown	0	0.0
Employed	239	97.6
Pursuing graduate degrees	2	0.8
Unemployed seeking employment	0	0.0
Unemployed not seeking employment	4	1.6

Type of Employment

# employed in law firms	165	69.0
# employed in business and industry	5	2.1
# employed in government	9	3.8
# employed in public interest	8	3.3
# employed as judicial clerks	52	21.8
# employed in academia	0	0.0

Geographic Location

# employed in state	65	27.2
# employed in foreign countries	3	1.3
# of states where employed		20

Bar Passage Rates

Jurisdiction	New York			Pennsylvania		
Exam	Sum 03	Win 04	Total	Sum 03	Win 04	Total
# from school taking bar for the first time	108	4	112	75	0	75
School's pass rate for all first-time takers	93%	75%	92%	87%		87%
State's pass rate for all first-time takers	78%	58%	75%			

University of Pennsylvania Law School

Philadelphia, PA 19104-6204
Phone: 215.898.7400; Fax: 215.573.2025
E-mail: admissions@law.upenn.edu; Website: www.law.upenn.edu

The information on these pages was provided by the law school

■ Introduction

Penn Law, one of the nation's most distinguished law schools, offers talented students a first-rate education in an intellectually stimulating, cross-disciplinary environment. The Law School takes advantage of its role as a professional school at Penn, an Ivy League institution and one of the world's preeminent research universities. Our faculty collaborate with world-renowned scholars in other disciplines. Our students enrich their legal education with study in other disciplines, via courses, a certificate program, including one at the Wharton School for Business, or formal joint-degree programs, either those currently defined or those self-initiated by the motivated student.

The rich university community is complemented by a collegial environment. We pride ourselves on our well-known reputation as a supportive environment for students as they engage in the rigors of legal study. Students develop close relationships with their faculty and colleagues. Penn Law staff are committed to getting to know students as individuals and to working with them to support their law school experiences.

Minutes from downtown Philadelphia, Penn Law enjoys a university-campus neighborhood and close proximity to one of the nation's most lively urban areas providing an exciting, invigorating, and affordable world.

■ Faculty

Penn Law's outstanding faculty are national leaders in every major area of the law. A majority hold joint degrees; many hold joint appointments with other schools at the university.

Their scholarship is recognized worldwide. Students have opportunities to engage in research in the classroom, as research assistants, and in faculty presentations.

Faculty commitment to students and the Law School's low student-faculty ratio allow the development of close personal and professional relationships, which often develop into life-long mentorships.

■ Libraries

Biddle Law Library is one of the world's premier law libraries. Our librarians help students make full use of the Biddle's and university's collections. They also teach legal research courses and provide research assistance to support students in their intellectual endeavors.

■ Curriculum

Penn Law's first-year curriculum includes the standard first-year law school courses and also allows students the choice of two first-year electives. Students receive small-group individualized legal writing and research instruction.

In the upper years, the work is elective, allowing an opportunity to concentrate in particular areas or to study more broadly. Penn Law students can take up to four graduate or professional courses, based on their relevance to that particular student's legal education.

Penn Law offers students a wide choice of clinical courses. And, Penn Law students enjoy participating in our ABA award-winning Pro Bono program; each student spends a total of 70 hours in pro bono service.

In addition to the JD, we offer the Master of Laws (LLM), Master of Comparative Law (LLCM), and Doctor of Juridical Science (SJD).

■ Special Programs

As noted, Penn Law is unique in its interrelatedness with the other graduate and professional programs on campus.

Students can engage these departments through individual courses; a certificate in Business and Public Policy (Wharton), Women's Studies (School of Arts & Sciences), Environmental Policy or Environmental Science (School of Arts & Sciences); or through a joint-degree program (JD/MBA, JD/MGA Government, JD/MBioethics, JD/MCP City Planning, JD/PhD Communications, JD/MSW, JD/MD in Medicine; MA programs in Criminology, Education, Environment, Administration, Philosophy, Public Health; and PhDs in economics, legal history, and philosophy); and other programs including Global Business (studying at the Panthéon-Sorbonne Law School & Institut d'Études Politiques). Student opportunities at Penn are limited only by their imaginations— we work with students interested to create possibilities given their intellectual curiosity and professional goals.

■ Student Body

Students come from all over the country and from more than 180 undergraduate institutions, creating one of the nation's most diverse student bodies. About 15 percent hold advanced degrees and, on average, 65 percent do not enroll directly from undergraduate studies. Approximately 33 percent of our student body is composed of students of color. The diversity of our community creates a dynamic and engaging classroom environment and enriches every aspect of the school.

■ Student Activities

The nation's oldest law review, now the *University of Pennsylvania Law Review*, was founded in 1852. Penn Law also publishes the *Journal of Constitutional Law*, the *Journal of International Economic Law*, and the *Journal of Labor and*

560 **University of Pennsylvania Law School**

Employment Law. Students also self-publish an additional journal, *Journal of Law and Social Change* (Hybrid).

Students are active in numerous moot court and mock trial activities and in a chapter of the Inns of Court.

The student government is particularly active, and council representatives serve as voting members of many faculty/student committees.

There are more than 50 student organizations.

■ Admission

The demand for a Penn Law legal education has risen dramatically in recent years. In the 2003–2004 admission cycle, more than 5,100 applicants sought admission for the JD program. Sixteen percent of those applicants were accepted, with a median LSAT score in the 98th percentile.

While academic excellence is of primary importance for admission, we take all factors in each application into consideration and do not have numeric cutoff points for LSAT or GPA. Instead, we read each individual file, including letters of recommendation, personal statements, and the résumé, to get a full picture of the applicant.

We begin processing applications on October 1. Applications received by November 1, and completed by November 15, will be considered for our early notification program; these applicants receive a decision in mid-December. The regular admission deadline is February 15. Our program is limited to fall semester full-time students.

■ Housing

Penn Law students select from the wide range of living arrangements both on campus and in private housing.

■ Expenses and Financial Aid

The Law School maintains a substantial program of need-based scholarship and loan aid, with over 80 percent of the student body receiving financial assistance.

Penn Law extends merit-based scholarships to a select group of applicants. Every applicant is considered.

Penn Law invites students with a demonstrated previous involvement in public service, who are committed to public-sector employment following graduation, to apply for one of several Public Interest Scholarships. Penn Law has a loan forgiveness program to assist graduates who choose public sector work.

■ Career Services

The Career Planning and Placement Office has a successful record of assisting law students in finding employment and counseling students and alumni on employment opportunities. The office offers specialized counseling for public interest work, first-year job searches, judicial clerkships, and alternate careers.

About 65–70 percent of graduates start their careers in private practice, 17–21 percent take judicial clerkships, 2–5 percent work in government or public interest positions, 2–5 percent in university or law school teaching or study, and 4–6 percent accept opportunities in the business world.

Applicant Profile

Penn Law has chosen not to include an admission profile here because a grid that contains only LSAT and GPA would not capture the other qualities that make our students so dynamic. We value their diverse backgrounds, rich life experiences, leadership, community service, professional accomplishments, advanced degrees and coursework, motivation, initiative, and exemplary writing skills. While admission to Penn Law is highly selective, the admission committee takes all of the factors mentioned above into consideration when reviewing applications.

Pepperdine University School of Law

24255 Pacific Coast Highway
Malibu, CA 90263
Phone: 310.506.4611; Fax: 310.506.7668
E-mail: soladmis@pepperdine.edu; Website: law.pepperdine.edu

ABA
Approved
Since
1972

The Basics

Type of school	Private
Term	Semester
Application deadline	3/1
Application fee	$50
Financial aid deadline	4/1
Can first year start other than fall?	No
Student to faculty ratio (fall)	19.7 to 1
Does the university offer:	
housing restricted to law students?	No
graduate housing for which law students are eligible?	Yes

Faculty and Administrators

	Total		Men		Women		Minorities	
	Fall	Spr	Fall	Spr	Fall	Spr	Fall	Spr
Full-time	29	27	21	19	8	8	4	4
Other Full-time	0	0	0	0	0	0	0	0
Deans, librarians, & others who teach	17	18	10	11	7	7	0	0
Part-time	45	47	28	34	17	13	1	4
Total	91	92	59	64	32	28	5	8

Curriculum

		Full-time	Part-time
Typical first-year section size		80	0
Is there typically a "small section" of the first-year class, other than Legal Writing, taught by full-time faculty		No	No
If yes, typical size offered last year		0	0
# of classroom course titles beyond 1st year curriculum		96	
# of upper division courses, excluding seminars with an enrollment:	Under 25	98	
	25-49	37	
	50-74	7	
	75-99	7	
	100+	7	
# of seminars		18	
# of seminar positions available		424	
# of seminar positions filled		346	0
# of positions available in simulation courses		1,428	
# of simulation positions filled		1,254	0
# of positions available in faculty supervised clinical courses		48	
# of faculty supervised clinical positions filled		43	0
# involved in field placements		145	0
# involved in law journals		120	0
# involved in moot court or trial competitions		149	0
# of credit hours required to graduate		88	

JD Enrollment and Ethnicity

	Men		Women		Full-time		Part-time		1st-year		Total		JD Degs. Awd.
	#	%	#	%	#	%	#	%	#	%	#	%	
African Amer.	13	3.7	12	3.3	25	3.5	0	0.0	10	4.0	25	3.5	7
Amer. Indian	0	0.0	2	0.5	2	0.3	0	0.0	0	0.0	2	0.3	2
Asian Amer.	26	7.3	46	12.6	72	10.0	0	0.0	25	9.9	72	10.0	15
Mex. Amer.	5	1.4	9	2.5	14	1.9	0	0.0	6	2.4	14	1.9	6
Puerto Rican	0	0.0	0	0.0	0	0.0	0	0.0	0	0.0	0	0.0	0
Hispanic	7	2.0	5	1.4	12	1.7	0	0.0	6	2.4	12	1.7	7
Total Minority	51	14.4	74	20.2	125	17.4	0	0.0	47	18.6	125	17.4	37
For. Nation.	0	0.0	0	0.0	0	0.0	0	0.0	0	0.0	0	0.0	0
Caucasian	217	61.3	222	60.7	439	61.0	0	0.0	144	56.9	439	61.0	112
Unknown	86	24.3	70	19.1	156	21.7	0	0.0	62	24.5	156	21.7	31
Total	354	49.2	366	50.8	720	100.0	0	0.0	253	35.1	720		180

Tuition and Fees

	Resident	Nonresident
Full-time	$29,690	$29,690
Part-time	$0	$0

Living Expenses

Estimated living expenses for singles

Living on campus	Living off campus	Living at home
$18,990	$18,990	$18,990

Pepperdine University School of Law

ABA Approved Since 1972

GPA and LSAT Scores

	Total	Full-time	Part-time
# of apps	3,456	3,456	0
# of admits	879	879	0
# of matrics	250	250	0
75% GPA	3.71	3.71	0.00
25% GPA	3.31	3.31	0.00
75% LSAT	161	161	0
25% LSAT	157	157	0

Grants and Scholarships (from prior year)

	Total #	Total %	Full-time #	Full-time %	Part-time #	Part-time %
Total # of students	680		680		0	
Total # receiving grants	475	69.9	475	69.9	0	0.0
Less than 1/2 tuition	355	52.2	355	52.2	0	0.0
Half to full tuition	73	10.7	73	10.7	0	0.0
Full tuition	18	2.6	18	2.6	0	0.0
More than full tuition	29	4.3	29	4.3	0	0.0
Median grant amount			$2,664		$0	

Informational and Library Resources

# of volumes and volume equivalents	365,044
# of titles	115,992
# of active serial subscriptions	3,603
Study seating capacity inside the library	495
# of professional librarians	6
Hours per week library is open	105
# of open, wired connections available to students	80
# of networked computers available for use by students	51
# of simultaneous wireless users	250
Require computer?	N

JD Attrition (from prior year)

	Academic #	Other #	Total #	Total %
1st year	12	15	27	9.9%
2nd year	0	0	0	0.0%
3rd year	0	0	0	0.0%
4th year	0	0	0	0.0%

Employment

	Total	Percentage
Employment status known	199	99.0
Employment status unknown	2	1.0
Employed	161	80.9
Pursuing graduate degrees	7	3.5
Unemployed seeking employment	25	12.6
Unemployed not seeking employment	6	3.0

Type of Employment

# employed in law firms	111	68.9
# employed in business and industry	19	11.8
# employed in government	9	5.6
# employed in public interest	0	0.0
# employed as judicial clerks	5	3.1
# employed in academia	5	3.1

Geographic Location

# employed in state	126	78.3
# employed in foreign countries	0	0.0
# of states where employed		17

Bar Passage Rates

Jurisdiction	California		
Exam	Sum 03	Win 04	Total
# from school taking bar for the first time	167	10	177
School's pass rate for all first-time takers	70%	70%	70%
State's pass rate for all first-time takers	63%	47%	60%

Pepperdine University School of Law

24255 Pacific Coast Highway
Malibu, CA 90263
Phone: 310.506.4611; Fax: 310.506.7668
E-mail: soladmis@pepperdine.edu; Website: law.pepperdine.edu

■ Introduction

Pepperdine School of Law is located in Malibu, California, just 30 miles from downtown Los Angeles, making it a conducive environment for the intense study of law. Malibu offers an almost rural setting, yet it is an integral part of greater Los Angeles, providing access to one of the largest legal communities in the world. Pepperdine is a Christian university committed to the highest standards of academic excellence and Christian values, where students are strengthened for lives of purpose, service, and leadership.

■ Student Body

Pepperdine students bring a broad spectrum of back-grounds. They share a strong desire to attain high levels of achievement, in academics, in their personal lives, and careers. Students come to Pepperdine from diverse socioeconomic, cultural, and religious backgrounds for the emphasis on integrity, service, and justice with a desire to become trusted leaders.

■ Faculty

Although the faculty have distinguished themselves through scholarly research and writing as well as leader-ship positions in prestigious legal organizations, the faculty's primary mission is to teach—to help students see the structure of legal thought and to be available as professional examples of a multifaceted profession. They demonstrate to their students that lawyers should be people-oriented individuals with strong moral character, capable of guiding their clients toward what is just and honorable as well as what is legally permissible.

■ Library and Physical Facilities

The School of Law occupies the Odell McDonnell Law Center, located on the university's 830-acre campus overlooking the Pacific Ocean. The Jerene Appleby Harnish Library is the focal point of the school, housing a collection of 365,000+ volumes and volume equivalents. Students enjoy access to online legal research services and the Internet via the law school's network in three computer resource centers and at 70 wired study carrels. Wireless network access is available throughout the Law Center. The faculty contains a high-tech courtroom, as well as lecture halls, seminar rooms, a bookstore, student dining area, and lounges.

■ Curriculum

Pepperdine offers a three-year, full-time JD program; four-year, full-time JD/MBA and JD/MPP joint-degree programs; a five-year, full-time JD/MDiv joint-degree program; a concurrent JD/MDR degree program, and a LLM in Dispute Resolution. A student enrolled in two summer sessions can accelerate graduation by one semester. The required core courses are complemented by an extensive selection of elective courses.

■ Center for Entrepreneurship and Technology Law

This innovative new certificate program is designed to prepare students for both the challenges and opportunities technology is presenting in areas such as business, entertainment law, securities regulation, and intellectual property rights. The center offers a fully integrated academic approach to law, business, and technology.

■ Straus Institute for Dispute Resolution

The Straus Institute is the most comprehensive program of its type in the nation. The institute's faculty involve-ment as mediators, continuing legal education educators, and consultants enriches the practical application of course materials. Students studying in the field of dispute resolution can complete a special certificate program as part of their Juris Doctor degree program or a Master of Dispute Resolution. The LLM in Dispute Resolution began January 2003.

■ London Program

Students have the opportunity to study law in London at Pepperdine's university-owned facility in the museum district of South Kensington. While in London, students may serve as externs in clinical placements.

■ Exchange Programs

Students have the opportunity to participate in exchange programs with the University of Copenhagen and the University of Augsburg.

■ Clinical Education

Clinical law programs provide students the opportunity to refine their skills under the supervision of faculty, lawyers, and judges. The majority of clinical law opportunities are with the district attorneys, public defenders, and state and federal court judges. There are a number of programs offering experience in corporate and securities law, tax law, juvenile law, family law, labor law, consumer protection, environmental law, and trade regulation. Placements are also available within the film, television, and music industries.

Public Interest Opportunities

Pepperdine has partnered with the Los Angeles Union Rescue Mission to develop the Pepperdine Union Rescue Mission Legal Aid Clinic. Located in downtown Los Angeles, the mission provides emergency food and shelter, health services, recovery programs, education, job training, and counseling within a Christian context. Students, professors, and alumni volunteer at the mission, where they meet with residents regarding legal concerns.

Student Activities

Pepperdine has earned a national reputation for excellence in Appellate Advocacy and Trial Advocacy Competitions. Editorial and staff positions are awarded with the *Pepperdine Law Review, Pepperdine Dispute Resolution Law Journal*, and the *National Association of Administrative Law Judges Journal*.

Admission

Admission is based on the applicant's academic record, LSAT score, a written personal statement as well as a response to the university's mission statement, and other information that reflects outstanding academic and professional promise. Applications are also evaluated on the basis of employment experience, extracurricular activities, community involvement, commitment to high standards of morality and ethics, maturity, initiative, and motivation. The admission process is guided by the view that a student body that reflects diversity provides a superior educational environment. Admission decisions may be based on consideration of factors that include racial and ethnic origin, unique work or service experience, a history of overcoming disadvantage, or unusual life experiences. First-year students are admitted only in the fall.

Housing

The George Page Residential Complex is located directly across the street from the Law Center. The 72-unit complex houses graduate students in two- and four-bedroom apartments. The Admission Office also provides an extensive housing referral service.

Expenses and Financial Aid

An active financial aid program provides over 85 percent of the student body with some type of assistance. Scholarship grants are available to students with outstanding academic credentials and to those with demonstrated financial need. The deadline for completed applications for financial aid is April 1 of the entering year.

Career Development Office

The Career Development Office is committed to helping every law student explore, define, and achieve their career goals through career-related workshops, guest speaker programs, and one-on-one counseling sessions. The office also sponsors a robust Alumni Mentoring Program. Annually, over 125 employers participate in Pepperdine recruiting programs.

Applicant Profile

Pepperdine University School of Law
This grid includes only applicants who earned 120-180 LSAT scores under standard administrations.

LSAT Score	3.75 + Apps	3.75 + Adm	3.50 - 3.74 Apps	3.50 - 3.74 Adm	3.25 - 3.49 Apps	3.25 - 3.49 Adm	3.00 - 3.24 Apps	3.00 - 3.24 Adm	2.75 - 2.99 Apps	2.75 - 2.99 Adm	2.50 -2.74 Apps	2.50 -2.74 Adm	2.25 - 2.49 Apps	2.25 - 2.49 Adm	2.00 - 2.24 Apps	2.00 - 2.24 Adm	Below 2.00 Apps	Below 2.00 Adm	No GPA Apps	No GPA Adm	Total Apps	Total Adm
175-180	1	1	1	1	0	0	0	0	1	1	0	0	0	0	0	0	0	0	0	0	3	3
170-174	7	7	6	6	6	5	4	3	4	2	1	0	0	0	2	0	0	0	0	0	30	23
165-169	33	32	49	45	20	19	15	14	11	3	5	0	2	0	2	0	0	0	2	0	139	113
160-164	62	60	109	100	119	112	75	57	58	9	21	2	14	0	6	0	1	0	5	0	470	340
155-159	117	71	192	121	265	116	223	26	143	6	63	4	27	0	8	0	1	0	13	0	1052	344
150-154	79	10	195	13	264	10	234	9	138	2	62	0	29	0	7	0	4	0	9	0	1021	44
145-149	31	0	82	0	103	0	125	6	95	1	54	0	33	0	4	0	3	0	8	0	538	7
140-144	6	0	11	0	39	0	50	0	48	1	28	0	19	0	8	0	2	0	7	0	218	1
135-139	0	0	8	0	13	0	14	0	17	0	6	0	11	0	3	0	2	0	1	0	75	0
130-134	0	0	1	0	1	0	4	0	4	0	6	0	3	0	4	0	1	0	3	0	27	0
125-129	0	0	0	0	0	0	0	0	1	0	2	0	3	0	2	0	0	0	1	0	9	0
120-124	0	0	0	0	0	0	0	0	0	0	0	0	0	0	0	0	0	0	0	0	0	0
Total	336	181	654	286	830	262	744	115	520	25	248	6	141	0	46	0	14	0	49	0	3582	875

Apps = Number of Applicants   Adm = Number Admitted   Reflects 99% of the total applicant pool.

University of Pittsburgh School of Law

3900 Forbes Avenue
Pittsburgh, PA 15260
Phone: 412.648.1413; Fax: 412.648.2647
E-mail: admissions@law.pitt.edu; Website: www.law.pitt.edu

ABA
Approved
Since
1923

The Basics

Type of school	Public
Term	Semester
Application deadline	3/1
Application fee	$55
Financial aid deadline	3/1
Can first year start other than fall?	No
Student to faculty ratio (fall)	13.7 to 1
Does the university offer:	
housing restricted to law students?	No
graduate housing for which law students are eligible?	No

Faculty and Administrators

	Total Fall	Total Spr	Men Fall	Men Spr	Women Fall	Women Spr	Minorities Fall	Minorities Spr
Full-time	44	39	29	25	15	14	6	5
Other Full-time	2	3	2	2	0	1	0	0
Deans, librarians, & others who teach	10	10	4	4	6	6	0	0
Part-time	43	47	32	35	11	12	3	3
Total	99	99	67	66	32	33	9	8

Curriculum

	Full-time	Part-time
Typical first-year section size	82	0
Is there typically a "small section" of the first-year class, other than Legal Writing, taught by full-time faculty	Yes	No
If yes, typical size offered last year	27	0
# of classroom course titles beyond 1st year curriculum	171	
# of upper division courses, excluding seminars with an enrollment: Under 25	100	
25-49	35	
50-74	18	
75-99	5	
100+	10	
# of seminars	18	
# of seminar positions available	219	
# of seminar positions filled	164	0
# of positions available in simulation courses	260	
# of simulation positions filled	229	0
# of positions available in faculty supervised clinical courses	169	
# of faculty supervised clinical positions filled	137	0
# involved in field placements	166	0
# involved in law journals	167	0
# involved in moot court or trial competitions	130	0
# of credit hours required to graduate	88	

JD Enrollment and Ethnicity

	Men #	Men %	Women #	Women %	Full-time #	Full-time %	Part-time #	Part-time %	1st-year #	1st-year %	Total #	Total %	JD Degs. Awd.
African Amer.	18	4.6	36	10.9	54	7.5	0	0.0	18	7.3	54	7.5	13
Amer. Indian	0	0.0	1	0.3	1	0.1	0	0.0	1	0.4	1	0.1	0
Asian Amer.	15	3.8	13	4.0	28	3.9	0	0.0	7	2.8	28	3.9	12
Mex. Amer.	3	0.8	0	0.0	3	0.4	0	0.0	0	0.0	3	0.4	0
Puerto Rican	0	0.0	0	0.0	0	0.0	0	0.0	0	0.0	0	0.0	1
Hispanic	3	0.8	5	1.5	8	1.1	0	0.0	2	0.8	8	1.1	0
Total Minority	39	9.9	55	16.7	94	13.0	0	0.0	28	11.4	94	13.0	26
For. Nation.	0	0.0	0	0.0	0	0.0	0	0.0	0	0.0	0	0.0	0
Caucasian	281	71.5	224	68.1	505	69.9	0	0.0	143	58.1	505	69.9	242
Unknown	73	18.6	50	15.2	123	17.0	0	0.0	75	30.5	123	17.0	0
Total	393	54.4	329	45.6	722	100.0	0	0.0	246	34.1	722		268

Tuition and Fees

	Resident	Nonresident
Full-time	$19,074	$27,970
Part-time	$0	$0

Living Expenses

Estimated living expenses for singles

Living on campus	Living off campus	Living at home
$13,700	$13,700	$10,700

University of Pittsburgh School of Law

*ABA
Approved
Since
1923*

GPA and LSAT Scores

	Total	Full-time	Part-time
# of apps	2,209	2,209	0
# of admits	670	670	0
# of matrics	248	248	0
75% GPA	3.64	3.64	0.00
25% GPA	3.05	3.05	0.00
75% LSAT	162	162	0
25% LSAT	157	157	0

Grants and Scholarships (from prior year)

	Total		Full-time		Part-time	
	#	%	#	%	#	%
Total # of students	721		721		0	
Total # receiving grants	335	46.5	335	46.5	0	0.0
Less than 1/2 tuition	192	26.6	192	26.6	0	0.0
Half to full tuition	139	19.3	139	19.3	0	0.0
Full tuition	3	0.4	3	0.4	0	0.0
More than full tuition	1	0.1	1	0.1	0	0.0
Median grant amount			$10,000		$0	

Informational and Library Resources

# of volumes and volume equivalents	430,924
# of titles	243,223
# of active serial subscriptions	4,266
Study seating capacity inside the library	438
# of professional librarians	8
Hours per week library is open	103
# of open, wired connections available to students	304
# of networked computers available for use by students	25
# of simultaneous wireless users	425
Require computer?	N

JD Attrition (from prior year)

	Academic	Other	Total	
	#	#	#	%
1st year	1	19	20	8.5%
2nd year	0	2	2	0.8%
3rd year	0	0	0	0.0%
4th year	0	0	0	0.0%

Employment

	Total	Percentage
Employment status known	235	99.2
Employment status unknown	2	0.8
Employed	212	90.2
Pursuing graduate degrees	5	2.1
Unemployed seeking employment	7	3.0
Unemployed not seeking employment	11	4.7

Type of Employment

# employed in law firms	134	63.2
# employed in business and industry	31	14.6
# employed in government	15	7.1
# employed in public interest	4	1.9
# employed as judicial clerks	18	8.5
# employed in academia	5	2.4

Geographic Location

# employed in state	154	72.6
# employed in foreign countries	1	0.5
# of states where employed		23

Bar Passage Rates

Jurisdiction	Pennsylvania		
Exam	Sum 03	Win 04	Total
# from school taking bar for the first time	174	12	186
School's pass rate for all first-time takers	82%	67%	81%
State's pass rate for all first-time takers	78%	66%	76%

University of Pittsburgh School of Law

3900 Forbes Avenue
Pittsburgh, PA 15260
Phone: 412.648.1413; Fax: 412.648.2647
E-mail: admissions@law.pitt.edu; Website: www.law.pitt.edu

■ Introduction

The University of Pittsburgh School of Law (Pitt), founded in 1895, is a leader in the world of legal education. It features a broad and varied curriculum, an internationally accomplished faculty, state-of-the-art physical facilities, and a talented and diverse student body hailing from all over the globe. The School of Law is located in its own modern six-story building on campus in Oakland, the cultural and educational center of Pittsburgh. State and federal courts, major corporate headquarters, and hundreds of law firms are located nearby in downtown Pittsburgh, only minutes from campus. The dynamic Oakland area is home to four colleges and universities, the world-renowned, multi-hospital University of Pittsburgh Medical Center, numerous scientific and high-tech offices and research centers, museums, art galleries, coffee houses, and libraries. The Pitt campus abuts a beautiful 429-acre city park. Desirable and affordable residential areas are situated nearby. Quality housing is readily available, and all mass transit in the city is free to Pitt students with ID cards.

■ Library and Physical Facilities

The newly renovated Barco Law Library is an attractive, 425,000-volume, open-stack research facility, housed on three floors of the School of Law building. Full of natural light, it contains two computer labs and ample carrel and seating space. The Fawcett Student Commons in the library is a comfortable gathering spot for students, faculty, and staff, and contains the Sidebar Café, featuring Starbucks coffee products. Faculty offices ring the perimeter of the first and third floors of the library, encouraging ease of interaction between students and faculty. Classrooms with state-of-the-art technology are located on the first and ground floors of the School of Law building. A spacious and comfortable student lounge and the elegant Teplitz Memorial Courtroom are located on the ground floor. Student computing is also supported through a wireless network and wired carrels and seating.

■ Law at Sea Summer Program

During the summer, Pitt sponsors its unique Law at Sea Program. Comparative and international law courses are taught to law students by Pitt Law and other international faculty members while sailing on the world-renowned Semester at Sea® Program, housed on its own large cruise ship, which docks in seven Pacific Rim countries.

■ Special Programs

- *Clinical Programs*—Academics and reality meet head-on in our legal clinics. Pitt law students have the opportunity to obtain hands-on experience in several different clinical programs, which include a Tax Clinic; an Environmental Law Clinic; a Civil Practice Clinic that selects a focus on either Health Law, Elder Law, or Family Law and Related Matters; and a Community Economic Development Clinic. With a supervising attorney, students do it all: pretrial preparation, negotiation, litigation, and counseling real-life clients about real-life legal concerns.
- *Certificate Programs*—One way to practice proficiently in an interdependent world is to develop specialized expertise. Pitt law students may seize that advantage through participation in our certificate programs; a collection of sharply focused courses that culminate in certification to specialize in a high-demand area of practice. Certificate programs currently exist in the areas of civil litigation; environmental law, science, and policy; health law; international and comparative law; and intellectual property and technology law. These certificate programs can be completed within the regular 88 credits.
- *Mellon Legal Writing Program*—The Mellon Program provides academic support to students at the law school who wish to improve their writing, exam-taking, and study skills. Exam preparation sessions include general discussion regarding the form and substance of law school exams as well as more specific guidance relating to particular topics and classes. All workshops are led by the Associate Dean for Student Affairs.

■ Center for International Legal Education (CILE)

In today's world, legal transactions inevitably involve many nations and many sets of laws. The successful lawyer—today's global lawyer—understands the political, cultural, and social influences on the legal systems of other countries and uses that knowledge for the benefit of his or her clients. CILE faculty prepare Pitt law students for successful futures in this modern world. Students study the workings of foreign legal systems and explore the wide array of issues facing practicing attorneys in the global marketplace. The center also coordinates international programs at Pitt with the University Center for International Studies and affiliated area studies programs, and it supervises a number of specialized language classes, for example, French for Lawyers, Spanish for Lawyers, German for Lawyers, Chinese for Lawyers, and Japanese for Lawyers.

■ Admission

Pitt Law is highly competitive and decisions are based upon several factors with the GPA and LSAT being the most important. A required personal statement gives the committee a view into the nonacademic world of the applicant. This is critical in our ability to enroll a diverse class. Letters of recommendation play an equally important role in this process as they can reveal the strengths of the academic achievements of the applicant.

■ Scholarships

If you are accepted to Pitt Law, we make every effort to assist you in securing the financial resources you will need in order to cover the cost of your legal education. Approximately 43 percent of the student body receives merit and/or need-based scholarship funds. The University of Pittsburgh School of Law also offers a Public Interest Scholarship and has several firm-sponsored scholarships available.

■ Student Activities

The *Law Review*, the *Journal of Law and Commerce*, and the *Journal of Law and Technology* are legal periodicals published by upper-class law students. In addition, more than 30 law student organizations exist under the auspices of the Student Bar Association, reflecting the diverse social and intellectual interests and experiences of our students. They include the Asian Law Students Association, the Black Law Students Association, the Environmental Law Council, the Federalist Society, the Hispanic Law Society, the Jewish Law Students Association, the Lesbian-Gay Rights Organization (OUTLAW), the Pitt Law Women's Association, and the Pitt Legal Income Sharing Foundation to name a few.

■ Career Services

The Career Service's Office provides year-round assistance to Pitt students and graduates. The office serves as a clearinghouse for information on summer, part-time, and permanent work with law firms, corporations, accounting firms, government agencies, judges, and other legal employers. It also helps students develop practical job search strategies, helps demystify the dynamics of the legal job market, offers strategies for finding the perfect job in that market, and offers information and counseling regarding nontraditional careers utilizing professional skills gained in law school. The placement rate for the class of 2003 was 96.5 percent.

Applicant Profile

University of Pittsburgh School of Law
This grid includes only applicants who earned 120-180 LSAT scores under standard administrations.

LSAT Score	GPA 3.75 + Apps	Adm	3.50 - 3.74 Apps	Adm	3.25 - 3.49 Apps	Adm	3.00 - 3.24 Apps	Adm	2.75 - 2.99 Apps	Adm	2.50 - 2.74 Apps	Adm	Below 2.50 Apps	Adm	No GPA Apps	Adm	Total Apps	Adm
165-180	25	23	29	27	26	26	19	15	8	6	8	7	6	2	2	2	123	108
160-164	66	65	64	53	87	66	59	50	36	25	16	9	14	7	1	0	343	275
155-159	103	47	147	63	177	82	132	43	75	14	38	4	13	2	8	1	693	256
150-154	73	6	122	4	148	14	149	13	54	3	33	1	23	2	5	0	607	43
145-149	20	0	45	1	73	6	61	3	28	1	13	1	22	0	4	0	266	12
Below 145	9	0	13	0	25	0	46	0	35	0	22	0	26	1	6	0	182	1
Total	296	141	420	148	536	194	466	124	236	49	130	22	104	14	26	3	2214	695

Apps = Number of Applicants
Adm = Number Admitted
Reflects 100% of the total applicant pool.

Pontifical Catholic University of Puerto Rico, School of Law

2250 Avenida Las Americas
Ponce, PR 00732
Phone: 787.841.2000, ext. 1836, 1837; Fax: 787.841.4620
E-mail: derecho@pucpr.edu; Website: www.pucpr.edu/derecho

ABA
Approved
Since
1967

The Basics

Type of school	Private
Term	Semester
Application deadline	4/15 9/30
Application fee	$75
Financial aid deadline	5/5
Can first year start other than fall?	Yes
Student to faculty ratio (fall)	15.8 to 1
Does the university offer:	
housing restricted to law students?	No
graduate housing for which law students are eligible?	No

Faculty and Administrators

	Total		Men		Women		Minorities	
	Fall	Spr	Fall	Spr	Fall	Spr	Fall	Spr
Full-time	23	22	18	17	5	5	23	22
Other Full-time	1	2	1	2	0	0	1	1
Deans, librarians, & others who teach	5	5	3	3	2	2	5	5
Part-time	14	18	13	16	0	1	14	18
Total	43	47	35	38	7	8	43	46

Curriculum

		Full-time	Part-time
Typical first-year section size		36	37
Is there typically a "small section" of the first-year class, other than Legal Writing, taught by full-time faculty		Yes	Yes
If yes, typical size offered last year		19	15
# of classroom course titles beyond 1st year curriculum		78	
# of upper division courses, excluding seminars with an enrollment:	Under 25	54	
	25-49	37	
	50-74	22	
	75-99	2	
	100+	0	
# of seminars		15	
# of seminar positions available		323	
# of seminar positions filled		86	188
# of positions available in simulation courses		152	
# of simulation positions filled		49	77
# of positions available in faculty supervised clinical courses		0	
# of faculty supervised clinical positions filled		6	0
# involved in field placements		0	0
# involved in law journals		98	2
# involved in moot court or trial competitions		0	0
# of credit hours required to graduate		94	

JD Enrollment and Ethnicity

	Men		Women		Full-time		Part-time		1st-year		Total		JD Degs. Awd.
	#	%	#	%	#	%	#	%	#	%	#	%	
African Amer.	0	0.0	0	0.0	0	0.0	0	0.0	0	0.0	0	0.0	0
Amer. Indian	0	0.0	0	0.0	0	0.0	0	0.0	0	0.0	0	0.0	0
Asian Amer.	0	0.0	0	0.0	0	0.0	0	0.0	0	0.0	0	0.0	0
Mex. Amer.	0	0.0	0	0.0	0	0.0	0	0.0	0	0.0	0	0.0	0
Puerto Rican	228	99.6	261	100.0	328	99.7	161	100.0	183	99.5	489	99.8	141
Hispanic	0	0.0	0	0.0	0	0.0	0	0.0	0	0.0	0	0.0	0
Total Minority	228	99.6	261	100.0	328	99.7	161	100.0	183	99.5	489	99.8	141
For. Nation.	1	0.4	0	0.0	1	0.3	0	0.0	1	0.5	1	0.2	0
Caucasian	0	0.0	0	0.0	0	0.0	0	0.0	0	0.0	0	0.0	0
Unknown	0	0.0	0	0.0	0	0.0	0	0.0	0	0.0	0	0.0	0
Total	229	46.7	261	53.3	329	67.1	161	32.9	184	37.6	490		141

Tuition and Fees

	Resident	Nonresident
Full-time	$12,736	$0
Part-time	$9,074	$0

Living Expenses

Estimated living expenses for singles

Living on campus	Living off campus	Living at home
$7,366	$9,482	$6,782

Pontifical Catholic University of Puerto Rico, School of Law

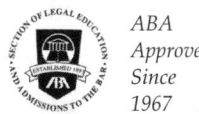

*ABA
Approved
Since
1967*

GPA and LSAT Scores

	Total	Full-time	Part-time
# of apps	503	335	168
# of admits	288	172	116
# of matrics	192	129	63
75% GPA	3.53	3.58	3.50
25% GPA	2.90	2.93	2.82
75% LSAT	138	139	138
25% LSAT	133	133	131

Grants and Scholarships (from prior year)

	Total		Full-time		Part-time	
	#	%	#	%	#	%
Total # of students	481		339		142	
Total # receiving grants	32	6.7	28	8.3	4	2.8
Less than 1/2 tuition	0	0.0	0	0.0	0	0.0
Half to full tuition	23	4.8	20	5.9	3	2.1
Full tuition	9	1.9	8	2.4	1	0.7
More than full tuition	0	0.0	0	0.0	0	0.0
Median grant amount			$5,400		$4,230	

Informational and Library Resources

# of volumes and volume equivalents	214,704
# of titles	27,846
# of active serial subscriptions	2,572
Study seating capacity inside the library	194
# of professional librarians	4
Hours per week library is open	92
# of open, wired connections available to students	60
# of networked computers available for use by students	60
# of simultaneous wireless users	250
Require computer?	N

JD Attrition (from prior year)

	Academic	Other	Total	
	#	#	#	%
1st year	13	17	30	18.4%
2nd year	1	4	5	3.9%
3rd year	0	1	1	0.6%
4th year	0	0	0	0.0%

Employment

	Total	Percentage
Employment status known	136	93.2
Employment status unknown	10	6.8
Employed	118	86.8
Pursuing graduate degrees	2	1.5
Unemployed seeking employment	16	11.8
Unemployed not seeking employment	0	0.0

Type of Employment

# employed in law firms	40	33.9
# employed in business and industry	10	8.5
# employed in government	45	38.1
# employed in public interest	1	0.8
# employed as judicial clerks	3	2.5
# employed in academia	0	0.0

Geographic Location

# employed in state	0	0.0
# employed in foreign countries	0	0.0
# of states where employed	0	

Bar Passage Rates

Jurisdiction	Puerto Rico		
Exam	Sum 03	Win 04	Total
# from school taking bar for the first time	112	28	140
School's pass rate for all first-time takers	45%	43%	44%
State's pass rate for all first-time takers	57%	38%	54%

Pontifical Catholic University of Puerto Rico, School of Law

2250 Avenida Las Americas
Ponce, PR 00732
Phone: 787.841.2000, ext. 1836, 1837; Fax: 787.841.4620
E-mail: derecho@pucpr.edu; Website: www.pucpr.edu/derecho

■ Introduction

The School of Law of the Pontifical Catholic University of Puerto Rico was founded in 1961. It is located within the main campus of the Pontifical Catholic University of Puerto Rico, on the southern part of the island in the historical city of Ponce, one of the most beautiful places in Puerto Rico.

The primary objective of the Pontifical Catholic University School of Law is the formation of lawyers imbued with a deep love and concern for their Catholic faith and imbedded in the redeeming truths of Christian philosophy and ethics. The law school of the Pontifical Catholic University of Puerto Rico hopes to contribute to upholding the high ethical, cultural, and literary accomplishments of the Puerto Rican bar, which historically represents a tradition of moral austerity, intellectual achievement, and professional competence.

■ Library and Physical Facilities

The School of Law occupies the Spellman Building. Its location on the campus of Pontifical Catholic University of Puerto Rico enables students to study related academic disciplines, to participate in the intellectual life, and to enjoy many other facilities of the university.

Among the materials in the library is a comprehensive and growing collection of legal treatises, tests, monographs, and periodicals, including the most important and recent publications in civil, common, and comparative law. Modern audiovisual equipment and computerized services are also available. The library is an authorized depository for the United Nations documents as well as for United States documents. In addition, it offers the services of the Westlaw and LexisNexis systems, which permit computer-assisted legal research.

■ Curriculum

The required subjects are Developments and Evolution of the Institutions of the Civil Law, Constitutional Law, Torts, Property Law, Legal Ethics and Professional Responsibility, Theology, Family Law, Successions and Donations, Penal Law, Criminal Procedure, Administrative Law, Obligations, Contracts, Notarial Law, Civil Procedure, Evidence, Mortgages, Trial Practice, Legal Aid Clinic, Corporations, Mercantile Law, Negotiable Instruments, Federal Jurisdiction, Analysis of Jurisprudence, Legal Document Workshop, and Legal Bibliography. The basic program covers three years in the day division or four years in the evening division.

The school curriculum includes a clinical program for third-year students. Pursuant to a rule approved by the

Supreme Court of the Commonwealth of Puerto Rico in 1974, students practice trial advocacy under the supervision of law school professors in the Courts of First Instance and in administrative agencies.

The Pontifical Catholic University of Puerto Rico also offers a combined JD/MBA degree. For the combined degree, students are required to complete 85 credit hours at the School of Law (79 required credits and 6 elective credits) plus 9 credit hours in electives completed at the Graduate Program of the School of Business Administration for a total of 94 credit hours. In addition, the students must complete 34 credit hours at the School of Business Administration (31 required credits and 3 electives) and an additional 9 approved elective credits in JD for a total of 43 credits, plus four hours of Theology.

■ Admission

Application for admission is open to men and women of good character who have received a bachelor's degree from a qualified institution and have obtained a 2.5 grade-point average.

The required forms for application for admission and all other information may be obtained from the registrar of the law school and should be filed with all supporting documents before April 15. The School of Law admits beginning students in August and January for both the full-time and part-time programs.

Applicants are required to take both the LSAT and the Prueba de Admision para Estudios Graduados (PAEG).

Test scores are not the only factor considered. Besides the objective factors, there are many intangible and personal considerations, such as strong motivation, disadvantaged circumstances, evidence of improving performance, and relevant work experience. A personal interview of the applicant by a committee is essential before a decision is made. Applicants of both sexes and from all religious, racial, social, and ethnic backgrounds are encouraged to apply.

All courses are offered only in Spanish. Consequently, students are required to be proficient in Spanish.

■ Student Activities

The law review, *Revista de Derecho Puertorriqueño*, is devoted to scholarly analysis and discussion of development of the law. It publishes student notes, comments and surveys, as well as articles of outstanding quality submitted by attorneys, judges, and other members of the legal profession. The school has a student council, a chapter of the National Association of Law Students of Puerto Rico, and an Association for Women's Rights. Local chapters of Phi Alpha Delta international law

Pontifical Catholic University of Puerto Rico, School of Law

fraternity, the Delta Theta Phi law fraternity, and the Law Student Division of the ABA are also active and well organized in the law school.

■ Housing

Students live either in university residences or private housing. Inquiries concerning housing facilities should be addressed to the Housing Office, Pontifical Catholic University of Puerto Rico, Ponce, Puerto Rico 00732.

■ Expenses and Financial Aid

There is a deferred plan for students who have financial difficulties at the time of registration. The university has made available for law students several full-tuition scholarships to be awarded on the basis of scholastic excellence. The university also has an office for student loans and other types of financial services.

Applicant Profile Not Available

University of Puerto Rico School of Law

PO Box 23349, UPR Station
San Juan, PR 00931-3349
Phone: 787.999.9595; Fax: 787.764.4360
E-mail: wperez@law.upr.edu

*ABA
Approved
Since
1945*

The Basics

Type of school	Public
Term	Semester
Application deadline	2/14
Application fee	$15
Financial aid deadline	4/30
Can first year start other than fall?	No
Student to faculty ratio (fall)	21.5 to 1
Does the university offer:	
housing restricted to law students?	Yes
graduate housing for which law students are eligible?	No

Faculty and Administrators

	Total		Men		Women		Minorities	
	Fall	Spr	Fall	Spr	Fall	Spr	Fall	Spr
Full-time	24	22	16	15	8	7	23	20
Other Full-time	2	4	0	1	2	3	1	2
Deans, librarians, & others who teach	4	4	1	1	3	3	4	4
Part-time	31	26	22	17	9	9	29	22
Total	61	56	39	34	22	22	57	48

Curriculum

		Full-time	Part-time
Typical first-year section size		45	55
Is there typically a "small section" of the first-year class, other than Legal Writing, taught by full-time faculty		No	No
If yes, typical size offered last year		0	0
# of classroom course titles beyond 1st year curriculum		80	
# of upper division courses, excluding seminars with an enrollment:	Under 25	19	
	25-49	28	
	50-74	22	
	75-99	8	
	100+	0	
# of seminars		32	
# of seminar positions available		473	
# of seminar positions filled		293	180
# of positions available in simulation courses		60	
# of simulation positions filled		56	0
# of positions available in faculty supervised clinical courses		182	
# of faculty supervised clinical positions filled	135		47
# involved in field placements		56	0
# involved in law journals		20	5
# involved in moot court or trial competitions	28		8
# of credit hours required to graduate		92	

JD Enrollment and Ethnicity

	Men		Women		Full-time		Part-time		1st-year		Total		JD Degs. Awd.
	#	%	#	%	#	%	#	%	#	%	#	%	
African Amer.	0	0.0	0	0.0	0	0.0	0	0.0	0	0.0	0	0.0	0
Amer. Indian	0	0.0	0	0.0	0	0.0	0	0.0	0	0.0	0	0.0	0
Asian Amer.	0	0.0	0	0.0	0	0.0	0	0.0	0	0.0	0	0.0	0
Mex. Amer.	0	0.0	0	0.0	0	0.0	0	0.0	0	0.0	0	0.0	0
Puerto Rican	306	100.0	403	98.8	427	99.1	282	99.6	196	100.0	709	99.3	171
Hispanic	0	0.0	1	0.2	0	0.0	1	0.4	0	0.0	1	0.1	0
Total Minority	306	100.0	404	99.0	427	99.1	283	100.0	196	100.0	710	99.4	171
For. Nation.	0	0.0	2	0.5	2	0.5	0	0.0	0	0.0	2	0.3	0
Caucasian	0	0.0	2	0.5	2	0.5	0	0.0	0	0.0	2	0.3	0
Unknown	0	0.0	0	0.0	0	0.0	0	0.0	0	0.0	0	0.0	0
Total	306	42.9	408	57.1	431	60.4	283	39.6	196	27.5	714		171

Tuition and Fees

	Resident	Nonresident
Full-time	$2,395	$3,570
Part-time	$1,720	$3,570

Living Expenses

Estimated living expenses for singles

Living on campus	Living off campus	Living at home
$9,138	$11,655	$8,150

University of Puerto Rico School of Law

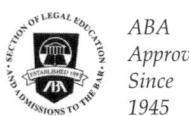

ABA
Approved
Since
1945

GPA and LSAT Scores

	Total	Full-time	Part-time
# of apps	724	464	260
# of admits	217	135	82
# of matrics	196	130	66
75% GPA	3.74	3.78	3.80
25% GPA	3.25	3.30	3.31
75% LSAT	149	149	149
25% LSAT	142	143	143

Grants and Scholarships (from prior year)

	Total #	Total %	Full-time #	Full-time %	Part-time #	Part-time %
Total # of students	679		452		227	
Total # receiving grants	1	0.1	1	0.2	0	0.0
Less than 1/2 tuition	1	0.1	1	0.2	0	0.0
Half to full tuition	0	0.0	0	0.0	0	0.0
Full tuition	0	0.0	0	0.0	0	0.0
More than full tuition	0	0.0	0	0.0	0	0.0
Median grant amount			$1,200		$0	

Informational and Library Resources

# of volumes and volume equivalents	392,585
# of titles	78,171
# of active serial subscriptions	5,140
Study seating capacity inside the library	407
# of professional librarians	9
Hours per week library is open	112
# of open, wired connections available to students	180
# of networked computers available for use by students	50
# of simultaneous wireless users	0
Require computer?	N

JD Attrition (from prior year)

	Academic #	Other #	Total #	Total %
1st year	6	21	27	14.1%
2nd year	2	6	8	3.4%
3rd year	0	3	3	1.4%
4th year	0	0	0	0.0%

Employment

	Total	Percentage
Employment status known	52	33.5
Employment status unknown	103	66.5
Employed	43	82.7
Pursuing graduate degrees	0	0.0
Unemployed seeking employment	8	15.4
Unemployed not seeking employment	1	1.9

Type of Employment

# employed in law firms	24	55.8
# employed in business and industry	4	9.3
# employed in government	7	16.3
# employed in public interest	0	0.0
# employed as judicial clerks	7	16.3
# employed in academia	1	2.3

Geographic Location

# employed in state	41	95.3
# employed in foreign countries	0	0.0
# of states where employed	2	

Bar Passage Rates

Jurisdiction	Puerto Rico		
Exam	Sum 03	Win 04	Total
# from school taking bar for the first time	132	10	142
School's pass rate for all first-time takers	72%	60%	71%
State's pass rate for all first-time takers	57%	38%	54%

University of Puerto Rico School of Law

PO Box 23349, UPR Station
San Juan, PR 00931-3349
Phone: 787.999.9595; Fax: 787.764.4360
E-mail: wperez@law.upr.edu

■ Introduction

The University of Puerto Rico School of Law was founded in 1913 at its present site on the University Campus at Rio Piedras, within the metropolitan area of San Juan. The School of Law has been accredited by the American Bar Association since 1945, and the University of Puerto Rico is accredited by the Middle States Colleges Association. In 1948, the school was approved by the Association of American Law Schools. It is also accredited by the Council on Higher Education and the Puerto Rico Supreme Court.

■ Library and Physical Facilities

The law library is the largest law library in the Caribbean. Its collection reflects both the Romano-Germanic civil law and Anglo-American common law traditions. The law library harbors a comprehensive collection of legal materials from the Caribbean Basin, including resources from Mexico, Central America, Venezuela, and Colombia, as well as the island jurisdictions. In addition to hard-copy and microform materials, the law library subscribes to a variety of computerized legal research services. The law library has been designated as a European Documentation Center by the European Union and is also a selective depository for US government documents.

■ Clinical Program

The curriculum includes clinical programs for third-year students. The Legal Aid Clinic handles upwards of 1,300 cases per year. Rules for the participation of students before the local courts were approved by the Puerto Rico Supreme Court in March 1974 and by the US District Court in 1991.

■ Special Programs

The law school has student exchange programs with the University of Arizona College of Law, the University of Connecticut Law School, and the University of Chile Law School. Under these programs, the students will register at their home institution but will take a full courseload at the host institution. The credits and grades earned during a single semester will be awarded by the home institution according to the standard procedure of the home law school.

Students also have a chance to attend two different law programs at the University of Barcelona, Spain. The first one is a summer law program. The other alternative is a four-year program: three years of study at the University of Puerto Rico School of Law and one year abroad at the University of Barcelona. At the end of this program, the student will receive a Juris Doctor from the University of Puerto Rico and a law degree from the University of Barcelona, which will enable the student to practice law in the European Union.

The law school also has three joint-degree programs: a JD/MBA program with the University of Puerto Rico Graduate School of Business Administration, a JD/MPP program with the Hubert H. Humphrey Institute of Public Policy of the University of Minnesota, and a JD/MD program with the University of Puerto Rico School of Medicine.

The law school offers an LLM Program for Latin American Lawyers.

■ Admission

In order to be admitted to the University of Puerto Rico School of Law, applicants must take the LSAT and the Examen de Admision a Estudios de Posgrado (EXADEP), administered by the Educational Testing Service, no later than February and March, respectively, the year of application. They must complete their undergraduate degree before enrolling in the law school. The LSAT, the EXADEP, and the graduating index are converted into the student's admission index.

The cases of applicants with disabilities, who, by reason of their disability, cannot take the required aptitude tests, are considered individually by the Admissions Committee.

The University of Puerto Rico does not discriminate against students on the basis of race, color, religion, gender, age, marital status, national origin, or disability.

■ Expenses and Financial Aid

Resident law students pay tuition and fees amounting to $75 per credit each semester. Nonresident students who are American citizens pay the same amount that would be required from Puerto Rican students if they were to study in the state from which the nonresidents come, thus establishing a reciprocity principle.

Regular fees for basic medical services amount to $337 for the first semester and $473 for the second semester, which includes summer. The medical fee for the summer session only is $135.

Nonresident students—Nonresident students who are not American citizens pay additional tuition and fees amounting to $1,750 for eight or more credits for each semester.

Additional regular fees for basic medical services amount to $115 for the first semester and $161 for the second semester, which includes summer.

All financial aid for the University of Puerto Rico School of Law is administered by the school's Office of Financial Aid. Each student is considered on his or her own merit and need. Awards are made only after an applicant has been admitted.

■ Career Services

Since 1981, the school has had an Office of Student Affairs under an assistant dean that offers a variety of services, including placement. The Placement Officer, with the aid of the Puerto Rico Bar Association, the Department of Justice, and other government agencies, helps students obtain part-time jobs, full-time jobs, or scholarships.

The Office of Student Affairs has initiated a series of statistical studies on the school's alumni, which include a former governor of Puerto Rico, the secretary of justice, Puerto Rico Supreme Court justices, and many cabinet members, judges, and legislators.

Applicant Profile

University of Puerto Rico School of Law
This grid includes only applicants who earned 120-180 LSAT scores under standard administrations.

LSAT Score	3.75 +		3.50 - 3.74		3.25 - 3.49		3.00 - 3.24		2.75 - 2.99		2.50 -2.74		2.25 - 2.49		2.00 - 2.24		Below 2.00		No GPA		Total	
	Apps	Adm	Apps	Adm	Apps	Adm	Apps	Adm	Apps	Adm	Apps	Adm	Apps	Adm	Apps	Adm	Apps	Adm	Apps	Adm	Apps	Adm
175-180	0	0	0	0	0	0	0	0	0	0	0	0	0	0	0	0	0	0	0	0	0	0
170-174	0	0	0	0	0	0	0	0	0	0	0	0	0	0	0	0	0	0	0	0	0	0
165-169	0	0	0	0	1	0	1	0	1	1	0	0	0	0	0	0	0	0	0	0	3	1
160-164	0	0	0	0	1	1	0	0	0	0	1	1	0	0	0	0	0	0	0	0	2	2
155-159	1	1	3	3	4	4	3	3	1	1	0	0	0	0	2	1	0	0	0	0	14	13
150-154	6	6	13	13	9	5	10	8	2	1	5	3	4	2	1	0	0	0	1	1	51	39
145-149	21	20	19	18	15	12	19	14	6	4	9	3	5	2	2	0	1	0	2	1	99	74
140-144	29	25	29	21	34	17	39	7	18	0	14	0	2	0	1	0	0	0	3	0	169	70
135-139	22	7	32	6	33	3	29	0	26	0	11	0	4	0	2	0	1	0	9	0	169	16
130-134	17	2	26	0	27	0	24	0	14	0	11	0	4	0	4	0	0	0	6	0	133	2
125-129	6	0	12	0	8	0	11	0	8	1	11	0	5	0	1	0	0	0	10	0	72	1
120-124	0	0	2	0	2	0	1	0	2	0	2	0	0	0	1	0	0	0	2	0	12	0
Total	102	61	136	61	134	42	137	32	78	8	64	7	24	4	14	1	2	0	33	2	724	218

Apps = Number of Applicants
Adm = Number Admitted
Reflects 99% of the total applicant pool.

Quinnipiac University School of Law

275 Mt. Carmel Avenue
Hamden, CT 06518
Phone: 203.582.3400; Fax: 203.582.3339
E-mail: ladm@quinnipiac.edu; Website: http://law.quinnipiac.edu

ABA Approved Since 1992

The Basics

Type of school	Private
Term	Semester
Application deadline	
Application fee	$40
Financial aid deadline	4/15
Can first year start other than fall?	No
Student to faculty ratio (fall)	15.4 to 1
Does the university offer:	
housing restricted to law students?	No
graduate housing for which law students are eligible?	No

Faculty and Administrators

	Total		Men		Women		Minorities	
	Fall	Spr	Fall	Spr	Fall	Spr	Fall	Spr
Full-time	32	33	19	20	13	13	3	3
Other Full-time	5	5	2	2	3	3	0	0
Deans, librarians, & others who teach	2	2	2	2	0	0	0	0
Part-time	33	40	25	29	8	11	0	1
Total	72	80	48	53	24	27	3	4

Curriculum

		Full-time	Part-time
Typical first-year section size		77	48
Is there typically a "small section" of the first-year class, other than Legal Writing, taught by full-time faculty		No	No
If yes, typical size offered last year		0	0
# of classroom course titles beyond 1st year curriculum		102	
# of upper division courses, excluding seminars with an enrollment:	Under 25	130	
	25-49	26	
	50-74	14	
	75-99	4	
	100+	0	
# of seminars		14	
# of seminar positions available		212	
# of seminar positions filled		62	83
# of positions available in simulation courses		537	
# of simulation positions filled		214	220
# of positions available in faculty supervised clinical courses		118	
# of faculty supervised clinical positions filled		76	10
# involved in field placements		125	0
# involved in law journals		105	50
# involved in moot court or trial competitions		30	11
# of credit hours required to graduate		86	

JD Enrollment and Ethnicity

	Men		Women		Full-time		Part-time		1st-year		Total		JD Degs. Awd.
	#	%	#	%	#	%	#	%	#	%	#	%	
African Amer.	5	1.4	7	2.3	7	1.5	5	2.7	5	2.5	12	1.8	13
Amer. Indian	1	0.3	1	0.3	1	0.2	1	0.5	1	0.5	2	0.3	0
Asian Amer.	9	2.6	11	3.6	15	3.2	5	2.7	9	4.4	20	3.1	4
Mex. Amer.	0	0.0	0	0.0	0	0.0	0	0.0	0	0.0	0	0.0	0
Puerto Rican	0	0.0	0	0.0	0	0.0	0	0.0	0	0.0	0	0.0	0
Hispanic	3	0.9	7	2.3	7	1.5	3	1.6	3	1.5	10	1.5	13
Total Minority	18	5.2	26	8.4	30	6.4	14	7.4	18	8.9	44	6.7	30
For. Nation.	1	0.3	2	0.6	3	0.6	0	0.0	0	0.0	3	0.5	0
Caucasian	296	85.5	258	83.5	387	82.9	167	88.8	152	74.9	554	84.6	137
Unknown	31	9.0	23	7.4	47	10.1	7	3.7	33	16.3	54	8.2	0
Total	346	52.8	309	47.2	467	71.3	188	28.7	203	31.0	655		167

Tuition and Fees

	Resident	Nonresident
Full-time	$30,280	$30,280
Part-time	$21,340	$21,340

Living Expenses

Estimated living expenses for singles

Living on campus	Living off campus	Living at home
N/A	$15,786	$10,972

Quinnipiac University School of Law

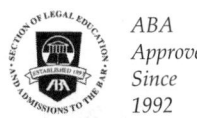

*ABA
Approved
Since
1992*

GPA and LSAT Scores

	Total	Full-time	Part-time
# of apps	2,679	2,146	533
# of admits	683	547	136
# of matrics	230	154	76
75% GPA	3.51	3.54	3.41
25% GPA	2.94	2.98	2.88
75% LSAT	155	156	154
25% LSAT	152	152	150

Grants and Scholarships (from prior year)

	Total		Full-time		Part-time	
	#	%	#	%	#	%
Total # of students	628		411		217	
Total # receiving grants	367	58.4	270	65.7	97	44.7
Less than 1/2 tuition	269	42.8	206	50.1	63	29.0
Half to full tuition	97	15.4	64	15.6	33	15.2
Full tuition	0	0.0	0	0.0	0	0.0
More than full tuition	1	0.2	0	0.0	1	0.5
Median grant amount			$9,000		$7,400	

Informational and Library Resources

# of volumes and volume equivalents	385,854
# of titles	123,494
# of active serial subscriptions	2,584
Study seating capacity inside the library	400
# of professional librarians	8
Hours per week library is open	99
# of open, wired connections available to students	395
# of networked computers available for use by students	117
# of simultaneous wireless users	610
Require computer?	N

JD Attrition (from prior year)

	Academic	Other	Total	
	#	#	#	%
1st year	8	28	36	20.1%
2nd year	0	0	0	0.0%
3rd year	0	0	0	0.0%
4th year	1	0	1	1.5%

Employment

	Total	Percentage
Employment status known	216	96.4
Employment status unknown	8	3.6
Employed	186	86.1
Pursuing graduate degrees	5	2.3
Unemployed seeking employment	21	9.7
Unemployed not seeking employment	4	1.9

Type of Employment

# employed in law firms	76	40.9
# employed in business and industry	43	23.1
# employed in government	37	19.9
# employed in public interest	2	1.1
# employed as judicial clerks	16	8.6
# employed in academia	2	1.1

Geographic Location

# employed in state	137	73.7
# employed in foreign countries	1	0.5
# of states where employed	11	

Bar Passage Rates

Jurisdiction	Connecticut		
Exam	Sum 03	Win 04	Total
# from school taking bar for the first time	147	22	169
School's pass rate for all first-time takers	81%	82%	81%
State's pass rate for all first-time takers	82%	78%	81%

Quinnipiac University School of Law

275 Mt. Carmel Avenue
Hamden, CT 06518
Phone: 203.582.3400; Fax: 203.582.3339
E-mail: ladm@quinnipiac.edu; Website: http://law.quinnipiac.edu

■ Introduction

Excellent law schools share many common traits—
faculty renowned for their scholarship and commitment
to teaching, academically rigorous courses, loyal successful alumni, and motivated focused students. All of these
are essential components of Quinnipiac Law's identity.
However, what sets Quinnipiac apart is its personal,
student-centered approach to the law school experience.
Contributing to this identity is a favorable 14:1 student-
faculty ratio, the extraordinary accessibility of the faculty,
and an environment that both challenges and supports
its students as they prepare for careers in law.

Nestled among the hills, woods, and waterways of
Connecticut on one of the most beautiful campuses in
New England, yet just 75 miles from New York City,
Quinnipiac's setting and location are ideal. The beautiful,
state-of-the-art law center, opened in 1995, with wireless
computer access in all classrooms and most study areas,
provides students with a modern, relaxed, and safe
environment for study.

■ Faculty

Our faculty's academic credentials span the nation's
leading law schools from Harvard, Yale, and Berkeley to
Chicago, Michigan, and Georgetown. They combine
excellence in scholarship and teaching with exceptional
accessibility. Indeed, the care with which faculty
members demonstrate their interest in each student's
progress and success is a distinguishing characteristic
of Quinnipiac Law. Most have an open-door policy and
generously share of their expertise, insights, and time.
The low student-faculty ratio (14:1) allows students to
work closely with faculty, and this translates into a
different kind of law school experience.

■ Library and Physical Facilities

The 50,000-square-foot law library is at the center of the
School of Law complex. With a collection of more than
380,000 volumes, it also provides comprehensive access
to numerous electronic resources and databases such as
LexisNexis, Westlaw/Dialog, JSTOR, and other
web-based services. Its interlibrary loan network makes
it possible to obtain materials from any library in the
world. The beautiful facility features spacious public
areas and numerous reading rooms and individual
study carrels, providing a comfortable and relaxing
environment for research and study.

■ Curriculum

The law school is fully approved by the ABA and is a
member of AALS. Full-time day and part-time evening
programs are offered beginning each fall. The academic
program is designed to prepare students to be generalists
or specialists. It provides a dynamic blend of traditional
classroom instruction and extensive experiential learning
opportunities. Students who wish to focus on a specific
area of study may choose from six different concentrations—**civil advocacy and dispute resolution, criminal
law and advocacy, family and juvenile law, health law,
intellectual property,** and **tax.** The law school also offers
a joint JD/MBA degree (with a health administration
track) and a summer study abroad program with Trinity
College in Dublin, Ireland.

■ Special Programs

Quinnipiac is recognized as having one of the premier
clinical and externship programs in the country, and
students often cite their experiences in these programs
as one of the highlights of their law school career. These
experiential learning opportunities allow students to
bridge the gap between theory and practice. A total of
16 clinical and externship programs are available to
students. The seven clinical programs include **civil, tax,
health law, advanced, evening** (for part-time students),
defense appellate, and **prosecution appellate.** The nine
externship programs are **Corporate Counsel, Criminal
Justice, Family and Juvenile Law, Judicial, Legal
Services, Legislative, Mediation, Public Interest,** and
Field Placement II.

Quinnipiac has established two centers in specialized
fields of law—the **Center for Health Law and Policy** and
the **Center on Dispute Resolution**—both of which draw
on considerable academic strengths and resources within
the law school community.

■ Admission

Admission is competitive and based upon a variety of
factors: undergraduate academic record, LSAT scores,
personal statement, letters of recommendation, and other
evidence such as advanced degrees, life and work
experience, and extracurricular activities. Applications
are welcomed from students of color, nontraditional
students, and all students who add to the diversity of the
student body. A rolling admission system is employed;
however, the priority application deadline for admission
and scholarship consideration is March 1.

Regent University School of Law

1000 Regent University Drive, RH239
Virginia Beach, VA 23464
Phone: 757.226.4584; Fax: 757.226.4139
E-mail: Lawschool@regent.edu; Website: www.regent.edu/law

ABA
Approved
Since
1989

The Basics

Type of school	Private
Term	Semester
Application deadline	6/1
Application fee	$40
Financial aid deadline	6/1
Can first year start other than fall?	No
Student to faculty ratio (fall)	20.3 to 1
Does the university offer:	
housing restricted to law students?	No
graduate housing for which law students are eligible?	Yes

Faculty and Administrators

	Total		Men		Women		Minorities	
	Fall	Spr	Fall	Spr	Fall	Spr	Fall	Spr
Full-time	20	19	15	14	5	5	5	5
Other Full-time	3	2	3	2	0	0	0	0
Deans, librarians, & others who teach	8	8	7	7	1	1	0	0
Part-time	16	15	12	11	4	4	0	1
Total	47	44	37	34	10	10	5	6

Curriculum

		Full-time	Part-time
Typical first-year section size		80	30
Is there typically a "small section" of the first-year class, other than Legal Writing, taught by full-time faculty		No	No
If yes, typical size offered last year		0	0
# of classroom course titles beyond 1st year curriculum		68	
# of upper division courses, excluding seminars with an enrollment:	Under 25	78	
	25-49	21	
	50-74	12	
	75-99	4	
	100+	0	
# of seminars		7	
# of seminar positions available		205	
# of seminar positions filled		60	13
# of positions available in simulation courses		569	
# of simulation positions filled		332	77
# of positions available in faculty supervised clinical courses		24	
# of faculty supervised clinical positions filled		16	1
# involved in field placements		31	4
# involved in law journals		32	3
# involved in moot court or trial competitions		46	0
# of credit hours required to graduate		90	

JD Enrollment and Ethnicity

	Men		Women		Full-time		Part-time		1st-year		Total		JD Degs. Awd.
	#	%	#	%	#	%	#	%	#	%	#	%	
African Amer.	8	3.0	34	14.0	35	8.0	7	9.7	12	6.5	42	8.2	14
Amer. Indian	2	0.7	0	0.0	2	0.5	0	0.0	0	0.0	2	0.4	1
Asian Amer.	5	1.9	8	3.3	11	2.5	2	2.8	7	3.8	13	2.5	1
Mex. Amer.	0	0.0	0	0.0	0	0.0	0	0.0	0	0.0	0	0.0	0
Puerto Rican	0	0.0	0	0.0	0	0.0	0	0.0	0	0.0	0	0.0	0
Hispanic	7	2.6	8	3.3	12	2.7	3	4.2	6	3.2	15	2.9	1
Total Minority	22	8.2	50	20.6	60	13.7	12	16.7	25	13.4	72	14.1	17
For. Nation.	2	0.7	2	0.8	3	0.7	1	1.4	1	0.5	4	0.8	2
Caucasian	233	86.9	185	76.1	361	82.2	57	79.2	153	82.3	418	81.8	106
Unknown	11	4.1	6	2.5	15	3.4	2	2.8	7	3.8	17	3.3	9
Total	268	52.4	243	47.6	439	85.9	72	14.1	186	36.4	511		134

Tuition and Fees

	Resident	Nonresident
Full-time	$23,014	$23,014
Part-time	$17,134	$17,134

Living Expenses

Estimated living expenses for singles

Living on campus	Living off campus	Living at home
$14,558	$14,558	$14,558

Regent University School of Law

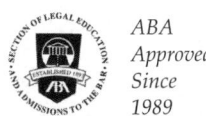

*ABA
Approved
Since
1989*

GPA and LSAT Scores

	Total	Full-time	Part-time
# of apps	734	664	70
# of admits	309	283	26
# of matrics	188	167	21
75% GPA	3.58	3.59	3.40
25% GPA	2.92	2.94	2.75
75% LSAT	155	156	153
25% LSAT	150	150	150

Grants and Scholarships (from prior year)

	Total		Full-time		Part-time	
	#	%	#	%	#	%
Total # of students	502		412		90	
Total # receiving grants	446	88.8	372	90.3	74	82.2
Less than 1/2 tuition	331	65.9	271	65.8	60	66.7
Half to full tuition	87	17.3	75	18.2	12	13.3
Full tuition	26	5.2	24	5.8	2	2.2
More than full tuition	2	0.4	2	0.5	0	0.0
Median grant amount			$4,300		$3,310	

Informational and Library Resources

# of volumes and volume equivalents	382,759
# of titles	44,423
# of active serial subscriptions	4,249
Study seating capacity inside the library	382
# of professional librarians	7
Hours per week library is open	105
# of open, wired connections available to students	192
# of networked computers available for use by students	136
# of simultaneous wireless users	80
Require computer?	N

JD Attrition (from prior year)

	Academic	Other	Total	
	#	#	#	%
1st year	21	18	39	21.5%
2nd year	1	8	9	6.1%
3rd year	0	2	2	1.4%
4th year	0	1	1	3.7%

Employment

	Total	Percentage
Employment status known	120	88.9
Employment status unknown	15	11.1
Employed	96	80.0
Pursuing graduate degrees	3	2.5
Unemployed seeking employment	18	15.0
Unemployed not seeking employment	3	2.5

Type of Employment

# employed in law firms	31	32.3
# employed in business and industry	25	26.0
# employed in government	21	21.9
# employed in public interest	4	4.2
# employed as judicial clerks	5	5.2
# employed in academia	9	9.4

Geographic Location

# employed in state	46	47.9
# employed in foreign countries	0	0.0
# of states where employed		19

Bar Passage Rates

Jurisdiction	Virginia		
Exam	Sum 03	Win 04	Total
# from school taking bar for the first time	43	16	59
School's pass rate for all first-time takers	60%	31%	53%
State's pass rate for all first-time takers	75%	60%	72%

Regent University School of Law

1000 Regent University Drive, RH239
Virginia Beach, VA 23464
Phone: 757.226.4584; Fax: 757.226.4139
E-mail: Lawschool@regent.edu; Website: www.regent.edu/law

■ Introduction

Regent University is distinctive among ABA-approved law schools because of the integration of Christian principles into the curriculum. It is this balance of professional legal training and affirmation of biblical principles that enables Regent graduates to provide excellent legal counsel to their clients while carrying forth the mission of the university—Christian Leadership to Change the World. Approximately 3,300 men and women are pursuing graduate degrees at Regent University. The law school is composed of approximately 500 students. The campus of Regent University is situated on a stately, Georgian-style campus in Virginia Beach, minutes from the Atlantic Ocean, less than a two-hour drive from Richmond, and less than four hours from Washington, DC.

■ Christian Distinction

The foremost distinction of Regent University School of Law is the Christian perspective. The School of Law is unique in that the mission embraces a Christian world-view and the school seeks to nurture students' faith. This mission provides a strong basis for teaching the highest ethical standards for lawyers.

■ Academic Program/Legal Skills

Regent law school places great emphasis on developing practical lawyering skills. Courses have been designed to provide in-depth training and opportunities to develop these skills. Regent law students enjoy tremendous success in student competitions, winning national and regional awards in negotiations, moot court, trial practice, client counseling, and appellate advocacy. The practical lawyering skills and strong ethical values of Regent graduates have enabled them to successfully obtain employment with top law firms, federal and state courts, business and technology companies, and national public interest law firms.

■ Clinical Opportunities—Public Interest Law

Regent law students are noted for their commitment to public service and fighting for equal justice for all. A recent survey ranked Regent as number two for "Quality of Life" and number nine for faculty teaching and accessibility among the "Best 117 Law Schools." The School of Law provides opportunities for hands-on, student-client contact through Litigation and Family Mediation clinics. Additionally, the School of Law enjoys a special relationship with the American Center for Law and Justice (ACLJ), the nation's foremost public interest law firm defending religious liberties. Selected law students may obtain volunteer and paid positions to assist staff attorneys involved in pro-family and pro-liberty cases and may participate in a semester in DC program.

■ Full- and Part-Time Programs

The School of Law offers full- and part-time 90 semester-hour Juris Doctor programs in-residence only. Students in the full-time program normally complete their degrees in three years; part-time students in four to five years.

■ Admission and the Bar

Applicants to the law school are required to submit a personal statement as part of the admission process. This personal statement, unique in style to Regent, is considered very carefully along with the applicant's LSAT score, undergraduate record, résumé, and letters of recommendation. The law school is committed to considering the entire application in the decision process, ultimately offering admission to prospective students who present a strong likelihood for success in law school. This commitment has resulted in a diverse student body. Applications from prospective students with LSAT scores of 150 and above and UGPA's above 3.0 are especially encouraged, as the law school has evidence that such students are very likely to succeed in law school and also very likely to pass the bar exam on their first attempt. Regent's bar passage rate for all graduates with LSAT scores of 150 or above was 73 percent, 155 or above 81 percent, and 160 and above 88 percent.

■ Academic Assistance

Regent University School of Law is on the cutting edge in offering academic assistance to its students. The law school employs a full-time faculty member who serves as the director of academic success and who oversees the three components of the school's Academic Success Program. Under the first component, the school invites selected first-year students to attend a two-week pre-enrollment program as a condition for admission into the school. The pre-enrollment program helps the students develop good law school study skills and introduces them to selected areas of the law in small sections taught by members of the full-time faculty. Under the second component, the director of academic assistance offers study skills workshops and one-on-one advising during the spring and fall semesters. These services are available to all students needing extra assistance in their studies. As the third component, the director teaches a for-credit course on advanced legal reasoning, analysis, and writing. The class, offered to third-year students, enables the students to fine-tune their analytical and writing skills in concrete ways that will benefit them in their future legal careers.

Regent University School of Law

■ The Law Library

Regent University law library occupies the entire third floor of the 150,000 square-foot university library building, immediately adjacent to the School of Law. The current collection contains approximately 375,000 volumes, substantial electronic resources, and an extensive microform collection.

■ International Law and Summer Abroad Program

Regent students are becoming increasingly interested in international law. The law school has established an *International Law Journal* and has a very active International Law Society. In addition, the School of Law hosts a summer program in Strasbourg, France, focusing on international law and human rights. Regent faculty and other distinguished scholars and practicing attorneys such as Jay Sekulow, Chief Counsel for the American Center for Law and Justice, teach in the program.

■ Housing

Regent Village is located three-quarters of a mile from campus. The apartment-style complex consists of 112 two-bedroom, one-bath units; 56 two-bedroom, two-bath units; and 56 three-bedroom, two-bath units. Rates are comparable to or less than similar apartment complexes in the nearby vicinity.

■ Financial Aid

The School of Law is committed to helping students finance their legal education. The Scholarship Committee awards approximately $2.3 million in scholarships and grants to law students, ranging in value from $250 to full tuition. In recent years, approximately 70 percent of law students receive some type of scholarship or grant. Scholarships are awarded on the basis of academic promise with attention given to the applicant's academic performance, LSAT scores, leadership, public service, and other factors indicative of the applicant's potential for law school success. Students not awarded financial assistance the first year of law school may qualify for assistance in future years based on academic performance. Residents of Virginia attending a private Virginia university may qualify for the Virginia Tuition Assistance Grant. A variety of loan programs exist to meet the tuition and living expenses related to law school.

■ Campus Visitations

Campus Visitations: *www.regent.edu/acad/schlaw/admissions/visit.cfm*.
   To RSVP for campus visitations or to arrange an alternate appointment, contact *lawschool@regent.edu* or telephone 757.226.4584.

Applicant Profile

Regent University School of Law
This grid includes only applicants who earned 120-180 LSAT scores under standard administrations

LSAT Score	GPA								
	3.75 +	3.50 - 3.74	3.25 - 3.49	3.00 - 3.24	2.75 - 2.99	2.50 - 2.74	2.25 - 2.49	2.00 - 2.24	Below 2.00
160-180									
153-159									
152									
151									
150									
149									
147-148									
120-146									

☐ Strong Possibility   ▨ Possible   ■ Unlikely

This grid is intended to provide prospective applicants a general sense of our admission standards, as based upon competition for entry into recent classes entering the law school. This grid does not adequately describe the numerous nonquantifiable factors that are considered by our Admission Committee. Prospective applicants are encouraged to review our admission materials for a fuller understanding of the admission-review standards used by Regent University School of Law.

Regent University School of Law   585

University of Richmond School of Law

28 Westhampton Way
University of Richmond, VA 23173
Phone: 804.289.8189; Fax: 804.287.6516
E-mail: lawadmissions@richmond.edu; Website: law.richmond.edu

ABA
Approved
Since
1928

The Basics

Type of school	Private
Term	Semester
Application deadline	1/15
Application fee	$35
Financial aid deadline	2/25
Can first year start other than fall?	Yes
Student to faculty ratio (fall)	15.4 to 1
Does the university offer:	
housing restricted to law students?	Yes
graduate housing for which law students are eligible?	Yes

Faculty and Administrators

	Total		Men		Women		Minorities	
	Fall	Spr	Fall	Spr	Fall	Spr	Fall	Spr
Full-time	26	26	17	18	9	8	4	3
Other Full-time	4	4	4	4	0	0	0	0
Deans, librarians, & others who teach	4	4	2	2	2	2	0	0
Part-time	44	48	30	31	14	16	4	1
Total	78	82	53	55	25	26	8	4

Curriculum

		Full-time	Part-time
Typical first-year section size		85	0
Is there typically a "small section" of the first-year class, other than Legal Writing, taught by full-time faculty		Yes	No
If yes, typical size offered last year		42	0
# of classroom course titles beyond 1st year curriculum		82	
# of upper division courses, excluding seminars with an enrollment:	Under 25	78	
	25-49	17	
	50-74	9	
	75-99	7	
	100+	0	
# of seminars		13	
# of seminar positions available		208	
# of seminar positions filled	143		0
# of positions available in simulation courses		494	
# of simulation positions filled	442		0
# of positions available in faculty supervised clinical courses		40	
# of faculty supervised clinical positions filled	22		0
# involved in field placements	61		0
# involved in law journals	178		0
# involved in moot court or trial competitions	333		0
# of credit hours required to graduate		86	

JD Enrollment and Ethnicity

	Men		Women		Full-time		Part-time		1st-year		Total		JD Degs. Awd.
	#	%	#	%	#	%	#	%	#	%	#	%	
African Amer.	7	2.8	13	5.8	20	4.2	0	0.0	9	5.7	20	4.2	6
Amer. Indian	1	0.4	0	0.0	1	0.2	0	0.0	0	0.0	1	0.2	0
Asian Amer.	11	4.3	5	2.2	16	3.3	0	0.0	5	3.2	16	3.3	3
Mex. Amer.	0	0.0	0	0.0	0	0.0	0	0.0	0	0.0	0	0.0	0
Puerto Rican	0	0.0	0	0.0	0	0.0	0	0.0	0	0.0	0	0.0	0
Hispanic	1	0.4	3	1.3	4	0.8	0	0.0	0	0.0	4	0.8	1
Total Minority	20	7.9	21	9.4	41	8.6	0	0.0	14	8.9	41	8.6	10
For. Nation.	0	0.0	4	1.8	4	0.8	0	0.0	1	0.6	4	0.8	0
Caucasian	234	92.1	199	88.8	433	90.6	0	0.0	142	89.9	433	90.6	136
Unknown	0	0.0	0	0.0	0	0.0	0	0.0	0	0.0	0	0.0	0
Total	254	53.1	224	46.9	478	100.0	0	0.0	158	33.1	478		146

Tuition and Fees

	Resident	Nonresident
Full-time	$25,510	$25,510
Part-time	$0	$0

Living Expenses

Estimated living expenses for singles

Living on campus	Living off campus	Living at home
$10,404	$12,840	$6,240

University of Richmond School of Law

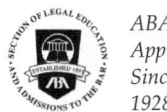

*ABA
Approved
Since
1928*

GPA and LSAT Scores

	Total	Full-time	Part-time
# of apps	2,400	2,400	0
# of admits	553	553	0
# of matrics	158	158	0
75% GPA	3.54	3.54	0.00
25% GPA	3.11	3.11	0.00
75% LSAT	163	163	0
25% LSAT	159	159	0

Grants and Scholarships (from prior year)

	Total		Full-time		Part-time	
	#	%	#	%	#	%
Total # of students	482		479		3	
Total # receiving grants	284	58.9	284	59.3	0	0.0
Less than 1/2 tuition	264	54.8	264	55.1	0	0.0
Half to full tuition	18	3.7	18	3.8	0	0.0
Full tuition	0	0.0	0	0.0	0	0.0
More than full tuition	2	0.4	2	0.4	0	0.0
Median grant amount			$4,210		$0	

Informational and Library Resources

# of volumes and volume equivalents	364,065
# of titles	156,169
# of active serial subscriptions	4,509
Study seating capacity inside the library	643
# of professional librarians	7
Hours per week library is open	106
# of open, wired connections available to students	1,051
# of networked computers available for use by students	36
# of simultaneous wireless users	210
Require computer?	Y

JD Attrition (from prior year)

	Academic	Other	Total	
	#	#	#	%
1st year	1	22	23	14.1%
2nd year	0	0	0	0.0%
3rd year	0	1	1	0.7%
4th year	0	0	0	0.0%

Employment

	Total	Percentage
Employment status known	158	97.5
Employment status unknown	4	2.5
Employed	145	91.8
Pursuing graduate degrees	7	4.4
Unemployed seeking employment	3	1.9
Unemployed not seeking employment	3	1.9

Type of Employment

# employed in law firms	80	55.2
# employed in business and industry	29	20.0
# employed in government	16	11.0
# employed in public interest	1	0.7
# employed as judicial clerks	19	13.1
# employed in academia	0	0.0

Geographic Location

# employed in state	0	0.0
# employed in foreign countries	0	0.0
# of states where employed	0	

Bar Passage Rates

Jurisdiction	Virginia		
Exam	Sum 03	Win 04	Total
# from school taking bar for the first time	92	14	106
School's pass rate for all first-time takers	74%	100%	77%
State's pass rate for all first-time takers	75%	60%	72%

University of Richmond School of Law

28 Westhampton Way
University of Richmond, VA 23173
Phone: 804.289.8189; Fax: 804.287.6516
E-mail: lawadmissions@richmond.edu; Website: law.richmond.edu

■ Introduction

The University of Richmond School of Law, founded in 1870, enjoys an established reputation for preparing its graduates for legal careers. Accredited by the ABA and a member of the AALS, its graduates are qualified to seek admission to the bar of all 50 states and the District of Columbia.

Situated on the beautiful 350-acre suburban campus, the school is only a 20-minute drive from downtown. In addition to being home to a number of international law firms, Richmond is the capital of the Commonwealth of Virginia, has numerous state and federal offices, and is the seat of both the Supreme Court of Virginia and the US Court of Appeals for the Fourth Circuit.

■ Library and Physical Facilities

The law school is housed in a collegiate gothic-style building, which includes a moot courtroom that is the site of many classes, events, and mock trials. A panel of federal judges from the Fourth Circuit hears oral arguments once a year in the moot courtroom. The building is outfitted with instructional technology, including wireless access. In 1994, the school was the first law school in the country to require laptop computers. Every student is assigned an individual study carrel bearing their name, that functions as their own office in the law library. The library's holdings are comprehensive and include several special collections.

■ Curriculum

Courses in environmental law, contracts, torts, criminal law, procedure, property, and constitutional law comprise the first-year curriculum. Required upper-level courses include professional responsibility and a third-year writing seminar. Elective courses in a variety of areas are available. In addition, all students complete a program in legal reasoning, writing, research, and fundamental lawyering skills and values. Often, justices of the Virginia Supreme Court teach in the lawyering skills program.

■ Special Programs

Several dual-degree programs are offered that allow students to earn the JD degree as well as a master's degree in a related discipline. Students can reduce the time and cost associated with obtaining two degrees while enjoying the study of two fields of interest. Dual-degree programs are available in Business Administration, Health Administration, Social Work, Urban Studies and Planning, and Public Administration.

The law school operates the Children's Law Center through which one may participate in the Delinquency Clinic, the Disabilities Clinic, and/or the Advanced Children's Clinic.

Exciting clinical placements are arranged for academic credit in courts, law offices, and corporations. Externships are available in civil, criminal, judicial, and business law.

■ International Programs

Richmond Law offers an extremely popular summer program at Emmanuel College in Cambridge, England, and an exchange program with the University of Paris as well as with more than 20 universities worldwide; 9 of which have acclaimed law programs. Additionally, Richmond Law has created a series of rotating visiting professorships to bring distinguished foreign scholars to the campus.

■ Academic Success Program

The goal of this program is to assist students to achieve at their highest level as well as to support our students toward a 100 percent bar passage. This goal was first achieved in February 2004.

■ Bar Passage

Students are enrolled from throughout the US and several foreign countries and therefore choose to take a variety of bar exams. Graduates who take the Virginia bar exam have exceeded the statewide rate on the exam year after year.

■ Student Activities

A student board publishes *The University of Richmond Law Review* on a quarterly basis. The *Richmond Journal of Law and Technology*, the first student-edited scholarly journal in the world to be published exclusively in electronic form, went online April 10, 1995. *The Richmond Journal of Law and the Public Interest* is a second online journal published by our students as an interdisciplinary journal dedicated to current and often controversial issues affecting the public. *The Richmond Journal of Global Law and Business* provides scholarly and practical insight into major legal and business issues affecting our global economy.

Richmond's moot court activities allow students to test their research, brief-writing, trial, and appellate advocacy skills. Students participate in intraschool tournaments that lead to membership on the Moot Court Board and on teams that represent the law school in regional and national competitions.

■ Admission

Applications are reviewed as they become complete. All decisions are released by May 15. The admission committee considers the UGPA and LSAT as two important items, although extracurricular and community-service activities and employment experience are also of interest. The law school provides an equal educational opportunity without regard to race, color, national origin, sex, handicap, or religion.

Admission conferences are available in November, December, and January. They are invaluable in providing information and answering questions. We encourage class visits, and, in keeping with our very personal approach to admission, we also encourage you to take advantage of meeting with a law student. Law students are available to give tours Monday through Saturday and may be reached at *LSAR@richmond.edu.*

■ Expenses and Financial Aid

Institutional aid in the form of grants and scholarships is available on the basis of need and merit. To qualify for grants based on need, one must file a completed FAFSA form which the federal processor must receive no later than February 25. Parental income is not considered in determining financial aid for students who are considered to be independent by the law school.

John Marshall Scholars Program—The law school's most prestigious awards offer $10,000 annual stipends, as well as other honors, and are renewable annually if criteria are met. The general application must be **completed** by February 1. If invited to compete for these awards, a separate application must be submitted in early March. Committee consideration for these scholarships is based solely on

merit and personal attributes. Some applicants may be able to demonstrate the required attributes by having successfully overcome serious disadvantages or obstacles. John Marshall Scholars will be awarded institutional grants and scholarships in addition to their JM Scholarship.

■ Housing

Limited on-campus housing is available on a first-come, first-served basis. Richmond offers an abundance of good, affordable housing in proximity to the law school. For information on housing, contact the Admissions Office.

■ Career Services

The role of the Career Services Office is to serve law students and alumni in obtaining employment by helping them develop the skills and the knowledge necessary to conduct successful job searches. The office organizes a comprehensive, on-campus interview program. It also participates in a number of regional and national job fairs.

Richmond has more types of courts than any city in the US outside of Washington, DC or Boston, which provide our students with a myriad of opportunities for part-time employment while in their second and third year of study, thereby giving our students the benefit of gaining crucial legal experience and producing income for educational purposes.

For the last several years, our graduates have reported between 98 and 100 percent employment within six months of graduation.

Applicant Profile

University of Richmond School of Law
This grid includes only applicants who earned 120-180 LSAT scores under standard administrations.

LSAT Score	3.75 +		3.50 - 3.74		3.25 - 3.49		3.00 - 3.24		2.75 - 2.99		2.50 - 2.74		2.25 - 2.49		2.00 - 2.24		Below 2.00		No GPA		Total	
	Apps	Adm	Apps	Adm	Apps	Adm	Apps	Adm	Apps	Adm	Apps	Adm	Apps	Adm	Apps	Adm	Apps	Adm	Apps	Adm	Apps	Adm
175-180	0	0	1	1	0	0	0	0	0	0	0	0	0	0	0	0	0	0	0	0	1	1
170-174	2	2	0	0	3	3	3	3	2	1	1	1	1	0	2	2	0	0	0	0	14	12
165-169	6	6	15	14	16	15	18	18	7	4	11	2	3	0	2	1	0	0	1	0	79	60
160-164	44	43	62	61	89	88	85	77	56	16	34	7	17	6	6	3	0	0	5	4	398	305
155-159	76	25	138	39	178	43	179	16	84	2	42	2	25	0	3	0	2	0	12	2	739	129
150-154	45	0	100	4	150	10	162	15	79	4	52	2	18	0	9	0	1	0	8	0	624	35
145-149	21	1	42	1	63	0	62	0	37	1	35	0	18	0	6	0	1	0	6	0	291	3
140-144	3	0	22	0	17	0	26	0	20	0	28	0	8	0	6	0	2	0	10	0	142	0
135-139	1	0	0	0	4	0	8	0	8	0	5	0	7	0	4	0	1	0	4	0	42	0
130-134	0	0	4	0	4	0	3	0	2	0	4	0	1	0	3	0	0	0	3	0	24	0
125-129	0	0	0	0	0	0	1	0	1	0	1	0	2	0	0	0	0	0	1	0	6	0
120-124	0	0	0	0	0	0	0	0	0	0	1	0	1	0	0	0	0	0	0	0	2	0
Total	198	77	384	120	524	159	547	129	296	28	214	14	101	6	41	6	7	0	50	6	2362	545

Apps = Number of Applicants   Adm = Number Admitted   Reflects 98% of the total applicant pool.

Roger Williams University, Ralph R. Papitto School of Law

Ten Metacom Avenue
Bristol, RI 02809-5171
Phone: 401.254.4555 or 800.633.2727; Fax: 401.254.4516
E-mail: admissions@law.rwu.edu; Website: law.rwu.edu

The Basics

Type of school	Private
Term	Semester
Application deadline	4/15
Application fee	$60
Financial aid deadline	3/15
Can first year start other than fall?	No
Student to faculty ratio (fall)	20.9 to 1
Does the university offer: housing restricted to law students?	Yes
graduate housing for which law students are eligible?	No

Faculty and Administrators

	Total		Men		Women		Minorities	
	Fall	Spr	Fall	Spr	Fall	Spr	Fall	Spr
Full-time	23	24	17	17	6	7	2	2
Other Full-time	7	7	1	1	6	6	0	0
Deans, librarians, & others who teach	11	11	4	4	7	7	0	0
Part-time	18	23	11	17	7	6	1	1
Total	59	65	33	39	26	26	3	3

Curriculum

		Full-time	Part-time
Typical first-year section size		77	39
Is there typically a "small section" of the first-year class, other than Legal Writing, taught by full-time faculty		No	No
If yes, typical size offered last year		0	0
# of classroom course titles beyond 1st year curriculum		129	
# of upper division courses, excluding seminars with an enrollment:	Under 25	52	
	25-49	14	
	50-74	15	
	75-99	3	
	100+	1	
# of seminars		31	
# of seminar positions available		770	
# of seminar positions filled		424	111
# of positions available in simulation courses		252	
# of simulation positions filled		175	52
# of positions available in faculty supervised clinical courses		57	
# of faculty supervised clinical positions filled		55	2
# involved in field placements		48	2
# involved in law journals		30	6
# involved in moot court or trial competitions		29	2
# of credit hours required to graduate		90	

JD Enrollment and Ethnicity

	Men		Women		Full-time		Part-time		1st-year		Total		JD Degs. Awd.
	#	%	#	%	#	%	#	%	#	%	#	%	
African Amer.	7	2.3	8	2.5	10	2.1	5	3.3	7	2.8	15	2.4	10
Amer. Indian	1	0.3	3	0.9	4	0.8	0	0.0	2	0.8	4	0.6	8
Asian Amer.	11	3.6	20	6.2	26	5.5	5	3.3	17	6.8	31	4.9	0
Mex. Amer.	0	0.0	1	0.3	1	0.2	0	0.0	1	0.4	1	0.2	0
Puerto Rican	0	0.0	0	0.0	0	0.0	0	0.0	0	0.0	0	0.0	0
Hispanic	6	2.0	7	2.2	12	2.5	1	0.7	7	2.8	13	2.1	7
Total Minority	25	8.2	39	12.0	53	11.1	11	7.2	34	13.6	64	10.2	25
For. Nation.	3	1.0	1	0.3	4	0.8	0	0.0	2	0.8	4	0.6	0
Caucasian	231	75.5	249	76.9	360	75.5	120	78.4	176	70.4	480	76.2	113
Unknown	47	15.4	35	10.8	60	12.6	22	14.4	38	15.2	82	13.0	18
Total	306	48.6	324	51.4	477	75.7	153	24.3	250	39.7	630		156

Tuition and Fees

	Resident	Nonresident
Full-time	$24,410	$24,410
Part-time	$17,400	$17,400

Living Expenses

Estimated living expenses for singles

Living on campus	Living off campus	Living at home
$14,972	$14,972	$14,972

Roger Williams University, Ralph R. Papitto School of Law

*ABA
Approved
Since
1995*

GPA and LSAT Scores

	Total	Full-time	Part-time
# of apps	1,618	1,450	168
# of admits	643	542	101
# of matrics	248	200	48
75% GPA	3.54	3.54	3.41
25% GPA	2.86	2.91	2.67
75% LSAT	155	155	154
25% LSAT	150	150	147

Grants and Scholarships (from prior year)

	Total		Full-time		Part-time	
	#	%	#	%	#	%
Total # of students	598		458		140	
Total # receiving grants	254	42.5	199	43.4	55	39.3
Less than 1/2 tuition	150	25.1	114	24.9	36	25.7
Half to full tuition	65	10.9	50	10.9	15	10.7
Full tuition	38	6.4	34	7.4	4	2.9
More than full tuition	1	0.2	1	0.2	0	0.0
Median grant amount			$10,000		$3,800	

Informational and Library Resources

# of volumes and volume equivalents	281,848
# of titles	122,566
# of active serial subscriptions	3,713
Study seating capacity inside the library	387
# of professional librarians	6
Hours per week library is open	110
# of open, wired connections available to students	164
# of networked computers available for use by students	56
# of simultaneous wireless users	300
Require computer?	N

JD Attrition (from prior year)

	Academic	Other	Total	
	#	#	#	%
1st year	12	29	41	18.1%
2nd year	3	2	5	2.9%
3rd year	0	0	0	0.0%
4th year	0	0	0	0.0%

Employment

	Total	Percentage
Employment status known	90	80.4
Employment status unknown	22	19.6
Employed	72	80.0
Pursuing graduate degrees	1	1.1
Unemployed seeking employment	16	17.8
Unemployed not seeking employment	1	1.1

Type of Employment

# employed in law firms	34	47.2
# employed in business and industry	11	15.3
# employed in government	11	15.3
# employed in public interest	4	5.6
# employed as judicial clerks	9	12.5
# employed in academia	1	1.4

Geographic Location

# employed in state	45	62.5
# employed in foreign countries	0	0.0
# of states where employed	11	

Bar Passage Rates

Jurisdiction	Rhode Island			Massachusetts		
Exam	Sum 03	Win 04	Total	Sum 03	Win 04	Total
# from school taking bar for the first time	57	6	63	47	6	53
School's pass rate for all first-time takers	70%	50%	68%	79%	33%	74%
State's pass rate for all first-time takers	67%	69%	67%	82%	82%	82%

Roger Williams University, Ralph R. Papitto School of Law

Ten Metacom Avenue
Bristol, RI 02809-5171
Phone: 401.254.4555 or 800.633.2727; Fax: 401.254.4516
E-mail: admissions@law.rwu.edu; Website: law.rwu.edu

■ Introduction

Roger Williams University School of Law is located on a peninsula in the historic seacoast town of Bristol, Rhode Island. Providence, the state's capital and legal center, is 20 minutes away and offers employment and externship opportunities. The resort town of Newport is located close by and is the hub of significant cultural, sporting, and recreational events. Boston is one hour to the north. The School of Law is the only law school in the state of Rhode Island. As a small school, the faculty is both accessible and approachable. While the academic environment is challenging, a collegial atmosphere exists.

■ Library and Physical Facilities

The School of Law is self-contained in a multimillion-dollar building designed exclusively for the study of law. The four-level facility contains class and seminar rooms and is equipped with state-of-the-art audiovisual and computer technology. The law library contains more than 280,000 volumes and equivalents, including wireless Internet access. The WebCatalog is available through the Internet, as are many library publications and resources. Access to the LexisNexis and Westlaw/Dialog services, Internet, and CD-ROM publications is provided in three separate computer labs. Word processing and research-related and instructional programs are available to students in the labs.

■ Curriculum

The curriculum integrates intellectual theory, case analysis, and practical lawyering skills. The fundamental building blocks of effective lawyering constitute the first- and second-year curriculum. Students learn the skills of traditional legal analysis and the ability to elicit and convey information that every lawyer must master. The Legal Methods Program and other required courses prepare students to become problem solvers; to comprehend, analyze, and synthesize complex material; and to communicate their positions effectively. In the latter years of their education, students gain expertise in legal specialties through clustering elective courses in particular fields of interest.

Beginning in August 2005, the School of Law is no longer enrolling a part-time Extended Division class.

■ Joint-Degree Programs

Roger Williams University offers a JD/Master of Science in Criminal Justice. This program is designed to prepare graduates to formulate system policy and serve effectively as administrators to United States justice system agencies.

The School of Law also offers three joint-degree programs in conjunction with the University of Rhode Island (URI). Graduates of the JD/Master of Community Planning program are prepared to practice in the public sector for agencies that set policies or regulate land use, or in the private sector for clients or corporations that focus on property-related concerns. The JD/Master of Marine Affairs program is geared toward students interested in maritime, admiralty, and environmental law. The JD/Master of Science in Labor Relations and Human Resources program is designed for students interested in issues relating to employment and labor relations.

■ Special Programs

Marine Affairs Institute—The institute is recognized as a distinguished focal point for the exploration of legal, economic, and policy issues raised by the development of the oceans and coastal zone. Students take elective courses in traditional admiralty law and practice, pollution and environmental regulation, coastal zoning, fisheries, and the international law of the sea.

Feinstein Institute—The school believes that lawyers should serve the communities that support them. Introducing students to volunteerism and public service as part of their legal education, therefore, sets the stage for a lifetime of commitment. Thus, students are required to complete 20 hours of community service.

■ Honors Program

The Honors Program is a three-year program of seminars, clinics, and externships. Scholarships of half to full tuition are awarded to students selected for the Honors Program. The Admissions Committee selects students, evaluating them on their academic records, LSAT scores, and recommendations.

■ Practical Experience

The School of Law operates a Criminal Defense Clinic, a Disability Law Clinic, and a Community Justice and Legal Assistance Clinic in Providence. These clinics provide a service to the community by helping indigent clients and at the same time provide an excellent opportunity for students to represent clients before courts and agencies under the supervision of a faculty member. Students may also engage in a semester-long supervised clerkship in a judge's chambers or in a public interest or governmental law office for academic credit.

Roger Williams University, Ralph R. Papitto School of Law

■ Study Abroad

The London Program on Comparative Advocacy provides a unique opportunity to participate in a mini-pupilage with a barrister. The Lisbon program is the only legal study-abroad program in Lisbon. The classes are taught in English by professors from the Catholic University of Portugal and Roger Williams University School of Law.

■ Admission

Admission is competitive and is based on the UGPA and the LSAT score, as well as other indicators of probable success in the study of law, such as graduate degree, work experience, undergraduate extracurricular activities, and community service. Applicants must register with LSDAS. A personal statement and the $60 fee must accompany all applications. Letters of recommendation will be considered.

■ Financial Aid

Merit-based scholarships of up to full tuition are available; no separate application is required. Federal and state governmental agencies, as well as private lenders, offer students loans at comparative rates and flexible repayment terms. Students must file the Free Application for Federal Student Aid (FAFSA) to be considered for federal loans.

■ Student Activities

Law Review—Membership on *The Roger Williams Law Review* is considered one of the most valuable and prestigious student activities available. The law review is staffed and primarily administered by students who are selected based upon superior academic achievement and writing ability.

Moot Court Honor Society—The Moot Court Honor Society is composed of students possessing superior appellate advocacy and writing ability. This prestigious organization sponsors speakers and programs on appellate advocacy, organizes an intraschool competition, and sends moot court teams to interschool competitions.

Extracurricular Activities—The Multi-Cultural Mentor Program pairs students of color with members of the bench and bar. Other student organizations include *The Docket* (student newspaper), Maritime Law Society, Women's Law Association, the Alliance (GLBT), the Association of Public Interest Law, and the American Trial Lawyers Association.

■ Career Services

The Office of Career Services is dedicated to serving the needs of law students, alumni, and the legal community. The office features a welcoming suite for career research, on-campus interviews, and mock interviews.

Applicant Profile

Roger Williams University, Ralph R. Papitto School of Law

LSAT Score	GPA								
	3.75 +	3.50 - 3.74	3.25 - 3.49	3.00 - 3.24	2.75 - 2.99	2.50 - 2.74	2.25 - 2.49	2.00 - 2.24	Below 2.00
175-180									
170-174									
165-169									
160-164									
155-159									
150-154									
145-149									
140-144									
135-139									
130-134									
125-129									
120-124									

■ Good Possibility   ■ Possible   □ Unlikely

Rutgers—The State University of New Jersey—School of Law—Camden

217 North Fifth Street
Camden, NJ 08102
Phone: 856.225.6102 or 800.466.7561; Fax: 856.969.7903
E-mail: admissions@camlaw.rutgers.edu; Website: www-camlaw.rutgers.edu/

ABA
Approved
Since
1950

The Basics

Type of school	Public
Term	Semester
Application deadline	4/1
Application fee	$50
Financial aid deadline	3/15
Can first year start other than fall?	Yes
Student to faculty ratio (fall)	17.2 to 1
Does the university offer:	
housing restricted to law students?	No
graduate housing for which law students are eligible?	Yes

Faculty and Administrators

	Total		Men		Women		Minorities	
	Fall	Spr	Fall	Spr	Fall	Spr	Fall	Spr
Full-time	35	36	24	23	11	13	2	2
Other Full-time	12	13	5	6	7	7	1	1
Deans, librarians, & others who teach	4	4	2	2	2	2	0	0
Part-time	40	45	25	35	15	10	6	4
Total	91	98	56	66	35	32	9	7

Curriculum

	Full-time	Part-time
Typical first-year section size	85	50
Is there typically a "small section" of the first-year class, other than Legal Writing, taught by full-time faculty	Yes	Yes
If yes, typical size offered last year	50	50
# of classroom course titles beyond 1st year curriculum	99	
# of upper division courses, excluding seminars with an enrollment: Under 25	103	
25-49	40	
50-74	23	
75-99	7	
100+	4	
# of seminars	17	
# of seminar positions available	238	
# of seminar positions filled	142	10
# of positions available in simulation courses	607	
# of simulation positions filled	429	91
# of positions available in faculty supervised clinical courses	73	
# of faculty supervised clinical positions filled	56	18
# involved in field placements	43	0
# involved in law journals	148	13
# involved in moot court or trial competitions	120	7
# of credit hours required to graduate	84	

JD Enrollment and Ethnicity

	Men #	Men %	Women #	Women %	Full-time #	Full-time %	Part-time #	Part-time %	1st-year #	1st-year %	Total #	Total %	JD Degs. Awd.
African Amer.	16	3.3	22	7.1	32	5.5	6	2.8	12	4.7	38	4.8	12
Amer. Indian	0	0.0	1	0.3	1	0.2	0	0.0	0	0.0	1	0.1	2
Asian Amer.	26	5.4	22	7.1	45	7.8	3	1.4	17	6.6	48	6.1	12
Mex. Amer.	4	0.8	0	0.0	4	0.7	0	0.0	1	0.4	4	0.5	3
Puerto Rican	3	0.6	6	1.9	6	1.0	3	1.4	3	1.2	9	1.1	4
Hispanic	13	2.7	9	2.9	19	3.3	3	1.4	10	3.9	22	2.8	9
Total Minority	62	12.8	60	19.5	107	18.5	15	7.0	43	16.7	122	15.4	42
For. Nation.	7	1.4	3	1.0	8	1.4	2	0.9	0	0.0	10	1.3	0
Caucasian	416	85.8	245	79.5	464	80.1	197	92.1	215	83.3	661	83.4	218
Unknown	0	0.0	0	0.0	0	0.0	0	0.0	0	0.0	0	0.0	0
Total	485	61.2	308	38.8	579	73.0	214	27.0	258	32.5	793		260

Tuition and Fees

	Resident	Nonresident
Full-time	$16,724	$23,755
Part-time	$13,318	$19,254

Living Expenses

Estimated living expenses for singles

Living on campus	Living off campus	Living at home
$12,609	$16,409	$6,509

Rutgers—The State University of New Jersey—School of Law—Camden

ABA
Approved
Since
1950

GPA and LSAT Scores

	Total	Full-time	Part-time
# of apps	2,554	N/A	N/A
# of admits	544	N/A	N/A
# of matrics	252	151	101
75% GPA	3.61	3.60	3.68
25% GPA	3.02	3.20	3.02
75% LSAT	162	163	161
25% LSAT	157	159	156

Grants and Scholarships (from prior year)

	Total #	Total %	Full-time #	Full-time %	Part-time #	Part-time %
Total # of students	770		570		200	
Total # receiving grants	259	33.6	239	41.9	20	10.0
Less than 1/2 tuition	250	32.5	231	40.5	19	9.5
Half to full tuition	6	0.8	5	0.9	1	0.5
Full tuition	1	0.1	1	0.2	0	0.0
More than full tuition	2	0.3	2	0.4	0	0.0
Median grant amount			$4,000		$1,500	

Informational and Library Resources

# of volumes and volume equivalents	433,420
# of titles	89,108
# of active serial subscriptions	4,187
Study seating capacity inside the library	403
# of professional librarians	7
Hours per week library is open	103
# of open, wired connections available to students	145
# of networked computers available for use by students	84
# of simultaneous wireless users	1,024
Require computer?	N

JD Attrition (from prior year)

	Academic #	Other #	Total #	Total %
1st year	1	13	14	6.2%
2nd year	0	0	0	0.0%
3rd year	0	2	2	0.8%
4th year	1	0	1	2.9%

Employment

	Total	Percentage
Employment status known	220	93.2
Employment status unknown	16	6.8
Employed	210	95.5
Pursuing graduate degrees	2	0.9
Unemployed seeking employment	6	2.7
Unemployed not seeking employment	2	0.9

Type of Employment

# employed in law firms	74	35.2
# employed in business and industry	29	13.8
# employed in government	15	7.1
# employed in public interest	1	0.5
# employed as judicial clerks	86	41.0
# employed in academia	0	0.0

Geographic Location

# employed in state	136	64.8
# employed in foreign countries	0	0.0
# of states where employed	16	

Bar Passage Rates

Jurisdiction	New Jersey		
Exam	Sum 03	Win 04	Total
# from school taking bar for the first time	178	23	201
School's pass rate for all first-time takers	78%	83%	79%
State's pass rate for all first-time takers	76%	59%	73%

Rutgers—The State University of New Jersey—School of Law—Camden

217 North Fifth Street
Camden, NJ 08102
Phone: 856.225.6102 or 800.466.7561; Fax: 856.969.7903
E-mail: admissions@camlaw.rutgers.edu; Website: www-camlaw.rutgers.edu/

■ Introduction

Chartered in 1766 by George III of Great Britain as the Queen's College, Rutgers—The State University of New Jersey is one of the oldest and largest state higher educational systems in the nation. The law school at the Camden campus is proud to continue this national reputation of excellence. With more than 100 faculty and staff members, the law school is a leading center of legal education. Noted for excellence in scholarship, the faculty is internationally recognized in fields as diverse as international law, health law, family and women's rights law, state constitutional law, and legal history.

Located at the base of the Benjamin Franklin Bridge, just minutes from the Liberty Bell and Independence Hall in Philadelphia, the law school is in one of the nation's largest legal markets. Rutgers' thriving, 25-acre, tree-lined urban campus in Camden, New Jersey, is a handsome blend of converted Victorian buildings and newly constructed facilities. A member of the Association of American Law Schools, the school is included on the list of approved schools of the American Bar Association.

■ Library and Physical Facilities

The law school building houses research facilities, seminar and reading rooms, student lounges, a clinical suite, computer labs, study areas, a cafeteria, classrooms, and faculty offices. A new law school building is being constructed and annexed to the existing 93,860-square-foot structure. The new building design includes courtrooms, state-of-the-art classrooms, and enhanced student spaces. A selective federal repository, the law library, with more than 420,000 bibliographic units is one of the largest in the state. In addition to the traditional materials, students are trained on a number of computerized research systems, including a myriad of databases available on the Internet. The library consists of three floors of book stacks, a bridge that overlooks the campus and Philadelphia skyline, and a large computer lab for LexisNexis and Westlaw training. Over 400 individual working areas, carrels, and lounge seats are available.

■ Faculty

Faculty scholarship has been cited by numerous courts, including the United States Supreme Court, and faculty members have authored numerous casebooks and significant legal works. Faculty members testify regularly before Congress and serve as consultants and reporters for the American Bar Association, the American Law Institute, and several federal and state commissions, and act as counsel in important public interest litigation.

■ Curriculum and Special Programs

The first-year curriculum includes the traditional core legal courses. Central to the curriculum is the lawyering program that engages students in simulated lawyering activities and practical applications of the law. Upper-class students can typically choose from more than 100 exciting elective courses each year, including cyberlaw, corporate counseling, trial advocacy, sports law, children's law, and international business transactions.

An outstanding Externship Program offers third-year students the opportunity to work with federal and state judges, public agencies, and public interest organizations. Other students participate in the Civil Practice Clinic and pro bono programs at the law school. Live client experiences include the Domestic Violence Project, the Pro Bono Bankruptcy Project, the Immigration Project, the Mediation Project, and the Elder Law Clinic, or representing clients in connection with the LEAP Charter School. Each of these programs constitutes a comprehensive initiative that reflects the law school's commitment to public service.

Students may pursue their legal studies in the full-time day program as well as the part-time program, available day or evening. Both programs are subject to the same rigorous admission and academic standards.

■ Joint-Degree Programs

Eight formal joint JD and master's or doctoral degree programs are available with the University of Medicine and Dentistry, Graduate School of Business, Bloustein School of Planning and Public Policy, School of Social Work, and Graduate School–Camden, including JD/MD, JD/DO, JD/MPA, JD/MBA, JD/MSW, and JD/MCRP. Upon approval of the faculty, students may also pursue self-designed joint-degree programs within Rutgers University or with other graduate institutions.

■ Admission

Although admission is highly competitive, the Committee on Admissions does consider each applicant's file individually, and special qualities may occasionally overcome lower numbers. Important factors to the committee include LSAT, undergraduate and graduate grade-point average, undergraduate and graduate institutions, work experience, and letters of recommendation. Typically, half of the entering class scores in the top quartile on the LSAT (162 or higher) with an average GPA of 3.4 or higher. The entering class size each fall is about 165 full- and 80 part-time day and evening students. The law school draws from 40 states, the District of Columbia, and seven foreign countries. More than 300 colleges and

Rutgers—The State University of New Jersey—School of Law—Camden

universities are represented in the student body. Decisions are made on a rolling basis beginning in early December. The law school has rolling admission and will consider candidates who take the February and June LSAT. However, early applicants have an enhanced opportunity for admission. Applicants may also apply for advanced standing as a transfer student only upon completion of one year of law study. Students may request an application from the law school or apply online at *www.camlaw.rutgers.edu/*.

■ Financial Aid

In the 2003-2004 academic year, over $14 million was distributed to law students through fellowships, grants, loans, and employment. The average financial aid package was approximately $23,000, with 92 percent of the student body receiving some form of assistance. The Federal Direct Loan Program, the largest financial aid program, provided almost $11 million to over 650 students in the last academic year. For fall consideration, the FAFSA should be submitted by March 1. Merit-based scholarships are also available for outstanding academic performance.

■ Housing

Air-conditioned and carpeted law school apartments are located on-campus. There are also abundant housing opportunities in the nearby suburbs and excellent public transportation systems. First-year admitted students are invited to utilize the law school's housing web page and to attend the Dean's Law and Housing Day in the spring.

■ Career Services

As a direct result of the quality of legal education at Rutgers, typically more than 96 percent of each year's class obtains employment in the legal profession within nine months of graduation. All major Philadelphia, New Jersey, and Delaware firms recruit from Rutgers, as do prestigious firms from New York City, California, and Washington, DC. The school's more than 7,000 alumni are leading members of the judiciary, government, and bar throughout this nation. The average salary of an associate who joins a private law firm is in excess of $76,000, with top students typically making in excess of $100,000. The school's placement rate is one of the best in the country (41 percent of last year's class) for highly desirable state and federal clerkships.

■ Student Activities

Among the numerous student organizations are the Latino Law Students Association, Asian/Pacific American Law Students Association, Association for Public Interest Law, Black Law Students Association, Christian Legal Society, Community Outreach Group, Cyberlaw, Environmental Law Students Association, Francis Deak International Law Society, OUTLAW Student Bar Association, Health Law Society, Italian-American Law Students Organization, Jewish Law Students Association, Law Journal (publishes the *Rutgers Law Journal*), *Journal of Law and Urban Policy*, *Rutgers Journal of Law and Religion*, Phi Alpha Delta law fraternity, Pro Bono/Public Interest Steering Committee, and the Women's Law Caucus.

Applicant Profile

Rutgers—The State University of New Jersey—School of Law—Camden
This grid includes only applicants who earned 120-180 LSAT scores under standard administrations.

LSAT Score	GPA								
	3.75 +	3.50 - 3.74	3.25 - 3.49	3.00 - 3.24	2.75 - 2.99	2.50 - 2.74	2.25 - 2.49	2.00 - 2.24	Below 2.00
170-180									
165-169									
161-164									
158-160									
155-157									
150-154									
Below 150									

Very Likely   Likely   Possible   Unlikely*

*Special attributes may sometimes overcome lower scores/GPAs.
This chart is to be used as a general guide only. Nonnumerical factors are strongly considered for all applicants.

Rutgers University School of Law—Newark

Center for Law and Justice, 123 Washington Street
Newark, NJ 07102
Phone: 973.353.5554/7; Fax: 973.353.3459
E-mail: nwklaw@rci.rutgers.edu; Website: law.newark.rutgers.edu

ABA Approved Since 1941

The Basics

Type of school	Public
Term	Semester
Application deadline	3/15
Application fee	$50
Financial aid deadline	3/15
Can first year start other than fall?	No
Student to faculty ratio (fall)	18.3 to 1
Does the university offer:	
housing restricted to law students?	No
graduate housing for which law students are eligible?	Yes

Curriculum

	Full-time	Part-time
Typical first-year section size	60	78
Is there typically a "small section" of the first-year class, other than Legal Writing, taught by full-time faculty	Yes	Yes
If yes, typical size offered last year	35	39
# of classroom course titles beyond 1st year curriculum	138	
# of upper division courses, excluding seminars with an enrollment: Under 25	75	
25-49	28	
50-74	18	
75-99	5	
100+	1	
# of seminars	30	
# of seminar positions available	600	
# of seminar positions filled	223	48
# of positions available in simulation courses	220	
# of simulation positions filled	128	71
# of positions available in faculty supervised clinical courses	220	
# of faculty supervised clinical positions filled	167	16
# involved in field placements	149	28
# involved in law journals	180	10
# involved in moot court or trial competitions	79	8
# of credit hours required to graduate	84	

Faculty and Administrators

	Total		Men		Women		Minorities	
	Fall	Spr	Fall	Spr	Fall	Spr	Fall	Spr
Full-time	33	42	19	21	14	21	9	9
Other Full-time	3	3	3	3	0	0	1	1
Deans, librarians, & others who teach	5	5	5	4	0	1	3	2
Part-time	21	28	13	20	7	7	3	4
Total	62	78	40	48	21	29	16	16

JD Enrollment and Ethnicity

	Men		Women		Full-time		Part-time		1st-year		Total		JD Degs. Awd.
	#	%	#	%	#	%	#	%	#	%	#	%	
African Amer.	55	11.9	59	16.9	76	13.5	38	15.3	56	19.7	114	14.1	40
Amer. Indian	4	0.9	0	0.0	2	0.4	2	0.8	1	0.4	4	0.5	1
Asian Amer.	55	11.9	47	13.5	80	14.3	22	8.8	37	13.0	102	12.6	21
Mex. Amer.	2	0.4	3	0.9	5	0.9	0	0.0	2	0.7	5	0.6	1
Puerto Rican	21	4.6	17	4.9	29	5.2	9	3.6	13	4.6	38	4.7	8
Hispanic	24	5.2	15	4.3	27	4.8	12	4.8	13	4.6	39	4.8	14
Total Minority	161	34.9	141	40.4	219	39.0	83	33.3	122	43.0	302	37.3	85
For. Nation.	8	1.7	9	2.6	8	1.4	9	3.6	5	1.8	17	2.1	2
Caucasian	292	63.3	199	57.0	334	59.5	157	63.1	157	55.3	491	60.6	154
Unknown	0	0.0	0	0.0	0	0.0	0	0.0	0	0.0	0	0.0	0
Total	461	56.9	349	43.1	561	69.3	249	30.7	284	35.1	810		241

Tuition and Fees

	Resident	Nonresident
Full-time	$16,525	$23,556
Part-time	$13,169	$19,105

Living Expenses

Estimated living expenses for singles

Living on campus	Living off campus	Living at home
$12,675	$16,475	$6,575

Rutgers University School of Law—Newark

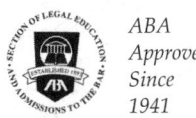

ABA
Approved
Since
1941

GPA and LSAT Scores

	Total	Full-time	Part-time
# of apps	3,480	2,821	659
# of admits	730	613	117
# of matrics	284	206	78
75% GPA	3.58	3.61	3.45
25% GPA	2.93	3.00	2.83
75% LSAT	161	162	159
25% LSAT	152	153	152

Grants and Scholarships (from prior year)

	Total		Full-time		Part-time	
	#	%	#	%	#	%
Total # of students	783		551		232	
Total # receiving grants	254	32.4	216	39.2	38	16.4
Less than 1/2 tuition	224	28.6	194	35.2	30	12.9
Half to full tuition	16	2.0	8	1.5	8	3.4
Full tuition	8	1.0	8	1.5	0	0.0
More than full tuition	6	0.8	6	1.1	0	0.0
Median grant amount			$3,000		$3,000	

Informational and Library Resources

# of volumes and volume equivalents	516,700
# of titles	180,948
# of active serial subscriptions	3,140
Study seating capacity inside the library	425
# of professional librarians	9
Hours per week library is open	108
# of open, wired connections available to students	510
# of networked computers available for use by students	178
# of simultaneous wireless users	600
Require computer?	N

JD Attrition (from prior year)

	Academic	Other	Total	
	#	#	#	%
1st year	0	20	20	8.0%
2nd year	0	6	6	2.6%
3rd year	0	1	1	0.4%
4th year	0	0	0	0.0%

Employment

	Total	Percentage
Employment status known	213	97.7
Employment status unknown	5	2.3
Employed	190	89.2
Pursuing graduate degrees	4	1.9
Unemployed seeking employment	9	4.2
Unemployed not seeking employment	10	4.7

Type of Employment

# employed in law firms	88	46.3
# employed in business and industry	15	7.9
# employed in government	13	6.8
# employed in public interest	6	3.2
# employed as judicial clerks	66	34.7
# employed in academia	2	1.1

Geographic Location

# employed in state	130	68.4
# employed in foreign countries	0	0.0
# of states where employed	10	

Bar Passage Rates

Jurisdiction	New Jersey			New York		
Exam	Sum 03	Win 04	Total	Sum 03	Win 04	Total
# from school taking bar for the first time	190	27	217	145	17	162
School's pass rate for all first-time takers	75%	56%	72%	76%	47%	73%
State's pass rate for all first-time takers	76%	59%	73%	78%	58%	75%

Rutgers University School of Law—Newark

Center for Law and Justice, 123 Washington Street
Newark, NJ 07102
Phone: 973.353.5554/7; Fax: 973.353.3459
E-mail: nwklaw@rci.rutgers.edu; Website: law.newark.rutgers.edu

■ Introduction

Rutgers School of Law—Newark is a leading center for the study of theory and practice of law, the advancement of law reform, and the application of law to promote equality and social justice. Four core principles shape the work of our faculty and students: academic excellence, scholarship, public service, and equal opportunity. Through a unique combination of traditional doctrinal courses and clinical education, we prepare our students to become highly skilled, ethical lawyers who will assume influential roles in the law and other disciplines. Our alumni have fulfilled that responsibility as practitioners, judges, legislators, public officials, and leaders in business. Our internationally recognized faculty regularly contribute to the development of legal theory and produce scholarship that addresses significant social issues from interdisciplinary perspectives. Through our clinical program and pro bono activities, faculty and students give the principles of justice and equality a practical significance. Rutgers—Newark is the home of the oldest chapter of the Order of the Coif in New Jersey.

■ The Center for Law and Justice

The Center for Law and Justice is one of the most attractive and technologically advanced law school buildings in the country. Design highlights include a light-filled library housing over 500,000 volumes and five computer labs; lecture rooms with excellent acoustics, sightlines, and power and data lines at every seat; a well-appointed courtroom complex where the Appellate Division of the Superior Court regularly hears cases; and numerous lounge and study areas with wireless Internet access. The building opens onto a pedestrian plaza and a garden terrace, favorite gathering spots for students and faculty.

■ Faculty

The faculty contributes to every aspect of the law school experience. They examine, shape, and resolve new and developing issues of law, such as gender and race studies, dispute resolution, international transactions, and new theories of the corporation. Faculty members engage students through teaching styles that range from traditional Socratic method to interactive problem solving. The faculty is diverse, ensuring the kind of intellectual inquiry that provides a rich foundation for a career in law.

■ Curriculum

The rigorous curriculum ensures the development of professional skills and values within a theoretical framework that promotes intellectual growth and a commitment to justice.

First-year students learn the essential conceptual, analytical, and research methods to be effective lawyers in complex environments. Upper-level students build on those skills through our extensive curriculum of over 200 class, clinic, and seminar options. The faculty reviews the curriculum regularly to ensure that the offerings prepare students for a rapidly changing legal environment.

The Global Legal Studies Program offers students interested in public and private international law a rich array of academic courses, clinical programs, and experiential learning opportunities, focusing on the human condition in an interconnected world. An accredited semester of study abroad sends students to Leiden University in The Netherlands for an intensive program in international law, European Union law, comparative law, legal history, and law and international economics. The Rutgers Center for Global Change and Governance, located in our building, also serves as a nexus for students interested in the international dimension.

Joint-degree programs are available with the Rutgers Graduate Schools of Business, Urban Planning, and Social Work, as well as the University of Medicine and Dentistry of New Jersey. Students are encouraged to take advantage of the rich curriculum offerings throughout the university through cross-disciplinary registration. The Foreign Lawyer Program permits persons with foreign law degrees to earn a JD in two years.

■ Clinics and Public Service

With nearly 35 years of pacesetting experience and a historic commitment to public service, Rutgers—Newark offers students rich opportunities for hands-on legal experience in real cases involving underrepresented clients, communities, or causes. Guided by talented and accomplished faculty with expertise in litigation, legislation, mediation, or transactional practice, our eight clinics are noted for their diversity, breadth and comprehensiveness of experiences, and involvement in cases and projects of social and community impact. Clinical experiences enable students to work for underserved clients and causes, and provide corporate, transactional, and intellectual property legal services to nonprofit corporations, start-up for-profit businesses, and other entities. Other opportunities include pro bono work, internships, fellowships, and summer placements. The Loan Repayment Assistance Program, one of the largest in the country, assists graduates pursuing careers in public service.

■ Students and Student Life

Rutgers enrolls students of extraordinary academic and professional promise who enrich the community with their intellectual strength and significant life and work experience. Many students have earned advanced degrees while others provide a global perspective to the classroom.

Diversity of views enlivens the classroom and creates an inclusive environment. Our Minority Student Program reflects the faculty's long-standing commitment to preserve the diversity of the law school and to improve diversity in the legal profession. Student-run organizations reflect myriad interests, political positions, and backgrounds, from the Lawyers Guild to the Sports and Entertainment Law Society. Student publications include the *Rutgers Law Review, Rutgers Computer and Technology Journal*, the *Women's Rights Law Reporter*, the *Rutgers Race and the Law Review*, and the online student newspaper, *The Rutgers Law Record*.

■ Admission

The faculty believes that diverse perspectives and backgrounds are essential to a complete understanding of the law and its relation to contemporary society. The law school seeks and attracts a talented student body with a breadth of experience, and provides unparalleled opportunities for those who have been historically excluded from the legal profession.

The Admission Committee considers a broad range of factors, including but not limited to educational and employment experiences, community service, LSAT, UGPA, race, ethnicity, socioeconomic background, and extraordinary family circumstances. Every applicant can choose to compete for admission with primary emphasis placed on numerical indicators (LSAT and UGPA), or nonnumerical indicators (experiences and accomplishments).

In each entering class, 35–40 percent of our students are people of color. All regions of the country and more than two dozen foreign countries are represented.

■ Housing

Graduate school university housing is located in close proximity to the law school. Other accommodations are available in nearby suburban areas. Public transportation is widely available.

■ Career Services

The Office of Career Services provides traditional and innovative services and programs, assisting students and graduates develop career goals and conduct successful job searches. Individual counseling, panels, workshops, networking events, and on- and off-campus interview programs which attract many of the nation's leading law firms are a few of a myriad of services offered.

Applicant Profile

Rutgers University School of Law—Newark

LSAT Score	GPA									
	3.75 +	3.50 - 3.74	3.25 - 3.49	3.00 - 3.24	2.75 - 2.99	2.50 - 2.74	2.25 - 2.49	2.00 - 2.24	Below 2.00	No GPA
175-180										
170-174										
165-169										
160-164										
157-159										
154-156										
150-153										
145-149										
140-144										
135-139										
130-134										
125-129										
120-124										

Highly Possible　　Possible　　Unlikely

The information contained in this grid should be used as an approximate gauge as to the likelihood of admission. The Admissions Committee gives considerable weight to individual accomplishments and other nonnumerical factors in the admissions process. LSAT and UGPA are not the sole determinants for admission.

St. John's University School of Law

8000 Utopia Parkway
Queens, NY 11439
Phone: 718.990.6474; Fax: 718.990.2526
E-mail: lawinfo@stjohns.edu; Website: www.law.stjohns.edu

*ABA
Approved
Since
1937*

The Basics

Type of school	Private
Term	Semester
Application deadline	4/1 12/1
Application fee	$60
Financial aid deadline	2/1
Can first year start other than fall?	Yes
Student to faculty ratio (fall)	17.3 to 1
Does the university offer:	
housing restricted to law students?	No
graduate housing for which law students are eligible?	Yes

Faculty and Administrators

	Total		Men		Women		Minorities	
	Fall	Spr	Fall	Spr	Fall	Spr	Fall	Spr
Full-time	43	46	28	31	15	15	8	8
Other Full-time	0	2	0	1	0	1	0	0
Deans, librarians, & others who teach	5	5	2	2	3	3	1	1
Part-time	42	50	34	42	8	8	2	4
Total	90	103	64	76	26	27	11	13

Curriculum

	Full-time	Part-time
Typical first-year section size	95	70
Is there typically a "small section" of the first-year class, other than Legal Writing, taught by full-time faculty	Yes	No
If yes, typical size offered last year	30	0
# of classroom course titles beyond 1st year curriculum		156
# of upper division courses, excluding seminars with an enrollment: Under 25		90
25-49		65
50-74		12
75-99		12
100+		5
# of seminars		51
# of seminar positions available		590
# of seminar positions filled	385	16
# of positions available in simulation courses		414
# of simulation positions filled	290	44
# of positions available in faculty supervised clinical courses		74
# of faculty supervised clinical positions filled	73	0
# involved in field placements	134	10
# involved in law journals	102	4
# involved in moot court or trial competitions	62	0
# of credit hours required to graduate		86

JD Enrollment and Ethnicity

	Men #	Men %	Women #	Women %	Full-time #	Full-time %	Part-time #	Part-time %	1st-year #	1st-year %	Total #	Total %	JD Degs. Awd.
African Amer.	24	4.8	39	8.5	37	4.9	26	12.9	22	7.6	63	6.6	16
Amer. Indian	1	0.2	1	0.2	1	0.1	1	0.5	1	0.3	2	0.2	0
Asian Amer.	40	8.0	43	9.4	67	8.8	16	7.9	32	11.0	83	8.6	31
Mex. Amer.	4	0.8	4	0.9	5	0.7	3	1.5	1	0.3	8	0.8	0
Puerto Rican	5	1.0	2	0.4	5	0.7	2	1.0	1	0.3	7	0.7	4
Hispanic	25	5.0	15	3.3	25	3.3	15	7.4	18	6.2	40	4.2	2
Total Minority	99	19.7	104	22.7	140	18.4	63	31.2	75	25.9	203	21.1	53
For. Nation.	9	1.8	12	2.6	15	2.0	6	3.0	12	4.1	21	2.2	2
Caucasian	342	68.1	298	64.9	531	70.0	109	54.0	138	47.6	640	66.6	187
Unknown	52	10.4	45	9.8	73	9.6	24	11.9	65	22.4	97	10.1	33
Total	502	52.2	459	47.8	759	79.0	202	21.0	290	30.2	961		275

Tuition and Fees

	Resident	Nonresident
Full-time	$30,500	$30,500
Part-time	$22,900	$22,900

Living Expenses

Estimated living expenses for singles

Living on campus	Living off campus	Living at home
$18,990	$18,990	$7,840

St. John's University School of Law

*ABA
Approved
Since
1937*

GPA and LSAT Scores

	Total	Full-time	Part-time
# of apps	4,370	3,655	715
# of admits	1,097	922	175
# of matrics	308	235	73
75% GPA	3.62	3.62	3.66
25% GPA	3.11	3.13	3.05
75% LSAT	162	163	157
25% LSAT	156	158	153

Grants and Scholarships (from prior year)

	Total #	Total %	Full-time #	Full-time %	Part-time #	Part-time %
Total # of students	969		780		189	
Total # receiving grants	506	52.2	452	57.9	54	28.6
Less than 1/2 tuition	282	29.1	248	31.8	34	18.0
Half to full tuition	130	13.4	119	15.3	11	5.8
Full tuition	83	8.6	75	9.6	8	4.2
More than full tuition	11	1.1	10	1.3	1	0.5
Median grant amount			$12,500		$8,250	

Informational and Library Resources

# of volumes and volume equivalents	481,475
# of titles	131,384
# of active serial subscriptions	4,923
Study seating capacity inside the library	571
# of professional librarians	7
Hours per week library is open	99
# of open, wired connections available to students	141
# of networked computers available for use by students	141
# of simultaneous wireless users	870
Require computer?	N

JD Attrition (from prior year)

	Academic #	Other #	Total #	Total %
1st year	5	27	32	9.2%
2nd year	1	3	4	1.3%
3rd year	1	0	1	0.3%
4th year	0	0	0	0.0%

Employment

	Total	Percentage
Employment status known	277	98.2
Employment status unknown	5	1.8
Employed	254	91.7
Pursuing graduate degrees	0	0.0
Unemployed seeking employment	7	2.5
Unemployed not seeking employment	16	5.8

Type of Employment

# employed in law firms	161	63.4
# employed in business and industry	36	14.2
# employed in government	44	17.3
# employed in public interest	2	0.8
# employed as judicial clerks	8	3.1
# employed in academia	1	0.4

Geographic Location

# employed in state	224	88.2
# employed in foreign countries	1	0.4
# of states where employed	15	

Bar Passage Rates

Jurisdiction	New York		
Exam	Sum 03	Win 04	Total
# from school taking bar for the first time	256	11	267
School's pass rate for all first-time takers	85%	73%	85%
State's pass rate for all first-time takers	78%	58%	75%

The information on these pages was provided by the law school

St. John's University School of Law

8000 Utopia Parkway
Queens, NY 11439
Phone: 718.990.6474; Fax: 718.990.2526
E-mail: lawinfo@stjohns.edu; Website: www.law.stjohns.edu

■ Introduction

St. John's University School of Law is a forceful presence and an integral part of the New York metropolitan area. It imparts to its students training and competency in the basic skills and techniques of the legal profession, a grasp of the history and the system of common law, and a familiarity with important statutes and decisions in federal and state jurisdictions, including the state of New York.

The recently completed expansion of the law school produced a state-of-the-art facility with a gross total square footage of 179,400, one of the highest space-per-student ratios in the country. Some highlights of the new addition include expanded facilities for student activities, new alumni function areas, a student lounge, faculty offices, and classrooms for teaching clinical and lawyering skills. Recently, St. John's School of Law introduced a wireless network, permitting high speed Internet accessibility from anywhere in the law school.

The School of Law is located on the Queens Campus of St. John's University. Situated on almost 100 rolling acres in a residential area, the campus boasts a spectacular view of the Manhattan skyline. St. John's School of Law is approved by the ABA and is a member of the AALS.

■ Library and Physical Facilities

The showpiece of the law school building is its beautiful law library, which incorporates the most recent advances in law library science and technology. It contains a 22-terminal computer classroom, a 30-terminal state-of-the-art computer laboratory, and eight study rooms for student conferences. The library occupies approximately 60,000 square feet on five of the eight building levels. It has been designated a depository library for US government and UN documents.

The School of Law has recently completed a major renovation of its moot court, producing a beautiful, state-of-the-art facility that incorporates technologies that further the teaching and research missions of St. John's.

■ Special Programs and LLM in Bankruptcy

Elective clinical programs that include a class component are available to second- and third-year full-time students (12–15 hours per week).

In the Civil Clinical Program, students work in (1) a legal services office assisting lawyers who provide legal representation to the poor; or (2) a public service or governmental agency such as the United States Attorney's Office, the Securities and Exchange Commission, or the New York Legal Aid Society.

In the Criminal Clinical Program, students work in a District Attorney's office, a Legal Aid office, or the law

department of the Supreme Court or Criminal Court. In the Judicial Clinical Program, students work in the federal, state, or city court system.

The Domestic Violence Clinical Program affords students the opportunity to work with agencies such as the Queens Legal Services Corporation and Domestic Violence Law and Advocacy Project. Students gain a greater understanding of the dynamics of domestic violence and of how the law can be used to combat it.

In the Elder Law Clinic, students represent elderly clients with legal problems that involve the danger of losing their homes, denial of disability benefits, unlawful collection practices, and illegal lending schemes.

Students in the Domestic Violence Litigation Clinic represent women who are victims of spousal abuse. The students perform services that include client interviews, negotiating settlements, and making court appearances.

The Prosecutors Clinic allows students to witness the criminal justice system at work—not just by observing, but by prosecuting real cases.

St. John's has started the nation's first master's program in bankruptcy. It is designed to meet an important and special educational need in the field of bankruptcy law. Matriculating students will be required to complete 30 credits, including the preparation and defense of a major thesis on a current significant bankruptcy topic. Students may matriculate on a full- or part-time basis. An advisory board, consisting of leading bankruptcy judges, practitioners, and insolvency professionals, will advise on the scope of the program and the course offerings.

■ Special Diversity Admissions Program

The School of Law sponsors a program for individuals who have suffered the effects of discrimination, chronic financial hardship, or other social, educational, or physical disadvantages to such an extent that their undergraduate performance or LSAT score would not otherwise warrant unconditional acceptance into the entering class. This Summer Institute program, which is available at no additional charge to the participants, consists of a substantive course taught and graded according to the same qualitative standard applied to all first-year courses, as well as a legal writing course. The program enables individuals whose LSAT score and GPA are not reliable predictors of their success to demonstrate that they have the ability to succeed in the study of law.

■ Vincentian Scholarship Program

The Mission Statement of St. John's University School of Law calls for the law school "to provide a superior legal education for a diverse population of students with special

St. John's University School of Law

awareness for economic fairness and equal opportunity, consistent with and in fulfillment of the Vincentian tradition and mission." In furtherance of this Vincentian tradition and mission, the School of Law provides five full-tuition Vincentian scholarships each year in its ongoing effort to achieve a diverse student body. These are in addition to the extensive need-based and academic financial scholarship aid provided to law students annually. Applicants seeking a Vincentian scholarship are encouraged to so indicate on their application for admission and to discuss their qualifications in an addendum to their application.

■ Student Activities

Publications—*St. John's Law Review, The Catholic Lawyer, Journal of Legal Commentary, International Law Review of the New York State Bar Association, American Bankruptcy Institute Law Review.*

Mock Trial and Appellate Activities—Moot Court, Criminal Law Institute, Civil Trial Institute.

Specialized Legal Activities—The Student Bar Association, Admiralty Law Society, Women's Law Association, Bankruptcy Law Society, Environmental Law Club, Entertainment and Sports Club, International Law Society, Intellectual Property, Labor and Employment Club, Real Property Club, the Black Law Students Association, the Asian American Law Students Association, the Latino American Law Students Association, and Client Counseling Competition. The school also maintains chapters in two legal societies, Phi Delta Phi and Phi Alpha Delta, and the Black, Asian, and Latino Law Students Association.

■ Expenses and Financial Aid

The School of Law provides extensive need-based and academic financial scholarship aid to students annually. There are new dormitory facilities on campus and many students find other suitable living accommodations in the vicinity of the university. In addition, the Admission Office coordinates a housing network for students. Students with housing needs are invited to contact the Admission Office for assistance and information.

■ Career Services

Career Services provides an array of services, including résumé and cover letter critiquing, mock interview coaching, career job openings and judicial clerkships, newsletters, lists of prospective employers, interview programs, and career education panels. Recent graduates have obtained employment in many areas of the legal profession. Annually, 5 to 8 percent accept federal and state judicial clerkships. For the class of 2003, the employment rate (nine months after graduation) was 97 percent.

Alumni of the law school are currently practicing throughout the United States and its territories. Many have achieved positions of prominence in executive and legislative branches of the government, as members of the judiciary, and in both private and corporate practice. Two recent governors of New York, a recent governor of the US Virgin Islands, a former governor of California, and recently three of the seven judges on the NYS Court of Appeals were graduates of St. John's School of Law.

Applicant Profile

St. John's University School of Law

LSAT Score	GPA								
	3.75 +	3.50 - 3.74	3.25 - 3.49	3.00 - 3.24	2.75 - 2.99	2.50 - 2.74	2.25 - 2.49	2.00 - 2.24	Below 2.00
175-180									
170-174									
165-169									
160-164									
155-159									
150-154									
145-149									
140-144									
135-139									
130-134									
125-129									
120-124									

■ Good Possibility   ▨ Possible   ▢ Unlikely

Saint Louis University School of Law

3700 Lindell Blvd.
St. Louis, MO 63108
Phone: 314.977.2800; Fax: 314.977.1464
E-mail: admissions@law.slu.edu; Website: law.slu.edu

*ABA
Approved
Since
1924*

The Basics

Type of school	Private
Term	Semester
Application deadline	3/1
Application fee	$55
Financial aid deadline	6/1
Can first year start other than fall?	No
Student to faculty ratio (fall)	18.9 to 1
Does the university offer:	
housing restricted to law students?	No
graduate housing for which law students are eligible?	No

Faculty and Administrators

	Total		Men		Women		Minorities	
	Fall	Spr	Fall	Spr	Fall	Spr	Fall	Spr
Full-time	35	36	25	25	10	11	3	2
Other Full-time	7	7	2	2	5	5	1	1
Deans, librarians, & others who teach	3	3	3	3	0	0	0	0
Part-time	35	12	24	9	11	3	2	0
Total	80	58	54	39	26	19	6	3

Curriculum

	Full-time	Part-time
Typical first-year section size	110	80
Is there typically a "small section" of the first-year class, other than Legal Writing, taught by full-time faculty	Yes	No
If yes, typical size offered last year	35	0
# of classroom course titles beyond 1st year curriculum	61	
# of upper division courses, excluding seminars with an enrollment: Under 25	42	
25-49	18	
50-74	15	
75-99	11	
100+	4	
# of seminars	25	
# of seminar positions available	300	
# of seminar positions filled	207	58
# of positions available in simulation courses	170	
# of simulation positions filled	135	26
# of positions available in faculty supervised clinical courses	60	
# of faculty supervised clinical positions filled	53	5
# involved in field placements	126	24
# involved in law journals	87	10
# involved in moot court or trial competitions	54	2
# of credit hours required to graduate	91	

JD Enrollment and Ethnicity

	Men		Women		Full-time		Part-time		1st-year		Total		JD Degs. Awd.
	#	%	#	%	#	%	#	%	#	%	#	%	
African Amer.	10	2.3	26	5.8	26	4.0	10	4.3	9	2.9	36	4.1	11
Amer. Indian	0	0.0	0	0.0	0	0.0	0	0.0	0	0.0	0	0.0	0
Asian Amer.	15	3.5	11	2.5	22	3.4	4	1.7	6	2.0	26	3.0	7
Mex. Amer.	0	0.0	0	0.0	0	0.0	0	0.0	0	0.0	0	0.0	0
Puerto Rican	0	0.0	0	0.0	0	0.0	0	0.0	0	0.0	0	0.0	0
Hispanic	7	1.6	13	2.9	16	2.5	4	1.7	6	2.0	20	2.3	0
Total Minority	32	7.5	50	11.2	64	10.0	18	7.7	21	6.9	82	9.4	18
For. Nation.	0	0.0	0	0.0	0	0.0	0	0.0	0	0.0	0	0.0	2
Caucasian	342	79.7	370	82.6	511	79.6	201	85.5	244	79.7	712	81.2	201
Unknown	55	12.8	28	6.3	67	10.4	16	6.8	41	13.4	83	9.5	1
Total	429	48.9	448	51.1	642	73.2	235	26.8	306	34.9	877		222

Tuition and Fees

	Resident	Nonresident
Full-time	$27,250	$0
Part-time	$19,890	$0

Living Expenses

Estimated living expenses for singles

Living on campus	Living off campus	Living at home
N/A	$11,750	$11,018

Saint Louis University School of Law

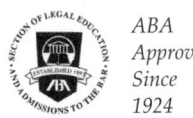

*ABA
Approved
Since
1924*

GPA and LSAT Scores

	Total	Full-time	Part-time
# of apps	2,121	1,675	446
# of admits	796	673	123
# of matrics	313	234	79
75% GPA	3.72	3.75	3.62
25% GPA	3.23	3.32	3.07
75% LSAT	159	160	156
25% LSAT	153	154	151

Grants and Scholarships (from prior year)

	Total		Full-time		Part-time	
	#	%	#	%	#	%
Total # of students	825		597		228	
Total # receiving grants	375	45.5	309	51.8	66	28.9
Less than 1/2 tuition	223	27.0	162	27.1	61	26.8
Half to full tuition	117	14.2	113	18.9	4	1.8
Full tuition	34	4.1	34	5.7	0	0.0
More than full tuition	1	0.1	0	0.0	1	0.4
Median grant amount			$12,000		$3,000	

Informational and Library Resources

# of volumes and volume equivalents	629,032
# of titles	293,496
# of active serial subscriptions	3,696
Study seating capacity inside the library	464
# of professional librarians	9
Hours per week library is open	101
# of open, wired connections available to students	702
# of networked computers available for use by students	58
# of simultaneous wireless users	900
Require computer?	N

JD Attrition (from prior year)

	Academic	Other	Total	
	#	#	#	%
1st year	9	19	28	9.6%
2nd year	7	5	12	4.4%
3rd year	2	0	2	1.0%
4th year	0	0	0	0.0%

Employment

	Total	Percentage
Employment status known	200	100.0
Employment status unknown	0	0.0
Employed	186	93.0
Pursuing graduate degrees	0	0.0
Unemployed seeking employment	3	1.5
Unemployed not seeking employment	11	5.5

Type of Employment

# employed in law firms	119	64.0
# employed in business and industry	30	16.1
# employed in government	16	8.6
# employed in public interest	8	4.3
# employed as judicial clerks	8	4.3
# employed in academia	5	2.7

Geographic Location

# employed in state	153	82.3
# employed in foreign countries	0	0.0
# of states where employed	15	

Bar Passage Rates

Jurisdiction	Missouri			Illinois		
Exam	Sum 03	Win 04	Total	Sum 03	Win 04	Total
# from school taking bar for the first time	137	26	163	35	54	89
School's pass rate for all first-time takers	77%	81%	78%	77%	87%	83%
State's pass rate for all first-time takers	83%	87%	84%	86%	78%	84%

Saint Louis University School of Law

3700 Lindell Blvd.
St. Louis, MO 63108
Phone: 314.977.2800; Fax: 314.977.1464
E-mail: admissions@law.slu.edu; Website: law.slu.edu

■ Introduction

The mission of Saint Louis University School of Law is to advance the understanding and the development of law, and prepare students to achieve professional success and personal satisfaction through leadership and service to others. The school is guided by the Jesuit tradition of academic excellence, freedom of inquiry, and respect for individual differences.

Located in beautiful midtown St. Louis, Saint Louis University School of Law is perfectly positioned to provide students with unparalleled exposure to the legal world. St. Louis boasts an impressive array of law firms, corporate offices, and governmental agencies; there are local, state, and federal courthouses throughout the city and surrounding counties, including the largest federal courthouse in the United States.

With an accomplished, accessible faculty and a diverse curriculum, the School of Law provides a challenging yet collegial environment designed to foster success for dedicated students. Whatever the interest—corporate and finance, health, international, intellectual property, tax, securities, real estate, labor and employment, litigation, sports and entertainment law—the school can help students achieve their desired career goals.

For those who work full-time and are unable to attend classes during the day, the school offers a challenging part-time **Evening Program**—the only program of its kind in the state of Missouri. Through this program, students can earn their law degree in four years with summer attendance or five years without summer attendance.

Regardless of the program in which a student enrolls, all first-year law students benefit from the school's unique small section program. Each small section is combined with every other section in courses throughout the first year. This allows for individualized instruction and focused student interaction, and, most importantly, builds a sense of community among classmates.

■ Special Academic Programs

Centers for Excellence—The school features one of the premier Health Law Studies programs in the nation along with specialized Centers in Employment Law and International and Comparative Law.

- The **Center for Health Law Studies** boasts a nationally recognized faculty, an unparalled curriculum, and some of the country's finest health law publications. Visit: *law.slu.edu/healthlaw*.
- The **Center for Employment Law** specializes in issues of labor disputes, benefits, hiring and discharging, and arbitration. Visit: *law.slu.edu/emplaw*.

- The **Center for International and Comparative Law** offers a specialized program of study in areas such as public international law, international criminal law, and international corporate law. Students receive instruction from faculty who have experienced and studied foreign legal systems. Visit: *law.slu.edu/cicl*.
- **Study Abroad**—Through the Center for International and Comparative Law, students can study law at Saint Louis University's campus in Madrid, Spain, earning up to six credit hours of comparative law with foreign and American professors who have extensive experience in the fields of foreign and American criminal law, civil law, and global human rights. The school also maintains cooperative agreements with the University College in Cork, Ireland, Université d'Orleans in France, University of Georgia in Brussels, Belgium, and the Ruhr University in Bochum, Germany.
- **Joint-Degree Programs**—The School of Law offers intensive joint-degree programs in cooperation with other university schools. Students must meet the admission requirements of both schools, including each school's entrance examination. Candidates in a joint-degree program must complete the first-year law curriculum before beginning the joint program; students enrolled in the JD/MBA program may begin in either program. Candidates must complete both degrees within the same semester. The joint-degree programs available are JD/MBA, JD/MHA, JD/MA in Public Administration, JD/MA in Urban Affairs, and JD/MPH.

■ Practical Skills Training

Students are presented with a variety of opportunities to practice law throughout their education. **Legal Clinics** provide immediate exposure to the legal world through a variety of service-oriented programs. Students represent clients in court, clerk for judges, and participate in externships at law firms, corporations, and government agencies. Visit: *law.slu.edu/clinics*. The **Trial Advocacy** program helps students develop skills in all aspects of trial preparation. Through the **Client Counseling** program, students learn to communicate with clients, learning how to ask the right questions, listen effectively, and encourage clients to talk. In the **Negotiation** program, students experience first-hand the practice of negotiation through a variety of simulation activities.

■ Cocurricular Activities

The school allows students to perfect their writing and editing skills by working on one of three law journals — *Saint Louis University Law Journal, Saint Louis University Public Law Review,* and the *Journal of Health Law.*

Qualifying students are invited to write and edit the collections of scholarly work submitted from lawyers and law professors across the world. The **Moot Court Competitions** hone a student's litigation skills in research, analysis, writing, and oral argument. Students interested in international law may participate in the **Jessup Moot Court Competition**. In addition, there is a **Health Law Moot Court** and an **Intellectual Property Moot Court**. The school also offers **Trial Advocacy Competitions** and **Client Counseling Competitions**.

■ Financial Aid/Scholarships

Saint Louis University School of Law awards a substantial number of merit-based scholarships to a select group of highly qualified admitted students, including 10 full-tuition scholarships through the 1843 Scholars program. The school has a variety of ways to help students meet their financial goals. Contact the School of Law's Financial Aid Coordinator at *fin_aid@law.slu.edu*.

■ Library

The Omer Poos Law Library serves as the center for legal research and information. The collection contains over 600,000 volumes and more than 6,400 serials covering federal and state primary law as well as international legal materials. The library currently ranks 27th in the country for size of collection. Visit: *law.slu.edu/library*.

■ Career Services

The Career Services Office, staffed by two licensed attorneys and a licensed professional counselor, assists students in identifying their career goals. Through a litany of career resources, students are able to pursue employment opportunities that meet their goals and suit their needs. The graduating classes within the past four years have averaged a 90 percent employment rate within six months of graduation. Visit: *law.slu.edu/community/careersvcs*.

Applicant Profile

Saint Louis University School of Law

LSAT Score	GPA						
	3.75 +	3.50 - 3.74	3.25 - 3.49	3.00 - 3.24	2.75 - 2.99	2.50 - 2.74	Below 2.50
175-180							
170-174							
165-169							
160-164							
155-159							
150-154							
145-149							
140-144							
135-139							
130-134							
125-129							
120-124							

Likely   Possible   Unlikely

Note: This chart is to be used as a general guide only. Nonnumerical factors are strongly considered for all applicants.

St. Mary's University School of Law

One Camino Santa Maria
San Antonio, TX 78228-8601
Phone: 210.436.3523; Toll-free: 866.639.5831; Fax: 210.431.4202
E-mail: lawadmissions@stmarytx.edu; Website: law.stmarytx.edu

*ABA
Approved
Since
1948*

The Basics

Type of school	Private
Term	Semester
Application deadline	3/1
Application fee	$55
Financial aid deadline	3/21
Can first year start other than fall?	No
Student to faculty ratio (fall)	23.4 to 1
Does the university offer:	
housing restricted to law students?	No
graduate housing for which law students are eligible?	Yes

Faculty and Administrators

	Total		Men		Women		Minorities	
	Fall	Spr	Fall	Spr	Fall	Spr	Fall	Spr
Full-time	28	29	21	22	7	7	6	7
Other Full-time	6	6	2	2	4	4	1	1
Deans, librarians, & others who teach	6	5	3	2	3	3	3	3
Part-time	64	56	34	32	30	24	24	18
Total	104	96	60	58	44	38	34	29

Curriculum

	Full-time	Part-time
Typical first-year section size	75	0
Is there typically a "small section" of the first-year class, other than Legal Writing, taught by full-time faculty	No	No
If yes, typical size offered last year	0	0
# of classroom course titles beyond 1st year curriculum		95

# of upper division courses, excluding seminars with an enrollment:		
	Under 25	51
	25-49	21
	50-74	14
	75-99	9
	100+	0

# of seminars		6
# of seminar positions available		72
# of seminar positions filled	30	0
# of positions available in simulation courses		208
# of simulation positions filled	201	0
# of positions available in faculty supervised clinical courses		33
# of faculty supervised clinical positions filled	33	0
# involved in field placements	23	0
# involved in law journals	86	0
# involved in moot court or trial competitions	65	0
# of credit hours required to graduate		90

JD Enrollment and Ethnicity

	Men		Women		Full-time		Part-time		1st-year		Total		JD Degs. Awd.
	#	%	#	%	#	%	#	%	#	%	#	%	
African Amer.	10	2.1	7	2.2	17	2.2	0	0.0	3	1.0	17	2.2	4
Amer. Indian	4	0.9	5	1.6	9	1.1	0	0.0	4	1.4	9	1.1	3
Asian Amer.	10	2.1	17	5.3	27	3.4	0	0.0	12	4.2	27	3.4	4
Mex. Amer.	83	17.8	64	20.0	147	18.7	0	0.0	35	12.1	147	18.7	55
Puerto Rican	0	0.0	2	0.6	2	0.3	0	0.0	0	0.0	2	0.3	0
Hispanic	18	3.9	8	2.5	26	3.3	0	0.0	18	6.2	26	3.3	2
Total Minority	125	26.8	103	32.2	228	29.0	0	0.0	72	24.9	228	29.0	68
For. Nation.	0	0.0	0	0.0	0	0.0	0	0.0	0	0.0	0	0.0	0
Caucasian	341	73.2	217	67.8	558	71.0	0	0.0	217	75.1	558	71.0	112
Unknown	0	0.0	0	0.0	0	0.0	0	0.0	0	0.0	0	0.0	0
Total	466	59.3	320	40.7	786	100.0	0	0.0	289	36.8	786		180

Tuition and Fees

	Resident	Nonresident
Full-time	$21,150	$21,150
Part-time	$0	$0

Living Expenses

Estimated living expenses for singles

Living on campus	Living off campus	Living at home
$12,398	$13,182	$13,182

St. Mary's University School of Law

ABA
Approved
Since
1948

GPA and LSAT Scores

	Total	Full-time	Part-time
# of apps	2,170	2,170	0
# of admits	685	685	0
# of matrics	295	295	0
75% GPA	3.40	3.40	0.00
25% GPA	2.78	2.78	0.00
75% LSAT	156	156	0
25% LSAT	152	152	0

Grants and Scholarships (from prior year)

	Total		Full-time		Part-time	
	#	%	#	%	#	%
Total # of students	732		732		0	
Total # receiving grants	277	37.8	277	37.8	0	0.0
Less than 1/2 tuition	248	33.9	248	33.9	0	0.0
Half to full tuition	26	3.6	26	3.6	0	0.0
Full tuition	0	0.0	0	0.0	0	0.0
More than full tuition	3	0.4	3	0.4	0	0.0
Median grant amount			$3,931		$0	

Informational and Library Resources

# of volumes and volume equivalents	408,069
# of titles	73,976
# of active serial subscriptions	4,257
Study seating capacity inside the library	395
# of professional librarians	7
Hours per week library is open	104
# of open, wired connections available to students	600
# of networked computers available for use by students	208
# of simultaneous wireless users	640
Require computer?	N

JD Attrition (from prior year)

	Academic	Other	Total	
	#	#	#	%
1st year	28	25	53	17.6%
2nd year	2	12	14	5.8%
3rd year	1	1	2	1.1%
4th year	0	0	0	0.0%

Employment

	Total	Percentage
Employment status known	181	83.4
Employment status unknown	36	16.6
Employed	138	76.2
Pursuing graduate degrees	5	2.8
Unemployed seeking employment	19	10.5
Unemployed not seeking employment	19	10.5

Type of Employment

# employed in law firms	83	60.1
# employed in business and industry	15	10.9
# employed in government	21	15.2
# employed in public interest	6	4.3
# employed as judicial clerks	5	3.6
# employed in academia	0	0.0

Geographic Location

# employed in state	115	83.3
# employed in foreign countries	4	2.9
# of states where employed		4

Bar Passage Rates

Jurisdiction	Texas		
Exam	Sum 03	Win 04	Total
# from school taking bar for the first time	160	22	182
School's pass rate for all first-time takers	74%	50%	71%
State's pass rate for all first-time takers	83%	69%	80%

St. Mary's University School of Law

One Camino Santa Maria
San Antonio, TX 78228-8601
Phone: 210.436.3523; Toll-free: 866.639.5831; Fax: 210.431.4202
E-mail: lawadmissions@stmarytx.edu; Website: law.stmarytx.edu

■ Introduction

St. Mary's University School of Law was founded in 1927, as part of the oldest and largest Catholic university in the Southwest. St. Mary's is located in the beautiful, unique, and legendary city of San Antonio. San Antonio combines a diverse blend of historic sites, natural beauty, charming vistas, and urban amenities. With its culturally rich population and environment, San Antonio is the perfect backdrop for the mission and goals of the School of Law. Enriched by the spirit of the Society of Mary (Marianists), the school imparts to its students the knowledge and attributes of mind and character essential to public service. St. Mary's is vigilant to the need to preserve a tradition of excellence in legal education, with development of new programs and methodologies for the changing world. St. Mary's is committed to academic excellence rooted in a deep tradition of faith and striving for attainment of justice within the legal system.

■ Library and Physical Facilities

The Sarita Kenedy East Law Library is a modern award-winning building. The collection includes primary legal documents from the federal government, all states and territories, the United Kingdom, and most commonwealth countries. St. Mary's Mexican collection is significant. Access to primary and secondary sources through the latest technology, including digital format and microfilm, is provided. The new library utilizes both DocuShare and wireless Internet.

The Law Classroom Building contains four amphitheater-style classrooms with electronically retractable walls and a modern courtroom as its center. Electrical outlets and data ports are at each student's seat and the public lounges provide wireless access.

The law school's four primary buildings are located around an oak-shaded quadrangle, forming a central gathering spot. The recently completed Alumni Athletic and Convocation Center provides 135,000-square-feet of wellness and fitness options. The center provides for ceremonial facilities as well as athletic endeavors.

■ Curriculum

Required first-year courses are constitutional law, contracts, criminal law, legal research and writing, federal procedure, property, and torts. All students must also take the following required courses: professional responsibility, evidence, and Texas civil procedure only required of those planning to take the Texas bar examination), and a specified number of courses from a menu-style core curriculum. Students must also complete a research paper. The size of first-year sections provides personalized attention and instruction from faculty.

■ Clinical Legal Education

The Clinical Program at St. Mary's offers three classes: Civil Justice, Criminal Justice, and Immigration/Human Rights. The clinics teach lawyering skills and responsibilities through supervised representation of low-income clients and through development of community based projects. Civil Justice offers three components: community development, homeless issues, and representation; crime victim issues and representation; and housing, including landlord-tenant. Students engage in office practice, family law, wills and probate, and housing law. Criminal Justice students defend low income individuals of any age in misdemeanor and low felony cases. Immigration/Human Rights students represent indigent foreign nationals and refugees. Students appear in Immigration Court and assist clients with applications for residence, asylum, and benefits under the Violence Against Women Act.

■ International Law

The St. Mary's Institute on World Legal Problems is conducted at the University of Innsbruck in Austria during July and August. The program is designed to provide law students with a broader understanding of global issues and the role that law can play in their peaceful resolution.

Five justices of the United States Supreme Court have participated in the program as distinguished visiting jurists (Chief Justice William H. Rehnquist, Justice Antonin Scalia, Justice John Paul Stevens, Justice Ruth Bader Ginsburg, and Justice Sandra Day O'Connor). The program draws students and faculty from all parts of the United States and abroad. It has included students from at least 100 American law schools, as well as from Austria, Hungary, China, and Russia. More than 40 visiting professors from law schools in the United States and several foreign countries have participated in the institute.

The Innsbruck Institute is part of the law school's program in international and comparative law, which also includes an LLM in international and comparative law and cooperation with Mexican law schools.

Housed in the Sarita Kenedy East Law Library at St. Mary's is the new **Center for Terrorism Law**, a nonpartisan, nonprofit institution dedicated to the study of legal issues associated with terrorism, with particular emphasis on cyberspace and information assurance technologies.

■ Judicial Internships

St. Mary's students participate in a wide range of pregraduation judicial internships with outstanding state and federal courts. Students work under the supervision of a judge or staff attorney performing legal research and writing projects, which often include the drafting of orders that will be used to decide pending cases, composing jury instructions, researching evidentiary questions, or attending settlement conferences.

■ Admission Standards

St. Mary's goal is to create an intellectually stimulating student body composed of persons with diverse backgrounds who share a desire for academic excellence and accomplishment in the practice of law. In addition to academic ability, St. Mary's seeks evidence of qualities such as leadership ability, maturity, community organization skills, knowledge of other languages and cultures, a history of overcoming disadvantage, public interest accomplishments, or success in a previous career. A faculty committee reviews all applications. No one is automatically rejected. All files are read.

■ Student Activities

St. Mary's has over 30 active student organizations. Student organizations are a key part of the collegial environment of the law school.

St. Mary's has two law reviews—the *St. Mary's Law Journal* and *The Scholar: St. Mary's Law Review on Minority Issues*. The reviews offer students excellent opportunities to develop advanced legal research and writing skills. The *Law Journal* has been cited as persuasive authority in hundreds of court decisions.

St. Mary's students are active in moot court and mock trial competitions. During the spring semester, first-year students participate in a school-wide moot court competition. Second- and third-year students can compete in on-campus tournaments and in St. Mary's External Advocacy Program (EAP). St. Mary's EAP students travel throughout the US to attend the ABA National Moot Court, National Mock Trial, ATLA Mock Trial, and negotiation competitions.

■ Career Services

The role of the Office of Career Services is to assist law students and graduates with their self-directed career searches by informing them of career options and job search strategies and connecting them with potential employers. Career Services does so by sponsoring programs designed to educate, facilitate, and connect students with potential employers during and after law school.

One-on-one confidential strategy sessions with the director provide a unique opportunity for students to develop a personal plan to assess and meet their career goals. The office maintains a job bank and a résumé bank. The office also publishes *Professional Pathways*, a weekly e-newsletter with job information and career advice. A Student Resource Center offers an extensive and up-to-date library of career resources and directories of attorneys, as well as computer terminals with employer databases to help students direct and begin their careers in legal and nontraditional positions. Students have extensive opportunities to interact with alumni, who assist with career programming throughout the year.

For the students in the class of 2003 who reported employment status, 74 percent are employed, with almost all of them in legal jobs.

Applicant Profile

St. Mary's University School of Law
This grid includes only applicants who earned 120-180 LSAT scores under standard administrations.

LSAT Score	3.75 +		3.50 - 3.74		3.25 - 3.49		3.00 - 3.24		2.75 - 2.99		2.50 - 2.74		2.25 - 2.49		2.00 - 2.24		Below 2.00		No GPA		Total	
	Apps	Adm	Apps	Adm	Apps	Adm	Apps	Adm	Apps	Adm	Apps	Adm	Apps	Adm	Apps	Adm	Apps	Adm	Apps	Adm	Apps	Adm
175-180	0	0	0	0	0	0	0	0	1	1	0	0	0	0	0	0	0	0	0	0	1	1
170-174	0	0	1	1	0	0	0	0	1	1	1	1	0	0	0	0	0	0	0	0	3	3
165-169	2	2	0	0	1	1	4	4	1	1	0	0	1	1	1	1	0	0	0	0	10	10
160-164	10	10	9	9	10	10	14	14	10	10	8	8	5	5	1	0	0	0	1	0	68	66
155-159	20	19	36	36	48	48	56	55	48	46	36	30	16	11	10	6	3	0	0	0	273	251
150-154	38	31	75	64	100	58	138	84	106	34	94	28	44	11	18	6	1	0	2	0	616	316
145-149	23	1	61	4	101	7	136	6	105	7	71	2	49	2	11	1	0	0	6	1	563	31
140-144	14	0	33	0	54	0	95	0	62	0	73	2	36	0	23	1	5	0	3	0	398	3
135-139	4	0	7	0	17	0	26	0	32	0	31	0	21	0	13	0	1	0	4	0	156	0
130-134	0	0	1	0	5	0	7	0	10	0	12	0	8	0	2	0	3	0	3	0	51	0
125-129	0	0	0	0	0	0	0	0	2	0	0	0	3	0	2	0	0	0	1	0	8	0
120-124	0	0	0	0	0	0	0	0	0	0	0	0	0	0	0	0	0	0	0	0	0	0
Total	111	63	223	114	336	124	476	163	378	100	326	71	183	30	81	15	13	0	20	1	2147	681

Apps = Number of Applicants (Reflects 99% of the total applicant pool.) Adm = Number Admitted

St. Thomas University School of Law

16401 NW 37th Avenue
Miami Gardens, FL 33054
Phone: 800.245.4569, 305.623.2310; Fax: 305.623.2357
E-mail: admitme@stu.edu; Website: www.stu.edu/lawschool/

*ABA
Approved
Since
1988*

The Basics

Type of school	Private
Term	Semester
Application deadline	4/30 10/31
Application fee	$45
Financial aid deadline	5/1
Can first year start other than fall?	Yes
Student to faculty ratio (fall)	27.3 to 1
Does the university offer:	
housing restricted to law students?	Yes
graduate housing for which law students are eligible?	Yes

Faculty and Administrators

	Total		Men		Women		Minorities	
	Fall	Spr	Fall	Spr	Fall	Spr	Fall	Spr
Full-time	22	22	12	12	10	10	2	2
Other Full-time	3	3	1	1	2	2	1	1
Deans, librarians, & others who teach	6	6	4	4	2	2	2	2
Part-time	47	54	28	34	19	20	15	16
Total	78	85	45	51	33	34	20	21

Curriculum

	Full-time	Part-time
Typical first-year section size	70	0
Is there typically a "small section" of the first-year class, other than Legal Writing, taught by full-time faculty	No	No
If yes, typical size offered last year	0	0
# of classroom course titles beyond 1st year curriculum	96	
# of upper division courses, excluding seminars with an enrollment: Under 25	88	
25-49	28	
50-74	13	
75-99	6	
100+	0	
# of seminars	13	
# of seminar positions available	197	
# of seminar positions filled	171	0
# of positions available in simulation courses	250	
# of simulation positions filled	183	0
# of positions available in faculty supervised clinical courses	24	
# of faculty supervised clinical positions filled	19	0
# involved in field placements	78	0
# involved in law journals	84	0
# involved in moot court or trial competitions	52	0
# of credit hours required to graduate	90	

JD Enrollment and Ethnicity

	Men		Women		Full-time		Part-time		1st-year		Total		JD Degs. Awd.
	#	%	#	%	#	%	#	%	#	%	#	%	
African Amer.	16	4.0	38	11.8	54	7.5	0	0.0	27	9.9	54	7.5	11
Amer. Indian	2	0.5	0	0.0	2	0.3	0	0.0	0	0.0	2	0.3	0
Asian Amer.	18	4.5	14	4.3	32	4.4	0	0.0	18	6.6	32	4.4	2
Mex. Amer.	7	1.8	4	1.2	11	1.5	0	0.0	6	2.2	11	1.5	2
Puerto Rican	5	1.3	8	2.5	13	1.8	0	0.0	3	1.1	13	1.8	2
Hispanic	81	20.4	109	33.7	190	26.4	0	0.0	42	15.3	190	26.4	45
Total Minority	129	32.4	173	53.6	302	41.9	0	0.0	96	35.0	302	41.9	62
For. Nation.	9	2.3	9	2.8	18	2.5	0	0.0	5	1.8	18	2.5	0
Caucasian	243	61.1	135	41.8	378	52.4	0	0.0	164	59.9	378	52.4	83
Unknown	17	4.3	6	1.9	23	3.2	0	0.0	9	3.3	23	3.2	3
Total	398	55.2	323	44.8	721	100.0	0	0.0	274	38.0	721		148

Tuition and Fees

	Resident	Nonresident
Full-time	$24,700	$24,700
Part-time	$0	$0

Living Expenses

Estimated living expenses for singles

Living on campus	Living off campus	Living at home
$15,595	$16,479	$8,100

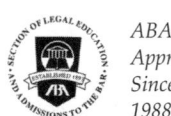

*ABA
Approved
Since
1988*

St. Thomas University School of Law

GPA and LSAT Scores

	Total	Full-time	Part-time
# of apps	2,116	2,116	0
# of admits	788	788	0
# of matrics	274	274	0
75% GPA	3.26	3.26	0.00
25% GPA	2.58	2.58	0.00
75% LSAT	153	153	0
25% LSAT	148	148	0

Grants and Scholarships (from prior year)

	Total		Full-time		Part-time	
	#	%	#	%	#	%
Total # of students	619		619		0	
Total # receiving grants	243	39.3	243	39.3	0	0.0
Less than 1/2 tuition	136	22.0	136	22.0	0	0.0
Half to full tuition	95	15.3	95	15.3	0	0.0
Full tuition	4	0.6	4	0.6	0	0.0
More than full tuition	8	1.3	8	1.3	0	0.0
Median grant amount		$0		$0		

Informational and Library Resources

# of volumes and volume equivalents	317,379
# of titles	87,970
# of active serial subscriptions	3,090
Study seating capacity inside the library	472
# of professional librarians	6
Hours per week library is open	106
# of open, wired connections available to students	57
# of networked computers available for use by students	51
# of simultaneous wireless users	1,652
Require computer?	N

JD Attrition (from prior year)

	Academic	Other	Total	
	#	#	#	%
1st year	18	59	77	25.8%
2nd year	2	5	7	4.0%
3rd year	2	0	2	1.4%
4th year	0	0	0	0.0%

Employment

	Total	Percentage
Employment status known	140	90.3
Employment status unknown	15	9.7
Employed	109	77.9
Pursuing graduate degrees	12	8.6
Unemployed seeking employment	12	8.6
Unemployed not seeking employment	7	5.0

Type of Employment

# employed in law firms	70	64.2
# employed in business and industry	12	11.0
# employed in government	15	13.8
# employed in public interest	5	4.6
# employed as judicial clerks	2	1.8
# employed in academia	3	2.8

Geographic Location

# employed in state	97	89.0
# employed in foreign countries	0	0.0
# of states where employed		10

Bar Passage Rates

Jurisdiction	Florida		
Exam	Sum 03	Win 04	Total
# from school taking bar for the first time	103	32	135
School's pass rate for all first-time takers	60%	47%	57%
State's pass rate for all first-time takers	76%	75%	76%

St. Thomas University School of Law

16401 NW 37th Avenue
Miami Gardens, FL 33054
Phone: 800.245.4569, 305.623.2310; Fax: 305.623.2357
E-mail: admitme@stu.edu; Website: www.stu.edu/lawschool/

■ Introduction

St. Thomas University School of Law, founded in 1984, is one of the most culturally diverse and technologically advanced law schools in the country. St. Thomas emphasizes professional ethics throughout its programs, provides intensive academic support on an individual and small-group basis, and offers a broad curriculum, including an array of clinical experiences.

St. Thomas University is located on a 140-acre campus several miles northwest of Miami. Fifteen miles southeast, in downtown Miami, stands the federal courthouse, the location of the United States District Court for the Southern District of Florida. State trial and appellate courts are several blocks away. Approximately 20 miles to the north of the law school is the city of Ft. Lauderdale, another venue for state and appellate courts.

■ Library and Physical Facilities

St. Thomas' law library has an integrated wireless network and TOMCAT, a state-of-the-art, web-based online catalog. The library meets the needs of students in the twenty-first century by hosting an extensive collection of digital material searchable in the online catalog.

The wireless network enables students, through their laptops or one of over 30 library workstations, to access digital information resources anywhere within the law school complex and across the Internet.

The library has over 312,000 volumes and volume equivalents and seating for over 300. A professional staff provides instruction in research and reference materials. Virtual reference service has been created to support students.

■ Clinical Legal Education Programs

The law school offers five clinical programs: the Bankruptcy Clinic, the Family Court Clinic, the Field Placement Clinic, the Immigration Clinic, and the Tax Clinic. Each clinic is a year-long program for which third-year students receive eight hours of credit.

In the **Bankruptcy Clinic**, students represent bankruptcy petitioners in Federal Court under the guidance of adjunct professors who are experienced bankruptcy practitioners.

In the **Family Court Clinic**, second-year students assist *pro se* litigants in family court matters, and third-year students, under the close supervision of a faculty member, represent victims of domestic violence.

The **Field Placement Clinic** involves 20 students working as interns in public defender, states attorneys, city and county attorneys, and legal services offices. In a

second section of this clinic, students clerk for federal judges, drafting opinions in actual cases.

In the **Immigration Clinic**, students, under the supervision of an experienced faculty member, represent indigent immigrants detained at a federal facility in deportation and exclusion hearings and other immigration matters before immigration judges.

In the **Tax Clinic**, students provide legal assistance to low-income taxpayers and handle controversies with the Internal Revenue Service.

■ Graduate Degree Programs

St. Thomas offers an online **LLM in International Taxation** delivered via the Internet. The program focuses on practical training in offshore finance, global commerce, and international taxation. The faculty includes experts from 20 jurisdictions and students from approximately 30 jurisdictions. For information, e-mail the program office at: *Williambyrnes@hotmail.com* or *www.llmprogram.org*.

The **LLM/MA in Intercultural Human Rights** offers in-depth instruction on the critical issue of our time: the protection of human dignity across political, cultural, and religious lines. The faculty of global distinction includes top-level United Nations experts, outstanding scholars, judges, and practitioners in the field.

■ Special Programs

- **Summer-in-Spain Program**—Law students have the opportunity to take six credits at The Royal College University Escorial Maria Cristina, a part of the University of Madrid. The program is designed to prepare students for practicing law in the globalized twenty-first century, broadening the understanding of foreign legal systems.
- **Summer Conditional Program**—Applicants who may not have strong academic credentials, but nonetheless possess the abilities necessary to succeed in a rigorous program of legal study, may be invited to participate in a summer conditional program. Students who successfully complete the Summer Conditional Program are offered admission in the fall entering class.
- **Joint-Degree Programs**—The law school offers four joint-degree programs in cooperation with other graduate divisions of the university. A JD/MBA in Accounting couples skills traditionally in great demand in the corporate, tax, and accounting worlds. The joint JD/MBA in International Business opens the burgeoning field of international transactional law to the new attorney. The JD/MS in Marriage and Family Counseling, one of the only programs of its kind in the country, fills a serious need in the family lawyer's repertory of skills. A joint JD/MS in Sports Administration prepares

participants for a diverse set of positions in the world of sports. St. Thomas was a pioneer in the sports administration field. The undergraduate sports program was started in 1973 and today offers one of the most esteemed programs in the country.

- **Academic Support Program**—The law school has a commitment to the success of its students. The school has a comprehensive program of Dean's fellows, tutors, practice examinations, lectures, and a Dean for Academic Support designed to assist students individually and in small groups. The law school also provides a program to assist graduates with the bar examination.

■ Career Services

The Office of Career Services is dedicated to assisting students in identifying and attaining their professional goals. It offers a range of traditional and innovative services, including a Career Services resource center; on-campus interviews with major law firms, corporations, and government agencies; interviewing and résumé-writing workshops; networking opportunities; and speakers drawn from various areas of legal practice.

■ Student Activities

The *St. Thomas Law Review* is a student-operated scholarly journal, publishing articles submitted by law faculty and members of the bench and bar nationwide. Membership is determined on the basis of academic excellence and demonstrated writing ability.

The Student Bar Association sponsors various social and educational programs for the student body and otherwise represents student interests. In the student-run Moot Court Program, teams of student advocates compete in interscholastic tournaments across the country, preparing written briefs and presenting oral arguments in simulated appellate cases presided over by members of the bench and bar. Numerous student organizations are active on campus.

■ Housing

Law students can reserve on-campus housing at the University Inn, which offers private rooms with private bath and a choice of meal plans.

For law students desiring to live off campus, numerous apartment complexes are located within minutes of the law school.

Applicant Profile

St. Thomas University School of Law
This grid includes only applicants who earned 120-180 LSAT scores under standard administrations.

LSAT Score	3.75 +		3.50 - 3.74		3.25 - 3.49		3.00 - 3.24		2.75 - 2.99		2.50 - 2.74		2.25 - 2.49		2.00 - 2.24		Below 2.00		No GPA		Total	
	Apps	Adm	Apps	Adm	Apps	Adm	Apps	Adm	Apps	Adm	Apps	Adm	Apps	Adm	Apps	Adm	Apps	Adm	Apps	Adm	Apps	Adm
175-180	0	0	0	0	0	0	0	0	0	0	0	0	0	0	0	0	0	0	0	0	0	0
170-174	0	0	0	0	0	0	0	0	0	0	0	0	1	1	0	0	0	0	0	0	1	1
165-169	1	1	0	0	0	0	0	0	0	0	1	1	3	2	0	0	0	0	0	0	5	4
160-164	2	2	3	2	5	5	3	3	5	5	3	3	2	2	1	1	0	0	0	0	24	23
155-159	6	6	16	15	24	24	21	20	23	21	12	10	21	19	7	4	5	4	1	0	136	123
150-154	16	14	31	30	66	61	79	78	74	66	56	55	37	32	23	19	6	3	2	2	390	360
145-149	24	19	74	53	108	79	151	96	137	71	113	50	75	29	24	6	10	1	10	3	726	407
140-144	14	5	43	13	79	19	120	26	92	14	94	8	63	1	27	1	5	1	16	1	553	89
135-139	5	0	18	4	28	5	43	4	45	4	40	1	28	1	17	1	3	0	7	0	234	20
130-134	1	0	0	0	5	0	9	1	11	0	19	1	8	0	8	0	4	0	9	0	74	2
125-129	0	0	0	0	1	0	1	0	2	0	3	0	2	0	0	0	0	0	6	0	15	0
120-124	0	0	0	0	0	0	0	0	1	0	0	0	0	0	0	0	0	0	0	0	1	0
Total	69	47	185	117	316	193	427	228	390	181	341	129	240	87	107	32	33	9	51	6	2159	1029

Apps = Number of Applicants
Adm = Number Admitted
Reflects 99% of the total applicant pool.

University of St. Thomas School of Law—Minneapolis

1000 LaSalle Avenue
Minneapolis, MN 55403
Phone: 651.962.4895
E-mail: lawschool@stthomas.edu; Website: www.stthomas.edu/law

The Basics

Type of school	Private
Term	Semester
Application deadline	7/1
Application fee	$50
Financial aid deadline	6/1
Can first year start other than fall?	No
Student to faculty ratio (fall)	15.0 to 1
Does the university offer:	
housing restricted to law students?	No
graduate housing for which law students are eligible?	No

Faculty and Administrators

	Total Fall	Total Spr	Men Fall	Men Spr	Women Fall	Women Spr	Minorities Fall	Minorities Spr
Full-time	20	19	12	12	8	7	2	1
Other Full-time	0	0	0	0	0	0	0	0
Deans, librarians, & others who teach	5	5	4	4	1	1	0	0
Part-time	29	46	17	32	12	14	1	3
Total	54	70	33	48	21	22	3	4

Curriculum

	Full-time	Part-time
Typical first-year section size	62	0
Is there typically a "small section" of the first-year class, other than Legal Writing, taught by full-time faculty	No	No
If yes, typical size offered last year	0	0
# of classroom course titles beyond 1st year curriculum	72	

# of upper division courses, excluding seminars with an enrollment:		
Under 25	68	
25-49	26	
50-74	7	
75-99	0	
100+	0	

# of seminars	5	
# of seminar positions available	97	
# of seminar positions filled	69	0
# of positions available in simulation courses	168	
# of simulation positions filled	108	0
# of positions available in faculty supervised clinical courses	62	
# of faculty supervised clinical positions filled	49	0
# involved in field placements	10	0
# involved in law journals	36	0
# involved in moot court or trial competitions	12	0
# of credit hours required to graduate	88	

JD Enrollment and Ethnicity

	Men #	Men %	Women #	Women %	Full-time #	Full-time %	Part-time #	Part-time %	1st-year #	1st-year %	Total #	Total %	JD Degs. Awd.
African Amer.	6	3.6	8	4.1	14	3.9	0	0.0	6	4.1	14	3.9	5
Amer. Indian	1	0.6	3	1.5	4	1.1	0	0.0	1	0.7	4	1.1	0
Asian Amer.	5	3.0	21	10.8	26	7.2	0	0.0	12	8.2	26	7.2	2
Mex. Amer.	0	0.0	1	0.5	1	0.3	0	0.0	1	0.7	1	0.3	0
Puerto Rican	0	0.0	1	0.5	1	0.3	0	0.0	1	0.7	1	0.3	0
Hispanic	2	1.2	6	3.1	8	2.2	0	0.0	1	0.7	8	2.2	0
Total Minority	14	8.4	40	20.5	54	15.0	0	0.0	22	15.1	54	15.0	7
For. Nation.	0	0.0	0	0.0	0	0.0	0	0.0	0	0.0	0	0.0	1
Caucasian	127	76.5	134	68.7	261	72.3	0	0.0	94	64.4	261	72.3	101
Unknown	25	15.1	21	10.8	46	12.7	0	0.0	30	20.5	46	12.7	0
Total	166	46.0	195	54.0	361	100.0	0	0.0	146	40.4	361		109

Tuition and Fees

	Resident	Nonresident
Full-time	$24,842	$24,842
Part-time	$0	$0

Living Expenses

Estimated living expenses for singles

Living on campus	Living off campus	Living at home
N/A	$12,960	$12,960

University of St. Thomas School of Law—Minneapolis

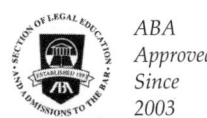

*ABA
Approved
Since
2003*

GPA and LSAT Scores

	Total	Full-time	Part-time
# of apps	746	746	0
# of admits	365	365	0
# of matrics	147	147	0
75% GPA	3.66	3.66	0.00
25% GPA	3.08	3.08	0.00
75% LSAT	160	160	0
25% LSAT	152	152	0

Grants and Scholarships (from prior year)

	Total		Full-time		Part-time	
	#	%	#	%	#	%
Total # of students	329		329		0	
Total # receiving grants	265	80.5	265	80.5	0	0.0
Less than 1/2 tuition	87	26.4	87	26.4	0	0.0
Half to full tuition	59	17.9	59	17.9	0	0.0
Full tuition	119	36.2	119	36.2	0	0.0
More than full tuition	0	0.0	0	0.0	0	0.0
Median grant amount			$15,000		$0	

Informational and Library Resources

# of volumes and volume equivalents	127,938
# of titles	36,420
# of active serial subscriptions	1,262
Study seating capacity inside the library	379
# of professional librarians	7
Hours per week library is open	83
# of open, wired connections available to students	595
# of networked computers available for use by students	103
# of simultaneous wireless users	0
Require computer?	N

JD Attrition (from prior year)

	Academic	Other	Total	
	#	#	#	%
1st year	0	0	0	0.0%
2nd year	0	3	3	3.2%
3rd year	0	0	0	0.0%
4th year	0	0	0	0.0%

Employment

	Total	Percentage
Employment status known	0	0.0
Employment status unknown	0	0.0
Employed	0	0.0
Pursuing graduate degrees	0	0.0
Unemployed seeking employment	0	0.0
Unemployed not seeking employment	0	0.0

Type of Employment

# employed in law firms	0	0.0
# employed in business and industry	0	0.0
# employed in government	0	0.0
# employed in public interest	0	0.0
# employed as judicial clerks	0	0.0
# employed in academia	0	0.0

Geographic Location

# employed in state	0	0.0
# employed in foreign countries	0	0.0
# of states where employed	0	

Bar Passage Rates

Jurisdiction

Exam	Sum 03	Win 04	Total
# from school taking bar for the first time	0	0	0
School's pass rate for all first-time takers			
State's pass rate for all first-time takers			

University of St. Thomas School of Law—Minneapolis

1000 LaSalle Avenue
Minneapolis, MN 55403
Phone: 651.962.4895
E-mail: lawschool@stthomas.edu; Website: www.stthomas.edu/law

■ Introduction

The University of St. Thomas integrates faith and reason into the search for truth through a focus on morality and social justice. The close-knit community, drawn by the mission of a faith-based, national law school, shares a distinctive vision of what law and the legal profession can be. University of St. Thomas students lead by personal example and understand that their responsibility is to serve their clients, the community, and those who are most in need of, and least able to pay for, legal assistance.

■ Curriculum

The School of Law offers more than 65 advanced, elective courses in addition to 20 required courses. The number of electives will increase substantially over the next several years. Students can pursue one of five joint-degree programs, including the College of Business (JD/MBA), Catholic Studies (JD/MA), Public Policy (JD/MA), Professional Psychology (JD/MA), and Social Work (JD/MSW).

No other law school has a structured mentor externship integrated into the curriculum that matches each student with an experienced lawyer or judge each year of law school. Mentors introduce students to a range of lawyering tasks. In addition to gaining practical knowledge, students talk with their mentors about the intellectual, ethical, and moral challenges facing attorneys.

At the Interprofessional Center for Counseling and Legal Services, law students work side-by-side with students from graduate programs in social work and professional psychology. The center allows students to work with actual clients on active cases and provides experience with the sum-total of a client's legal problems.

■ Special Programs

All students are required to perform 50 hours of community service work. The School of Law expects all students to explore a variety of ways in which their interests, skills, and talents can best serve the public.

■ The Area

The University of St. Thomas School of Law is located in downtown Minneapolis, the regional center for business and culture. Minneapolis and the nearby capital city of St. Paul make up the core of the Twin Cities metropolitan area—a metro area of more than 3.5 million residents. The Twin Cities are home to a vibrant business community that features 12 of FORTUNE 500's largest corporations. The Twin Cities are also home to a lively legal community that has embraced the School of Law through the mentor program and summer employment opportunities.

The seemingly limitless recreational opportunities and distinctive beauty of the region add immeasurably to the quality of life. The Twin Cities boast 949 lakes in the metropolitan area. Outdoor enthusiasts have plenty of options from which to choose.

■ Admission

The School of Law seeks to identify students who show the potential to distinguish themselves academically and to integrate the fundamental characteristics of faith and values into their professional character and identity.

The Admission Committee reviews applications with the goal of understanding the strengths, skills, and unique perspectives of each applicant. While the committee examines quantitative criteria such as LSAT scores and undergraduate transcripts, it also focuses on evidence of writing skills, leadership experience and potential, motivation, and commitment to our mission.

The committee carefully examines all materials submitted to determine whether the university and the student is a good fit. A student's personal statement, letters of recommendation, and other subjective information play an important role in assisting the committee with its goal.

■ Faculty

The faculty are a distinguished group of scholars with an impressive mixture of skills, expertise, and experience. Faculty members are recognized for their professional and scholarly proficiency; all have experience as teachers and as practicing lawyers or expert witnesses, and 11 have advanced degrees in other disciplines.

Of equal importance, faculty members have demonstrated a commitment to service and leadership. All have developed reputations as caring, accessible mentors for students, and each has an inspiring record of service to the community. Faculty members share a strong commitment to a faith-based legal education and a dedication to assisting each student in his or her formation as an accomplished servant leader.

Each academic year, the full-time faculty is supplemented by approximately 50 practicing attorneys and judges who serve as adjunct professors.

■ Enrollment/Student Body

The student body is diverse. In the fall 2004 entering class alone, students represent 18 states and 8 countries, and have received degrees from more than 70 undergraduate institutions. While many students come to the School of Law directly from undergraduate institutions, others have earned postgraduate degrees or have work experience.

University of St. Thomas School of Law—Minneapolis

■ Library and Physical Facilities

In July 2003, the School of Law moved into a new 114,334-square-foot building in downtown Minneapolis. The building combines a state-of-the-art education center with the unique character of the School of Law.

Modern technology enhances the classrooms, library, group study areas, moot courtroom, and private offices. A computer lab and training center accommodate student research needs. Twelve group study rooms are available in the library as are a number of individual study spaces.

The 39,289-square-foot library includes shelving for up to 210,000 books and storage space for 250,000 microform volume-equivalents. New technologies and alternative information formats supplement the collection. Students have access to major legal related databases.

■ Financial Aid

St. Thomas is committed to making high-quality legal education available to students by offering scholarships, grants, employment, and loans. The School of Law administers two scholarship programs that acknowledge applicants who have outstanding academic records, who contribute to our dedicated diversity effort, or who are particularly likely to contribute to the school's mission. All incoming students are automatically considered for scholarship awards.

The Loan Repayment Assistance Program (LRAP) will provide up to $6,000 in annual assistance for up to 10 years for qualifying applicants. In general, graduates who undertake public service jobs benefitting the poor and underserved will be eligible to receive assistance.

■ Career Services

Alumni and students work with federal and state judges; international, national, and local public interest organizations; corporations; banks; and law firms of all sizes.

The Office of Career and Professional Development supports students wherever they are in their career path and encourages them to consider how their career choices complement their spiritual and ethical beliefs. Available resources include résumé and cover-letter writing workshops and individual review, interviewing skills seminars, mock interviews, online job center, resource center, practice area panel discussions with local attorneys, networking events, career fairs, and on-campus interviewing.

■ Student Activities

Students are encouraged to form and join student organizations that help them integrate their faith or passion for social justice with their image of themselves as lawyers. Students have created several unique student organizations dedicated to integrating faith and reason in the search for truth with an emphasis on social justice.

The *University of St. Thomas Law Journal* gives students the opportunity to contribute to the development of legal scholarship and further hone their research, analysis, and writing abilities. The Board of Advocates oversees interscholastic competitions in moot court, trial advocacy, client counseling, and negotiation.

Applicant Profile

University of St. Thomas School of Law—Minneapolis
This grid includes only applicants who earned 120-180 LSAT scores under standard administrations.

LSAT Score	3.75 +		3.50 - 3.74		3.25 - 3.49		3.00 - 3.24		2.75 - 2.99		2.50 - 2.74		2.25 - 2.49		2.00 - 2.24		Below 2.00		No GPA		Total	
	Apps	Adm	Apps	Adm	Apps	Adm	Apps	Adm	Apps	Adm	Apps	Adm	Apps	Adm	Apps	Adm	Apps	Adm	Apps	Adm	Apps	Adm
175-180	0	0	0	0	0	0	0	0	0	0	0	0	0	0	0	0	0	0	0	0	0	0
170-174	1	1	0	0	0	0	0	0	0	0	0	0	1	1	0	0	0	0	0	0	2	2
165-169	5	4	2	2	1	1	2	2	0	0	0	0	0	0	0	0	0	0	0	0	10	9
160-164	15	15	23	21	14	14	12	12	7	7	7	6	1	1	2	2	1	0	0	0	82	78
155-159	19	19	37	36	31	30	31	28	14	13	4	2	2	2	1	0	0	0	2	2	141	132
150-154	22	17	53	37	47	27	36	19	25	6	11	2	6	0	4	1	0	0	0	0	204	109
145-149	9	3	18	4	40	2	28	1	25	3	16	3	9	1	3	0	2	0	0	0	150	17
140-144	3	0	7	1	14	1	15	1	15	0	11	0	4	0	1	0	0	0	2	0	32	0
135-139	1	0	1	0	5	0	7	0	1	0	8	0	3	0	2	0	2	0	0	0	15	0
130-134	0	0	1	0	0	0	3	0	2	0	3	0	2	0	2	0	2	0	0	0	1	0
125-129	0	0	0	0	1	0	0	0	0	0	0	0	0	0	0	0	0	0	0	0	0	0
120-124	0	0	0	0	0	0	0	0	0	0	0	0	0	0	0	0	0	0	0	0	0	0
Total	75	59	142	101	153	75	134	63	89	29	60	13	28	5	15	3	7	0	4	2	707	350

Apps = Number of Applicants   Adm = Number Admitted   Reflects 99% of the total applicant pool.

Samford University, Cumberland School of Law

800 Lakeshore Drive
Birmingham, AL 35229
Phone: 800.888.7213, 205.726.2702; Fax: 205.726.2057
E-mail: law.admissions@samford.edu; Website: http://cumberland.samford.edu

ABA
Approved
Since
1949

The Basics

Type of school	Private	
Term	Semester	
Application deadline	2/28	5/1
Application fee	$50	
Financial aid deadline	3/1	
Can first year start other than fall?	No	
Student to faculty ratio (fall)	20.4 to 1	
Does the university offer:		
housing restricted to law students?		No
graduate housing for which law students are eligible?		No

Faculty and Administrators

	Total		Men		Women		Minorities	
	Fall	Spr	Fall	Spr	Fall	Spr	Fall	Spr
Full-time	22	23	18	18	4	5	3	3
Other Full-time	1	1	0	0	1	1	0	0
Deans, librarians, & others who teach	3	4	2	2	1	2	1	1
Part-time	23	28	19	19	4	9	1	2
Total	49	56	39	39	10	17	5	6

Curriculum

	Full-time	Part-time
Typical first-year section size	65	0
Is there typically a "small section" of the first-year class, other than Legal Writing, taught by full-time faculty	No	No
If yes, typical size offered last year	0	0
# of classroom course titles beyond 1st year curriculum	67	

# of upper division courses, excluding seminars with an enrollment:	Under 25	39
	25-49	29
	50-74	20
	75-99	6
	100+	0

# of seminars		9
# of seminar positions available		225
# of seminar positions filled	106	0
# of positions available in simulation courses		308
# of simulation positions filled	250	0
# of positions available in faculty supervised clinical courses	0	
# of faculty supervised clinical positions filled	0	0
# involved in field placements	34	0
# involved in law journals	88	0
# involved in moot court or trial competitions	250	0
# of credit hours required to graduate		90

JD Enrollment and Ethnicity

	Men		Women		Full-time		Part-time		1st-year		Total		JD Degs. Awd.
	#	%	#	%	#	%	#	%	#	%	#	%	
African Amer.	9	2.7	21	10.2	29	5.4	1	20.0	18	10.3	30	5.6	3
Amer. Indian	3	0.9	1	0.5	4	0.7	0	0.0	1	0.6	4	0.7	0
Asian Amer.	3	0.9	1	0.5	4	0.7	0	0.0	1	0.6	4	0.7	1
Mex. Amer.	0	0.0	0	0.0	0	0.0	0	0.0	0	0.0	0	0.0	0
Puerto Rican	0	0.0	0	0.0	0	0.0	0	0.0	0	0.0	0	0.0	0
Hispanic	1	0.3	4	1.9	5	0.9	0	0.0	0	0.0	5	0.9	1
Total Minority	16	4.8	27	13.1	42	7.9	1	20.0	20	11.5	43	8.0	5
For. Nation.	0	0.0	0	0.0	0	0.0	0	0.0	0	0.0	0	0.0	0
Caucasian	301	90.1	169	82.0	466	87.1	4	80.0	139	79.9	470	87.0	160
Unknown	17	5.1	10	4.9	27	5.0	0	0.0	15	8.6	27	5.0	0
Total	334	61.9	206	38.1	535	99.1	5	0.9	174	32.2	540		165

Tuition and Fees

	Resident	Nonresident
Full-time	$23,758	$23,758
Part-time	$14,255	$14,255

Living Expenses

Estimated living expenses for singles

Living on campus	Living off campus	Living at home
N/A	$16,156	$16,156

Samford University, Cumberland School of Law

*ABA
Approved
Since
1949*

GPA and LSAT Scores

	Total	Full-time	Part-time
# of apps	1,397	1,381	16
# of admits	386	380	6
# of matrics	174	170	4
75% GPA	3.49	3.49	3.16
25% GPA	2.90	2.90	2.69
75% LSAT	157	157	157
25% LSAT	154	154	152

Grants and Scholarships (from prior year)

	Total		Full-time		Part-time	
	#	%	#	%	#	%
Total # of students	536		534		2	
Total # receiving grants	187	34.9	187	35.0	0	0.0
Less than 1/2 tuition	109	20.3	109	20.4	0	0.0
Half to full tuition	22	4.1	22	4.1	0	0.0
Full tuition	43	8.0	43	8.1	0	0.0
More than full tuition	13	2.4	13	2.4	0	0.0
Median grant amount			$7,500		$0	

Informational and Library Resources

# of volumes and volume equivalents	284,085
# of titles	36,779
# of active serial subscriptions	2,005
Study seating capacity inside the library	474
# of professional librarians	7
Hours per week library is open	107
# of open, wired connections available to students	248
# of networked computers available for use by students	42
# of simultaneous wireless users	0
Require computer?	N

JD Attrition (from prior year)

	Academic	Other	Total	
	#	#	#	%
1st year	3	8	11	5.5%
2nd year	1	0	1	0.6%
3rd year	0	0	0	0.0%
4th year	0	0	0	0.0%

Employment

	Total	Percentage
Employment status known	156	99.4
Employment status unknown	1	0.6
Employed	145	92.9
Pursuing graduate degrees	4	2.6
Unemployed seeking employment	5	3.2
Unemployed not seeking employment	2	1.3

Type of Employment

# employed in law firms	115	79.3
# employed in business and industry	7	4.8
# employed in government	8	5.5
# employed in public interest	1	0.7
# employed as judicial clerks	13	9.0
# employed in academia	1	0.7

Geographic Location

# employed in state	102	70.3
# employed in foreign countries	0	0.0
# of states where employed	12	

Bar Passage Rates

Jurisdiction	Alabama		
Exam	Sum 03	Win 04	Total
# from school taking bar for the first time	107	15	122
School's pass rate for all first-time takers	90%	87%	89%
State's pass rate for all first-time takers	83%	72%	81%

Samford University, Cumberland School of Law

800 Lakeshore Drive
Birmingham, AL 35229
Phone: 800.888.7213, 205.726.2702; Fax: 205.726.2057
E-mail: law.admissions@samford.edu; Website: http://cumberland.samford.edu

■ Introduction

The Cumberland School of Law, established in 1847 as a part of Cumberland University in Lebanon, Tennessee, is one of the oldest law schools in the country. The law school was acquired by Samford University in 1961. Today, Samford University is the largest privately supported and fully accredited institution of higher learning in Alabama. The beautiful campus is located in a suburban area of Birmingham, Alabama's largest city. Birmingham is the state's industrial, business, and cultural center. The Cumberland School of Law has been a member of the AALS since 1952 and has been accredited by the ABA since 1949.

■ Library and Physical Facilities

The Lucille Stewart Beeson Law Library, an $8.4 million, freestanding, Georgian structure, opened in March 1995. The library is visually stunning, as well as superbly functional. This 61,000-square-foot, three-and-one-half story building is connected to the law school by a second-story breezeway. The building's design is intended to make all facilities easily accessible to students with disabilities.

Complete training on Westlaw, LexisNexis, and LegalTrac is part of the first-year curriculum through the Lawyering and Legal Reasoning course. All study carrels and conference rooms are wired for data transmission. In addition, law students have full access to the university's four campus libraries, as well as six computer labs.

■ Joint-Degree Programs

To broaden their thinking or help them prepare for careers in special fields, Cumberland students may opt to pursue six different joint degrees: JD/MAcc, JD/MBA, JD/MPH, JD/MPA, JD/MDivinity, and JD/MS in Environmental Management.

■ Center for Biotechnology, Law, and Ethics

Dedicated to furthering practical training in the legal disciplines critical to biotechnology, Cumberland's unique program builds on a base of intellectual property, health care, environmental, tort, and natural resources law. The center's specific focus on biotechnology includes issues related to the medical, pharmaceutical, and agricultural sectors and offers students research opportunities.

■ International Law

Cumberland conducts two ABA-approved international summer programs that are offered at the University of Durham, England, and the University of Victoria, British

Columbia. The graduate degree of Master of Comparative Law (MCL) is offered to international law school graduates.

■ Advocacy and Skills Training

Cumberland's emphasis on teaching students the art and science of courtroom advocacy begins in the first-year curriculum, where a six-credit, two-semester course titled Lawyering and Legal Reasoning provides students hands-on, practical instruction in prelitigation skills, such as client interviewing, counseling, memorandum preparation, and negotiation; pretrial litigation skills, including summary judgment motions and making compelling oral arguments; and appellate litigation skills. This intensive course prepares students to work effectively in their first summer clerkships, where they may be expected to research cases and write briefs in their first week.

Cumberland has an exceptional record of recent trial-advocacy competition victories, winning both the ABA and ATLA national championships (including several national second- and third-place awards); winning 31 regional championships; and winning the coveted American College of Trial Lawyers' Emil Gumpert Award for Excellence in Teaching Trial Advocacy. The law school also offers a Certificate in Trial Advocacy to recognize students' achievements. Cumberland students have the chance to get class credit and a professional leg up working for Birmingham's major law firms, judges' offices, and corporate legal departments. The clinical curriculum offers second- and third-year students judicial and corporate externships, as well as externships in the offices of the IRS, US Attorney, and organizations that serve underrepresented or economically disadvantaged groups. In addition, the Alabama Third-Year Practice Rule gives third-year students a chance to practice law under the supervision of a licensed attorney.

■ Flex Program

Cumberland's flex program allows students a maximum of five years to complete their studies. A limited number of students will be enrolled in the flex program, which requires students to take a minimum of eight credit hours each semester. Flex students attend classes during the day and pay the hourly tuition rate.

■ Admission

Cumberland School of Law does not use a number index system or formula when choosing who will be admitted. Every applicant's file is thoroughly reviewed by the

Samford University, Cumberland School of Law

Faculty Admissions Committee. In addition to the LSAT score and undergraduate GPA, other important factors considered are undergraduate school; grade trend and difficulty of major; extracurricular activities and/or employment while in undergraduate school; whether economic, physical, or other challenges have been overcome; graduate work; scholarly achievements; employment experience; personal statement; and letters of recommendation. Applicants, who because of their backgrounds will bring to the School of Law different and enlightening perspectives, will be recognized by the committee. The law school seeks a diverse student body that will make a contribution to the law school and to the legal profession.

Admitted applicants are required to pay a nonrefundable $400 seat deposit that is credited toward tuition. The first installment of $150 is due April 1; the second installment of $250 is due June 15.

■ Student Activities

The Student Bar Association (SBA) functions as the first professional organization of a law student's career. Student Bar chapters keep students in touch with job opportunities and bar requirements. Since many students in the entering class come from other states, the SBA actively assists each student who desires help in relocating to Birmingham.

In addition to many outstanding organizations, students may also be invited to join one of three national legal fraternities and be inducted into two honorary societies, Order of the Barrister and Curia Honoris. Student-run publications include *Cumberland Law Review, American Journal of Trial Advocacy,* and *Pro Confesso.*

■ Scholarships

All admitted applicants are automatically considered for merit- and recruiting-scholarship awards. Various other scholarships are available to outstanding students who distinguish themselves academically, or who make outstanding contributions through leadership in the law school's program, or who demonstrate financial need.

■ Career Services

Through the Career Services Office, the law school assists all law students in locating summer clerkships and part-time and permanent employment upon graduation. Students also receive individual counseling and take part in workshops. The office schedules on-campus interview programs during the fall and spring semesters. Cumberland students and graduates are encouraged to attend well-known recruiting conferences in Chicago, Atlanta, Nashville, and Washington, DC. The Career Services Office surveys each graduating class nine months after graduation, and based on data collected from the most recent graduates (Class of 2003), 96 percent had successfully obtained employment or were attending graduate school.

Applicant Profile

Samford University, Cumberland School of Law

LSAT Score	GPA								
	3.75 +	3.50 - 3.74	3.25 - 3.49	3.00 - 3.24	2.75 - 2.99	2.50 - 2.74	2.25 - 2.49	2.00 - 2.24	Below 2.00
175-180									
170-174									
165-169									
160-164									
155-159									
150-154									
145-149									
140-144									
135-139									
130-134									
125-129									
120-124									

■ Good Possibility   □ Possible   ▨ Unlikely

University of San Diego—School of Law

Warren Hall, 5998 Alcalá Park
San Diego, CA 92110-2492
Phone: 619.260.4528; Fax: 619.260.2218
E-mail: jdinfo@sandiego.edu; Website: www.law.sandiego.edu

ABA Approved Since 1961

The Basics

Type of school	Private
Term	Semester
Application deadline	2/1
Application fee	$50
Financial aid deadline	3/1
Can first year start other than fall?	No
Student to faculty ratio (fall)	14.8 to 1
Does the university offer:	
housing restricted to law students?	No
graduate housing for which law students are eligible?	Yes

Faculty and Administrators

	Total		Men		Women		Minorities	
	Fall	Spr	Fall	Spr	Fall	Spr	Fall	Spr
Full-time	53	56	40	45	13	11	6	6
Other Full-time	5	5	0	0	5	5	0	0
Deans, librarians, & others who teach	12	13	5	5	7	8	2	2
Part-time	39	27	34	23	5	4	3	2
Total	109	101	79	73	30	28	11	10

Curriculum

	Full-time	Part-time
Typical first-year section size	85	85
Is there typically a "small section" of the first-year class, other than Legal Writing, taught by full-time faculty	Yes	Yes
If yes, typical size offered last year	43	43
# of classroom course titles beyond 1st year curriculum	119	
# of upper division courses, excluding seminars with an enrollment: Under 25	142	
25-49	43	
50-74	16	
75-99	16	
100+	2	
# of seminars	36	
# of seminar positions available	683	
# of seminar positions filled	476	54
# of positions available in simulation courses	465	
# of simulation positions filled	397	51
# of positions available in faculty supervised clinical courses	143	
# of faculty supervised clinical positions filled	131	12
# involved in field placements	119	11
# involved in law journals	152	27
# involved in moot court or trial competitions	98	15
# of credit hours required to graduate	85	

JD Enrollment and Ethnicity

	Men		Women		Full-time		Part-time		1st-year		Total		JD Degs. Awd.
	#	%	#	%	#	%	#	%	#	%	#	%	
African Amer.	12	2.1	11	2.4	13	1.7	10	3.9	6	1.8	23	2.2	10
Amer. Indian	4	0.7	3	0.6	6	0.8	1	0.4	5	1.5	7	0.7	1
Asian Amer.	79	14.0	79	17.0	120	15.5	38	14.7	49	14.5	158	15.3	53
Mex. Amer.	26	4.6	28	6.0	37	4.8	17	6.6	17	5.0	54	5.2	14
Puerto Rican	3	0.5	4	0.9	4	0.5	3	1.2	3	0.9	7	0.7	0
Hispanic	21	3.7	20	4.3	32	4.1	9	3.5	13	3.9	41	4.0	7
Total Minority	145	25.6	145	31.3	212	27.5	78	30.2	93	27.6	290	28.2	85
For. Nation.	3	0.5	2	0.4	3	0.4	2	0.8	2	0.6	5	0.5	4
Caucasian	418	73.9	317	68.3	557	72.2	178	69.0	242	71.8	735	71.4	226
Unknown	0	0.0	0	0.0	0	0.0	0	0.0	0	0.0	0	0.0	0
Total	566	55.0	464	45.0	772	75.0	258	25.0	337	32.7	1030		315

Tuition and Fees

	Resident	Nonresident
Full-time	$30,796	$30,796
Part-time	$21,896	$21,896

Living Expenses

Estimated living expenses for singles

Living on campus	Living off campus	Living at home
$16,854	$16,854	$8,326

University of San Diego—School of Law

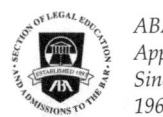

*ABA
Approved
Since
1961*

GPA and LSAT Scores

	Total	Full-time	Part-time
# of apps	6,020	5,428	592
# of admits	1,374	1,144	230
# of matrics	352	245	107
75% GPA	3.54	3.60	3.37
25% GPA	3.11	3.19	2.96
75% LSAT	163	164	159
25% LSAT	158	160	156

Grants and Scholarships (from prior year)

	Total		Full-time		Part-time	
	#	%	#	%	#	%
Total # of students	1,026		761		265	
Total # receiving grants	390	38.0	326	42.8	64	24.2
Less than 1/2 tuition	139	13.5	111	14.6	28	10.6
Half to full tuition	200	19.5	169	22.2	31	11.7
Full tuition	42	4.1	37	4.9	5	1.9
More than full tuition	9	0.9	9	1.2	0	0.0
Median grant amount			$14,000		$9,900	

Informational and Library Resources

# of volumes and volume equivalents	515,841
# of titles	284,419
# of active serial subscriptions	5,026
Study seating capacity inside the library	600
# of professional librarians	8
Hours per week library is open	112
# of open, wired connections available to students	235
# of networked computers available for use by students	59
# of simultaneous wireless users	2,254
Require computer?	N

JD Attrition (from prior year)

	Academic	Other	Total	
	#	#	#	%
1st year	9	32	41	11.4%
2nd year	1	7	8	2.6%
3rd year	0	7	7	2.1%
4th year	0	0	0	0.0%

Employment

	Total	Percentage
Employment status known	267	94.7
Employment status unknown	15	5.3
Employed	238	89.1
Pursuing graduate degrees	20	7.5
Unemployed seeking employment	7	2.6
Unemployed not seeking employment	2	0.7

Type of Employment

# employed in law firms	155	65.1
# employed in business and industry	31	13.0
# employed in government	24	10.1
# employed in public interest	12	5.0
# employed as judicial clerks	8	3.4
# employed in academia	2	0.8

Geographic Location

# employed in state	205	86.1
# employed in foreign countries	0	0.0
# of states where employed		18

Bar Passage Rates

Jurisdiction	California		
Exam	Sum 03	Win 04	Total
# from school taking bar for the first time	225	33	258
School's pass rate for all first-time takers	83%	55%	79%
State's pass rate for all first-time takers	63%	47%	60%

University of San Diego—School of Law

Warren Hall, 5998 Alcalá Park
San Diego, CA 92110-2492
Phone: 619.260.4528; Fax: 619.260.2218
E-mail: jdinfo@sandiego.edu; Website: www.law.sandiego.edu

■ Introduction

Only 50 years old, USD School of Law is already recognized as a leading center of legal education. Set in a landmark location overlooking San Diego's shoreline, the School of Law fosters a climate of stimulating and rigorous intellectual exchange. The university and the community offer a wealth of cultural, social, and athletic activities. The graceful Spanish Renaissance architecture and ideal climate make this an attractive place to live and study. The law school is part of a private, values-based university, and the educational environment supports the broader personal and ethical development of students.

■ Admission

The educational mission of the School of Law embraces a commitment to academic excellence, individual dignity, and the need to develop the knowledge, values, and skills of its students to prepare them for service to their professional, global, civic, and faith communities. As a Roman Catholic institution, USD has a moral and theological commitment to educating a diverse student body. USD recognizes that diversity of viewpoint, background, and experience, including race, ethnicity, cultural diversity, gender, religion, age, socioeconomic status, and disability, among its student body is essential to the full and informed exchange of ideas and to the quality of legal education it seeks to provide.

■ Accreditation and Membership

Accredited: ABA, Committee of Bar Examiners—State of California. Membership: AALS, Order of the Coif.

■ Legal Research Center

Regarded as one of the finest academic law libraries in the nation, USD's Pardee Legal Research Center offers state-of-the-art services and facilities to law students. The School of Law holds one of the major legal research collections in Southern California. It features an instructional multimedia computer lab with fully networked computers; access to local and global online resources; and other electronic sources. Internet access is also available on personal laptops through wired and wireless connections.

■ Special Programs

Institute on International and Comparative Law—The institute conducts summer law programs in England, France, Ireland, Italy, Russia, Spain, and Mexico. The programs introduce American law students to foreign law and legal institutions and provide intensive study.

Clinical Education Program—The Clinical Education Program is recognized as one of the most extensive and successful in the nation. The law school received the Emil Gumpert Award from the American College of Trial Lawyers for excellence in trial advocacy training. Students interview, counsel, and represent clients under the supervision of a clinical professor.

Research and Advocacy Institutes—The Center for Public Interest Law and Children's Advocacy Institute offer unique research and clinical opportunities.

Joint Degrees—Students desiring to concentrate in business or international relations may concurrently pursue the JD/MBA, JD/International MBA, or JD/MA in International Relations.

Lawyering Skills—Students receive extensive training in a variety of legal skills, including first-year legal writing and research, interviewing, counseling, discovery, trial advocacy, and alternative dispute resolution. In addition, the law school provides an outstanding Academic Support Program.

Oral Advocacy—The National Mock Trial Team is evidence of USD's commitment to trial advocacy. Trial teams consistently rank among the finest teams in the nation. The trial team has taken first place in the prestigious American Inns of Court's National Tournament of Champions. The trial team has won the Western Regional Championship of the Association of Trial Lawyers of America nine times and has been selected as the best team in the Ninth Circuit for seven of the last nine years. The USD Mock Trial Team competes in the ABA's National Trial competitions and has placed first in the Western Regional for many years. The USD Moot Court hosts several prestigious oral advocacy tournaments throughout the year, including the McLennon Honors competition, which has featured justices of the United States Supreme Court as presiding judges.

■ Campus Highlights

The University of San Diego's Joan B. Kroc Institute for Peace and Justice joined the ranks of the world's most important centers for promoting global peace and social justice. The institute hosts international conferences and workshops, as well as service-learning programs and conflict resolution and mediation services. The institute offers an interdisciplinary master's degree in peace studies. A recent gift from the estate of Joan B. Kroc will lead to the establishment of a School of Peace Studies on campus.

The Jenny Craig Pavillion showcases Division 1 athletics and hosts special events. The Donald P. Shiley Center for Science and Technology, a 150,000-square-foot science center, opened in fall 2003. The Degheri Alumni Center opened in spring 2004.

■ Distinguished Visitors and Speakers

The School of Law hosts annual conferences, symposia, and speakers series to enhance the classroom experience, provide an environment in which legal scholars can work on cutting-edge and interdisciplinary issues, and promote the exchange of ideas. Among these are the *Journal of Contemporary Legal Issues* Conference, the Annual Tax Conference, and the distinguished Nathanson Memorial Lecture Series, a forum for justices of the US Supreme Court. New this year are the Joan E. Bowes-James Madison Distinguished Speaker Series and the Jane Ellen Bergman Lecture on Women, Children, and Human Rights. The Law, Economics, and Politics Workshop Series is presented in conjunction with the University of California at San Diego.

■ Student Activities

Approximately 38 organizations serve the student body by developing a sense of community, and activities range from writing for a legal journal and doing scholarly research to participating in the student/faculty intramural sports activities. The *San Diego Law Review* is a student-run law journal addressing major issues and topics in law.

Students also submit to the *San Diego International Law Journal* articles, comments, book reviews, and case notes concerning important international law topics.

■ Financial Aid

The School of Law is committed to providing financial assistance to eligible students through a comprehensive financial aid program. Entering students are automatically considered for merit- and need-based scholarships. In awarding scholarship assistance, the admission committee focuses on students with academic merit or promise, or potential for service to the community, and for contribution to the diversity of the USD community. The law school expects to award more than 350 scholarships and grants to entering and continuing students.

■ Career Services

The Career Services Office offers the opportunity to learn about law careers, define personal career objectives, consider and apply for a broad range of legal employment opportunities, and plan for a successful transition into the legal profession. Annually, 225 interviewers from 30 states participate in the recruiting process. USD's students and graduates work throughout the nation and internationally with prestigious law firms and with government, public interest, corporate, and academic employers.

■ Housing

USD Housing Office and School of Law Admission Office assist in providing information and resources in locating on- and off-campus accommodations.

Applicant Profile

University of San Diego—School of Law
(Note: This chart is to be used as a general guide only. Nonnumerical factors are also considered.)

LSAT Score	GPA								
	3.75 +	3.50 - 3.74	3.25 - 3.49	3.00 - 3.24	2.75 - 2.99	2.50 - 2.74	2.25 - 2.49	2.00 - 2.24	Below 2.00
175-180									
170-174									
165-169									
160-164									
155-159									
150-154									
145-149									
140-144									
135-139									
130-134									
125-129									
120-124									

■ Very Likely   ■ Possible   □ Unlikely

University of San Francisco School of Law

2130 Fulton Street
San Francisco, CA 94117-1080
Phone: 415.422.6586; Fax: 415.422.6433
E-mail: lawschool@usfca.edu; Website: www.law.usfca.edu

*ABA
Approved
Since
1935*

The Basics

Type of school	Private
Term	Semester
Application deadline	2/1 4/1
Application fee	$60
Financial aid deadline	2/15
Can first year start other than fall?	No
Student to faculty ratio (fall)	17.5 to 1
Does the university offer:	
housing restricted to law students?	No
graduate housing for which law students are eligible?	Yes

Faculty and Administrators

	Total		Men		Women		Minorities	
	Fall	Spr	Fall	Spr	Fall	Spr	Fall	Spr
Full-time	32	26	24	18	8	8	8	6
Other Full-time	0	0	0	0	0	0	0	0
Deans, librarians, & others who teach	5	5	3	3	2	2	1	1
Part-time	35	37	20	24	15	13	8	6
Total	**72**	**68**	**47**	**45**	**25**	**23**	**17**	**13**

Curriculum

	Full-time	Part-time
Typical first-year section size	95	66
Is there typically a "small section" of the first-year class, other than Legal Writing, taught by full-time faculty	Yes	No
If yes, typical size offered last year	48	0
# of classroom course titles beyond 1st year curriculum	86	
# of upper division courses, excluding seminars with an enrollment: Under 25	57	
25-49	25	
50-74	12	
75-99	7	
100+	1	
# of seminars	14	
# of seminar positions available	280	
# of seminar positions filled	205	20
# of positions available in simulation courses	182	
# of simulation positions filled	147	17
# of positions available in faculty supervised clinical courses	140	
# of faculty supervised clinical positions filled	113	11
# involved in field placements	96	6
# involved in law journals	77	2
# involved in moot court or trial competitions	92	4
# of credit hours required to graduate	86	

JD Enrollment and Ethnicity

	Men		Women		Full-time		Part-time		1st-year		Total		JD Degs. Awd.
	#	%	#	%	#	%	#	%	#	%	#	%	
African Amer.	20	5.7	23	6.3	33	5.6	10	7.9	16	6.3	43	6.0	9
Amer. Indian	2	0.6	2	0.6	1	0.2	3	2.4	2	0.8	4	0.6	1
Asian Amer.	51	14.4	68	18.7	101	17.1	18	14.3	60	23.8	119	16.6	38
Mex. Amer.	12	3.4	14	3.9	21	3.6	5	4.0	9	3.6	26	3.6	7
Puerto Rican	2	0.6	1	0.3	2	0.3	1	0.8	1	0.4	3	0.4	1
Hispanic	16	4.5	12	3.3	21	3.6	7	5.6	15	6.0	28	3.9	10
Total Minority	103	29.2	120	33.1	179	30.3	44	34.9	103	40.9	223	31.1	66
For. Nation.	1	0.3	0	0.0	1	0.2	0	0.0	0	0.0	1	0.1	0
Caucasian	200	56.7	211	58.1	341	57.8	70	55.6	111	44.0	411	57.4	136
Unknown	49	13.9	32	8.8	69	11.7	12	9.5	38	15.1	81	11.3	4
Total	353	49.3	363	50.7	590	82.4	126	17.6	252	35.2	716		206

Tuition and Fees

	Resident	Nonresident
Full-time	$29,057	$29,057
Part-time	$20,785	$20,785

Living Expenses

Estimated living expenses for singles

Living on campus	Living off campus	Living at home
$14,480	$17,026	$7,350

University of San Francisco School of Law

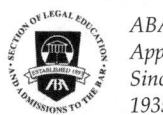

*ABA
Approved
Since
1935*

GPA and LSAT Scores

	Total	Full-time	Part-time
# of apps	4,581	4,121	460
# of admits	1,122	997	125
# of matrics	257	190	67
75% GPA	3.51	3.54	3.43
25% GPA	2.95	2.98	2.88
75% LSAT	162	162	160
25% LSAT	157	157	157

Grants and Scholarships (from prior year)

	Total		Full-time		Part-time	
	#	%	#	%	#	%
Total # of students	712		575		137	
Total # receiving grants	349	49.0	308	53.6	41	29.9
Less than 1/2 tuition	147	20.6	119	20.7	28	20.4
Half to full tuition	192	27.0	181	31.5	11	8.0
Full tuition	0	0.0	0	0.0	0	0.0
More than full tuition	10	1.4	8	1.4	2	1.5
Median grant amount			$13,000		$3,500	

Informational and Library Resources

# of volumes and volume equivalents	344,992
# of titles	160,729
# of active serial subscriptions	3,243
Study seating capacity inside the library	428
# of professional librarians	6
Hours per week library is open	98
# of open, wired connections available to students	1,285
# of networked computers available for use by students	69
# of simultaneous wireless users	0
Require computer?	N

JD Attrition (from prior year)

	Academic	Other	Total	
	#	#	#	%
1st year	23	20	43	15.9%
2nd year	3	1	4	1.9%
3rd year	1	0	1	0.5%
4th year	0	0	0	0.0%

Employment

	Total	Percentage
Employment status known	178	96.7
Employment status unknown	6	3.3
Employed	161	90.4
Pursuing graduate degrees	1	0.6
Unemployed seeking employment	15	8.4
Unemployed not seeking employment	1	0.6

Type of Employment

# employed in law firms	93	57.8
# employed in business and industry	17	10.6
# employed in government	21	13.0
# employed in public interest	3	1.9
# employed as judicial clerks	5	3.1
# employed in academia	2	1.2

Geographic Location

# employed in state	138	85.7
# employed in foreign countries	0	0.0
# of states where employed	6	

Bar Passage Rates

Jurisdiction	California		
Exam	Sum 03	Win 04	Total
# from school taking bar for the first time	162	15	177
School's pass rate for all first-time takers	65%	60%	64%
State's pass rate for all first-time takers	63%	47%	60%

University of San Francisco School of Law

2130 Fulton Street
San Francisco, CA 94117-1080
Phone: 415.422.6586; Fax: 415.422.6433
E-mail: lawschool@usfca.edu; Website: www.law.usfca.edu

■ Introduction

Founded in 1912, the School of Law is located on the University of San Francisco's 55-acre hilltop campus in a quiet residential part of San Francisco. It overlooks Golden Gate Park, the Pacific Ocean, and downtown San Francisco. The campus is only minutes by public transportation from the many educational, cultural, social, and recreational choices the San Francisco Bay Area offers.

The city and surrounding communities extend the classroom, providing an extraordinary laboratory for the study of law. The law school is in close proximity to San Francisco's civic center and financial district, where numerous private law practices have offices, where federal, state, and local governmental agencies are located, and where both federal and state trial and appellate courts, including the California Supreme Court, are in session. All of this provides exceptional learning, practice, placement, and service opportunities.

The law school is fully accredited by the American Bar Association and is a member of the Association of American Law Schools.

■ A School with a Mission

USF's law school has a tradition of excellence in educating skilled and effective lawyers with high ethical standards, a global perspective, and a social conscience. We train professionals who care about the well-being of others. We believe that law is a noble profession and that lawyers are capable of doing enormous good. Consistent with our mission, the law school has developed an array of programs dedicated to serving communities throughout the United States and around the globe. The law school has also developed a unique curriculum for ethics and professional responsibility which helps put into practice what we teach.

■ Degree Programs

The law school offers both full-time and part-time instructional programs leading to the JD degree. Students entering through the part-time program may accelerate their studies and complete the degree in seven semesters or they may convert to the full-time program after the first year and complete their degree in three years. Either option requires attendance at one or more summer sessions. In conjunction with the university's School of Business and Management, the law school offers a four-year, full-time concurrent JD and MBA degree program. The law school also offers a Master of Laws (LLM) in International Transactions and Comparative Law for foreign lawyers who have earned first degrees in law from a non-American university, as well as a Master of Laws (LLM) in Intellectual Property and Technology Law.

■ Facilities

The University of San Francisco School of Law's Koret Law Center includes Kendrick Hall and the Dorraine Zief Law Library. The Dorraine Zief Law Library, opened in August 2000, more than doubled the amount of law library space, enhancing services and bringing significantly expanded study and research facilities to the law school. It features a comfortable, flexible, and fully wired environment with hundreds of data connections, including tables, carrels, and lounge seating. There are numerous individual and group study rooms, as well as computer classrooms, laboratories, and specially designed training and research rooms with the latest in demonstration, hands-on training, and distance learning technology.

Kendrick Hall, built in the 1960s, has been thoroughly renovated to provide a twenty-first century infrastructure and expanded student services and programming space. The classrooms include power and data connections at every seat, and state-of-the-art equipment is available throughout the building, including the new Moot Court Room featuring the latest in trial practice technology.

Because the law school is located on USF's campus, students have available to them all of the amenities and facilities one expects to find at a major urban university.

■ The Curriculum

The core curriculum, concentrated in the first year of the full-time program and the first and second years of the part-time program, includes courses essential to a solid understanding of dominant legal concepts. It orients students to central areas of the law and ensures mastery of basic doctrine and the fundamental analytical and communication skills demanded in the practice of law. It is also designed to make students aware of basic social interests and the role of law in ordering them. The core curriculum is complemented by a rich offering of specialized courses and programs providing almost unlimited opportunities for specialized study and practical experience. Elective courses are constantly updated to reflect changes in the law and legal practice, to meet the relentless pace of technological change, and to match student interest.

There are JD certificate programs and curricular concentrations in several areas of law. Notable among these are courses in International and Comparative Law; Public Interest Law; Advocacy and Alternative Dispute Resolution; and Intellectual Property and Cyberspace Law. There are also opportunities for participation in unique clinical programs, including a Mediation Clinic, an Investor Justice Clinic, and an International Human Rights Clinic.

■ International Programs

The law school has summer study-abroad programs in Budapest, Dublin, and Prague. Our Center for Law and Global Justice sponsors many legal assistance projects, including programs in Cambodia and Vietnam. The law school also has faculty exchange programs with sister schools in Ireland, the Czech Republic, China, and Hungary. These programs bring to the law school faculty from around the globe to teach international law subjects in which they have unique expertise.

■ Student Activities

Through the Student Bar Association, students take part in numerous activities and organizations. Student representatives participate at faculty meetings and on many law school committees. Students serve as editors and publish the *USF Law Review*, the *USF Maritime Law Journal*, and the *USF Intellectual Property Law Bulletin*. A student Board of Directors organizes the Moot Court Program and the advanced intra- and interschool competitions.

■ Faculty

The law school's faculty members are accomplished scholars as well as dedicated teachers committed to quality education and to developing each student's fullest potential. Faculty members are especially accessible outside the classroom, welcoming interaction with students. They create an intellectually challenging but supportive atmosphere in which each student may grow as a professional and as an individual. Full-time faculty members achieved numerous scholastic accomplishments, graduating from the most elite law schools, earning honors, and serving as editors of prestigious law journals. Almost all have had substantial practical experience and continue to be involved in service to the community and the profession. Collectively, they have authored hundreds of treatises, casebooks, practice guides, law review articles, and book reviews. Yet, they remain passionate about teaching, which is each faculty member's highest priority.

The full-time faculty is augmented by approximately 60 adjunct professors, including federal and state court judges, attorneys from many public agencies, and other distinguished members of the bar who are in private practice or serving as counsel for leading business ventures. The availability in the San Francisco Bay Area legal community of so many talented and experienced people allows the law school to expand its curriculum with specialized courses and provide students access to a wealth of practical expertise.

Applicant Profile

University of San Francisco School of Law
This grid includes only applicants who earned 120-180 LSAT scores under standard administrations.

LSAT Score	3.75 +		3.50 - 3.74		3.25 - 3.49		3.00 - 3.24		2.75 - 2.99		2.50 - 2.74		2.25 - 2.49		2.00 - 2.24		Below 2.00		No GPA		Total	
	Apps	Adm	Apps	Adm	Apps	Adm	Apps	Adm	Apps	Adm	Apps	Adm	Apps	Adm	Apps	Adm	Apps	Adm	Apps	Adm	Apps	Adm
175-180	0	0	0	0	2	2	1	1	1	1	0	0	0	0	0	0	0	0	0	0	4	4
170-174	2	2	5	5	5	5	6	6	5	4	3	2	0	0	1	0	0	0	1	1	28	25
165-169	15	14	24	23	33	32	24	22	25	21	17	9	4	2	2	1	1	0	4	4	149	128
160-164	56	55	134	128	174	157	140	98	78	42	37	17	20	7	9	5	0	0	8	7	656	516
155-159	114	72	244	127	328	92	272	46	168	15	85	5	33	4	11	3	1	0	13	5	1269	369
150-154	82	8	206	9	324	16	319	11	170	7	111	4	45	2	19	0	1	0	17	0	1294	57
145-149	29	0	86	6	145	7	176	6	127	1	66	1	42	0	16	0	1	0	17	1	705	22
140-144	8	0	32	0	53	0	70	0	59	0	44	0	29	0	5	0	2	0	5	0	307	0
135-139	2	0	10	0	12	0	23	0	14	0	18	0	6	0	5	0	1	0	4	0	95	0
130-134	0	0	1	0	1	0	4	0	4	0	6	0	4	0	2	0	0	0	4	0	26	0
125-129	0	0	1	0	0	0	2	0	3	0	1	0	0	0	1	0	1	0	0	0	9	0
120-124	0	0	0	0	0	0	0	0	0	0	1	0	0	0	0	0	0	0	0	0	1	0
Total	308	151	743	298	1077	311	1037	190	654	91	389	38	183	15	71	9	8	0	73	18	4543	1121

Apps = Number of Applicants
Adm = Number Admitted
Reflects 99% of the total applicant pool.

Santa Clara University School of Law

500 El Camino Real
Santa Clara, CA 95053
Phone: 408.554.5048; Fax: 408.554.7897
E-mail: lawadmissions@scu.edu; Website: www.scu.edu/law

ABA
Approved
Since
1937

The Basics

Type of school	Private
Term	Semester
Application deadline	2/1
Application fee	$75
Financial aid deadline	3/1
Can first year start other than fall?	No
Student to faculty ratio (fall)	19.7 to 1
Does the university offer: housing restricted to law students?	Yes
graduate housing for which law students are eligible?	Yes

Faculty and Administrators

	Total		Men		Women		Minorities	
	Fall	Spr	Fall	Spr	Fall	Spr	Fall	Spr
Full-time	38	38	22	23	16	15	8	10
Other Full-time	14	15	3	3	11	12	0	0
Deans, librarians, & others who teach	5	5	3	3	2	2	1	1
Part-time	24	32	15	18	9	14	2	2
Total	81	90	43	47	38	43	11	13

Curriculum

	Full-time	Part-time
Typical first-year section size	82	64
Is there typically a "small section" of the first-year class, other than Legal Writing, taught by full-time faculty	Yes	No
If yes, typical size offered last year	40	0
# of classroom course titles beyond 1st year curriculum	233	
# of upper division courses, excluding seminars with an enrollment: Under 25	144	
25-49	44	
50-74	17	
75-99	15	
100+	1	
# of seminars	43	
# of seminar positions available	880	
# of seminar positions filled	589	0
# of positions available in simulation courses	375	
# of simulation positions filled	325	0
# of positions available in faculty supervised clinical courses	165	
# of faculty supervised clinical positions filled	147	0
# involved in field placements	191	0
# involved in law journals	84	0
# involved in moot court or trial competitions	102	0
# of credit hours required to graduate	86	

JD Enrollment and Ethnicity

	Men		Women		Full-time		Part-time		1st-year		Total		JD Degs. Awd.
	#	%	#	%	#	%	#	%	#	%	#	%	
African Amer.	19	4.0	29	5.8	43	5.8	5	2.2	24	7.5	48	4.9	6
Amer. Indian	3	0.6	6	1.2	7	0.9	2	0.9	2	0.6	9	0.9	0
Asian Amer.	106	22.1	156	31.4	202	27.0	60	26.2	77	24.2	262	26.8	75
Mex. Amer.	0	0.0	0	0.0	0	0.0	0	0.0	0	0.0	0	0.0	0
Puerto Rican	0	0.0	0	0.0	0	0.0	0	0.0	0	0.0	0	0.0	0
Hispanic	45	9.4	50	10.1	74	9.9	21	9.2	41	12.9	95	9.7	22
Total Minority	173	36.1	241	48.5	326	43.6	88	38.4	144	45.3	414	42.4	103
For. Nation.	0	0.0	0	0.0	0	0.0	0	0.0	0	0.0	0	0.0	0
Caucasian	273	57.0	221	44.5	370	49.5	124	54.1	137	43.1	494	50.6	139
Unknown	33	6.9	35	7.0	51	6.8	17	7.4	37	11.6	68	7.0	10
Total	479	49.1	497	50.9	747	76.5	229	23.5	318	32.6	976		252

Tuition and Fees

	Resident	Nonresident
Full-time	$30,750	$30,750
Part-time	$21,525	$21,525

Living Expenses

Estimated living expenses for singles

Living on campus	Living off campus	Living at home
$18,098	$18,098	$18,098

Santa Clara University School of Law

*ABA
Approved
Since
1937*

GPA and LSAT Scores

	Total	Full-time	Part-time
# of apps	5,288	4,856	432
# admits	1,608	1,433	167
# of matrics	324	250	74
75% GPA	3.59	3.61	3.52
25% GPA	3.20	3.23	3.12
75% LSAT	160	160	159
25% LSAT	155	156	154

Grants and Scholarships (from prior year)

	Total		Full-time		Part-time	
	#	%	#	%	#	%
Total # of students	940		726		214	
Total # receiving grants	240	25.5	195	26.9	45	21.0
Less than 1/2 tuition	179	19.0	153	21.1	26	12.1
Half to full tuition	50	5.3	37	5.1	13	6.1
Full tuition	10	1.1	5	0.7	5	2.3
More than full tuition	1	0.1	0	0.0	1	0.5
Median grant amount			$12,000		$10,000	

Informational and Library Resources

# of volumes and volume equivalents	332,981
# of titles	138,597
# of active serial subscriptions	4,026
Study seating capacity inside the library	483
# of professional librarians	7
Hours per week library is open	106
# of open, wired connections available to students	831
# of networked computers available for use by students	49
# of simultaneous wireless users	240
Require computer?	N

JD Attrition (from prior year)

	Academic	Other	Total	
	#	#	#	%
1st year	23	25	48	15.3%
2nd year	1	6	7	2.3%
3rd year	1	1	2	0.7%
4th year	0	1	1	2.6%

Employment

	Total	Percentage
Employment status known	282	98.3
Employment status unknown	5	1.7
Employed	230	81.6
Pursuing graduate degrees	5	1.8
Unemployed seeking employment	40	14.2
Unemployed not seeking employment	7	2.5

Type of Employment

# employed in law firms	106	46.1
# employed in business and industry	26	11.3
# employed in government	19	8.3
# employed in public interest	4	1.7
# employed as judicial clerks	7	3.0
# employed in academia	2	0.9

Geographic Location

# employed in state	192	83.5
# employed in foreign countries	1	0.4
# of states where employed		15

Bar Passage Rates

Jurisdiction	California		
Exam	Sum 03	Win 04	Total
# from school taking bar for the first time	238	31	269
School's pass rate for all first-time takers	69%	42%	66%
State's pass rate for all first-time takers	63%	47%	60%

Santa Clara University School of Law

500 El Camino Real
Santa Clara, CA 95053
Phone: 408.554.5048; Fax: 408.554.7897
E-mail: lawadmissions@scu.edu; Website: www.scu.edu/law

■ Introduction

Santa Clara University School of Law is located 46 miles from San Francisco, near the southern tip of San Francisco Bay. It is situated on the university campus, which was founded by the Jesuit fathers in 1851 and which surrounds the Mission of Santa Clara de Asis, the eighth of California's original 21 missions. The School of Law was added to the Santa Clara College in 1912 when the college became a university. The school is approved by the ABA and is a member of the AALS.

For 150 years, Santa Clara has fostered an exceptional academic program based on the Jesuit tradition. Located adjacent to San Jose and situated in the midst of one of the nation's greatest concentrations of high technology industry, internationally known as Silicon Valley, the law school has established a curriculum that addresses the fundamental demands of law practice and the evolving needs of society.

■ Enrollment/Student Body

Over 40 percent of the applicants were from outside California, including applicants from 50 states and 60 foreign countries. Santa Clara is consistently among the top 10 law schools nationwide in terms of ethnic diversity. The entering class of 2004 was 49 percent minority and 54 percent women.

■ Library and Physical Facilities

The School of Law is on the 105-acre university campus. Towering palm trees, spacious lawns, and extensive flower gardens surround the Heafey Law Library. A traditional moot courtroom provides the setting for advocacy training and activities of the Edwin A. Heafey Jr. Center for Trial and Appellate Advocacy. Other facilities include Bergin Hall faculty office building, Bannan Hall with its technologically equipped classrooms, and Law House where law career services is located. Students also have access to other campus facilities, including computer laboratories, Cowell Student Health Center, Benson Memorial Center, and Pat Malley Fitness Center with its pool; basketball, volleyball, and racquetball courts; and steam room and sauna.

■ Curriculum

Full-time and part-time programs, Academic Success Program, 86 semester units required to graduate, over 200 courses available. Degrees available: JD, JD/MBA, JD/MST, LLM in International Law, LLM in US Law for Foreign Attorneys, and LLM in Intellectual Property. An academic orientation introduces first-year students to the study of law. The first-year curriculum is prescribed.

JD/MBA Combined-Degree program is a powerful union of Santa Clara's nationally recognized School of Law and Leavey School of Business. This is an opportunity to earn both degrees in a full-time program lasting three and one-half to four years. The **JD/MST** is done in conjunction with San Jose State University. Students enrolled in this joint-degree program would take sufficient courses to satisfy both SJSU's MS in Taxation degree and the SCU's JD degree. Full-time students would be able to complete this joint program in three and one-half to four years.

■ International Law Certificate

A specialized curriculum allows students to earn a Certificate in International Law. The Institute of International and Comparative Law sponsors summer law study programs in Munich, Germany; Strasbourg, France; Geneva, Switzerland; Oxford, England; Hong Kong; Singapore; Seoul, Korea; Bangkok, Thailand; Ho Chi Minh City, Socialist Republic of Vietnam; Beijing, People's Republic of China; Kuala Lumpur, Malaysia; Tokyo, Japan; and Sydney, Australia. The institute is exploring opportunities for additional programs in Latin America and Eastern Europe. All of the programs, with the exception of Oxford, offer internships with law offices, corporations, or groups particularly suited to give students on-site observation and participation in areas of international law.

■ Computer and High Technology Law Certificate

Santa Clara has capitalized on its Silicon Valley location by establishing a specialized curriculum that emphasizes computer and high technology law. Students seeking an emphasis on high technology issues can enroll in courses such as patent law, copyright, biotechnology law, and technology licensing. They may also intern with a leading high tech firm and may earn a certificate in High Technology Law.

■ Public Interest and Social Justice Law Certificate

Students concerned with social issues, social justice, and public service can earn a Certificate in Public Interest. Santa Clara's Center for Social Justice and Public Service offers an impressive array of resources for students who want to focus on social justice and public interest work during their legal education and in practice. Santa Clara University is distinctive in making explicit its intention to evoke from students "a commitment to fashioning a more humane and just world."

■ Clinical Programs

The Santa Clara University Law Clinic allows students to practice law under the supervision of an experienced attorney. Students participate in all phases of a case from the initial client interview through the trial. Students have the opportunity to earn credit for work as law clerks with public agencies such as the district attorney or public defender, with legal aid offices, or with private law offices. Students may also work as judges' clerks in appellate courts, including the California Supreme Court; or trial courts, including the United States District Court and local superior court. Northern California Innocence Project (NCIP) is a clinical program developed by the Santa Clara University Criminal Defense Clinic. NCIP identifies prisoners with innocence claims and provides direct services to them. NCIP serves as a resource center for the legal community in innocence cases. Law students in the NCIP program investigate, evaluate, and where possible, pursue relief for claims of wrongful conviction.

■ Student Activities

The school's quarterly, *Santa Clara Law Review*, is published by a student editorial board. The *Computer and High Technology Law Journal* provides a practical resource for high technology industry and the corresponding legal community. The new *Journal of International Law* is an Internet-based publication. Through the Student Bar Association and student-faculty committees, students participate in the decision processes of the law school.

■ Admission

A faculty committee reviews all applications. No one is automatically accepted or rejected. When the LSAT is repeated, the highest score received is used.

Recognizing the critical need for persons from underrepresented groups to gain access to the legal profession, the School of Law has adopted a policy for special admission. Applicants may request a special consideration because of race, disadvantaged background, or other factors. Over 49 percent of the entering class is composed of students of color and 54 percent are women.

Applicants are encouraged to visit the School of Law. Arrangements can be made through the Admissions Office to attend a law class, meet with an admission counselor, or tour the campus.

■ Career Services

The Career Services Office serves as a liaison between students and prospective employers. Firms, businesses, and government agencies interview on campus each year. Graduates find employment in the legal profession throughout the 50 states. Office services include individual career counseling and a series of workshops in job-search strategies. Strong alumni support assists students in all stages of their career exploration and development. Current employment statistics are on the school's website: *www.scu.edu/law*.

Applicant Profile

Santa Clara University School of Law
This grid includes only applicants who earned 120-180 LSAT scores under standard administrations.

LSAT Score	3.75 + Apps	Adm	3.50 - 3.74 Apps	Adm	3.25 - 3.49 Apps	Adm	3.00 - 3.24 Apps	Adm	2.75 - 2.99 Apps	Adm	2.50 - 2.74 Apps	Adm	2.25 - 2.49 Apps	Adm	2.00 - 2.24 Apps	Adm	Below 2.00 Apps	Adm	No GPA Apps	Adm	Total Apps	Adm
175-180	2	2	1	1	5	5	0	0	0	0	0	0	0	0	0	0	0	0	0	0	8	8
170-174	6	6	15	15	5	5	12	12	8	4	1	1	3	0	1	0	0	0	1	1	52	44
165-169	42	42	55	54	50	50	37	32	27	7	23	4	8	1	4	0	0	0	6	6	252	196
160-164	118	116	192	188	199	185	152	113	91	16	50	8	14	1	8	1	0	0	14	12	838	640
155-159	131	96	276	166	374	150	298	80	186	15	83	5	30	2	10	1	1	0	26	5	1415	520
150-154	93	17	254	43	375	49	378	39	206	15	90	1	37	1	15	0	3	0	30	4	1481	169
145-149	46	3	104	5	144	5	172	6	115	2	71	0	37	0	16	0	3	0	24	0	732	21
140-144	10	0	28	0	59	0	66	0	54	0	32	0	33	0	8	0	1	0	8	0	299	0
135-139	2	0	8	0	12	0	18	0	22	0	19	0	11	0	4	0	1	0	7	0	104	0
130-134	0	0	3	0	4	0	4	0	5	0	5	0	6	0	7	0	0	0	3	0	37	0
125-129	0	0	1	0	0	0	2	0	2	0	1	0	1	0	2	0	0	0	1	0	10	0
120-124	0	0	0	0	0	0	0	0	0	0	0	0	1	0	0	0	0	0	0	0	1	0
Total	450	282	937	472	1227	449	1139	282	716	59	375	19	181	5	75	2	9	0	120	28	5229	1598

Apps = Number of Applicants   Adm = Number Admitted   Reflects 99% of the total applicant pool.

Seattle University School of Law

901 12th Avenue, Sullivan Hall
Seattle, WA 98122-1090
Phone: 206.398.4200; Fax: 206.398.4058
E-mail: lawadmis@seattleu.edu; Website: www.law.seattleu.edu

ABA Approved Since 1994

The Basics

Type of school	Private
Term	Semester
Application deadline	4/1 4/1
Application fee	$50
Financial aid deadline	
Can first year start other than fall?	Yes
Student to faculty ratio (fall)	16.6 to 1
Does the university offer:	
housing restricted to law students?	No
graduate housing for which law students are eligible?	Yes

Faculty and Administrators

	Total		Men		Women		Minorities	
	Fall	Spr	Fall	Spr	Fall	Spr	Fall	Spr
Full-time	51	46	31	27	20	19	11	11
Other Full-time	1	1	1	1	0	0	0	0
Deans, librarians, & others who teach	7	8	3	3	4	5	1	1
Part-time	37	34	21	24	16	10	4	3
Total	96	89	56	55	40	34	16	15

Curriculum

	Full-time	Part-time
Typical first-year section size	86	77
Is there typically a "small section" of the first-year class, other than Legal Writing, taught by full-time faculty	No	No
If yes, typical size offered last year	0	0
# of classroom course titles beyond 1st year curriculum	116	
# of upper division courses, excluding seminars with an enrollment: Under 25	82	
25-49	51	
50-74	26	
75-99	11	
100+	2	
# of seminars	31	
# of seminar positions available	516	
# of seminar positions filled	268	163
# of positions available in simulation courses	455	
# of simulation positions filled	253	169
# of positions available in faculty supervised clinical courses	196	
# of faculty supervised clinical positions filled	136	20
# involved in field placements	94	17
# involved in law journals	95	4
# involved in moot court or trial competitions	29	0
# of credit hours required to graduate	90	

JD Enrollment and Ethnicity

	Men		Women		Full-time		Part-time		1st-year		Total		JD Degs. Awd.
	#	%	#	%	#	%	#	%	#	%	#	%	
African Amer.	23	4.6	21	3.5	30	3.5	14	5.5	12	3.5	44	4.0	11
Amer. Indian	6	1.2	11	1.8	10	1.2	7	2.7	7	2.0	17	1.5	4
Asian Amer.	43	8.6	79	13.1	96	11.3	26	10.2	44	12.9	122	11.1	30
Mex. Amer.	13	2.6	11	1.8	18	2.1	6	2.4	9	2.6	24	2.2	12
Puerto Rican	5	1.0	4	0.7	7	0.8	2	0.8	2	0.6	9	0.8	1
Hispanic	10	2.0	10	1.7	14	1.7	6	2.4	2	0.6	20	1.8	7
Total Minority	100	20.0	136	22.6	175	20.7	61	23.9	76	22.2	236	21.4	65
For. Nation.	9	1.8	14	2.3	20	2.4	3	1.2	7	2.0	23	2.1	3
Caucasian	369	73.9	425	70.5	621	73.3	173	67.8	237	69.3	794	72.1	239
Unknown	21	4.2	28	4.6	31	3.7	18	7.1	22	6.4	49	4.4	7
Total	499	45.3	603	54.7	847	76.9	255	23.1	342	31.0	1102		314

Tuition and Fees

	Resident	Nonresident
Full-time	$24,676	$24,676
Part-time	$16,452	$16,452

Living Expenses

Estimated living expenses for singles

Living on campus	Living off campus	Living at home
$14,983	$14,983	$8,170

Seattle University School of Law

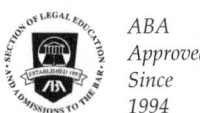

*ABA
Approved
Since
1994*

GPA and LSAT Scores

	Total	Full-time	Part-time
# of apps	2,920	2,660	260
# of admits	817	710	107
# of matrics	344	268	76
75% GPA	3.65	3.65	3.62
25% GPA	3.15	3.16	3.13
75% LSAT	159	159	159
25% LSAT	152	152	151

Grants and Scholarships (from prior year)

	Total		Full-time		Part-time	
	#	%	#	%	#	%
Total # of students	1,067		809		258	
Total # receiving grants	456	42.7	393	48.6	63	24.4
Less than 1/2 tuition	443	41.5	380	47.0	63	24.4
Half to full tuition	13	1.2	13	1.6	0	0.0
Full tuition	0	0.0	0	0.0	0	0.0
More than full tuition	0	0.0	0	0.0	0	0.0
Median grant amount			$6,000		$5,000	

Informational and Library Resources

# of volumes and volume equivalents	348,513
# of titles	71,404
# of active serial subscriptions	3,240
Study seating capacity inside the library	369
# of professional librarians	8
Hours per week library is open	119
# of open, wired connections available to students	2,140
# of networked computers available for use by students	25
# of simultaneous wireless users	9,999
Require computer?	Y

JD Attrition (from prior year)

	Academic	Other	Total	
	#	#	#	%
1st year	3	18	21	6.2%
2nd year	0	11	11	3.3%
3rd year	0	0	0	0.0%
4th year	0	1	1	1.8%

Employment

	Total	Percentage
Employment status known	300	100.0
Employment status unknown	0	0.0
Employed	284	94.7
Pursuing graduate degrees	12	4.0
Unemployed seeking employment	0	0.0
Unemployed not seeking employment	4	1.3

Type of Employment

# employed in law firms	101	35.6
# employed in business and industry	94	33.1
# employed in government	51	18.0
# employed in public interest	13	4.6
# employed as judicial clerks	19	6.7
# employed in academia	6	2.1

Geographic Location

# employed in state	253	89.1
# employed in foreign countries	0	0.0
# of states where employed	11	

Bar Passage Rates

Jurisdiction	Washington		
Exam	Sum 03	Win 04	Total
# from school taking bar for the first time	209	68	277
School's pass rate for all first-time takers	70%	79%	72%
State's pass rate for all first-time takers	71%	79%	74%

Seattle University School of Law

901 12th Avenue, Sullivan Hall
Seattle, WA 98122-1090
Phone: 206.398.4200; Fax: 206.398.4058
E-mail: lawadmis@seattleu.edu; Website: www.law.seattleu.edu

■ Introduction

Seattle University School of Law is a vital part of Seattle University, the Northwest's largest independent university. Here, students are trained to lead and serve others with integrity and compassion by faculty dedicated to their growth in the law. In our community, curriculum, and programs, as a Jesuit institution the School of Law seeks to reflect a tradition of academic distinction and open inquiry.

The School of Law serves an impressive body of students, whose diversity encompasses age, life experience, and cultural heritage. Fittingly, the law school has been recognized nationally for its diverse faculty and welcoming environment for older students. Home to the only part-time legal education program in the state of Washington, and programs and initiatives that examine law at the service of justice, the School of Law is dedicated to educating the whole person.

The law school is fully accredited by the ABA and holds full membership in AALS. Students may pursue a Juris Doctor or an LLM in American Legal Studies (limited to students with law degrees from non-US institutions).

Sullivan Hall, home to the School of Law, lies on the eastern boundary of Seattle University's 42-acre campus. The five-floor, handsomely appointed structure features a street-front law clinic, media-equipped classrooms, a modern and impressive law library, a spacious courtroom, and comfortable activity areas. Wireless connectivity is available throughout the entire building, allowing students to use laptops anywhere to connect to classes, the SU Law community, and the Internet. Together, these amenities provide an attractive and accommodating setting in which students can learn and thrive.

■ Location

Seattle University School of Law sits in a landscaped, urban setting in the First Hill neighborhood of Seattle, less than a mile from downtown. A sophisticated city, Seattle is also one of the most livable cities in the United States, offering a rich mix of business, culture, adventure, and industry that provides a natural extension of our classrooms.

Being minutes from a vibrant downtown only enhances prospects for students seeking career-building opportunities. We are part of a strong legal community that welcomes new talent, and our students pursue summer and school-year employment with multinational and regional law firms, public agencies, private corporations, and boutique partnerships whose legal specialties reflect the special interests of Northwest natives.

■ Focus Area Curriculum

After completion of rigorous first-year studies that emphasize sound legal analytical skills, the law school curriculum allows students to select a primary area of interest and support that interest with enrollment in a prescribed range of courses. Students may focus their upper-division legal studies in one of 14 substantive areas, including Civil Advocacy, Criminal Practice, Environmental Law, Health Law, Labor and Employment, and Real Estate Law.

■ Faculty

Seattle University law faculty always places teaching first. This means instruction using numerous pedagogical styles, from Socratic classroom dialogue to drafting laboratories and seminar discussion.

While emphasizing the importance of teaching, faculty also recognize the critical role that scholarship plays in academic excellence. Since 1997, law school faculty have published 21 books, over 25 book chapters, and over 100 articles that have appeared in law reviews—including several of the most frequently cited publications—and specialized journals.

■ Academic Enrichment Programs

Access to Justice Institute—The Access to Justice Institute is an outgrowth of the law school's dedication to social justice and the need to deliver legal services to underrepresented communities. Through the institute and under the supervision of an attorney, students can work at one of AtJI's Community Justice Centers directly serving low-income persons. The institute also sponsors in-house projects, including the Immigration Court Project, the Language Bank, and the Unemployment Insurance for Battered Women Project. Over 300 law students volunteer with AtJI each year.

Center on Corporations, Law and Society—The Center on Corporations, Law and Society serves as a platform for enhanced scholarly inquiry while providing a forum for sustained discussion among academics, legal practitioners, business leaders, activists, policymakers, and citizens on the complex and important relationships between business enterprises and their many stakeholders.

International Initiatives—Recognizing the reach of global issues and the value international outreach adds to legal education, the School of Law consistently seeks regional and international connections that will enhance the educational experiences of both students and faculty, and heighten the school's profile internationally. The School of Law has established programs and connections with Alaska, British Columbia, Japan, Korea, Mexico, Nicaragua, and Russia.

■ Admission and Financial Aid

In admission decisions, the law school places equal emphasis on three factors: (1) LSAT performance; (2) the undergraduate academic record; and (3) personal achievements, especially talents or factors that contribute to our law school community in special and significant ways.

We also admit a limited group of applicants annually through a wholly discretionary process. The law school's **Alternative Admission Program** addresses those cases where traditional admission criteria are inadequate predictors of success in law school and in the practice of law. Members of historically disadvantaged, underrepresented, or physically challenged groups are among those individuals considered for this program (limited to no more than 10 percent of the entering class).

The law school's **Scholarship Program** is among the most ambitious in the region, awarding over $2 million per year to approximately 350 students. Its objectives are twofold: to offer to all students—regardless of economic or social background—the advantages of a private legal education; and second, to recognize and reward—regardless of financial need—the achievements and outstanding potential of the most highly qualified students in the applicant pool. Upon admission to the School of Law, all entering students are considered for scholarships automatically.

Consistent with the School of Law's mission of preparing students who are committed to contributing to the common good by shaping an equitable legal system, the **Loan Repayment Assistance Program** assists School of Law graduates who choose full-time public interest legal careers as licensed attorneys doing law-related, public interest work in both content and spirit. Through this program, the School of Law lends funds to qualifying graduates to assist with loan repayment, and under very specific conditions, forgives those loans.

Applicant Profile

Seattle University School of Law

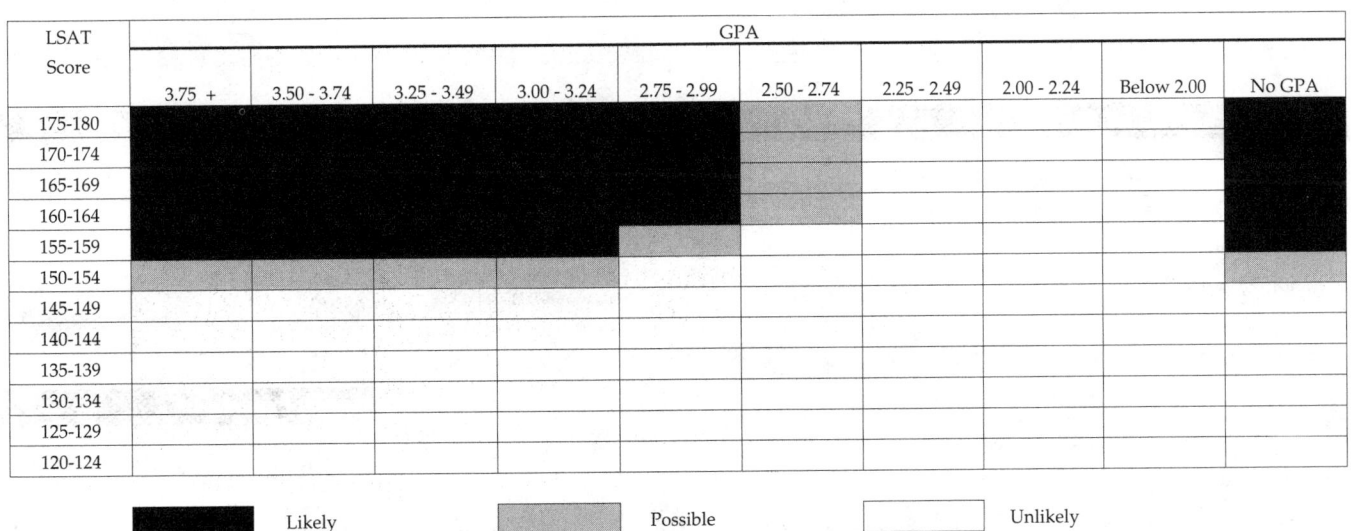

LSAT Score	GPA									
	3.75 +	3.50 - 3.74	3.25 - 3.49	3.00 - 3.24	2.75 - 2.99	2.50 - 2.74	2.25 - 2.49	2.00 - 2.24	Below 2.00	No GPA
175-180										
170-174										
165-169										
160-164										
155-159										
150-154										
145-149										
140-144										
135-139										
130-134										
125-129										
120-124										

■ Likely   ▨ Possible   □ Unlikely

Of applicants in the Unlikely category, about one in 20 candidates was admitted to the Alternative Admission Program.

Seton Hall University School of Law

One Newark Center
Newark, NJ 07102-5210
Phone: 888.415.7271, 973.642.8747; Fax: 973.642.8876
E-mail: admitme@shu.edu; Website: http://law.shu.edu

ABA
Approved
Since
1951

The Basics

Type of school	Private
Term	Semester
Application deadline	4/4
Application fee	$65
Financial aid deadline	4/1
Can first year start other than fall?	No
Student to faculty ratio (fall)	17.1 to 1
Does the university offer:	
housing restricted to law students?	No
graduate housing for which law students are eligible?	Yes

Faculty and Administrators

	Total		Men		Women		Minorities	
	Fall	Spr	Fall	Spr	Fall	Spr	Fall	Spr
Full-time	54	58	33	36	21	22	13	13
Other Full-time	1	1	1	1	0	0	0	0
Deans, librarians, & others who teach	6	6	2	2	4	4	1	1
Part-time	84	76	56	55	28	21	9	10
Total	145	141	92	94	53	47	23	24

Curriculum

	Full-time	Part-time
Typical first-year section size	80	80
Is there typically a "small section" of the first-year class, other than Legal Writing, taught by full-time faculty	No	No
If yes, typical size offered last year	0	0
# of classroom course titles beyond 1st year curriculum	163	
# of upper division courses, excluding seminars with an enrollment: Under 25	87	
25-49	51	
50-74	39	
75-99	12	
100+	0	
# of seminars	104	
# of seminar positions available	1,658	
# of seminar positions filled	736	501
# of positions available in simulation courses	1,238	
# of simulation positions filled	753	306
# of positions available in faculty supervised clinical courses	87	
# of faculty supervised clinical positions filled	76	11
# involved in field placements	100	8
# involved in law journals	136	10
# involved in moot court or trial competitions	210	15
# of credit hours required to graduate	85	

JD Enrollment and Ethnicity

	Men		Women		Full-time		Part-time		1st-year		Total		JD Degs. Awd.
	#	%	#	%	#	%	#	%	#	%	#	%	
African Amer.	17	2.5	39	7.2	27	3.1	29	7.8	16	4.7	56	4.5	7
Amer. Indian	3	0.4	2	0.4	3	0.3	2	0.5	2	0.6	5	0.4	1
Asian Amer.	50	7.3	50	9.2	68	7.9	32	8.6	37	10.8	100	8.1	24
Mex. Amer.	0	0.0	2	0.4	1	0.1	1	0.3	2	0.6	2	0.2	1
Puerto Rican	12	1.7	12	2.2	11	1.3	13	3.5	9	2.6	24	1.9	4
Hispanic	26	3.8	34	6.2	39	4.5	21	5.7	9	2.6	60	4.9	17
Total Minority	108	15.7	139	25.5	149	17.3	98	26.4	75	21.8	247	20.0	54
For. Nation.	16	2.3	15	2.8	24	2.8	7	1.9	7	2.0	31	2.5	12
Caucasian	565	82.0	391	71.7	690	80.0	266	71.7	262	76.2	956	77.5	257
Unknown	0	0.0	0	0.0	0	0.0	0	0.0	0	0.0	0	0.0	0
Total	689	55.8	545	44.2	863	69.9	371	30.1	344	27.9	1234		323

Tuition and Fees

	Resident	Nonresident
Full-time	$29,950	$29,950
Part-time	$21,914	$21,914

Living Expenses

Estimated living expenses for singles

Living on campus	Living off campus	Living at home
N/A	$15,985	$10,385

Seton Hall University School of Law

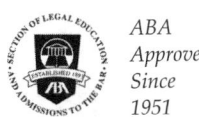

GPA and LSAT Scores

	Total	Full-time	Part-time
# of apps	3,528	2,883	645
# of admits	1,199	702	497
# of matrics	344	189	155
75% GPA	3.51	3.52	3.48
25% GPA	2.90	2.91	2.87
75% LSAT	160	162	156
25% LSAT	154	158	152

Grants and Scholarships (from prior year)

	Total		Full-time		Part-time	
	#	%	#	%	#	%
Total # of students	1,277		932		345	
Total # receiving grants	539	42.2	474	50.9	65	18.8
Less than 1/2 tuition	392	30.7	328	35.2	64	18.6
Half to full tuition	140	11.0	139	14.9	1	0.3
Full tuition	7	0.5	7	0.8	0	0.0
More than full tuition	0	0.0	0	0.0	0	0.0
Median grant amount			$10,000		$3,000	

Informational and Library Resources

# of volumes and volume equivalents	453,163
# of titles	90,479
# of active serial subscriptions	9,989
Study seating capacity inside the library	540
# of professional librarians	9
Hours per week library is open	91
# of open, wired connections available to students	124
# of networked computers available for use by students	234
# of simultaneous wireless users	1,600
Require computer?	N

JD Attrition (from prior year)

	Academic	Other	Total	
	#	#	#	%
1st year	26	17	43	9.7%
2nd year	10	3	13	2.9%
3rd year	1	0	1	0.3%
4th year	0	0	0	0.0%

Employment

	Total	Percentage
Employment status known	333	97.9
Employment status unknown	7	2.1
Employed	306	91.9
Pursuing graduate degrees	3	0.9
Unemployed seeking employment	22	6.6
Unemployed not seeking employment	2	0.6

Type of Employment

# employed in law firms	93	30.4
# employed in business and industry	45	14.7
# employed in government	24	7.8
# employed in public interest	4	1.3
# employed as judicial clerks	128	41.8
# employed in academia	1	0.3

Geographic Location

# employed in state	253	82.7
# employed in foreign countries	0	0.0
# of states where employed	15	

Bar Passage Rates

Jurisdiction	New Jersey			New York		
Exam	Sum 03	Win 04	Total	Sum 03	Win 04	Total
# from school taking bar for the first time	263	38	301	178	20	198
School's pass rate for all first-time takers	81%	63%	79%	87%	85%	86%
State's pass rate for all first-time takers	76%	59%	73%	78%	58%	75%

Seton Hall University School of Law

Office of Admissions, One Newark Center
Newark, NJ 07102-5210
Phone: 888.415.7271, 973.642.8747; Fax: 973.642.8876
E-mail: admitme@shu.edu; Website: http://law.shu.edu

■ Introduction

Founded in 1951, Seton Hall University School of Law is the only private law school in the state of New Jersey. While it values its Catholic identity as a division of the university, the law school is a pluralistic community representing a diversity of racial, cultural, religious, and socioeconomic backgrounds. The school is consistently recognized for its high level of student satisfaction and its high rate of judicial clerkship placement. The law school building is architecturally dynamic, fostering a congenial atmosphere and incorporating technological sophistication for the study of law. The school location is in the midst of federal, appellate, state, and county courts; the legal center; hundreds of law firms and legal agencies; and the New Jersey Performing Arts Center. The school is also conveniently located near all forms of major transportation. It is just 15 minutes from New York City by train.

■ Curriculum

The JD requires 85 credits to graduate and may be completed as a full-time or a part-time program. The school offers both a day and an evening program following a semester calendar. The program emphasizes humanistic principles and encourages their synthesis with knowledge of the law and professional responsibility. The law school is committed to in-depth training in legal writing and research.

In addition to the core required courses, more than 150 courses are offered in a wide range of areas grouped as follows: Commercial Law, Corporate Law, Criminal Justice, Environmental Law, Health Law, History and Philosophy of Law, Intellectual Property and Entertainment Law, International Legal Studies, Labor and Employment Law, Personal and Family Law, Procedure and Remedies, Properties and Estates Law, Public Law—Government, Public Law—Protection of Rights, Legislation, and Taxation. Externships, journals, legal writing, and moot court programs are also included in the school's offerings.

Graduate-degree programs: a Master of Laws (LLM) and a Master of Science in Jurisprudence are also offered in the areas of health law and science and technology.

■ Joint-Degree Programs

JD/MBA Program—A four-year program with Seton Hall University Stillman School of Business.

JD/MADIR Program—A four-year program with Seton Hall School of Diplomacy and International Relations.

JD/MD Program—A six-year program with Robert Wood Johnson Medical School of the University of Medicine and Dentistry of New Jersey.

MSJ/MD Program—A five-year program with the Robert Wood Johnson Medical School of the University of Medicine and Dentistry of New Jersey.

■ Special Programs

Clinics—Seton Hall School of Law is committed to clinical education and is at its forefront. The 25 years of service performed by the law school's clinics were recognized by Congress and the president in the form of a $5.4 million grant. With the grant, the school has created the Center for Social Justice, a clinical education center that serves as a national model. The school's litigation clinics presently represent more than 3,000 disadvantaged and underrepresented clients each year in a wide range of litigation such as civil litigation, family law, housing and homelessness, immigration and human rights, impact litigation, and juvenile justice.

Judicial Internships—The law school offers judicial internships with justices of the New Jersey Supreme Court, judges of the New Jersey Appellate Division, Chancery and Law Courts, the Third Circuit Court of Appeals, the US District Courts, and the US Bankruptcy Courts. There are internship programs with the Environmental Protection Agency, and the Internal Revenue Service.

Externships—Externship offerings include environmental law, health law, entertainment law, international organizations, the European Court of Justice or Court of First Instance, the Federal Public Defender, Securities and Exchange Commission, New York Stock Exchange, Internal Revenue Service, National Labor Relations Board, and US Attorney.

Concentrations—The law school offers concentrations with certificates in health and intellectual property law.

Journals—The law school offers students an opportunity to advance legal scholarship through four student journals—the *Seton Hall Law Review, Seton Hall Legislative Journal, Seton Hall Sports and Entertainment Law Journal,* and the *Circuit Review.*

International Study—Each summer the law school cosponsors, with the University of Parma, a course of international studies for American law students in Parma, Italy. The law school also offers a summer program for the study of law in the Middle East at the American University of Cairo in Egypt and a program at Galway University in Ireland, focusing on Intellectual Property.

Health Law—Seton Hall offers an LLM degree in health law, which provides attorneys the opportunity to broadly explore health law and policy or focus more narrowly on courses designed for the lawyer planning to represent the health provider, payer, or regulator; the pharmaceutical company; or the biotechnology company.

Seton Hall also offers a Master of Science in Jurisprudence (MSJ) degree in Health Law, Science, and

Technology which provides professionals with a solid foundation in legal aspects of health care and intellectual property regulation. Such a concentrated exposure to health law issues can be vital to medical directors, regulatory and contract compliance officers, risk and case managers, employee benefits personnel, lobbyists, and pharmaceutical employees. Full- and part-time programs are available for both the LLM and MSJ degrees.

Moot Court Program—Students represent the law school in the National Moot Court competition as well as in 10 interschool competitions focusing on specific areas of law.

LEO Institute—The Monsignor Thomas Fahy Legal Education Opportunities Institute provides an intense, summer-long classroom experience for educationally disadvantaged students. Applicants from disadvantaged groups, regardless of race, religion, age, sex, sexual orientation, or national origin, may wish to inquire about this program.

■ Student Activities

There are approximately 30 student organizations at Seton Hall Law, representing various personal and professional interests. The Student Bar Association (SBA) and other student organizations sponsor a variety of practical, social, and educational events. The SBA plays a major role in orientation, sponsors a holiday party each November in Newark and a Barristers' Ball in the spring. Organizations sponsor career seminars focused on different areas of the law, host symposiums and panel discussions that focus on current legal and societal issues, and plan annual banquets and networking receptions during the year.

■ Career Services

Seton Hall School of Law maintains a Career Services Office staffed by four full-time counselors who assist students in defining their career objectives and goals and establishing contact with employers. Each fall and spring, law firms, accounting firms, and public interest and governmental employers conduct interviews through the school's On-Campus Interview Program. The class of 2003 employment rate was 92 percent. Alumni are practicing nationwide.

Applicant Profile

Seton Hall University School of Law
This grid includes only applicants who earned 120-180 LSAT scores under standard administrations.

LSAT Score	3.75 +		3.50 - 3.74		3.25 - 3.49		3.00 - 3.24		2.75 - 2.99		2.50 - 2.74		2.25 - 2.49		2.00 - 2.24		Below 2.00		No GPA		Total	
	Apps	Adm	Apps	Adm	Apps	Adm	Apps	Adm	Apps	Adm	Apps	Adm	Apps	Adm	Apps	Adm	Apps	Adm	Apps	Adm	Apps	Adm
175-180	0	0	0	0	0	0	0	0	0	0	0	0	0	0	0	0	0	0	0	0	0	0
170-174	0	0	0	0	1	1	2	2	1	1	1	1	0	0	1	1	0	0	0	0	6	6
165-169	9	9	11	11	14	13	18	18	9	8	6	6	8	7	2	2	0	0	1	1	78	75
160-164	33	32	52	50	60	55	66	64	48	48	38	37	20	18	5	5	0	0	7	6	329	315
155-159	63	51	136	117	166	142	173	134	114	51	67	30	49	22	16	2	3	0	14	12	801	561
150-154	62	17	196	60	221	51	242	46	173	14	102	15	65	13	15	1	4	0	12	3	1092	220
145-149	35	6	90	4	142	3	167	5	138	8	77	1	48	3	22	0	1	0	17	1	737	31
140-144	11	0	34	0	56	1	70	2	73	4	60	0	36	0	9	1	1	0	6	0	353	8
135-139	5	0	13	0	14	0	35	1	32	0	38	0	20	0	12	0	1	0	6	0	176	1
130-134	1	0	1	0	5	0	12	0	10	0	13	0	8	0	6	0	2	0	7	0	65	0
125-129	0	0	0	0	0	0	0	0	2	0	5	0	1	0	2	0	1	0	4	0	15	0
120-124	0	0	1	0	0	0	0	0	0	0	0	0	2	0	0	0	0	0	0	0	3	0
Total	219	115	534	242	679	266	785	272	600	134	407	90	257	63	90	12	13	0	71	23	3655	1217

Apps = Number of Applicants
Adm = Number Admitted
Reflects 99% of the total applicant pool.

SMU Dedman School of Law

PO Box 750110
Dallas, TX 75275-0110
Phone: 214.768.2550, 888.768.5291; Fax: 214.768.2549
E-mail: lawadmit@smu.edu; Website: www.law.smu.edu

*ABA
Approved
Since
1927*

The Basics

Type of school	Private
Term	Semester
Application deadline	2/15
Application fee	$50
Financial aid deadline	4/15
Can first year start other than fall?	No
Student to faculty ratio (fall)	15.7 to 1
Does the university offer:	
housing restricted to law students?	No
graduate housing for which law students are eligible?	Yes

Faculty and Administrators

	Total		Men		Women		Minorities	
	Fall	Spr	Fall	Spr	Fall	Spr	Fall	Spr
Full-time	43	43	27	28	16	15	8	10
Other Full-time	2	2	2	2	0	0	0	0
Deans, librarians, & others who teach	2	2	1	1	1	1	0	0
Part-time	26	39	20	30	6	9	2	2
Total	73	86	50	61	23	25	10	12

Curriculum

		Full-time	Part-time
Typical first-year section size		93	91
Is there typically a "small section" of the first-year class, other than Legal Writing, taught by full-time faculty		No	No
If yes, typical size offered last year		0	0
# of classroom course titles beyond 1st year curriculum		120	
# of upper division courses, excluding seminars with an enrollment:	Under 25	66	
	25-49	34	
	50-74	16	
	75-99	15	
	100+	6	
# of seminars		20	
# of seminar positions available		377	
# of seminar positions filled		340	0
# of positions available in simulation courses		349	
# of simulation positions filled		314	0
# of positions available in faculty supervised clinical courses		173	
# of faculty supervised clinical positions filled	173		0
# involved in field placements		71	0
# involved in law journals		212	0
# involved in moot court or trial competitions		69	0
# of credit hours required to graduate		87	

JD Enrollment and Ethnicity

	Men		Women		Full-time		Part-time		1st-year		Total		JD Degs. Awd.
	#	%	#	%	#	%	#	%	#	%	#	%	
African Amer.	13	2.9	29	7.3	32	4.6	10	7.2	19	6.7	42	5.0	4
Amer. Indian	4	0.9	5	1.3	8	1.1	1	0.7	5	1.8	9	1.1	4
Asian Amer.	29	6.6	29	7.3	49	7.0	9	6.5	22	7.8	58	6.9	15
Mex. Amer.	1	0.2	7	1.8	5	0.7	3	2.2	6	2.1	8	1.0	0
Puerto Rican	0	0.0	0	0.0	0	0.0	0	0.0	0	0.0	0	0.0	0
Hispanic	22	5.0	24	6.0	42	6.0	4	2.9	15	5.3	46	5.5	17
Total Minority	69	15.6	94	23.5	136	19.4	27	19.4	67	23.7	163	19.4	40
For. Nation.	4	0.9	4	1.0	7	1.0	1	0.7	3	1.1	8	1.0	4
Caucasian	338	76.6	282	70.5	530	75.5	90	64.7	163	57.6	620	73.7	237
Unknown	30	6.8	20	5.0	29	4.1	21	15.1	50	17.7	50	5.9	0
Total	441	52.4	400	47.6	702	83.5	139	16.5	283	33.7	841		281

Tuition and Fees

	Resident	Nonresident
Full-time	$29,722	$29,722
Part-time	$22,784	$22,784

Living Expenses

Estimated living expenses for singles

Living on campus	Living off campus	Living at home
$14,000	$14,000	N/A

SMU Dedman School of Law

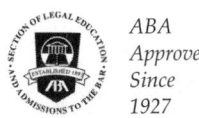

ABA
Approved
Since
1927

GPA and LSAT Scores

	Total	Full-time	Part-time
# of apps	3,301	2,650	651
# of admits	563	405	158
# of matrics	287	175	112
75% GPA	3.81	3.84	3.57
25% GPA	3.21	3.32	3.11
75% LSAT	163	164	160
25% LSAT	155	156	152

Grants and Scholarships (from prior year)

	Total		Full-time		Part-time	
	#	%	#	%	#	%
Total # of students	866		791		75	
Total # receiving grants	535	61.8	535	67.6	0	0.0
Less than 1/2 tuition	398	46.0	398	50.3	0	0.0
Half to full tuition	101	11.7	101	12.8	0	0.0
Full tuition	30	3.5	30	3.8	0	0.0
More than full tuition	6	0.7	6	0.8	0	0.0
Median grant amount			$10,000		$0	

Informational and Library Resources

# of volumes and volume equivalents	591,773
# of titles	213,665
# of active serial subscriptions	4,598
Study seating capacity inside the library	744
# of professional librarians	8
Hours per week library is open	104
# of open, wired connections available to students	0
# of networked computers available for use by students	117
# of simultaneous wireless users	1,053
Require computer?	N

JD Attrition (from prior year)

	Academic	Other	Total	
	#	#	#	%
1st year	0	15	15	4.8%
2nd year	0	0	0	0.0%
3rd year	0	0	0	0.0%
4th year	0	0	0	0.0%

Employment

	Total	Percentage
Employment status known	220	96.9
Employment status unknown	7	3.1
Employed	197	89.5
Pursuing graduate degrees	6	2.7
Unemployed seeking employment	9	4.1
Unemployed not seeking employment	8	3.6

Type of Employment

# employed in law firms	137	69.5
# employed in business and industry	15	7.6
# employed in government	19	9.6
# employed in public interest	4	2.0
# employed as judicial clerks	14	7.1
# employed in academia	2	1.0

Geographic Location

# employed in state	170	86.5
# employed in foreign countries	0	0.0
# of states where employed		15

Bar Passage Rates

Jurisdiction		Texas	
Exam	Sum 03	Win 04	Total
# from school taking bar for the first time	197	0	197
School's pass rate for all first-time takers	92%		92%
State's pass rate for all first-time takers	83%	69%	80%

SMU Dedman School of Law

Office of Admissions, PO Box 750110
Dallas, TX 75275-0110
Phone: 214.768.2550, 888.768.5291; Fax: 214.768.2549
E-mail: lawadmit@smu.edu; Website: www.law.smu.edu

■ Introduction

Founded in 1925, SMU Dedman School of Law is located on a magnificent tree-lined campus in a beautiful residential neighborhood just five miles north of downtown Dallas. SMU offers an intimate learning community within a vibrant urban center.

With a relatively small entering class size, an outstanding teaching faculty, and distinguished guest lecturers, SMU offers a scholarly community with fantastic opportunities both inside and outside the classroom. SMU also has a well-rounded, diverse student body from more than 160 colleges and universities, over 30 states, and 13 countries.

■ Law School Campus

SMU offers a beautiful setting to pursue legal studies. The Law School Quadrangle, a six-acre self-contained corner of the campus, offers students convenient access to all law school facilities. The larger SMU campus offers students a variety of housing options, a childcare facility, a health center, and a fitness/wellness center.

SMU recently completed a multimillion-dollar renovation to all of the law school classrooms. A four-story parking garage with 500 spaces is available exclusively for law student parking and a new dining hall is under construction.

■ Curriculum

SMU offers seven degree programs: JD (full-time day or part-time evening), JD/MBA, JD/MA in Economics, LLM (General), LLM (Taxation), LLM (International and Comparative Law—for foreign attorneys only), and SJD.

Students find a sophisticated curriculum that complements SMU's wide breadth of class offerings with extensive depth of focus. The JD curriculum is designed to achieve the goal of producing lawyers who are capable and responsible professionals through its emphasis on providing substantive knowledge, ethical and moral training, and practical skills to serve their clients in local, national, and global communities.

Each JD student must complete 87 hours. Thirty-one of these hours comprise the mandatory first-year curriculum. After the first year, students must complete a course in professional responsibility and two upper-level writing courses (including an edited writing seminar in which an extensive scholarly, expository writing project is reviewed and critiqued by the professor).

SMU offers many small classes in which students will get to know their classmates and professors. Each entering class is divided into three sections (two full-time day and one part-time evening) of approximately 85 students each. Each semester, first-year students are assigned to a legal research, writing, and advocacy class of approximately 25 students. One-half of SMU's upper-division courses have fewer than 25 students, and over three-fourths have fewer than 50 students.

SMU's rich upper-division curricular offerings, with over 150 upper-division courses per year, offer students a wide range of courses and the freedom to tailor a program of study that furthers their professional and personal goals. With traditional strengths in business, litigation, tax, and international law, the curriculum extends to many areas, including intellectual property, health care, environmental, and family law.

SMU's tax, international, and general LLM programs are intended to enhance careers in the private practice of law, teaching, and public service by providing the opportunity for students who already have their basic law degree to increase their understanding of legal theory and policies. The LLM program in Comparative and International Law is the largest graduate program, enrolling approximately 40 students from about 20 countries each year. SMU has over 1,300 international alumni from over 70 countries, including many who hold significant positions in major international corporations, in the highest courts of their nations, and in other key government and private entities.

■ Public Service

All students are required to perform 30 hours of public service prior to graduation. This model public-service program not only allows the student to learn in a hands-on setting, but also provides an early exposure to pro bono practice, which is integral to the US legal system. SMU professors voluntarily hold themselves to this same requirement.

■ Externships and Clinics

Externships offer students the opportunity to work at a government agency for up to two hours of course credit. Popular externships include those with the US Attorney, the SEC, and the EPA.

Clinics offer students an opportunity to engage in the practice of law for up to five hours of course credit. Currently SMU has five clinical programs: civil litigation, criminal defense, criminal prosecution, tax, and child advocacy.

■ Overseas Study

SMU offers students an opportunity to study law for six weeks at University College at Oxford University in England.

■ Admission

SMU looks for excellent, well-rounded students with strong academic backgrounds and life experiences and perspectives that will enrich its educational community. Each application is considered in its entirety: LSAT score, undergraduate performance, graduate studies, work experience, activities, a personal statement, and letters of recommendation are all read and evaluated. Applications can be downloaded from the web.

■ Student Activities and Law Reviews

Students are able to enhance their legal education by participating in numerous programs and conferences sponsored by various faculty and student groups and centers. Selected law students serve on five major journals for which they receive academic credit. Law students are able to expand their legal education experience through participating in over 20 moot court, trial advocacy, client counseling, and negotiation competitions held at the local, regional, national, and international level and by becoming active members in over 25 student organizations.

■ Scholarships

SMU provides approximately 50 percent of its entering class with scholarship assistance. SMU law scholarships, including three full-tuition Hutchison scholarships, are awarded on the basis of the admission application, including the applicant's answer to an optional question

(question 15 on the application). In addition, two private foundations, the Hatton W. Sumners Foundation and the Dallas Bar Foundation, fund and select five to nine additional full-tuition scholarships per entering class. Both foundations require a separate scholarship application available from the SMU Admissions Office. The Sarah T. Hughes Scholarships are awarded to outstanding minority applicants. The Sumners Scholars are selected from a competitive pool of applicants with strong academics and extracurricular activities. Both foundations require that the SMU application, the respective scholarship application, and all supporting documents be submitted no later than February 15. The law firm of Haynes and Boone, LLP also awards scholarships to two exceptional minority students. A separate scholarship application is due by June 30.

■ Career Services and Bar Passage

SMU provides students with job placement assistance throughout their legal careers. The Career Services Office helps students develop their job search and career development skills and partners with students in locating summer and permanent job opportunities.

SMU graduates fare very well in the legal market. Within nine months of graduation, 93.5 percent of the class of 2003 was employed. They had an average starting salary of $81,100 in the private sector and an average starting salary of $72,700 overall.

In July 2003, over 92 percent of SMU first-time test takers passed the Texas Bar Exam, while the average bar passage rate in Texas was less than 83 percent.

Applicant Profile

SMU Dedman School of Law
This grid includes only applicants who earned 120-180 LSAT scores under standard administrations.

LSAT Score	3.75 +		3.50 - 3.74		3.25 - 3.49		3.00 - 3.24		2.75 - 2.99		2.50 - 2.74		2.25 - 2.49		2.00 - 2.24		Below 2.00		No GPA		Total	
	Apps	Adm	Apps	Adm	Apps	Adm	Apps	Adm	Apps	Adm	Apps	Adm	Apps	Adm	Apps	Adm	Apps	Adm	Apps	Adm	Apps	Adm
175-180	0	0	1	1	0	0	1	1	1	1	0	0	0	0	1	0	0	0	0	0	4	3
170-174	4	4	4	4	2	2	7	7	0	0	1	1	2	1	0	0	0	0	0	0	20	19
165-169	31	31	21	21	23	22	21	21	16	13	6	5	4	2	2	1	0	0	3	3	127	119
160-164	96	77	89	41	82	27	77	29	54	19	33	9	12	2	1	0	1	0	2	0	447	204
155-159	106	47	166	26	180	14	166	11	78	2	44	3	14	0	4	0	1	0	9	3	768	106
150-154	77	28	152	22	189	9	166	6	84	0	69	3	20	0	5	0	4	0	10	1	776	69
145-149	34	13	59	9	72	4	94	1	55	0	48	1	25	1	13	0	1	0	13	0	414	29
140-144	10	1	25	0	58	0	44	1	52	0	44	0	18	0	12	0	4	0	12	3	279	5
135-139	4	0	6	0	9	0	18	0	13	0	16	0	13	0	4	0	0	0	6	0	89	0
130-134	1	0	1	0	2	0	4	0	2	0	6	0	3	0	3	0	0	0	6	0	28	0
125-129	0	0	0	0	0	0	0	0	2	0	2	0	1	0	1	0	0	0	1	0	7	0
120-124	0	0	0	0	0	0	0	0	0	0	0	0	0	0	0	0	0	0	1	0	1	0
Total	363	201	524	124	617	78	598	77	357	35	269	22	112	6	46	1	11	0	63	10	2960	554

Apps = Number of Applicants
Adm = Number Admitted
Reflects 99% of the total applicant pool.

University of South Carolina School of Law

701 South Main Street
Columbia, SC 29201
Phone: 803.777.6605; Fax: 803.777.7751
E-mail: usclaw@law.law.sc.edu; Website: www.law.sc.edu

ABA
Approved
Since
1925

The Basics

Type of school	Public
Term	Semester
Application deadline	4/15
Application fee	$60
Financial aid deadline	4/15
Can first year start other than fall?	No
Student to faculty ratio (fall)	20.8 to 1
Does the university offer:	
housing restricted to law students?	No
graduate housing for which law students are eligible?	Yes

Faculty and Administrators

	Total		Men		Women		Minorities	
	Fall	Spr	Fall	Spr	Fall	Spr	Fall	Spr
Full-time	33	34	28	30	5	4	2	2
Other Full-time	1	1	1	1	0	0	0	0
Deans, librarians, & others who teach	5	5	4	4	1	1	1	1
Part-time	0	0	0	0	0	0	0	0
Total	39	40	33	35	6	5	3	3

Curriculum

		Full-time	Part-time
Typical first-year section size		75	0
Is there typically a "small section" of the first-year class, other than Legal Writing, taught by full-time faculty		No	No
If yes, typical size offered last year		0	0
# of classroom course titles beyond 1st year curriculum		99	
# of upper division courses, excluding seminars with an enrollment:	Under 25	48	
	25-49	23	
	50-74	22	
	75-99	16	
	100+	4	
# of seminars		10	
# of seminar positions available		174	
# of seminar positions filled		167	0
# of positions available in simulation courses		305	
# of simulation positions filled		305	0
# of positions available in faculty supervised clinical courses		52	
# of faculty supervised clinical positions filled		44	0
# involved in field placements		9	0
# involved in law journals		183	0
# involved in moot court or trial competitions		22	0
# of credit hours required to graduate		90	

JD Enrollment and Ethnicity

	Men		Women		Full-time		Part-time		1st-year		Total		JD Degs. Awd.
	#	%	#	%	#	%	#	%	#	%	#	%	
African Amer.	25	6.0	25	7.4	50	6.7	0	0.0	19	7.9	50	6.6	12
Amer. Indian	0	0.0	0	0.0	0	0.0	0	0.0	0	0.0	0	0.0	0
Asian Amer.	1	0.2	3	0.9	4	0.5	0	0.0	2	0.8	4	0.5	1
Mex. Amer.	0	0.0	0	0.0	0	0.0	0	0.0	0	0.0	0	0.0	0
Puerto Rican	0	0.0	0	0.0	0	0.0	0	0.0	0	0.0	0	0.0	0
Hispanic	4	1.0	5	1.5	9	1.2	0	0.0	2	0.8	9	1.2	1
Total Minority	30	7.2	33	9.8	63	8.4	0	0.0	23	9.5	63	8.4	14
For. Nation.	0	0.0	0	0.0	0	0.0	0	0.0	0	0.0	0	0.0	2
Caucasian	378	90.6	297	88.1	672	89.5	3	100.0	212	88.0	675	89.5	222
Unknown	9	2.2	7	2.1	16	2.1	0	0.0	6	2.5	16	2.1	1
Total	417	55.3	337	44.7	751	99.6	3	0.4	241	32.0	754		239

Tuition and Fees

	Resident	Nonresident
Full-time	$14,288	$28,704
Part-time	$606	$1,206

Living Expenses

Estimated living expenses for singles

Living on campus	Living off campus	Living at home
$13,358	$13,358	$7,365

University of South Carolina School of Law

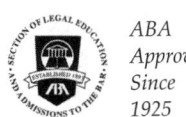

ABA
Approved
Since
1925

GPA and LSAT Scores

	Total	Full-time	Part-time
# of apps	1,612	1,612	0
# of admits	480	480	0
# of matrics	238	238	0
75% GPA	0.00	3.70	0.00
25% GPA	0.00	3.22	0.00
75% LSAT	0	160	0
25% LSAT	0	156	0

Grants and Scholarships (from prior year)

	Total		Full-time		Part-time	
	#	%	#	%	#	%
Total # of students	739		739		0	
Total # receiving grants	109	14.7	109	14.7	0	0.0
Less than 1/2 tuition	75	10.1	75	10.1	0	0.0
Half to full tuition	31	4.2	31	4.2	0	0.0
Full tuition	3	0.4	3	0.4	0	0.0
More than full tuition	0	0.0	0	0.0	0	0.0
Median grant amount			$3,000		$0	

Informational and Library Resources

# of volumes and volume equivalents	503,365
# of titles	76,522
# of active serial subscriptions	3,436
Study seating capacity inside the library	606
# of professional librarians	4
Hours per week library is open	111
# of open, wired connections available to students	52
# of networked computers available for use by students	56
# of simultaneous wireless users	700
Require computer?	N

JD Attrition (from prior year)

	Academic	Other	Total	
	#	#	#	%
1st year	1	6	7	2.9%
2nd year	0	6	6	2.5%
3rd year	0	1	1	0.4%
4th year	0	0	0	0.0%

Employment

	Total	Percentage
Employment status known	214	97.7
Employment status unknown	5	2.3
Employed	200	93.5
Pursuing graduate degrees	10	4.7
Unemployed seeking employment	2	0.9
Unemployed not seeking employment	2	0.9

Type of Employment

	Total	Percentage
# employed in law firms	114	57.0
# employed in business and industry	10	5.0
# employed in government	22	11.0
# employed in public interest	2	1.0
# employed as judicial clerks	52	26.0
# employed in academia	0	0.0

Geographic Location

	Total	Percentage
# employed in state	170	85.0
# employed in foreign countries	3	1.5
# of states where employed	14	

Bar Passage Rates

Jurisdiction	South Carolina			North Carolina		
Exam	Sum 03	Win 04	Total	Sum 03	Win 04	Total
# from school taking bar for the first time	183	18	201	11	0	11
School's pass rate for all first-time takers	81%	89%	82%	82%		82%
State's pass rate for all first-time takers	78%	76%	78%	78%	64%	76%

University of South Carolina School of Law

701 South Main Street
Columbia, SC 29201
Phone: 803.777.6605; Fax: 803.777.7751
E-mail: usclaw@law.law.sc.edu; Website: www.law.sc.edu

■ Introduction

The University of South Carolina School of Law, established in 1867, is located in Columbia, SC. With a metropolitan population of more than 450,000, Columbia combines the advantages of a progressive, growing area with the pace of a smaller city. The School of Law is located two blocks from the state capitol building. As the seat of state government, the SC Supreme Court, the State Court of Appeals, federal district court, and criminal, civil, and special jurisdiction courts meet in Columbia. There are also numerous law firms in proximity of the law school. Situated in the center of the state, there is easy access to the mountains and the coast. The School of Law enjoys the unique advantage of being the only law school in South Carolina that is accredited by the ABA. The School of Law has been a member of the Association of American Law Schools since 1924.

■ Library and Physical Facilities

Since its founding, the School of Law has provided excellent preparation for students of the law. The curriculum combines traditional teaching methods and courses with modern, state-of-the-art studies. The School of Law houses a major research library with a collection of about 450,000 volumes and extensive computer-assisted research capabilities including LexisNexis, Westlaw, Loislaw, Dialog, RLIN, OCLC, and USCAN, the online card catalog. The library also includes the SC Legal History Collection. A well-trained staff of librarians provides assistance and instruction in research and reference techniques. The library is open more than 111 hours per week and for extended hours during the examination period. The computer lab and two electronic resource learning centers are also located within the library. Individual closed study carrels are available for assignment to students, and larger study rooms and open carrels are also available for students.

The School of Law offers a full-time only day program leading to the Juris Doctor degree. In order to earn the JD, a student must successfully complete 90 semester hours of coursework. In each semester, a student must register for a minimum of 12 credit hours. The School of Law offers one 7-week summer session each year.

In addition to all first-year courses, students are required to take Constitutional Law II, criminal procedures, professional responsibility, and a perspectives course, and satisfy an upper-level writing requirement. The School of Law offers advanced courses that allow detailed study in corporate and commercial law, tax and estate planning, and litigation. The peer-assistance tutoring program provides academic support to first-year students, and a mentoring program pairs a first-year student with an upper-class student. Every effort is made to assist students in succeeding academically.

■ Dual-Degree Programs

The School of Law, in cooperation with other graduate programs at USC, currently offers dual JD and master's degrees in the following: international master of business administration (IMBA), human resource management, accounting, economics, public administration, criminal justice, social work, earth and environmental resource management, and health administration.

The USC School of Law and Vermont Law School offer a dual degree in environmental law. Students earn a JD from USC and a Master of Studies in Environmental Law (MSEL) degree from Vermont Law School.

■ Special Programs

The School of Law recognizes that experiential learning in the area of professional skills is essential to a well-rounded legal education. Under special court rule, third-year law students in South Carolina may represent clients and appear in court when enrolled in a clinical legal education course. The clinical education program offers courses designed to develop critical lawyering skills. The program offers training in trial advocacy, interviewing, counseling, negotiation, alternative dispute resolution, and legal drafting. Clinics include environmental law, criminal practice, juvenile justice, domestic practice, bankruptcy, and federal litigation. Judicial internships place students with trial and appellate court judges.

The Pro Bono Program, one of the longest operating programs of its type, has an outstanding national and local reputation. Under the leadership of a full-time director and a student board, the program offers students an opportunity to be involved in activities such as income tax assistance, Habitat for Humanity, and legal research.

The National Judicial Advocacy Center and the National College of District Attorneys are located on the USC campus. The Advocacy Center, operated by the US Department of Justice, provides intensive training to approximately 15,000 federal prosecutors and attorneys from across the country. The National College of District Attorneys provides training to nearly 2,000 prosecutors.

■ Admission

The School of Law seeks to enroll qualified students who will enhance and embrace the school's rigorous educational environment and, as graduates, make positive societal contributions to South Carolina, the region, and the nation. In making decisions, the Faculty Committee on Admissions employs a holistic approach, taking into account all information available about each candidate. No single factor is conclusive. While undergraduate GPA and the Law School Admission Test (LSAT) are emphasized, the committee's decision is also influenced by other factors including the applicant's personal statement, employment or other life experience, residency, letters of recommendation, and contribution to a diverse educational environment.

■ Student Activities

The School of Law publishes the *South Carolina Law Review*; the *ABA Real Property, Probate, and Trust Journal*; and the *Environmental Law Journal*. Moot court teams are sponsored in the national, international, ABA, and labor law competitions. Students who have obtained high academic achievement are eligible for membership in the Order of the Coif, a national legal honorary society, and the Order of Wig and Robe, a local scholastic organization founded in 1935. Other student organizations include the Student Bar Association, Black Law Students Association, Women in Law, Christian Legal Society, and the Environmental Law Society.

■ Expenses and Financial Aid

While most students will depend on federal student loans to finance a legal education, the School of Law does offer both merit- and need-based scholarships. Candidates who want to be considered for the merit scholarships should submit their applications in early December and the file must be complete by February 1. The application to law school is the application for merit scholarships.

■ Office of Career Services

The Office of Career Services serves as liaison between students and legal employers and offers services to equip students with the skills and information necessary for a successful employment search. The Office of Career Services uses E-Attorney/OCI+. Services available include individual counseling, résumé writing and interviewing seminars, on-campus interviews, and participation in job fairs. The School of Law regularly participates in the Southeastern Law Placement Consortium in Atlanta, GA; the Mid-Atlantic Recruiting Conference in Washington, DC; the Southeastern Minority Job Fair; the Patent Law Interview Program; the Atlanta Legal Hiring Conference; and the National Public Interest Career Fair.

Applicant Profile

University of South Carolina School of Law
This grid includes only applicants who earned 120-180 LSAT scores under standard administrations.

LSAT Score	3.75 + Apps	Adm	3.50 - 3.74 Apps	Adm	3.25 - 3.49 Apps	Adm	3.00 - 3.24 Apps	Adm	2.75 - 2.99 Apps	Adm	2.50 - 2.74 Apps	Adm	2.25 - 2.49 Apps	Adm	2.00 - 2.24 Apps	Adm	Below 2.00 Apps	Adm	No GPA Apps	Adm	Total Apps	Adm
175-180	0	0	0	0	0	0	0	0	0	0	0	0	0	0	0	0	0	0	0	0	0	0
170-174	5	5	2	1	1	1	0	0	2	2	0	0	0	0	0	0	0	0	0	0	10	9
165-169	9	9	10	9	10	10	6	4	4	4	6	4	3	2	2	0	0	0	1	0	48	42
160-164	27	26	64	62	38	34	34	31	16	11	9	2	15	0	6	0	2	0	3	0	197	167
155-159	53	45	81	51	115	60	89	28	47	8	23	1	13	1	7	0	3	0	2	0	431	192
150-154	49	13	102	12	120	12	89	4	67	6	23	0	16	0	2	0	7	1	2	0	475	49
145-149	22	2	50	6	53	4	44	3	38	0	23	0	16	0	2	0	1	0	2	0	257	16
140-144	8	1	20	2	19	0	24	0	19	0	14	0	9	0	3	0	1	0	0	0	119	3
135-139	0	0	4	0	3	0	10	0	12	0	8	0	7	0	0	0	0	0	0	0	44	0
130-134	1	0	2	0	1	0	7	0	7	0	1	0	3	0	3	0	1	0	0	0	26	0
125-129	0	0	0	0	0	0	2	0	0	0	0	0	1	0	0	0	0	0	1	0	4	0
120-124	0	0	0	0	0	0	0	0	0	0	0	0	0	0	0	0	0	0	0	0	0	0
Total	174	101	335	143	360	121	305	70	212	31	104	7	73	4	23	0	9	0	16	1	1611	478

Apps = Number of Applicants
Adm = Number Admitted
Reflects 99% of the total applicant pool.

The University of South Dakota School of Law

414 E Clark
Vermillion, SD 57069-2390
Phone: 605.677.5443; Fax: 605.677.5417
E-mail: lawreq@usd.edu; Website: www.usd.edu/law

ABA
Approved
Since
1923

The Basics

Type of school	Public
Term	Semester
Application deadline	3/1
Application fee	$35
Financial aid deadline	3/1
Can first year start other than fall?	No
Student to faculty ratio (fall)	17.4 to 1
Does the university offer:	
housing restricted to law students?	No
graduate housing for which law students are eligible?	Yes

Faculty and Administrators

	Total		Men		Women		Minorities	
	Fall	Spr	Fall	Spr	Fall	Spr	Fall	Spr
Full-time	12	11	10	9	2	2	0	0
Other Full-time	3	3	2	2	1	1	0	0
Deans, librarians, & others who teach	2	3	2	3	0	0	0	0
Part-time	1	1	1	1	0	0	0	0
Total	18	18	15	15	3	3	0	0

Curriculum

	Full-time	Part-time
Typical first-year section size	91	0
Is there typically a "small section" of the first-year class, other than Legal Writing, taught by full-time faculty	Yes	No
If yes, typical size offered last year	46	0
# of classroom course titles beyond 1st year curriculum	41	

# of upper division courses, excluding seminars with an enrollment:		
	Under 25	23
	25-49	12
	50-74	9
	75-99	2
	100+	0

# of seminars	0	
# of seminar positions available	0	
# of seminar positions filled	0	0
# of positions available in simulation courses	193	
# of simulation positions filled	190	0
# of positions available in faculty supervised clinical courses	0	
# of faculty supervised clinical positions filled	0	0
# involved in field placements	17	0
# involved in law journals	39	0
# involved in moot court or trial competitions	35	0
# of credit hours required to graduate	90	

JD Enrollment and Ethnicity

	Men		Women		Full-time		Part-time		1st-year		Total		JD Degs. Awd.
	#	%	#	%	#	%	#	%	#	%	#	%	
African Amer.	0	0.0	1	0.9	1	0.4	0	0.0	0	0.0	1	0.4	1
Amer. Indian	2	1.4	2	1.8	4	1.6	0	0.0	1	1.3	4	1.6	3
Asian Amer.	4	2.8	1	0.9	5	2.0	0	0.0	1	1.3	5	2.0	0
Mex. Amer.	0	0.0	1	0.9	1	0.4	0	0.0	0	0.0	1	0.4	0
Puerto Rican	0	0.0	0	0.0	0	0.0	0	0.0	0	0.0	0	0.0	0
Hispanic	2	1.4	2	1.8	4	1.6	0	0.0	1	1.3	4	1.6	1
Total Minority	8	5.7	7	6.4	15	6.0	0	0.0	3	4.0	15	6.0	5
For. Nation.	2	1.4	0	0.0	2	0.8	0	0.0	0	0.0	2	0.8	0
Caucasian	131	92.9	103	93.6	231	93.1	3	100.0	72	96.0	234	93.2	71
Unknown	0	0.0	0	0.0	0	0.0	0	0.0	0	0.0	0	0.0	0
Total	141	56.2	110	43.8	248	98.8	3	1.2	75	29.9	251		76

Tuition and Fees

	Resident	Nonresident
Full-time	$7,498	$15,230
Part-time	$3,749	$7,615

Living Expenses

Estimated living expenses for singles

Living on campus	Living off campus	Living at home
$8,200	$11,354	$8,200

The University of South Dakota School of Law

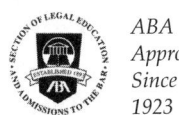

*ABA
Approved
Since
1923*

GPA and LSAT Scores

	Total	Full-time	Part-time
# of apps	469	469	0
# of admits	169	169	0
# of matrics	73	73	0
75% GPA	0.00	3.65	0.00
25% GPA	0.00	2.93	0.00
75% LSAT	0	156	0
25% LSAT	0	150	0

Grants and Scholarships (from prior year)

	Total		Full-time		Part-time	
	#	%	#	%	#	%
Total # of students	255		250		5	
Total # receiving grants	61	23.9	61	24.4	0	0.0
Less than 1/2 tuition	55	21.6	55	22.0	0	0.0
Half to full tuition	2	0.8	2	0.8	0	0.0
Full tuition	3	1.2	3	1.2	0	0.0
More than full tuition	1	0.4	1	0.4	0	0.0
Median grant amount			$0		$0	

Informational and Library Resources

# of volumes and volume equivalents	202,427
# of titles	40,548
# of active serial subscriptions	1,856
Study seating capacity inside the library	227
# of professional librarians	6
Hours per week library is open	168
# of open, wired connections available to students	227
# of networked computers available for use by students	37
# of simultaneous wireless users	0
Require computer?	N

JD Attrition (from prior year)

	Academic	Other	Total	
	#	#	#	%
1st year	0	4	4	4.3%
2nd year	0	0	0	0.0%
3rd year	0	0	0	0.0%
4th year	0	0	0	0.0%

Employment

	Total	Percentage
Employment status known	52	100.0
Employment status unknown	0	0.0
Employed	44	84.6
Pursuing graduate degrees	2	3.8
Unemployed seeking employment	5	9.6
Unemployed not seeking employment	1	1.9

Type of Employment

# employed in law firms	17	38.6
# employed in business and industry	1	2.3
# employed in government	10	22.7
# employed in public interest	0	0.0
# employed as judicial clerks	15	34.1
# employed in academia	0	0.0

Geographic Location

# employed in state	37	84.1
# employed in foreign countries	0	0.0
# of states where employed		6

Bar Passage Rates

Jurisdiction	South Dakota		
Exam	Sum 03	Win 04	Total
# from school taking bar for the first time	43	9	52
School's pass rate for all first-time takers	74%	67%	73%
State's pass rate for all first-time takers	79%	67%	76%

The University of South Dakota School of Law

414 E Clark
Vermillion, SD 57069-2390
Phone: 605.677.5443; Fax: 605.677.5417
E-mail: lawreq@usd.edu; Website: www.usd.edu/law

■ Introduction

The School of Law, located on the university campus in Vermillion, is noted for its contributions in training distinguished leaders for the bench, the bar, and the lawmaking bodies of the state and region. Founded in 1901, the school is accredited by the ABA and is an AALS member. The city of Vermillion, with a population of approximately 10,000, provides a small-town atmosphere for students, faculty, and staff.

■ Library and Physical Facilities

The three-story McKusick Law Library is equipped to meet the research needs of students, faculty, and members of the bar. Students, staff, and faculty have access to the law school facility 7 days a week, 24 hours a day through swipe-card access. It is South Dakota's largest and most complete law library, providing essential research services to the courts, legislature, government agencies, lawyers, private citizens, and students conducting interdisciplinary research. The book and microform collections include court reports, statutes, and other legal authorities.

The School of Law building, completed in 1981, has received national recognition for its design. The law school's balconied courtroom, situated in the middle of the building, is the architectural focal point within the law school. The courtroom is fully wired with state-of-the-art videoconferencing technologies and has an adjoining audiovisual control room and Judges' Chambers. The building also contains two large classrooms, two smaller classrooms, a computer laboratory, a student lounge and locker area, and suites of offices for faculty, administration, and student organizations. The law school building is equipped for wireless network connectivity. The student organization suites contain study carrels for member use. The law library has 227 study seats, including 166 carrels assigned to members of the student body.

■ Curriculum

Ninety semester credits are required for the JD degree. The first-year curriculum is required of all students. In the second and third years, electives are available in addition to required courses. During the summer, an externship program is offered for six credit hours. Externs learn by doing under the close supervision of an attorney and the externship director. Skills training is also available to second- and third-year students in the trial techniques course, negotiations, and other courses, each of which utilizes to the fullest extent the technological capabilities of the law school.

■ Special Programs

- Joint-degree Programs—There are nine programs with other graduate departments, with master's degrees available in professional accountancy, business administration, history, English, psychology, education administration, political science, public administration, and administrative studies. Students may transfer nine hours of approved interdisciplinary coursework for JD credit and must complete both programs in three years.

- Interdisciplinary Study—For upper-division students not in a joint-degree program, up to six graduate credits in other university divisions may be taken and applied toward the hours required for the JD degree. This allows a law student to broaden his or her education by the pursuit of new disciplines.

- Curricular Emphases—Two areas of emphasis are identified. Instruction in these areas is informally structured and encompasses curricular, cocurricular, and extracurricular opportunities for enhancement. Emphasis is offered in environmental and natural resources law, as well as Indian law.

- Flex-time Program—This program permits certain well-qualified students to take less than the normal load of credits each semester and obtain a JD in five years instead of three. The program admits a limited number of students who could not attend law school on a full-time basis. The law school does not offer evening or weekend courses.

- Accelerated Admission—An applicant may apply for accelerated admission, and be admitted to and enroll in law school without final completion of the requirements for the applicant's undergraduate degree. The undergraduate degree must be attained by the applicant prior to graduation from law school.

- Law Honors Scholars Program—High school seniors who are accepted as USD undergraduate Honors Scholars may apply for and receive provisional (automatic) admission to the law school upon successful completion of their undergraduate degree in four years with a 3.5 GPA, fulfillment of Honors Program requirements, and completion of the LSAT for statistical purposes only.

- Summer Screening Program—Applicants who are not regularly admitted may be invited to participate in the Summer Screening Program. The program consists of two courses, agency and personal property, offered in five weeks of lecture and finals during the sixth week. Participants are admitted or denied admission on the basis of their performance on final exams, which are graded anonymously.

The University of South Dakota School of Law

■ Student Activities

The *South Dakota Law Review* publishes articles by legal scholars, lawyers, jurists, and students three times a year. The *Great Plains Natural Resources Journal* publishes articles on environmental law and natural resources law topics. Other cocurricular activities include a Moot Court Board, Client Counseling and Negotiations Board, and Trial Advocacy teams. Boards successfully compete at the intramural, regional, and national levels. The school is active in the Law Student Division of the ABA. Other organizations include Women in Law, Native American Law Students Association, Black Law Students Association, Christian Legal Society, Environmental Law Society, International Law Students Association, Law School Democrats, Federalist Society, Delta Theta Phi, Phi

Alpha Delta, Phi Delta Phi, R.D. Hurd Pro Bono Society (pro bono legal work under the supervision of legal services attorneys in surrounding communities and reservations), and the South Dakota Innocence Project.

■ Career Services

The placement opportunities for third-year law students are excellent in South Dakota, the surrounding areas, and throughout the United States. Approximately 34 percent of the graduates are placed in judicial clerkships, and one-fourth are employed outside South Dakota. The law school has an active program to place first- and second-year students in summer internship programs with law firms.

Applicant Profile

The University of South Dakota School of Law

LSAT Score	GPA								
	3.75 +	3.50 - 3.74	3.25 - 3.49	3.00 - 3.24	2.75 - 2.99	2.50 - 2.74	2.25 - 2.49	2.00 - 2.24	- 2.00
165 +									
160-164									
155-159									
150-154									
145-149									
140-144									
- 140									

▨ Good Possibility   ▨ Possible   ☐ Unlikely

USD School of Law considers many factors beyond LSAT score and GPA. This chart should be used only as a general rule.

For Fall 2004:

Applicants:	479
Completed applications:	469
Regularly admitted:	154
Accepted from Summer Screening or PLSI:	15
Total accepted:	169
Matriculated full-time:	73

75th/25th percentile for the 154 regular admits:
LSAT: 157/151
GPA: 3.75/3.03

South Texas College of Law

1303 San Jacinto Street
Houston, TX 77002-7000
Phone: 713.659.8040; Fax: 713.646.2906
E-mail: admissions@stcl.edu; Website: www.stcl.edu

ABA
Approved
Since
1959

The Basics

Type of school	Private
Term	Semester
Application deadline	2/25 10/1
Application fee	$50
Financial aid deadline	5/1 10/1
Can first year start other than fall?	Yes
Student to faculty ratio (fall)	20.0 to 1
Does the university offer:	
housing restricted to law students?	No
graduate housing for which law students are eligible?	No

Faculty and Administrators

	Total		Men		Women		Minorities	
	Fall	Spr	Fall	Spr	Fall	Spr	Fall	Spr
Full-time	48	43	32	29	16	14	4	4
Other Full-time	1	0	1	0	0	0	0	0
Deans, librarians, & others who teach	7	7	4	4	3	3	2	2
Part-time	47	37	36	26	11	11	4	5
Total	103	87	73	59	30	28	10	11

Curriculum

		Full-time	Part-time
Typical first-year section size		90	60
Is there typically a "small section" of the first-year class, other than Legal Writing, taught by full-time faculty		No	No
If yes, typical size offered last year		0	0
# of classroom course titles beyond 1st year curriculum		125	
# of upper division courses, excluding seminars with an enrollment:	Under 25	91	
	25-49	48	
	50-74	23	
	75-99	34	
	100+	4	
# of seminars		32	
# of seminar positions available		640	
# of seminar positions filled		104	313
# of positions available in simulation courses		724	
# of simulation positions filled		349	375
# of positions available in faculty supervised clinical courses		42	
# of faculty supervised clinical positions filled		32	10
# involved in field placements		144	46
# involved in law journals		228	72
# involved in moot court or trial competitions		68	21
# of credit hours required to graduate		90	

JD Enrollment and Ethnicity

	Men		Women		Full-time		Part-time		1st-year		Total		JD Degs. Awd.
	#	%	#	%	#	%	#	%	#	%	#	%	
African Amer.	19	2.8	39	6.7	21	2.2	37	12.5	30	4.6	58	4.6	30
Amer. Indian	5	0.7	3	0.5	6	0.6	2	0.7	2	0.3	8	0.6	1
Asian Amer.	51	7.6	46	7.9	73	7.6	24	8.1	61	9.3	97	7.7	23
Mex. Amer.	35	5.2	23	4.0	44	4.6	14	4.7	25	3.8	58	4.6	29
Puerto Rican	4	0.6	1	0.2	3	0.3	2	0.7	2	0.3	5	0.4	0
Hispanic	27	4.0	28	4.8	44	4.6	11	3.7	29	4.4	55	4.4	16
Total Minority	141	21.0	140	24.1	191	19.9	90	30.4	149	22.8	281	22.4	99
For. Nation.	1	0.1	0	0.0	1	0.1	0	0.0	1	0.2	1	0.1	1
Caucasian	530	78.9	442	75.9	766	80.0	206	69.6	504	77.1	972	77.5	283
Unknown	0	0.0	0	0.0	0	0.0	0	0.0	0	0.0	0	0.0	0
Total	672	53.6	582	46.4	958	76.4	296	23.6	654	52.2	1254		383

Tuition and Fees

	Resident	Nonresident
Full-time	$19,770	$19,770
Part-time	$13,380	$13,380

Living Expenses

Estimated living expenses for singles

Living on campus	Living off campus	Living at home
N/A	$14,382	$10,158

South Texas College of Law

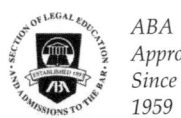

ABA
Approved
Since
1959

GPA and LSAT Scores

	Total	Full-time	Part-time
# of apps	3,188	2,808	380
# of admits	984	863	121
# of matrics	415	348	67
75% GPA	3.49	3.50	3.42
25% GPA	3.03	3.04	3.01
75% LSAT	156	157	156
25% LSAT	151	152	151

Grants and Scholarships (from prior year)

	Total		Full-time		Part-time	
	#	%	#	%	#	%
Total # of students	1,289		949		340	
Total # receiving grants	431	33.4	336	35.4	95	27.9
Less than 1/2 tuition	406	31.5	318	33.5	88	25.9
Half to full tuition	20	1.6	15	1.6	5	1.5
Full tuition	4	0.3	2	0.2	2	0.6
More than full tuition	1	0.1	1	0.1	0	0.0
Median grant amount			$1,543		$1,079	

Informational and Library Resources

# of volumes and volume equivalents	485,404
# of titles	79,719
# of active serial subscriptions	4,326
Study seating capacity inside the library	849
# of professional librarians	10
Hours per week library is open	103
# of open, wired connections available to students	1,017
# of networked computers available for use by students	100
# of simultaneous wireless users	100
Require computer?	N

JD Attrition (from prior year)

	Academic	Other	Total	
	#	#	#	%
1st year	41	41	82	12.7%
2nd year	7	6	13	3.7%
3rd year	1	2	3	1.3%
4th year	0	0	0	0.0%

Employment

	Total	Percentage
Employment status known	304	94.4
Employment status unknown	18	5.6
Employed	249	81.9
Pursuing graduate degrees	6	2.0
Unemployed seeking employment	45	14.8
Unemployed not seeking employment	4	1.3

Type of Employment

# employed in law firms	179	71.9
# employed in business and industry	26	10.4
# employed in government	27	10.8
# employed in public interest	3	1.2
# employed as judicial clerks	9	3.6
# employed in academia	1	0.4

Geographic Location

# employed in state	240	96.4
# employed in foreign countries	0	0.0
# of states where employed	6	

Bar Passage Rates

Jurisdiction	Texas		
Exam	Sum 03	Win 04	Total
# from school taking bar for the first time	249	98	347
School's pass rate for all first-time takers	78%	60%	73%
State's pass rate for all first-time takers	83%	69%	80%

South Texas College of Law

1303 San Jacinto Street
Houston, TX 77002-7000
Phone: 713.659.8040; Fax: 713.646.2906
E-mail: admissions@stcl.edu; Website: www.stcl.edu

■ Introduction

South Texas College of Law, situated at the very core of Houston's vibrant downtown legal and financial centers, is a private, nonprofit, independent law school founded in 1923. South Texas is the oldest law school in Houston and one of the largest in the nation, accredited by the American Bar Association and a member of the AALS. The college offers full- and part-time programs leading to the Doctor of Jurisprudence degree.

■ Admission

Students are admitted to STCL both in the fall and spring semesters. Admission application deadlines are February 25 for fall consideration and October 1 for spring. Early application is encouraged. A bachelor's degree is required as well as taking the LSAT and registering with LSDAS.

Students are admitted primarily on the basis of their LSAT score and undergraduate GPA. However, a significant percentage of each incoming class is selected on the basis of additional factors. Every attempt is made to evaluate each applicant as an individual, a prospective student, and a future professional.

■ Curriculum

The curriculum at South Texas combines traditional classroom instruction with a broad range of innovative simulated and clinical courses. The college offers a class scheduling system whereby students may select convenient class times rather than having to choose between day and evening divisions. To accommodate part-time working students, a complete curriculum of classes is scheduled after 5:30 PM, with a few classes also scheduled on Saturdays.

For students interested in the increased globalization of law, South Texas offers a variety of foreign programs throughout the year. Two ABA-approved cooperative exchange programs allow students to study for a semester in The Netherlands and Denmark. Summer programs are offered in Valletta, Malta; London, England; Istanbul, Turkey; Galway, Ireland; Durham, England; Prague, Czech Republic; and Cuernavaca, Mexico.

■ Special Programs

Development of strong legal and advocacy skills is important at South Texas, evidenced by its various institutes and its skills and clinical programs.

The Frank Evans Center for Conflict Resolution promotes conflict resolution outside the traditional litigation system, fostering opportunities for students to develop skills in alternative dispute resolution procedures.

The Law Institute for Medical Studies places students in corporate counsel offices of major hospitals where they confront issues facing the contemporary hospital administrator, including bioethics and labor and contract disputes.

Clinics. South Texas offers off-site clinics that place students in the real world of lawyering, including state and federal trial and appellate court chambers, prosecutors' and defenders' offices, public interest legal service providers, and state and federal government agencies. In the International Criminal Process Clinic, students work with defenders involved with the United Nations' Ad Hoc International Criminal Tribunal for the former Yugoslavia. In the General Civil Clinic, students work in an on-site clinic while providing direct representation for clients in a variety of administrative and state court settings.

Academic Assistance and Counseling. Students are encouraged to participate in the varied programs and services offered and designed to help them reach their fullest academic potential.

The **Langdell Scholar Program**, conducted by course-proficient upperclassmen, continues to benefit eligible students in mastering the framework of legal analysis, while garnering a proficiency in effective outlining, study skills, and exam-taking techniques. Students are selected into the program based on their LSAT performance, undergraduate GPA, and academic assistance diagnostic test.

Competitions—Unparalleled Achievement. South Texas is represented by student teams each year at various moot court and mock trial competitions. Since 1980, these teams have outperformed all other law school teams in the nation by winning an array of state, regional, and national championship victories.

■ Student Activities

Students at South Texas have the opportunity to become members of 28 active student organizations representing a wide range of interests.

■ Scholarly Publications

The *South Texas Law Review* is a scholarly periodical published and edited by a staff of law school students selected for membership on the basis of outstanding scholarship or writing ability. In addition, South Texas law students edit and publish *CURRENTS: International Trade Law Journal* and the *Corporate Counsel Review*.

■ Library and Physical Facilities

Recent additions to the South Texas campus ensure that students have access to and are trained with state-of-the-art tools now used in the legal profession. The T. Gerald Treece Courtroom was opened in November 2003 and houses a nine-seat judges' bench and the very latest courtroom technology available for trial attorneys. The courtroom is heavily used by the school's nationally recognized advocacy program for practice and competition. It is also available to the members of Houston's legal community, including the judiciary.

The Fred Parks Law Library encompasses more than 72,000 square feet. Each of the 780 seats in the six-story facility is wired for data and power. The building is crowned with a conference center and rooftop terrace perfect for student congregating and campus events.

The college is also the home of the First and Fourteenth Texas Courts of Appeals, distinguishing South Texas as only one of two American law schools housing appellate courts on a permanent basis.

■ Financial Assistance

South Texas offers an extensive financial aid program, in terms of both scholarships and outside funding options. Depending on qualifications, Texas residents are eligible for state and federal tuition assistance grants, which have amounted to as much as several thousand dollars in prior years. In addition, the Office of Scholarships and Financial Aid administers financial assistance through the federal work-study program, federal and private loans, and a variety of scholarship offerings. Incoming students are considered for merit scholarships based on UGPA and LSAT achievement. Continuing students are eligible for both merit- and need-based scholarships. Contact the Office of Scholarships and Financial Aid for eligibility and documentation requirements (713.646.1820).

■ Career Services

In light of today's competitive job market, the Career Resources Center (CRC) continues providing its students and graduates with the edge and direction needed to succeed. The CRC offers a full range of services to meet the current employment needs of students, while at the same time being responsive to the changes in hiring trends and patterns. The office serves as a counseling and resource center for students seeking employment on either a full- or part-time basis and assists graduates pursuing permanent employment. In addition to on-campus recruiting, the CRC also offers workshops on résumé preparation and courses on developing skills that will help in the interviewing process. The objective of the CRC staff is to aid students in exploring career options, while building valuable job search skills utilizing their strengths and abilities. For those taking advantage of the many programs and services offered by the CRC, students are afforded the luxury of taking their career planning and job search to a higher level.

Applicant Profile

South Texas College of Law
This grid includes only applicants who earned 120-180 LSAT scores under standard administrations.

LSAT Score	GPA 3.75 +		3.50 - 3.74		3.25 - 3.49		3.00 - 3.24		2.75 - 2.99		2.50 - 2.74		2.25 - 2.49		2.00 - 2.24		Below 2.00		No GPA		Total	
	Apps	Adm	Apps	Adm	Apps	Adm	Apps	Adm	Apps	Adm	Apps	Adm	Apps	Adm	Apps	Adm	Apps	Adm	Apps	Adm	Apps	Adm
170-180	0	0	2	2	0	0	0	0	2	2	0	0	0	0	0	0	0	0	0	0	4	4
165-169	3	3	4	4	4	4	8	7	1	1	2	1	3	1	1	1	0	0	0	0	26	22
160-164	9	9	17	16	19	18	24	21	27	22	20	13	9	4	1	1	0	0	0	0	126	104
155-159	25	25	60	57	69	62	93	83	65	44	45	13	27	1	2	0	1	0	0	0	387	285
150-154	41	37	99	87	143	95	167	105	117	24	108	10	44	2	20	0	1	0	10	4	750	364
145-149	34	13	63	14	131	16	159	9	127	5	97	2	42	0	17	0	2	0	15	4	687	63
140-144	11	0	36	1	63	0	105	1	87	0	93	0	34	0	21	0	3	0	10	0	463	2
Below 140	2	0	10	0	16	0	38	0	40	0	45	0	30	0	19	0	8	0	11	0	219	0
Total	125	87	291	181	445	195	594	226	466	98	410	39	189	8	81	2	15	0	46	8	2662	844

Apps = Number of Applicants
Adm = Number Admitted
Reflects 99% of the total applicant pool.

University of Southern California Law School

USC Law School, University of Southern California
Los Angeles, CA 90089-0074
Phone: 213.740.2523; Fax: 213.740.4570
E-mail: admissions@law.usc.edu; Website: www.usc.edu/law

ABA
Approved
Since
1924

The Basics

Type of school	Private
Term	Semester
Application deadline	2/1
Application fee	$70
Financial aid deadline	2/15
Can first year start other than fall?	No
Student to faculty ratio (fall)	13.1 to 1
Does the university offer:	
housing restricted to law students?	No
graduate housing for which law students are eligible?	Yes

Faculty and Administrators

	Total		Men		Women		Minorities	
	Fall	Spr	Fall	Spr	Fall	Spr	Fall	Spr
Full-time	40	38	27	26	13	12	3	3
Other Full-time	2	2	0	0	2	2	1	1
Deans, librarians, & others who teach	10	10	5	5	5	5	2	2
Part-time	54	64	34	44	20	19	11	23
Total	106	114	66	75	40	38	17	29

Curriculum

		Full-time	Part-time
Typical first-year section size		70	0
Is there typically a "small section" of the first-year class, other than Legal Writing, taught by full-time faculty		No	No
If yes, typical size offered last year		0	0
# of classroom course titles beyond 1st year curriculum		84	
# of upper division courses, excluding seminars with an enrollment:	Under 25	55	
	25-49	17	
	50-74	6	
	75-99	3	
	100+	9	
# of seminars		18	
# of seminar positions available		394	
# of seminar positions filled		198	0
# of positions available in simulation courses		341	
# of simulation positions filled		227	0
# of positions available in faculty supervised clinical courses		90	
# of faculty supervised clinical positions filled	86		0
# involved in field placements		107	0
# involved in law journals		154	0
# involved in moot court or trial competitions	71		0
# of credit hours required to graduate		88	

JD Enrollment and Ethnicity

	Men		Women		Full-time		Part-time		1st-year		Total		JD Degs. Awd.
	#	%	#	%	#	%	#	%	#	%	#	%	
African Amer.	16	4.9	39	12.9	55	8.7	0	0.0	20	9.9	55	8.7	21
Amer. Indian	0	0.0	0	0.0	0	0.0	0	0.0	0	0.0	0	0.0	0
Asian Amer.	56	17.1	77	25.5	133	21.1	0	0.0	49	24.1	133	21.1	35
Mex. Amer.	28	8.5	22	7.3	50	7.9	0	0.0	20	9.9	50	7.9	20
Puerto Rican	0	0.0	0	0.0	0	0.0	0	0.0	0	0.0	0	0.0	0
Hispanic	11	3.4	10	3.3	21	3.3	0	0.0	6	3.0	21	3.3	5
Total Minority	111	33.8	148	49.0	259	41.1	0	0.0	95	46.8	259	41.1	81
For. Nation.	1	0.3	1	0.3	2	0.3	0	0.0	1	0.5	2	0.3	1
Caucasian	182	55.5	129	42.7	311	49.4	0	0.0	85	41.9	311	49.4	118
Unknown	34	10.4	24	7.9	58	9.2	0	0.0	22	10.8	58	9.2	17
Total	328	52.1	302	47.9	630	100.0	0	0.0	203	32.2	630		217

Tuition and Fees

	Resident	Nonresident
Full-time	$36,025	$36,025
Part-time	$0	$0

Living Expenses

Estimated living expenses for singles

Living on campus	Living off campus	Living at home
$14,596	$14,596	$6,032

University of Southern California Law School

*ABA
Approved
Since
1924*

GPA and LSAT Scores

	Total	Full-time	Part-time
# of apps	7,677	7,677	0
# of admits	1,376	1,376	0
# of matrics	203	203	0
75% GPA	3.76	3.76	0.00
25% GPA	3.54	3.54	0.00
75% LSAT	167	167	0
25% LSAT	163	163	0

Grants and Scholarships (from prior year)

	Total		Full-time		Part-time	
	#	%	#	%	#	%
Total # of students	645		645		0	
Total # receiving grants	367	56.9	367	56.9	0	0.0
Less than 1/2 tuition	319	49.5	319	49.5	0	0.0
Half to full tuition	31	4.8	31	4.8	0	0.0
Full tuition	13	2.0	13	2.0	0	0.0
More than full tuition	4	0.6	4	0.6	0	0.0
Median grant amount			$10,000		$0	

Informational and Library Resources

# of volumes and volume equivalents	405,787
# of titles	169,720
# of active serial subscriptions	5,603
Study seating capacity inside the library	281
# of professional librarians	7
Hours per week library is open	100
# of open, wired connections available to students	60
# of networked computers available for use by students	115
# of simultaneous wireless users	650
Require computer?	N

JD Attrition (from prior year)

	Academic	Other	Total	
	#	#	#	%
1st year	1	10	11	5.0%
2nd year	0	3	3	1.5%
3rd year	0	1	1	0.5%
4th year	0	0	0	0.0%

Employment

	Total	Percentage
Employment status known	210	100.0
Employment status unknown	0	0.0
Employed	203	96.7
Pursuing graduate degrees	2	1.0
Unemployed seeking employment	1	0.5
Unemployed not seeking employment	4	1.9

Type of Employment

# employed in law firms	141	69.5
# employed in business and industry	37	18.2
# employed in government	10	4.9
# employed in public interest	8	3.9
# employed as judicial clerks	3	1.5
# employed in academia	4	2.0

Geographic Location

# employed in state	179	88.2
# employed in foreign countries	1	0.5
# of states where employed		15

Bar Passage Rates

Jurisdiction	California		
Exam	Sum 03	Win 04	Total
# from school taking bar for the first time	177	8	185
School's pass rate for all first-time takers	81%	38%	79%
State's pass rate for all first-time takers	63%	47%	60%

University of Southern California Law School

USC Law School, University of Southern California
Los Angeles, CA 90089-0074
Phone: 213.740.2523; Fax: 213.740.4570
E-mail: admissions@law.usc.edu; Website: www.usc.edu/law

■ Introduction

The University of Southern California Law School is a private, highly selective national law school with a 100-year history and a reputation for academic excellence. Under the leadership of a stellar, energetic faculty, the school's rigorous, interdisciplinary program focuses on the law as an expression of social values and an instrument for implementing social goals. USC is known for its diverse student body, its leadership in clinical education, and its tight-knit alumni network composed of national leaders in the legal profession, business, and the public sector. With 200 students in each class, the school is small, informal, and collegial.

The Law School is located on the beautiful main campus of the University of Southern California, just south of downtown Los Angeles and in the heart of the city's exciting "Arts and Education Corridor." A dynamic laboratory for legal training, Los Angeles is a center of state, national, and international commerce and government, and the city's legal market is among the most extensive in the world. The Law School is housed in a five-level, technologically advanced facility that provides a superb setting for professional training and sophisticated legal research.

■ Curriculum

USC's curriculum is comprehensive, uniquely inter-disciplinary, and designed to challenge. Courses provide a solid foundation in all substantive areas of law as well as extensive opportunities to explore specializations in traditional and emerging fields. Many faculty members have expertise in both law and other disciplines, such as economics, communication, public policy, medicine, history, psychology, and philosophy. The first-year curriculum consists of courses that examine the foundation of the legal system. The second and third years of study allow students to pursue individual interests in such areas as international law, intellectual property, corporations and business-government relationships, taxation, bioethics, civil rights and liberties, and judicial administration.

■ Special Programs

Dual Degrees: The Law School offers 17 dual-degree programs in coordination with USC graduate and professional schools and the California Institute of Technology. These programs enable qualified students to earn a law degree and a master's degree in the following fields: Business Administration, Business Taxation, Economics, Communications Management, Gerontology, International Relations, Philosophy, Political Science, Public Administration, Public Policy, Real Estate Development,

Religion, and Social Work. A JD/PhD program in Political Science, a JD/PharmD program, and a JD/PhD program in Social Science with the California Institute of Technology are also offered.

Legal Clinics: The nationally recognized Post-Conviction Justice Project, the Children's Legal Issues Clinic, the Employer Legal Advice Clinic, the Domestic Violence Clinic, and the Immigration Law Clinic enable students to gain valuable advocacy and lawyering skills by representing real clients under faculty supervision. Students in the Intellectual Property Clinic review technology contracts, engage in patent evaluation and application, assist with litigation, and perform film clearance work. The Law School sponsors more than 60 clinical internship programs, allowing students to earn academic credit while working for government and public interest agencies and federal and state judges.

Research Centers: Law students participate in the scholarly activities of several interdisciplinary research centers: the Center for Communications Law and Policy; the Pacific Center for Health Policy and Ethics; the Center for Law, Economics, and Organization; the USC-Caltech Center for the Study of Law and Politics; the Center for Law, History, and Culture; and the Center for Law and Philosophy.

Continuing Legal Education: Students help coordinate the Law School's practice-oriented programs and serve as research assistants for the Entertainment Law Institute and the Intellectual Property Institute.

■ Student Activities and Cocurricular Programs

Academic life is exciting and fast-paced, and students are often engaged in numerous scholarly pursuits and cocurricular programs. The *Southern California Law Review* has one of the largest circulations in the country. Students also publish the *Southern California Interdisciplinary Law Journal* and the *Review of Law and Women's Studies*. The Moot Court honors program sends participants to national and state competitions.

Public-service activities abound. The Public Interest Law Foundation is one of the largest in the country, providing summer grants for public-service employment as well as the Irmas Fellowship for Public Interest Law, which awards a year's salary to a third-year student committed to postgraduate work in public interest.

The Law School has a long tradition of student participation in governance, and elected student members serve on most committees and attend and vote at faculty meetings. The Student Bar Association allocates funds to support voluntary student organizations. Asian, African American, and Latino law students are represented by associations. Other student organizations include international and entertainment law societies, Women's

Law Association, Middle Eastern and South Asian Law Association, Gay and Lesbian Law Union, Christian Legal Society, Jewish Law Students, and chapters of the ACLU and the Federalist Society.

■ Professional Careers

USC graduates accept job offers in all regions of the country, with New York and Washington, DC, the most popular placement locations outside the West Coast. A significant percentage of graduates begin their professional careers as judicial law clerks to federal and state judges. Each year, several hundred private firms, government agencies, public interest organizations, and corporations from throughout the country come to USC to recruit students for summer and permanent employment. An off-campus recruiting program helps coordinate interviews with East Coast employers. The school's enthusiastic network of alumni is a valuable tool in the job-search process. The Alumni Mentor Program pairs first-year students with a graduate who practices in the student's field of interest, and other programs bring alumni from a range of fields to campus to discuss career opportunities. Overall placement statistics are consistently strong; historically, more than 95 percent of each graduating class finds employment. Average starting salaries are among the highest in the nation.

■ Housing

Housing is available in an apartment-style residence located within easy walking distance of the Law School.

The apartments are fully furnished and equipped with high-speed Ethernet lines. A roommate referral service is available to help incoming students arrange shared housing in various LA neighborhoods.

■ Admission and Financial Aid

Admission decisions are made on the basis of the student's academic record, LSAT score, personal statement, letters of recommendation, and other information in the file. The Admissions Committee gives primary consideration to outstanding academic and professional promise and to qualities that will enhance the diversity of the student body or enrich the Law School educational environment. Two letters of recommendation are required; applicants are strongly urged to submit at least one academic recommendation letter. The Law School operates on a semester basis and admits only full-time students. USC is committed to helping students successfully finance their legal education. In addition to various loan programs, the Law School offers substantial scholarship awards to a large percentage of the incoming class. Most scholarships are based on merit and need, although a number of scholarships are awarded based solely on the applicant's potential as indicated by the admission file. In addition, the Loan Assistance Repayment Program assists graduates who accept employment with low-paying public interest organizations. Prospective applicants should not allow financial concerns to deter their interest in USC.

Applicant Profile

University of Southern California Law School
This grid includes only applicants who earned 120-180 LSAT scores under standard administrations.

LSAT Score	3.75 +		3.50 - 3.74		3.25 - 3.49		3.00 - 3.24		2.75 - 2.99		Below 2.75		No GPA		Total	
	Apps	Adm	Apps	Adm	Apps	Adm	Apps	Adm	Apps	Adm	Apps	Adm	Apps	Adm	Apps	Adm
175-180	24	24	23	21	10	1	8	2	3	1	1	0	0	0	69	49
170-174	142	135	145	125	62	19	36	1	12	0	8	0	5	1	410	281
165-169	394	353	480	352	281	55	134	6	68	1	35	1	16	3	1408	771
160-164	347	71	664	67	524	21	265	14	106	0	72	1	32	1	2010	175
155-159	232	19	440	34	437	24	283	4	127	0	90	0	32	0	1641	81
150-154	110	6	226	10	248	0	222	0	117	0	102	0	20	0	1045	16
Below 150	48	0	136	0	178	0	204	0	175	0	214	0	54	0	1009	0
Total	1297	608	2114	609	1740	120	1152	27	608	2	522	2	159	5	7592	1373

Apps = Number of Applicants
Adm = Number Admitted
Reflects 99% of the total applicant pool.

Southern Illinois University School of Law

School of Law Welcome Center, 1209 W Chautauqua, Mailcode 6811
Carbondale, IL 62901
Phone: 800.739.9187 or 618.453.8858; Fax: 618.453.8921
E-mail: lawadmit@siu.edu; Website: www.law.siu.edu

ABA
Approved
Since
1974

The Basics

Type of school	Public
Term	Semester
Application deadline	3/1
Application fee	$50
Financial aid deadline	3/1
Can first year start other than fall?	No
Student to faculty ratio (fall)	14.1 to 1
Does the university offer:	
housing restricted to law students?	No
graduate housing for which law students are eligible?	Yes

Faculty and Administrators

	Total		Men		Women		Minorities	
	Fall	Spr	Fall	Spr	Fall	Spr	Fall	Spr
Full-time	23	24	12	13	11	11	0	1
Other Full-time	2	2	1	1	1	1	0	0
Deans, librarians, & others who teach	8	8	3	3	5	5	2	2
Part-time	14	3	9	2	5	1	3	0
Total	47	37	25	19	22	18	5	3

Curriculum

	Full-time	Part-time
Typical first-year section size	72	0
Is there typically a "small section" of the first-year class, other than Legal Writing, taught by full-time faculty	No	No
If yes, typical size offered last year	0	0
# of classroom course titles beyond 1st year curriculum	74	
# of upper division courses, excluding seminars with an enrollment: Under 25	51	
25-49	24	
50-74	10	
75-99	3	
100+	0	
# of seminars	6	
# of seminar positions available	72	
# of seminar positions filled	60	0
# of positions available in simulation courses	455	
# of simulation positions filled	281	0
# of positions available in faculty supervised clinical courses	88	
# of faculty supervised clinical positions filled	53	0
# involved in field placements	32	0
# involved in law journals	62	0
# involved in moot court or trial competitions	24	0
# of credit hours required to graduate	90	

JD Enrollment and Ethnicity

	Men		Women		Full-time		Part-time		1st-year		Total		JD Degs. Awd.
	#	%	#	%	#	%	#	%	#	%	#	%	
African Amer.	3	1.2	3	2.1	6	1.5	0	0.0	1	0.8	6	1.5	4
Amer. Indian	0	0.0	1	0.7	1	0.3	0	0.0	0	0.0	1	0.3	0
Asian Amer.	10	4.0	3	2.1	13	3.3	0	0.0	4	3.1	13	3.3	1
Mex. Amer.	3	1.2	1	0.7	4	1.0	0	0.0	0	0.0	4	1.0	0
Puerto Rican	0	0.0	0	0.0	0	0.0	0	0.0	0	0.0	0	0.0	0
Hispanic	0	0.0	0	0.0	0	0.0	0	0.0	0	0.0	0	0.0	0
Total Minority	16	6.4	8	5.7	24	6.2	0	0.0	5	3.9	24	6.2	6
For. Nation.	0	0.0	0	0.0	0	0.0	0	0.0	0	0.0	0	0.0	1
Caucasian	207	82.8	126	90.0	332	85.3	1	100.0	115	89.8	333	85.4	92
Unknown	27	10.8	6	4.3	33	8.5	0	0.0	8	6.3	33	8.5	3
Total	250	64.1	140	35.9	389	99.7	1	0.3	128	32.8	390		102

Tuition and Fees

	Resident	Nonresident
Full-time	$9,004	$24,184
Part-time	$0	$0

Living Expenses

Estimated living expenses for singles

Living on campus	Living off campus	Living at home
$10,165	$10,165	$4,985

Southern Illinois University School of Law

*ABA
Approved
Since
1974*

GPA and LSAT Scores

	Total	Full-time	Part-time
# of apps	754	754	0
# of admits	291	291	0
# of matrics	129	129	0
75% GPA	3.64	3.64	0.00
25% GPA	3.15	3.15	0.00
75% LSAT	156	156	0
25% LSAT	151	151	0

Grants and Scholarships (from prior year)

	Total		Full-time		Part-time	
	#	%	#	%	#	%
Total # of students	383		380		3	
Total # receiving grants	156	40.7	156	41.1	0	0.0
Less than 1/2 tuition	132	34.5	132	34.7	0	0.0
Half to full tuition	20	5.2	20	5.3	0	0.0
Full tuition	2	0.5	2	0.5	0	0.0
More than full tuition	2	0.5	2	0.5	0	0.0
Median grant amount			$3,100		$0	

Informational and Library Resources

# of volumes and volume equivalents	382,740
# of titles	73,388
# of active serial subscriptions	3,892
Study seating capacity inside the library	355
# of professional librarians	5
Hours per week library is open	78
# of open, wired connections available to students	14
# of networked computers available for use by students	40
# of simultaneous wireless users	500
Require computer?	N

J.D. Attrition (from prior year)

	Academic	Other	Total	
	#	#	#	%
1st year	4	23	27	17.5%
2nd year	1	2	3	2.4%
3rd year	0	0	0	0.0%
4th year	0	0	0	0.0%

Employment

	Total	Percentage
Employment status known	100	97.1
Employment status unknown	3	2.9
Employed	89	89.0
Pursuing graduate degrees	5	5.0
Unemployed seeking employment	4	4.0
Unemployed not seeking employment	2	2.0

Type of Employment

	Total	Percentage
# employed in law firms	59	66.3
# employed in business and industry	4	4.5
# employed in government	19	21.3
# employed in public interest	2	2.2
# employed as judicial clerks	4	4.5
# employed in academia	1	1.1

Geographic Location

	Total	Percentage
# employed in state	56	62.9
# employed in foreign countries	0	0.0
# of states where employed		15

Bar Passage Rates

Jurisdiction		Illinois	
Exam	Sum 03	Win 04	Total
# from school taking bar for the first time	63	18	81
School's pass rate for all first-time takers	79%	72%	78%
State's pass rate for all first-time takers	86%	78%	84%

Southern Illinois University School of Law

Office of Admissions, School of Law Welcome Center, 1209 W Chautauqua, Mailcode 6811
Carbondale, IL 62901
Phone: 800.739.9187 or 618.453.8858; Fax: 618.453.8921
E-mail: lawadmit@siu.edu; Website: www.law.siu.edu

■ Introduction

Southern Illinois University School of Law is located in a community of 27,000 people in one of the most scenic areas of Illinois. National forests, state parks, historic sites, and campgrounds, theaters, festivals, and cultural events, make Carbondale's quality of life among the highest in small cities in Illinois. The School of Law is one of many colleges of Southern Illinois University Carbondale, a 130-year-old university with a tradition of excellence as well as a diverse, multicultural student body of 23,000. The 12-1 student to faculty ratio at the School of Law is among the best in the nation. The School of Law is fully accredited by the ABA and the AALS.

■ Library and Physical Facilities

Students enjoy a completely renovated library, courtroom, and classrooms. Technological improvements include 24-hour keypad access to the law building and library, a wireless network allowing Internet access anywhere in or near the building, and distance-learning capabilities allowing live correspondence with national law schools. The new courtroom and classrooms are stocked with the latest computers, televisions, video cameras, and digital projectors to enhance learning. The vast collection of legal authorities the law library houses meets the demanding research needs of the prospective lawyer. All facilities are accessible to individuals with disabilities.

■ Curriculum

All students have a uniform first-year curriculum. A broad range of courses and seminars are offered in the second and third years. Throughout the curriculum, the faculty emphasizes professional skills such as writing, oral argumentation, drafting documents, interviewing, negotiating, and counseling.

An innovative first-year Lawyering Skills Program gives students a strong foundation in basic lawyering skills, including legal research and writing, oral advocacy, client interviewing and counseling, and negotiation.

The school has a very strong health law curriculum and is the site for the National Health Law Moot Court Competition as well as a Center for Health Law and Policy. The school also has groups of courses in trial/litigation skills, international, intellectual property, criminal, labor, corporate, family, and environmental law.

■ Special Programs

Clinical programs enable senior law students to represent/ assist clients in administrative and court hearings under the supervision of clinical faculty members, judges, and licensed attorneys. The Elderly Clinic provides direct legal assistance to persons 60 years of age and older in the 13 southernmost counties of Illinois. Students may participate in the externship program and obtain academic credit while working at local, state, or federal legal offices. The Alternative Dispute Resolution Clinic allows students to develop mediation skills and use them through community, peer, and in-court mediation services. The Domestic Violence Clinic provides legal assistance to victims of domestic violence. Students can also gain valuable experience through work in the Illinois Agriculture Mediation Program and the award-winning Self Help Legal Center.

The school provides a comprehensive student-run moot court program with teams that have competed in the National Moot Court, ABA Moot Court, all-Illinois Moot Court, and Philip C. Jessup International Law Moot Court competitions. The school also provides an annual intra-school Client Interviewing and Counseling competition and a Negotiation competition. SIU law students have enjoyed tremendous success in these competitions.

As a part of its mission to emphasize leadership skills, the school sponsors an active public speakers' program focusing on important national and regional issues. In addition, the school sponsors a major symposium each year bringing a large number of prominent legal educators to Carbondale. Recent speakers and symposia have addressed issues involving human rights, school violence, tobacco litigation, hate speech, and managed care.

■ Joint-Degree Programs

Concurrent JD/Master's Degree programs are offered in conjunction with the Graduate School in education, social work, public administration, accounting, and business administration. A concurrent PhD program is available in political science. A six-year program offered in cooperation with the School of Medicine permits students to concurrently obtain JD and MD degrees.

■ Career Services

The Career Services Office reports 94 percent of the 2003 graduating class was employed or seeking an advanced degree within nine months of graduation. The office provides services for both enrolled students and alumni, including individual career counseling, on-campus interviews, a research-pool service, career workshops, a job-listing service, subscriptions to a variety of job news-letters, a biweekly job-vacancy bulletin, and job-bulletin exchanges with other law schools. Special presentations that cover a variety of career and employment topics are offered throughout the year, and students have the opportunity to participate in a variety of regional and national job fairs and career conferences. The Career Library contains diverse career materials, including firm résumés, corporate brochures, and directories. Students can contact the Career Services Office at 618.453.8707 or by e-mail at *lawjobs@siu.edu*.

■ Expenses, Scholarships, and Financial Aid

Due to a generous program of scholarships for both current and existing students, graduates of the SIU School of Law enjoy an average debt load that is over 33 percent below the national law school average. Students can qualify for the in-state resident tuition rate after they have been an Illinois resident for six consecutive months. Student loans, work-study opportunities, and most other forms of financial aid are administered by the university's Financial Aid Office. Information concerning loans and financial aid procedures may be obtained from the Financial Aid Office at 618.453.4334 or by e-mail at *fao@siu.edu*.

■ Admission

Admission decisions are based on a number of factors, the LSAT score and undergraduate GPA being the most important. The highest LSAT score is used for repeat test takers. Other factors considered by the Admission Committee include trends in academic performance, writing ability, leadership and maturity, letters of recommenda-

tion, work experience, community and public service, and obstacles imposed by religious, ethnic, gender, or disability discrimination.

■ Student Activities

The school publishes the *SIU Law Journal*, which provides editorial and writing experience for a number of upper-class students. Students with a particular interest in health law can also publish articles in *The Journal of Legal Medicine.*

All students belong to the Student Bar Association. The SBA schedules lectures and social affairs, provides services to its members, and serves as a channel of communication between students and faculty. Students play an active role in law school governance, serving on most faculty committees. Past and current student organizations include Equal Justice Works, Phi Alpha Delta, International Law Society, Women's Law Forum, Environmental Law Society, Parents as Law Students, Animal Legal Defense Fund, Business Law Society, Black Law Student Association, Federalist Society, Law School Democrats, Law School Republicans, Media Law Society, Lesbian and Gay Law Students, Sports Law Society, Phi Delta Phi, Law and Medicine Society, Christian Legal Society, Hispanic Law Student Association, Asian Pacific Law Student Association, and law student divisions of the Illinois State Bar Association and the American Bar Association.

Applicant Profile

Southern Illinois University School of Law
This grid includes only applicants who earned 120-180 LSAT scores under standard administrations.

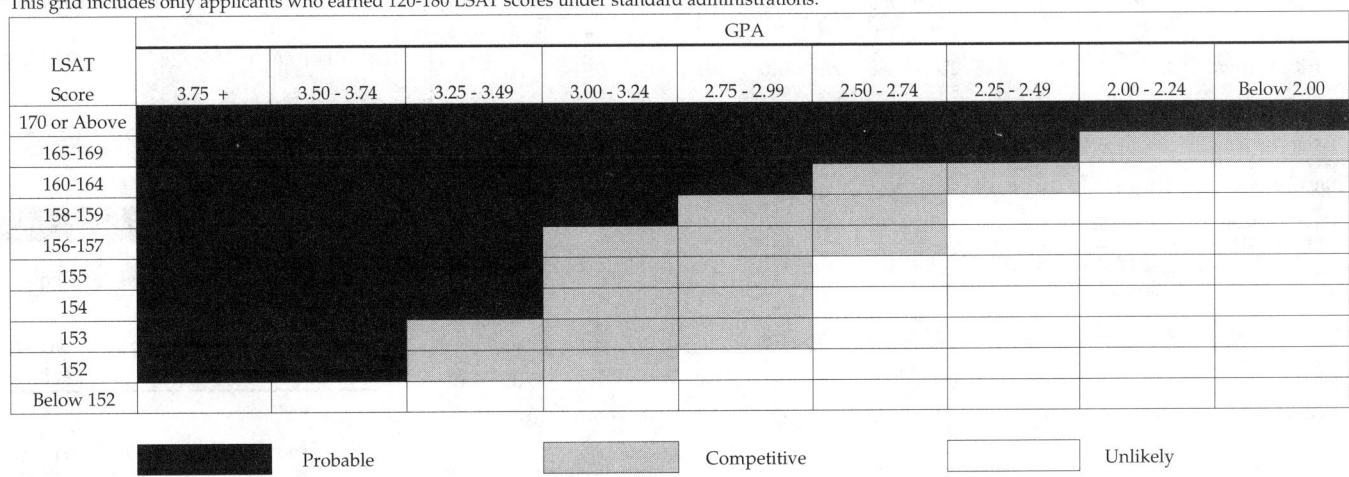

LSAT Score	3.75 +	3.50 - 3.74	3.25 - 3.49	3.00 - 3.24	2.75 - 2.99	2.50 - 2.74	2.25 - 2.49	2.00 - 2.24	Below 2.00
170 or Above									
165-169									
160-164									
158-159									
156-157									
155									
154									
153									
152									
Below 152									

■ Probable   ▨ Competitive   ☐ Unlikely

Southern University Law Center

PO Box 9294, Southern Branch Post Office
Baton Rouge, LA 70813
Phone: 225.771.5340 or 800.537.1135; Fax: 225.771.2121
E-mail: admissions@sulc.edu; Website: www.sulc.edu

ABA Approved Since 1953

The Basics

Type of school	Public
Term	Semester
Application deadline	2/28 2/28
Application fee	$25
Financial aid deadline	4/15
Can first year start other than fall?	No
Student to faculty ratio (fall)	13.3 to 1
Does the university offer:	
housing restricted to law students?	No
graduate housing for which law students are eligible?	No

Faculty and Administrators

	Total		Men		Women		Minorities	
	Fall	Spr	Fall	Spr	Fall	Spr	Fall	Spr
Full-time	28	28	15	15	13	13	17	17
Other Full-time	0	0	0	0	0	0	0	0
Deans, librarians, & others who teach	5	5	4	4	1	1	4	4
Part-time	18	18	9	9	9	9	15	15
Total	51	51	28	28	23	23	36	36

Curriculum

	Full-time	Part-time
Typical first-year section size	50	0
Is there typically a "small section" of the first-year class, other than Legal Writing, taught by full-time faculty	No	No
If yes, typical size offered last year	0	0

# of classroom course titles beyond 1st year curriculum		36
# of upper division courses, excluding seminars with an enrollment:	Under 25	27
	25-49	26
	50-74	4
	75-99	0
	100+	0

# of seminars		4
# of seminar positions available		65
# of seminar positions filled	47	0
# of positions available in simulation courses		192
# of simulation positions filled	115	0
# of positions available in faculty supervised clinical courses		122
# of faculty supervised clinical positions filled	73	0
# involved in field placements	4	0
# involved in law journals	10	0
# involved in moot court or trial competitions	16	0
# of credit hours required to graduate		96

JD Enrollment and Ethnicity

	Men		Women		Full-time		Part-time		1st-year		Total		JD Degs. Awd.
	#	%	#	%	#	%	#	%	#	%	#	%	
African Amer.	123	51.0	171	76.7	274	66.8	20	37.0	109	56.2	294	63.4	74
Amer. Indian	0	0.0	0	0.0	0	0.0	0	0.0	0	0.0	0	0.0	0
Asian Amer.	1	0.4	2	0.9	2	0.5	1	1.9	1	0.5	3	0.6	2
Mex. Amer.	0	0.0	0	0.0	0	0.0	0	0.0	0	0.0	0	0.0	0
Puerto Rican	0	0.0	0	0.0	0	0.0	0	0.0	0	0.0	0	0.0	0
Hispanic	1	0.4	2	0.9	3	0.7	0	0.0	3	1.5	3	0.6	0
Total Minority	125	51.9	175	78.5	279	68.0	21	38.9	113	58.2	300	64.7	76
For. Nation.	0	0.0	0	0.0	0	0.0	0	0.0	0	0.0	0	0.0	0
Caucasian	116	48.1	48	21.5	131	32.0	33	61.1	81	41.8	164	35.3	45
Unknown	0	0.0	0	0.0	0	0.0	0	0.0	0	0.0	0	0.0	0
Total	241	51.9	223	48.1	410	88.4	54	11.6	194	41.8	464		121

Tuition and Fees

	Resident	Nonresident
Full-time	$5,724	$10,324
Part-time	$3,604	$5,904

Living Expenses

Estimated living expenses for singles

Living on campus	Living off campus	Living at home
$12,313	$12,313	$12,313

Southern University Law Center

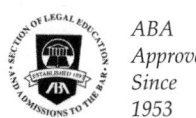

ABA
Approved
Since
1953

GPA and LSAT Scores

	Total	Full-time	Part-time
# of apps	1,343	1,143	200
# of admits	304	251	53
# of matrics	194	148	46
75% GPA	3.25	3.25	3.25
25% GPA	2.64	2.66	2.55
75% LSAT	150	149	151
25% LSAT	144	144	144

Grants and Scholarships (from prior year)

	Total		Full-time		Part-time	
	#	%	#	%	#	%
Total # of students	439		419		20	
Total # receiving grants	142	32.3	142	33.9	0	0.0
Less than 1/2 tuition	0	0.0	0	0.0	0	0.0
Half to full tuition	0	0.0	0	0.0	0	0.0
Full tuition	0	0.0	0	0.0	0	0.0
More than full tuition	142	32.3	142	33.9	0	0.0
Median grant amount			$3,725		$0	

Informational and Library Resources

# of volumes and volume equivalents	460,154
# of titles	66,301
# of active serial subscriptions	4,587
Study seating capacity inside the library	284
# of professional librarians	6
Hours per week library is open	99
# of open, wired connections available to students	25
# of networked computers available for use by students	41
# of simultaneous wireless users	0
Require computer?	N

JD Attrition (from prior year)

	Academic	Other	Total	
	#	#	#	%
1st year	23	13	36	20.3%
2nd year	3	2	5	4.0%
3rd year	0	2	2	1.5%
4th year	0	0	0	0.0%

Employment

	Total	Percentage
Employment status known	95	88.8
Employment status unknown	12	11.2
Employed	86	90.5
Pursuing graduate degrees	5	5.3
Unemployed seeking employment	2	2.1
Unemployed not seeking employment	2	2.1

Type of Employment

# employed in law firms	45	52.3
# employed in business and industry	2	2.3
# employed in government	11	12.8
# employed in public interest	1	1.2
# employed as judicial clerks	23	26.7
# employed in academia	2	2.3

Geographic Location

# employed in state	71	82.6
# employed in foreign countries	0	0.0
# of states where employed		6

Bar Passage Rates

Jurisdiction	Louisiana		
Exam	Sum 03	Win 04	Total
# from school taking bar for the first time	87	10	97
School's pass rate for all first-time takers	37%	10%	34%
State's pass rate for all first-time takers	62%	60%	61%

Southern University Law Center

Admission Office, PO Box 9294
Baton Rouge, LA 70813
Phone: 225.771.5340 or 800.537.1135; Fax: 225.771.2121
E-mail: admissions@sulc.edu; Website: www.sulc.edu

■ Introduction

In September 1947, the Southern University school of law was officially opened and was redesignated as a law center in 1985. Accredited by the American Bar Association, the Supreme Court of Louisiana, and the Southern Association of Colleges and Secondary Schools, the Law Center maintains a high standard of professional education. It is fully approved by the Veterans Administration for the training of eligible veterans. The Southern University Law Center adheres to the principle of equal opportunity without regard to race, sex, color, creed, national origin, age, handicap, or marital status.

The Law Center is located in Baton Rouge, the capital of Louisiana. With a population of over 500,000, this seat of state government includes state agencies and courts. As a hub of legal activity, Baton Rouge offers law students many opportunities to participate in state government through interaction with legislature, state agencies, and private law firms.

■ Library

The law library contains more than 450,000 volumes, 1,000,000 microfiche, 40,000 rolls of microfilm, and 800 law reviews. The library offers research assistance and reference service to students, faculty, and the public. Its collection adequately supports the curriculum and conforms to the standards of the American Bar Association. Both federal and Louisiana state governments have designated Southern University Law Center Library as an official depository for government documents. A complete collection of Louisiana legal materials, including continuing legal education materials of the Louisiana Bar Association, is provided in the library. Although library acquisitions reflect the civil law tradition of Louisiana, sufficient materials for research in the common law and a substantial number of basic legal reference works are available. Media equipment in the library includes copying machines for printed materials and microform.

The library occupies a 30,000-square-foot area, which includes computer and multimedia law learning labs. Cooperative arrangements with the Louisiana State University Law Center Library provide access to one of the largest Anglo-American and civil law resource collections in the southern region. Interlibrary loans from other libraries can be made through the Southern University Law Library.

■ Curriculum

The program of study is designed to give students a comprehensive knowledge of both the civil law and common law. While emphasis is given to the substantive and procedural law of Louisiana with its French and Spanish origins, Anglo-American law is strongly integrated into the curriculum. Fundamental differences in method and approach and the results reached in the two systems are analyzed.

The civil system of Louisiana offers the law student a unique educational opportunity. The program of instruction examines the historical background of the Anglo-American setting. Students are trained in the art of advocacy, legal research, and the sources and social purposes of legal principles. Techniques to discipline the students' minds in legal reasoning are an integral part of the educational objectives of the Law Center. Students are instructed in the ethics of the legal profession and the professional responsibility of the lawyer to society.

The Juris Doctor (JD) degree through a full-time and a part-time day/evening program is offered at the Southern University Law Center. The JD program has a three-year curriculum requiring 96 hours of academic credits and six semesters of residency. The part-time program requires enrollment in at least eight credit hours a semester and a minimum of eight regular semesters in residence. A JD and Master of Public Administration joint degree is also offered by the Law Center and the Southern University Nelson Mandela School of Public Policy and Urban Affairs. The JD/MPA joint-degree program requires 123 hours of academic credit and can be completed in four years.

■ Admission

The Law Center does not prescribe any prelegal courses but strongly recommends a foundation in such courses as English, speech, political science, history, economics, psychology, logic, mathematics and analytical courses, and science.

Students beginning the study of law are admitted only in the fall semester. Applicants are advised to take the LSAT prior to the February test date of the expected year of enrollment. Under no circumstances will a score received on the test administered more than three years prior to the anticipated date of acceptance be considered. All applications for admission are reviewed by a special committee. Many variables are taken into consideration for admission, including, but not limited to, the undergraduate grade-point average and the LSAT. Work experience and past pursuits are also reviewed.

Completed application forms, in addition to two letters of recommendation and one copy of an official transcript, should be filed with the Admission Office during the fall semester prior to the year in which admission is sought.

Student Activities

Students with advanced standing are eligible to enroll in the Clinical Education Program, which allows students to handle cases under the direct supervision of a full-time faculty member of the Law Center.

The *Southern University Law Review* is a scholarly periodical published under the auspices of the Southern University Law Center. Editorial administration and managerial responsibilities are handled by the student members of the *Law Review* staff with guidance from a faculty advisor. Membership is conditional on the submission, by each candidate, or other interested students, of a manuscript deemed by the editorial board to be publishable. *Law Review* membership provides eligible students with a wealth of experience in legal research and writing.

The purpose of the Student Bar Association is to promote the general welfare of the Law Center, encourage among its members high scholarship, and cultivate rapport and cooperation among the students, faculty, and members of the legal profession.

Housing

Limited dormitory accommodations are available for law students. All students desiring to live in campus housing are required to submit an application to the Housing Office, in addition to a security deposit of $50.

Applications should be made to the Director of Housing, Southern University, as early as possible.

Other Student Organizations

Other student organizations include Moot Court Board; Law Student Division, ABA; Black Law Students Association; Delta Theta Phi Law Fraternity; Phi Alpha Delta Law Fraternity, International; Women in Law; Environmental Law Society; Sports and Entertainment Legal Association; Student Trial Lawyers Association; Christians at Law Society; International Law Student Association; Southern Student Association of Criminal Defense Lawyers; Public Interest Law Society; and Phi Delta Phi International Legal Fraternity.

Career Services

The Office of Career Counseling and Development assists students and alumni in obtaining meaningful employment opportunities. Information on part-time employment before graduation is available through this office. Assistance is also given in job-seeking skills and interviewing techniques. The Law Center is a member of the National Association for Law Placement and pre-scribes to its standards for promoting career planning and development activities.

Applicant Profile Not Available

Southwestern University School of Law

675 South Westmoreland Avenue
Los Angeles, CA 90005-3992
Phone: 213.738.6717; Fax: 213.383.1688
E-mail: admissions@swlaw.edu; Website: www.swlaw.edu

ABA
Approved
Since
1970

The Basics

Type of school	Private
Term	Semester
Application deadline	6/30
Application fee	$50
Financial aid deadline	6/1
Can first year start other than fall?	No
Student to faculty ratio (fall)	16.7 to 1
Does the university offer:	
housing restricted to law students?	No
graduate housing for which law students are eligible?	No

Faculty and Administrators

	Total		Men		Women		Minorities	
	Fall	Spr	Fall	Spr	Fall	Spr	Fall	Spr
Full-time	43	44	31	32	12	12	7	9
Other Full-time	6	6	1	1	5	5	1	1
Deans, librarians, & others who teach	8	8	5	5	3	3	1	1
Part-time	18	25	15	20	3	5	6	2
Total	75	83	52	58	23	25	15	13

Curriculum

		Full-time	Part-time
Typical first-year section size		76	90
Is there typically a "small section" of the first-year class, other than Legal Writing, taught by full-time faculty		No	No
If yes, typical size offered last year		0	0
# of classroom course titles beyond 1st year curriculum		114	
# of upper division courses, excluding seminars with an enrollment:	Under 25	80	
	25-49	40	
	50-74	30	
	75-99	11	
	100+	1	
# of seminars		20	
# of seminar positions available		405	
# of seminar positions filled		238	61
# of positions available in simulation courses		740	
# of simulation positions filled		411	104
# of positions available in faculty supervised clinical courses		0	
# of faculty supervised clinical positions filled		0	0
# involved in field placements		249	24
# involved in law journals		78	16
# involved in moot court or trial competitions		72	14
# of credit hours required to graduate		87	

JD Enrollment and Ethnicity

	Men		Women		Full-time		Part-time		1st-year		Total		JD Degs. Awd.
	#	%	#	%	#	%	#	%	#	%	#	%	
African Amer.	18	3.8	28	5.6	25	3.8	21	6.8	16	4.7	46	4.8	14
Amer. Indian	3	0.6	8	1.6	4	0.6	7	2.3	4	1.2	11	1.1	1
Asian Amer.	88	18.7	110	22.2	142	21.5	56	18.2	62	18.4	198	20.5	33
Mex. Amer.	23	4.9	41	8.3	35	5.3	29	9.4	27	8.0	64	6.6	19
Puerto Rican	2	0.4	2	0.4	1	0.2	3	1.0	1	0.3	4	0.4	1
Hispanic	16	3.4	16	3.2	22	3.3	10	3.3	12	3.6	32	3.3	14
Total Minority	150	31.8	205	41.3	229	34.7	126	41.0	122	36.2	355	36.7	82
For. Nation.	11	2.3	4	0.8	12	1.8	3	1.0	9	2.7	15	1.6	6
Caucasian	281	59.7	253	51.0	372	56.4	162	52.8	149	44.2	534	55.2	154
Unknown	29	6.2	34	6.9	47	7.1	16	5.2	57	16.9	63	6.5	6
Total	471	48.7	496	51.3	660	68.3	307	31.7	337	34.9	967		248

Tuition and Fees

	Resident	Nonresident
Full-time	$28,600	$0
Part-time	$18,150	$0

Living Expenses

Estimated living expenses for singles

Living on campus	Living off campus	Living at home
N/A	$15,600	$9,714

Southwestern University School of Law

*ABA
Approved
Since
1970*

GPA and LSAT Scores

	Total	Full-time	Part-time
# of apps	4,116	3,524	592
# of admits	916	769	147
# of matrics	347	253	94
75% GPA	3.62	3.64	3.52
25% GPA	3.11	3.13	3.07
75% LSAT	157	157	156
25% LSAT	152	153	151

Grants and Scholarships (from prior year)

	Total		Full-time		Part-time	
	#	%	#	%	#	%
Total # of students	979		693		286	
Total # receiving grants	243	24.8	201	29.0	42	14.7
Less than 1/2 tuition	192	19.6	161	23.2	31	10.8
Half to full tuition	44	4.5	35	5.1	9	3.1
Full tuition	3	0.3	3	0.4	0	0.0
More than full tuition	4	0.4	2	0.3	2	0.7
Median grant amount			$8,000		$5,000	

Informational and Library Resources

# of volumes and volume equivalents	457,960
# of titles	129,508
# of active serial subscriptions	4,469
Study seating capacity inside the library	610
# of professional librarians	9
Hours per week library is open	104
# of open, wired connections available to students	442
# of networked computers available for use by students	118
# of simultaneous wireless users	400
Require computer?	N

JD Attrition (from prior year)

	Academic	Other	Total	
	#	#	#	%
1st year	42	21	63	17.5%
2nd year	12	4	16	5.5%
3rd year	4	1	5	1.8%
4th year	1	0	1	2.0%

Employment

	Total	Percentage
Employment status known	188	88.7
Employment status unknown	24	11.3
Employed	170	90.4
Pursuing graduate degrees	0	0.0
Unemployed seeking employment	5	2.7
Unemployed not seeking employment	13	6.9

Type of Employment

	Total	Percentage
# employed in law firms	95	55.9
# employed in business and industry	24	14.1
# employed in government	19	11.2
# employed in public interest	2	1.2
# employed as judicial clerks	1	0.6
# employed in academia	0	0.0

Geographic Location

	Total	Percentage
# employed in state	161	94.7
# employed in foreign countries	0	0.0
# of states where employed	9	

Bar Passage Rates

Jurisdiction	California		
Exam	Sum 03	Win 04	Total
# from school taking bar for the first time	161	27	188
School's pass rate for all first-time takers	58%	52%	57%
State's pass rate for all first-time takers	63%	47%	60%

Southwestern University School of Law

675 South Westmoreland Avenue
Los Angeles, CA 90005-3992
Phone: 213.738.6717; Fax: 213.383.1688
E-mail: admissions@swlaw.edu; Website: www.swlaw.edu

■ Introduction

With a long-standing emphasis on diversity; a mid-city campus featuring a world-renowned Art Deco landmark; strong ties to the legal, business, and civic sectors as well as the entertainment industry; and the most technologically advanced courtroom, Southwestern reflects the vibrancy of LA and provides an ideal setting for law study. To accommodate the needs of a diverse student population, Southwestern is the only law school to offer four courses of study leading to the JD that differ in scheduling and instruction, including traditional full- and part-time programs as well as a unique two-year curriculum. The law school's 10,000 alumni include prominent public officials—from members of Congress to mayors, and over 200 judges—as well as founders of major law firms and general counsels of multinational corporations. Founded in 1911 as an independent, non-profit, nonsectarian institution, Southwestern is approved by the ABA and is a member of the AALS.

■ Diverse and Talented Student Body

Students come to Southwestern from virtually every state and a dozen foreign countries, and represent over 250 undergraduate institutions. About two-thirds have prior work experience or have already completed advanced degrees in diverse disciplines from accounting to urban planning. The most recent entering class is equally divided between women and men, while minorities make up 37 percent, and students report fluency in over 25 foreign languages. The average age is 25 in the full-time programs and 30 in the part-time programs.

■ Distinguished Faculty

Southwestern's faculty focus on enhancing the quality of both the classroom experience and the attention provided to students as individuals. Bringing rich backgrounds in both legal practice and teaching, the full-time faculty include nationally recognized experts in antitrust, criminal justice, entertainment and media, environmental, family, housing and urban development, intellectual property, and international law, among other areas. The adjunct faculty of distinguished judges and attorneys are known for their expertise in specialized practices and enjoy sharing their real-world knowledge with students.

■ Award-Winning Campus Facilities

Southwestern's award-winning campus includes the extraordinary **Bullocks Wilshire** building that is listed on the National Register of Historic Places. The facilities feature state-of-the-art multimedia technology and wireless Internet access, spacious dining facilities and student lounges in restored historic areas, large terraces with panoramic city views, and tranquil student commons and promenade plazas, as well as a 10,000-square-foot spa-quality fitness center. Southwestern's law library is the second largest academic law library facility in California. The law school's new **Julian C. Dixon Courtroom and Advocacy Center** is the most technologically sophisticated center of its kind in the country.

■ Two-, Three-, and Four-Year JD Programs

Four JD programs are offered: three-year, full-time day; four-year, part-time evening; four-year, part-time day (**PLEAS**—Part-time Legal Education Alternative at Southwestern), for students with child-care responsibilities; and an intensive two-year alternative program (**SCALE**®—Southwestern's Conceptual Approach to Legal Education). SCALE presents the law as an integrated whole, utilizes simulated client files and externships to develop practical lawyering skills, and is completed in two calendar years that are equivalent to three traditional academic years.

■ Comprehensive Curriculum

The required traditional curriculum includes 19 courses. Over 140 elective courses and more than 150 externship placements allow students to design a broad-based legal education or emphasize an area of law. As a result of Southwestern's location, faculty expertise, alumni presence in the profession, and history, the law school has developed a reputation for leading innovation and excellence in several areas, including four burgeoning fields: entertainment and media law, international law, criminal law, and trial advocacy/litigation. Southwestern sponsors summer law programs in Argentina, Canada, England, and Mexico. Academic Support Programs are offered in the summer and during the academic year.

■ Entertainment and Media Law Institute

Taking advantage of its position in the heart of the Entertainment Capital of the World and the Digital Coast, Southwestern established the Biederman Entertainment and Media Law Institute. The law school has the largest contingent of full-time entertainment and media law faculty of any law school, and benefits from an extensive network of alumni and adjunct faculty who hold prominent positions in these industries. The institute sponsors over 50 courses, 40 externships, a special law firm practicum, and summer programs in Los Angeles and London, and presents lectures and symposia with industry leaders. Southwestern also offers the only LLM program in Entertainment and Media Law.

Student Activities

Southwestern has earned a reputation for having one of the most active and successful interscholastic Moot Court honors programs, with teams earning numerous awards in the 15 competitions entered each year. Teams also compete through the Interscholastic Trial Advocacy Program and in national client counseling and negotiation competitions. The *Southwestern University Law Review* and the *Southwestern Journal of Law and Trade in the Americas* feature scholarly articles and commentary on current legal issues and sponsor Distinguished Lecture Series and symposia on campus. Southwestern's Student Bar Association sponsors award-winning student welfare programs and community outreach projects. There are also over 35 on-campus student organizations, including three legal fraternities; minority, cultural, political, and religious groups; and societies concerned with specific areas of law.

Public Interest Involvement

Southwestern encourages students to pursue public interest service through special scholarship funds, a loan forgiveness program, the Silbert Public Interest Fellowship Program, and other summer grants for students working with public-service agencies; extensive student volunteer work with local schools and community organizations; and a variety of externships. The law school's annual Public Interest Law Week activities raise funds and awareness on campus.

Career Services

The Career Services Office coordinates career planning, counseling, workshops, and panel presentations as well as the Alumni Resource Network to help students prepare for and secure legal employment. The office sponsors intensive on- and off-campus interview programs and maintains extensive online job listings through LawMatch and eAttorney. Although the majority of Southwestern graduates choose to practice in California, alumni can be found in 47 states and 15 foreign countries.

Admission Criteria

Admission to Southwestern is highly competitive, with a recent acceptance rate of less than 22 percent. Emphasis is placed upon undergraduate GPA and LSAT scores earned within the past three years. Employment experience, community involvement, motivation, recommendations, and diversity are also major factors. Transfer applications are considered from students who have successfully completed at least one year at another ABA-approved law school.

Scholarships for Entering Students

Among the more than 50 institutional scholarship funds are the Paul W. Wildman Scholarship and the John J. Schumacher Minority Leadership Scholarship programs, which provide up to full-tuition renewable scholarships to members of the entering class who demonstrate exceptional academic and leadership potential.

Applicant Profile

Southwestern University School of Law

GPA	LSAT Score										
	120-124	125-129	130-134	135-139	140-144	145-149	150-154	155-159	160-164	165-169	170 +
3.75 +											
3.50-3.74											
3.25-3.49											
3.00-3.24											
2.75-2.99											
2.50-2.74											
2.25-2.49											
2.00-2.24											
Below 2.00											
No GPA											

Unlikely   Possible   Likely

Note: This chart is to be used as a general guide only in determining chances for admittance. Nonnumerical factors are seriously considered for all applicants.

Stanford University Law School

559 Nathan Abbott Way
Stanford, CA 94305-8610
Phone: 650.723.4985; Fax: 650.723.0838
E-mail: Admissions@law.stanford.edu; Website: www.law.stanford.edu

ABA Approved Since 1923

The Basics

Type of school	Private
Term	Semester
Application deadline	2/1
Application fee	$65
Financial aid deadline	3/15
Can first year start other than fall?	No
Student to faculty ratio (fall)	9.5 to 1
Does the university offer:	
housing restricted to law students?	No
graduate housing for which law students are eligible?	Yes

Faculty and Administrators

	Total		Men		Women		Minorities	
	Fall	Spr	Fall	Spr	Fall	Spr	Fall	Spr
Full-time	45	44	32	30	13	14	7	8
Other Full-time	8	10	1	2	7	8	3	3
Deans, librarians, & others who teach	3	3	3	3	0	0	1	1
Part-time	22	18	15	9	7	9	0	0
Total	78	75	51	44	27	31	11	12

Curriculum

	Full-time	Part-time
Typical first-year section size	56	0
Is there typically a "small section" of the first-year class, other than Legal Writing, taught by full-time faculty	Yes	No
If yes, typical size offered last year	28	0
# of classroom course titles beyond 1st year curriculum	131	

# of upper division courses, excluding seminars with an enrollment:	Under 25	76
	25-49	20
	50-74	8
	75-99	6
	100+	2

# of seminars	45	
# of seminar positions available	792	
# of seminar positions filled	628	0
# of positions available in simulation courses	340	
# of simulation positions filled	340	0
# of positions available in faculty supervised clinical courses	131	
# of faculty supervised clinical positions filled	118	0
# involved in field placements	31	0
# involved in law journals	344	0
# involved in moot court or trial competitions	48	0
# of credit hours required to graduate	86	

JD Enrollment and Ethnicity

	Men #	Men %	Women #	Women %	Full-time #	Full-time %	Part-time #	Part-time %	1st-year #	1st-year %	Total #	Total %	JD Degs. Awd.
African Amer.	20	7.4	24	9.9	44	8.6	0	0.0	13	7.8	44	8.6	12
Amer. Indian	6	2.2	1	0.4	7	1.4	0	0.0	2	1.2	7	1.4	4
Asian Amer.	18	6.6	37	15.3	55	10.7	0	0.0	20	12.0	55	10.7	18
Mex. Amer.	33	12.1	25	10.3	58	11.3	0	0.0	18	10.8	58	11.3	19
Puerto Rican	1	0.4	4	1.7	5	1.0	0	0.0	1	0.6	5	1.0	3
Hispanic	0	0.0	4	1.7	4	0.8	0	0.0	1	0.6	4	0.8	2
Total Minority	78	28.7	95	39.3	173	33.7	0	0.0	55	33.1	173	33.7	58
For. Nation.	7	2.6	5	2.1	12	2.3	0	0.0	6	3.6	12	2.3	6
Caucasian	161	59.2	118	48.8	279	54.3	0	0.0	90	54.2	279	54.3	102
Unknown	26	9.6	24	9.9	50	9.7	0	0.0	15	9.0	50	9.7	11
Total	272	52.9	242	47.1	514	100.0	0	0.0	166	32.3	514		177

Tuition and Fees

	Resident	Nonresident
Full-time	$34,230	$0
Part-time	$0	$0

Living Expenses

Estimated living expenses for singles

Living on campus	Living off campus	Living at home
$18,290	$23,798	N/A

Stanford University Law School

ABA
Approved
Since
1923

GPA and LSAT Scores

	Total	Full-time	Part-time
# of apps	5,040	5,040	0
# of admits	390	390	0
# of matrics	166	166	0
75% GPA	3.94	3.94	0.00
25% GPA	3.77	3.77	0.00
75% LSAT	172	172	0
25% LSAT	166	166	0

Grants and Scholarships (from prior year)

	Total		Full-time		Part-time	
	#	%	#	%	#	%
Total # of students	519		519		0	
Total # receiving grants	219	42.2	219	42.2	0	0.0
Less than 1/2 tuition	140	27.0	140	27.0	0	0.0
Half to full tuition	74	14.3	74	14.3	0	0.0
Full tuition	5	1.0	5	1.0	0	0.0
More than full tuition	0	0.0	0	0.0	0	0.0
Median grant amount			$12,907		$0	

Informational and Library Resources

# of volumes and volume equivalents	538,715
# of titles	210,541
# of active serial subscriptions	8,068
Study seating capacity inside the library	591
# of professional librarians	8
Hours per week library is open	96
# of open, wired connections available to students	274
# of networked computers available for use by students	117
# of simultaneous wireless users	9,999
Require computer?	Y

JD Attrition (from prior year)

	Academic	Other	Total	
	#	#	#	%
1st year	0	3	3	1.8%
2nd year	0	0	0	0.0%
3rd year	0	0	0	0.0%
4th year	0	0	0	0.0%

Employment

	Total	Percentage
Employment status known	192	99.5
Employment status unknown	1	0.5
Employed	188	97.9
Pursuing graduate degrees	2	1.0
Unemployed seeking employment	1	0.5
Unemployed not seeking employment	1	0.5

Type of Employment

# employed in law firms	122	64.9
# employed in business and industry	7	3.7
# employed in government	4	2.1
# employed in public interest	5	2.7
# employed as judicial clerks	50	26.6
# employed in academia	0	0.0

Geographic Location

# employed in state	84	44.7
# employed in foreign countries	4	2.1
# of states where employed	24	

Bar Passage Rates

Jurisdiction	California			New York		
Exam	Sum 03	Win 04	Total	Sum 03	Win 04	Total
# from school taking bar for the first time	97	5	102	44	6	50
School's pass rate for all first-time takers	92%	60%	90%	98%	100%	98%
State's pass rate for all first-time takers	63%	47%	60%	78%	58%	75%

Stanford University Law School

Office of Admissions, 559 Nathan Abbott Way
Stanford, CA 94305-8610
Phone: 650.723.4985; Fax: 650.723.0838
E-mail: Admissions@law.stanford.edu; Website: www.law.stanford.edu

■ Introduction

Stanford Law School is part of one of the world's leading research institutions, providing plentiful opportunities for interdisciplinary cooperation. Stanford University is a private university located in the heart of Silicon Valley, just 35 miles south of San Francisco. The university's 8,180 acres stretch between the foothills of the Santa Cruz Mountains and the cities of Palo Alto and Menlo Park, in a part of the country that offers an ideal, Mediterranean climate of dry, warm summers and wet but temperate winters.

Current enrollment at the university is approximately 14,000 students, of whom about 7,500 are graduate students. The Law School is small, with about 520 JD students, 30 LLM and JSM students, and a faculty of 40-plus permanent members. The school has teaching and research ties with schools and departments across campus. Law School courses are taught in 16 beautiful recently renovated multimedia classrooms with full wireless Internet connectivity.

Stanford Law School offers a unique combination of the classic and cutting edge in legal education. The school is preparing its students for a rich and varied professional life in an era of great excitement and rapid change—much of it generated by the remarkable innovations in information technology pioneered in Silicon Valley—and for careers in an increasingly global community.

■ Faculty

Stanford Law School has an exceptional faculty, distinguished not only for its scholarship, but also for its commitment to teaching and curricular innovation. The school's unusually low student/faculty ratio creates an intimate, collegial environment that fosters students' intellectual and professional development both in and out of the classroom. Students have many opportunities to work closely with faculty members as research assistants on scholarly projects; indeed, the faculty actively encourages interested students to develop their own scholarship for future academic careers. The relationships formed between Stanford faculty and students often last a lifetime.

Instruction at Stanford takes place primarily in small classes and seminars and through individually directed research. It also takes innovative forms: Stanford is a leader in the development of simulation and individualized feedback. And case studies, similar to those of business schools, challenge Stanford law students to consider the interaction of legal and nonlegal factors involved in a given situation. A growing clinical faculty is bringing dynamic new courses in live-client representation to the school.

■ Library and Physical Facilities

Stanford Law School is housed at the center of the university campus in Crown Quadrangle, a four-building complex. Housed within Crown Quad is the Robert Crown Law Library, which holds more than 500,000 books and more than 8,000 current serial subscriptions. The Crown Library has recently undergone a renovation to create a spacious modern reading room. Features such as computer-based legal information systems, facilities for online data retrieval, and wireless Internet access make this library one of the nation's most complete and efficient legal research centers. As a member of the Research Libraries Group, Crown Library provides access to the holdings of other leading universities as well.

■ Special Programs

Stanford Law School students are able to participate in a number of interdisciplinary programs, including joint-degree options with Stanford's Graduate School of Business (JD/MBA) and several other Stanford departments. Joint-degree programs are also offered with the Woodrow Wilson School of Public and International Affairs at Princeton University and the School of Advanced International Studies at Johns Hopkins University. In addition, the school will consider requests for joint programs on an individually designed basis. Students may engage in graduate-level research and policy-oriented study through the Stanford Center on Conflict and Negotiation, and the Programs in Law, Economics, and Business; Law, Science, and Technology; and International Law, Business, and Policy.

Stanford's clinical courses offer students the opportunity to undertake, under the close supervision of experienced practitioners, the roles and responsibilities of practicing lawyers. Such training includes witness examination, deposition and discovery, negotiation, mediation, planning, pleading, drafting, investigation, and analysis of tactical and ethical problems. Supervised work with clients may take place under the auspices of the Stanford Community Law Clinic, the Earthjustice Legal Defense Fund, or other legal service entities.

Through the school's externship program, students spend 20 to 40 hours per week in criminal law, environmental law, direct legal services, and civil rights and public policy practices. Past externship placements have included the American Civil Liberties Union, Natural Resources Defense Council, Mexican American Legal Defense and Educational Fund, and various district attorney and public defender offices.

Housing

Stanford provides a variety of subsidized on-campus housing options. Housing is guaranteed to all new, matriculated students who apply for housing by the early-May deadline and are willing to live in any graduate residence. The university maintains listings of off-campus housing opportunities. More information about housing is available at the Housing Assignment Services website *www.stanford.edu/dept/hds/has/*.

Student Activities

Forty-eight student organizations enrich the law school experience. Opportunities for scholarly work are provided through the *Stanford Law Review; Stanford Journal of Civil Rights and Civil Liberties; Stanford Journal of International Law; Stanford Journal of Law, Business and Finance; Stanford Law and Policy Review; Stanford Technology Law Review;* and *Stanford Environmental Law Journal.* Advocacy skills are developed in moot court.

Students who are female, Asian, African American, Latino, Native American, Christian, Jewish, bisexual, gay, or lesbian will all find groups with their particular concerns. Other organizations focus on environmental law, international law, law and technology, and public interest law. Local affiliates of the Federalist Society, the American Constitution Society, and the National Lawyers Guild are present.

Expenses and Financial Aid

Estimated expenses are as follows: For 2004–2005, full-time tuition was $33,870, with additional expenses including housing estimated at $18,650 for single students living on campus and $24,150 for single students living off campus. Scholarships are awarded on the basis of financial need. The purpose of financial aid is to assist students who would otherwise be unable to pursue a legal education at Stanford. Approximately 81 percent of the student body receives tuition fellowship or loan assistance.

Stanford law students planning public service careers may apply for Public Service Fellowships for their second and third years of school. The school also offers funding to students who dedicate a law school summer to qualified public service work. And for graduates who take low-paying public interest jobs and have substantial educational debt, the school has an excellent Loan Repayment Assistance Program.

Career Services

The Office of Career Services helps students find employment. More than 300 employers representing 600 offices worldwide participate in the spring and fall on-campus interview programs. The office also offers counseling and information on traditional and nontraditional careers and employers. The school encourages students to consider public interest and public-sector employment and assists students to secure such positions.

A survey of students graduating in the class of 2003 shows the following employment patterns: law firm associates, 65 percent; judicial clerks, 27 percent; and business (legal and nonlegal), public interest, government, or law teaching, 8 percent.

Applicant Profile

Our admission process takes into consideration many factors besides the undergraduate GPA and LSAT score. A statistical grid, as is typically provided here, only takes into consideration these two factors. We have chosen not to provide applicants with such a grid because our admission process would not be accurately portrayed.

Stetson University College of Law

1401 61st Street South
Gulfport, FL 33707
Phone: 727.562.7802; Fax: 727.343.0136
E-mail: lawadmit@law.stetson.edu; Website: www.law.stetson.edu

*ABA
Approved
Since
1930*

The Basics

Type of school	Private
Term	Semester
Application deadline	3/1 8/15
Application fee	$55
Financial aid deadline	
Can first year start other than fall?	Yes
Student to faculty ratio (fall)	17.7 to 1
Does the university offer:	
housing restricted to law students?	Yes
graduate housing for which law students are eligible?	No

Faculty and Administrators

	Total		Men		Women		Minorities	
	Fall	Spr	Fall	Spr	Fall	Spr	Fall	Spr
Full-time	41	45	22	25	19	20	6	6
Other Full-time	0	0	0	0	0	0	0	0
Deans, librarians, & others who teach	7	7	3	3	4	4	1	1
Part-time	47	54	32	39	15	15	3	4
Total	95	106	57	67	38	39	10	11

Curriculum

	Full-time	Part-time
Typical first-year section size	69	72
Is there typically a "small section" of the first-year class, other than Legal Writing, taught by full-time faculty	No	No
If yes, typical size offered last year	0	0
# of classroom course titles beyond 1st year curriculum	141	
# of upper division courses, excluding seminars with an enrollment: Under 25	250	
25-49	64	
50-74	48	
75-99	14	
100+	0	
# of seminars	20	
# of seminar positions available	337	
# of seminar positions filled	291	4
# of positions available in simulation courses	848	
# of simulation positions filled	744	30
# of positions available in faculty supervised clinical courses	129	
# of faculty supervised clinical positions filled	128	1
# involved in field placements	235	0
# involved in law journals	81	2
# involved in moot court or trial competitions	56	1
# of credit hours required to graduate	88	

JD Enrollment and Ethnicity

	Men		Women		Full-time		Part-time		1st-year		Total		JD Degs. Awd.
	#	%	#	%	#	%	#	%	#	%	#	%	
African Amer.	14	3.2	49	9.9	46	6.2	17	9.2	27	7.3	63	6.8	12
Amer. Indian	2	0.5	5	1.0	6	0.8	1	0.5	3	0.8	7	0.8	0
Asian Amer.	14	3.2	15	3.0	26	3.5	3	1.6	13	3.5	29	3.1	6
Mex. Amer.	4	0.9	6	1.2	9	1.2	1	0.5	9	2.4	10	1.1	1
Puerto Rican	7	1.6	5	1.0	10	1.3	2	1.1	5	1.4	12	1.3	4
Hispanic	33	7.6	47	9.5	66	8.8	14	7.6	30	8.2	80	8.6	15
Total Minority	74	16.9	127	25.7	163	21.8	38	20.7	87	23.6	201	21.6	38
For. Nation.	1	0.2	2	0.4	3	0.4	0	0.0	1	0.3	3	0.3	1
Caucasian	351	80.3	354	71.7	563	75.4	142	77.2	267	72.6	705	75.7	238
Unknown	11	2.5	11	2.2	18	2.4	4	2.2	13	3.5	22	2.4	2
Total	437	46.9	494	53.1	747	80.2	184	19.8	368	39.5	931		279

Tuition and Fees

	Resident	Nonresident
Full-time	$24,940	$24,940
Part-time	$17,240	$17,240

Living Expenses

Estimated living expenses for singles

Living on campus	Living off campus	Living at home
$13,541	$16,755	$7,854

Stetson University College of Law

*ABA
Approved
Since
1930*

GPA and LSAT Scores

	Total	Full-time	Part-time
# of apps	3,180	2,844	336
# of admits	850	727	123
# of matrics	371	299	72
75% GPA	3.65	3.66	3.41
25% GPA	3.06	3.16	2.73
75% LSAT	157	157	157
25% LSAT	151	151	149

Grants and Scholarships (from prior year)

	Total		Full-time		Part-time	
	#	%	#	%	#	%
Total # of students	875		745		130	
Total # receiving grants	103	11.8	100	13.4	3	2.3
Less than 1/2 tuition	24	2.7	24	3.2	0	0.0
Half to full tuition	26	3.0	26	3.5	0	0.0
Full tuition	10	1.1	7	0.9	3	2.3
More than full tuition	43	4.9	43	5.8	0	0.0
Median grant amount			$12,462		$10,000	

Informational and Library Resources

# of volumes and volume equivalents	394,552
# of titles	118,826
# of active serial subscriptions	4,061
Study seating capacity inside the library	609
# of professional librarians	7
Hours per week library is open	103
# of open, wired connections available to students	1,255
# of networked computers available for use by students	113
# of simultaneous wireless users	1,800
Require computer?	Y

JD Attrition (from prior year)

	Academic	Other	Total	
	#	#	#	%
1st year	6	25	31	8.6%
2nd year	2	1	3	1.3%
3rd year	0	1	1	0.4%
4th year	0	0	0	0.0%

Employment

	Total	Percentage
Employment status known	232	98.7
Employment status unknown	3	1.3
Employed	210	90.5
Pursuing graduate degrees	7	3.0
Unemployed seeking employment	10	4.3
Unemployed not seeking employment	5	2.2

Type of Employment

# employed in law firms	118	56.2
# employed in business and industry	16	7.6
# employed in government	60	28.6
# employed in public interest	3	1.4
# employed as judicial clerks	8	3.8
# employed in academia	5	2.4

Geographic Location

# employed in state	189	90.0
# employed in foreign countries	0	0.0
# of states where employed	13	

Bar Passage Rates

Jurisdiction	Florida		
Exam	Sum 03	Win 04	Total
# from school taking bar for the first time	149	100	249
School's pass rate for all first-time takers	83%	76%	80%
State's pass rate for all first-time takers	76%	75%	76%

Stetson University College of Law

1401 61st Street South
Gulfport, FL 33707
Phone: 727.562.7802; Fax: 727.343.0136
E-mail: lawadmit@law.stetson.edu; Website: www.law.stetson.edu

■ Introduction

Founded in 1900, Stetson University College of Law is Florida's first law school. The college's main campus is located in Gulfport, which is a suburb of St. Petersburg. Located in a former resort hotel, the main campus provides an outstanding environment in which to study law. A new satellite campus in downtown Tampa hosts some classes in our part-time JD program and judges on Florida's Second District Court of Appeal. This campus places us in the center of legal and business activity in the region. Stetson is fully accredited by the American Bar Association and has been an Association of American Law Schools member since 1931. The college is an equal opportunity education institution. For additional information, visit *www.law.stetson.edu*.

■ Library and Physical Facilities

Buildings at the college feature Spanish architecture with plazas, palm trees, and fountains. Modern in every educational aspect, the facilities include five courtrooms, with a sixth under construction. A new Student Center opened in 2002. The Law Library and Legal Information Center is one of the most advanced research and communications technology centers in the southeast. It contains 394,552 volumes and is equipped for instant access to computerized databases and the Internet. The Tampa Law Center includes a satellite library. There is a laptop requirement for all admitted students.

■ Admission

The college received more than 3,420 applications, offered admission to 849 applicants, and enrolled 371 first-year students: 299 full-time and 72 part-time. The 2004 entering class is the most diverse in Stetson history with 25 percent students of color and 55 percent women. There are 142 undergraduate institutions and 33 states/territories represented. These numbers represent the spring, summer, and fall full-time and part-time 2004 entering classes. The student body consists of approximately 920 JD students and 16 LLM students (from 11 countries). Our students, faculty, and staff work together toward one common goal: preparing our students to be the best lawyers and leaders possible.

■ Faculty

The intellectual exchange among students and faculty is continuous, both inside and outside the classroom. The 53 full-time professors are engaged in projects that bring them regional and national prominence but make teaching and working with students their top priority. Each semester, full-time faculty is supplemented by approximately 50 practicing attorneys and judges who serve as adjunct professors in specialized areas.

■ Curriculum

Academic Success Programs: The college offers many programs, including academic advising, an academic orientation, a semester-long academic skills workshop, a Writing Clinic, and a Dean's Fellows program, designed to assist all students in achieving their academic potential.

Lawyering Skills: Stetson's academic program focuses on the lawyering process. Stetson is a pioneer and national leader in advocacy and clinical training.

Additional Academic Offerings: Stetson offers a part-time JD program that allows a student to earn a law degree in four years by taking classes in the evenings. Classes will be taken at both the Gulfport campus and our new facility in downtown Tampa. The college also offers a joint JD/MBA program that prepares students for careers in law and business. The Master of Laws (LLM) program in International Law and Business has included lawyers from 33 different countries. Stetson offers summer abroad opportunities in Buenos Aires, Argentina; Tallinn, Estonia; and Granada, Spain. Stetson also has Centers for Excellence in Advocacy, Elder Law, Higher Education Law and Policy, and International Law and Business.

■ Special Programs

Trial Advocacy: Stetson is recognized as one of the best law schools for advocacy. Stetson's teams routinely win national, regional, and state mock trial, moot court, and client skills competitions. Stetson was the first law school to win all five major national mock trial competitions in a single academic year.

Clinics and Internships: Stetson offers upper-level students a wide variety of opportunities to work closely with attorneys and judges, and, in some cases, actually represent clients and try cases. Clinical opportunities include Alternative Dispute Resolution, Civil Government, Civil Poverty Law, Elder Consumer Protection, Employment Discrimination, Labor Law, Local Government, Prosecution, and Public Defender. Internships include Bankruptcy Judicial Internship, Environmental Law Internship, Federal Litigation Internship, Health Law Internship, In-House Counsel Internship, Intellectual Property Internship, and Federal and State Judicial Internships.

Certificates of Concentration: Students can apply to a certificate program in which they focus their elective credits on advocacy, elder law, health law, or international law.

Law Review: The *Stetson Law Review* publishes three issues each year. Students are selected based on grades and writing ability. Stetson serves as headquarters for the National Conference of Law Reviews. Stetson also publishes the *Journal of International Aging Law and Policy* in cooperation with AARP.

Honors Program: Students with a 3.5 GPA after their first or second semester are invited to join the Honors Program, which features a special colloquium and seminar. Honors students also are invited to attend a wide variety of faculty colloquia and other special events.

Continuing Legal Education: Students are encouraged to attend the numerous seminars and conferences sponsored by the college for practicing attorneys, judges, and other professionals.

■ Expenses and Financial Aid

Full-time tuition for 2004–2005 (fall/spring) is $24,760, and part-time tuition for 2004–2005 (fall/spring/summer) is $21,325. Partial and full merit and diversity scholarships are offered on a competitive basis. Need and endowed scholarships are offered for continuing students. There is no financial aid deadline and completion of the FAFSA is the only required form.

■ Housing

The college has limited on-campus dormitories, as well as approximately 50 single-family homes and 32 apartments located within a few blocks of the campus. For more information, contact the Stetson Housing Office at 727.562.7886, or visit *www.law.stetson.edu/housing/default.htm*.

■ Career Services

The college's firm commitment to helping students achieve their goals is reflected in its strong career services program. The Office of Career Services assists students and alumni in securing all types of legal and law-related employment and provides group seminars and individual counseling on subjects ranging from interviewing techniques to résumé writing. More than 94 percent of the 2003 graduating class reported that they found employment within nine months of graduation. Approximately 90 percent of recent Stetson graduates practice within Florida; however, alumni are located in 47 states and 17 countries.

■ Office for Student Life

The Office for Student Life promotes and supports over 35 student organizations on campus. Each organization provides a way for students to develop social and legal skills. These programs are used to enrich the classroom experience and to provide personal growth. The Office for Student Life also promotes leadership through its Ambassador Program and Leadership Development Committee. Students who attend Stetson College of Law are able to develop leadership skills to advance them in the legal community. Overall, these multiple opportunities allow students to obtain a rich and meaningful law school experience.

Applicant Profile

Stetson University College of Law
This grid includes only applicants who earned 120-180 LSAT scores under standard administrations.

LSAT Score	3.75 +		3.50 - 3.74		3.25 - 3.49		3.00 - 3.24		2.75 - 2.99		2.50 - 2.74		2.25 - 2.49		2.00 - 2.24		Below 2.00		No GPA		Total	
	Apps	Adm	Apps	Adm	Apps	Adm	Apps	Adm	Apps	Adm	Apps	Adm	Apps	Adm	Apps	Adm	Apps	Adm	Apps	Adm	Apps	Adm
175-180	0	0	0	0	0	0	0	0	0	0	0	0	0	0	0	0	0	0	0	0	0	0
170-174	2	2	0	0	1	1	0	0	0	0	1	1	1	1	0	0	0	0	0	0	5	5
165-169	7	6	5	4	3	3	2	2	2	2	1	1	1	0	0	0	0	0	0	0	21	18
160-164	18	17	17	14	24	24	25	22	25	14	13	6	5	0	0	0	0	0	2	1	129	98
155-159	40	37	52	48	81	61	94	34	50	9	27	7	25	7	4	1	1	0	2	0	376	204
150-154	69	63	144	85	180	30	180	20	131	15	66	10	34	2	17	1	2	0	7	1	830	227
145-149	44	17	105	16	169	7	164	8	109	4	66	3	38	0	11	0	6	0	10	1	722	56
140-144	14	1	43	0	53	3	62	1	66	0	43	0	29	0	12	0	1	0	12	0	335	5
135-139	3	0	13	0	18	0	25	0	23	0	19	0	10	0	6	0	3	0	9	0	129	0
130-134	1	0	1	0	2	0	5	0	8	0	3	0	4	0	5	0	1	0	1	0	31	0
125-129	1	0	0	0	0	0	1	0	2	0	1	0	2	0	2	0	0	0	3	0	12	0
120-124	0	0	0	0	0	0	0	0	0	0	0	0	0	0	0	0	0	0	0	0	0	0
Total	199	143	380	167	531	129	558	87	416	44	240	28	149	10	57	2	14	0	46	3	2590	613

Apps = Number of Applicants   Adm = Number Admitted   Reflects 99% of the total applicant pool.

Suffolk University Law School

David J. Sargent Hall, 120 Tremont Street
Boston, MA 02108-4977
Phone: 617.573.8144; Fax: 617.523.1367
E-mail: lawadm@suffolk.edu; Website: www.law.suffolk.edu

ABA Approved Since 1953

The Basics

Type of school	Private
Term	Semester
Application deadline	3/1
Application fee	$60
Financial aid deadline	3/1
Can first year start other than fall?	No
Student to faculty ratio (fall)	17.4 to 1
Does the university offer:	
housing restricted to law students?	No
graduate housing for which law students are eligible?	No

Faculty and Administrators

	Total		Men		Women		Minorities	
	Fall	Spr	Fall	Spr	Fall	Spr	Fall	Spr
Full-time	70	71	49	49	21	22	7	7
Other Full-time	6	6	1	1	5	5	2	2
Deans, librarians, & others who teach	7	8	6	6	1	2	0	0
Part-time	65	76	52	56	13	20	3	5
Total	148	161	108	112	40	49	12	14

Curriculum

	Full-time	Part-time
Typical first-year section size	92	90
Is there typically a "small section" of the first-year class, other than Legal Writing, taught by full-time faculty	Yes	Yes
If yes, typical size offered last year	45	45
# of classroom course titles beyond 1st year curriculum	285	
# of upper division courses, excluding seminars with an enrollment: Under 25	112	
25-49	51	
50-74	25	
75-99	15	
100+	14	
# of seminars	65	
# of seminar positions available	940	
# of seminar positions filled	359	316
# of positions available in simulation courses	1,285	
# of simulation positions filled	627	445
# of positions available in faculty supervised clinical courses	99	
# of faculty supervised clinical positions filled	86	13
# involved in field placements	70	12
# involved in law journals	122	28
# involved in moot court or trial competitions	84	30
# of credit hours required to graduate	84	

JD Enrollment and Ethnicity

	Men		Women		Full-time		Part-time		1st-year		Total		JD Degs. Awd.
	#	%	#	%	#	%	#	%	#	%	#	%	
African Amer.	22	2.7	20	2.4	25	2.4	17	2.8	18	3.4	42	2.5	19
Amer. Indian	2	0.2	4	0.5	4	0.4	2	0.3	4	0.7	6	0.4	3
Asian Amer.	43	5.2	58	6.9	63	5.9	38	6.3	43	8.0	101	6.1	15
Mex. Amer.	0	0.0	0	0.0	0	0.0	0	0.0	0	0.0	0	0.0	0
Puerto Rican	0	0.0	0	0.0	0	0.0	0	0.0	0	0.0	0	0.0	0
Hispanic	20	2.4	25	3.0	26	2.4	19	3.1	20	3.7	45	2.7	8
Total Minority	87	10.5	107	12.7	118	11.1	76	12.6	85	15.9	194	11.6	45
For. Nation.	10	1.2	15	1.8	12	1.1	13	2.2	7	1.3	25	1.5	6
Caucasian	675	81.7	669	79.5	860	80.9	484	80.1	405	75.6	1344	80.6	404
Unknown	54	6.5	50	5.9	73	6.9	31	5.1	39	7.3	104	6.2	18
Total	826	49.6	841	50.4	1063	63.8	604	36.2	536	32.2	1667		473

Tuition and Fees

	Resident	Nonresident
Full-time	$29,980	$29,980
Part-time	$22,486	$22,486

Living Expenses

Estimated living expenses for singles

Living on campus	Living off campus	Living at home
N/A	$16,095	$7,721

Suffolk University Law School

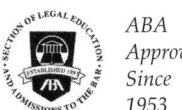

ABA
Approved
Since
1953

GPA and LSAT Scores

	Total	Full-time	Part-time
# of apps	3,278	2,657	621
# of admits	1,317	1,042	275
# of matrics	542	356	186
75% GPA	3.45	3.50	3.40
25% GPA	2.95	3.00	2.90
75% LSAT	159	159	158
25% LSAT	153	154	152

Grants and Scholarships (from prior year)

	Total		Full-time		Part-time	
	#	%	#	%	#	%
Total # of students	1,668		1,039		629	
Total # receiving grants	697	41.8	549	52.8	148	23.5
Less than 1/2 tuition	639	38.3	498	47.9	141	22.4
Half to full tuition	58	3.5	51	4.9	7	1.1
Full tuition	0	0.0	0	0.0	0	0.0
More than full tuition	0	0.0	0	0.0	0	0.0
Median grant amount			$3,000		$2,000	

Informational and Library Resources

# of volumes and volume equivalents	352,497
# of titles	175,570
# of active serial subscriptions	6,567
Study seating capacity inside the library	880
# of professional librarians	11
Hours per week library is open	103
# of open, wired connections available to students	2,663
# of networked computers available for use by students	231
# of simultaneous wireless users	75
Require computer?	N

JD Attrition (from prior year)

	Academic	Other	Total	
	#	#	#	%
1st year	32	1	33	5.9%
2nd year	0	19	19	3.8%
3rd year	0	2	2	0.4%
4th year	0	2	2	1.3%

Employment

	Total	Percentage
Employment status known	473	98.7
Employment status unknown	6	1.3
Employed	420	88.8
Pursuing graduate degrees	5	1.1
Unemployed seeking employment	45	9.5
Unemployed not seeking employment	3	0.6

Type of Employment

# employed in law firms	221	52.6
# employed in business and industry	91	21.7
# employed in government	61	14.5
# employed in public interest	4	1.0
# employed as judicial clerks	29	6.9
# employed in academia	10	2.4

Geographic Location

# employed in state	350	83.3
# employed in foreign countries	2	0.5
# of states where employed		21

Bar Passage Rates

Jurisdiction	Massachusetts		
Exam	Sum 03	Win 04	Total
# from school taking bar for the first time	366	41	407
School's pass rate for all first-time takers	81%	83%	81%
State's pass rate for all first-time takers	82%	82%	82%

Suffolk University Law School

David J. Sargent Hall, 120 Tremont Street
Boston, MA 02108-4977
Phone: 617.573.8144; Fax: 617.523.1367
E-mail: lawadm@suffolk.edu; Website: www.law.suffolk.edu

■ Introduction

Suffolk University Law School was founded by Gleason Archer in 1906. His mission was that Suffolk Law School would be a welcoming portal for all who wished to study the law, regardless of economic status, education, or place of birth. In a city where the cobblestones and gas lamps of Beacon Hill coexist with cutting-edge organizations that include education, medicine, high technology, and finance, Suffolk University Law School is woven into Boston's rich past and bright future. Boston offers the authenticity of what was, with the very best of what is—and Sargent Hall is a grand and visible extension of the city's two faces. Our students are steps away from city, state, and federal courthouses, governmental agencies, and the legal community, where they obtain valuable training in one of our many internship or clinical placements.

This fall, our incoming class consisted of students from approximately 200 different colleges and universities, 35 states, and 19 foreign countries.

All applicants for admission must submit a completed application, a personal statement, one letter of recommendation, and a Dean's Certification of Good Standing, and must have obtained a bachelor's degree from a four-year accredited college or university. The application deadline is March 1.

■ Technology and Physical Facilities

In 1999, we opened a new, state-of-the-art law school building, Sargent Hall, that is one of the most technologically advanced law schools in the country. The technology includes a high speed data network with over 3,000 data nodes, and every seat in each classroom, the library, and common area has direct access to the high-speed network. Additionally the library now has wireless connections.

All classrooms contain multimedia capability, including electric screens, LCD projectors, automated lighting controls, wireless microphones, hearing assistance, advanced speaker systems, and auxiliary computer connections for laptop computer presentations, and are equipped for teleconferencing/distance learning.

■ Concentrations and Joint-Degree Programs

Students may enroll in one of five area concentrations in Intellectual Property Law, Civil Litigation, Health Care/Biomedical Law, Financial Services, or International Law. In addition, there are five joint-degree programs that combine a Juris Doctor with a Master of Business Administration, Public Administration, International Economics, Finance, or Criminal Justice.

■ Clinical and Internship Programs

Students are encouraged to enroll in one of our clinical programs such as the Battered Women's Advocacy Program, Disability Advocacy Clinic, Evening Landlord and Tenant Clinic, Family Advocacy Clinic, Housing and Consumer Protection Clinic, Juvenile Justice Center, Suffolk Defenders, Suffolk Prosecutors, or one of over 500 internship placements, including AIDS and the Law Internship, Children and the Law Internship, Government Lawyer Internship, Immigration Law Internship, Judicial Internship, Labor and Employment Law Internship, Legal Profession Internship, Prosecutors Internship, The Reflective Lawyer: Peace-Training for Lawyers, and the International Human Rights Project.

■ Foreign and Graduate Programs

Suffolk University Law School, in conjunction with the University of Lund, offers a summer study-abroad program held in June and July in Lund, Sweden. The program combines the strengths of the international law curriculum of Suffolk University Law School with the international expertise offered by members of the University of Lund law faculty and the Swedish Bar and Judiciary.

Suffolk University Law School offers an LL.M. program in Global Technology which offers concentrations in Intellectual Property, Biomedicine, and Information Technology.

■ Academic Support Programs

Academic Success Program. This program offers skills evaluation, exam-skills training, and writing guidance to both first-year and upper-level students. Students are introduced to the technology that accommodates the learning styles and needs of all students, as well as an English as a second language program for students whose primary language is not English.

■ Student Activities, Publications, and Opportunities

Students have a number of opportunities to develop legal skills outside of the classroom through participation in the *Suffolk University Law Review*, the *Suffolk Transnational Law Review*, the *Suffolk Journal of Trial and Appellate Advocacy*, the *Journal of High Technology Law* (which is online at *www.law.suffolk.edu/stuservices/jhtl*), and *Suffolk Journal of Health and Biomedical Law*. Students may also participate in moot court competitions such as the National Trial Competition, ATLA Trial Team, Constitutional Law Team, Information Technology and Privacy Law Team, Intellectual Property Law Team, Jessup International Law Team, National Invitational Trial Tournament of Champions,

National Moot Court Team, Securities Law Team, Sports Law Team, and Tax Law Team. Students may also join one of our 30 student organizations or participate in our Student Bar Association.

■ Scholarships and Loans

Suffolk University Law School participates in a number of student financial aid programs in order to assist students in financing the costs of their legal education. Both need-based and merit-based aid is available. Financial aid awards (scholarships, grants, loans, and employment awards) are made to assist students in financing educational costs when their personal and family resources may not be sufficient. Merit-based scholarships are awarded by the Law School's Admissions Committee at the time a candidate is admitted to the Law School. These awards are made to students based on outstanding academic achievement.

Suffolk University Law School also has a loan repayment assistance program for students who, upon graduation, pursue low-income, public service, law-related employment. The committee selects two recent graduates each year for this program.

■ Office of Career Development

Suffolk University Law School is committed to preparing students for the increasingly complex and rapidly changing world in which they will serve their clients and communities. Suffolk's balanced curriculum provides a solid foundation essential for a successful practitioner, and offers ample opportunities for individual concentration in specialized areas of the law. We are very proud of the school's rich diversity. Almost 30 percent of our students speak a foreign language. Our 17,000 graduates practice law throughout the United States, as well as in 20 foreign countries. They can be found in private practice, corporations, public interest organizations, the military, and the executive, judicial, and legislative branches of government.

The Office of Career Development coordinates the fall recruiting program, résumé collection, and web page links to job postings and national employment information. The office arranges an off-campus interview program and hosts, in conjunction with other law schools, several placement programs that serve students with special interests or special needs.

Applicant Profile

Suffolk University Law School

LSAT Score	GPA								
	3.75 +	3.50 - 3.74	3.25 - 3.49	3.00 - 3.24	2.75 - 2.99	2.50 - 2.74	2.25 - 2.49	2.00 - 2.24	Below 2.00
175-180									
170-174									
165-169									
160-164									
155-159									
150-154									
145-149									
140-144									
135-139									
130-134									
125-129									
120-124									

■ Very Likely   □ Possible   ▨ Unlikely

Syracuse University College of Law

Syracuse, NY 13244-1030
Phone: 315.443.1962; Fax: 315.443.9568
E-mail: admissions@law.syr.edu; Website: www.law.syr.edu

The Basics

Type of school	Private
Term	Semester
Application deadline	4/1
Application fee	$50
Financial aid deadline	2/15
Can first year start other than fall?	No
Student to faculty ratio (fall)	16.8 to 1
Does the university offer:	
housing restricted to law students?	Yes
graduate housing for which law students are eligible?	Yes

Faculty and Administrators

	Total		Men		Women		Minorities	
	Fall	Spr	Fall	Spr	Fall	Spr	Fall	Spr
Full-time	39	34	23	21	15	13	6	3
Other Full-time	10	10	5	5	5	5	1	1
Deans, librarians, & others who teach	7	8	4	5	3	3	1	1
Part-time	24	42	19	33	5	9	4	3
Total	80	94	51	64	28	30	12	8

Curriculum

	Full-time	Part-time
Typical first-year section size	80	0
Is there typically a "small section" of the first-year class, other than Legal Writing, taught by full-time faculty	Yes	No
If yes, typical size offered last year	40	0
# of classroom course titles beyond 1st year curriculum	140	

# of upper division courses, excluding seminars with an enrollment:		
	Under 25	110
	25-49	35
	50-74	11
	75-99	34
	100+	2

# of seminars		8
# of seminar positions available		128
# of seminar positions filled	78	0
# of positions available in simulation courses		545
# of simulation positions filled	519	0
# of positions available in faculty supervised clinical courses		120
# of faculty supervised clinical positions filled	117	0
# involved in field placements	60	0
# involved in law journals	184	0
# involved in moot court or trial competitions	83	0
# of credit hours required to graduate		87

JD Enrollment and Ethnicity

	Men		Women		Full-time		Part-time		1st-year		Total		JD Degs. Awd.
	#	%	#	%	#	%	#	%	#	%	#	%	
African Amer.	9	2.1	25	6.8	34	4.4	0	0.0	10	4.0	34	4.3	13
Amer. Indian	2	0.5	4	1.1	6	0.8	0	0.0	3	1.2	6	0.8	1
Asian Amer.	30	7.1	25	6.8	54	6.9	1	9.1	24	9.6	55	6.9	22
Mex. Amer.	4	0.9	5	1.4	9	1.2	0	0.0	3	1.2	9	1.1	7
Puerto Rican	2	0.5	4	1.1	6	0.8	0	0.0	1	0.4	6	0.8	0
Hispanic	17	4.0	13	3.5	29	3.7	1	9.1	15	6.0	30	3.8	0
Total Minority	64	15.1	76	20.7	138	17.7	2	18.2	56	22.5	140	17.7	43
For. Nation.	17	4.0	14	3.8	31	4.0	0	0.0	8	3.2	31	3.9	17
Caucasian	258	60.8	237	64.4	486	62.2	9	81.8	141	56.6	495	62.5	144
Unknown	85	20.0	41	11.1	126	16.1	0	0.0	44	17.7	126	15.9	38
Total	424	53.5	368	46.5	781	98.6	11	1.4	249	31.4	792		242

Tuition and Fees

	Resident	Nonresident
Full-time	$31,642	$31,642
Part-time	$27,329	$27,518

Living Expenses

Estimated living expenses for singles

Living on campus	Living off campus	Living at home
$15,790	$15,790	$15,790

Syracuse University College of Law

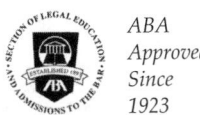

*ABA
Approved
Since
1923*

GPA and LSAT Scores

	Total	Full-time	Part-time
# of apps	3,212	3,158	54
# of admits	783	782	1
# of matrics	250	249	1
75% GPA	3.56	3.56	0.00
25% GPA	3.15	3.15	0.00
75% LSAT	156	156	0
25% LSAT	152	152	0

Grants and Scholarships (from prior year)

	Total		Full-time		Part-time	
	#	%	#	%	#	%
Total # of students	835		828		7	
Total # receiving grants	683	81.8	683	82.5	0	0.0
Less than 1/2 tuition	601	72.0	601	72.6	0	0.0
Half to full tuition	51	6.1	51	6.2	0	0.0
Full tuition	0	0.0	0	0.0	0	0.0
More than full tuition	31	3.7	31	3.7	0	0.0
Median grant amount			$8,000		$0	

Informational and Library Resources

# of volumes and volume equivalents	443,277
# of titles	78,685
# of active serial subscriptions	3,248
Study seating capacity inside the library	433
# of professional librarians	8
Hours per week library is open	104
# of open, wired connections available to students	25
# of networked computers available for use by students	70
# of simultaneous wireless users	1,000
Require computer?	Y

JD Attrition (from prior year)

	Academic	Other	Total	
	#	#	#	%
1st year	0	1	1	0.3%
2nd year	9	18	27	10.2%
3rd year	0	0	0	0.0%
4th year	0	0	0	0.0%

Employment

	Total	Percentage
Employment status known	236	95.9
Employment status unknown	10	4.1
Employed	205	86.9
Pursuing graduate degrees	11	4.7
Unemployed seeking employment	11	4.7
Unemployed not seeking employment	9	3.8

Type of Employment

	Total	Percentage
# employed in law firms	114	55.6
# employed in business and industry	22	10.7
# employed in government	27	13.2
# employed in public interest	5	2.4
# employed as judicial clerks	30	14.6
# employed in academia	2	1.0

Geographic Location

	Total	Percentage
# employed in state	90	43.9
# employed in foreign countries	3	1.5
# of states where employed	30	

Bar Passage Rates

Jurisdiction	New York		
Exam	Sum 03	Win 04	Total
# from school taking bar for the first time	129	16	145
School's pass rate for all first-time takers	84%	50%	80%
State's pass rate for all first-time takers	78%	58%	75%

Syracuse University College of Law

Office of Admissions and Financial Aid, Suite 340
Syracuse, NY 13244-1030
Phone: 315.443.1962; Fax: 315.443.9568
E-mail: admissions@law.syr.edu; Website: www.law.syr.edu

■ Introduction

Syracuse University College of Law was established in 1895. The college is a charter member of the AALS and is fully approved by the ABA. It is one of the oldest of the 12 schools and colleges comprising Syracuse University, a major teaching and research institution. The College of Law complex is located on the 200-acre Syracuse University campus overlooking scenic Central New York and the city of Syracuse.

■ Curriculum

Syracuse University College of Law's mission is guided by the philosophy that the best way to train lawyers to practice in today's world is to teach them to apply what they learn in the classroom to real legal issues, problems, and clients. Beginning in the first year and continuing throughout the curriculum, the Syracuse Applied Learning Program creates educational settings that integrate opportunities for students to acquire an understanding of legal theory and doctrine, develop professional skills, and get exposure to the values and ethics of the legal profession. The Applied Learning Program does not replace the traditional educational program. Rather, it adds experiences that allow students to draw on all that they have studied. As a result, Syracuse students are better prepared for the practice of law.

■ Applied Learning Centers/Institute

- **Center for Law and Business Enterprise**—provides students with comprehensive and professional training for careers in corporate law, business, or general practice. In addition to courses, students participate in either a skills seminar, clinic, or externship related to business or general practice. Students may focus their coursework to earn a certificate in the Law and Market Economy Program or the Corporate Counsel Program.
- **Family Law and Social Policy Center**—provides a dynamic way for students to combine in-depth classroom learning with actual problem solving. Through courses, programs, and research, the center blends an interdisciplinary group of students, faculty members, and practitioners interested in a range of issues from divorce, domestic violence, and mediation to children's rights and bioethics.
- **Center for Global Law and Practice**—provides a broad variety of opportunities both in and out of the classroom for students interested in global law. Course offerings are broad and cocurricular activities include moot court competitions, the International Law Society, and the *Syracuse Journal of International Law and Commerce*. A summer abroad program is offered in London.
- **Law, Technology, and Management Center**—emphasizes interdisciplinary and applied learning approaches to commercial development of new technology. Coursework is developed around a business curriculum. Students work in cross-disciplinary teams on real-world developments arranged through SU's Technology Transfer Research Center with companies and research organizations.
- **Institute for National Security and Counterterrorism**—is dedicated to the promotion of interdisciplinary research, teaching, and public service that concerns national security and counterterrorism. While law and policy are at the center of its activities, the institute seeks to include in its endeavors government officials, practitioners from a variety of fields, and professors and students from a wide range of disciplines. The institute, established in 2003–2004, is engaged in a variety of projects, including the preparation of an assessment of the state of homeland security preparedness in New York State.
- **Center for Indigenous Law, Governance, and Citizenship**—newly established in 2003–2004, will focus on programmatic activities which include conducting research relating to citizenship, rights, and responsibilities of indigenous peoples and governance of indigenous nations in the United States and Canada; providing technical assistance to indigenous nations seeking to reform their governing institutions and administrative laws and to federal, state, local, and provincial governments seeking to reform their Indian affairs laws; and promoting a greater understanding of the law, governance, and history of the Haudenosaunee ("People of the Longhouse").

■ Other Opportunities for Specialization

- **Clinical Programs**—Students enrolled in our clinical programs work on real cases under faculty supervision for course credit. Diverse clinical opportunities at the College of Law include the Criminal Law Clinic, the Community Development Law Clinic, the Children's Rights and Family Law Clinic, the Public Interest Law Firm, the Low Income Taxpayer Clinic, and the Securities Arbitration Clinic. The college also offers several externship courses.
- **Joint-Degree Programs**—Interdisciplinary study is an integral part of academic life in the college. Students who desire a greater degree of specialization may select from a number of joint-degree opportunities. Formal joint-degree programs are offered with many graduate programs of Syracuse University, including the Maxwell School of Citizenship and Public Affairs,

the S.I. Newhouse School of Public Communications, and the School of Management, among many others. Joint degrees may also be designed to fit special career objectives. Joint degrees available include JD/MPA, JD/MBA, JD/MA, JD/MS, and JD/PhD.

- **Advocacy Skills**—Syracuse Law is recognized for its exceptional advocacy programs. Students are actively involved and have been highly successful in national moot court competitions. Syracuse students participate in intraschool programs throughout the year in trial and appellate competitions covering a wide variety of areas.

■ Library

The library spans four spacious levels within the College of Law complex. The main floor of the library epitomizes its commitment to student service in an ever-changing information environment. The library adds approximately 2,500 new titles to its catalog each year, including a growing number of licensed electronic databases. All holdings—print, microform, audio, video, and CD-ROM—are accessible through the university-wide online public catalog.

■ Admission

History reveals that undergraduate grades and LSAT scores are reliable measures, in most cases, for predicting probable success in law study. Thus, an index combining grades and test scores becomes a factor in most admission decisions. However, recognizing that numerical

indicators are not always the best predictors of success in law school—even when considered in combination with other factors—the college admits a limited number of students each year through its Legal Education Opportunity (LEO) Program. A goal of the LEO program is the admission of persons who may have been deprived of equal education opportunities for reasons of race, gender, poverty, or other factors beyond their control.

■ Financial Aid

The college makes available awards from a variety of sources, including merit-based scholarships and need-based tuition grants, university fellowships, and federal sources such as the work-study program and the Perkins and Stafford Loan Programs. Private loan programs are available to assist law students with supplemental financing for legal education expenses.

■ Career Services

Syracuse graduates are employed throughout the United States and overseas. The Office of Career Services is dedicated to assisting current students and alumni with their individual job searches. Career Services staff administer a comprehensive program that utilizes the most current resources available to assist students in developing a career plan and employment search strategy. The office provides a full range of services to students, including a broad mix of innovative and traditional support, empowering students with the confidence and skills necessary to conduct an effective job search.

Applicant Profile

Syracuse University College of Law
This grid includes only applicants who earned 120-180 LSAT scores under standard administrations.

LSAT Score	3.75 +		3.50 - 3.74		3.25 - 3.49		3.00 - 3.24		2.75 - 2.99		2.50 - 2.74		2.25 - 2.49		2.00 - 2.24		Below 2.00		No GPA		Total	
	Apps	Adm	Apps	Adm	Apps	Adm	Apps	Adm	Apps	Adm	Apps	Adm	Apps	Adm	Apps	Adm	Apps	Adm	Apps	Adm	Apps	Adm
170-180	0	0	2	2	1	0	0	0	2	0	1	0	1	0	1	0	0	0	0	0	8	2
165-169	6	5	6	6	3	2	2	2	0	0	5	2	5	0	0	0	0	0	0	0	27	17
160-164	15	11	30	18	25	18	27	15	18	8	10	3	4	0	1	0	1	0	0	0	131	73
155-159	44	31	89	57	126	87	118	88	83	32	31	4	16	0	8	1	0	0	4	2	519	302
150-154	81	44	174	82	244	93	266	45	163	18	80	6	31	1	14	0	2	0	12	3	1067	292
145-149	46	11	151	17	182	17	222	14	140	4	70	2	40	0	11	0	3	0	14	2	879	67
120-144	21	0	52	1	93	3	121	0	114	2	74	0	44	0	12	0	5	0	27	1	563	7
Total	213	102	504	183	674	220	756	164	520	64	271	17	141	1	47	1	11	0	57	8	3194	760

Apps = Number of Applicants
Adm = Number Admitted
Reflects 99% of the total applicant pool.

This chart is provided as a general guide in assessing an applicant's possibility of admission based solely on quantitative factors. It should be noted that nonquantitative factors are also considered in all admission decisions.

Temple University—James E. Beasley School of Law

1719 North Broad Street
Philadelphia, PA 19122
Phone: 800.560.1428; Fax: 215.204.9319
E-mail: lawadmis@temple.edu; Website: www.temple.edu/lawschool

*ABA
Approved
Since
1933*

The Basics

Type of school	Public
Term	Semester
Application deadline	3/1
Application fee	$60
Financial aid deadline	3/1
Can first year start other than fall?	No
Student to faculty ratio (fall)	16.5 to 1
Does the university offer:	
housing restricted to law students?	No
graduate housing for which law students are eligible?	Yes

Faculty and Administrators

	Total		Men		Women		Minorities	
	Fall	Spr	Fall	Spr	Fall	Spr	Fall	Spr
Full-time	49	48	32	30	17	18	12	12
Other Full-time	0	0	0	0	0	0	0	0
Deans, librarians, & others who teach	17	17	9	9	8	8	2	2
Part-time	109	126	69	88	40	38	8	12
Total	**175**	**191**	**110**	**127**	**65**	**64**	**22**	**26**

Curriculum

	Full-time	Part-time
Typical first-year section size	65	71
Is there typically a "small section" of the first-year class, other than Legal Writing, taught by full-time faculty	No	No
If yes, typical size offered last year	0	0
# of classroom course titles beyond 1st year curriculum	169	
# of upper division courses, excluding seminars with an enrollment:	Under 25	141
	25-49	53
	50-74	24
	75-99	13
	100+	3
# of seminars	56	
# of seminar positions available	729	
# of seminar positions filled	478	157
# of positions available in simulation courses	857	
# of simulation positions filled	580	189
# of positions available in faculty supervised clinical courses	0	
# of faculty supervised clinical positions filled	0	0
# involved in field placements	249	13
# involved in law journals	172	15
# involved in moot court or trial competitions	30	1
# of credit hours required to graduate	87	

JD Enrollment and Ethnicity

	Men		Women		Full-time		Part-time		1st-year		Total		JD Degs. Awd.
	#	%	#	%	#	%	#	%	#	%	#	%	
African Amer.	24	4.4	57	11.3	64	8.0	17	6.8	32	9.6	81	7.7	28
Amer. Indian	5	0.9	0	0.0	3	0.4	2	0.8	1	0.3	5	0.5	0
Asian Amer.	53	9.7	46	9.1	80	10.0	19	7.6	37	11.1	99	9.4	22
Mex. Amer.	3	0.5	5	1.0	6	0.7	2	0.8	5	1.5	8	0.8	1
Puerto Rican	8	1.5	2	0.4	8	1.0	2	0.8	4	1.2	10	0.9	4
Hispanic	12	2.2	9	1.8	17	2.1	4	1.6	10	3.0	21	2.0	8
Total Minority	105	19.2	119	23.5	178	22.2	46	18.4	89	26.8	224	21.3	63
For. Nation.	0	0.0	8	1.6	6	0.7	2	0.8	5	1.5	8	0.8	0
Caucasian	438	80.1	376	74.3	615	76.6	199	79.6	237	71.4	814	77.3	257
Unknown	4	0.7	3	0.6	4	0.5	3	1.2	1	0.3	7	0.7	5
Total	547	51.9	506	48.1	803	76.3	250	23.7	332	31.5	1053		325

Tuition and Fees

	Resident	Nonresident
Full-time	$13,312	$22,800
Part-time	$10,752	$18,342

Living Expenses

Estimated living expenses for singles

Living on campus	Living off campus	Living at home
$19,254	$19,254	$14,220

Temple University—James E. Beasley School of Law

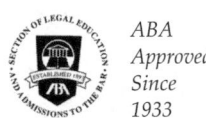

ABA
Approved
Since
1933

GPA and LSAT Scores

	Total	Full-time	Part-time
# of apps	4,484	4,088	396
# of admits	1,269	1,149	120
# of matrics	331	257	74
75% GPA	3.60	3.62	3.58
25% GPA	3.15	3.17	3.02
75% LSAT	162	163	160
25% LSAT	157	158	156

Grants and Scholarships (from prior year)

	Total		Full-time		Part-time	
	#	%	#	%	#	%
Total # of students	1,065		796		269	
Total # receiving grants	390	36.6	347	43.6	43	16.0
Less than 1/2 tuition	127	11.9	113	14.2	14	5.2
Half to full tuition	242	22.7	217	27.3	25	9.3
Full tuition	21	2.0	17	2.1	4	1.5
More than full tuition	0	0.0	0	0.0	0	0.0
Median grant amount			$6,039		$4,831	

Informational and Library Resources

# of volumes and volume equivalents	563,059
# of titles	109,805
# of active serial subscriptions	3,019
Study seating capacity inside the library	685
# of professional librarians	10
Hours per week library is open	96
# of open, wired connections available to students	421
# of networked computers available for use by students	150
# of simultaneous wireless users	508
Require computer?	N

JD Attrition (from prior year)

	Academic	Other	Total	
	#	#	#	%
1st year	2	8	10	2.9%
2nd year	2	9	11	3.4%
3rd year	2	2	4	1.2%
4th year	0	2	2	3.0%

Employment

	Total	Percentage
Employment status known	304	96.2
Employment status unknown	12	3.8
Employed	289	95.1
Pursuing graduate degrees	0	0.0
Unemployed seeking employment	10	3.3
Unemployed not seeking employment	5	1.6

Type of Employment

# employed in law firms	147	51.0
# employed in business and industry	46	15.9
# employed in government	39	13.5
# employed in public interest	17	5.9
# employed as judicial clerks	28	9.7
# employed in academia	5	1.7

Geographic Location

# employed in state	218	75.7
# employed in foreign countries	1	0.3
# of states where employed		16

Bar Passage Rates

Jurisdiction	Pennsylvania			New Jersey		
Exam	Sum 03	Win 04	Total	Sum 03	Win 04	Total
# from school taking bar for the first time	236	22	258	169	28	197
School's pass rate for all first-time takers	84%	68%	83%	90%	57%	85%
State's pass rate for all first-time takers	78%	66%	76%	76%	59%	73%

Temple University—James E. Beasley School of Law

1719 North Broad Street
Philadelphia, PA 19122
Phone: 800.560.1428; Fax: 215.204.9319
E-mail: lawadmis@temple.edu; Website: www.temple.edu/lawschool

■ Introduction

Temple law school is distinguished by our conviction that the best way to learn the practice of law is to do the work of lawyers. Our unique student centered curriculum integrates both critical thinking and practical legal skills. Students at Temple build lawyering skills both in the classroom and in the law firms, courts, civic organizations, and financial institutions of Philadelphia, the fifth largest city in the nation. As a result, our students graduate with a head start, ready to perform skillfully in the legal marketplace.

■ Student Body and Faculty

Temple seeks to maintain and strengthen its longstanding tradition of accessibility and diversity to pursue the goals of excellence in higher education and equal justice under the law. Temple offers both day and evening programs and students may enroll on either a full- or part-time basis. Of the 1,053 students enrolled at the law school, 21 percent are minority students and 48 percent are women. The faculty is an outstanding group of teacher-scholars who embody the law school's philosophical diversity. Twenty-three percent of the full-time faculty are minorities and 36 percent are women. While their accomplishments are many, it is their commitment to teaching that many students note as their greatest achievement.

■ Curriculum

Temple has a national reputation for its prize-winning **trial advocacy** programs including the distinction of being the only two-time winner of the American College of Trial Lawyers Emil Gumpert Award for Excellence in Teaching Trial Advocacy. Temple's record in law school trial competitions is unmatched. In the last ten years, Temple has earned the best record and scored the most points in the country in major law school tournaments and won more national championships than any other law school. Temple's successful trial advocacy curriculum is anchored by the innovative "Integrated Program," which combines the teaching of trial advocacy, evidence, and civil procedure.

Temple students have access to an extensive array of programs preparing them to practice law in an increasingly global society. Temple's strength in **international law** includes opportunities for summer study in Rome and Tel Aviv and a **semester-abroad program in Tokyo, Japan,** that is the only ABA-accredited semester abroad program offered by an American law school in Asia; a distinguished international law faculty; a diverse curriculum in international and comparative law; a Master of Laws

program for international students holding foreign law degrees; and active student organizations, such as the international law journal and International Law Society. Temple's strong reputation in international law has been enhanced by the JD/LLM in Transnational Law for American law students, an LLM program in Beijing, China, in which Chinese lawyers study American law, and the creation of the Institute for International Law and Public Policy.

Temple is a pioneer in the uncharted territory of **intellectual property and technology law**, preparing students to learn and succeed in the virtual world. Temple has expanded the boundaries of traditional intellectual property law by integrating bodies of law that bear on the rapid expansion of the Internet, electronic commerce, biotechnologies and other newly emerging legal issues. Through hands-on activities outside the classroom, and faculty members who are experts in the field, students learn how to meet the challenges of practicing law in a world without borders.

Temple offers superior training in **business and tax law**, including a creative program which combines the teaching of professional responsibility, substantive law courses, and business skills, such as interviewing, negotiating, and drafting. Prospective business lawyers can also pursue the JD/MBA dual-degree program, offered in conjunction with the Fox School of Business and Management, or the JD/LLM in Taxation.

Public service is a Temple tradition. Students provide legal services in the Philadelphia area through the clinical program, the Temple Legal Aid Office, and the Law, Education, and Participation Program, which offers programs designed to teach children about the law. Public interest careers are supported by the Student Public Interest Network, which provides grants for summer internships; the Public Interest Scholars Program, which provides scholarships to entering students with a demonstrated commitment to public service; and the Barrack Public Interest Fellowships, a loan repayment assistance program for graduates in public interest jobs.

■ Technology and Facilities

The law school complex consists of three newly renovated buildings designed to provide students with a state-of-the-art educational environment. "Smart" classrooms equipped with cutting-edge technology, including video, audio, and Internet access, allow faculty to use technology in all of the classrooms. The law school is committed to ensuring that our students have optimal access to electronic resources and has implemented an "anytime, anywhere" computer access program. The program includes a combination of wired and wireless network access, wired study carrels, and state-of-the-art computer labs. The faculty and administration regularly communicate with students via e-mail, and the law school uses a sophisticated course management system that allow the faculty to post assignments, syllabi, announcements, and links to a variety of additional resources for each class. Electronic study groups and discussion boards offer a unique way for students to learn outside the classroom. In addition to the vast technological resources available to students, the law library houses over 540,000 volumes, making it among the largest in the nation.

Student Activities

Students are an integral part of policymaking and governance at the law school. The Student Bar Association is the umbrella organization that oversees the over 30 student organizations that flourish at Temple, including the Black Law Students Association, the Latino Law Students Association, the Asian/Pacific Islander American Law Student Association, the Women's Law Caucus, and OUTLaw. Student publications include the *Temple Law Review*, the *Temple Journal of Science, Technology and Environmental Law*, the *Temple International and Comparative Law Journal*, and the *Temple Political and Civil Rights Law Review*. Students who excel in advocacy may participate in the National Trial Team or the Moot Court Honor Society.

Career Planning

The Career Planning Office provides one-on-one counseling, administers numerous on-campus and off-campus interviewing programs, publishes an online weekly newsletter, sponsors workshops and programs on job search skills, and maintains the Career Planning Resource Center. The 2003 graduating class had a placement rate of 95 percent.

Admissions and Financial Aid

Temple has a highly competitive admission process which is designed to look at the whole person. In keeping with Temple's commitment to diversity and its mission of offering opportunities to students who might otherwise be foreclosed from pursuing a high quality legal education, the faculty Admissions Committee may consider an application under our discretionary admission process, the Sp.A.C.E. program. Under this program, the faculty carefully selects applicants who have outstanding performance records and exceptional aptitudes for the study and practice of law, not necessarily reflected by grades and LSAT scores alone.

Our financial aid program supports the admission process with loans and both need- and merit-based scholarships, including the Beasley Scholars program, Conwell Law Scholarships, Law Faculty Scholarships, the Public Interest Scholars program, and First Year Scholar Awards.

Applicant Profile

Temple University—James E. Beasley School of Law
This grid includes only applicants who earned 120-180 LSAT scores under standard administrations.

LSAT Score	3.75 +		3.50 - 3.74		3.25 - 3.49		3.00 - 3.24		2.75 - 2.99		2.50 - 2.74		2.25 - 2.49		2.00 -2.24		Below 2.00		No GPA		Total	
	Apps	Adm	Apps	Adm	Apps	Adm	Apps	Adm	Apps	Adm	Apps	Adm	Apps	Adm	Apps	Adm	Apps	Adm	Apps	Adm	Apps	Adm
170-180	10	10	11	11	19	19	14	14	6	5	1	0	1	0	0	0	0	0	0	0	62	59
165-169	42	42	53	52	53	52	57	50	25	16	5	4	8	4	2	0	0	0	3	3	248	223
160-164	144	124	224	179	233	163	216	111	81	34	30	11	15	9	3	3	0	0	10	8	956	642
155-159	137	56	239	57	298	71	245	55	151	24	43	6	22	2	5	0	2	0	11	2	1153	273
150-154	95	13	189	18	207	7	216	7	109	1	69	2	30	2	8	0	4	0	14	2	941	52
145-149	37	1	75	2	117	7	113	1	79	2	67	0	32	0	5	0	1	0	9	0	535	13
140-144	15	0	29	0	55	0	86	0	58	0	46	0	31	0	12	0	1	0	12	0	345	0
Below 140	4	0	20	0	27	0	45	0	43	0	46	0	31	0	12	0	5	0	13	0	246	0
Total	484	246	840	319	1009	319	992	238	552	82	307	23	170	17	47	3	13	0	72	15	4486	1262

Apps = Number of Applicants
Adm = Number Admitted
Reflects 99% of the total applicant pool.

University of Tennessee College of Law

1505 W Cumberland Avenue, Suite 161
Knoxville, TN 37996-1810
Phone: 865.974.4131; Fax: 865.974.1572
E-mail: lawadmit@libra.law.utk.edu; Website: www.law.utk.edu

The Basics

Type of school	Public
Term	Semester
Application deadline	3/1
Application fee	$15
Financial aid deadline	3/1
Can first year start other than fall?	No
Student to faculty ratio (fall)	12.6 to 1
Does the university offer:	
housing restricted to law students?	No
graduate housing for which law students are eligible?	Yes

Faculty and Administrators

	Total		Men		Women		Minorities	
	Fall	Spr	Fall	Spr	Fall	Spr	Fall	Spr
Full-time	30	30	18	18	8	8	7	7
Other Full-time	0	0	0	0	0	0	0	0
Deans, librarians, & others who teach	13	13	5	5	7	7	1	1
Part-time	37	42	24	27	13	15	1	2
Total	80	85	47	50	28	30	9	10

Curriculum

		Full-time	Part-time
Typical first-year section size		52	0
Is there typically a "small section" of the first-year class, other than Legal Writing, taught by full-time faculty		No	No
If yes, typical size offered last year		0	0
# of classroom course titles beyond 1st year curriculum		102	
# of upper division courses, excluding seminars with an enrollment:	Under 25	82	
	25-49	15	
	50-74	13	
	75-99	4	
	100+	1	
# of seminars		7	
# of seminar positions available		112	
# of seminar positions filled		60	0
# of positions available in simulation courses		369	
# of simulation positions filled		282	0
# of positions available in faculty supervised clinical courses		72	
# of faculty supervised clinical positions filled		62	0
# involved in field placements		26	0
# involved in law journals		137	0
# involved in moot court or trial competitions		4	0
# of credit hours required to graduate		89	

JD Enrollment and Ethnicity

	Men		Women		Full-time		Part-time		1st-year		Total		JD Degs. Awd.
	#	%	#	%	#	%	#	%	#	%	#	%	
African Amer.	15	6.6	37	16.4	52	11.5	0	0.0	24	15.3	52	11.5	19
Amer. Indian	1	0.4	0	0.0	1	0.2	0	0.0	0	0.0	1	0.2	0
Asian Amer.	1	0.4	2	0.9	3	0.7	0	0.0	0	0.0	3	0.7	3
Mex. Amer.	0	0.0	0	0.0	0	0.0	0	0.0	0	0.0	0	0.0	0
Puerto Rican	0	0.0	0	0.0	0	0.0	0	0.0	0	0.0	0	0.0	0
Hispanic	3	1.3	1	0.4	4	0.9	0	0.0	3	1.9	4	0.9	0
Total Minority	20	8.8	40	17.8	60	13.3	0	0.0	27	17.2	60	13.3	22
For. Nation.	0	0.0	0	0.0	0	0.0	0	0.0	0	0.0	0	0.0	0
Caucasian	207	91.2	185	82.2	392	86.7	0	0.0	130	82.8	392	86.7	133
Unknown	0	0.0	0	0.0	0	0.0	0	0.0	0	0.0	0	0.0	0
Total	227	50.2	225	49.8	452	100.0	0	0.0	157	34.7	452		155

Tuition and Fees

	Resident	Nonresident
Full-time	$8,396	$21,384
Part-time	$0	$0

Living Expenses

Estimated living expenses for singles

Living on campus	Living off campus	Living at home
$13,690	$13,690	$9,484

University of Tennessee College of Law

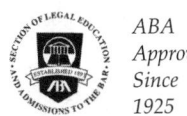

ABA
Approved
Since
1925

GPA and LSAT Scores

	Total	Full-time	Part-time
# of apps	1,556	1,556	0
# of admits	316	316	0
# of matrics	156	156	0
75% GPA	3.83	3.83	0.00
25% GPA	3.39	3.39	0.00
75% LSAT	161	161	0
25% LSAT	155	155	0

Grants and Scholarships (from prior year)

	Total		Full-time		Part-time	
	#	%	#	%	#	%
Total # of students	459		459		0	
Total # receiving grants	173	37.7	173	37.7	0	0.0
Less than 1/2 tuition	53	11.5	53	11.5	0	0.0
Half to full tuition	42	9.2	42	9.2	0	0.0
Full tuition	6	1.3	6	1.3	0	0.0
More than full tuition	72	15.7	72	15.7	0	0.0
Median grant amount			$7,168		$0	

Informational and Library Resources

# of volumes and volume equivalents	544,317
# of titles	109,863
# of active serial subscriptions	6,701
Study seating capacity inside the library	437
# of professional librarians	9
Hours per week library is open	112
# of open, wired connections available to students	164
# of networked computers available for use by students	98
# of simultaneous wireless users	900
Require computer?	N

JD Attrition (from prior year)

	Academic	Other	Total	
	#	#	#	%
1st year	0	10	10	6.3%
2nd year	1	5	6	4.2%
3rd year	0	0	0	0.0%
4th year	0	0	0	0.0%

Employment

	Total	Percentage
Employment status known	157	97.5
Employment status unknown	4	2.5
Employed	138	87.9
Pursuing graduate degrees	2	1.3
Unemployed seeking employment	4	2.5
Unemployed not seeking employment	13	8.3

Type of Employment

	Total	Percentage
# employed in law firms	104	75.4
# employed in business and industry	9	6.5
# employed in government	7	5.1
# employed in public interest	3	2.2
# employed as judicial clerks	14	10.1
# employed in academia	1	0.7

Geographic Location

	Total	Percentage
# employed in state	94	68.1
# employed in foreign countries	0	0.0
# of states where employed	16	

Bar Passage Rates

Jurisdiction	Tennessee		
Exam	Sum 03	Win 04	Total
# from school taking bar for the first time	100	12	112
School's pass rate for all first-time takers	89%	75%	88%
State's pass rate for all first-time takers	81%	79%	81%

University of Tennessee College of Law

Admissions Office, 1505 W Cumberland Avenue, Suite 161
Knoxville, TN 37996-1810
Phone: 865.974.4131; Fax: 865.974.1572
E-mail: lawadmit@libra.law.utk.edu; Website: www.law.utk.edu

■ Introduction

For more than a century, the University of Tennessee College of Law has offered a strong combination of practical and theoretical legal training. Established in 1890, the College of Law is a charter member of the AALS and is ABA-approved.

■ Enrollment/Student Body

The College of Law enrolls a diverse class each August. The 2004 entering class was composed of 156 students, of which 54 percent were women, 46 percent were men, and 18 percent were students of color. Entering students were graduates of 76 colleges and universities across the nation and the world and are residents of 18 states. Although many members of each entering class are pursuing a law degree directly from undergraduate school, a number of law students have advanced degrees and have had careers in fields as diverse as engineering, teaching, medicine, journalism, and business.

Tennessee has a relatively small law school: The total population is fewer than 500 students. Tennessee residents are approximately 80 percent of the student body, but students are from every part of the US.

■ Faculty

The quality of our faculty is evidenced by their legal training at some of the finest law schools in the US, the significance of their scholarly writings, their activity in professional associations, and their involvement with public service. Current students at UT tell potential candidates for admission that they find the faculty to be effective, accessible, and caring.

■ College of Law, Library, and Physical Facilities

The law center at the University of Tennessee—a melding of the old with the new—is an exceptional setting for legal education in the twenty-first century. The 110,000-square-foot facility was completed in 1997 and is located on Cumberland Avenue, just across from the University Center, in the heart of the campus. The law center includes the Joel A. Katz Law Library, dedicated in 1999 to a distinguished corporate and entertainment lawyer and alumnus.

■ Location

The College of Law is located on the main campus of the University of Tennessee at Knoxville, the largest city in eastern Tennessee and the third largest in the state. More than 28,000 students attend UTK. Knoxville has the natural advantage of being located in the foothills of the Great Smoky Mountains, making hiking, biking, golf, and fishing popular and accessible activities. The law school community enjoys access to campus facilities for sports and recreation, leisure, the performing arts, entertainment, and other activities.

■ Curriculum

First-year students begin law school with a week-long introductory period; a series of minicourses to introduce students to the study of law. Second- and third-year students may choose from over 70 elective courses. Two dual-degree programs are offered—the JD/MBA and the JD/MPA (Masters in Public Administration).

The College of Law offers two optional concentrations for students. The **Center for Entrepreneurial Law** allows second- and third-year students to focus on the legal aspects of the conduct of public and private enterprise, emphasizing the needs of small- and intermediate-sized business concerns. A **Business Clinic** is offered for students seeking practical experience working with business clients.

The **Center for Advocacy and Dispute Resolution** allows interested students to focus their second- and third-year experience toward a career in advocacy, commonly thought of as litigation or trial practice. UT was recognized by the American College of Trial Lawyers for the 1996 Emil Gumpert Award for Excellence in Teaching Trial Advocacy.

The **Charles H. Miller Legal Clinic** is the site for our clinical programs in advocacy and mediation. Established in 1947, this is one of the oldest continually operating clinical programs in the US. UT also offers a **Mediation Clinic**, in which students work in teams to mediate real civil and misdemeanor cases in the lower courts.

■ Student Activities and Programs

Students can choose from a variety of student programs, activities, publications, and organizations. A complete listing is available on our website.

UT moot court teams have distinguished themselves in competitions. Tennessee has won three Jerome Prince Evidence Moot Court national championships and was the first team in the history of that competition to win back-to-back titles in 2000 and 2001.

The *Tennessee Law Review* offers participants an excellent opportunity to conduct legal research and produce writings of a scholarly and practical nature. The *Transactions Business Journal* provides an opportunity for students to write about topical issues and legal developments of interest to the business bar. The Student Bar Association and various other student organizations offer numerous programs, services, and special events. The national honor fraternity, Order of the Coif, and two leading professional fraternities, Phi Delta Phi and Phi Alpha Delta, have local chapters here.

■ Admission

Admission to the College of Law is competitive. The Admissions Committee places substantial emphasis on traditional indicators of performance—UGPA and LSAT score. The committee also considers factors such as improvement in undergraduate grades and graduate school performance, strength of undergraduate institution and major course of study, extracurricular activities, community service, and employment and professional experience. Also considered are circumstances that may have affected an applicant's grades or LSAT score; economic, social, or cultural background; and success in overcoming social or economic disadvantage. Applicants are required to submit two letters of recommendation and write a personal statement and an essay.

The College of Law recognizes its obligation to assure legal education to qualified applicants who are members of historically underrepresented groups in the legal profession. The College of Law encourages applications from such students.

Successful completion of the CLEO summer institute and the Tennessee Institute for Pre-Law Program may also be considered by the Admissions Committee.

■ Expenses, Financial Aid, and Housing

The College of Law offers a number of scholarships for entering students. Scholarships may be based on academic credentials (LSAT score and UGPA), records of leadership and community service, or other factors as established by the scholarship donor. Several scholarships may be awarded for which financial need, as established by the university after the FAFSA process is complete, is a primary criteria. Candidates for admission should complete the FAFSA process as soon as possible after the first of the year to be considered for scholarships in which financial need is a factor. Candidates for admission will automatically be considered for all scholarships for which they are eligible, with the exception of the William M. Leech, Jr. Memorial Scholarship, the Graduate Research Assistantships, and the Clarence and Augusta Kolwyck Memorial Achievement Award, for which specific application is required. Please check our website or our Applicant Guide for more information and application guidelines. Campus apartment housing is open to law students. Knoxville also offers ample private apartment housing at a reasonable cost. Knoxville Place, a new campus living community, is adjacent to the law school.

■ Career Services

Career Services helps students research, select, and seek the right career path for them. These efforts have contributed to consistently high employment rates for UT graduates, well above the national average in recent years. Most graduates choose to stay in the southeastern US, but recent graduates have accepted associate positions and judicial clerkships from Portland, Oregon, to Los Angeles, and from New York City to the US Virgin Islands.

Applicant Profile

University of Tennessee College of Law
This grid includes only applicants who earned 120-180 LSAT scores under standard administrations.

LSAT Score	3.75 +		3.50 - 3.74		3.25 - 3.49		3.00 - 3.24		2.75 - 2.99		2.50 - 2.74		2.25 - 2.49		2.00 - 2.24		Below 2.00		No GPA		Total	
	Apps	Adm	Apps	Adm	Apps	Adm	Apps	Adm	Apps	Adm	Apps	Adm	Apps	Adm	Apps	Adm	Apps	Adm	Apps	Adm	Apps	Adm
175-180	0	0	0	0	0	0	0	0	0	0	0	0	0	0	0	0	0	0	0	0	0	0
170-174	0	0	1	1	1	1	1	1	0	0	1	1	0	0	0	0	0	0	0	0	4	4
165-169	7	7	5	4	8	7	7	6	4	1	2	0	2	0	1	0	0	0	1	0	37	25
160-164	41	36	51	40	47	36	33	13	14	4	10	1	8	1	2	0	0	0	3	1	209	132
155-159	84	46	102	41	111	30	80	4	42	0	25	2	6	0	5	0	1	0	2	1	458	124
150-154	63	11	77	5	75	3	72	4	58	3	25	2	9	0	3	0	0	0	5	1	387	29
145-149	27	5	33	3	58	3	35	0	37	4	24	1	10	0	6	0	3	0	8	0	241	16
140-144	4	0	16	1	21	2	26	1	19	0	15	0	15	0	4	0	2	0	2	0	124	4
135-139	2	0	2	0	5	0	14	0	3	0	9	0	7	0	7	0	0	0	4	0	53	0
130-134	1	0	0	0	0	0	3	0	2	0	5	0	2	0	1	0	0	0	3	0	17	0
125-129	0	0	0	0	1	0	4	0	0	0	2	0	0	0	1	0	0	0	2	0	10	0
120-124	0	0	0	0	0	0	0	0	0	0	0	0	0	0	0	0	0	0	0	0	0	0
Total	229	105	287	95	327	82	275	29	179	12	118	7	59	1	30	0	6	0	30	3	1540	334

Apps = Number of Applicants   Adm = Number Admitted   Reflects 97% of the total applicant pool.

The University of Texas School of Law

727 East Dean Keeton
Austin, TX 78705
Phone: 512.232.1200; Fax: 512.471.2765
E-mail: admissions@mail.law.utexas.edu; Website: www.utexas.edu/law/

Official ABA Data

ABA Approved Since 1923

The Basics

Type of school	Public
Term	Semester
Application deadline	11/1 2/1
Application fee	$70
Financial aid deadline	3/31
Can first year start other than fall?	No
Student to faculty ratio (fall)	17.1 to 1
Does the university offer:	
housing restricted to law students?	No
graduate housing for which law students are eligible?	Yes

Faculty and Administrators

	Total		Men		Women		Minorities	
	Fall	Spr	Fall	Spr	Fall	Spr	Fall	Spr
Full-time	69	62	48	41	21	21	7	6
Other Full-time	3	4	0	1	3	3	0	0
Deans, librarians, & others who teach	7	7	4	4	3	3	1	1
Part-time	45	84	32	54	13	30	5	8
Total	124	157	84	100	40	57	13	15

Curriculum

	Full-time	Part-time
Typical first-year section size	126	0
Is there typically a "small section" of the first-year class, other than Legal Writing, taught by full-time faculty	Yes	No
If yes, typical size offered last year	31	0
# of classroom course titles beyond 1st year curriculum	140	
# of upper division courses, excluding seminars with an enrollment: Under 25	132	
25-49	52	
50-74	30	
75-99	10	
100+	23	
# of seminars	59	
# of seminar positions available	768	
# of seminar positions filled	654	0
# of positions available in simulation courses	438	
# of simulation positions filled	397	0
# of positions available in faculty supervised clinical courses	237	
# of faculty supervised clinical positions filled	198	0
# involved in field placements	186	0
# involved in law journals	652	0
# involved in moot court or trial competitions	240	0
# of credit hours required to graduate	86	

JD Enrollment and Ethnicity

	Men		Women		Full-time		Part-time		1st-year		Total		JD Degs. Awd.
	#	%	#	%	#	%	#	%	#	%	#	%	
African Amer.	24	2.9	47	7.1	71	4.8	0	0.0	22	5.0	71	4.8	15
Amer. Indian	4	0.5	6	0.9	10	0.7	0	0.0	5	1.1	10	0.7	3
Asian Amer.	42	5.1	61	9.2	103	6.9	0	0.0	28	6.4	103	6.9	34
Mex. Amer.	99	11.9	75	11.3	174	11.7	0	0.0	60	13.7	174	11.7	32
Puerto Rican	0	0.0	0	0.0	0	0.0	0	0.0	0	0.0	0	0.0	0
Hispanic	37	4.5	21	3.2	58	3.9	0	0.0	24	5.5	58	3.9	7
Total Minority	206	24.8	210	31.6	416	27.9	0	0.0	139	31.8	416	27.9	91
For. Nation.	0	0.0	0	0.0	0	0.0	0	0.0	0	0.0	0	0.0	0
Caucasian	514	62.0	409	61.6	923	61.8	0	0.0	233	53.3	923	61.8	335
Unknown	109	13.1	45	6.8	154	10.3	0	0.0	65	14.9	154	10.3	40
Total	829	55.5	664	44.5	1493	100.0	0	0.0	437	29.3	1493		466

Tuition and Fees

	Resident	Nonresident
Full-time	$13,955	$25,003
Part-time	$10,836	$18,956

Living Expenses

Estimated living expenses for singles

Living on campus	Living off campus	Living at home
$11,290	$11,792	$6,096

The University of Texas School of Law

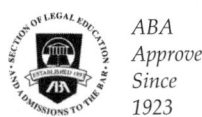

*ABA
Approved
Since
1923*

GPA and LSAT Scores

	Total	Full-time	Part-time
# of apps	6,098	6,098	0
# of admits	955	955	0
# of matrics	425	425	0
75% GPA	3.79	3.79	0.00
25% GPA	3.40	3.40	0.00
75% LSAT	167	167	0
25% LSAT	162	162	0

Grants and Scholarships (from prior year)

	Total		Full-time		Part-time	
	#	%	#	%	#	%
Total # of students	1,532		1,532		0	
Total # receiving grants	852	55.6	852	55.6	0	0.0
Less than 1/2 tuition	795	51.9	795	51.9	0	0.0
Half to full tuition	2	0.1	2	0.1	0	0.0
Full tuition	32	2.1	32	2.1	0	0.0
More than full tuition	23	1.5	23	1.5	0	0.0
Median grant amount			$1,250		$0	

Informational and Library Resources

# of volumes and volume equivalents	1,010,074
# of titles	339,045
# of active serial subscriptions	7,977
Study seating capacity inside the library	1,321
# of professional librarians	15
Hours per week library is open	99
# of open, wired connections available to students	310
# of networked computers available for use by students	215
# of simultaneous wireless users	3,500
Require computer?	N

JD Attrition (from prior year)

	Academic	Other	Total	
	#	#	#	%
1st year	0	7	7	1.4%
2nd year	0	9	9	1.6%
3rd year	0	2	2	0.4%
4th year	0	0	0	0.0%

Employment

	Total	Percentage
Employment status known	489	100.0
Employment status unknown	0	0.0
Employed	467	95.5
Pursuing graduate degrees	5	1.0
Unemployed seeking employment	4	0.8
Unemployed not seeking employment	13	2.7

Type of Employment

# employed in law firms	291	62.3
# employed in business and industry	33	7.1
# employed in government	55	11.8
# employed in public interest	21	4.5
# employed as judicial clerks	55	11.8
# employed in academia	8	1.7

Geographic Location

# employed in state	352	75.4
# employed in foreign countries	6	1.3
# of states where employed	34	

Bar Passage Rates

Jurisdiction	Texas			New York		
Exam	Sum 03	Win 04	Total	Sum 03	Win 04	Total
# from school taking bar for the first time	347	46	393	27	3	30
School's pass rate for all first-time takers	93%	89%	93%	96%	67%	93%
State's pass rate for all first-time takers	83%	69%	80%	78%	58%	75%

The University of Texas School of Law

727 East Dean Keeton
Austin, TX 78705
Phone: 512.232.1200; Fax: 512.471.2765
E-mail: admissions@mail.law.utexas.edu; Website: www.utexas.edu/law/

■ Introduction

The School of Law is located at The University of Texas at Austin. This location in the heart of the capital city provides ready access to the state legislature, the Supreme Court of Texas, federal trial and appellate court, offices of state and federal agencies, and the libraries and other main campus facilities. Recognized for its distinguished faculty and rich academic program, the law school has been a member of AALS since 1907, was approved by the ABA in 1923, and is fully accredited.

Situated on the banks of the Colorado River, Austin is an eclectic town noted for its politics, scholars, rolling hills, film industry, and live music and restaurant scene. The University of Texas plays an important role in this metropolitan area of over one million people, and many entertainment and cultural activities cater to the student population.

■ Enrollment/Student Body

As a Texas public institution, the Texas legislature limits nonresident enrollment to 20 percent of the population. We currently have over 250 undergraduate institutions, 48 states, and the District of Columbia represented in our student body. Please refer to the statistical information for details as to the strength of the student body and the competition for admission.

■ Library and Physical Facilities

The Tarlton Law Library of the Joseph D. Jamail Center for Legal Research, with over one million volumes, is the seventh largest academic law library in the United States and the finest legal research center in the Southwest. It houses working collections from many other countries, with special strength in primary legal materials from Latin America and Western European nations, as well as a full depository for European Union documents. A suite of rooms in the law library houses rare books, manuscripts, law school archives, and special collections of materials ranging from a fifteenth century Roman law codex to the papers of former Supreme Court Justice Tom C. Clark. The Hyder Collection, a 4,000-item collection of law-related artifacts, makes the library an unusually welcoming place for study.

■ Faculty

The University of Texas School of Law has long had one of the outstanding faculties in the nation, both in terms of scholarly distinction of the faculty members and their success in the classroom. More than a third of the faculty is elected to the American Law Institute, one of the highest percentage memberships in the nation. Texas is also one of only a dozen schools with three active faculty elected to the American Academy of Arts and Sciences, the nation's most prestigious learned society. The law school has consistently hired the best and brightest younger scholars, including eight former clerks for justices of the United States Supreme Court.

Texas enjoys a leadership position in many areas of legal study. The breadth and depth of offerings in several areas—constitutional law, environmental law, wills and estates, admiralty and maritime law, torts and product liability, labor law, jurisprudence and philosophy—is matched by few schools in the country. With one of the largest faculties in the country, Texas is able to offer students coverage of all fields of law and exposure to truly diverse scholarly perspectives on legal questions.

■ Curriculum

All first-year students are required to take a full courseload, averaging 15 hours per week, in contracts, property, torts, civil procedure, criminal law, constitutional law, brief writing and oral advocacy, and legal research and writing. After the first year, the only required courses are professional responsibility, advanced constitutional law, and a writing and research seminar. A student may design his or her course of study from an array of course offerings in many fields of law. These offerings include interdisciplinary and advanced public and private law courses.

■ Special Programs

The school offers clinical education courses for credit in such fields as capital punishment, children's rights, criminal defense, domestic violence, housing, immigration, juvenile justice, mediation, and mental health. Internships are available to qualified students with the Texas Supreme Court, the Texas Court of Criminal Appeals, and the Third Court of Appeals. A limited number of externships are available for credit in the public-service area. The law school also has an extensive trial-advocacy program boasting several national championships. There are a number of joint-degree programs: JD/MPAff; JD/MBA; JD/Master of Arts in Latin American Studies; JD/Master of Science in Community and Regional Planning; JD/Master of Arts in Russian, East European, and Eurasian Studies; and JD/Master of Arts in Middle Eastern Studies, in addition to several combined programs with a PhD.

■ Admission

Admission to the JD program at UT Law is competitive. For the entering class of 2004, more than 6,000 applicants competed for the 450 seats in the entering class. As a general rule, there are no presumptive numbers. Every application completed and submitted is reviewed in its entirety. Each applicant must take the LSAT and have earned a baccalaureate degree from an accredited college or university with a minimum grade-point average of 2.2 as calculated by the Law School Admission Council (LSAC), or have completed the equivalent of six semesters and expect to graduate during the current academic year. Each candidate must complete all application forms and fulfill all mandatory attachments as described in the application.

■ Student-Edited Journals

The School of Law offers many student-administered, cocurricular activities that enhance the law students' regular studies. Student-edited journals include *American Journal of Criminal Law, Texas Environmental Law Journal, Texas Forum on Civil Liberties and Civil Rights, Texas Hispanic Journal of Law and Policy, Texas Intellectual Property Law Journal, Texas International Law Journal, Texas Journal of Business Law, Texas Journal of Women and the Law, Texas Law Review, Texas Review of Entertainment and Sports Law, Texas Review of Law and Politics,* and *The Review of Litigation.*

■ Financial Aid

A limited number of scholarships are available for first-year students on the basis of performance and financial need. The prestigious Townes-Rice Scholarship

is offered to eight outstanding law students with full-tuition and fees plus stipends for all three years of law school. Scholarships and research assistantships are available for second- and third-year students. The law school administers several short-term and long-term loan funds for students with financial need, and the university offers substantial federally funded loan programs.

■ Housing

Approximately 95 percent of all law students live off-campus. The Division of Housing and Food Services (Box 7666, University Station, Austin, TX 78713; telephone 512.471.3136) has information regarding on-campus living. Other sources of information are classified ads in the student newspaper, the *Daily Texan,* apartment management services, rental agencies, and current students.

■ Career Services

Each year, nearly 400 employers representing over 550 offices participate in career services programs and recruit our students for summer and full-time positions through on-campus interviews, recruit-by-mail opportunities, and off-campus job fairs. Over 50 percent of on-campus employers are from outside the state of Texas. For the past three years, more than 99 percent of graduates who are actively seeking employment have secured it within nine months of graduation.

Applicant Profile

The University of Texas School of Law
This grid includes only applicants who earned 120-180 LSAT scores under standard administrations.

LSAT Score	3.75 +		3.50 - 3.74		3.25 - 3.49		3.00 - 3.24		2.75 - 2.99		2.50 - 2.74		2.25 - 2.49		2.00 - 2.24		Below 2.00		No GPA		Total	
	Apps	Adm	Apps	Adm	Apps	Adm	Apps	Adm	Apps	Adm	Apps	Adm	Apps	Adm	Apps	Adm	Apps	Adm	Apps	Adm	Apps	Adm
175-180	10	10	14	13	8	3	6	4	4	1	1	0	0	0	0	0	0	0	0	0	43	31
170-174	79	77	65	43	62	21	28	10	12	1	6	0	4	0	1	0	0	0	3	1	260	153
165-169	264	232	245	132	197	51	104	23	42	3	21	0	7	0	2	0	1	0	6	3	889	444
160-164	425	100	543	60	380	37	210	12	107	6	54	2	14	1	2	0	0	0	20	3	1755	221
155-159	279	13	366	28	329	15	212	8	99	3	54	0	24	0	2	0	2	0	16	0	1383	67
150-154	142	7	203	8	194	5	169	1	93	3	59	2	24	0	6	0	1	0	7	0	898	26
145-149	47	1	108	2	90	0	93	2	48	0	42	0	13	1	10	0	0	0	9	0	460	6
140-144	18	0	38	1	47	1	62	0	38	2	34	0	10	0	3	0	1	0	5	0	256	4
135-139	3	0	7	0	13	0	8	0	11	0	15	0	14	1	7	0	0	0	0	0	78	1
130-134	1	0	0	0	2	0	6	0	5	0	5	0	3	0	1	0	1	0	3	0	27	0
125-129	0	0	1	0	0	0	0	0	2	0	1	0	1	0	1	0	0	0	0	0	6	0
120-124	0	0	0	0	0	0	0	0	0	0	0	0	0	0	0	0	0	0	0	0	0	0
Total	1268	440	1590	287	1322	133	898	60	461	19	292	4	114	3	35	0	6	0	69	7	6055	953

Apps = Number of Applicants
Adm = Number Admitted
Reflects 99% of the total applicant pool.

Texas Southern University—Thurgood Marshall School of Law

3100 Cleburne
Houston, TX 77004
Phone: 713.313.7114; Fax: 713.313.7297
E-mail: tsimmons@tsulaw.edu; Website: www.tsu.edu/academics/law

ABA
Approved
Since
1949

The Basics

Type of school	Public
Term	Semester
Application deadline	4/1
Application fee	$50
Financial aid deadline	4/1
Can first year start other than fall?	No
Student to faculty ratio (fall)	15.6 to 1
Does the university offer:	
housing restricted to law students?	No
graduate housing for which law students are eligible?	No

Faculty and Administrators

	Total		Men		Women		Minorities	
	Fall	Spr	Fall	Spr	Fall	Spr	Fall	Spr
Full-time	34	34	18	18	16	16	28	28
Other Full-time	2	2	1	1	1	1	2	2
Deans, librarians, & others who teach	10	10	4	4	6	6	9	9
Part-time	7	12	7	10	0	2	6	10
Total	53	58	30	33	23	25	45	49

Curriculum

		Full-time	Part-time
Typical first-year section size		66	0
Is there typically a "small section" of the first-year class, other than Legal Writing, taught by full-time faculty		No	No
If yes, typical size offered last year		0	0
# of classroom course titles beyond 1st year curriculum		119	
# of upper division courses, excluding seminars with an enrollement:	Under 25	43	
	25-49	18	
	50-74	19	
	75-99	0	
	100+	0	
# of seminars		18	
# of seminar positions available		20	
# of seminar positions filled		156	0
# of positions available in simulation courses		18	
# of simulation positions filled		164	0
# of positions available in faculty supervised clinical courses		10	
# of faculty supervised clinical positions filled		6	0
# involved in field placements		54	0
# involved in law journals		7	0
# involved in moot court or trial competitions		30	0
# of credit hours required to graduate		90	

JD Enrollment and Ethnicity

	Men		Women		Full-time		Part-time		1st-year		Total		JD Degs. Awd.
	#	%	#	%	#	%	#	%	#	%	#	%	
African Amer.	90	32.8	217	61.3	307	48.9	0	0.0	142	53.4	307	48.9	99
Amer. Indian	3	1.1	0	0.0	3	0.5	0	0.0	1	0.4	3	0.5	0
Asian Amer.	16	5.8	21	5.9	37	5.9	0	0.0	18	6.8	37	5.9	5
Mex. Amer.	74	27.0	55	15.5	129	20.5	0	0.0	52	19.5	129	20.5	25
Puerto Rican	0	0.0	0	0.0	0	0.0	0	0.0	0	0.0	0	0.0	0
Hispanic	10	3.6	8	2.3	18	2.9	0	0.0	7	2.6	18	2.9	3
Total Minority	193	70.4	301	85.0	494	78.7	0	0.0	220	82.7	494	78.7	132
For. Nation.	0	0.0	0	0.0	0	0.0	0	0.0	0	0.0	0	0.0	0
Caucasian	65	23.7	43	12.1	108	17.2	0	0.0	34	12.8	108	17.2	24
Unknown	16	5.8	10	2.8	26	4.1	0	0.0	12	4.5	26	4.1	0
Total	274	43.6	354	56.4	628	100.0	0	0.0	266	42.4	628		156

Tuition and Fees

	Resident	Nonresident
Full-time	$9,664	$12,856
Part-time	$0	$0

Living Expenses

Estimated living expenses for singles

Living on campus	Living off campus	Living at home
$11,026	$11,026	$11,026

Texas Southern University—Thurgood Marshall School of Law

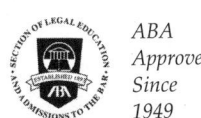

ABA
Approved
Since
1949

GPA and LSAT Scores

	Total	Full-time	Part-time
# of apps	2,102	2,102	0
# of admits	512	512	0
# of matrics	265	265	0
75% GPA	0.00	3.23	0.00
25% GPA	0.00	2.66	0.00
75% LSAT	147	147	0
25% LSAT	142	142	0

Grants and Scholarships (from prior year)

	Total		Full-time		Part-time	
	#	%	#	%	#	%
Total # of students	570		570		0	
Total # receiving grants	456	80.0	456	80.0	0	0.0
Less than 1/2 tuition	19	3.3	19	3.3	0	0.0
Half to full tuition	209	36.7	209	36.7	0	0.0
Full tuition	0	0.0	0	0.0	0	0.0
More than full tuition	228	40.0	228	40.0	0	0.0
Median grant amount			$3,000		$0	

Informational and Library Resources

# of volumes and volume equivalents	580,628
# of titles	131,665
# of active serial subscriptions	2,626
Study seating capacity inside the library	378
# of professional librarians	8
Hours per week library is open	108
# of open, wired connections available to students	945
# of networked computers available for use by students	41
# of simultaneous wireless users	500
Require computer?	N

JD Attrition (from prior year)

	Academic	Other	Total	
	#	#	#	%
1st year	29	20	49	19.3%
2nd year	0	4	4	2.5%
3rd year	0	0	0	0.0%
4th year	0	0	0	0.0%

Employment

	Total	Percentage
Employment status known	146	88.0
Employment status unknown	20	12.0
Employed	134	91.8
Pursuing graduate degrees	4	2.7
Unemployed seeking employment	8	5.5
Unemployed not seeking employment	0	0.0

Type of Employment

	Total	Percentage
# employed in law firms	66	49.3
# employed in business and industry	16	11.9
# employed in government	2	1.5
# employed in public interest	8	6.0
# employed as judicial clerks	5	3.7
# employed in academia	3	2.2

Geographic Location

	Total	Percentage
# employed in state	109	81.3
# employed in foreign countries	2	1.5
# of states where employed	13	

Bar Passage Rates

Jurisdiction	Texas		
Exam	Sum 03	Win 04	Total
# from school taking bar for the first time	117	24	141
School's pass rate for all first-time takers	50%	42%	49%
State's pass rate for all first-time takers	83%	69%	80%

Texas Southern University—Thurgood Marshall School of Law

Office of Admissions, 3100 Cleburne
Houston, TX 77004
Phone: 713.313.7114; Fax: 713.313.7297
E-mail: tsimmons@tsulaw.edu; Website: www.tsu.edu/academics/law

■ Introduction

The Thurgood Marshall School of Law, a state institution founded in 1947, seeks to provide a legal education and an opportunity to excel to students from a wide range of backgrounds, including those who otherwise would not have an opportunity for legal training. The law school is accredited by the ABA. The student body is truly multi-ethnic and multicultural. The law school is housed in a trilevel structure and is located just outside downtown Houston. Near-campus housing is available in the form of modern apartments for single and married students. The school makes extensive use of legal facilities in Houston through its clinical programs.

■ Enrollment/Student Body

A majority of the students are from Texas, but all parts of the country are represented. Approximately 49 percent of the students are black, 23 percent Chicano, 17 percent Caucasian, and 6 percent Asian and Native American. The median age range is about 26 to 36 years.

■ Library and Physical Facilities

Students receive individual or group orientation and intensive training in the use of the library. The law school has undergone approximately $16 million in renovations, expanding the available space from 103,000 to 108,000 square feet.

■ Curriculum

Upon entry to the School of Law, all students in the first-year class are required to attend a week-long orientation program. Attention is given to examinations, briefing cases, outlining, and an overview of law school life and expectations.

The law school offers a three-year, full-time JD program. The minimum courseload is 12 hours. Required courses for the first year are Lawyering Process I and II, Civil Procedure, Property, Contracts, Torts, and Criminal Law. Second-year students must take Constitutional Law, Evidence, Criminal Procedure, Trial Simulation, Business Associations, Commercial Law, Professional Responsibility, and Wills and Trusts. Second- or third-year students are required to take Federal Jurisdiction and Procedure, a seminar/independent research project, and Basic Federal Taxation. Third-year students are required to take Consumer Rights and Texas Practice. The remaining hours required to complete the degree may be selected from a number of areas of interest.

The law school operates a full-time, in-house clinic in which students work under the supervision of faculty and adjunct faculty members. Internships are available with the Harris County District Attorney's Office, the Federal Magistrates, Gulf Coast Legal Foundation, the Federal Bankruptcy Court, the Harris County Attorney's Office, the Internal Revenue Service, and the US District Court. The school operates a number of clinics, including advanced skills, basic skills, civil and criminal externships, environmental justice, family law, and housing law. A judicial externship with state and federal judges is available to academically outstanding third-year students.

■ Admission

The GPA and LSAT (or average LSAT if attempted more than once on same scale) are factored into a formula that places more weight on the LSAT. The number derived, the index, is used to determine an applicant's initial competitiveness.

No particular undergraduate major is preferred, but the school looks for applicants with broad backgrounds in the social sciences, natural sciences, humanities, and business sciences. Admission decisions are based primarily on the applicant's motivation and intellectual capacity, undergraduate GPA, and LSAT scores. Newly admitted students must send two seat deposits ($150 upon acceptance and $100 in June), which are refundable upon matriculation. The law school's student body represents one of the most culturally and ethnically diverse student bodies in the country. Transfer applications are accepted; students must submit a transcript and letter from the dean of their former law school stating that they are in good standing. All newly admitted students must submit an official transcript from the baccalaureate degree-granting institution as well as all law schools attended. No application will be evaluated by the Admissions Committee until the LSDAS report has been received.

In order to ensure complete review, applications must be received by the Office of Admissions no later than April 1, although earlier submission is encouraged. Entering students are admitted only in August (fall semester). Students are notified of acceptance after the Admissions Committee has reviewed the complete file. Admission decisions are made on a rolling basis.

■ Student Activities

Numerous law school organizations are active on campus. A student board edits the *Thurgood Marshall Law Review*. Moot court competitions are held in trial and appellate work, labor law, and client counseling.

Texas Southern University—Thurgood Marshall School of Law

■ Expenses and Financial Aid

About 90 percent of the students receive some form of aid. The law school administers its own scholarship program, which is competitive. Scholarships are awarded on the basis of both need and merit, and may range up to full tuition. The university also offers additional scholarship aid, and the law school and the university offer loan assistance. Ten to fifteen percent of the students hold assistantships. The aid application deadline is April 1.

The scholarship program makes several awards (approximately 60) each year. The awards have enabled out-of-state residents to qualify for resident-tuition rates. In addition, a number of law students each year qualify for the federal work-study and loan programs. Additional limited scholarship aid is available to students after they have completed a year of law study. An applicant in need of other financial assistance should make arrangements for financial aid through the Law School Financial Aid Counselor by either calling 713.313.7243 or e-mail *mabraxton@tsulaw.edu*.

■ Career Development

The law school employs a full-time career development officer. Graduates are placed primarily with law firms, federal and state agencies, legal services, judges, and businesses. The Career Development Office also conducts a major national effort to encourage legal employers in every major city in the United States to recruit Texas Southern University—Thurgood Marshall School of Law graduates.

Applicant Profile

Texas Southern University—Thurgood Marshall School of Law
This grid includes only applicants who earned 120-180 LSAT scores under standard administrations.

LSAT Score	3.75 +		3.50 - 3.74		3.25 - 3.49		3.00 - 3.24		2.75 - 2.99		2.50 - 2.74		2.25 - 2.49		2.00 - 2.24		Below 2.00		No GPA		Total	
	Apps	Adm	Apps	Adm	Apps	Adm	Apps	Adm	Apps	Adm	Apps	Adm	Apps	Adm	Apps	Adm	Apps	Adm	Apps	Adm	Apps	Adm
175-180	0	0	0	0	0	0	0	0	0	0	0	0	0	0	0	0	0	0	0	0	0	0
170-174	0	0	1	0	0	0	0	0	0	0	0	0	0	0	0	0	0	0	0	0	1	0
165-169	0	0	0	0	0	0	0	0	0	0	0	0	1	0	0	0	0	0	0	0	1	0
160-164	1	1	0	0	0	0	2	2	4	2	0	0	1	0	1	1	0	0	0	0	9	6
155-159	0	0	3	2	9	4	12	9	9	5	10	7	6	1	5	0	2	0	1	0	57	28
150-154	12	9	16	8	16	12	33	21	30	16	30	14	18	6	14	7	2	1	2	0	173	94
145-149	8	5	19	6	42	21	67	35	79	37	67	22	45	16	26	10	7	0	8	3	368	155
140-144	17	11	46	22	76	40	151	60	128	37	128	30	108	17	53	5	7	0	22	1	736	223
135-139	7	2	31	3	54	4	76	2	93	0	77	1	61	0	29	0	13	1	15	0	456	13
130-134	3	0	6	0	12	0	17	0	34	1	29	0	27	0	16	1	5	0	16	0	165	2
125-129	0	0	0	0	1	0	3	0	3	0	5	0	4	0	8	0	1	0	3	0	28	0
120-124	0	0	0	0	0	0	1	0	0	0	0	0	1	0	0	0	0	0	1	0	3	0
Total	48	28	122	41	210	81	362	129	380	98	346	74	272	40	152	24	37	2	68	4	1997	521

Apps = Number of Applicants
Adm = Number Admitted
Reflects 99% of the total applicant pool.

Texas Tech University School of Law

1802 Hartford Avenue
Lubbock, TX 79409
Phone: 806.742.3791; Fax: 806.742.1629
E-mail: donna.williams@ttu.edu; Website: www.law.ttu.edu

ABA
Approved
Since
1969

The Basics

Type of school	Public
Term	Semester
Application deadline	11/1 2/1
Application fee	$50
Financial aid deadline	4/15
Can first year start other than fall?	Yes
Student to faculty ratio (fall)	19.6 to 1
Does the university offer:	
housing restricted to law students?	No
graduate housing for which law students are eligible?	Yes

Faculty and Administrators

	Total		Men		Women		Minorities	
	Fall	Spr	Fall	Spr	Fall	Spr	Fall	Spr
Full-time	29	28	19	16	10	12	6	6
Other Full-time	0	0	0	0	0	0	0	0
Deans, librarians, & others who teach	8	7	5	5	3	2	3	2
Part-time	15	20	14	17	1	3	3	3
Total	52	55	38	38	14	17	12	11

Curriculum

	Full-time	Part-time
Typical first-year section size	74	0
Is there typically a "small section" of the first-year class, other than Legal Writing, taught by full-time faculty	No	No
If yes, typical size offered last year	0	0
# of classroom course titles beyond 1st year curriculum	91	
# of upper division courses, excluding seminars with an enrollment: Under 25	60	
25-49	32	
50-74	12	
75-99	6	
100+	8	
# of seminars	16	
# of seminar positions available	296	
# of seminar positions filled	262	0
# of positions available in simulation courses	302	
# of simulation positions filled	236	0
# of positions available in faculty supervised clinical courses	79	
# of faculty supervised clinical positions filled	70	0
# involved in field placements	64	0
# involved in law journals	103	0
# involved in moot court or trial competitions	45	0
# of credit hours required to graduate	90	

JD Enrollment and Ethnicity

	Men		Women		Full-time		Part-time		1st-year		Total		JD Degs. Awd.
	#	%	#	%	#	%	#	%	#	%	#	%	
African Amer.	8	2.3	9	2.7	17	2.5	0	0.0	8	3.3	17	2.5	5
Amer. Indian	2	0.6	3	0.9	5	0.7	0	0.0	4	1.6	5	0.7	2
Asian Amer.	7	2.0	8	2.4	15	2.2	0	0.0	11	4.5	15	2.2	3
Mex. Amer.	33	9.6	46	13.6	79	11.6	0	0.0	33	13.5	79	11.6	16
Puerto Rican	0	0.0	0	0.0	0	0.0	0	0.0	0	0.0	0	0.0	0
Hispanic	0	0.0	0	0.0	0	0.0	0	0.0	0	0.0	0	0.0	0
Total Minority	50	14.5	66	19.5	116	17.0	0	0.0	56	22.9	116	17.0	26
For. Nation.	0	0.0	1	0.3	1	0.1	0	0.0	0	0.0	1	0.1	0
Caucasian	293	84.9	264	78.1	557	81.6	0	0.0	185	75.5	557	81.6	191
Unknown	2	0.6	7	2.1	9	1.3	0	0.0	4	1.6	9	1.3	0
Total	345	50.5	338	49.5	683	100.0	0	0.0	245	35.9	683		217

Tuition and Fees

	Resident	Nonresident
Full-time	$11,126	$17,454
Part-time	$0	$0

Living Expenses

Estimated living expenses for singles

Living on campus	Living off campus	Living at home
$12,196	$12,196	N/A

Texas Tech University School of Law

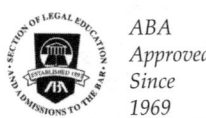

*ABA
Approved
Since
1969*

GPA and LSAT Scores

	Total	Full-time	Part-time
# of apps	1,550	1,550	0
# of admits	504	504	0
# of matrics	244	244	0
75% GPA	3.78	3.78	0.00
25% GPA	3.33	3.33	0.00
75% LSAT	157	157	0
25% LSAT	150	150	0

Grants and Scholarships (from prior year)

	Total		Full-time		Part-time	
	#	%	#	%	#	%
Total # of students	672		672		0	
Total # receiving grants	458	68.2	458	68.2	0	0.0
Less than 1/2 tuition	344	51.2	344	51.2	0	0.0
Half to full tuition	22	3.3	22	3.3	0	0.0
Full tuition	76	11.3	76	11.3	0	0.0
More than full tuition	16	2.4	16	2.4	0	0.0
Median grant amount			$5,508		$0	

Informational and Library Resources

# of volumes and volume equivalents	289,344
# of titles	61,339
# of active serial subscriptions	2,597
Study seating capacity inside the library	539
# of professional librarians	7
Hours per week library is open	168
# of open, wired connections available to students	621
# of networked computers available for use by students	326
# of simultaneous wireless users	260
Require computer?	N

JD Attrition (from prior year)

	Academic	Other	Total	
	#	#	#	%
1st year	6	11	17	7.6%
2nd year	1	1	2	0.8%
3rd year	1	0	1	0.5%
4th year	0	0	0	0.0%

Employment

	Total	Percentage
Employment status known	200	91.3
Employment status unknown	19	8.7
Employed	197	98.5
Pursuing graduate degrees	1	0.5
Unemployed seeking employment	2	1.0
Unemployed not seeking employment	0	0.0

Type of Employment

	Total	Percentage
# employed in law firms	139	70.6
# employed in business and industry	14	7.1
# employed in government	34	17.3
# employed in public interest	1	0.5
# employed as judicial clerks	9	4.6
# employed in academia	0	0.0

Geographic Location

	Total	Percentage
# employed in state	191	97.0
# employed in foreign countries	0	0.0
# of states where employed	4	

Bar Passage Rates

Jurisdiction	Texas		
Exam	Sum 03	Win 04	Total
# from school taking bar for the first time	177	43	220
School's pass rate for all first-time takers	90%	67%	85%
State's pass rate for all first-time takers	83%	69%	80%

Texas Tech University School of Law

1802 Hartford Avenue
Lubbock, TX 79409
Phone: 806.742.3791; Fax: 806.742.1629
E-mail: donna.williams@ttu.edu; Website: www.law.ttu.edu

■ Introduction

The school, which accepted its first class in 1967, is located on the main campus of Texas Tech University in Lubbock. It is fully accredited with the Supreme Court of Texas and the ABA and is a member of the AALS. Its graduates are eligible to take the bar examination in any state in the nation. In 1974, a chapter of the Order of the Coif was established, a distinction accorded to only one-third of American law schools. The faculty embraces an open-door policy, enabling students to ask questions beyond formal class hours.

■ Library and Physical Facilities

The school is designed to meet the needs of a contemporary legal education. The law library supports the research and academic needs of the students and faculty as evinced by superb computer resources and wireless Internet access, complementing a substantial collection of printed materials. All students have 24/7 access to the library and assigned library carrels that serve as computer-based workstations. All classrooms are equipped with state-of-the-art technology, including individual connections to power and/or network in every room.

■ Curriculum

The program of study equips students to practice law as advocates, counselors, judges, or law teachers, and the school recognizes that legal education is also a stepping-stone to careers in government, politics, or business. The required curriculum provides a broad-based legal education. Elective courses afford students the opportunity to create an area of concentration, ranging from business law to emerging areas such as health law, natural resources law, and law and bioterrorism. The School of Law offers an Academic Success Program to assist students in developing the skills to succeed in the study and practice of law.

■ Programs of Study

Qualified students may elect to pursue one of several joint-degree programs: the JD/MBA; the JD/MPA; the JD/MS in Agriculture and Applied Economics; the JD/MS in Accounting (Taxation); the JD/Master of Environmental Toxicology; the JD/Master of Biotechnology; the JD/MS in Personal Financial Planning; and the JD/MS in Crop Science/Horticulture/Soil Science/Entomology. Successful completion of the JD/MS in Personal Financial Planning qualifies students to sit for the Certified Financial Planning exam. The joint-degree programs allow students to complete the requirements for both degrees in three to four academic years. Also, in 2004, the school initiated a Law & Science Certificate Program that allows for specialization in several areas.

■ Admission

The school uses a rolling admission policy. The Admissions Committee admits applicants from a wide range of backgrounds and experiences. While an applicant's LSAT and GPA figure significantly, the committee also considers other factors, including extracurricular activities, public interest service, previous employment, and leadership qualities. A bachelor's degree from an accredited college or university is required.

The school offers a binding Early Decision Program with an application deadline of November 1 and an LSDAS report deadline of November 10. The deadline for regular decision applicants is February 1. Some students may be admitted through a Summer Entry Program.

Written recommendations are required. Anyone filing an application after February 1 will be at a disadvantage. Those applicants accepted in the Early Decision Program will be required to pay a nonrefundable deposit of $750, and those accepted in the regular admission process must pay a deposit of $300 to hold their place.

■ Legal Publication and Research Opportunities

Texas Tech has several student organizations that allow students to hone their research and writing skills. The *Texas Tech Law Review* publishes articles written by students and leading jurists, practitioners, and academics.

In 1999, the State Bar of Texas selected the school to publish the *Texas Tech Journal of Texas Administrative Law*. The *Texas Bank Lawyer* publishes articles about banking and commercial law.

The school is home to the Center for BioDefense, Law, and Policy, which provides research and scholarship opportunities. See *www.ttu.edu/biodefense*.

Students take the lead in writing and producing the school's alumni magazine, the *Texas Tech Lawyer*.

■ Clinical Program

The school boasts a newly remodeled clinic facility that includes a state-of-the-art multimedia teleconference room. Students have the opportunity to represent clients and participate in real cases through four clinical courses. Full-time tenure-track faculty members teach the clinical courses. Students enrolled in the Civil Litigation Clinic represent clients in a wide range of civil matters. The Criminal Justice Clinic provides a unique opportunity for third-year law students to represent actual clients charged with misdemeanors and felonies in state and federal courts in and around Lubbock. In the Tax

Clinic, students represent taxpayers in disputes with the IRS. The Alternative Dispute Resolution Clinic focuses on resolving legal issues without litigation. A wide array of externship opportunities are also available.

■ Advocacy Program

The school has an excellent reputation in various competitions. The school boasts 10 national titles and numerous top finishes in competitions, including the 2003 John Marshall Moot Court National Championship.

Students gain advocacy experience in simulated practice settings and through intraschool competitions.

■ Student Activities

The Student Bar Association is the focal point for many student activities. The school also has over 30 student organizations and 3 legal fraternities. Transitional groups are designed to assist students in their adjustment to law school.

■ Semester Abroad Programs

Texas Tech is a consortium partner in the Summer Law Institute, a cooperative teaching program with the historic University of Guanajuato, Mexico. The Summer Law Institute offers an introduction to Mexican law, international law, and legal subjects of interest to both US and Mexican lawyers such as NAFTA. See *www.law.ttu.edu* for additional information.

French or Spanish fluent students are offered legal study for credit through cooperative programs with the Universidad de Pablo Olavide in Seville, Spain, and the University of Lyon in France. Students learn firsthand about the legal systems in these countries.

■ Expenses and Financial Aid

Last year more than 46 percent of entering students received scholarships. The school awards In-State Tuition Scholarships to many nonresident applicants. Additional scholarships are available for second- and third-year students.

Long-term educational loan funds are available through the Office of Student Financial Aid, and short-term loans are available through the Law School Foundation.

■ Housing

Information about campus housing may be obtained from the Housing Office, *www.housing.ttu.edu*.

■ Career Services

The school is a member of NALP. The school participates in on- and off-campus interviewing programs. Historically, 91–99 percent of graduates are employed within six months of graduation.

Please contact *www.law.ttu.edu*, or 806.742.3990, ext. 273, for applications or additional information.

Applicant Profile

Texas Tech University School of Law
This grid includes only applicants who earned 120-180 LSAT scores under standard administrations.

LSAT Score	3.75 +		3.50 - 3.74		3.25 - 3.49		3.00 - 3.24		2.75 - 2.99		2.50 - 2.74		2.25 - 2.49		2.00 - 2.24		Below 2.00		No GPA		Total	
	Apps	Adm	Apps	Adm	Apps	Adm	Apps	Adm	Apps	Adm	Apps	Adm	Apps	Adm	Apps	Adm	Apps	Adm	Apps	Adm	Apps	Adm
175-180	0	0	0	0	0	0	0	0	0	0	0	0	0	0	0	0	0	0	0	0	0	0
170-174	1	1	0	0	0	0	1	1	0	0	0	0	0	0	0	0	0	0	0	0	2	2
165-169	5	5	6	3	4	4	5	5	3	3	1	1	1	0	1	1	0	0	0	0	26	22
160-164	16	15	17	13	20	18	12	10	18	7	9	1	7	1	0	0	0	0	2	0	101	65
155-159	41	40	54	48	67	52	88	34	44	8	24	3	12	1	2	0	1	0	1	0	334	186
150-154	60	44	90	59	94	27	120	9	52	4	49	2	18	0	10	1	1	0	4	3	498	149
145-149	31	17	61	20	75	11	81	6	59	2	37	0	15	0	3	0	0	0	6	2	368	58
140-144	9	4	22	2	37	8	52	3	34	0	27	1	9	0	7	0	1	0	4	0	202	18
135-139	3	0	5	0	10	0	9	0	11	0	8	0	9	0	5	0	1	0	1	0	62	0
130-134	1	0	1	0	0	0	3	0	0	0	2	0	2	0	0	0	0	0	1	0	10	0
125-129	0	0	0	0	0	0	0	0	0	0	0	0	0	0	1	0	0	0	0	0	1	0
120-124	0	0	0	0	0	0	0	0	0	0	0	0	0	0	0	0	0	0	0	0	0	0
Total	167	126	256	145	307	120	371	68	221	24	157	8	73	2	29	2	4	0	19	5	1604	500

Apps = Number of Applicants   Adm = Number Admitted   Reflects 99% of the total applicant pool.

Texas Wesleyan University School of Law

1515 Commerce Street
Fort Worth, TX 76102
Phone: 800.733.9529; 817.212.4000; Fax: 817.212.4002
E-mail: lawadmissions@law.txwes.edu; Website: www.law.txwes.edu

ABA Approved Since 1994

The Basics

Type of school	Private
Term	Semester
Application deadline	3/31
Application fee	$50
Financial aid deadline	5/15
Can first year start other than fall?	No
Student to faculty ratio (fall)	22.6 to 1
Does the university offer:	
housing restricted to law students?	No
graduate housing for which law students are eligible?	No

Faculty and Administrators

	Total		Men		Women		Minorities	
	Fall	Spr	Fall	Spr	Fall	Spr	Fall	Spr
Full-time	22	22	15	15	7	7	2	2
Other Full-time	4	4	3	3	1	1	0	0
Deans, librarians, & others who teach	8	8	3	3	5	5	0	0
Part-time	24	29	17	20	6	8	6	5
Total	58	63	38	41	19	21	8	7

Curriculum

	Full-time	Part-time
Typical first-year section size	84	55
Is there typically a "small section" of the first-year class, other than Legal Writing, taught by full-time faculty	No	No
If yes, typical size offered last year	0	0
# of classroom course titles beyond 1st year curriculum	0	
# of upper division courses, excluding seminars with an enrollment: Under 25	65	
25-49	28	
50-74	10	
75-99	6	
100+	1	
# of seminars	16	
# of seminar positions available	256	
# of seminar positions filled	120	66
# of positions available in simulation courses	332	
# of simulation positions filled	212	92
# of positions available in faculty supervised clinical courses	138	
# of faculty supervised clinical positions filled	85	53
# involved in field placements	92	46
# involved in law journals	43	17
# involved in moot court or trial competitions	15	3
# of credit hours required to graduate	88	

JD Enrollment and Ethnicity

	Men		Women		Full-time		Part-time		1st-year		Total		JD Degs. Awd.
	#	%	#	%	#	%	#	%	#	%	#	%	
African Amer.	11	3.4	35	9.8	23	5.4	23	8.8	15	6.4	46	6.7	20
Amer. Indian	4	1.2	3	0.8	5	1.2	2	0.8	2	0.8	7	1.0	2
Asian Amer.	15	4.6	23	6.5	27	6.4	11	4.2	13	5.5	38	5.6	6
Mex. Amer.	18	5.5	25	7.0	26	6.1	17	6.5	13	5.5	43	6.3	12
Puerto Rican	0	0.0	0	0.0	0	0.0	0	0.0	0	0.0	0	0.0	0
Hispanic	9	2.7	2	0.6	9	2.1	2	0.8	5	2.1	11	1.6	4
Total Minority	57	17.4	88	24.7	90	21.3	55	21.1	48	20.3	145	21.2	44
For. Nation.	0	0.0	0	0.0	0	0.0	0	0.0	0	0.0	0	0.0	0
Caucasian	247	75.3	252	70.8	310	73.3	189	72.4	173	73.3	499	73.0	138
Unknown	24	7.3	16	4.5	23	5.4	17	6.5	15	6.4	40	5.8	8
Total	328	48.0	356	52.0	423	61.8	261	38.2	236	34.5	684		190

Tuition and Fees

	Resident	Nonresident
Full-time	$19,520	$19,520
Part-time	$14,090	$14,090

Living Expenses

Estimated living expenses for singles

Living on campus	Living off campus	Living at home
$10,532	$10,532	$7,220

Texas Wesleyan University School of Law

ABA
Approved
Since
1994

GPA and LSAT Scores

	Total	Full-time	Part-time
# of apps	2,097	1,708	389
# of admits	698	545	153
# of matrics	269	176	93
75% GPA	3.43	3.43	3.34
25% GPA	2.87	2.88	2.91
75% LSAT	156	157	156
25% LSAT	151	151	151

Grants and Scholarships (from prior year)

	Total		Full-time		Part-time	
	#	%	#	%	#	%
Total # of students	695		429		266	
Total # receiving grants	123	17.7	79	18.4	44	16.5
Less than 1/2 tuition	98	14.1	57	13.3	41	15.4
Half to full tuition	22	3.2	19	4.4	3	1.1
Full tuition	1	0.1	1	0.2	0	0.0
More than full tuition	2	0.3	2	0.5	0	0.0
Median grant amount			$4,500		$2,000	

Informational and Library Resources

# of volumes and volume equivalents	215,519
# of titles	133,749
# of active serial subscriptions	4,787
Study seating capacity inside the library	254
# of professional librarians	7
Hours per week library is open	112
# of open, wired connections available to students	5
# of networked computers available for use by students	38
# of simultaneous wireless users	100
Require computer?	N

JD Attrition (from prior year)

	Academic	Other	Total	
	#	#	#	%
1st year	33	35	68	28.5%
2nd year	3	9	12	6.3%
3rd year	0	0	0	0.0%
4th year	0	0	0	0.0%

Employment

	Total	Percentage
Employment status known	144	94.7
Employment status unknown	8	5.3
Employed	123	85.4
Pursuing graduate degrees	2	1.4
Unemployed seeking employment	19	13.2
Unemployed not seeking employment	0	0.0

Type of Employment

# employed in law firms	67	54.5
# employed in business and industry	16	13.0
# employed in government	22	17.9
# employed in public interest	3	2.4
# employed as judicial clerks	2	1.6
# employed in academia	3	2.4

Geographic Location

# employed in state	118	95.9
# employed in foreign countries	0	0.0
# of states where employed		6

Bar Passage Rates

Jurisdiction		Texas	
Exam	Sum 03	Win 04	Total
# from school taking bar for the first time	102	55	157
School's pass rate for all first-time takers	78%	73%	76%
State's pass rate for all first-time takers	83%	69%	80%

Texas Wesleyan University School of Law

1515 Commerce Street
Fort Worth, TX 76102
Phone: 800.733.9529; 817.212.4000; Fax: 817.212.4002
E-mail: lawadmissions@law.txwes.edu; Website: www.law.txwes.edu

■ Introduction

Established in 1989, the law school became part of Texas Wesleyan University in 1992. A comprehensive university, Texas Wesleyan was founded in 1890 and offers degrees in business, education, fine arts, humanities, sciences, and law. The law school is fully approved by the ABA and offers both full-time and part-time studies leading to the juris doctor degree. The law school is located in downtown Fort Worth, Texas, in close proximity to the legal and judicial communities. The Fort Worth/Dallas Metroplex, with approximately 5.8 million residents, has rapidly grown to be one of the largest and most diversified metropolitan areas in the country, offering a relatively low cost of living, a growing economy, and extensive opportunities for professional advancement.

■ Student Body

Texas Wesleyan is committed to educating students of diverse backgrounds, varied life experiences, and educational perspectives. Although a large number of students enter the law school directly from their undergraduate institutions, many are seeking a legal education at a later stage in their lives and come from a variety of professional backgrounds. Students in the fall 2004 class range in age from 21 to 59. The median age for the day class is 24, evening class is 31, and overall is 25.

■ Faculty

Texas Wesleyan has a highly qualified, energetic, accessible faculty. The 31 members of the faculty hold degrees from the top law schools across the country, including Yale, Harvard, Georgetown, Columbia, Chicago, Virginia, University of Southern California, and George Washington. In addition to their academic backgrounds, diverse professional and community interests are represented in the experiences and activities of the Wesleyan faculty. They have served in a variety of high-level governmental positions and in the judiciary and state legislatures. Faculty members endeavor to stay current in legal developments and have published in prestigious law reviews. Several faculty members have book credits as well. The student-to-faculty ratio of approximately 24:1 ensures that students have the attention they need, both inside and outside of class, from the school's well-qualified faculty.

■ Library and Physical Facilities

The law school boasts first-rate facilities, including spacious classrooms, impressive courtrooms, an in-house law clinic, and an accessible library. The Wesleyan law library contains 204,000 volumes and equivalents. The law library's mission is to support the educational, instructional, curricular, and research needs of the faculty, students, and staff. In addition to its law book collection, the law library subscribes to major online electronic legal information services, including LexisNexis, Westlaw, legal research Internet sites, and several CD-ROM legal research tools.

Complementing book and electronic sources, an extensive collection of US Congressional documents, including full transcripts of all congressional hearings from 1970, are available on microfiche. The law library has 7 full-time librarians and a staff of 13 and is open 111.5 hours per week, 81 of which reference services are available.

■ Curriculum

Eighty-eight hours of academic instruction are required for completion of the juris doctor degree. Students may choose between full-time day and part-time day or evening courseloads. The part-time program and Wesleyan's flexible scheduling make it possible for those with continuing business and family responsibilities to meet their obligations while obtaining a legal education. The law school offers over 100 courses divided among traditional law courses and advanced courses that provide training in a variety of specialized law areas. Starting with the fall 2002 entering class, students are required to complete 30 hours of pro bono activities prior to graduation. Texas Wesleyan is the second law school in Texas and one in a handful in the nation to require pro bono work for graduation.

■ Skills Training

In order to allow students to develop necessary practical lawyering skills, Texas Wesleyan has developed a series of courses in its juris doctor curriculum, each termed a practicum, in discrete substantive areas, and in particular skills areas. The term practicum identifies courses involving the supervised practical application of previously studied theory.

The law school offers a variety of externships with trial and appellate courts as well as government agencies. For academic credit, students perform legal tasks and apply their academic studies to real client cases, gaining valuable insight into the operation of legal institutions. Wesleyan also has an in-house legal clinic that functions as an actual law office where students represent indigent clients in court under the direction of a faculty supervisor. All skills programs are coordinated by a full-time professor, ensuring significant legal experience in interviewing, negotiating, counseling clients, or alternative dispute resolutions.

Student Life

Texas Wesleyan student organizations provide a broad spectrum of opportunities for student involvement. Our enthusiastic law students have held many offices at the state, regional, and national levels. Students have won numerous awards, including the Top Speaker Award in the ABA Regional Moot Court Competition, Most Outstanding Senate Award in the Nation, and the Most Outstanding Student Leader in the Nation.

Career Services

The Wesleyan law school Career Services Office assists students, graduates, and employers in their mutual efforts to link those seeking legal positions with those providing employment opportunities. Career Services also supports students securing part-time or temporary employment while attending law school. A range of services, such as career counseling, résumé writing, and on-campus interviewing are available. The law school also offers a career planning library. The school is a member of the National Association of Law Placement.

Expenses and Financial Aid

Texas Wesleyan offers a relatively low private tuition. Tuition and general costs vary by courseload. For 2004/2005, annual tuition for full-time students was $18,960; for part-time students, $13,530; and for extended students, $640 per credit hour. Fees are an additional $280 per semester. The university works with individual students to provide the best financial aid package the student is eligible to receive. The financial aid package may include several types of assistance for financing a law school education, including scholarships, grants, employment opportunities, and loan programs. A majority of law students receive some form of financial assistance.

Admission

To be considered for admission, an applicant to Texas Wesleyan School of Law must hold a baccalaureate degree from a regionally accredited college or university prior to enrollment. A Law School Admission Test score is also required.

The law school offers full-time, part-time, and evening programs. Students are admitted only in the fall. March 31 of each year is the suggested application deadline; however, the School of Law uses a rolling admission process.

The admission committee will endeavor to determine the academic and professional promise of each applicant. Accordingly, the admission committee evaluates all factors relevant to an applicant's potential to be successful in meeting the academic standards of the juris doctor program, as well as potential for success on the bar examination and in other professional endeavors.

Traditional criteria, such as undergraduate academic achievement, LSAT performance, graduate studies, work experience, life experience, activities, honors, personal statement, recommendation letters, and other experiences, are used in the admission evaluation process.

Applicant Profile

Texas Wesleyan University School of Law
This grid includes only applicants who earned 120-180 LSAT scores under standard administrations.

LSAT Score	3.75 +		3.50 - 3.74		3.25 - 3.49		3.00 - 3.24		2.75 - 2.99		2.50 - 2.74		2.25 - 2.49		2.00 - 2.24		Below 2.00		No GPA		Total	
	Apps	Adm	Apps	Adm	Apps	Adm	Apps	Adm	Apps	Adm	Apps	Adm	Apps	Adm	Apps	Adm	Apps	Adm	Apps	Adm	Apps	Adm
175-180	0	0	0	0	0	0	0	0	0	0	0	0	0	0	0	0	0	0	0	0	0	0
170-174	0	0	0	0	0	0	2	2	0	0	0	0	0	0	0	0	0	0	0	0	2	2
165-169	0	0	0	0	0	0	2	1	3	3	1	1	1	1	0	0	0	0	0	0	7	6
160-164	8	8	6	4	13	13	7	6	7	6	10	8	6	6	2	2	0	0	0	0	59	53
155-159	12	11	26	25	37	35	58	54	43	37	35	32	12	8	8	3	2	1	3	2	236	208
150-154	35	34	63	56	95	82	118	85	103	44	85	20	29	6	17	1	4	0	0	0	549	328
145-149	25	20	59	28	80	14	126	14	118	5	79	2	41	0	20	0	4	0	13	1	565	84
140-144	11	0	36	1	66	1	78	2	72	0	66	1	40	0	16	0	3	0	10	1	398	6
135-139	3	0	11	0	12	0	37	0	31	0	29	0	22	0	10	0	3	0	8	0	166	0
130-134	2	0	2	0	3	0	3	0	12	0	12	0	4	0	5	0	4	0	5	0	52	0
125-129	0	0	0	0	0	0	0	0	4	0	2	0	0	0	1	0	0	0	2	0	9	0
120-124	0	0	0	0	0	0	0	0	0	0	1	0	0	0	0	0	0	0	0	0	1	0
Total	96	73	203	114	306	145	431	164	393	95	320	64	155	21	79	6	20	1	41	4	2044	687

Apps = Number of Applicants   Adm = Number Admitted   Reflects 98% of the total applicant pool.

The Thomas M. Cooley Law School

PO Box 13038, 300 S Capitol Avenue
Lansing, MI 48901
Phone: 517.371.5140, ext. 2244; Fax: 517.334.5718
E-mail: admissions@cooley.edu; Website: www.cooley.edu

*ABA
Approved
Since
1975*

The Basics

Type of school	Private
Term	Semester
Application deadline	8/15 1/3 5/1
Application fee	$0
Financial aid deadline	
Can first year start other than fall?	Yes
Student to faculty ratio (fall)	21.1 to 1
Does the university offer:	
housing restricted to law students?	No
graduate housing for which law students are eligible?	No

Faculty and Administrators

	Total		Men		Women		Minorities	
	Fall	Spr	Fall	Spr	Fall	Spr	Fall	Spr
Full-time	81	71	52	44	29	27	10	10
Other Full-time	4	4	2	2	2	2	0	0
Deans, librarians, & others who teach	15	15	7	7	8	8	1	1
Part-time	184	152	116	108	67	44	23	12
Total	284	242	177	161	106	81	34	23

Curriculum

		Full-time	Part-time
Typical first-year section size		68	68
Is there typically a "small section" of the first-year class, other than Legal Writing, taught by full-time faculty		No	No
If yes, typical size offered last year		0	0
# of classroom course titles beyond 1st year curriculum		132	
# of upper division courses, excluding seminars with an enrollment:	Under 25	258	
	25-49	52	
	50-74	29	
	75-99	43	
	100+	18	
# of seminars		121	
# of seminar positions available		2,627	
# of seminar positions filled		322	1,689
# of positions available in simulation courses		2,136	
# of simulation positions filled		265	1,392
# of positions available in faculty supervised clinical courses		204	
# of faculty supervised clinical positions filled		21	111
# involved in field placements		51	270
# involved in law journals		20	105
# involved in moot court or trial competitions		34	184
# of credit hours required to graduate		90	

JD Enrollment and Ethnicity

	Men		Women		Full-time		Part-time		1st-year		Total		JD Degs. Awd.
	#	%	#	%	#	%	#	%	#	%	#	%	
African Amer.	117	8.0	314	22.4	45	9.5	386	16.1	220	12.7	431	15.0	72
Amer. Indian	6	0.4	3	0.2	2	0.4	7	0.3	5	0.3	9	0.3	2
Asian Amer.	82	5.6	94	6.7	29	6.1	147	6.1	114	6.6	176	6.1	16
Mex. Amer.	25	1.7	27	1.9	4	0.8	48	2.0	24	1.4	52	1.8	13
Puerto Rican	11	0.7	11	0.8	3	0.6	19	0.8	12	0.7	22	0.8	6
Hispanic	48	3.3	39	2.8	12	2.5	75	3.1	55	3.2	87	3.0	16
Total Minority	289	19.7	488	34.8	95	20.0	682	28.5	430	24.9	777	27.1	125
For. Nation.	38	2.6	39	2.8	11	2.3	66	2.8	41	2.4	77	2.7	12
Caucasian	1098	74.8	833	59.5	356	74.9	1575	65.8	1190	68.9	1931	67.3	274
Unknown	42	2.9	41	2.9	13	2.7	70	2.9	66	3.8	83	2.9	0
Total	1467	51.2	1401	48.8	475	16.6	2393	83.4	1727	60.2	2868		411

Tuition and Fees

	Resident	Nonresident
Full-time	$22,160	$22,160
Part-time	$15,840	$15,840

Living Expenses

Estimated living expenses for singles

Living on campus	Living off campus	Living at home
$10,520	$10,520	$10,520

The Thomas M. Cooley Law School

*ABA
Approved
Since
1975*

GPA and LSAT Scores

	Total	Full-time	Part-time
# of apps	5,215	4,387	828
# of admits	2,921	2,616	305
# of matrics	1,428	387	1,041
75% GPA	3.30	3.39	3.29
25% GPA	2.67	2.67	2.66
75% LSAT	149	151	148
25% LSAT	143	144	142

Grants and Scholarships (from prior year)

	Total		Full-time		Part-time	
	#	%	#	%	#	%
Total # of students	2,303		422		1881	
Total # receiving grants	1122	48.7	268	63.5	854	45.4
Less than 1/2 tuition	723	31.4	168	39.8	555	29.5
Half to full tuition	353	15.3	90	21.3	263	14.0
Full tuition	46	2.0	10	2.4	36	1.9
More than full tuition	0	0.0	0	0.0	0	0.0
Median grant amount			$5,625		$4,500	

Informational and Library Resources

# of volumes and volume equivalents	523,422
# of titles	181,722
# of active serial subscriptions	5,891
Study seating capacity inside the library	915
# of professional librarians	20
Hours per week library is open	124
# of open, wired connections available to students	270
# of networked computers available for use by students	175
# of simultaneous wireless users	3,000
Require computer?	N

JD Attrition (from prior year)

	Academic	Other	Total	
	#	#	#	%
1st year	159	180	339	24.1%
2nd year	69	57	126	22.7%
3rd year	12	1	13	3.8%
4th year	0	0	0	0.0%

Employment

	Total	Percentage
Employment status known	353	80.6
Employment status unknown	85	19.4
Employed	272	77.1
Pursuing graduate degrees	12	3.4
Unemployed seeking employment	67	19.0
Unemployed not seeking employment	2	0.6

Type of Employment

	Total	Percentage
# employed in law firms	127	46.7
# employed in business and industry	41	15.1
# employed in government	52	19.1
# employed in public interest	4	1.5
# employed as judicial clerks	31	11.4
# employed in academia	11	4.0

Geographic Location

	Total	Percentage
# employed in state	132	48.5
# employed in foreign countries	3	1.1
# of states where employed	28	

Bar Passage Rates

Jurisdiction	Michigan		
Exam	Sum 03	Win 04	Total
# from school taking bar for the first time	81	81	162
School's pass rate for all first-time takers	49%	53%	51%
State's pass rate for all first-time takers	77%	71%	75%

The Thomas M. Cooley Law School

PO Box 13038, 300 S Capitol Avenue
Lansing, MI 48901
Phone: 517.371.5140, ext. 2244; Fax: 517.334.5718
E-mail: admissions@cooley.edu; Website: www.cooley.edu

■ Introduction

The Thomas M. Cooley Law School's mission is to educate law students in the knowledge, skills, and ethics needed for successful practice. The school carries out that vision by developing a rigorous and practical curriculum with a solid academic foundation, a strong emphasis on plain-English writing, and an outstanding array of clinical opportunities. Offering classes days, evenings, and weekends, in three locations, provides flexibility to qualified students. Cooley's main campus is blocks from Michigan's capitol. Classes are also offered at two additional campuses: at suburban Oakland University, minutes from Detroit, and in Grand Rapids, at Western Michigan University's downtown Graduate Center. Cooley has been fully accredited by the ABA since 1978, and by the North Central Association since 2001. Cooley/Oakland, 472 O'Dowd Hall, Rochester, MI 48309, 248.370.3148; Cooley/Grand Rapids, Law Center, 111 Commerce Avenue, SW, Grand Rapids, MI 49503, 616.301.6800.

■ Enrollment/Student Body

2,868 total students: over 80 percent part-time, 33 percent minority, 49 percent women. Of Thomas Cooley's diverse student body, 66 percent are from out-of-state. The median age of entering students is 26.

■ Admission

Bachelor's degree required; two-year and 3/4 admission considered; rolling admission. LSAT, LSDAS required, no application fee. Cooley Law School uses a fair and objective formula to determine eligibility (UGPA x 15 + Highest LSAT = Admission Index). Meeting the index may determine eligibility, but the Faculty Admissions Committee may deny candidates for negative character and fitness factors. A few students are selected each term through our qualifying program. Please refer to the Cooley website at *www.cooley.edu* for the most current admission requirements.

■ Library and Physical Facilities

Over 500,000 volumes and equivalents; open 124 hours/week including weekends; LexisNexis, Westlaw, CALI, LoisLaw; and 21 full-time librarians. Cooley's research facility is designed to meet the research needs of today's law student, including web-based chat reference and a toll-free phone number to support students' reference needs, and reference services available 100 hours/week. Campus libraries at Oakland and Grand Rapids offer on-site services to local students.

■ Expenses, Financial Aid, and Scholarships

Tuition—$790/credit hour in 2005; fees—$20/term; estimated additional expenses—$10,150 (room & board, books, personal, transportation); scholarships and financial aid available. Honors Scholarships of up to 100 percent of tuition are awarded to incoming students in two ways.

1. Admission index levels:

Index	Honors Scholarship
215+	100%
210-214	75%
205-209	50%
195-204	25%

2. Student's highest LSAT score:

LSAT	Honors Scholarship
163+	100%
158-162	75%
153-157	50%
150-152	25%

Students can both earn or increase an Honors Scholarship based on their Cooley class ranking. Students retain their highest scholarship award as long as they remain in good standing.

■ Flexible Scheduling

Cooley offers more scheduling options than any other law school in the country, including the first and largest ABA-approved weekend program. Students may choose from full- or part-time schedules ranging from two to five years; morning, afternoon, evening, and on the weekend. New students are admitted three times a year: January, May, and September. The full-time faculty teach all required courses, including those offered evenings and weekends.

■ Curriculum

Cooley has nearly 100 full-time faculty and more than 100 adjunct professors, with a student-faculty ratio of 24:1. The Cooley curriculum has been carefully designed by its faculty and deans to provide students with the substantive law and skills needed for bar examinations, law practice, and further graduate study. **Concentrations**—Students may choose to focus their elective coursework in any of the Cooley Concentrations: Business Transactions, General Practice/Solo and Small Firm, Litigation, and Public and International Law, including tracks in Administrative Law, Constitutional Law and Civil Rights, Environmental Law, and International Law. **Clinical Opportunities**—Cooley believes students immersed in a dynamic, hands-on learning environment learn and understand the law more fully and are better prepared to serve their clients. Our rich variety of clinical offerings include the award-winning Sixty Plus Elderlaw Clinic, and the Innocence Project. The Estate Planning Clinic also gives real-client experience to night and weekend students. More than 1,000 faculty-approved extern sites across the nation allow students to gain supervised practical experience in nearly any legal setting. Cooley opened its $2.8 million, 18,480-square-foot state-of-the-art courtroom complex in fall 2003, and it is devoted to building trial and appellate skills. Cooley students have won numerous awards in national competitions. **Writing Programs**—Thomas M. Cooley is recognized as a world leader in the plain-language movement. Legal writing is taught by full-time, tenure-track professors. Students complete a six-credit sequence that provides a solid foundation in researching and drafting law office memorandums, contracts, pleadings, briefs, and statutes. **International Studies**—Cooley Law School offers students the opportunity to study law abroad in a number of locations worldwide. Cooley has two programs of its own—13 weeks in Australia/New Zealand in January and a summer term in Toronto, Canada. Cooley also cooperates with other law schools to provide students opportunities to study in Europe. **Online Prelaw Program**—Cooley's Prelaw Program is offered online and helps incoming students understand what to expect in law school and what skills they will need during their first year of law school. For details, see *www.cooley.edu*. **Master of Laws (LLM) Program**—Cooley offers graduate law degrees in Tax and Intellectual Property at Cooley's Rochester/Oakland University Campus. Find out more about Cooley's growing LLM programs by visiting *www.cooley.edu* and clicking on graduate programs. **Joint Degrees**—Students may enroll in joint-degree programs with cooperating universities.

■ Academic Success

The Academic Resource Center (ARC) is designed as a resource for students who desire to improve themselves academically. With the assistance of computer lab and written resources, the ARC includes a PhD reading specialist, a Cooley faculty member, and three other attorneys. The ARC is a place for students to work with faculty, staff, and fellow students for assistance in achieving their academic goals.

■ Housing

The main campus is in Lansing, the capital city of Michigan. Private housing is nearby in all price ranges, some within walking distance, others are on public transportation routes. The Career Services Office also has housing options for Cooley's Grand Rapids/Western Michigan University and Rochester/Oakland University Campuses.

■ Career Services

The Career Services Office provides a wide variety of services to students and graduates of the Law School. Job postings (updated weekly) provide listings for full-time positions across the United States, as well as listings for local legally related part-time work. Workshops and seminars, focusing on topics ranging from Law Student to Lawyer: Becoming a Trial Attorney to Professional Sports Management: An Alternative to the Practice of Law, are open to all students and graduates. Services for alumni include roundtable group discussions regarding job searching and career strategies, and a job-bulletin exchange with over 100 law schools.

Applicant Profile

The Thomas M. Cooley Law School

Academic Success Rates at Cooley Law School January 1996–January 2003	
LSAT	Academic Success
*171-180	100%
*166-170	100%
*161-165	100%
*156-160	95%
*151-155	90%
146-150	81%
145	79%
144	78%

The Law School Admission Test and undergraduate grades are good overall predictors of first-year law school performance, although they do not predict individual results. Mainly, these factors predict relative first-year class rank for large groups of first-year students. Students are urged to assess their own potential before making the commitment to law school.

*Law School Admission Test scores of 150 and above may qualify for an honors scholarship from 25 to 100 percent of tuition based on LSAT score only.

Thomas Jefferson School of Law

2121 San Diego Avenue
San Diego, CA 92110
Phone: 619.297.9700; 800.956.5070; Fax: 619.294.4713
E-mail: adm@tjsl.edu; Website: www.tjsl.edu

ABA
Approved
Since
1996

The Basics

Type of school	Private
Term	Semester
Application deadline	
Application fee	$35
Financial aid deadline	4/30
Can first year start other than fall?	Yes
Student to faculty ratio (fall)	27.6 to 1
Does the university offer:	
housing restricted to law students?	No
graduate housing for which law students are eligible?	No

Faculty and Administrators

	Total		Men		Women		Minorities	
	Fall	Spr	Fall	Spr	Fall	Spr	Fall	Spr
Full-time	23	26	10	12	13	14	1	2
Other Full-time	0	0	0	0	0	0	0	0
Deans, librarians, & others who teach	4	4	2	2	2	2	0	0
Part-time	27	27	22	20	5	7	2	1
Total	**54**	**57**	**34**	**34**	**20**	**23**	**3**	**3**

Curriculum

	Full-time	Part-time
Typical first-year section size	70	35
Is there typically a "small section" of the first-year class, other than Legal Writing, taught by full-time faculty	No	No
If yes, typical size offered last year	0	0
# of classroom course titles beyond 1st year curriculum	72	
# of upper division courses, excluding seminars with an enrollment: Under 25	33	
25-49	48	
50-74	7	
75-99	14	
100+	1	
# of seminars	14	
# of seminar positions available	280	
# of seminar positions filled	154	76
# of positions available in simulation courses	503	
# of simulation positions filled	302	123
# of positions available in faculty supervised clinical courses	25	
# of faculty supervised clinical positions filled	13	0
# involved in field placements	161	20
# involved in law journals	38	8
# involved in moot court or trial competitions	43	4
# of credit hours required to graduate	88	

JD Enrollment and Ethnicity

	Men #	Men %	Women #	Women %	Full-time #	Full-time %	Part-time #	Part-time %	1st-year #	1st-year %	Total #	Total %	JD Degs. Awd.
African Amer.	7	1.4	10	3.0	5	0.8	12	5.7	6	1.5	17	2.0	7
Amer. Indian	2	0.4	0	0.0	0	0.0	2	0.9	1	0.3	2	0.2	0
Asian Amer.	36	7.3	32	9.5	48	7.7	20	9.5	31	8.0	68	8.2	9
Mex. Amer.	27	5.4	15	4.5	26	4.2	16	7.6	20	5.2	42	5.0	11
Puerto Rican	3	0.6	2	0.6	5	0.8	0	0.0	2	0.5	5	0.6	0
Hispanic	7	1.4	9	2.7	13	2.1	3	1.4	4	1.0	16	1.9	7
Total Minority	82	16.5	68	20.2	97	15.6	53	25.1	64	16.5	150	18.0	34
For. Nation.	0	0.0	0	0.0	0	0.0	0	0.0	0	0.0	0	0.0	0
Caucasian	414	83.5	269	79.8	525	84.4	158	74.9	324	83.5	683	82.0	152
Unknown	0	0.0	0	0.0	0	0.0	0	0.0	0	0.0	0	0.0	0
Total	496	59.5	337	40.5	622	74.7	211	25.3	388	46.6	833		186

Tuition and Fees

	Resident	Nonresident
Full-time	$26,950	$26,950
Part-time	$16,950	$16,950

Living Expenses

Estimated living expenses for singles

Living on campus	Living off campus	Living at home
N/A	$18,392	$18,392

Thomas Jefferson School of Law

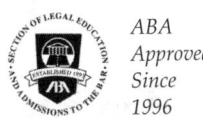

*ABA
Approved
Since
1996*

GPA and LSAT Scores

	Total	Full-time	Part-time
# of apps	4,430	4,046	384
# of admits	1,072	936	136
# of matrics	281	223	58
75% GPA	3.34	3.35	3.32
25% GPA	2.68	2.67	2.65
75% LSAT	155	157	157
25% LSAT	150	150	149

Grants and Scholarships (from prior year)

	Total		Full-time		Part-time	
	#	%	#	%	#	%
Total # of students	832		613		219	
Total # receiving grants	433	52.0	343	56.0	90	41.1
Less than 1/2 tuition	255	30.6	212	34.6	43	19.6
Half to full tuition	87	10.5	55	9.0	32	14.6
Full tuition	91	10.9	76	12.4	15	6.8
More than full tuition	0	0.0	0	0.0	0	0.0
Median grant amount			$6,000		$6,000	

Informational and Library Resources

# of volumes and volume equivalents	229,304
# of titles	114,790
# of active serial subscriptions	3,376
Study seating capacity inside the library	272
# of professional librarians	4
Hours per week library is open	115
# of open, wired connections available to students	50
# of networked computers available for use by students	44
# of simultaneous wireless users	500
Require computer?	N

JD Attrition (from prior year)

	Academic	Other	Total	
	#	#	#	%
1st year	38	32	70	14.2%
2nd year	5	6	11	6.1%
3rd year	1	1	2	1.5%
4th year	0	0	0	0.0%

Employment

	Total	Percentage
Employment status known	105	74.5
Employment status unknown	36	25.5
Employed	95	90.5
Pursuing graduate degrees	3	2.9
Unemployed seeking employment	5	4.8
Unemployed not seeking employment	2	1.9

Type of Employment

	Total	Percentage
# employed in law firms	51	53.7
# employed in business and industry	21	22.1
# employed in government	5	5.3
# employed in public interest	1	1.1
# employed as judicial clerks	7	7.4
# employed in academia	1	1.1

Geographic Location

	Total	Percentage
# employed in state	65	68.4
# employed in foreign countries	2	2.1
# of states where employed	20	

Bar Passage Rates

Jurisdiction	California		
Exam	Sum 03	Win 04	Total
# from school taking bar for the first time	71	37	108
School's pass rate for all first-time takers	46%	49%	47%
State's pass rate for all first-time takers	63%	47%	60%

Thomas Jefferson School of Law

2121 San Diego Avenue
San Diego, CA 92110
Phone: 619.297.9700; 800.956.5070; Fax: 619.294.4713
E-mail: adm@tjsl.edu; Website: www.tjsl.edu

■ Introduction

The Thomas Jefferson School of Law is a private, nonprofit, independent law school that emphasizes an individualized approach to legal education. This approach features small classes, written feedback on student performance during the semester, close student/faculty interaction in a supportive environment, and a flexible curriculum that allows students to attend full or part time and accelerate graduation by attending classes in the summer.

The mission of the School of Law is to provide an outstanding legal education for a nationally based student body in a collegial and supportive environment with attention to newly emerging areas of law, particularly those related to technological development, globalization, and the quest for social justice.

San Diego boasts what many consider to be the finest climate in the continental United States. The seventh largest city in the nation offers all of the professional, social, and cultural opportunities of a major metropolitan area.

■ Faculty

The Thomas Jefferson faculty is distinguished by three features: its qualifications, youth, and commitment to teaching. Members of the faculty were educated at many of the finest law schools in the nation and all practiced law before turning to academic careers.

The youth and vitality of the faculty are suggested by the fact that more than 85 percent of the faculty have joined Thomas Jefferson since 1990. All contribute to creating the student-centered environment that is a defining characteristic of Thomas Jefferson.

The full-time faculty is very unusual in that nearly half of its members are women.

■ Library and Physical Facilities

The law school is housed in two modern buildings situated in the beautiful and historic Old Town section of San Diego. The library includes the law school's two computer labs and numerous private study rooms that students may reserve for group or individual study. Our classrooms utilize natural and artificial light and are wired for laptop use. The campus has wireless access to its network throughout.

■ Curriculum

Students may commence their studies at Thomas Jefferson in either August or January. The law school offers a three-year full-time program and a four-year part-time program which students may attend.

All programs have the same admission standards and graduation requirements. Students who take additional classes during the summer may accelerate graduation by one semester. The full-time faculty teaches more than two-thirds of the coursework in both the day and evening divisions.

The curriculum is highly interactive and collaborative between the faculty and the students. During their first semester, entering students have the opportunity, in all their courses, to receive feedback from the faculty on their written legal analytical skills in order to enhance their understanding of the course material and hone their performance prior to final exams. First-year students are assigned faculty advisors, but all members of the faculty emphasize being available to students outside of class. The law school has an extensive Academic Support Program that permits students in all three years of law school to meet individually with special tutors who can help them excel as law students.

■ Special Programs

The law school has acquired special strength in the areas of law that most reflect our changing world. To provide an institutional framework for the study of technological change and globalization and their effects on both traditional areas of practice and emerging new fields, the law school has established three academic centers. In addition to a broad program of course offerings, each center represents substantial engagement by faculty in scholarly research, speaker programs, and opportunities for student participation beyond the classroom.

The Center for Law, Technology, and Communications prepares students for careers in fields of law related to high technology and communications. Course offerings include traditional intellectual property law, emerging new specialties such as cyberspace law, biotechnology law and bioethics, media and telecommunications law, and sports and entertainment law.

The Center for Global Legal Studies prepares students for the transborder aspects of contemporary legal practice and offers a wide variety of courses in international law, including international business law, international environmental law, international criminal law, and international human rights.

The Center for Law and Social Justice prepares students for a law practice geared toward the preservation of the values of liberty and equality in a changing working world. Recent activity has focussed on issues related to gender and the law, especially the problems of women, gays, lesbians, intersexuals, and the transgendered.

Each year the law school also offers a large number of courses that train students in professional skills, supplemented by a variety of field placement programs.

The judicial internship program allows students to work for a semester with local federal and state judges, gaining experience in drafting opinions and observing courtroom proceedings. Students also may work for credit at a variety of public agencies and private law firms. California law allows students who have completed certain coursework to obtain certification to appear in court.

■ Admission

Thomas Jefferson conducts a rolling admission process under which applicants are considered when their applications are complete. Because the law school admits two entering classes each year, the admission committee meets continuously throughout the year, and there are no formal application deadlines. Early applications are encouraged, however, and those who apply early increase their chance of a favorable decision.

The admission committee gives each applicant careful, thorough, and personalized consideration. In addition to the LSAT score, the committee considers the applicant's undergraduate record, extracurricular activities, work experience, and history of overcoming adversity.

The law school accepts applications from transfer students in both the fall and spring semesters. Transfer students must be in good academic standing.

■ Expenses and Financial Aid

All entering students with an average LSAT score of 150 or higher automatically receive a partial or full scholarship renewable for the second and third years. Partial- and full-tuition scholarships also are automatically awarded after the first year but are based on academic performance at the end of the prior year. Generally, all students in the top 30 percent are on partial or full scholarship.

Student loans and work-study funds also are available. Students interested in these programs should apply as early as possible and should not wait for an admission decision before applying for financial assistance.

■ Student Activities

The most prestigious cocurricular activity is the *Thomas Jefferson Law Review*, a journal of legal scholarship edited and managed by students.

Cocurricular programs include the moot court and mock trial competitions. Extracurricular activities serve a variety of student interests and needs. Some student organizations are formed as a result of heightened student interest in substantive areas of law practice, such as the International Law Society, the Entertainment and Sports Law Societies, the Law and Medicine Society, and the Public Interest Law Foundation. Many student organizations provide a source of mutual support for various groups of students, including the Black Students Association, La Raza, and the Pan Asian Law Students Association.

■ Career Services

The Career Services Office assists students and alumni in finding temporary and permanent law-related employment. The office maintains listings of employment opportunities and schedules on-campus interviewing. It also assists students in obtaining placement with state and federal judges and with various public agencies, where they can work during the year for academic credit.

The Career Services Office has developed an alumni mentoring program, through which Thomas Jefferson students can obtain advice and assistance from some of the law school's more than 4,000 alumni.

Applicant Profile Not Available

The University of Toledo College of Law

2801 West Bancroft Street
Toledo, OH 43606-3390
Phone: 419.530.4131; Fax: 419.530.4345
E-mail: law.admissions@utoledo.edu; Website: www.utlaw.edu

The Basics

Type of school	Public
Term	Semester
Application deadline	7/1
Application fee	$40
Financial aid deadline	8/1
Can first year start other than fall?	No
Student to faculty ratio (fall)	13.5 to 1
Does the university offer:	
housing restricted to law students?	No
graduate housing for which law students are eligible?	No

Faculty and Administrators

	Total		Men		Women		Minorities	
	Fall	Spr	Fall	Spr	Fall	Spr	Fall	Spr
Full-time	29	29	18	18	11	11	2	2
Other Full-time	0	0	0	0	0	0	0	0
Deans, librarians, & others who teach	3	3	2	2	1	1	0	0
Part-time	17	21	11	16	6	5	0	0
Total	49	53	31	36	18	17	2	2

Curriculum

	Full-time	Part-time
Typical first-year section size	59	27
Is there typically a "small section" of the first-year class, other than Legal Writing, taught by full-time faculty	No	No
If yes, typical size offered last year	0	0
# of classroom course titles beyond 1st year curriculum	79	

# of upper division courses, excluding seminars with an enrollment:		
	Under 25	95
	25-49	33
	50-74	7
	75-99	3
	100+	0

# of seminars	0	
# of seminar positions available	0	
# of seminar positions filled	0	0
# of positions available in simulation courses	433	
# of simulation positions filled	299	65
# of positions available in faculty supervised clinical courses	130	
# of faculty supervised clinical positions filled	48	2
# involved in field placements	89	1
# involved in law journals	41	3
# involved in moot court or trial competitions	33	0
# of credit hours required to graduate	89	

JD Enrollment and Ethnicity

	Men		Women		Full-time		Part-time		1st-year		Total		JD Degs. Awd.
	#	%	#	%	#	%	#	%	#	%	#	%	
African Amer.	11	3.8	9	4.0	13	3.8	7	4.0	8	3.7	20	3.9	6
Amer. Indian	0	0.0	0	0.0	0	0.0	0	0.0	0	0.0	0	0.0	0
Asian Amer.	4	1.4	8	3.6	6	1.7	6	3.5	7	3.3	12	2.3	3
Mex. Amer.	0	0.0	0	0.0	0	0.0	0	0.0	0	0.0	0	0.0	0
Puerto Rican	0	0.0	0	0.0	0	0.0	0	0.0	0	0.0	0	0.0	0
Hispanic	3	1.0	3	1.3	5	1.5	1	0.6	2	0.9	6	1.2	1
Total Minority	18	6.1	20	8.9	24	7.0	14	8.1	17	7.9	38	7.4	10
For. Nation.	2	0.7	1	0.4	3	0.9	0	0.0	0	0.0	3	0.6	0
Caucasian	200	68.3	169	75.4	249	72.4	120	69.4	139	64.7	369	71.4	115
Unknown	73	24.9	34	15.2	68	19.8	39	22.5	59	27.4	107	20.7	4
Total	293	56.7	224	43.3	344	66.5	173	33.5	215	41.6	517		129

Tuition and Fees

	Resident	Nonresident
Full-time	$12,852	$23,096
Part-time	$10,177	$18,286

Living Expenses

Estimated living expenses for singles

Living on campus	Living off campus	Living at home
N/A	$12,576	$6,691

The University of Toledo College of Law

*ABA
Approved
Since
1939*

GPA and LSAT Scores

	Total	Full-time	Part-time
# of apps	1,352	1,099	253
# of admits	374	251	123
# of matrics	190	86	104
75% GPA	3.64	3.76	3.37
25% GPA	2.94	3.07	2.86
75% LSAT	157	159	155
25% LSAT	151	153	151

Grants and Scholarships (from prior year)

	Total		Full-time		Part-time	
	#	%	#	%	#	%
Total # of students	503		353		150	
Total # receiving grants	181	36.0	168	47.6	13	8.7
Less than 1/2 tuition	44	8.7	35	9.9	9	6.0
Half to full tuition	18	3.6	17	4.8	1	0.7
Full tuition	59	11.7	59	16.7	0	0.0
More than full tuition	60	11.9	57	16.1	3	2.0
Median grant amount			$10,609		$800	

Informational and Library Resources

# of volumes and volume equivalents	341,575
# of titles	52,117
# of active serial subscriptions	3,351
Study seating capacity inside the library	471
# of professional librarians	5
Hours per week library is open	113
# of open, wired connections available to students	27
# of networked computers available for use by students	62
# of simultaneous wireless users	200
Require computer?	N

JD Attrition (from prior year)

	Academic	Other	Total	
	#	#	#	%
1st year	12	29	41	20.3%
2nd year	3	1	4	2.5%
3rd year	0	2	2	1.7%
4th year	0	1	1	4.5%

Employment

	Total	Percentage
Employment status known	106	98.1
Employment status unknown	2	1.9
Employed	102	96.2
Pursuing graduate degrees	0	0.0
Unemployed seeking employment	4	3.8
Unemployed not seeking employment	0	0.0

Type of Employment

	Total	Percentage
# employed in law firms	51	50.0
# employed in business and industry	18	17.6
# employed in government	21	20.6
# employed in public interest	1	1.0
# employed as judicial clerks	3	2.9
# employed in academia	3	2.9

Geographic Location

	Total	Percentage
# employed in state	65	63.7
# employed in foreign countries	1	1.0
# of states where employed		14

Bar Passage Rates

Jurisdiction	Ohio			Michigan		
Exam	Sum 03	Win 04	Total	Sum 03	Win 04	Total
# from school taking bar for the first time	61	19	80	14	9	23
School's pass rate for all first-time takers	77%	89%	80%	93%	89%	91%
State's pass rate for all first-time takers	81%	72%	79%	77%	71%	75%

The University of Toledo College of Law

2801 West Bancroft Street
Toledo, OH 43606-3390
Phone: 419.530.4131; Fax: 419.530.4345
E-mail: law.admissions@utoledo.edu; Website: www.utlaw.edu

■ Introduction

The University of Toledo is a state university of more than 22,000 students, conveniently located on the western edge of Toledo, Ohio, in one of the city's nicest residential areas.

The College of Law, located on the main campus of The University of Toledo, is accredited by the ABA and is a member of the AALS and the League of Ohio Law Schools. It has been training lawyers since 1906 and, in 1984, was awarded a chapter of the Order of the Coif. The college provides a quality legal education with a personal touch at an affordable price. The nationally recognized faculty emphasizes classroom teaching and student accessibility as its primary function. The College of Law is committed to its open-door policy that provides total student support.

■ Student Body

The college seeks a diverse student body. Nearly two-thirds of the students hail from outside the local area. More than 200 undergraduate institutions are represented. This diversity exposes students to an interesting, stimulating, and creative atmosphere where insights and ideas flourish. Diversity is reflected in student groups and activities representing a broad spectrum of social, political, ethnic, and religious perspectives.

■ Faculty

The full-time faculty earned law degrees from some of the most outstanding universities in the country. Many have advanced degrees.

While legal scholarship is important and many faculty members have national reputations for scholarship, the faculty places a high priority on effective teaching and accessibility to students.

■ Library and Physical Facilities

The spacious, newly renovated Law Center includes tiered classrooms, a striking student lounge, a state-of-the-art moot courtroom, and an amphitheater-style auditorium. The entire building supports wireless web technology.

Occupying four levels within the Law Center, the library contains group-study rooms, videotaping facilities, and a modern computer lab for use by law students. All first-year students are trained in the use of two vast electronic law libraries—LexisNexis and Westlaw.

■ Curriculum

The College of Law requires the successful completion of 89 semester hours for graduation. The curriculum in the first year of the full-time and the first two years of the part-time program consists of required courses. An extensive and ever-growing curriculum covers traditional subjects as well as cutting-edge environmental law, international law, and cyberlaw subjects and incorporates the development of professional legal skills and values.

Our academic success program provides teaching assistants for students in all basic required courses and offers tutors for any student who requests academic support. Students can graduate with certificates in environmental, intellectual property, international law, and labor/employment law.

The College of Law has joint-degree programs with the Colleges of Engineering, Business, and Arts and Sciences leading to a Master of Science in Engineering, PhD in Engineering, Master of Business Administration, Master of Public Administration, or Master of Criminal Justice. Students may also design individual joint-degree programs.

■ Special Programs

Cybersecurities Law Institute—The institute focuses on the impact of Internet technology on securities and investment law. The institute sponsors conferences, research, lectures, symposia, and the development of courses and online resources.

Legal Clinics—A pioneer in clinical legal education, the college provides an atmosphere for learning basic lawyering techniques and allows students the opportunity to further sharpen their skills in live client settings. Advanced students appear in court under close supervision in both civil and criminal cases.

Through the Dispute Resolution Clinic, mediation experience is available in a variety of matters, including unruly child complaints and custody and visitation issues in parentage cases in juvenile court. Students in the Public Service Externship Clinic are assigned to public service legal entities such as the judiciary, legal services offices, pro bono programs, public defender offices, legislative bodies, government agencies, and public interest organizations.

Legal Institute of the Great Lakes—The institute supports research, publishes a scholarly journal, and sponsors conferences on the legal, economic, and social issues of importance to the Great Lakes region of the United States and Canada. The highlight of these discussions is an annual symposium on the national and international water crisis and the need for fresh water.

■ Admission

A bachelor's degree from an accredited institution is required. Grades and LSAT scores are the most important determinants of admission. However, the Admission

Committee carefully considers each application on its own merits. Letters of recommendation are important.

Prospective students are encouraged to visit the law school, talk to our students and faculty, and sit in on a class. Appointments can be made through the Admission Office.

■ Student Activities

The *University of Toledo Law Review* is published four times a year by students selected on the basis of scholarship. Students may also qualify by submitting a publishable article. Training and practice in brief writing and oral argument beyond the required appellate advocacy course are obtained through the Moot Court Program, in the Charles Fornoff Intramural Moot Court Competition, and in several national and regional competitions.

The Student Bar Association, American Civil Liberties Union, Black Law Students Association, Business Law Society, Christian Legal Society, Environmental Law Society, Federalist Society, Health Law Association, Hispanic Law Students Association, International Law Society, Jewish Law Students Association, OUTLAW, Sports Law Association, and Women Law Students Association are among many active organizations.

■ Financial Aid

The College of Law strives to provide an affordable legal education without sacrificing quality. Every effort is made to ensure that students graduate without large financial obligations that may take years to repay. The College of Law awards scholarships totaling in excess of $1,000,000 each year. Monroe County, Michigan, residents are treated as in-state residents for tuition purposes. The goal of the financial aid program is to ensure that graduates become the lawyers they want to be and not the lawyers they have to be to repay financial obligations.

■ Career Services

The college places top priority on providing comprehensive career planning and placement for its students and graduates. The Law Career Services Office assists students through workshops, videotapes, and counseling and provides guest speakers on legal career options.

As a result of both on- and off-campus interviews, second- and third-year students accept summer or attorney positions in all major cities of Ohio and Michigan as well as locations throughout the US.

The college's Judicial Clerkship Program places graduates as clerks with federal and state courts around the country. Graduates are successfully practicing in major law firms, government offices, the judiciary, and in public interest positions in nearly every state. Graduates also can be found in Asia, Europe, and Africa.

Graduates are a valuable resource for current students as they pursue employment opportunities nationwide.

Applicant Profile

The University of Toledo College of Law

GPA	LSAT (10) Percentile Intervals								
	0-20	21-30	31-40	41-50	51-60	61-70	71-80	81-90	91-99
3.75 Above									
3.74 3.50									
3.49 3.25									
3.24 3.00									
2.99 2.75									
2.74 2.50									
2.49 2.25									
2.24 2.00									
Below 2.00									

■ Highly Likely   ▨ Possible   ☐ Unlikely

Touro College—Jacob D. Fuchsberg Law Center

300 Nassau Road
Huntington, NY 11743
Phone: 631.421.2244, ext. 312; Fax: 631.421.9708
E-mail: admissions@tourolaw.edu; Website: www.tourolaw.edu

*ABA
Approved
Since
1983*

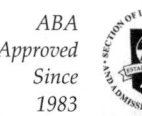

The Basics

Type of school	Private
Term	Semester
Application deadline	
Application fee	$50
Financial aid deadline	4/15
Can first year start other than fall?	No
Student to faculty ratio (fall)	17.3 to 1
Does the university offer:	
housing restricted to law students?	Yes
graduate housing for which law students are eligible?	No

Faculty and Administrators

	Total		Men		Women		Minorities	
	Fall	Spr	Fall	Spr	Fall	Spr	Fall	Spr
Full-time	32	30	20	18	12	12	3	3
Other Full-time	3	3	1	1	2	2	0	0
Deans, librarians, & others who teach	5	5	3	3	2	2	0	0
Part-time	17	17	14	12	3	5	3	1
Total	57	55	38	34	19	21	6	4

Curriculum

	Full-time	Part-time
Typical first-year section size	71	75
Is there typically a "small section" of the first-year class, other than Legal Writing, taught by full-time faculty	No	No
If yes, typical size offered last year	0	0
# of classroom course titles beyond 1st year curriculum	62	

# of upper division courses, excluding seminars with an enrollment:	Under 25	62
	25-49	28
	50-74	21
	75-99	1
	100+	2

# of seminars	14	
# of seminar positions available	277	
# of seminar positions filled	141	62
# of positions available in simulation courses	272	
# of simulation positions filled	119	101
# of positions available in faculty supervised clinical courses	180	
# of faculty supervised clinical positions filled	115	26
# involved in field placements	5	2
# involved in law journals	18	9
# involved in moot court or trial competitions	20	11
# of credit hours required to graduate	87	

JD Enrollment and Ethnicity

	Men		Women		Full-time		Part-time		1st-year		Total		JD Degs. Awd.
	#	%	#	%	#	%	#	%	#	%	#	%	
African Amer.	29	7.1	46	13.4	34	7.0	41	15.4	23	8.5	75	9.9	17
Amer. Indian	3	0.7	1	0.3	1	0.2	3	1.1	2	0.7	4	0.5	0
Asian Amer.	30	7.3	26	7.6	41	8.4	15	5.6	29	10.7	56	7.4	9
Mex. Amer.	0	0.0	0	0.0	0	0.0	0	0.0	0	0.0	0	0.0	0
Puerto Rican	0	0.0	0	0.0	0	0.0	0	0.0	0	0.0	0	0.0	0
Hispanic	15	3.6	29	8.4	24	4.9	20	7.5	11	4.0	44	5.8	12
Total Minority	77	18.7	102	29.7	100	20.4	79	29.7	65	23.9	179	23.7	38
For. Nation.	3	0.7	3	0.9	6	1.2	0	0.0	3	1.1	6	0.8	0
Caucasian	303	73.7	224	65.1	360	73.6	167	62.8	178	65.4	527	69.8	119
Unknown	28	6.8	15	4.4	23	4.7	20	7.5	26	9.6	43	5.7	1
Total	411	54.4	344	45.6	489	64.8	266	35.2	272	36.0	755		158

Tuition and Fees

	Resident	Nonresident
Full-time	$25,660	$25,660
Part-time	$20,000	$20,000

Living Expenses

Estimated living expenses for singles

Living on campus	Living off campus	Living at home
$20,851	$20,851	$9,832

Touro College—Jacob D. Fuchsberg Law Center

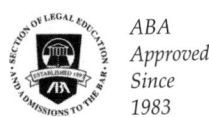

*ABA
Approved
Since
1983*

GPA and LSAT Scores

	Total	Full-time	Part-time
# of apps	2,251	1,731	520
# of admits	684	546	138
# of matrics	273	200	73
75% GPA	3.34	3.32	3.37
25% GPA	2.73	2.74	2.62
75% LSAT	152	153	152
25% LSAT	149	150	148

Grants and Scholarships (from prior year)

	Total		Full-time		Part-time	
	#	%	#	%	#	%
Total # of students	719		432		287	
Total # receiving grants	343	47.7	221	51.2	122	42.5
Less than 1/2 tuition	309	43.0	200	46.3	109	38.0
Half to full tuition	29	4.0	17	3.9	12	4.2
Full tuition	4	0.6	3	0.7	1	0.3
More than full tuition	1	0.1	1	0.2	0	0.0
Median grant amount			$4,000		$2,500	

Informational and Library Resources

# of volumes and volume equivalents	437,797
# of titles	67,693
# of active serial subscriptions	4,503
Study seating capacity inside the library	375
# of professional librarians	7
Hours per week library is open	86
# of open, wired connections available to students	56
# of networked computers available for use by students	56
# of simultaneous wireless users	700
Require computer?	N

JD Attrition (from prior year)

	Academic	Other	Total	
	#	#	#	%
1st year	27	45	72	25.3%
2nd year	8	5	13	6.4%
3rd year	2	0	2	1.2%
4th year	1	0	1	1.5%

Employment

	Total	Percentage
Employment status known	135	95.7
Employment status unknown	6	4.3
Employed	99	73.3
Pursuing graduate degrees	3	2.2
Unemployed seeking employment	33	24.4
Unemployed not seeking employment	0	0.0

Type of Employment

# employed in law firms	63	63.6
# employed in business and industry	15	15.2
# employed in government	14	14.1
# employed in public interest	6	6.1
# employed as judicial clerks	1	1.0
# employed in academia	0	0.0

Geographic Location

# employed in state	91	91.9
# employed in foreign countries	1	1.0
# of states where employed	4	

Bar Passage Rates

Jurisdiction	New York		
Exam	Sum 03	Win 04	Total
# from school taking bar for the first time	96	39	135
School's pass rate for all first-time takers	63%	56%	61%
State's pass rate for all first-time takers	78%	58%	75%

Touro College—Jacob D. Fuchsberg Law Center

300 Nassau Road
Huntington, NY 11743
Phone: 631.421.2244, ext. 312; Fax: 631.421.9708
E-mail: admissions@tourolaw.edu; Website: www.tourolaw.edu

■ The School

Established in 1980, Touro Law Center is fully accredited by the American Bar Association and is a member of the Association of American Law Schools. The Law Center's campus is located in Huntington, Long Island, in the heart of a vibrant suburban community—one hour by car or train from New York City.

Huntington and neighboring communities boast a wide variety of affordable housing options, ranging from apartments and condominiums to single-family homes. Students may also use the Office of Admissions' Housing Information Network, which provides current listings of accommodations, as well as information regarding car pools and shared living arrangements. On-campus parking is plentiful and free of charge.

■ Students and Faculty

The Law Center's students, coming from diverse backgrounds and experiences, represent over 125 undergraduate institutions and a broad mix of majors. Women make up 46 percent of the total enrollment; African Americans, Hispanics, and Asians comprise 25 percent of the student body.

Students play an active role in governing the entire institution through the Student Bar Association and service on faculty committees, where they enjoy voting rights. There are two honor societies: the *Touro Law Review* and the Moot Court Board. There are also 30 student organizations devoted to specialized professional and social concerns.

Of Touro's 35 full-time faculty members, many have advanced degrees in other disciplines, including medicine, philosophy, business, and finance. Almost all have extensive practice backgrounds, ranging from the bench, major law firms, criminal prosecution and defense, government agencies, and public interest organizations.

While they embody a unique mix of talents and achievements, the faculty shares one common characteristic: accessibility to students. Every entering student is assigned a faculty advisor, matched by common background or interest area, for discussions on any aspect of the law school experience: study strategy, course selection, career goals, and so on. With an open-door policy and a student faculty ratio of 16:1, everyone reaps the benefits of a personal and dynamic educational experience.

■ Academic Programs

Juris Doctor (JD): Touro offers the JD degree full time in the day, part time in the day (10:00 AM to 2:00 PM, Monday—Friday), and part time in the evening (6:30 PM to 9:45 PM, Monday—Thursday). Students wishing to accelerate may graduate within two and a half years (full time) and three and a half years (part time), by attending summer sessions.

Dual Degrees: The JD may be combined with a Master of Business Administration (MBA), a Master of Public Administration (MPA) in Health Care, or a Master of Social Work (MSW), allowing students to complete the two degrees with significant time and cost savings.

Master of Laws (LLM): The Law Center also offers a 24-credit general LLM, full time or part time, and a 27-credit LLM in US Legal Studies (for foreign law graduates), full time or part time.

■ Curriculum

Touro's curriculum is focused on bridging the gap between law school and law practice, between the classroom and the courtroom.

Areas of Specialization: Students may choose elective courses to create legal specialties in business, criminal, family, health care, intellectual property, international, and public interest law.

Practice Modules: In conjunction with courses in Business Organizations, Family Law, and Trusts and Estates, students handle simulated cases from initial client contact to successful resolution.

Clinics: Touro offers five in-house clinics, where clients bring real cases to on-campus offices: Civil Rights Litigation; Elder Law; Family Law; International Human Rights/Asylum Litigation; and Not-for-Profit Corporation Law, with the last two designed for part-time evening students. There are four field-placement clinics in which students work off campus: Business, Law, and Technology (law firms and high-tech corporations); Civil Practice (law firms, corporations, and public and private agencies); Criminal Law (District Attorneys' and Legal Aid/Public Defenders' offices); and Judicial Clerkship (state and federal judges' chambers). In addition, Touro offers two "rotations," mirroring the medical school model, where students work intensively in practice groups at the US Attorney's office and at a regional legal services agency.

Externships: The Law Center provides externships through its Domestic Violence, Housing Rights, and Social Justice projects, as well as placements in private law firms, corporate law departments, government agencies, the courts, and public interest organizations.

Institutes: Touro hosts the Institute for Business, Law, and Technology (technology-related legal issues); the Local and Suburban Law Institute (research in municipal law); the Jewish Law Institute (the Jewish legal tradition); and the Institute on the Holocaust and the Law (the role of law/legal institutions in the Holocaust).

Summer Programs: In addition to the Law Center's on-site summer program, which features special programs on New York law, there are opportunities for work and study abroad: Moscow, Russia (Russian legal system in transition); Shimla and Dharamsala, India (India's religious and cultural pluralism); Xiamen, China (historical, philosophical, and sociological underpinnings of Chinese society); and Berlin, Germany (justice and human rights). Touro also offers summer internships in law firms, courts, and government offices in Europe and in Israel.

■ Academic Support and Enrichment

The Law Center provides a unique program of outside-the-classroom assistance. Teaching Assistants (TAs) review material covered in class and conduct small-group sessions on effective study methods and test-taking techniques. The Writing Resources Center offers workshops and tutorials to assist students in producing a professional work product. In addition, the Legal Education Access Program (LEAP) enhances the experience of students of color, through a four-week summer program for new students and mentoring during the academic year.

The Honors Program, beginning in the second year, allows outstanding students to become Faculty Fellows, where they receive additional scholarship assistance and access to academic enrichment seminars.

■ Career Services

The Career Services Office finds students and graduates part-time, full-time, and summer employment. In addition to placing students in national, regional, and local law firms, there are opportunities in federal, state, and local courts and government agencies, and in the legal departments of corporations and municipalities.

■ Admission and Financial Aid

Touro Law Center declines to provide an Applicant Pool Grid because such data fail to reflect the complexity of the selection process. At no point on a purely objective scale is an applicant assured of a particular decision. Among the most important criteria are the LSAT score and UGPA. The selection process, however, is based upon evaluation of all factors that may be indicative of potential for success—college major and course selection, graduate study, work experience, community involvement, and character.

In order to finance law school, Touro provides access to federal loans and work study, New York State loan and assistance programs, and need-based Touro Grants. Most students receive some form of financial aid, and over 50 percent of entering students receive scholarships.

■ Scholarships

Institutional aid is available to entering students (based on LSAT/UGPA) and to continuing students (based on academic performance). Assistance includes Dean's Fellowships (full tuition remission), Merit Scholarships (up to 75 percent tuition remission), and Incentive Awards (up to $7,000 per year). In addition, the Law Center offers Public Interest Law Fellowships for summer employment and a Loan Repayment Assistance Program for graduates employed in public interest law.

Applicant Profile Not Available

Tulane University Law School

John Giffen Weinmann Hall, 6329 Freret Street
New Orleans, LA 70118
Phone: 504.865.5930; Fax: 504.865.6710
E-mail: admissions@law.tulane.edu; Website: www.law.tulane.edu

ABA
Approved
Since
1925

The Basics

Type of school	Private
Term	Semester
Application deadline	5/1
Application fee	$60
Financial aid deadline	2/15
Can first year start other than fall?	No
Student to faculty ratio (fall)	18.8 to 1
Does the university offer:	
housing restricted to law students?	No
graduate housing for which law students are eligible?	Yes

Faculty and Administrators

	Total		Men		Women		Minorities	
	Fall	Spr	Fall	Spr	Fall	Spr	Fall	Spr
Full-time	43	41	34	32	9	9	4	2
Other Full-time	10	10	3	3	7	7	1	1
Deans, librarians, & others who teach	6	6	2	2	4	4	1	1
Part-time	26	46	25	38	1	8	1	1
Total	85	103	64	75	21	28	7	5

Curriculum

	Full-time	Part-time
Typical first-year section size	85	0
Is there typically a "small section" of the first-year class, other than Legal Writing, taught by full-time faculty	No	No
If yes, typical size offered last year	0	0
# of classroom course titles beyond 1st year curriculum	203	
# of upper division courses, excluding seminars with an enrollment: Under 25	86	
25-49	65	
50-74	19	
75-99	12	
100+	12	
# of seminars	30	
# of seminar positions available	508	
# of seminar positions filled	507	0
# of positions available in simulation courses	442	
# of simulation positions filled	409	0
# of positions available in faculty supervised clinical courses	90	
# of faculty supervised clinical positions filled	90	0
# involved in field placements	25	0
# involved in law journals	254	0
# involved in moot court or trial competitions	130	0
# of credit hours required to graduate	88	

JD Enrollment and Ethnicity

	Men		Women		Full-time		Part-time		1st-year		Total		JD Degs. Awd.
	#	%	#	%	#	%	#	%	#	%	#	%	
African Amer.	21	4.3	56	11.4	77	7.9	0	0.0	21	6.9	77	7.9	27
Amer. Indian	3	0.6	4	0.8	7	0.7	0	0.0	1	0.3	7	0.7	0
Asian Amer.	12	2.5	37	7.5	49	5.0	0	0.0	19	6.2	49	5.0	17
Mex. Amer.	4	0.8	5	1.0	9	0.9	0	0.0	4	1.3	9	0.9	0
Puerto Rican	3	0.6	4	0.8	7	0.7	0	0.0	1	0.3	7	0.7	0
Hispanic	14	2.9	13	2.6	26	2.7	1	50.0	11	3.6	27	2.8	13
Total Minority	57	11.7	119	24.2	175	17.9	1	50.0	57	18.7	176	18.0	57
For. Nation.	12	2.5	9	1.8	21	2.2	0	0.0	3	1.0	21	2.1	9
Caucasian	384	79.0	344	70.1	727	74.6	1	50.0	224	73.4	728	74.5	257
Unknown	33	6.8	19	3.9	52	5.3	0	0.0	21	6.9	52	5.3	13
Total	486	49.7	491	50.3	975	99.8	2	0.2	305	31.2	977		336

Tuition and Fees

	Resident	Nonresident
Full-time	$31,210	$31,210
Part-time	$0	$0

Living Expenses

Estimated living expenses for singles

Living on campus	Living off campus	Living at home
$14,662	$14,662	$7,692

Tulane University Law School

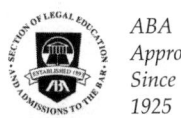

*ABA
Approved
Since
1925*

GPA and LSAT Scores

	Total	Full-time	Part-time
# of apps	4,126	4,126	0
# of admits	1,055	1,055	0
# of matrics	300	300	0
75% GPA	3.73	3.73	0.00
25% GPA	3.28	3.28	0.00
75% LSAT	163	163	0
25% LSAT	158	158	0

Grants and Scholarships (from prior year)

	Total #	Total %	Full-time #	Full-time %	Part-time #	Part-time %
Total # of students	1,018		1,018		0	
Total # receiving grants	605	59.4	605	59.4	0	0.0
Less than 1/2 tuition	398	39.1	398	39.1	0	0.0
Half to full tuition	186	18.3	186	18.3	0	0.0
Full tuition	19	1.9	19	1.9	0	0.0
More than full tuition	2	0.2	2	0.2	0	0.0
Median grant amount			$10,000		$0	

Informational and Library Resources

# of volumes and volume equivalents	553,972
# of titles	298,370
# of active serial subscriptions	5,023
Study seating capacity inside the library	557
# of professional librarians	10
Hours per week library is open	113
# of open, wired connections available to students	295
# of networked computers available for use by students	108
# of simultaneous wireless users	1,000
Require computer?	N

JD Attrition (from prior year)

	Academic #	Other #	Total #	Total %
1st year	4	23	27	8.0%
2nd year	1	6	7	2.1%
3rd year	0	0	0	0.0%
4th year	0	0	0	0.0%

Employment

	Total	Percentage
Employment status known	316	96.6
Employment status unknown	11	3.4
Employed	276	87.3
Pursuing graduate degrees	16	5.1
Unemployed seeking employment	13	4.1
Unemployed not seeking employment	11	3.5

Type of Employment

# employed in law firms	158	57.2
# employed in business and industry	18	6.5
# employed in government	20	7.2
# employed in public interest	9	3.3
# employed as judicial clerks	29	10.5
# employed in academia	0	0.0

Geographic Location

# employed in state	62	22.5
# employed in foreign countries	3	1.1
# of states where employed	30	

Bar Passage Rates

Jurisdiction	Louisiana			New York		
Exam	Sum 03	Win 04	Total	Sum 03	Win 04	Total
# from school taking bar for the first time	78	15	93	64	5	69
School's pass rate for all first-time takers	71%	67%	70%	86%	80%	86%
State's pass rate for all first-time takers	62%	60%	61%	78%	58%	75%

Tulane University Law School

John Giffen Weinmann Hall, 6329 Freret Street
New Orleans, LA 70118
Phone: 504.865.5930; Fax: 504.865.6710
E-mail: admissions@law.tulane.edu; Website: www.law.tulane.edu

■ Introduction

Tulane Law School, established in 1847, is the 12th oldest law school in the United States. The Law School is centrally located on the main university campus in a picturesque neighborhood of uptown New Orleans. New Orleans itself offers a reasonable cost of living and a surprising number of legal resources, including the US Court of Appeals for the Fifth Circuit, Federal District Court, the Louisiana Supreme Court, and lower state civil, criminal, and specialized courts. In addition to numerous events at Tulane University, students enjoy the advantages of city life and the richness of New Orleans culture. On-campus housing is available. Off-campus housing is also plentiful and nearby.

The Law School curriculum offers a complete selection of common law and federal subjects. In addition, Tulane offers electives in the civil law, with the result that students have the opportunity to pursue comparative education in the world's two major legal systems. The breadth and depth of the curriculum permit students to survey a broad range of subject areas or to concentrate in one or more.

■ Facilities

The Law School's 160,000-square-foot building, John Giffen Weinmann Hall, was completed in 1995. Designed to integrate classrooms, other student spaces, excellent computer facilities, faculty offices, and a state-of-the-art library that contains both national and international collections, the building is centrally located on campus.

Immediately adjacent to Weinmann Hall is the Law School's Career Development Office. A 13,000-square-foot addition and renovation project will soon bring the Career Development Office into Weinmann Hall. Within minutes of the Law School building are the university's Howard-Tilton Library, housing over one million volumes, various university dining facilities, the bookstore, the Reily Student Recreation Center, the Freeman School of Business, the Newcomb Art Gallery, and various auditoriums and performance venues.

■ The Academic Program

Six semesters in residence, completion of 88 credits with at least a C average, and fulfillment of a 20-hour community service obligation are required for graduation from the JD degree program. The first-year curriculum comprises eight required courses and one elective. Thereafter, all courses are elective, except for a legal ethics course. All first-year and many upper-class courses are taught in multiple sections to allow for smaller classes. The first-year Legal Research and Writing Program is taught by instructors with significant experience as lawyers and writers, each assisted by senior fellows. The legal analysis course is an optional invitational program during the first semester in which students work closely with faculty and senior fellows on writing and analysis skills.

At the graduate level, the Law School offers a general LLM program; LLM programs in Admiralty, Energy and Environmental Law, American Business Law, and International and Comparative Law; and the PhD.

■ Special Programs

The school offers five optional concentration programs that allow JD students to receive a certificate of completion of successful studies in (a) European Legal Studies, (b) Environmental Law, (c) Maritime Law, (d) Sports Law, or (e) Civil Law. Tulane's Eason-Weinmann Center for Comparative Law, its Maritime Law Center, and its Institute for Environmental Law and Policy add depth to the curriculum. Tulane also offers strong programs in intellectual property law and business, corporate, and commercial law.

Tulane conducts a summer school in New Orleans and offers summer-study programs abroad in Canada, England, The Netherlands, France, Italy, Germany, and Greece. It offers semester-long exchange programs with select law schools in a number of countries throughout the world.

■ Clinical Programs

The school offers six live clinical programs: civil, criminal, juvenile, domestic violence, environmental, and legislative and administrative advocacy. In addition, there is a Trial Advocacy program, and third-year students may do externships with federal and state judges, with a local death penalty project, or with certain administrative agencies. The school was the first to institute a mandatory pro bono program requiring that each student complete at least 20 hours of community-service work prior to graduation.

■ Joint-Degree Programs

Joint-degree programs are offered in conjunction with Tulane's Freeman School of Business, (JD/MBA and JD/MACCT), School of Public Health and Tropical Medicine, (JD/MHA and JD/MPH), School of Social Work (JD/MSW), and Graduate School (JD/MS in International Development; JD/MA in a variety of fields including Latin American Studies and International Affairs). Proposals for additional programs are considered on an ad hoc basis.

Tulane University Law School

■ Admission

Competition is keen, and a combination of the objective factors, the LSAT score and the UGPA, is relied upon heavily. In the case of multiple LSAT scores, the school looks at the average score. Tulane seeks to individualize the admission process by also considering subjective factors such as grade trends, courseload, undergraduate school, nonacademic activities, the student's background and experience, barriers overcome, and the personal statement. The Law School processes applications for admission beginning October 1 and starts to announce decisions after December 1.

■ Student Activities

Journals published or edited at Tulane Law School include the *Tulane Law Review, Tulane Maritime Law Journal, Tulane Environmental Law Journal, Journal of Law & Sexuality, Tulane European and Civil Law Forum, Tulane Journal of International and Comparative Law, Journal of Technology and Intellectual Property*, and *Sports Lawyer's Journal*, published by the national Sports Lawyers Association. An active moot court program holds trial and appellate competitions within the school and fields teams for a variety of interschool competitions. The Law School has a chapter of the Order of the Coif. Over 40 student organizations are active at Tulane, including Tulane Law Women, Black Law Students Association, La Alianza, Asian Pacific American Law Students Association, Environmental Law Society, and several legal fraternities. The Tulane Public Interest Law Foundation raises funds, matched by the Law School, to support as many as 30 students each summer in public interest fellowships with a variety of organizations.

■ Career Services

The Career Development Office at the Law School assists both students and alumni in finding employment in the legal profession. A large career-services library is available to students, as well as a full range of counseling services. Tulane offers both on- and off-campus interview programs. Each student is assigned a career counselor. In addition to working individually with students, career counselors engage in employer development activities and develop expertise in a variety of job search skills and in particular practice areas and settings. The office takes a proactive stance in assisting students with their job searches, with the result that Tulane graduates find law-related employment throughout the United States.

Applicant Profile

Tulane University Law School

LSAT Score	GPA									
	3.75 +	3.50 - 3.74	3.25 - 3.49	3.00 - 3.24	2.75 - 2.99	2.50 - 2.74	2.25 - 2.49	2.00 - 2.24	Below 2.00	No GPA
175-180										
170-174										
165-169										
160-164										
155-159										
150-154										
145-149										
140-144										
135-139										
130-134										
125-129										
120-124										

Excellent　　Possible　　Unlikely

The University of Tulsa College of Law

3120 East Fourth Place
Tulsa, OK 74104-3189
Phone: 918.631.2406; Fax: 918.631.3630
E-mail: george-justice@utulsa.edu; Website: www.law.utulsa.edu

*ABA
Approved
Since
1950*

The Basics

Type of school	Private
Term	Semester
Application deadline	2/1
Application fee	$30
Financial aid deadline	
Can first year start other than fall?	Yes
Student to faculty ratio (fall)	22.7 to 1
Does the university offer:	
housing restricted to law students?	Yes
graduate housing for which law students are eligible?	Yes

Faculty and Administrators

	Total		Men		Women		Minorities	
	Fall	Spr	Fall	Spr	Fall	Spr	Fall	Spr
Full-time	20	22	10	12	10	10	3	3
Other Full-time	2	2	0	0	2	2	0	0
Deans, librarians, & others who teach	12	12	6	6	6	6	2	3
Part-time	38	27	30	20	8	7	1	1
Total	72	63	46	38	26	25	6	7

Curriculum

	Full-time	Part-time
Typical first-year section size	76	60
Is there typically a "small section" of the first-year class, other than Legal Writing, taught by full-time faculty	Yes	No
If yes, typical size offered last year	45	40
# of classroom course titles beyond 1st year curriculum		94
# of upper division courses, excluding seminars with an enrollment: Under 25		97
25-49		34
50-74		12
75-99		1
100+		0
# of seminars		15
# of seminar positions available		187
# of seminar positions filled	79	33
# of positions available in simulation courses		644
# of simulation positions filled	317	238
# of positions available in faculty supervised clinical courses		72
# of faculty supervised clinical positions filled	60	3
# involved in field placements	55	4
# involved in law journals	93	4
# involved in moot court or trial competitions	91	11
# of credit hours required to graduate		88

JD Enrollment and Ethnicity

	Men		Women		Full-time		Part-time		1st-year		Total		JD Degs. Awd.
	#	%	#	%	#	%	#	%	#	%	#	%	
African Amer.	9	2.4	9	3.7	12	2.4	6	5.2	6	3.1	18	2.9	9
Amer. Indian	15	4.0	27	11.2	31	6.2	11	9.5	9	4.7	42	6.8	14
Asian Amer.	4	1.1	6	2.5	9	1.8	1	0.9	3	1.6	10	1.6	2
Mex. Amer.	14	3.7	5	2.1	16	3.2	3	2.6	8	4.2	19	3.1	8
Puerto Rican	0	0.0	0	0.0	0	0.0	0	0.0	0	0.0	0	0.0	0
Hispanic	0	0.0	0	0.0	0	0.0	0	0.0	0	0.0	0	0.0	0
Total Minority	42	11.1	47	19.5	68	13.5	21	18.1	26	13.5	89	14.4	33
For. Nation.	4	1.1	0	0.0	3	0.6	1	0.9	1	0.5	4	0.6	3
Caucasian	303	80.4	169	70.1	388	77.3	84	72.4	147	76.6	472	76.4	122
Unknown	28	7.4	25	10.4	43	8.6	10	8.6	18	9.4	53	8.6	10
Total	377	61.0	241	39.0	502	81.2	116	18.8	192	31.1	618		168

Tuition and Fees

	Resident	Nonresident
Full-time	$22,777	$22,777
Part-time	$15,967	$15,967

Living Expenses

Estimated living expenses for singles

Living on campus	Living off campus	Living at home
$11,966	$15,400	$8,690

The University of Tulsa College of Law

ABA
Approved
Since
1950

GPA and LSAT Scores

	Total	Full-time	Part-time
# of apps	1,328	1,236	92
# of admits	535	501	34
# of matrics	233	216	17
75% GPA	3.57	3.56	3.47
25% GPA	2.95	3.00	2.85
75% LSAT	154	154	159
25% LSAT	148	148	150

Grants and Scholarships (from prior year)

	Total		Full-time		Part-time	
	#	%	#	%	#	%
Total # of students	614		515		99	
Total # receiving grants	181	29.5	157	30.5	24	24.2
Less than 1/2 tuition	127	20.7	114	22.1	13	13.1
Half to full tuition	40	6.5	33	6.4	7	7.1
Full tuition	14	2.3	10	1.9	4	4.0
More than full tuition	0	0.0	0	0.0	0	0.0
Median grant amount			$4,250		$6,000	

Informational and Library Resources

# of volumes and volume equivalents	375,359
# of titles	181,591
# of active serial subscriptions	3,253
Study seating capacity inside the library	685
# of professional librarians	9
Hours per week library is open	110
# of open, wired connections available to students	420
# of networked computers available for use by students	158
# of simultaneous wireless users	2,000
Require computer?	N

JD Attrition (from prior year)

	Academic	Other	Total	
	#	#	#	%
1st year	15	19	34	15.0%
2nd year	3	14	17	7.4%
3rd year	0	0	0	0.0%
4th year	0	0	0	0.0%

Employment

	Total	Percentage
Employment status known	159	98.1
Employment status unknown	3	1.9
Employed	125	78.6
Pursuing graduate degrees	12	7.5
Unemployed seeking employment	22	13.8
Unemployed not seeking employment	0	0.0

Type of Employment

# employed in law firms	86	68.8
# employed in business and industry	20	16.0
# employed in government	17	13.6
# employed in public interest	1	0.8
# employed as judicial clerks	1	0.8
# employed in academia	0	0.0

Geographic Location

# employed in state	82	65.6
# employed in foreign countries	0	0.0
# of states where employed		20

Bar Passage Rates

Jurisdiction	Oklahoma		
Exam	Sum 03	Win 04	Total
# from school taking bar for the first time	66	25	91
School's pass rate for all first-time takers	88%	80%	86%
State's pass rate for all first-time takers	82%	83%	82%

The University of Tulsa College of Law

3120 East Fourth Place
Tulsa, OK 74104-3189
Phone: 918.631.2406; Fax: 918.631.3630
E-mail: george-justice@utulsa.edu; Website: www.law.utulsa.edu

■ Introduction

Expect the extraordinary from the University of Tulsa. You will not be disappointed. The people at TU prove daily that it is possible for friendliness, challenge, respect, and excellence to coexist in law school. Housed in beautiful and technologically enhanced John Rogers Hall on the University of Tulsa campus, and fully accredited by the ABA, the law school presents a forum for study and exploration of legal issues enhanced impressively by professors with exemplary credentials. A true open-door policy encouraged by professors invites students to expand their legal education from the classroom to one-on-one accessibility and interaction. Students are celebrated as the unique, gifted individuals they are. We honor that talent with scholarships ranging up to full tuition. With most students coming to Tulsa from states other than Oklahoma, a rich fabric of diversity expands the learning experience of every student. Located in the beautiful, culturally diverse, and extraordinarily friendly city of Tulsa, law students can enjoy award-winning theater, national touring concerts, world-class museums, gorgeous parks, and vibrant neighborhood shopping areas. The city also boasts an internationally recognized burgeoning environment for high-tech industry and commerce.

■ Library and Physical Facilities

The $11.5 million state-of-the-art, award-winning Mabee Legal Information Center is much more than a library. The brand-new center was designed for students. Enter the center and you are immediately surrounded with the warmth of burnished mahogany, bayberry, and sienna. It would be very difficult to find a more attractive, pleasant place to spend your hours of study, research, and, yes, even relaxation. The center is just the latest proof that students are our highest priority at Tulsa.

Eight professional librarians are ready to help with legal research in the 300,000-volume collection. Numerous electronic resources are accessible to the students onsite or from home. With over 700 seats available and miles of shelving space, there is plenty of space for students, alumni, and books. The Native American Law Center and the International/Comparative Law Center offer inviting forums for study, research, and the exchange of ideas with impressive artwork contributing to the rich heritage represented by these two very strong programs. The 301 carrels and two grand main reading rooms reflect inviting, wide-open spaces. The new-century library has 269 open, wired network connections for laptops, with all tables and carrels wired to the network.

Three computer labs offer 59 workstations with impressive credentials: flat screen displays, 500 MHz Pentium IIIs with 128 MB RAM, 6 GB hard drives, and 100 MB zip drives. Another 38 PCs are available for use throughout the information center. Student staffing offices for the Board of Advocates, the *Tulsa Law Review*, the *Energy Law Journal*, and *The Journal of Comparative and International Law* provide generous working space for these important enterprises at the College of Law. Specialized classrooms include a laptop lab complete with 24 laptops for students and the Alternative Dispute Resolution Center, where negotiation exercises are possible within a variety of simulation configurations.

The College of Law is a wireless facility. Electronic classrooms throughout the College of Law are wired for laptop utilization by students from their desks with access for instruction from a variety of computerized configurations, including smart podiums, large-screen projection, and Internet feeds. A new law clinic center and wireless renovation of the moot courtroom by the same architectural design firm that completed work on the Mabee Legal Information Center bring the same state-of-the-art capacities to the study and training for trial and appellate advocacy. They are outstanding laboratories in which the best in preparation may ensue for Tulsa law students as they prepare for many regional and national moot court competitions as well as future legal practice.

■ Curriculum and Specialization

Full-time and part-time programs are available, as well as summer classes and the ability for new students to begin their study in August or in January. Students may choose either general legal study covering a broad expanse of expertise or specialization. Eight areas of concentrated study include the Native American Law Certificate, the Health Law Certificate, the Public Policy and Regulation Certificate, the Practical Skills Certificate, the Comparative and International Law Certificate, the Center for Dispute Resolution Certificate, the Center for Entrepreneurial Law Certificate, and the National Energy-Environmental Law and Policy Certificate.

Summer- and semester-abroad programs ensure that Tulsa students will have the opportunity to become immersed in the excitement of broadening international horizons for legal training and personal exploration. The University of Tulsa International Law Program is augmented by exciting summer programs in Edinburgh (Scotland), Dublin (Ireland), Geneva (Switzerland), Leuven (Belgium), and Buenos Aires (Argentina), plus a semester of study in London.

Students at Tulsa have a great variety of career choices available to them, including interdisciplinary study. The following joint-degree programs are available: JD/MBA, JD/MA in Anthropology, JD/MA in History, JD/MA in Industrial/Organizational Psychology, JD/MA in English, JD/Master of Accountancy, JD/MS in Biological

Sciences, JD/MA in Clinical Psychology, JD/MS in Geosciences, and JD/MS in Taxation.

■ Professors

Knowledge and experience, matched by the passion for teaching, typifies the character of the professors at the University of Tulsa. Recognized nationally and internationally for their expertise, Tulsa professors are always accessible to their students. Specializations and strong experiential expertise in areas as diverse as international trade, energy regulation, family and juvenile law, sports law, Native American tribal jurisdiction, trial advocacy, and bioethics confirm the rich learning available to Tulsa law students. The ability to develop strong relationships with professors will strengthen Tulsa students' law school experience and their future legal practice in remarkable ways.

■ Housing

Law students at Tulsa may choose to live on or off campus. On-campus housing includes apartments that are less than five years old. Each apartment unit includes computer connections and large, spacious floor plans. With a very attractive low cost of living, the city of Tulsa offers a great variety of affordable housing opportunities. Information about housing may be obtained by calling 918.631.5249 or by contacting the Office of Law Admissions at 918.631.2406.

■ Career Services

Students at Tulsa gain significant personalized assistance in career counseling. On-campus interview coordination, résumé/dossier preparation services, informative seminar offerings, and summer and permanent job placement make the Office of Career Services an invaluable resource for future success. Tulsa graduates practicing in all 50 states and internationally make networking a vital resource in the enhancement of employment potential for students and alumni.

■ Practical Experience

Tulsa law students gain firsthand training beyond the classroom. The Tulsa Legal Clinic is housed conveniently in a beautiful, spacious new facility across the street from John Rogers Hall. The Legal Clinic offers programs such as the Indian Law Clinic, the Older American Law Project, and the Health Law Project. Federal and state judicial internships are available as well as the Legal Internship Program, which enables a student to represent clients in criminal and civil cases, subject to rules authorized by the Oklahoma Supreme Court.

Applicant Profile

The University of Tulsa College of Law

GPA	LSAT Score						
	120-147	147-151	151-153	153-157	157-163	163-170	170-180
3.75 + Above	Unlikely	Possible	Likely	Likely	Likely	Likely	Likely
3.74 3.50-	Unlikely	Possible	Likely	Likely	Likely	Likely	Likely
3.49 3.25-	Unlikely	Possible	Likely	Likely	Likely	Likely	Likely
3.24 3.00-	Unlikely	Possible	Likely	Likely	Likely	Likely	Likely
2.99 2.75-	Unlikely	Unlikely	Possible	Likely	Likely	Likely	Likely
2.74 2.50-	Unlikely	Unlikely	Unlikely	Possible	Likely	Likely	Likely
2.49 2.25-	Unlikely	Unlikely	Unlikely	Unlikely	Possible	Likely	Likely
2.24 2.00-	Unlikely	Unlikely	Unlikely	Unlikely	Unlikely	Possible	Likely

☐ Unlikely*   ▨ Possible   ■ Likely

* Individual accomplishments crucial

This chart is to be used as a general guide in determining the chances for admittance.

University of Utah S.J. Quinney College of Law

332 South 1400 East, Room 101
Salt Lake City, UT 84112-0730
Phone: 801.581.6833; Fax: 801.581.6897
E-mail: admissions@law.utah.edu; Website: www.law.utah.edu

ABA
Approved
Since
1927

The Basics

Type of school	Public
Term	Semester
Application deadline	2/1
Application fee	$50
Financial aid deadline	3/15
Can first year start other than fall?	No
Student to faculty ratio (fall)	12.9 to 1
Does the university offer:	
housing restricted to law students?	No
graduate housing for which law students are eligible?	Yes

Faculty and Administrators

	Total		Men		Women		Minorities	
	Fall	Spr	Fall	Spr	Fall	Spr	Fall	Spr
Full-time	26	23	19	16	7	7	6	5
Other Full-time	5	5	3	3	2	2	0	0
Deans, librarians, & others who teach	6	7	2	3	4	4	0	0
Part-time	16	23	12	18	4	5	1	0
Total	53	58	36	40	17	18	7	5

Curriculum

		Full-time	Part-time
Typical first-year section size		42	0
Is there typically a "small section" of the first-year class, other than Legal Writing, taught by full-time faculty		Yes	No
If yes, typical size offered last year		21	0
# of classroom course titles beyond 1st year curriculum		103	
# of upper division courses, excluding seminars with an enrollment:	Under 25	47	
	25-49	26	
	50-74	9	
	75-99	2	
	100+	0	
# of seminars		18	
# of seminar positions available		270	
# of seminar positions filled		149	0
# of positions available in simulation courses		0	
# of simulation positions filled		406	0
# of positions available in faculty supervised clinical courses		0	
# of faculty supervised clinical positions filled		0	0
# involved in field placements		216	0
# involved in law journals		95	0
# involved in moot court or trial competitions		112	0
# of credit hours required to graduate		88	

JD Enrollment and Ethnicity

	Men		Women		Full-time		Part-time		1st-year		Total		JD Degs. Awd.
	#	%	#	%	#	%	#	%	#	%	#	%	
African Amer.	1	0.4	1	0.7	2	0.5	0	0.0	1	0.8	2	0.5	0
Amer. Indian	5	2.0	0	0.0	5	1.2	0	0.0	2	1.5	5	1.2	4
Asian Amer.	9	3.5	6	4.1	15	3.7	0	0.0	9	6.9	15	3.7	9
Mex. Amer.	4	1.6	2	1.4	6	1.5	0	0.0	3	2.3	6	1.5	0
Puerto Rican	1	0.4	0	0.0	1	0.2	0	0.0	0	0.0	1	0.2	1
Hispanic	5	2.0	2	1.4	7	1.7	0	0.0	2	1.5	7	1.7	5
Total Minority	25	9.8	11	7.4	36	9.0	0	0.0	17	13.0	36	9.0	19
For. Nation.	1	0.4	2	1.4	3	0.7	0	0.0	0	0.0	3	0.7	2
Caucasian	204	80.3	121	81.8	325	80.8	0	0.0	103	78.6	325	80.8	115
Unknown	24	9.4	14	9.5	38	9.5	0	0.0	11	8.4	38	9.5	1
Total	254	63.2	148	36.8	402	100.0	0	0.0	131	32.6	402		137

Tuition and Fees

	Resident	Nonresident
Full-time	$9,746	$20,742
Part-time	$0	$0

Living Expenses

Estimated living expenses for singles

Living on campus	Living off campus	Living at home
$15,080	$15,080	$8,366

University of Utah S.J. Quinney College of Law

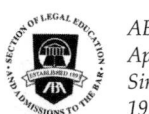

ABA
Approved
Since
1927

GPA and LSAT Scores

	Total	Full-time	Part-time
# of apps	1,263	1,263	0
# of admits	321	321	0
# of matrics	132	132	0
75% GPA	3.78	3.78	0.00
25% GPA	3.37	3.37	0.00
75% LSAT	162	162	0
25% LSAT	156	156	0

Grants and Scholarships (from prior year)

	Total		Full-time		Part-time	
	#	%	#	%	#	%
Total # of students	410		410		0	
Total # receiving grants	160	39.0	160	39.0	0	0.0
Less than 1/2 tuition	143	34.9	143	34.9	0	0.0
Half to full tuition	17	4.1	17	4.1	0	0.0
Full tuition	0	0.0	0	0.0	0	0.0
More than full tuition	0	0.0	0	0.0	0	0.0
Median grant amount			$950		$0	

Informational and Library Resources

# of volumes and volume equivalents	327,907
# of titles	128,816
# of active serial subscriptions	4,838
Study seating capacity inside the library	356
# of professional librarians	7
Hours per week library is open	100
# of open, wired connections available to students	612
# of networked computers available for use by students	39
# of simultaneous wireless users	400
Require computer?	N

JD Attrition (from prior year)

	Academic	Other	Total	
	#	#	#	%
1st year	0	6	6	4.8%
2nd year	0	0	0	0.0%
3rd year	0	0	0	0.0%
4th year	0	0	0	0.0%

Employment

	Total	Percentage
Employment status known	117	97.5
Employment status unknown	3	2.5
Employed	109	93.2
Pursuing graduate degrees	4	3.4
Unemployed seeking employment	2	1.7
Unemployed not seeking employment	2	1.7

Type of Employment

# employed in law firms	60	55.0
# employed in business and industry	18	16.5
# employed in government	18	16.5
# employed in public interest	2	1.8
# employed as judicial clerks	10	9.2
# employed in academia	1	0.9

Geographic Location

# employed in state	78	71.6
# employed in foreign countries	0	0.0
# of states where employed		13

Bar Passage Rates

Jurisdiction		Utah		
Exam	Sum 03	Win 04	Total	
# from school taking bar for the first time	80	13	93	
School's pass rate for all first-time takers	90%	77%	88%	
State's pass rate for all first-time takers	93%	87%	92%	

University of Utah S.J. Quinney College of Law

332 South 1400 East, Room 101
Salt Lake City, UT 84112-0730
Phone: 801.581.6833; Fax: 801.581.6897
E-mail: admissions@law.utah.edu; Website: www.law.utah.edu

■ Introduction

Established in 1913, the University of Utah S.J. Quinney College of Law is nationally recognized for its academic reputation, innovative curriculum, and favorable faculty/student ratio. Among the students, there is a prevailing sense of community fostered by a faculty and administration that is friendly, open, and service-oriented.

The College of Law is situated in the foothills of the picturesque Wasatch Range of the Rocky Mountains. The law school is less than a 10-minute drive or light rail ride from downtown Salt Lake City, the seat of federal, state, and local governmental bodies. This location provides ample professional opportunities for our students and a strong cultural scene. Recently voted one of America's most livable cities, Salt Lake City and the University of Utah campus hosted the 2002 Winter Olympics.

■ Library and Physical Facilities

The S.J. Quinney Law Library and the law building provide first-year students with their own study hall and personal carrels. The building is set up for wired and wireless laptop computer access. Advanced students are provided a personal study carrel, which also has laptop access in the adjacent Quinney Law Library—a modern, spacious facility with the latest technological equipment and library research services.

The library contains more than 325,000 volumes of law and law-related material and serves as a depository of US Government documents. CD-ROM and web-based databases provide access to primary legal materials, journal indexes, directories, and other law-related information.

In the law building and library, there are two student computing labs, other computer support, and recently remodeled classrooms and a moot courtroom auditorium with state-of-the-art video-computer projection equipment.

■ Curriculum

The Quinney law school's innovative academic programs blend theory and practice skills. Our program prepares graduates to practice law in any jurisdiction. The curriculum is designed to allow more efficient and rational sequencing of legal education that responds to the evolving legal, social, and ethical needs of our society.

The entering students are first offered an intensive four-day Introduction to Law course before they begin the required first-year curriculum. The first-year doctrinal courses include a small section in which enrollment is limited to no more than 25 students, as well as a spring-semester elective. Second-year students select from a variety of foundational courses. In the third year, students may take year-long intensive courses that

provide the opportunity for in-depth study, research, and a practicum in a focused area of law.

Additionally, students may select from more than 50 advanced courses and seminars, a variety of clinical and skills courses, and numerous cocurricular opportunities.

■ Special Programs

The Wallace Stegner Center for Land, Resources, and the Environment provides opportunities for JD candidates to engage in academic courses and related law activities focusing on public lands, environmental and natural resources law, and energy law. A certificate in Environmental and Natural Resources Law is awarded to candidates who complete a sequence of approved courses with a specified GPA. Courses regularly offered include Natural Resources Law, Oil and Gas, Mining and Minerals, Water Law, Public Land Use, and Environmental Law. The law school also offers a specialized LLM degree in natural resources and environmental law.

The clinical programs offer both live and simulated opportunities for students to assume the lawyering role. In the Civil Clinic and the Criminal Clinic, students represent clients, investigate cases, and appear in court. In the Judicial Clinic, students act as clerks to judges, researching issues and drafting opinions in pending cases. The Judicial Extern Program allows students to spend a semester away from school working as full-time clerks for certain courts.

Through the London Law Consortium, students may engage in study abroad during spring semester. This academic program consists of courses taught by visiting consortium faculty members residing in London and courses on the English legal system and law of the European Union taught by law lecturers from British universities.

The College of Law maintains two formal joint-degree programs. Students may earn joint degrees in the areas of business (JD/MBA) or public administration (JD/MPA).

The college's Academic Support Program provides assistance to students whose backgrounds and experiences before law school indicate a need for such assistance. Students apply to participate in the program after admission to the College of Law.

■ Admission Standards

No applicant is accepted or rejected without members of the Admission Committee having first fully considered the entire application. The personal statement should expand on the applicant's biographic and academic background and motivations for seeking a legal education. The College of Law makes a special effort to attract students from diverse cultural, educational, economic, ethnic, racial, and nontraditional backgrounds. Each applicant is evaluated for the contribution that person can make to the student body or the legal profession, in addition to evidence of demonstrated high academic ability.

■ Student Activities

The *Utah Law Review*, the *Journal of Law and Family Studies*, and the *Journal of Land, Resources, and Environmental Law* are professional journals edited and published by students. For the *Utah Law Review*, staff members are selected on the basis of academic achievement and a writing competition. The journals select staff members based on a writing competition.

Student organizations include the Student Bar Association, the Women's Law Caucus, Natural Resources Law Forum, the Moot Court Society, the Minority Law Caucus, the International Law Society, Health Law Coalition, American Constitution Society, Intramural Sports, the Federalist Society, the Gay and Lesbian Law Student Alliance, Native American Law Student Association, the Public Interest Law Organization, and Student Intellectual Property Law Association.

■ Expenses and Financial Aid

Tuition reported on the official ABA data page represents a three-year average. Students interested in need-based scholarships or long-term loans such as Perkins, Stafford, or private educational loans must submit a FAFSA and should contact the University of Utah, Office of Financial Aid, 201 S 1460 E, Room 105, Salt Lake City, Utah 84112-9055, 801.581.6211. The FAFSA deadline to begin the financial aid process is March 15. Merit scholarships are awarded to selected candidates based on information contained in their application materials. The law school also has a Loan Forgiveness Program for qualified graduates who practice in the public sector or the public interest field.

■ Career Services

The College of Law and its graduates have access to one of the most technologically advanced Legal Career Services programs in the country. The LCS office transmits information to prospective employers, both on and off campus. The LCS office also offers personal counseling, maintains a resource library, and sponsors numerous seminars throughout the year.

Applicant Profile

University of Utah S. J. Quinney College of Law
This grid includes only applicants who earned 120-180 LSAT scores under standard administrations.

LSAT Score	3.75 +		3.50 - 3.74		3.25 - 3.49		3.00 - 3.24		2.75 - 2.99		2.50 - 2.74		2.25 - 2.49		2.00 - 2.24		Below 2.00		No GPA		Total	
	Apps	Adm	Apps	Adm	Apps	Adm	Apps	Adm	Apps	Adm	Apps	Adm	Apps	Adm	Apps	Adm	Apps	Adm	Apps	Adm	Apps	Adm
175-180	0	0	0	0	0	0	0	0	0	0	0	0	0	0	0	0	0	0	0	0	0	0
170-174	2	2	4	4	2	2	3	2	3	0	0	0	1	1	1	0	0	0	0	0	16	11
165-169	22	22	19	18	17	13	10	6	1	0	0	0	0	0	0	0	0	0	0	0	69	59
160-164	53	45	72	46	62	30	36	9	26	6	8	2	2	0	0	0	1	0	0	0	260	138
155-159	79	38	91	24	91	11	69	6	29	1	13	0	4	0	3	1	1	0	2	0	382	81
150-154	41	5	72	4	65	5	61	5	41	2	17	1	4	0	4	0	0	0	0	0	305	22
145-149	11	0	35	4	39	3	29	1	22	0	13	1	2	1	3	0	0	0	2	0	156	10
140-144	1	1	7	0	13	0	11	0	12	1	4	0	3	0	0	0	0	0	1	0	52	2
135-139	0	0	3	0	1	0	7	0	4	0	5	0	0	0	0	0	0	0	3	0	23	0
130-134	0	0	0	0	0	0	0	0	0	0	0	0	1	0	0	0	0	0	2	0	3	0
125-129	0	0	0	0	0	0	0	0	2	0	1	0	0	0	0	0	1	0	0	0	4	0
120-124	0	0	0	0	0	0	0	0	0	0	0	0	0	0	0	0	0	0	0	0	0	0
Total	209	113	303	100	290	64	226	29	140	10	61	4	17	2	11	1	3	0	10	0	1270	323

Apps = Number of Applicants
Adm = Number Admitted
Reflects 100% of the total applicant pool.
Note: This chart is to be used as a general guide only. Nonnumerical factors are strongly considered for all applicants.

Valparaiso University School of Law

656 S Greenwich—Wesemann Hall
Valparaiso, IN 46383-6493
Phone: 888.ValpoLaw, 219.465.7829; Fax: 219.465.7808
E-mail: valpolaw@valpo.edu; Website: www.valpo.edu/law/

ABA Approved Since 1929

The Basics

Type of school	Private
Term	Semester
Application deadline	4/1
Application fee	$50
Financial aid deadline	3/1
Can first year start other than fall?	No
Student to faculty ratio (fall)	16.8 to 1
Does the university offer:	
housing restricted to law students?	No
graduate housing for which law students are eligible?	No

Faculty and Administrators

	Total		Men		Women		Minorities	
	Fall	Spr	Fall	Spr	Fall	Spr	Fall	Spr
Full-time	27	26	16	15	11	11	1	1
Other Full-time	1	1	1	1	0	0	0	0
Deans, librarians, & others who teach	9	9	5	5	4	4	0	0
Part-time	19	27	13	19	6	8	0	0
Total	56	63	35	40	21	23	1	1

Curriculum

	Full-time	Part-time
Typical first-year section size	98	0
Is there typically a "small section" of the first-year class, other than Legal Writing, taught by full-time faculty	Yes	No
If yes, typical size offered last year	65	0
# of classroom course titles beyond 1st year curriculum		90

# of upper division courses, excluding seminars with an enrollment:	Under 25	56
	25-49	17
	50-74	8
	75-99	8
	100+	4

# of seminars		12
# of seminar positions available		168
# of seminar positions filled	148	10
# of positions available in simulation courses	747	
# of simulation positions filled	474	6
# of positions available in faculty supervised clinical courses		90
# of faculty supervised clinical positions filled	76	1
# involved in field placements	158	9
# involved in law journals	42	0
# involved in moot court or trial competitions	54	0
# of credit hours required to graduate		90

JD Enrollment and Ethnicity

	Men		Women		Full-time		Part-time		1st-year		Total		JD Degs. Awd.
	#	%	#	%	#	%	#	%	#	%	#	%	
African Amer.	6	2.2	18	6.3	20	3.9	4	8.7	10	5.1	24	4.3	7
Amer. Indian	2	0.7	0	0.0	2	0.4	0	0.0	0	0.0	2	0.4	0
Asian Amer.	9	3.3	4	1.4	13	2.5	0	0.0	2	1.0	13	2.3	4
Mex. Amer.	3	1.1	3	1.1	5	1.0	1	2.2	4	2.0	6	1.1	0
Puerto Rican	1	0.4	1	0.4	2	0.4	0	0.0	1	0.5	2	0.4	0
Hispanic	9	3.3	3	1.1	10	1.9	2	4.3	4	2.0	12	2.1	3
Total Minority	30	10.9	29	10.2	52	10.1	7	15.2	21	10.7	59	10.6	14
For. Nation.	4	1.5	2	0.7	6	1.2	0	0.0	2	1.0	6	1.1	2
Caucasian	240	87.6	254	89.1	455	88.7	39	84.8	173	88.3	494	88.4	132
Unknown	0	0.0	0	0.0	0	0.0	0	0.0	0	0.0	0	0.0	0
Total	274	49.0	285	51.0	513	91.8	46	8.2	196	35.1	559		148

Tuition and Fees

	Resident	Nonresident
Full-time	$25,282	$25,282
Part-time	$15,766	$15,766

Living Expenses

Estimated living expenses for singles

Living on campus	Living off campus	Living at home
N/A	$9,950	$4,850

Valparaiso University School of Law

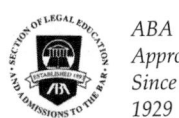

*ABA
Approved
Since
1929*

GPA and LSAT Scores

	Total	Full-time	Part-time
# of apps	2,494	2,386	108
# of admits	623	581	42
# of matrics	189	164	25
75% GPA	3.62	3.62	3.48
25% GPA	3.01	3.01	2.91
75% LSAT	155	155	150
25% LSAT	150	150	145

Grants and Scholarships (from prior year)

	Total		Full-time		Part-time	
	#	%	#	%	#	%
Total # of students	563		514		49	
Total # receiving grants	263	46.7	263	51.2	0	0.0
Less than 1/2 tuition	108	19.2	108	21.0	0	0.0
Half to full tuition	45	8.0	45	8.8	0	0.0
Full tuition	58	10.3	58	11.3	0	0.0
More than full tuition	52	9.2	52	10.1	0	0.0
Median grant amount			$11,525		$0	

Informational and Library Resources

# of volumes and volume equivalents	314,012
# of titles	119,200
# of active serial subscriptions	2,059
Study seating capacity inside the library	351
# of professional librarians	5
Hours per week library is open	113
# of open, wired connections available to students	55
# of networked computers available for use by students	15
# of simultaneous wireless users	2,500
Require computer?	N

JD Attrition (from prior year)

	Academic	Other	Total	
	#	#	#	%
1st year	11	25	36	17.2%
2nd year	2	3	5	2.5%
3rd year	0	0	0	0.0%
4th year	0	0	0	0.0%

Employment

	Total	Percentage
Employment status known	109	89.3
Employment status unknown	13	10.7
Employed	94	86.2
Pursuing graduate degrees	2	1.8
Unemployed seeking employment	11	10.1
Unemployed not seeking employment	2	1.8

Type of Employment

# employed in law firms	60	63.8
# employed in business and industry	7	7.4
# employed in government	12	12.8
# employed in public interest	1	1.1
# employed as judicial clerks	7	7.4
# employed in academia	4	4.3

Geographic Location

# employed in state	49	52.1
# employed in foreign countries	0	0.0
# of states where employed		16

Bar Passage Rates

Jurisdiction	Indiana		
Exam	Sum 03	Win 04	Total
# from school taking bar for the first time	51	16	67
School's pass rate for all first-time takers	78%	81%	79%
State's pass rate for all first-time takers	79%	76%	79%

Valparaiso University School of Law

656 S Greenwich—Wesemann Hall
Valparaiso, IN 46383-6493
Phone: 888.ValpoLaw, 219.465.7829; Fax: 219.465.7808
E-mail: valpolaw@valpo.edu; Website: www.valpo.edu/law/

■ Introduction

Valparaiso University School of Law was founded in 1879. Throughout its 125 year history, and more so today, its renown is threefold: a personal manner of legal education; enduring core competencies; and exceptional legal research and writing.

Truly Personal: The teaching and learning style of Valpo Law is highly collaborative and integrated. You interact with faculty both in and out of the classroom. They know who you are and strive to provide a legal education that is tailored to you and your aspirations. The class sizes are smaller by design. Every pedagogical component is designed to encourage individualized attention.

Enduring Core Competencies: No matter how much the world and laws change, no matter how often attorneys change their practice, there is one constant: the ability to engage in critical, analytical, and creative thinking. This quality is the cornerstone of the law curriculum.

Exceptional Legal Research and Writing: According to a survey by the American Bar Foundation, hiring partners at law firms ranked research and writing skills as the most important skill set a new lawyer can bring to the job. It is common for law schools to have one-year of legal writing, as part of the first-year curriculum. We have three years of research and writing. The program boasts a faculty of experts. Visit *www.valpo.edu/law/academics/legalresearch/.*

■ Curriculum

Valpo provides a comprehensive and intensive study of the foundations of the law, an introduction to the substantive areas of the law, and the opportunity for advanced study in specific areas. The curriculum provides a grounding in legal analysis, legal writing and research, practical skills training, perspectives on the law, and ethics.

The Valpo Law curriculum may be segmented into six areas: **General Practice, Business Law, Public Interest Representation, Property, Litigation, and Taxation.** To learn more, visit *www.valpo.edu/law/academics/courses/* and *www.valpo.edu/law/bulletin/.*

Students may participate in externships and internships and enhance their skills in our law clinic. No matter how you choose to apply your education, you will have the tools and foundation to succeed.

Upon completing the required first-year curriculum, students are given the opportunity to explore various avenues of study. During the second year, students begin to select electives. By the third year, almost all required courses will be completed and students select courses for general skills competency or focus on areas of interest.

The School of Law is committed to the highest standards of professional ethics and to an inquiry into values, and is concerned that students not view the legal system as unchangeable and untouched by their own ethical and intellectual analysis. A 20-hour commitment of pro bono legal service is required of all students. Valpo Law is one of the few schools requiring pro bono work.

■ Degree Programs

We have full-time, part-time day, and two one-half year options for our JD program. In addition, we offer dual-degree programs such as: JD/MA Psychology; JD/MA Clinical Mental Health; JD/MA Liberal Studies in either Gerontology, English, Ethics and Values, History, Human Behavior and Society, or Theology; JD/MBA; JD/MSSA, Sports Administration; and JD/MSICP, International Commerce and Policy. Valpo Law also has a one year full-time LLM program for international students, who already have a law degree.

■ Special Programs

Clinical Law Program—Students enrolled in the live-client law clinic represent indigent clients and participate in all stages of representation. The five clinics based on practice areas are criminal, civil, mediation, juvenile, and tax.

Current Representation—Faculty members invite students to work on cases in which they are providing legal representation.

Externships—The School of Law currently sponsors over 50 externships throughout the US, including semester-away externships. To learn more, visit *www.valpo.edu/law/academics/externships/.*

Summer Study Abroad—Valparaiso's interest in international and comparative law is enhanced with its Summer Study Abroad Program in Cambridge, England.

Honors Program—The Honors Program offers an academic challenge to talented students. Visit *www.valpo.edu/law/academics/honors/.* Candidates are selected based on academic credentials and demonstrated leadership skills. Personal interviews are required.

Summer Public Interest Scholarships—Each summer we award students who work in a public interest capacity a Summer Public Interest Scholarship. Visit *www.valpo.edu/law/admissions/financialaid/summerpublicinterestscholarship/.* Valpo Law has a Loan Repayment Assistance program. This program is designed to offer financial assistance to graduates who have chosen to go into public service employment, and who have accumulated substantial debt from educational loans. Grants range from $1,000 to $6,000 each year. This program is available to alumni who have graduated within three years from the law school.

Academic Success Program—The Academic Success Program is available for assistance with the transition from college or the work-force to law school.

■ Career Planning

Our service mission is to assist all students and graduates in planning career paths, preparing for the job market, and identifying or creating opportunities; and to work closely with employers in developing career-related networks for all our law students.

Our programs help you identify, define, and verbalize your goals; build the confidence to overcome obstacles; and articulate your skills and accomplishments.

■ Faculty

Our professors have been Fulbright scholars and clerks to federal appellate and state supreme court judges, and have served in government. They bring to their teaching practical experience in public and private sectors. Their scholarship interests span a broad range. Professors practice an open-door policy and each student is paired with a faculty advisor in the first year.

Visit *www.valpo.edu/law/academics/faculty/program/.*

■ Library and Physical Facilities

The law library is the largest legal research facility in Northwest Indiana. Individual and group study carrels are available for student use. Two computer labs provide facilities for word processing, Internet, and web access and offer access to LexisNexis, Westlaw, CALI, FolioViews, LOIS, and Dialog. Wired and wireless network ports are available for student use throughout the campus. The School of Law occupies two buildings that house classrooms, the law library, a state-of-the-art courtroom and a jury room, the law clinic, and administration and faculty offices.

■ Student Activities

The *Valparaiso University Law Review* is a scholarly journal published three times per year. Because of Valpo's emphasis on legal writing, membership on the *Law Review* is based upon academic achievement as well as a writing competition.

Students interested in enhancing their advocacy skills may try out for the Client Counseling, Mock Trial, Negotiation teams, and Moot Court Society (a program that provides the opportunity for study in persuasive writing and oral arguments at the appellate level).

Valpo Law has over 25 student organizations. Just as the students represent a wide cross section of society, so too do the organizations on campus—Visit *www.valpo.edu/law/studentlife/studentorganizations/.*

■ Student Body Profile

Our student body is ethnically and religiously diverse averaging a composition of students from 87 different colleges and universities, 27 states, and 5 foreign countries. The average age is 25 with an age range from 19 to 60.

■ Expenses and Financial Aid

Approximately 65 percent of the student body received merit scholarships or need-based grants. The School of Law awards approximately $3 million annually in financial aid. In addition, 90 percent of all law students received assistance through loan programs. Valparaiso also offers a Public Interest Loan Repayment Assistance program and a Summer Public Interest Scholarship program.

Applicant Profile

We seek highly motivated and talented individuals; therefore LSAT scores and GPAs do not guarantee admission or denial.

Vanderbilt University Law School

131 21st Avenue South
Nashville, TN 37203
Phone: 615.322.6452; Fax: 615.322.1531
E-mail: admissions@law.vanderbilt.edu; Website: law.vanderbilt.edu

ABA
Approved
Since
1925

The Basics

Type of school	Private
Term	Semester
Application deadline	3/15
Application fee	$50
Financial aid deadline	2/15
Can first year start other than fall?	No
Student to faculty ratio (fall)	16.0 to 1
Does the university offer:	
housing restricted to law students?	No
graduate housing for which law students are eligible?	Yes

Faculty and Administrators

	Total		Men		Women		Minorities	
	Fall	Spr	Fall	Spr	Fall	Spr	Fall	Spr
Full-time	33	32	24	23	9	9	5	4
Other Full-time	4	4	3	3	1	1	2	2
Deans, librarians, & others who teach	4	5	3	4	1	1	0	0
Part-time	26	36	16	23	10	13	5	3
Total	67	77	46	53	21	24	12	9

Curriculum

		Full-time	Part-time
Typical first-year section size		99	0
Is there typically a "small section" of the first-year class, other than Legal Writing, taught by full-time faculty		Yes	No
If yes, typical size offered last year		50	0
# of classroom course titles beyond 1st year curriculum		126	
# of upper division courses, excluding seminars with an enrollment:	Under 25	69	
	25-49	24	
	50-74	24	
	75-99	6	
	100+	7	
# of seminars		16	
# of seminar positions available		256	
# of seminar positions filled		186	0
# of positions available in simulation courses		174	
# of simulation positions filled		153	0
# of positions available in faculty supervised clinical courses		75	
# of faculty supervised clinical positions filled		75	0
# involved in field placements		105	0
# involved in law journals		192	0
# involved in moot court or trial competitions		153	0
# of credit hours required to graduate		88	

JD Enrollment and Ethnicity

	Men		Women		Full-time		Part-time		1st-year		Total		JD Degs. Awd.
	#	%	#	%	#	%	#	%	#	%	#	%	
African Amer.	18	5.5	60	19.8	78	12.3	0	0.0	24	10.6	78	12.3	22
Amer. Indian	1	0.3	1	0.3	2	0.3	0	0.0	1	0.4	2	0.3	2
Asian Amer.	17	5.2	18	5.9	35	5.5	0	0.0	19	8.4	35	5.5	13
Mex. Amer.	0	0.0	0	0.0	0	0.0	0	0.0	0	0.0	0	0.0	0
Puerto Rican	0	0.0	0	0.0	0	0.0	0	0.0	0	0.0	0	0.0	0
Hispanic	16	4.9	10	3.3	26	4.1	0	0.0	12	5.3	26	4.1	6
Total Minority	52	15.8	89	29.4	141	22.3	0	0.0	56	24.7	141	22.3	43
For. Nation.	11	3.3	11	3.6	22	3.5	0	0.0	8	3.5	22	3.5	7
Caucasian	264	80.2	200	66.0	464	73.4	0	0.0	160	70.5	464	73.4	145
Unknown	2	0.6	3	1.0	5	0.8	0	0.0	3	1.3	5	0.8	0
Total	329	52.1	303	47.9	632	100.0	0	0.0	227	35.9	632		195

Tuition and Fees

	Resident	Nonresident
Full-time	$32,194	$32,194
Part-time	$0	$0

Living Expenses

Estimated living expenses for singles

Living on campus	Living off campus	Living at home
N/A	$17,876	N/A

Vanderbilt University Law School

ABA
Approved
Since
1925

GPA and LSAT Scores

	Total	Full-time	Part-time
# of apps	3,770	3,770	0
# of admits	763	763	0
# of matrics	227	227	0
75% GPA	3.80	3.80	0.00
25% GPA	3.50	3.50	0.00
75% LSAT	166	166	0
25% LSAT	164	164	0

Grants and Scholarships (from prior year)

	Total		Full-time		Part-time	
	#	%	#	%	#	%
Total # of students	595		595		0	
Total # receiving grants	346	58.2	346	58.2	0	0.0
Less than 1/2 tuition	238	40.0	238	40.0	0	0.0
Half to full tuition	93	15.6	93	15.6	0	0.0
Full tuition	2	0.3	2	0.3	0	0.0
More than full tuition	13	2.2	13	2.2	0	0.0
Median grant amount			$13,000		$0	

Informational and Library Resources

# of volumes and volume equivalents	565,553
# of titles	120,614
# of active serial subscriptions	6,962
Study seating capacity inside the library	291
# of professional librarians	6
Hours per week library is open	109
# of open, wired connections available to students	377
# of networked computers available for use by students	49
# of simultaneous wireless users	1,000
Require computer?	N

JD Attrition (from prior year)

	Academic	Other	Total	
	#	#	#	%
1st year	0	12	12	6.1%
2nd year	0	0	0	0.0%
3rd year	0	0	0	0.0%
4th year	0	0	0	0.0%

Employment

	Total	Percentage
Employment status known	183	99.5
Employment status unknown	1	0.5
Employed	174	95.1
Pursuing graduate degrees	4	2.2
Unemployed seeking employment	1	0.5
Unemployed not seeking employment	4	2.2

Type of Employment

# employed in law firms	115	66.1
# employed in business and industry	7	4.0
# employed in government	19	10.9
# employed in public interest	3	1.7
# employed as judicial clerks	29	16.7
# employed in academia	0	0.0

Geographic Location

# employed in state	41	23.6
# employed in foreign countries	4	2.3
# of states where employed	32	

Bar Passage Rates

Jurisdiction	Tennessee			New York		
Exam	Sum 03	Win 04	Total	Sum 03	Win 04	Total
# from school taking bar for the first time	44	1	45	18	3	21
School's pass rate for all first-time takers	82%	100%	82%	94%	100%	95%
State's pass rate for all first-time takers	81%	79%	81%	78%	58%	75%

Vanderbilt University Law School

131 21st Avenue South
Nashville, TN 37203
Phone: 615.322.6452; Fax: 615.322.1531
E-mail: admissions@law.vanderbilt.edu; Website: law.vanderbilt.edu

■ At a Glance

Vanderbilt University Law School is an intellectual community in which students and faculty members engage in the rigorous study of law, both in and out of the classroom. The Law School's location, adjacent to Vanderbilt's Business School and College of Arts and Sciences and two miles from the state capital, fosters both interdisciplinary studies and interaction with Nashville's legal and business communities. Intellectual inquiry combined with a focus on the problems addressed by the legal system gives Vanderbilt students the skills necessary for a successful legal career.

Vanderbilt's tradition of sustained inquiry conducted in an atmosphere of respect for both individuals and ideas is maintained by a student/faculty ratio of 16:1 and the faculty's open-door policy. The Law School building offers state-of-the-art facilities and a comfortable learning environment.

■ Faculty

Vanderbilt's faculty is composed of nationally recognized scholars dedicated to training future leaders of the legal community. The faculty regularly present their scholarship at law schools and conferences throughout the world. They have long recognized that research enhances the classroom experience, allowing students to explore current legal issues and tensions facing the law. Vanderbilt faculty draw on various perspectives, including economic, historical, and philosophical, in both their scholarship and their teaching.

■ Library and Physical Facilities

The Alyne Queener Massey Law Library, one of the primary legal research centers in the Southeast, supports the curriculum needs and research interests of the law faculty and students. The law school building, including the library, is equipped for wireless connectivity. Students have a variety of spaces within the library for study and research, including two reading rooms and nearly 200 carrels. The service-oriented library staff of 20 includes 8 full-time librarians. The law library collection contains more than 550,000 volumes and provides onsite and remote access to over 250 law and non-law electronic databases. All other Vanderbilt University libraries, containing more than 2.3 million volumes, are available to law students.

■ Curriculum

Degrees available include JD, JD/MBA, JD/MDiv, JD/MTS, JD/MD, JD/MPP, JD/MA, JD/PhD, LLM for international lawyers, and LLM/MA in Latin American

Studies. First-year required courses include the foundation courses of legal study in addition to an innovative course on legal process and the institutions of lawmaking. The yearlong legal writing course in which students learn the fundamentals of writing, analysis, and research is taught in small groups of 24 students. With the exception of professional responsibility and an independent research writing class or seminar, all upper-level courses are electives. The curriculum is broad, offering students the opportunity to gain exposure to the fundamental knowledge necessary to become a competent professional, while focusing on areas of special interest.

A highly innovative Law and Business Program offers an interdisciplinary curriculum, taught by both law school and business faculty. Through this program, students may earn a certificate in law and business in three years. The Joe C. Davis Foundation Program in Law and Economics features regular workshops involving leading scholars from around the nation. Vanderbilt University is home to the First Amendment Center, a nationally recognized institute where journalists and legal scholars research and write on issues involving freedoms granted by the First Amendment to the Constitution. The Vanderbilt Institute for Policy Studies offers faculty and students from departments throughout the university a place to work cooperatively on issues ranging from health care policy to international trade. Clinical programs offer students the chance to represent clients in civil, family, criminal, domestic violence, business, and juvenile cases while earning academic credit.

■ Student Activities

Students continue their learning outside the classroom through opportunities to serve on the editorial boards of the *Vanderbilt Law Review*, the *Journal of Entertainment Law and Practice*, and the *Journal of Transnational Law*; through participation on moot court teams and the moot court board; and through the activities of more than 40 student organizations. The Hyatt Speakers Fund has been established to enhance the intellectual experience of students by supporting symposia and educational programs run by student organizations.

■ Expenses and Financial Aid

Full-time tuition: $31,900. Estimated additional expenses: $18,170 (housing, food, books, travel, etc.). Need-based and merit-based scholarships are available. FAFSA, Need Access, and Vanderbilt Law School Financial Aid Statement are required for financial aid consideration and should be submitted by February 15.

A substantial amount of scholarship aid is available for law students. Financial aid packages are awarded before the admission response deadlines. Scholarship awards are made for three years, conditioned on good standing. Approximately 85 percent of entering students receive financial aid. Vanderbilt participates in federal, university, and private loan programs to assist students in funding their legal education. A good credit history is essential for borrowing private loans. Vanderbilt offers a loan forgiveness program to graduates who serve in public-interest positions.

■ Career Services

Vanderbilt graduates enjoy an outstanding reputation in the legal profession. In addition to the on-campus recruiting program, hundreds of employers write annually to solicit résumés from Vanderbilt students. In the fall of 2004, over 500 employers visited Vanderbilt to recruit students participating in the on-campus recruiting program. They came from more than 38 states, and Vanderbilt graduates accepted positions throughout the country. The Career Services Office maintains a staff of professional counselors to assist students individually with their career goals. The placement rate nine months following graduation is 97 percent. Ninety-five percent of students worked in law-related jobs during the summer following their second year. An on-campus interviewing program is held for first-year students in the spring. More than 97 percent of first-year students had a legal job last summer.

■ Housing

Law students live in apartments and other off-campus housing. The admission office assists incoming students during the summer months with roommate lists and housing information.

■ Admission

A bachelor's degree from an accredited college or university is required. JD application deadline: March 15; LLM application deadline: March 15; early decision deadline: November 1. LSAT and LSDAS are required. Application fee: $50.

The admission committee thoroughly evaluates each application, considering the candidate's academic record, LSAT score, letters of recommendation, personal statement, extracurricular/civic activities, GPA, and work experience. The committee takes into account any elements in the applicant's background that will add depth to the student body or that indicate leadership promise. The full-file review process yields a group of students that have developed the ability to speak and write clearly, to think precisely, and to analyze complex issues. Maintaining cultural diversity is also important to the Law School as lawyers must serve a multifaceted society. The entering class is limited to approximately 195 students. Because the students work in a cooperative and mutually respectful environment, Vanderbilt attracts students with diverse interests, who are academically serious about studying law.

Applicant Profile

Vanderbilt University Law School
This grid includes only applicants who earned 120-180 LSAT scores under standard administrations.

LSAT Score	3.75 +		3.50 - 3.74		3.25 - 3.49		3.00 - 3.24		2.75 - 2.99		2.50 - 2.74		2.25 - 2.49		2.00 - 2.24		Below 2.00		No GPA		Total	
	Apps	Adm	Apps	Adm	Apps	Adm	Apps	Adm	Apps	Adm	Apps	Adm	Apps	Adm	Apps	Adm	Apps	Adm	Apps	Adm	Apps	Adm
175-180	5	5	2	2	4	4	4	0	1	0	0	0	0	0	1	0	0	0	0	0	17	11
170-174	24	24	18	18	28	18	12	2	3	0	5	0	0	0	1	0	0	0	2	2	93	64
165-169	154	153	193	177	135	43	69	8	33	0	9	0	3	0	1	0	1	0	5	5	603	386
160-164	311	90	425	91	286	32	145	13	69	0	16	0	5	0	1	0	1	0	12	4	1271	230
155-159	215	5	272	9	184	7	109	7	55	1	21	0	5	0	1	0	0	0	10	0	872	29
150-154	76	5	112	8	104	13	87	10	37	0	24	0	10	0	6	0	1	0	8	0	465	36
145-149	34	0	52	1	48	0	40	0	35	0	14	0	8	0	2	0	1	0	6	0	240	1
140-144	11	0	17	0	21	0	16	0	15	0	9	0	9	0	6	0	0	0	5	0	109	0
135-139	4	0	3	0	9	0	11	0	7	0	7	0	2	0	3	0	1	0	2	0	49	0
130-134	0	0	1	0	2	0	1	0	2	0	3	0	1	0	2	0	1	0	1	0	14	0
125-129	0	0	0	0	0	0	0	0	0	0	1	0	0	0	0	0	0	0	0	0	1	0
120-124	0	0	0	0	0	0	0	0	0	0	0	0	0	0	0	0	0	0	1	0	1	0
Total	834	282	1095	306	821	117	494	40	257	1	109	0	43	0	24	0	6	0	52	11	3735	757

Apps = Number of Applicants   Adm = Number Admitted   Reflects 99% of the total applicant pool.

Vermont Law School

Chelsea Street, PO Box 96
South Royalton, VT 05068
Phone: 888.277.5985 (toll-free) or 802.831.1239; Fax: 802.763.7071
E-mail: admiss@vermontlaw.edu; Website: www.vermontlaw.edu

ABA
Approved
Since
1975

The Basics

Type of school	Private
Term	Semester
Application deadline	3/1
Application fee	$50
Financial aid deadline	3/1
Can first year start other than fall?	No
Student to faculty ratio (fall)	17.5 to 1
Does the university offer:	
housing restricted to law students?	Yes
graduate housing for which law students are eligible?	No

Faculty and Administrators

	Total		Men		Women		Minorities	
	Fall	Spr	Fall	Spr	Fall	Spr	Fall	Spr
Full-time	26	24	14	12	12	12	0	0
Other Full-time	11	10	4	3	7	7	0	0
Deans, librarians, & others who teach	12	11	5	4	7	7	2	2
Part-time	12	17	7	12	5	5	0	2
Total	**61**	**62**	**30**	**31**	**31**	**31**	**2**	**4**

Curriculum

	Full-time	Part-time
Typical first-year section size	68	0
Is there typically a "small section" of the first-year class, other than Legal Writing, taught by full-time faculty	Yes	No
If yes, typical size offered last year	45	0
# of classroom course titles beyond 1st year curriculum	108	

# of upper division courses, excluding seminars with an enrollment:	Under 25	72
	25-49	24
	50-74	11
	75-99	6
	100+	0

# of seminars	17	
# of seminar positions available	307	
# of seminar positions filled	205	0
# of positions available in simulation courses	263	
# of simulation positions filled	235	0
# of positions available in faculty supervised clinical courses	67	
# of faculty supervised clinical positions filled	55	0
# involved in field placements	130	0
# involved in law journals	88	0
# involved in moot court or trial competitions	157	0
# of credit hours required to graduate	84	

JD Enrollment and Ethnicity

	Men #	Men %	Women #	Women %	Full-time #	Full-time %	Part-time #	Part-time %	1st-year #	1st-year %	Total #	Total %	JD Degs. Awd.
African Amer.	17	6.5	23	8.1	40	7.3	0	0.0	14	6.9	40	7.3	5
Amer. Indian	3	1.1	3	1.1	6	1.1	0	0.0	4	2.0	6	1.1	2
Asian Amer.	5	1.9	12	4.2	17	3.1	0	0.0	9	4.4	17	3.1	5
Mex. Amer.	1	0.4	0	0.0	1	0.2	0	0.0	0	0.0	1	0.2	0
Puerto Rican	0	0.0	0	0.0	0	0.0	0	0.0	0	0.0	0	0.0	0
Hispanic	10	3.8	14	4.9	24	4.4	0	0.0	8	3.9	24	4.4	4
Total Minority	36	13.8	52	18.3	88	16.1	0	0.0	35	17.2	88	16.1	16
For. Nation.	1	0.4	1	0.4	2	0.4	0	0.0	0	0.0	2	0.4	0
Caucasian	210	80.5	222	78.2	432	79.3	0	0.0	159	77.9	432	79.3	141
Unknown	14	5.4	9	3.2	23	4.2	0	0.0	10	4.9	23	4.2	0
Total	261	47.9	284	52.1	545	100.0	0	0.0	204	37.4	545		157

Tuition and Fees

	Resident	Nonresident
Full-time	$26,747	$26,747
Part-time	$0	$0

Living Expenses

Estimated living expenses for singles

Living on campus	Living off campus	Living at home
N/A	$16,675	N/A

Vermont Law School

ABA
Approved
Since
1975

GPA and LSAT Scores

	Total	Full-time	Part-time
# of apps	1,015	1,015	0
# of admits	532	532	0
# of matrics	203	203	0
75% GPA	3.54	3.54	0.00
25% GPA	3.02	3.02	0.00
75% LSAT	157	157	0
25% LSAT	151	151	0

Grants and Scholarships (from prior year)

	Total		Full-time		Part-time	
	#	%	#	%	#	%
Total # of students	513		513		0	
Total # receiving grants	315	61.4	315	61.4	0	0.0
Less than 1/2 tuition	291	56.7	291	56.7	0	0.0
Half to full tuition	21	4.1	21	4.1	0	0.0
Full tuition	3	0.6	3	0.6	0	0.0
More than full tuition	0	0.0	0	0.0	0	0.0
Median grant amount			$6,000		$0	

Informational and Library Resources

# of volumes and volume equivalents	234,436
# of titles	43,745
# of active serial subscriptions	1,860
Study seating capacity inside the library	360
# of professional librarians	7
Hours per week library is open	110
# of open, wired connections available to students	100
# of networked computers available for use by students	45
# of simultaneous wireless users	240
Require computer?	N

JD Attrition (from prior year)

	Academic	Other	Total	
	#	#	#	%
1st year	0	12	12	6.5%
2nd year	0	1	1	0.6%
3rd year	0	0	0	0.0%
4th year	0	0	0	0.0%

Employment

	Total	Percentage
Employment status known	153	100.0
Employment status unknown	0	0.0
Employed	133	86.9
Pursuing graduate degrees	9	5.9
Unemployed seeking employment	5	3.3
Unemployed not seeking employment	6	3.9

Type of Employment

# employed in law firms	48	36.1
# employed in business and industry	27	20.3
# employed in government	23	17.3
# employed in public interest	9	6.8
# employed as judicial clerks	19	14.3
# employed in academia	2	1.5

Geographic Location

# employed in state	41	30.8
# employed in foreign countries	4	3.0
# of states where employed	35	

Bar Passage Rates

Jurisdiction	Vermont		
Exam	Sum 03	Win 04	Total
# from school taking bar for the first time	33	1	34
School's pass rate for all first-time takers	70%	100%	71%
State's pass rate for all first-time takers	77%	87%	80%

Vermont Law School

Chelsea Street, PO Box 96
South Royalton, VT 05068
Phone: 888.277.5985 (toll-free) or 802.831.1239; Fax: 802.763.7071
E-mail: admiss@vermontlaw.edu; Website: www.vermontlaw.edu

■ Introduction

Five features distinguish legal education at Vermont Law School—a core JD curriculum that emphasizes the broader social context of the law in addition to focusing on legal doctrine and analysis; clinical/experiential programs that complement traditional classroom instruction; the internationally recognized Master of Studies in Environmental Law and LLM in Environmental Law programs; the informal atmosphere of a beautiful rural setting; and a real sense of community and commitment to public service. The school is accredited by the American Bar Association, the Association of American Law Schools, and the New England Association of Schools and Colleges.

Situated in a National Register Historic District along Vermont's scenic White River, the school's 13-acre campus is an integrated complex of renovated turn-of-the-century buildings, a new computer center, and a modern library and community center. A 25,000-square-foot classroom building was completed in summer 1998. Nearby Dartmouth College complements the Law School's social and cultural offerings. Ample housing is available in the area, and the Law School maintains an extensive landlord list.

■ Enrollment/Student Body

Vermont Law School is one of the most geographically diverse law schools in the country. Students bring a remarkable range of experience and backgrounds. Their ages range from 20 to over 50 years, with the average being 27.

Organizations that further support Vermont Law School's commitment to diversity include the Lesbian, Gay, Bisexual, Transgender, and Straight Alliance; Asian Pacific American Law Students Association; Black Law Students Association; Jewish Students Group; National Latino Law Students Association; Native American Law Society; and Women's Law Group.

■ Faculty

Vermont Law School attracts faculty who are committed to teaching and scholarship. Recent faculty publications have included the topics of capital punishment, national security and the environment, Oliver Wendell Holmes, publicity and privacy, environmental law, and federal taxation.

■ Library and Technology

Opened in 1991, the 33,000-square-foot Cornell Library houses all primary sources needed for student research.

The library subscribes to some 2,461 periodicals and serials and features an exceptionally fine environmental law collection. It also serves as a selective depository for United States government documents. The library catalog is online and accessible from all computers on the network. Vermont Law School has a fully networked computer environment with web accessed e-mail. Six classrooms contain electronic teaching stations. All classrooms have easily accessible power outlets and wireless Internet access.

■ Curriculum

The curriculum prepares graduates to practice law in all 50 states. A wide variety of clinical programs, electives, seminars, and opportunities for supervised independent research are important adjuncts to a strong core curriculum.

Environmental Law Center—Vermont Law School's Environmental Law Center is recognized internationally as a preeminent center for the study of environmental law and policy. The Environmental Law Center offers one-year programs leading to either the Master of Studies (MSEL) or Master of Laws (LLM) in Environmental Law degree based upon a multidisciplinary curriculum of law, science, policy, and economics. The center offers over 50 environmental courses and an **Environmental Semester in Washington, DC**, and sponsors conferences and research. Through the **Environmental and Natural Resources Law Clinic**, students work on significant environmental law and policy issues and learn from some of the best environmental lawyers in the country and around the world.

General Practice Program—The optional General Practice Program has classes structured to operate as a law firm with professors in the role of senior partners. Because it teaches the range of skills generally required of new associates in most types of legal environments, the program is also valuable to students who ultimately plan to specialize.

Special Programs—The **Semester in Practice Program** allows students to participate in a full-credit, supervised clinical program in a legal environment outside the law school. Students currently work throughout the Northeast, including New York, Boston, and Washington, DC. In the **Legislation Clinic**, students work under the direction of a legislative committee chair on research and draft projects directly related to legislation pending before the Vermont General Assembly. Students working with the **South Royalton Legal Clinic** develop legal skills while providing legal assistance to low-income clients. The **Dispute Resolution Project** introduces students to nonlitigious approaches to dispute resolution, such as arbitration, mediation, and negotiation. Through the **Law School**

Exchange Program, students may spend a semester at one of eight participating law schools across the US, McGill University (Canada), Trento University (Italy), and University of Paris 13 (France).

Joint-Degree Programs—The joint JD/MSEL program can be completed in three academic years and two summers. The joint JD/MEM program, in collaboration with the Yale University School of Forestry and Environmental Studies, is a four-year program.

■ Admission

The school seeks candidates who will bring diverse perspectives and talents to the Law School community and the community-at-large. Successful applicants demonstrate substantial ability, motivation, life experience, and unique personal attributes. Two of the more important admission criteria are the academic record and application personal statements. Multiple LSAT scores are averaged. The school responds favorably to community and college involvement and work experience, and is committed to attracting people traditionally underrepresented in the legal profession.

■ Student Activities

A community-oriented and active student body supports more than 30 official organizations, including *Vermont Law Review*, *Vermont Journal of Environmental Law*, Douglas M. Costle Environmental Moot Court Competition, *Guardians ad Litem*, Habitat for Humanity,

International Law Society, National Lawyers Guild, Thomas M. Debevoise Moot Court Competition, and Volunteer Income Tax Assistance Program, among others. Student organizations and the Law School sponsor a full range of social, cultural, and academic events. Students also field several athletic teams.

■ Expenses and Financial Aid

Combinations of merit scholarships, loans, tuition grants, and work-study employment are used to meet demonstrated financial need. About 90 percent of the student body receives some form of assistance and about 40–45 percent receive VLS grant aid. The Vermont Law School Loan Repayment Assistance Program aids graduates entering lower-paying public interest positions to repay educational debts.

■ Career Services

The Career Services office is directed by an attorney and provides a broad range of counseling and placement services. The school aggressively pursues employment opportunities nationwide, and graduates work in a full range of legal and nonlegal positions throughout the US. A Cooperative Legal Education program facilitates the transition from academics to legal practice.

Graduates in the class of 2003 are working in over 30 states; 89.5 percent either held full-time positions or were enrolled in academic programs within six months of graduation.

Applicant Profile

Vermont Law School
This grid includes only applicants who earned 120-180 LSAT scores under standard administrations.

LSAT Score	GPA 3.75 +		3.50 - 3.74		3.25 - 3.49		3.00 - 3.24		2.75 - 2.99		2.50 - 2.74		Below 2.50		No GPA		Total	
	Apps	Adm	Apps	Adm	Apps	Adm	Apps	Adm	Apps	Adm	Apps	Adm	Apps	Adm	Apps	Adm	Apps	Adm
170-180	0	0	2	2	2	1	1	1	1	1	2	2	0	0	0	0	8	7
165-169	5	5	4	3	8	7	2	2	0	0	1	1	1	0	2	2	23	20
160-164	9	9	23	23	25	20	11	10	7	6	4	4	5	2	1	0	85	74
155-159	20	18	29	27	47	45	47	36	37	27	15	7	9	6	2	2	206	168
150-154	21	19	42	33	62	39	62	36	56	19	26	6	22	2	4	2	295	156
145-149	9	6	29	15	56	11	48	5	44	9	27	3	25	1	6	0	244	50
140-144	1	0	8	3	16	2	20	1	17	0	21	1	14	1	1	0	98	8
Below 140	2	0	4	1	8	2	10	2	12	1	8	2	10	1	3	0	57	9
Total	67	57	141	107	224	127	201	93	174	63	104	26	86	13	19	6	1016	492

Apps = Number of Applicants
Adm = Number Admitted
Reflects 99% of the total applicant pool.

Vermont Law School does not use cutoff LSAT scores or GPAs.

Villanova University School of Law

299 North Spring Mill Road
Villanova, PA 19085
Phone: 610.519.7010; Fax: 610.519.6291
E-mail: admissions@law.villanova.edu; Website: www.law.villanova.edu

ABA
Approved
Since
1954

The Basics

Type of school	Private
Term	Semester
Application deadline	3/1
Application fee	$75
Financial aid deadline	
Can first year start other than fall?	No
Student to faculty ratio (fall)	18.1 to 1
Does the university offer:	
housing restricted to law students?	No
graduate housing for which law students are eligible?	No

Faculty and Administrators

	Total		Men		Women		Minorities	
	Fall	Spr	Fall	Spr	Fall	Spr	Fall	Spr
Full-time	35	34	23	23	12	11	3	2
Other Full-time	8	10	1	2	7	8	1	3
Deans, librarians, & others who teach	9	9	2	2	7	7	3	3
Part-time	41	54	32	34	9	19	2	3
Total	93	107	58	61	35	45	9	11

Curriculum

		Full-time	Part-time
Typical first-year section size		90	0
Is there typically a "small section" of the first-year class, other than Legal Writing, taught by full-time faculty		Yes	No
If yes, typical size offered last year		30	0
# of classroom course titles beyond 1st year curriculum		110	
# of upper division courses, excluding seminars with an enrollment:	Under 25	78	
	25-49	27	
	50-74	9	
	75-99	11	
	100+	9	
# of seminars		15	
# of seminar positions available		255	
# of seminar positions filled		227	0
# of positions available in simulation courses		323	
# of simulation positions filled		309	0
# of positions available in faculty supervised clinical courses		66	
# of faculty supervised clinical positions filled		66	0
# involved in field placements		129	0
# involved in law journals		145	0
# involved in moot court or trial competitions		6	0
# of credit hours required to graduate		87	

JD Enrollment and Ethnicity

	Men #	Men %	Women #	Women %	Full-time #	Full-time %	Part-time #	Part-time %	1st-year #	1st-year %	Total #	Total %	JD Degs. Awd.
African Amer.	6	1.6	23	6.1	29	3.8	0	0.0	12	4.9	29	3.8	10
Amer. Indian	2	0.5	1	0.3	3	0.4	0	0.0	1	0.4	3	0.4	0
Asian Amer.	21	5.4	43	11.5	64	8.4	0	0.0	21	8.6	64	8.4	8
Mex. Amer.	0	0.0	0	0.0	0	0.0	0	0.0	0	0.0	0	0.0	0
Puerto Rican	0	0.0	0	0.0	0	0.0	0	0.0	0	0.0	0	0.0	0
Hispanic	19	4.9	15	4.0	34	4.5	0	0.0	8	3.3	34	4.5	8
Total Minority	48	12.4	82	21.9	130	17.1	0	0.0	42	17.1	130	17.1	26
For. Nation.	0	0.0	0	0.0	0	0.0	0	0.0	0	0.0	0	0.0	0
Caucasian	339	87.6	292	77.9	631	82.8	0	0.0	202	82.4	631	82.8	221
Unknown	0	0.0	1	0.3	1	0.1	0	0.0	1	0.4	1	0.1	0
Total	387	50.8	375	49.2	762	100.0	0	0.0	245	32.2	762		247

Tuition and Fees

	Resident	Nonresident
Full-time	$26,380	$26,380
Part-time	$0	$0

Living Expenses

Estimated living expenses for singles

Living on campus	Living off campus	Living at home
N/A	$14,110	$5,020

Villanova University School of Law

ABA
Approved
Since
1954

GPA and LSAT Scores

	Total	Full-time	Part-time
# of apps	2,924	2,924	0
# of admits	921	921	0
# of matrics	247	247	0
75% GPA	3.69	3.69	0.00
25% GPA	3.25	3.25	0.00
75% LSAT	162	162	0
25% LSAT	157	157	0

Grants and Scholarships (from prior year)

	Total		Full-time		Part-time	
	#	%	#	%	#	%
Total # of students	780		780		0	
Total # receiving grants	114	14.6	114	14.6	0	0.0
Less than 1/2 tuition	85	10.9	85	10.9	0	0.0
Half to full tuition	20	2.6	20	2.6	0	0.0
Full tuition	9	1.2	9	1.2	0	0.0
More than full tuition	0	0.0	0	0.0	0	0.0
Median grant amount			$6,000		$0	

Informational and Library Resources

# of volumes and volume equivalents	507,734
# of titles	143,066
# of active serial subscriptions	3,540
Study seating capacity inside the library	368
# of professional librarians	9
Hours per week library is open	168
# of open, wired connections available to students	327
# of networked computers available for use by students	151
# of simultaneous wireless users	640
Require computer?	N

JD Attrition (from prior year)

	Academic	Other	Total	
	#	#	#	%
1st year	0	9	9	3.3%
2nd year	0	28	28	10.8%
3rd year	0	0	0	0.0%
4th year	0	0	0	0.0%

Employment

	Total	Percentage
Employment status known	233	99.6
Employment status unknown	1	0.4
Employed	211	90.6
Pursuing graduate degrees	11	4.7
Unemployed seeking employment	9	3.9
Unemployed not seeking employment	2	0.9

Type of Employment

# employed in law firms	123	58.3
# employed in business and industry	27	12.8
# employed in government	20	9.5
# employed in public interest	6	2.8
# employed as judicial clerks	33	15.6
# employed in academia	3	1.4

Geographic Location

# employed in state	135	64.0
# employed in foreign countries	2	0.9
# of states where employed	16	

Bar Passage Rates

Jurisdiction	Pennsylvania		
Exam	Sum 03	Win 04	Total
# from school taking bar for the first time	176	7	183
School's pass rate for all first-time takers	84%	71%	83%
State's pass rate for all first-time takers	78%	66%	76%

Villanova University School of Law

299 North Spring Mill Road
Villanova, PA 19085
Phone: 610.519.7010; Fax: 610.519.6291
E-mail: admissions@law.villanova.edu; Website: www.law.villanova.edu

■ Introduction

Today, as never before, there is a need for law schools to teach far more than the letter of the law. They must give future lawyers a sense of the importance of their role in the larger society, and they must prepare lawyers to work in an environment of burgeoning technology with issues of global importance.

With its Catholic roots, Villanova offers a legal education designed to teach the rules of law and their application; to demonstrate how lawyers analyze legal issues and express arguments and conclusions; to inculcate the skills of the counselor, advocate, and decision maker; and to explore the ethical and moral dimensions of law practice and professional conduct. The school is also providing leadership in information technology, law and psychology, taxation, and international law, among other fields.

Few law schools are located in a more beautiful and tranquil environment. Adjacent to the university campus is Philadelphia's Main Line. The school is at the approximate midpoint of east coast legal centers in New York and Washington and only 20 minutes by commuter rail from the center of Philadelphia.

Opened in 1953, the school is approved by the American Bar Association and is a member of the Association of American Law Schools. Students are graduates of more than 124 colleges and universities; many have significant work experience outside the law. The atmosphere of the school is noted for its collegiality.

■ Faculty

While Villanova faculty members are recognized nationally and internationally for their legal scholarship and for their contributions to the study and practice of law, they are also deeply committed to teaching. The student-faculty ratio is 18 to 1.

■ Library and Physical Facilities

In the law library, students have access to 130 computer workstations located in a state-of-the-art computer lab and throughout the library's stacks. There are an additional 40 computers dedicated to student usage throughout the remainder of the law school. In addition, all students with laptops can access Villanova University's high-speed Internet connection and all technology resources throughout the law school via wired and wireless connections. Finally, the law library contains more than 500,000 volume-equivalents in books and microforms, along with subscriptions to numerous legal databases to which students have ready access.

■ Joint JD/MBA Program

The Villanova University School of Law and College of Commerce and Finance offer a joint program permitting simultaneous study for the Juris Doctor and the Master of Business Administration degrees. The College of Commerce and Finance is one of the few colleges of business in the nation whose Master of Business Administration and Department of Accountancy program have been approved by the Association to Advance Collegiate Schools of Business.

Credit is given in the program for certain courses by both the School of Law and the College of Commerce and Finance. Degrees may be completed in less time than it would take to obtain them separately.

■ Joint JD/PhD Program in Law and Psychology

In cooperation with Drexel University, Villanova Law School offers an integrated program in law and psychology leading to a Juris Doctor from Villanova and a PhD in clinical psychology from Drexel. Villanova offers the only program in the country with a PhD component in clinical psychology, which is fully accredited by the American Psychological Association. The program has three major purposes—(1) to produce lawyer-psychologists who can participate in the development of mental health policy in the legislature and the courts; (2) to develop scientist-practitioners who will produce legally sophisticated social science research to assist the legal system in making better, more empirically based decisions; and (3) to educate highly trained clinicians who can contribute to the advancement of forensic psychology in such areas as criminal law, domestic relations, and civil commitment.

■ LLM in Taxation

This interdisciplinary program is conducted under the auspices of the School of Law and Villanova's College of Commerce and Finance. The program enriches the tax curriculum available to JD candidates, who are able to enroll in LLM courses, as well as participate in the joint JD/LLM program.

■ Special Programs

Beyond the skills of written and oral expression developed in the first-year writing program and the required upper-level moot court program, drafting, and seminar courses, Villanova students acquire the fundamental skills of the practicing lawyer—including counseling, negotiation, advocacy, mediation, dispute resolution, conciliation, and mature judgment. Hands-on clinical opportunities allow students to apply classroom experiences to real-world client representation, often while performing public service. Clinical programs include the Tax, Civil Justice, Asylum, Refugee and Emigrant Services, and Farmworkers Legal Aid.

■ Student Activities

The *Villanova Law Review* is a scholarly journal prepared and edited by law students. Members are selected on the basis of academic rank or through an open writing competition.

The *Villanova Environmental Law Journal* publishes both student and outside articles dealing with environmental issues. Students are selected for membership by an open writing competition.

The *Villanova Sports and Entertainment Law Journal* contains articles prepared by practitioners and professors in sports and entertainment law as well as by students. Membership is earned by selection through an open writing competition.

Each year, second- and third-year students have the opportunity to practice lawyering skills through the Client Interviewing and Counseling Competition, the Reimel Moot Court Competition, and several outside moot court competitions.

Student organizations include Asian-Pacific American Law Students, Black Law Students Association, Civil Rights Law Society, Corporate Law Society, Criminal Law Society, Environmental Law Society, Family Law Society, Gay-Straight Alliance, Health Law Society, Intellectual Property Protection Society, International Law Society, Jewish Law Students Association, Latin American Law Student Association, Justinian Society, Phi Delta Phi, Public Interest Law Society, St. Thomas More Society, Sports and Entertainment Law Society, Tax Law Society, and Women's Caucus.

■ Career Strategy and Advancement

The mission of the Career Strategy and Advancement Office is to provide career planning education, recruitment programs, and individual counseling as the foundation for future career development and satisfaction of our students. Distinctive features and programs include three attorney-advisors, including a public service/pro bono specialist; open-door policy, including daily "on call" advisor for walk-ins and "quick questions"; small group workshops for 1Ls; dozens of career workshops and panel programs on topics ranging from interviews, résumés, and networking, to public interest careers, judicial clerkships, and a multitude of practice specialty areas; "Practice Specialty Expo," which brings nearly 100 attorneys to the law school for a festive networking experience; recruitment programs throughout the year, including a diverse array of employers in private practice (large and small firms), government, nonprofits, the judiciary, and corporations; special recruitment programs designed to enhance diversity in the profession; job fairs targeting unique geographic or practice preferences; job search coaching for new graduates on the job market; pro bono programs such as "Lawyering Together" and other projects, providing students with the opportunity to serve the disadvantaged while developing skills and positive relationships with practicing attorneys.

Admission

Villanova has chosen not to provide prospective students with an admission profile based on individual undergraduate GPAs and LSAT scores. The Admissions Committee seeks to create a diverse community by adhering to a comprehensive evaluation of a candidate's file that includes academic performance as well as professional promise. Each candidate's background, interests, accomplishments, and goals are considered before a decision is made.

University of Virginia School of Law

580 Massie Road
Charlottesville, VA 22903-1789
Phone: 434.924.7351; Fax: 434.982.2128
E-mail: lawadmit@virginia.edu; Website: www.law.virginia.edu

ABA
Approved
Since
1923

The Basics

Type of school	Public
Term	Semester
Application deadline	1/15
Application fee	$70
Financial aid deadline	2/15
Can first year start other than fall?	No
Student to faculty ratio (fall)	13.6 to 1
Does the university offer:	
housing restricted to law students?	No
graduate housing for which law students are eligible?	Yes

Faculty and Administrators

	Total		Men		Women		Minorities	
	Fall	Spr	Fall	Spr	Fall	Spr	Fall	Spr
Full-time	67	72	50	53	17	19	7	5
Other Full-time	0	0	0	0	0	0	0	0
Deans, librarians, & others who teach	3	3	2	2	1	1	1	1
Part-time	64	76	56	65	8	11	1	5
Total	**134**	**151**	**108**	**120**	**26**	**31**	**9**	**11**

Curriculum

		Full-time	Part-time
Typical first-year section size		60	0
Is there typically a "small section" of the first-year class, other than Legal Writing, taught by full-time faculty		Yes	No
If yes, typical size offered last year		30	0
# of classroom course titles beyond 1st year curriculum			213
# of upper division courses, excluding seminars with an enrollment:	Under 25		71
	25-49		31
	50-74		20
	75-99		10
	100+		20
# of seminars			100
# of seminar positions available			1,371
# of seminar positions filled		1,193	0
# of positions available in simulation courses			811
# of simulation positions filled		754	0
# of positions available in faculty supervised clinical courses			53
# of faculty supervised clinical positions filled		51	0
# involved in field placements		107	0
# involved in law journals		500	0
# involved in moot court or trial competitions		225	0
# of credit hours required to graduate			86

JD Enrollment and Ethnicity

	Men		Women		Full-time		Part-time		1st-year		Total		JD Degs. Awd.
	#	%	#	%	#	%	#	%	#	%	#	%	
African Amer.	29	4.5	42	9.2	71	6.5	0	0.0	32	8.9	71	6.5	22
Amer. Indian	2	0.3	2	0.4	4	0.4	0	0.0	1	0.3	4	0.4	5
Asian Amer.	39	6.1	53	11.6	92	8.4	0	0.0	24	6.7	92	8.4	22
Mex. Amer.	0	0.0	0	0.0	0	0.0	0	0.0	0	0.0	0	0.0	0
Puerto Rican	0	0.0	0	0.0	0	0.0	0	0.0	0	0.0	0	0.0	0
Hispanic	8	1.2	5	1.1	13	1.2	0	0.0	4	1.1	13	1.2	6
Total Minority	78	12.1	102	22.3	180	16.4	0	0.0	61	16.9	180	16.4	55
For. Nation.	2	0.3	3	0.7	5	0.5	0	0.0	0	0.0	5	0.5	1
Caucasian	433	67.4	288	62.9	721	65.5	0	0.0	232	64.4	721	65.5	240
Unknown	129	20.1	65	14.2	194	17.6	0	0.0	67	18.6	194	17.6	63
Total	642	58.4	458	41.6	1100	100.0	0	0.0	360	32.7	1100		359

Tuition and Fees

	Resident	Nonresident
Full-time	$26,100	$31,100
Part-time	$0	$0

Living Expenses

Estimated living expenses for singles

Living on campus	Living off campus	Living at home
$15,100	$15,100	$15,100

University of Virginia School of Law

ABA Approved Since 1923

GPA and LSAT Scores

	Total	Full-time	Part-time
# of apps	5,475	5,475	0
# of admits	1,024	1,024	0
# of matrics	360	360	0
75% GPA	3.82	3.82	0.00
25% GPA	3.49	3.49	0.00
75% LSAT	171	171	0
25% LSAT	166	166	0

Grants and Scholarships (from prior year)

	Total		Full-time		Part-time	
	#	%	#	%	#	%
Total # of students	1,087		1,087		0	
Total # receiving grants	440	40.5	440	40.5	0	0.0
Less than 1/2 tuition	354	32.6	354	32.6	0	0.0
Half to full tuition	68	6.3	68	6.3	0	0.0
Full tuition	3	0.3	3	0.3	0	0.0
More than full tuition	15	1.4	15	1.4	0	0.0
Median grant amount			$8,500		$0	

Informational and Library Resources

# of volumes and volume equivalents	870,251
# of titles	268,421
# of active serial subscriptions	11,378
Study seating capacity inside the library	802
# of professional librarians	12
Hours per week library is open	112
# of open, wired connections available to students	86
# of networked computers available for use by students	76
# of simultaneous wireless users	1,424
Require computer?	Y

JD Attrition (from prior year)

	Academic	Other	Total	
	#	#	#	%
1st year	0	10	10	2.7%
2nd year	0	8	8	2.2%
3rd year	0	0	0	0.0%
4th year	0	0	0	0.0%

Employment

	Total	Percentage
Employment status known	348	100.0
Employment status unknown	0	0.0
Employed	336	96.6
Pursuing graduate degrees	4	1.1
Unemployed seeking employment	1	0.3
Unemployed not seeking employment	7	2.0

Type of Employment

# employed in law firms	256	76.2
# employed in business and industry	4	1.2
# employed in government	16	4.8
# employed in public interest	10	3.0
# employed as judicial clerks	45	13.4
# employed in academia	0	0.0

Geographic Location

# employed in state	44	13.1
# employed in foreign countries	5	1.5
# of states where employed	33	

Bar Passage Rates

Jurisdiction	Virginia			New York		
Exam	Sum 03	Win 04	Total	Sum 03	Win 04	Total
# from school taking bar for the first time	96	7	103	89	5	94
School's pass rate for all first-time takers	94%	86%	93%	97%	60%	95%
State's pass rate for all first-time takers	75%	60%	72%	78%	58%	75%

University of Virginia School of Law

Admissions Office, 580 Massie Road
Charlottesville, VA 22903-1789
Phone: 434.924.7351; Fax: 434.982.2128
E-mail: lawadmit@virginia.edu; Website: www.law.virginia.edu

■ Introduction

Founded in 1826, the University of Virginia School of
Law is a world-renowned training ground for distinguished lawyers and public servants. As identified by
American Lawyer magazine, Virginia is one of only two
law schools in the country with graduates practicing in
each of the nation's top 100 law firms. But the law school
also is dedicated to upholding Thomas Jefferson's
conviction that lawyers must serve the public interest
and provides special career counseling and placement
assistance, operates pro bono programs, and administers
a loan assistance and forgiveness program.

At Virginia, law in its origins, impact, and implications
is analyzed and debated in classes, workshops, lecture
programs, student organizations, and faculty-student
informal exchanges. Students are challenged to determine
how and why the law developed in a certain way, whether
it accomplishes its purpose, and how changes might affect
social behavior. Faculty are fully committed to teaching,
scholarship, and public service. They meet with and
mentor students, explore ideas, and foster understanding.
A third of the faculty hold advanced degrees in fields such
as psychology, economics, philosophy, history, and the
social study of science and technology.

■ Curriculum and Degrees

Intellectual rigor, dynamic teaching, and rich diversity
distinguish the Virginia curriculum. Each first-year
student takes a first-semester class in a small section of
30 students. Other first-year classes range from 60 to 90
students. During the second semester, students choose
five to seven hours of electives. In addition, the law
school offers annually nearly 200 different courses and
seminars beyond the first-year curriculum.

The law school has strength in corporate and
commercial law rooted in exceptional faculty and
enhanced by close relationships with the Darden
Graduate Business School. The Law and Business
program uniquely integrates business and legal analysis
throughout a range of courses. Virginia's prominence in
international law is built on a long tradition, with
notable faculty in areas of immigration, human rights,
environment, and constitutional law in other countries,
as well as private and commercial law in a global
community. Its reputation in legal and constitutional
history stems from highly visible and influential faculty,
many of whom hold doctorates in history. Environmental
endeavors draw strength from the Center for
Environmental Studies, the *Virginia Environmental Law
Journal*, and opportunities for joint study and practice
with others within and outside the university.

Students may enroll in several joint-degree programs.
The JD-MBA program is a four-year program in conjunction
with the Darden Graduate Business School. Other
combined degree programs include a JD-MA in bioethics,
economics, English, government and foreign affairs, history,
philosophy, or sociology; a JD-MS in accounting; a JD-MP
in planning; and a JD-MPH in public health. In addition,
students may combine a law degree from Virginia with the
MPA from Princeton, MALD from the Fletcher School at
Tufts, or MA in International Relations and International
Economics from Johns Hopkins.

■ Facilities

The Law Grounds, a complex of integrated buildings,
offers an expansive and attractive setting reflecting Jefferson's position that an intellectual community in a
beautiful environment fosters learning and personal
growth. The library, with more than 870,000 volumes, is
one of the largest law libraries in the country. But, more
than a repository of books, the library is the law school's
central research facility. Professional librarians provide
research support for faculty and assistance and training
for students. The library is committed to a dynamic
concept of information in which the traditional printed
text is merely one of many learning tools. It is fully
computerized and offers full LAN access, both wired
and wireless, throughout the facility.

■ Admission

The Admission Committee believes that absolute standards
based on a combination of LSAT score and GPA cannot be
the only criteria for selection. Recognizing that the real
meaning of GPA will vary with such factors as quality of
the institution attended, rigor of courses selected, and
degree of grade inflation, the committee considers an array
of elements in addition to the essential LSAT and GPA, with
a view toward assembling a diverse class while arriving at
a fair appraisal of the individual applicant.

While the LSAT and GPA remain the primary
determinants for admission, the committee takes other
elements into account, including the maturing effect of
some years away from formal education, trends in
academic performance, employment history, significant
personal achievement or unusual prior training, background, or ethnicity, which promises a contribution to the
law school community. Successfully overcoming economic,
social, or educational obstacles is viewed favorably.

The law school seeks to maintain a diverse student
body in which the free exchange of ideas and viewpoints
can flourish, creating a rich learning experience for all
law school students. Therefore, the active recruitment of
minority students is important to our admission process.

While individual interviews are not a part of the admission process, prospective students are encouraged to visit the School of Law. When classes are in session, student-led tours are available and classes are open to visitors. On most Friday afternoons throughout the summer and during the fall semester, the School of Law holds admission information sessions. Check our website at *www.law.virginia.edu/admissions* for details.

■ Financial Aid

The University of Virginia School of Law assists its students in financing their legal education through a variety of resources, including scholarship assistance; Title IV federally sponsored programs such as Stafford Student Loans, Perkins Loans, and College Work-Study funding; and private sector educational loans. Most scholarship assistance is awarded on a combined basis of academic merit and financial need. Some scholarships are awarded solely on merit. The Financial Aid Office works individually with students to develop realistic budgets that meet the costs of obtaining a legal education and to identify sources of financial support that will enable students to achieve their educational and professional goals.

Students who choose less financially lucrative positions in the public sector can benefit from a variety of financial assistance programs offered by Virginia. Summer fellowships are available for students who accept unpaid or low-paid summer internships with public sector employers. The Mortimer Caplin and Linda Fairstein Public Service Fellowships provide tuition assistance for the third year of law school as well as a living stipend for the first two years of a graduate's public sector legal practice. The Powell Fellowship in Legal Services awards

$35,000 to a graduating student or judicial clerk to enable him or her to work under the sponsorship of a public interest organization to enhance the delivery of civil legal services to the poor. The law school also has a generous Loan Forgiveness Program available to graduates who choose qualifying employment.

■ Career Services

The law school boasts one of the most successful career services programs in legal education. An online job-search system gives students 24-hour, web-based access to employment opportunities and employer information and provides the vehicle for interview sign-up and scheduling. Over 800 public and private sector law offices, from every region of the United States, annually conduct nearly 8,000 interviews with second- and third-year students. University of Virginia School of Law graduates are employed in all 50 states, the District of Columbia, and many foreign countries.

■ Student Life

The law school is continually enriched and diversified by student organizations, extracurricular activities, and community spirit. Intellectual challenges are complemented by cooperation and camaraderie, all integrated under Virginia's 160-year-old, student-run honor system. The array of opportunity includes eight academic journals, 40 interest-centered organizations, student governance, and social and athletic activities. The university and local community are large enough to offer something to meet anyone's interests and small enough to make active participation compatible with the rigors of an academic schedule.

Admission Profile

The University of Virginia School of Law has elected not to provide an admission profile based only on GPA and LSAT, as these numbers cannot be the sole criteria for selecting an entering class. Each applicant is assessed as an individual, taking into account not only LSAT scores and undergraduate grades, but also the strength of an applicant's undergraduate or graduate curriculum, trends in grades, the maturing effect of experiences since college, the nature and quality of any work experience, significant achievement in extracurricular activities, service in the military, contributions to campus or community through service and leadership, and personal qualities displayed.

Wake Forest University School of Law

PO Box 7206, Reynolda Station
Winston-Salem, NC 27109
Phone: 336.758.5437; Fax: 336.758.3930
E-mail: admissions@law.wfu.edu; Website: www.law.wfu.edu

ABA
Approved
Since
1936

The Basics

Type of school	Private
Term	Semester
Application deadline	3/1
Application fee	$60
Financial aid deadline	
Can first year start other than fall?	No
Student to faculty ratio (fall)	12.0 to 1
Does the university offer:	
housing restricted to law students?	No
graduate housing for which law students are eligible?	No

Faculty and Administrators

	Total		Men		Women		Minorities	
	Fall	Spr	Fall	Spr	Fall	Spr	Fall	Spr
Full-time	33	32	22	23	11	9	5	3
Other Full-time	7	7	1	1	6	6	3	3
Deans, librarians, & others who teach	5	5	2	2	3	3	0	0
Part-time	12	16	11	12	1	4	2	0
Total	57	60	36	38	21	22	10	6

Curriculum

	Full-time	Part-time
Typical first-year section size	40	0
Is there typically a "small section" of the first-year class, other than Legal Writing, taught by full-time faculty	Yes	No
If yes, typical size offered last year	40	0
# of classroom course titles beyond 1st year curriculum		85
# of upper division courses, excluding seminars with an enrollment: Under 25		53
25-49		35
50-74		10
75-99		0
100+		0
# of seminars		26
# of seminar positions available		521
# of seminar positions filled	358	0
# of positions available in simulation courses		741
# of simulation positions filled	615	0
# of positions available in faculty supervised clinical courses		70
# of faculty supervised clinical positions filled	67	0
# involved in field placements	12	0
# involved in law journals	61	0
# involved in moot court or trial competitions	51	0
# of credit hours required to graduate		89

JD Enrollment and Ethnicity

	Men		Women		Full-time		Part-time		1st-year		Total		JD Degs. Awd.
	#	%	#	%	#	%	#	%	#	%	#	%	
African Amer.	8	3.0	22	10.3	30	6.5	0	0.0	15	9.6	30	6.3	12
Amer. Indian	0	0.0	0	0.0	0	0.0	0	0.0	0	0.0	0	0.0	0
Asian Amer.	5	1.9	6	2.8	9	1.9	2	11.1	2	1.3	11	2.3	1
Mex. Amer.	0	0.0	0	0.0	0	0.0	0	0.0	0	0.0	0	0.0	0
Puerto Rican	0	0.0	0	0.0	0	0.0	0	0.0	0	0.0	0	0.0	0
Hispanic	16	6.0	10	4.7	26	5.6	0	0.0	16	10.2	26	5.4	1
Total Minority	29	10.9	38	17.8	65	14.1	2	11.1	33	21.0	67	14.0	14
For. Nation.	4	1.5	1	0.5	5	1.1	0	0.0	1	0.6	5	1.0	2
Caucasian	233	87.6	175	81.8	392	84.8	16	88.9	123	78.3	408	85.0	133
Unknown	0	0.0	0	0.0	0	0.0	0	0.0	0	0.0	0	0.0	0
Total	266	55.4	214	44.6	462	96.3	18	3.8	157	32.7	480		149

Tuition and Fees

	Resident	Nonresident
Full-time	$26,400	$0
Part-time	$0	$0

Living Expenses

Estimated living expenses for singles

Living on campus	Living off campus	Living at home
N/A	$14,125	N/A

Wake Forest University School of Law

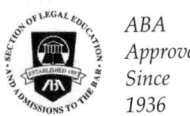

ABA
Approved
Since
1936

GPA and LSAT Scores

	Total	Full-time	Part-time
# of apps	2,433	2,433	0
# of admits	493	493	0
# of matrics	157	157	0
75% GPA	3.60	3.60	0.00
25% GPA	3.15	3.15	0.00
75% LSAT	165	165	0
25% LSAT	160	160	0

Grants and Scholarships (from prior year)

	Total #	Total %	Full-time #	Full-time %	Part-time #	Part-time %
Total # of students	489		470		19	
Total # receiving grants	146	29.9	146	31.1	0	0.0
Less than 1/2 tuition	41	8.4	41	8.7	0	0.0
Half to full tuition	46	9.4	46	9.8	0	0.0
Full tuition	41	8.4	41	8.7	0	0.0
More than full tuition	18	3.7	18	3.8	0	0.0
Median grant amount			$18,825		$0	

Informational and Library Resources

# of volumes and volume equivalents	412,011
# of titles	229,627
# of active serial subscriptions	5,424
Study seating capacity inside the library	574
# of professional librarians	7
Hours per week library is open	108
# of open, wired connections available to students	650
# of networked computers available for use by students	91
# of simultaneous wireless users	0
Require computer?	Y

JD Attrition (from prior year)

	Academic #	Other #	Total #	Total %
1st year	1	4	5	2.6%
2nd year	6	11	17	11.1%
3rd year	0	1	1	0.7%
4th year	0	0	0	0.0%

Employment

	Total	Percentage
Employment status known	151	95.0
Employment status unknown	8	5.0
Employed	142	94.0
Pursuing graduate degrees	5	3.3
Unemployed seeking employment	4	2.6
Unemployed not seeking employment	0	0.0

Type of Employment

# employed in law firms	85	59.9
# employed in business and industry	14	9.9
# employed in government	10	7.0
# employed in public interest	2	1.4
# employed as judicial clerks	23	16.2
# employed in academia	2	1.4

Geographic Location

# employed in state	63	44.4
# employed in foreign countries	0	0.0
# of states where employed	22	

Bar Passage Rates

Jurisdiction	North Carolina		
Exam	Sum 03	Win 04	Total
# from school taking bar for the first time	78	6	84
School's pass rate for all first-time takers	86%	100%	87%
State's pass rate for all first-time takers	78%	64%	76%

Wake Forest University School of Law

PO Box 7206, Reynolda Station
Winston-Salem, NC 27109
Phone: 336.758.5437; Fax: 336.758.3930
E-mail: admissions@law.wfu.edu; Website: www.law.wfu.edu

■ Introduction

Wake Forest University School of Law, established in 1894, is located in Winston-Salem, North Carolina. It is a member of the AALS and is ABA approved. In 1998, the law school was awarded a chapter of the Order of the Coif, a national honorary society.

Wake Forest offers students a solid and personalized legal education. Class sizes are smaller than virtually any other law school in the nation, with approximately 40 students in each first-year section and about 20 students in first-year legal writing sections.

Faculty members are nationally renowned teachers and scholars. The director of trial advocacy was awarded the Roscoe Pound Foundation's Jacobson Award for Excellence in Teaching Trial Advocacy, and recently Wake Forest received the prestigious Emil Gumpert Award from the American College of Trial Lawyers for its outstanding trial advocacy program. Faculty chairs are held by six of the nation's most respected authorities in the areas of administrative law, commercial law, sports and entertainment law, constitutional law, torts and product liability, and health care law and policy.

Wake Forest law school embraces seven principal commitments: (1) to maintain a school of the right size that begins with a first-year class of approximately 160 students composed of four sections of about 40 students each; (2) to develop and retain a faculty strong in teaching, experience, and current scholarly writing; (3) to assure that students are taught substantive law and how to research through the maximum use of leading-edge technology; (4) to continue the school's emphasis on dispute resolution and litigation skills through instruction, competition, and clinical practice; (5) to build a bridge between law and management communities by an enhanced curriculum, the sharing of resources, and collaborative instruction; (6) to seek to provide career opportunities for our students and graduates that match their potential; and (7) to teach the transcendence of ethics and to inculcate in graduates the importance of doing good while doing well throughout their professional lives.

■ Admission

Requirements: Bachelor's degree from accredited college or university, application with dean's certification and academic recommendation, LSAT and LSDAS, application fee—$60, application deadline—March 1. First-year students are admitted only in the fall semester for full-time study. The law school has a rolling admission policy. Completed files are individually reviewed to select a diverse group of students who are likely to succeed in law school and contribute to the legal profession. The LSAT and undergraduate GPA, as well as a number of subjective factors—including personal talents, work experience, community service, leadership potential, graduate study, and a history of overcoming social or economic hardship—indicating intellectual capacity, character, motivation, and maturity are considered. For multiple LSAT scores, the average of the test scores will be used. Applicants should explain disparate scores.

A $300 nonrefundable deposit is due by April 15, and a tuition deposit must be paid by June 15 (both fees are applicable toward tuition). Personal interviews are not required; however, we encourage all applicants to visit the law school.

Transfer students meeting the admission requirements are accepted on a space-available basis after the successful completion of one year at an AALS or ABA-approved law school.

■ Expenses and Financial Aid

Tuition/fees—$26,400, estimated living expenses—$7,000-$9,000.

Merit, need-based, and diversity scholarships available. FAFSA due April 1.

■ Clinical Programs

Two exceptional clinical programs allow students to gain hands-on legal experience. In the Litigation Clinic, students are placed in offices such as the US Attorney's Office, the district attorney's office, the public defender's office, legal aid, the National Labor Relations Board, private law firms, and corporate counsel. While receiving classroom instruction and skills training in interviewing, counseling, negotiation, and discovery, students represent clients under the supervision of an experienced attorney.

The Elder Law Clinic is an in-house clinic representing low- to moderate-income clients over the age of 60. Located at the Wake Forest University Baptist Medical Center, the classroom component is jointly taught by members of the law and medical school faculties. Students draft essential documents, such as wills, and handle administrative representation and state court litigation with a clinic professor/attorney.

■ Technology

Wake Forest prepares students to embrace the rapidly changing technological environment of the legal profession. Classrooms have been upgraded to multimedia theaters allowing technology to augment classroom teaching. Many professors routinely use web pages to distribute essential course information and provide online discussion forums outside of the classroom.

Students are required to have a laptop. The law school wireless network gives students instant access to e-mail, essential legal research systems, the Internet, and a variety of other resources. A university-wide network allows students to register for courses, receive grades, obtain transcripts, and interact with university offices.

■ Joint-Degree Programs

The law school offers a joint JD/MBA program with the Babcock Graduate School of Management. Admission and scholarship decisions are made independently at each school. The law school also offers an LLM in American Law for graduates of foreign law schools. A separate (LLM) application is required and may be obtained at *LLM-admissions@Law.wfu.edu* or by writing the director of the LLM program.

■ Foreign Study

Students in good standing may participate in a four-week program offered each summer at the Worrell House, the university's residential center near Regent's Park in London, England; in Italy at Casa Artom on the Grand Canal; and at the University of Vienna in Vienna, Austria. Students participating in the programs can earn up to six hours of academic credit.

■ Career Services

The Career Services Office aggressively seeks opportunities for students in both summer and permanent legal positions. Knowledgeable staff members personally counsel students to assist them in developing solid career portfolios. The office also conducts workshops in résumé preparation, interviewing, and career planning. Faculty and staff expand career opportunities by visiting law firms, corporations, and agencies throughout the country to acquaint them with the exceptional Wake Forest program. A large number of employers interview students on campus each year or request that résumés be forwarded by the Career Services Office. Wake Forest law graduates are located throughout the country.

Applicant Profile

Wake Forest University School of Law
This grid includes only applicants who earned 120-180 LSAT scores under standard administrations.

LSAT Score	3.75 +		3.50 - 3.74		3.25 - 3.49		3.00 - 3.24		2.75 - 2.99		2.50 - 2.74		2.25 - 2.49		2.00 - 2.24		Below 2.00		No GPA		Total	
	Apps	Adm	Apps	Adm	Apps	Adm	Apps	Adm	Apps	Adm	Apps	Adm	Apps	Adm	Apps	Adm	Apps	Adm	Apps	Adm	Apps	Adm
175-180	1	1	0	0	1	1	1	1	0	0	0	0	0	0	0	0	0	0	0	0	3	3
170-174	5	4	5	5	7	7	3	3	1	1	2	1	1	1	2	0	0	0	0	0	26	22
165-169	21	20	32	32	35	35	32	29	11	3	12	7	5	0	2	0	0	0	2	1	152	127
160-164	101	66	169	106	156	59	124	32	61	9	26	4	8	0	3	0	0	0	1	0	649	276
155-159	125	2	206	9	215	9	161	9	53	3	23	0	12	0	3	0	0	0	1	0	799	32
150-154	43	2	81	6	114	12	91	7	52	2	17	2	13	1	4	0	1	0	1	0	417	32
145-149	16	1	29	0	38	1	49	6	29	0	4	0	9	0	1	0	1	0	0	0	176	8
140-144	7	0	9	0	23	0	32	0	20	0	13	0	4	0	2	0	0	0	3	0	113	0
135-139	0	0	3	0	5	0	7	0	5	0	4	0	4	0	1	0	2	0	2	0	33	0
130-134	0	0	1	0	2	0	5	0	3	0	1	0	2	0	2	0	0	0	0	0	16	0
125-129	0	0	0	0	0	0	0	0	0	0	0	0	1	0	1	0	0	0	0	0	2	0
120-124	0	0	0	0	0	0	0	0	0	0	0	0	0	0	0	0	0	0	0	0	0	0
Total	319	96	535	158	596	124	505	87	235	18	102	14	59	2	21	0	4	0	10	1	2386	500

Apps = Number of Applicants
Adm = Number Admitted
Reflects 99% of the total applicant pool.

Washburn University School of Law

1700 SW College Avenue
Topeka, KS 66621-1140
Phone: 800.WASHLAW or 800.927.4529; Fax: 785.231.1120
E-mail: admissions@washburnlaw.edu; Website: washburnlaw.edu

ABA
Approved
Since
1923

The Basics

Type of school	Public
Term	Semester
Application deadline	4/1 11/1 4/1
Application fee	$40
Financial aid deadline	4/1 11/1 4/1
Can first year start other than fall?	Yes
Student to faculty ratio (fall)	14.8 to 1
Does the university offer:	
housing restricted to law students?	No
graduate housing for which law students are eligible?	Yes

Faculty and Administrators

	Total		Men		Women		Minorities	
	Fall	Spr	Fall	Spr	Fall	Spr	Fall	Spr
Full-time	26	24	16	15	10	9	7	6
Other Full-time	2	2	1	1	1	1	0	0
Deans, librarians, & others who teach	4	4	3	3	1	1	0	0
Part-time	20	20	15	19	5	1	0	0
Total	52	50	35	38	17	12	7	6

Curriculum

	Full-time	Part-time
Typical first-year section size	75	0
Is there typically a "small section" of the first-year class, other than Legal Writing, taught by full-time faculty	Yes	No
If yes, typical size offered last year	37	0
# of classroom course titles beyond 1st year curriculum	74	
# of upper division courses, excluding seminars with an enrollment: Under 25	29	
25-49	21	
50-74	14	
75-99	11	
100+	1	
# of seminars	17	
# of seminar positions available	424	
# of seminar positions filled	280	0
# of positions available in simulation courses	349	
# of simulation positions filled	203	0
# of positions available in faculty supervised clinical courses	67	
# of faculty supervised clinical positions filled	67	0
# involved in field placements	41	0
# involved in law journals	63	0
# involved in moot court or trial competitions	34	0
# of credit hours required to graduate	90	

JD Enrollment and Ethnicity

	Men		Women		Full-time		Part-time		1st-year		Total		JD Degs. Awd.
	#	%	#	%	#	%	#	%	#	%	#	%	
African Amer.	9	3.5	12	5.8	21	4.5	0	0.0	10	6.6	21	4.5	8
Amer. Indian	4	1.6	5	2.4	9	1.9	0	0.0	2	1.3	9	1.9	1
Asian Amer.	8	3.1	5	2.4	13	2.8	0	0.0	7	4.6	13	2.8	6
Mex. Amer.	7	2.7	2	1.0	9	1.9	0	0.0	1	0.7	9	1.9	1
Puerto Rican	0	0.0	1	0.5	1	0.2	0	0.0	1	0.7	1	0.2	1
Hispanic	4	1.6	2	1.0	6	1.3	0	0.0	5	3.3	6	1.3	3
Total Minority	32	12.5	27	13.1	59	12.8	0	0.0	26	17.1	59	12.8	20
For. Nation.	4	1.6	2	1.0	6	1.3	0	0.0	4	2.6	6	1.3	5
Caucasian	213	83.2	172	83.5	385	83.3	0	0.0	110	72.4	385	83.3	123
Unknown	7	2.7	5	2.4	12	2.6	0	0.0	12	7.9	12	2.6	0
Total	256	55.4	206	44.6	462	100.0	0	0.0	152	32.9	462		148

Tuition and Fees

	Resident	Nonresident
Full-time	$10,766	$17,682
Part-time	$0	$0

Living Expenses

Estimated living expenses for singles

Living on campus	Living off campus	Living at home
$12,984	$12,984	$12,984

Washburn University School of Law

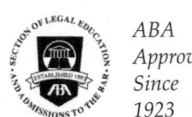

*ABA
Approved
Since
1923*

GPA and LSAT Scores

	Total	Full-time	Part-time
# of apps	1,172	1,172	0
# of admits	370	370	0
# of matrics	157	157	0
75% GPA	3.60	3.60	0.00
25% GPA	2.95	2.95	0.00
75% LSAT	156	156	0
25% LSAT	151	151	0

Grants and Scholarships (from prior year)

	Total		Full-time		Part-time	
	#	%	#	%	#	%
Total # of students	473		473		0	
Total # receiving grants	209	44.2	209	44.2	0	0.0
Less than 1/2 tuition	135	28.5	135	28.5	0	0.0
Half to full tuition	15	3.2	15	3.2	0	0.0
Full tuition	37	7.8	37	7.8	0	0.0
More than full tuition	22	4.7	22	4.7	0	0.0
Median grant amount			$3,000		$0	

Informational and Library Resources

# of volumes and volume equivalents	372,265
# of titles	237,650
# of active serial subscriptions	4,032
Study seating capacity inside the library	432
# of professional librarians	7
Hours per week library is open	101
# of open, wired connections available to students	18
# of networked computers available for use by students	88
# of simultaneous wireless users	3,060
Require computer?	N

JD Attrition (from prior year)

	Academic	Other	Total	
	#	#	#	%
1st year	5	9	14	8.5%
2nd year	1	10	11	6.6%
3rd year	1	2	3	2.1%
4th year	0	0	0	0.0%

Employment

	Total	Percentage
Employment status known	123	98.4
Employment status unknown	2	1.6
Employed	109	88.6
Pursuing graduate degrees	5	4.1
Unemployed seeking employment	5	4.1
Unemployed not seeking employment	4	3.3

Type of Employment

# employed in law firms	56	51.4
# employed in business and industry	14	12.8
# employed in government	20	18.3
# employed in public interest	10	9.2
# employed as judicial clerks	7	6.4
# employed in academia	2	1.8

Geographic Location

# employed in state	79	72.5
# employed in foreign countries	0	0.0
# of states where employed	13	

Bar Passage Rates

Jurisdiction	Kansas		
Exam	Sum 03	Win 04	Total
# from school taking bar for the first time	82	15	97
School's pass rate for all first-time takers	78%	80%	78%
State's pass rate for all first-time takers	81%	85%	83%

Washburn University School of Law

1700 SW College Avenue
Topeka, KS 66621-1140
Phone: 800.WASHLAW or 800.927.4529; Fax: 785.231.1120
E-mail: admissions@washburnlaw.edu; Website: washburnlaw.edu

■ Introduction

The Washburn University School of Law is celebrating its second century of providing students with quality legal education. Washburn Law opened in 1903, became a member of the AALS in 1905, and, in 1923, appeared on the first list of law schools fully accredited by the ABA. Today it boasts a diverse and accessible faculty, a dynamic student community, and top-flight electronic library resources. Students enjoy a comparatively low cost of living in Topeka. The city offers a wide range of opportunities for clerkships, externships, and employment.

■ Curriculum

Students may begin their study in either the fall or spring semester. The first-year curriculum is prescribed and includes an intensive course in legal analysis, research, and writing. More than 90 percent of first-year students participate in the Academic Success Program, a small-group supplemental class discussion facilitated by academically successful upper-level students. Second- and third-year students satisfy advanced writing and oral presentation requirements and take one or more classes from a group of perspectives in law courses.

■ Centers of Excellence

Washburn has a long tradition of excellence in teaching, producing some of the finest practicing attorneys in the region. Washburn's curriculum is enhanced by its three signature programs in advocacy, business and transactional law, and children and family law.

Business and Transactional Law Center—The center offers students an innovative education in all aspects of transactional law, including coursework in crucial skills. Whether a student is interested in corporate and securities law, agribusiness law, banking, financial institution regulation, entrepreneurial law, real estate development law, oil and gas law, or a general business practice, students will be able to prepare themselves for a successful career.

Center for Excellence in Advocacy—The center trains law students in the persuasive and skilled use of advocacy techniques. The center also supports research in trial behavior, trial process, and effective advocacy. Students hone their advocacy skills in Washburn's live client law clinic and in a variety of advocacy skills courses. The center coordinates student participation in trial advocacy, negotiation, and client counseling. The center also sponsors national and regional advocacy conferences and hosts a jurist in residence each year.

Children and Family Law Center—The center supports education, interdisciplinary research, advocacy, and

training services focused on children and families involved in the legal system. Washburn houses the American Bar Association's *Family Law Quarterly*. Students working in the center have the opportunity to take a range of courses related to children and families and to participate in the Washburn Law Clinic representing clients in divorce, child in need of care, and other family law cases.

■ Certificate Programs

Washburn Law offers certificates of specialization in natural resources law, family law, and tax law. The certificate programs allow students to fully develop their legal interests in these fields. Students who earn certificates graduate with a highly developed working knowledge of the practice area.

■ Law Clinic

In 1970, Washburn became one of the first law schools in the nation to offer a program of clinical legal education. Clinical education is the study of law through faculty-supervised representation of real clients with real problems. Students provide a full range of legal services, including new programs in Native American law and transactional law.

■ Externships

Washburn's externship program allows students to earn course credit through placement in legal settings outside the law school. Students can experience the practice of law in a wide variety of settings tailored to their specific interests and needs. Students are closely supervised by an attorney and by the externship director.

■ International Programs

Washburn Law offers two international programs. The summer study abroad program is at the University of Utrecht in The Netherlands. The law school also has a student exchange program with the University of Limerick in Ireland, allowing students to take one semester of law classes at that university.

■ January Start Program

Washburn's January Start Program permits students to begin law school in January. These students may either complete law school at the normal pace or they may participate in the Accelerated Degree Program.

Washburn University School of Law

■ Accelerated Degree Program

This program allows students to complete law school in two and a half years by taking courses during both summers.

■ Facilities and Technology

The law library, one of the best law libraries in the country according to *National Jurist* magazine, is a leader in the use of information technology. Students have wireless access throughout the building. Classrooms are equipped with audio, video, and computer technology. The renovated Robinson Courtroom/Bianchino Technology Center provides a state-of the-art high-tech courtroom.

■ Admission

While an applicant's LSAT score and GPA are significant factors, there is no bright-line cutoff. The Admission Committee carefully considers other factors, including life and work experience, graduate coursework, cultural background, and extracurricular activities. Washburn welcomes applications from qualified individuals without regard to race, color, religion, age, national origin, ancestry, disability, gender, sexual orientation, or marital or parental status.

■ Student Activities

There are more than 25 active student organizations; two law fraternities; Black, Hispanic, Asian, and Native American Law Student Associations; the Women's Legal Forum; the Lesbian and Gay Network; Volunteer Society; and societies for students interested in environmental, tax, international, and public interest law specialties.

Students are selected for membership on the Board of Editors of the *Washburn Law Journal*. Students also have opportunities to be student editors for the *Family Law Quarterly*, a publication of the ABA Family Law Section.

■ Expenses and Financial Aid

Scholarships are awarded based upon a combination of academic performance and need. Contribution to diversity is considered in making scholarship awards. Resident status for tuition purposes can be established with a primary Kansas residence after six months. The Financial Aid Office assists law students in procuring federal loans and financial aid. Housing costs are reasonable. Most students live in the residential areas surrounding the campus.

■ Career Services

The Career Services office offers programs that emphasize assessment of career goals, exploration of varied applications of a legal education, and support for the transition into the professional marketplace. The office makes available extensive resources regarding local, regional, national, and international legal employment in the public and private sectors, graduate and foreign study, and judicial clerkships.

Washburn graduates enjoy great success in seeking employment. Washburn law school alumni reside in every state in the nation, the District of Columbia, and several foreign countries.

Applicant Profile

Washburn University School of Law
This chart is to be used for general purpose information only. Nonnumerical factors are weighed heavily in all admission decisions.

LSAT Score	3.75 + Apps	Adm	3.50 - 3.74 Apps	Adm	3.25 - 3.49 Apps	Adm	3.00 - 3.24 Apps	Adm	2.75 - 2.99 Apps	Adm	2.50 - 2.74 Apps	Adm	2.25 - 2.49 Apps	Adm	Below 2.25 Apps	Adm	Total Apps	Adm
175-180	0	0	0	0	0	0	0	0	0	0	0	0	0	0	0	0	0	0
170-174	1	1	0	0	0	0	0	0	0	0	0	0	0	0	0	0	1	1
165-169	0	0	1	1	2	2	0	0	1	1	1	1	0	0	1	0	6	5
160-164	8	8	6	6	6	6	5	4	2	1	1	0	0	0	3	2	31	27
155-159	15	14	20	20	12	12	13	13	14	12	11	9	1	0	3	1	89	81
150-154	33	26	40	32	43	29	53	39	44	21	19	8	20	2	12	4	264	161
145-149	22	5	42	5	60	4	67	9	59	6	36	7	21	0	2	1	309	37
140-144	2	0	24	1	37	4	55	3	39	4	21	2	18	0	15	1	211	15
Below 140	4	0	10	0	10	0	21	0	26	0	14	0	15	0	13	0	113	0
Total	85	54	143	65	170	57	214	68	185	45	103	27	75	2	49	9	1024	327

Apps = Number of Applicants
Adm = Number Admitted
Reflects 99% of the total applicant pool.

University of Washington School of Law

William H. Gates Hall, Box 35-3020
Seattle, WA 98195-3020
Phone: 206.543.4078
E-mail: lawadm@u.washington.edu; Website: www.law.washington.edu

ABA
Approved
Since
1924

The Basics

Type of school	Public
Term	Quarter
Application deadline	1/15
Application fee	$50
Financial aid deadline	2/28
Can first year start other than fall?	No
Student to faculty ratio (fall)	11.0 to 1
Does the university offer:	
housing restricted to law students?	No
graduate housing for which law students are eligible?	Yes

Faculty and Administrators

	Total		Men		Women		Minorities	
	Fall	Spr	Fall	Spr	Fall	Spr	Fall	Spr
Full-time	42	43	26	27	16	16	7	7
Other Full-time	5	6	2	3	3	3	0	0
Deans, librarians, & others who teach	5	5	2	2	3	3	1	1
Part-time	16	56	11	39	5	17	0	5
Total	68	110	41	71	27	39	8	13

Curriculum

	Full-time	Part-time
Typical first-year section size	62	0
Is there typically a "small section" of the first-year class, other than Legal Writing, taught by full-time faculty	Yes	No
If yes, typical size offered last year	30	0
# of classroom course titles beyond 1st year curriculum		105

# of upper division courses, excluding seminars with an enrollment:	Under 25	48
	25-49	29
	50-74	7
	75-99	4
	100+	4

# of seminars		13
# of seminar positions available		290
# of seminar positions filled	234	0
# of positions available in simulation courses	208	
# of simulation positions filled	180	0
# of positions available in faculty supervised clinical courses	113	
# of faculty supervised clinical positions filled	92	0
# involved in field placements	174	0
# involved in law journals	108	0
# involved in moot court or trial competitions	72	0
# of credit hours required to graduate	135	

JD Enrollment and Ethnicity

	Men		Women		Full-time		Part-time		1st-year		Total		JD Degs. Awd.
	#	%	#	%	#	%	#	%	#	%	#	%	
African Amer.	7	3.3	7	2.1	14	2.5	0	0.0	5	2.8	14	2.5	2
Amer. Indian	6	2.8	11	3.2	17	3.1	0	0.0	4	2.2	17	3.1	2
Asian Amer.	19	9.0	45	13.2	64	11.6	0	0.0	20	11.0	64	11.6	18
Mex. Amer.	0	0.0	1	0.3	1	0.2	0	0.0	0	0.0	1	0.2	9
Puerto Rican	0	0.0	0	0.0	0	0.0	0	0.0	0	0.0	0	0.0	1
Hispanic	3	1.4	4	1.2	7	1.3	0	0.0	2	1.1	7	1.3	5
Total Minority	35	16.5	68	20.0	103	18.7	0	0.0	31	17.1	103	18.7	37
For. Nation.	3	1.4	15	4.4	18	3.3	0	0.0	6	3.3	18	3.3	6
Caucasian	174	82.1	256	75.3	430	77.9	0	0.0	143	79.0	430	77.9	127
Unknown	0	0.0	1	0.3	1	0.2	0	0.0	1	0.6	1	0.2	5
Total	212	38.4	340	61.6	552	100.0	0	0.0	181	32.8	552		175

Tuition and Fees

	Resident	Nonresident
Full-time	$13,634	$19,934
Part-time	$0	$0

Living Expenses

Estimated living expenses for singles

Living on campus	Living off campus	Living at home
$14,688	$14,688	$7,176

University of Washington School of Law

ABA Approved Since 1924

GPA and LSAT Scores

	Total	Full-time	Part-time
# of apps	2,413	2,413	0
# of admits	502	502	0
# of matrics	181	181	0
75% GPA	0.00	3.84	0.00
25% GPA	0.00	3.47	0.00
75% LSAT	0	166	0
25% LSAT	0	159	0

Grants and Scholarships (from prior year)

	Total		Full-time		Part-time	
	#	%	#	%	#	%
Total # of students	555		555		0	
Total # receiving grants	275	49.5	275	49.5	0	0.0
Less than 1/2 tuition	140	25.2	140	25.2	0	0.0
Half to full tuition	121	21.8	121	21.8	0	0.0
Full tuition	1	0.2	1	0.2	0	0.0
More than full tuition	13	2.3	13	2.3	0	0.0
Median grant amount			$5,500		$0	

Informational and Library Resources

# of volumes and volume equivalents	569,887
# of titles	122,217
# of active serial subscriptions	5,419
Study seating capacity inside the library	389
# of professional librarians	14
Hours per week library is open	89
# of open, wired connections available to students	0
# of networked computers available for use by students	111
# of simultaneous wireless users	500
Require computer?	N

JD Attrition (from prior year)

	Academic	Other	Total	
	#	#	#	%
1st year	0	8	8	4.2%
2nd year	0	0	0	0.0%
3rd year	0	0	0	0.0%
4th year	0	0	0	0.0%

Employment

	Total	Percentage
Employment status known	152	98.7
Employment status unknown	2	1.3
Employed	133	87.5
Pursuing graduate degrees	11	7.2
Unemployed seeking employment	0	0.0
Unemployed not seeking employment	8	5.3

Type of Employment

	Total	Percentage
# employed in law firms	68	51.1
# employed in business and industry	10	7.5
# employed in government	22	16.5
# employed in public interest	8	6.0
# employed as judicial clerks	19	14.3
# employed in academia	5	3.8

Geographic Location

	Total	Percentage
# employed in state	106	79.7
# employed in foreign countries	0	0.0
# of states where employed	13	

Bar Passage Rates

Jurisdiction	Washington		
Exam	Sum 03	Win 04	Total
# from school taking bar for the first time	121	19	140
School's pass rate for all first-time takers	84%	89%	85%
State's pass rate for all first-time takers	71%	79%	74%

University of Washington School of Law

William H. Gates Hall, Box 35-3020
Seattle, WA 98195-3020
Phone: 206.543.4078
E-mail: lawadm@u.washington.edu; Website: www.law.washington.edu

■ Introduction

Established in 1899, the School of Law is part of the main campus of the University of Washington, approximately four miles from downtown Seattle. The university, the largest single campus institution in the western United States, with an enrollment of 33,500 students, offers nearly every discipline for study. The School of Law has 46 full-time faculty members and about 500 JD students. Because of the favorable student-to-faculty ratio, classes are generally small, with frequent opportunities for student-teacher contacts. Each first-year student is usually in at least one class of 30 or fewer students, in addition to the Basic Legal Skills course. The school is a member of the AALS, is approved by the ABA, and has a chapter of the Order of the Coif.

■ Curriculum

The first-year curriculum is prescribed. After that, except for an advanced writing requirement and a class in professional responsibility, all courses in the second and third years are elective. In addition to traditional courses and seminars, advanced students may participate in one of 11 clinics: Innocence Project Northwest, Berman Environmental Law, Mediation, Child Advocacy, Unemployment Compensation, Disability, Immigration, Tribal Court Criminal Defense, Refugee and Immigrant Advocacy, Technology Law and Public Policy, or Low-Income Taxpayer clinic; or in courses in trial advocacy. Judicial, legislative, agency, and public-interest externships are available. Students must also perform 60 hours of public service legal work.

Students are encouraged to rely on their initiative and to develop their own powers of perception. Classroom discussion, in which students participate fully, is one means used to assist this development. Independent research projects, either in the context of a seminar or through individualized study under faculty supervision, are also emphasized. Although it is a state law school, Washington state law is not emphasized unduly. Graduates of the school are prepared to practice law anywhere in the United States or in other common law countries.

■ Special Programs

Concentration tracks are available in Asian law, dispute resolution, environmental law, health law, intellectual property, and international and comparative law.

There are Centers for Advanced Study and Research on Intellectual Property (CASRIP), Indian Law, and Law, Commerce, and Technology.

Students studying for the JD program may take courses in any of the LLM programs during the second and third years. The UW also offers a master's degree in Law Librarianship.

■ Admission Standards

In selecting the entering class, the law school does not make all of its admission decisions solely on the basis of predicted academic performance. Important academic objectives are furthered by classes composed of students having talents and skills derived from diverse backgrounds believed to be relevant to a rich and effective study of law.

About 20 percent of the incoming class are students of color, for whom the school provides student, faculty, and professional mentoring programs.

■ Student Activities

The *Washington Law Review, Pacific Rim Law and Policy Journal,* and *Shidler Journal of Law, Commerce & Technology* are edited and published by students. The University of Washington is consistently among the top scoring moot court teams in the nation.

Through the Student Bar Association and student/faculty committees, students participate in the decision processes of the law school. Student organizations include the American Bar Association/ Law Student Division; American Constitution Society; American Civil Liberties Union; Asian/Pacific American Law Student Association; Black Law Students Association; Center for Human Rights and Justice; Center for Labor and Employment Justice; Christian Legal Society; European Law Initiative; Federalist Society; GreenLaw; Student Health Law Organization; Immigrant Families Advocacy Project; Innocence Project Northwest; International Law Society; Jewish Legal Society; Latino/Latina Law Students Association; Law and Alternative Dispute Resolution; Law Students for Choice; Law Women's Caucus; Military Law Students' Association; Minority Law Students' Association; Moot Court Honor Board; National Lawyers Guild; Native American Law Student Association; Outlaws; *Pacific Rim Law & Policy Journal*; PALS: Parents Attending Law School; Phi Alpha Delta; Phi Delta Phi; Public Interest Law Association; *Shidler Journal of Law Commerce & Technology*; Sports and Entertainment Law Club; Street Youth Legal Advocates of Washington; Student Bar Association; Students for Sensible Drug Policy; Technology Law Society; and *Washington Law Review*.

■ Career Services

The Career Services Office serves as a liaison between students and prospective employers. Firms, agencies,

University of Washington School of Law

and other potential employers are invited to interview at the school and to list job openings in the regularly published placement bulletin. About 80 percent of the graduates choose to remain in Washington state.

■ William H. Gates Hall

The law school moved into its $80 million new facility in September 2003. The new building, named for one of its most distinguished graduates, features the latest technology, including wireless access, to educate lawyers for the twenty-first century.

■ Visitation

The law school invites prospective students to visit a large section first-year class. The schedule can be found at *law.washington.edu/Admissions/Visit.html*.

Applicant Profile

University of Washington School of Law
This grid includes only applicants who earned 120-180 LSAT scores under standard administrations.

LSAT Score	3.75 +		3.50 - 3.74		3.25 - 3.49		3.00 - 3.24		2.75 - 2.99		2.50 - 2.74		Below 2.00		No GPA		Total	
	Apps	Adm	Apps	Adm	Apps	Adm	Apps	Adm	Apps	Adm	Apps	Adm	Apps	Adm	Apps	Adm	Apps	Adm
169-180	27	27	44	43	31	26	17	7	13	2	4	1	2	1	2	2	140	109
166-168	43	42	46	37	35	17	18	2	10	0	4	1	4	0	2	2	162	101
163-165	78	65	96	48	80	14	42	3	18	0	2	0	2	0	6	5	324	135
160-162	85	31	163	30	114	6	61	5	29	1	9	0	4	0	8	2	473	75
157-159	73	15	127	15	119	5	48	1	26	0	10	0	2	0	7	3	412	39
154-156	56	10	80	5	92	2	56	0	17	0	12	1	8	0	8	4	329	22
120-153	66	8	129	3	133	4	95	3	76	0	29	2	14	0	25	1	567	21
Total	428	198	685	181	604	74	337	21	189	3	70	5	36	1	58	19	2407	502

Apps = Number of Applicants
Adm = Number Admitted

Washington and Lee University School of Law

Sydney Lewis Hall
Lexington, VA 24450
Phone: 540.458.8503; Fax: 540.458.8586
E-mail: lawadm@wlu.edu; Website: www.law.wlu.edu

ABA
Approved
Since
1923

The Basics

Type of school	Private
Term	Semester
Application deadline	2/1
Application fee	$50
Financial aid deadline	2/15
Can first year start other than fall?	No
Student to faculty ratio (fall)	11.7 to 1
Does the university offer:	
housing restricted to law students?	Yes
graduate housing for which law students are eligible?	Yes

Faculty and Administrators

	Total		Men		Women		Minorities	
	Fall	Spr	Fall	Spr	Fall	Spr	Fall	Spr
Full-time	31	33	22	25	9	8	4	4
Other Full-time	0	0	0	0	0	0	0	0
Deans, librarians, & others who teach	3	3	2	2	1	1	1	1
Part-time	8	27	7	23	1	4	1	1
Total	42	63	31	50	11	13	6	6

Curriculum

	Full-time	Part-time
Typical first-year section size	58	0
Is there typically a "small section" of the first-year class, other than Legal Writing, taught by full-time faculty	Yes	No
If yes, typical size offered last year	21	0
# of classroom course titles beyond 1st year curriculum	74	

# of upper division courses, excluding seminars with an enrollment:	Under 25	37
	25-49	15
	50-74	9
	75-99	5
	100+	0

# of seminars	20	
# of seminar positions available	298	
# of seminar positions filled	211	0
# of positions available in simulation courses	180	
# of simulation positions filled	180	0
# of positions available in faculty supervised clinical courses	54	
# of faculty supervised clinical positions filled	54	0
# involved in field placements	47	0
# involved in law journals	95	0
# involved in moot court or trial competitions	120	0
# of credit hours required to graduate	85	

JD Enrollment and Ethnicity

	Men		Women		Full-time		Part-time		1st-year		Total		JD Degs. Awd.
	#	%	#	%	#	%	#	%	#	%	#	%	
African Amer.	10	4.4	26	15.0	36	9.0	0	0.0	10	7.8	36	9.0	12
Amer. Indian	1	0.4	2	1.2	3	0.8	0	0.0	1	0.8	3	0.8	1
Asian Amer.	13	5.8	8	4.6	21	5.3	0	0.0	7	5.5	21	5.3	3
Mex. Amer.	1	0.4	0	0.0	1	0.3	0	0.0	0	0.0	1	0.3	0
Puerto Rican	0	0.0	0	0.0	0	0.0	0	0.0	0	0.0	0	0.0	0
Hispanic	3	1.3	0	0.0	3	0.8	0	0.0	2	1.6	3	0.8	1
Total Minority	28	12.4	36	20.8	64	16.0	0	0.0	20	15.6	64	16.0	17
For. Nation.	2	0.9	6	3.5	8	2.0	0	0.0	3	2.3	8	2.0	3
Caucasian	196	86.7	131	75.7	327	82.0	0	0.0	105	82.0	327	82.0	102
Unknown	0	0.0	0	0.0	0	0.0	0	0.0	0	0.0	0	0.0	0
Total	226	56.6	173	43.4	399	100.0	0	0.0	128	32.1	399		122

Tuition and Fees

	Resident	Nonresident
Full-time	$25,771	$0
Part-time	$0	$0

Living Expenses

Estimated living expenses for singles

Living on campus	Living off campus	Living at home
$14,679	$14,679	$1,200

Washington and Lee University School of Law

ABA
Approved
Since
1923

GPA and LSAT Scores

	Total	Full-time	Part-time
# of apps	3,710	3,710	0
# of admits	713	713	0
# of matrics	128	128	0
75% GPA	3.77	3.77	0.00
25% GPA	3.11	3.11	0.00
75% LSAT	167	167	0
25% LSAT	162	162	0

Grants and Scholarships (from prior year)

	Total		Full-time		Part-time	
	#	%	#	%	#	%
Total # of students	389		389		0	
Total # receiving grants	317	81.5	317	81.5	0	0.0
Less than 1/2 tuition	126	32.4	126	32.4	0	0.0
Half to full tuition	179	46.0	179	46.0	0	0.0
Full tuition	11	2.8	11	2.8	0	0.0
More than full tuition	1	0.3	1	0.3	0	0.0
Median grant amount			$13,300		$0	

Informational and Library Resources

# of volumes and volume equivalents	416,341
# of titles	157,793
# of active serial subscriptions	4,114
Study seating capacity inside the library	540
# of professional librarians	7
Hours per week library is open	168
# of open, wired connections available to students	325
# of networked computers available for use by students	78
# of simultaneous wireless users	750
Require computer?	N

JD Attrition (from prior year)

	Academic	Other	Total	
	#	#	#	%
1st year	0	1	1	0.8%
2nd year	0	7	7	5.0%
3rd year	1	1	2	1.6%
4th year	0	0	0	0.0%

Employment

	Total	Percentage
Employment status known	115	99.1
Employment status unknown	1	0.9
Employed	105	91.3
Pursuing graduate degrees	2	1.7
Unemployed seeking employment	3	2.6
Unemployed not seeking employment	5	4.3

Type of Employment

# employed in law firms	52	49.5
# employed in business and industry	7	6.7
# employed in government	12	11.4
# employed in public interest	2	1.9
# employed as judicial clerks	30	28.6
# employed in academia	0	0.0

Geographic Location

# employed in state	26	24.8
# employed in foreign countries	0	0.0
# of states where employed		24

Bar Passage Rates

Jurisdiction	Virginia		
Exam	Sum 03	Win 04	Total
# from school taking bar for the first time	36	3	39
School's pass rate for all first-time takers	78%	100%	79%
State's pass rate for all first-time takers	75%	60%	72%

Washington and Lee University School of Law

Office of Admissions, Sydney Lewis Hall
Lexington, VA 24450
Phone: 540.458.8503; Fax: 540.458.8586
E-mail: lawadm@wlu.edu; Website: www.law.wlu.edu

■ Introduction

Washington and Lee University School of Law, founded in 1849, is located on the historic campus of Washington and Lee University in Lexington, Virginia, approximately three hours southwest of Washington, DC, in the Blue Ridge Mountains. The School of Law is fully accredited by the ABA and is a member of the AALS. Washington and Lee is known for providing its students with an academically rigorous and professionally challenging legal education in an environment characterized by a commitment to students, small classes, a generous student-to-faculty ratio, and a collegial community.

■ The Honor System

The Washington and Lee community is governed by an Honor System that is the foundation for academic and student life at the university. In the School of Law, the Honor System is an integral part of a professional education that fosters a sensitivity to the ethical imperatives of the legal profession. The Honor System means that the library is always open, exams are unproctored, the exam schedule for upper class students is flexible, and some professors choose to give take-home examinations. The Honor System contributes significantly to a law school environment characterized by mutual respect, trust, and collegiality.

■ Curriculum and Clinical Programs

All first-year classes are required. The second- and third-year curriculum is almost entirely elective, and students choose from over 120 upper-class courses. Offerings in corporate and business law, international law, health law, public policy and regulatory reform, and civil and criminal litigation are particularly strong. A wide variety of public interest clinical programs and externships provide students with opportunities for hands-on client contact experience as part of the academic program. Clinics include the Virginia Capital Case Clearinghouse, established to provide research and litigation support to attorneys appointed to represent persons charged with capital crimes or who are appealing a death penalty conviction; the Black Lung Administrative Law Clinic, in which students represent coal miners seeking disability benefits in federal administrative hearings or appeals in federal court; the Community Legal Practice Center, which provides qualified low- and moderate-income Rockbridge area residents legal services in a range of areas including domestic violence, end-of-life planning; and landlord-tenant and government benefits; the Legal Aid Society, providing legal services to indigent clients in domestic relations, and landlord-tenant, consumer, government

benefits, and other civilian matters; the United States Attorney's Program, in which students assist with investigations and trial preparation, pretrial and trial practice, and appeals in federal court; and the Judicial Clerkship Program, which offers students the opportunity to clerk for trial, appellate, juvenile and domestic relations, or federal bankruptcy judges.

■ Student Activities

Students have four journal opportunities: the *Washington and Lee Law Review*, a quarterly journal for scholarly discussion of legal issues; the *Race and Ethnic Ancestry Law Journal*, focusing on legal issues with an impact on racial and ethnic minorities; the *Capital Defense Journal*, reviewing developments in the law of capital punishment; and the *Environmental Law News*, a practitioner-oriented newsletter covering environmental case law and legislation in Virginia and the Fourth Circuit. A variety of moot court and advocacy competitions allow upper-level students to hone advocacy, counseling, negotiation, and trial skills.

Law students also participate in university intramural sports, drama, music, and political programs. Within the law school, students have established numerous groups such as Black Law Students Association, Asian American Law Students Association, Women Law Students Organization, GayLaw, Jewish Law Students Association, Christian Legal Society, Agnostic and Atheist Law Students Organization, Law Families, Federalist Society, American Constitution Society, National Lawyers Guild, and chapters of three national professional fraternities. Practice-oriented groups include the Environmental Law Forum, International Law Society, Tax Law Society, Sports and Entertainment Law Society, Public Interest Law Students Association, and Intellectual Property and Tech Law Society. Student groups foster a rich intellectual environment at the School of Law by presenting programs addressing issues of special concern to their members.

■ Admission and Financial Aid

The School of Law actively seeks a diverse student body whose members are of different religious, racial, ethnic, economic, and geographic backgrounds. The admission process at Washington and Lee is highly individualized. Students are not ranked by any index number, nor is there a weight assigned to any objective or subjective factor presented in the application. The Admissions Committee considers not only the cumulative undergraduate grade-point average, but also trends in grades, the rigor of an applicant's academic program and the quality of the school attended, the LSAT score, extra-curricular activities, community service, evidence of leadership, graduate study, work experience, assessments of recommenders, and any information presented in the applicant's personal statement. An applicant may request an interview with a member of the admission office staff. Applicants are encouraged to visit the school to sit in on classes, tour the facility, and talk with students and faculty.

A generous scholarship endowment allows the School of Law to assist about 60 percent of its students with grant funds. Scholarships may be based on a combination of need and merit or on merit alone.

■ Career Services

Washington and Lee graduates practice in every state and throughout the world. More than 97 percent of the 2003 graduating class was employed within a few months of bar passage. Twenty-five percent of a typical graduating class accepts a judicial clerkship; 50–60 percent enter private practice; the remainder choose careers in business, government, the military or public interest, or pursue an advanced legal degree. More than 70 percent of recent graduates practice outside Virginia.

The Office of Career Services educates students about opportunities in the legal profession and acts as a liaison between students and legal employers. OCS' two counseling professionals hold JD degrees. OCS listed

nearly 800 employment opportunities in the 2003–2004 academic year; listing employers hailed from 43 states and several foreign countries. W&L Law students interview with prospective employers on campus, at fall programs in New York, Dallas, New Hampshire, Delaware, Chicago, Atlanta, and Los Angeles, and at spring programs in Richmond, Williamsburg, and Washington, DC. An active alumni network assists students with contacts in every state.

■ Law Library and Physical Facilities

Sydney Lewis Hall, home of the School of Law, was built in 1976 and expanded in 1991 with the addition of the Lewis F. Powell, Jr. Archives, which house the Supreme Court and professional papers of retired Supreme Court Justice Powell, a graduate of the university's college and law school. Each student is provided his or her own reserved study carrel or office space, which is open 24 hours a day, 365 days a year. Students have access to the library collection on an open-stack basis. The law school makes extensive use of state-of-the-art technology in the library, computer-equipped classrooms, and the moot court room. Law students have access from on or off campus to the library's electronic holdings, catalogs, and database search services.

Applicant Profile

Washington and Lee University School of Law
This grid includes only applicants who earned 120-180 LSAT scores under standard administrations.

LSAT Score	3.75 +		3.50 - 3.74		3.25 - 3.49		3.00 - 3.24		2.75 - 2.99		2.50 - 2.74		2.25 - 2.49		2.00 - 2.24		Below 2.00		No GPA		Total	
	Apps	Adm	Apps	Adm	Apps	Adm	Apps	Adm	Apps	Adm	Apps	Adm	Apps	Adm	Apps	Adm	Apps	Adm	Apps	Adm	Apps	Adm
175-180	1	1	3	3	4	3	2	2	1	1	1	1	0	0	0	0	0	0	0	0	12	11
170-174	26	23	27	25	29	29	21	17	15	6	4	3	2	1	2	1	0	0	1	0	127	105
165-169	152	125	165	120	138	82	100	50	35	8	17	5	6	0	3	0	0	0	1	0	617	390
160-164	309	96	369	43	333	6	181	4	84	7	40	3	11	0	4	0	1	0	9	0	1341	159
155-159	118	5	186	10	182	4	132	6	59	0	26	0	11	1	4	0	0	0	9	0	727	26
150-154	67	2	89	5	135	4	135	4	69	1	22	1	8	0	5	0	1	0	3	0	534	17
145-149	16	2	35	1	45	0	35	1	30	0	14	0	8	0	3	0	1	0	1	0	188	4
140-144	2	0	14	0	18	0	21	0	14	0	16	0	9	0	1	0	0	0	0	0	95	0
135-139	2	0	1	0	7	0	3	0	6	0	5	0	5	0	1	0	0	0	1	0	31	0
130-134	1	0	3	0	0	0	4	0	1	0	2	0	3	0	1	0	1	0	0	0	16	0
125-129	0	0	0	0	1	0	1	0	0	0	1	0	1	0	0	0	0	0	1	0	5	0
120-124	0	0	0	0	0	0	0	0	0	0	0	0	0	0	0	0	0	0	0	0	0	0
Total	694	254	892	207	892	128	635	84	314	23	148	13	64	2	24	1	4	0	26	0	3693	712

Apps = Number of Applicants
Adm = Number Admitted
Reflects 99% of the total applicant pool.

Washington University School of Law

Box 1120, One Brookings Drive
St. Louis, MO 63130-4899
Phone: 314.935.4525; Fax: 314.935.8778
E-mail: admiss@wulaw.wustl.edu; Website: http://law.wustl.edu

ABA
Approved
Since
1923

The Basics

Type of school	Private
Term	Semester
Application deadline	3/1 3/1
Application fee	$70
Financial aid deadline	3/1
Can first year start other than fall?	No
Student to faculty ratio (fall)	13.6 to 1
Does the university offer:	
housing restricted to law students?	Yes
graduate housing for which law students are eligible?	Yes

Faculty and Administrators

	Total		Men		Women		Minorities	
	Fall	Spr	Fall	Spr	Fall	Spr	Fall	Spr
Full-time	46	45	23	23	23	22	4	4
Other Full-time	1	1	0	0	1	1	0	0
Deans, librarians, & others who teach	9	9	7	7	2	2	1	1
Part-time	60	56	45	44	15	12	9	3
Total	**116**	**111**	**75**	**74**	**41**	**37**	**14**	**8**

Curriculum

	Full-time	Part-time
Typical first-year section size	87	0
Is there typically a "small section" of the first-year class, other than Legal Writing, taught by full-time faculty	Yes	No
If yes, typical size offered last year	42	0
# of classroom course titles beyond 1st year curriculum	121	

# of upper division courses, excluding seminars with an enrollment:	Under 25	85
	25-49	30
	50-74	16
	75-99	6
	100+	6

# of seminars		19
# of seminar positions available		313
# of seminar positions filled	281	0
# of positions available in simulation courses		962
# of simulation positions filled	811	0
# of positions available in faculty supervised clinical courses		76
# of faculty supervised clinical positions filled	73	0
# involved in field placements	83	0
# involved in law journals	226	0
# involved in moot court or trial competitions	180	0
# of credit hours required to graduate		85

JD Enrollment and Ethnicity

	Men		Women		Full-time		Part-time		1st-year		Total		JD Degs. Awd.
	#	%	#	%	#	%	#	%	#	%	#	%	
African Amer.	21	4.8	26	8.3	46	6.1	1	25.0	15	6.3	47	6.2	12
Amer. Indian	6	1.4	1	0.3	7	0.9	0	0.0	2	0.8	7	0.9	2
Asian Amer.	42	9.5	29	9.2	71	9.4	0	0.0	24	10.1	71	9.4	19
Mex. Amer.	1	0.2	2	0.6	3	0.4	0	0.0	0	0.0	3	0.4	0
Puerto Rican	1	0.2	0	0.0	1	0.1	0	0.0	0	0.0	1	0.1	0
Hispanic	7	1.6	1	0.3	8	1.1	0	0.0	2	0.8	8	1.1	2
Total Minority	78	17.7	59	18.7	136	18.1	1	25.0	43	18.1	137	18.1	35
For. Nation.	21	4.8	15	4.8	36	4.8	0	0.0	3	1.3	36	4.8	16
Caucasian	275	62.4	214	67.9	486	64.6	3	75.0	156	65.5	489	64.7	194
Unknown	67	15.2	27	8.6	94	12.5	0	0.0	36	15.1	94	12.4	1
Total	441	58.3	315	41.7	752	99.5	4	0.5	238	31.5	756		246

Tuition and Fees

	Resident	Nonresident
Full-time	$33,189	$33,189
Part-time	$0	$0

Living Expenses

Estimated living expenses for singles

Living on campus	Living off campus	Living at home
N/A	$18,500	$8,796

Washington University School of Law

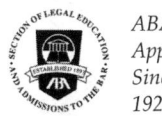

*ABA
Approved
Since
1923*

GPA and LSAT Scores

	Total	Full-time	Part-time
# of apps	3,113	3,113	0
# of admits	802	802	0
# of matrics	238	238	0
75% GPA	3.70	3.70	0.00
25% GPA	3.20	3.20	0.00
75% LSAT	167	167	0
25% LSAT	162	162	0

Grants and Scholarships (from prior year)

	Total		Full-time		Part-time	
	#	%	#	%	#	%
Total # of students	742		737		5	
Total # receiving grants	468	63.1	468	63.5	0	0.0
Less than 1/2 tuition	299	40.3	299	40.6	0	0.0
Half to full tuition	130	17.5	130	17.6	0	0.0
Full tuition	10	1.3	10	1.4	0	0.0
More than full tuition	29	3.9	29	3.9	0	0.0
Median grant amount			$12,000		$0	

Informational and Library Resources

# of volumes and volume equivalents	661,447
# of titles	144,016
# of active serial subscriptions	6,094
Study seating capacity inside the library	485
# of professional librarians	5
Hours per week library is open	120
# of open, wired connections available to students	760
# of networked computers available for use by students	96
# of simultaneous wireless users	600
Require computer?	N

JD Attrition (from prior year)

	Academic	Other	Total	
	#	#	#	%
1st year	0	16	16	6.8%
2nd year	0	0	0	0.0%
3rd year	0	0	0	0.0%
4th year	0	0	0	0.0%

Employment

	Total	Percentage
Employment status known	244	97.6
Employment status unknown	6	2.4
Employed	236	96.7
Pursuing graduate degrees	7	2.9
Unemployed seeking employment	0	0.0
Unemployed not seeking employment	1	0.4

Type of Employment

# employed in law firms	161	68.2
# employed in business and industry	11	4.7
# employed in government	29	12.3
# employed in public interest	15	6.4
# employed as judicial clerks	13	5.5
# employed in academia	1	0.4

Geographic Location

# employed in state	76	32.2
# employed in foreign countries	2	0.8
# of states where employed		33

Bar Passage Rates

Jurisdiction	Missouri			Illinois		
Exam	Sum 03	Win 04	Total	Sum 03	Win 04	Total
# from school taking bar for the first time	88	14	102	53	27	80
School's pass rate for all first-time takers	90%	86%	89%	89%	93%	90%
State's pass rate for all first-time takers	83%	87%	84%	86%	78%	84%

Washington University School of Law

Box 1120, One Brookings Drive
St. Louis, MO 63130-4899
Phone: 314.935.4525; Fax: 314.935.8778
E-mail: admiss@wulaw.wustl.edu; Website: http://law.wustl.edu

■ Introduction

Washington University School of Law offers its students an outstanding legal education in an intellectually challenging and collegial environment. Our faculty members are recognized for their excellent teaching and scholarship and are highly accessible to our students. The School of Law curriculum blends traditional theory with opportunities to participate in a wide variety of clinical programs and cocurricular activities that encourage the development of practical skills and interdisciplinary learning.

■ Library and Physical Facilities

The law school moved into its state-of-the-art facility, Anheuser-Busch Hall, in 1997. While Anheuser-Busch Hall itself appears to be traditional, the latest computing and multimedia technologies are incorporated in its design. Cutting-edge information technology provides students with quick access to the Internet where they can register for courses, view grades, order transcripts, view a photo directory of classmates, access their e-mail, and enhance their legal research capabilities. Wireless connections are available throughout the law school. The law library is the focal point for much of the intellectual activity in the law school. It has a collection of over 600,000 volumes with particularly strong collections in the areas of international law, environmental law, land use planning, urban law, tax law, and Chinese law.

■ Curriculum

Washington University law school offers a traditional, broad-based curriculum that highlights applied lawyering skills. A three-year, full-time course of study leads to the JD degree. All first-year students have half their courses in small sections of approximately 40 students or less. These small classes increase the opportunities for participation in class discussions and individualized teacher-student contact. Second- and third-year students choose their own classes and can tailor them to fit their own particular interests. Students may also opt to enroll in a course from another graduate program at the university and apply the credit toward the JD requirements. In addition, our Center for Interdisciplinary Studies, the Whitney R. Harris Institute for Global Legal Studies, and other school-sponsored conferences and symposia expose our students to a wide range of nationally and internationally renowned legal scholars.

■ Clinical Opportunities

The School of Law's exceptional Clinical Education Program provides law students opportunities to learn professional skills and values by working with clients, attorneys, judges, and legislators under the close supervision of experienced and expert faculty. Every interested student is guaranteed at least one clinical course during his or her second or third year of law school. The School of Law offers a wide variety of clinical courses including Civil Justice, Interdisciplinary Environmental, Civil Rights and Community Justice, Government Lawyering, Criminal Justice, Appellate, Judicial Clerkship and Intellectual Property and Business Formation Legal Clinics. In addition, the Congressional and Administrative Law Clinic, founded in 1977, offers students the opportunity to spend their final semester working in Washington, DC, for a member of the United States Congress, a congressional committee, or a federal administrative agency.

■ Special Degree Programs

Washington University complements its outstanding JD program with many different joint-degree opportunities. In addition to our formal joint-degree programs, students may design their own joint degrees, combining law and another course of study that leads to a master's degree. Joint degrees offered include a JD/MBA, JD/MSW, JD/MHA, JD/MA-Economics, and JD/PhD-Political Science. We are one of only a very few joint-degree programs in the nation combining law with an MA in East Asian Studies. The School of Law also offers LLM programs in Intellectual Property and Technology, Taxation, and US and International Law for international students.

■ Study Abroad Opportunities

The School of Law offers students the opportunity to study abroad for a semester and for international law students to study at our law school. Our students take regular courses in leading international institutions, studying under the legal scholars of the country. Washington University has exchange or study abroad agreements in place with each of the following law schools: Utrecht University, Utrecht, The Netherlands; Inns of Court School of Law, London, UK; The Gerd Bucerius Law School, Hamburg, Germany; Monash University Faculty of Law, Melbourne, Australia; National University of Singapore; Tribhuvan University, Kathmandu, Nepal; Kobe University Graduate School of Law, Japan; and the University of KwaZulu-Natal, Durban, South Africa.

■ Student Activities

The School of Law publishes three student-edited law review periodicals, the *Washington University Law Quarterly*, the *Washington University Journal of Law and Policy*, and the *Washington University Global Studies Law Review*. The Trial and Advocacy Program includes a very active moot court program, mock trial competitions, and competitions in negotiation and client counseling. Students are actively involved in over 40 student organizations, including the Women's Law Caucus, Student Bar Association, Black Law Students Association, Latin American Law Students Association, Asian American Law Students Association, Native American Law Students Association, and OUTLAW (gay and lesbian alliance). Students also participate in a number of volunteer public service projects through student organizations or the school's Public Service Project Program.

■ Public Interest

The School of Law has a longstanding commitment to public service and lawyering in the public interest. In addition to its nine clinics, public interest law is supported in a number of different ways: the Webster Society provides full tuition public interest scholarships; public interest summer stipends provide funding for students engaged in public interest work; a loan repayment assistance program helps graduates beginning their careers in public service positions; a public service director coordinates the Public Service Project; a Director of Public Service Advising is part of the Career Services Office professional staff; and the popular Public Interest Law Speakers Series is offered.

■ Housing

Students find the cost of living in St. Louis is much less than in other large metropolitan areas. There is a wide range of affordable housing available near the School of

Law. For university-owned housing information, students should contact Parkview Properties at 800.874.4330. For privately owned housing, contact Apartment Referral Service at 314.935.5092.

■ Scholarship and Financial Aid

The school offers merit scholarships that are awarded to entering students with exceptional credentials without regard to financial need. Most student aid is in the form of government and privately sponsored loans. Over one-half of the students receive some scholarship assistance; two-thirds receive loans. (Virtually all of those receiving scholarships also receive loans.) The school also offers loan repayment assistance for students who choose qualifying public interest law jobs upon graduation.

■ Career Services

With individual counseling a high priority, each student is assigned one of five attorneys in the Career Services Office as his or her primary contact. The CSO professionals help students investigate and strategize career paths and goals. In addition to providing both on-campus and off-campus interviewing programs, the CSO offers programs on networking and skill development, clerkships, fellowships, researching employers, and a variety of informational sessions on different practice areas. Within six months of graduation, 98 percent of the class of 2003 were employed in 32 different states, the District of Columbia, and two foreign countries.

Applicant Profile

Washington University School of Law
This grid includes only applicants who earned 120-180 LSAT scores under standard administrations.

Good Possibility   Possible   Unlikely

Reflects 98% of the total applicant pool.

Wayne State University Law School

471 W Palmer Street
Detroit, MI 48202
Phone: 313.577.3937; Fax: 313.993.8129
E-mail: lawinquire@wayne.edu; Website: www.law.wayne.edu

ABA Approved Since 1937

The Basics

Type of school	Public
Term	Semester
Application deadline	3/15
Application fee	$50
Financial aid deadline	6/30
Can first year start other than fall?	No
Student to faculty ratio (fall)	20.4 to 1
Does the university offer:	
housing restricted to law students?	No
graduate housing for which law students are eligible?	Yes

Faculty and Administrators

	Total		Men		Women		Minorities	
	Fall	Spr	Fall	Spr	Fall	Spr	Fall	Spr
Full-time	27	26	18	18	9	8	4	3
Other Full-time	4	4	1	1	3	3	0	0
Deans, librarians, & others who teach	6	6	2	2	4	4	2	2
Part-time	20	32	16	26	4	6	0	0
Total	57	68	37	47	20	21	6	5

Curriculum

	Full-time	Part-time
Typical first-year section size	89	31
Is there typically a "small section" of the first-year class, other than Legal Writing, taught by full-time faculty	No	No
If yes, typical size offered last year	0	0
# of classroom course titles beyond 1st year curriculum	74	
# of upper division courses, excluding seminars with an enrollment: Under 25	46	
25-49	22	
50-74	14	
75-99	6	
100+	5	
# of seminars	14	
# of seminar positions available	251	
# of seminar positions filled	145	47
# of positions available in simulation courses	349	
# of simulation positions filled	213	99
# of positions available in faculty supervised clinical courses	52	
# of faculty supervised clinical positions filled	25	17
# involved in field placements	114	38
# involved in law journals	67	15
# involved in moot court or trial competitions	118	17
# of credit hours required to graduate	86	

JD Enrollment and Ethnicity

	Men		Women		Full-time		Part-time		1st-year		Total		JD Degs. Awd.
	#	%	#	%	#	%	#	%	#	%	#	%	
African Amer.	19	5.1	53	15.2	45	8.4	27	14.5	23	11.0	72	10.0	20
Amer. Indian	5	1.3	6	1.7	9	1.7	2	1.1	3	1.4	11	1.5	0
Asian Amer.	12	3.2	24	6.9	24	4.5	12	6.5	9	4.3	36	5.0	7
Mex. Amer.	1	0.3	2	0.6	3	0.6	0	0.0	0	0.0	3	0.4	1
Puerto Rican	0	0.0	0	0.0	0	0.0	0	0.0	0	0.0	0	0.0	1
Hispanic	8	2.1	5	1.4	11	2.0	2	1.1	5	2.4	13	1.8	1
Total Minority	45	12.0	90	25.8	92	17.1	43	23.1	40	19.0	135	18.7	30
For. Nation.	3	0.8	2	0.6	4	0.7	1	0.5	3	1.4	5	0.7	0
Caucasian	317	84.8	245	70.2	424	79.0	138	74.2	146	69.5	562	77.7	190
Unknown	9	2.4	12	3.4	17	3.2	4	2.2	21	10.0	21	2.9	0
Total	374	51.7	349	48.3	537	74.3	186	25.7	210	29.0	723		220

Tuition and Fees

	Resident	Nonresident
Full-time	$12,707	$25,418
Part-time	$6,869	$13,648

Living Expenses

Estimated living expenses for singles

Living on campus	Living off campus	Living at home
$11,544	$19,290	$11,302

Wayne State University Law School

*ABA
Approved
Since
1937*

GPA and LSAT Scores

	Total	Full-time	Part-time
# of apps	1,610	1,434	176
# of admits	556	512	44
# of matrics	210	184	26
75% GPA	3.69	3.71	3.52
25% GPA	3.29	3.32	3.06
75% LSAT	158	158	159
25% LSAT	152	152	151

Grants and Scholarships (from prior year)

	Total		Full-time*		Part-time*	
	#	%	#	%	#	%
Total # of students	745		529		216	
Total # receiving grants	493	66.2	469	88.7	24	11.1
Less than 1/2 tuition	477	64.0	453	85.6	24	11.1
Half to full tuition	10	1.3	10	1.9	0	0.0
Full tuition	5	0.7	4	0.8	1	0.5
More than full tuition	1	0.1	1	0.2	0	0.0
Median grant amount			$2,000		$1,000	

Informational and Library Resources

# of volumes and volume equivalents	605,671
# of titles	246,539
# of active serial subscriptions	4,841
Study seating capacity inside the library	461
# of professional librarians	5
Hours per week library is open	97
# of open, wired connections available to students	151
# of networked computers available for use by students	82
# of simultaneous wireless users	360
Require computer?	N

*Wayne State University Law School does not collect Grants and Scholarship information by full-time or part-time programs.

JD Attrition (from prior year)

	Academic	Other	Total	
	#	#	#	%
1st year	2	4	6	2.7%
2nd year	3	13	16	7.0%
3rd year	0	4	4	1.7%
4th year	0	0	0	0.0%

Employment

	Total	Percentage
Employment status known	183	100.0
Employment status unknown	0	0.0
Employed	164	89.6
Pursuing graduate degrees	2	1.1
Unemployed seeking employment	17	9.3
Unemployed not seeking employment	0	0.0

Type of Employment

# employed in law firms	105	64.0
# employed in business and industry	22	13.4
# employed in government	19	11.6
# employed in public interest	8	4.9
# employed as judicial clerks	7	4.3
# employed in academia	2	1.2

Geographic Location

# employed in state	157	95.7
# employed in foreign countries	3	1.8
# of states where employed		3

Bar Passage Rates

Jurisdiction	Michigan		
Exam	Sum 03	Win 04	Total
# from school taking bar for the first time	160	31	191
School's pass rate for all first-time takers	83%	87%	83%
State's pass rate for all first-time takers	77%	71%	75%

Wayne State University Law School

Admissions Office, 471 W Palmer Street
Detroit, MI 48202
Phone: 313.577.3937; Fax: 313.993.8129
E-mail: lawinquire@wayne.edu; Website: www.law.wayne.edu

■ Introduction

Wayne State University Law School in Detroit is the only public law school in the nation's eighth largest metropolitan area. Located on a beautiful 185-acre campus in the heart of Michigan's legal, economic, and cultural capital, the Law School blends cutting-edge legal theory with real-world practice skills, all at an affordable cost.

Wayne State law graduates serve at the highest levels of law and government. Fully one quarter of Michigan's judges earned their law degrees from Wayne State, as did the managing partners of many of the state's leading law firms and the directors of many of its nonprofit and community organizations. The Wayne State law faculty is made up of dedicated teachers and distinguished scholars known nationally and internationally for their contributions to legal study; they have published articles in the nation's top law journals, authored leading casebooks and treatises, litigated cases in the Supreme Court, and served with distinction in state and federal government. The Law School's location—minutes away from state and federal courts, major law firms, government agencies, and multinational corporate headquarters—offers its students unrivaled opportunities in employment, hands-on experience, and public service.

Established in 1927, Wayne State University Law School is accredited by the ABA, is a member of the AALS, and has a chapter of the Order of the Coif, the national honor society of the legal profession.

■ The Law School's Setting and Facilities

The Law School is a flagship unit of Wayne State University, a major metropolitan research university located in the Cultural Center district about four miles from downtown Detroit. Within blocks of the Law School are the Detroit Public Library, the Detroit Institute of Arts, the Charles H. Wright Museum of African-American History, the Detroit Science Center, and other cultural attractions. State and federal courts are concentrated nearby in the downtown area. The Law School complex sits at the north end of the university's main campus, a leafy urban oasis featuring several famous Yamasaki-designed buildings.

■ The Arthur Neef Law Library

The Arthur Neef Law Library is the second largest academic law library in Michigan and the twenty-third largest in the United States. With over 550,000 volumes, it serves as a major center of legal research in the Detroit and Michigan legal communities and is a designated federal government depository.

The total combined collections of the university's seven libraries exceed 2.9 million volumes. The Detroit Public Library and the library of the Detroit Institute of Arts are within walking distance and lend to Wayne State students and faculty as part of the Detroit Area Library Network.

The majority of the study space in the recently renovated law library makes use of natural light. Comfortable reading tables and wired carrels are available throughout the building. The law library has recently installed a wireless network that can accommodate up to 340 simultaneous computer users; in addition, many study spaces are equipped with communication ports and electrical outlets for the convenient use of notebook computers.

A significant feature of the law library is the new 24-station computer laboratory, featuring personal computers available for the exclusive use of Wayne State law students. Mobile laptop carts are available for use by law students.

■ Clinical and Internship Programs

Wayne State University Law School offers its students a broad range of opportunities for practical legal training through its live-client clinics and its internship programs. The Law School operates five clinics: a Civil Rights Litigation Clinic, a Criminal Appellate Practice Clinic, a Disability Law Clinic, a Free Legal Aid Clinic, and a Nonprofit Corporations and Urban Development Law Clinic. These clinical offerings give students a chance to take first-chair responsibility in a choice of settings while serving the needs of Detroit's urban community. Students also have the chance to serve as interns for state and federal judges, for public prosecutors, for the State Appellate Defender's Office, and for many nonprofit organizations. The work of student interns is supervised directly by practicing attorneys and results in academic credit.

■ Joint-Degree Programs

Students may pursue joint-degree programs in one of five different areas: business administration, dispute resolution, history, political science, and economics. Joint-degree students must be admitted separately to the Law School and to the appropriate master's degree program at the university. Each joint-degree program requires a student to spend his or her first year taking exclusively law courses, followed by two and a half to three years of concurrent studies.

■ Intellectual Property Law Institute

Intellectual property (IP) law and related fields, such as the emerging area of electronic commerce, are among the strengths of the Wayne State law faculty. The Law School offers a tremendous variety of courses and seminars on IP-related subjects. Wayne State law students may take courses at the University of Detroit Mercy and the University of Windsor, just across the river in Canada, through the Intellectual Property Law Institute (IPLI). IPLI, which was created in 1987 as a cooperative effort of these three law schools, offers a rich curriculum for IP-focused students, including courses and seminars in patent, copyright, trademark, computer and related technology, communications and media, and entertainment law. Wayne State law students who enroll in IPLI pay tuition to Wayne State and receive transfer credit for IPLI courses taken at other schools.

■ International Law and Foreign Study Programs

International and comparative law is another area of curricular strength at Wayne State. The Law School offers a wide variety of courses in these fields, taught by faculty with global reputations. In addition, Wayne State law students have the opportunities to enroll in international and comparative law courses at the University of Windsor in Canada; to participate in one of the Law School's two international student exchange programs, at the University of Utrecht in The Netherlands or at the University of Warwick in England; and to apply for a summer study fellowship at the Hague.

■ Student Activities

Student-Edited Law Journals—Wayne State University Law School publishes two student-edited law journals.

The Wayne Law Review, a scholarly legal journal with a nationwide circulation, has been published since 1954 by upper-class law students selected on the basis of superior academic achievement and writing ability. The *Journal of Law in Society* publishes articles drawn from an annual spring symposium on topics such as affirmative action, environmental justice, reparations for slavery, school vouchers, and gentrification. Both journals offer an opportunity for students to enhance their research and writing skills and further their knowledge of the law while earning law school course credit.

Moot Court—Founded in 1949, Wayne State University's Moot Court program, which helps students hone their written and oral advocacy skills, has evolved into one of the most competitive appellate advocacy programs in the country. In 2003, a student team from Wayne State won first place in the 53rd annual National Moot Court Competition, beating out 188 teams from law schools across the nation.

Student Trial Advocacy Program—The Student Trial Advocacy Program (STAP) complements Wayne State's extensive offering of skills courses by providing students with instruction and experience in the techniques of trial litigation. Wayne State STAP members have successfully competed in trial advocacy competitions across the country.

Other Student Organizations—Wayne State University Law School has more than 25 other active student organizations, offering students a diverse mixture of opportunities for study, advocacy, debate, entertainment, and fellowship with their colleagues.

Applicant Profile

Wayne State University Law School
This grid includes only applicants who earned 120-180 LSAT scores under standard administrations.

LSAT Score	GPA																					Total	
	3.75 +		3.50 - 3.74		3.25 - 3.49		3.00 - 3.24		2.75 - 2.99		2.50 - 2.74		2.25 - 2.49		2.00 - 2.24		Below 2.00		No GPA				
	Apps	Adm	Apps	Adm	Apps	Adm	Apps	Adm	Apps	Adm	Apps	Adm	Apps	Adm	Apps	Adm	Apps	Adm	Apps	Adm	Apps	Adm
175-180	0	0	0	0	0	0	0	0	0	0	0	0	0	0	0	0	0	0	0	0	0	0
170-174	0	0	1	1	2	2	0	0	0	0	0	0	0	0	0	0	0	0	0	0	3	3
165-169	9	9	6	4	7	6	3	2	8	8	1	1	1	1	0	0	1	0	0	0	36	31
160-164	26	24	41	40	37	34	23	21	15	5	7	3	6	1	1	0	0	0	0	0	156	128
155-159	38	37	79	77	85	67	69	22	33	3	26	6	9	0	1	0	3	0	6	4	349	216
150-154	37	35	74	41	119	25	110	13	54	9	26	3	17	2	5	0	1	0	8	2	451	130
145-149	16	5	53	9	64	11	77	8	57	7	35	1	16	0	4	0	0	0	11	4	333	45
140-144	6	0	16	0	49	1	46	0	39	0	29	0	17	0	4	0	0	0	6	0	212	1
135-139	1	0	7	0	8	0	18	0	24	0	17	0	11	0	3	0	1	0	4	0	94	0
130-134	0	0	3	0	3	0	5	0	7	0	8	0	4	0	1	0	0	0	1	0	32	0
125-129	1	0	2	0	0	0	0	0	2	0	4	0	2	0	2	0	0	0	2	0	15	0
120-124	0	0	0	0	0	0	0	0	0	0	0	0	0	0	0	0	0	0	1	0	1	0
Total	134	110	282	172	374	146	351	66	239	32	153	14	83	4	21	0	6	0	39	10	1682	554

Apps = Number of Applicants   Adm = Number Admitted   Reflects 98% of the total applicant pool.

West Virginia University College of Law

PO Box 6130
Morgantown, WV 26506-6130
Phone: 304.293.5301; Fax: 304.293.8102
E-mail: wvulaw.admissions@mail.wvu.edu; Website: www.wvu.edu/~law

ABA
Approved
Since
1923

The Basics

Type of school	Public
Term	Semester
Application deadline	2/1
Application fee	$50
Financial aid deadline	
Can first year start other than fall?	No
Student to faculty ratio (fall)	17.5 to 1
Does the university offer:	
housing restricted to law students?	No
graduate housing for which law students are eligible?	Yes

Faculty and Administrators

	Total		Men		Women		Minorities	
	Fall	Spr	Fall	Spr	Fall	Spr	Fall	Spr
Full-time	22	23	15	15	7	8	4	4
Other Full-time	1	2	1	2	0	0	0	0
Deans, librarians, & others who teach	5	5	3	3	2	2	0	0
Part-time	26	16	19	10	7	6	0	0
Total	**54**	**46**	**38**	**30**	**16**	**16**	**4**	**4**

Curriculum

	Full-time	Part-time
Typical first-year section size	75	0
Is there typically a "small section" of the first-year class, other than Legal Writing, taught by full-time faculty	No	No
If yes, typical size offered last year	0	0
# of classroom course titles beyond 1st year curriculum	72	
# of upper division courses, excluding seminars with an enrollment: Under 25	31	
25-49	32	
50-74	10	
75-99	2	
100+	1	
# of seminars	15	
# of seminar positions available	235	
# of seminar positions filled	218	0
# of positions available in simulation courses	239	
# of simulation positions filled	213	0
# of positions available in faculty supervised clinical courses	28	
# of faculty supervised clinical positions filled	28	0
# involved in field placements	6	0
# involved in law journals	38	0
# involved in moot court or trial competitions	34	0
# of credit hours required to graduate	91	

JD Enrollment and Ethnicity

	Men		Women		Full-time		Part-time		1st-year		Total		JD Degs. Awd.
	#	%	#	%	#	%	#	%	#	%	#	%	
African Amer.	8	3.4	10	4.4	18	3.9	0	0.0	6	3.5	18	3.9	11
Amer. Indian	0	0.0	2	0.9	2	0.4	0	0.0	0	0.0	2	0.4	0
Asian Amer.	1	0.4	5	2.2	6	1.3	0	0.0	2	1.2	6	1.3	0
Mex. Amer.	0	0.0	1	0.4	1	0.2	0	0.0	1	0.6	1	0.2	0
Puerto Rican	0	0.0	0	0.0	0	0.0	0	0.0	0	0.0	0	0.0	0
Hispanic	2	0.8	1	0.4	3	0.7	0	0.0	1	0.6	3	0.6	2
Total Minority	11	4.7	19	8.3	30	6.6	0	0.0	10	5.9	30	6.5	13
For. Nation.	2	0.8	3	1.3	5	1.1	0	0.0	2	1.2	5	1.1	0
Caucasian	223	94.5	206	90.4	421	92.3	8	100.0	158	92.9	429	92.5	137
Unknown	0	0.0	0	0.0	0	0.0	0	0.0	0	0.0	0	0.0	0
Total	236	50.9	228	49.1	456	98.3	8	1.7	170	36.6	464		150

Tuition and Fees

	Resident	Nonresident
Full-time	$8,216	$19,342
Part-time	$0	$0

Living Expenses

Estimated living expenses for singles

Living on campus	Living off campus	Living at home
$11,244	$11,244	$11,244

West Virginia University College of Law

ABA
Approved
Since
1923

GPA and LSAT Scores

	Total	Full-time	Part-time
# of apps	752	750	2
# of admits	297	295	2
# of matrics	172	170	2
75% GPA	3.19	3.19	0.00
25% GPA	3.77	3.77	0.00
75% LSAT	149	149	0
25% LSAT	156	156	0

Grants and Scholarships (from prior year)

	Total		Full-time		Part-time	
	#	%	#	%	#	%
Total # of students	468		459		9	
Total # receiving grants	149	31.8	149	32.5	0	0.0
Less than 1/2 tuition	113	24.1	113	24.6	0	0.0
Half to full tuition	8	1.7	8	1.7	0	0.0
Full tuition	7	1.5	7	1.5	0	0.0
More than full tuition	21	4.5	21	4.6	0	0.0
Median grant amount			$2,000		$0	

Informational and Library Resources

# of volumes and volume equivalents	340,725
# of titles	57,904
# of active serial subscriptions	3,221
Study seating capacity inside the library	274
# of professional librarians	5
Hours per week library is open	96
# of open, wired connections available to students	170
# of networked computers available for use by students	43
# of simultaneous wireless users	100
Require computer?	N

JD Attrition (from prior year)

	Academic	Other	Total	
	#	#	#	%
1st year	7	10	17	10.5%
2nd year	0	0	0	0.0%
3rd year	0	0	0	0.0%
4th year	0	0	0	0.0%

Employment

	Total	Percentage
Employment status known	135	94.4
Employment status unknown	8	5.6
Employed	127	94.1
Pursuing graduate degrees	4	3.0
Unemployed seeking employment	1	0.7
Unemployed not seeking employment	3	2.2

Type of Employment

# employed in law firms	66	52.0
# employed in business and industry	8	6.3
# employed in government	12	9.4
# employed in public interest	2	1.6
# employed as judicial clerks	30	23.6
# employed in academia	7	5.5

Geographic Location

# employed in state	107	84.3
# employed in foreign countries	1	0.8
# of states where employed	9	

Bar Passage Rates

Jurisdiction	West Virginia		
Exam	Sum 03	Win 04	Total
# from school taking bar for the first time	112	8	120
School's pass rate for all first-time takers	74%	63%	73%
State's pass rate for all first-time takers	73%	57%	72%

West Virginia University College of Law

PO Box 6130
Morgantown, WV 26506-6130
Phone: 304.293.5301; Fax: 304.293.8102
E-mail: wvulaw.admissions@mail.wvu.edu; Website: www.wvu.edu/~law

■ Introduction

The College of Law, established in 1878, is the oldest professional school in West Virginia. The university is located in Morgantown, WV. Within a 500-mile radius of Morgantown is half of the population of the US and one-third of the population of Canada. The College of Law has been a member of the AALS since 1914 and was fully accredited by the ABA in 1923. The college has had a chapter of the Order of the Coif since 1925.

■ Library and Physical Facilities

The College of Law facility measures 131,966 square feet and provides a spacious learning community for law students. The law center is home to six classrooms, two courtrooms, a distance learning center, financial aid, career services, and a law bookstore. Ample parking at the law center is available by permit for all law students.

The George R. Farmer, Jr., Law Library, a three-story, 32,476-square-foot facility with 40,386 feet of shelving space, is home to the largest law library in the state of West Virginia. The law library is comprehensive in scope with a collection of over 300,000 volumes and equivalents. The library provides access to 42 networked computers, including the Carlin Computer Lab, a 16-computer teaching lab.

The Student Recreation Center is a $34 million, 177,000-square-foot facility complete with two swimming pools, a massive 50-foot climbing wall that stretches up through the center of the three-story building. The center also houses a wellness center, a resource library, a study area, a food-service operation, a small classroom, a meeting/conference room, and socialization areas.

■ Curriculum

Subject to modification, 91 hours are required for graduation. The 31-hour, first-year curriculum, is specified. The second- and third-year programs offer a number of course options and possibilities for concentration.

Students have the option, after being admitted, to request enrollment in the part-time program that offers day-time courses congruently with the full-time program. There is not a separate nighttime track.

■ Student Activities

West Virginia University College of Law has various student organizations. The Student Bar Association is the student government of the school. The *West Virginia Law Review*, the fourth oldest law review in the nation, selects members on the basis of performance during their first year in law school and a writing competition. An active Moot Court Program is conducted at the law school.

■ Opportunities for Minority Students

The College of Law is committed to maintaining a diverse student body by welcoming students who are members of groups traditionally underrepresented in the legal profession. The Meredith Career Services Center assists minority students with securing summer employment through a Minority Clerkship Program. The College of Law also participates in the Southeast Minority Job Fair in Atlanta, a regional job fair that brings together employers and minority students. Student organizations, such as Black Law Students Association, provide additional opportunities for minority students.

■ Placement

Our graduates are employed at the major law firms in West Virginia, are members of the judiciary, and hold important positions in government. They are also in major law firms from New York City to Hong Kong, Rome to Pittsburgh, and San Diego to Richmond. Many graduates also run their own offices and work tirelessly for those who have little or no money but desperately need legal representation. Please visit the Meredith Career Services Center on our website for more information.

■ Admission

The College of Law admits first-year students only in the first (fall) semester. No specific prelaw curriculum is required for admission. The college subscribes to the suggestions on prelaw study in this book and stresses the value of college courses that require extensive analytic skills and writing assignments.

Persons are admitted to the College of Law on the basis of previous academic performance, scores on the Law School Admission Test, personal statements, letters of recommendation, and such other factors that bear upon the potential professional qualifications of the applicant as are determined by the College of Law.

Applications are accepted beginning in September of each year for the class to be admitted in the following August. Those accepted are required to make a deposit of $100 against tuition and fees within a designated period, but not before April 1.

West Virginia University College of Law

■ Expenses and Financial Aid

Although WVU's reasonable tuition and fees are an excellent value, the College of Law recognizes that many students may not be able to afford the full cost of a legal education without financial assistance. Limited funds in the form of tuition waivers, scholarships, and college work-study are available each year through the university. Even if the student has not been accepted to the College of Law, he or she should apply for financial aid by March 1. The Free Application for Federal Student Aid (FAFSA) must be completed in order to receive any financial assistance, including all need-based scholarships. Students must complete the FAFSA each year in order to be considered for financial aid.

More information may be obtained by contacting Joanna Hastings, Financial Aid Counselor, PO Box 6130, Morgantown, WV 26506-6130; phone: 304.293.5302; *joanna.hastings@mail.wvu.edu.*

■ Housing

WVU Law students select from a wide range of living arrangements both on campus and in private housing. Contact the University Housing Office, located in Bennett Tower, Evansdale Residential Complex at 304.293.3621, for information concerning university-owned dormitories and apartments. Information concerning off-campus, privately owned housing may be obtained by calling the Office of Student Affairs in E. Moore Hall at 304.293.5613.

Applicant Profile

West Virginia University College of Law
This grid includes only applicants who earned 120-180 LSAT scores under standard administrations.

LSAT Score	3.75 +		3.50 - 3.74		3.25 - 3.49		3.00 - 3.24		2.75 - 2.99		2.50 - 2.74		2.25 - 2.49		2.00 - 2.24		Below 2.00		No GPA		Total	
	Apps	Adm	Apps	Adm	Apps	Adm	Apps	Adm	Apps	Adm	Apps	Adm	Apps	Adm	Apps	Adm	Apps	Adm	Apps	Adm	Apps	Adm
175-180	0	0	0	0	0	0	0	0	0	0	0	0	0	0	0	0	0	0	0	0	0	0
170-174	1	1	0	0	0	0	0	0	0	0	0	0	1	1	0	0	0	0	0	0	2	2
165-169	0	0	1	1	2	1	0	0	1	1	0	0	0	0	1	0	0	0	0	0	5	3
160-164	11	11	10	10	6	5	1	1	6	3	5	4	2	2	0	0	0	0	1	1	42	37
155-159	17	17	14	13	16	13	20	19	10	4	8	4	2	0	2	2	0	0	1	1	90	73
150-154	31	26	39	28	48	30	38	20	25	5	13	2	15	3	3	1	1	0	2	1	215	116
145-149	19	12	32	14	51	5	45	5	32	4	27	0	9	0	2	0	0	0	3	0	220	40
140-144	15	4	17	6	21	1	25	2	20	0	11	1	9	1	6	0	0	0	3	0	127	15
135-139	3	0	4	0	8	0	6	0	7	0	6	0	3	0	0	0	1	0	0	0	38	0
130-134	1	0	1	0	0	0	0	0	2	0	0	0	0	0	1	0	0	0	1	0	6	0
125-129	0	0	0	0	0	0	0	0	0	0	0	0	0	0	0	0	0	0	1	0	1	0
120-124	0	0	0	0	0	0	0	0	0	0	0	0	0	0	0	0	0	0	0	0	0	0
Total	98	71	118	72	152	55	135	47	103	17	70	11	41	7	15	3	2	0	12	3	746	286

Apps = Number of Applicants
Adm = Number Admitted
Reflects 99% of the total applicant pool.

Western New England College School of Law

1215 Wilbraham Road
Springfield, MA 01119-2684
Phone: 800.782.6665, 413.782.1406; Fax: 413.796.2067
E-mail: admissions@law.wnec.edu; Website: www.law.wnec.edu

ABA Approved Since 1974

The Basics

Type of school	Private
Term	Semester
Application deadline	3/15
Application fee	$50
Financial aid deadline	
Can first year start other than fall?	No
Student to faculty ratio (fall)	18.9 to 1
Does the university offer:	
housing restricted to law students?	No
graduate housing for which law students are eligible?	Yes

Faculty and Administrators

	Total		Men		Women		Minorities	
	Fall	Spr	Fall	Spr	Fall	Spr	Fall	Spr
Full-time	23	25	16	16	7	9	2	2
Other Full-time	5	4	1	1	4	3	2	1
Deans, librarians, & others who teach	3	3	3	3	0	0	0	0
Part-time	18	22	13	13	5	9	0	0
Total	49	54	33	33	16	21	4	3

Curriculum

		Full-time	Part-time
Typical first-year section size		72	53
Is there typically a "small section" of the first-year class, other than Legal Writing, taught by full-time faculty		No	No
If yes, typical size offered last year		0	0
# of classroom course titles beyond 1st year curriculum		84	
# of upper division courses, excluding seminars with an enrollment:	Under 25	62	
	25-49	41	
	50-74	7	
	75-99	1	
	100+	0	
# of seminars		5	
# of seminar positions available		83	
# of seminar positions filled		44	11
# of positions available in simulation courses		329	
# of simulation positions filled		170	94
# of positions available in faculty supervised clinical courses		76	
# of faculty supervised clinical positions filled		61	5
# involved in field placements		25	6
# involved in law journals		30	9
# involved in moot court or trial competitions		15	6
# of credit hours required to graduate		88	

JD Enrollment and Ethnicity

	Men		Women		Full-time		Part-time		1st-year		Total		JD Degs. Awd.
	#	%	#	%	#	%	#	%	#	%	#	%	
African Amer.	10	3.2	18	6.6	10	2.5	18	9.8	6	3.1	28	4.8	8
Amer. Indian	0	0.0	0	0.0	0	0.0	0	0.0	0	0.0	0	0.0	0
Asian Amer.	7	2.3	11	4.0	16	4.0	2	1.1	10	5.1	18	3.1	3
Mex. Amer.	0	0.0	0	0.0	0	0.0	0	0.0	0	0.0	0	0.0	0
Puerto Rican	0	0.0	0	0.0	0	0.0	0	0.0	0	0.0	0	0.0	0
Hispanic	6	1.9	10	3.6	13	3.2	3	1.6	8	4.1	16	2.7	2
Total Minority	23	7.4	39	14.2	39	9.7	23	12.5	24	12.2	62	10.6	13
For. Nation.	7	2.3	12	4.4	17	4.2	2	1.1	6	3.1	19	3.2	3
Caucasian	201	64.6	169	61.7	256	63.8	114	62.0	118	60.2	370	63.2	83
Unknown	80	25.7	54	19.7	89	22.2	45	24.5	48	24.5	134	22.9	29
Total	311	53.2	274	46.8	401	68.5	184	31.5	196	33.5	585		128

Tuition and Fees

	Resident	Nonresident
Full-time	$27,060	$27,060
Part-time	$20,002	$20,002

Living Expenses

Estimated living expenses for singles

Living on campus	Living off campus	Living at home
$15,140	$15,140	$7,200

Western New England College School of Law

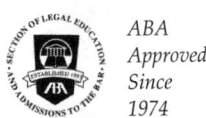

ABA
Approved
Since
1974

GPA and LSAT Scores

	Total	Full-time	Part-time
# of apps	1,641	1,402	239
# of admits	674	565	109
# of matrics	194	141	53
75% GPA	3.38	3.41	3.03
25% GPA	2.76	2.80	2.65
75% LSAT	156	157	152
25% LSAT	150	151	147

Grants and Scholarships (from prior year)

	Total		Full-time		Part-time	
	#	%	#	%	#	%
Total # of students	554		365		189	
Total # receiving grants	288	52.0	229	62.7	59	31.2
Less than 1/2 tuition	159	28.7	110	30.1	49	25.9
Half to full tuition	111	20.0	102	27.9	9	4.8
Full tuition	18	3.2	17	4.7	1	0.5
More than full tuition	0	0.0	0	0.0	0	0.0
Median grant amount			$13,000		$4,000	

Informational and Library Resources

# of volumes and volume equivalents	375,209
# of titles	46,142
# of active serial subscriptions	5,503
Study seating capacity inside the library	401
# of professional librarians	7
Hours per week library is open	103
# of open, wired connections available to students	17
# of networked computers available for use by students	43
# of simultaneous wireless users	253
Require computer?	N

JD Attrition (from prior year)

	Academic	Other	Total	
	#	#	#	%
1st year	9	21	30	13.8%
2nd year	1	0	1	0.6%
3rd year	0	0	0	0.0%
4th year	0	0	0	0.0%

Employment

	Total	Percentage
Employment status known	118	88.7
Employment status unknown	15	11.3
Employed	96	81.4
Pursuing graduate degrees	3	2.5
Unemployed seeking employment	17	14.4
Unemployed not seeking employment	2	1.7

Type of Employment

# employed in law firms	29	30.2
# employed in business and industry	31	32.3
# employed in government	16	16.7
# employed in public interest	5	5.2
# employed as judicial clerks	11	11.5
# employed in academia	3	3.1

Geographic Location

# employed in state	36	37.5
# employed in foreign countries	0	0.0
# of states where employed	20	

Bar Passage Rates

Jurisdiction	Massachusetts			Connecticut		
Exam	Sum 03	Win 04	Total	Sum 03	Win 04	Total
# from school taking bar for the first time	54	12	66	39	25	64
School's pass rate for all first-time takers	59%	92%	65%	64%	72%	67%
State's pass rate for all first-time takers	82%	82%	82%	82%	78%	81%

Western New England College School of Law

Office of Admissions, 1215 Wilbraham Road
Springfield, MA 01119-2684
Phone: 800.782.6665, 413.782.1406; Fax: 413.796.2067
E-mail: admissions@law.wnec.edu; Website: www.law.wnec.edu

■ Introduction

For more than three-quarters of a century, Western New England College School of Law has been preparing men and women to enter the legal profession. We are fully accredited by the ABA and are a member of the AALS. Our 6,000 alumni live in nearly all 50 states and several foreign countries and include judges, private practice attorneys, corporate lawyers, and armed services personnel. We offer both full- and part-time programs and are conveniently located 90 miles west of Boston and 150 miles north of New York City. Western New England College School of Law offers a full, well-rounded curriculum taught by experts and scholars in their respective fields—faculty who are interested in helping you learn and understand the law to your fullest ability. Our first-year section size is purposely among the smallest in the country in order to promote collegiality and effective learning. During the first year, day students are in sections of 50 students, and the evening section features a section of 40 students. These small sections encourage greater class participation and allow the students to interact more with each other and with their professors.

■ Admission and Scholarships

Every application is read by members of the Admissions Committee. All facets of the application are carefully considered, including race, gender, language, educational, social, and economic obstacles overcome in the applicant's pursuit of higher education. We seek candidates with well-developed writing ability and analytical skills who will contribute to classroom discussions and the law school community.

Each year partial- and full-tuition scholarships are awarded to applicants whose credentials and backgrounds suggest they are likely to enrich the life of the School of Law. Several students are awarded full-tuition Oliver Wendell Holmes Jr. Scholarships. The Holmes Scholars usually score in the top 20 percent of the LSAT nationally and finish very near the top of their undergraduate classes.

Partial tuition scholarships are also awarded on the basis of academic merit and to applicants who demonstrate potential for success and who have overcome cultural, economic, societal, physical, or educational obstacles. All admitted applicants receive automatic scholarship consideration. Typically, 40 percent of the entering class receives scholarships of some type.

■ Faculty

The School of Law's 34 full-time faculty members have been educated at many of the nation's most prestigious law schools. All have practiced law prior to joining our faculty, with most having practiced in the fields of law that they now teach. They all share a love of teaching and take pride in their ability to engage students in rigorous law study in a collaborative, collegial environment. They are productive scholars who are consistently praised by our students for their accessibility.

■ Curriculum

All required courses, both day and evening, are taught by full-time faculty members. Some upper-level courses are taught through classroom discussions of judicial decisions and statutes. Others are taught through simulations in which students perform the roles of lawyers in lifelike situations and through clinics where students represent actual clients. Part-time day and evening programs are also available.

Our broad-based curriculum allows students the opportunity to focus their legal studies in many different areas of the law, including tax, public interest, and corporate law. For a full list, please reference our website or bulletin.

We also offer three joint-degree programs:
- JD/MBA (Master of Business Administration) with Western New England College
- JD/MSW (Master of Social Work) with Springfield College
- JD/MRP (Master of Regional Planning) with the University of Massachusetts at Amherst

In the fall of 2005, Western New England College School of Law will offer its first-ever postgraduate degree with the introduction of the Master of Laws (LLM) degree in Estate Planning and Elder Laws. The part-time evening program will prepare both new and established attorneys to meet the growing demand for estate planning and taxation counseling resulting from the aging baby boomer generation.

■ Experiential Learning

Clinics provide an opportunity for upper-class students to represent clients with actual legal problems. Currently, the School of Law offers five different clinics in which students can gain valuable lawyering skills such as legal writing, interviewing, and negotiating. The following clinical opportunities are offered:
- Criminal Law Clinic, students prosecute cases for the Hampden County District Attorney's Office;
- Legal Services Clinic, students work in the office of Western Massachusetts Legal Services, Inc.;
- Consumer Protection Clinic, students work in the City of Springfield's Consumer Protection Program;
- Real Property Practicum, students work with practitioners in the real estate area; and

- Small Business Clinic, students help start-up businesses at the Springfield Enterprise Center's business incubator.

Moot court competitions give our students the opportunity to hone their research, writing, and oral advocacy skills. Western New England College School of Law participates in many national trial, negotiation, and moot court competitions each year. In the past several years our students have been strong competitors and have earned many honors including national champions in 2004 at the First Amendment Moot Court Competition in Nashville, Tennessee; national champions in 2001 at the ABA Negotiation Moot Court Competition, and national finalists in 2002, 2003, and 2004 at the ABA Negotiation Competition.

■ Library, Facilities, and the Area

Our spacious law library with its 370,000-volume collection is enhanced by participation in the New England Law Library Consortium. This arrangement allows students access to 20 academic, 1 private, and 4 government law libraries.

The law school building is located on Western New England College's 215-acre campus in a residential section of Springfield. Ample, on-campus, free parking is available to all students.

Springfield is a small city offering a wide array of recreational, social, and cultural attractions. The Pioneer Valley provides our students with a range of affordable housing options in a variety of settings. Attending the only law school in Western Massachusetts, Western New England College School of Law students have accessibility to a host of externship and clinical opportunities throughout the region.

The School of Law's location places you within reach of a rich and diverse legal community. State and federal courthouses; offices of the Attorney General, District Attorney, and Public Defender; and many small and medium sized law firms in Springfield, Northampton, and nearby Hartford, Connecticut, represent opportunities for externships and full and part-time employment in traditional legal careers.

■ Student Activities

The Student Bar Association (SBA) is the student government of the School of Law. Officers are elected by the student body and representatives are elected by class from both the full-time and part-time divisions. The SBA plays a significant role in the administration of the School of Law with representation at the Faculty Meeting and on the Faculty/Student Committees.

The Multi-Cultural Law Students Association, the Women's Law Association and OUTLaw are some of the student groups created around the common experience and interests of our students. They are important in assisting new students in becoming part of our community, and are active in bringing to the entire student body the experiences and views of their individual communities.

Applicant Profile

Western New England College School of Law
This grid includes only applicants who earned 120-180 LSAT scores under standard administrations.

LSAT Score	3.75 +		3.50 - 3.74		3.25 - 3.49		3.00 - 3.24		2.75 - 2.99		2.50 - 2.74		2.25 - 2.49		2.00 - 2.24		Below 2.00		No GPA		Total	
	Apps	Adm	Apps	Adm	Apps	Adm	Apps	Adm	Apps	Adm	Apps	Adm	Apps	Adm	Apps	Adm	Apps	Adm	Apps	Adm	Apps	Adm
175-180	0	0	0	0	0	0	0	0	0	0	0	0	0	0	0	0	0	0	0	0	0	0
170-174	1	1	2	2	0	0	0	0	0	0	0	0	0	0	0	0	0	0	0	0	3	3
165-169	0	0	0	0	3	3	1	1	0	0	1	1	2	2	0	0	0	0	0	0	7	7
160-164	6	6	7	7	10	10	9	9	8	8	7	7	5	5	0	0	1	1	0	0	53	53
155-159	9	9	31	31	40	40	41	41	31	31	23	22	12	12	8	7	1	0	3	2	199	195
150-154	26	25	39	36	60	59	86	79	65	49	50	37	27	16	18	8	3	1	8	7	382	317
145-149	25	14	45	18	84	25	101	30	90	13	77	6	54	1	19	2	6	0	3	1	505	110
140-144	10	1	19	0	49	0	63	0	64	0	59	0	33	0	12	0	4	0	5	0	316	1
135-139	5	0	8	0	11	0	26	0	22	0	19	0	12	0	5	0	6	0	4	0	118	0
130-134	1	0	1	0	4	0	3	0	9	0	9	0	4	0	3	0	3	0	0	0	37	0
125-129	0	0	0	0	1	0	0	0	0	0	0	0	2	0	2	0	0	0	2	0	7	0
120-124	0	0	0	0	0	0	0	0	0	0	1	0	0	0	1	0	0	0	0	0	2	0
Total	83	56	152	94	262	137	330	160	289	101	246	73	152	36	67	17	24	2	25	10	1629	686

Apps = Number of Applicants   Adm = Number Admitted
Reflects 99% of the total applicant pool.

Whittier Law School

3333 Harbor Boulevard
Costa Mesa, CA 92626
Phone: 714.444.4141 or 800.808.8188, ext. 123; Fax: 714.444.0250
E-mail: info@law.whittier.edu; Website: www.law.whittier.edu

ABA
Approved
Since
1978

The Basics

Type of school	Private
Term	Semester
Application deadline	3/15 10/1
Application fee	$50
Financial aid deadline	5/1
Can first year start other than fall?	Yes
Student to faculty ratio (fall)	19.6 to 1
Does the university offer:	
housing restricted to law students?	No
graduate housing for which law students are eligible?	No

Faculty and Administrators

	Total		Men		Women		Minorities	
	Fall	Spr	Fall	Spr	Fall	Spr	Fall	Spr
Full-time	38	37	22	22	16	15	5	5
Other Full-time	0	0	0	0	0	0	0	0
Deans, librarians, & others who teach	4	4	3	3	1	1	1	1
Part-time	52	29	25	12	27	17	4	6
Total	94	70	50	37	44	33	10	12

Curriculum

		Full-time	Part-time
Typical first-year section size		76	94
Is there typically a "small section" of the first-year class, other than Legal Writing, taught by full-time faculty		No	No
If yes, typical size offered last year		0	0
# of classroom course titles beyond 1st year curriculum		82	
# of upper division courses, excluding seminars with an enrollment:	Under 25	70	
	25-49	35	
	50-74	26	
	75-99	3	
	100+	0	
# of seminars		13	
# of seminar positions available		195	
# of seminar positions filled		100	53
# of positions available in simulation courses		600	
# of simulation positions filled		388	181
# of positions available in faculty supervised clinical courses		51	
# of faculty supervised clinical positions filled		26	13
# involved in field placements		140	55
# involved in law journals		75	36
# involved in moot court or trial competitions	62	20	
# of credit hours required to graduate		87	

JD Enrollment and Ethnicity

	Men		Women		Full-time		Part-time		1st-year		Total		JD Degs. Awd.
	#	%	#	%	#	%	#	%	#	%	#	%	
African Amer.	16	3.4	46	8.6	32	4.8	30	8.9	21	5.4	62	6.2	13
Amer. Indian	3	0.6	3	0.6	2	0.3	4	1.2	1	0.3	6	0.6	1
Asian Amer.	86	18.3	100	18.7	129	19.3	57	17.0	68	17.4	186	18.5	40
Mex. Amer.	24	5.1	29	5.4	34	5.1	19	5.7	21	5.4	53	5.3	8
Puerto Rican	1	0.2	1	0.2	1	0.1	1	0.3	0	0.0	2	0.2	0
Hispanic	29	6.2	42	7.8	48	7.2	23	6.8	18	4.6	71	7.1	12
Total Minority	159	33.8	221	41.2	246	36.7	134	39.9	129	33.1	380	37.8	74
For. Nation.	8	1.7	6	1.1	11	1.6	3	0.9	7	1.8	14	1.4	0
Caucasian	300	63.8	308	57.5	410	61.2	198	58.9	252	64.6	608	60.4	81
Unknown	3	0.6	1	0.2	3	0.4	1	0.3	2	0.5	4	0.4	1
Total	470	46.7	536	53.3	670	66.6	336	33.4	390	38.8	1006		156

Tuition and Fees

	Resident	Nonresident
Full-time	$27,790	$27,790
Part-time	$16,690	$16,690

Living Expenses

Estimated living expenses for singles

Living on campus	Living off campus	Living at home
N/A	$16,160	$16,160

Whittier Law School

ABA
Approved
Since
1978

GPA and LSAT Scores

	Total	Full-time	Part-time
# of apps	3,070	2,446	624
# of admits	1,010	836	174
# of matrics	390	297	93
75% GPA	3.33	3.35	3.34
25% GPA	2.70	2.69	2.74
75% LSAT	154	155	154
25% LSAT	150	150	149

Grants and Scholarships (from prior year)

	Total #	Total %	Full-time #	Full-time %	Part-time #	Part-time %
Total # of students	884		562		322	
Total # receiving grants	346	39.1	289	51.4	57	17.7
Less than 1/2 tuition	250	28.3	212	37.7	38	11.8
Half to full tuition	55	6.2	45	8.0	10	3.1
Full tuition	28	3.2	23	4.1	5	1.6
More than full tuition	13	1.5	9	1.6	4	1.2
Median grant amount			$4,000		$3,000	

Informational and Library Resources

# of volumes and volume equivalents	390,164
# of titles	171,978
# of active serial subscriptions	6,750
Study seating capacity inside the library	386
# of professional librarians	4
Hours per week library is open	103
# of open, wired connections available to students	368
# of networked computers available for use by students	77
# of simultaneous wireless users	0
Require computer?	N

JD Attrition (from prior year)

	Academic #	Other #	Total #	Total %
1st year	61	62	123	31.2%
2nd year	11	7	18	6.9%
3rd year	2	0	2	1.1%
4th year	0	0	0	0.0%

Employment

	Total	Percentage
Employment status known	189	97.4
Employment status unknown	5	2.6
Employed	163	86.2
Pursuing graduate degrees	3	1.6
Unemployed seeking employment	17	9.0
Unemployed not seeking employment	6	3.2

Type of Employment

	Total	Percentage
# employed in law firms	87	53.4
# employed in business and industry	48	29.4
# employed in government	12	7.4
# employed in public interest	8	4.9
# employed as judicial clerks	2	1.2
# employed in academia	6	3.7

Geographic Location

	Total	Percentage
# employed in state	144	88.3
# employed in foreign countries	2	1.2
# of states where employed	14	

Bar Passage Rates

Jurisdiction	California		
Exam	Sum 03	Win 04	Total
# from school taking bar for the first time	144	25	169
School's pass rate for all first-time takers	31%	24%	30%
State's pass rate for all first-time takers	63%	47%	60%

Whittier Law School

3333 Harbor Boulevard
Costa Mesa, CA 92626
Phone: 714.444.4141 or 800.808.8188, ext. 123; Fax: 714.444.0250
E-mail: info@law.whittier.edu; Website: www.law.whittier.edu

■ Introduction

Whittier College is a nationally recognized, independent liberal arts college founded in 1887 in Whittier, California. The Law School, located in the city of Costa Mesa in Orange County, California, was established in 1966. Orange County, ranked among the top business centers in the United States, is home to over 10,000 lawyers, more lawyers than half the states in the nation. Ideally situated between Los Angeles County and San Diego County, the Law School enjoys the vibrant economies each area produces as well as within Orange County. The Law School is 30 miles south of downtown Los Angeles, 100 miles north of San Diego, and minutes away from the local beach cities such as Huntington Beach and Newport Beach.

The Whittier tradition stresses concern for individual students' intellectual and ethical development. This tradition is reflected in admission practices stressing diversity, a small student-to-faculty ratio, small elective classes, and individual student counseling and placement services. Whittier faculty members recognize that their teaching obligation includes considerable interaction with students.

■ Accelerated and Part-Time Programs

In addition to the traditional three year full-time program, the JD can also be completed in four years, including two summer sessions, in the flexible day or evening programs. First- and second-year part-time students generally attend classes three days a week. Standards for admission and retention are identical for all students, and the full-time faculty serves both programs.

To accommodate students who want to accelerate their law school career, the Law School offers the Spring Admission program beginning in January. Students enroll in a schedule of day and evening courses that enable them to complete their degree in two and one-half years.

■ Admission and Scholarships

Whittier Law School is nationally recognized as one of the most ethnically diverse law school student bodies in the country and is committed to maintaining a diverse student body. In addition to the LSAT score and undergraduate GPA, subjective factors such as undergraduate school, major, graduate work, ethnic and economic background, work experience, and personal accomplishments are considered. Applicants are encouraged to discuss these factors in their written personal statements.

The admission office automatically considers all applicants for merit-based scholarships.

■ Special Programs

Center for Children's Rights—The center enrolls up to 20 students yearly who receive fellowships and summer stipends to prepare for careers in children's rights advocacy. Fellows participate in special classes, symposia, and externships. The center also sponsors the National Juvenile Law Moot Court Competition.

Center for Intellectual Property Law—The center provides students and practitioners with academic instruction in intellectual property law, including Patent Law, Trademark Law, Copyright Law, Internet Law, and Entertainment Law. The cornerstones of the center are the Certificate Program, the Summer Institute, and the Distinguished Speaker Series. The center also awards IP Fellowships to incoming students enrolled in an IP-oriented legal writing program.

Center for International and Comparative Law—The center allows students to participate in a specialized legal writing course, attend the International Law Symposium and Colloquia series, and receive a certificate by enrolling in courses offered through the center. The center also awards CICL Fellowships to incoming students enrolled in an international law oriented legal writing program.

Clinics—Whittier Law School boasts five clinics: the Children's Advocacy Clinic, the Special Education Clinic, the Family Violence Clinic, the Health Care Access Clinic, and the "clientless" Legal Policy Clinic.

Exchange Programs in France and Spain—Students with some knowledge of French or Spanish can spend one semester at the University of Paris X in Nanterre, France, or the University of Cantabria in Santander, Spain, or the University of Seville, Spain.

Summer Abroad Programs—The Law School offers summer study abroad programs at the prestigious Bar-Ilan University in Tel Aviv, Israel; the University of Cantabria in Santander, Spain; the University of Toulouse in Toulouse, France; and Sun Yat-sen University in Zhuhai, China. Additionally, a tentative program in Amsterdam, Netherlands, is scheduled for Summer 2005.

LLM Degree in US Legal Studies for Foreign Lawyers—Foreign lawyers admitted to the LLM program may enroll in any course offered in the regular JD program. Applicants must have a degree in law from a recognized foreign university and must demonstrate their proficiency in English.

Academic Success Program—The program, administered by a full-time director, allows students to participate in workshops, small seminars, and individual sessions all designed to teach students skills essential for law school success. Also, students may take part in a first-year summer program to enhance basic study skills and a 13-week Bar Exam Preparation Program.

■ Library and Physical Facilities

Now in its fourth decade, Whittier Law School has established a permanent home in the city of Costa Mesa on a beautiful 15-acre campus with exceptional facilities, including the largest academic law research library in the region. The Law School is comprised of four completely handicap accessible buildings totaling 130,000 square feet and offers plentiful on-site parking.

With over 380,000 volumes, the library has a rapidly growing legal research collection and serves as a state and federal depository. Three student computer labs support a variety of software to aid students with computer-assisted instruction, online legal research, and Internet access. Numerous conference rooms are available for group study. The entire facility is equipped with Internet access for individual study.

■ Student Activities

The *Whittier Law Review*-is open to students on the bashs of grades and a writing competition. The *Review* publishes the annual Health Law and International Law Symposia.

The *Whittier Journal of Child and Family Advocacy*, a student-run scholarly publication focusing on topics related to juvenile and family law, is one of the few journals of its kind in the nation.

Members of the Moot Court Honors Board and the Trial Advocacy Honors Board utilize written and oral advocacy skills to represent the Law School in regional and national trial and appellate advocacy competitions.

The Student Bar Association's activities include publication of the school newspaper, support of various social functions, and participation in student-faculty committees for school governance. Numerous other student organizations represent various ethnic groups and legal specialties.

■ Externships and Career Services

Whittier Law School provides assistance to students and alumni in obtaining clerkships, externships, and attorney positions. The Law School offers a variety of externships with trial and appellate judges, governmental agencies, and public interest organizations. The Career Services Office assists in résumé building exercises, career goal identification, and career planning strategies. Additional services include on-campus interviews, mentor program, panels and symposia on career-related topics, student newsletter, a comprehensive library of career resources, and mock interview program.

Whittier Law School alumni, approximately 4,000 strong, work in 48 states and 14 nations across a multitude of fields within and outside the legal community.

Applicant Profile

Whittier Law School
This grid includes only applicants who earned 120-180 LSAT scores under standard administrations.

LSAT Score	3.75 +		3.50 - 3.74		3.25 - 3.49		3.00 - 3.24		2.75 - 2.99		2.50 - 2.74		2.25 - 2.49		2.00 - 2.24		Below 2.00		No GPA		Total	
	Apps	Adm	Apps	Adm	Apps	Adm	Apps	Adm	Apps	Adm	Apps	Adm	Apps	Adm	Apps	Adm	Apps	Adm	Apps	Adm	Apps	Adm
175-180	0	0	0	0	0	0	0	0	0	0	0	0	0	0	0	0	0	0	0	0	0	0
170-174	0	0	1	1	0	0	1	1	0	0	0	0	0	0	1	0	0	0	0	0	3	2
165-169	1	0	2	2	2	2	3	2	4	3	1	1	1	1	0	0	0	0	0	0	14	11
160-164	7	7	15	14	18	13	18	18	12	9	10	9	5	3	1	1	0	0	1	1	87	75
155-159	19	18	33	32	61	49	63	51	67	52	37	28	25	20	8	5	4	2	5	5	322	262
150-154	31	22	87	71	148	124	134	99	140	87	90	50	54	29	21	7	2	0	7	3	714	492
145-149	29	4	84	24	134	22	172	32	161	17	108	5	65	4	18	1	7	0	15	3	793	112
140-144	6	0	43	0	78	1	109	0	98	0	75	1	55	0	22	0	4	0	6	0	496	2
135-139	5	0	13	0	18	0	37	0	41	0	33	0	19	0	4	0	1	0	7	0	178	0
130-134	1	0	1	0	5	0	4	0	7	0	10	0	9	0	7	0	5	0	4	0	53	0
125-129	0	0	0	0	0	0	1	0	2	0	1	0	3	0	2	0	0	0	0	0	9	0
120-124	0	0	0	0	0	0	0	0	0	0	0	0	0	0	0	0	0	0	0	0	0	0
Total	99	51	279	144	464	211	542	203	532	168	365	94	236	57	84	14	23	2	45	12	2669	956

Apps = Number of Applicants
Adm = Number Admitted
Reflects 99% of the total applicant pool.

Widener University School of Law—Delaware

4601 Concord Pike, PO Box 7474
Wilmington, DE 19803-0474
Phone: 302.477.2162, Fax: 302.477.2224
E-mail: law.admissions@law.widener.edu; Website: www.law.widener.edu

*ABA
Approved
Since
1975*

The Basics

Type of school	Private
Term	Semester
Application deadline	5/15
Application fee	$60
Financial aid deadline	4/15
Can first year start other than fall?	Yes
Student to faculty ratio (fall)	20.1 to 1
Does the university offer:	
housing restricted to law students?	Yes
graduate housing for which law students are eligible?	Yes

Faculty and Administrators

	Total		Men		Women		Minorities	
	Fall	Spr	Fall	Spr	Fall	Spr	Fall	Spr
Full-time	41	41	26	26	15	15	2	2
Other Full-time	10	10	1	1	9	9	3	3
Deans, librarians, & others who teach	12	11	5	4	7	7	0	0
Part-time	47	64	33	45	14	19	0	3
Total	**110**	**126**	**65**	**76**	**45**	**50**	**5**	**8**

Curriculum

	Full-time	Part-time
Typical first-year section size	80	60
Is there typically a "small section" of the first-year class, other than Legal Writing, taught by full-time faculty	Yes	No
If yes, typical size offered last year	67	0
# of classroom course titles beyond 1st year curriculum		124
# of upper division courses, excluding seminars with an enrollment: Under 25		200
25-49		45
50-74		24
75-99		9
100+		3
# of seminars		30
# of seminar positions available		600
# of seminar positions filled	212	121
# of positions available in simulation courses		767
# of simulation positions filled	358	242
# of positions available in faculty supervised clinical courses		108
# of faculty supervised clinical positions filled	74	34
# involved in field placements	40	25
# involved in law journals	64	20
# involved in moot court or trial competitions	64	6
# of credit hours required to graduate		87

JD Enrollment and Ethnicity

	Men		Women		Full-time		Part-time		1st-year		Total		JD Degs. Awd.
	#	%	#	%	#	%	#	%	#	%	#	%	
African Amer.	27	4.5	39	7.1	25	3.7	41	8.7	27	6.9	66	5.7	11
Amer. Indian	1	0.2	0	0.0	0	0.0	1	0.2	0	0.0	1	0.1	0
Asian Amer.	28	4.6	28	5.1	39	5.7	17	3.6	30	7.7	56	4.9	7
Mex. Amer.	0	0.0	0	0.0	0	0.0	0	0.0	0	0.0	0	0.0	0
Puerto Rican	0	0.0	0	0.0	0	0.0	0	0.0	0	0.0	0	0.0	0
Hispanic	4	0.7	8	1.5	8	1.2	4	0.9	5	1.3	12	1.0	10
Total Minority	60	10.0	75	13.7	72	10.6	63	13.4	62	15.9	135	11.7	28
For. Nation.	6	1.0	2	0.4	1	0.1	7	1.5	6	1.5	8	0.7	0
Caucasian	433	71.8	377	68.9	499	73.3	311	66.3	266	68.0	810	70.4	152
Unknown	104	17.2	93	17.0	109	16.0	88	18.8	57	14.6	197	17.1	63
Total	603	52.4	547	47.6	681	59.2	469	40.8	391	34.0	1150		243

Tuition and Fees

	Resident	Nonresident
Full-time	$26,870	$26,870
Part-time	$20,170	$20,170

Living Expenses

Estimated living expenses for singles

Living on campus	Living off campus	Living at home
$13,240	$13,240	$8,740

Widener University School of Law—Delaware

ABA
Approved
Since
1975

GPA and LSAT Scores

	Total	Full-time	Part-time
# of apps	2,629	1,939	690
# of admits	1,101	764	337
# of matrics	391	221	170
75% GPA	3.41	3.42	3.41
25% GPA	2.79	2.84	2.71
75% LSAT	154	155	153
25% LSAT	150	151	148

Grants and Scholarships (from prior year)

	Total		Full-time		Part-time	
	#	%	#	%	#	%
Total # of students	1,144		663		481	
Total # receiving grants	276	24.1	213	32.1	63	13.1
Less than 1/2 tuition	217	19.0	170	25.6	47	9.8
Half to full tuition	44	3.8	29	4.4	15	3.1
Full tuition	14	1.2	13	2.0	1	0.2
More than full tuition	1	0.1	1	0.2	0	0.0
Median grant amount			$3,000		$5,000	

Informational and Library Resources

# of volumes and volume equivalents	393,395
# of titles	70,828
# of active serial subscriptions	4,635
Study seating capacity inside the library	432
# of professional librarians	10
Hours per week library is open	107
# of open, wired connections available to students	75
# of networked computers available for use by students	112
# of simultaneous wireless users	250
Require computer?	N

JD Attrition (from prior year)

	Academic	Other	Total	
	#	#	#	%
1st year	22	60	82	17.6%
2nd year	10	1	11	3.2%
3rd year	0	0	0	0.0%
4th year	0	0	0	0.0%

Employment

	Total	Percentage
Employment status known	263	90.4
Employment status unknown	28	9.6
Employed	221	84.0
Pursuing graduate degrees	5	1.9
Unemployed seeking employment	29	11.0
Unemployed not seeking employment	8	3.0

Type of Employment

# employed in law firms	79	35.7
# employed in business and industry	45	20.4
# employed in government	32	14.5
# employed in public interest	0	0.0
# employed as judicial clerks	43	19.5
# employed in academia	4	1.8

Geographic Location

# employed in state	54	24.4
# employed in foreign countries	0	0.0
# of states where employed	7	

Bar Passage Rates

Jurisdiction	Pennsylvania			New Jersey		
Exam	Sum 03	Win 04	Total	Sum 03	Win 04	Total
# from school taking bar for the first time	164	45	209	151	28	179
School's pass rate for all first-time takers	62%	44%	58%	74%	71%	74%
State's pass rate for all first-time takers	78%	66%	76%	76%	59%	73%

Widener University School of Law—Harrisburg

3800 Vartan Way, PO Box 69381
Harrisburg, PA 17106-9381
Phone: 717.541.3903; Fax: 717.541.3999
E-mail: law.admissions@law.widener.edu; Website: www.law.widener.edu

ABA Approved Since 1994

The Basics

Type of school	Private
Term	Semester
Application deadline	5/15
Application fee	$60
Financial aid deadline	4/15
Can first year start other than fall?	No
Student to faculty ratio (fall)	19.9 to 1
Does the university offer:	
housing restricted to law students?	No
graduate housing for which law students are eligible?	No

Faculty and Administrators

	Total		Men		Women		Minorities	
	Fall	Spr	Fall	Spr	Fall	Spr	Fall	Spr
Full-time	19	21	12	13	7	8	0	1
Other Full-time	2	2	0	0	2	2	0	0
Deans, librarians, & others who teach	4	4	1	1	3	3	0	0
Part-time	18	26	13	19	5	7	1	0
Total	43	53	26	33	17	20	1	1

Curriculum

		Full-time	Part-time
Typical first-year section size		70	50
Is there typically a "small section" of the first-year class, other than Legal Writing, taught by full-time faculty		No	No
If yes, typical size offered last year		0	0
# of classroom course titles beyond 1st year curriculum		58	
# of upper division courses, excluding seminars with an enrollment:	Under 25	50	
	25-49	20	
	50-74	14	
	75-99	1	
	100+	0	
# of seminars		5	
# of seminar positions available		100	
# of seminar positions filled		27	25
# of positions available in simulation courses		200	
# of simulation positions filled		120	64
# of positions available in faculty supervised clinical courses		60	
# of faculty supervised clinical positions filled	23	10	
# involved in field placements		11	9
# involved in law journals		27	2
# involved in moot court or trial competitions		15	5
# of credit hours required to graduate		87	

JD Enrollment and Ethnicity

	Men		Women		Full-time		Part-time		1st-year		Total		JD Degs. Awd.
	#	%	#	%	#	%	#	%	#	%	#	%	
African Amer.	4	1.5	7	2.9	7	2.1	4	2.3	0	0.0	11	2.1	2
Amer. Indian	0	0.0	1	0.4	0	0.0	1	0.6	1	0.5	1	0.2	0
Asian Amer.	7	2.6	11	4.6	11	3.2	7	4.1	7	3.8	18	3.5	0
Mex. Amer.	0	0.0	0	0.0	0	0.0	0	0.0	0	0.0	0	0.0	0
Puerto Rican	0	0.0	0	0.0	0	0.0	0	0.0	0	0.0	0	0.0	0
Hispanic	4	1.5	7	2.9	6	1.8	5	2.9	5	2.7	11	2.1	2
Total Minority	15	5.5	26	10.9	24	7.0	17	9.9	13	7.0	41	8.0	4
For. Nation.	2	0.7	0	0.0	1	0.3	1	0.6	1	0.5	2	0.4	0
Caucasian	197	71.9	173	72.4	246	72.1	124	72.1	139	74.7	370	72.1	58
Unknown	60	21.9	40	16.7	70	20.5	30	17.4	33	17.7	100	19.5	23
Total	274	53.4	239	46.6	341	66.5	172	33.5	186	36.3	513		85

Tuition and Fees

	Resident	Nonresident
Full-time	$26,870	$26,870
Part-time	$20,170	$20,170

Living Expenses

Estimated living expenses for singles

Living on campus	Living off campus	Living at home
$13,240	$13,240	$8,740

Widener University School of Law—Harrisburg

ABA
Approved
Since
1994

GPA and LSAT Scores

	Total	Full-time	Part-time
# of apps	964	779	185
# of admits	408	309	99
# of matrics	186	132	54
75% GPA	3.50	3.52	3.48
25% GPA	2.86	2.89	2.75
75% LSAT	153	152	153
25% LSAT	149	149	150

Grants and Scholarships (from prior year)

	Total		Full-time		Part-time	
	#	%	#	%	#	%
Total # of students	493		310		183	
Total # receiving grants	103	20.9	82	26.5	21	11.5
Less than 1/2 tuition	87	17.6	69	22.3	18	9.8
Half to full tuition	8	1.6	6	1.9	2	1.1
Full tuition	8	1.6	7	2.3	1	0.5
More than full tuition	0	0.0	0	0.0	0	0.0
Median grant amount			$3,000		$1,500	

Informational and Library Resources

# of volumes and volume equivalents	206,115
# of titles	26,756
# of active serial subscriptions	3,503
Study seating capacity inside the library	341
# of professional librarians	4
Hours per week library is open	106
# of open, wired connections available to students	10
# of networked computers available for use by students	52
# of simultaneous wireless users	100
Require computer?	N

JD Attrition (from prior year)

	Academic	Other	Total	
	#	#	#	%
1st year	12	25	37	20.0%
2nd year	2	4	6	3.5%
3rd year	1	0	1	1.0%
4th year	0	0	0	0.0%

Employment

	Total	Percentage
Employment status known	100	99.0
Employment status unknown	1	1.0
Employed	88	88.0
Pursuing graduate degrees	1	1.0
Unemployed seeking employment	10	10.0
Unemployed not seeking employment	1	1.0

Type of Employment

# employed in law firms	35	39.8
# employed in business and industry	11	12.5
# employed in government	21	23.9
# employed in public interest	0	0.0
# employed as judicial clerks	20	22.7
# employed in academia	0	0.0

Geographic Location

# employed in state	60	68.2
# employed in foreign countries	0	0.0
# of states where employed	7	

Bar Passage Rates

Jurisdiction	Pennsylvania		
Exam	Sum 03	Win 04	Total
# from school taking bar for the first time	77	13	90
School's pass rate for all first-time takers	70%	54%	68%
State's pass rate for all first-time takers	78%	66%	76%

Widener University School of Law

4601 Concord Pike, PO Box 7474, Wilmington, DE 19803-0474, Phone: 302.477.2162; Fax: 302.477.2224
3800 Vartan Way, PO Box 69381, Harrisburg, PA 17106-9381; Phone: 717.541.3903; Fax: 717.541.3999
E-mail: law.admissions@law.widener.edu; Website: www.law.widener.edu

■ Introduction

Widener University School of Law is unique among American law schools. Widener has two campuses—one in Wilmington, Delaware, the corporate and banking center of the United States, and the other in Harrisburg, Pennsylvania, the state capital and a major center of government and commerce. Each campus offers a comprehensive curriculum of basic and advanced courses complemented by one of the most extensive clinical and skills programs in the country. The Harrisburg campus features a unique admission and academic cooperative program with the Pennsylvania State System of Higher Education.

Widener's first-year curriculum provides greater emphasis on individual work in legal writing and more concentrated study in courses essential to current developments in legal practice. The intensity of study throughout the curriculum is balanced by the strong commitment of faculty members to personal attention and individual counseling so that all students will be encouraged to fulfill their potential. The school is a member of the AALS and is accredited by the ABA.

■ Library and Physical Facilities

The Legal Information Center houses one of the most significant legal collections in the region. The combined collections of the Delaware and Harrisburg campuses exceed 600,000 volumes. The library is a selective depository for United States government documents.

The attractive 40-acre Delaware campus is located in the heart of the beautiful Brandywine River Valley. The law building houses the Legal Information Center, state-of-the-art computer facilities, faculty offices, traditional and technologically enhanced classrooms, Delaware Volunteer Legal Services offices, and the Ruby R. Vale Moot Courtroom. The scenic 21-acre Harrisburg campus is located in three modern buildings among the foothills of the Blue Ridge Mountains. The contemporary complex is located within minutes of the state capital.

■ Special Programs and Institutes

Widener is a leader in developing a coordinated lawyering skills program. The program includes clinical practice, externship placements, and comprehensive simulations.

Clinics are designed to permit students to represent actual clients under the supervision of the clinic director before courts and administrative boards. Widener operates Environmental Law, Criminal Defense, Delaware Civil, Pennsylvania Civil, and Harrisburg Civil Clinics. The Veterans Assistance Program provides representation to disabled veterans and their dependents. A large number of supervised externships permit students to work as lawyers-in-training with state and county government agencies and nonprofit corporations. An extensive judicial externship program places students with state and federal courts at both the trial and appellate levels in DC, Delaware, Maryland, New Jersey, Pennsylvania, and Virginia. Additional public interest service opportunities are also available.

Widener offers certificate programs for specialized study in health law, law and government, business organizations law, and trial advocacy.

The Health Law Institute on the Delaware campus provides research, policy analysis, and specialty education for those seeking expertise in the area of health law. The Law and Government Institute on the Harrisburg campus provides hands-on experience with the operation and structure of government and practice before government agencies. The Institute of Delaware Corporate Law on the Delaware campus provides a fundamental knowledge of business law through participation in the Business Organizations Law concentration that serves as a predicate to advanced practice in business and corporate law. The Trial Advocacy Institute on the Delaware campus provides extensive litigation skills essential to being a competent, professionally responsible trial advocate. Additionally, both campuses offer a seven-day Intensive Trial Advocacy Program supervised by outstanding local trial lawyers and judges.

Widener offers four joint-degree programs. The JD/MBA is offered in conjunction with the university's School of Business Administration. The JD/PsyD is offered in conjunction with the university's Institute for Graduate Clinical Psychology. The JD/MSLS is offered in conjunction with Clarion University of Pennsylvania. The JD/MMP is offered in conjunction with The University of Delaware.

■ International Law Programs

Widener students have the opportunity to study international and comparative law while living abroad. Widener offers summer-abroad programs in Nairobi, Kenya; Geneva, Switzerland; Sydney, Australia; and Venice, Italy.

■ Student Activities

Selected Delaware students publish *The Delaware Journal of Corporate Law* and the *Widener Law Review*. Selected Harrisburg students publish the *Widener Law Journal*. Students at both campuses compete in regional and national interschool moot court and trial competitions.

Student organizations provide opportunities for intra-scholastic and interscholastic competitions, public service, and association with others who share the same interests.

■ Admission

While there are no fixed admission criteria, great weight is given to the applicant's LSAT score and undergraduate grade-point average. The Admissions Committee carefully considers an applicant's personal statement. Graduate degrees, writing samples, extracurricular activities, and community and professional service may enhance the application. The law school encourages those with diverse backgrounds to apply.

Applications for admission must be received by May 15. Admission decisions are made on a rolling basis, and applicants are encouraged to apply early.

Each summer, Widener conducts the Trial Admissions Program (TAP) for a small number of carefully selected applicants who show potential for success in law school despite a relatively low score on the LSAT or a lower undergraduate grade-point average. TAP is a conditional admittance program. Participants who successfully complete the six-week program are offered admission to the fall entering class.

■ Financial Aid

The Office of Financial Aid works with any student wishing assistance in finding appropriate sources of funding. Additionally, all applicants are considered for Widener's merit- and need-based scholarships.

■ Career Development

The Career Development Office is strongly committed to helping students obtain the positions that best suit their individual needs and ambitions.

Widener's placement statistics evidence its success in helping graduates find a niche in the contemporary job market. Widener alumni have become judges in Delaware, New Jersey, New York and Pennsylvania; members of the legislature; partners in major regional law firms; hospital administrators; legal educators; and broadcast journalists.

Applicant Profile

Widener University School of Law
This grid includes only applicants who earned 120-180 LSAT scores under standard administrations.

LSAT Score	GPA 3.75 +		3.50 - 3.74		3.25 - 3.49		3.00 - 3.24		2.75 - 2.99		2.50 - 2.74		2.25 - 2.49		2.00 - 2.24		Below 2.00		No GPA		Total	
	Apps	Adm	Apps	Adm	Apps	Adm	Apps	Adm	Apps	Adm	Apps	Adm	Apps	Adm	Apps	Adm	Apps	Adm	Apps	Adm	Apps	Adm
175-180	0	0	0	0	0	0	0	0	0	0	0	0	0	0	0	0	0	0	0	0	0	0
170-174	2	2	1	1	0	0	0	0	0	0	0	0	1	1	0	0	0	0	0	0	4	4
165-169	4	4	3	3	1	1	4	3	5	4	1	1	3	3	0	0	0	0	0	0	21	19
160-164	9	9	10	10	25	24	19	17	12	10	13	13	6	6	3	3	0	0	5	4	102	96
155-159	40	39	50	48	76	74	71	65	61	59	30	28	29	28	9	8	2	2	1	0	369	351
150-154	61	59	119	112	165	154	185	170	117	101	91	66	53	43	31	25	6	3	13	2	841	735
145-149	46	12	119	31	185	48	233	64	196	21	153	22	100	12	28	0	7	0	23	3	1090	213
140-144	18	0	54	0	95	2	164	2	135	1	107	1	72	0	27	0	4	0	22	0	698	6
135-139	8	0	10	0	32	0	60	1	60	0	51	0	36	0	24	0	9	0	17	0	307	1
130-134	0	0	5	0	8	0	12	0	16	0	20	0	15	0	13	0	6	0	6	0	101	0
125-129	0	0	0	0	1	0	3	0	1	0	3	0	5	0	1	0	1	0	1	0	16	0
120-124	0	0	0	0	0	0	0	0	0	0	1	0	1	0	1	0	0	0	0	0	3	0
Total	188	125	371	205	588	303	751	322	603	196	470	131	321	93	137	36	35	5	88	9	3552	1425

Apps = Number of Applicants
Adm = Number Admitted
Reflects 98% of the total applicant pool.

The grid includes applicants admitted based upon successful completion of our Trial Admissions Program, rather than upon their LSAT score and undergraduate grade-point average.

Willamette University College of Law

Truman Wesley Collins Legal Center, 245 Winter Street SE
Salem, OR 97301
Phone: 503.370.6282; Fax: 503.370.6087
E-mail: law-admission@willamette.edu; Website: www.willamette.edu/wucl

ABA Approved Since 1938

The Basics

Type of school	Private
Term	Semester
Application deadline	4/1
Application fee	$50
Financial aid deadline	
Can first year start other than fall?	No
Student to faculty ratio (fall)	18.3 to 1
Does the university offer:	
housing restricted to law students?	No
graduate housing for which law students are eligible?	Yes

Faculty and Administrators

	Total		Men		Women		Minorities	
	Fall	Spr	Fall	Spr	Fall	Spr	Fall	Spr
Full-time	21	22	17	18	4	4	3	4
Other Full-time	5	5	2	2	3	3	0	0
Deans, librarians, & others who teach	2	2	1	1	1	1	0	0
Part-time	10	10	8	6	2	4	0	1
Total	**38**	**39**	**28**	**27**	**10**	**12**	**3**	**5**

Curriculum

		Full-time	Part-time
Typical first-year section size		90	0
Is there typically a "small section" of the first-year class, other than Legal Writing, taught by full-time faculty		Yes	No
If yes, typical size offered last year		25	0
# of classroom course titles beyond 1st year curriculum		98	
# of upper division courses, excluding seminars with an enrollment:	Under 25	60	
	25-49	23	
	50-74	8	
	75-99	5	
	100+	2	
# of seminars		16	
# of seminar positions available		276	
# of seminar positions filled	176		0
# of positions available in simulation courses		168	
# of simulation positions filled	151		0
# of positions available in faculty supervised clinical courses		32	
# of faculty supervised clinical positions filled	23		0
# involved in field placements	23		0
# involved in law journals	49		0
# involved in moot court or trial competitions	123		0
# of credit hours required to graduate		90	

JD Enrollment and Ethnicity

	Men #	Men %	Women #	Women %	Full-time #	Full-time %	Part-time #	Part-time %	1st-year #	1st-year %	Total #	Total %	JD Degs. Awd.
African Amer.	3	1.1	1	0.5	4	0.9	0	0.0	2	1.1	4	0.9	4
Amer. Indian	1	0.4	7	3.7	8	1.7	0	0.0	5	2.8	8	1.7	0
Asian Amer.	10	3.6	8	4.2	18	3.9	0	0.0	6	3.3	18	3.9	4
Mex. Amer.	1	0.4	3	1.6	4	0.9	0	0.0	1	0.6	4	0.9	2
Puerto Rican	0	0.0	0	0.0	0	0.0	0	0.0	0	0.0	0	0.0	0
Hispanic	3	1.1	3	1.6	6	1.3	0	0.0	2	1.1	6	1.3	0
Total Minority	18	6.5	22	11.6	40	8.7	0	0.0	16	8.8	40	8.6	10
For. Nation.	4	1.4	2	1.1	6	1.3	0	0.0	0	0.0	6	1.3	1
Caucasian	222	80.1	136	72.0	354	76.8	4	80.0	136	75.1	358	76.8	100
Unknown	33	11.9	29	15.3	61	13.2	1	20.0	29	16.0	62	13.3	6
Total	277	59.4	189	40.6	461	98.9	5	1.1	181	38.8	466		117

Tuition and Fees

	Resident	Nonresident
Full-time	$24,280	$0
Part-time	$0	$0

Living Expenses

Estimated living expenses for singles

Living on campus	Living off campus	Living at home
$12,650	$12,650	$12,650

Willamette University College of Law

ABA
Approved
Since
1938

GPA and LSAT Scores

	Total	Full-time	Part-time
# of apps	1,264	1,264	0
# of admits	504	504	0
# of matrics	181	181	0
75% GPA	3.57	3.57	0.00
25% GPA	3.13	3.13	0.00
75% LSAT	158	158	0
25% LSAT	153	153	0

Grants and Scholarships (from prior year)

	Total #	Total %	Full-time #	Full-time %	Part-time #	Part-time %
Total # of students	445		442		3	
Total # receiving grants	205	46.1	204	46.2	1	33.3
Less than 1/2 tuition	142	31.9	141	31.9	1	33.3
Half to full tuition	59	13.3	59	13.3	0	0.0
Full tuition	3	0.7	3	0.7	0	0.0
More than full tuition	1	0.2	1	0.2	0	0.0
Median grant amount			$9,500		$4,500	

Informational and Library Resources

# of volumes and volume equivalents	282,907
# of titles	39,061
# of active serial subscriptions	3,174
Study seating capacity inside the library	492
# of professional librarians	3
Hours per week library is open	113
# of open, wired connections available to students	122
# of networked computers available for use by students	43
# of simultaneous wireless users	700
Require computer?	N

JD Attrition (from prior year)

	Academic #	Other #	Total #	Total %
1st year	11	24	35	19.9%
2nd year	3	4	7	4.7%
3rd year	0	0	0	0.0%
4th year	0	0	0	0.0%

Employment

	Total	Percentage
Employment status known	136	100.0
Employment status unknown	0	0.0
Employed	118	86.8
Pursuing graduate degrees	6	4.4
Unemployed seeking employment	6	4.4
Unemployed not seeking employment	6	4.4

Type of Employment

	Total	Percentage
# employed in law firms	60	50.8
# employed in business and industry	21	17.8
# employed in government	19	16.1
# employed in public interest	2	1.7
# employed as judicial clerks	11	9.3
# employed in academia	1	0.8

Geographic Location

	Total	Percentage
# employed in state	73	61.9
# employed in foreign countries	1	0.8
# of states where employed	16	

Bar Passage Rates

Jurisdiction	Oregon		
Exam	Sum 03	Win 04	Total
# from school taking bar for the first time	76	7	83
School's pass rate for all first-time takers	79%	43%	76%
State's pass rate for all first-time takers	78%	76%	78%

Willamette University College of Law

Truman Wesley Collins Legal Center, 245 Winter Street SE
Salem, OR 97301
Phone: 503.370.6282; Fax: 503.370.6087
E-mail: law-admission@willamette.edu; Website: www.willamette.edu/wucl

■ Introduction

Willamette University College of Law is one of the nation's oldest and smallest law schools. It is situated on the campus of Willamette University in the historic riverfront capital city of Salem, Oregon. Willamette University, an independent institution historically related to The United Methodist Church, first began educating lawyers in 1883. Today, the 430 students in the College of Law are members of a distinguished university community of 2,500 students enrolled in the undergraduate College of Liberal Arts and in graduate programs offered by its School of Education and the Atkinson Graduate School of Management. Intellectual intimacy is the hallmark of a Willamette education.

Willamette's location, Salem, Oregon, is home to a large, active legal community. The state capitol complex, where Willamette graduates preside over the state supreme court and court of appeals, lies adjacent to the university. Members of Salem's large legal community readily employ and actively mentor Willamette law students. With 137,000 residents, Salem is neither a college town nor a big city. This historic riverfront city boasts world-class vineyards, a vibrant downtown, beautiful parks, an innovative children's museum, an art museum, coffeehouses, microbreweries, and a minor league baseball team. Salem is the gateway to the urban distractions of metropolitan Portland and the natural distractions of Oregon's breathtaking mountains, forests, rivers, lakes, and Pacific beaches.

■ Faculty

Students enjoy close relationships with professors. Willamette's talented teachers are internationally recognized scholars. Faculty expertise is particularly noteworthy in international and comparative law, labor and employment law, dispute resolution, business, and government. Together, Willamette faculty bring almost 250 years of practice and over 500 years of teaching experience.

■ Academic Programs

The Doctor of Jurisprudence program (JD) requires three years of full-time study. After successfully completing the first year, in which all courses are prescribed, students may choose to create an individual program electing courses from Willamette's broad-based curriculum. For students interested in specialization, four certificate programs are offered: International and Comparative Legal Studies, Business Law, Law and Government, and Dispute Resolution. (A separate application is required during the first year of law school to gain admission to the certificate programs.)

The College of Law, in concert with the Willamette University Atkinson Graduate School of Management, offers a joint-degree program that leads to the JD and MBA for Business, Government, and Not-for-Profit Management after four years, saving students one additional year of study. Students must apply separately for admission to each degree program and may begin the program either in the College of Law or in the Atkinson School. Students may apply prior to matriculating to Willamette or while in their first year of either the JD or MBA program.

Willamette also offers the LLM in Transnational Law, an advanced degree available to those who have completed the JD at an ABA-accredited American law school or its equivalent from a foreign law school. The one-year program is small and selective. For more information see *www.willamette.edu/wucl/llm"*.

■ Facility

The College of Law is housed in the award-winning Truman Wesley Collins Legal Center on Willamette's peaceful 65-acre campus.

Willamette was the first law school in the region to offer a wireless network, allowing network access from any point in the College of Law. The facility includes faculty and administrative offices, 10 spacious classrooms (including a small seminar room), a teaching courtroom with video capability, several student lounge areas, game room, locker area, and organization offices. Lee House, one-half block from the College of Law, is home to the Clinical Law Program.

The J.W. Long Library, which anchors the north wing of the Collins Center, is open to students 24 hours a day. Through a library consortium, an online shared catalog gives Willamette students access to a remarkably vast array of resources. Long Law Library houses special collections in public international law, tax law, and labor law. It is a Selective Federal Government Repository.

■ International Study Programs

The summer China Program acquaints students with Chinese law and Pacific Rim legal issues. It is based in Shanghai at the East China University of Politics and Law. The Ecuador Program provides students with an intensive semester immersion in the fundamentals of a civil law system and Latin American legal institutions. Students take courses at the Pontifical Catholic University of Ecuador in Quito. Proficiency in Spanish is required. The semester-long Germany Program is at the Bucerius Law School in Hamburg, the first private institution for legal study in Germany.

Academic Centers and Other Resources

The nationally recognized Center for Dispute Resolution produces research on conflict theory and problem solving, serving various constituencies ranging from the federal government to the local school district. The center teaches the theory and practice of negotiation, mediation, arbitration, and other methods of resolving disputes. It also administers the certificate program in dispute resolution. The Willamette Center for Law and Government provides an impartial forum for the study, discussion, and improvement of government and public policy. It also administers the certificate program in law and government. The Oregon Law Commission was established by statute to provide academic and practical support for ongoing law revision, reform, and improvement. It is housed at Willamette and is led by an executive director who is also an associate dean of the College of Law. The Clinical Law Program, under the direction of full-time supervising attorneys, provides legal assistance to needy Oregonians while offering practical legal experience for our law students. The Externship program, based on a partnership between the College of Law and offices employing lawyers in governmental, in house, and nonprofit capacities, offers students experiential learning environments that develop skills and values of the legal profession.

Admission

Applicants are urged to apply the fall prior to the year they intend on entering law school. Willamette enrolls a first-year law class with a wide range of goals and backgrounds that also is distinguished by its academic achievement. Applications are reviewed closely and in their entirety to ensure an informed and fair decision. Though April 1 is the deadline for applications, students begin receiving admission decisions from Willamette in January.

Scholarships

Generous merit-based scholarships reward applicants whose accomplishments suggest continuing success in law school. Scholarships are renewable with a 2.90 cumulative law GPA. Every student is automatically considered for a scholarship when the application for admission is initially reviewed. All applicants to the College of Law should also complete and submit the Free Application for Federal Student Aid (FAFSA) prior to March 1. Federal and private loan monies may also be available.

Employment and Career Services

Historically, most Willamette graduates choose careers in private practice. Graduates in government-related practice (including judicial clerkships) comprise the next largest group. Business and industry attract the third largest group. Most graduates remain in the Pacific Northwest because of the region's unique lifestyle and natural environment. While the Willamette alumni network is strongest in Oregon and Washington, the Career Services Office provides a comprehensive service enabling students to tailor their employment search. Thus, Willamette graduates practice nationwide, from Hawaii to Washington, DC, from Alaska to Florida, and internationally, as well.

Applicant Profile Not Available

William & Mary Law School

613 South Henry Street
Williamsburg, VA 23185
Phone: 757-221-3785; Fax: 757-221-3261
E-mail: lawadm@wm.edu; Website: www.wm.edu/law/

The Basics

Type of school	Public
Term	Semester
Application deadline	3/1
Application fee	$40
Financial aid deadline	2/15
Can first year start other than fall?	No
Student to faculty ratio (fall)	15.7 to 1
Does the university offer:	
housing restricted to law students?	No
graduate housing for which law students are eligible?	Yes

Curriculum

		Full-time	Part-time
Typical first-year section size		71	0
Is there typically a "small section" of the first-year class, other than Legal Writing, taught by full-time faculty		No	No
If yes, typical size offered last year		0	0
# of classroom course titles beyond 1st year curriculum		107	
# of upper division courses, excluding seminars with an enrollment:	Under 25	115	
	25-49	28	
	50-74	13	
	75-99	3	
	100+	3	
# of seminars		30	
# of seminar positions available		455	
# of seminar positions filled		344	0
# of positions available in simulation courses		892	
# of simulation positions filled		895	0
# of positions available in faculty supervised clinical courses		0	
# of faculty supervised clinical positions filled		0	0
# involved in field placements		147	0
# involved in law journals		244	0
# involved in moot court or trial competitions		51	0
# of credit hours required to graduate		86	

Faculty and Administrators

	Total		Men		Women		Minorities	
	Fall	Spr	Fall	Spr	Fall	Spr	Fall	Spr
Full-time	31	28	21	19	10	9	5	5
Other Full-time	0	0	0	0	0	0	0	0
Deans, librarians, & others who teach	4	4	2	2	2	2	0	0
Part-time	62	72	30	42	32	30	3	2
Total	97	104	53	63	44	41	8	7

JD Enrollment and Ethnicity

	Men		Women		Full-time		Part-time		1st-year		Total		JD Degs. Awd.
	#	%	#	%	#	%	#	%	#	%	#	%	
African Amer.	19	5.8	24	9.2	43	7.4	0	0.0	22	10.8	43	7.4	15
Amer. Indian	2	0.6	1	0.4	3	0.5	0	0.0	0	0.0	3	0.5	1
Asian Amer.	11	3.4	11	4.2	22	3.8	0	0.0	7	3.4	22	3.8	8
Mex. Amer.	0	0.0	0	0.0	0	0.0	0	0.0	0	0.0	0	0.0	0
Puerto Rican	0	0.0	0	0.0	0	0.0	0	0.0	0	0.0	0	0.0	0
Hispanic	8	2.5	2	0.8	10	1.7	0	0.0	2	1.0	10	1.7	3
Total Minority	40	12.3	38	14.6	78	13.3	0	0.0	31	15.2	78	13.3	27
For. Nation.	1	0.3	1	0.4	2	0.3	0	0.0	1	0.5	2	0.3	2
Caucasian	241	74.2	189	72.7	430	73.5	0	0.0	147	72.1	430	73.5	156
Unknown	43	13.2	32	12.3	75	12.8	0	0.0	25	12.3	75	12.8	10
Total	325	55.6	260	44.4	585	100.0	0	0.0	204	34.9	585		195

Tuition and Fees

	Resident	Nonresident
Full-time	$14,160	$24,400
Part-time	$420	$760

Living Expenses

Estimated living expenses for singles

Living on campus	Living off campus	Living at home
$13,550	$13,550	$13,550

William & Mary Law School

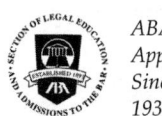

ABA
Approved
Since
1932

GPA and LSAT Scores

	Total	Full-time	Part-time
# of apps	4,243	4,243	0
# of admits	848	848	0
# of matrics	206	206	0
75% GPA	3.82	3.82	0.00
25% GPA	3.36	3.36	0.00
75% LSAT	165	165	0
25% LSAT	160	160	0

Grants and Scholarships (from prior year)

	Total		Full-time		Part-time	
	#	%	#	%	#	%
Total # of students	582		582		0	
Total # receiving grants	301	51.7	301	51.7	0	0.0
Less than 1/2 tuition	122	21.0	122	21.0	0	0.0
Half to full tuition	178	30.6	178	30.6	0	0.0
Full tuition	1	0.2	1	0.2	0	0.0
More than full tuition	0	0.0	0	0.0	0	0.0
Median grant amount			$5,000		$0	

Informational and Library Resources

# of volumes and volume equivalents	384,198
# of titles	162,819
# of active serial subscriptions	4,369
Study seating capacity inside the library	427
# of professional librarians	7
Hours per week library is open	168
# of open, wired connections available to students	41
# of networked computers available for use by students	47
# of simultaneous wireless users	275
Require computer?	N

JD Attrition (from prior year)

	Academic	Other	Total	
	#	#	#	%
1st year	0	7	7	3.4%
2nd year	0	2	2	1.1%
3rd year	0	2	2	1.0%
4th year	0	0	0	0.0%

Employment

	Total	Percentage
Employment status known	168	98.8
Employment status unknown	2	1.2
Employed	151	89.9
Pursuing graduate degrees	7	4.2
Unemployed seeking employment	2	1.2
Unemployed not seeking employment	8	4.8

Type of Employment

# employed in law firms	70	46.4
# employed in business and industry	20	13.2
# employed in government	27	17.9
# employed in public interest	4	2.6
# employed as judicial clerks	28	18.5
# employed in academia	2	1.3

Geographic Location

# employed in state	58	38.4
# employed in foreign countries	1	0.7
# of states where employed		25

Bar Passage Rates

Jurisdiction	Virginia		
Exam	Sum 03	Win 04	Total
# from school taking bar for the first time	85	5	90
School's pass rate for all first-time takers	75%	100%	77%
State's pass rate for all first-time takers	75%	60%	72%

William & Mary Law School

613 South Henry Street
Williamsburg, VA 23185
Phone: 757-221-3785; Fax: 757-221-3261
E-mail: lawadm@wm.edu; Website: www.wm.edu/law/

■ Introduction

Established in 1779 at the request of Thomas Jefferson, William & Mary Law School is the nation's oldest. At William & Mary, concern for students' intellectual development is accompanied by concern that they develop the character and values of constructive citizens who will do their part in society. The Law School is small enough for people to know one another by name, but large enough to form a critical mass for learning and scholarship. Members of the 2004–2005 student body earned undergraduate degrees from 237 colleges and universities and represent 46 states, DC, and 9 countries. The Law School is located a few blocks from Colonial Williamsburg, within easy driving distance of the metropolitan areas of Washington, DC, Richmond, and Norfolk. Visits and student tours are encouraged as well as attendance at one of three Friday information sessions. The dates for the information sessions are noted in the *Viewbook* and on our website.

■ Library and Physical Facilities

The library's collection of nearly 400,000 volumes, its comfortable building, and its service-oriented staff provide an excellent setting for study and research. The library has legal materials in all formats, including an extensive treatise collection that covers all areas of law, with particular strengths in constitutional and environmental law, public and private international law, jurisprudence, legal history, Roman law, commercial law, intellectual property, and taxation. The library has two computer labs, with additional PCs and iMacs available throughout the library. Students can reach the Internet with laptop computers via networked study carrels and study rooms, or through our wireless network.

The McGlothlin Courtroom at the Law School is the world's most technologically advanced trial and appellate chamber. The courtroom is designed to permit trials with multiple remote appearances and web-based evidence. It has a wide variety of technologies, including all available major court record systems, evidence presentation technologies, assistive and foreign language interpretation technologies, and critical infrastructure technologies.

The Law School is located between the National Center for State Courts and William & Mary's graduate apartment complex. The Law School employs wireless technology for e-mail and web access throughout the building. All classrooms accommodate instructional technology and laptop computers.

■ Curriculum

The required first-year curriculum includes constitutional law, contracts, torts, civil procedure, property, criminal

law, and legal skills. Through the two-year Legal Skills Program, which begins with a week-long concentrated introduction to the legal system and law study before classes begin, students experience and refine lawyering skills such as interviewing, negotiating, trial techniques, and oral advocacy. This innovative program utilizes simulated law offices, client representation, and mock trials to teach the skills necessary for the practice of law as well as legal research and writing and professional responsibility. To earn a Juris Doctor degree, students must successfully complete 86 credit hours, 90 residency weeks, all required courses, and a significant paper of publishable quality. Students may choose yearly from more than 90 upper-level courses covering a broad range of contemporary and traditional areas of law. The Law School offers three clinical programs (legal aid clinic, domestic violence clinic, and federal tax clinic) and a wide variety of externships, including externships at the Supreme Court of Virginia, the Virginia Court of Appeals, the Attorney General's Office, and the Department of Employment Dispute Resolution. Students can also gain practical experience through the Judicial Clerk Externship, the Non-Profit Organization Externship, and the General Practice Externship. In addition, second- and third-year students are encouraged to gain legal experience working in private firms and public law offices.

■ Joint-Degree Programs

There are three joint-degree programs: JD/MBA, JD/MPP, and JD/MA in American Studies. The JD/MBA and the JD/MPP combine traditional five-year programs into four years of study with one entire year spent in each program followed by two years of coursework at both schools. Students may complete the JD/MA in either three or four years.

■ International Programs

A summer session in Madrid, Spain, offers a five-week program in which students can earn up to six credits studying various topics in international law. William & Mary professors and prominent Spanish professors and practitioners of law teach the courses in English. In addition, students fluent in Spanish can complete a one-week externship in a Spanish law firm.

The Law School also offers an LLM in the American Legal System for students from outside the US who take courses with the JD students and bring the richness of their legal traditions to the classroom.

■ Special Programs

Through the Institute of Bill of Rights Law, the Law School has become one of the preeminent institutions studying the US Constitution's Bill of Rights. The institute sponsors lectures, symposia, and publications that entice scholars from around the country to examine important constitutional issues. The Law School's McGlothlin Courtroom is at the cutting edge of courtroom technology, research, and application. It attracts an international audience of judges, administrators, and lawyers, and offers our students hands-on training in the use of state-of-the-art courtroom technology.

■ Housing

Students may live next to the Law School in the university's graduate apartment complex or choose from a wide variety of housing options in the Williamsburg area. For more information about campus housing, visit *www.wm.edu/reslife/residenceHalls/graduate.php*.

■ Student Activities

Legal scholars and practitioners frequently cite articles from our student-managed academic journals. These publications include *William and Mary Law Review, William & Mary Bill of Rights Journal, William and Mary Environmental Law and Policy Review,* and *William and Mary Journal of Women and the Law.* The Law School has a highly competitive Moot Court Program and National Trial Team. The more than 25 student organizations reflect the diverse interests of the student body. Student organizations include the

Asian Law Students Association, the Black Law Students Association, the Christian Legal Society, the Federalist Society, the Intellectual Property Society, the International Law Society, the Jewish Law Students Association, the Lesbian and Gay Law Association, the Military Law Society, the Public Service Fund, the Sports and Entertainment Law Society, Student Legal Services, and the Phi Delta Phi and Phi Alpha Delta legal fraternities.

■ Career Services

Employers from 31 states and the District of Columbia conducted on-campus interviews during 2004. Through our Video Interview Program, William & Mary also used video technology to bring students and employers together. The Office of Career Services posted notices from more than 3,000 nonvisiting employers from all 50 states, the District of Columbia, and several countries. William & Mary students also had the opportunity to participate in 26 off-campus job fairs with a national employer base, including events in Atlanta, Chicago, Dallas, Los Angeles, and New York and specialized programs for intellectual property law, public interest and governmental positions, and small regional firms. The Law School awarded 77 fellowships to assist students working in low-paying or nonpaying public-service positions during the summer of 2004. Ninety-nine percent of the class of 2003 are employed throughout the US and abroad or pursuing advanced degrees.

Applicant Profile

William & Mary Law School
This grid includes only applicants who earned 120-180 LSAT scores under standard administrations, and represents 99% of the total applicant pool.

LSAT Score	3.75 +		3.50 - 3.74		3.25 - 3.49		3.00 - 3.24		2.75 - 2.99		2.50 - 2.74		2.25 - 2.49		2.00 - 2.24		Below 2.00		No GPA		Total	
	Apps	Adm	Apps	Adm	Apps	Adm	Apps	Adm	Apps	Adm	Apps	Adm	Apps	Adm	Apps	Adm	Apps	Adm	Apps	Adm	Apps	Adm
175-180	2	2	9	8	7	4	5	4	1	0	1	0	1	0	1	0	0	0	0	0	27	18
170-174	35	31	33	30	49	33	32	19	19	2	5	1	3	0	1	0	0	0	2	1	179	117
165-169	189	173	189	141	187	62	135	25	59	3	35	1	15	0	2	0	0	0	3	0	814	405
160-164	252	111	381	69	330	21	211	9	100	4	49	1	12	1	4	0	0	0	8	0	1347	216
155-159	167	21	227	9	244	4	156	7	74	4	23	1	12	1	3	0	1	0	8	0	915	47
150-154	68	9	109	9	116	3	88	4	51	1	27	0	10	0	3	0	3	0	5	0	480	26
145-149	26	1	38	1	44	3	54	1	39	1	17	0	7	0	7	1	1	0	5	0	238	8
140-144	5	0	21	0	18	0	18	0	22	0	28	0	11	0	4	0	0	0	5	0	132	0
135-139	1	0	7	0	7	0	5	0	8	0	6	0	11	0	5	0	0	0	2	0	52	0
130-134	0	0	2	0	4	0	3	0	3	0	2	0	1	0	1	0	0	0	1	0	17	0
125-129	0	0	0	0	2	0	1	0	2	0	0	0	1	0	2	0	0	0	0	0	8	0
120-124	0	0	0	0	0	0	0	0	0	0	0	0	0	0	0	0	0	0	0	0	0	0
Total	745	348	1016	267	1008	130	708	69	378	15	193	4	84	2	33	1	5	0	39	1	4209	837

Apps = Number of Applicants
Adm = Number Admitted

William Mitchell College of Law

875 Summit Avenue
St. Paul, MN 55105
Phone: 651.290.6476; toll-free: 888.WMCL.LAW; Fax: 651.290.7535
E-mail: admissions@wmitchell.edu; Website: www.wmitchell.edu

*ABA
Approved
Since
1938*

The Basics

Type of school	Private
Term	Semester
Application deadline	6/1
Application fee	$45
Financial aid deadline	3/15
Can first year start other than fall?	No
Student to faculty ratio (fall)	22.9 to 1
Does the university offer:	
housing restricted to law students?	No
graduate housing for which law students are eligible?	No

Faculty and Administrators

	Total		Men		Women		Minorities	
	Fall	Spr	Fall	Spr	Fall	Spr	Fall	Spr
Full-time	34	33	23	21	11	12	5	5
Other Full-time	0	0	0	0	0	0	0	0
Deans, librarians, & others who teach	4	4	2	2	2	2	1	1
Part-time	200	205	113	115	87	89	37	39
Total	238	242	138	138	100	103	43	45

Curriculum

		Full-time	Part-time
Typical first-year section size		78	50
Is there typically a "small section" of the first-year class, other than Legal Writing, taught by full-time faculty		No	No
If yes, typical size offered last year		0	0
# of classroom course titles beyond 1st year curriculum		119	
# of upper division courses, excluding seminars with an enrollment:	Under 25	52	
	25-49	65	
	50-74	25	
	75-99	4	
	100+	0	
# of seminars		44	
# of seminar positions available		865	
# of seminar positions filled		336	315
# of positions available in simulation courses		1,221	
# of simulation positions filled		729	376
# of positions available in faculty supervised clinical courses		204	
# of faculty supervised clinical positions filled	100		87
# involved in field placements		67	41
# involved in law journals		45	22
# involved in moot court or trial competitions		72	36
# of credit hours required to graduate		86	

JD Enrollment and Ethnicity

	Men		Women		Full-time		Part-time		1st-year		Total		JD Degs. Awd.
	#	%	#	%	#	%	#	%	#	%	#	%	
African Amer.	22	4.1	20	3.7	21	3.2	21	4.9	8	2.5	42	3.9	17
Amer. Indian	2	0.4	3	0.6	2	0.3	3	0.7	2	0.6	5	0.5	3
Asian Amer.	27	5.0	20	3.7	27	4.1	20	4.7	14	4.5	47	4.4	17
Mex. Amer.	0	0.0	5	0.9	2	0.3	3	0.7	2	0.6	5	0.5	1
Puerto Rican	0	0.0	2	0.4	1	0.2	1	0.2	1	0.3	2	0.2	0
Hispanic	9	1.7	7	1.3	9	1.4	7	1.6	4	1.3	16	1.5	2
Total Minority	60	11.2	57	10.5	62	9.5	55	12.9	31	9.9	117	10.9	40
For. Nation.	5	0.9	1	0.2	2	0.3	4	0.9	1	0.3	6	0.6	2
Caucasian	427	79.5	445	82.3	529	81.0	343	80.7	230	73.2	872	80.9	266
Unknown	45	8.4	38	7.0	60	9.2	23	5.4	52	16.6	83	7.7	1
Total	537	49.8	541	50.2	653	60.6	425	39.4	314	29.1	1078		309

Tuition and Fees

	Resident	Nonresident
Full-time	$24,550	$24,550
Part-time	$17,780	$17,780

Living Expenses

Estimated living expenses for singles

Living on campus	Living off campus	Living at home
N/A	$14,300	N/A

William Mitchell College of Law

*ABA
Approved
Since
1938*

GPA and LSAT Scores

	Total	Full-time	Part-time
# of apps	1,570	1,570	0
# of admits	823	742	81
# of matrics	320	214	106
75% GPA	3.64	3.67	3.57
25% GPA	3.10	3.14	3.04
75% LSAT	158	158	157
25% LSAT	150	153	147

Grants and Scholarships (from prior year)

	Total		Full-time		Part-time	
	#	%	#	%	#	%
Total # of students	1,076		630		446	
Total # receiving grants	369	34.3	194	30.8	175	39.2
Less than 1/2 tuition	147	13.7	85	13.5	62	13.9
Half to full tuition	179	16.6	86	13.7	93	20.9
Full tuition	43	4.0	23	3.7	20	4.5
More than full tuition	0	0.0	0	0.0	0	0.0
Median grant amount			$3,505		$2,558	

Informational and Library Resources

# of volumes and volume equivalents	331,340
# of titles	111,414
# of active serial subscriptions	4,118
Study seating capacity inside the library	674
# of professional librarians	8
Hours per week library is open	106
# of open, wired connections available to students	240
# of networked computers available for use by students	89
# of simultaneous wireless users	1,048
Require computer?	Y

JD Attrition (from prior year)

	Academic	Other	Total	
	#	#	#	%
1st year	10	26	36	10.3%
2nd year	0	1	1	0.3%
3rd year	0	0	0	0.0%
4th year	0	0	0	0.0%

Employment

	Total	Percentage
Employment status known	224	77.8
Employment status unknown	64	22.2
Employed	189	84.4
Pursuing graduate degrees	3	1.3
Unemployed seeking employment	28	12.5
Unemployed not seeking employment	4	1.8

Type of Employment

# employed in law firms	104	55.0
# employed in business and industry	34	18.0
# employed in government	20	10.6
# employed in public interest	3	1.6
# employed as judicial clerks	25	13.2
# employed in academia	3	1.6

Geographic Location

# employed in state	172	91.0
# employed in foreign countries	1	0.5
# of states where employed	12	

Bar Passage Rates

Jurisdiction	Minnesota		
Exam	Sum 03	Win 04	Total
# from school taking bar for the first time	216	58	274
School's pass rate for all first-time takers	93%	79%	90%
State's pass rate for all first-time takers	92%	75%	89%

William Mitchell College of Law

Office of Admissions, 875 Summit Avenue
St. Paul, MN 55105
Phone: 651.290.6476; toll-free: 888.WMCL.LAW; Fax: 651.290.7535
E-mail: admissions@wmitchell.edu; Website: www.wmitchell.edu

■ Introduction

For more than 100 years, William Mitchell College of Law has been committed to legal education of the highest quality. The college provides practical legal skills training in addition to a strong traditional academic curriculum. We offer innovative clinic, practicum, and legal writing programs; a nationally recognized and experienced faculty; and a network of accomplished alumni. We offer students the flexibility to attend law school full time or part time, and we offer evening courses. Among the college's 12,000 alumni are distinguished members of the judiciary: Warren E. Burger, 15th chief justice of the United States; Douglas Amdahl, former chief justice of the Minnesota Supreme Court; Rosalie Wahl and Esther Tomljanovich, former justices of the Minnesota Supreme Court; and Sam Hanson and Helen Meyer, current justices of the Minnesota Supreme Court.

The college is accredited by the ABA, is a member of the Association of American Law Schools, and is approved by the US Veterans Administration.

■ Faculty

William Mitchell's full-time faculty members are educators, advocates, lawyers, and scholars. While their highest priority is effective teaching and learning, they have earned regional, national, and international respect for their extensive research and writing, as well as recognition for their significant practice experience and leadership roles in national bar and legal education organizations. They are accessible to students and ensure that graduates are well prepared to enter the world of legal work. The judges and attorneys who are members of our adjunct faculty teach many elective courses and offer legal expertise and real-world examples fresh from their experience.

■ Academics

William Mitchell's academic program integrates legal theory with practical legal skills to prepare students to practice law. Our Juris Doctor program is rigorous, providing students with the tools and skills essential to a successful legal career. The traditional theoretical curriculum is supplemented with coursework in legal ethics and prepares students for the workforce with practical coursework, as well as 14 clinical and externship options. Students choose from an extensive course list and can specialize in many areas, such as intellectual property law, corporate law, tax law, public interest law, and family law.

Our nationally recognized clinical program was one of the first to be established at a US law school. Since its inception in 1972, William Mitchell's law clinic program has become a national leader in trial advocacy and clinical education. Full-time professors and supervisory attorneys teach the clinics. Students can also participate in the Legal Practicum, in which students working as two-person law firms handle a series of simulated cases, learning the essential skills they will need for their law careers. While at William Mitchell, students further shape their trial skills through regional, national, and international competitions.

William Mitchell's legal writing program is praised widely by law school faculty throughout the country. The legal writing text, written by William Mitchell's faculty members, has been adopted by many law schools nationwide. One of the strengths of the program is the low student-faculty ratio.

■ Flexible Scheduling

William Mitchell offers a flexible schedule that enables students to take advantage of clerkships or other law-related employment opportunities while obtaining their degrees or continue working in their chosen careers while they attend law school. Students can choose to attend law school part time or full time. The college offers many evening courses. Summer courses are also available.

■ Library and Physical Facilities

The Warren E. Burger Library has a strong core collection, with electronic access to thousands of additional resources and a professional staff whose first priority is helping law students. The library was designed around the newest technologies in legal research.

William Mitchell's campus is located in St. Paul near the capitol, and is one block from one of the Twin Cities' most popular shopping, dining, and entertainment areas. Minneapolis and St. Paul are widely regarded as among the most livable cities in the United States. Boasting one of the highest employment rates in the country, the Twin Cities is home to numerous major law firms and international and Fortune 500 companies.

The campus has many high-tech classrooms and courtrooms. Wireless technology is available throughout the campus, and laptop accessibility is prevalent. The campus also includes computer labs, seminar rooms, moot courtrooms, the Law Clinics, a new student lounge and cafeteria, and offices for student organizations.

■ Public Service Opportunities

William Mitchell students have many opportunities to provide community service. The law school partners with the Minnesota Justice Foundation, through which students provide more than 6,000 hours of supervised pro bono legal service per year. In addition, students perform approximately 14,000 hours of pro bono service annually through the college's for-credit legal clinical program.

■ Special Programs

William Mitchell's Law in London program provides students an opportunity to study English and European Union law and practice for up to five weeks during the summer.

William Mitchell's Summer Excellence Program is an intensive orientation to law school, including an introduction to resources such as the library and study and exam skills, for a limited number of entering students.

Through the Consortium of Innovative Legal Education, in which William Mitchell is a member, students can enroll in a number of summer study abroad programs.

■ Student Body

William Mitchell's student population ranges from age 20 to 59. Students in our most recent entering class represented 25 states and 13 foreign countries. Approximately 27 percent of students come directly from undergraduate institutions, while others come from professional careers, parenting, or both.

Students can participate in more than 25 on-campus student organizations, including the Student Bar Association and the *William Mitchell Law Review*.

■ Career Services

William Mitchell graduates are highly employable. Because the college's curriculum combines practical skills with legal theory, our students have the experience employers are looking for. Nine months after graduating, 93.3 percent of William Mitchell's class of 2003 who were seeking employment were employed, and more than 90 percent of William Mitchell graduates pass the Minnesota bar exam on their first try.

William Mitchell's Career Services office provides on-campus interviews and personalized, proactive career counseling, and programming, publications, and online job postings.

■ Scholarship/Financial Aid

William Mitchell offers a substantial number of scholarships to both new and continuing students each year. Students can receive significant need- and merit-based scholarships. Approximately 90 percent of all William Mitchell students receive some type of financial aid in the form of scholarships, loans, and employment.

Applicant Profile

William Mitchell College of Law
This grid includes only applicants who earned 120-180 LSAT scores under standard administrations.

LSAT Score	3.75 +		3.50 - 3.74		3.25 - 3.49		3.00 - 3.24		2.75 - 2.99		2.50 - 2.74		2.25 - 2.49		2.00 - 2.24		Below 2.00		No GPA		Total	
	Apps	Adm	Apps	Adm	Apps	Adm	Apps	Adm	Apps	Adm	Apps	Adm	Apps	Adm	Apps	Adm	Apps	Adm	Apps	Adm	Apps	Adm
175-180	0	0	0	0	0	0	0	0	0	0	0	0	0	0	0	0	0	0	0	0	0	0
170-174	2	2	1	1	2	2	0	0	0	0	0	0	0	0	0	0	0	0	0	0	5	5
165-169	9	9	8	8	7	7	7	7	2	2	2	2	2	2	1	0	0	0	1	0	39	37
160-164	29	29	31	31	38	38	25	25	16	16	10	9	1	1	2	0	0	0	1	0	153	149
155-159	40	40	73	73	70	69	62	60	31	28	22	21	10	8	7	0	1	0	2	1	318	300
150-154	41	40	67	57	103	62	89	33	51	12	27	7	16	5	5	0	1	0	3	2	357	88
145-149	26	17	54	22	74	27	77	13	49	7	36	1	23	0	12	0	2	0	4	1	167	26
140-144	5	3	15	7	24	6	40	3	34	3	26	0	15	2	5	0	2	0	1	0	55	0
135-139	1	0	2	0	6	0	13	0	12	0	9	0	5	0	3	0	2	0	2	0	24	0
130-134	0	0	1	0	1	0	4	0	6	0	4	0	2	0	3	0	3	0	0	0	6	0
125-129	0	0	0	0	0	0	1	0	0	0	1	0	1	0	2	0	1	0	0	0	0	0
120-124	0	0	0	0	0	0	0	0	0	0	0	0	0	0	0	0	0	0	0	0	0	0
Total	153	140	252	199	325	211	318	141	201	68	137	42	75	18	40	0	12	0	14	4	1527	823

Apps = Number of Applicants
Adm = Number Admitted
Represents 93% of the total applicant pool.

University of Wisconsin Law School

975 Bascom Mall
Madison, WI 53706
Phone: 608.262.5914; Fax: 608.263.3190
E-mail: admissions@law.wisc.edu; Website: www.law.wisc.edu

ABA Approved Since 1923

The Basics

Type of school	Public
Term	Semester
Application deadline	2/1
Application fee	$45
Financial aid deadline	3/1
Can first year start other than fall?	No
Student to faculty ratio (fall)	12.5 to 1
Does the university offer:	
housing restricted to law students?	No
graduate housing for which law students are eligible?	Yes

Faculty and Administrators

	Total		Men		Women		Minorities	
	Fall	Spr	Fall	Spr	Fall	Spr	Fall	Spr
Full-time	55	52	33	31	22	21	8	8
Other Full-time	8	8	6	6	2	2	2	2
Deans, librarians, & others who teach	7	7	6	6	1	1	0	0
Part-time	58	50	28	24	30	26	12	15
Total	128	117	73	67	55	50	22	25

Curriculum

	Full-time	Part-time
Typical first-year section size	75	0
Is there typically a "small section" of the first-year class, other than Legal Writing, taught by full-time faculty	Yes	No
If yes, typical size offered last year	21	0
# of classroom course titles beyond 1st year curriculum	158	
# of upper division courses, excluding seminars with an enrollment: Under 25	110	
25-49	40	
50-74	12	
75-99	8	
100+	4	
# of seminars	78	
# of seminar positions available	1,425	
# of seminar positions filled	844	0
# of positions available in simulation courses	528	
# of simulation positions filled	372	0
# of positions available in faculty supervised clinical courses	500	
# of faculty supervised clinical positions filled	306	0
# involved in field placements	220	0
# involved in law journals	164	0
# involved in moot court or trial competitions	126	0
# of credit hours required to graduate	90	

JD Enrollment and Ethnicity

	Men #	Men %	Women #	Women %	Full-time #	Full-time %	Part-time #	Part-time %	1st-year #	1st-year %	Total #	Total %	JD Degs. Awd.
African Amer.	23	5.0	49	12.5	65	8.1	7	13.7	22	7.7	72	8.5	9
Amer. Indian	6	1.3	10	2.6	15	1.9	1	2.0	9	3.1	16	1.9	8
Asian Amer.	30	6.5	33	8.4	61	7.6	2	3.9	28	9.8	63	7.4	22
Mex. Amer.	32	7.0	12	3.1	43	5.4	1	2.0	21	7.3	44	5.2	1
Puerto Rican	7	1.5	5	1.3	11	1.4	1	2.0	5	1.7	12	1.4	0
Hispanic	8	1.7	8	2.0	15	1.9	1	2.0	1	0.3	16	1.9	9
Total Minority	106	23.0	117	29.9	210	26.3	13	25.5	86	30.1	223	26.2	49
For. Nation.	12	2.6	8	2.0	18	2.3	2	3.9	5	1.7	20	2.4	4
Caucasian	329	71.5	256	65.5	549	68.6	36	70.6	174	60.8	585	68.7	189
Unknown	13	2.8	10	2.6	23	2.9	0	0.0	21	7.3	23	2.7	0
Total	460	54.1	391	45.9	800	94.0	51	6.0	286	33.6	851		242

Tuition and Fees

	Resident	Nonresident
Full-time	$10,734	$26,952
Part-time	$8,945	$22,461

Living Expenses

Estimated living expenses for singles

Living on campus	Living off campus	Living at home
$12,960	$12,960	$7,260

*Part-time tuition and fees per credit.

University of Wisconsin Law School

*ABA
Approved
Since
1923*

GPA and LSAT Scores

	Total	Full-time	Part-time
# of apps	3,411	3,411	0
# of admits	747	747	0
# of matrics	282	274	8
75% GPA	3.64	3.64	0.00
25% GPA	3.15	3.15	0.00
75% LSAT	163	163	0
25% LSAT	155	155	0

Grants and Scholarships (from prior year)

	Total		Full-time		Part-time	
	#	%	#	%	#	%
Total # of students	819		767		52	
Total # receiving grants	282	34.4	282	36.8	0	0.0
Less than 1/2 tuition	49	6.0	49	6.4	0	0.0
Half to full tuition	135	16.5	135	17.6	0	0.0
Full tuition	32	3.9	32	4.2	0	0.0
More than full tuition	66	8.1	66	8.6	0	0.0
Median grant amount			$12,560		$0	

Informational and Library Resources

# of volumes and volume equivalents	547,354
# of titles	282,862
# of active serial subscriptions	6,169
Study seating capacity inside the library	615
# of professional librarians	10
Hours per week library is open	104
# of open, wired connections available to students	309
# of networked computers available for use by students	71
# of simultaneous wireless users	1,000
Require computer?	Y

JD Attrition (from prior year)

	Academic	Other	Total	
	#	#	#	%
1st year	0	5	5	1.7%
2nd year	0	14	14	4.7%
3rd year	0	11	11	4.7%
4th year	0	0	0	0.0%

Employment

	Total	Percentage
Employment status known	243	95.7
Employment status unknown	11	4.3
Employed	231	95.1
Pursuing graduate degrees	6	2.5
Unemployed seeking employment	2	0.8
Unemployed not seeking employment	4	1.6

Type of Employment

# employed in law firms	148	64.1
# employed in business and industry	25	10.8
# employed in government	32	13.9
# employed in public interest	4	1.7
# employed as judicial clerks	20	8.7
# employed in academia	2	0.9

Geographic Location

# employed in state	121	52.4
# employed in foreign countries	3	1.3
# of states where employed	22	

Bar Passage Rates

Jurisdiction	Wisconsin			Illinois		
Exam	Sum 03	Win 04	Total	Sum 03	Win 04	Total
# from school taking bar for the first time	222	24	246	35	4	39
School's pass rate for all first-time takers	100%	100%	100%	97%	100%	97%
State's pass rate for all first-time takers	82%	69%	79%	86%	78%	84%

All graduates were admitted to the Wisconsin bar via the diploma privilege.

University of Wisconsin Law School

975 Bascom Mall
Madison, WI 53706
Phone: 608.262.5914; Fax: 608.263.3190
E-mail: admissions@law.wisc.edu; Website: www.law.wisc.edu

■ A Preeminent Law School; A World-Class University; A Beautiful City

The UW Law School is one of the most intellectually exciting law schools in the country, attracting students from around the world. Students represent a variety of backgrounds, ages, interests, races, nationalities, and life experiences which encourage a robust exchange of ideas.

Top students are drawn to the UW Law School because of its tradition of excellence, its beautiful setting in the heart of one of the world's leading research universities, and its *law-in-action* philosophy, an approach that differentiates it from other law schools.

The UW Law School is located in Madison, an affordable city strategically and conveniently situated in the middle of a triangle formed by Chicago, Minneapolis, and Milwaukee. As the state capital, Madison is home to many courts and state and federal government agencies—all within walking distance of the Law School.

■ A Commitment to Diversity and Community

A major indicator of the strength of any law school is its student body. The fall 2004 entering class of 274 students represents 31 states and 114 undergraduate institutions. Forty-one percent are from outside of Wisconsin; 48 percent are women; and 35 percent are students of color. The UW Law School's admission policies enhance the diversity, vigor, social concern, and academic ability of the student community. There is a special feeling of community in the school and an informal, supportive atmosphere, reflecting a strong commitment by faculty and administrators to student learning, morale, and well-being.

■ The Faculty: Leading Scholars and Outstanding Teachers

The UW Law School's nationally recognized faculty comes from a wide range of backgrounds and offers students strong role models and a variety of experiences. They are leading scholars who are also actively involved in the law. They advise on stem cell issues, represent clients on death row, work with congressional staffers to draft legislation, provide legal advice to poor farmers in the South, and work with the European Union on monetary policy. They are interesting lawyers doing interesting things, but first and foremost, they are excellent teachers who are committed to their students. A superb clinical faculty and an experienced adjunct faculty provide additional teaching resources.

■ The Curriculum: Law in Action

Students at the UW Law School have many opportunities to experience *law in action*. An extensive curriculum places an emphasis on the dynamics of the law (how the law relates to social change and to society as a whole) while at the same time emphasizing skill development, particularly legal analysis and writing. The first-year small-section program teaches the fundamentals of legal analysis and reasoning in a supportive setting. In the first semester, two of a student's five classes—a substantive law class and a legal research and writing class—are small sections. Students receive one-to-one feedback, and it is easy to form study groups and friendships because students from these small sections take all of their other classes together.

In the second and third years of law school, students have time both to explore the curriculum and to develop the lawyering skills they need. The UW Law School is a national law school that prepares students to practice wherever they choose. Students choose courses from an extraordinary breadth and depth of offerings, affording them the opportunity to explore cutting-edge legal issues in the classroom and to apply their knowledge in one of the many clinical programs.

■ Dual-Degree Programs

Renowned for its interdisciplinary approach, the UW Law School offers many opportunities for students to combine the study of law with a graduate degree in another subject. There are many existing dual-degree programs. If one of the existing programs does not meet a student's academic needs, the Law School will help create an individualized curriculum.

■ Clinicals and Skills Training: Hands-on Learning

The UW Law School is committed to practical experience as a part of legal education. With one of the largest clinical programs in the country, the UW Law School offers a wide variety of hands-on lawyering experiences with real clients and excellent supervision. From representing low-income clients to teaming up with medical students as advocates for newly diagnosed cancer patients or assisting inmates in state and federal prisons, these experiences are invaluable opportunities. Judicial internships, externships, and our innovative lawyering skills program provide additional hands-on learning experiences.

■ Going Global: International Law and Study Abroad

Ten professors devote their scholarship and teaching primarily to international or comparative law, and many others integrate analysis of foreign legal developments into their domestic law courses. The Law School hosts international students and professors, bringing diverse international perspectives to the classroom, and the university has one of the largest groups of international students in the country. Students can also study with one of the eight foreign law faculties with which the Law School has exchange agreements or participate in foreign study programs of other US law schools. Additional international opportunities are available through the Law School's East Asian Legal Studies Center, established to formalize and increase the Law School's interaction in East and Southeast Asia.

■ Student Activities

More than 30 organizations provide outstanding opportunities for students to pursue their talents and interests. Several moot court competitions at the UW Law School enable students to gain experience with brief writing and oral advocacy, and several student journals—*Wisconsin Law Review, Wisconsin International Law Journal,* and *Wisconsin Women's Law Journal*—give students an opportunity to contribute to the Law School's scholarly publications and gain invaluable training in legal research and writing.

■ Career Opportunities

Leading law firms, government agencies, businesses, and public interest organizations seek to hire UW Law School graduates. A broad range of legal employers from many major cities participate in the on-campus interview program. The Law School also participates in nine off-campus job fairs each year in New York, Washington, DC, Los Angeles, Chicago, and Minneapolis. Our students receive assistance from many of our more than 12,000 alumni throughout the country, and our graduates typically accept jobs in more than 20 different states from New York to California.

Applicant Profile

Admission to the University of Wisconsin Law School is competitive. The most recent entering class had a median LSAT score of 160 and a median GPA of 3.38. The Law School does not provide a profile chart because its admission decisions involve many factors that are not represented by undergraduate GPA and LSAT scores.

The UW Law School Admissions Committee looks at an applicant's credentials taken as a whole. While candidates with higher grades and scores tend to be admitted at higher rates, GPA and LSAT scores alone are not necessarily good predictors of admission decisions on individual applications.

University of Wyoming College of Law

Dept. 3035, 1000 E University Ave.
Laramie, WY 82071
Phone: 307.766.6416; Fax: 307.766.6417
E-mail: lawadmis@uwyo.edu; Website: www.uwyo.edu/law

ABA
Approved
Since
1923

The Basics

Type of school	Public
Term	Semester
Application deadline	3/1
Application fee	$50
Financial aid deadline	3/1
Can first year start other than fall?	No
Student to faculty ratio (fall)	15.9 to 1
Does the university offer:	
housing restricted to law students?	No
graduate housing for which law students are eligible?	Yes

Faculty and Administrators

	Total		Men		Women		Minorities	
	Fall	Spr	Fall	Spr	Fall	Spr	Fall	Spr
Full-time	12	12	7	8	5	4	2	3
Other Full-time	0	0	0	0	0	0	0	0
Deans, librarians, & others who teach	6	5	2	1	4	4	0	0
Part-time	6	12	2	6	4	6	0	0
Total	24	29	11	15	13	14	2	3

Curriculum

		Full-time	Part-time
Typical first-year section size		78	0
Is there typically a "small section" of the first-year class, other than Legal Writing, taught by full-time faculty		No	No
If yes, typical size offered last year		0	0
# of classroom course titles beyond 1st year curriculum		48	
# of upper division courses, excluding seminars with an enrollment:	Under 25	27	
	25-49	7	
	50-74	8	
	75-99	3	
	100+	0	
# of seminars		3	
# of seminar positions available		34	
# of seminar positions filled		34	0
# of positions available in simulation courses		118	
# of simulation positions filled		89	0
# of positions available in faculty supervised clinical courses		66	
# of faculty supervised clinical positions filled	62		0
# involved in field placements	49		0
# involved in law journals	24		0
# involved in moot court or trial competitions	16		0
# of credit hours required to graduate		88	

JD Enrollment and Ethnicity

	Men		Women		Full-time		Part-time		1st-year		Total		JD Degs. Awd.
	#	%	#	%	#	%	#	%	#	%	#	%	
African Amer.	1	0.8	0	0.0	1	0.4	0	0.0	0	0.0	1	0.4	1
Amer. Indian	1	0.8	3	3.1	4	1.7	0	0.0	2	2.6	4	1.7	1
Asian Amer.	0	0.0	2	2.0	2	0.9	0	0.0	1	1.3	2	0.9	1
Mex. Amer.	2	1.5	1	1.0	3	1.3	0	0.0	1	1.3	3	1.3	2
Puerto Rican	2	1.5	0	0.0	2	0.9	0	0.0	1	1.3	2	0.9	0
Hispanic	2	1.5	2	2.0	4	1.7	0	0.0	1	1.3	4	1.7	3
Total Minority	8	6.1	8	8.2	16	7.0	0	0.0	6	7.7	16	7.0	8
For. Nation.	2	1.5	2	2.0	4	1.7	0	0.0	2	2.6	4	1.7	1
Caucasian	103	78.6	83	84.7	186	81.2	0	0.0	63	80.8	186	81.2	72
Unknown	18	13.7	5	5.1	23	10.0	0	0.0	7	9.0	23	10.0	3
Total	131	57.2	98	42.8	229	100.0	0	0.0	78	34.1	229		84

Tuition and Fees

	Resident	Nonresident
Full-time	$5,269	$10,869
Part-time	$0	$0

Living Expenses

Estimated living expenses for singles

Living on campus	Living off campus	Living at home
$11,662	$11,662	$5,447

University of Wyoming College of Law

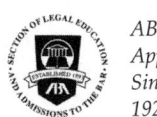

ABA
Approved
Since
1923

GPA and LSAT Scores

	Total	Full-time	Part-time
# of apps	765	765	0
# of admits	191	191	0
# of matrics	78	78	0
75% GPA	3.66	3.66	0.00
25% GPA	3.04	3.04	0.00
75% LSAT	156	156	0
25% LSAT	149	149	0

Grants and Scholarships (from prior year)

	Total		Full-time		Part-time	
	#	%	#	%	#	%
Total # of students	243		243		0	
Total # receiving grants	178	73.3	178	73.3	0	0.0
Less than 1/2 tuition	151	62.1	151	62.1	0	0.0
Half to full tuition	16	6.6	16	6.6	0	0.0
Full tuition	3	1.2	3	1.2	0	0.0
More than full tuition	8	3.3	8	3.3	0	0.0
Median grant amount			$1,000		$0	

Informational and Library Resources

# of volumes and volume equivalents	284,770
# of titles	25,171
# of active serial subscriptions	1,898
Study seating capacity inside the library	250
# of professional librarians	3
Hours per week library is open	107
# of open, wired connections available to students	189
# of networked computers available for use by students	25
# of simultaneous wireless users	180
Require computer?	N

JD Attrition (from prior year)

	Academic	Other	Total	
	#	#	#	%
1st year	1	2	3	3.8%
2nd year	0	3	3	3.8%
3rd year	0	0	0	0.0%
4th year	0	0	0	0.0%

Employment

	Total	Percentage
Employment status known	60	98.4
Employment status unknown	1	1.6
Employed	51	85.0
Pursuing graduate degrees	2	3.3
Unemployed seeking employment	3	5.0
Unemployed not seeking employment	4	6.7

Type of Employment

	Total	Percentage
# employed in law firms	20	39.2
# employed in business and industry	6	11.8
# employed in government	9	17.6
# employed in public interest	2	3.9
# employed as judicial clerks	12	23.5
# employed in academia	0	0.0

Geographic Location

	Total	Percentage
# employed in state	28	54.9
# employed in foreign countries	1	2.0
# of states where employed	13	

Bar Passage Rates

Jurisdiction	Wyoming			Colorado		
Exam	Sum 03	Win 04	Total	Sum 03	Win 04	Total
# from school taking bar for the first time	34	8	42	10	2	12
School's pass rate for all first-time takers	65%	38%	60%	70%	100%	75%
State's pass rate for all first-time takers	72%	47%	65%	75%	73%	75%

University of Wyoming College of Law

Dept. 3035, 1000 E University Ave.
Laramie, WY 82071
Phone: 307.766.6416; Fax: 307.766.6417
E-mail: lawadmis@uwyo.edu; Website: www.uwyo.edu/law

■ Introduction

The University of Wyoming College of Law is located on the campus of the University of Wyoming in Laramie. The university, the only four-year institution of higher learning in Wyoming, comprises seven colleges, a graduate school, and several organized research units. The university has a student body of 13,000.

The College of Law, founded in 1920, is a member of the AALS and is accredited by the ABA. An excellent faculty of 16 full-time professors and several lecturers instructs a student body of about 225. The limited size of the student body and the favorable student-faculty ratio create an atmosphere of friendliness and informality, and students enjoy a degree of access to faculty that students would rarely find at a larger institution.

Laramie is a town of 30,000 located in the southeastern part of Wyoming at an altitude of 7,200 feet on the high plains between two mountain ranges. Laramie's proximity to the mountains provides a variety of recreational activities, including skiing, backpacking, rock climbing, hiking, mountain-biking, camping, fishing, and hunting. Denver is two hours to the south.

■ Library and Physical Facilities

The College of Law first occupied its current building in 1977. The facility provides ample classroom, library, and student study space, and furnishes a pleasant environment for study. A new three-story library addition was completed in the fall of 1993. This addition doubled the existing square footage of the law library, providing individual carrel space for students. All law students are trained in computerized legal research, as well as in traditional research methods. Two of the four major classrooms were renovated in 2004, to provide the latest in technological instruction aids and power/data ports to each seat.

■ Curriculum

The first year consists entirely of required courses. During the second year, students must take additional required courses, including evidence, professional responsibility, and a second semester of constitutional law and civil procedure. Students must also complete an advanced writing requirement prior to graduation. As a condition of graduation from the College of Law, all students must successfully complete at least two of the following three courses—administrative law, business organizations, and trusts and estates. In addition, all students must successfully complete at least one of the following three courses—creditors' rights, income taxation, or secured transactions.

In both the second and third years, practical legal training is available through courses in legal research, legal skills and problems, trial practice, and clinical work. The college has only limited non-classroom offerings in it's summer session; however, graduation may be accelerated one semester by attending two summer sessions at other accredited law schools.

■ Special Programs

The College of Law has a strong program of elective courses in natural resources law. Courses are regularly offered in environmental law, hazardous waste and water pollution, oil and gas, mining law, public land resources, and water rights. Other electives include coverage of trial and appellate practice, business planning, estate planning, corporate and commercial law, administrative law, consumer law, and Indian law.

Students may obtain practical experience and receive academic credit for work in five clinical programs: (1) a defender aid program in which students brief and argue criminal appeals on behalf of indigent persons and assist penitentiary inmates in post-conviction cases; (2) a prosecution assistance program in which students work directly with prosecuting attorneys in criminal cases; (3) a legal services program in which students provide legal assistance to economically disadvantaged persons; (4) a clinic dealing with victims of domestic violence; and (5) a clinic providing legal services in civil matters to University of Wyoming students. All clinical programs operate under faculty supervision. Under a special state rule, students working in the clinics frequently brief and argue cases before the Wyoming Supreme Court, an opportunity that is rare—if not unique—among law schools.

■ Admission Standards

The College of Law generally restricts the entering class to 75–80 students. The school does not discriminate on the basis of race, color, religion, sex, national origin, disability, age, veteran status, sexual orientation, or political belief in making admission decisions.

Students are admitted only for the fall semester. The college begins to accept applications in October for the class entering the following August. The entering class is selected from applications completed and on file by March 1. To meet the March 1 deadline, applicants should take the LSAT no later than February and should register for the LSDAS and arrange for forwarding of official transcripts no later than mid-January.

As a general rule, applicants must have received an undergraduate degree prior to registration. Applicants may submit up to three letters of recommendation. Selection of the entering class is based on consideration of applicants' undergraduate records, LSAT scores, and other criteria relevant to success in the study and practice of law.

■ Student Activities

The College of Law publishes the *Wyoming Law Review*, a student-edited journal. Other student organizations include Potter Law Club, which provides student government and social activities with the Law Student Division of the ABA, three legal fraternities, Christian Legal Society, Intellectual Property Club, International Law Students Association, Minority Law Student Association, Natural Resources Law Forum, Women's Law Forum, and the Wyoming Trial Lawyers Association. Students represent the college each year in the National Moot Court Competition, National Environmental Law Moot Court Competition, National Client Counseling Competition, and the ATLA National Student Trial Advocacy Competition. Student organizations also include two law school honorary societies, the Order of the Coif, and the Order of Barristers.

■ Career Services

About 75 percent of graduates remain in the Rocky Mountain region, but the College of Law alumni around the globe. The curriculum is broad in scope, providing a core foundation of legal knowledge to prepare graduates to practice in a wide range of legal and geographic areas.

Graduates of the UW College of Law practice in primarily small private firms or are employed by state, local, tribal, and national governments. They also find work in public service, public interest organizations, and many alternative careers related to law. Twenty-five percent of graduates consistently work in state and federal judicial clerkships following law school. This is an extraordinary achievement since national placement statistics in judicial clerkships are around 11 percent according to the National Association of Law Placement.

As with other aspects of the college's operation, the small size of the student body permits the Career Services Office to provide students with a level of personal attention that may not be feasible at larger institutions. Students receive one-on-one career counseling and job searching for permanent or summer employment. Career Services also works with students and alumni to develop insightful career panels and résumé cover letter workshops. A network of loyal alums hires often exclusively at the University of Wyoming College of Law. Plus fall and spring on-campus interviews provide many firms and students a chance to interview one another. An online posting system allows national and local organizations to post legal positions for UW students across the country.

Applicant Profile

University of Wyoming College of Law
This grid includes only applicants who earned 120-180 LSAT scores under standard administrations.

LSAT Score	3.75 +		3.50 - 3.74		3.25 - 3.49		3.00 - 3.24		2.75 - 2.99		2.50 - 2.74		2.25 - 2.49		2.00 - 2.24		Below 2.00		No GPA		Total	
	Apps	Adm	Apps	Adm	Apps	Adm	Apps	Adm	Apps	Adm	Apps	Adm	Apps	Adm	Apps	Adm	Apps	Adm	Apps	Adm	Apps	Adm
175-180	0	0	0	0	0	0	0	0	0	0	0	0	0	0	0	0	0	0	0	0	0	0
170-174	0	0	0	0	0	0	0	0	0	0	0	0	0	0	0	0	0	0	0	0	0	0
165-169	0	0	1	1	0	0	2	1	0	0	0	0	1	0	0	0	0	0	0	0	4	2
160-164	8	7	1	1	9	6	6	3	6	2	4	2	1	0	1	0	0	0	1	1	37	22
155-159	12	9	21	8	23	10	36	14	26	8	12	2	2	1	2	0	0	0	0	0	134	52
150-154	20	11	42	20	43	8	53	15	43	6	21	1	5	0	2	0	2	0	2	1	233	62
145-149	17	5	31	10	41	8	45	5	29	4	22	3	12	2	4	0	1	0	5	0	207	37
140-144	4	1	21	4	21	2	13	2	13	1	14	0	12	1	1	0	0	0	3	3	102	14
135-139	1	0	5	0	4	0	5	0	4	0	2	0	1	0	0	0	0	0	1	0	23	0
130-134	0	0	0	0	2	0	2	0	1	0	0	0	0	0	0	0	1	0	1	0	7	0
125-129	0	0	0	0	0	0	0	0	0	0	1	0	1	0	0	0	0	0	0	0	2	0
120-124	0	0	0	0	0	0	0	0	0	0	0	0	0	0	0	0	0	0	0	0	0	0
Total	62	33	122	44	143	34	162	40	122	21	76	8	35	4	10	0	4	0	13	5	749	189

Apps = Number of Applicants
Adm = Number Admitted
Reflects 99% of the total applicant pool.

Yale Law School

PO Box 208329
New Haven, CT 06520-8329
Phone: 203.432.4995
E-mail: admissions.law@yale.edu; Website: www.law.yale.edu

The Basics

Type of school	Private
Term	Semester
Application deadline	2/1
Application fee	$70
Financial aid deadline	3/15
Can first year start other than fall?	No
Student to faculty ratio (fall)	7.9 to 1
Does the university offer:	
housing restricted to law students?	Yes
graduate housing for which law students are eligible?	Yes

Faculty and Administrators

	Total		Men		Women		Minorities	
	Fall	Spr	Fall	Spr	Fall	Spr	Fall	Spr
Full-time	61	58	50	50	11	8	9	8
Other Full-time	4	4	1	1	3	3	2	2
Deans, librarians, & others who teach	10	10	5	5	5	5	2	2
Part-time	43	41	27	28	16	13	5	5
Total	**118**	**113**	**83**	**84**	**35**	**29**	**18**	**17**

Curriculum

	Full-time	Part-time
Typical first-year section size	68	0
Is there typically a "small section" of the first-year class, other than Legal Writing, taught by full-time faculty	Yes	No
If yes, typical size offered last year	17	0
# of classroom course titles beyond 1st year curriculum	148	

# of upper division courses, excluding seminars with an enrollment:		
	Under 25	22
	25-49	22
	50-74	13
	75-99	8
	100+	3

# of seminars	80	
# of seminar positions available	1,120	
# of seminar positions filled	891	0
# of positions available in simulation courses	210	
# of simulation positions filled	181	0
# of positions available in faculty supervised clinical courses	468	
# of faculty supervised clinical positions filled	400	0
# involved in field placements	37	0
# involved in law journals	441	0
# involved in moot court or trial competitions	125	0
# of credit hours required to graduate	82	

JD Enrollment and Ethnicity

	Men		Women		Full-time		Part-time		1st-year		Total		JD Degs. Awd.
	#	%	#	%	#	%	#	%	#	%	#	%	
African Amer.	21	6.5	28	10.9	49	8.4	0	0.0	19	10.1	49	8.4	16
Amer. Indian	0	0.0	1	0.4	1	0.2	0	0.0	0	0.0	1	0.2	1
Asian Amer.	35	10.8	39	15.2	74	12.8	0	0.0	21	11.1	74	12.7	17
Mex. Amer.	10	3.1	9	3.5	18	3.1	1	100.0	5	2.6	19	3.3	4
Puerto Rican	4	1.2	4	1.6	8	1.4	0	0.0	2	1.1	8	1.4	1
Hispanic	18	5.6	11	4.3	29	5.0	0	0.0	12	6.3	29	5.0	7
Total Minority	88	27.2	92	35.8	179	30.9	1	100.0	59	31.2	180	31.0	46
For. Nation.	10	3.1	8	3.1	18	3.1	0	0.0	7	3.7	18	3.1	7
Caucasian	215	66.4	152	59.1	367	63.3	0	0.0	117	61.9	367	63.2	126
Unknown	11	3.4	5	1.9	16	2.8	0	0.0	6	3.2	16	2.8	4
Total	324	55.8	257	44.2	580	99.8	1	0.2	189	32.5	581		183

Tuition and Fees

	Resident	Nonresident
Full-time	$36,490	$36,490
Part-time	$0	$0

Living Expenses

Estimated living expenses for singles

Living on campus	Living off campus	Living at home
$13,500	$13,500	$13,500

Yale Law School

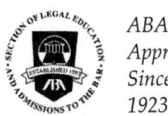

GPA and LSAT Scores

	Total	Full-time	Part-time
# of apps	3,783	3,783	0
# of admits	246	246	0
# of matrics	189	189	0
75% GPA	3.96	3.96	0.00
25% GPA	3.79	3.79	0.00
75% LSAT	175	175	0
25% LSAT	168	168	0

Grants and Scholarships (from prior year)

	Total		Full-time		Part-time	
	#	%	#	%	#	%
Total # of students	582		582		0	
Total # receiving grants	263	45.2	263	45.2	0	0.0
Less than 1/2 tuition	152	26.1	152	26.1	0	0.0
Half to full tuition	108	18.6	108	18.6	0	0.0
Full tuition	2	0.3	2	0.3	0	0.0
More than full tuition	1	0.2	1	0.2	0	0.0
Median grant amount			$14,810		$0	

Informational and Library Resources

# of volumes and volume equivalents	1,104,485
# of titles	320,569
# of active serial subscriptions	10,873
Study seating capacity inside the library	414
# of professional librarians	18
Hours per week library is open	133
# of open, wired connections available to students	1,009
# of networked computers available for use by students	111
# of simultaneous wireless users	540
Require computer?	N

JD Attrition (from prior year)

	Academic	Other	Total	
	#	#	#	%
1st year	0	0	0	0.0%
2nd year	0	1	1	0.5%
3rd year	0	1	1	0.5%
4th year	0	0	0	0.0%

Employment

	Total	Percentage
Employment status known	216	99.5
Employment status unknown	1	0.5
Employed	205	94.9
Pursuing graduate degrees	6	2.8
Unemployed seeking employment	3	1.4
Unemployed not seeking employment	2	0.9

Type of Employment

	Total	Percentage
# employed in law firms	96	46.8
# employed in business and industry	5	2.4
# employed in government	5	2.4
# employed in public interest	10	4.9
# employed as judicial clerks	86	42.0
# employed in academia	3	1.5

Geographic Location

	Total	Percentage
# employed in state	11	5.4
# employed in foreign countries	7	3.4
# of states where employed	30	

Bar Passage Rates

Jurisdiction	New York		
Exam	Sum 03	Win 04	Total
# from school taking bar for the first time	90	6	96
School's pass rate for all first-time takers	96%	83%	95%
State's pass rate for all first-time takers	78%	58%	75%

Yale Law School

PO Box 208329
New Haven, CT 06520-8329
Phone: 203.432.4995
E-mail: admissions.law@yale.edu; Website: www.law.yale.edu

■ Introduction

Yale Law School is an extraordinary community in which to study law. Standing at the intersection of the worlds of thought and action, Yale seeks not only to promote an intellectual understanding of the law, but also to sustain the moral commitments that justice requires.

Extensive student-faculty interactions and institutional flexibility are hallmarks of the Yale Law School experience. Students enjoy countless opportunities for research and writing with professors. Our unmatched faculty-to-student ratio allows us to offer a wide range of courses and small classes, with an average class size of under 20 students.

The school is also part of one of the world's great research universities. Yale University is home to an abundance of intellectual, cultural, social, and athletic activities, all of which are accessible to Yale Law students.

■ Students

The vitality of Yale Law School depends as much on the knowledge, experience, and interests of the students as it does on the faculty, the library, or the alumni. The school selects its entering class from applicants with the highest academic qualifications. Within this exceptional group, Yale seeks a diversity of backgrounds, experiences, and interests. This diversity is reflected in the many thriving student organizations and student-run journals found at the school.

■ Faculty

The faculty at Yale Law School is as broad-ranging in its interests and expertise as it is distinguished. It includes prominent scholars of economics, philosophy, and the social sciences as well as leading specialists in every area of law. Sixty-eight full-time professors are joined each year by visiting lecturers, adjunct professors from other parts of the university, and practicing lawyers. Additionally, dozens of guest lecturers from around the world—ranging from Kofi Annan to Greta Van Susteren—help to make Yale Law School a vibrant intellectual community.

■ Facilities and Housing

The Sterling Law Building occupies one city block in the heart of Yale University and downtown New Haven. The recently renovated building was modeled on the English Inns of Court, with classrooms, a dining hall, faculty offices, the law library, and a dormitory surrounding three pleasant courtyards. All classrooms are Internet-accessible, and a wireless network is available in the common areas. A daycare center is located on-site.

Forty remodeled dormitory rooms are available by lottery. Other Yale campus housing is also available, but most students live off-campus, within a 10-minute walk of the Law School.

■ Curriculum and Grading

The Yale Law School curriculum is very flexible. Students are able to shape their own course of study to satisfy their unique intellectual interests and goals. In the fall semester, all first-year students take classes in constitutional law, contracts, procedure, and torts. One of these classes is a small group of about 16 students, which includes instruction in legal research and writing. After the first term, students may select any classes they wish, including independent studies, clinics, and courses outside the Law School. Two major writing projects and courses in criminal law and professional responsibility are required for graduation.

In order to allow students to concentrate on learning, rather than on GPAs, Yale Law School does not use grades in the traditional sense. During the fall of first year, all classes are credit/fail. In subsequent terms, grades are honors, pass, low pass, and fail, with credit/fail options available. Yale Law School does not calculate class rankings.

■ Joint Degrees, Special Programs, and Clinical Opportunities

Yale Law School sees the study of law as interrelated with other intellectual disciplines and with practical experience. The Law School offers a number of joint degrees with other schools and departments at Yale, including JD/MBAs, JD/PhDs, and JD/MDs. Joint degrees with other universities and opportunities for intensive semester experiences outside the Law School are available.

Yale Law School also offers a number of clinical opportunities to all students beginning in the first year. For example, students participate in international human rights work under the auspices of the Lowenstein International Human Rights Clinic. Other clinics including advocacy for prisoners, people with disabilities, children, and immigrants, provide opportunities for Yale law students to work on behalf of clients who cannot afford private attorneys.

■ Transfer Students and Advanced Degrees

Students who have completed two semesters of study at another law school may apply to transfer to Yale Law School. Transfer students must complete at least two years of work at Yale Law School.

In addition to the JD, Yale Law School offers an LLM degree for foreign lawyers who are interested in teaching law. The Master of Studies in Law (MSL) is a one-year program designed for professionals in other fields who desire an intensive introduction to the law. Yale also offers a JSD program for the school's LLM students.

■ Financial Aid and Loan Forgiveness

Financial aid is awarded solely on the basis of need, and admission decisions are made independently of financial aid decisions. Approximately 80 percent of the student body now receives some form of financial aid. A financial aid award may consist of a portion in grant and portion in loan; typically, the higher the total financial need, the higher the proportion of grant.

In addition to financial aid during law school, Yale has the most generous loan forgiveness program in the country: the Career Options Assistance Program (COAP). COAP provides grants to help repay the educational loans of graduates who take relatively low-paying jobs. Unlike many loan forgiveness programs, Yale's COAP includes not only law school loans, but some undergraduate loans as well. Last year, COAP covered over $2.2 million worth of loan payments for over 300 graduates.

■ Career Development

Yale Law School graduates occupy leadership positions in a tremendous range of endeavors. The Law School Career Development Office helps students explore the unparalleled diversity of opportunities available to them. Most students work for public interest organizations, private firms, or government entities during summer breaks. After graduation, a large number of students obtain judicial clerkships. Others work for law firms or corporations, while still others take advantage of public service fellowships available to Yale Law School graduates. In addition, many graduates pursue careers in academia.

■ The Admission Process

The admission process at Yale Law School is intensely competitive. No single element in an application is decisive; the totality of available information about the applicant is taken into account. A 250-word essay, on a subject of the applicant's choice, is required. Personal statements are also welcome, and applicants are encouraged to bring aspects of their personal background or other special characteristics to the attention of the admission committee. Two letters of recommendation are required; additional letters are also welcome.

Each application file is first read by the Dean or Director of Admissions. A group of the most highly rated files is then considered by faculty. Each faculty member rates applications on the basis of the faculty member's unique criteria; the weight given to various factors is within each reader's discretion.

The Law School issues most of its decisions by the beginning of April, but decisions continue to be made throughout the spring. Use of the wait list varies from year to year, and the list is not ranked until offers are made.

Applicant Profile

Yale Law School

Undergraduate GPA	Average LSAT Score on the 120-180 Scale													
	Below 155		155-159		160-164		165-169		170-174		175-180		Total	
	Apps	Adm	Apps	Adm	Apps	Adm	Apps	Adm	Apps	Adm	Apps	Adm	Apps	Adm
3.75 +	107	1	110	2	271	10	456	41	399	100	139	62	1482	216
3.50-3.74	112	1	99	0	226	1	306	13	214	15	79	8	1036	38
3.25-3.49	123	0	83	0	131	2	152	3	95	5	18	4	602	14
3.00-3.24	105	0	42	0	63	1	40	0	14	0	8	0	272	1
Below 3.00	110	0	39	1	32	0	18	0	15	0	4	0	218	1
No GPA	36	0	18	0	25	0	25	0	12	2	3	0	119	2
Total	593	2	391	3	748	14	997	57	749	122	251	74	3729	272

Totals reflect 99 percent of applicant pool.
Apps = Number of Applicants
Adm = Number Admitted

Appendix A: Legal Education Statistics

Law School Attendance Figures, Fall 2004

		Full-time	Part-time	Total
First Year	Total	39,924	8,315	48,239
	Women	18,971	3,933	22,904
Second Year	Total	39,658	5,248	44,906
	Women	18,991	2,553	21,544
Third Year	Total	38,647	4,709	43,356
	Women	18,868	2,288	21,156
Fourth Year	Total	0	3,875	3,875
	Women	0	1,834	1,834
JD Total	Total	118,229	22,147	140,376
	Women	56,830	10,608	67,438
Post-JD	Total	4,260	2,247	6,507
	Women	1,814	1,026	2,840
Other	Total	699	587	1,286
	Women	374	340	714
Grand Total	Total	123,188	24,981	148,169
	Women	59,018	11,974	70,992

Professional Degrees Conferred, 2004

		Full-time	Part-time	Total
JD/LLB	Total	35,349	4,674	40,023
	Women	17,524	2,294	19,818
LLM	Total	3,506	554	4,060
	Women	1,442	256	1,698
MCL/MCJ	Total	23	0	23
	Women	11	0	11
SJD/JSD	Total	61	9	70
	Women	14	6	20
Other	Total	427	193	620
	Women	206	113	319
Total	Total	39,366	5,430	44,796
	Women	19,197	2,669	21,866

Teachers in Law Schools, 2004–2005

	Women	Minorities	Total
Full-time	2,393	1,074	6,959
Part-time	2,145	721	6,975
Deans & Administrators	2,239	707	3,553
Librarians	1,064	242	1,631

Total Minority Enrollment

Academic Year	Number of Schools Reporting*	First Year	Second Year	Third Year	Fourth Year	Total
2004–05	188	10,694	9,280	8,766	749	29,489
2003–04	187	10,468	9,144	8,062	721	28,318
2002–03	187	10,224	8,326	7,898	721	27,169
2001–02	184	9,557	8,172	7,785	743	26,257
2000–01	183	9,335	8,052	7,690	676	25,753
1999–00	182	9,079	7,876	7,547	751	25,253
1998–99	181	9,076	7,635	7,761	794	25,266
1997–98	178	8,493	7,740	7,705	747	24,685
1996–97	179	8,722	8,009	7,869	679	25,279
1995–96	178	9,119	8,402	7,411	622	25,554
1994–95	177	9,249	7,633	7,124	605	24,611
1993–94	176	8,595	7,244	6,409	551	22,799
1992–93	176	8,070	6,682	6,032	482	21,266
1991–92	176	7,575	6,155	5,255	425	19,410
1990–91	175	6,933	5,325	4,676	396	17,330
1989–90	175	6,172	4,890	4,264	394	15,720
1988–89	174	5,565	4,408	3,911	411	14,295
1987–88	175	5,130	3,994	3,717	409	13,250
1986–87	175	4,738	3,839	3,648	325	12,550
1985–86	175	4,534	3,810	3,625	388	12,357

*Please note that the minority enrollment charts on pages 25 through 34 do not include students from the three Puerto Rican schools. JD Enrollment for the law schools in Puerto Rico was 1,962 for fall 2004.

American Indian or Alaskan Native Enrollment

Academic Year	Number of Schools Reporting	First Year	Second Year	Third Year	Fourth Year	Total
2004–05	188	387	366	325	28	1,106
2003–04	187	396	341	291	20	1,048
2002–03	187	375	318	317	11	1,021
2001–02	184	365	323	275	27	990
2000–01	183	348	293	290	21	952
1999–00	182	342	294	312	30	978
1998–99	181	361	307	351	45	1,064
1997–98	178	355	348	355	27	1,085
1996–97	179	391	397	310	18	1,116
1995–96	178	436	338	294	17	1,085
1994–95	177	377	283	290	12	962
1993–94	176	336	280	243	14	873
1992–93	176	313	243	206	14	776
1991–92	176	286	219	176	11	692
1990–91	175	224	185	129	16	554
1989–90	175	220	147	143	17	527
1988–89	174	177	165	149	8	499
1987–88	175	189	144	148	11	492
1986–87	175	176	155	148	9	488
1985–86	174	183	146	124	10	463

Asian or Pacific Islander Enrollment

Academic Year	Number of Schools Reporting	First Year	Second Year	Third Year	Fourth Year	Total
2004–05	188	3,982	3,440	3,217	217	10,856
2003–04	187	3,881	3,279	2,685	195	10,040
2002–03	187	3,602	2,819	2,578	182	9,181
2001–02	184	3,052	2,646	2,541	182	8,421
2000–01	183	2,924	2,570	2,510	169	8,173
1999–00	182	2,772	2,519	2,401	191	7,883
1998–99	181	2,762	2,403	2,497	215	7,877
1997–98	178	2,562	2,463	2,394	180	7,599
1996–97	179	2,695	2,451	2,380	180	7,706
1995–96	178	2,773	2,572	2,225	149	7,719
1994–95	177	2,740	2,247	2,087	122	7,196
1993–94	176	2,432	2,101	1,789	136	6,458
1992–93	176	2,235	1,873	1,618	97	5,823
1991–92	176	2,019	1,621	1,306	82	5,028
1990–91	175	1,753	1,343	1,134	76	4,306
1989–90	175	1,501	1,151	946	78	3,676
1988–89	174	1,282	954	825	72	3,133
1987–88	175	1,064	804	724	64	2,656
1986–87	175	929	685	650	39	2,303
1985–86	175	799	678	622	54	2,153

African American Enrollment

Academic Year	Number of Schools Reporting	First Year	Second Year	Third Year	Fourth Year	Total
2004–05	188	3,457	2,873	2,845	313	9,488
2003–04	187	3,300	3,007	2,786	342	9,435
2002–03	187	3,491	2,875	2,773	297	9,436
2001–02	184	3,474	2,867	2,737	334	9,412
2000–01	183	3,402	2,890	2,757	305	9,354
1999–00	182	3,353	2,903	2,700	316	9,272
1998–99	181	3,478	2,728	2,754	311	9,271
1997–98	178	3,126	2,752	2,887	367	9,132
1996–97	179	3,223	3,013	2,991	315	9,542
1995–96	178	3,474	3,161	2,855	289	9,542
1994–95	177	3,600	3,000	2,771	310	9,681
1993–94	176	3,455	2,846	2,573	282	9,156
1992–93	176	3,303	2,603	2,465	267	8,638
1991–92	176	3,169	2,556	2,196	228	8,149
1990–91	175	2,982	2,222	2,023	205	7,432
1989–90	175	2,628	2,128	1,816	219	6,791
1988–89	174	2,463	1,913	1,728	217	6,321
1987–88	175	2,339	1,761	1,690	238	6,028
1986–87	175	2,159	1,800	1,735	200	5,894
1985–86	175	1,800	1,838	1,791	240	6,052

Mexican American Enrollment

Academic Year	Number of Schools Reporting	First Year	Second Year	Third Year	Fourth Year	Total
2004–05	188	938	855	819	53	2,665
2003–04	187	923	831	738	47	2,539
2002–03	187	906	771	680	55	2,412
2001–02	184	896	705	686	47	2,334
2000–01	183	883	757	734	43	2,417
1999–00	182	901	772	750	60	2,483
1998–99	181	885	734	764	68	2,451
1997–98	178	859	766	777	50	2,452
1996–97	179	861	768	751	49	2,429
1995–96	178	896	820	743	36	2,495
1994–95	177	902	739	719	42	2,402
1993–94	176	838	698	639	28	2,203
1992–93	176	807	744	683	24	2,258
1991–92	176	770	644	584	29	2,027
1990–91	175	768	624	527	31	1,950
1989–90	175	640	531	469	23	1,663
1988–89	174	656	510	458	33	1,657
1987–88	175	610	528	472	34	1,644
1986–87	176	564	486	431	31	1,512
1985–86	175	609	503	500	23	1,635

Puerto Rican Enrollment

Academic Year	Number of Schools Reporting	First Year	Second Year	Third Year	Fourth Year	Total
2004–05	188	181	206	182	25	594
2003–04	187	228	204	194	29	655
2002–03	187	208	198	204	29	639
2001–02	184	221	216	222	30	689
2000–01	183	249	213	191	27	680
1999–00	182	243	188	192	23	646
1998–99	181	206	205	196	25	632
1997–98	178	224	198	188	26	636
1996–97	179	206	213	238	29	686
1995–96	178	236	238	214	17	705
1994–95	177	263	244	186	25	718
1993–94	176	275	195	177	17	664
1992–93	176	202	193	177	15	587
1991–92	176	208	177	140	14	539
1990–91	175	183	153	158	12	506
1989–90	175	171	150	156	6	483
1988–89	174	168	156	141	13	478
1987–88	175	178	134	140	7	459
1986–87	175	183	152	130	6	471
1985–86	175	171	126	108	7	412

Other Hispanic American Enrollment

Academic Year	Number of Schools Reporting	First Year	Second Year	Third Year	Fourth Year	Total
2004–05	188	1,749	1,540	1,378	113	4,780
2003–04	187	1,724	1,430	1,328	135	4,617
2002–03	187	1,642	1,345	1,346	147	4,480
2001–02	184	1,549	1,415	1,324	123	4,411
2000–01	183	1,529	1,329	1,208	111	4,177
1999–00	182	1,468	1,200	1,192	131	3,991
1998–99	181	1,384	1,258	1,199	130	3,971
1997–98	178	1,367	1,213	1,104	97	3,781
1996–97	179	1,346	1,167	1,199	88	3,880
1995–96	178	1,304	1,273	1,079	114	3,770
1994–95	177	1,367	1,120	1,071	94	3,652
1993–94	176	1,259	1,124	988	74	3,445
1992–93	176	1,210	966	883	65	3,124
1991–92	176	1,123	938	853	61	2,975
1990–91	175	1,023	798	705	56	2,582
1989–90	175	1,019	783	734	51	2,587
1988–89	174	819	710	610	68	2,207
1987–88	175	750	623	543	55	1,971
1986–87	175	727	561	554	40	1,882
1985–86	175	589	516	477	50	1,632

Legal Education Statistics, 1982–2004

Academic Year	Number of Schools	Total LSAT Administrations	Applicants	First-year Enrollment	Total JD Enrollment	Total[1] Overall Enrollment	JD or LLB Awarded
2004–05	189	145,258	*	48,239	140,376	148,169	40,023
2003–04	187	147,617	99,504	48,867	137,676	145,088	38,314
2002–03	186	148,014	90,853	48,433	132,901	139,366	38,605
2001–02	184	134,251	77,235	45,070	127,610	135,091	37,687
2000–01	183	109,030	74,550	43,518	125,173	132,464	38,157
1999–00	182	107,153	74,380	43,152	125,184	132,276	39,071
1998–99	181	104,236	71,726	42,804	125,627	131,833	39,455
1997–98	178[2]	103,991	72,340	42,186	125,886	131,801	40,114
1996–97	179	105,315	76,715	43,245	125,623	134,949	39,920
1995–96	178	114,756	84,305	43,676	129,397	135,595	39,271
1994–95	177	128,553	89,633	44,298	128,989	134,784	39,710
1993–94	176	132,028	91,892	43,644	127,802	133,339	40,213
1992–93	176	140,054	97,720	42,793	128,212	133,783	39,425
1991–92	176	145,567	99,327	44,050	129,580	135,157	38,800
1990–91	175	152,685	92,958	44,104	127,261	132,433	36,385
1989–90	175	138,865	87,288	43,826	124,471	129,698	35,520
1988–89	174	137,088	78,930	42,860	120,694	125,870	35,701
1987–88	175	115,988	68,804	41,055	117,997	123,198	35,478
1986–87	175	101,235	65,168	40,195	117,813	132,277	36,121
1985–86	175	91,848	60,338	40,796	118,700	124,092	36,829
1984–85	174	95,563	63,801	40,747	119,847	125,698	36,687
1983–84	173	105,076	71,755	41,159	121,201	127,195	36,389
1982–83	172	112,125	72,912	42,034	121,791	127,828	34,846

Note: Enrollment is in American Bar Association-approved law schools as of October 1, 2004. The LSAT year begins in June and ends in February of the following year. JD or LLB degrees are those awarded by approved schools for the academic year ending in the first year stated. Total new admissions to the bar include those admitted by office study, diploma privilege, and examination and study at an unapproved law school. The great bulk of those admitted were graduated from approved schools.

[1] Total overall enrollment includes post-JD and other.

[2] The District of Columbia School of Law is not included in this figure.

[3] Data were not complete for these years; this figure is lower than prior years.

*Data not available.

Appendix B: Post-JD Programs

Standard 308 of the ABA *Standards: Rules of Procedure for Approval of Law Schools* states that an ABA-approved law school may not establish a degree program in addition to its JD degree program unless the school is fully approved, and the quality of its JD degree program meets the requirements of the Standards, and the additional degree program may not detract from a law school's ability to maintain a sound JD degree program, and finally, the school must obtain the Council's acquiescence.

For additional information about post-JD programs you should visit the Section of Legal Education and Admissions to the Bar's website at *www.abanet.org/legaled*. However, for specific information about post-JD programs you should contact the school(s) directly. In addition, if you have not obtained a JD from an ABA-approved law school you may wish to contact the bar admission authorities in the state(s) in which you intend to practice for more information on whether graduation from a post-JD program will qualify you to take the bar examination in that state. Please note, however, that it is the ABA Section of Legal Education and Admissions to the Bar Council's position that no graduate degree in law is or should be a substitute for the first professional degree in law (JD) and should not serve as the same basis for bar admission purposes as the JD degree.

For updates or corrections to the following list, please visit the Section's website: *www.abanet.org/legaled*.

■ Graduate Degrees Defined

While an individual law school's degree may differ slightly by name to similar programs elsewhere, most degrees offered through law schools fall into three general categories:

1) Academic master's degrees for nonlawyers, such as:

   MS   Master of Science or Master of Studies
   MPS   Master of Professional Studies

2) Post-JD law degrees for practicing lawyers and/or foreign lawyers seeking to practice in the US, such as:
   LLM   Master of Laws

   JM   Juris Master
   MCL   Master of Comparative Law
   MJ   Master of Jurisprudence

3) Research and academic-based doctorate level degrees, such as:
   JSD   Doctor of Jurisprudence
   SJD   Doctor of Juridical Science
   DCL   Doctor of Comparative Law

For questions regarding specific degree descriptions, contact the school directly.

■ Post-JD Programs By School

Akron, University of
Intellectual Property, LLM

Alabama, University of
Taxation, LLM
General, LLM

Albany Law School
General, LLM; MLS

American University
International Legal Studies, LLM
Government and Public Policy, LLM
General, SJD

Arizona, University of
International Trade Law, LLM
Indigenous Peoples Law and Policy, LLM

Arkansas (Fayetteville), University of
Agricultural Law, LLM

Baltimore, University of
Taxation, LLM

Boston University
Taxation, LLM
Banking and Financial Law, LLM
American Law (for foreign lawyers), LLM
Intellectual Property, LLM

Brigham Young University
Comparative Law (for foreign lawyers), LLM

Buffalo State University of New York, University at
Criminal Law, LLM

California—Berkeley, University of
General, LLM; JSD

California—Davis, University of
US Law (for foreign lawyers), LLM

California—Hastings, University of
US Law (for foreign lawyers), LLM

California at Los Angeles, University of
As Approved (for foreign lawyers), LLM

California Western
Comparative Law (for foreign lawyers), LLM; MCL
Advocacy (with specialization in federal criminal law), LLM

Capital University
Taxation, LLM; MT
Taxation and Business, LLM
Taxation, JD/LLM
Business, JD/LLM; LLM

Cardozo School of Law
Intellectual Property Law, LLM
General, LLM

Case Western Reserve University
Taxation, LLM
US Legal Studies (for foreign lawyers), LLM

Catholic University of America
As Approved, LLM

Chapman University
Taxation, LLM

Chicago, University of
General, LLM; MCL; DCL; JSD

Chicago-Kent—Illinois Institute of Technology
Taxation, LLM
International and Comparative Law, LLM
Financial Services Law, LLM
International Intellectual Property, LLM

Cleveland State University
General, LLM

Columbia University
General, LLM; JSD

Connecticut, University of
Insurance Law, LLM
US Legal Studies (for foreign lawyers), LLM

Cornell Law School
General, LLM; JSD
International and Comparative Law, LLM

Denver, University of
Natural Resources, LLM
American and Comparative Law (for foreign lawyers), LLM
Taxation, LLM

DePaul, University of
Taxation, LLM
Health Law, LLM
Intellectual Property, LLM

Duke University
Research, SJD
US Law for International Students and International
Comparative Law, LLM

Emory University
General, LLM

Florida, University of
Taxation, LLM; SJD
Comparative Law, LLM

Florida State University
American Law (for foreign lawyers), LLM

Fordham University
Banking, Corporate, and Finance Law, LLM
International Business and Trade Law, LLM

Franklin Pierce Law Center
Intellectual Property, Commerce and Technology, LLM; MIP
Education Law, MEL

George Mason University
Policy Analysis, JM
Intellectual Property, LLM
Law and Economics, LLM

George Washington University
General, LLM
Environmental Law, LLM
Intellectual Property Law, LLM
Government Procurement Law, LLM
International and Comparative Law, LLM
Various, SJD
Litigation and Dispute Resolution, LLM

Georgetown University
General, LLM
Taxation, LLM
International and Comparative Law, LLM
Securities and Financial Regulation, LLM
Advocacy, LLM
International Legal Studies (or general studies), LLM
As Approved (for foreign lawyers), SJD

Georgia, University of
General, LLM

Golden Gate University
Taxation, LLM
International Legal Studies, LLM; SJD
US Legal Studies (for foreign lawyers), LLM
Environmental Law, LLM
Intellectual Property, LLM

Hamline University
Foreign Lawyers, LLM

Harvard Law School
General, LLM; SJD

Hawai'i, University of
Foreign Lawyers, LLM

Hofstra University
American Legal Studies (for foreign lawyers), LLM
International Law, LLM

Houston, University of
International Law, LLM
Energy, Environment and Natural Resources, LLM
Tax Law, LLM
Foreign Scholars Program, LLM
Health Law, LLM
Intellectual Property and Information Law, LLM

Howard University
International Law, LLM

Illinois, University of
General, JSD; LLM

Indiana University—Bloomington
As Approved, LLM; SJD
Comparative Law, MCL
Research, SJD

Indiana University—Indianapolis
American Law (for foreign lawyers), LLM

Iowa, University of
International and Comparative Law, LLM

John Marshall Law School
Taxation, LLM
Intellectual Property, LLM
Comparative Legal Studies, LLM
Real Estate, LLM
Information Technology, LLM; MS

International Business and Trade Law, LLM
Employee Benefits, LLM

Judge Advocate General's School
Military Law, LLM

Lewis & Clark Law School
Environmental/Natural Resources, LLM

Louisiana State University
As Approved, BCL; LLM; MCL

Loyola Law School (Los Angeles)
Taxation, LLM

Loyola University—Chicago
Health Law, LLM; MJ
Child Law, LLM; MJ
Corporate Law, MJ
Business Law, LLM
Taxation, LLM
Health Law and Policy, DL; SJD

Miami, University of
Taxation, LLM
Estate Planning, LLM
Ocean and Coastal Law, LLM
International Law, LLM
Inter-American Law, LLM
Real Property, Land Development, and Finance Law, LLM
Comparative Law, LLM

Michigan State University
American Legal System (for foreign lawyers), LLM
Intellectual Property, LLM

Michigan, University of
As Approved, LLM; MCL; SJD

Minnesota, University of
American Law (for foreign lawyers), LLM

Missouri—Columbia, University of
Dispute Resolution, LLM

Missouri—Kansas City, University of
General, LLM
Taxation, LLM
Urban Affairs, LLM
Estate Planning, LLM

Nebraska, University of
Law/Psychology, MLS

New England School of Law
US Law (for foreign lawyers), LLM

New York Law School
Taxation, LLM

New York University
As Approved, JSD
Corporate Law, LLM
International Legal Studies, LLM
Taxation, LLM
Trade Regulation, LLM
General Studies, LLM
International Taxation, LLM
Comparative Jurisprudence, MCJ
Labor and Employment Law, LLM
International Public Interest, LLM

Northern Kentucky University
Law/Business, JD

Northwestern University
Research, SJD
As Approved, LLM

Notre Dame Law School
International and Comparative Law, LLM
International Human Rights, JSD; LLM

Pace University
Environmental Law, LLM; SJD
Comparative Legal Studies, LLM

Pacific, McGeorge, University of
Taxation, LLM
Business and Taxation, LLM
Transnational Business Practice, LLM
Government and Public Policy, LLM
International Water Resources Law, JSD; LLM

Penn State University
Comparative Law, LLM

Pennsylvania, University of
As Approved, LLCM; LLM; SJD

Pepperdine University
Dispute Resolution, MDR, LLM

Pittsburgh, University of
International and Comparative Law, LLM

Puerto Rico, University of
General (for foreign lawyers), LLM

Regent University
International Tax, LLM

St. John's University
Bankruptcy, LLM

Saint Louis University
Health Law, LLM
American Law (for foreign lawyers), LLM

St. Mary's University
International and Comparative Law, LLM
American Legal Studies (for foreign lawyers), LLM

St. Thomas University
International Taxation, LLM
Intercultural Human Rights, LLM

Samford University
Comparative Law, MCL
General, SJD

San Diego, University of
Taxation, LLM
Comparative Law, LLM
General, LLM
International Law, LLM
Business and Corporate Law, LLM

San Francisco, University of
International Transactions and Comparative Law, LLM
Intellectual Property and Technology Law, LLM

Santa Clara University
Comparative Law (for foreign lawyers), LLM
Intellectual Property Law, LLM
Comparative and International Law, LLM

Seton Hall University
Health Law, LLM

SMU Dedman
General, LLM; SJD
Comparative and International Law, LLM
Taxation, LLM

Southern California Law School
General (for foreign lawyers), LLM

Southwestern University
Entertainment/Media Law, LLM

Stanford University
As Approved, JSD; JSM
Corporate Governance, LLM
Law, Science, and Technology, LLM

Stetson University
International Law and Business, LLM

Suffolk University
International Intellectual Property, Comparative
    Biomedicine and Healthcare, Global Information
    Technology, LLM

Temple University
General, LLM
Taxation, LLM
American Common Law Legal System, LLM
International and Comparative Law (for foreign
    lawyers), LLM
Law and Humanities, LLM
Clinical Legal Education, LLM
Trial Advocacy, LLM
General (in China), LLM

Texas, University of
General, LLM

Thomas M. Cooley Law School
Taxation, LLM
Intellectual Property, LLM

Touro College
American Legal Studies (for foreign lawyers), LLM
General, LLM

Tulane University
General, LLM; SJD
Admiralty, LLM
Energy and Environment, LLM
Comparative Law, MCL
Comparative Law and Latin American Studies, MCL-MA
International and Comparative Law, LLM

Tulsa, University of
Comparative and International Law (for foreign
    lawyers), LLM
American Indian and Indigenous Law, LLM

Utah, University of
Environmental and Natural Resources Law, LLM

Valparaiso University
General, LLM

Vanderbilt University
Research, LLM

Vermont Law School
Environmental Law and Policy, LLM; MSEL

Villanova University
Taxation, LLM

Virginia, University of
General, LLM; SJD
Judicial Process, LLM

Wake Forest University
American Law (for foreign lawyers), LLM

Washington & Lee University
United States Law, LLM

Washington, University of
Asian and Comparative Law, LLM; PhD
Law and Marine Affairs, LLM
International Environmental Law, LLM
Sustainable International Development, LLM
Taxation, LLM
Intellectual Property and Technology Law, LLM

Washington University
Taxation, LLM
Research, JSD
Urban Studies, LLM
US Law, LLM
Intellectual Property and Technology Law, LLM

Wayne State University
General, LLM
Corporate and Finance Law, LLM
Labor Law, LLM
Taxation, LLM

Whittier Law School
US Legal Studies (for foreign lawyers), LLM

Widener University
Corporate Law and Finance, LLM
Health Law, DL; LLM; MJ; SJD

William & Mary Law School
American Legal System (for foreign lawyers), LLM

Wisconsin, University of
Research, LLM; MLI; SJD

Yale Law School
General, LLM; JSD

■ Post-JD Programs by Category

Admiralty/Marine Affairs
Tulane University, LLM
Washington, University of, LLM

Agricultural Law
Arkansas (Fayetteville), University of, LLM

Asian and Comparative Law
Washington, University of, LLM; PhD

Banking, Corporate, and Finance Law/Financial Services/Securities
Boston University, LLM
Chicago-Kent—Illinois Institute of Technology, LLM
Fordham University, LLM
Loyola University—Chicago, MJ
New York University, LLM
Stanford University, LLM
Wayne State University, LLM
Widener University, LLM

Bankruptcy Law
St. John's University, LLM

Business and Taxation
Capital University, LLM
Pacific, McGeorge, University of, LLM

Business Law
Capital University, JD/LLM; LLM
Loyola University—Chicago, LLM
Northern Kentucky University, LLM
San Diego, University of, LLM

Child and Family Law
Loyola University—Chicago, LLM; MJ

Clinical Legal Education
Temple University, LLM

Comparative Biomedicine and Healthcare
Suffolk University, LLM

Comparative Law and Latin American Studies
Tulane University, MCL-MA

Comparative Law/Comparative Legal Studies/Comparative Jurisprudence
Florida, University of, LLM
Indiana University—Bloomington, MCL
John Marshall Law School, LLM
Miami, University of, LLM
New York University, MCJ
Pace University, LLM

Penn State University, LLM
Samford University, MCL
San Diego, University of, LLM
Tulane University, MCL

Criminal Law
Buffalo, State University of New York, University at, LLM

Dispute Resolution
Missouri—Columbia, University of, LLM
Pepperdine University, MDR

Education Law
Franklin Pierce Law Center, MEL

Employee Benefits
John Marshall Law School, LLM

Energy, Environment/Natural Resources
Denver, University of, LLM
George Washington University, LLM
Golden Gate University, LLM
Houston, University of, LLM
Lewis & Clark Law School, LLM
Pace University, LLM; SJD
Pacific, McGeorge, University of, JSD; LLM
Tulane University Law School, LLM
Utah, University of, LLM
Vermont Law School, LLM; MSEL

Entertainment/Media Law
Southwestern University, LLM

Estate Planning
Miami, University of, LLM
Missouri—Kansas City, University of, LLM

General or As Approved
Alabama, University of, LLM
Albany Law School, University of, LLM; MLS
American University, SJD
California—Berkeley (Boalt Hall), University of, LLM; JSD
Cardozo School of Law, LLM
Catholic University of America—School of Law, LLM
Chicago, University of, LLM; MCL; DCL; JSD
Cleveland State University, LLM
Columbia University, LLM; JSD
Cornell Law School, LLM; JSD
Emory University, LLM
George Washington University, LLM; SJD
Georgetown University, LLM
Georgia, University of, LLM
Harvard Law School, LLM; SJD

Illinois, University of, JSD; LLM
Indiana University—Bloomington, LLM; SJD
Louisiana State University, BCL; LLM; MCL
Michigan, University of, LLM; MCL; SJD
Missouri—Kansas City, University of, LLM
New York University, LLM; JSD
Northwestern University, LLM
Pennsylvania, University of, LLCM; LLM; SJD
Samford University, SJD
San Diego, University of, LLM
SMU Dedman, LLM; SJD
Stanford University, JSD; JSM
Temple University, LLM
Texas, University of, LLM
Touro College, LLM
Tulane University, LLM; SJD
Valparaiso University, LLM
Virginia, University of, LLM; SJD
Wayne State University, LLM
Yale Law School, LLM; JSD

Global Technology
Suffolk University, LLM

Government and Public Policy
American University, LLM
George Mason University, JM
George Washington University, LLM
Pacific, McGeorge, University of, LLM

Health Law
DePaul University, LLM
Houston, University of, LLM
Loyola University—Chicago, LLM; MJ; DL; SJD
Saint Louis University, LLM
Seton Hall University, LLM
Suffolk University, LLM
Widener University, DL; LLM; MJ; SJD

Indigenous Law
Arizona, University of, LLM
Tulsa, University of, LLM

Insurance Law
Connecticut, University of, LLM

Intellectual Property/Technology/Information Technology Law
Akron, University of, LLM
Boston University, LLM
Cardozo School of Law, LLM
DePaul University, LLM
Franklin Pierce Law Center, LLM; MIP
George Mason University, LLM

George Washington University, LLM
Golden Gate University, LLM
Houston, University of, LLM
John Marshall Law School, LLM; MS
Michigan State University, LLM
San Francisco, University of, LLM
Santa Clara University, LLM
Suffolk University, LLM
Washington, University of, LLM
Washington University, LLM

Inter-American Law
Miami, University of, LLM

Intercultural/International Human Rights/International Public Interest
New York University, LLM
Notre Dame Law School, JSD; LLM
St. Thomas University, LLM

International Business and Trade Law/Transnational Business Practice
Arizona, University of, LLM
Fordham University, LLM
John Marshall Law School, LLM
New York University, LLM
Pacific, McGeorge, University of, LLM
San Francisco, University of, LLM
Stetson University, LLM

International Environmental Law
Washington, University of, LLM

International Taxation
New York University, LLM
Regent University, LLM
St. Thomas University, LLM

International/International and Comparative Law/Comparative and International Law/International Legal Studies
American University, LLM
Chicago-Kent—Illinois Institute of Technology, LLM
Cornell Law School, LLM
George Washington University, LLM
Georgetown University, LLM
Golden Gate University, LLM; SJD
Hofstra University, LLM
Houston, University of, LLM
Howard University, LLM
Iowa, University of, LLM
Miami, University of, LLM
New York University, LLM
Notre Dame Law School, LLM

Pittsburgh, University of, LLM
St. Mary's University, LLM
San Diego, University of, LLM
Santa Clara University, LLM
SMU Dedman, LLM
Tulane University, LLM

Judicial Process
Virginia, University of, LLM

Labor Law/Employment Law
New York University, LLM
Wayne State University, LLM

Law and Economics
George Mason University, LLM

Law, Science, and Technology
Stanford University, LLM

Law/Psychology
Nebraska, University of, MLS

Litigation/Trial Advocacy/Advocacy
California Western, LLM
Emory University, LLM
George Washington University, LLM
Georgetown University, LLM
Temple University, LLM

Military Law
Judge Advocate General's School, LLM

Ocean and Coastal Law
Miami, University of, LLM

Policy Analysis
George Mason University, LLM

Real Estate/Land Development
John Marshall Law School, LLM
Miami, University of, LLM

Research
Duke University, SJD
Indiana University—Bloomington, SJD
Northwestern University, SJD
Vanderbilt University, LLM
Washington University, JSD
Wisconsin, University of, LLM; MLI; SJD

Securities and Financial Regulation
Georgetown University, LLM

Sustainable International Development
Washington, University of, LLM

Taxation
Alabama, University of, LLM
Baltimore, University of, LLM
Boston University, LLM
Capital University, JD/LLM; LLM; MT
Case Western Reserve University, LLM
Chapman University, LLM
Chicago-Kent—Illinois Institute of Technology, LLM
Denver, University of, LLM
DePaul University, LLM
Emory University, LLM
Florida, University of, LLM; SJD
Georgetown University, LLM
Golden Gate University, LLM
Houston, University of, LLM
John Marshall Law School, LLM
Loyola Law School (Los Angeles), LLM
Loyola University—Chicago, LLM
Miami, University of, LLM
Missouri—Kansas City, University of, LLM
New York Law School, LLM
New York University, LLM
Pacific, McGeorge, University of, LLM
San Diego, University of, LLM
SMU Dedman, LLM
Temple University, LLM
Thomas M. Cooley, LLM
Villanova University, LLM
Washington, University of, LLM
Washington University, LLM
Wayne State University, LLM

Urban Affairs
Missouri—Kansas City, University of, LLM
Washington University, LLM

Programs for Foreign Lawyers or International Students
Boston University, LLM
Brigham Young University, LLM
California—Davis, University of, LLM
California—Hastings, University of, LLM
California at Los Angeles, University of, LLM
California Western, LLM; MCL
Case Western Reserve University, LLM
Connecticut, University of, LLM
Denver, University of, LLM
Duke University, LLM
Florida State University, LLM
Georgetown University, SJD
Golden Gate University, LLM
Hamline University, LLM

Hawai'i, University of, LLM
Hofstra University, LLM
Houston, University of, LLM
Indiana University—Indianapolis, LLM
Minnesota, University of, LLM
New England School of Law, LLM
Puerto Rico, University of, LLM
Saint Louis University, LLM
St. Mary's University, LLM
Santa Clara University, LLM

Southern California, University of, LLM
Temple University, LLM
Touro College, LLM
Tulsa, University of, LLM
Wake Forest University, LLM
Washington University, LLM
Whittier Law School, LLM
William & Mary Law School, LLM

■ A Note to Graduates of Law Schools Located Outside the United States:

Degrees Other Than a JD and Bar Admission

In order to obtain a license to practice law in the United States, all candidates must apply for bar admission through a state board of bar examiners. Although this board is ordinarily an agency of the highest court in the jurisdiction, occasionally the board is connected to the state's bar association. The criteria for eligibility to take the bar examination or to otherwise qualify for bar admission are set by each state, not by the ABA or the Council of the Section of Legal Education and Admissions to the Bar.

In order to sit for the bar examination, most states require an applicant to hold a Juris Doctor (JD) degree from a law school that meets established educational standards. A JD earned at an ABA-approved law school meets the educational requirements in every jurisdiction in the United States. For those individuals who have not earned a JD degree from an ABA-approved law school, bar admission authorities have developed varying requirements and criteria to ascertain if such individuals meet the minimum educational requirements for bar admission. In most jurisdictions individuals who lack such a JD will find that they do not satisfy the minimum educational requirements for bar admission and are ineligible to take the bar exam. In some of the remaining states, graduates of foreign law schools will find that additional schooling such as an LLM is required, and a few others recognize with regularity the sufficiency of a specific foreign legal education. A number offer an alternative licensure mechanism known as a Foreign Legal Consultant, which is a limited license to practice. And finally, some jurisdictions will allow individuals to be eligible for admission without examination under certain conditions if they have been admitted to the bar in another US jurisdiction.

In the past few years, there has been a large increase in the number of graduates from schools located outside the United States enrolled in advanced degree programs

(such as the LLM). In fact, roughly half of all the individuals currently enrolled in LLM programs are graduates of foreign law schools. Upon graduating, many of these individuals return to their home country without seeking or obtaining bar licensure in the United States. However, an increasing number of these individuals seek to be admitted to a state bar.

Unlike the JD degree bestowed by an ABA-approved law school, which carries the indicia that the holder of that degree has completed a course of study imparting standards entitling him or her to engage in the practice of law, advanced degree programs at ABA-approved law schools are not regulated, and thus, not "approved." As a result, such degrees vary in content and rigor. In other words, the American Bar Association does NOT accredit degrees of any kind other than the JD.

It is the position of the Council of the Section of Legal Education and Admissions to the Bar of the American Bar Association that no graduate degree in law (LLM, MCL, SJD, etc.) is or should be a substitute for the first professional degree in law (JD) and that no graduate degree should substitute for the JD in order to meet the legal education requirements for admission to the bar.

As a result of the variance in state bar admission rules, the ABA strongly encourages individuals to contact the state board of bar examiners in the state(s) in which they are interested in being admitted to ascertain its requirements to sit for the bar examination. Contact information for all the state board of bar examiners is available at *www.abanet.org/legaled*; in the *Comprehensive Guide to Bar Admission Requirements*, which is available online at the website above or through the ABA Service Center at 800.285.2221, Product Code: 5290087 (05ED).

Appendix C: Other Organizations

You may have questions concerning a variety of issues while you are applying to law school, once you are in law school, and even after you have your degree.

The following organizations may provide you with the answers you need.

American Association of Law Libraries (AALL)

The American Association of Law Libraries exists to provide leadership in the field of legal information, to foster the professional growth of law librarians, to develop the profession of law librarianship, and to enhance the value of law libraries to the legal community and to the public. AALL members come from all sizes and types of libraries: the Library of Congress, legislative libraries, academic law libraries, law firm libraries, bar association libraries, county law libraries, court libraries, and law libraries in business and industry. The association publishes a quarterly journal (*Law Library Journal*), a monthly magazine (*AALL Spectrum*), and an annual directory and handbook (which includes a minority law librarians directory).

For more information, contact:

American Association of Law Libraries
53 W Jackson Boulevard, Suite 940
Chicago, IL 60604
Phone: 312.939.4764
URL: *www.aallnet.org*

American Bar Association (ABA)

The American Bar Association is the national organization of the legal profession. It is composed principally of practicing lawyers; judges; court administrators; law teachers; public service attorneys; many nonpracticing lawyers (such as business executives, government officials, etc.); and law students. Although the ABA does not have the power to discipline attorneys or enforce rules, the association leads by serving as the national voice of the profession.

The ABA, with over 405,348 members and 50,000 law student members, is the world's largest voluntary professional association. It serves a dual role as advocate for the profession and for the public. During the past decade, the association has initiated hundreds of programs addressing a wide range of public concerns. Response to these concerns is made possible by thousands of volunteers who contribute both time and money.

The Council of the Section of Legal Education and Admissions to the Bar of the ABA is identified by the US Department of Education as the "nationally recognized accrediting agency for professional schools of law." The role that the American Bar Association plays as a central accrediting body has allowed accreditation to become national in scope rather than fragmented among the 50 states, District of Columbia, the Commonwealth of Puerto Rico, and other territories. Most admitting jurisdictions require applicants for admission to be graduates of law schools approved by the American Bar Association.

The ABA may be contacted for information on the accreditation of law schools and the role of lawyers in the legal profession:

Office of the Consultant on Legal Education
American Bar Association
321 North Clark Street
Chicago, IL 60610
Phone: 312.988.6738
URL: *www.abanet.org/legaled*

Association of American Law Schools (AALS)

The Association of American Law Schools was founded for "the improvement of the legal profession through legal education." It is an association of law schools that serves as the law teachers' learned society. The association requires quality teaching and scholarship of its 166 member schools.

The organization provides a range of services to law schools. Among them are professional development workshops and conferences for law faculty, facilitation of law faculty recruitment, publication of the *AALS Directory of Law Teachers*, and interpretation of the mission and needs of legal education as the principal representative to other national higher education organizations, the federal government, and learned societies.

The AALS may be contacted for specific information about the role of legal education in the profession:

Association of American Law Schools
1201 Connecticut Avenue, NW
Suite 800
Washington, DC 20036-2605
Phone: 202.296.8851
URL: *www.aals.org*

HEATH Resource Center

The George Washington University operates the HEATH Resource Center, the national clearinghouse on postsecondary education for individuals with disabilities. HEATH provides information about disability-related accommodations, physical and programmatic access available at institutions of higher education, and issues related to choosing and applying to the most appropriate programs. Publications from The George Washington University HEATH Resource Center are available at no charge online at *www.heath.gwu.edu*.

For more information:

The George Washington University
HEATH Resource Center
2121 K Street, NW
Suite 220
Washington, DC 20037
Phone (Voice/TTY): 800.544.3284 and 202.973.0904
URL: *www.heath.gwu.edu*

Law School Admission Council

The Law School Admission Council (LSAC) is a non-profit corporation whose members are more than 200 law schools in the United States and Canada. It was founded in 1947 to coordinate, facilitate, and enhance the law school admission process. The organization also provides programs and services related to legal education. All law schools approved by the American Bar Association (ABA) are LSAC members. Canadian law schools recognized by a provincial or territorial law society or government agency are also included in the voting membership of the Council.

The services provided by LSAC include: The Law School Admission Test (LSAT); the Law School Data Assembly Service (LSDAS); the Candidate Referral Service (CRS); and various publications and LSAT preparation tools. The LSAT, the LSDAS, and the CRS are provided to assist law schools in serving and evaluating applicants. LSAC does not engage in assessing an applicant's chances for admission to any law school; all admission decisions are made by individual law schools.

LSAC exists to serve both the law schools and their candidates for admission. Last year, LSAC administered 147,617 tests, and processed 200,000 transcripts, 555,000 law school report requests, 810,000 law school reports, and 194,000 letters of recommendation.

For more information on the LSAT, the LSDAS, and law school admission, contact:

Law School Admission Council
662 Penn Street
Box 2000
Newtown, PA 18940-0998
Phone: 215.968.1001
URL: *www.LSAC.org*

For information on minority opportunities in law, contact:

Law School Admission Council
Minority Opportunities in Law
662 Penn Street
Box 40
Newtown, PA 18940-0040
Phone: 215.968.1338
URL: *www.LSAC.org*

NALP

NALP is a professional organization of law schools and legal employers. NALP provides information, coordination, and standards for fair recruiting for all of the participants in the legal employment process. NALP provides a forum for discussion of recruiting trends and practices among school and employer representatives; provides professional education and resources for law school career services professionals, legal employers, recruiting directors, lawyer professional development administrators, and hiring attorneys; and conducts research on legal employment.

NALP offers information and resources related to law careers through its website and online bookstore at *www.nalp.org*. In addition, NALP publishes an online directory of legal employers and their hiring criteria at *www.nalpdirectory.com*, and offers an extensive database of public opportunities for law students and lawyers through *www.pslawnet.org* (NALP's Public Service Law Network Worldwide). NALP is not an employment agency and does not offer placement or career counseling services.

NALP believes that each law school offers unique programs and opportunities and, like the American Bar Association and the Law School Admission Council, does not rank law schools or career services offices.

For further information, contact:

NALP
Suite 1110
1025 Connecticut Avenue, NW
Washington, DC 20036-5413
Phone: 202.835.1001
URL: *www.nalp.org*

Appendix D: Resources for the Prelaw Candidate

The following list of prelaw readings offers prospective law students an overview of selected classics and current titles in certain subjects: law school and legal education, the legal profession, biography, jurisprudence and legal issues, and financing a law school education. Some of these publications list sources for financial aid, but students will need to call or write the individual organizations for the most up-to-date information.

This list should not be construed as the official bibliography of Law School Admission Council or ABA; it is beyond the scope of those organizations to provide any sort of definitive catalog of prelaw readings.

Some of these books have already withstood the test of time, and are as relevant today as when they were first written and published, generations ago. Examples are Richard Kluger's *Simple Justice*—a rare glimpse into the private workings and deliberations of the Supreme Court; and Karl Llewellyn's *The Bramble Bush*—a classic study of how legal education shapes our legal institutions.

Some titles simply reflect the most current writing on the subjects listed above and are not necessarily recommended simply because they appear on this list. It will be up to you to search out the titles that pique your interest and make your own determination of their worth. The aim of our list is merely to give you a head start. We hope that those interested in pursuing legal studies will find the issues raised and the ideas discussed in these works helpful in making the decision to choose law as a career.

■ Law School and Legal Education

African American Lawyers: Trailblazers and Role Models. DVD, 23 mins. Newtown, PA: Law School Admission Council, 2004.

Barber, David H. *Winning in Law School: Stress Reduction.* 2d ed. Dillon, CO: Spectra, 1986.

Bay, Monica. *Careers in Civil Litigation.* Chicago: American Bar Association/Law Student Division, 1990.

Becoming a Lawyer: A Video Collection. DVD, includes seven videos. Newtown, PA: Law School Admission Council, 2004.

Bell, Susan J. *Full Disclosure: Do You Really Want to Be a Lawyer?* Princeton, NJ: Peterson's Guides, 1989.

Bell, Susan J. *Interviewing for Success and Satisfaction.* Chicago: American Bar Association/Young Lawyers Division, 1989.

Boyer, Paul. *College Rankings Exposed.* Lawrenceville, NJ: Peterson's, 2003.

Briggs, Amy Thompson. *Degrees of Difference: A How-to Guide to Choosing a Law School.* Washington, DC: National Association of Law Placement, 1998.

Carter, Lief H. and **Thomas F. Burke.** *Reason in Law.* 6th ed. Boston: Addison-Wesley, 2001.

Chase, William C. *The American Law School and the Rise of Administrative Government.* Madison, WI: University of Wisconsin Press, 1982.

Curry, Boykin and **Brian Kasbar**, eds. *Essays That Worked for Law Schools (Revised): 40 Essays from Successful Applications to the Nation's Top Law Schools.* Ontario, Canada: Ballantine Books, 2003.

Deaver, Jeff. *The Complete Law School Companion: How to Excel at America's Most Demanding Post-Graduate Curriculum.* New York: John Wiley & Sons, 1992.

Dvorkin, Elizabeth, Jack Himmelstein, and **Howard Lesnick.** *Becoming a Lawyer: A Humanistic Perspective on Legal Education and Professionalism.* St. Paul, MN: West Publishing, 1989.

Farnsworth, Edward A. *An Introduction to the Legal System of the United States.* 2d ed. Dobbs Ferry, NY: Oceana Publications, 1983.

Financing a Legal Education: Investing in Your Future. DVD, 20 mins. Newtown, PA: Law School Admission Council, 2004.

Getting There: Four Paths to Law School. Videocassette, 20 min. Newtown, PA: Law School Admission Council, 2001.

Goldfarb, Sally F. and **Carol-June Cassidy.** *Inside the Law Schools: A Guide by Students for Students.* New York: Plume, 1998.

Goodrich, Chris. *Anarchy and Elegance: Confessions of a Journalist at Yale Law School.* Lincoln, NE: iUniverse, 2003.

Hirshman, Linda. *A Woman's Guide to Law School.* Bergenfield, NJ: Viking Penguin, 1999.

Kaplin, William A. *The Concepts and Methods of Constitutional Law.* Durham, NC: Carolina Academic Press, 1992.

Legal Education and Professional Development—An Educational Continuum. Report of the Task Force on Law Schools and the Profession: Narrowing the Gap. Chicago: American Bar Association, Section of Legal Education and Admissions to the Bar, July 1992.

Llewellyn, Karl N. *The Bramble Bush: On Our Law and Its Study.* (Rev. ed.). Dobbs Ferry, NY: Oceana Publications, 1981.

Margulies, Sheldon and **Kenneth Lasson.** *Learning Law: The Mastery of Legal Logic.* Durham, NC: Carolina Academic Press, 1993.

Mayfield, Craig K. *Reading Skills for Law Students.* Charlottesville, VA: Michie Co., 1980.

Miller, Robert H. *Law School Confidential—A Complete Guide to the Law School Experience: By Students, for Students.* New York: St. Martin's Griffin, 2000.

Moliterno, James E. and **Frederic Lederer.** *An Introduction to Law, Law Study, and the Lawyer's Role.* Durham, NC: Carolina Academic Press, 2004.

Morgan, Rick L. and **Kurt Snyder.** *Official American Bar Association Guide to Approved Law Schools.* New York: Macmillan, 1999.

OutLooks. DVD, 27 min. Newtown, PA: Law School Admission Council, 1998.

Schlag, Pierre and **David Skover.** *Tactics of Legal Reasoning.* Durham, NC: Carolina Academic Press, 1986.

Shapo, Helene and **Marshall Shapo.** *Law School Without Fear: Strategies for Success.* (2d ed.) New York: Foundation Press, 2002.

Simonhoff, Mark, ed. *My First Year as a Lawyer.* New York: Walker & Company, 1994.

Stevens, Robert. *Law School: Legal Education in America from the 1850s to the 1980s.* Chapel Hill, NC: University of North Carolina Press, 1987.

Stover, Robert V. *Making It and Breaking It: The Fate of Public Interest Commitment During Law School.* Urbana, IL: University of Illinois Press, 1989.

Swygert, Michael I. and **Robert Batey**, eds. *Maximizing the Law School Experience: A Collection of Essays.* St. Petersburg, FL: Stetson University College of Law, 1983.

Turow, Scott. *One L: The Turbulent True Story of a First Year at Harvard Law School.* New York: Warner Books, 1997.

Vanderbilt, Arthur T. *Law School: Briefing for a Legal Education.* New York: Penguin Books, 1981.

VerSteeg, Russ. *Essential Latin for Lawyers.* Durham, NC: Carolina Academic Press, 1990.

Williams, Glanville and **A. T. H. Smith.** *Learning the Law.* 12th ed. London: Stevens, 2002.

Wydick, Richard C. *Plain English for Lawyers.* 4th ed. Durham, NC: Carolina Academic Press, 1998.

■ Legal Profession

American Bar Association Center for Pro Bono. *Law School Public Interest Law Support Programs: A Directory.* Chicago: ABA, 2000.

Abel, Richard L. *American Lawyers.* New York: Oxford University Press, 1991.

Abrams, Lisa L. *The Official Guide to Legal Specialties: An Insider's Guide to Every Major Practice Area.* Chicago: The BarBri Group in association with the National Association for Law Placement (NALP), 2000.

Arron, Deborah. *Running from the Law: Why Good Lawyers Are Getting Out of the Legal Profession.* Berkeley, CA: Ten Speed Press, 1991.

Arron, Deborah. *What Can You Do With a Law Degree? A Lawyer's Guide to Career Alternatives Inside, Outside & Around the Law.* Seattle: Decision Books, 2003.

Bailey, F. Lee. *To Be a Trial Lawyer.* New York: John Wiley & Sons, 1985.

Bellow, Gary and **Martha Minow**, eds. *Law Stories.* Ann Arbor: University of Michigan Press, 1998.

Caplan, Lincoln. *Skadden: Inside the Business of Law in America.* New York: Farrar, Straus & Giroux, 1993.

Couric, Emily. *The Trial Lawyers: The Nation's Top Litigators Tell How They Win.* New York: St. Martin's Press, 1988.

Delaney, John. *Learning Legal Reasoning: Briefings, Analysis and Theory.* (Rev. ed.). Bogota, NJ: John Delaney Publications, 1987.

Epstein, Cynthia Fuchs. *Women in Law.* 2d ed. Urbana, IL: University of Illinois Press, 1993.

Foonberg, Jay G. *How to Start and Build a Law Practice.* 3d ed. Chicago: American Bar Association/Law Student Division, 1991.

Fox, Ronald W. *Lawful Pursuit: Careers in Public Interest Law.* Chicago: American Bar Association, Career Series, 1995.

Galanter, Marc and **Thomas Palay.** *Tournament of Lawyers: The Transformation of the Big Law Firm.* Chicago: University of Chicago Press, 1991.

Glendon, Mary Ann. *A Nation Under Lawyers: How the Crisis in the Legal Profession is Transforming American Society.* New York: Farrar, Straus & Giroux, 1994.

Greene, Robert Michael. *Making Partner: A Guide for Law Firm Associates.* Chicago: American Bar Association, Section of Law Practice Management, 1992.

Harrington, Mona. *Women Lawyers: Rewriting the Rules.* New York: Alfred A. Knopf, 1994.

Henslee, William D. *Careers in Entertainment Law.* Chicago: American Bar Association/Law Student Division, 1990.

Horn, Carl, III. *Lawyer Life: Finding a Life and Higher Calling in the Practice of Law.* Chicago: American Bar Association, 2003.

Kelly, Michael J. *Lives of Lawyers: Journeys in the Organizations of Practice.* Ann Arbor: University of Michigan Press, 1994.

Killoughey, Donna M. ed. *Breaking Traditions: Work Alternatives for Lawyers.* Chicago: American Bar Association, Section of Law Practice Management, 1993.

Kronman, Anthony T. *The Lost Lawyer: Failing Ideals of the Legal Profession.* Cambridge, MA: Harvard University Press (Belknap Press), 1993.

Linowitz, Sol M., with **Martin Mayer.** *The Betrayed Profession: Lawyering at the End of the Twentieth Century.* New York: Charles Scribner's Sons, 1994.

López, Gerald P. *Rebellious Lawyering: One Chicano's Vision of Progressive Law Practice.* Boulder, CO: Westview Press, 1992.

Luney, Percy R., Jr. *Careers in Natural Resources and Environmental Law.* Chicago: American Bar Association/Law Student Division, 1987.

Mayer, Martin. *The Lawyers.* Westport, CT: Greenwood Press, 1980.

Moll, Richard W. *The Lure of the Law: Why People Become Lawyers, and What the Profession Does to Them.* New York: Penguin Books, 1990.

Munneke, Gary A. *The Legal Career Guide: From Law Student to Lawyer.* Chicago: American Bar Association Career Series, 1992.

Munneke, Gary A. and **William D. Henslee.** (4th ed.) *Nonlegal Careers for Lawyers.* Chicago: American Bar Association, 2002.

O'Neill, Suzanne B. and **Catherine Gerhauser Sparkman.** *From Law School to Law Practice: The New Associate's Guide.* Philadelphia: American Law Institute/American Bar Association Committee on Continuing Professional Education, 1989.

Shaffer, Thomas L., with **Mary M. Shaffer.** *American Lawyers and Their Communities: Ethics in the Legal Profession.* Notre Dame, IN: University of Notre Dame Press, 1991.

Shropshire, Kenneth. *Careers in Sports Law.* Chicago: American Bar Association/Law Student Division, 1990.

Smith, Janet. *Beyond L.A. Law: Break the Traditional "Lawyer" Mold.* Chicago: Harcourt, Brace, 1998.

Smith, J. Clay, Jr. *Rebels in Law: Voices in History of Black Women Lawyers.* Ann Arbor: The University of Michigan Press, 1998.

Speiser, Stuart M. *Lawyers and the American Dream.* New York: M. Evan and Co., 1993.

Stewart, James B. *The Partners.* New York: Simon & Schuster, 1983.

Strauss, Debra M. *Behind the Bench: The Guide to Judicial Clerkships.* Chicago: The BarBri Group, 2002.

Thorner, Abbie Willard, ed. *Now Hiring: Government Jobs for Lawyers (1990-1991 edition).* Chicago: American Bar Association/Law Student Division, 1990.

Wayne, Ellen. *Careers in Labor Law.* Chicago: American Bar Association/Law Student Division, 1985.

■ Biography

Auchincloss, Louis. *Life, Law and Letters: Essays and Sketches.* Boston: Houghton Mifflin Co., 1979.

Baker, Leonard. *John Marshall: A Life in Law.* New York: Macmillan, 1974.

Barth, Alan. *Prophets With Honor: Great Dissents and Great Dissenters in the Supreme Court.* New York: Vintage Books, 1975.

Cray, Ed. *Chief Justice: A Biography of Earl Warren.* New York: Simon & Schuster, 1997.

Darrow, Clarence. *The Story of My Life.* New York: Charles Scribner's Sons, 1932.

Davis, Deane C. *Justice in the Mountains: Stories & Tales by a Vermont Country Lawyer.* Shelburne, VT: New England Press, 1980.

Davis, Lenwood G. *I Have a Dream: The Life and Times of Martin Luther King.* Westport, CT: Negro Universities Press, 1973.

Davis, Michael D. and **Hunter R. Clark.** *Thurgood Marshall: Warrior at the Bar, Rebel on the Bench.* New York: Birch Lane Press/Carol Publishing Group, 1993.

Douglas, William O. *Go East Young Man: The Early Years.* New York: Random House, 1974.

Douglas, William O. *Court Years, 1939-1975: The Autobiography of William O. Douglas.* New York: Random House, 1980.

Dunne, Gerald T. *Hugo Black and the Judicial Revolution.* New York: Simon & Schuster, 1977.

Frankfurter, Felix. *Felix Frankfurter Reminisces.* New York: Reynal & Co., 1960.

Goldman, Roger, with **David Gallen.** *Justice William J. Brennan, Jr.: Freedom First.* New York: Carroll & Graf Publishers, Inc., 1994

Griffith, Kathryn. *Judge Learned Hand and the Role of the Federal Judiciary.* Norman, OK: University of Oklahoma Press, 1973.

Griswold, Erwin N. *Ould Fields, New Corne: The Personal Memoirs of a Twentieth Century Lawyer.* St. Paul, MN: West Publishing, 1992.

Gunther, Gerald. *Learned Hand: The Man and the Judge.* New York: Alfred A. Knopf, 1994.

Howe, Mark deWolfe. *Justice Oliver Wendell Holmes.* Cambridge, MA: Harvard University Press, 1957 (vol. 1), 1963 (vol. 2).

Jeffries, John, Jr. *Justice Lewis F. Powell.* New York: Scribner, 1994.

Kahlenberg, Richard D. *Broken Contract: A Memoir of Harvard Law School.* New York: Farrar, Straus & Giroux, 1992.

Lynn, Conrad J. *There Is a Foundation: The Autobiography of a Civil Rights Lawyer.* Westport, CT: Hill & Company, 1978.

Marke, Julius J. *The Holmes Reader.* Dobbs Ferry, NY: Oceana Publications, 1964.

Mason, Alpheus. *Harlan Fiske Stone: Pillar of the Law.* New York: Viking Press, 1956.

Nizer, Louis. *Reflections Without Mirrors: An Autobiography of the Mind.* New York: Doubleday, 1978.

Noonan, John T., Jr. *Persons and Masks of the Law: Cardozo, Holmes, Jefferson, and Wythe as Makers of the Masks.* New York: Farrar, Straus & Giroux, 1976.

Pusey, Merlo J. *Charles Evans Hughes.* New York: Macmillan, 1951.

Rosenkranz, E. Joshua and **Bernard Schwartz.** *Reason and Passion: Justice Brennan's Enduring Influence.* New York: Norton, 1997.

Rowan, Carl T. *Dream Makers, Dream Breakers. The World of Justice Thurgood Marshall.* Boston: Little Brown & Company, 1993.

Schwartz, Bernard. *Super Chief, Earl Warren and His Supreme Court—A Judicial Biography.* New York: New York University Press, 1983.

Simon, James F. *Independent Journey: The Life of William O. Douglas.* New York: Harper & Row, 1980.

Strum, Phillippa. *Brandeis: Beyond Progressivism.* Lawrence, KS: University Press of Kansas, 1993.

Thomas, Evan. *The Man to See: Edward Bennett Williams, Ultimate Insider; Legendary Trial Lawyer.* New York: Simon & Schuster, 1991.

Urofsky, Melvin I. *Louis D. Brandeis and the Progressive Tradition.* Boston: Little, Brown and Company, 1981.

Westin, Alan F. *Autobiography of the Supreme Court: Off-the-Bench Commentary by the Justices.* Westport, CT: Greenwood Press, 1978.

White, G. Edward. *Earl Warren: A Public Life.* New York: Oxford University Press, 1982.

White, G. Edward. *Justice Oliver Wendell Holmes: Law and the Inner Self.* New York: Oxford University Press, 1993.

Wigdor, David. *Roscoe Pound: Philosopher of Law.* Westport, CT: Greenwood Press, 1974.

Williams, Juan. *Thurgood Marshall: American Revolutionary.* New York: Time Books, 1998.

■ Jurisprudence and Legal Issues

Berry, Mary Frances. *Black Resistance, White Law: A History of Constitutional Racism in America.* New York: Allen Lane/Penguin Press, 1994.

Bickel, Alexander M. *The Least Dangerous Branch: The Supreme Court at the Bar of Politics.* 2d ed. New Haven: Yale University Press, 1986.

Bodenhamer, David J. and **James E. Ely, Jr.,** eds. *The Bill of Rights in Modern America.* Bloomington, IN: Indiana University Press, 1993.

Cahn, Edmond. *The Moral Decision: Right and Wrong in the Light of American Law.* Bloomington, IN: Indiana University Press, 1955.

Cardozo, Benjamin N. *The Nature of the Judicial Process.* New Haven: Yale University Press, 1921.

Fine, Toni M. *American Legal Systems: A Resource and Reference Guide.* Cincinnati, OH: Anderson Publishing, 1997.

Finkel, Norman J. *Insanity on Trial.* New York: Plenum, 1988.

Friedman, Lawrence M. *Law in America: A Short History.* New York: Modern Library, 2002.

Friedman, Lawrence M. and **Harry N. Scheiber,** eds. *Legal Culture and the Legal Profession.* Boulder, CO: Westview Press, 1996.

Greenberg, Jack. *Crusaders in the Courts: How a Dedicated Band of Lawyers Fought for the Civil Rights Revolution.* New York: Basic Books, 1994.

Guinier, Lani. *The Tyranny of the Majority: Fundamental Fairness in Representative Democracy.* New York: Martin Kessler Books (The Free Press), 1994.

Hoban, Thomas More and Richard Oliver Brooks. *Green Justice: The Environment and the Courts.* Boulder, CO: Westview Press, 1996.

Irons, Peter and Stephanie Guitton, eds. *May It Please the Court: The Most Significant Oral Arguments Made Before the Supreme Court Since 1955.* Audiocassette. New York: New Press, 1993.

Kennedy, Caroline and Ellen Aldeman. *The Right to Privacy.* New York: Knopf, 1995.

Kluger, Richard. *Simple Justice: The History of Brown vs. Board of Education and Black America's Struggle for Equality.* New York: Alfred A. Knopf, 1976.

Lewis, Anthony. *Gideon's Trumpet.* New York: Random House, 1964.

Lewis, Anthony. *Make No Law: The Sullivan Case and the First Amendment.* New York: Random House, 1991.

Pound, Roscoe. *Law and Morals.* South Hackensack, NJ: Rothman Reprints, 1969.

Rehnquist, William H. *The Supreme Court: How It Was, How It Is.* New York: Quill Press, 1987.

Savage, David. *Turning Right: The Making of the Rehnquist Supreme Court.* New York: John Wiley & Sons, 1992.

Schwartz, Bernard. *A History of the Supreme Court.* New York: Oxford University Press, 1992.

Shapiro, Fred R. *The Oxford Dictionary of American Legal Quotations.* New York: Oxford University Press, 1993.

Shapiro, Joseph P. *No Pity: People With Disabilities Forging a New Civil Rights Movement.* New York: Random House, 1993.

Simon, James F. *The Antagonists: Hugo Black, Felix Frankfurter and Civil Liberties in Modern America.* New York: Simon & Schuster, 1989.

Spence, Gerry. *With Justice for None.* New York: Penguin, 1990.

Stone, Geoffrey R., Richard Epstein, and Cass R. Sunstein, eds. *The Bill of Rights in the Modern State.* Chicago: University of Chicago Press, 1992.

Sunstein, Cass R. *Democracy and the Problem of Free Speech.* New York: The Free Press, 1993.

Treanor, Richard Bryant. *We Overcame: The Story of Civil Rights for Disabled People.* Falls Church, VA: Regal Direct Publishing, 1993.

Tribe, Laurence H. *God Save This Honorable Court: How the Choice of Supreme Court Justices Shapes Our History.* New York: Penguin/Mentor, 1986.

Tushnet, Mark V. *Making Civil Rights Law: Thurgood Marshall and the Supreme Court, 1936-1961.* New York: Oxford University Press, 1994.

Tushnet, Mark, ed. *The Warren Court in Historical and Political Perspective.* Charlottesville, VA: University Press of Virginia, 1993.

Vandevelde, Kenneth J. *Thinking Like a Lawyer: An Introduction to Legal Reasoning.* Boulder, CO: Westview Press, 1996.

Walker, Samuel. *Hate Speech: The History of an American Controversy.* Lincoln, NE: University of Nebraska Press, 1994.

Walker, Samuel. *In Defense of American Liberties: A History of the ACLU.* New York: Oxford University Press, 1990.

Williams, Patricia J. *The Alchemy of Race and Rights.* Cambridge, MA: Harvard University Press, 1991.

Wishman, Seymour. *Anatomy of a Jury.* New York: Penguin, 1987.

■ Financing Law School

Schlachter, Gail Ann. *Financial Aid for Women, 2005–2007.* El Dorado Hills, CA: Reference Service Press.

Schlachter, Gail Ann and R. David Weber. *Financial Aid for African Americans, 2005–2007.* El Dorado Hills, CA: Reference Service Press.

Schlachter, Gail Ann and R. David Weber. *Financial Aid for Asian Americans, 2005–2007.* El Dorado Hills, CA: Reference Service Press.

Schlachter, Gail Ann and R. David Weber. *Financial Aid for Hispanic Americans, 2005–2007.* El Dorado Hills, CA: Reference Service Press.

Schlachter, Gail Ann and R. David Weber. *Financial Aid for Native Americans, 2005–2007.* El Dorado Hills, CA: Reference Service Press.

Schlachter, Gail Ann and R. David Weber. *Financial Aid for the Disabled and Their Families, 2004–2006.* El Dorado Hills, CA: Reference Service Press.

Schlachter, Gail Ann and R. David Weber. *Financial Aid for Veterans, Military Personnel, and Their Dependents, 2004–2006.* El Dorado Hills, CA: Reference Service Press.

Schlachter, Gail Ann and **R. David Weber.** *How to Pay for Your Law Degree, 2004–2006.* El Dorado Hills, CA: Reference Service Press.

Scholarships, Fellowships, and Loans, 2004. Detroit: Gale Research, Inc.

Appendix E: Canadian LSAC-Member Law Schools

University of Alberta
Faculty of Law
Room 480, Admissions Office
Edmonton, Alberta
CANADA T6G 2H5

University of British Columbia
Faculty of Law
1822 East Mall
Vancouver, British Columbia
CANADA V6T 1Z1

University of Calgary
Faculty of Law
Murray Fraser Hall
Calgary, Alberta
CANADA T2N 1N4

Dalhousie Law School
6061 University Avenue
Halifax, Nova Scotia
CANADA B3H 4H9

University of Manitoba, Faculty of Law
Robson Hall
Winnipeg, Manitoba
CANADA R3T 2N2

McGill University
Faculty of Law
3644 Peel Street
Montreal, Quebec
CANADA H3A 1W9

University of New Brunswick
Faculty of Law
PO Box 44271
Fredericton, New Brunswick
CANADA E3B 6C2

University of Ottawa
Faculty of Law
57 Louis Pasteur Street
Ottawa, Ontario
CANADA K1N 6N5

Queen's University
Faculty of Law
Director of Admissions, MacDonald Hall
Kingston, Ontario
CANADA K7L 3N6

University of Saskatchewan
College of Law
Admissions Committee
15 Campus Drive
Saskatoon, Saskatchewan
CANADA S7N 5A6

University of Toronto
Faculty of Law
78 Queen's Park
Toronto, Ontario
CANADA M5S 2C5

University of Victoria
Faculty of Law
PO Box 2400, STN CSC
Victoria, British Columbia
CANADA V8W 3H7

University of Western Ontario
Faculty of Law
London, Ontario
CANADA N6A 3K7

University of Windsor
Faculty of Law
401 Sunset Avenue
Windsor, Ontario
CANADA N9B 3P4

York University
Osgoode Hall Law School
4700 Keele Street
North York, Ontario
CANADA M3J 1P3

Publications Available from the ABA's Section

The Section publishes a number of books, reports, newsletters, and brochures to inform and educate its members and the public. All of the following publications are available by calling the ABA Service Center at 1.800.285.2221 or 312.988.5522. In addition, several publications (Bar Admission Requirements, Standards, Chairpersonsí Reflections) are available unabridged through the Section website: www.abanet.org/legaled.

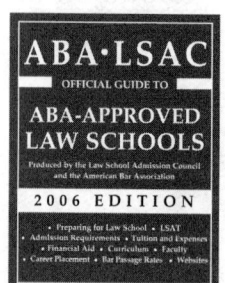

THE OFFICIAL GUIDE TO ABA-APPROVED LAW SCHOOLS, 2006 EDITION

The Official Guide is published in cooperation with the Law School Admission Council and pursuant to the Section's Standard 509, modeled after Department of Education regulations requiring law schools to "publish basic consumer information in a fair and accurate manner reflective of actual practice."
Admission data, tuition, fees, living costs, financial aid, enrollment data, graduation rates, composition and number of faculty and administrators, curricular offerings, library resources, physical facilities, placement rates, bar passage data, and post-J.D. programs are only some of the many categories covered in this comprehensive guide. Also available at major bookstores.

Product Code: 5290085 (06ED), Price: $24.00

STANDARDS: RULES OF PROCEDURE FOR APPROVAL OF LAW SCHOOLS

ABA Standards: Rules of Procedure for Approval of Law Schools sets forth the standards that a law school must meet to obtain or retain ABA Approval. The book is divided into several parts: Standards & Interpretations; Rules of Procedure; Criteria for Approval of Summer Foreign Programs of ABA Approved Schools; Criteria for Student Study at a Foreign Institution; Criteria for Approval of Semester Abroad Programs for Credit Granting Foreign Segment of Approved J.D. Program; Statement of Ethical Practices in the Process of Law School Accreditation; Internal Operating Practices; Council Statements.

Product Code: 5290084 (04ED), Price: $15.00

OCCASIONAL PAPER #9:

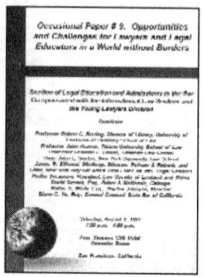

OPPORTUNITIES AND CHALLENGES FOR LAWYERS AND LEGAL EDUCATORS IN A WORLD WITHOUT BORDERS

A transcript of a 1997 discussion during the ABA Annual Meeting organized by the Section of Legal Education & Admissions to the Bar, International Law Section, and the Young Lawyers Division.

Product Code: 5290092 (0009), Price: $4.00

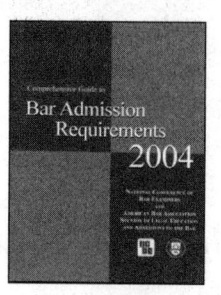

COMPREHENSIVE GUIDE TO BAR ADMISSION REQUIREMENTS, 2005 EDITION

The Comprehensive Guide to Bar Admission Requirements is published each year by the Section and the National Conference of Bar Examiners. It sets out the rules and practices of all U.S. jurisdictions for admission to the bar by examination and on motion; that is, legal education, character and fitness, bar examinations, and special licenses. Supplemental information follows each chart.

Product Code: 5290087 (05ED), Price: $12.50

TEACHING AND LEARNING PROFESSIONALISM

This is a 1996 report by the ABA Section of Legal Education and Admissions to the Bar Professionalism Committee. It examines the recent decline in professionalism and makes a number of recommendations designed to increase the level of professionalism among American law students, practicing lawyers, and judges.

Product Code: 5290083, Price: $3.75

TEACHING AND LEARNING PROFESSIONALISM: SYMPOSIUM PROCEEDINGS

The publication of this monograph brings to a conclusion the professionalism projects of the Section and the ABA Professionalism Committee. The initial Committee report entitled "Teaching and Learning Professionalism" and this publication, which reproduces the papers presented at and summarizes the discussion from a national invitational Symposium on Teaching and Learning Professionalism in October 1996 contains a broad range of ideas and recommendations for enhancing the level of professionalism among American law students and lawyers. Serious discussion and implementation of these ideas and recommendations by law faculties, judges, practitioners, and bar association officials will be the true test of this project's success.

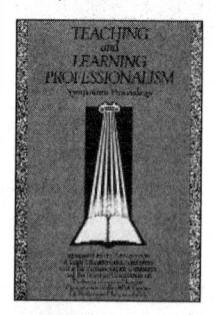

Product Code: 5290086, Price: $3.75

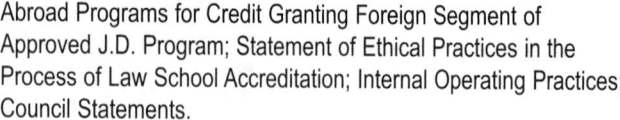

# of Legal Education & Admissions to the Bar

SYLLABUS

Syllabus is the news publication of the Section of Legal Education and Admissions to the Bar. Three times a year readers learn about Section conferences and workshops, as well as contemporary legal education topics. Statistical information pertaining to legal education is also included.

Product Code: 5290002, Price: $15.00 per year

ANNUAL REPORT OF THE CONSULTANT ON LEGAL EDUCATION TO THE ABA

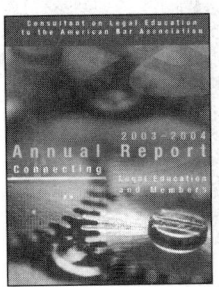

The Consultant's Office Annual Report is a brief overview of the events and activities of the Section and the Consultant's Office for the year. The current year edition is now available as are limited quantities of editions from previous years. 56 pages.

Product Code: 5290089 (0304), Price: $2.00

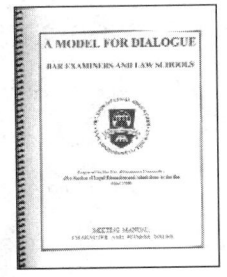

THE ABA'S FIRST SECTION: ASSURING A QUALIFIED BAR

This book was created by Susan Boyd as part of the Centennial Celebration of the Section in 1993. It is 148 pages in length and provides a history of the Section of Legal Education and Admissions to the Bar for the American Bar Association.

Product Code: 5290058, Price: $10.00

A MODEL FOR DIALOGUE: BAR EXAMINERS AND LAW SCHOOLS

In the Spring of 2002 the Bar Admissions Committee updated this manual to be used as a tool to inform as well as encourage and facilitate dialogue between bar examiners, law schools, and supreme courts. The 70 page publication contains several provocative and realistic hypotheticals to facilitate discussion among these entities.

Product Code: 5290093 (02ED), Price: $4.00

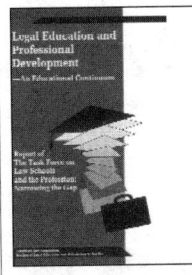

LEGAL EDUCATION AND PROFESSIONAL DEVELOPMENT - AN EDUCATIONAL CONTINUUM ("MACCRATE REPORT")

In August 1992, the Council received the "Report of the Task Force on Law Schools and the Profession: Narrowing the Gap" chaired by Robert MacCrate. The report was distributed to deans and members of law school faculties, chief justices, bar presidents, and members of the Section. All were asked to discuss the recommendations of the Task Force. During the upcoming year we expect to revisit the MacCrate report by requesting schools, states, and individuals to report on the impact of MacCrate on legal education and the profession.

Product Code: 5290052, Price: $10.00

SOURCEBOOK ON LEGAL WRITING PROGRAMS

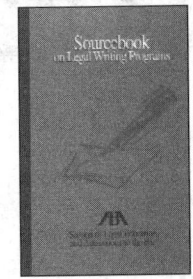

This 174 page book is packed full of information relating to directing, running, and implementing a successful legal writing program. The Sourcebook was drafted by five current or former legal writing program directors who were members of the Communication Skills Committee, who collectively had experience with a wide variety of programs, and who each had more than a decade of experience as a director.

Product Code: 5290091, Price: $10.00

CHAIRPERSONS' REFLECTIONS

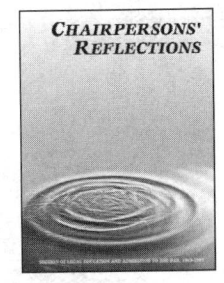

Chairpersons' Reflections contains thoughtful articles by former Section chairpersons from 1969 to 1993, including ABA President Phillip S. Anderson, Norman Redlich, Jose Garcia-Pedrosa, Judge Henry Ramsey, Jr., and Dean Nina S. Appel. It is a wonderful historic publication that shows the progress of legal education and the role of the Section and its Council from 1969 to 1993. The short essays of reflection by former Section Chairpersons give insights and perspectives on the work of the Section and the changing nature of legal education and the legal profession.

Product Code: 5290088, Price: $10.00